RESCUE PLATFORM™

Emergency Flotation for 10 Adults

. . . . an idea and a price you can live with.

Originally designed for use by airport crash/rescue teams, the Rescue Platform is an affordable way to keep 10 adults afloat and out of the water until help arrives. Its now available to operators of motor yachts, sport fishermen, and center console boats. Inflated by CO_2, its reversible configuration is ready for boarding no matter which side is up. Weighing less than 40 lbs., the Rescue Platform is available in compact soft valise or fiberglass container with an optional stainless steel cradle.

  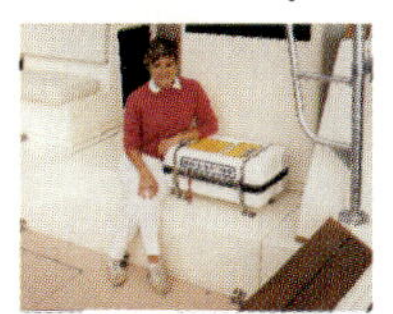 

INFLATED DIMENSIONS	9 ft. 6 in. (octagonal)
BUOYANCY TUBE DIAMETER	12 inches
BUOYANCY	1306 lbs.
SOFT VALISE	38 lb. (8″ hi. × 13″ wd. × 24″ lg.)
FIBERGLASS CONTAINER	43 lb. (10″ hi. × 13″ wd. × 24″ lg.)

Standard Features and Equipment:

- interior and exterior grasp lines
- 2 over pressure relief valves
- 2 water activated locator lights
- heaving ring and line • sea anchor
- floating safety knife
- 3 day/night U.S.C.G. approved distress flares
- emergency flag • whistle
- repair kit and hand pump • flashlight and batteries

Ask Your Dealer For Further Information

SWITLIK PARACHUTE CO., INC.

P.O. Box 1328   1325 East State Street   Trenton, N.J. 08607   (609)587-3300   Telex: 843 421: SPECO

Crow's Nest

MARINE SUPPLIES

EVERYTHING FOR THE BOAT OWNER

✔**MARINE ATLAS VOLUMES 1& 2**
✔**CHARTS AND NAVIGATION SUPPLIES**
✔**FOULWEATHER GEAR**
✔**SAILING HARDWARE**
✔**HARKEN FURLING**
✔**MARINE ELECTRONICS**
✔**AVON INFLATABLES**

✔**PAINTS, VARNISHES & COATING SYSTEMS**
✔**3M PRODUCTS**
✔**MORSE CONTROLS**
✔**ANCHORS, CHAIN & WINDLASSES**
✔**PUMPS AND PLUMBING**
✔**PREVAILER BATTERIES**
✔**YACHTING CORDAGE**

CALL US FOR FAST DELIVERY OF REPAIR PARTS - WE SHIP ANYWHERE

SEATTLE
Shilshole
6010 Seaview Ave. N.W.
(206) 783-6262

SEATTLE
Lake Union
1900 N. Northlake Way
(206) 632-3555

EVERETT
14th St. Yacht Basin
(206) 745-6242
(206) 258-9202

A Division of Fisheries Supply Co., exclusive distributor of the *Marine Atlas*

The friendly waters of the Northwest look a lot more friendly with a Marine Atlas on board.

Marine Atlas

VOLUME 1— OLYMPIA TO MALCOLM ISLAND
VOLUME 2— PORT HARDY TO SKAGWAY

THE ORIGINAL
PACIFIC
NORTHWEST
SKIPPERS' PILOTING GUIDE.

- ☐ Updated Charts
- ☐ Proven Course Lines
- ☐ Convenient Size For Use On Small Boats
- ☐ Aerial Photos Of Popular Harbors
- ☐ Location Index
- ☐ Up-To-Date Marine Facility Location And Information
- ☐ Compass Rose On Every Chart
- ☐ Non-Magnetic Plastic Coil

Marine Atlas has been the standard marine guide for over 30 years. Each 14"x11½" volume provides a wealth of Northwest cruising information for safe and enjoyable boating.

Each detailed cruise chart comes with pre-plotted compass courses. Aerial photos give you a bird's-eye view of unfamiliar harbors. Marine facilities and parks are conveniently listed and keyed to their corresponding chart.

Both volumes are well printed and designed for easy reading. The flexible spiral bindings allow easy on-deck use while the heavy, plastic laminated covers provide durability and protection.

To order the Marine Atlas by mail: indicate the volume number(s) and quantity you would like, enclose $35.95 each in U.S. funds plus $2.00 each for postage and handling. Add state and local taxes where applicable. You may examine your order for 15 days and return, if not completely satisfied, for a prompt refund.

Mail to:

Bayless BE Enterprises

501 S.W. SEVENTH • 226-6395 • RENTON, WASHINGTON 98055

VOL #'s/QUANTITY EA. ___________

NAME ___________

STREET ___________

CITY/STATE/ZIP ___________

Boats & Brokers

COMPLETE YACHT BUYERS GUIDE & BROKER MULTIPLE LISTING SERVICE

NOT JUST FOR BROKERS ANYMORE!

SZ	MANUFACTURER	YR	TY	CO	PW	LO	PRICE	KY
46	SPINDRIFT	85	MY	FG	TD	NB	229,000	NH
46	SPINDRIFT	86	MY	FG	TD	MR	239,900	MD
47	CHRIS CRAFT	52	AC	WD	TD	WL		NE
47	CHRIS CRAFT	66	MY	FG	TD	NB	140,000	PM
47	CHRIS CRAFT	66	MY	FG	TD	SP	140,000	NC
47	CHRIS CRAFT	67	MY	FG	TG	RC	139,000	IA
47	CHRIS CRAFT	69	FD	FG	TD	PO	139,000	BS
47	CLASSIC	12	CR	WD	SD	SF	89,000	GT
47	HOME BUILT	78	TR	WD	SD	AN	94,000	AV
47	HUNTER	66	CR	FG	TG	SD	35,000	YJ
47	INT'L. OFFSHOR	81	PH	FG	TD	NB	185,000	PN
47	JONES-GOODEL	68	TR	WD	TD	WL	134,500	NE
47	NEWPORT	70	PH	FG	TD	SK	148,500	IH
47	NEWPORT	70	TR	FG	TD		148,500	KK
47	NEWPORT	70	TR	FG	TD	SK	165,000	YG
47	PACEMAKER	68	MY	WD	TD	MR	68,000	MW
47	PACEMAKER	68	MY	WD	TD	MR	75,000	MA
47	PACEMAKER	69	MY	WD	TD	MR	67,000	MF
47	PACEMAKER	69	AC	WD	TD	SD	129,500	YJ
47	SEA RANGER	87	PH	FG	TD	AO	195,000	GV
47	SPINDRIFT	86	FB	FG	TD	MR	279,000	MV
47	VENTARE	89	SF	FG	TD	SE	249,000	AV
48	CALIFORIAN	86	MY	FG	TD	MR	365,000	MU
48	CALIFORNIA	88	MY	FG	TD	MR	370,000	MU
50	GRAND BANKS	71	TR	WD	TD	MR	215,000	MR
50	GRAND BANKS	71	TR	WD	TD	NB	215,000	NH
50	GRAND BANKS	71	TR	FG	TD	MR	225,000	NJ
50	GRAND BANKS	72	MY	WD	TD	SD	285,000	YL
50	GRAND BANKS	73	TR	WD	TD	MR	239,500	PK
50	GRAND BANKS	74	TR	WD	D	SD	249,000	YY
50	HATTERAS	66	YF	FG	TD	WL	250,000	NF
50	HATTERAS	68	SF	FG	TD	SD	150,000	YL
50	HATTERAS	68	SF	FG	TD	HB	215,000	YG
50	HATTERAS	80	SF	FG	TD	HB	365,000	MV
50	HATTERAS	80	SF	FG	TD	HB	460,000	KD
50	HAWTHORNE	70	SF	FG	TD	SD	175,000	YL
50	HOROKAWA	20	TR	WD	SD	SD	69,000	YA
50	HOROKAWA	20	TR	WD	SD	SD	83,000	YA
50	JOHNSON	89	MY	FG	TD	OX	395,000	KG
50	JONES/GODDELL	79	SF	FG	TD	SD	395,000	YG
50	KHA SHING	84	YF	FG	TD	NB	249,000	PN
50	LIEN HWA	90	FD		TD	SF	275,000	GZ
50	OCEAN	79	PH	FG	TD	HV	189,900	PN
50	OCEAN ALEXANDE	82	MY	FG	TD	WL	340,000	NE
50	PACIFICA	85	SF	FG	TD	MR	575,000	NH
50	PHILBROOK	61	MY	WD	TD	BE	128,800	AT
50	ROMO	57	MY	WD	TD	OX	69,900	MD
50	SPOILER	80	SE	FG	TD		139,000	PN

PLEASE SEND ME A SUBSCRIPTION TO BOATS & BROKERS

☐ 3 years: $55.00   ☐ 2 years: $39.00   ☐ 1 year: $21.00

PLEASE ENCLOSE PAYMENT: ☐ Check enclosed   Charge my: ☐ MasterCard   ☐ VISA

Account No.________________________________ Expiration Date________________________________

Signature____

Name____

Address____

____

City/State/Zip____

BOATS & BROKERS   PO BOX 341668   LOS ANGELES, CA 90034
(213) 287-2833

Editor
Peter L. Griffes

Production
Susan Willson
Kathy Helman

Design Director
Roger Gordon

Advertising
Ping Hart
Dan Davis

Typesetting
Teri Schrader

Radio & Electronics
Gordon West

Medical
Robert Kahn M.D.

Regional Reporters
Henry Kehler
Lane Anderson

MEMBER

Copyright 1991 by Western Marine Ent. Inc.
All rights reserved ISSN 0899 9368
ISBN 0-930030-66-4
Address all editorial mail to
P.O. Box 341668, Los Angeles, CA 90034
PACIFIC BOATING ALMANAC
published annually in three separate
regional editions: Southern California,
Arizona, and Baja; Northern California
& Nevada; Pacific Northwest, British
Columbia & Alaska. Each volume is $15.95
plus $2.75 per order for shipping.
California residents please add sales tax.
For a complete catalog of boating books,
write to P.O. Box 341668, Los Angeles, CA
90034 (213) 287-2830

1991 PACIFIC BOATING ALMANAC

Pacific Northwest & Alaska

On the cover: An aerial view of the San Juan Islands at dusk, from 60' above the water.
— **Photo by Leonard Aube**

Published annually since 1965

INTERNATIONAL FLAGS AND PENNANTS
Including International Morse Code

ALPHABET FLAGS			NUMERAL PENNANTS
Alfa (• —)	**K**ilo (— • —)	**U**niform (• • —)	1 (• — — — —)
Bravo (— • • •)	**L**ima (• — • •)	**V**ictor (• • • —)	2 (• • — — —)
Charlie (— • — •)	**M**ike (— —)	**W**his-key (• — —)	3 (• • • — —)
Delta (— • •)	**N**ovem-ber (— •)	**X**ray (— • • —)	4 (• • • • —)
Echo (•)	**O**scar (— — —)	**Y**ankee (— • — —)	5 (• • • • •)
Foxtrot (• • — •)	**P**apa (• — — •)	**Z**ulu (— — • •)	6 (— • • • •)
Golf (— — •)	**Q**uebec (— — • —)	REPEATER 1st Repeater	7 (— — • • •)
Hotel (• • • •)	**R**omeo (• — •)	2nd Repeater	8 (— — — • •)
India (• •)	**S**ierra (• • •)	3rd Repeater	9 (— — — — •)
Juliett (• — — —)	**T**ango (—)	CODE (Answering Pennant or Decimal Point)	0 (— — — — —)

Boating Laws and Rules Handbook Now Available

A 60-page handbook on Washington state's recreational watercraft laws and regulations now is available for only $15 from the NMTA office.

The booklet, assembled in a three-ring binder notebook for easy updating on an annual basis, was prepared by John Woodring, NMTA's legislative counsel.

It emphasizes four areas: Registration and titling of recreational vessels; Vessel dealer registration; Recreational vessel taxation; and Boating safety.

Contained in the handbook are both the statutes passed by the Legislature and the implementing rules adopted by state agencies to carry out the statutes. There are introductory materials highlighting important aspects of the law. Contact persons in various state agencies are also listed.

It is NMTA's intent to update the handbook on an annual basis to reflect statutory and rules changes.

Anyone interested in ordering the handbook should contact the NMTA office at 1900 North Northlake Way, Suite 233, Seattle WA 98103, or call (206) 634-0911.

Imagine the idyllic majesty of the San Juan Islands; it's rocky islets, quiet coves and sleepy towns. Sail north to the islands of Canada and experience the magnificent solitude of Desolation Sound, deep fjords, plunging waterfalls, soaring eagles. Relax in steamy hot springs, or watch killer whales cavort off shore.

We're Anacortes Yacht Charters, the unrivalled experts at the art of northwest cruising. We'll tell you where the great spots are and send you off in one of our meticulously prepared yachts. Power or sail, from 28' to 58', we have a boat that will make your next vacation the experience of a lifetime.

P.O. Box 69
Anacortes, WA 98221
1-800-842-4002
in WA 1-800-233-3004

National Safe Boating Council

Up ahead, there's Texaco...

You'll get a warm welcome at the more than 600 independently owned and operated Texaco StarPorts and marinas. They're strategically located on the East and West Coasts, Florida, the Gulf of Mexico and many inland waterways. Check your Pacific Boating Almanac for locations.

At Texaco StarPorts, you're certain to find outstanding facilities. And of course, you can fill up on quality Texaco fuels and lubricants.

Tie up at a Texaco StarPort and get "Texaco Star Treatment" for you and your boat.

BEFORE CASTING OFF...

Get in the habit of performing these brief steps:

▶ **"Sniff" your bilges.** Your nose is usually the best fuel/vapor detector. It'll mean getting down on your hands and knees, but it's the best way to do it.

▶ **Operate the bilge blower for AT LEAST FOUR (4) MINUTES** before starting an inboard engine. If you still smell fumes, try to find out what is causing them and make repairs **before** starting the engine.

▶ **Make sure** the locations of your **fire extinguishers** are known to **all** passengers.

▶ **When refueling,** close all hatches, ports and other openings; shut off all engines and motors; and refrain from smoking. Fill all portable tanks on the dock.

▶ **After refueling,** wipe up or wash off any excess or spilled fuel; open all hatches and ports; and let the boat air out. "Sniff" your bilges. Operate the bilge blower for at least four (4) minutes before starting an inboard engine.

Make these suggestions part of your boating routine. There's no question about it — a shipshape boat is a firesafe boat.

Supplied by the United States Coast Guard and the U.S. Department of Transportation

Nautical Chart Catalog

Chart Number	Title	Scale
18400	Strait of Georgia and Strait of Juan	
	de Fuca	1:200,000
18421	Str. of Juan de Fuca to Str. of Georgia	1:80,000
	Drayton Harbor	1:30,000
18423 SC	FOLIO SMALL-CRAFT	
	Bellingham to Everett including San Juan	
	Islands	1:80,000
	Blaine	1:30,000
18424	Bellingham Bay	1:40,000
	Bellingham Harbor	1:20,000
18427	Anacortes to Skagit Bay	1:25,000
18428	Oak and Crescent Harbors	1:10,000
18429	Rosario Strait—southern part	1:25,000
18430	Rosario Strait—northern part	1:25,000
18431	Rosario Strait to Cherry Point	1:25,000
18432	Boundary Pass	1:25,000
18433	Haro Strait—Middle Bank to	
	Stuart Island	1:25,000
18434	San Juan Channel	1:25,000
18440	Admiralty Inlet and Puget Sound	1:150,000
18441	Admiralty Inlet and Puget Sound to Seattle	1:80,000
18443	Approaches to Everett	1:40,000
18444	Everett Harbor	1:10,000
18445 SC	FOLIO SMALL-CRAFT	
	Puget Sound—Possession Sound to Olympia	
	including Hood Canal	1:80,000
18446	Puget Sound—Apple Cove Pt. to Keyport	1:25,000
	Agate Passage	1:10,000
18447 SC	Lake Washington Ship Canal	1:10,000
	Lake Washington	1:25,000
18448	Puget Sound—Seattle to Olympia	1:80,000
18449	Puget Sound—Seattle to Bremerton	1:25,000
18450	Seattle Harbor, Elliott Bay and Duwamish	
	Waterway	1:10,000
18452	Sinclair Inlet	1:10,000
18453	Tacoma Harbor	1:15,000
18456	Olympia Harbor and Budd Inlet	1:20,000
18457	Puget Sound—Hammersley In. to Shelton	1:10,000
18458	Hood Canal—South Point to Quatsap Point	
	including Dabob Bay	1:25,000
Ⓒ 18460	Strait of Juan de Fuca Entrance	1:100,000
18461	Hood Canal—Port Ludlow to South Point	1:20,000
18464	Port Townsend	1:20,000
18465	Strait of Juan de Fuca—eastern part	1:80,000
18468	Port Angeles	1:10,000
18471	Approaches to Admiralty Inlet—	
	Dungeness to Oak Bay	1:40,000
18473	Puget Sound—Oak Bay to	
	Shilshole Bay	1:40,000

Chart Number	Title	Scale
Ⓒ 18480	Approaches to Strait of Juan de Fuca—	
	Destruction Is. to Amphitrite Pt.	1:176,253
	Quillayute River Entrance	1:10,000
18484	Neah Bay	1:10,000
18485	Cape Flattery	1:40,000
Ⓒ 18500	Columbia River to Destruction Island	1:180,789
18502	Grays Harbor	1:40,000
	Westport Harbor	1:10,000
18504	Willapa Bay	1:40,000
Ⓒ 18520	Yaquina Head to Columbia River	1:185,238
	Netarts Bay	1:30,000
	COLUMBIA RIVER	
18521	Pacific Ocean to Harrington Point	1:40,000
	Ilwaco Harbor	1:20,000
18523	Harrington Point to Crims Island	1:40,000
18524	Crims Island to Vancouver	1:40,000
18526	Port of Portland, including Vancouver	1:20,000
	Multhomah Channel—southern part	1:10,000
18527	Willamette River—Swan Island Basin	1:5,000
18528	Willamette River—Portland to Newberg	1:15,000
18531	Vancouver to The Dalles	1:40,000
	Bonneville Dam	1:10,000
	The Dalles	1:10,000
	Hood River	1:10,000
18533	Lake Celilo	1:20,000
18535	John Day Dam to Blalock	1:20,000
18536	Sundale to Heppner Junction	1:20,000
18537	Alderdale to Blalock Islands	1:20,000
18539	Blalock Island to McNary Dam	1:20,000
18541	McNary Dam to Juniper	1:20,000
18542	Juniper to Pasco	1:20,000
18545 PF	Lake Sacajawea	1:20,000
18546 SC	Snake River—Lake Herbert G. West	1:20,000
18547 PF	Snake River—Lake Bryan	1:20,000
18548 PF	Snake River—Lower Granite Lake	1:20,000
	FRANKLIN D. ROOSEVELT LAKE	
18551	Southern part	1:50,000
18553	Northern part	1:50,000
18554	Pend Oreille Lake	1:50,000
18556	Nehalem River	1:20,000
18558	Tillamook Bay	1:20,000
18561	Approaches to Yaquina Bay	1:50,000
	Depoe Bay	1:10,000
Ⓒ 18580	Cape Blanco to Yaquina Head	1:191,730
18581	Yaquina Bay and River	1:10,000
	Continuation of Yaquina River	1:25,000

Ⓒ Includes LORAN-C Lines of Position

Nautical Chart Catalog

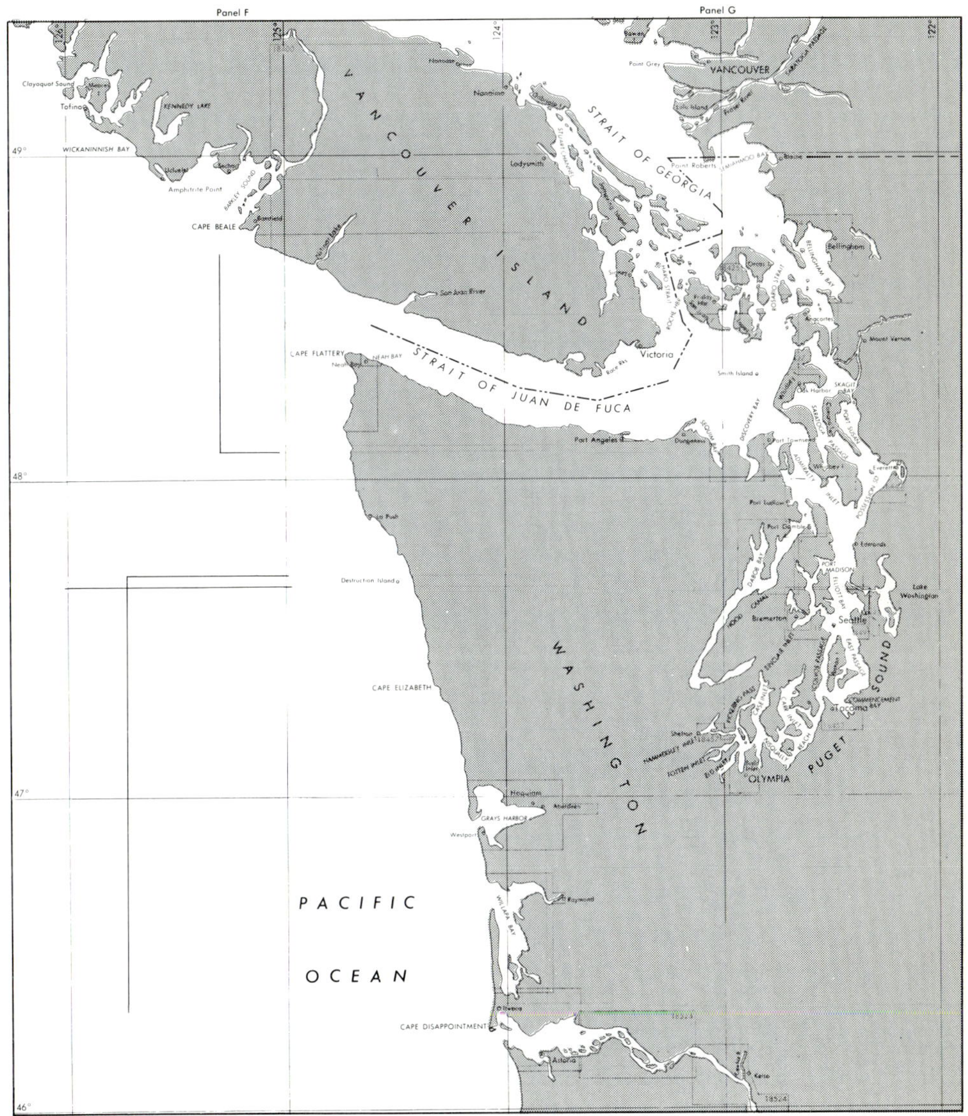

ALL CHARTS
$13.00 each

Charts listed here may be ordered from the Distribution Branch (N/CG33), National Ocean Service, Riverdale, Maryland 20737, (301) 436-6990 or from authorized sales agents listed in the ALMANAC. Orders mailed to Riverdale, Maryland should be accompanied by a check or money order payable to NOS, Department of Commerce. Visa / Mastercard accepted on phone in orders. Call for free chart catalogs.

"A little cruise is just like life. It may, if you are lucky, contain a bit of everything you need. Moments of fear, moments of exhilaration, singing moments of perception, spells of relaxation, toil and change. It may end at any moment in disaster. It may make a fool of you, or it may make you feel momentarily rather clever and even rather good. It will assuredly show you to yourself. Nearly all the problems of life on land are present on the sea and some are magnified; but on the sea it is possible to escape for a time from the congestion and contagion of the world."

— Maurice Wiggin

WE NEED YOUR HELP

The ALMANAC has always relied on its Regional Reporters for accurate, mile-by-mile information on travel throughout the West Coast -- but we don't rely only on staffers for information. Each year (for 25 years now) we've found that some of our best travel information has come from readers -- you and your fellow travelers.

If, during your travels, you find changes such as the opening of a new facility, the closure of a fuel dock or other changes that will be helpful to fellow travelers, please give us the details on the form that follows (or on a separate sheet of paper) and mail it to The Editor, The Pacific Boating Almanac, P.O. Box 341668, Los Angeles, CA 90034 We'll take note of your report when we prepare the 1992 ALMANAC.

Please feel free to elaborate -- we're always anxious to hear about your travel experiences on the West Coast (favorite attractions, routes traveled, areas that might deserve more editorial coverage next year or whatever).

Have a fantastic trip . . . and let us know how it goes!

- The Editor

On **Page** _______ of the 1991 ALMANAC, So. Cal No. Cal PNW Edition, in
column _______ (1 or 2) we suggest that you make the following change(s):

____
____
____
____
____

On Page _______ of the 1991 ALMANAC, So. Cal No. Cal PNW Edition, in
column _______ (1 or 2) we suggest that you make the following change(s):

____
____
____
____
____

On Page _______ of the 1991 ALMANAC, So. Cal No. Cal PNW Edition, in
column _______ (1 or 2) we suggest that you make the following change(s):

____
____
____
____
____

On Page _______ of the 1991 ALMANAC, So. Cal No. Cal PNW Edition, in
column _______ (1 or 2) we suggest that you make the following change(s):

____
____
____
____
____

On Page _______ of the 1991 ALMANAC, So. Cal No. Cal PNW Edition, in
column _______ (1 or 2) we suggest that you make the following change(s):

____
____
____
____
____

HOW TO USE THE FACILITY DATA

To provide the most complete and current description, marine facilities on the Pacific Coast are reviewed annually and the material updated. Wherever pertinent, the following is listed in concise form:

Name and location • Postal address and phone number • Open part or all year • Hours open • Slips, moorings, storage • Ramp - number of lanes, type of surface with hours of use • Hoist, elevator, travelift, marine railway and capacity • Boat and engine repairs • New and used boat and engine sales • Fuel available • Marine hardware • Water skiing permitted • Fishing: licenses, bait, tackle, boats and motors available • Special features: restaurant, bar, coffee shop, ice, groceries, beverages, food-to-go, hotel or motel, trailer or campsites, etc.

DOCKSIDE ELECTRICITY: The code system below, numbered from 1 to 10, illustrates the outlets with the proper voltage and amperage. Where available, we have tried to indicate the rating and the plug-in configuration by using the code number. For example: the code number (2) following the facility description indicates a 2-prong plug, 15 amps., 125 volts, as shown in the diagram.

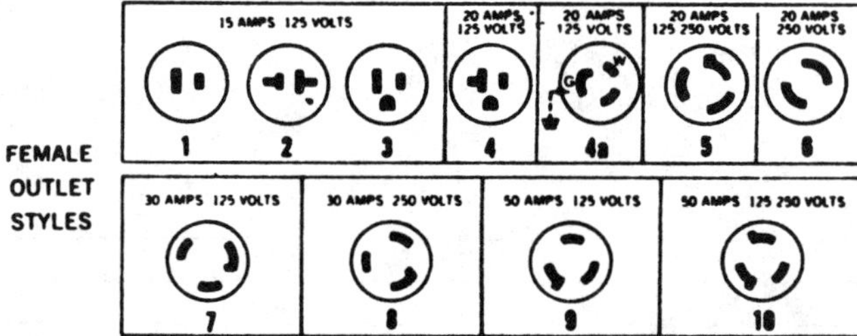

U.S. COAST PILOT INFORMATION

UNITED STATES COAST PILOT 7 – Twenty-fourth Edition - June 1988 † Extract from this latest edition of the COAST PILOT are reprinted in the ALMANAC in Italics at the beginning of each chapter. The 1988 COAST PILOT cancels the preceding 1987 Edition and is corrected from U.S. Coast Guard Local Notices to Mariners through No. 41 (11th Coast Guard District) dated October 3, 1988 and No. 40 (13th Coast Guard District) dated October 4, 1988.

CAUTION † The COAST PILOT should not be used without reference to the Notices to Mariners issued subsequent to the above dates.

For coastal waters and tributaries in California south of 34°58'N; Commander Eleventh Coast Guard District, 400 Oceangate, Long Beach, CA 90822.

For Coastal waters and tributaries in Oregon, Washington and Idaho; Commander Thirteenth Coast Guard District 915, Second Avenue, Seattle, WA 98174.

For Alaska: Seventeenth Coast Guard District, FPO Seattle, WA 98771.

Notices to Mariners may be obtained free by applying to the Commander of the local Coast Guard District.

TABLE OF CONTENTS

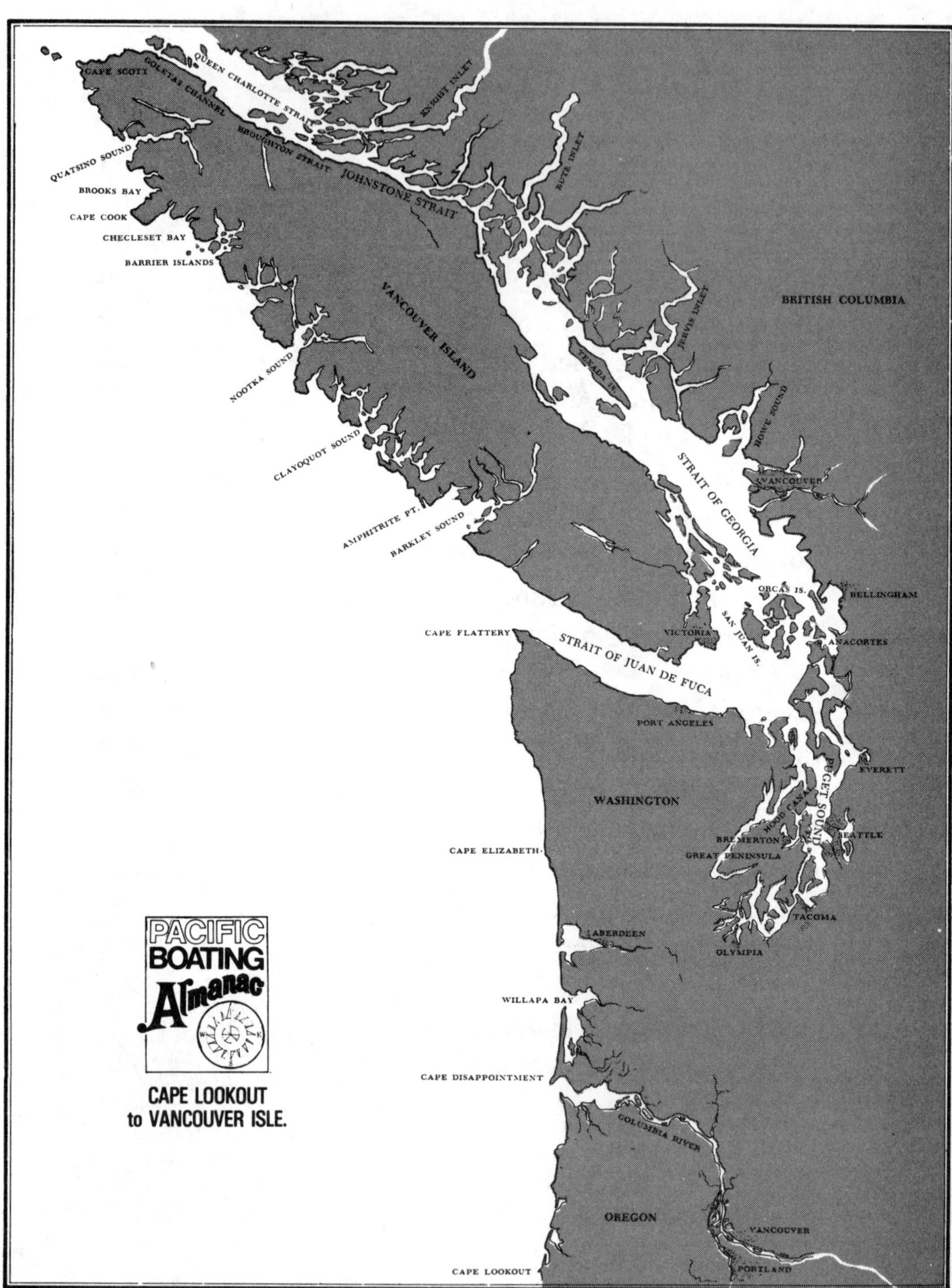

CAPE SCOTT
GOLETAS CHANNEL
QUEEN CHARLOTTE STRAIT
KNIGHT INLET
QUATSINO SOUND
BROOKS BAY
CAPE COOK
CHECLESET BAY
BARRIER ISLANDS
BROUGHTON STRAIT
JOHNSTONE STRAIT
BUTE INLET
JERVIS INLET
BRITISH COLUMBIA
VANCOUVER ISLAND
NOOTKA SOUND
TEXADA IS.
HOWE SOUND
VANCOUVER
CLAYOQUOT SOUND
STRAIT OF GEORGIA
AMPHITRITE PT.
BARKLEY SOUND
ORCAS IS.
BELLINGHAM
CAPE FLATTERY
VICTORIA
SAN JUAN IS.
ANACORTES
STRAIT OF JUAN DE FUCA
PORT ANGELES
EVERETT
WASHINGTON
PUGET SOUND
HOOD CANAL
SEATTLE
BREMERTON
CAPE ELIZABETH
GREAT PENINSULA
TACOMA
ABERDEEN
OLYMPIA
WILLAPA BAY
CAPE DISAPPOINTMENT
COLUMBIA RIVER
OREGON
VANCOUVER
PORTLAND
CAPE LOOKOUT
PACIFIC BOATING Almanac
CAPE LOOKOUT to VANCOUVER ISLE.

1
RIVER BARS & COASTAL INLETS
OREGON COAST TO WASHINGTON

Smuggler's Cove. Last natural anchorage along Oregon Coast.

CROSSING THE BAR

The Oregon coast runs north to south nearly all its length. Very few natural lees exist on this windswept stretch. All the major ports lie past the mouths of rivers. All the entrances become impassable in certain conditions. This coast is home to a hardy band of seafarers, from salmon and crab fishermen to recreational boating enthusiasts. All have learned to cope with this coast and its vagaries of wind and weather.

A few common sense practices are followed by knowledgeable sailors. At the top of the list is preparation, which begins with the boat itself. Space does not allow for much elaboration on the selection of a boat for these waters, but it must be stout, seaworthy and reliable if it is to survive. Size does not always provide safety because when conditions are really bad, even the largest ships come to a standstill.

Proper gear is essential. Lifejackets are required, while a good radio is cheap life insurance. Flares and smoke signals are also required, but an EPIRB can signal your position even if you are out of sight. (EPIRB stands for "emergency position indicating radio beacon." EPIRBS send out a continual distress signal that can be picked up by aircraft.) Warm clothes, plenty of water and provisions and spare parts are a must. An exposure suit will provide protection against the elements in severe cases of exposure.

CROSSING THE BAR. † Before venturing out to sea, listen to the marine weather forecast and station reports. If you have any doubts, don't go out. Check the tides, too. Try to plan on returning during the flood. Many river bars can be seen from nearby observation points on land. If possible, drive out to the point and check out conditions. Finally, the harbor entrances have *Rough Bar Advisory Signs.* These are diamond-shaped, with an International Orange border and bold black letters that say "Rough Bar." If the two amber or yellow lights on the signs are flashing, this means the bar is breaking and that you should not attempt to cross. Even when the sign is not flashing, this does not necessarily mean that it is safe to cross. In the final analysis, the decision is yours.

Getting out is often easier than returning. If conditions look marginal, chances are they will not improve. If conditions are favorable, leave the harbor quickly, following the main channel, preferably behind a local boat with a deeper draft than yours. Remember that although every effort is made to mark the channels, shoaling does occur rapidly and the channel buoys may not mark the safest course. Check with the Coast Guard, Pilot or Harbormaster before setting out.

A float plan is a very good idea. Include when you plan on leaving, where you will be and when you will return. Leave the plan with a responsible person and if you fail to return within a reasonable time, he can telephone the Coast Guard and advise them that you are overdue.

On returning, check your tide table again. Plan on coming in on the flood. Check the entrance from well offshore, allowing time for sets of waves to develop. Note where they break. Also, check the Rough Bar Advisory Sign. See if other boats are coming and going. If all looks well, head in, planning on crossing the bar as quickly as possible and during a lull between sets of waves. Again, follow a local boat with a deeper draft than yours if possible.

If you have any doubts, do not attempt to cross. Radio the Coast Guard on VHF Channel 16, or call for a pilot if one is available. If it's a matter of waiting for the tide, simply run offshore where there is plenty of sea room and await the change.

If the weather is worsening, you may face a tough decision. Run for another port or wait it out offshore? Or take your chances on the bar? If you decide to run for another port, be sure you have enough fuel. Also, be sure you can get there before the weather gets any worse. If you decide to wait it out offshore, you must have a very seaworthy boat.

Should you decide to cross the bar, lash everything down and have everyone put on life preservers. Call the Coast Guard and advise them that you are going to attempt to cross. Often they can talk you in if they have a better vantage point from which to judge the breakers on the bar.

Try to come in on the back of the waves, keeping your boat at right angles to them. A careful hand on the throttle will often keep you from overtaking a breaking wave, or from being overtaken.

If you do get dumped, stay with the boat and stay together. Ignite any flares, lights, or EPIRBS you are carrying and await rescue.

The following material on river bars and harbor entrances in Washington and Oregon is taken from BOATING IN COASTAL WATERS, published by the Oregon State Marine Board, Salem, Oregon 97310 and the U.S. Coast Guard GUIDE TO HAZARDOUS BARS, 1982 Edition, issued by Commander, 13th Coast Guard District, 915 Second Ave., Seattle, WA 98174.

REGULATED BOATING AREAS † The U.S. Coast Guard, in accordance with provisions in Part 177 of Subchapter S, Title 33, Code of Federal Regulations Chapter 1, has provided for the termination of use of boats during especially hazardous conditions on certain river bars and coastal inlets along the Pacific coastline of the State of Washington and Oregon. These regulated boating areas are:

1. Quillayute River Entrance, Wash.
2. Grays Harbor Entrance, Wash.
3. Willapa Bay, Wash.
4. Columbia River Bar, Wash.-Ore.
5. Nehalem River Bar, Ore.
6. Tillamook Bay Bar, Ore.
7. Netarts Bay Bar, Ore.
8. Siletz Bay Bar, Ore.
9. Depoe Bay Bar, Ore.
10. Yaquina Bay Bar, Ore.
11. Siuslaw River Bar, Ore.
12. Umpqua River Bar, Ore.
13. Coos Bay Bar, Ore.
14. Coquille River Bar, Ore.
15. Rogue River Bar, Ore.
16. Chetco River Bar, Ore.

CHETCO RIVER DANGER AREAS

Use Chart 18602.

A. WEST JETTY ROCKY AREA. This area is dangerous because of the many rocks and shoaling. At high tide the rocks are covered by water and the area appears to be navigable, but is extremely dangerous. This area is to be avoided at all times.

B. EAST & WEST JETTY SHOAL AREAS. These areas are extremely dangerous at all times because of submerged rocks and breakers. Rocks in these areas may be seen at low tide. Avoid these areas at all times.

BAR WARNING † A ROUGH BAR ADVISORY SIGN is located on the fuel dock at the Coast Guard station and faces approximately NNW.

BAR CONDITION REPORTS † Radio station KURY (910 kHz) gives bar condition reports every hour during daylight in the summer only.

JETTIES † In general jetties continue seaward for several yards past the visible end. By all means AVOID CROSSING OVER A SUBMERGED JETTY. Navigate with extreme caution near jetties particularly when wind and sea are setting you toward the jetty.

RANGE MARKERS † The Front Range Marker consists of a red rectangular shape with a vertical white stripe and the Rear Range Marker, a red square shape with a vertical white stripe. By steering a course which keeps the two range markers in line, the boatman will remain within the approximate channel. Because the entrance channel is constantly shifting, the range markers do not always mark the exact channel.

CHETCO RIVER/ BROOKINGS † This is unique among Oregon ports with bars to cross in that it faces north-south. Although it is a small port , it is fairly easy to enter in moderate conditions. Plenty of rocks exist offshore, so stay at least $1\frac{1}{2}$ miles offshore. When coming in, bring both jetties to view, then head straight in. Do not wander east or west because numerous foul areas line either side.

Several state parks lie on either side of the town of Brookings. Every Memorial Day an Azalea Festival is held. Events include a barbecue, seafood luncheon, flower and art shows and numerous other activities.

MACK ARCH, some 12 miles north of Chetco, is a prominent rock less than a mile offshore (see Chart 18602). A fair day anchorage lies about ½ mile east-southeast of the rock in about 65 feet of water, sand bottom. Approach with caution because the area has not been thoroughly charted.

The best anchorage is in MACK ARCH COVE, above the rock and east of the reefs. To reach it, approach from about 150 yards southwest of Mack Arch. Watch for a submerged rock about 125 yards south of the east end of the arch. After you pass the rock, steer for the highest rock at the north end of the reef, about 352° magnetic. Anchor about ½ mile north of Mack Arch in a sand channel about 35 to 45 feet deep.

HUNTERS COVE lies under the southeast corner of Cape Sebastian. Enter the anchorage from the west keeping Hunters Island to port and dropping your hook to the northeast of the island. Watch for a wash rock in the east part of Hunters Cove. This is a fair day anchorage in settled condition.

Charleston, Oregon

26

ROGUE RIVER
DANGER AREAS

Use Chart 18601.

Rogue River channel lies along the North Jetty. This bar is unstable with frequent changes in the channel. Local knowledge is required to cross the bar. Boaters are urged to use and stay within the channel.

A. SHOAL WATER, SOUTH SIDE. Alongside the south side of the Rogue River channel are shoal water and gravel bars. This shoal water breaks to a height of 6 feet when a well is running. Many boats fishing inside the river, trolling between the jetties, find themselves set into this dangerous area by northwest winds. If a vessel breaks down in the channel and is not anchored, the northwest wind and ebb tide will set it into this dangerous area in a matter of a few minutes.

B. OUTER END NORTH JETTY. Breakers are almost always present in the area. Even when it appears to be calm, there may be occasional breakers 1,000 feet outside the South Jetty. When the sea is running from the west or southwest this area is very dangerous.

Small boats which do not usually go out into the ocean fish inside the bar, trolling in an area between the North and South jetties. Freqently there are a great number of boats in this small area and these boats tend to crowd each other. Because trolling is the method of fishing most frequently used, lines are sometimes accidently caught in boat propellers. Should this happen, the disabled boat should immediately anchor or call for aid. A northwest wind or ebb current could set your boat into a dangerous area in a matter of minutes.

BAR WARNINGS † A small boat ROUGH BAR ADVISORY SIGN is located on a building at position 42°25.6'N and 124°25.4'W.
JETTIES † In general , jetties continue seaward for several yards past the visible end. By all means AVOID CROSSING OVER A SUBMERGED JETTY. Navigate with extreme caution near jetties particularly when wind and sea are setting you toward the jetty.

PORT ORFORD
HARBOR OF REFUGE
(42°44'N., 124°30'W.)

PORT ORFORD † This is the only natural lee that has become a real port without needing major improvements. It is also the only coastal Oregon port without a bar to cross. Port Orford is no place to be in southerly winter conditions, however, because it then becomes a treacherous lee shore.

The forests around Port Orford are renowed for their Port Orford cedar. This fine wood was once widely used for planking and decking as well as for furniture. In World War II, however, huge stands of Port Orfords cedars were leveled; the wood to be used as separators in storage batteries in the war effort. Fortunately, plastics came along in time to save this stately tree.

COQUILLE RIVER
DANGER AREAS
(43°07'N., 124°25'W.)

Use Chart 18588.

A. SOUTH JETTY. It is always dangerous to get too close to the end of a jetty. An unexpected breaker could carry a small boat onto the end of the jetty with great force. The inside of the South Jetty is a dangerous area. Boaters should remain clear of this area. The prevailing north west wind could set a powerless boat onto the jetty.

B. NORTH JETTY. Stay clear of the end of this jetty. The sea breaks almost continuously in this area. A shallow area with partially submerged rocks extends from the abandoned lighthouse to the end of the jetty. Large swells which occur in this area could put a boat onto these rocks.

C. SOUTH SIDE OF COQUILLE RIVER ENTRANCE. The area to the south of the entrance can be very dangerous. There are several rocks just below the surface that cannot be seen except during heavy seas. There is a prevailing northwest wind during the summer months; also the sea currents run to the south . These two conditions may cause a powerless boat in this area to drift onto these rocks.

BAR CONDITIONS REPORTS † Note: The Coast Guard Station on the Coquille River is manned during the summer months only from May 15 to Octobe 15. Information concerning the Coquille River Bar should be directed to the Coquille River Coast Guard Station when it is manned. Otherwise contact Coast Guard Station Coos Bay.

JETTIES † In general jetties continue seaward for several yards past the visible end. By all means AVOID CROSSING OVER A SUBMERGED JETTY. Navigate with extreme caution near jetties particularly when wind and sea are setting you toward the jetty.

RANGE MARKERS † The front Range Marker consists of a white square daymark with a red triangle on a skeleton tower. The Rear Range Marker consists of a white square daymark with a red inverted triangle on a skeleton tower. By steering a course which keeps the two Range Markers in line the boatman will remain within the channel.

COQUILLE RIVER / BANDON † Also boasts a treacherous bar crossing, although plans are being considered to improve the entrance. The harbor itself has already been considerably improved with the construction of a new marina, launch ramp and fishing pier.

No visit to Bandon would be complete without a taste tour of the Bandon Cheese Factory. Here, fine aged cheddar is made that will stand up to any of the wider known brands. The factory is within easy walking distance of the marina.

Another must is a visit to Andrea's Old Town Cafe. The coffee must be tasted to be believed. It is far better than any coffee should be, while the meals would satisfy a lumberjack or salmon fisherman. Quality and quantity go hand in hand at Andrea's. And the prices are right. It's only a block off the waterfront.

Bandon's Annual Cranberry Festival, held in September, is a spectacle that shouldn't be missed. The whole town cuts loose at this time and if you like cranberries, you'll find yourself at home in Bandon.

SOUTH COVE, just below Cape Arago (pronounced "air-uh-go"), is a tight little summer anchorage sometimes used by locals. It is in a picturesque setting and is a fine spot, but cannot be recommended for strangers because of the gauntlet of reefs and rocks guarding the entrance.

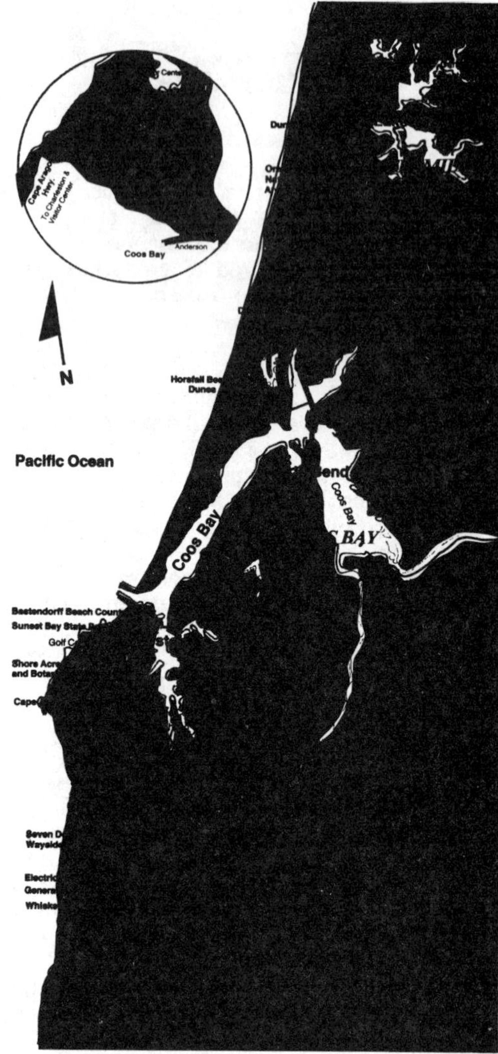

Coos Bay, a harbor of refuge, can be entered at any time in extreme weather.

COOS BAY
DANGER AREAS
(43°22'N., 124°13'W.)

Use Chart 18587.

A. SAND SPIT, SOUTH SLOUGH. As you leave the Charleston Boat Basin, the South Slough Sand Spit is on your left. This area can be crossed by small craft at high water. It extends North, parallel to the channel from South Slough Buoy #14 approximately 450 yards toward South Slough Light #2. Presently, Nun Buoy #2T marks the North end of the sand spit. This area should not be crossed.

B. SUBMERGED JETTY. Proceeding out from the Charleston Boat Basin in the South Slough channel, when you are directly between South Slough Light #2 and Can Buoy #3, directly ahead will be South Slough Light #1 which is marking the end of the submerged jetty. This jetty is only visible at low water. When departing the Charleston Boat Basin, stay to the left of Light #1 at all times.

C. SAND SPIT, NORTH BEACH. This area is dangerous because of shoal waters and submerged jetties. Occasionally, on a strong ebb, there will be breakers in this area. This area should be avoided because of the possibility of going aground or striking submerged jetties and pillings. Also noted are inbound and outbound tugs with tows, freighters etc., that pass close aboard this area and cannot stop for obstructions in the channel; i.e. small vessels in the channel.

D. SOUTH JETTY, GUANO ROCK AREA. This is a very dangerous area due to shoals extending out from the South Jetty to the Entrance Channel. Breaks are frequently experienced from Coos Buoy #4 extending out to a little past the end of the South Jetty. Extreme care must be exercised in this area at all times, especially on ebb tides.

E. NORTH JETTY SUBMERGED. The North Jetty was extended approximately 300 yards to the West. The outward end of the jetty is submerged from the visible end of the jetty out towards Buoy #3. This area should never be crossed. There are breakers in this area most of the time. When departing the Bar North bound, be sure to pass Buoy #3 before turning to the North.

F. AREA NORTH OF BUOY #5. This area can be very dangerous when there are any large swells on the Bar or during ebb tide. Freak breakers are common in this area. Many boats transit this area on occasion although it is stongly not recommended.

BAR WARNING † A ROUGH BAR ADVISORY SIGN is located 12 feet above the water on the newly constructed jetty just north of the Charleston Boat Basin. The advisory is a two part Bar Sign facing (1) toward the Charleston Boat Basin and (2) north toward South Slough Light #2.

BAR CONDITION REPORTS † Weather and bar conditions are recorded twice daily at the Coast Guard Station in Charleston. This can be obtained by calling (503) 888-3102. Radio station KBBR (1340 kHz) broadcasts bar conditions once each hour during the summer months. Current weather advisories are also posted at the Coast Guard Station in Charleston.

UMPQUA RIVER DANGER AREAS
(43°41'N., 124°11'W.)

Use Chart 18584.

The Umpqua River Bar has a fairly complicated channel. The bar can change drastically and local knowledge should be obtained from the Coast Guard or local operators by personnel unfamiliar with the bar.

Umpqua River, 19.5 miles north of Coos Bay. Entrance to Salmon Harbor.

A. MIDDLE GROUND AND NORTH SPIT. The North Spit is to your right as you proceed down the Umpqua River, starting from the first rock spar jetty and long pier on the east side of the channel. The North Spit area has small breakers when a swell is running and gets rougher as you proceed along the north jetty. The North Spit is very dangerous because large breakers may come into this area from the Middle Ground. The Middle Ground area extends from the north jetty to the black bell buoy. This area is dangerous because a little swell can create large breakers which may capsize your vessel. Boatman should not linger near the mouth of the river during ebb tide, for if your power fails, your boat could be carried out to sea before an anchor would be effective or oars put to work.

B. SOUTH JETTY AND SOUTH JETTY COVE. There is a light and bell on the end of the south jetty. The area south of the south jetty can be very dangerous. Whenever breakers are observed boatmen should avoid this area.

BAR CONDITION REPORTS † Bar condition reports for Umpqua River are given hourly during daylight hours by radio station KDUN (1470 kHz) during summer months.

JETTIES † In general, jetties continue seaward for several yards past the visible end. By all means AVOID CROSSING OVER A SUBMERGED JETTY. Navigate with extreme caution near jetties particularly when wind and sea are setting you toward the jetty.

RANGE MARKERS † The Range Marker consists of a red rectangular shape with a white vertical stripe mounted on a skeleton tower. By steering a course which keeps the two Range Markers in line, the boatman will remain approximately within the channel.

Suislaw River, Oregon.

Because the entrance channel is constantly shifting, the Range Markers do not always mark the exact channel.

SUISLAW RIVER DANGER AREAS

Use Chart 18583

Siuslaw River bar has a very narrow channel extending out past the jetties. Unlike the larger bars on the Oregon coast, the Siuslaw River Bay may be rendered impassable for small boats by a moderate swell, particularly at ebb tide. Boaters should use extreme caution when operating near this bar.

DANGER SHOALING SIUSLAW RIVER † Siuslaw River Bar is experiencing heavy shifts of sand which have caused low water depths of 8 feet reported on the Bar Entrance Range. Mariners are urged to navigate with caution in this area.

A. SHOAL WATER NORTHEAST SIDE OF THE CHANNEL has a depth of $2\frac{1}{2}$ to 3 feet of water at high tide.

B. SHOAL WATER, SOUTH SIDE OF THE CHANNEL extends from buoy #17, well inside the bar, almost out to buoy #5 (lighted gong). Breakers in this area are common, even with a small swell running.

C. OUTER END OF THE SOUTH JETTY. Breakers are almost always present in this area. When the seas are from the southwest or west, breakers may extend out past the lighted gong buoy.

D. OUTER END OF THE NORTH JETTY. Breakers are almost always present in this area. When the seas are from the west, the breakers may extend all the way out to the lighted gong buoy.

Yaquina Bay, Newport lies just inside the N entrance point.

BAR WARNING † A ROUGH BAR ADVISORY SIGN is mounted on the Coast Guard lookout tower and faces 150° true.

JETTIES † In general, jetties continue seaward for several yards past the visable end. By all means, AVOID CROSSING OVER A SUBMERGED JETTY. Navigate with extreme caution near jetties particularly when wind and sea are setting you toward the jetty.

RANGE MARKERS † The Siuslaw River entrance range consists of two white rectangular daymarks with red vertical stripes. The Siuslaw River channel lies along the northern half of the river entrance. Water depth ranges from 6 to 20 feet. Boaters are urged to stay on the north side of this channel, as breakers are prevalent on the south side. Although the channel is constantly shifting, the boatman will remain in the approximate channel by steering a course which keeps the range markers in line.

ALSEA
(44°26'N., 124°04'W.)

ALSEA / WALDPORT † A sheltered bay and river much favored by clammers and anglers. No jetties protect the river mouth, however and even the locals in small boats brave the bar only rarely.

YAQUINA BAY DANGER AREAS

Use Chart 18581.

A. SOUTH JETTY AND GROINS IN RUINS. The groins or short jetties along the south side of the entrance are completely submerged at high tide, but are bare at other stages. In addition, there are submerged rocks in the vicinity which are close to the surface at all times. There are submerged rocks along the entire length close to the jetty. NEVER CROSS OVER THE SUBMERGED END and do not hug the jetty on either side. Remain in the channel

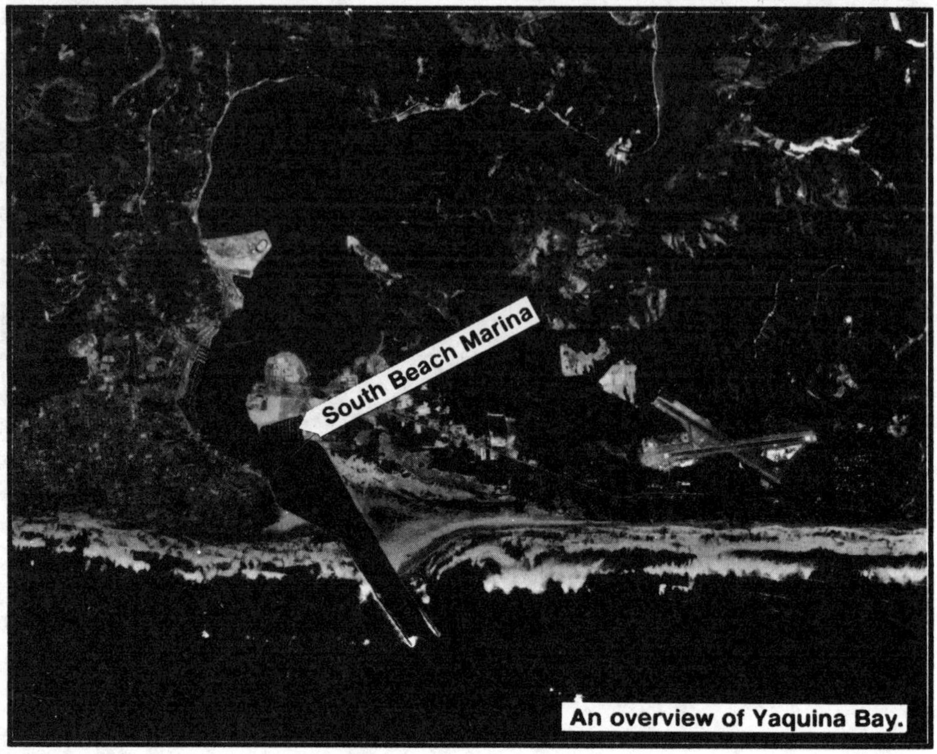

entering and leaving the river, so that if your engine should fail, you'll have enough time to anchor before the current or wind sweeps you onto the rocks.

B. **NORTH JETTY** has excellent protection from northerly winds. However, the same caution should be exercised in running close to it as with the south jetty. On the ebb tide stay well clear of the end of the north jetty as there is danger of being swept into the breakers at the extreme end. Remain in the channel outbound until you have passed buoy #3 at the south end of Yaquina Reef. This applies to entering the river as well as leaving.

C. **SOUTH REEF** can be considered an extension of Yaquina Reef and is equally dangerous due to the same surf conditions as are encountered on Yaquina Reef. When going south continue out of the channel to the lighted bell buoy #1 before turning south.

D. **YAQUINA REEF** is always extremely dangerous, even when the winds are light and few breakers are seen. A large swell coming from seaward can cause a tremendous breaker on this reef with little or no warning, even when the sea is otherwise calm. Never fish too close to the reef and do not turn north between the end of the north jetty and buoy #3.

BAR WARNING † A ROUGH BAR ADVISORY SIGN is on the west end of the Coast Guard pier and faces 040° true.

BAR CONDITION REPORTS † Radio station KNPT (1310 kHz) gives bar condition reports in the summer three times daily and upon Coast Guard request; in the winter twice daily and upon Coast Guard request.

JETTIES † In general, jetties continue seaward for several yards past the

Fixed bridge at Depoe, Oregon.

visible end. By all means AVOID CROSSING A SUBMERGED JETTY! Navigate with extreme caution near jetties particularly when wind and sea are setting you toward the jetty.

RANGE MARKERS † The Front Range Marker consists of a white square daymark with a red vertical stripe on a dolphin. The Rear Range Marker consists of a white diamond daymark with a red vertical stripe on a skeleton tower on a pile structure. By steering a course which keeps the two Range Markers in line, the boatman will remain within the channel.

DEPOE BAY
DANGER AREAS

Use Chart 18561

Depoe Bay Channel has been widened from 35 feet to 50 feet to make passing less dangerous. This channel has a depth of 8 feet at low water. Under normal conditions, small craft can enter and leave the harbor with little difficulty. However, even under good conditions, the area between the breakwater and the bridge should be navigated with extreme caution.

Under adverse conditions, only mariners thoroughly familiar with the channel should attempt to enter this harbor. Depoe Bay has the only flood lighted entrance on the coast. However, it should not be entered at night unless the boat operator is well acquainted with the channel entrance and range lights.

A. NORTH REEF. Once a boat has cleared the entrance any waters to the north are hazardous until the red bell buoy is reached. The seas break from the northwest and southwest at the same time so this area must be avoided at all times.

B. SOUTH REEF. Better known as "Flat Rock" this area lies just south of the channel. Breakers are almost always present in this area. Boats coming from the south should never use this area as a short cut to the channel. This area should be avoided by boats at all times.

C. CHANNEL FROM RED BELL BUOY IN. (Approximately 1,000 yards.) Because the north and south reefs are so close to the channel, this area sometimes becomes very hazardous. During adverse conditions, breakers from the North Reef will cross the channel and run into the entrance. When this condition exists, it is better to standby at the entrance buoy until the Coast Guard either advises that it is safe to enter, or is there to escort boats in. An important rule at Depoe Bay: NEVER FISH BETWEEN THE ENTRANCE AND THE RED BELL BUOY!

BAR WARNING † A ROUGH BAR ADVISORY SIGN has been established 25 feet above the water, visible from the channel looking seaward, on a building on the north side of the entrance channel.

JETTIES † In general jetties continue seaward for several yards past the visible end. By all means AVOID CROSSING OVER A SUBMERGED JETTY. Navigate with extreme caution near jetties, particularly when wind and seas are setting you toward the jetty.

RANGE MARKERS † The Front Range Marker consists of a white square shape with a red vertical stripe. The Rear Range Marker is a white diamond shape with a red vertical stripe. By steering a course which keeps the two Range Markers in line, the boatman will remain within the channel.

DEPOE BAY † Was named after an Indian who lived at an old Army depot there. "Charlie's Depot's" name now graces what locals call the world's smallest harbor. But good things do come in small packages and Depoe Bay is no exception. It has about everything you could want in the way of facilities and once inside, it's a snug little port. ONE FLEW OVER THE CUCKOO'S NEST, starring Jack Nicholson, was filmed here, or at least the part where all the mentally disturbed patients go out for a day of salmon fishing.

Tillamook Bay, entrance to Garibaldi.

TILLAMOOK BAY DANGER AREAS

Use Chart 18558.

The Tillamook Bay channel lies just south of the north jetty. Boaters are urged to navigate with extreme caution as this channel changes constantly. The range markers do not necessarily mark the correct channel location.

A. BAR AREA. The entire area between the beach and the 20-foot curve is BAR AREA and breaks on the ebbing current. The water runs out from 4 to 6 knots on the average and is very strong. Boats proceeding out should stop in the channel eastward of the seaward end of the breakwater and carefully evaluate the bar. If a decision is made to cross, proceed out but DO NOT ATTEMPT TO TURN AROUND IF THE BAR IS BREAKING.

B. NORTH JETTY. About 800 yards of the outer end of the north jetty is submerged. This area and the portion of the channel just south is extremely hazardous. Avoid the sunken jetty and use caution in the channel south of it.

BAR WARNING † A ROUGH BAR ADVISORY SIGN has been established 28 feet above the water, visible from the channel looking seaward, on the structure of the Tillamook Bay Entrance Front Light.
BAR CONDITION REPORTS † Radio station KTIL (1590) kHz) gives bar condition reports twice daily and when conditions change.
JETTIES † In general, jetties continue seaward for several yards past the visible end. By all means AVOID CROSSING OVER A SUBMERGED JETTY. Navigate with extreme caution near jetties particularly when wind and sea are setting you toward the jetty.
A new jetty is being constructed on the south side of the channel, extending

out from Kincheloe Point. As the jetty progresses, the channel depth is subject to change by shifting sand. A tug towing a dock barge uses the channel frequently. Use caution and stay clear of tug and tow.

RANGE MARKERS † The Range Markers consist of an orange background with a black center.

SEASONAL FOG HORN AND LIGHT † A seasonal fog horn and light on the tip of the North Jetty will be in operation from May 1 to October 1.

TILLAMOOK BAY † Is guarded by two brawny breakwaters that stretch seaward a considerable distance. A huge "G" has been placed on the hill to the north so visitors will have no doubt where the town of Garibaldi is.

Garibaldi boasts numerous slips and complete facilities for visitors, although space can be limited during the short salmon season. Call ahead to be certain space is available. The launch ramp is in good condition.

Along the waterfront, seafood restaurants vie for customers. All serve hearty meals. Nearby is the famous Tillamook Cheese Factory, where you can watch them making the ever-popular cheddar.

NEHALEM RIVER DANGER AREAS

Use Chart 18556

The Nehalem River entrance lies between two deteriorated and partially sunken jetties. The best water is close to the South Jetty. The channel seaward of the jetties is continually shifting and local knowledge is needed to cross it safely. The range markers do not necessarily show the exact channel.

A. CRAB ROCK is located about 150 yards southwest of Jetty Fisheries Resort docks and is a hazard to small boats when it is covered by water. There is a red buoy just westward of the rock. Stay to the right of this buoy when outbound and to the left when inbound.

B. BAR AREA. The entire area between the beach and the 30-foot curve is BAR AREA and breaks on the ebbing current. The safest channel across the bar is subject to frequent change. Boats proceeding out should stop just inside the entrance and carefully evaluate the bar. If a decision is made to cross, pick the calmest area and proceed but do not attempt to turn around if the bar is breaking.

BAR CONDITION REPORTS † Radio station KTIL (1590 kHz) gives bar condition reports twice daily and when conditions change.

WASHINGTON COAST

THE WASHINGTON COAST † North of Ilwaco, at the mouth of the Columbia, has only three ports: Willapa Bay, Grays Harbor and La Push. The Coast Pilot Number 7 lists two "indifferent" anchorages; otherwise, the coast offers virtually no protection.

The same precautions outlined in the beginning of this chapter should be heeded here as well. The Washington Coast is no place for the unwary.

WILLAPA BAY † 24 miles north of the Columbia River mouth, is a haven for foreigners: Japanese oysters have found the mudflats of Willapa Bay to their liking. Several firms farm the oysters, pawning their wares to passing motorists and boating enthusiasts, or shipping them to gourmet cooks and seafood restaurants along the west coast. In March, the oysters receive their just desserts during the Willapa Bay Annual Raw Oyster-Eating Contest. The current record stands at a stomach-turning 121 LIVE oysters.

Willapa Bay has more to offer than oysters. Small marinas are found at Nahcotta, Bay Center, South Bend, Raymond and Tokeland. Some of these are run-down and facilities are limited, but you can usually find what you need.

GRAYS HARBOR, north of Willapa Bay, boasts a large, well-equipped marina called Westport. Here, complete facilities await the visitor. The marina is well protected by a massive breakwater on the channel side along with stout walls on the bay side. Westport was home to one of the fastest, best-equipped charter fleets on the west coast, but the salmon industry, which made the fleet what it was, has had severe problems of late. The fleet has been reduced to a fourth of its size and is still dwindling. Careful management may turn the tide.

WILLAPA BAY DANGER AREAS
(46°41'N., 123°45'W.)

Use Chart 18504.

Most of the water in Willapa Harbor is "DANGEROUS AREA". This is due to large amounts of shoal water, effect of ocean wind and swells and the fact that bars and shoals are constantly changing. The sea can break into a dangerous surf at any time in this area. If your boat should swamp, help may not be able to reach you because the sea breaks into shoal water.

The channel into Willapa Bay is subject to frequent change. The channel buoys may be moved or changed to reflect changes in the channel.

A. SOUTH SPIT is located on your left as you leave Willapa Bay. During ebb currents it generally breaks with swells 4 to 6 feet high. In addition to the danger of capsizing in this area, there is the added hazard of fouling your propeller on one of the many crab pot floats set by the local fishermen.

B. NORTH SPIT lies to your right as you leave Willapa Bay. This area is dangerous due to shallow water and there is generally an 8 to 10 foot swell running. During ebb currents it is usually breaking and great caution should be used while fishing near this area. The drift rate is very fast and the turbulence may cause your boat to capsize.

BAR CONDITION REPORTS † Radio station KAPA (1340 kHz) gives bar condition reports Monday through Saturday at 6:30 AM, 9 AM, 3 PM and 6 PM and on Sundays at 8 AM, noon and 4 PM.

Westport Marina, Grays Harbor, at the shore terminus of S Jetty on Point Chehalis. Full services are available.

GRAYS HARBOR DANGER AREA

Use Chart 18502

A. OUTER WHITCOMB FLATS is to your right as you leave Westport. This is a shoal area and breakers sometimes exist causing a dangerous situation.

B. THE MIDDLE GROUND is shoal water and a possible danger area where breakers may exist. Stay to the south of this area when crossing the bar.

C. THE SOUTH JETTY is submerged from the exposed end to about 4,500 feet seaward. Usually the sunken rocks are not visible and the danger of grounding is always present. In other than very calm weather conditions, breakers exist on the sunken jetty creating the possibility of capsizing and grounding. The sunken or seaward end of the jetty is marked by a red buoy #8. Always avoid the area between buoy #8 and the raised or exposed end of the south jetty. This area has been the cause of most boating mishaps in the bar in recent years.

D. THE NORTH JETTY and the area north of it are dangerous because of shallow water and breaking surf.

BAR WARNING † A ROUGH BAR ADVISORY SIGN is on the point of land NE of the Islander Motel and Restaurant. The sign faces 070° true.

BAR CONDITION REPORTS † Bar condition reports are given by the radio and TV stations listed below:

KGHO (1200 kHz) - three times daily and when conditions change.

KXRO (1320 kHz) - three times daily and when conditions change.

TV-Channel 6 - (local) Continuous.

JETTIES † In general, jetties continue seaward for several yards past the visible end. By all means AVOID

CROSSING OVER A SUBMERGED JETTY. Navigate with extreme caution near jetties particularly when wind and sea are setting you toward the jetty.

RANGE MARKERS † The Bar Range Front Marker consists of a white rectangular daymark with a red vertical stripe on a skeleton tower. The Bar Range Rear Marker consists of a white rectangular daymark with a red vertical stripe. By steering a course which keeps the two range markers in line, the boatman will remain within the channel.

QUILLAYUTE RIVER DANGER AREAS

Use Chart 18480

The river entrance lies between James Island and a rock breakwater. The depth is about ten feet but is subject to extreme variations. The usual width to the entrance is about 70 feet. While inside the entrance (north of the breakwater) stay on the jetty side of mid-channel and keep a sharp eye out for Indian fish nets especially between mid August and early June. During the summer months there is very little danger of breakers on the bar except when a storm is passing through the area. The entrance to the river is hazardous after dark and entering should not be attempted unless one is familiar with the area. The radio beacon is now located directly on James Island and emits code characteristics "JI" on 288 kHz in minute two of a six minute sequence. The radio beacon has a range of 50 miles.

A. ROCK DIKE AND NORTH SIDE OF JAMES ISLAND. A rock dike, exposed at low water, runs from the northeastern side of James Island northeastward to the beach. It should be given a wide berth because of the danger of being swept upon it by river currents. The area northward of James Island is fouled with many submergbed rocks just below the surface. This area should be avoided.

B. OUTER END OF THE BREAK-WATER. The end of the breakwater is slowly settling and the area around it is shoaling up (becoming shallower). Breakers are likely and the area should be avoided.

C. WASH ROCK. Wash Rock, 4 feet above the water at mean low tide, lies about 55 feet off the southeast corner of James Island. In calm weather it can be passed fairly close, but care must be taken not to hit it. In rough weather there is considerable turbulence around it which affects the boat.

D. AREA EAST OF BREAKWATER. This area is very shallow and breaks in almost all weather. It should be avoided.

BAR WARNING † A ROUGH BAR ADVISORY SIGN has been established 34 feet above the water, facing 016° true, on the northwest corner of the Coast Guard boathouse.

BAR CONDITION REPORT † Radio station KVAC (1490 kHz) gives bar condition reports at 6 AM, noon & 5 PM and when conditons change.

JETTIES † In general, jetties continue seaward for several yards past the visible end. By all means AVOID CROSSING OVER A SUBMERGED JETTY. Navigate with extreme caution near jetties particularly when wind and sea are setting you toward the jetty.

Nahalem River, 5 miles N of Tillamook Bay.

CAPE FLATTERY/NEAH BAY DANGER AREAS

Use Charts 18485 / 18484.

DANGER † The Coast Guard units in the Neah Bay-Cape Flattery area reported that seven sport fishermen lost their lives in this area from 1970 to 1972. This is especially dangerous to the small boat operator who is not familiar with the region. Listed below are some of the hazardous areas along with some basic characteristics of the region:

CAPE FLATTERY † A bold rocky head with cliffs 120 feet high, rises to nearly 1500 feet about 2 miles back from the beach. From southward it looks like an island because of the low land in the valley of WAATCH RIVER. Numerous rocks and reefs border the cliffs south and east of the cape. These sheer cliffs along the southern coast rise straight from the water and prevent the use of the coast for a beaching area. There is no place to put in during rough weather.

NEAH BAY † Five miles eastward of Cape Flattery is used by small craft as a harbor of refuge in foul weather. Its proximity to Cape Flattery and ease of access at any time makes anchorage very useful. It is protected from all but easterly weather.

A rubblestone breakwater extends from the western side of the bay to almost the middle of WAADAH ISLAND. Anchorage is in a 4 to 6 fathoms sandy bottom.

Since logging is one of the main industries of the region, free floating logs and submerged deadheads or sinkers are a constant source of danger in the Strait of Juan de Fuca. Deadheads or sinkers are logs which have become adrift from rafts or booms, have become water logged and float in a vertical position with one end awash, rising and falling with the tide.

A. TATOOSH ISLAND, 0.4 mile northwest-ward of Cape Flattery, is about 0.2 mile in diameter, 108 feet high, flattopped and bare. It is the largest of the group of rocks and reefs making out 0.9 NW from the cape. The passage between Tatoosh Island and the cape is dangerous and constricted by two rocks awash near its center. Although sometimes used by local small craft, it cannot be recommended. The currents are strong and treacherous.

DUNCAN ROCK and DUNTZE ROCK, the two principal dangers north-northwestward of Tatoosh Island, lie respectively, 1 mile and 1.3 miles from Tatoosh Island. Duncan Rock is small and low while Duntze Rock is covered by $3\frac{1}{4}$ fathoms. Ledges and rocks constrict the passage between Duncan Rock and Tatoosh Island to less then 0.5 miles, and strong currents and tide rips make it hazardous.

B. THE COASTLINE on the south side of the Strait of Juan de Fuca trends eastnorth eastward for four miles from Cape Flattery to Koitlah Point (the western point at the entrance to Neah Bay). The shores are rugged and provide little refuge from foul weather. The coast is lined with submerged boulders and reefs.

C. WAADAH ISLAND. 0.5 miles long, forms the northeastern side of the bay; it is 0.3 miles northward of Baadah Point and is high and wooded with a reef and foul ground extending 0.2 miles from its southwestern side.

TIDES AND CURRENTS † TIDES are the vertical rise and fall of the water. TIDAL CURRENT is the horizontal flow. As the tide rises and falls, the tidal current FLOODS (the movement toward the shore) and EBBS (the movement away from shore). When there is no horizontal movement it is SLACK WATER.

The currents, which are influenced by strong winds, can attain velocities of 2 to 4 knots. This may vary with the range of the tide.

The flood current entering the Strait of Juan de Fuca sets with considerable velocity over Duncan and Duntze Rocks. Instead of running in the channel

direction there is a continued set toward the Vancouver Island shore. The flood current velocity is greater on the northern shore of the strait than on the southern shore.

The ebb current is felt most along the southern shore and there is a decided set southward and westward, especially during the large tides. With the wind and swell against the current, a short, choppy sea is raised near the entrance to the strait.

Tide rips occur off the prominent points and in the vicinity of the banks. During periods of maximum tides these rips are heavy and can be dangerous to small craft. During periods of moderate to heavy swells breakers are formed. These swells can ground small craft on the many rocks and reefs in the area.

WEATHER † In summer, prevailing northwesterly winds draw into the strait, increasing toward evening and at times blowing a 10-knot breeze before midnight. This occurs, however, only when the winds are strong outside. In winter, southeasterly winds draw out of the strait, causing a confused cross-seas off the entrance, the heavy southwesterly swell meeting that coming out. Under these conditions small outbound vessels, especially sail, often make Neah or Clallam Bays and await more favorable weather. The weather off the entrance as a rule is exceptionally severe and wrecks are of frequent occurance.

FACILITIES

BROOKINGS

BECCO INC., P.O. Box 1220, Brookings, 607 Railroad St., OR 97415. (503) 469 - 2113. All year 8:30 AM - 5:30 PM, Mon - Fri. Electronic sales and service. Marine Operator. 24 hour dispatch.

LORING'S LIGHTHOUSE SPORTING GOOD (on Hwy. 101) Box L., 554 Chetco Ave., Brookings, OR 97415. (503) 469 - 2148. Marine hardware. Charts. Electronics. Boat and motor sales. Engine maintenance and repairs. Fishing: bait and tackle. President: Alden M. Loring.

ROUGE RIVER

ROUGE RIVER / GOLD BEACH † has been considerably improved over the years. New launch ramps and a new marina have been constructed. The bar is unpredictable, however, for it is subject to rapid shoaling. When the bar is breaking, many people stay on the river instead. Crab, salmon and steelhead fishing can be outstanding in season. Bottom fishing offshore ranks with the best anywhere along this coast.

It was the great fishing that brought Zane Grey, the famous Western novelist, to the Rogue River. The river itself called him back many times. Today the Rogue is a National Wild and Scenic River, one of only a dozen in America. Several jet boat tour operators have become established at the mouth of the Rogue. Each offers a 64 and a 104-mile round trip excursion from Gold Beach up the Rogue. The trips are well worth it as a busman's holiday for visiting yachtsmen. Overnight stays in quaint lodges can be arranged.

CHALLENGER MARINE, Box 1339, Waterffront, Gold Beach, OR 97444. (503) 247 - 4583. Aluminum boat builders. Boat and engine maintenance and repairs. Engine parts. Custom welding. Owners: J & P Shepherd.

JOT'S RESORT (at north end of Rogue River Bridge on Hwy. 101) Box J, Gold Beach, OR 97444. (503) 247 - 6676. All year. Ramp: 2-lanes, concrete. Open daylight hours. Fuel dock: gas and outboard mix, open 6 AM - 10 PM. Slips. Engine parts and repairs. Marine hardware. Snack bar. Restaurant. Overnight accommodations. Fishing: bait and tackle. Rental boats and motors. Guided river fishing and charter boats. Manager: Lou Giottonini.

PORT OF GOLD BEACH, P.O. Box 1126, Gold Beach, OR 97444. (503) 247 - 6269. All year. 6 AM - 6 PM. Picnic area, RV campsites. Ramp: 2-lane, concrete launch. Hoist cap.: 15,000 lbs. Slips and boat storage yard. Dockside electricty. Fuel dock: gas, diesel. Port Manager: H. E. Teague.

ROGUE RIVER MAIL BOAT SERVICE INC. ($\frac{1}{4}$ mile upstream from the north end of the Rogue River Bridge) Box 1165, Gold Beach, OR 97444. (503) 247 - 7033. Slips. Picnic area. Daily river trips. President: Edward G. Kammer.

COOS BAY

COOS BAY † A deep draft port, one of the few along this coast. The bar here remains passable much of the time, but when it closes out in heavy winter weather, it can be a terrible place to be. Fortunately, this seldom happens.

Charleston, just to the south of the inside of the entrance channel, is the most popular place for small boats. The inner basin is well-protected and well-maintained. Complete facilities are available here, including a marine railway capable of hauling out boats up to 70 feet long and 22 feet wide. A new fishing pier is being built which should be open this year.

September is the time for the annual Bay Area Fun Festival, or BAFF as it is called. Events range from a yacht races to the beer keg Olympics, from a clam bake to BAFF tub races -- that's what they call them. The four-day festival is full of fun activities.

CHARLESTON MARINE COMPLEX, Box 5409, Charleston, OR 97420. (503) 888 - 2548. All year. Ramp: 6-lane, concrete, open 24 hours. Fuel dock: gas, diesel and outboard mix, open 7 AM - 7 PM. Moorings. Boat maintenance, repairs, hoist, marine rail ways and 500' repair dock. Engine parts and repairs. Prop and shaft repair. Marine hardware and RV park. Charts. Groceries. Waste pumpout. Brokerage. Overnight accommodations. Showers. Restaurants. Ice. Fishing: license, bait and tackle. Rental / Charter boats. Dockside electricity. Owned/operated by Oregon Int'l Port of Coos Bay.

COOS BAY MARINE, 1201 Ocen Blvd., Coos Bay, OR 97420. (503) 888 - 2535. Boat motor and trailer sales and service. Owners: Norm Nichols and Harry Andrews Van Messner.

DICK'S SPORTHAVEN MARINA (one block off Hwy. 101) Box 2215, Harbor, OR 97415. (503) 469 - 3301. Dry storage. Ice. River guide and charter boat trips. Fishing: licenses, bait and tackle. Half-day fishing boats. Owner: Dick Pendleton.

ENGLUND MARINE SUPPLY CO., P.O. Box 387, Westport, WA 98595. (206) 268 - 9311. All year. 8 AM - 5:30 PM daily. Charts. Electronic sales. Marine hardware. Ramp: 4-lanes, paved, open 24 hours. Fishing: tackle and supplies. Skin and scuba diving. Year round commercial fishing fleet unloading daily. Manager: Barney Towle.

FLETCHER'S MARINE FUEL & SUPPLY (Charleston Boat Basin), Box 5018, Charleston, OR 97420. (503) 888 - 4711. All year. Fuel dock: gas and diesel. Open Summer, 6 AM - 8 PM; Winter, 8 AM - 5 PM. Manager: Kevin Fletcher.

GARY'S AUTO ELECTRIC, 405 Newmark Avenue, Coos Bay, OR 97420. (503) 888 - 6188. Marine alternators, generators and starters, sales and service.

GEORGE'S MARINE ELECTRONICS, 4831 Charleston Avenue, Coos Bay, OR 97420. (503) 888 - 5209. Marine electronic sales and service.

HARBOR MARINE & SUPPLY, Box 487, Westport, WA 98585. (206) 268-9116. Charts. New and used motor sales. Marine hardware. Engine maintenance, parts and repairs. Prop and shaft repairs. Electronic and instrument repairs. Fishing: tackle. Owner: Virgil Smith.

KNUTSON DIESEL & MACHINE, 580 North Front Street, Coos Bay, OR 97420. (503) 267 - 2016. Boat maintenance and repairs. Engine repairs. Dockside electricity: (3). Owner: Harold and John Knutson.

ROGER SPAUGH ELECTRONICS (in shipyard, one block east of Hwy. 101) 912 N. Front Street, Coos Bay, OR 97420. (503) 267 - 6029. Marine electronics sales and service. Owner: Roger Spaugh.

WEST COAST PROPELLER SERVICE, 5135 Troller Road, Coos Bay, OR 97420. (503) 888 - 5723. Prop and shaft repairs and replacements. Columbian and MerCruiser Propellers. Machine shop. Welding and heli-arc. Owner: John R. Kalander.

WRIGHT'S ELECTRIC MOTOR REPAIRS, 1023 S. Broadway, Coos Bay, OR 97420. (503) 269 - 5343. Marine electrical devices. Sales and service. 24-hour emergency service. Owner: John N. Wright, Jr.

UMPQUA RIVER AREA

UMPQUA RIVER / WINCHESTER BAY / SALMON HARBOR † (43°41'N., 124°11'W.) The Umpqua (pronounced "um-kwah") River mouth has been tamed somewhat by two long jetties sprawling out to sea. Nonetheless, it commands respect. Conditions can change swiftly there, so up-to-date local knowledge is a must.

Along the river mouth lies Winchester Bay and Salmon Harbor, two marinas side by side, each quite handy to the channel. Facilities are not as complete here as at Coos Bay, but you can still find most of what you need.

Farther upriver is Reedsport, a deep draft lumber port noted for its Storm Festival held in February. Activities include sandcastle building contests, driftwood and glass ball hunting and a crab relay race: live Dungeness crabs are passed from runner to runner in lieu of the tamer batons.

NORTH LAKE RESORT & MARINA (about 1 mile nórth of Lakeside) 2090 North Lake Road, Lakeside, OR 97449. (503) 759 - 3515. All year. Ramp: 1-lane, concrete. Fuel dock: gas and outboard mix. LP refills. Slips. Dry storage. Groceries. Snack Bar. Fishing: bait and tackle. Rental motorboats. Camping.

REEDSPORT MACHINE & FABRICATIONS (at Small Boat Basin) Box 508, Reedsport, OR 97467. (503) 271 - 2466. Travelift cap.: 60 tons. Custom aluminum boats. Boat and engine maintenance and repairs. Prop and shaft repair. Owner: Oley Nelson.

SALMON HARBOR (Port of Umpqua) Box 7, Whinchester Bay, OR 97467. (503) 271 - 3407. Ramp: 2-lanes, concrete. Open daylight hours. Hoist cap.: 8 tons. Fuel dock: gas, diesel, outboard mix and LP refills, open 5 AM - 8 PM. Guest dock and slips. Hull and engine maintenance, parts and repairs. Boat and motor sales. Marine hardware. Electronic sales and service. Instrument repairs. Overnight accommodations. Trailer and campsites. Picnic area. Restaurant. Groceries. Ice. Laundry. Fishing: bait and tackle. Rental tackle. Charter boats. Dockside electricity: (5).

SIUSLAW RIVER AREA
(43°58'N., 124°07'W.)

SIUSLAW RIVER AREA † The Suislaw (pronounced "sigh-yew-slaw") River bar has been improved recently. The two jetties are twice as long as they once were. Be sure to check with the Coast Guard for the latest conditions on the bar. However, it is nothing to fool with even though it has been greatly improved. Inside the entrance, privately owned slips can be rented at Florence. Check locally for details. The Oregon Dunes National Recreation Area provides a pleasant diversion for visitors. Lovely dunes, brushed clean every afternoon by the northwesterlies, extend along some 40 miles of coast. Pines flourish among the dunes, astounding travelers from the south.

C & D FISHING DOCK & TRAILER PARK (on Siuslaw River 10 miles east of Florence) 9634 Hwy. 126, Florence, OR 97439. (503) 268 - 9950. Hoist cap.: 5 tons, open daylight hours. Fuel dock open daylight hours. Moorings. Snack bar. Ice. Overnight accommodations. Trailer sites. Showers. Camping. Fishing: bait and tackle. Rental boats, motors. Manager: Nlta Brooks.

DARLINGS RESORT, 4879 Darlings Loop, Florence, OR 97439. (503) 997 - 2841. (on Siltcoos Lake, ½ mile east of Hwy 101 on North Beach Rd.) Ramp: 2-lanes, concrete. All year, 7 AM - 12 AM. Gas. Overnight guest dock, moorings. RV campsites. Groceries. Ice. Deli. Tavern. Fishing: license, bait, tackle. Trout, large mouthed bass, perch, salmon. Rental boats. Water skiing. Open for year round fishing, large mouth bass tournaments. ½ mile east of Oregon Dunes. Close to ocean. Tent camping also available. Owner: Dusty and Sandra Ambrosio.

PORT OF SIUSLAW RIVER MARINA (1st and Harbor St's) Box 1220, Florence, OR 97439. (503) 997 - 3040. Ramp: 2-lanes, concrete. Open 24 hours. Slips. Guest dock. Open and covered dry storage. Engine maintenance, parts and repairs. Marine hardware. Groceries. Ice. RV campsites. Picnic area. Laundry. Fishing: licenses, bait and tackle.

SILTCOOS LAKE RESORT (2 blocks off Hwy. 101 at Westlake Junction, 6 miles south of Florence), Box 36, Westlake, OR 97439. (503) 997 - 3741. All year. Ramp: 1 - lane, concrete. Slips. Overnight accommodations. Showers. Trailer sites. Motel, kitchen units. Fishing: bait and tackle. Boat and motor rentals. Owners: R. & C. Beckmann.

SIUSLAW MARINA (on the Siuslaw River, 3 miles east of Florence on Hwy. 126 at Cushman) 06516 Hwy. 126, Florence, OR 97439. (503) 997 - 3254. All year. Hoist cap.: 2 tons. Marine railway open 24 hours. Cap.: 50 tons. Slips. Guest dock. Boat and engine maintenance and repairs; motor sales. Electronics. Marine hardware. Welding, sandblasting and painting. Salvage diving. Commercial gear. Fishing: rental boats, motor and tackle. Dockside electricity: (3). Owner: Kirby Hansen.

ALSEA

DRIFT CREEK LANDING ($3\frac{1}{2}$ miles east of Waldport on Hwy. 34), 3851 Alsea Hwy., Waldport, OR 97394. (503) 563 - 3610. All year. Ramp: 1 - lane, paved. Fuel dock: gas and outboard mix. Propane. Moorings. Snack bar. Overnight accommodations. Trailer sites. Showers. Laundry. Fishing: licenses, bait and tackle. Rental boats, motors and tackle. Owners: Chet and Dee Waldo.

KOZY KOVE MARINA (on the Alsea River on Hwy. 34, 9 miles east of Hwy. 101) 9464 Alsea Highway, Tidewater, OR 97390. (503) 528-3251. Ramp: 2-lanes, paved. Fuel dock: gas, outboard mix ,propane. Dry storage. Cafe. Groceries. Marine hardware. Ice. Showers. Camping. RV sites. Fishing: bait & tackle. Floats, boats, motors. Restaurant, lounge. Dockside electricity.

OAKLAND'S (4 miles east of Waldport on Hwy. 34) 4173 Alsea Hwy., Waldport, OR 97394. (503) 563 - 2122. Open all year: 7 AM - 4 PM. Fuel dock. Covered slips and moorings. Marine supplies and hardware. Snack bar. Overnight accommodations. Showers. Fishing: licenses, bait and tackle. Rental boats. Managers: Mark & Laura Walters.

PORT OF ALSEA, P.O. Box 1060, Waldport, OR 97394. (503) 563 - 3872. (one mile east of Hwy 101) Picnic area & restaurant. Ramp: 2-lancs, concrete. 24 hours. Moorings. Outboard motor rentals. Engine maintenance, repairs and parts. Prop and shaft repairs. Fishing: bait and tackle. Perch, salmon, trout, crabbing. Water skiing. New crabbing and moorage dock facility. Superb crabbing. Good windsurfing. Good fishing. Several nearby RV parks. Manager: Michael Taylor.

TAYLORS LANDING, 7164 Alsea Hwy, Waldport, OR 97394. (503) 528 - 3388. All year. Restaurant. Laundry. Marine hardware. Picnic area. RV campsite. Hoist. Guest dock with electricity. Slips and moorings. Boat storage. Fuel: gas and mix. Fishing: bait and tackle. Rental boats. Owner: J. & P. Petersen.

YAQUINA BAY
(44°38'N., 124°03'W.)

YAQUINA BAY / NEWPORT † Yaquina (pronounced "yuh-keen-uh") Bay is a broad, well-sheltered bay with a wide entrance. The north jetty extends all the way out to Yaquina Reef, transforming a hazard into an asset.

Across the bay from Newport is the new South Beach Marina, a handsomely set-up facility with all the amenities. Here, the Swiftsure, a retired lightship that saw many years of service off the Swiftsure Banks of Washington, now reposes as a restaurant. The cuisine is excellent, the service friendly. Also on the south bank is the Marine Science Center with its colorful displays of living marine life.

The north bank is host to an older marina, many shops and restaurants, a few fish processing plants, and the Embarcadero, a resort hotel and marina. Sailing is popular on Yaquina Bay because it is large and well-protected from the boisterous seas offshore. A shopping mall is under construction along the south bank, along with a 200-unit hotel and restaurant.

B & B BOATBUILDING & WELDING, Port Dock #7, Newport, OR 97365. (503) 265 - 2057. Boat construction and repair. Welding. Marine hydraulic repair.

B & F MARINE ELECTRONICS, 134 SW Bay Blvd., Newport, OR 97365. (503) 265 - 8839. Marine electronic sales and service.

CURRY MARINE, 396 SE Benson Rd, Newport, OR 97365. (503) 265 - 7955. All year. New and used boat and motor sales. Elecronics. Marine hardware. Marine surveyor. Generators. Pumps. Engine repairs and parts. Owner: John Curry.

EMBARCADERO MARINA (from Hwy. 101 to Hwy. 20 east to stoplight at foot of Moore Road) 1000 S.E. Bay Blvd., Newport, OR 97365. (503) 265 - 5435. Fuel dock: gas and diesel. Open Summer: 5 AM - 9 PM; Winter: daylight hours. Slips. Guest dock. Marine hardware. Groceries. Picnic area. Swimming pool. Restaurant. Overnight accommodations. Fishing: licenses, bait and tackle. Rental boats and tackle. Deep-sea charters. Dockside electricity: (4a) (7). Marina Manager: Rhonda Hamstreet.

FAIR LINE MARINE INC., Yaquina Bay Road, Newport, OR 97365. (503) 265 - 7819. Full service repair facilities. Marine ways. Haulouts to 500 tons.

NEWPORT MARINA AT SOUTH BEACH, 600 SE Bay Blvd., Newport, OR 97365. (503) 867 - 3321. Summer hours: 5 AM - 9 PM. Winter hours: 8 AM - 5 PM. Groceries. Ice. Laundry. Picnic area. RV campsites. Snack bar. Waste disposal pumpout. Ramp: 4-lane. Hoist. Overnight docks with electricity. Slips. Fuel dock: gas and diesel. Fishing: licenses, bait, tackle, charter boats. Operations Manager: Russ Crabtree.

RIVERBEND MOORAGE, 5262 Yaquina Bay Road, Newport, OR 97365. (503) 265 - 9243. Travelift cap.: 70 tons. Slips. Guest dock. Open and covered dry storage. Fuel dock: gas only. Boat and engine maintenance, parts and repairs. Marine hardware. New and used boats and motors. Owner: Schlesser Properties, Inc.

SAWYER'S LANDING (3 miles upriver from Newport Port docks) Yaquina Bay Road, Newport, OR 97365. (503) 265 - 3907. Monorail launch to 23 feet. Guest moorage. Groceries. Parking. Fishing: bait and tackle. Rental boats.

SCHIEWE MARINE SUPPLY, 103 S.E. Bay Blvd., Newport, OR 97365. (503) 265 - 7382. Marine hardware. Charts. Foulweather gear.

YAQUINA BAY MARINE SUPPLY, 424 S.W. Bay Blvd., Newport OR, 97365. (503) 265 - 9275. Marine hardware. Electronic sales/service. Instrument repairs. Foulweather gear.

YAQUINA MARINA (5 miles upriver from the Newport Port Docks) 4504 Yaquina Bay Road, Newport, OR 97365. (503) 265 - 2941. Guest dock. Gas and propane. Restaurant.

DEPOE BAY

DEPOE BAY CITY MARINA, City Hall, Depoe Bay, OR 97341. (503) 765-2363. Ramp. Fuel dock. Guest moorage. Charter boats. Stores & park nearby. Parking. dockside electricity.

IMPERIAL MARINE SERVICE, Box 363, Depoe Bay, OR 97341. (503) 765 - 2535. Open year round. Hoist cap.: 3 tons. Open 6 AM - 6 PM. Fuel dock: gas, diesel and outboard mix. Open 6 AM - 6 PM. Boat maintenance and repairs. Marine hardware. Snack bar. Fishing: bait and tackle. Manager: W.W. Wahl.

SUNSET TRUE VALUE, 234 S.E. Hwy. 101, Box 307, Depoe Bay, OR 97341. (503) 765 - 2534. Marine hardware. Charts. Fishing: bait and tackle. Manager: Tom MacDougall.

SILETZ BAY

SILETZ BAY / LINCOLN CITY † A haven for outboard enthusiasts, because the bay is too shallow to allow deep draft vessels. Like Alsea Bay, it has no jetties at its mouth. Lincoln City is actually a conglomeration of five little towns along the bay.

PACIFIC CITY is host to well-known fleet of dories. Just south of Cape Kiwanda, which is pictured on nearly every postcard rack of the Oregon Coast, a protected beach is found. Here the dorymen launch their boats through the surf, fishing for bottom fish, crabs or salmon as the season dictates. Watching them dashing in and out of the breakers is a treat for all boating enthusiasts. A few of the dorymen are licensed skippers and will take you fishing with them for a modest fee.

CAPE LOOKOUT is the most contrary feature of the Oregon coast. Here a rugged promontory stretches due west out to sea from the north-south coast. Behind the protective arm of this cape is a fair anchorage in about 35 to 50 feet of water. Closer to shore, the bottom becomes rockstrewn and dangerous.

NETARTS BAY is another quiet body of water with virtually no way of reaching the sea. Like Alsea and Siletz bays, it is popular with clammers, anglers and outboarders.

SILETZ MOORAGE (on the Siletz River, 2 miles south of Lincoln City on Hwy. 229) 82 Siletz Highway, Lincoln City, OR 97367. (503) 996 - 3671. Open year round. Ramp: asphalt. Open: Summer, 6 AM - 5 PM; Winter, 7 AM - 5 PM. Fuel dock: gas and outboard mix. Engine parts and repairs. Marine hardware. Fishing: bait and tackle. Rental boats, motors and tackle.

TILLAMOOK BAY

GARIBALDI AUTO PARTS & MACHINE SHOP, P.O. Box 288, Garibaldi, OR 97118. (503) 322 - 3512. (on Hwy 101 in Garibaldi) All Year, 8 AM - 5:30 PM weekdays. 8:30 AM - 4 PM Sat. No Sunday. Electronic sales. Engine maintenance and repairs. Engine parts. Full service Napa parts jobber. Machine shop and Radio Shack dealer within walking distance of the port docking facilities. Owner: Lowrie A. St. James.

GARIBALDI MARINA, Box 497, Garibaldi, OR 97118. (503) 322 - 3312. Ramp. Guest Moorage.

GREG'S MARINE SERVICE, INC., Drawer B, Old Mill Marina, Garibaldi, OR 97118. (503) 322 - 3643. (on 3rd St. off Hwy 101 in Garibaldi) Boat and motor sales. Marine hardware. Minor hull maintenance and repairs. Engine maintenance, repairs and parts. All year. Owners: Greg and Deb Iseri.

OLD MILL MARINA RESORT, INC., 210 So. 3rd Street, Garibaldi, OR 97118. (503) 322 - 3243. All year. Ramp. Guest dock. Dry storage. Showers. Fishing: bait and tackle.

PACIFIC PINES MARINA (on Tillamook River near bay), 64 Netarts Hwy. West, Netarts, OR 97143. (503) 842 - 3553. Ramp. Fuel dock. Guest moorage. Outboard engine repairs. Guide service.

PORT OF BAY CITY, (Garibaldi Boat Basin). (503) 322 - 3292. Guest moorage. Port Manager: Henry DuPrey.

NEHALEM BAY

NEHALEM RIVER has its jetties, but the entrance is quite shallow and breaks almost all the time. It is not recommended for seafarers, but the river itself is fun for a small boat or canoe in moderate condition.

SMUGGLER COVE is the last natural anchorage along the Oregon coast. After this comes the mouth of the Columbia, with its great upriver seaports. (See Chapters 2, 3 and 4 for detailed information on Columbia River ports).

Smuggler Cove lies beneath the south flank of Cape Falcon. The best area to anchor is in 25 to 35 feet of water. Rocks rise precipitously from the sea floor 150 feet down near the entrance, so newcomers must be extremely careful in approaching Smuggler Cove.

BRIGHTON MOORAGE, 29200 Hwy. 101 North, Rockaway, OR 97136. (503) 368 - 5745. Slips. Fuel dock: gas. Fishing: bait and tackle. Rental boats.

JETTY FISHERY, 27550 Hwy 101 N., Rockaway Beach, OR 97136. (503) 368 - 5746. Boats and motors. Groceries.

The entrance to Siletz Bay, 15 miles N of Yaquina Head, is limited to shallow draft vessels of 4 or 5 feet.

Ice. Marine hardware. Picnic area. Snack Bar. Ramp. Moorings. Boat Storage. Fuel: gas and mix. RV campsite. Fishing: licenses, bait and tackle. Boat rentals. Water skiing. Owner: Jean and Shirley Laviolette.

MILBURN'S MOORAGE (on North Fork Road from Hehalem), 37395 No. Fork Road, Nehalem, OR 97131. (503) 358 - 5577. Open year round. RV Park and moorage. Fuel dock: gas only.

NEHALEM PUBLIC DOCKS, docks located at the ends of "H" Street and Tohl Street on the river. Nearby ramp located $\frac{1}{4}$ mile S of Nehalem on Hwy. 101.

WHEELER MARINA Box 72, Wheeler, OR 97147. (503) 368 - 5780. 6:30 - DARK. New and used boat and motor sales. Marine hardware. Ramp: 24 hours. Overnight guest dock. Slips and moorings. Boat and engine parts and repairs. Fuel dock: gas and mix. Rental boats. Boat storage, covered. Fishing: licenses, bait and tackle. Salmon, trout, bottom fish, crabbing and clamming. Great windsurfing. One of the best crabbing bays in Oregon. Outstanding fall runs of Chincok and Coho Salmon. Owners: James and Marjorie Neilson.

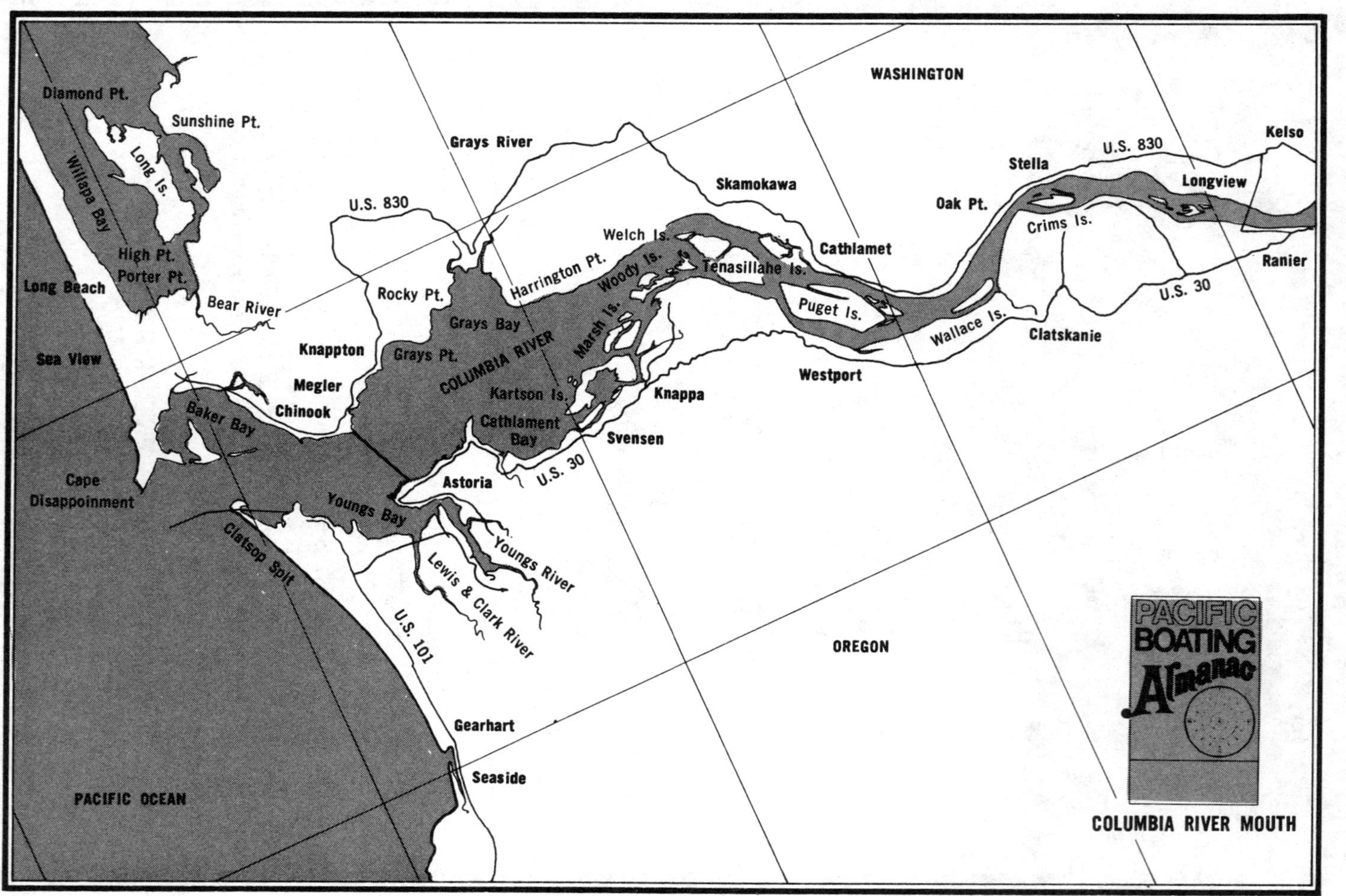

WASHINGTON
OREGON
PACIFIC OCEAN
Diamond Pt.
Sunshine Pt.
Willapa Bay
Long Is.
High Pt.
Porter Pt.
Long Beach
Sea View
Cape Disappoinment
Bear River
Rocky Pt.
Knappton
Megler
Chinook
Baker Bay
Clatsop Spit
Grays River
U.S. 830
Grays Bay
Grays Pt.
COLUMBIA RIVER
Harrington Pt.
Welch Is.
Woody Is.
Marsh Is.
Kartson Is.
Cathlament Bay
Astoria
Youngs Bay
Youngs River
Lewis & Clark River
U.S. 101
U.S. 30
Svensen
Knappa
Tenasillahe Is.
Puget Is.
Cathlamet
Skamokawa
Westport
Wallace Is.
Clatskanie
Oak Pt.
Crims Is.
Stella
U.S. 830
U.S. 30
Longview
Kelso
Ranier
Gearhart
Seaside
PACIFIC
BOATING
Almanac
COLUMBIA RIVER MOUTH

2
COLUMBIA RIVER ENTRANCE TO ASTORIA

DISTANCES ON COLUMBIA RIVER SYSTEM

Figure at interaction of columns opposite ports in question is the nautical/statute mileage between the two. Example: Astoria, Oreg. , is 85 nautical miles (98 statute miles) from Portland, Oreg.

Ports (in chart order), with coordinates:

- Columbia River Mouth, 46°14. 8'N., 124°05. 5'W.
- Ilwaco, Wash. 46°18. 3'N., 124°02. 2'W.
- Warrenton, Oreg. 46°10. 1'N., 123°55. 0'W.
- Astoria, Oreg. 46°11. 7'N., 123°50. 0'W.
- Longview, Wash. 46°06. 3'N., 122°57. 7'W.
- St. Helens, Oreg. 45°51. 7'N., 122°47. 6'W.
- Vancouver, Wash. 45°37. 6'N., 122°41. 3'W.
- Bonneville Lock & Dam 45°38. 3'N., 121°56. 8'W.
- Hood River (town), Oreg. 45°43. 0'N., 121°30. 0'W.
- The Dalles Lock & Dam 45°36. 9'N., 121°08. 3'W.
- John Day Lock & Dam 45°42. 9'N., 120°41. 5'W.
- Arlington, Oreg. 45°43. 6'N., 120°12. 2'W.
- Umatilla, Oreg. 45°55. 4'N., 119°20. 5'W.
- McNary Lock & Dam 45°56. 4'N., 119°17. 9'W.
- Port of Walla Walla, Wash. 46°06. 0'N., 118°55. 3'W.
- Pasco, Wash. 46°13. 2'N., 119°05. 9'W.
- Richland, Wash. 46°16. 5'N., 119°16. 1'W.
- Portland, Oreg. 45°33. 0'N., 122°41. 7'W.
- Oregon City, Oreg. 45°21. 5'N., 122°36. 5'W.
- Salem, Oreg. 44°56. 2'N., 123°03. 1'W.
- Albany, Oreg. 44°38. 3'N., 123°06. 2'W.
- Corvallis, Oreg. 44°34. 0'N., 123°15. 3'W.
- Harrisburg, Oreg. 44°16. 0'N., 123°10. 2'W.
- Ice Harbor Dam, Wash. 46°15. 1'N., 118°52. 7'W.
- Central Ferry, Wash. 46°37. 6'N., 117°46. 6'W.
- Lewiston, Idaho 46°25. 1'N., 116°59. 9'W.
- Johnson Bar Landing, Idaho 45°27. 6'N., 116°33. 8'W.

River labels on chart: Columbia River; Willamette River; Snake River. Axis labels: Nautical Miles (lower left); Statute Miles (right).

Upper (statute miles) portion of the chart, rows as printed top to bottom:

7	13	14	67	86	106	145	170	191	216	242	289	292	318	328	337	112	127	186	221	234	265	335	407	465	556
14	15	68	87	107	146	171	192	217	243	290	292	318	329	338	113	128	188	222	234	265	336	409	465	557	
5	58	77	97	136	161	183	207	232	261	283	308	319	328	102	119	177	212	224	255	326	398	456	547		
52	71	92	131	157	177	203	228	275	277	303	314	323	98	113	171	207	219	250	320	394	450	541			
20	39	78	104	124	150	175	222	224	250	261	270	45	60	120	154	166	197	268	341	397	489				
23	63	87	109	135	159	207	209	235	246	255	29	45	104	139	151	182	252	325	382	473					
40	64	86	110	136	184	186	212	222	232	15	30	89	124	136	167	229	302	359	450						
25	46	71	97	144	146	171	183	192	54	70	129	163	176	207	189	262	319	410							
21	46	71	119	122	147	158	167	79	94	154	189	200	231	165	237	295	386								
25	51	98	100	125	137	146	100	116	175	211	222	253	143	216	273	364									
25	72	75	100	112	121	125	142	200	235	247	278	117	191	247	338										
48	51	76	86	96	150	166	224	260	272	303	93	166	223	314											
2	28	39	48	198	214	273	308	320	351	45	119	175	266												
25	37	46	200	216	275	311	322	353	43	116	173	264													
12	21	226	242	300	336	348	379	17	91	147	238														
9	237	253	312	346	359	390	14	86	144	235															
246	262	321	356	368	399	23	96	153	244																
16	75	110	122	153	243	316	373	464																	
59	94	106	137	259	331	389	480																		
36	47	78	318	391	448	539																			
12	43	353	426	483	574																				
31	365	437	495	586																					
396	466	526	617																						
72	130	221																							
58	148																								
91																									

Lower (nautical miles) portion of the chart, rows as printed top to bottom:

6																									
11	12																								
12	13	4																							
58	59	50	45																						
75	76	67	62	17																					
92	93	84	80	34	20																				
126	127	118	114	68	55	35																			
148	149	140	136	90	76	56	22																		
166	167	159	154	108	95	75	40	18																	
188	189	180	176	130	117	96	62	40	22																
210	211	202	198	152	138	118	84	62	44	22															
251	252	244	239	193	180	160	125	103	85	63	42														
254	254	246	241	195	182	162	127	106	87	65	44	2													
276	276	268	263	217	204	184	149	128	109	87	66	24	22												
285	286	277	273	227	214	193	159	137	119	97	75	34	32	10											
293	294	285	281	235	222	202	167	145	127	105	83	42	40	18	8										
97	98	89	85	39	25	13	47	69	87	109	130	172	174	196	206	214									
110	111	103	98	52	39	26	61	82	101	123	144	186	188	210	220	228	14								
162	163	154	149	104	90	77	112	134	152	174	195	237	239	261	271	279	65	51							
192	193	184	180	134	121	108	142	164	183	204	226	268	270	292	301	309	96	82	31						
203	203	195	190	144	131	118	153	174	193	215	236	278	280	302	312	320	106	92	41	10					
230	230	222	217	171	158	145	180	201	220	242	263	305	307	329	339	347	133	119	68	37	27.				
291	292	283	278	233	219	199	164	143	124	102	81	39	37	15	12	20	211	225	276	307	317	344			
354	355	346	342	296	282	262	228	206	188	166	144	103	101	79	75	83	275	288	340	370	380	407	63		
404	404	396	391	345	332	312	277	256	237	215	194	152	150	128	125	133	324	338	389	420	430	457	113	50	
483	484	475	470	425	411	391	356	335	316	294	273	231	229	207	204	212	403	417	468	499	509	536	192	129	79

COLUMBIA RIVER DANGER AREAS

A.

CHINOOK SPUR, UPPER LOWER AND MIDDLE SAND ISLAND SPURS are built on two rows of staggered pilings. Currents flowing through these pilings attain a velocity of up to 5 knots. A boat which becomes disabled or is maneuvered in such a way as to let it come in contact with any of these spurs is almost sure to suffer damage. Even large boats have been capsized in these areas. Give these spurs a wide berth and never get close to them on the up current side.

B.

CLATSOP SPIT is the most unpredictable area on the river entrance. During flood currents and slacks it may be calm with only a gentle swell breaking far in on the spit. Yet 5 or 10 minutes later, when the current has started to ebb, it can become a roaring monster with breakers extending far out toward the channel. You should remain north of the red buoys in this area, particularly just before or during the ebb. The South Jetty has a section broken away on the outer end. The broken section is under water close to the surface. Boats should use extra caution in the area from the visible tip of the Jetty out to Buoy 2SJ. Peacock and Clatsop Spits are called the graveyard of the Pacific for good reason.

C.

JETTY A, which is southwest of Cape Disappointment, presents a particular danger when the current is ebbing. Water, flowing out of the river, is deflected by the jetty and frequently the current reaches 8 knots. This often causes waves up to 8 feet high. Boats proceeding into Baker Bay West Channel make very little speed against the swift current and are exposed to the rough water or surf on rough days for long periods of time. The shallow, sandy area should be avoided by small craft when heavy seas are running because of the surf which breaks on the beach.

D.

PEACOCK SPIT. Breakers are heavy in any type of current. Sports craft leaving the river should never be on the north side of the black buoys. When rounding Peacock Spit, give the breakers at least a half-mile clearing. Many times unusually large swells coming in from the sea suddenly commence breaking $\frac{1}{4}$ to $\frac{1}{2}$ mile outside the usual break on the end of the north jetty.

E.

MIDDLE GROUND. This is a more shallow area between the North Jetty and main Ship Channel that is subject to breaking seas when swells as small as 4 feet are present and conditions can change in minutes with tidal current changes.

BAR CONDITION REPORTS † Radio stations KVAS (1230 kHz) and KAST (1370 kHz) give bar condition reports 15 minutes before and after the hour.

NOTE: The nautical charts covering the Columbia, Willamette, and Snake Rivers show statue mile designations. However, the distances given in the text for these waterways are the nautical miles above their respective mouths with the statue mile equivalents shown in parentheses. Unless otherwise indicated, all other distances are given in nautical miles.

MILE 0.0 on the Columbian River, is at the junction of the Main Channel Range and a line joining the outer ends of the jetties. The distance to the mouth of the Columbia River from a position 0.5 mile W of the Columbia River Approach Lighted Horn Buoy CR is 5.8 (6.6) miles.

CAUTION † The Volcanic eruptions of Mount Saint Helens in mid-1980 caused extensive flooding with resulting heavy siltation in the lower Columbia River. Large amounts of mud, logs and other debris entered Columbia River from Cowlitz River, just E of Longview at Mile 59 (68). In late 1980, dredging was done in the aforementioned area, however, mariners are advised to use caution in the Columbia River and its tributaries.

Rice Island, Miller Sands, Jim Crow Sands and Cottonwood Islands are used for dredging disposal sites. Elevations of these islands constantly change, as well as the overall shape and dimensions.

CHART 18003, 18007 † COLUMBIA RIVER rises in British Columbia, Canada, through which it flows for some 370 (425) miles before entering the continental United States in NE Washington. Thence it flows S to its junction with Snake River, from which it curves W and forms the boundary between the States of Washington and Oregon for the remainder of its course to the Pacific Ocean. Its entrance is 548 miles N of San Francisco and 145 miles S of the Strait of Juan de Fuca. The length of the river is 647 (745) miles in the United States. Between the Cascade Mountains, the river flows through a canyon averaging about 5 miles wide between high cliffs on each side; of this width, the river occupies about 1 mile, the rest being marsh, low islands, and lowlands, Near the mouth, the river becomes wider, and in some places is 5 miles across.

Columbia and Willamette Rivers are navigable by deep-draft vessels to Vancouver, Wash., and Portland, Oreg. Barges navigate the Columbia River to Pasco and Kennewick, Wash., 268 (329) miles above the mouth.

Navigation on the tributary Snake River, which joins the Columbia at Pasco, is possible to Lewiston, Idaho. The hydro-electric powerplants at the dams on the Columbia provide the major supply of electricity for the entire Northwest.

There are numerous settlements and landings, but Astoria, Oreg.; Longview, Wash.; Vancouver, Wash.; and Portland, Oreg.; are the principal shipping points. The distances above the mouth of the Columbia River to these ports are, respectively, 12 (14) miles, 58 (66) miles, 92 (106) miles, and 97 (112) miles; Portland is on the Willamette River 9 (10.5) miles above its junction with the Columbia. A U.S. or Interstate Highway closely follows the S side of the Columbia River from Astoria to Portland to Pasco, Wash., and a Washington State Highway extends along or near the N bank from Skamokawa to Richland, Wash.

PROMINENT FEATURES † COLUMBIA RIVER APPROACH LIGHTED HORN BUOY CR (46°11.1'N., 124°11.0' W.), Replacing Columbia lightship, is a large navigational buoy (LNB) about 5.3 miles SW of the entrance to Columbia River. The buoy shows a light 42 feet above the water. A fog signal, radiobeacon, and radar beacon (Racon) are at the buoy.

MOUNT SAINT HELENS, nearly 8,500 feet high with a truncated-cone shape, is about 75 miles E of the entrance to the river. On a clear day it is visible when looking up the valley from seaward. MOUNT HOOD and MOUNT ADAMS are lofty snow-covered peaks, which are also visible from parts of the Columbia River on a clear day.

In 1980, several volcanic eruptions occurred from Mt. St. Helens. Mt. St. Helens' eruptions were the first in the continental U.S. since the volcanic eruption of Mt. Lassen in northern California in 1915; both volcanoes are part of the Cascade Range.

CHART 18521 † CLATSOP SPIT, on the S side of the entrance, is a low sand beach, extending about 2.5 miles NW from Point Adams. There is a tendency for the shoal N of the spit to build up to the NW because of spring freshets and NW storms; vessels are cautioned to keep informed about conditions at the spit. A Coast Guard lookout tower, on the NW end of the spit, is prominent from the entrance.

POINT ADAMS, just inside Clatsop Spit, is a low sandy point covered with spruce and undergrowth to the edge of the sand beach and low dunes. The point usually shows well from seaward, particularly as it is hazy inside.

CAPE DISAPPOINTMENT, the rugged N point at the Columbia River entrance , is the first major headland along the 20 miles of sand beach N from Tillamook Head. It comprises a group of rounding hills covering an area 2.5 miles long and 1 mile wide, divided by a narrow valley extending NNW. The seaward faces of these hills are precipitous cliffs with jagged, rocky points and small strips of sand beach. CAPE DISAPPOINTMENT LIGHT

(46°16.6'N., 124°03.1'W.), 220 feet above the water, is shown from a 53-foot white conical tower with white horizontal band at the top and bottom, and black horizontal band in the middle, on the S point of the cape; a radiobeacon is at the station. A Coast Guard station is at Fort Canby on the E side of the cape.

STORM WARNING SIGNALS ARE DISPLAYED. (See chart.)

From the S, Cape Disppointment shows as three low knobs, separated by low flat ridges. North Head Light shows on the W slope of the W knob. From the W, the cape is not prominent, but it stands out clearly when there is fog, haze, or smoke inside the cape. From NW, the cape appears as a flat island with a slight depression in the center and a timbered knob at each end. From this direction, a low, flat hill with gently sloping sides between the cape and high ridges E appears as an island from a distance.

McKENZIE HEAD, 0.8 mile NW of Cape Disppointment Light, is 190 feet high and nearly round. On its seaward face it is covered with grass and fern; bare of trees. On its E face it is heavily wooded with spruce.

NORTH HEAD, the extreme W point of the cape, is 270 feet high, with a very jagged, precipitous cliff, backed by a narrow grassy strip; the higher ground behind it is covered with trees. NORTH HEAD LIGHT (46° 18.0'N., 124°04.6'W.), 194 feet above the water, is shown from a 65-foot white conical tower on the W point.

The entrance to Columbia River is marked by two jetties. The S jetty extends 2.7 miles seaward from the NW end of Clatsop Spit; the westernmost mile of the jetty is submerged. The N jetty extends 800 yards seaward from the shoreline on the N side of the entrance. Lighted ranges, lights, buoys, and daybeacons mark the channels.

CHANNELS † Federal project depths in the Columbia River are 48 feet over the bar, thence 40 feet to the Broadway Bridge at Portland, Oregon; 40 feet from the confluence of the Willamette and Columbia Rivers through the lower turning basin at Vancouver; and thence 35 feet through the upper turning basin at Vancouver. (See Notice to Mariners and latest editions of charts for controlling depths.) Additional information can be obtained from the Corps of Engineers, Portland, Oregon.

Above Vancouver the Federal project depth is 27 feet for about 75 (86) miles to The Dalles, thence 14 feet for about 87 (100) miles to McNary Dam. The Federal project also provides for a 15-foot alternate barge channel which extends SE from the S side of the upper turning basin at Vancouver and connects with the 27-foot channel about 1 (1.2) mile upriver. Controlling depths may be considerably less than project depths. The depths over the lower sills of the locks at The Dalles, John Day, and McNary Dams may be the controlling depth for this stretch of the river; the least sill depth (at McNary Dam) will usually exceed 12 feet at normal pool level. In the pool above McNary Dam to Pasco and Kennewick, depths range from 14 to 115 feet. Navigation on the Snake River is possible to Lewiston, Idaho. (See Notice to Mariners and latest editions of charts for controlling depths.) Additional information can be obtained from the Corps of Engineers, Portland, Oregon and Walla Walla, Washington.

DEPTHS † Minimum depths are given at mean lower low water from the entrance to the Columbia River to Harrington Point, thence at Columbia River Datum to Bonneville Dam on the Columbia River, and Willamette Falls Locks at Oregon City on the Willamette River. COLUMBIA RIVER DATUM is the mean lower low water during lowest river stages. The staff gage at the Columbia River Pilots' Office, at the foot of 14th Street at Astoria, Oregon., is set with zero at mean lower low water. The staff gages on the bars from Harrington Point to Portland, Oregon, are set with zero at Columbia River Datum. Above the Willamette Falls Locks, at Oregon City, depths of the Willamette River are at WILLAMETTE RIVER DATUM. Above Bonneville Dam depths of the Columbia River are referred to the normal pool level of the various dams on the Columbia River.

BRIDGES AND CABLES † Clearances of bridges and cables over

Columbia River and its tributaries are at mean lower low water below Harrington Point and at COLUMBIA RIVER DATUM between Harrington Point and Bonneville Dam. Above Bonneville Dam the clearances are referred to the normal pool level of the various dams on the Columbia River. On the Willamette River above the Willamette Falls Locks, at Oregon City, clearances are referred to the datum of NEWBURG POOL. Minimum clearance of cable crossing the main channel of the Columbia and Willamette Rivers to Portland and Vancouver is 216 feet.

CAUTION REGARDING AIDS TO NAVIGATION † During the seasonal high-water conditions, aids to navigation may be destroyed or rendered unreliable. Mariners are warned to exercise caution in navigating the river and to obtain the latest information regarding aids to navigation by local inquiry and through local Notice to Mariners, available upon request to the Commander, 13th Coast Guard District, Seattle, Wash. Every effort is made to restore the aids to operating condition as soon as possible.

WEATHER † The maritime climate near the Columbia River's mouth slowly turns continental as you head upstream. Temperatures become warmer in summer and colder in winter. Daily temperatures vary more. Rain and fog are less frequent, but the chance of snow is greater. In the Columbia River Gorge, winds are deflected and channeled by topography.

Average winter daytime temperatures vary from the upper forties near the mouth to the upper thirties near the Snake River junction. At night, this range is from the midthirties to the midtwenties. Cold spells occur with an outbreak of frigid Canadian air. Extreme temperatures range from the low teens near the coast to below zero upriver. Snow, of a significant amount, falls on 2 to 5 days each year, and is most likely upriver. Occasionally, an ice storm or "silver thaw" will occur; this happens most often between the Gorge and Vancouver. While winds are strongest in late fall and winter, they seldom reach gale force along the Columbia. Extremes of 75 knots have occured;

strongest winds are usually out of the S or SW. Wind flow is generally from the E through SE in winter, and wind speeds reach 17 knots or more about 5 to 10 percent of the time. However, locally at Troutdale, winds blow at 17 knots or more up to 30 percent of the time. Fog drops winter visibilities below 0.5 mile on about 3 to 6 days per month.

Spring temperatures rise slowly near the mouth of the Columbia, compared to the rise upriver. By April, daytime temperatures upriver average in the midsixties, while those near the mouth are in the midfifties. Average low temperatures are near 40° F everywhere. Rain and fog become less frequent than they were in winter. Gales are rare and winds of 17 knots or more blow less than 5 percent of the time except locally around The Dalles, where winds of 17 knots or more occur 18 to 25 percent of the time from April through August. By April, winds are generally out of the W through NW. Flooding on the Columbia is most likely to occur from April through June, when snowmelt at its headwater is most rapid. While flooding is kept under control to a great extent by multi-purpose dams, heavy rains during the melting season can trigger floods.

Summer winds remain W through NW and generally light. Near the mouth of the river, these maritime winds have a cooling effect. They keep average daytime temperatures below 70° F at Astoria and below 80° F at Portland. This effect diminishes upstream, and E of the Cascades daytime temperatures average close to 90° F. Lows at night fall into the low fifties near the coast and upper fifties inland. Rain falls on only a few days per month, usually in the form of showers or thunderstorms. Toward late summer, fog becomes a hazard near the mouth. At Astoria, visibilities fall below 0.5 mile on about 4 days in August.

Fog spreads upstream to Portland and Troutdale by September. During the fall, fog reduces visibilities to less than 0.5 mile on 4 to 8 days per month, W of the Columbia River Gorge. The difference in fog E and W of the Gorge does not extend to temperatures. The temperature range is smallest in fall. In October, daytime high temperatures range from the low sixties near the mouth to the midsixties upriver, while average low temperatures vary from the midforties near the coast to the low forties inland. By October, winds begin to blow more out of the E through SE and become stronger. While gales are infrequent, winds of 17 knots or more occur 4 to 10 percent of the time. Rain falls on about 5 to 15 days per month W of the Cascades and 2 to 6 days per month to the E.

ROUTES, COLUMBIA RIVER APPROACH † The lights at the entrance and at Willapa Bay 28 miles N, are distinguishing marks for determining a vessel's position and subsequent shaping of her course.

In thick weather, great caution is essential on the approach from any direction. The currents are variable and uncertain. Velocities of 3 to 3.5 knots have been observed between Blunts Reef and Swiftsure Bank, and velocities considerably in excess of those amounts have been reported. Under such condition vessels should keep outside the 30-fathom curve until Columbia River Approach Lighted Horn Buoy CR (LNB) has been made. Care should be taken not to mistake the low sand beach N of Cape Disappointment for that S of Point Adams. Nearly all the vessels which have gone ashore attempting the entrance have been wrecked N of the mouth, in the vicinity of Peacock Spit.

In clear weather, vessels should have no difficulty in entering the river as the aids to navigation are numerous. In thick weather, however, when aids cannot be seen, strangers should not attempt to enter without a pilot.

Local vessels entering in thick weather and with a rising tide, as a rule, do not attempt to pass beyond Desdemona Sands Light, because of the difficulty under such circumstances of avoiding vessels anchored in the narrow channel above the light. Strangers should not attempt to navigate the river at night.

Dredges will usually be found at work in the channels; these dredges should be passed with caution and reduced speed.

WEATHER † An estimate of bar conditions, visibility, and weather may be obtained by radio from the Coast Guard station at Cape Disappointment.

TIDES † Mean ranges of tides on the Columbia River ranges from 6.7 feet at Young Bay, E of Astoria, to 3.3 feet at Longview, Wash., to 1.3 feet at Vancouver, Wash. (See Tidal Current Tables for mean and diurnal ranges at selected points along the Columbia River.) These are contained in this edition of the PACIFIC BOATING ALMANAC.

CURRENTS † The Currents in the Columbia River and approaches are described in the Tidal Current Tables included in this edition of the PACIFIC BOATING ALMANAC.

CAUTION † The Columbia River bar is reported to be very dangerous because of sudden and unpredictable changes in the currents often accompanied by breakers. It is reported that ebb currents on the N side of the bar attain velocities of 6 to 8 knots, and that strong NW winds sometimes cause currents that set N or against the wind in the area outside the jetties.

In the entrance the currents are variable, and at times reach a velocity of over 5 knots on the ebb; on the flood they seldom exceed a velocity of 4 knots. The current velocity is 3.5 knots, but this tidal current is always modified both as to velocity and time of slack water by the river discharge. On the flood there is a dangerous set toward Clatsop Spit, its direction being approximately ESE; on the ebb the current sets along the line of buoys. Heavy breakers have been reported as far inside the entrance as Buoy 20, N of Clatsop Spit.

FRESHETS † The annual high-water freshet stage on the Columbia occurs in the latter part of May, but on Willamette River the peak-flow period usually begins mid-December and continues through February, according to measurements taken by the U.S. Geological Survey over the past 70 years. Thus, the Willamette is low, or nearly so, at the time of the peak flow on the Columbia in late May. This causes the Willamette to apparently change direction under the influence of the stronger flow or "backup" from the Columbia, with the change apparent at least as far up the Willamette as the city of Portland.

On Columbia River, the freshet flow causes some shoaling in the dredged cuts, but redredging is done to maintain project depths.

Since logging is one of the main industries of the region, free floating logs and submerged deadheads or sinkers are a constant source of danger in the Columbia and Willamette Rivers. The danger is increased during spring freshets. DEADHEADS or SINKERS are logs which have become adrift from rafts or booms. One end of the sinker settles to the bottom while the other end floats just awash, rising and falling with the tide.

Ice forms occasionally in both the Willamette and Columbia Rivers, but it is seldom heavy enough to affect navigation seriously.

A fixed amber light is maintained by the Columbia Bar Pilots, atop the pilot office of Astoria. When this light is exhibited it will inform outward bound vessels that desire a bar pilot that the bar is not passable and that the vessel should anchor.

BAKER BAY is a shoal open bight, E of Cape Disappointment, formed by the cape and the recession of the land N. SAND ISLAND, low and flat, fronts the bay on the SW side.

A dredged channel leads N from the Columbia River along the W side of Sand Island thence to the Port of Ilwaco mooring basin about 3 miles above the entrance. The entrance is between two detached jetties marked at the channel ends by lights. The channel is marked by lights and daybeacons.

In July 1986, the controlling depth was 6 feet (10 feet at midchannnel) to Fort Canby, then 5 feet to the Port of Ilwaco mooring basin. In 1980, depths in the mooring basin varied considerably, ranging from 7 to 16 feet in the W part to 4 to 1 foot in the E part. The entrance is subject to continual change. As there is usually a swell here, the channel should be navigated only at high water with local knowledge. The rest of Baker Bay is covered with shoals and abandoned fish traps.

ILWACO is the base for a large commercial and sport fishing fleet.

Berths with electricity, gasoline, diesel fuel, ice, water and other supplies are available. The largest marine railway can handle vessels up to 75 feet, 50 tons. Machine and carpentry shops are at this boatyard. The PORT OF ILWACO administers the docks and facilities of the port.

DESDEMONA SANDS, marked by a light near the W end is a shoal area extending SE for about 8 (9.2) miles from just inside the entrance to Columbia River. Desdemona Sands has the main river channel to the S and a secondary channel to the N.

FORT STEVENS WHARF, at Mile 7.3 (8.4) on the Oregon side, is marked by a light and fog signal on a dolphin off the end. A special radio direction finder calibration station is at the light. (See Light List for details.) The wharf is in ruins. A boat basin is at HAMMOND, 0.2 mile SSE of the wharf. Its entrance is marked by a light and a day-beacon on the east and west jetties, respectively. Depths inside are about 6 feet. Berths with electricity, for about 140 craft, gasoline, diesel fuel, water, ice, and a launching ramp are available at the basin.

The pier of the former Coast Guard station is just E of the Hammond boat basin. A packing plant wharf is E of the former Coast Guard pier.

WARRENTON, (46°10'N., 123°55'W.) on the SKIPANON WATERWAY Mile 9.5 (11), is the base of a large sport fishing fleet. The largest marine railway here can handle vessels up to 80 feet, 150 tons, 23-foot wide, or 12 feet in draft for hull and engine repairs. Several marinas are on the waterway, and a mooring basin is in the E part of the waterway about 1.2 miles above the entrance. Floats for about 300 craft, gasoline, diesel fuel, water, ice and marine supplies are available.

In January 1987, the midchannel controlling depth from the entrance of Skipanon Waterway to the turning basin 1 mile above the entrance was 13 feet. The channel to the turning basin is marked by a 198°30' lighted range; lights mark the channel entrance.

Above the waterfront area, the river is crossed by a railroad swing bridge and a fixed highway bridge; the least clearance is 10 feet above mean lower low water, and the least width is 33 feet. A power cable at the second bridge has a reported clearance of 25 feet.

SCARBORO HILL, 820 feet high, is on the Washington side about 7 (8) miles E of Cape Disappointment. It is a long, gradually rising ridge, covered with grass, fern, and some trees. A number of conspicuous light-colored buildings of the historical Fort Columbia State Park may be seen near the base of the hill.

A dredged marked channel leads from Columbia River near the E end of Baker Bay to a basin at CHINOOK, on the Washington side. In January 1986, the controlling depth was 9 feet on the centerline. Berths, gasoline, diesel fuel, water, ice, a launching ramp and some marine supplies are available at the basin. A packing company wharf is at the basin. A 6-ton hoist is available for handling small craft, and a tidal grid for engine repair work. Wet winter storage is available in the basin.

SMITH POINT, at Mile 11.3 (13.0) on the Oregon side, is the W termination of a high, wooded ridge; it is the first prominent point on the S bank SE of Point Adams. The ridge culminates in COXCOMB HILL, 595 feet high, behind Astoria. The ASTORIA COLUMN on the top of the hill is prominent.

YOUNGS BAY is a shoal body of water just W of Smith Point. It receives the water of YOUNGS RIVER and LEWIS AND CLARK RIVER. The docks of a marine repair yard are 0.5 mile above the highway bridge crossing the Lewis and Clark River. The yard can handle vessels up to 350 tons in weight, 33 feet wide, and 15-foot draft for hull and engine repairs. Traffic on the two rivers is confined chiefly to tugs handling log rafts just above the highway bridges. Small tugs operate to the town of OLNEY on Youngs River at high tide. A powerhouse with a prominent white concrete stack is on the N shore of the bay, just W of the highway bascule bridge.

Reported depths of about 7 feet can be taken to and inside Lewis and Clark River . In January 1987, the controlling depth was 6 feet in the improved channel through Youngs Bay to the bascule highway bridge at the entrance

to Youngs River; deeper water can be found inside.

Youngs Bay is crossed by U.S. Route 26/101 vertical-lift bridge, with clearances of 45 feet down and 80 feet up, about 0.3 mile above the mouth. The bridgetender monitors VHF-FM channel 16 (156.80 MHz) and works on channel 13 (156.65 MHz); call sign WHG-914. The railroad swing bridge, just above the the lift bridge, has a clearance of 17 feet. The highway bascule bridge, 2.1 miles above the bay entrance at the entrance to Youngs River, has a clearance of 24 feet. The least clearance of overhead cables across Youngs River to about the mouth is 103 feet.

Over Lewis and Clark River, 0.8 miles above the mouth, is a highway bascule bridge with a clearance of 25 feet. The power cable at the bridge and the one 1.8 miles above the mouth have a least clearance of 64 feet. The highway bridge, 4.8 miles above the mouth, has a fixed span 18 feet wide with clearance of 10 feet. Clearances and depths of Youngs River and Lewis and Clark River are at MEAN LOWER LOW WATER.

POINT ELLICE, on the Washington side 11 (12.7) miles inside the entrance, is the termination of a spur from the mountain ridge back of Scarboro Hill. The point is rounding and rocky, but not high. Two high hillocks lie behind the point. In this area there are many abandoned fish traps and pike structures that extend into the river.

ASTORIA, (46°12'N., 123°50'W.) at Mile 12 (14) on the Oregon side, extends from Youngs Bay to Tongue Point. It is the principal city on the Columbia River below Longview, Wash. It has connections with the interior by both rail and highway.

GENERAL ANCHORAGES are N and W of Tongue Point. Harbor regulations prohibit vessels from anchoring more than 1 hour within an area bounded on the S by the Astoria waterfront and on the N by the main channel buoys. Temporary anchorage may be had by any vessel of suitable draft just E of Buoy 19, NW of Desdemona Sands Light. The fixed highway bridge between Astoria and

Point Ellice has a clearance of 205 feet at the center over the main channel and 48 feet over the N channel. A private fog signal is sounded from the bridge support pier just N of the main ship channel.

TIDES † The mean range of tide at Astoria is 6.6 feet, and the diurnal range of tide is 8.4 feet. A range of about 12 feet may occur at the time of maximum tides. (see the Tide Tables for daily prediction at Astoria [Tongue Point] contained in this edition of the PACIFIC BOATING ALMANAC.)

CURRENTS † Above Astoria the current velocity is 1 to 3 knots except during the freshet period when the ebb is considerably increased although not enough to affect navigation seriously.

WEATHER † Astoria's perenially verdant landscape is hemmed by rather low mountains on the N, E, and S. On the W it is open to the Pacific Ocean over 4 miles or more of low green dunelands and the last 10 miles of the Columbia River.

Weather hazards occasionally occur. Storms may sink or wreck ships. Even in fair weather, wind and wave may combine to produce a type of breaker known as the "widow-maker" and swamp a boat. Heavy rains inundate lowlands, and high tides aggravated by gales may push seawater across highways and up beaches. Rains may cause earthslides, mostly in highway cuts. Storms may fell trees or break power and phone lines. Lightning strikes are rare. Showers of small hail may briefly whiten the ground during many of the months. Occasionally in winter there may be rather brief periods of freezing temperatures, with snow or ice.

The climate is generally healthful, except for dampness and a dearth of isolation in winter. Even then, the gloomy spells of cloud and driving rain may be broken by bright sunshine. Also relaxing are the cool breezes, waters, fog, and warm sands of summer; and the roaring seas and storms with their rainy balmy nights in winter. Heat waves are uncommon and usually brief. The washed atmosphere stays remarkably clean and fresh.

COAST GUARD † Two Coast Guard Cutters are stationed at Astoria.

Astoria Coast Guard Air Station is at Clatsop County Airport.

HARBOR REGULATIONS are prescribed by the Port of Astoria Board of Commissioners. The direct operation of the port is controlled by a port manager who is appointed by the board.

SMALL-CRAFT FACILITIES † Two mooring basins for small craft and fishing vessels are maintained by the Port of Astoria. The West, 0.3 (0.3) mile W of the S end of the Astoria Bridge, has 15 feet reported through the entrance and depths of about 5 feet at the floats. The entrance to the basin is marked by private lights. About 425 berths with electricity, gasoline, diesel fuel, water, ice and some marine supplies are available. Engine repairs can be made at several private firms on the basin. A 10-ton hoist at a packing company just W of the basin can handle small craft in emergencies. The East Basin, 2 (2.3) miles E of the Astoria Bridge, has berths for about 50 craft and a launching ramp; however, no services are available. Reported depths of 15 feet through the entrance and 10 feet at the floats are available.

TONGUE POINT, (46°12'N., 123°45'W.) at Mile 16 (18) on the Oregon side, is a bold, rocky peninsula, 308 feet high, covered with trees and connected with the S bank by a low, narrow neck; it projects into the river for 0.8 mile. A buoy depot of the Coast Guard is on the W side of the peninsula near its inner end. On the E side are the concrete piers of the former naval base.

CATHLAMET BAY lies E of Tongue Point and S of Main Ship Channel. There are many islands which are covered with tule in the summer, but in the winter they are almost indiscernible. The JOHN DAY CHANNEL extends between Tongue Point and JOHN DAY RIVER, just N of the point, the name changes to SOUTH CHANNEL, which follows the shore closely to and around SETTLER POINT to SVENSEN. These channels are marked along John Day River. The E part of Cathlamet Bay (chart 18523) is used mostly for logging operations and log store.

GRAYS BAY on the Washington side extends from GRAYS POINT to HARRINGTON POINT N of the Main

Ship Channel. In the NE section of the bay are extensive mud flats. In 1978, a submerged rock was reported in about 46°17'16"N., 123°43'34"W.; caution is advised. DEEP RIVER flows into the N part of the bay. The channel is marked and follows the shore from Grays Point around PORTUGESE POINT and ROCKY POINT. This river is used only by small pleasure craft and sport fisherman and for logging operations. Depths of about 6 feet are available for about 2 miles above the mouth, above which it is shoal and probably good for no more than 2 feet.

GRAYS RIVER, entered just E of Deep River, is another small stream used only by pleasure craft. Depths are not more than 2 feet, and much of the stream is blocked by snags and sunken logs.

-U.S. COAST PILOT 7
25th edition. August 1989
Corrected thru 10.22.90
Local Notice to Mariners

PENDLETON

MC NARY YACHT CLUB, P.O. Box 463, Pendleton, OR 97801. All year. 24 hours. Picnic area. RV campsite. Ice. Ramp: 1-lane. Overnight guest dock. Slips. Fuel dock: gas. Water skiing. Commodore: Glen Brogoitti.

Columbia river entrance. The largest river on the continent emptying into the Pacific.

Fisherman's Dock and Marina. Operated by Port of Astoria.

FACILITIES

ILWACO
(46°18'N., 124°03'W.)

ED'S OUTBOARD, 2nd and Lake Streets, Box 251, Ilwaco, WA 98624. (206) 642 - 3243. Outboard motor service. Marine hardware. Fishing: tackle and supplies. Open Feb. - Oct.

ENGLUND MARINE SUPPLY CO., INC., Mooring Basin, Box 426, Ilwaco, Wa 98624. (206) 642 - 2308. Marine hardware, wholesale and retail. Fishing: tackle and supplies.

ILWACO BOAT WORKS, P.O. Box 830, Ilwaco, WA 98624. (206) 642 - 2712. All year. Marine railway to 50 tons. Travelift cap.: 50 tons. Boat maintenance and repairs. Prop and shaft repairs. Do-it-yourself. General Manager: Steven L. Bellinger.

PORT OF ILWACO, (Mouth of the Columbia River), Box 307, Ilwaco, Wa 98624. (206) 642 - 3143. 2 hoists, cap: 7 tons. Travelift cap: 50 ton. Fuel dock: gas, diesel and outboard mix. Slips. Boat maintenance and repairs. Engine parts and repairs. Prop and shaft repair. Marine hardware. Snack bar. Restaurant. Groceries. Ice. Overnight accommodations. Laundry. Fishing: bait and tackle. Rental tackle. Dockside electricity: (1), (2) and (3). Port Manager: Robert C. Petersen.

WIRKKALA MARINE REPAIR (on Hwy. 101), Box 490, Ilwaco, WA 98624. (206) 642 - 2414. Boat and motor sales. Marine hardware. Boat and engine maintenance and repairs. Prop and shaft repairs. Boat hauling. Owner: Gary and Larry Wirkkala.

WARRENTON
(46°10'N., 123°55'W.)

D & D MARINA, Box 343, 280 SE Main, Warrenton, OR 97146. (503) 861 - 1821. Inboard, outboard and I/O engine repairs and parts.

HAMMOND MOORING BASIN, Town of Hammond, P.O. Box 161, Hammond, OR 97121. (503) 861 - 1461. Year round. 24 hours a day through Oct., 10 hours a day in winter. Picnic area. Ramp: 6-lane asphalt, 24 hours. Slips. Overnight guest dock with electricity. Fuel dock: gas, diesel and mix. Largest state park in Oregon. Harbormaster: Ken Smith.

WARRENTON BOAT YARD, NE Bay and Harbor Ct., Warrenton, OR 97146. (503) 861 - 1311. All year. 8 AM - 5 PM. 24 hour emergency. Marine hardware. Marine railway, 100 feet. Hull maintenance and repairs. Engine and prop repairs. Managing Operator: Elmer Salmi.

WARRENTON MOORING BASIN (on Skipanon Waterway), Box 250 Warrenton, OR 97146. (503) 861 - 3822 or 861 - 2233. Fuel dock. Ramp: 2 - lane, concrete. Guest moorage. Tidal grid. Showers. Charter boats. Dockside electricity. Harbormaster: Jack Zimmerman.

WEST COAST PROPELLER SERVICE, 827 NE Harbor Street, Box 190, Warrenton, OR 97146. (503) 861 - 1483 or 325 - 3099. Prop and shaft repairs and replacements. Machine shop. Outboard and inboard propellers. Welding and heli-arc. Owner: John R. Kalander.

CHINOOK

PORT OF CHINOOK, Box 185, Chinook, WA 98614. (206) 777 - 8797. All year. Launching ramp: 2-lanes, concrete. Open daylight hours. Hoist cap: 5 tons. Open daylight hours. Fuel dock: gas and diesel. Open daylight hours. Fishing: bait and tackle. Dockside electricity. Some moorage available. Port Manager: Glen Easer.

ASTORIA

AIRPORT CRABPOT CO., Rt. 1, Box 777, Astoria, OR 97103. (503) 325 - 7876. Commercial and sport crab pots. Owners: E.J. Mattson and L.R. Mattson.

ASTORIA MARINE SUPPLY, Foot of 12th street, Astoria, OR 98103. (503) 325 - 2521. Marine hardware. Fishing supplies.

CARMICHAEL OIL / CHEVRON FUEL DOCK, 10-5th Street, Astoria, OR 97103. (503) 325 - 3122. All year. Fuel dock: gas and diesel. Manager: Tom Carmichael.

COLUMBIA RIVER MARITIME MUSEUM, 1792 Marine Drive, Astoria, OR 97103. (503) 325 - 2323. Open daily 9:30 AM - 5 PM, Ship models and marine artifacts portraying history of the Pacific Northwest. Historic lightship *COLUMBIA* open for inspection. Admission: $3/adults, $2/Seniors, $1.50/Students, children free.

ENGLUND MARINE SUPPLY CO., INC., Foot of 15th Street, Box 296, Astoria, OR 97103. (503) 325 - 4341. Marine hardware, wholesale and retail. Fishing: tackle and supplies. Commercial and sport.

JENSEN COMMUNICATIONS, 2158 Exchange Street, Astoria, OR 97103. (503) 325 - 5917. Marine radio and electronic sales and service.

McGREGOR'S SUPPLY CO., 207 7th Street, Astoria, OR 97103. (503) 325 - 1612. Alternator and starter sales and service. Marine electrical services.

NORTHWEST PROPELLER WORKS, 421 Industry Street, Astoria, OR 97103. (503) 325 - 0832. All year. Prop repair. Machine shop, general repair of machinery and hydraulic systems. Marine products. Owner: Warren and Brad Junes.

PORTWAY MACHINE WORKS, 401 Industry Street, Astoria, OR 97103. (503) 325 - 2151. Welding, trailer repair.

POWER TRANSMISSION PRODUCTS, Box 360, 750 Astor Street, Astoria, OR 97103. (503) 325 - 3341. Hydraulics, welding supplies.

WEST MOORING BASIN, Foot of Industry Street, Astoria, OR 97103. (503) 325 - 8279. Fuel dock: gas and diesel. Open 8 AM - 5 PM June through Sept.; daylight hours the rest of the year. Hoist cap: 2.5 ton. Bathrooms and showers. Harbormaster: Bill Cook.

3

ASTORIA TO BONNEVILLE DAM

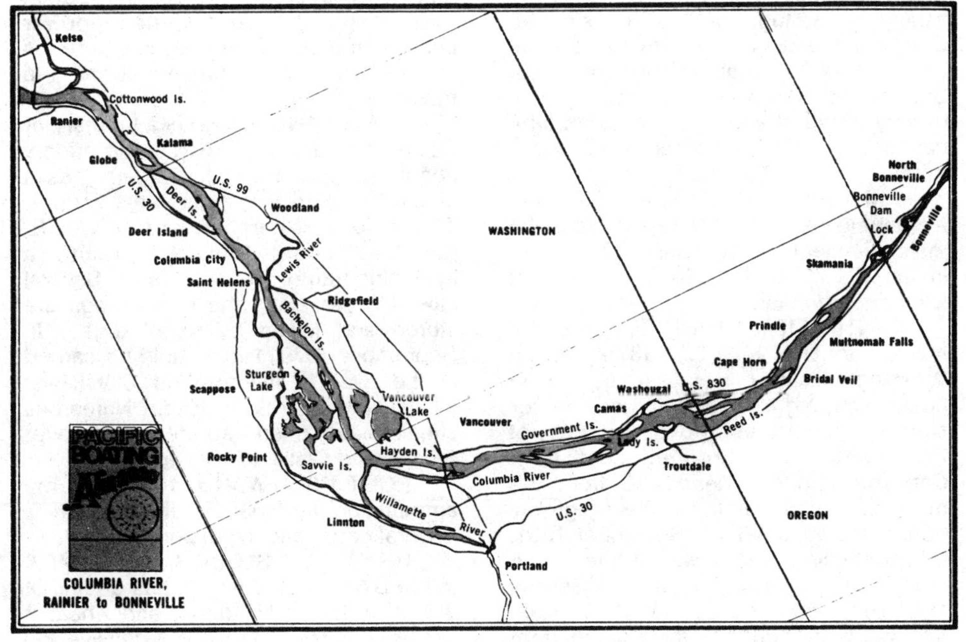

CHART 18523 † Between HARRINGTON POINT, Mile 20.5 (23.6), and CRIMS ISLAND, Mile 47.5 (54.6), Columbia River main channel follows the N bank to THREE TREE POINT, then swings around the bend, holding to the NE shore as far as HUNTING ISLANDS, where it swings along the S shore until off the SE end of PUGET ISLAND; then it follows the N bank from CAPE HORN past ABERNATHY POINT and N of Crims Island and GULL ISLAND.

CURRENTS † In this section the current velocity is about 1 knot. Because of the river flow, which combines with the current, the upstream flow is weak or nonexistent and the downstream flow attains velocities of 2 to 3 knots.

LOCAL MAGNETIC DISTURBANCE † Differences of as much as 3° from the normal variation have been observed along this section of the river.

STEAMBOAT SLOUGH, NE of PRICE ISLAND at Mile 29.3 (33.7) on the Washington Side, and ELOCHOMAN SLOUGH, on the E side of Hunting Islands at Mile 31.3 (36), are used by fishing boats, tugs, and for log storage. Gasoline and diesel fuel are available at SKAMOKAWA just above the NW end of Steamboat Slough. A small marine railway, owned by a private packing firm, can be used if prior arrangements are made.

At Mile 35 (39.9), a power cable with a least clearance of 221 feet crosses the main channel to Puget Island. The tower in the E side of the channel on Puget Island is prominent.

CATHLAMET CHANNEL joins the main channel at Mile 32.3 (37.2) on the Washington side. It is used by fishing boats, tugs, log rafts, and barges, and for some log storage above the city of CATHLAMET. A dredged section of Cathlamet Channel leads SE from the main river channel to a fixed highway bridge at Cathlamet. In November 1981, the controlling depth was 10 feet. A mooring basin is at Cathlamet; gasoline and diesel fuel are available. A fixed highway bridge crosses the channel from Cathlamet to PUGET ISLAND; the clearance is 74 feet for the N span. A power cable, 0.5 (0.6) mile above the bridge, has a clearance of 97 feet.

WESTPORT SLOUGH, at Mile 37.3 (43) on the Oregon side, leads to a ferry dock at the village of WESTPORT. A lumbermill wharf, in ruins, is just E of the ferry slip. In November 1979, the midchannel controlling depth to the ferry dock was 27 feet. The ferry operates between Westport and the ferry landing 0.5 mile N of PANCAKE POINT on Puget Island and carries passengers and automobiles. Above Westport the slough is used for log storage; about 7 feet can be carried to KERRY, 2.4 miles above the mouth. Overhead power cables 0.8 and 1 mile above the mouth of the slough have clearances of 74 and 75 feet, respectively.

WALLACE SLOUGH, at Mile 41 (47) S of Wallace Island, is used by cannery tenders, fishing boats and house floats. A depth of 4 to 5 feet can be carried through the slough.

BEAVER SLOUGH enters Wallace Slough near the SE end of Wallace Island. The slough is used by fishing boats and house floats. A fixed bridge with a 14-foot span and clearance of 6 feet crosses the W arm of the slough near its mouth. An overhead power cable with a clearance of 68 feet crosses the slough about 2 miles above the mouth.

CLATSKANIE RIVER is a tributary of Beaver Slough. A railroad swing bridge, about 0.6 mile above the mouth, has a clearance of 16 feet through the E draw. There is a wharf at CLATSKANIE; gasoline diesel fuel, water and a launching ramp are available. Several sawmills are along the river. Logs are stored and towed by small tugs. In September 1979, 1 foot could be carried in the river to the town of Clatskanie; local knowledge is advised. Numerous shoals have been reported in Beaver Slough and Clatskanie River.

PORT WESTWARD, a former Army ammunition terminal, is the site of a general cargo and log export terminal.

BRADBURY SLOUGH, at Mile 46.6 (53.6) SW of Crims Island, has depths of 9 feet as far as the upper end where it shoals to 3 feet. There is extensive log storage along the Crims Island shore.

CHART 18524 † Between Crims Island and Saint Helens, Mile 75 (86), the main channel starts its SE swing, passing S of FISHER ISLAND and HUMP ISLAND and N of WALKER ISLAND and LORD ISLAND; then, under the Longview fixed bridge, then W of COTTONWOOD ISLAND, E of SANDY ISLAND and W of MARTIN ISLAND and BURKE ISLAND. Numerous jetties along this stretch are usually marked by lights or daybeacons.

CURRENTS † In his section the average velocity on the ebb is 2.0 knots; current usually does not flood.

LOCAL MAGNETIC DISTURBANCE † Differences of as much as 8° from the normal variation have been observed along this section of the Columbia River.

COAL CREEK SLOUGH, at Mile 48.9 (56.3) on the Washington side, empties into the river at STELLA. Gasoline is available. The slough is used for log-raft storage and moorage of small craft. Depths over the bar are 3 to 4 feet, but deeper water extends nearly 3 miles above the entrance. Power cables over the deeper part of the slough have a least clearance of 65 feet.

FISHER ISLAND SLOUGH, N of Fisher Island, is used as the Longview Yacht Basin, by small fishing vessels, and as log-storage grounds. A depth of 7 feet may be carried through the channel.

Power cables over the main channel at Mile 54.2 (62.4), at LORD ISLAND, have at least clearance of 216 feet.

The channel between WALDER ISLAND and the Oregon shore is used for log-raft storage. The shoal area, N of DIBBLEE POINT, limits the maximum depth which may be carried through the entire channel to about 7 feet. The power cables S of Lord Island have a least clearance of 115 feet.

The LONGVIEW BRIDGE, at Mile 57.3 (66.0) between Longview and Rainier, has a fixed span with a clearance of 185 feet. Fog signals are on the two piers of the bridge.

LONGVIEW, (48°08'N., 122°56'W.) at Mile 57.3 (66) on the Washington side is a major river port. Papermills, lumbermills, and an aluminum plant are in the city. The lumber mills here are said to be the world's largest.

PROMINENT FEATURES † The Longview Bridge with its high towers is easily the most prominent feature in approaching Longview from either up or down the river. Upon close approach, the many stacks and tanks of the mills can be identified; most are charted.

TIDES AND CURRENTS † The mean range of tide at Longview is 3.3 feet. Average current velocity, on the ebb, at Longview is 2.0 knots.

HARBOR REGULATIONS † The Port of Longview is a municipal corporation governed by a board of commissioners and administered by a port manager.

COWLITZ RIVER flows into Columbia River at Mile 59 (68), just E of Longview. Only small craft and pleasure craft ply the river. In July 1981, the controlling depth in the entrance channel was 3 feet to the railroad bascule bridge about 1.4 miles above the entrance, thence with local knowledge 1 foot to Kelso. The controlling depth is less than I foot above Kelso. A light marks the entrance to the river. The tide varies from 4 feet at the mouth to zero at OSTRANDER, 7.8 miles above the mouth. At Kelso a stage of 20 feet is reached during ordinary freshets and a stage of 25 feet at extreme floods.

Minimum clearance of the drawbridges across Cowlitz River between the mouth and Ostrander is 25 feet; minimum clearance for fixed bridges is 63 feet. Several overhead power and television cables cross the river between the entrance and Ostrander; least clearance is 67 feet.

At KELSO there are several private wharfs including a sand and gravel wharf, a public landing, and several small craft floats, at one of which gasoline is available.

RAINIER, (46°05'N., 122°56'W) on the Oregon side opposite Longview, has a large sawmill. Lumber is shipped from a 475-foot wharf with reported depths of 30 feet alongside and a deck height of 22 feet. The town of Rainier operates a small-craft basin; berths, gasoline, water, ice and a launching ramp are available. Diesel fuel may be obtained at the tugboat moorage just E of the city basin. A marine railway that can handle vessels to 100 feet in length is at Rainier. In November 1982, a side channel leading to the waterfront facilities had a controlling depth of 24 feet.

CARROLLS CHANNEL, between Cottonwood Island and the Washington shore of Columbia River, is used for log storage and fishing boats. About 13 feet can be carried through the channel.

Two State fish hatcheries are on KALAMA RIVER at Mile 63.5 (73.1). KALAMA, (46°01'N., 122°51'W.) on the E bank about 3 (3.5) miles above Cottonwood Island is the site of several shingle and plywood mills. A marina and mooring basin are at Kalama. Berths with electricity, gasoline, diesel fuel, water, ice, marine suppiles, a launching ramp, a pumpout station, and wet and dry winter boat storage are available at the marina.

The 500-foot-tall cooling tower of the TROJAN NUCLEAR POWER PLANT is on the S side of the river opposite the mouth of the Kalama River. This tower is conspicuous for many miles both up and down the river.

The channel circling the W side of SANDY ISLAND is used by tugs hauling log rafts and barges; the controlling depth is about 7 feet.

MARTIN SLOUGH, between MARTIN ISLAND and BURKE ISLAND and the Washington shore, is used in log rafting operations, as is BURKE SLOUGH between Burke Island and the Washington shore.

COLUMBIA CITY is a municipality at Mile 73 (84) on the Oregon side. The main channel follows along the waterfront

At the S end of DEER ISLAND SLOUGH, about 1.5 miles N of Columbia City, is the pier of a chemical plant.

SAINT HELENS, (45°52'N., 122°48'W.) at Mile 75 (86) opposite the mouth of Lewis River, is the site of paper and lumber mills, the products of which are occasionally shipped by deep-draft vessel from the mill's wharf.

Berths, gasoline, diesel fuel, water, ice, and some marine supplies are available at two floating marine stations at Saint Helens. Outboard engine repairs can be made. There are a large number of houseboats and boathouses in the vicinity of the marine stations.

The stacks of a cement plant and a plywood plant are conspicuous S of Saint Helens along the W side of the N end of Multnomah Channel. A dredged channel with a reported controlling depth of 7 feet in July 1973 leads to a marina in SCAPPOOSE BAY, SW of Saint Helens. This marina, owned by the Port of Saint Helens, has berths, gasoline, water and ice available. A marine railway here can handle craft up to 40 feet for hull and engine repairs.

LEWIS RIVER enters Columbia River at AUSTIN POINT, Mile 75.7 (87.0), on the Washington side. Depths are about 3 feet over the mouth, but just below the first bridge a bar reduces the depth to less than 1 foot. Some logging and other traffic move up to WOODLAND, 5.7 miles about the mouth, at high water. The railroad swing bridge 1.8 miles above the mouth remains in the closed position and has a clearance of 28 feet. The other bridges, all fixed, have clearances of 34 feet or more.

From Saint Helens, Columbia River follows a S course to the mouth of the Willamette River, Mile 88 (101.2), and then turns SE to Vancouver, Mile 92 (106).

MULTNOMAH CHANNEL is a 19-mile waterway separated from the Columbia River near Saint Helens and from the Willamette River near Portland by SAUVIE ISLAND. It is used by tows and small river boats during the winter when the main channel is discharging floe ice; logs are stored along the channel. Depths are 20 feet or more at the entrances, but decrease to 6 feet inside. A power cable about midway through the channel has a clearance of 100 feet. A small-boat landing is 1 mile S from the power cable. Covered berths, with electricity, gasoline, water, ice, a launching ramp, and marine supplies are available. Minor hull and engine repairs can be made. A fixed highway bridge near the S end has a clearance of 78 feet.

WARRIOR ROCK, the point on the E side of WARRIOR POINT at the N end of SAUVIE ISLAND, is marked by a light. In thick fog vessels seldom attempt to pass the light; they anchor either above or below the point until the weather clears.

LOCAL MAGNETIC DISTURBANCE † Differences of as much as 6° from the normal variation have been reported between Warrior Rock and the light off DUCK CLUB 1.5 miles S.

LAKE RIVER, the outlet for VANCOUVER LAKE, flows N for 9.5 miles to its junction with Columbia River at the N end of Bachelor Island, Mile 76 (88). The reported controlling depth was 6 feet in July 1973 to the small-craft harbor at RIDGEFIELD, 2.5 miles about the mouth. There are two marinas at Ridgefield; about 200 berths, gasoline, water, ice, a launching ramp and some marine supplies are available. Hull and engine repairs can be made. The town of Ridgefield operates a public small-craft moorage just S of the marinas. A wood-treating plant is near the boat harbor.

A marina, in the channel behind the elongated island W of Shillapoo Lake, has berths, with electricity, gasoline, water, ice, a launching ramp and marine supplies. A 2½-ton hoist is available for launching small craft. Reported depths of 5 feet can be carried through the channel and to the river N of the marina. However, the channel S of the marina is closed by shoals.

CHART 18526 † The main channel of the Columbia River favors the Washington shore, N of HAYDEN ISLAND and TOMAHAWK ISLAND, from MATHEWS POINT to Ryan Point. Overhead clearances are at COLUMBIA RIVER DATUM. Overhead power cables with a least clearance of 220 feet cross at Mile 90.6 (104.2). Two bridges cross the main channel between Vancouver and Hayden Island. The Burlington Northern Railroad swing bridge at Mile 91.8 (105.7) has a clearance of 39 feet. The bridgetender monitors VHF-FM channel 16 (156.80 MHz) and works on channel 13 (156.65 MHz); call sign KQ-9049. The interstate 5 highway bridge, Mile 92.5 (106.5) has twin lift spans with clearances of 39 feet down and 178 feet up, and twin fixed spans with a clearance of 58 feet at the center and 46 feet elsewhere crossing the alternate barge channel S of the main channel. The bridgetender monitors VHF-FM channel 16 and works on channel 13; call sign KBM Interstate.

NORTH PORTLAND HARBOR is that portion of the river channel between the Oregon shore and Hayden Island. The lower or W entrance is at Mile 89.0 (102.5); the upper or E entrance is at Mile 94.5 (108.8).

A Federal project provides for a 40-foot turning basin at the W entrance to North Portland Harbor, a 40-foot channel for about 1.3 miles above the W entrance, and thence a 20-foot channel to the project limit about 2 miles farther upstream. In June 1981, the midchannel controlling depth was 40 feet for about 1.3 miles above the W entrance; thence in 1977-78, the controlling depth was 7 feet to the end of the project. The federal project for the E entrance to North Portland Harbor provides for a channel 10 feet deep from the main channel in Columbia River SW to just S of the E end of Tomahawk Island. In December 1980, the midchannel controlling depth was 8 feet from the junction with Columbia River to just off the channel range from the light, thence 2 feet (10 feet in the S quarter) to the project limit. A 241° lighted range marks the channel for about 0.6 mile from the junction with Columbia River. Two bridges cross North Portland Harbor. The railroad bridge, 2.6 miles E of the W entrance, has a swing span with a clearance of 39 feet. A fixed highway bridge (Interstate 5) about 0.8 mile E has a clearance of 34 feet. A large marina is on the S side of Hayden Island just E of the Interstate highway bridge. Berths, gasoline, diesel fuel, water, ice and marine supplies are available. Hull, engine, and electronic repairs can be made. A large repair facility, just W of this marina, has a 70-ton drydock that can handle craft up to 55 feet long and 16 feet wide for hull, engine and electronic repairs. A private yacht club is near the E end of Tomahawk Island. Many houseboats are moored in North Portland Harbor.

VANCOUVER, (45°38'N., 122°41'W.) is on the Washington side of the Columbia River at Mile 92 (106). The port is a water outlet for a large lumber-producing section in SW Washington, as well as a distributing point for a fair share of the grain produced in the interior of Washington and Oregon.

The Port of Vancouver is controlled by a board of commissioners and a general manager.

SUPPLIES † Complete marine supplies and services are available from Portland. Fuel oil must be delivered by barge. Small-craft supplies are available in North Portland Harbor and at other places on the Columbia River E of Vancouver.

REPAIRS † Complete repairs for large and small vessels are available at Portland. Vancouver has no facilities for repair work on large ocean going vessels. Small-craft repairs on craft up to 70 tons or 55 feet can be made in North Portland Harbor; there are no repair facilities on the N side of the river at Vancouver.

CHART 18531 † From Vancouver to Bonneville, Mile 126 (145), Columbia River passes through the impressive COLUMBIA RIVER GORGE, flanked on each side by railroads and highways. Commerce on the river in this section consists mostly of pleasure craft and barges.

There are more than 35 dike dolphins along this portion, some are marked with lights at their ends. All the dikes are completely covered at higher stages, but bare about 6 feet at datum level.

RYAN POINT, 1.4 miles ESE of the Vancouver Interstate 5 highway bridge, is the site of a former shipyard and is now an industrial park. A public launching ramp is at the park.

There are many marinas, yacht clubs, and moored houseboats along the Oregon shore from Tomahawk Island to the E end of Government Island. Berths, gasoline, diesel fuel, water, ice and marine supplies are available at several of these facilities.

A 107°-287° MEASURED NAUTICAL MILE has been established at LIESER POINT, 3.6 (4.1) miles above the Interstate bridge at Vancouver. Each range marker is painted yellow with black stripes.

At Mile 97.9 (112.7), the river is crossed by a fixed highway bridge with a clearance of 136 feet (144 feet for the center 300 feet) over the channel.

A SPECIAL ANCHORAGE is between Sand Island and Government Island.

CAMAS, (45°35'N., 122°24'W.) at Mile 104.3 (120.0) on the Washington side, has a large papermill which maintains its own wharf on CAMAS SLOUGH, N of LADY ISLAND. About 8 feet can be taken from the Columbia River through the W entrance to the papermill wharf near the E end of the slough; the channel is marked by lights, a buoy, and a lighted range. The E entrance to the slough is foul and bares at low water. Most of the traffic in the slough is for the papermill, which barges its products to Portland for reshipment. At high flood stages a current of as much as 5 knots prevails in the slough.

Two fixed highway bridges cross Camas Slough from the mainland to Lady Island; the W one has a clearance of 69 feet, and the E one has a clearance of 37 feet.

A marina at mile 105.7 (121.6) just E of Camas, has about 250 berths, open and covered and with electricity, gasoline, water, a launching ramp and complete marine supplies. A marine sales and repair facility adjacent to the marina has a 12-ton hoist that can handle craft to 42 feet for hull and engine repairs. A sawmill is just E of the marina.

There are five power cables crossing at IONE REEF, S of Lady Island. The least clearance is 133 feet.

The entrance to SANDY RIVER, on the Oregon side opposite Camas, bares at low water. At higher flood stages, passage up Sandy River as far as TROUTDALE is possible.

LOCAL MAGNETIC DISTURBANCE † Differences of as much as 8° from the normal variation have been observed between TUNNEL POINT and POINT VANCOUVER, E of REED ISLAND.

DANGERS † In this section of the river, the principal hazards to navigation are the strong currents, rocks and rocky banks, winds, and an accumulation of ice.

CURRENTS † In general, currents run fair with the main channels with considerable intensity, increasing in regions upstream toward Bonneville. Exceptions are the turn in the channel at

Washougal Light 50, where a NW set prevails, SW of CAPE HORN, where a W set is experienced; and the region between Fashion Reef and Multnomah Falls, where a S set is experienced.

WEATHER † Between CORBETT, Mile 110.3 (127), and The Dalles, Mile 165 (189.8), the river flows between the bold, mountains of the CASCADE RANGE. In this stretch, winds of considerable force prevail during much of the time; generally they blow upstream in summer and downstream in winter. Daily peak velocities vary from 6 to 42 knots, but Corps of Engineers officials at Bonneville Dam measures gusts as high as 76 knots during 1960-62.

Near WARRENDALE, Mile 123 (141.5), the river becomes very constricted within less than a mile and continues so almost to the approach to the locks of Bonneville Dam, at the lower end of BRADFORD ISLAND.

BEACON ROCK, 840 feet high and 300 yards inshore, is on the Washington side opposite Warrendale. It is a prominent dark gray rock outcropping of volcanic origin. A State park of the same name surrounds the rock. The park maintains a mooring float just inside the entrance to the channel W of PIERCE ISLAND; moorage is restricted to pleasure boats and to periods not to exceed 36 hours. Water and ice are available at the park.

BONNEVILLE, on the Oregon side at Mile 126 (145), is the headquarters of the U.S. Army Corps of Engineers in charge of the Bonneville Lock and Dam.

BONNEVILLE LOCK AND DAM, 126.3 (145.3) miles above the mouth of the Columbia River, is in two parts. The spillway is between the Washington shore and Bradford Island. The powerhouse and lock are between Bradford Island and the Oregon shore. The dam has a single lift ship lock with a vertical lift of about 59 feet. Restricted areas are above and below the spillway.

The strong current toward the power-house makes it difficult to approach Bonneville Lock from upstream, particularly if the lock is approached at an angle and if a turn is to be executed in time to avoid an accident. Therefore, all craft approaching the lock from the E and pushing one or more barges should steer as close to the Oregon mainland shore as safety will permit, should be in line with the lock upon reaching the E end of the guide wall and should continue at a steady but reduced speed if the lock is prepared for entrance and the signal for entrance has been given.   -U.S. COAST PILOT 7
25th edition, August 1989
Corrected thru 10 22 90
Local Notice to Mariners

FACILITIES

CATHLAMET

ELOCHOMAN SLOUGH MARINA, Box 651, Cathlamet, WA 98612. (206) 795 - 3501. Ramp: 3 - lanes, concrete. Fuel dock: gas and diesel. Slips. Guest dock. Showers. Dockside electricity. TV and cable. Picnic area. Harbormaster: Jim Mast.

KELSO

KELSO MARINE SUPPLY, 3rd and Oak, Kelso, WA 98626. (206) 636-3000. All year. Engine parts and repairs. Marine hardware. Fishing: licenses and tackle.

KALAMA

PORT OF KALAMA MARINA (on I-5, 9 miles S of Kelso/Longview), Box 7, 380 West Marine Drive, Kalama, Wa 98625. (206) 673 - 2325. Ramp: 2 - lanes, asphalt. Open 24 hours. Fuel dock: gas, diesel and mix. Open 8 AM - 4:45 PM. Guest dock. Open and covered slips. covered dry storage. Pumpout station. Picnic area. RV sites. Dockside electricity: (7). Marina Mgr: J. Wicker.

SAINT HELENS

BAYPORT MARINA INC., Box 959, St. Helens, OR 97051. (503) 397 - 0001. All year. Ramp: 2 - lanes, asphalt. Fuel dock open daylight hours. Open and covered berths. Outboard/inboard repairs. Overnight accommodations. Camping. Snacks. Ice. Bait and tackle. Owners: Jack and Jan Gronholm.

SCIPIO'S GOBLE LANDING (NW of Portland at Columbia River Mile 74.4), 70360 Columbia River Hwy., Rainier, OR 97048. (503) 556 - 6510. All year. Ramp: 1 - lane, concrete. Open 24 hours. Fuel dock. Slips. Dry storage. RV campsites. Groceries. Fishing: licenses, bait and tackle. Manager: Ray Ryder.

ST. HELENS MARINA (foot of columbia Blvd.), Box 1054, St. Helens, OR 97051. (503) 397 - 4162. Ramp: 2 - lane, concrete. Open daylight hours only. Fuel dock: gas only. Open daylight hours. Moorings. Marine hardware. Engine sales and service. Electronic sales and service. Snack bar. Fishing: licenses, bait and tackle. Dockside electricity: (1). Owner: J. & M. Calnon.

MULTNOMAH CHANNEL

BROWN'S LANDING (on Multnomah Channel at end of Dike Road), 50565 Browns Landing Ct., Scappoose, OR 97056. (503) 543 - 6526. Open 7 days. Launching facility. Fuel dock: gas. Moorings. Engine repairs. Marine hardware. Fishing: bait and tackle. Rental boats and motors, canoes. Restaurant adjacent. Owners: Jerry and Joan Blair.

FRED'S MARINA (at mouth of Multnomah Channel), 12800 NW Marina Way, Portland, OR 97231. (503) 286 - 5537. Ramp: 2 - lanes, asphalt. OPen 24 hours. Fuel dock: gas. Open Spring, 7 AM - 5 PM; Summer 9 AM - 6 PM. Slips. Guest dock. Hull and engine maintenance, parts and repairs. Prop and shaft repairs. Used boats. New & used motor sales Marine hardware. Charts. Electronics. Ice. Snack bar. Water skiing. Fishing: bait and tackle. Rental tackle, boats and motors. Owner: Alexander E. Fredrick.

LARSON'S MARINA, 14444 NW Larson Road, Portland, OR 97231. (503) 286 - 1233. Ramp: 1 - lane, asphalt. Fuel dock: gas only. Open 7 AM - 8 PM. Guest dock. New and used motor sales. Marine hardware. Ice. Fishing bait and tackle. Owner: Earl Larson.

LARSON'S MARINE SERVICES, 14452 NW Larson Road, Portland, OR 97231. (503) 286 - 0793. Marine Construction and towing.

LARSON'S MOORAGE, 144426 NW Larson Road, Portland, OR 97231. (503) 286 - 1233. Covered and open moorage.

RON'S MARINE REPAIR, 34415 E. Columbia Avenue, Scappoose, OR 97056. (503) 543 - 7586. Engine maintenance, parts and repairs. Gas and arc welding. Marine hardware. Owner: Ron Waterman.

SCAPPOOSE MOORAGE, 50900 A Dike Road, Scappoose, OR 97056. (503) 543 - 3939. (1 mile from Hwy. 30 on Dike Rd.) Open year round. Overnight guest dock. Slips: 50 feet, some covered. Managers: Bob and Shirley Farrell.

WASHOUGAL

PORT OF CAMAS / WASHOUGAL, 24 A Street, Washougal, WA 98761. (206) 835 - 2196. All year. Ramp: 4-lanes, concrete, 24 hours. Guest dock. Slips. Fuel dock: gas and diesel. Picnic area. Waste disposal pumpout. Charts. Restaurant.

4

BONNEVILLE DAM TO PRIEST RAPIDS DAM

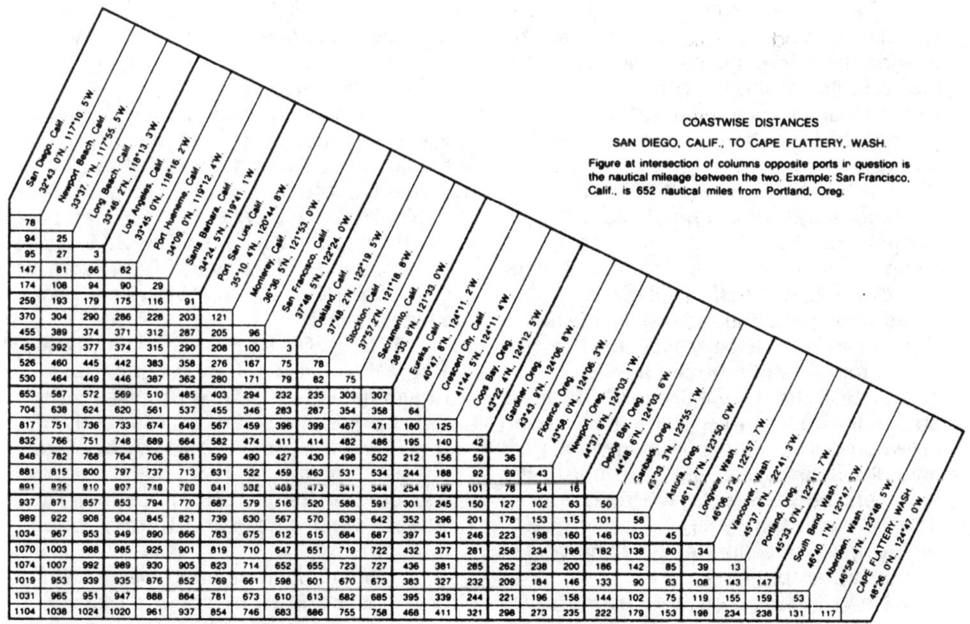

COASTWISE DISTANCES

SAN DIEGO, CALIF., TO CAPE FLATTERY, WASH.

Figure at intersection of columns opposite ports in question is the nautical mileage between the two. Example: San Francisco, Calif., is 652 nautical miles from Portland, Oreg.

Ports (with positions):

1. San Diego, Calif. 32°43.0'N., 117°10.5'W.
2. Newport Beach, Calif. 33°37.1'N., 117°55.5'W.
3. Long Beach, Calif. 33°46.2'N., 118°13.3'W.
4. Los Angeles, Calif. 33°45.0'N., 118°16.2'W.
5. Port Hueneme, Calif. 34°09.0'N., 119°12.4'W.
6. Santa Barbara, Calif. 34°24.5'N., 119°41.1'W.
7. Port San Luis, Calif. 35°10.4'N., 120°44.8'W.
8. Monterey, Calif. 36°36.5'N., 121°53.0'W.
9. San Francisco, Calif. 37°48.5'N., 122°24.0'W.
10. Oakland, Calif. 37°48.2'N., 122°19.5'W.
11. Stockton, Calif. 37°57.2'N., 121°18.8'W.
12. Sacramento, Calif. 38°33.8'N., 121°33.0'W.
13. Eureka, Calif. 40°47.8'N., 124°11.2'W.
14. Crescent City, Calif. 41°44.5'N., 124°11.4'W.
15. Coos Bay, Oreg. 43°22.4'N., 124°12.5'W.
16. Gardiner, Oreg. 43°43.9'N., 124°06.8'W.
17. Florence, Oreg. 43°58.0'N., 124°06.3'W.
18. Newport, Oreg. 44°37.8'N., 124°03.1'W.
19. Depoe Bay, Oreg. 44°48.6'N., 124°03.6'W.
20. Garibaldi, Oreg. 45°33.3'N., 123°55.1'W.
21. Astoria, Oreg. 46°11.7'N., 123°50.0'W.
22. Longview, Wash. 46°06.3'N., 122°57.7'W.
23. Vancouver, Wash. 45°37.6'N., 122°41.3'W.
24. Portland, Oreg. 45°33.0'N., 122°41.7'W.
25. South Bend, Wash. 46°40.1'N., 123°47.5'W.
26. Aberdeen, Wash. 46°58.4'N., 123°48.5'W.
27. Cape Flattery, Wash. 48°26.0'N., 124°47.0'W.

Distances (columns 1–13):

Port	San Diego	Newport Beach	Long Beach	Los Angeles	Port Hueneme	Santa Barbara	Port San Luis	Monterey	San Francisco	Oakland	Stockton	Sacramento	Eureka
Newport Beach	78												
Long Beach	94	25											
Los Angeles	95	27	3										
Port Hueneme	147	81	66	62									
Santa Barbara	174	108	94	90	29								
Port San Luis	259	193	179	175	116	91							
Monterey	370	304	290	286	228	203	121						
San Francisco	455	389	374	371	312	287	205	96					
Oakland	458	392	377	374	315	290	208	100	3				
Stockton	526	460	445	442	383	358	276	167	75	78			
Sacramento	530	464	449	446	387	362	280	171	79	82	75		
Eureka	653	587	572	569	510	485	403	294	232	235	303	307	
Crescent City	704	638	624	620	561	537	455	346	283	287	354	358	64
Coos Bay	817	751	736	733	674	649	567	459	396	399	467	471	180
Gardiner	832	766	751	748	689	664	582	474	411	414	482	486	195
Florence	848	782	768	764	706	681	599	490	427	430	498	502	212
Newport	881	815	800	797	737	713	631	522	459	463	531	534	244
Depoe Bay	891	825	810	807	748	720	641	531	468	473	541	544	254
Garibaldi	937	871	857	853	794	770	687	579	516	520	588	591	301
Astoria	989	922	908	904	845	821	739	630	567	570	639	642	352
Longview	1034	967	953	949	890	866	783	675	612	615	684	687	397
Vancouver	1070	1003	988	985	925	901	819	710	647	651	719	722	432
Portland	1074	1007	992	989	930	905	823	714	652	655	723	727	436
South Bend	1019	953	939	935	876	852	769	661	598	601	670	673	383
Aberdeen	1031	965	951	947	888	864	781	673	610	613	682	685	395
Cape Flattery	1104	1038	1024	1020	961	937	854	746	683	686	755	758	468

Distances (columns 14–26):

Port	Crescent City	Coos Bay	Gardiner	Florence	Newport	Depoe Bay	Garibaldi	Astoria	Longview	Vancouver	Portland	South Bend	Aberdeen
Coos Bay	125												
Gardiner	140	42											
Florence	156	59	36										
Newport	188	92	69	43									
Depoe Bay	199	101	78	54	16								
Garibaldi	245	150	127	102	63	50							
Astoria	296	201	178	153	115	101	58						
Longview	341	246	223	198	160	146	103	45					
Vancouver	377	281	258	234	196	182	138	80	34				
Portland	381	285	262	238	200	186	142	85	39	13			
South Bend	327	232	209	184	146	133	90	63	108	143	147		
Aberdeen	339	244	221	196	158	144	102	75	119	155	159	53	
Cape Flattery	411	321	298	273	235	222	179	153	198	234	238	131	117

Entrance buoy (32°37. 3'N., 117°14. 7'W.) to San Diego, 8. 3 miles.
Entrance buoy (33°42. 7'N., 118°11. 0'W.) to Long Beach, 4.3 miles.
Entrance buoy (33°42. 0'N., 118°14. 5'W.) to Los Angeles, 3.8 miles.
Entrance buoy (37°45. 0'N., 122°41. 5'W.) to San Francisco, 15.0
  miles; Oakland, 18.5 miles; Stockton, 87 miles; Sacramento, 91 miles.
Humboldt Bay entrance buoy (40°46. 4'N., 124°16. 2'W.) to Eureka, 5.5 miles.

Entrance buoy (43°22. 2'N., 124°23. 0'W.) to Coos Bay (city), 13. 3 miles.
Yaquina Bay entrance buoy (44°35. 9'N., 124°06. 7'W.) to Newport, 3.3 miles.
Columbia River LNB (46°11. 1'N., 124°11. 0'W.) to: Astoria, 17.8 miles;
  Longview, 64 Miles; Vancouver, 98 miles; Portland, 103 miles.
Willapa Bay entrance buoy (46°44. 3'N., 124°10. 4'W.) to South Bend, 19 miles.
Grays Harbor entrance buoy (46°51. 4'N., 124°14. 1'W.) to Aberdeen, 21 miles.

CHART 18531 † From Bonneville to The Dalles, the channel is through the pool created by Bonneville Dam, which extends 40 (46) miles to The Dalles Dam. Depths and overhead clearances are at NORMAL POOL LEVEL.

Although there is deep water in much of the pool, the controlling depth to The Dalles Dam navigation lock is about 14 feet. The channels are marked by navigation.

An overhead power cable with a clearance of 190 feet crosses the river 1 (1.1) mile above the dam.

Tugs use the dolphins on the S side of the river 1.2 (1.5) miles above the lock for mooring and shifting barges and log rafts. Small craft can find refuge in the mouth of EAGLE CREEK, 0.6 (0.7) miles above the lock, if the creek is not in flood.

CURRENTS † From the lock at Bonneville through Cascade Rapids, constant piloting is necessary because of the strong currents. From Cascade Rapids E, a set of 1° to 3° may be experienced depending on the angle that the course makes with the general direction of the river, the strength of the current, and the direction and strength of the wind.

LOCAL MAGNETIC DISTURBANCE † Differences of as much as 6° from normal variation have been observed along this section of the Columbia River.

BRIDGE OF THE GODS, 2. 6 (2.8) miles above the Bonneville Dam, has a fixed span with a clearance of 135 feet over a middle width of 284 feet.

CASCADE LOCKS, 3 (3.3) miles above the Bonneville Dam, have been drowned out. At normal stages of Pool level the sides of the old chamber of the lock bare about 3 feet. A strong current flows through the lock. A marina, just E of the lock, has berths, gasoline and a launching ramp.

Along this section are several inlets or rivers, generally used for log storage, where small craft may find refuge. Most are behind fixed bridges. These places, and their distances above the Bonneville Dam are: ROCK CREEK at STEVENSON Wash., 4.2 (4.8) miles; the bridge clearance is 18 feet. GOVERNMENT COVE, on the Oregon side, 5.6 (6.4) miles. WIND RIVER at HOME VALLEY, WA, 8.1 (8.3) miles; the minimum bridge clearance is 26 feet. DRANO LAKE, near COOK, Wash., 14.5 (16.7) miles; the bridge clearance is 19 feet. RUTHTON, Oreg., 17.8 (20.4) miles, WHITE SALMON RIVER at UNDERWOOD, WA, 20.9 (24) miles; the bridge clearance is 26 feet.

Rock Creek, Wind River and Drano Lake have log rafts and booms used by nearby sawmills.

HOOD RIVER, OR.,21.7 (25) miles above the Bonneville Dam, is a town at the junction of Columbia and Hood Rivers. There are two boat basins at Hood River; the W basin is privately owned and is used by a repair yard for building and repairing steel barges and tugs. The E basin, operated by the Port of Hood River Commission, has about 55 berths. Gasoline and water are available. The entrance to the E basin is marked by private lights. In 1976, depths of 7 to 12 feet were reported available in the E basin. A shoal, covered 2 feet, is reported to extend NW from the W side of the E basin entrance to near the entrance to Hood River.

The highway bridge over Columbia River just above the small-craft basin has a lift span with a clearance of 67 feet down and 148 feet up. There are power cables with clearance of 155 feet over the river at STANLEY ROCK, 22.9 (26.4) miles above Bonneville Dam and at CRATES POINT, 13 (15) miles above Stanley Rock.

THE DALLES, (45°36'N., 121°11'W.) is on the Oregon side of Columbia River, 39 (44.8) miles above the Bonneville Dam. River traffic, between the town and Vancouver, consists mainly of petroleum products and general freight bound upstream and wheat, wool and rafted logs bound downstream.

A small-boat mooring basin with a breakwater and shear boom protection is just E of the city wharf. Depths inside are 4 to 8 feet. The basin has a small-craft launching ramp. Gasoline, ice and marine supplies are available. Engine repairs can be made.

The city wharf is over 1,000 feet long and has two warehouses; depths alongside are about 20 feet. There are also private facilities for handling petroleum Products, bulk grain, and fresh fruit. An aluminum mill is at West The Dalles.

CHARTS 18533, 18535 † THE DALLES LOCK AND DAM, 40 (46) miles above Bonneville Dam, has a single lift lock with a vertical lift of about 87.5 feet. RESTRICTED AREAS are above and below the dam. LAKE CELILO, the pool created by The Dalles Dam, provides slack water navigation with a controlling depth of about 14 feet for 22 (25.33) miles upstream to the John Day Dam. Depths and overhead clearances are at NORMAL POOL LEVEL.

Traffic above The Dalles Dam consists mostly of grain and petroleum products.

Ice occasionally interferes with navigation for 2 weeks or more, usually in January or February.

A fixed highway bridge across the downstream approach to the lock at The Dalles Dam has a clearance of 100 feet.

A railroad bridge, 7 (8.1) miles above The Dalles Dam, has a lift span with clearance of 20 feet down and 79 feet up.

The Celilo Park basin 7.7 (8.9) miles above The Dalles Dam, offers shelter to small boats, but there are no facilities except a launching ramp. The entrance to the basin is marked by a light.

At MILLER ISLAND, 10.5 (12) miles above The Dalles Dam, the N and S channels are marked by ranges. The main channel is along the N side of the island; however it is reported that the S channel is more frequently used.

On the Oregon side just S of Miller Island is DESCHUTES RIVER, crossed by a fixed bridge with clearance of 20 feet. Small craft occasionally seek shelter here during unfavorable weather.

The BIGGS BRIDGE, 13.6 (17) miles above The Dalles Dam, has a clearance of 88 feet at the center of the fixed highway span. The bridge joins MARYHILL, WA, and BIGGS JUNCTION, OR.

CHARTS 18535, 18536, 18537, 18539 † JOHN DAY DAM, 188 (216.3) miles above The Dalles Dam, has a single lift lock with a vertical lift of about 105 feet. RESTRICTED AREAS are above and below the dam. Depths and overhead clearances are at NORMAL POOL LEVEL.

The rock awash near the E approach to John Day Locks in 45°43'25"N., 120°41'20"W. is marked by a light and sign; mariners are urged to exercise caution when passing N of Lake Umatilla Lighted Buoy 2, so as to avoid being carried to the NW and striking the rock awash.

LAKE UMATILLA, the pool created by John Day Dam, extends 65 (75) miles to McNary Dam. Depths are generally great, but there are many shoals. The winding channel through the lake has a controlling depth of about 19 feet and is marked by aids to navigation. The chart is the best guide. An overhead power cable with a clearance of 90 ft. is about 41 (47.2) miles above John Day Dam.

JOHN DAY RIVER is 2.3 miles above John Day Dam on the S side of the Columbia. Just S of the highway bridges over the entrance to the river is the JOHN DAY RIVER RECREATION AREA. There are floats here for about 40 craft and a launching ramp. The fixed highway bridges have a clearance of 19 feet. Small craft moorage and a launching ramp are available at Arlington.

At BOARDMAN, 45.6 (52.2) miles above the John Day Dam, there is a small-craft basin protected by a stone breakwater and a jetty. Berths and a launching ramp are available here.

UMATILLA is on the Oregon side 62 (71.3) miles above the John Day Dam.

There is a small-craft basin about 500 yards W of the highway bridge. The E side of the entrance is marked by a light. About 80 covered and uncovered berths, electricity, gasoline, diesel fuel, water and ice are available. A concrete launching ramp is at the basin.

The fixed highway bridge across the river, 63 (72.5) miles above the John Day Dam, near Umatilla, has two navigational spans, each with a clearance of 85 feet. The N opening is generally used during high water as there is less current, but during low water it is unsafe. The power cables E of the bridge have a least clearance of 82 feet.

CHARTS 18541, 18542 † McNARY LOCK AND DAM, 254.5 (292.9) miles above the mouth of the Columbia River and just above Umatilla, has a single lift lock with a vertical lift of about 75 feet. A RESTRICTED AREA is above the dam. Depths and overhead clearances are at NORMAL POOL LEVEL.

LAKE WALLULA, the pool created by McNary Dam, provides slack-water navigation from McNary Dam to the junction with the Yakima River, a distance of about 37 (43) miles. Depths in the lake are generally deep, but there are shoal spots; depths range from 14 to 115 feet. The channel is marked by aids to navigations as far as Richland, 40 (46) miles above McNary Dam.

The PORT OF UMATILLA, on the Oregon side, about 0.4 miles above the McNary Lock and Dam, has a 218-foot port wharf with 918 feet of berthing space with dolphins; reported depths of 20 feet are available alongside.

HAT ROCK STATE PARK, on the S side about 5.5 (6.3) miles above McNary Dam, has a public launching ramp and offers excellent protection for small craft. Gasoline is available here.

PORT KELLEY, on the E side of Columbia River, 16 (19.5) miles above McNary Dam, has a large grain elevator and facilities for handling bulk grain by rail, truck or water. Unlighted ranges lead clear of the rock and shoal area in the middle ground 0.4 mile W of the facility.

A small boat moorage is in the bight just NE of Port Kelley. Berths, electricity, gasoline, and water are available.

The PORT OF WALLA WALLA river enters Columbia river on the E side 18.4 (21.2) miles above McNary Dam. There is a public launching ramp on the S side of the river just E of the highway bridges at the entrance.

The Union Pacific Railroad bridge crossing Columbia River, 27 (31) miles above McNary Dam, has a vertical lift span with a clearance of 11 feet down and 72 feet up. The bridgetender monitors VHF-FM channel 16 (156.80 MHz) and works on channels 13 (156.65 MHz); call sign KTD-561.

CHART 18542 † PASCO, on the N side of the Columbia River 286 (329) miles above its mouth, is 32 (36.8) miles above McNary Dam. The Port of Pasco is a municipal corporation with a Board of Commissioners and a General Manager. In addition to the marine terminal and industrial park, the port operates an airport.

The Pasco Yacht Basin, on the E side just below the railroad lift bridge, has berths, gasoline, diesel fuel and marine supplies. Engine and electronic repairs can be made. An 8-ton hoist and a launching ramp are available at the basin.

At CLOVER ISLAND, there is a large small-craft harbor. About 80 berths with electricity, gasoline, diesel fuel, water and marine supplies are available. Hull, engine, and electronic repairs can be made. A 12-ton crane is at a marina occupying the center section of the island. A private yacht club is on the S side, and a Coast Guard station is on the E end of the island.

Four bridges cross the river in this area; the railroad lift bridge clearance is 18 feet down and 70 feet up. The two fixed highway bridges 0.35 (0.4) mile W of the railroad bridge have a least clearance of 49 feet. The fixed highway bridge 1.7 (2.) miles W of the railroad bridge has a clearance of 61 feet. An overhead power cable crossing the river at the E end of Clover Island has a least clearance of 54 feet.

COLUMBIA PARK RECREATION AREA, 3.8 (4.4) miles above the upper fixed highway bridge at Pasco, has a small-craft marina at which berths, electricity, gasoline, water, a launching ramp and marine supplies are available. Engine repairs can be made. Diesel fuel is available in the town of Richland, just above the recreation area.

PRIEST RAPIDS DAM, 68 (78.3) miles above McNary Dam and 353 (407) miles above the mouth of Columbia River, completed and dedicated in 1962, is the head of navigation, although in its construction providing was made for later building of a navigation lock if needed. However, Richland is the present practical head of navigation.

FACILITIES

BONNEVILLE

COVERT'S LANDING (River Mile 140 on Columbia River), Star Rt. Box 40, Bonneville, OR 97014. (503) 374 - 8577. Ramp: 3 - lanes, asphalt. Open 24 hours. Fuel dock: gas only. Open daylight hours. Guest dock. Slips. Dry storage. Marine hardware. Electronics. RV campsites. Groceries. Picnic area. Fishing: Licenses, bait and tackle. Owner: Ken Covert.

CASCADE LOCKS

CASCADE LOCKS MARINE PARK, Box 307, Cascade Locks, OR 97014. (503) 374 - 8619. Open year round. Waste disposal pump. Picnic area. RV campsite. Ramp: 1-lane, paved. Overnight guest dock with electricity. Moorings. Fuel dock: gas, diesel and mix. Water skiing. The Sternwheeler Columbia Gorge is located in Cascade Locks at the Marina from mid-June until the end of September. General Manager: Dana E. Walker.

HOOD RIVER

MID-COLUMBIA MARINA (at junction of Hwy. 84 and Hwy 35), Port Marina Park, Hood River, OR 97031. (503) 386 - 2477. Ramp: 2 0 lanes, asphalt. Open 24 hours. Slips to 35 feet. Guest dock. Fuel dock: gas and diesel. Open Summer, 8:30 AM - 5:30 PM; Winter, 8 :30 AM - 5 PM. Open Sundays in Summer. Manager: Kenneth Franklin.

PORT OF HOOD RIVER (adjacent to I-84), Box 239, Hood River, OR 97031. (503) 386 - 1645. All year. Ramp: 2 - lanes, asphalt. Open daylight hours. Fuel dock: gas and diesel. Pumpout. Overnight accommodations. Port Manager: James S. O'Banion.

THE DALLES

THE COLUMBIA GORGE MARINE, 2720 W. 2nd Street, The Dalles, WA 97058. (503) 296 - 4206. Complete boat shop. New boat sales and repairs.

THE DALLES YACHT CLUB, Box 775, The Dalles, OR 97058. Ramp: asphalt. Open 24 hours. Fuel available. Contact a member.

FUN COUNTRY INC., 1318 W. 2nd, Box 58, The Dalles, OR 97058. (503) 298 - 1161. Marine hardware. Charts.

HAT ROCK

HAT ROCK ARMINA (McNary Yacht Club at Hat Rock State Park, 10 miles east of McNary Dam on Oregon shore), Rt. 3, Box 3748, Hermiston, OR 97838. (503) 567 - 3784. All year. Ramp: 1-lane, concrete. Fuel dock: gas and outboard mix. Open 9 AM - 6 PM. Moorings. Camping.

UMATILLA

UMATILLA MARINA, 1710 Quincy, Box 1138, Umatilla, OR 97882. (503) 922 - 3939. Open all year 7 AM - 9 PM. Ramp: 2-lane, 24 hours. Overnight guest dock with electricity. Slips and moorings. Storage. Charts. Beverages and ice. Picnic area. Waste disposal pumpout. RV campsite, tent areas. Fuel dock: gas, diesel and mix. Bait and tackle. Water skiing. Skin and scuba diving. Operator: David W. Barnes.

WESTLAKE

WESTLAKE RESORT, Box 25, Westlake, OR 97493. (503) 997 - 3722. Open March to October 8 AM - 5 PM. Overnight guest dock. Accommodations. Rental rowboats with outboard motors. Fishing: licenses, bait and tackle. Owners: Charles and Barbara Doran.

WALLA WALLA

WALLA WALLA YACHT CLUB, Port Kelly, Box 1223, Walla Walla, Wa 99362. (509) 547-4946. Caretaker, year round. Launching facility. Fuel dock: gas and outboard mix. Open 9 AM - 5 PM.

PASCO

WATER WORLD MARINA, INC. (at Pasco Boat Basin), 1315 S. 4th Ave., Pasco, Wa 99301. (509) 547 - 9455. Slips. Fuel dock open daylight hours in summer. Ramp: 4 - lanes, concrete. New and used boat sales. Inboard, outboard engine sales and service. President: David H. Chambers.

KENNEWICK

METZ MARINA INC., 206 Clover Island, Kennewick, Wa 99336. (509) 582 - 8709. Fuel dock: gas, diesel and outboard mix. Moorings. Hull and engine repairs. Prop and shaft repair. Instrument repairs. Marine hardware. Electronics. Ice. Laundry. Pumpout.

WILLAMETTE RIVER & PORTLAND

CHART 18526, 18527 † At Mile 88 (101.2), Columbia River is joined by WILLAMETTE RIVER, its largest tributary below the Cascade Mountains. The Willamette drains a large territory and is important as the site of the city of Portland, 9 (10.4) miles above its mouth. The Federal Project depth in Willamette River is 40 feet to the Broadway Bridge in Portland, thence, maintained by the Port of Portland, 30 feet between Broadway Bridge and Ross Island. (See Notice to Mariners and latest editions of charts for controlling depths on the Willamette River to the Broadway Bridge.) Additional information can be obtained from the Corps of Engineers, Portland, Oreg. Contact the Port of Portland for the controlling depths of the section of the channel maintained by the port.

From the entrance of the Willamette River to the Willamette Falls Locks at Oregon City, overhead clearances and depths are at COLUMBIA RIVER DATUM. Above the Willamette Falls Locks depths of the Willamette River are at WILLAMETTE RIVER DATUM and clearances are at the datum of NEWBURG POOL.

KELLEY POINT JUNCTION LIGHT (45°39.2'N., 122°45.7'W.), 21 feet above the water, is shown from a pile structure with a red and green triangular daymark on the end of the dike extending from KELLEY POINT on the E side of the entrance to the river.

COLUMBIA SLOUGH, a narrow back channel roughly parallel to Columbia River, empties into the Willamette about 0.4 (0.5) mile above its mouth. Least depth in the slough is about 2 feet. A dam has been constructed across the slough about 7.3 miles above the mouth.

The fixed bridges over the slough have a least clearance of 27 feet. The least clearance of the overhead power and telephone cables is 42 feet.

In the vicinity of POST OFFICE BAR RANGE, 2 (2.4) miles above the mouth of Willamette River, deep-draft vessels favor the W side of the river, while smaller vessels and tows usually hug the E side because of lesser current. A 311°06' lighted range marks the river channel near the Burlington Northern Railroad Bridge, about 6 (6.9) miles above the mouth. This range may present a confused image if height of eye is less than 50 feet. Overhead power cables with a least clearance of 230 feet cross the river 0.3 mile above the junction with Multnomah Channel. The twin towers supporting the cables are the most conspicuous features in this area.

PORTLAND, (45°31'N., 122°40'W.) on Willamette River about 9 (10.4) miles from its mouth, is the principal city of the Columbia River system and one of the major ports on the Pacific coast. The port has over 25 deep-draft piers and wharves on both sides of the Willamette River between its junction with the Columbia and Ross Island. In addition, there are extensive facilities for small vessels and barges S of Hawthorne Bridge and at North Portland Harbor, S of Hayden Island.

BRIDGES † The minimum clearance of the drawbridges is 26 feet at the Glisan Street vertical-lift bridge, 10.4 (12.0) miles above the mouth; the raised clearance of both decks of the bridge is 161 feet, and of the lower deck alone, 71 feet up. The minimum fixed-span clearance is 120 feet for the central, 100 feet at the Ross Island highway bridge. The Marquam fixed highway bridge, midway between the Hawthorne and Ross Island bridges, has a clearance of 120 feet for a center 220-foot width. The river is crossed near the N end of Ross Island by a power cable with clearances of 123 feet over the main channel and 83 feet over the E channel. About 0.4 mile S, over the E channel, are cables with least clearance of 75 feet.

MEASURED NAUTICAL MILE † Two 127°33' - 307°33' measured nautical mile courses are on the Willamette River, the first just SE of Doane Point and the second W of Swan Island.

TIDES † The mean range of tide at Portland is 1.8 feet and the diurnal range of tide is 2.4 feet.

WEATHER † The coast range provides limited shielding from the maritime influence of the Pacific Ocean. The Cascade Range provides a steep high slope for the lift of moisture-laden W winds and consequent heavy rainfall in the Western Cascade Piedmont and also forms a barrier containing the Interior Columbia Basin with its continental airmasses. Airflow is usually NW in Portland in spring and summer and SE in fall and winter, interrupted occasionally by outbreaks of dry continental air E through Cascade passes and across ridge tops. When such an outbreak occurs, extreme high or low temperatures are usually experienced in the Portland area.

Portland has a very definite winter rainfall climate. About 88 percent of the annual total occurs in October through May, 9 percent in June and September, while only 3 percent comes in July and August. Precipitation is mostly rain; on the average only 5 days each year have measurable snow. Snowfall is seldom more than a couple of inches, and it generally lasts only a few days. The greatest measured snowfall in period of record is 15 inches.

Each season is clearly marked. Winter is mild, cloudy, and wet with SE surface winds predominating. Summer is marked by mild temperature, with prevailing NW winds and very little precipitation. Fall and spring are transitional in nature, with frequent periods of ground fog. At all times, incursions of marine-tempered air are a frequent moderating influence. Outbreaks of continental air from E of the Cascade Mountains flow through the Columbia Gorge at near sea level and spread into the Portland area associated with the movement of Pacific storms offshore on a NE storm track. In winter this brings the coldest weather and the extremes of low temperature are registered in the cold airmass. Freezing rain and ice glaze often are transitional effects. In summer the hot, dry, continental air brings the highest temperatures. Extreme temperatures below zero are very infrequent. The absolute lowest ever reached is 3° F below zero. Extreme temperatures above 100° F have occurred several times; the absolute highest temperature is 107° F. Temperatures 90° F or higher are reached every year, but seldom persist for more than 2 or 3 days before the warm spell is broken by a flow of cool, moist air from the ocean.

Destructive storms are infrequent in the Portland area. Surface winds seldom exceed gale force and only once in the period of record have winds reached higher than 75 m.p.h. Thunderstorms are infrequent. Tornadoes with the funnel cloud reaching the ground have yet to be observed. There are rare occurrences of heavy rain even though winter rains may persist for days at a time.

Ice forms occasionally, but it is seldom heavy enough to affect navigation seriously, although navigation by small craft may be difficult.

SMALL-CRAFT FACILITIES † Most of the small-craft facilities, including practically all of the moorage, is in North Portland harbor and along the S bank of the Columbia River between the E end of Tomahawk Island and the W end of Government Island. Complete facilities are available. Berths, electricity, gasoline, diesel fuel, water, ice and marine supplies can be obtained at many marinas. Hull, engine, and electronic repairs can be made. Drydocks to 70 tons, 55 feet long, and 16 feet wide are available in North Portland Harbor.

CHART 18528 † Navigation of Willamette River above Portland is hazardous due to the rocks, shoaling bars and strong currents. Local knowledge and midchannel courses are recommended. Depths of about 6 feet can be carried to Oregon City, 22.6 (26.0) miles above the mouth, thence about 2 feet to Corvallis, 115 (132) miles above the mouth. Present chart coverage extends only to Newberg, 43.4 (50) miles above the mouth. Many of the daybeacons in the Willamette River are seasonal. The navigational aids above Newberg are not maintained. Navigation should be with local knowledgd only. The Portland Coast Guard should be contacted for the latest information concerning navigation of the Willamette River above Salem.

Below the falls at Oregon City, ordinary fluctuation of stage of water is 15 feet and extreme fluctuation due to flood conditions is 30 to 50 feet. Above Oregon City, ordinary fluctuation is 12 to 20 feet and extreme is 20 to 27 feet.

Depths and clearances of bridges and cables are at COLUMBIA RIVER DATUM below the Willamette Falls Locks. Above the Willamette Falls Locks depths of the Willamette River are at WILLAMETTE RIVER DATUM and clearances are at the datum of NEWBERG POOL.

The minimum clearances of the overhead power cables crossing the river from Portland to Newberg are: 77 feet to Willamette Falls Canal; 72 feet over Willamette Falls Canal; and 75 feet to Newberg.

Between Portland and Willamette Falls most of the terminals are privately owned mill wharves and oil-receiving facilities. Above the falls are small privately owned wharves or natural landings.

Sellwood fixed highway bridge, 14.5 (16.7) miles about the mouth, has a clearance of 72 feet. A marina, on the W bank of the river just N of the bridge, can provide berths, gasoline, and marine supplies. Craft up to 36 feet can be handled for hull, engine, or electronic repairs. Another marina, on the E bank of the river just S of the bridge, can provide berths, gasoline and marine supplies. A marina at Milwaukie, 16.2 (28.6) miles above the mouth, has a launching ramp. Minor engine repairs can be made.

A fixed railroad bridge, 17.4 (20) miles above the mouth, has a clearance of 74 feet.

The channel passes E of HOG (ROCKY) ISLAND, 1.6 (1.8) miles above the railroad bridge. COPELEYS ROCK, 150 yards E of the S end of the island, is covered 10 feet and should be avoided.

OREGON CITY, on the E bank 22.6 (26) miles above the mouth, is connected with WEST LINN by two fixed highway bridges; one, about 0.2 (0.2) mile below the Willamette Falls canal locks, has a vertical clearance of 74 feet. The second, 0.6 (0.7) miles below the N end of the locks, has a clearance of 76 feet.

A marina, on the E bank just above the lower highway bridge, has about 350 berths, gasoline, diesel fuel, a launching ramp and marine supplies. Outboard engine repairs can be made.

WILLAMETTE FALLS CANAL, on the W bank 22.8 (26.2) miles above the mouth, has four locks with a total lift of 50 feet; usable lock dimensions are 175 feet long, 37 feet wide, and 6 feet deep over the miter sills at low water. The least clearance of the power cables and pipeline that cross the canal is 72 feet. Upbound vessels may expect a delay at the approach to the locks and through the locks during weekdays because of the downbound traffic from the papermills. The lock is equipped with a radiotelephone. The dockmaster can be contacted on VHF-FM channel 14 (156.70 MHz); call sign, WUJ 363.

A marina, on the E bank opposite WILLAMETTE and 24.3 (27.9) miles above the mouth, has about 50 berths, with electricity, gasoline, diesel fuel and water available. This marina has an elevator lift that can handle craft to 5 tons or 30 feet for hull and engine repairs.

From the entrance to TUALATIN RIVER, 24.8 (28.5) miles above the mouth for over 4 miles, Willamette River is shallow and winding; buoys and unlighted ranges mark the channel.

Small craft can tie up at SHANKS LANDING, 28.8 (33.1) miles above the mouth.

WALNUT EDDY is on the E bank 29.4 (33.8) miles above the mouth.

CABLE FERRY † The Canby ferry crosses the river about 1.1 (1.3) miles above Walnut Eddy. The ferry carries passengers and vehicles, and operates from 0600 to 2200 daily except during periods of high water. When the ferry is underway, the cable is suspended below the water surface at varying depths. When the ferry is docked, the cable is dropped to the bottom. DO NOT ATTEMPT TO PASS A MOVING CABLE FERRY.

Near WILSONVILLE, 33.7 (38.8) miles above the mouth, there are twin fixed highway bridges and a fixed railroad bridge, with clearances of 74 feet and 76 feet, respectively. A marina, on the S bank under the railroad bridge, has about 115 berths, with electricity, gasoline, water, ice, and marine supplies. The marina has a launching ramp and can make hull and engine repairs.

Marine towing service for small craft is also available at this marina.

A quarry is on the N side of the river about 300 yards W of the railroad bridge. Mariners are advised to exercise caution because barges and tugs may be operating in the area.

Near BUTTEVILLE, 37.3 (43.0) miles above the mouth, there is a small-craft marina with about 35 berths, electricity, gasoline, water, ice, a launching ramp and some marine supplies available. Minor engine repairs can be made. The fixed bridge, 42.1 (48.4) miles above the mouth, has a clearance of 68 feet at the main span. At Newberg, 43.4 (50.0) miles above the mouth, there is a fixed highway bridge with a clearance of 88 feet. An overhead power cable with a clearance of 55 feet, crosses the river 44.9 (51.7) miles above the mouth.

From Newberg to Corvallis, Willamette River is more tortuous and turning, but not considered difficult for the small craft and occasional log-rafting tugs that use this section. The tributary YAMHILL RIVER empties into Willamette River about 3 miles above Newberg. Depths in Yamhill River of about 3 feet are reported to Dayton, 4 miles above its mouth.

CABLE FERRY † The Wheatland ferry crosses Willamette River about 63 (72.5) miles above the mouth. The ferry carries passengers and vehicles and operates between 0600 and 2145 daily except when the river level exceeds 16 feet. Warning signs and warning lights mark the crossing. The ferry is guided by two cables. The upper cable, 80 feet above the river level, controls the ferry during normal condition. The low water cable, near the bottom at all times, controls the ferry when the river level drops below 12 feet. The low water cable is dropped to the bottom when the ferry is not operating. DO NOT ATTEMPT TO PASS A MOVING CABLE FERRY.

SALEM, capital of the State of Oregon, is 74.4 (85.6) miles above the mouth. Several moorings and floats for log-rafts and small craft are here; berths, gasoline, diesel fuel, water, ice and marine supplies are available at several small marina. Hull engine, and electronic repairs can be made in Salem.

A power cable at the N city limits of Salem has a clearance of 86 feet. Minimum clearance of the bridges is 68 feet at the fixed highway bridges, and 42 feet down and 87 feet up at the railroad lift bridge. The railroad lift bridge is maintained in the closed position.

At INDEPENDENCE, 83 (95.5) miles above the mouth, there is a small-craft launching ramp, but no facilities.

The town of BUENA VISTA is 92 (106) miles above the mouth of the river.

CABLE FERRY † A cable ferry crosses the river near Buena Vista. The self-propelled ferry carries passengers and vehicles, and operates from 0700 to 2100 daily except Saturdays, Sundays and holidays. Both when the ferry is underway and when docked the guide cables are suspended approximately 80 feet above the water. When underway, the ferry shows the required navigation lights. DO NOT ATTEMPT TO PASS A MOVING CABLE FERRY.

The river is crossed at ALBANY, 104 (119.8) miles above the mouth, by three bridges: a railroad swing bridge with a clearance of 40 feet, a fixed highway bridge with a clearance of 55 feet and a fixed highway bridge with a clearance of 60 feet in the center of the N span and 58 feet in the center of the S span. The railroad swing bridge is maintained in the closed position.

CORVALLIS, 114.6 (131.9) miles above the mouth, is the limit of the Federal project of the river. Navigation above Corvallis is dangerous and should not be attempted.

There are small-craft finger piers and marginal facilities at Corvallis; gasoline and water are available. A highway bridge has a swing span with a clearance of 35 feet.

-U.S. COAST PILOT
25th edition. August 1989
Corrected thru 10 22 90
Local Notice to Mariners

FACILITIES

PORTLAND

BEAVER MARINE SERVICES, 121-3 NE Victory, Gresham, OR 97030. (503) 661 - 1177. Propeller specialists. Sales and service. Skeg repair. Owners: Mel and Mary LInn.

BIG EDDY MARINA, 19609 NE Marine Drive, Portland, OR 97230. (503) 666 - 3515. Open 8 AM - 6 PM. Slips. Closed Thursdays.

CAPTAIN'S NAUTICAL SUPPLIES, 138 NW 10th St., Portland, OR. (503) 227-1648. Nautical charts and books. Instruments and instrument repairs. Manager: Lance Howard.

CHARLOT MARINA, 303 NE Tomahawk Island Drive, POrtland, OR 97217. (503) 289 - 1855. Open 8 AM - 5 PM, Mon. - Fri. Marine ways. Dry storage. Hull repairs. Custom building. Prop and shaft repair. Do-it-yourself facilities. Marine hardware. Emergency repairs. Painting: (503) 287 - 9797. Owner: D.W. Charlot.

COLUMBIA MARINE ELECTRONICS (at McCuddy's), 2913 NE Marine Drive, Portland, OR 97211. (503) 287 - 1560. Open 9:30 AM - 5 PM weekdays. Electronic sales and service. Owner: Max E. Coyne.

COOK ENGINE CO., 530 NE Tomahawk Island Drive, Portland, OR 97217. (503) 289 - 8466. Engine sales and service. Transmission repairs.

COLUMBIA RIDGE MARINA (from Portland, take Banfield Freeway to 181st Street East; 181st N to Sandy Blvd., then east to 185th St. and N to Marine Drive), 18525 NE Marine Drive, Portland, OR 97230. (503) 665 - 3705. All year. Fuel dock: gas and oubtoard mix. Open 11 AM - 7 PM. Slips. Snack bar. Ice. Dockside electricity: (3). managers: Larry and Sylvia Cameron.

DONALDSON MARINA, 3501 NE Marine Drive, Portland, OR 97211. (503) 288 - 6169. Covered moorage. Dry dock and repairs. Convenience store. Fuel dock: gas only. Managers: Margi and Gordon Sahnow, Jr.

DUCK'S MOORAGE, 18699 NE Marine Drive, Portland, OR 97230. (503) 665 - 8348. Boat and houseboat moorage. Slips. Houseboat and float construction. Diving service. Owner: Thomas E.W. Olson.

FISHERMAN'S MARINE SUPPLY (at I-5 Columbia Blvd. exit), 901 N. Columbia Blvd., Portland, OR 97217. (503) 283 - 0044. Marine hardware and accessories. Charts. Electronics. Fishing: bait and tackle. Manager: Dan Grogan.

H2O BOAT BARN (on Sauvies Island), 31421 NW Reeder Road, Portland, Or 97231. (503) 621-3293. Inboard/ outboard sales and service. New and used boat sales.

HARBOR I MARINE CENTER INC., 3307 NE Marine Drive, Portland, OR 97211. (503) 289 - 3509. Hoist cap: 10 tons. Open 10 AM - 6 PM. Slips. Guest dock. Dry storage. Hull and engine maintenance and repairs. New and used boat and engine sales. Snack bar. Ice. Laundry. Dockside electricity. Sailing school and club. Boat rentals. Manager: Dick Semmes.

HARRY A. WHITE MARINE SERVICE, 1132 N. Jantzen, Portland, OR 97217. (503) 285 - 4407. Open 8 AM - 4:30 PM, Mon. - Fri. Drydock cap.: 75 tons and 50'. Shipyard repairs. Boat and engine maintenance and repairs. Engine parts. Prop and shaft repairs. Fiberglass repairs. Manager: Harry A. White.

JANTZEN BEACH GAS DOCK, 1058 N. Jantzen, Portland, OR 97217. (503) 289 - 3265. Fuel dock: gas and diesel. Open daily 9 AM - 6 PM, Mon. - Thurs.; 8 AM - 8 PM, Fri. - Sun. Marine hardware. Scrubomatic bottom washer.

LUCKY LANDING, 12900 NW Marina Way, Portland, OR 97231. (503) 240 - 9190. Covered and open slips, liveaboards, launch ramp and dry storage.

MONTE'S BOAT TOPS, 303 NE Tomahawk Island Drive, Portland, OR 97217. (503) 289 - 0796. Boat tops. Canvas repairs. Owner: Monte Bentley.

O'CASA INC., SAILING CENTER, 50 NE Tomahawk Island Drive, Portland, OR 97217. (503) 283 - 0160. Brokerage. Sailing lessons and charters. Closed Wednesdays. President: Wm. E. Downey.

PACIFIC MARINE CENTER, 1130 N. Jantzen Ave, Portland, OR 97217. (503) 289 - 9881. All year. 9 AM - 6 PM Mon. - Sat. Boats and motors. Marine hardware. Engine maintenance and parts. Owner: Tom Dropchinski.

PACIFIC MARINE SURVEY, 1406 Jantzen Beach center, Portland, OR 97217. (503) 289 - 4973. Boat and engine maintenance and repairs. Engine parts. Prop and shaft repairs. Fiberglass repairs. Marine surveys. Manager: Terry O'Neill.

PORTAGE MARINE INC., 4141 NE Marine Drive, Portland, OR 97211. (503) 288 - 6306. Engine parts and repairs. Boat and motor sales. Owner: J. Wolff.

PORTLAND PRECISION INSTRUMENT CO., 1111 SE Pint, Portland, Or 97214. (503) 233 - 5159. Marine instrument sales and repairs. Charts. President: Joan L. Peterson.

PROGRESS ELECTRONICS COMPANY, 2725 NE Columbia Blvd., Portland, Or 97211. (503) 287 - 0581. Open Mon. - Fri., 8 AM - 4:30 PM; 24 hour emergency service. Marine electronic sales and service. V. President: John Cauduro.

RICHMOND BOAT WORKS, 535 NE Bridgeton Road, Portland, OR 97211. (503) 283 - 3653. Drydock cap.: 60 tons. Wood, fiberglass and metal hull maintenance and repairs.

RODGER'S MARINE ELECTRONICS, 3445 NE Marine Dr, Portland, OR 97211. (503) 287-1101. All year. 9 AM - 5 PM, Mon - Sat. Electronics sales and service. Radio, radar, loran, etc. Charts. Instrument repairs. Owner: Rodger Jenkins.

RYAN'S MARINE SERVICE, 3335 NE Marine Drive, Portland, OR 97211. (503) 282 - 8807. Boat and engine repairs. Inboard/outboard sales and service. (Columbia Corinthian Marina. 60 slips. Moorage: 288-3988.) Owner: Steve Ryan.

SELLS MARINE SERVICE (Portland Yacht Club), 1111 NE Marine Drive, Portland, OR 97211. (503) 285 - 3838. All year. Floating dry dock. Cap.: 50 tons and 55'. Hull and engine repairs. Owner: Dick Wilson.

SEXTON'S CHANDLERY, 303 NE Tomahawk Island Drive, Portland, OR,97217. (503) 289 - 9358. All year. Marine hardware, maintenance supplies, stove repair and parts. Located on the Columbia River.

SHEFFIELD MARINE PROPELLER, INC., 10002 N. Vancouver Way, Portland, OR 97217. (503) 289 - 2620. Factory authorized station for sales and service for Michigan Wheel Co. We can service all your propulsion needs -- shafts, struts, rudders, couplings and related marine hardware. Since 1956. President: Walter Sheffield

STAFF JENNINGS, INC., (2 Portland locations: #1 on Willamette River under the west end of Sellwood Bridge,) Box 02176 Portland, OR 97202. (503) 244 - 7505. Ramp. Fuel dock. Slips. Crane cap.: 7 tons. Open daily. To order parts only, please call. #2: on Columbia River at 33rd and Mairne Drive, 2900 NE Marine Drive, Portland, OR 97202. (503) 284 - 6050. Marine sales, service and parts. Marine hardware. Open daily. To order parts only, please call. Manager: Jeffrey S. Jennings.

Willamette River through Downtown Portland.

SUNDANCE MOORAGE (Hayden Island) 570 NE tomahawk Island Drive, Portland, OR 97217. (503) 283 - 3216. Slips. Crane cap.: 50 tons. Full service marina. New and used boat sales. Do-it-yourself yard. Owner: Bob Buck.

TOMAHAWK BAY MOORAGE, 515 NE Tomahawk Island Dr, Portland, OR 97217. (503) 286 - 1578. Open all year. New/used boat/motor sales. Electronic sales. Ice. Laundry. Marine hardware. Waste disposal pumpout. Overnight guest dock. Dockside electricity. Slips. Boat storage. Water skiing. Harbormaster: G. McAllister.

TOMAHAWK BOAT WORKS, INC, 303 NE Tomahawk Is. Dr, Portland, OR 97217. (503) 283 - 5200. All year. Marine hardware. Building supplies. Electronic sales and repairs. Hauling service. Boat storage. Hull maintenance and repairs. Do-it-yourself repair yard. Canvas/upholstery services. President: G. Katke.

TOMAHAWK ISLAND MARINA, 300 NE Tomahawk Is. Dr, Portland, OR 97217. (503) 289 - 5511. Elevator: 30-ton, 8 AM - 5 PM. Guest dock with electricity. Boat storage. Hull maintenance. Prop and shaft repairs. Covered slips. Manager: Philip Baudoin.

TOMAHAWK LIFT AND CRADLE, 152 NE Tomahawk Is. Dr, Portland, OR 97217. (503) 283-3000. Open all year. Mon - Fri, 7 AM - 7 PM. Sat 8 AM - 4:30 PM. Closed holidays. Overnight guest dock. Hull repairs. Prop and shaft repairs. Survey lifts. Painting. Cradling. Moorage. Owner: Kevin Miller.

WAVERLY YACHT CLUB, 600 SE Marion, Portland, OR 97202. (503) 232 - 7633. Open all year. 7 days a week. 9 AM - 5 PM. Overnight guest dock. Covered slips. Dockside electricity. Fuel dock: gas, diesel and mix. Manager: Sandy McCann.

WEST MARINE PRODUCTS, 12055 N. Center Avenue, Portland, OR 97217. (503) 289 - 9822. All year. Weekdays: 9 AM - 6 PM except Thursday, 9 AM - 8 PM. Saturdays and Sundays, 9 AM - 5 PM. Motor sales. Charts. Electronic sales. Marine hardware. Paint and supplies. Discount prices. Regional Manager: Brian Gallagher.

GRESHAM

BEAVER MARINE SERVICES, 121-3 N.E. Victory, Gresham, OR 97030. (503) 661 - 1177. Open 8 AM - 6 PM. Mon. - Sat. Merc-stern drive/prop repair. Engine parts. Owner: Mel Linn.

OREGON CITY

OREGON CITY MARINA INC., 18649 S. Hwy 99 E, Oregon City, OR 97045. (503) 656 - 4276. All year. Summer: daily 9 AM - 6 PM, Sundays 10 AM - 6 PM. Winter: daily 9 AM - 5 PM, Sundays 10 AM - 5 PM. New and used boat and motor sales. Charts, electronics and marine hardware. Engine maintenance, parts and repairs. Prop and shaft repairs. Slips. Fuel dock: gas only. Water skiing. President: Ron Criteser.

SPORTCRAFT LANDING, 1701 Clackamette Drive, Oregon City, Or 97045. (503) 655 - 0981. Covered and open moorage to 100'. Owners: Ken and Kathy Dye.

SPORTCRAFT MARINA, 1701 Clackamette Drive, Oregon City, OR 97045. (503) 656 - 6484. Ramp, open 24 hours. Slips. Fuel dock. Gas and mix. New and used boats and motors. Sales and service. Fishing: licenses, bait and tackle. Rental boats and motors. Owner: Larry J. Bigbee.

SALEM

ALLEN MARINE CENTER, 1125 Boone Road SE, Salem, OR 97306. (503) 399 - 1161. Engine repairs. Marine hardware. Electronics. Boat and motor sales. Owner: Gil Allen.

WESTERN OREGON MARINE (on the Willamette River 20 miles south of Portland and 22 miles north of Salem), 26177 NE Boones Ferry Landing, Aurora, OR 97002. (503) 678 - 5433 or 682 - 0515. River moorage April 1 to Oct. 1. Ramp: 3 - lanes, asphalt. Open daylight hours. Fuel dock: gas and outboard mix. Open 8 AM - 8 PM. Slips. Dry storage. Boat maintenance and repairs. Engine parts and repairs. Boat and motor sales. Water skiing. Rental skis. Marine hardware. Deli. Owner: Tom Reid.

Willamette River and Portland

PORTLAND, OREGON (45°36'N., 122°36'W.) Elevation 21 ft. (6.4m)

WEATHER ELEMENTS	JAN.	FEB.	MAR.	APR.	MAY	JUNE	JULY	AUG.	SEPT.	OCT.	NOV.	DEC.	YEAR	YEARS OF RECORD
SEA LEVEL PRESSURE														
Mean (Millibars)	1018.5	1018.6	1017.5	1018.1	1017.7	1016.8	1017.2	1016.6	1016.3	1017.9	1018.4	1018.0	1017.6	24
TEMPERATURE (DEGREES F)														
Mean	38.1	42.8	45.7	50.6	56.7	62.0	67.1	66.6	62.2	53.8	45.3	40.7	52.6	30
Mean Daily Maximum	43.6	50.1	54.3	60.3	67.0	72.1	79.0	78.1	73.9	62.9	52.1	46.0	61.6	30
Mean Daily Minimum	32.5	35.5	37.0	40.8	46.3	51.8	55.2	55.0	50.5	44.7	38.5	35.3	43.6	30
Extreme Highest	62	70	80	87	92	100	107	104	101	90	73	64	107	35
Extreme Lowest	−2	−3	19	29	29	39	43	44	34	26	13	6	−3	35
RELATIVE HUMIDITY														
Average Percentage (1000 l.s.t.)	82	79	72	68	66	65	61	64	66	79	82	84	72	35
Average Percentage (1600 l.s.t.)	76	68	60	55	53	49	45	46	49	64	74	79	60	35
CLOUD COVER														
Average Amount (Tenths)	8.6	8.3	8.1	7.7	7.1	6.8	4.5	5.1	5.4	7.2	8.3	8.9	7.2	27
Mean Number of Days with Clear Skies	2	3	3	4	5	6	14	11	11	5	3	2	69	27
Mean Number of Days with Cloudy Skies	26	22	24	21	19	17	9	10	12	19	23	27	229	27
PRECIPITATION														
Mean Amount (Inches)	5.88	4.06	3.64	2.22	2.09	1.59	0.47	0.82	1.60	3.59	5.61	6.04	37.61	30
Greatest Amount (Inches)	12.83	9.46	7.52	4.72	4.57	3.58	2.01	4.53	3.96	8.04	11.57	11.12	51.09	35
Least Amount (Inches)	1.02	0.78	1.10	0.53	0.57	0.03	0.00	t	t	0.72	1.44	1.90	23.37	35
Maximum in 24 hrs. (Inches)	2.61	2.00	1.83	1.47	1.47	1.82	0.91	1.38	2.23	2.18	2.62	2.17	2.62	35
Mean Amount of Snow (Inches)	4.4	0.8	0.6	t	t	0.0	0.0	0.0	t	t	0.2	1.5	7.5	35
Maximum Snowfall in 24 hrs. (Inches)	10.6	3.2	7.7	t	0.5	0.0	0.0	0.0	t	0.2	4.5	8.0	10.6	35
Mean Number of Days with Snow (One Inch or More)	1	**	**	0	**	0	0	0	0	0	**	1	2	35
0.01 Inch or More, Mean Number of Days	19	16	17	14	11	9	3	5	7	13	18	19	153	35
WIND														
Mean Wind Speed (Knots) (0700 l.s.t.)	8.0	6.7	6.4	5.3	4.7	4.4	4.5	4.2	4.1	4.9	6.5	7.8	0	24
Mean Wind Speed (Knots) (1300 l.s.t.)	9.7	9.0	9.0	8.0	7.0	7.0	7.4	6.9	7.1	7.3	8.7	9.5	0	24
Direction (Percentage of Obs.): at 0700 l.s.t.														
North	1.0	1.0	1.0	1.8	4.3	6.9	11.1	7.3	3.6	1.8	1.6	1.3	0	24
North Northeast	0.6	1.0	0.3	0.8	1.6	1.5	2.8	2.2	1.4	0.6	0.9	0.9	0	24
Northeast	1.5	1.3	0.7	0.8	1.5	1.8	2.7	1.9	1.0	0.8	1.2	1.0	0	24
East Northeast	2.0	1.3	0.8	0.7	1.1	1.5	1.7	0.9	0.9	0.8	1.2	1.1	0	24
East	9.4	6.2	5.1	3.4	3.8	2.8	2.1	2.2	2.4	3.1	4.0	5.6	0	24
East Southeast	25.4	23.1	16.2	13.1	6.8	5.4	3.8	4.4	8.3	14.3	20.2	26.5	0	24
Southeast	10.1	9.8	7.8	6.7	4.7	4.0	2.6	5.3	8.7	9.9	11.2	10.2	0	24
South Southeast	5.7	4.2	5.5	5.4	3.2	4.1	2.6	5.2	5.3	5.0	5.7	4.5	0	24
South	8.8	7.8	10.3	9.4	7.0	7.4	4.3	6.5	7.4	9.3	8.5	8.6	0	24
South Southwest	8.2	9.1	12.5	10.3	8.4	6.7	3.5	3.9	4.7	6.5	8.1	10.2	0	24
Southwest	4.2	4.8	5.0	5.0	4.3	4.1	2.5	2.9	4.9	5.4	4.3	5.3	0	24
West Southwest	1.8	2.1	3.3	2.9	3.3	1.8	1.9	1.8	2.9	3.2	2.8	2.3	0	24
West	3.2	3.5	4.2	4.6	4.5	3.7	2.9	3.9	6.0	5.5	3.7	3.3	0	24
West Northwest	3.3	3.4	4.7	8.3	8.6	6.2	8.8	8.5	8.9	6.2	5.1	2.9	0	24
Northwest	3.1	3.4	4.6	6.8	14.4	14.9	19.6	17.6	11.2	6.6	5.4	1.8	0	24
North Northwest	1.5	1.5	1.6	3.3	7.6	11.0	15.8	9.9	5.4	2.7	1.4	1.2	0	24
Calm	10.1	16.7	16.5	16.7	14.9	16.2	11.4	15.4	17.2	18.3	14.8	13.3	0	24
Direction (Percentage of Obs.): at 1300 l.s.t.														
North	1.6	2.3	3.7	5.1	5.9	7.0	6.4	6.2	6.1	2.7	2.0	1.7	0	24
North Northeast	0.6	1.0	1.3	2.4	2.8	2.7	1.8	1.8	2.2	1.1	1.2	0.8	0	24
Northeast	1.2	2.4	1.6	3.5	2.7	2.9	2.0	3.1	2.3	2.2	1.2	0.7	0	24
East Northeast	1.8	2.0	2.9	2.8	3.3	2.3	1.6	2.2	3.3	1.8	1.7	2.0	0	24
East	10.1	6.7	7.5	5.1	5.3	2.8	2.1	2.3	6.5	5.2	6.2	7.0	0	24
East Southeast	23.1	18.1	9.1	5.0	3.6	2.3	1.1	1.4	3.2	11.7	19.1	24.6	0	24
Southeast	9.1	8.0	5.6	2.3	2.2	0.9	0.7	1.6	2.2	5.7	9.8	9.5	0	24
South Southeast	4.5	3.4	2.5	2.5	1.5	1.2	1.0	1.0	2.0	2.3	3.6	3.2	0	24
South	8.6	7.8	8.6	7.1	4.3	4.4	1.9	3.6	4.5	9.4	9.3	8.1	0	24
South Southwest	10.8	12.0	12.7	10.2	6.3	5.4	2.2	3.3	4.4	8.3	9.9	12.9	0	24
Southwest	4.8	5.8	7.9	7.4	6.0	5.0	3.3	3.2	4.0	5.8	5.4	5.8	0	24
West Southwest	4.3	4.2	6.3	6.7	5.0	3.5	2.3	2.8	4.8	3.1	2.6	3.2	0	24
West	3.9	6.0	5.7	6.7	6.2	7.6	8.4	7.7	7.0	7.1	4.8	3.4	0	24
West Northwest	4.9	6.8	9.5	11.6	16.8	18.7	26.0	25.0	19.2	12.6	6.8	4.2	0	24
Northwest	3.7	6.0	7.8	12.1	17.9	21.0	26.5	23.8	18.2	11.6	7.3	5.5	0	24
North Northwest	1.9	3.2	4.3	7.1	8.5	10.7	11.7	9.8	7.6	4.7	2.8	2.2	0	24
Calm	4.9	4.4	3.0	2.5	1.6	1.6	1.2	1.3	2.5	4.6	6.2	5.2	0	24
VISIBILITY														
Days with Visibility equal to or less than 1/4 mile	4	4	2	1	**	**	**	**	3	8	6	5	33	33

6

STRAIT OF JUAN DE FUCA

AIR TRANSPORTATION
Kenmore Air Harbor: (206) 486-1257
Lake Union Air: (800) 692-2993

CHAMBER OF COMMERCE
Port Angeles: (206) 452-2363
Port Townsend: (206) 385-2722
Sequim: (206) 683-6197

COAST GUARD
VHF 16 or 22
Port Angeles: (206) 457-4404
Port Ludlow: (206) 385-3070
Port Townsend: (206) 457-4404
Seattle: (206) 442-7070
Search and Rescue: (206) 457-4404

CUSTOMS
Neah Bay: (206) 645-2311
Port Angeles: (206) 457-4311
Port Townsend: (206) 385-3777
After hours: (800) 562-5943

DECOMPRESSION CHAMBER
Bremerton: (206) 396-5111
Virginia Mason, Seattle:
(206) 624-1144

FERRY TRANSPORTATION
Washington State: (800) 542-0812

RED TIDE HOTLINE: (800) 562-5632

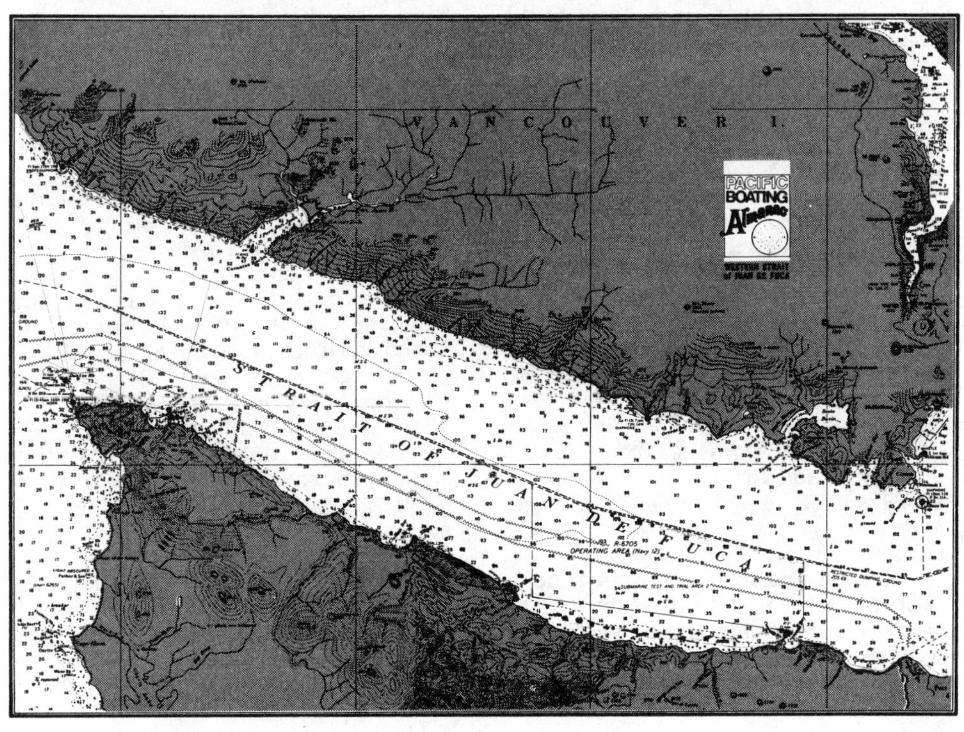

CHART 18400 † This includes the Strait of Juan de Fuca, Sequim Bay, Port Discovery, the San Juan Islands and its various passages and straits, Deception Pass, Fidalgo Island, Skagit and Similk Bays, Swinomish Channel, Fidalgo, Padilla and Bellingham Bays, Lummi Bay, Semiahmoo Bay and Drayton Harbor and the Strait of Georgia as far N as Burrard Inlet. The more important US. harbors described are Neah Bay, Port Angeles, Friday Harbor, La Conner, Anacortes, Bellingham and Blaine Harbor. Deep-draft vessels use the harbors at Port Angeles, Anacortes and Bellingham, the principal cities in the area. The Canadian coasts are only briefly described. (See Pub 154, Sailing Directions (enroute) for British Columbia, published by the Defense Mapping Agency Hydrographic / Topographic Center and the Sailing Directions, British Columbia Coast, (South Portion) Vol. 1, published by the Canadian Hydrographic Service, for complete information on Canadian water.)

STRAIT OF JUAN DE FUCA separates the S shore of Vancouver Island, Canada, from the N coast of the State of Washington. The entrance to the strait lies between parallels 48°23'N. and 48°36'N., on the meridian of 124°45'W. This important body of water is the connecting channel between the ocean and the inter-island passages extending S to Puget Sound and N to the inland waters of British Columbia and southeastern Alaska.

At its entrance and for 50 miles E to Race Rocks, the strait is about 12 miles wide and then widens to about 16 miles for 30 miles E to Whidbey Island, its E boundary. The waters as a rule are deep until near the shore with few outlying dangers, most of which are in the E part. The shores on both sides are heavily wooded, rising rapidly to elevations of considerable height and except in a few places, are bold and rugged.

The navigation of these waters is relatively simple in clear weather. The aids to navigation are numerous. In thick weather, because of strong and irregular currents, extreme caution and vigilance must be exercised.

The STRAIT OF JUAN DE FUCA TRAFFIC SEPARATION SCHEME has been established in the Strait of Juan de Fuca. Another system, the Haro Strait and Strait of Georgia Traffic Separation Scheme, has been established by the U.S. Coast Guard and Canadian Department of Transport. These schemes connect with each other and, although not a part of the mandatory PUGET SOUND VESSEL TRAFFIC SERVICE, described later in this chapter, both schemes are connected to that service. Vessels so desiring may while transiting the Strait, contact the Puget Sound Vessel Traffic Service by calling SEATTLE TRAFFIC on VHF-FM channel 14 (156.70 MHz) to receive desired information on known traffic, aids to navigation descrepancies and locally hazardous weather conditions. Preliminary calls to SEATTLE TRAFFIC on VHF-FM channel 16 (156.80 MHz) are not required or desired.

The Canadian Government recommends that ships conduct themselves in accordance with the navigational procedures set forth in the Ship Routing Regulations when navigating in or near the traffic separation scheme in Canadian waters. Mariners are advised that the Canadian Ship Routing Regulations are based upon the International Maritime Organization's "General Principles of Ships' Routing", except for a relaxation that permits vessels engaged in fishing to proceed in any direction in or near traffic lanes and on the high seas. (Canadian Ship Routing Regulations are published in the Annual Edition of Canadian Notices to Mariners.)

The Canadian waters S and E of Vancouver Island are a VESSEL TRAFFIC MANAGEMENT ZONE.

Complete details of the traffic separation schemes and the vessel traffic management and information system for the coastal waters of southern British Columbia are given in pub. No 152, Sailing Directions, Planning Guide for the North Pacific Ocean, published by the Defense Mapping Agency Hydrographic/ Topographic Center, Sailing Directions, British Columbia Coast (South Portion), Volume 1, published by the Canadian Hydrographic

Service and the Annual Edition of Canadian Notices to Mariners, published by the Canadian Coast Guard.

The TRAFFIC SEPARATION SCHEME (STRAIT OF JUAN DE FUCA) consists of five schemes: the WESTERN APPROACH and the SOUTHWESTERN APPROACH from the ocean and in the Strait, the WESTERN LANES, the SOUTHERN NORTHERN LANES to Victoria; and two precautionary areas, one NNW of Cape Flattery and the other N of Port Angeles. Each scheme consists of inbound and outbound traffic lanes separated by separation zones. Each precautionary area is marked by a lighted orange and white horizontally striped buoy. The lighted buoy marking the center of the precautionary area NNW of Cape Flattery is equipped with a radar transponder beacon (Racon). The purpose of these buoys is to assist in the separation of inbound and outbound vessels transiting the Strait of Juan de Fuca to eliminate as much as possible the cross vessel traffic that now occurs between the entrance to the Strait of Juan de Fuca at Cape Flattery and the pilot stations at Port Angeles and Victoria, B.C. It is recommended that all vessels navigate so as to leave these buoys to port.

The HARO STRAIT AND STRAIT OF GEORGIA TRAFFIC SEPARATION SCHEME, consisting of INBOUND and OUTBOUND TRAFFIC LANES separated by SEPARATION ZONES, continues E from the Victoria Approach segment of STRAIT OF JUAN DE FUCA TRAFFIC SEPARATION SCHEME to Victoria B.C., thence through Haro Strait, Boundary Pass and the Strait of Georgia, to Vancouver, B.C. Two abbreviated traffic separation schemes, also consisting of inbound and outbound traffic separation lanes, separated by separation zones, connect the Haro Strait and Strait of Georgia Scheme with the VESSEL TRAFFIC SERVICE (PUGET SOUND) described later in this chapter. One leads NW from the precautionary area E of Hein Bank into Haro Strait and the other leads NW from the precautionary area S of Alden Bank into the strait of Georgia. These abbreviated schemes are voluntary.

CAUTION † Since logging is one of the main industries of the region, free-floating logs and submerged deadheads or sinkers are a constant source of danger in the Strait of Juan de Fuca and Puget Sound. The danger is increased during freshets after storms, and unusually high tides. DEADHEADS or SINKERS are logs which have become adrift from rafts or booms, have become waterlogged, and float in a vertical position with one end just awash, rising and falling with the tide.

A VESSEL TRAFFIC SERVICE (PUGET SOUND), operated by the U.S. Coast Guard, has been established in the Strait of Juan de Fuca, E of Port Angeles and in the waters of Rosario Strait, Admiralty Inlet, Puget Sound and navigable waters adjacent to these areas. The System is designed to prevent collisions and groundings and to protect the navigable waters concerned from environmental harm resulting from such collisions and groundings.

The PUGET SOUND VESSEL TRAFFIC SERVICE comprises three major components: A TRAFFIC SEPARATION SCHEME, a VESSEL MOVEMENT REPORTING SYSTEM and RADAR SURVEILLANCE. The Traffic Separation Scheme comprises a network of one-way traffic lane separation zones in between and precautionary areas. The traffic lanes are each 1,000 yards wide and are separated by 500-yard-wide separation zones.

The Vessel Movement Reporting System is based upon a VHF-FM communications network maintained continuously by the Coast Guard Vessel Traffic Center in Seattle. This center will process information received from vessels in required and voluntary reports and will, in turn, disseminate navigational safety information to vessels participating in the service. The mariner is cautioned that information provided by the vessel traffic center is, with the exception of radar information, largely generated from these reports by vessels and can be no more accurate than that received. Additionally, the Coast Guard may not have firsthand knowledge of hazardous circumstances existing in the Vessel Traffic Service Area, and unreported hazards may confront the mariner at any time. The Vessel Traffic Service is shown on the appropriate nautical charts of the area.

CURRENTS, CAPE FLATTERY TO RACE ROCKS † The currents may attain velocities of 2 to 4 knots, varying with the range of tide and are influenced by strong winds. E of Race Rocks, in the wider portion of the strait, the velocity is considerably less. At Race Rocks and Discovery Island the velocity may be 6 knots or more.

The FLOOD CURRENT entering the Strait of Juan de Fuca sets with considerable velocity over Duncan and Duntze Rocks, but, instead of running in the direction of the channel, it has a continued set toward the Vancouver Island shore which is experienced as far as Race Rocks. The flood current velocity is greater on the N shore of the strait than on the S.

The EBB CURRENT is felt most along the S shore of the strait, and between New Dungeness Light and Crescent Bay there is a decided set S and W, especially during large tides. With the wind and swell against the current, a short choppy sea is raised near the entrance to the strait.

The current movement is complicated by a large daily inequality. The Tidal Current Tables should be consulted for times and velocities.

TIDE RIPS occur off the prominent points and in the vicinity of the banks. These are particularly heavy off Cape Flattery, Race Rocks, Dungeness Spit and Point Wilson, at times becoming dangerous to small vessels.

WINDS AND VISIBILITY † Winds are strongest from October through March. This results from the numerous winter storms that move through these waters; this is also an area where storms tend to intesify. As low-pressure systems approach the coast, winds strengthen and back to the SE quandrant, sometimes reaching gale force. After the storm passes, winds veer to the SW or NW. Gales usually last less than 1 day whereas the interval between storms normally varies from 1 to 5 days or up to 2 weeks when a strong high-pressure system settles in. These systems can also prevent local wind problems in the Georgia Strait. The

mountainous terrain of this region plays an important part in determining the direction and speed of the wind. There are normally two wind seasons - winter lasts from October through March, while a summer regime covers the other 6 months.

From October through March, winds at the Pacific entrance to the Strait of Juan de Fuca blow mostly out of the SE through SW. Gales blow on 4 to 6 days per month. They can come from any direction, however, SE winds are consistently the strongest, averaging about 18 knots. Strong SE winds raise dangerous confused seas off Cape Flattery, when they meet the long, rolling SW swells that frequent these waters. The frequent strong winds from a S quarter make the Vancouver coast between Cape Cook and Port San Juan a dangerous lee shore. When gales blow from the SW through W, it is usually safer inside the Strait than out. In general, winds are strongest and gales more frequent in the W end of the Strait. In the open water of the middle of the Strait, winter winds blow mostly out of the E through SE. Gales occur on about 2 to 4 days per month in the E half. The S shore is protected from the SE gales; Port Angeles provides good shelter. An approaching storm often sets up strong E winds in the central part of the Strait. This, in turn, sets up a drainage of air from the Georgia Strait, so that winds near the E entrance are frequently from the N through NE. As the storm moves inland, it produces a reversal of this flow. Winds blow from the W through most of the strait, backing to the SW in the E. Winds near the W entrance have reached 65 knots with gusts to 90 knots. In the strait, 50-knot winds and 80-knot gusts have been reported.

Summer winds at sea blow mainly from the SW through NW around the subtropical Pacific high. Heating of the North American continent helps draw air into the Strait of San Juan de Fuca. This sea breeze reinforces the prevailing flow and results in winds up to 30 knots in the late afternoon. The land breeze opposes the normal flow and calms are often the rule in early morning. SW through W winds are most frequent in the Strait of Juan de Fuca.

In few parts of the world is the vigilance of the mariner more called upon than when entering the Strait of Juan de Fuca from the Pacific in fog. Sea fog is the most common type, and it's at its worst from about July through October. Local land fog extends the visibility hazard into the winter. Fog is most frequent at the W end of the Strait. Here, visibilities drop to less than 0.75 mile on about 55 days annually, compared to about 35 days in the E end. Dense fog sometimes hangs over the ocean entrance to the Strait for days at a time; this is most likely during calms or light breezes. It gives the appearance of a wall and ships entering often run into clear, bright weather before they pass Tatoosh Island. Often the fog is carried E on the W sea breeze. When this happens, the fog usually penetrates farther E along the S shore. It is much more likely to reach Port Angeles or Port Townsend than Victoria. In spring, the E penetration of an infrequent fog is usually limited to Crescent or Freshwater Bays. Often when thick weather prevails in the Strait of Juan de Fuca, skies are clear N of Race Rocks.

CHARTS 18480, 18460 † Strait of JUAN DE FUCA, N SHORE (CANADA).-Carmanah Point has been described previously. BONILLA POINT, the N entrance point at the W end of the strait, is about 1.8 miles ESE from Carmanah Light. Bonilla Point is marked by a light. Inland of Bonilla Point which slopes gradually to the sea, the mountains attain heights over 3,500 feet and are heavily wooded. A reef extends 0.5 mile off the Point, and the shores should be given berth of at least 1.5 miles.

From Bonilla Point the coast trends in a SE direction for 9.5 miles to Owen Point. It is nearly straight, rocky and bluff, with high mountains rising immediately behind it; all are heavily wooded.

PORT SAN JUAN offers the first anchorage on the N shore within the entrance to the Strait of Juan de Fuca. The port is conspicuous from seaward, appearing as a deep gap between two mountain ranges.

The entrance between OWEN POINT and SAN JUAN POINT, 1.7 miles wide and 3.5 miles long, is 13 miles NE of Cape Flattery Light. It is marked by a lighted whistle buoy. San Juan Point is marked by a light and fog signal.

The port is open to SW winds and a heavy sea rolls in when a moderate gale is blowing from that direction. Though it is possible that a vessel with good ground tackle could ride out a gale if anchored in the most sheltered part, it is recommended that with any indication of SW gales a vessel should weigh anchor immediately and if the vessel's draft is 16 feet or less, seek shelter in Neah Bay: vessels of deeper draft should proceed to Port Angeles.

Anchorage may be had in 6 to 9 fathoms anywhere in Port San Juan: a good position is 5¼ fathoms about 1 mile from the beach at the head of the port.

CERANTES ROCKS, about 300 yards SW from San Juan Point, include several high pinnacle rocks with a few trees growing on them. About 800 yards N of these rocks and 300 yards from shore is another reef partly uncovered.

PORT RENFREW, is a settlement on the SE side of Port San Juan, about 2 miles NE of San Juan Point. A T-head pier has depths of 15 feet alongside.

From Port San Juan the coast trends SE for 23.5 miles to Sheringham Point. This stretch of coast presents no prominent features. The country is thickly wooded and the land rises to a considerable elevation. The points, some of which are bare on their extremities, are not prominent nor are they easily identified, except from close inshore.

A Canadian Armed Forces FIRING and PRACTICE EXERCISE AREA is established in the vicinity of Sheringham Point and San Simon Point about 8 miles to the W. (See Annual Edition of Canadian Notices to Mariners, for area limits, types of practice, warning signals, etc.)

Between Port San Juan and Race Rocks, fish traps and broken piles are reported to extend 0.5 mile offshore in places.

CHART 18465 † SHERINGHAM POINT is marked by a light. A fog signal is at a white square building close S of the light. Victoria marine radio station (VAK) is at Sheringham Point.

From Sheringham Point the coast continues in a series of bays and inlets for 16.5 miles to Race Rocks.

BEECHEY HEAD, 11.5 miles ESE of Sheringham Point is bold, wooded, and steep-to. Vessels bound up the strait and passing outside Race Rocks should give Beechey Head a berth of 2 miles.

RACE ROCKS, 5 miles E of Beechey Head, are a cluster of bare low rocks from 0.5 mile to almost 1.5 miles from shore. Foul ground extends for 0.5 miles in all directions from the light; dangerous overfalls and races occur during bad weather. A light, fog signal and radiobeacon are on the largest rock of the group and a lighted buoy marks the SE rock of the group. The tidal currents in Race Passage and in the vicinity of Race Rocks attain a velocity of 4 to 6 knots at times and dangerous tide rips are formed.

FIRING PRACTICE and EXERCISE AREAS of the Canadian Armed Forces are E of Race Rocks in the approaches to Esquimalt and Victoria Harbors. (See the Annual Edition of Canadian Notices to Mariners.)

Foul ground, due to dumping of heavy steel wire mesh material, is 3.2 miles W from Race Rocks Light.

E of Race Rocks the Strait of Juan deFuca expands to a width of about 16 miles and extends for 30 miles ENE to the entrance to Admiralty Inlet on the S and Rosaro Strait on the N.

A 25-fathom bank lies 8.5 miles SE of Race Rocks along the steamer track from Race Rocks Light to Point Wilson Light. The W edge of this bank is sometimes sharply defined by a line of ripples with glassy calm water to the E.

BENTINCK ISLAND, 1 mile NW of Race Rocks Light, is fringed with kelp on its S and E sides. PEDDER BAY, PARRY BAY, and ROYAL ROADS, separated by Eilliam Head and ALBERT HEAD, form the coast between the Bentinck Island and the W entrance to Esquimalt Harbor.

A 027°43'-207°43' MEASURED NAUTICAL MILE has been established on the NW shore of Parry Bay. Range beacons, consisting of fluorescent orange diamond-shaped daymarks, mark the NE and SW ends of the measured course.

A PROHIBITED AREA has been established in Parry Bay by the Canadian Government. No vessel may anchor in the area without permission.

WILLIAM HEAD is a comparatively low promontory extending about 0.5 mile NE of NED POINT. It is marked by a light and fog signal. Close W of William Head is QUARANTINE COVE, on the E shore of which are the conspicuous red brick buildings of the former quarantine station, now used as a penitentiary. Unauthorized vessels should not approach William Head within 200 yards.

Anchorage affording protection from W weather may be had in 7 fathoms about 0.5 mile N of William Head and about 1,200 yards from the mainland.

CONSTANCE BANK, 6.8 miles E of Wilson Head light, has general depths of 8 to 13 fathoms. It is about 2 miles long and 1 mile wide, within the 20 fathom curve. The bottom is rocky and tide rips form in this vicinity. Vessels should not attempt to anchor on the bank.

ALBERT HEAD, 3.3 miles NE of William Head, is marked by a light. FISGARD ISLAND, on the W side of the entrance to Esquimalt Harbor, is marked by a light. Its red sector covers SCROGGS ROCKS off the E entrance point. Scroggs Rocks are marked by a light.

ESQUIMALT HARBOR, about 3 miles NNE of Albert Head, affords safe and ample anchorage and can be entered at any time. The entrance channel has general depths of 8 fathoms. Depths within the entrance gradually decrease for 1.5 miles N to COLE ISLAND, above which the head of the harbor dries.

VICTORIA HARBOR, landlocked and well protected, is about 2 miles ESE of Esquimalt Harbor and can accommodate large vessels. A U.S. Immigration station is in Victoria.

Victoria Harbor is entered between MACAULAY POINT on the W and the breakwater extending from OGDEN

POINT on the E; the breakwater is marked by a light with a fog signal. The harbor extends for more than 0.5 mile N to SHOAL POINT on the E side and thence trends E to JAMES BAY. From the N part of James Bay, the upper harbor, which is crossed by three bridges, extends about 0.8 mile NNW to SELKIRK WATER, the W extremity of which is connected to PORTAGE INLET.

BROTCHIE LEDGE, the only outlying danger, about 200 yards long within the 5 fathom curve, lies 0.6 mile S of Ogden Point. The ledge has a least depth of 12 feet, and is marked by a light and fog signal.

CLOVER POINT, 2 miles ESE of the entrance to Victoria Harbor, is low, bare of trees and steep-to. Strong tide rips form off the point.

TRIAL ISLANDS, 4 miles E of Victoria Harbor, are bare and rocky; from most directions the two islands appear as one. The islands are marked by a light and fog signal. The S and larger island is 80 feet high and from STAINES POINT, its S extremity, a rocky ledge that uncovers 2 feet extends about 100 yards. Severe tide rips form off Staines Point, especially on the flood tidal current, which attains a velocity of 3 to 6 knots during large tides. The point should be given wide berth.

DISCOVERY ISLAND, 2 miles ENE of GONZALES POINT, lies off the junction of Haro Strait and the Strait of Juan de Fuca. The island is wooded and near its SE tip, PANDORA HILL attains a height of about 125 feet. The island is marked by a light and fog signal. The shore on all sides of the island is fringed with rocks in some places extending as far as 600 yards offshore.

CHARTS 18465, 18421, 18429   †
STRAIT OF JUAN FUCA, E END - HEIN BANK, with a least depth of 2¼ fathoms, lies 8.5 miles SE of Discovery Island; it is about 2 miles long in a N direction, within the 10-fathom curve, and 0.8 mile wide. The shoalest part of the bank is covered with thick kelp in the summer. It is marked by a lighted bell buoy equipped with a radar transponder beacon (Racon).

SMITH ISLAND, 5 miles W of Whidbey Island and 8 miles ESE of Hein Bank, is irregular in shape and about 0.5 mile long. The E end is low, but rises abruptly to an elevation of 55 feet at its W end, terminating in a white perpendicular cliff composed of sand and gravel. Kelp extends about 1.5 miles W of the island, with a width of about 1.5 miles over depths of 4 to 6 fathoms; a rock covered 3¼ fathoms lies about 1.8 miles W of the light. A rock that bares at lowest tides is about 0.3 mile W of the light. Strong currents set in and around the shoal area, especially on the flood and deep-draft vessels should keep well outside the 10-fathom curve to avoid being set into danger. SMITH ISLAND LIGHT (48°19.1'N, 122°50.6'W), 97 feet above the water, is shown from a 45-foot skeleton tower near the W extremity of the island; a radiobeacon is at the station.

A RESTRICTED AREA of air-to-surface weapon range is W of Smith Island.

MINOR ISLAND, small, low and rocky, lies 1 mile NE of Smith Island, and at lowest tide is connected with it by a gravel and boulder spit. A light and fog signal are on the island.

The N part of WHIDBEY ISLAND forms the E side of the Strait of Juan de Fuca. This part of the island has uniform sandy shore backed by low and rolling upland of farm and wooded areas.

The aerolight (48°20.9'N., 122°40.2'W.) at Ault Field is conspicuous.

-U S COAST PILOT 7
25th edition. August 1989
Corrected thru 10 22 90
Local Notice to Mariners

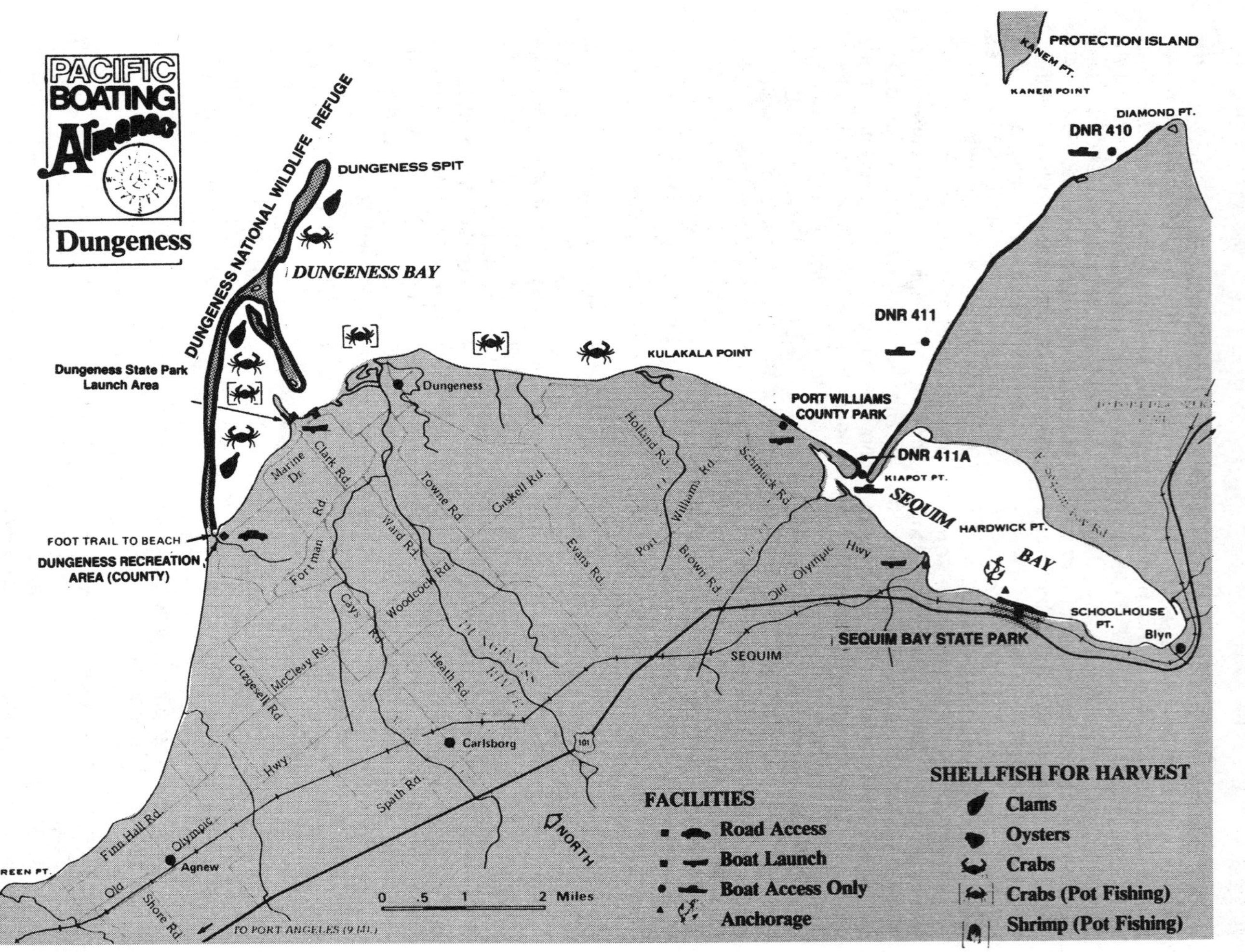

PACIFIC BOATING Almanac
Dungeness
PROTECTION ISLAND
KANEM PT.
KANEM POINT
DIAMOND PT.
DNR 410
DNR 411
DNR 411A
KIAPOT PT.
HARDWICK PT.
SCHOOLHOUSE PT.
Blyn
SEQUIM BAY
SEQUIM BAY STATE PARK
PORT WILLIAMS COUNTY PARK
KULAKALA POINT
DUNGENESS SPIT
DUNGENESS BAY
DUNGENESS NATIONAL WILDLIFE REFUGE
Dungeness State Park Launch Area
FOOT TRAIL TO BEACH
DUNGENESS RECREATION AREA (COUNTY)
Dungeness
Marine Dr
Clark Rd.
Fortman Rd
Ward Rd.
Towne Rd.
Giskell Rd.
Evans Rd.
Holland Rd
Port Williams Rd.
Brown Rd.
Schmuck Rd.
Cays Rd.
Woodcock Rd.
Heath Rd.
Lotzgesell Rd.
McCleay Rd.
Spath Rd.
Old Olympic Hwy
SEQUIM
Hwy
Carlsborg
101
Finn Hall Rd.
Old Olympic
Shore Rd.
GREEN PT.
Agnew
TO PORT ANGELES (9 MI.)
NORTH
0 .5 1 2 Miles
FACILITIES
Road Access
Boat Launch
Boat Access Only
Anchorage
SHELLFISH FOR HARVEST
Clams
Oysters
Crabs
Crabs (Pot Fishing)
Shrimp (Pot Fishing)

7

NEAH BAY TO PORT ANGELES

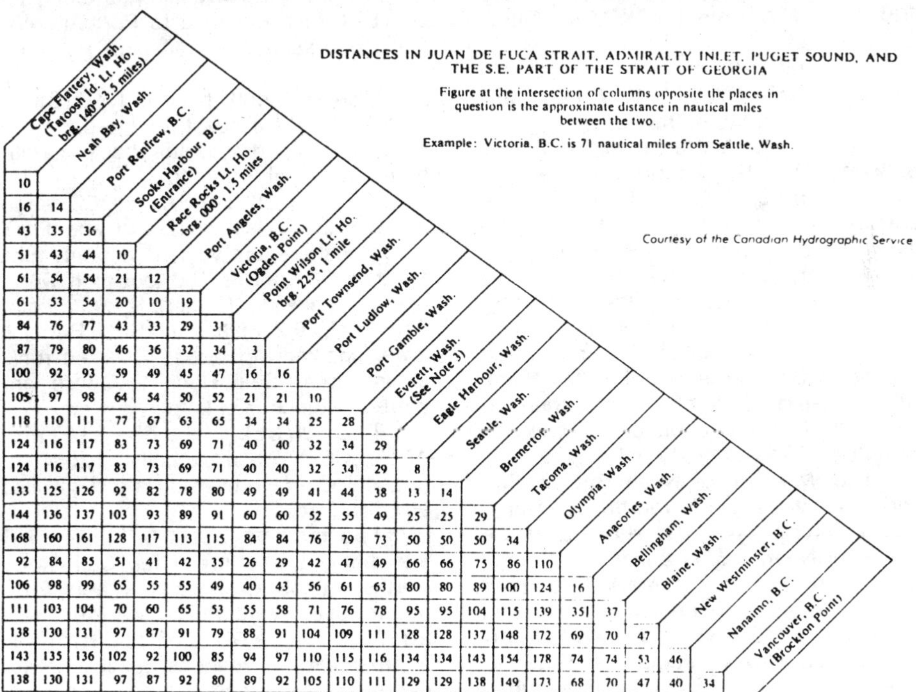

DISTANCES IN JUAN DE FUCA STRAIT, ADMIRALTY INLET, PUGET SOUND, AND THE S.E. PART OF THE STRAIT OF GEORGIA

Figure at the intersection of columns opposite the places in question is the approximate distance in nautical miles between the two.

Example: Victoria, B.C. is 71 nautical miles from Seattle, Wash.

Courtesy of the Canadian Hydrographic Service

Column places (left to right): 1 = Cape Flattery, Wash. (Tatoosh Id. Lt. Ho. brg. 140°, 3.5 miles); 2 = Neah Bay, Wash.; 3 = Port Renfrew, B.C.; 4 = Sooke Harbour, B.C. (Entrance); 5 = Race Rocks Lt. Ho. brg. 000°, 1.5 miles; 6 = Port Angeles, Wash.; 7 = Victoria, B.C. (Ogden Point); 8 = Point Wilson Lt. Ho. brg. 225°, 1 mile; 9 = Port Townsend, Wash.; 10 = Port Ludlow, Wash.; 11 = Port Gamble, Wash.; 12 = Everett, Wash. (See Note 3); 13 = Eagle Harbour, Wash.; 14 = Seattle, Wash.; 15 = Bremerton, Wash.; 16 = Tacoma, Wash.; 17 = Olympia, Wash.; 18 = Anacortes, Wash.; 19 = Bellingham, Wash.; 20 = Blaine, Wash.; 21 = New Westminster, B.C.; 22 = Nanaimo, B.C.; 23 = Vancouver, B.C. (Brockton Point).

From \ To	Cape Flattery	Neah Bay	Port Renfrew	Sooke Harbour	Race Rocks	Port Angeles	Victoria	Point Wilson	Port Townsend	Port Ludlow	Port Gamble	Everett	Eagle Harbour	Seattle	Bremerton	Tacoma	Olympia	Anacortes	Bellingham	Blaine	New Westminster	Nanaimo
Neah Bay	10																					
Port Renfrew	16	14																				
Sooke Harbour	43	35	36																			
Race Rocks	51	43	44	10																		
Port Angeles	61	54	54	21	12																	
Victoria	61	53	54	20	10	19																
Point Wilson	84	76	77	43	33	29	31															
Port Townsend	87	79	80	46	36	32	34	3														
Port Ludlow	100	92	93	59	49	45	47	16	16													
Port Gamble	105	97	98	64	54	50	52	21	21	10												
Everett	118	110	111	77	67	63	65	34	34	25	28											
Eagle Harbour	124	116	117	83	73	69	71	40	40	32	34	29										
Seattle	124	116	117	83	73	69	71	40	40	32	34	29	8									
Bremerton	133	125	126	92	82	78	80	49	49	41	44	38	13	14								
Tacoma	144	136	137	103	93	89	91	60	60	52	55	49	25	25	29							
Olympia	168	160	161	128	117	113	115	84	84	76	79	73	50	50	50	34						
Anacortes	92	84	85	51	41	42	35	26	29	42	47	49	66	66	75	86	110					
Bellingham	106	98	99	65	55	55	49	40	43	56	61	63	80	80	89	100	124	16				
Blaine	111	103	104	70	60	65	53	55	58	71	76	78	95	95	104	115	139	35	37			
New Westminster	138	130	131	97	87	91	79	88	91	104	109	111	128	128	137	148	172	69	70	47		
Nanaimo	143	135	136	102	92	100	85	94	97	110	115	116	134	134	143	154	178	74	74	53	46	
Vancouver	138	130	131	97	87	92	80	89	92	105	110	111	129	129	138	149	173	68	70	47	40	34

Notes: 1. Distances from ports in Juan de Fuca Strait to New Westminster, Nanaimo, and Vancouver are via Boundary Pass. For distances via Active Pass *deduct* 8 miles for Nanaimo, and 7 miles for New Westminster and Vancouver.
2. Distances from ports in Admiralty Inlet and Puget Sound to ports in the S.E. part of the Strait of Georgia are via Rosario Strait and adjacent channels.
3. Distances from Everett, Wash. to Anacortes, Bellingham, and ports in the S.E. part of the Strait of Georgia are by way of Saratoga Passage and Deception Pass. For distances over route west of Whidbey Island and via Rosario Strait *add* 11 miles.

CHARTS 18485, 18484 † On the S side of the Strait of Juan de Fuca the coast trends E for 4 miles from Cape Flattery to KOITLAH POINT, the W point of Heah Bay. The shores are rugged and the country is heavily timbered.

NEAH BAY, (48°22'N., 124°37'W.) about 5 miles E of Cape Flattery, is used extensively by small vessels as a harbor of refuge in foul weather. Its proximity to Cape Flattery and ease of access at any time make the anchorage very useful. It is protected from all but E weather.

BAADAH POINT, the E entrance point to Neah Bay, is rocky and grass-covered for some distance back from the WAADAH ISLAND, 0.3 mile N of Baadah Point, is 0.5 mile long, high and wooded. A rubblestone breakwater extends from the W side of the bay to about the middle of Waadah Island. A reef and foul ground extend 0.2 mile from the SW side of the island. A wharf, used by the Coast Guard, is on the S end of the island. A light and fog signal are at each end of the island. A reef that bares, marked by a lighted bell buoy, extends 500 yards NW from DTOKOAH POINT, SE of the entrance.

The buildings of the Coast Guard station, 0.4 mile SW of Baadah Point, are prominent from the entrance.

The buoyed entrance to the bay is between Waadah Island and Baadah Point. Depths of 14 to 16 feet can be carried into the bay. The careful navigator can carry 16 feet through the entrance by use of the chart and by favoring the S side of the entrance, passing the lights close aboard that mark the ends of the Makah Indian T-head pier about 375 yards W of Baadah Point. After passing the lights let the chart be the guide to the best water. Anchorage is in 20 to 40 feet, sandy bottom.

The W shore of Neah Bay is high and precipitous and bordered by craggy rock outcroppings. The shore E of the village of Neah Bay is a low sand beach to Baadah Point. Unmarked sunken wrecks are near the center of the bay in 48°22'25"N., 124°36'50"W. and in the N part of the bay in about 48°22'38"N., 124°36'32"W. Caution is advised when anchoring in the vicinity of the wrecks.

The Indian village of NEAH BAY, on the SW shore of the bay, is the site of considerable sport fishing and logging. Logs are trucked to a boom on the breakwater, 900 yards from the W end, where rafts are made up.

Neah Bay is a CUSTOMS PORT OF ENTRY. The customs officer also performs IMMIGRATION duties.

The Makah Indian T-head pier with a 300-foot face and privately marked at each end by a light, and the ruins of a T-head pier no longer visible, are about 375 and 500 yards SW of Baadah Point. Caution is advised in the vicinity of the pier in ruins, as submerged piles may exist. The Coast Guard pier is 0.5 mile W of Baadah Point.

Two cooperative fish piers, 1 mile and 1.2 miles SW of Baadah Point, have facilities for icing and supplying fishing boats. Limited berthage, electricity, gasoline, diesel fuel, water and ice are available. Both piers have reported depths of 12 feet off the ends. There are many small-craft floats extending along the S shore of the bay. Neah Bay has no public haulout or repair facilities.

A paved highway extends along the Strait of Juan de Fuca to Port Angeles; telephone service is available.

CHART 18460 † From Neah Bay to Clallam Bay, the coast for more than 14 miles is rugged and the back country high and heavily wooded.

SEAL ROCK and SAIL ROCK, about 2 miles E of Neah Bay and about 600 yards offshore, are very prominent. Seal Rock, the W one is 100 feet high with a flat top showing E, and light in color. Sail Rock, 0.2 mile E of Seal Rock, is lower and more pointed. Covered rocks extend from Seal Rock to shore and there are patches of kelp in this area.

The wreck of the steamer ANDALUCIA, once partially visible but now completely covered, is just off Seal and Sail Rocks.

Two marinas, about 0.1 mile apart, are along the shore near Sail Rock. Berths, gasoline, water, ice and 2-ton hoists are available. Mariners are advised to exercise caution in approaching the marinas because of the numerous rocks and ledges. The floats at the marinas bare at low water. SAIL RIVER empties near Seal and Sail Rocks. SEKIU RIVER, about 6.5 miles

Neah Bay, 5 miles east of Cape Flattery.

SE of Sail River, has some logging operations. The bridge over the river shows prominently through the trees.

CLALLAM BAY, about 15 miles SE of Neah Bay, is a broad open bight about 2 miles long and 1 mile wide. It affords anchorage in 6 to 10 fathoms, sandy bottom and is used to some extent in S or thick weather.

SLIP POINT, the E point of the bight, is high and wooded; there is a light-colored streak like a landslip down its face, which is visible for a long distance. A reef, extending 0.2 mile W of the point, is marked by a bell buoy. SLIP POINT LIGHT (48°15.9'N., 124°14.9'W.), 55 feet above the water, is shown from a 50-foot white square tower on a pile structure on the W extremity of the point; a fog signal is at the light.

SEKIU, (48°16'N., 124°18'W.) is a resort and sport fishing town on the W end of Clallam Bay and S of Sekiu Point. A resort at the N end of the town has berths within a stone breakwater with gasoline, water, ice, a launching ramp, and limited marine supplies available. The floats bare at low water. A small-craft basin, protected by a curved stone breakwater, is at the center of the S

shore of the bay. Gasoline, berths, water, ice and a launching ramp are available. CLALLAM BAY, a small town on the E side of Clallam Bay, has no waterfront facilities.

In entering Clallam Bay, give Slip Point a berth of more than 0.2 mile to avoid the reef projecting W of it. Stormbound vessels generally anchor abreast the rocky point near the middle of the long semicircular beach on the S shore of the bay.

PILLAR POINT, 6.7 miles ESE of Slip Point, is bold, 700 feet high, wooded up to its summit, with a dark pillar-shaped rock more than 100 feet high lying close under its E face. The rock shows prominently from W. Good anchorage may be had in 9 to 12 fathoms, sticky bottom, about 0.8 mile SE of Pillar Point. This anchorage offers good shelter from the heavy W swell, but gives no protection from the brisk E and NE winds that prevail in winter.

TWIN RIVERS are two small streams that flow into the strait about 7 miles E of Pillar Point. An earth filled barge-loading facility, 0.3 mile W of the West Twin River, has a reported depth of 15 feet alongside. The facility is owned by a cement company and used for barging clay to Seattle. A private unlighted range marks the approach to the facility.

CHART 18465 † Shoal water makes out a considerable distance from LOW POINT (48°09.6'N., 123°49.5'W.), 5 miles E of Twin Rivers and vessels should not approach this point closer than 0.8 mile. Many boulders that uncover are W of the point.

AGATE BAY, 3.5 miles E of Low Point, is clear and deep; 10 fathoms can be carried to within 0.2 mile of the shore.

CRESCENT BAY, 4.2 miles E of Low Point, is a small semicircular bight 1 mile in diameter. The E part is shoal and near the W shore the remains of a wharf should be avoided. This is not a good landing place in N weather. The anchorage is of limited extent and suitable only for small vessels. A resort at the W end of the bay has floats with berths for about 80 craft. Electricity, gasoline, diesel fuel, water, ice and a 2-ton hoist are avilable. CRESCENT ROCK, covered $\frac{1}{4}$ fathom and marked by a buoy, is 0.4 mile N of the W entrance point of Crescent Bay. The rock extends 0.4 mile in E direction, with a narrow channel between it and the point. The channel has a reported depth of 10 fathoms and is not recommended without local knowledge. A reef extends about 400 yards NW from TONGUE POINT, the E entrance point of Crescent Bay. A shoal, covered $1\frac{1}{4}$ fathoms, lies about 0.3 mile W of Tongue Point. A

wreck lies off the entrance about 0.3 mile N of Tongue Point.

OBSERVATION POINT is 3 miles E of Tongue Point. Between these points is a wooded ridge which, because of the lower land behind it, makes this area appear as an island when raised from E or W. The ridge attains an elevation of 1,135 feet, and is known as STRIPED PEAK. A rock, 20 feet high, lies close off Observatory Point; the rock and the point are almost joined at low water.

FRESHWATER BAY, about 4 miles E of Crescent Bay, is a broad open bight, affording anchorage in 6 to 10 fathoms. The bay and adjacent waters are designated as an EMERGENCY EXPLOSIVES ANCHORAGE.

ANGELES POINT, on the E side of Freshwater Bay, is low, sandy and covered with alders. The ELWHA RIVER empties into the strait at this point.

A microwave tower, marked by aircraft warning lights and a good landmark by day and night, is on Angeles Point.

CAUTION † The U.S. Navy advises that the Strait of Juan de Fuca Calibration Lighted Bell Buoy (48°14'15"N., 123°21'45"W.), about 6 miles NNE of Ediz Hook, is used by naval vessels to make equipment calibration tests. Mariners transiting this area are requested to proceed with caution.

-U S COAST PILOT 7
25th edition. August 1989
Corrected thru 10 22 90
Local Notice to Mariners

FACILITIES

NEAH BAY

FARWEST RESORT AND CHARTERS, Box 131, Neah Bay, WA 98357. (206) 645 - 2270. Open April - Sept. Fuel dock open 5AM - 8PM. Gas and outboard oil. Slips. Ice. Fishing: bait, tackle. Rental boats and motors. Charter boats. Features: Makah Museum, Cape Flattery and Swifsure Bank. Owners: Joan and Pete Hanson.

MAKAH RESORT, Box 757, Neah Bay, WA 98357. (206) 645 - 2366. All year. Overnight accommodations. Restaurant. Ice. Manager: Charlotte Venske.

MORTON'S RESORT (southerly portion of Neah Bay), Box 136, Neah Bay, WA 98357. (206) 645 - 2250. All year. Overnight accommodations. Restaurant. Trailer and campsites. Picnic area. Groceries. Ice. Laundry. Charts.

PETER'S NEAH BAY RESORT, P.O. Bxo 97, Neah Bay, WA 98357. (206) 645 - 2288. Open May 1 to Sept. 30. Boat hoist. Moorage. Dry storage. Cabins. Camping and RV sites. Ice. Cafe, groceries. Fishing: bait, tackle and rental boats. Owners: Don and Jean Anderson.

SNOW CREEK RESORT (on the Olympic Peninsula. Take Hwy. 112, 15 miles west of Sekiu or $4\frac{1}{2}$ miles E of Neah Bay) P.O. Box 248, Neah Bay, WA 98657. (206) 645-2284. Hoist cap.: 6 tons to 26 feet, open daylight hours. Fuel dock: gas and outboard mix. Moorings. Dry storage. Ice. Trailer sites. Showers. Camping. Fishing: bait and tackle. Rental boats.

SEKIU

COVE RESORT, P.O. Box 189, Sekiu, WA 98381. (206) 963 - 2321. Open May - Sept. 7AM - 12PM. Accommodations. Picnic area. Ice. Restaurant. Overnight guest dock. Boat rentals. Fishing: bait and tackle. Hiking. Skin and scuba diving. Owner: R. Little.

OLSON'S RESORT (on Hwy. 112) Box 216, Sekiu, WA 98381. (206) 963 - 2311. Open Feb. through Sept. Ramp: 6-lanes, concrete. Open 4 AM - 10 PM. Fuel dock: gas and outboard diesel mix, open same hours. Guest dock and moorings. Overnight accommodations. Trailer and RV campsites. Restaurant. Groceries. Ice. Fishing: bait and tackle. Rental boats and motors. Charter boats. Owner: Arlen A. Olson.

RICE'S RESORT, Box 180, Sekiu, WA 98381. (206) 963 - 2300. Moorage. Guest dock. Rental boats and motors. Cabins and RV sites. Pumpout station. Fishing: licenses, bait and tackle. Rental tackle. Owners: Skip and Kathy Mason.

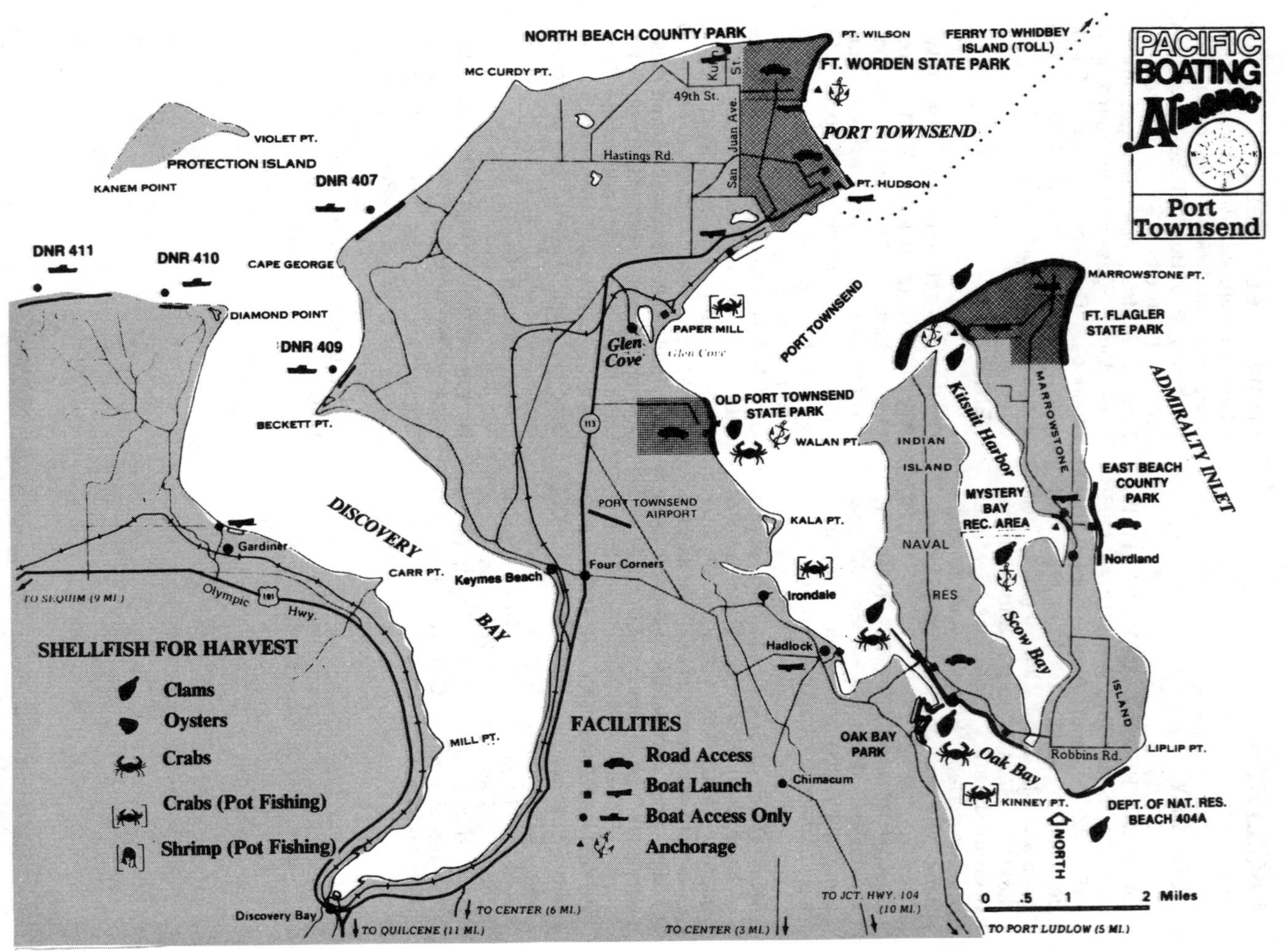

PACIFIC BOATING Almanac
Port Townsend
NORTH BEACH COUNTY PARK
PT. WILSON
FERRY TO WHIDBEY ISLAND (TOLL)
MC CURDY PT.
FT. WORDEN STATE PARK
49th St.
Kuhn St.
San Juan Ave.
PORT TOWNSEND
PT. HUDSON
VIOLET PT.
PROTECTION ISLAND
DNR 407
KANEM POINT
Hastings Rd.
DNR 411
DNR 410
CAPE GEORGE
DIAMOND POINT
DNR 409
MARROWSTONE PT.
FT. FLAGLER STATE PARK
PAPER MILL
PORT TOWNSEND
Glen Cove
Glen Cove
ADMIRALTY INLET
OLD FORT TOWNSEND STATE PARK
BECKETT PT.
WALAN PT.
Kitsuit Harbor
MARROWSTONE
EAST BEACH COUNTY PARK
INDIAN ISLAND
MYSTERY BAY REC. AREA
DISCOVERY
KALA PT.
NAVAL
Nordland
PORT TOWNSEND AIRPORT
RES
Scow Bay
ISLAND
BAY
Four Corners
Irondale
CARR PT.
Keymes Beach
TO SEQUIM (9 MI.)
Olympic Hwy.
101
Gardiner
Hadlock
OAK BAY PARK
Oak Bay
Robbins Rd.
LIPLIP PT.
MILL PT.
Chimacum
SHELLFISH FOR HARVEST
Clams
Oysters
Crabs
Crabs (Pot Fishing)
Shrimp (Pot Fishing)
FACILITIES
Road Access
Boat Launch
Boat Access Only
Anchorage
KINNEY PT.
NORTH
DEPT. OF NAT. RES. BEACH 404A
Discovery Bay
TO QUILCENE (11 MI.)
TO CENTER (6 MI.)
TO CENTER (3 MI.)
TO JCT. HWY. 104 (10 MI.)
TO PORT LUDLOW (5 MI.)
0 .5 1 2 Miles
113

8

PORT ANGELES TO HOOD CANAL
(48°07'N., 123°26'W., 48°07'N., 122°45'W.)
PORT ANGELES, PORT TOWNSEND, PORT LUDLOW

AIR TRANSPORTATION
Kenmore Air Harbor: (206) 486-1257
Lake Union Air: (800) 692-2993

CHAMBER OF COMMERCE
Port Angeles: (206) 452-2363
Port Townsend: (206) 385-2722
Sequim: (206) 683-6197

COAST GUARD
VHF 16 or 22
Port Angeles: (206) 457-4404
Port Ludlow: (206) 385-3070
Port Townsend: (206) 457-4404
Seattle: (206) 442-7070
Search and Rescue: (206) 457-4404

RED TIDE HOTLINE
(800) 562-5632

CUSTOMS
Neah Bay: (206) 645-2311
Port Angeles: (206) 457-4311
Port Townsend: (206) 385-3777
After hours: (800) 562-5943

DECOMPRESSION CHAMBER
Bremerton: (206) 396-5111
Virginia Mason, Seattle:
(206) 624-1144

FERRY TRANSPORTATION
Coho Ferry: (206) 457-4491
Washington State: (800) 542-0812
Port Angeles: (206) 457-4491

HOOD CANAL BRIDGE
(206) 779-3377

PORT TOWNSEND, immediately S of Point Wilson, is entered between Point Hudson and Marrowstone Point. Use chart 18441.

CHART 18468 † PORT ANGELES, 6.5 miles E of Freshwater Bay and 56 miles from Cape Flattery, is entered between EDIZ HOOK, a low, narrow, and bare sandspit 3 miles long, and the main shore to the S. The harbor, about 2.5 miles long, is easy access by the largest vessels, which frequently use it when awaiting orders or a tug, or are weatherbound.

The harbor is protected from all except E winds, which occasionally blow during the winter. During SE winter gales, the wind is not usually felt but some swells roll in. The depths are greatest on the N shore and decrease from 30 to 15 fathoms in the middle of the harbor; from the middle, the depths decrease regularly to the S shore, where the 3-fathom curve in some places in the E part is nearly 0.2 mile from the beach. A rock covered 19 feet is reported in the approach to the harbor in about 48°07'25"N., 123°23'00"W. A depth of 25 feet is off the Rayonier, Inc. Pier, the easternmost pier on the waterfront, and a shoal with a least depth of 3 fathoms lies 350 yards NW of the NW corner of the pier. A buoy is 225 yards off the NW corner of the pier.

Extra caution in navigating the waters inside Ediz Hook should be exercised because of the large number of submerged deadheads or sinkers in the area. The best anchorage is off the wharves, in 7 to 12 fathoms, sticky bottom. A NON ANCHORAGE AREA has been established in the E part of Port Angeles harbor. Extensive log booming grounds in the N part of the harbor extend more than 1 mile from the W shore. Care must be taken when anchoring at night to avoid the rafted logs; the booming grounds are charted.

EDIZ HOOK LIGHT (48°08.4'N., 123°24.5'W.), 70 feet above the water, is shown from the top of the Coast Guard air station control tower, 0.3 mile W of the E extremity of Ediz Hook. A radiobeacon and a fog signal are near the E end of the point. Shoals extend to about 75 yards E of the E extremity of Ediz Hook. A lighted buoy is about 150 yards E of the outer limits of the shoals. Coast Guard radio station NOW is at the air station. An unmarked shoal with a least depth of 44 feet is about 3.4 miles WNW of Ediz Hook Light.

PORT ANGELES, (48°07'N., 123°26'W.) is on the S shore of the harbor. Logs, lumber, plywood, newsprint, pulp, shakes and shingles, and petroleum products are the principal commodities handled.

COAST GUARD † A Coast Guard station is on Ediz Hook, about 0.3 mile W of the E extremity.

HARBOR REGULATIONS † The Port of Port Angeles Manager's office is at the Port docks.

SMALL-CRAFT FACILITIES † Port Angeles Boat Haven, operated by the port, is a large, well-equipped small-craft basin in the SW part of the harbor that can accommodate a large fleet of fishing boats and some pleasure craft. The basin is marked by lights. In July 1986, a controlling depth of 20 feet was in the entrance, and depths of 14 to 50 feet in the NW part of the basin with $9\frac{1}{2}$ to 14 feet in the SE part except for shoaling along the edges. About 500 berths, electricity, gasoline, diesel fuel, water, ice and marine supplies are available. A boat yard at the E end of the basin has a marine railway that can handle craft to 125 tons or 70 feet long and a 40-ton mobile hoist that can handle craft to 65 feet long or 22 feet wide. An 83-foot port-operated tidal grid is also available at the yard. Hull and engine repairs can be made at the yard and electronic repair work can be arranged. The harbormaster controls the moorings in the basin and the use of the tidal grid.

A 121°16'-301°16' MEASURED NAUTICAL MILE and a 200-yard MEASURED COURSE are in the SW part of the harbor close N of Port Angeles Boat Haven.

CHART 18465, 18471, † From Port Angeles the coast trends E for 13 miles to end of DUNGENESS SPIT, which borders the W side of DUNGENESS BAY. This bay affords shelter in W winds, but is open E; in N weather, the protection afforded is only fair. It is a dangerous place in winter gales, especially from the SE. The bay is formed by a sandspit extending NE 4 miles and forming, in addition to

Dungeness Bay, a small lagoon at the head of the harbor that can be entered by light-draft vessels with local knowledge.

A 75°-255° MEASURED NAUTICAL MILE has been established on the strait side of Dungeness Spit; the range markers are in the small lagoon at the head of the harbor.

NEW DUNGENESS LIGHT (48°10.9'N., 123°06.6'W.), 67 feet above the water, is shown from a 63-foot white conical tower on a dwelling on the outer end of the spit. A radiobeacon and fog signal are at the light.

From the end of the spit a shoal extends NE for 0.8 mile from the light. This has been reported as extending farther N, and it should be passed with caution. A lighted bell buoy marks the shoal but it may be submerged during periods of strong current; vessels should not pass between the buoy and the light. A shoal makes out about 1 mile from the S side of the bay.

The best anchorage is in 5 to 9 fathoms, sticky bottom, about 1 mile SE of the light, clear of the cable area.

DUNGENESS is a small town on the S shore of the bay. The ruins of a former wharf extend about 1,000 yards out across the flats.

SEQUIM BAY, 6 miles SE of Dungeness Bay is a landlocked bay 3.8 miles long. From the NE corner of the bay a sandspit extends W almost to the W shore and terminates in KIAPOT POINT, leaving only a narrow, winding channel marked by buoys, through which 9 feet can be taken with local knowledge. N of this point a shoal, marked on the end by a buoy, extends about 800 yards E from the W shore, and S of Kiapot Point a bar extends across the fairway. Inside is a good anchorage anywhere in 6 to 21 fathoms, muddy bottom. The harbor is seldom used and should be approached only by those with local knowledge. Buoys in the entrance to the bay are reported to sometimes tow under during strong currents. A marina with lights at the E ends of the entrance breakwaters is in the small cove just N of PITSHIP POINT on the W side of the bay. A marine research center of the Battelle Memorial Institute, with conspicuous white buildings, is on the W

side of the entrance to the harbor abreast the sandspit. Some log rafts are made up in the bay. SEQUIM BAY STATE PARK is at the SW end of the bay.

DISCOVERY BAY is 2 miles SSE of Protection Island. George Vancouver, the English explorer, anchored and refitted his ships here for his exploration of these regions in 1792. The bay trends in a SE direction for about 8 miles. The entrance is masked from seaward by Protection Island, which protects it from NW winds. There are no outlying dangers, and the depths are great.

A dangerous sunken wreck is on the W side of the bay about 300 yards S of Mill Point in 48°00'53"N., 122°51'27"W.

In August 1980, a sunken wreck was reported on the E side of the bay in about 48°03'17"N., 122°51'08"W.

DIAMOND POINT is the W point at the entrance to Discovery Bay. A wharf in ruins is just inside the point.

The shore from CAPE GEORGE, the E entrance point of Discovery Bay, for 3 miles to McCURDY POINT, consists of high, bare clay bluffs, sparsely wooded on top, attaining a height of 400 feet near the NE end. A shoal covered 2 fathoms extends 0.6 mile NW of McCurdy Point; it is marked by a buoy. Vessels are cautioned not to pass between the buoy and the point.

CHART 18441 † From McCurdy Point the shore trends E for 3.5 miles to Point Wilson, the W point at the entrance to Admiralty Inlet, and consists of high, bare clay bluffs, sparsely wooded on top, decreasing in height near McCurdy Point, and ending abruptly close W to Point Wilson.

POINT WILSON LIGHT (48°08.7'N., 122°45.2'W.), 51 feet above the water, is shown from a white octagonal tower on a building on the E extremity of the low point. A radiobeacon and fog signal are at the light.

Shoals extend 0.5 mile NW of Point Wilson to the 5-fathom curve over irregular bottom; these are generally indicated by kelp. The E edge of the shoals rises rather abruptly from deep water. Heavy tide rips extend N of these shoals, being especially heavy with a W wind and ebb current. A buoy marking the shoals is about 0.7 mile NW of Point Wilson Light.

In approaching Point Wilson in thick or foggy weather, especially if the fog signal is not heard, soundings should be taken continuosly.

POINT PARTRIDGE, the W point of Whidbey Island, has a yellow face and is prominent from the N or S; it is rounding and not easily identified from the W. A light and fog signal are on the point. A rocky ledge, marked by a lighted bell buoy, extends 0.5 mile W from the point. In the summer, the ledge is usually marked by kelp.

The W shore of Whidbey Island, between Admiralty Head, and Point Partridge, is mostly a sandy beach rising sharply to bluffs 100 to 250 feet high, backed by pine trees. The shoreline is generally strewn with logs.

A naval RESTRICTED AREA is off the W shore of Whidbey Island.

ADMIRALTY HEAD, 80 feet high, on Whidbey Island, is the E entrance point of Admiralty Inlet and the SE extremity of a succession of light bare bluffs which extend N of Point Partridge, where they attain their highest elevation. About 0.5 mile N of Admiralty Head an abandoned lighthouse tower 39 feet high stands on top of a bluff.

From Point Partridge the NW coast of Whidbey Island extends NNE for 11.5 miles to Deception Pass. It is free of flying dangers, but should not be approached closer than 1 mile.

PARTRIDGE BANK, within the 10-fathom curve, is about 3 miles long and 1.5 miles wide; the SE end reaches within 2 miles of Point Partridge. The N and E sides fall off abruptly to 20 and 30 fathoms. The shoalest part, $2\frac{3}{4}$ fathoms, lies near the N side about midway between the ends; it is marked by a buoy. A lighted bell buoy is about 0.6 mile SSE of the $2\frac{3}{4}$ fathom spot. A considerable part of the bank is covered with kelp, which is usually drawn under by currents. This generally extends to the 7-fathom curve, except toward the E end where the shoal narrows, and no kelp exists beyond a depth of 4 fathoms.

Fort Worden, formerly an Army base, about 0.6 mile SSW of Point Wilson, is a State Park. An unused 438-foot pier in good condition, with reported depths of 14 feet and shoaling along the face, is located here.

PORT TOWNSEND, (48°07'N., 122°45'W.) immediately S of Point Wilson, is entered between Point Hudson and Marrowstone Point. It extends in a general SSW direction for 2.5 miles, and then turns SSE for 3 miles, with a reduced width to its head. Inside Point Hudson, depths generally range from 5 to 20 fathoms. It is an excellent harbor with good anchorage throughout and is easily entered. The prevailing winds in summer are from W to SW, and in winter are generally in the SE quadrant.

The large pulpmill at GLEN COVE, (48°05'N., 122°47'W.) on the W shore of PORT TOWNSEND, emits a continuous whitish smoke, which acts like fog, but is more persistent. At times the visibility in Admiralty Inlet is reduced to about 0.5 mile by the smoke as far N and W as Dungeness with E winds, and as far S as Point No Point with N winds. The smoke has a characteristic sulfurous odor. Visibility is particularly reduced when natural fog occurs at the same time.

POINT HUDSON, on the W shore 1.7 miles SSE of Point Wilson, is low and sandy. It is marked by a light and fog signal. The outer limits of the shoal making out from the point are marked by a lighted bell buoy NE of the light.

MARROWSTONE POINT, the E point at the entrance to Port Townsend, is low at its extremity, but rises abruptly to a bluff about 120 feet high. The buildings of the former Fort Flager, now a recreation area of the Washington Park system, are about 0.5 mile to the S. The fort pier, with depths of about 20 feet at its face, is in poor condition. MARROWSTONE POINT LIGHT (48°06.1'N., 122°41.w'W.), 28 feet above the water, is shown from a 20-foot white square structure on the E edge of the point; a fog signal is at the light. Piling of former piers and anchor piling for wartime submarine nets extend up to 500 yards offshore 0.6 mile and 1.6 miles W of the light.

MIDCHANNEL BANK, covered $4\frac{3}{4}$ to 10 fathoms, extends NW from Marrowstone Point about 2 miles toward Point Wilson.

PORT TOWNSEND, the principal town, is on the W shore immediately W of Point Hudson. The depths at the wharves range from 12 to 20 feet along the faces. The only commercial traffic, other than fishing boats and occasional oil barges, is at the large Crown Zellerbach papermill SW of the town just N of Glen Cove.

TIDES † The mean range of tide at Port Twnsend is 5.2 feet, and the diurnal range of tide is 8.4 feet. Because of the large daily inequality in this vicinity there may be only one high water and one low water a day. Reference should be made to the Tide Tables which give daily tide predictions for Port Townsend contained in this edition of the PACIFIC BOATING ALMANAC.

STORM WARNING SIGNALS ARE DISPLAYED (See chart.)

Port Townsend is a CUSTOMS PORT OF ENTRY.

The graystone Custom House-Post Office Building, built in 1893, is conspicuous on the bluff overlooking the waterfront. This building was the customs headquarters for Puget Sound until 1913, when headquarters was moved to Seattle. Deep-draft vessels are inspected alongside the pulpmill wharf; tugs, after leaving their tows, and some small craft go to the Standard Oil pier SE of the Post Office Building for inspection. Most small craft are inspected either at the Point Hudson Boat Harbor or the Port Townsend Boat Haven.

POINT HUDSON HARBOR, just W of Point Hudson, is leased by the Port of Port Townsend to a private company. The entrance, protected by jetties, is marked by a private light on the end of the S jetty. Over 100 small-craft berths, electricity, gasoline, diesel fuel, water, ice and marine supplies are available. A 25-ton mobile hoist at the harbor can handle craft up to 50 feet for hull and engine repairs. A launching ramp is adjacent to the hoist. In June 1973, reported depths of 15 feet were available through the entrance of the harbor and to the hoist at the NW end of the basin. The town business district is adjacent to the harbor.

The terminus of Port Townsend-Keystone ferry is 0.2 mile WSW of Point Hudson Harbor.

The 440-foot long Union Wharf, 0.1 mile WSW of the ferry slip, has depths of 9 to 22 feet reported alongside and a deck height of 18 feet; receipt of fish, fueling and icing fishing vessels, mooring government vessels; owned and operated by Union Wharf Corp. Numerous shops and a restaurant are on the Wharf. Diesel fuel and water are available.

PORT TOWNSEND BOAT HAVEN † 1.1 miles SW from Point Hudson, is operated by the Port of Port Townsend. The entrance is marked by lights; in July-August 1985, the midchannel controlling depth was 11 feet in the entrance with depths of 10 to 12 feet in the basins. There are floats for about 375 small craft. A seafood packing company, several boat building and boat repair firms, and an electronic equipment repair firm are at the basin. Electricity, gasoline, diesel fuel, water, ice and marine supplies are available. Two mobile cranes, 40- and 60-ton capacities, are at the basin for launching and hauling out small craft. A launching ramp is at the SW end of the basin.

A 042°-222° MEASURED NAUTICAL MILE has been established off Port Townsend. The range markers, on the Port Townsend Boat Haven breakwater and on the Crown Zellerbach Pier, are orange and square daymarks with a black stripe.

SUPPLIES † Gasoline and diesel fuel are available at Point Hudson Harbor, and at Port Townsend Boat Haven. Water, ice and marine supplies are available at these facilities and in the town.

REPAIRS † Only minor above-the-waterline repairs can be made to large vessels. A 40-ton and a 60-ton mobile straddle crane are available at Port Townsend Boat Haven; a 25-ton hoist is at Point Hudson Harbor. Hull, engine and electronic repairs can be made.

COMMUNICATIONS † A passenger and automobile ferry operates between Port Townsend and Keystone Harbor, just E of Admiralty Head,

Whidbey Island. The town is served by a State highway and two railroads.

GLEN COVE, about 2.2 miles SW of Point Hudson, is the site of the large Crown Zellerbach papermill, at the N end of the cove. The 480-foot-long pier has reported depths of 30 feet alongside and a deck height of 18 feet. A private light and fog signal, on the seaward end of the pier, are maintained by the mill. A slight current may be encountered, and the use of an anchor is recommended in docking. The large white building and tall stacks of the mill are prominent, as is the smoke.

A Naval restricted area is in the E part of the harbor off WALAN POINT (48°04'18'N., 122°44'47'W.)

IRONDALE, on the W shore about 1.5 miles from the head of the bay, is the site of a former iron foundry. Shoal water extends nearly 0.3 mile from the shore at this place. Log booms extend N 0.8 mile to KALA POINT, which is marked by a light.

HADLOCK, a village at the head of the harbor, has landings with depths of 10 and 12 feet. A mooring float is maintained here during the summer by the Port of Townsend. Gasoline is available in the town. A marine railway here can handle craft to 20 tons, 42 feet long, and 12 feet wide for hull repairs. Submerged pilings are in the vicinity of the mooring float, and local knowledge is necessary to avoid them.

PORT TOWNSEND CANAL, a dredged Passage giving access to Oak Bay to the SE: is subject to considerable shoaling. In February-September 1984, the controlling depth was 14 feet. The S entrance is jettied; a light and daybeacon mark the S entrance. A light is at the N entrance.

Currents through the canal are strong at times, although there is no particular danger from them as the channel is wide and straight; there are, however, strong eddies at the S end on the ebb current.

The canal is crossed by a fixed highway bridge with a clearance of 58 feet. Power cables nearby have clearances of 90 feet.

KILISUT HARBOR, between INDIAN ISLAND on the W and MARROWSTONE ISLAND on the E, is a narrow inlet extending about 4 miles in a SSE direction. A Navy ammunition depot is on Indian Island. The entrance to Kilisut Harbor is 2.5 miles WSW of Marrowstone Point. The entrance channel is winding. In October 1981, a reported depth of 5 feet was in the entrance channel. A submerged pile is N of the entrance in about 48°05'13"N., 122°44'24"W.; caution is advised when approaching Kilidut Harbor from N. Inside the harbor is good anchorage in 4 to 5 fathoms. At the S end of the harbor the two islands are connected by an earth filled causeway and narrow strip of beach. The village of NORLAND is on the E side of MYSTERY BAY, a small shallow cove midway on the E side of Kilisut Harbor. A small-craft float is maintained in the cove by the Washington State Park Sysem. Water is available. The short pier on an oyster company is just SW of the State Park float. The head of the cove is used as a log dump. Caution should be exercised to avoid two concrete blocks located 20 to 30 feet off the E end of the State Park pier.

CHARTS 18448, 18477 †
ADMIRALTY INLET extends from the Strait of Juan de Fuca to Foulweather Bluff.

ADMIRALTY HEAD, 80 feet high, on Whidbey Island, is the E entrance point of Admiralty Inlet and the SE extremity of a succession of light bare bluffs which extend N of Point Partridge, where they attain their highest elevation. About 0.5 mile N of Admiralty Head an abandoned lighthouse tower 39 feet high stands on top of a bluff.

ADMIRALTY BAY, E of Admiralty Head, is used only occasionally as an anchorage as it is exposed to SW winds and has a hard bottom and strong current.

KEYSTONE HARBOR (see also Chart 18464) is entered through a dredged channel just NE of Admiralty Head. A ferry landing is at the head of the harbor. This landing is the Whidbey Island terminus of the passenger and automobile ferry that operates to Port Townsend. In April 1986, the midchannel controlling depth in the entrance channel was 18 feet, then 14 to

18 feet in the harbor basin except for shoaling along the edges. A breakwater, marked by a light, protects the E side of the entrance. A private light on a concrete pile marks the W side of the entrance.

A tall, narrow grayish green tank is prominent on LAGOON POINT, 5.5 miles SSE of Admiralty Head.

BUSH POINT, 8 miles SSE of Admiralty Head, is marked by a light at the end of a low sandspit. Back of the spit the land shows a low timbered point from N or S. The flood current is reported to set strongly toward Bush Point. In July 1983, Puget Sound Traffic Lane Separation Lighted Buoy SC, about 1.1 miles W of Bush Point, was reported to submerge during periods of strong currents. Tidal Current Charts for this area should be consulted. They are contained in this edition of the PACIFIC BOATING ALMANAC. Several rocks lie nearly 0.2 mile offshore 1.1 miles SE of Bush Point.

OAK BAY is a cove on the W side of Admiralty Inlet, W of the S ends of Marrowstone and Indian Islands. A $\frac{3}{4}$-fathom shoal, marked by a buoy, extends S of the E entrance point.

MUTINY BAY, between Bush Point and Double Bluff, affords temporary anchorage near the center in 10 to 20 fathoms. This anchorage is useful if overtaken by fog. The extremities are clay bluffs, and the center is low with extensive flats. Several sport fishing resorts are in the bay. Some have marine railways and can make minor repairs to outboard engines, and most have gasoline, water, and ice. Strong tide rips, at times dangerous for small craft, occur off Double Bluff, particularly on the ebb with strong NW winds. There is frequently an eddy in Mutiny Bay; tidal current charts should be consulted. They are contained in this edition of the PACIFIC BOATING ALMANAC.

DOUBLE BLUFF, marked by a light, consists of bare, white cliffs, 300 to 400 feet high on its E face, but much lower on its SW face. A lighted buoy marks the extremity of the shoals 600 yards W of the bluff. The shoals are usually marked by kelp.

CHART 18477 † Foulweather Bluff, on the E side of the entrance of Hood Canal, is one of the most prominent cliffs in Puget Sound. The N face, which is bare, is 0.5 mile broad and consists of vertical, grayish sand and clay cliffs, 225 feet high, sloping off on the E side to a bluff 40 feet high, but on the Hood Canal side the point is steep and high. A marsh, enclosed by a sandspit and marked by a light, extends about 500 yards from the base of the bluff on the hood Canal side. The top of the bluff is fir and underbrush. There are several boulders which bare within 100 yards N of the highest part of the bluff, and a shoal covered 2 to 18 feet extends 200 yards E from the extremity and in line with the face of the bluff. If overtaken by fog, a vessel can find temporary anchorage 0.5 mile N of Foulweather Bluff, in not less than 60 feet. A lighted bell buoy marks the shoal 0.4 mile N of the bluff.

At times the tide rips N of and around Foulweather Bluff are sufficiently heavy to be dangerous to small craft and to break up log rafts. This is most dangerous when the ebb current from the main body of Puget Sound meets that of Hood Canal off the point, and particularly so with the ebb against a strong N or NW wind.

KALAS ROCK, 0.2 mile from the W shore and 0.7 mile SSE of OLELE POINT, marks the entrance to Mats Mats Bay to the W and to PORT LUDLOW to the S. It is of small extent and awash at high water. The rock, marked by kelp, is surrounded by deep water with depths up to 100 feet between it and the shore. Klas Rock is marred on the N side by a lighted bell bouy, and on the S side by a buoy.

MATS MATS BAY, SW of Klas Rock, is a small, nearly landlocked lagoon offering excellent protection from the wind to small craft. The entrance to the bay is about 100 yards wide at high water. A dredged channel, marked by a 261°15' lighted range, buoys, and lights, leads from the entrance to the NE corner of the bay. In June 1977, the controlling depth in the entrance channel was 5 feet for a midwidth of 100 feet. Good anchorage may be had in the bay with general depths of 4 to 12 feet.

The three COLVOS ROCKS, 0.7 mile off Klas Rock and about 0.3 mile off the W shore, mark the N extremity of the bank covered by 7 to 28 feet which extends in an arc S to TALA POINT. The NW rock, 28 feet high and of small extent with deep water around it, is marked by a light. The SE point of the shoal extending SE from the rocks is marked by a buoy. Tala Point is a bluff, wooded, and about 310 feet high. A light is about 200 yards NE of the point.

SNAKE ROCK is 0.4 mile SW of the W Colvos Rock and 300 yards offshore.

The entrance to PORT LUDLOW, in the W part of Admiralty Inlet, is just W of Colvos Rocks on the W side at the entrance the bay extends in a general S direction 2.5 miles, terminating in a basin 0.5 mile in diameter. The basin affords good anchorage in 40 to 50 feet, soft bottom; the shores are fairly steep.

The town of PORT LUDLOW, once a major Puget Sound lumber port, is on the N shore of the inner portion of the bay. The former Port Ludlow townsite is now occupied by a housing development and resort of the same name. All that remains of the once thriving lumber industry here are the ruins of the municipal wharf, the concrete foundation of a sawmill slash burner, and a log dumping ground at the head of the bay. A few private small-craft floats are in the bay.

The resort has berths for nearly 100 craft; electricity, gasoline, diesel fuel, water, and ice are available. Reported depths of 16 feet can be taken to the floats. Lodging and a beautiful eighteen hole golf course are available.

THE TWINS are two islands at the extreme SW portion of Port Ludlow. The small bay S of the Twins is sometimes used as an anchorage for small craft in rough weather.

HANSVILLE, about 2.5 miles ESE of Foulweather Bluff, is a small village with stores and several waterfront resorts. Berthage is not available; however two of the resorts have marine railways and 2-ton hoists that can handle craft up to 19 feet. Gasoline, water, and ice are available. During the fishing season, many purse seiners operate just off the beach in the Hansvile area.

NORWEGIAN POINT, low and rounding, is about 0.2 mile NW of Hansville. A conspicuous privately owned lighthouse, 210 feet above the water and built from plans of the original lighthouse at Mukilteo, is about 1 mile W of Hansville.

POINT NO POINT, on the W shore of the sound about 3.5 miles SE of Foulweather Bluff, is a low sandspit. POINT NO POINT LIGHT (47°54.7'N., 122°31.5'W.), 27 feet above the water, is shown from a 20-foot white octagonal tower on the end of the point; a fog signal is at the station.

-U.S. COAST PILOT 7
25th edition, August 1989
Corrected thru 10/22/90
Local Notice to Mariners

SEQUIM

JOHN WAYNE MARINA, 615 W Sequim Bay Rd., Sequim, WA 98382. (206) 683 - 9898. Open all year. 8 AM - 5 PM, 7 days a week. Charts. Electronic and marine hardware sales. Waste disposal pumpout. Groceries and ice. Picnic area. Laundry. Snack bar. Ramp: 2 - lane, asphalt. 24 hours. Overnight guest dock with electricity. Slips. Boat rentals. Fuel dock: gas and diesel. Fishing: licenses, bait and tackle. Water skiing. Great clamming and crabbing. Harbormaster: Jan Hardin.

SEQUIM MARINE CO., 106 Gilbert Rd., Sequim, WA 98382. (206) 683 - 8800. All year. Boat and motor sales. Charts. Electronic and marine hardware sale. Prop repairs. Fishing tackle. Full service shop for all makes of sterndrives. Owners: Elden and Joan Ross.

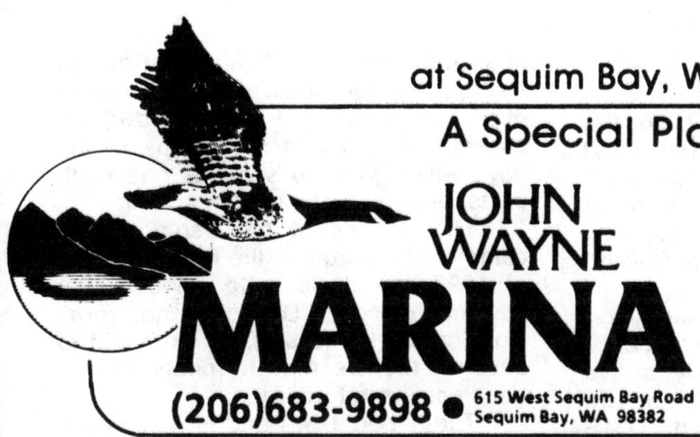

PORT ANGELES AREA

PORT ANGELES † Protected by the solid arm of Ediz Hook, Port Angeles Boat Haven offers a secure and pleasant moorage for pleasurecraft cruising the Strait of Juan de Fuca. Slips are doubly protected behind a man-made peninsula that parallels the shoreline.

Weather is the principal hazard here, even in summer. Afternoon westerlies sweep up the Strait, endangering novice skippers. Fishing is usually excellent in this area, especially in the mornings. Well-built launch ramps in the boat basin and on Ediz Hook make this harbor invaluable to trailerboatmen. The Olympics are close, snow-frosted and full of wildlife, all protected by law in this national park. A side trip up these spectacular heights is rewarding, if you can arrange it.

A direct crossing from Port Angeles to Victoria, B.C., lets you reach Canada's protected inland waters quickly, but rough chop is to be expected in midchannel unless it is a very calm day. Increasing numbers of skippers from Puget Sound and the San Juan Islands are finding that a run down Juan de Fuca Strait to Port Angeles can constitute an excellent, enjoyable cruise.

FACILITIES

PORT ANGELES

CHEVRON MARINE DOCK (at Port Angeles Boat Haven) 832 Boat Haven Drive, Port Angeles, WA 98362. (206) 457 - 4505. All year. Fuel dock: gas, diesel and mix, open 8 AM - 5 PM.

FAIRHOLM GENERAL STORE, HC 62 Box 35, Port Angeles, WA 98362. (206) 928 - 3217. Open April - Oct. 8 AM - 9 PM. Picnic area. Groceries. Ice. Snack bar. RV campsites. Ramp: 1-lane, concrete, 24 hours. Rental boats. Fuel dock: gas only. Fishing: bait and tackle. Water skiing. Skin and scuba diving. Hiking. Owners: Gary and Karen Johnson.

PORT ANGELES BOAT HAVEN, 832 Boat Haven Drive, Port Angeles, WA 98362. (206) 457 - 4505. Ramp: 2-lanes asphalt, open 24 hours. Fuel dock: gas, diesel and mix, open daily 8AM - 5 PM. Hoist cap.: 1-ton, open daylight hours. Marine railway: 125-tons. Travel lift 40 ton. Slips. Guest dock. Dockside electricity. Tidal grid. Mooring buoys. Pumpout station. Engine and hull repair. Fishing: bait. Charter boats. Operated by Port of Port Angeles. Harbormaster: Charles W. Faires.

PORT TOWNSEND

PORT TOWNSEND † In 1986 the Washington State Centennial Commission designated Port Townsend as one of six of the State's most significant historic Victorian seaports. Originally named by Captain George Vancouver for the Marquis of Townshend, a British nobleman, Port Townsend (or Kah Tai, as it was called by the Klallam Indians) already had a thriving maritime culture when Vancouver arrived aboard HMS Discovery in May of 1792. The Klallam and other area tribes fished, hunted, and traded from dugout canoes ranging in size from 30 to 100 feet.

Settlement of the area wouldn't take place fo another fifty years. In 1860 Port Townsend, the second city in the Puget Sound area, was established. The years that followed revealed Port Townsend as a city of great ambition, with an economy firmly abased on trade, but swollen by speculation. In 1854 the customs office was moved from Olympia to Port Townsend, and all vessels entering and leaving the Puget Sound were required to clear customs through Port Townsend. In anticipation of Port Townsend's becoming the New York of the west coast, a building boom began, leading to the construction of the dramatic nineteenth-century architecture of Port Townsend. Many of the town's most notable buildings were built during this time by prominent financiers and sea captains.

In its heyday during the Days of Sail, Port Townsend rivaled Seattle and Olympia in prominence, and in the 1880's was second only to New York in the number of ship clearances. The morning paper announced one day in 1889 that there wer 81 vessels presently loading 79,103 tons of goods in Port Townsend Bay. The city could only be described as diverse: different types of people, international cultures, and lumber barks, schooners, square riggers, clippers, and steam passenger vessels all arriving at the port.

It was a sailor's town, complete with bars, brothels, smuggling, and shanghaiing. In fact, Port Townsend was known as one of the most notorious shanghai ports. The practice of shanghaiing (or pressing unsuspecting men into service) was regarded as essential in order to man ships in the days when going to sea was one of th eleast pleasant ways to earn a living.

The decline of the aspiring port came on three fronts: the financial crisis of 1893, the decision to relocate the customs office to Olympia, and, most significantly, the loss of the city's bid to become the western terminus of the trans-continental railroad.

Today port Townsend in recognized by the Naitonal Trust for Historic Preservation as one of the country's only three remaining historic Victorian seaports. A sense of its maritime history is relived each year during the Port Townsend Wooden Boat Festival.

1st PLACE PROPELLER, 2730- Washington Street, POrt Townsend, WA 98368. (206) 385 - 7326.

ADMIRAL MARINE WORKS, INC., 919 Haines Street, Port Townsend, WA 98368. (206) 385 - 4670. Seattle: (206) 622 - 3144. FAX: (206) 385 - 4256.

FIRST CABIN MARINE INC., 2900 Washington Street, Port Townsend, WA 98368. (206) 385 - 7508. Finest yacht quality marine construction adn repair. Complete Full-service marine repair. Sterling polyurethane coatings; anti-fouling propeller coatings; preventive maintenance programs, 70 to haulout capacity; inside storage facility; customer moorage.

FLEET MARINE INC, (at Pt Hudson Marina), 419 Jackson, Port Townsend, WA 98368. (206) 385 - 4000. All year. 7 DAYS. 8 AM - 6 PM. Complete service shipyard and open yard. Travelift cap. 25 tons. Fiberglass and wood repairs. Painting. Osmosis and extensions. Retail supply store, bait and ice. Brokerage. Owners: Gary and Nadine Jonientz and Bernie Donanberg.

HARPER'S SUPER SERVICE
P.O. Box 227, Port Townsend
Washington 98368
(206) 385-1240
PORT FUEL DOCK

Shell Gasoline
& Diesel Fuel

Hours 8:00 to 4:30 - 7 days
Shell, Visa & Mastercard

GEM HYDRAULICS, 130 Cedar Avenue, P.O. Box 114, Hadlock, WA 98339. (206) 385 - 2560. Quality hoses and hydraulic components sales and service.

HARBOR MARINE CENTER, 2800-A Washington Street, Port Townsend, WA 98368. (206) 385 - 3020. Gas and diesel repair. Owner: Phil Hayes.

HARPER OIL CO./ HARPER'S SUPER SERVICE, (Port Fuel Dock) P.O. Box 227, Port Townsend, WA 98368. (206) 385 - 1240. Shell gasoline and diesel. 8 AM - 4:30 PM. 7 DAYS. Owner: R.C. Harper.

HASSE & PETRICH / PORT TOWNSEND SAILS, 315 Jackson, Port Townsend, WA 98368. (206) 385 - 1640. Custom sail-making. Canvas work. Repairs and service. Owners: Carol Hasse and Nora Petrich.

J & S FABRICATION, INC., 419 Haines Place, Industrial Park, Port Townsend. (206) 385 - 3003. Precision machine work. General fabrication. MIG-TIG-Portable welding. Steel, stainless and aluminum. GR8 and stainless nuts/bolts. Davits, bow rolelrs, shafts, cutlass bearing, repairs.

KEY ELECTRIC, 2227 Washington Street, Port Townsend, WA. (206) 385 - 4077. Mairne alternators and starters.

LA FONDA - A Mexican Restaurant, 2330 Washington St, Box 565, Port Townsend, WA 98368. (206) 385 - 4627. Open daily for lunch and dinner: 11:30 AM - 9 PM. Sat and Sun, 4 PM - 9 PM. Owner: G. Wall.

M & N CANVAS AND WELDING, 2900 Washington STreet, Port Townsend, WA 98368. (206) 385 - 7058. Nonie Crager and Mike Roth.

MOBILE LOGIC, INC., 3362-A State Hwy 20, P.O. Box 389, Port Townsend, WA 98368. (206) 385 - 3509. Steel Fabrication. Custom trailers. Trailer hitches. Sheet Metal. Steel and aluminum supplies.

OSAL MARINE SERVICES, 1541 29th Street, Port Townsend, WA 98368. (206) 385 - 0306. Porfessional salvage, diving, and towning. Moorings and boathouse float repairs.

PENINSULA ENGINE, 651 Old Eaglemount Road, Port Townsend, WA 98368. (206) 732 - 4723. Complete mechanical service for marine. Machine Scho. Electrical, installations, repowering, hydraulics.

PENINSULA YACHT MOVING & STORAGE, 305 8th street / 240 2nd Street, Port Townsend, WA 98368. (206) 385 - 2485 (keep trying). Load and unload land service. Storage.

POINT HUDSON HARBOR, Point Hudson, Port Townsend, WA, 98368. (206) 385 - 2828. All year. Ramp: 1-lane concrete, 24 hours. Moorings. Slips. Dockside electricity. Boat maintenance/repairs. Marine hardware. Overnight accommodations. Showers. Laundry. Trailer sites. Groceries. Charts. Picnic area. Restaurant. Fishing: bait/tackle. Mgr: Wade Osmer.

PORT OF PORT TOWNSEND, (at entrance to Port Townsend off Hwy 9). Harbormaster: (206) 385 - 2355. All year. Ramp: concrete, 24 hours. Hoist cap.: 60 and 70 tons, open 8 AM - 5 PM. Available anytime for emergency. Fuel dock open 8 AM - 4:30 PM. Sun, 10 AM - 4 PM. Slips. Dockside electricity. Dry storage. Boat maintenance and repairs. Engine parts and repairs. Marine hardware. Brokerage. Restaurant. Groceries. Ice. Laundry. Showers. U.S. Customs Port of Entry. Operated by the Port of Port Townsend. P.O. Box 1180, Port Townsend, WA 98368. Harbormaster: Bill Toskey.

PORT TOWNSEND'S FULL SERVICE BOATYARD, 731 Kuhn, Port Townsend Boat Haven; P.O. Box 577, Port Townsend, WA 98368. (206) 385 - 1523. Major hull repair, marine electrical, mechanical installations, metal fabrication. Haulouts to 70 tons. Dockside: 100 ft.

PORT TOWNSEND SHIPWRIGHTS CO-OP, 403 Belle Street, Port Townsend Boat Haven, Port Townsend. (206) 385 - 6138. Decking. Dustom interiors. Design. Stems. Keels. Caulking. Complete welding and metal fabrication. Planking. Rigging. Haulouts to 70 tons. Covered storage.

SKOOKUM MARINE, INC. (Port Townsend Boat Haven) 2800 Washington St., Port Townsend, WA 98368. (206) 385 - 2224. Custom boatbuilders, sail and power. President: Julian Arthur.

MYSTERY BAY

NORDLAND GROCERY (on east side of Mystery Bay) 5180 Flagler Road, Box 111, Nordland, WA 98358. (206) 385 - 0777. Fuel dock: gas only, open 9 AM - 9 PM. Moorings. Picnic area. Charts. Groceries. Ice. Fishing: bait and tackle.

PORT LUDLOW

PORT LUDLOW. † The little harbor of Port Ludlow is an incision in the Olympic Peninsula not far from Foulweather Bluff and the mouth of Hood Canal. Its outstanding modern feature is the stylish set of luxury condominium apartments sheltering among the trees on the north shore of the harbor. Owners of these handsome one and two-story rim-of-the-Pacific apartments also have the privilege of owning slips in the marina that stretches out beneath the restaurant building. But there seem to be enough slips to offer temporary moorage to transient pleasure craft.

Site of an early lumber operation, Port Ludlow was primarily a log storage inlet, almost abandoned, until the condos appeared. It remains a charming, two-mile-long sheet of water in which to anchor, to explore with dinghy or kayak, or to spend a quiet night. A most favored anchorage is in the southwestern section of the harbor behind the little Twin Islands that lie close to shore. Watch your depth finder when making your way back into this serene hideaway.

PORT LUDLOW MARINA at the Resort of Port Ludlow, (on Admiralty Inlet close to mouth of Hood Canal) 421 Marine View Drive, Port Ludlow, WA 98365. (206) 437 - 2222. All year. Fuel dock: gas, diesel and outboard mix, open Summer: 7 AM - 8 PM; Winter: 9 AM - 4 PM. Rental slips by reservation. Rental power and sailboats. Overnight accommodations. See your travel agent. Restaurant. Public golf course. Fishing: bait, and tackle. Rental boats. Pumpout station. Dockside electricity: (4). Dockmaster: Carol A. Franke.

MARINE PARKS

FORT FLAGLER MARINE PARK (on Marrowstone Island, 8 miles northeast of hadlock) Nordland, WA 98358. (206) 385-1259. 783 acres. Ramp. 7 mooring buoys, 212 feet of float space. Picnic areas. Campsites. Showers. Toilets. Groceries. Fishing: bait and tackle.

FORT WORDEN STATE PARK (at the north limits of Port Townsend) P.O. Box 574, Port Townsend, WA 98368. (206) 385-4730. 339 acres. Ramp. 8 mooring buoys, 140 feet of float space. Underwater park. Picnic areas. Campsites. Overnight accommodations. Toilets. Showers.

MYSTERY BAY BOAT STATE PARK (west side of Marrowstone Island in Kilisut harbor) Nordland, WA 98358. (206) 385-1259. 10 acres. Ramp: 1 - lane, concrete, open 24 hours. 7 mooring buoys, 194 feet of float space. Dock. Toilets. Picnic facilities.

PORT ANGELES MUNICIPAL PARK (on shoreline near ferry landing) 2 acre park with pier. Moorage. Guest floats. Maritime museum. Observation tower overlooking Strait of Juan de Fuca. Public beach, toilets, public phone.

OLD FORT TOWNSEND STATE PARK (3 miles south of Port Townsend, east from hwy. 20) P.O. Box 574, Port Townsend, WA 98368. (206) 385-4730. 377 acres. 4 mooring buoys. Picnic area. Campsites. Group camping. Toilets.

SEQUIM BAY STATE PARK (4 miles south of Sequim on Nwy. 101) 92 acres. Ramp. 6 mooring buoys. 405 feet float space. Picnic area. Campsites. Toilets. Showers.

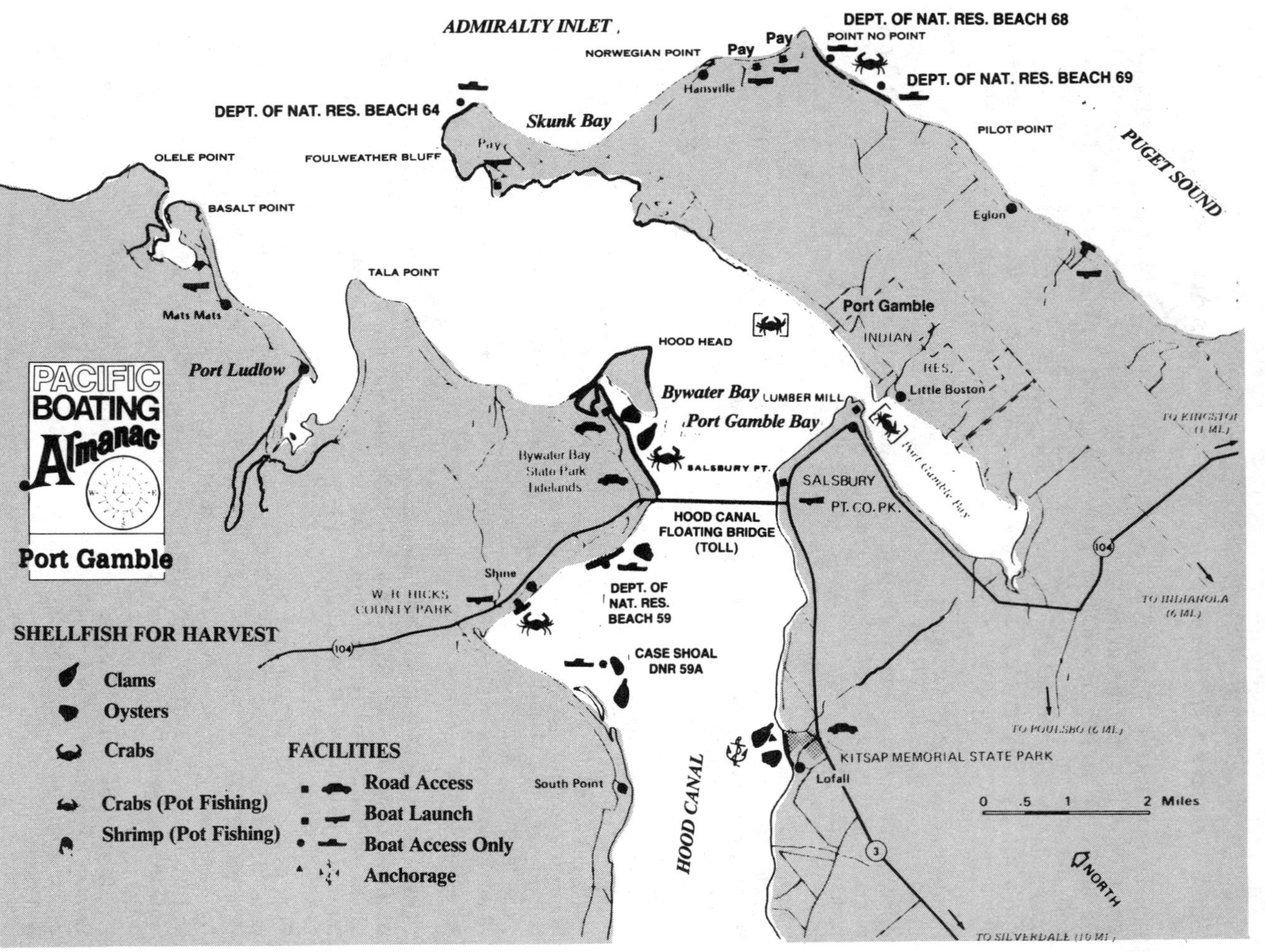

ADMIRALTY INLET
DEPT. OF NAT. RES. BEACH 68
POINT NO POINT
NORWEGIAN POINT
Pay
Pay
Hansville
DEPT. OF NAT. RES. BEACH 69
DEPT. OF NAT. RES. BEACH 64
Skunk Bay
PILOT POINT
PUGET SOUND
OLELE POINT
FOULWEATHER BLUFF
Pay
BASALT POINT
Eglon
TALA POINT
Port Gamble
INDIAN
RES.
Mats Mats
HOOD HEAD
Little Boston
Port Ludlow
Bywater Bay
LUMBER MILL
Port Gamble Bay
Port Gamble Bay
PACIFIC
BOATING
Almanac
Port Gamble
Bywater Bay
State Park
tidelands
SALSBURY PT.
SALSBURY
PT. CO. PK.
TO KINGSTON
(1 MI.)
HOOD CANAL
FLOATING BRIDGE
(TOLL)
104
TO INDIANOLA
(6 MI.)
Shine
W. H. HICKS
COUNTY PARK
DEPT. OF
NAT. RES.
BEACH 59
104
CASE SHOAL
DNR 59A
TO POULSBO (6 MI.)
SHELLFISH FOR HARVEST
Clams
Oysters
Crabs
FACILITIES
Crabs (Pot Fishing)
Shrimp (Pot Fishing)
Road Access
Boat Launch
Boat Access Only
Anchorage
South Point
HOOD CANAL
KITSAP MEMORIAL STATE PARK
Lofall
3
0   .5   1   2 Miles
NORTH
TO SILVERDALE (10 MI.)

9

HOOD CANAL

AIR TRANSPORTATION
  Kenmore Air Harbor: (206) 486-1257
  Lake Union Air: (800) 692-2993

CHAMBER OF COMMERCE
  Port Angeles: (206) 452-2363
  Port Townsend: (206) 385-2722
  Sequim: (206) 683-6197

COAST GUARD
  VHF 16 or 22
  Port Angeles: (206) 457-4404
  Port Ludlow: (206) 385-3070
  Port Townsend: (206) 457-4404
  Seattle: (206) 442-7070
  Search and Rescue: (206) 457-4404

RED TIDE HOTLINE
  (800) 562-5632

CUSTOMS
  Neah Bay: (206) 645-2311
  Port Angeles: (206) 457-4311
  Port Townsend: (206) 385-3777
  After hours: (800) 562-5943

DECOMPRESSION CHAMBER
  Bremerton: (206) 396-5111
  Virginia Mason, Seattle:
    (206) 624-1144

FERRY TRANSPORTATION
  Coho Ferry: (206) 457-4491
  Washington State: (800) 542-0812
  Port Angeles: (206) 457-4491

HOOD CANAL
  (206) 779-3377

Reaching 85 miles from Foulweather Bluff to Belfais, Hood Canal shelters birds, fish, shellfish, and other marine life. Hood Canal is an extensive cruising gound used by over 40,000 boaters each year. It is especially popular for its rcreational shrimping when over 20,000 boaters may be found in the canal on opening day of shrimp season.

Hood Canal is naturally flushed by tidal action once every 350 days and some areas near Belfair take six years to flush. Because of Hood Canal's tremendous vulnerability to both land-based and water-based pollution, it is important for recreational boaters to pay strict attention to existing boater regulations and laws. You can make a difference and keep the area from being spoiled.

Rivers and Harbors Act of 1899. Sec. 407 prohibits the throwing, discharging or deposition of any refuse matter into the nabigable waters of the United States.

Plastic Pollution Research and Control Act of 1987. This law prohibits the dumping of plastics at sea after January 1, 1989 and severely restricts the legality of dumping other ship-generated garbage both at sea and int he navigable waters of the United States.

These and other laws have enabled the Hood Canal Coordinating Council to work cooperateively toward protecting Hood Canal from degradation. As concerned boaters, we can do our part to protect the Canal by following these guidelines: (1) Take extra care to comply with the laws; (2) Inform others who may not be aware of the rules; (3) If necessary, report offenders to the appropriate authority.

CHARTS 18440, 18477, 18476. The entrance to HOOD CANAL is at the lower end of Admiralty Inlet, between Foulweather Bluff and Tala Point, about 10 miles S of Marrowstone Point. It extends in a general S direction for about 44 miles and then bends sharply NE for 11 miles, terminating in flats bare at low water. The head of Case Inlet, in the S part of Puget Sound, is less than 2 miles from the head of Hood Canal. The shores are high, bold, and wooded, and the water is deep, except at the heads of the bays and at the mouths of the streams. Many small craft ply these waters. There are mostly small float landings and private docks in the canal. Gasoline, is available at numerous resorts and marinas.

U.S. Highway 101 follows much of the W shore of Hood Canal, and a connecting highway to Port Orchard follows the S shore of the S part of the canal around The Great Bend. There are road connections with Port Orchard and with the Puget Sound highway system from all the settlements on the E shore of the canal.

Water traffic in general is confined to tugs with log rafts, naval vessels in the upper part, and many pleasure craft. Hood Canal is a vacation area. Numerous private houses and summer cottages with small piers and floats are on both sides of the canal. There are relatively few public floats or piers, and the only commercial activities are logging and some oystering.

Regulations governing vessels wishing to transit gill net fishing areas are given at the beginning of chapter 6. THE TIDAL CURRENTS in Hood Canal at times attain velocities exceeding 1.5 knots. In some places in the canal the currents are too weak and variable to predict. At times there are heavy tide rips N of and around Foulweather Bluff, sufficiently heavy to be dangerous to small boats and to break up log rafts. This is most pronounced when the ebb current from the main body of Puget Sound meets that from Hood Canal off the point, and particularly so with the ebb against a strong N or NW wind. Off Point Hannon and Hazel Point, tide rips occur at times sufficiently strong to be troublesome to

tugs with log tows. Current observations taken at a station in mid-channel E of Hazel Point show that directions of both flood and ebb vary considerably at that location. At times SW windsfrom Hood Canal and N wins from Dabob Bay cause a chop dangerous for small boats. Under these conditions smoother water is found near either shore.

The dangers are few and generally close in shore. A few low sandspits from 100 to 300 yards long are difficult to see at night, but most of them have been made into resorts and the buildings nearby show up well against the background of trees. Flats off the mouths of streams extend as much as 0.5 mile offshore and are extensive at the heads of some of the bays. A mid-channel course is clear until reaching The Great Bend, where the canal turns E. Here the N shore just E of Ayres Point should be favored to clear the flats extending from the E part of Annas Bay.

CHART 18477 † TWIN SPITS are two long, low sand points, 0.5 mile and 1 mile S of Foulweather Bluff. When waiting for smooth weather to round Foulweather Bluff, tugs with log tows often anchor in 50 feet a mile SE of the S spit, in a bight known locally as RACES COVE, with Colvos Rock Light slightly clear of the end of the S point of Twin Spits. There is a small resort on the S spit; gasoline is available from the northernmost of two piers. A marine railway for small-craft, ice, and some marine supplies are available.

HOOD HEAD, on the W side of Hood Canal 3 miles S of the entrance, is almost an island, having only a narrow strip of low sand connecting it with the W shore. The head is 220 feet high, steep and wooded, and is a prominent feature in the entrance.

A rocky ledge, marked by some kelp and covered 4 to 26 feet, extends more than 500 yards S of Hood Head; rocks covered 4 feet are near the S end of this ledge about 325 yards S of Hood Head. An aquaculture site, marked by lighted private buoys, is about 0.4 mile S of Hood Head.

COON BAY, 2.5 miles S of Foulweather Bluff, is a small, nearly landlocked harbor offering excellent protection to small craft during periods of rough weather. The privately dredged entrance channel is narrow and has a reported controlling depth of about 3 feet. There are several private piers inside the entrance, but no facilities are available.

POINT HANNON is at the E extension of Hood Head; it is marked by a light. A low sandy spit with shoal water extends about 200 yards E of the light.

LOCAL MAGNETIC DISTURBANCE † Differences of more than 2° from normal variation have been observed in Hood Canal at Point Hannon.

TERMINATION POINT, 1.6 miles E of the village of SHINE, is 1.7 miles SW of Point Hannon. A lighted transformer substation is on Termination Point. An aquaculture site, about 400 yards ENE of the point, is marked by private lighted buoys.

HOOD CANAL BRIDGE, a pontoon highway bridge crossing the canal between Termination Point and Salsbury Point W of Port Gamble has two fixed openings; the clearance of the W opening is 35 feet, an that of the E opening is 55 feet. In the 600-foot center opening there are pontoons which are retracted for larger vessels. The bridgetender monitors VHF-FM channel 16 (156.80 MHz) and works on channel 13 (156.65 MHz); call sign KZJ-376. A pivate fog signal is at each opening. Anchor cables, extending from the bridge pontoons to the canal bottom, extend nearly 500 yards both N and S of the bridge; anchoring should not be attempted in this area.

SISTERS, two rocks 200 yards apart, 0.5 mile S of Termination Point, are awash at about half tide. A light is on the S rock, 0.4 mile from the N entrance point to SQUAMISH HARBOR, an open bight just SW of Termination Point. Tugs frequently anchor near the head of the harbor in about 6 fathoms, muddy bottom.

CASE SHOAL, partly bare at low water, is about 0.6 mile from and parallel with the W shore of Squamish Harbor. The shoal is marked at its N end by a daybeacon and on its SE side by a light. A clam tract, marked at the N and S ends by private buoys, is in the SW part of the harbor between Case Shoal and W shore.

PORT GAMBLE BAY is a small bay on the E shore of Hood Canal 5 miles from the entrance. It is 2 miles long with a narrow entrance.

A dredged entrance channel leads from deep water in Hood Canal into deep water in Port Gamble Bay. In October 1982, the controlling depth was 24 feet. The channel is marked by a 001°-181° lighted range and two lights on the E side of the channel.

PORT GAMBLE, (47°51'N., 122°35'W.) the town on the W shore at the entrance, is owned by the lumber company which maintains all facilities including the local housing, church, and store. The mill has been in operation for more than a century. The white church steeple and flagpole in the town are prominent. A shoal covered 4 feet is about 500 yards NE from the N end of the lumbermill wharf.

Excellent anchorage may be had in the bay in 24 to 54 feet, muddy bottom.

CAUTION † The entrance channel to Port Gamble is quite constricted by shoals on both sides of the channel. The two lights on the E side of the channel are in shoal water and do not mark the edge of the channel.

A bridge pontoon storage area is on the W side of Port Gamble about 0.4 mile S of Port Gamble.

CHARTS 18458, 18476, 18477, 18441 † THORNDYKE BAY is a small bight on the W side of Hood Canal about 4 miles S of Squamish Harbor. An EXPLOSIVES ANCHORAGE is S of the bay.

BANGOR WHARF on the E side of the canal, 3.5 miles S of Thorndyke Bay, is the property of the Bangor U.S. Naval Submarine Base. A NAVAL RESTRICTED AREA surrounds the wharf and other naval docking facilities along the E side of Hood Canal. Keyport Naval Undersea Wafare Engineering Station, 0.9 mile SSW of Bangor Wharf, is also within the restricted areas. A 500 foot radio tower, marked by red aircraft warning lights, is on Bangor Wharf and is prominent. A 459 foot red and white radio tower, marked by red aircraft warning lights, is on the wharf 0.3 mile

NNE of Bangor Wharf; this tower is also prominent. It is reported that vessels southbound from Hood Canal Bridge can use the towers as a 200.6° range. Strong currents are in the vicinity of the piers at Keyport Naval Undersea Warfare Engineering Station.

BANGOR, a small residential community about 2 miles of Bangor Wharf, has no facilities.

SEABECK, about 6 miles SW of Bangor, is a settlement and resort at the head of SEABECK BAY, a small cove on the E shore. A marina, protected by a breakwater awash at high water, is on the S side of the bay. Berths, gasoline, diesel fuel, water, ice, supplies and a 1½ ton hoist are available. Shoal water extends 0.5 mile from the head of the bay. Good anchorage, well protected from SE to SW weather, is available in the bay in 35 to 50 feet. Shoal water extends more than 200 yards off MISERY POINT, at the W side of the entrance of the bay. A light is about 300 yards NE of Misery Point, and a fish haven is close NW of the light.

OAK HEAD, 2 miles NNE of Misery Point and marked by a light, is the S point of TOANDOS PENINSULA. HAZEL POINT, 1.8 miles ENE of Oak Head, is the turning point where the canal bends sharply from the S to SW.

FISHERMAN HARBOR is a cove on the S end of Toandos Peninsula, just E of Oak Head. It is very narrow, with a constricted entrance which is practically bare at low water. A sandspit extends partly across the entrance form the W shore.

BRINNON is a village on the S side of Dosewallips River 3.5 miles W of Oak Head, at the entrance of Dabob Bay. It has a general store and service station. Gasoline, water, and ice are available, but there is no landing pier. A log booming ground is close offshore at Brinnon.

DABOB BAY, the largest inlet in the canal and separated from it by Toandos Peninsula, extends 9 miles in a N direction. The entrance is between TSKUTSKO POINT and SYLOPASH POINT just N of the mouth of Dosewallips River. A light is off Tskutdko Point. The W shore of Dabob Bay is particularly steep and bold,

reaching an elevation of over 2,600 feet in less than 2 miles from the coast.

A NAVAL OPERATING AREA is in the bay. Navy maintained warning lights are shown from WHITNEY POINT and Sylopash Point on the W side of the bay, and from POINT ZELATCHED on the E side of the bay; flashing green lights will be shown when naval operations in the area require caution, and flashing red lights will be shown when naval operations close the area to navigation. Mariners are advised to pass no closer than 1 mile of naval vessels engaged in bottom operations unless directed otherwise by radiotelephone or other signal from the shore, picket boat, or surveillance aircraft.

A RESTRICTED AREA is off Whitney Point.

QUILCENE BAY is a small inlet on the W side of Dabob Bay N of Whitney Point. A light marks the E side of the entrance to the bay. The N half of the bay is filled with flats which bare. This part of the bay has two log booms and log storage areas. An oyster farm is on the E side of the bay just inside the entrance. Floats with mooring buoys evenly spaced along the E edge mark the oyster farm. Quilcene, a small town on the W side and near the head of the bay, is about 0.5 mile inland. The town has hotels, restaurants, and stores.

QUILCENE BOAT HAVEN, operated by the Port of Port Townsend, is on the W side of the bay about 1.4 miles S of the town. The entrance to the haven is protected by a stone breakwater; mooring floats and gasoline are available. The basin has a reported controlling depth of 10 feet. Two oyster farms are near the haven.

PLEASANT HARBOR is a small cove on the W shore of Hood Canal about 3 miles W of Misery Point. It is about 300 yards wide, and has a narrow shallow entrance. Doing to the narrowness of the entrance, boats should keep in mid-channel until clear of the 6 foot shoal. A large marina inside the harbor has berths for about 90 craft, electricity, gasoline, water, ice, and limited marine supplies. Anchorage in about 36 feet, mud bottom is available inside the harbor. A large log dump and

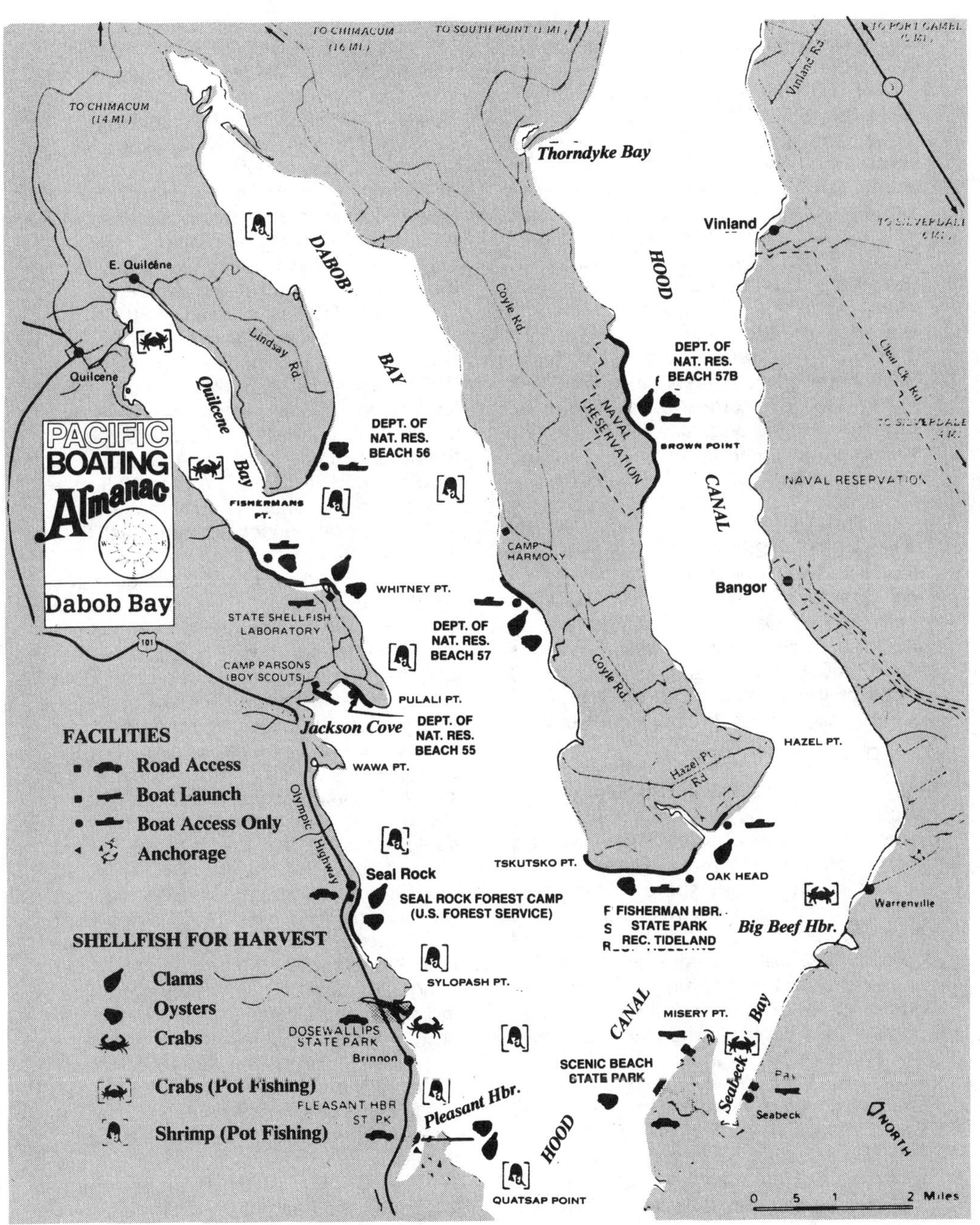

TO CHIMACUM
(16 MI.)
TO SOUTH POINT (1 MI.)
TO PORT GAMBLE
(6 MI.)
Thorndyke Bay
Vinland Rd.
TO CHIMACUM
(14 MI.)
Vinland
TO SILVERDALE
DABOB
E. Quilcene
HOOD
Coyle Rd.
DEPT. OF
NAT. RES.
BEACH 57B
Lindsay Rd.
BAY
Quilcene
Clear Ck. Rd.
Quilcene Bay
TO SILVERDALE
(4 MI.)
PACIFIC
BOATING
Almanac
BROWN POINT
DEPT. OF
NAT. RES.
BEACH 56
CANAL
NAVAL RESERVATION
W E
Dabob Bay
FISHERMANS
PT.
NAVAL RESERVATION
CAMP
HARMONY
Bangor
101
WHITNEY PT.
STATE SHELLFISH
LABORATORY
DEPT. OF
NAT. RES.
BEACH 57
Coyle Rd.
CAMP PARSONS
(BOY SCOUTS)
PULALI PT.
HAZEL PT.
FACILITIES
Jackson Cove
DEPT. OF
NAT. RES.
BEACH 55
Hazel Pt. Rd.
Road Access
WAWA PT.
Boat Launch
Olympic Highway
Boat Access Only
Anchorage
Seal Rock
TSKUTSKO PT.
OAK HEAD
SEAL ROCK FOREST CAMP
(U.S. FOREST SERVICE)
Warrenville
SHELLFISH FOR HARVEST
F FISHERMAN HBR.
S STATE PARK
R REC. TIDELAND
Big Beef Hbr.
Clams
SYLOPASH PT.
Oysters
Crabs
CANAL
MISERY PT.
Seabeck Bay
Crabs (Pot Fishing)
DOSEWALLIPS
STATE PARK
SCENIC BEACH
STATE PARK
Seabeck
Brinnon
Shrimp (Pot Fishing)
HOOD
PLEASANT HBR
ST PK
Pleasant Hbr.
NORTH
QUATSAP POINT
0 5 1 2 Miles

log boom, and a state park pier are in the harbor.

TRITON HEAD, on the W shore, is 8.2 miles SW of Oak Head. It is low, rocky, and timbered, with a reef that bares extending 200 yards N from the point. TRITON COVE is a small cove formed by the head and the W shore, which affords anchorage for small craft against S winds. Oyster bed, marked by stakes and brush, are about 0.8 mile N from Triton Head on the flat which extends off the mouth of FULTON CREEK. Two resorts just S of Triton Head have berths, gasoline, diesel fuel, water, ice, dry storage, and marine supplies. Hoists and railways to 10 tons are available, and outboard engine repairs can be made.

CHARTS 18448, 18476 † HOLLY (47°33.5'N., 122°58.6'W.), on the E shore of Hood Canal, is a settlement on the S side of a small bight about 10 miles SW of Oak Head. There are no facilities here. Shoal water extends about 300 yards N and E from the S shore of the bight. ANDERSON COVE is the shallow cove directly N of Holly. It is used for rafting logs.

ELDON is a W shore settlement on the S bank of HAMMA HAMMA RIVER, about 3 miles SW of Holly. There is a large tourist camp here. The delta flats of the Hamma Hamma River extend nearly 0.5 mile from shore. Unmarked jetties extend from the river through the flats into Hood Canal and constitute a potential hazard to small craft. There is an extensive log booming ground and dump at the mouth of Jorsted Creek, about 1 mile S of Hamma Hamma River.

LILLIWAUP is a village on the S shore of LILLIWAUP BAY, a small shallow cove on the W shore of Hood Canal about 6 miles SW of Eldon.

About 1 mile S, there is a resort at which berths, electricity, gasoline, diesel fuel, water, ice, and marine supplies are available. A 1½ ton elevator at the resort can handle craft to 19 feet long for hull and engine repairs.

DEWATTO is a small settlement on the S side of DEWATTO BAY, a small, shallow cove on the E shore opposite Lilliwaup.

HOODSPORT (47°25'N., 123°08'W.), the largest town on Hood Canal, is on the W shore 4 miles SW of Dewatto. It has a State fish hatchery.

HOODSPORT MARINA, with a pier, floats, and a 3½ ton elevator, has depths of 24 feet reported off the end of the lift area. Berths, electricity, water, ice, and marine supplies are available. Hull and engine repairs can be made. Just N of the marina is a public pier with floats.

POTLATCH is a small town on the W side of the canal about 2 miles S of Hoodsport and opposite THE GREAT BEND, where Hood Canal turns NE. The large gray building of a hydroelectric powerplant, connected to a standpipe on the mountain above by three pipelines, is very prominent on the W shore 0.5 mile S of the town. There is a recreation park and small-craft launching ramp just S of the powerplant.

UNION is a town with several stores on the S shore of The Great Bend. There are two marinas here; one has a 4 ton hoist that can handle craft to 30 feet long for hull and engine repairs. Both have berths, electricity, gasoline, water, ice, marine supplies, and facilities for making hull and engine repairs. Depths alongside the floats at these marinas are reported sufficient for small craft at all stages of the tide; however, the westernmost of the tow marinas should be approached from the NE to avoid shoal water and snags. A large resort in the cove on the S shore 1.3 miles E of Union has a T-pier with a 600 foot face and reported depths of 15 feet alongside. Berths, electricity, gasoline, and water are available at the resort. A large motel and restaurant are here.

ANNAS BAY, immediately W of Union, is a broad, open bight; the E half is flat and bare at low water. This flat extends about 0.2 mile into the canal immediately W of Union and is formed by the SKOKOMISH RIVER, which empties at the head of the bay.

TAHUYA, a small town on the N shore of The Great Bend 1.8 miles NE of Union, has a resort with a pier and floats. Electricity, gasoline, water, a 1½ ton hoist, and a launching ramp are available. Reported depths of 2½ feet are off the floats. TWANOH STATE PARK, about 6 miles E of Union on the S shore, has three launching ramps and a pier with reported depths of 2½ feet off the end. A small marina, operated during the summer is about 2 miles E of Twanoh State Park on the N shore. A pier with mooring floats, gasoline, and water are available. A float where gasoline is available is about 2.5 miles from the head of Lynch Cove on the N shore, and about 0.5 mile SW is a public pier with floats operated by the PORT OF ALLYN. The end of the pier is marked by lights. A reported depth of 10 feet is off the end of the float.

Hood Canal terminates in LYNCH COVE. Flats, mostly bare at low tide, extend for about 2.2 miles from the head of the cove.   -U S COAST PILOT 7
25th edition, August 1989
Corrected thru 10 22 90
Local Notice to Mariners

HOOD CANAL

HOOD CANAL † The Hood Canal is not so much a harbor as a complete cruising ground. It has marinas and harbors along its length, but since it is 55 miles long, and somewhere between ½ and 6¼ miles wide, these harbors are scarcely neighbors. Fishing and shellfishing are longtime favorite recreations in this hook-shaped fjord, but the Department of Fisheries regulates the sportfisherman's catch with open and closed intervals as well as bag limits, so you have to keep track of the official regulatory announcements as they are issued.

U.S. Navy installations at Bangor place parts of the Canal off limits to pleasurecraft, but an up-to-date NOAA chart will enable you to pass outside these reserved waters without difficulty.

The Olympic Mountains to the northwest and Mount Rainier to the east supply a regal frame for this body of water, making it one of the most beautiful, unimpeded cruising areas south of the Strait of Juan de Fuca.

ALDERBROOK INN, RESORT & CONFERENCE CENTER, E. 7101 Hwy. 106 Union, WA 98592. (206) 898-2200. Seattle Direct 622-2404. 82 hotel rooms, 22 cottages, restaurant, lounge, Convention Center, saltwater swimming, indoor swimming, jacuzzi, saunas, ice, daily/monthly moorage with facilities, seaplane landing, golf, tennis, scuba diving, water skiing, gift shops, beauty salon and boutique. No moorage fee when hotel guest. Operations Manager: Bob Allen

HOOD CANAL MARINE CORP., E 5101 Hwy. 106, P.O. Box 86, Union, WA 98592. (206) 898 - 2252. All year. Ramp. Fuel dock: gas and mix. Moorings. Slips. Dockside electricity. Dry storage. Boat maintenance and repairs. Engine repairs. Picnic area. Marine hardware. Owner: Steve Whiton.

SCENIC BEACH STATE PARK (on Hood Canal 3 miles southwest of Seabeck.), P.O. Box 7, Seabeck, WA 98380. (206) 830-5079. 90 acre park. Ramp. Picnic area, camping, hiking trails. Playground, public beach. Scuba diving. showers and toilets. Good anchoring ground. Fishing.

MARINE PARKS

KITSAP MEMORIAL STATE PARK (south of Hood Canal Bridge on the east shore.), 202 N.W. Park Street, Poulsbo, WA 98370. (206) 279-3205. 58 acres. Two mooring buoys. Picnic areas. Campsites. Showers. Toilet.

PLEASANT HARBOR STATE PARK (2 miles south of Brinnon.), P.O. Box K, Brinnon, WA 98320. (206) 796-4415. 0.8 acre. Moorings. Dock. Floats. Good anchorage. Pit toilets.

POTLATCH STATE PARK (on the Hood Canal near Potlatch, 18 miles north of Shelton.) 57 acres. Ramp. Five mooring buoys. Picnic areas. Campsites. Showers. toilets. Playground. Hiking trails. Public beach. Fishing.

TWANOH STATE PARK (Hood Canal on Hwy. 106.), E12190 Hwy. 106, Union, WA 98592. (206) 275 - 2222. From April 1 to Sept. 30, open 6:30 AM - 10 PM; Oct. 1 to March 31, closed except boat ramp. Ramp: 2-lane, concrete. 182 acres. Five mooring buoys, 200 feet of float space. Guest dock. Snack bar open Memorial Day to Labor Day. Groceries. Ice. Picnic area and RV campsites. Playground, swimming area. Showers. Toilets. Park Ranger: Larry Otto.

PACIFIC BOATING Almanac
Edmonds-Kingston
TO HANSVILLE 2.5 MILES
Eglon
PUGET SOUND
APPLE COVE PT.
TO PORT GAMBLE 3.6 MILES
TO BREMERTON 21.5 MILES
104
KINGSTON
PAY SLINGS
Appletree Cove
FERRY
SEATTLE - VICTORIA FERRY
PRESIDENT PT.
PT. JEFFERSON
Miller Bay
Indianola
Port Madison
Suquamish
TO MUKILTIO 4.5 MILES
525
99
NORTH
TO EVERETT 7.2 MILES
TO EVERETT (U.S. 2) 9 MILES
PICNIC PT.
B.N.R.R.
NORMA BEACH
0 .5 1 2 Miles
PREPARED BY KEN SIMKINS
Browns Bay
FACILITIES
Road Access
Boat Launch
Boat Access
Anchorage
524
196th St.
524
LYNNWOOD
EDMONDS
EDWARDS PT.
99
104
5
SHELLFISH FOR HARVEST
Clams
Oysters
Crabs
Crabs (Pot Fishing)
Shrimp (Pot Fishing)
PT. WELLS
RICHMOND BEACH
104
Lake Ballanger Wy
LAKE FOREST PARK
Aurora Ave
Holman Rd
B.N.R.R.
99
SEATTLE
522
Bothell Wy
LAKE WASHINGTON
TO BOTHELL 2.5 MILES

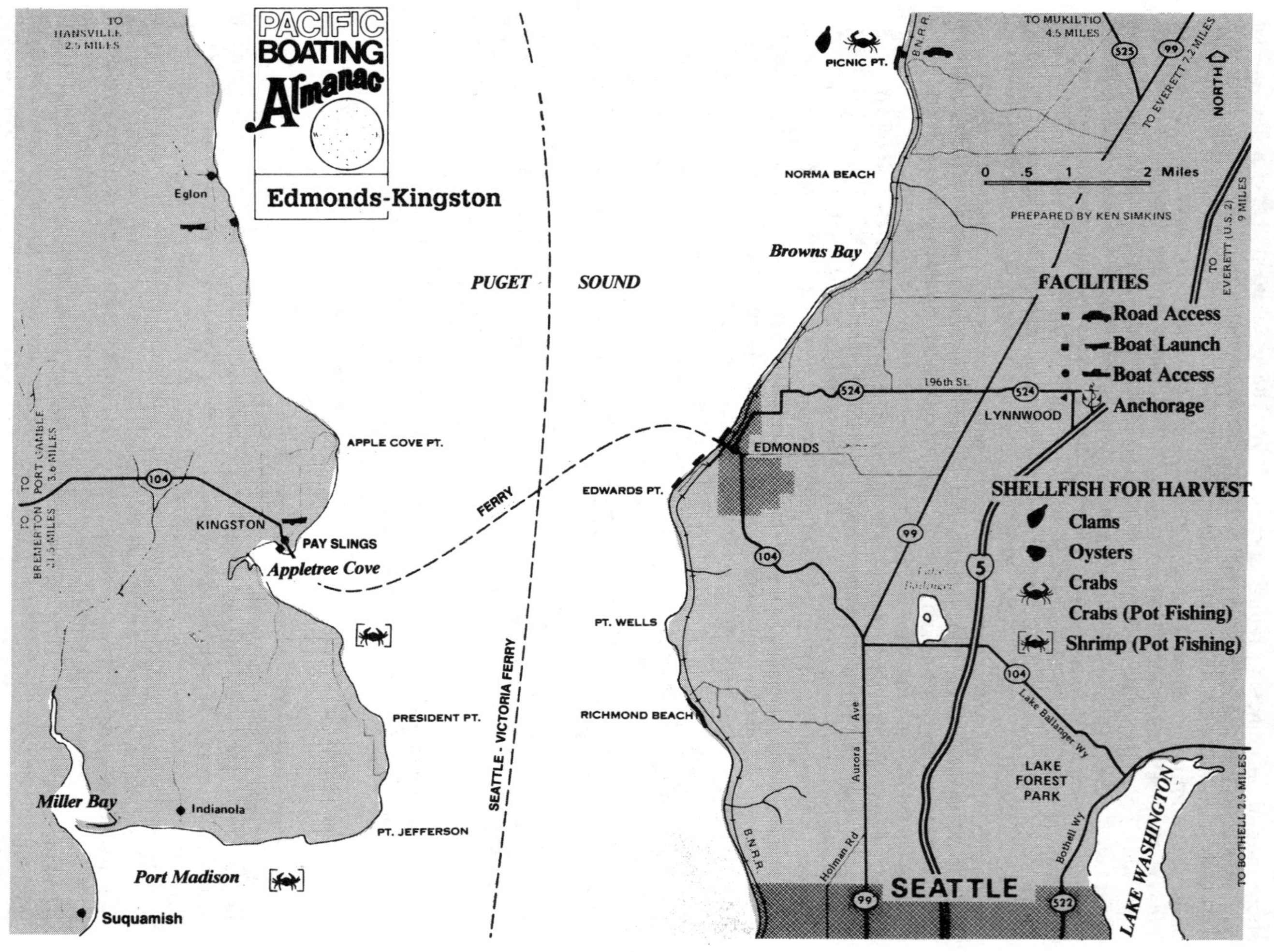

124

10

PUGET SOUND – NORTHERN PART
EDMONDS, KINGSTON, BAINBRIDGE ISLAND

AIR TRANSPORTATION
Kenmore Air Harbor: (206) 486-1257
Lake Union Air: (800) 692-2993

CHAMBER OF COMMERCE
Central Whidbey: (206) 678-5434
Edmonds: (206) 776-6711
Everett: (206) 252-5181
Freeland: (206) 321-4838
Langley: (206) 321-6765
North Whidbey: (206) 675-3535

COAST GUARD
VHF 16 or 22
Emergencies: (800) 592-9911
Snohomish County: (206) 252-5281
Seattle: (206) 442-7070

DECOMPRESSION CHAMBER
Virginia Mason, Seattle:
  (206) 624-1144

FERRY TRANSPORTATION
Washington State: (800) 542-0812

MARINE OPERATOR
Bellingham: VHF 28, 85
Everett: VHF 24
Seattle: VHF 25

RED TIDE HOTLINE
(800) 562-5632

STATE PARK INFORMATION
(800) 562-0990

CHART 18441 † USELESS BAY indenting Whidbey Island E of Double Bluff, is open to the SW. The shores are bluff, brush covered and low with a marshy area surrounding the bay. The N and SE sides of the bay are spotted with homes. At night, the lighted antenna about 2 miles NE of the head of Useless Bay is prominent.

SCATCHET HEAD and POSSESSION POINT, at the S end of Whidbey Island, are both prominent, especiallly from S; the white bluffs are visible for a considerable distance. A lighted bell buoy is 0.5 miles S of Possession Point. A fish haven, marked by private buoys, is close W of the lighted bell buoy. Shoals extend 0.5 mile offshore immediately W of Scatchet Head and over 0.2 mile offshore from the head to Possession Point. A lighted gong buoy is about 0.5 mile off Scatchet Head. CULTUS BAY, just W of Possession Point is shoal, much of the bay bares at low water. A private mooring basin is on the E side of the bay. A channel, marked by private buoys and daymarks, leads to the basin. Possession Sound and its tributaries are described later in this chapter.

CHART 18446 † APPLE COVE POINT is a low sandspit projecting 220 yards from the high, wooded land of the peninsula. The point is steep-to, but a shoal makes out nearly 0.5 mile SE from it. Just off the point is a light. Heavy tide rips caused by strong NW winds and a strong ebb current are encountered in the vicinity of the light.

A microwave tower, on the high ground about 0.6 mile SW from Apple Cove Point Light, is prominent from offshore.

APPLETREE COVE is the open bight on the W side of the sound about 1.5 miles S of Apple Cove Point. It affords anchorage in 30 to 60 feet inside the line of the entrance points, with some shelter from winds drawing in or out of the sound, but not from N and SE. Shoaling to 18 feet exists about 0.2 mile S to SE of the end of Kingston breakwater.

KINGSTON, a town on the N side of the cove, has a large, well-equipped small-craft basin and a pier with a ferry slip at its end. The ferry runs between Kingston and Edmonds. The basin is used by tugs, fishing boats, and pleasure craft. The harbor is protected by a stone breakwater that extends about 340 yards SW from the ferry pier; the end of the breakwater is marked by a light. The entrance to the harbor is marked by day-beacons. In October 1982, the controlling depth was 12 feet through the entrance and in the E part of the basin with 8½ feet in the W part of the basin. Berths for 275 craft, electricity, gasoline, diesel fuel, water, ice, dry storage, and marine supplies are available. A tidal grid that can handle craft up to 65 feet, and a 4-ton hoist are also available. Hull and engine repairs can be made.

EDWARDS POINT, (47°48'N., 122°24'W.) is a high, wooded point on the E side of Puget Sound 3.6 miles ESE of Apple Cove Point. It is a turning point for vessels running from Seattle N into Possession Sound and adjoining waters. An oil storage and distributing plant of the Union Oil Company of California is on the point. Many large tanks on and below the bluff make the point prominent from seaward. Dock lights, a lighted sign, and a fog signal are maintained by the company. Fuel barges are loaded here, and ships may be bunkered, but there are no provisions for the replenishment of stores.

EDMONDS is an incorporated city 1 mile NE of Edwards Point with a small boat basin and marina under the administration of the PORT OF EDMONDS. The basin, protected on its N, W, and S sides by a breakwater, is entered from the W at about midpoint of the W section of the breakwater. The breakwater is marked by lights and a daybeacon. In May 1985, shoaling to an unknown extent was reported in the entrance to the basin near the breakwater. In 1982, the midchannel controlling depth was 11 feet through the entrance; thence depths of 10 to 12 feet were inside the basin with lesser depths at the sides. Open and covered berths for about 700 craft to 50 feet, including 50 transient berths, are available. Berth assignments are made by the harbormaster. Electricity, gasoline, diesel fuel, water, ice, marine supplies, and a 35-foot marine railway and a 4-

ton hoist are available in the basin. A private boatyard is also available for minor hull and engine repairs.

Just NE of the boat basin are a fish haven, the Edmonds and Kingston ferry landings, and a scuba diving area. The fish haven is marked by private buoys near the boat basin breakwater N section; private buoys also mark the W side of the scuba diving area.

POINT WELLS (47°47'N., 122°24'W.), is a low, sandy point projecting 450 yards from the high land 1.5 miles S of Edwards Point on the E side of the sound. It is distinguished by prominent oil tanks. It is a water terminal and storage plant of Chevron USA, Inc.

The current at Point Wells is unpredictable being inconsistent for similar tidal conditions.

RICHMOND BEACH is a community on the E shore just S of Point Wells. A tall, charted radio tower (KGDN), marked by aircraft warning lights, is about 1.5 miles inshore from Richmond Beach; it is an excellent landmark, especially at night. A fish haven marked by private buoys, is off the mouth of Boeing Creek, about 1.9 miles S of Point Wells.

CHARTS 18446, 18449 †
BAINBRIDGE ISLAND, 9 miles long and heavily wooded, forms part of the W shore of Puget Sound. There are several towns on the island.

PORT MADISON indents the W shore between the N end of Bainbridge Island and POINT JEFFERSON. It is about 2.5 miles long and deep; not until within 0.5 mile of the beach can anchorage be found in 90 or 100 feet, sticky bottom. Its SW part connects with Port Orchard through Agate Passage.

The N shore is formed by broken white bluffs, with low beaches between, and bordered by sand and shingle beaches that bare in some cases as much as 0.2 mile off. The Bluffs on the W shore are moderately low; the buildings of the Indian reservation near the entrance to Agate Passage are prominent. INDIANOLA, a village on the N shore, has a long pier. The water E of the end of this pier is shoal.

MILLER BAY, in the NW part of Port Madison, is used by shallow-draft pleasure craft. The channel, privately marked, should not be used at low tide because of the very irregular bottom. Anchorage in 6 to 7 feet, sticky mud bottom, may be had N of the second buoy. The controlling depth to this anchorage is about 1 foot.

SQUAMISH is a small town N of Agate Passage.

POINT MONROE, the S point at the entrance of Port Madison, is a low, narrow sandspit, curving W and S and marked by a light. A small cove is between the sandspit and the shore to the S. The entrance dries at low water.

The S shore of Port Madison is composed of broken bluffs, except where it is indented by the narrow arm extending 1 mile S. The entrance to this narrow arm is 0.7 mile W of Point Monroe Light. The town of PORT MADISON, once the county seat, is a summer resort with many cottages and private piers along its shores. The moorings here are private, and there are no fueling facilities. The narrow channel through the arm has a least depth of about 14 feet, and local knowledge is necessary to keep in the best water. A submerged rock, covered 6 feet and marked by a daybeacon, is in (47°41'51"N., 122°32'07"W.), about 220 yards SSW of TREASURE ISLAND; caution should be exercised. An old ballast dump, nearly bare at low water, lies 75 yards offshore 400 yards in from the E entrance point. Care should be taken to avoid the cluster of covered rocks 100 yards off the E entrance point. Sheltered anchorage for small craft may be had in up to 21 feet, mudbottom.

MEADOW POINT, on the E side of Puget Sound nearly opposite Point Monroe, is a low, grassy point, with a high tree and brush-covered bluff behind it. A buoy is 550 yards NW of the point.

MURDEN COVE is an open bight on the W side of the sound about 3.5 miles S of Point Monroe. An extensive flat which bares extends almost 0.5 mile from the head of the cove, and outside of it the depth increases rapidly. SKIFF POINT, the N entrance point, has low yellow bluffs to the S. A shoal covered by kelp, extends about 250 yards from the point; this shoal is reported to be building out and should be given a wide berth. YEOMALT POINT, the S entrance point, is a low, grassy sandspit, 150 yards wide, rising gradually to the general level of the high land. The radio towers about 0.9 mile SW of Skiff Point are prominent from offshore.

WING POINT, on the N side of the entrance to Eagle Harbor, is a bluff point 30 feet high, covered with trees to the edge. A reef extends SSE for 0.5 mile from Wing Point and gerally marked by kelp. The S extremity of the reef is marked by a buoy. TYEE SHOAL 0.7 mile SSE of Wing Point, with a least depth of 15 feet, is marked by a light with a fog signal.

Foul ground extends as much as 500 yards off the S point at the entrance; a light and buoy mark its outer limits.

EAGLE HARBOR indents the E shore of Bainbridge Island opposite Elliott Bay. It is 2 miles long and affords excellent anchorage in 30 to 39 feet, muddy bottom. It narrows at the head to 300 yards.

The entrance is deep, but caution is necessary in entering because the natural channel is only 200 yards wide between the reef S of Wing Point and the spit on the W side of the channel entrance. The channel is marked by lights and buoys.

WINSLOW is the largest town on Bainbridge Island. It is on the N shore of Eagle Harbor, and is a major ferry port on the routes out of Seattle to the W. About 0.2 mile W of the ferry slip is a large building and two piers which were once part of a shipyard. The facilities are now used by the Washington State Ferry. System for ferry mooring and maintenance. A small marina and machine shop are just W of the W pier. Berths, water, and limited engine repairs are available. Another marina, farther westward, has berths, gasoline, diesel fuel, electricity, water, ice, marine supplies, and pump-out facilities.

BLAKELY ROCK, the highest of four rocks, is prominent in approaching Blakely Harbor; it it 0.7 mile N of Restoration Point and at high water shows about 15 feet at its highest point. It is 300 yards long, with shoal water,

BAINBRIDGE ISLAND

well marked by kelp, extending over 250 yards N. A light is on the S side of the rock.

BLAKELY HARBOR is a small inlet on the E shore of Bainbridge Island near its S end. It is 1 mile long. Depths range from 145 feet at the entrance to 25 feet near the head. The usual anchorage is near the entrance in 54 to 96 feet, sticky bottom, slightly favoring the S shore. There are many old pilings and dolphins in the shoal waters near the shores. There are no usable wharves in Blakely Harbor. One of the world's largest sawmills once operated here.

RESTORATION POINT is flat and about 10 feet high for 300 yards from the shore, then it rises abruptly to a wooded knoll about 100 feet high, on which a number of large buildings are prominent. DECATUR REEF. Partly bare, extends 300 yards E of Restoration Point. The outer end of the reef is marked by a light.

CHART 18440 † PUGET SOUND, a bay with numerous channels and branches, extends about 90 miles S from the Strait of Juan de Fuca to Olympia. The N boundary of the sound is formed, at its main entrance, by a line between Point Wilson on the Quimper Peninsula and Point Partridge on Whidbey Island; at a second entrance between West Point on Whidbey Island, Deception Island, and Sares Head on Fidalgo Island; at a third entrance, at the S end of Swinomish Channel between Fidalgo Island and McGlinn Island. Puget Sound was named by George Vancouver for Lieutenant Peter Puget, who explored the S end in May 1792. Deep-draft traffic is considerable in the larger passages, and small craft operate throughout the area. Unusually deep water and strong currents characterize these waters.

Navigation of the area is comparatively easy in clear weather; the outlying dangers are few and marked by aids. The currents follow the general direction of the channels and have considerable velocity. In thick weather, because of the uncertainty of the currents and the great depths which render soundings useless in many places, strangers are advised to take a pilot.

VESSEL TRAFFIC SERVICE (PUGET SOUND), operated by the U.S. Coast Guard, has been established in the Strait of Juan De Fuca, E of Port Angeles, and in the waters of Rosario Strait, Admiralty Inlet, Puget Sound, and the navigable waters adjacent to these areas.

Note: In April 1983, Commander, Thirteenth Coast Guard District, authorized that the Vessel Movement Reporting System (VMRS) requirements contained in CFR 161.128, 161.131, and 161.142 be waived upon the waters within and among the San Juan Islands, W of Rosario Strait; on the waters E of Whidbey Island, N of the N tip of Gedney Island; inside Hood Canal, S of Foulweather Bluff; within Tacoma Narrows (The Narrows) and upon all adjacent waters S of Point Defiance; and within Bellingham Bay N of the N tip of Eliza Island. There is little traffic, no radar coverage, and no Traffic Separation Scheme (TSS) in these areas.

Floating logs and DEADHEADS or SINKERS may be encountered anywhere in Puget Sound; caution should be exercised.

The large tides of Puget Sound are very complex and variable; use of the Tide Tables is advised. These are contained in this edition of the PACIFIC BOATING ALMANAC.

CURRENTS † The Tidal Current Charts, Puget Sound, Northern Part, show the direction and velocity of the tidal current for each hour of its cycle in the waterways of Puget Sound from Admiralty Inlet to Seattle. They are designed for use with the current predictions for Admiralty Inlet contained in the Tidal Current Tables. A similar publication, entitled Tidal Current Charts, Puget Sound, Southern Part, covers the sound from Seattle to Olympia. Both sets of Tidal Current Charts for Puget Sound are included in this edition of the PACIFIC BOATING ALMANAC.

In Admiralty Inlet and Puget Sound, the tidal currents are subjected to daily inequalities similar to those of the tides. Velocities of 2 to 7 knots occur from Point Wilson to Point No Point. In the more open waters of the sound S of Point No Point the velocities are much less.

At Point Wilson and at Marrowstone Point, slack water occurs from one-half to 1 hour earlier near shore than in midchannel.

In the winter, when S winds prevail, there is generally a N surface drift which increases the ebb current and decreases the flood current. This effect is about 0.5 knot between Nodule and Bush Points.

The tidal currents in the S entrance of Possession Sound are weak and variable.

Between Foulweather Bluff and Misery Point, the tidal currents have a velocity of about 0.8 knot, while in the S part of Hood Canal, the velocity is only about 0.5 knot; at times of tropic tides, however, the greater ebbs may attain velocities more than double these values.

The tidal currents have velocities up to about 6 knots or more in Agate Passage and in The Narrows.

WINDS AND VISIBILITY † Puget Sound is open to the N and S and protected to the W and E by mountains. Winds are mainly SE through SW from September through April and NW through N in late spring and summer. However, winter directions are still common in summer, as are summer directions in winter. From fall through spring, lows moving through or near the Puget Sound are responsible for the mainly S flow. Intense storms can generate sustained winds of 40 knots with 50-knots gusts over the area. These strong winds are almost always from a S direction. In the Seattle area, sustained winds of 56 knots and gusts of 60 knots have been recorded. Winds are strongest in winter and early spring, on the average. Also calm conditions are frequent in fall and winter, reflecting the lull between storm passages. In late spring and summer, winds flow into Puget Sound from the Pacific High. Often, winds are light and variable at night, then pick up to 8 to 15 knots during the afternoon, reflecting a sea breeze effect over the Sound. Occasionally, a low or front will bring a return to a S flow during the summer,

and these winds remain the strongest, on the average.

Fog in the Puget Sound area causes visibility problems on about 25 to 40 days each year. It most likely hinders navigation in autumn and again during January and February. This fog is mainly a land type that forms on cool, clear, calm nights, drifts out over the water, then dissipates during the day. It can hang on for several days if a stagnant condition develops. Fog can form in any month, but is least likely during April and May.

Poor visibilities are encountered more often N and S of Puget Sound than in the Sound itself. In Admiralty Inlet, fog signals at Point Wilson and Double Bluff and Point No Point blow about 8 to 15 percent of the time, during the late summer and fall. Fog lowers visibilities on this part of the coast to less than 0.5 mile on about 4 to 8 days per month. South of Point Robinson, in the East Passage, the fog signals operate about 8 to 15 percent of the time in fall and midwinter. In Puget Sound, fog signals, even during the heart of the season, blow less than 8 percent of the time; less than 5 percent in Elliott Bay. Waters of Point Wells and Point Pully are among the most fog free in the area; fog signals there operate just a few hours a month for most of the year. In the Seattle area, visibility falls below 0.5 mile on about 3 to 6 days per month during the foggy season.

-U.S. COAST PILOT 7
25th edition, August 1989
Corrected thru 10 22 90
Local Notice to Mariners

FACILITIES

KINGSTON AREA

KINGSTON COVE † The little town of Kingston serves the primary purpose of linking a major road from the Olympic Peninsula to the short Puget Sound ferry crossing from Edmonds. In the cove behind the ferry dock is a smallcraft marina that has had ups and downs. In the past few years the trend has definitely been up. Once privately owned, the floats and other equipment of the marina have recently been converted into a municipal facility, and much-needed facelifting is taking place. A small park, a hoist, various marine services and some shoreside restaurants now make Kingston Cove a very appealing and useful waystop, especially if you are headed into Port Madison on the way to Poulsbo.

APPLETREE BOATWORKS, Box 599, Kingston, WA 98346. (206) 297 - 4048. All year. Marine hardware. Hull maintenance. Spar and rigging. Woodwork. Interior remodeling. Mechanical and electrical installation and repair. Diver services. Marine surveyor. Owner: David Bennett.

APPLE TREE PHARMACY (in the Kingston Shopping Center) 26287 First Ave., N.E., Kingston, WA 98346. (206) 297 - 3355. Gifts, cards, photo finishing, dry cleaning, etc. Owners: Quentin E. and Mary E. Gilman.

BAY MARINA (on Miller Bay Road) Box 396, Squamish, WA 98392. (206) 598 - 4900. Open 9 AM - 5 PM, Tuesday through Saturday. Ramp: 2-lanes, concrete, open 24 hours. Slips. Guest dock. Open and covered dry storage. Fuel dock: gas and mix. Engine maintenance, parts and repairs. Marine hardware. Charts. New and used boats and motors. Electronics. Fishing: tackle. Manager: Dale Kramer.

KINGSTON MARINE (at port of Kingston) Kingston, WA 98346. (206) 297 - 3541. Inboard, stern drive and outboard repair. Chandlerey, food and beer. Owners: Bill Sibbett, Wayne and Terry Funk.

PORT OF KINGSTON (at the breakwater, west of the Kingston-Edmonds ferry terminal. Access by Kingston-Edmonds ferry) Box 559, Kingston, WA 98346. (206) 297 - 3545. Hoist cap.: 4 tons. Fuel dock: gas, diesel and outboard mix, open Summer: 5 AM - 10 PM weekends; 6 AM - 10 PM weekdays; Winter: 8 AM - 5 PM. Slips. Dry storage. Showers. Dockside electricity. Manager: Polly Harvey.

VIKING MARINE CENTER, (Downtown) Kingston, WA 98346. (206) 297 - 3838. Open seven days. Boat sales. Chandlery. Nautical gifts and books. Manager: Jim Xenos.

BAINBRIDGE ISLAND

BAINBRIDGE ISLAND † Primarily owned by individual residential families, and edged with water frontage that is also privately owned, Bainbridge Island offers the vacationing boatmen very little except pleasant scenery he can coast along and enjoy. Its one commercially developed inlet is Eagle Harbor at the south end of the island. Here, beyond another terminus for ferries from Seattle, are two smallcraft marinas, one (Winslow Wharf Marina) a longtime presence in Eagle Harbor, the other (Eagle Harbor Marina) which used be a modest little moorage mostly for Seattle-based boat owners and has now become a lavish set of condominium floats.

Closer to Seattle than neighbors like Port Washington Marina or the private facilities in Gig Harbor, Eagle Harbor Marina gives absentee owners quick access via ferry to their stored boats. From Eagle Harbor, it's pleasant to run westward through Rich Passage to visit Port Orchard, Bremerton, Brownsville or Poulsbo, to enjoy the amenities of Illahee State Park, or, almost on your doorstep, the compact recreational possibilities of Blake Island State Park.

BAINBRIDGE RENTALS, (Island Center) 8780 Fletcher Bay Road N.E., Bainbridge Island, WA 98110. (206) 842 - 3303. Two hoists. Engine repairs. Manager: Andy Cainion.

THE CHANDERLY (at Winslow Wharf), 133 Parfitt Way SW, Bainbridge Island, WA 98110. (206) 842 - SAIL. Open daily 10AM - 6:30 PM. Marine hardware and supplies. Nautical clothing and gifts. Beer and wine. Groceries. Ice. Owner: John M. Jay, Jr.

EAGLE HARBOR MARINA (opposite ferry dock on south side of harbor) 5834 Ward Ave NE, Bainbridge Island, WA 98110. (206) 842 - 4003. Transient or permanent rental moorage and condominium slips. Dockside electricity. Waste disposal pumpout. Laundry. Showers. Clubhouse. Manager: Dan Hornick.

WINSLOW WHARF MARINA, P.O. Box 10297. 141 Parfitt Way SW, Winslow, WA, 98110. (206) 842 - 4202. All year. Winter: 9 AM - 5 PM Tues. - Sun. Summer: 9 AM - 5 PM. 7 days a week. Charts. Electronics. Groceries. Ice. Laundry. Marine hardware. Restaurant. Waste disposal pumpout. Dockside electricity. Fuel dock: gas and diesel. Manager: C.W. Fry.

EDMONDS

EDMONDS † One of Seattle's bedroom communities Edmonds has developed a marina more for the use of its own residents than for transient boatmen. Consequently dock space for visitors is quite limited during the cruising season and is available only on a first-come, first-served basis. Very near the Port of Edmonds marina is a state-of-the-art fishing pier, which is built above an artificial reef attractive to rock fish. And along the shore are sandy beaches and small municipal parks equipped with picnic facilities which are used during the summer. The waterfront features several first-rate restaurants, and the downtown shopping district is within easy walking distance. As the eastern terminus of the cross-sound ferry, Edmonds serves as the embarking point for vacationers headed for Kingston and other destinations on the north end of the Great Peninsula.

In the waters next to the Edmonds ferry dock is an area reserved for divers and diving classes. This site houses a number of sunken vessels and even a submerged pier, all of which offer excellent opportunities for underwater exploration.

ALL SEASONS CHARTERS 300 Admiral Way, Edmonds, WA 98020. (206) 771-3277. Fishing Charters.

EDMONDS HARBOR MARINE (in Harbor Square) 190 West Dayton, Suite 101, Edmonds, WA 98020. (206) 775-7501. Open daily 9 AM - 6 PM. Marine hardware and supplies. Nautical clothing. Charts. Electronics. Inflatables. Owner: Lee Bondurant.

PORT OF EDMONDS, 336 Admiral Way, Edmonds, WA 98020. (206) 774-0549. Open daylight hours year round. Full service marina. Fuel dock: gas, diesel and accessory oils. Public launcher: 7000 pounds, 27 feet. 35 ton marine travel lift. Public workyard. Over 1200 linear feet of guest moorage available. Dockside electricity and showers. Over 1000 permanent moorage spaces. Nearby services include shopping centers, restaurants, and marine sales, services and repair businesses. Port Manager: Bill Stevens.

WILSON MARINE-EDMONDS, 471 Admiral Way, Edmonds, WA 98020. (206) 775-8111. Open all year 4 AM-9PM. Boat and motor sales. Electronic sales. Instrument repairs. Marine hardware. Hoist cap.: 30 tons. Hull and engine maintenance. Engine parts and service. Charter service. General Manager: Terry Roehl.

MARINE ENGINE SPECIALISTS (in Port of Edmonds Harbor Square). 180 West Dayton #101, Edmonds, WA 98020. (206) 778-2275. Open daily, Monday - Friday 8:30 AM - 5:30 PM; Saturday 9 AM - 1 PM. Marine hardware. Sterndrive, outboard and inboard parts, sales and service. Mobile dockside service. Owners: Don Starbuck.

MEADOWDALE MARINE, 16111-76th Place West, Edmonds, WA 98020. (206) 743 - 2211. Fuel dock: gas and mix. Open daylight hours. Haulouts cap.: 3 tons. Covered dry storage. Marine hardware. Ice. Fishing: licenses, bai, tackle. Rental boats. Mgr: Ron Hansen.

NORMA BEACH BOATHOUSE (3 miles east of Possession Pt. on Puget Sound), 14725 Norma Beach Road, Edmonds, WA 98020. (206) 743 - 0821. All year. Gas and outboard mix. Dry storage. Fishing: bait and tackle. Rental tackle, boats and motors.

SEA CHARTERS TACKLE AND MARINE, 115 W. Dayton, Edmonds, WA 98020. (206) 776 - 5611. "The boater's convenience store": food mart, bait and ice. Tackle, repairs, downriggers, marine supplies, skippered charters. Manager, Edmonds store: Tom Stansbery.

MARINE PARKS

FAY BAINBRIDGE STATE PARK, (north end of Bainbridge Island) 15446 Sunrise Drive NE, Bainbridge Island, WA 98110. (206) 842-3931. 17 acres. Campsites. Kitchens. Sand beach. Launching ramp. Mooring buoys. Showers and toilets.

BLAKE ISLAND STATE MARINE PARK (5 miles W of Seattle; 2 miles S of Bainbridge Island). 475 acres. 19 mooring buoys, 848 feet of float space. Picnic facilities. Campsites. Showers. Toilets. Hiking trails. Artificial fishing reef. A reader warns not to enter the state park dock area from the east on other than a high tide – "the west entrance is well marked, but a stranger might not see the real entrance if approaching from the south."

EAGLE HARBOR WATERFRONT PARK (at Winslow). Playground. Picnic area. Moor at Winslow Wharf.

FORT WARD STATE PARK (southwest of Winslow on Bainbridge Island, off Hwy. 305.) 137 acres. Ramp. Two mooring buoys. Underwater park. Picnic area. No water available. Toilets.

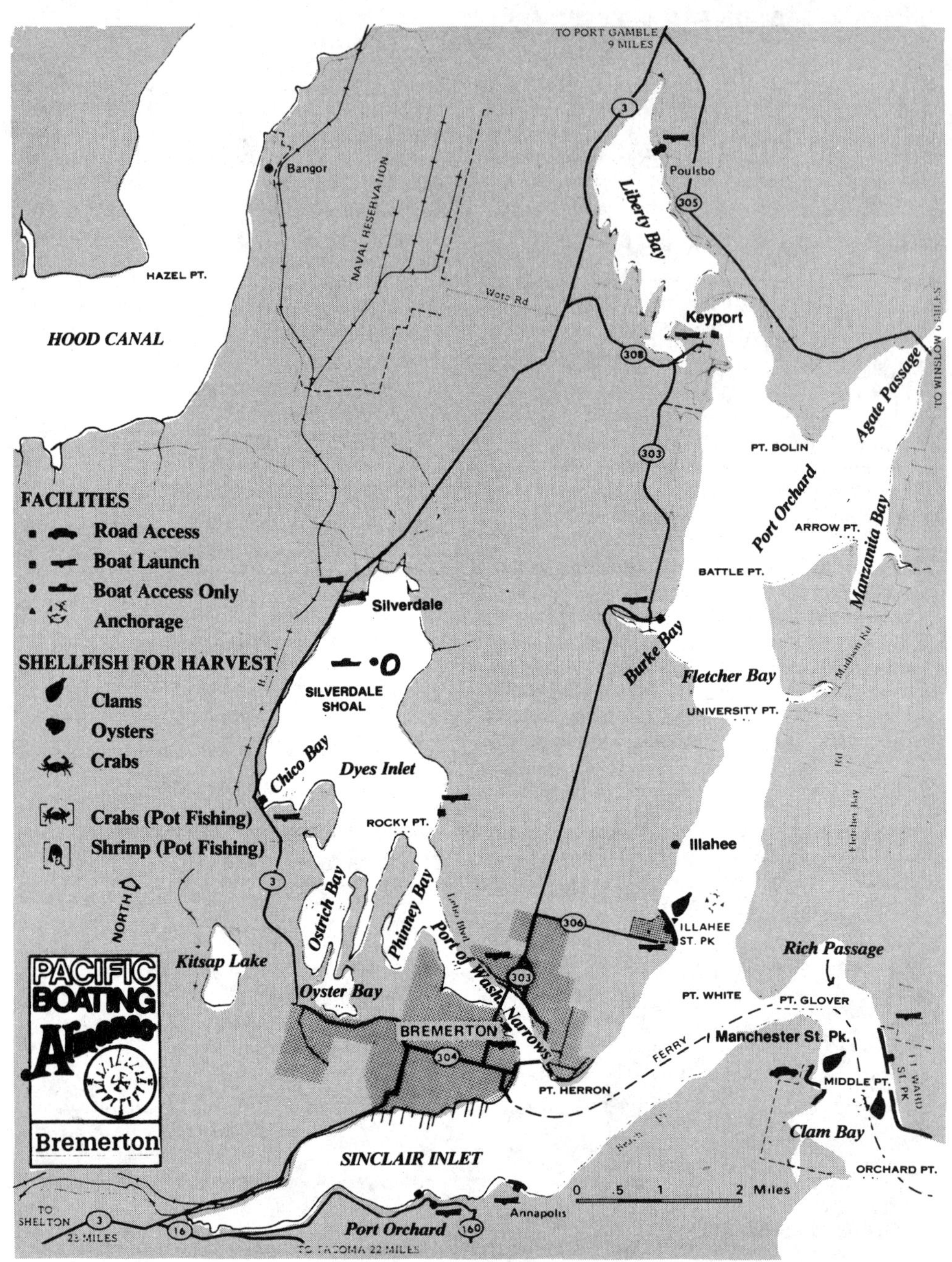

TO PORT GAMBLE
9 MILES
3
Bangor
Poulsbo
Liberty Bay
305
HAZEL PT.
Wato Rd
Keyport
HOOD CANAL
308
Agate Passage
303
PT. BOLIN
TO WINSLOW 8 MILES
FACILITIES
Road Access
Boat Launch
Boat Access Only
Anchorage
Port Orchard
ARROW PT.
Manzanita Bay
BATTLE PT.
Silverdale
Burke Bay
SHELLFISH FOR HARVEST
Clams
Oysters
Crabs
Crabs (Pot Fishing)
Shrimp (Pot Fishing)
SILVERDALE
SHOAL
Fletcher Bay
UNIVERSITY PT.
Madison Rd
Chico Bay
Dyes Inlet
Fletcher Bay Rd
ROCKY PT.
Illahee
NORTH
3
Ostrich Bay
Phinney Bay
306
ILLAHEE
ST. PK
Rich Passage
Kitsap Lake
Port of Wash.
303
PT. WHITE
PT. GLOVER
PACIFIC
BOATING
Almanac
Bremerton
Oyster Bay
Narrows
BREMERTON
304
FERRY
Manchester St. Pk.
WARD ST. PK
PT. HERRON
MIDDLE PT.
Clam Bay
SINCLAIR INLET
ORCHARD PT.
0   .5   1   2 Miles
TO
SHELTON
3
23 MILES
16
Port Orchard
160
Annapolis
TO TACOMA 22 MILES

11
POULSBO, BREMERTON AND PORT ORCHARD

AIR TRANSPORTATION
Kenmore Air Harbor: (206) 486-1257
Lake Union Air: (800) 692-2993

CHAMBER OF COMMERCE
Bainbridge Island: (206) 842-3700
Bremerton: (206) 479-3579
Bremerton/Kitsap Visitors:
(206) 479-3588
Central Kitsap: (206) 692-6800
South Kitsap: (206) 876-3505

COAST GUARD
VHF 16
Emergengies: (800) 592-9911
Seattle: (206) 442-7070

DECOMPRESSION CHAMBER
Keyport: (206) 396-5111
Virginia Mason, Seattle:
(206) 624-1144

FERRY TRANSPORTATION
Washington State: (800) 542-0812
Port Orchard-Bremerton:
(206) 876-2300

FISHING INFORMATION
(206) 753-6600

HOOD CANAL BRIDGE
(206) 779-3377

MARINE OPERATOR
VHF 28

POISON INFORMATION
(800) 732-6985

RED TIDE HOTLINE
(800) 562-5632

STATE PARK INFORMATION
(800) 562-0990

Poulsbo was founded in the 1880's by Norwegian fishermen. With most of its population still Norwegian, expect to see a "Little Norway on the Fjord" when traveling there. The town still celebrates Norway's Independence Day on May 17. Poulsbo is a picturesque adventure.

Port Orchard and Bremerton have long histories as navy towns. Port Orchard was the first city incorporated in Kitsap County and was originally named Sidney. Today, the community of approximately 5,000 has been restored and is a shoppers paradise. Bremerton was founded by William Bremer and today hosts the world's oldest cannon along with the Naval Shipyard Museum. This shipbuilding city can be reached by the ferry running to Port Orchard and back.

CHARTS 18446, 18449 † PORT ORCHARD (47°32'N., 122°38'W.), is an extensive body of water, W of Bainbridge Island, 15 miles long. Its N end connects with Port Madison through Agate Passage. At its S end Port Orchard connects with Puget Sound through Rich Passage. The depths in the main body of Port Orchard range from 36 to 150 feet with few dangers and these, as a rule, are close inshore. The shores are moderately low and wooded. Villages and numerous cottages line the shores.

CURRENT observations taken in mid-channel about 1 mile S of TOLO indicate that the tidal current in that locality is very weak.

CHART 18446 † AGATE PASSAGE is the N entrance to Port Orchard and connects it with Port Madison. The channel extends a mile in a SW direction. The depth is about 20 feet. The passage is straight; the shores are wooded and fairly steep to; the shoreline is mostly rocky and fringed with kelp to Point Bolin. The currents have velocities up to 6 knots; the flood sets SW and the ebb NE.

The passage is obstructed by a shoal, marked by a buoy, near the middle of the N end with depths of 9 to 10 feet, and there are other depths of 14 to 18 feet almost in midchannel.

The N entrance is marked by a light on the W side of the channel opposite AGATE POINT; a lighted buoy marks the channel through the passage and a light marks a shoal NE of Point Bolin.

A fixed highway bridge 0.7 mile S of Agate Point, has a clearance of 75 feet for a midwidth of 300 feet. Overhead power cables cross the pasage on both sides of the bridge; least clearance is 96 feet.

LIBERTY BAY is a narrow inlet extending about 4 miles in a N direction from the NW part of Port Orchard. The SE half of the bay is narrow and tortuous. The shore is low and wooded; the shoreline is mostly sand and gravel. There are mudflats at the head of the bay and in the small bight on the S side of the bay. Mud is the predominating bottom characteristic. The current velocity is 0.8 knot N of Keyport in the narrow entrance to the bay. Velocities exceeding 1 knot occur at times.

The KEYPORT NAVAL UNDERWATER WARFARE ENGINEERING STATION (NUWES) on the W side of the entrance to Liberty Bay has two piers. A seaplane float extends 100 feet NW from the end of the N pier. Mariners are requested not to exceed 5 knots when passing the S pier and not to exceed 3 knots when passing the N pier. Several buildings are prominent at the station.

A TORPEDO TEST AREA extends off the shore between Brownsville and Keyport NUWES. Flashing red lights on Navy range vessels between Keyport and Brownsville and atop the building at the seaward end of the S pier at Keyport NUWES indicate torpedo firings, that noise measurement tests are in progress, or that conditions are generally hazardous to mariners. When lights are flashing, mariners should not enter the test area. Mariners near the area should stop engines, or other equipment generating underwater noise. such as depth sounders, because some torpedos are guided by noise and may be attracted to the boat noises.

KEYPORT (47°42'N., 122°37'W.), is on the S side of the passage leading to Liberty Bay. A power cable with a clearance of 90 feet crosses the passage at Keyport. There is a pier with a float for small craft. A store with gasoline pumps is at the head of the pier. A marine railway that can handle craft to 42 feet is available for repairs.

POULSBO (47°44'N., 122°39'W.), a fishing and pleasure resort on the E shore at the head of Liberty Bay, is the principal town of the area. The small-craft harbor at Poulsbo, protected on the S and W sides by an angled timbered breakwater, can accommodate about 270 fishing boats and pleasure craft. The breakwater is well marked by private lights. Piers and floats are in the harbor; depths are about 12 feet at the outer floats. Electricity, water, ice, a launching ramp, a pump-out facility, a marine railroad to 30 tons, a 50 foot tidal grid, and hull repairs are available at the basin. A yacht club and a restaurant are here. The stores of the town business district are nearby, and all types of supplies may be obtained. A tall church steeple on the hill NE of the harbor is prominent.

Oysters are cultivated on the flats at the head of the bay. There is an oyster company plant about 0.6 mile SE of the Poulsbo. A covered rock is about 175 yards SE of the oyster wharf.

MANZANITA is a settlement on the W side of Bainbridge Island in a small cove about 2 miles S from Agate Passage. MANZANITA BAY, S of the town, affords an excellent anchorage for small craft in 27 feet, mud bottom. There are several private wharves and floats in the bay. Caution is urged to avoid rows of submerged pilings on each side of the bay, about midway in from the entrance.

BATTLE POINT, a sandy spit on the E side of Port Orchard about 1.7 miles S of Point Bolin, marks the turn in the direction of the channel from SW to S. A light is off the end of the spit.

BROWNSVILLE, on the W shore of Port Orchard, is on the N shore of BURKE BAY, about 1.2 miles SW of Battle Point. Brownsville has a marina with berths for about 250 vessels. Transient berths are available. The reported depth alongside is 8 feet. Electricity, gasoline diesel fuel, water, ice, and supplies are available. The marina has a marine railway that can handle craft for hull and engine repairs up to 26 feet. The harbormaster's office is on the second floor of the town store. All of Burke Bay bares, but it may be entered by a small craft at about half tide.

CHART 18449 † ILLAHEE is a small settlement on the W shore of Port Orchard about 3.0 miles S of Battle Point. The town has a wharf and stores. A fish haven, marked by buoys and extending about 140 feet from the outer end of the wharf, provides marine habitat improvement for scuba diving and public fishing; mariners are advised to use caution. About a mile S of Illahee at ILLAHEE STATE PARK is a public pier with floats for small craft and a launching ramp. A rock awash was reported about 50 yards SE of the pier in about 47°35'59.8"N., 122°35'32.1"W., caution is advised in the area.

FLETCHER BAY is a village on the E shore of Port Orchard about 1.2 miles S of Battle Point. Small boats can enter the bay at three quarter tide and find anchorage in 12 feet, mud bottom; the swinging area is limited. The bar across the entrance bares at half tide.

ORCHARD POINT, the S point at the entrance to Rich Passage, is marked by a light and fog signal. A GENERAL ANCHORAGE is in the vicinity of the point. RICH PASSAGE is about 3 miles long, with a sharp bend near its W end, where it narrows to 0.2 mile. ORCHARD ROCKS, some 400 yards in extent, are on the N side of the channel just inside the E entrance. A small area near the center of the reef, which uncovers, is marked by a daybeacon. The rocks are marked off their S end by a lighted buoy. The reef off POINT GLOVER is marked by a light and fog signal. WATERMAN POINT, at the W entrance, is marked by a light and fog signal. A light marks the S edge of the shoal extending from POINT WHITE, the N point at the W entrance.

CURRENTS † Continuous observations in mid-channel between Point Glover and Point White and at other points in the passage indicate that: Current velocities increase from E to W in Rich Passage reaching a maximum average velocity of 2.4 knots on the flood and 3.1 knots on the ebb of the W end off POINT WHITE. The strongest observed currents were 4 knots on the flood and 5 knots on the ebb. Ferry pilots on the regular daily run between Seattle and Bremerton advised that on rare occasions they have experienced ebb currents of "at least" 6 knots in the vicinity of Light 10.

Near the time of slack, the average period when the velocity does not exceed 0.2 knot is about 20 minutes. For strong currents these periods will be decreased; for weak currents they will be increased.

In the channel off Orchard Point, at the E end of Rich Passage, the velocity of the flood is 0.8 knot and on the ebb, 1.1 knots. Off Pleasant Beach the velocity of the flood is 1.3 knots and on the ebb, 2.8 knots.

On the flood, the lines of stream flow are nearly uniform except off the bight just NW of Middle Point and in the large cove on the N shore opposite Point Glover. Eddies do form in those two places, but they do not extend outward to the usual vessel track. On the ebb, however, extensive eddies and counter-currents do occur, owing to the funnel-shaped configuration of the passage.

Between Middle Point and Point Glover, an extensive eddy extends from shore almost to mid-channel, and will frequently be encountered by vessels on the track between Orchard Rocks and Point Glover buoys.

An eddy fills the cove on the N shore opposite Point Glover, but does not extend outward to the vessel track.

An eddy occurs about 0.2 mile SSW of Point White and a little N of mid-channel at the W entrance to the passage. A weak counter current occurs inshore along the SE side of Point White.

These eddies and counter currents on the ebb greatly diminish the effective width of the passage, and so increase the velocities in the channel.

Strangers should not attempt to navigate Port Orchard, and particularly Rich Passage, in thick weather on account of the strong tidal currents. In clear weather, however, the navigation of these waters presents no unusual difficulty.

CAUTION † RICH PASSAGE, because of activities of the Puget Sound Naval Shipyard, has a large volume of traffic. Many ferries a day each way, tugs with hawser tows, and various types of naval crafts all contribute to create a considerable collision hazard in the passage, particularly at the sharp bend off Point Glover. Strong tidal conditions prevail in this vicinity, and deep-draft outbound vessels making the sharp turn may be unavoidable set well over toward the E shore, necessitation a two-blast, starboard-to-starboard meeting with inbound vessels. Vessesl approaching Point Glover from either direction should sound one long blast when within 0.5 mile of the point as a warning to any vessel approaching from the opposite direction.

FORT WARD, (47°35'N., 122°31'W.) formerly a military post and now a State park on Bainbridge Island, is near the E entrance to Rich Passage, just inside Beans Point. There is a wharf here built out to 18 feet. A fish pen off the end of the wharf is marked by private light. A rocky patch covered 11 feet, 150 yards S of the wharf, is dangerous to vessels approaching from southward. A radio tower just NE of Fort Ward and a large white house on BEANS POINT are prominent from the E end of Rich Passage.

CHART 18452 † SINCLAIR INLET, site of the city of Bremerton and the Puget Sound Naval Shipyard, is entered from Rich Passage and Port Orchard on the E, and Port Washington Narrows on the N. The inlet is 3.5 miles long, extending in a WSW direction from POINT HERRON, which is at the junction of Port Washington Narrows and Port Orchard. The point is marked by a light and fog signal. Several Navy maintained unlighted mooring buoys, used at times by unlighted craft, are in Sinclair Inlet. Mariners are advised to exercise caution at night.

EAST BREMERTON, (47°34'N., 122°37'W.) is the community back of Point Herron, on the E side of the Port Washington Narrows entrance. The fixed highway bridge crossing the narrows here has a clearance of 82 feet.

Sinclair Inlet is a NAVAL RESTRICTED AREA. ANNAPOLIS is a village on the S shore of Sinclair Inlet directly S of Point Herron. A foot pier extends out to a float which is used by a passenger ferry between the village and Bremerton. E of the ferry pier is a public float and a launching ramp. The float grounds at low water. The buildings of a veterans' home on the bluff above the town are prominent.

A flat that bares extends about 0.2 mile from shore in the bight between Annapolis and Port Orchard.

The town of PORT ORCHARD is on the S shore just W of Annapolis. It has a ferry pier, float landing, and a marina. Passenger ferry service is maintained with Bremerton. A marina, W of the ferry pier and marked at its entrance by private lights, has covered and open berths for about 330 small craft. Transient berths are available at the marina. Electricity, water, gasoline, diesel fuel, and pumpout facilities are at the marina; ice and suplies can be obtained nearby. A small-craft moorage and boatyard have berthing for about 25 vessels on the W side of town; electricity, water, and diesel fuel are available. The yard has a marine railway that can handle craft up to 65 feet. Hull and engine repairs can be done at the boatyard; a machine shop and carpentry shop are available. Port Orchard Yacht Club has its moorings W of the boatyard. A floating breakwater in ruins, a wreck, and other sunken debris are about 75 yards off the ends of the Yacht Club floats. Another marina and boatyard, just W of Port Orchard Yacht Club, can accommodate about 25 vessels. A mobile hoist with a 30 ton capacity can handle craft up to 55 feet. Electricity, gasoline, water, and limited marine supplies are available at the marina.

A marina and boatyard, about 1.5 miles W of Port Orchard, has berths for about 50 fishing boats and small craft. Electricity, gasoline, water and limited marine supplies are available. The boatyard has three marine railways, the largest of which can handle craft to 30 tons for hull repairs.

PUGET SOUND NAVAL SHIPYARD occupies most of the N shore of the inlet. The hammerhead crane near the offshore end of Pier 6 of the yard is one of the most conspicuous objects from any direction.

BREMERTON adjoins the shipyard, and most of the city's business and affairs are keyed to the needs of the Navy establishment. The city limits include East Bremerton and Point Herron. Frequent ferry service connects with Seattle. Floats for small craft are adjacent the N ferry slip.

CHART 18448 † PORT WASHINGTON NARROWS, 3 miles long, joins Sinclair and Dyes Inlets. Tidal currents in the narrows attain velocities in excess of 4 knots at times. (See Tidal Current Tables and Tidal Current Charts for detailed information. These are contained in this edition of PACIFIC BOATING ALMANAC.)

There are a number of petroleum distribution facilities with storage tanks and receiving wharves along the W shore of Port Washington Narrows between the S bridge over the narrows and Phinney Bay.

The fixed highway bridges and two power cables cross the narrows. The Bremerton East Bremerton Bridge at East Bremerton. Gasoline, water, ice, and some marine supplies are available. A marine railway here can handle craft to 42 feet for minor hull and engine repairs.

ANDERSON COVE is a small bight on the S shore about 1.5 miles above the East Bremerton Bridge. The cove is shoal; however, it has several private piers and a public launching ramp. A small-craft moorage is 250 yards E of Anderson Cove. Oil wharves are on both sides of the moorage.

PHINNEY BAY, 0.8 mile long, makes into the W shore near the N end of the narrows. Bremerton Yacht Club has its moorage with floats on the W side of the bay. ROCKY POINT is on the W side of the N entrance of the narrows. There are tide rips off this point.

DYES INLET extends about 3 miles NNW from the N end of the narrows to the village of SILVERDALE, (47°39'N., 122°42'W.) on the W side of the head of the inlet. The inlet is used by fishing boats and pleasure craft. There are several villages and many houses on its shores. The ruins of a large wharf are at Silverdale. Some local fishing boats are hauled out by crane for repairs, but there are no facilities. The village of TRACYTON is on the E shore just N of the narrows. The town has a public boat launching ramp.

CHICO is a small residential town on the SW side of Dyes Inlet, close W of Chico Bay.

OSTRICH BAY is an inlet in the SW part of Dyes Inlet. A covered rock is reported in Ostrich Bay 500 yards S of ELWOOD POINT inside the breakwater extending S of the point.

That part of the W shore of Ostrich Bay extending about 0.5 mile S from Elwood Point is an annex of the Puget Sound Naval Shipyard. The wharves and shops are in ruins.

A depth of 6 feet can be carried from Ostrich Bay into OYSTER BAY on mid-channel courses. There is 4 feet or more in Oyster Bay.

-U.S. COAST PILOT 7
25th edition. August 1989
Corrected thru 10 22 90
Local Notice to Mariners

FACILITIES

POULSBO

FRED 'N SONS MOBILE MARINE SERVICE (at Liberty Bay Marine), Poulsbo, WA 98370. (206) 697 - 3828 or 779 - 6861. Open 7 days a week. Engine repairs and emergency calls. Owners: The Villopoto Family.

GOLDEN DRAGON RESTAURANT & LOUNGE, 2nd floor Xenos Viking Mall, Poulsbo Wharf, Box 1881, Poulsbo, WA 98370. (206) 779-7673. Open 7 days a week. Chinese and American food. Banquet room. Take out.

LIBERTY BAY MARINA, 17791 Fjord Drive N.E., Poulsbo, WA 98370. (206) 779 - 7762. Slips. Transient berths. Showers. Laundry. Dockside electricity. Manager: Earl Miller.

NORTHSTAR SPORTSWEAR, Waterfront, Poulsbo, WA 98370. (206) 697-3293. Custom group orders, silkscreening and embroidery sportswear. Official military com-mand ball caps in stock or special order. Owners: B. & L. Lidyard.

PORT OF POULSBO MARINA, Box 732, Poulsbo, WA 98370. (206) 779-3505. Ramp: 1-lane, concrete. Slips. Guest dock. Tidal grid. Opposite Liberty Bay Park with picnic area. Pumpout station. Showers and restrooms. Manager: Bud Kirkman . Dockside electricity.

VIKING MARINE CENTER, (on the Wharf), Viking Mall, Poulsbo, WA 98370. (206) 779 - 4656. Open 7 days. Marine hardware. Clothing and footwear. Nautical books and gifts. Boat and motor sales. Fishing: bait and tackle. Owner: E.J. Xenos.

VIKING HOUSE RESTAURANT (on the water at Poulsbo Wharf), Xenos Viking Mall, Poulsbo, WA 98370. (206) 779 - 9882 (Seattle and Bainbridge Island 283 - 0920.) Serving breakfast, lunch and dinner. Cocktails, beer and wine. Open 7 days.

BREMERTON

BROWNSVILLE MARINA, 9790 Ogle Road NE, Bremerton, WA 98310. (206) 692 - 5498. Ramps: 2-single lane, concrete. Slips. Guest dock. Fuel dock: gas and diesel. Open daily. Marine railway cap.: to 26 feet. Two tidal grids. Deli. Ice. Groceries. Showers. Laundry. Fishing: bait, tackle. Dockside electricity: (4). Harbormaster: Dick Laut.

PORT WASHINGTON MARINA (at Port Washington Narrows), 1805 Thompson Drive, Bremerton, WA 98310. (206) 479-3037. Guest moorage. Sauna. Showers. Laundry. Pumpout station. Dockside electricity. Harbormaster: Gale Durst.

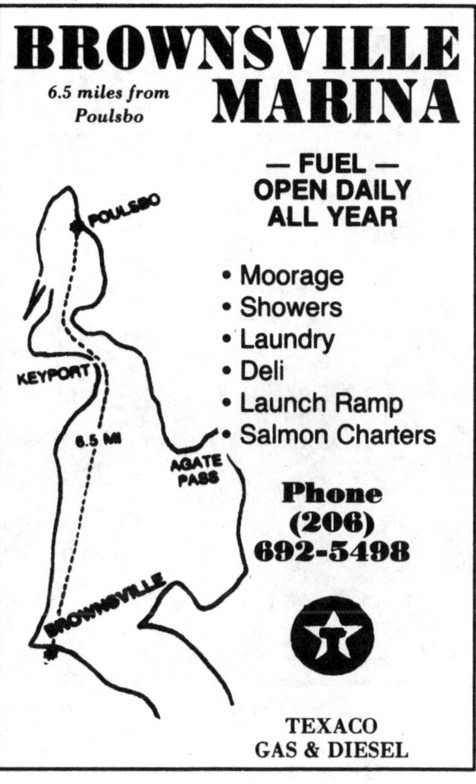

Port Orchard Marina showing the new guest dock.

PORT ORCHARD

BACKDOOR MALL (close to ferry and public moorage), 701 Prospect Street, Port Orchard, WA 98366. (206) 895 - 1729. Sixty-five country cottages in historic Howe Warehouse. Open 7 days. Mon. - Thurs. and Sat. 10 AM - 6 PM; Fri. 10 AM - 8 PM; Sun. 10 AM - 5 PM.

DOCKSIDE SALES AND SERVICE, Box 1028, Port Orchard, WA 98366. (206) 876 - 9016. All year. Travelift cap.: 30 ton. Slips to 45 feet. Boat storage. Marine hardware and electronics. Dry storage. Hull and engine maintenance, parts and repairs. Prop and shaft repairs. Used boat and motor sales. Owner: Don Morrison.

GEIGER REXALL PHARMACY (one block from Marina office next to Kitsap County Bank), 567 Bay Street, Port Orchard, WA 98366. (206) 876-4021. Drug store, gifts, cards, jewelry. Mon. - Fri. 9 AM - 7 PM; Sat. 9 AM - 6 PM; Owner: Robert G. Geiger.

KITSAP MARINA, 1595 SW Hwy 160, Port Orchard, WA 98366. (206) 895 - 2193. New and used boat and motor sales. Boat storage. Marine hardware. Engine maintenance, parts and repairs. Inboard / outboard gas and diesel engine service. Owner: Orrin Nelson.

OLDE CENTRAL ANTIQUE MALL (one block from guest dock), 801 Bay Street, Port Orchard, WA 98366. (206) 895 - 1902. Open daily 10 - 6. Friday until 8, Sunday 10 - 5. Owner/Manager: Gerry H. Bruckart.

PORT ORCHARD MARINA (next to small ferry landing), 8850 State Hwy. 3, Port Orchard, WA 98366. (206) 876 - 5535. Fuel dock: diesel, gas and outboard mix. Open and covered slips. Guest slips. Pumpout station. Showers. Operated by Port of Bremerton. Dockside electricity: (4a).

PORT ORCHARD YACHT SALES (300 yards from Port Orchard Marine), 551 Bay Street, Port Orchard, WA 98366. (206) 876 - 4584. Complete marine hardware and accessories. CHG. Ice. Yacht brokerage. Fishing: bait. Owner: Gary Blockus.

PUBLIC DOCK (between the Seattle and Port Orchard ferry docks.) Visitors' area for foot traffic at waterfront of 1st Street, Bremerton. Floats for transient boats adjoining. Small park adjacent. Operated by Port of Bremerton: 8850 State Hwy. 3, Port Orchard, WA 98366. Harbormaster: Darryl C. Piercy. (206) 876 - 5535.

SIDNEY VILLAGE MALL (one block from public moorage and ferry), 702 Bay Street, Port Orchard, WA 98336. (206) 876 - 4622. Sixty shops of new merchandise. Open 7 days. M, T, W, Th, Sat.: 10 AM - 6 PM. Fri.: 10 AM - 8 PM. Sun.: 10 AM - 5 PM.

SOO HOY RESTAURANT, 632 Bay Street (across from Port Orchard marina), Port Orchard, WA 98366. (206) 876-9913. Tues. - Thur. 11 AM - 2 AM; Fri. - Sat. 11 AM - 3 AM; Sun. 3 PM - 9:30 PM. Closed Monday.

SULDAN'S BOAT WORKS, INC, 1343 SW State Hwy 160, Port Orchard, WA 98366. (206) 876 - 4435. All year. Three marine railways cap.: 55 feet or 35 tons. Slips to 55 feet. Dockside electricity. Hull and engine maintenance, parts and repair. Prop and shaft repairs. Full line marine supplies. Fuel dock: gas only. President: Byron J. Suldan.

MARINE PARKS

ILLAHEE STATE PARK (Port Orchard Bay, 3 miles NW of Bremerton), 3540 Bahia Vista N.W., Bremerton, WA 98310. (206) 478- 6460. 75 acres. Ramp: 1-lane, concrete/sand, open 6:30 AM - dusk, April 1 to Sept. 15. Balance of year open 8 AM to dusk. Guest dock. Five mooring buoys, 311 feet of float space. Picnic area. RV campsites. Showers. Toilets.

SILVERDALE WATERFRONT PARK (at head of Dyes Inlet in town of Silverdale), Two ramps. Picnic area, playground. Historical museum. Toilets. Use extreme caution in approach. Foreshore dries at low tide.

FACILITIES
Road Access
Boat Launch
Boat Access Only
Anchorage
SHELLFISH FOR HARVEST
Clams
Oysters
Crabs
Crabs (Pot Fishing)
Shrimp (Pot Fishing)
Christianson Cove
PT. RICHMOND
Paradise Cove
COLVOS PASSAGE
Spring Beach Co. Park (undeveloped)
TO PORT ORCHARD 14.5 MILES
16
Gig Harbor
Dalco Passage
PT. DALCO
The Narrows
POINT DEFIANCE PK.
PT. DEFIANCE
OWENS BEACH
FERRY
BEACH 36
PT. EVANS
CITY
Wollochet Rd
Stone Rd
Wollochet Bay
Hale Passage
TACOMA NARROWS BRIDGE
BEACH 1A
PT. FOSDICK
DEPT. OF NAT. RES. BEACH 1
VASHON ISLAND
PAY
BURTON ACRES CO. PK.
Quartermaster Hbr.
MAURY ISL.
DOCKTON CO PK.
PINER PT.
DEPT. OF NAT. RES. BEACH 79
NEILL PT.
DEPT. OF NAT. RES. BEACH 83
ROBINSON PT.
PUGET SOUND
Lakota Beach Co. Park (undeveloped)
Dumas Bay Co. Pk.
DASH PT. CNTY. PK.
DASH PT.
DASH PT. STATE PK.
Drive
BROWNS PT. BEACH
BROWNS PT.
COMMENCEMENT BAY
Tacoma
NORTH
PAY
TO SEATTLE 16 MILES
516
509
99
SALTWATER STATE PK.
Poverty Bay
Redondo
509
FEDERAL WAY
TACOMA
B.N.R.R.
Pearl Street
Ruston Wy
6th Ave
Sprague Ave
0 .5 1 2 Miles
16
PAY
509
S 11th St.
Puyallup R.
99
5
TO OLYMPIA 30 MILES

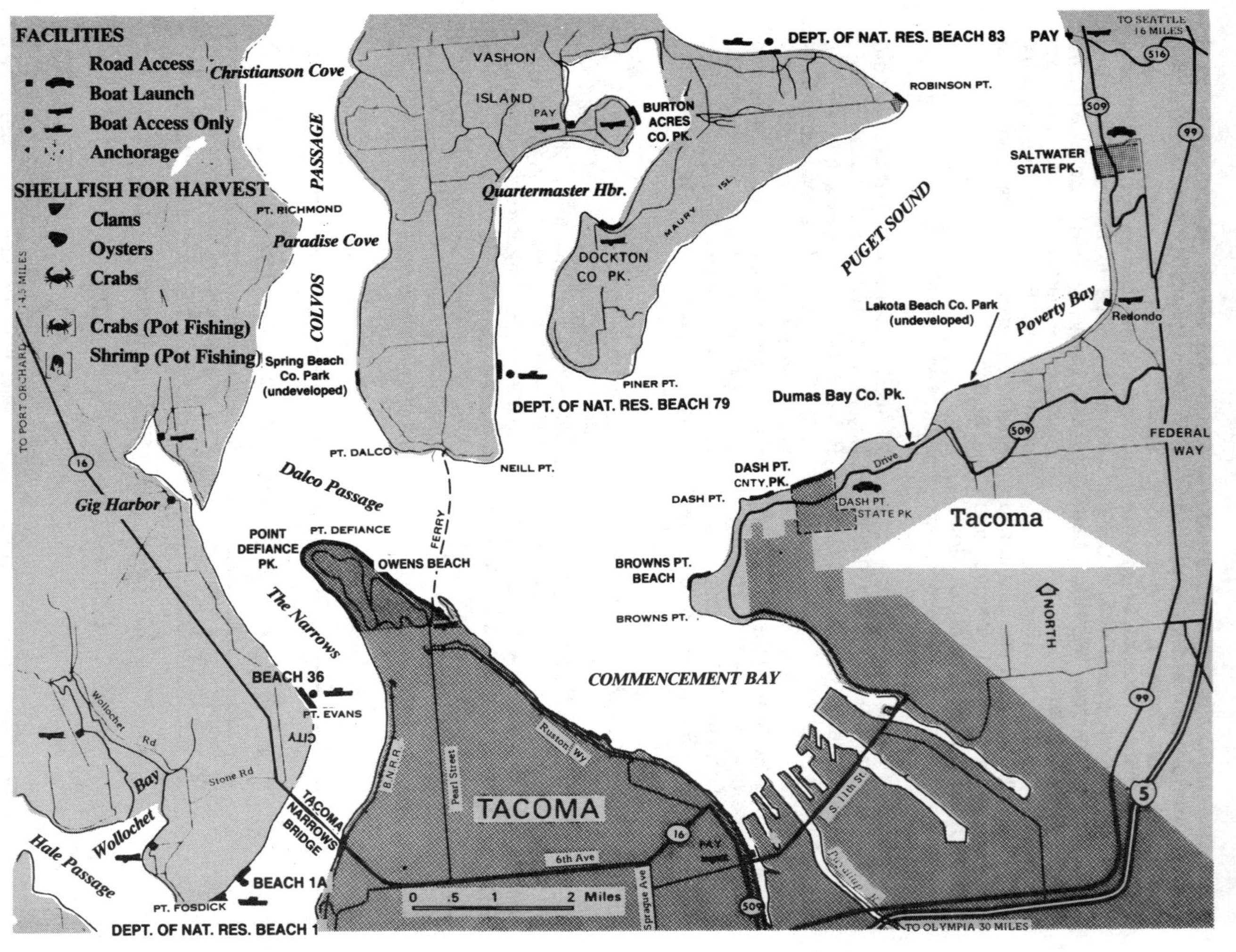

146

12

VASHON & MAURY ISLAND / GIG HARBOR

AIR TRANSPORTATION
Kenmore Air Harbor: (206) 486-1257
Lake Union Air: (800) 692-2993

CHAMBER OF COMMERCE
Olympia: (206) 357-3362
Olympia Visitor's Bureau:
    (206) 357-3370
Shelton: (206) 426-2021
Tacoma Visitor's Bureau:
    (206) 627-2175

COAST GUARD
VHF 16
Emergengies: (800) 592-9911
Seattle: (206) 442-7070

CUSTOMS
Tacoma/Olympia: (206) 593-6338

DECOMPRESSION CHAMBER
Keyport: (206) 396-5111
Virginia Mason, Seattle:
    (206) 624-1144

FERRY INFORMATION
Washington State: (800) 542-0812

FISHING INFORMATION
(206) 753-6600

MARINE OPERATOR
VHF 85

POISON INFORMATION
(800) 732-6985

RED TIDE HOTLINE
(800) 562-5632

STATE PARK INFORMATION
(800) 562-0990

TAXI
Olympia: (206) 357-3700
Shelton: (206) 426-4446
Tacoma: (206) 627-2525
Vashon: (206) 463-3815

CHART 18448, 18449, 18474 †
EAST PASSAGE, on the E side of Vashon and Maury Islands, extends from Alki Point SSE for 12.5 miles to Robinson Point, and then SW for 6 miles to Browns Point. The waters throughout are deep and free from dangers, which in no case extend as much as 0.5 mile from shore.

FAUNTLEROY COVE, 3.5 miles S of Alki Point, is the site of the landing for the automobile ferry plying from there to Vashon Heights and Southworth.

A GENERAL ANCHORAGE is on the W side of the passage in the bight included between Orchard Point and Point Southworth and protected on the E side by Blake Island. Several settlements and resort villages are along the shores of Yukon Harbor; mostly fishermen and pleasure boaters use the waterfront facilities. MANCHESTER has a short wharf with a float landing and a launching ramp. Two large wharves, one on the S side of MIDDLE POINT and the other on the S side of ORCHARD POINT, are included in the oil storage area of the Puget Sound U.S. Naval Supply Center. HARPER, a mile WNW of Point Southworth, is the site of a former ferry pier now in ruins. The ferry from Seattle, Fauntleroy and Vashon Island docks at the slip on Point Southworth.

BLAKE ISLAND, about 1 mile long, 249 feet high, and covered with trees, is off the N entrance to Colvos Passage. Heavy tide rips, strongest with a flood current, and strong S winds are encountered at the N entrance to Colvos Passage S of Blake Island. Shallow, irregular bottom extends about 0.5 mile off the N shre of the island. A light is on the NE point of the island. Just S of the NE point of the island are the ruins of a wharf. A State marine park small-craft basin, protected by a breakwater, is at the NE end of the island. The entrance to the basin is marked by a private light and daybeacons.

A fish haven, marked by a private buoy, is on the reef about 260 yards off the S side of Blake Island.

YUKON HARBOR, about 2 miles SW of Blake Island, affords anchorage in 30 to 50 feet, with protection from S winds.

VASHON ISLAND is 11 miles long in a N direction. MAURY ISLAND, actually a peninsula of Vashon Island at its SE extremity, is connected to it by a highway on a narrow neck of land. Maury Island is about 5 miles long.

On these islands the land is of moderate rolling elevation and in places rugged, and most of the country is heavily wooded. The islands have numerous orchards and houses. There is some farming and cattle and poultry are raised. The transmitting towers of Seattle broadcasting stations are on the islands; two groups of towers are on Vashon Island and tow on Maury Island. The shores on all sides have numerous settlements. The county wharves, formerly used to ship farm produce, are no longer kept in repair and shipments are now by truck.

POINT VASHON, the NW tip of Vashon Island, is 305 feet high, steep, and wooded. Shoal water extends 0.2 mile N from the point and nearly as far along the N shore as DOLPHIN POINT, 1 mile E. A light is 300 yards N of Point Vashon.

VASHON HEIGHTS LANDING, 0.5 mile ESE of Point Vashon, has a combination ferry slip and landing wharf out to 14 feet. An automobile ferry runs to Point Southworth and Fauntleroy.

The tall radio towers of station KOMO are on Point Beals. The town of VASHON is on high land 1.5 miles SW of Point Beals.

A 159°58'-339°58' MEASURED NAUTICAL MILE is E of Point Beals. The range markers are steel towers with round orange targets.

THREE TREE POINT about 7.8 miles S of Alki Point, is a sharp low spit, projecting 300 yards from the high land which in 1 mile rises to an elevation of 430 feet. On the low part of the point is a grassy knoll, 30 feet high, with several trees on it. A light and fog signal are on the point.

TRAMP HARBOR, formed by the easternmost part of Vashon Island and the N end of Maury Island, has shoal water extending about 0.2 mile out from shore along its entire length. It is bounded on the N by POINT HEYER, a sandspit behind which the ground rises rapidly. A shoal extends 0.2 mile SE from the point. A radio tower on this point is about 450 feet high. Private buoys mark a fish haven off Point Heyer, and private lighted buoys mark an aquaculture site on the SW side of the harbor.

PORTAGE is a village extending over both sides of the low isthmus that connects Vashon and Maury Islands. Two radio towers about 526 feet high are 0.6 mile S of the isthmus, and three other radio towers are one mile SE of the isthmus.

There is a large small-craft marina at DES MOINES, about 4 miles SE of Three Tree Point. A 2,200 foot rock breakwater, marked by a light at each end, offers shelter for over 700 craft in depths ranging from a reported 13 feet at the enctrance to 10 feet at the S end. Electricity, gasoline, diesel fuel, water, ice, launching ramps, wet and dry storage, and marine supplies are available. Two 40 ton sling-type launchers are at the harbor and a tidal grid is available for minor hull repair work.

STORM WARNING SIGNALS ARE DISPLAYED. (See chart.)

ROBINSON POINT, the eastern-most end of Maury Island and the major turning point in the passage, is a low spit projecting 140 yards from the wooded high land. ROBINSON POINT LIGHT (47°23.3'N., 122°22.4'W.), 40 feet above the water, is shown from a 38 foot white octagonal tower on the point; a fog signal is at the station.

There are tow barge loading berths at gravel pits about 1 mile SW of Robinson Point. Conveyors load the barges. The gravel pits are prominent from the S end of East Passage. These facilities are the only commercial wharves on Vashon and Maury Islands, except for oil receiving wharves.

REDONDO, on POVERTY BAY, about 6.8 miles SSE of Three Tree Point, is a suburban village. DUMAS, BAY, 2 miles W of Redondo, has a small wharf which bares alongside at low water.

QUARTERMASTER HARBOR, (47°23'N., 122°28'W.) extends 5 miles NNE between the S parts of Vashon and Maury Islands, opposite Commence-ment Bay. Its shores are low and wooded, with numerous clearings, and several landings and private piers.

Quartermaster Harbor affords excellent anchorage about 2 miles inside the entrance in 5 to 10 fathoms, muddy bottom. The harbor is easy of access, and a mid-channel course may be followed with safety.

A shoal just inside the entrance, between NEILL POINT and PINER POINT, extends 300 yards from the E shore and is marked by a buoy. In an area just N of Neill Point, shoal spots extend 400 yards offshore, covered $2\frac{1}{4}$ to $2\frac{3}{4}$ fathoms. Depths of $4\frac{1}{4}$ fathoms are near mid-channel W of Dockton.

Many settlements and summer resorts are along the shores of the harbor, but the landing wharves, for the most part, are in disrepair.

BURTON is a town on BURTON PENINSULA which projects E from the W side about 3 miles form the entrance. It has several stores and a marina. The marina has a pier with floats for a sizable number of pleasure craft; electricity gasoline, water, and ice are available. A 4 ton hoist at the marina can handle craft to 32 feet for hull, engine or electronic repairs. Some marine supplies are available in the town. The Quartermaster Yacht Club has its moorage just N of the marina. There are several private mooring buoys in this part of the harbor.

An oil receiving wharf and storage tanks are on the W side of the harbor about 0.7 mile N of Burton at the mouth of Judd Creek. The storage tanks are on the hill N of the harbor.

DOCKTON, in the bight on the E side about 2.5 miles from the entrance, is a village with a store. The County Park, on tho E side of the bight, has a public pier and mooring float. There are several piers in ruins and pilings in the bight.

In the upper part of the harbor, N of the Burton Peninsula, are several private wharves and floats.

COLVOS PASSAGE, on the W side of Washon Island, extends about 11 miles in a general S direction, with an average width of 1 mile. The passage is free of dangers. The N entrance is about 4.5 miles SW of Alki Point, and the S entrance is abreast Point Defiance. The passage is used principally by tugs

The narrow entrance to Gig Harbor requires care to avoid the sandspit at the lower left. Use Chart 18449.

hauling logs for the sawmills. A mid-channel course can be followed with safety. The passage is marked by lights.

The current in Colvos Passage favors a N set and at times advantage is taken of this fact by vessels bound from Tacoma to Seattle. The current in the middle of Dalco Passage and along the SW ashore of Commencement Bay sets W or NW almost continuously.

To obtain full advantage of the peculiar currents in Colvos Passage and connecting waterways, use should be made of the Tidal Current Charts, Puget Sound, Southern Part contained in this edition of the PACIFIC BOATING ALMANAC.

POINT SOUTHWORTH, on the W side of the N entrance, is high and wooded. A ferry slip is 0.2 mile NW of the point. An automobile ferry runs to Fauntleroy and Vashon Heights.

FRAGARIA and OLALLA, on the W shore of Colvos Passage, are small residential communities. Only isolated piling remain of their former wharves. A rock which bares at half tide lies 400 yards N of the former wharf at Olalla. Olalla has a small-craft float landing and a general store. Gasoline, water, ice, and some marine supplies are available.

COVE and LISABEULA, on the E shore, are summer resort areas. There are no facilities at either area. The wharf at Cove is in ruins. Several pilings formerly used as moorings for log rafts, are adjacent to the wharf. Lisabeula consists of a single waterfront resort with no facilities for small craft.

TAHLEQUAH is a small residential community on the S shore of Vashon Island between Neill Point and Point Dalco. A ferry operates between Tahlequah and Tacoma. A marina with a 280 foot pier is just N of the ferry slip. Berths, gasoline, water, and ice are available.

GIG HARBOR is an inlet about 1 mile long on the W side of the S entrance of Colvos Passage abreast Point Defiance. A light is on the S end of the sandspit, at the E side of the entrance, which makes out for 220 yards and constricts the entrance to less than 100 yards wide. A narrow 10 foot channel in the middle has currents of considerable velocity. Inside the entrance the basin has from 4 to 6 fathoms. The surrounding land, partially cleared of timber, slopes gently toward the shores and is thickly settled.

The town of GIG HARBOR extends along the W shore and the head of the harbor. It is the home port of many pleasure craft and fishing boats. The town has two boatyards, each with marine railways. The larger of the two can handle craft to 150 tons for hull and engine repairs. The second boatyard is smaller and specializes in yacht construction and repair. A machine shop is in the town. There are many private piers and wharves, including three oil wharves. There are several marinas here. Berths, gasoline, diesel fuel, water, ice, launching ramps, and marine supplies are available in the harbor. Most of the pleasure craft moor at a large marina at the head of the harbor. A Coast Guard patrol vessel is stationed at Gig Harbor.

On entering Gig Harbor, hold midway between the spit on the E side and the W shore until just inside the entrance. The swing right toward the E shore until past the short spit extending from the W shore, and steer a course just S of midchannel into the harbor.

-U.S. COAST PILOT 7
25th edition. August 1989
Corrected thru 10/22/90
Local Notice to Mariners

FACILITIES

GIG HARBOR

GIG HARBOR † This atttractive little basin on the Great Peninsula is one of the most popular cruising destinations for boatmen from Seattle and Tacoma. Sheltered from virtually all winds, Gig Harbor provides excellent overnight anchorage. And a public pier at Jerisich Park on the southwest shore allows about two dozen pleasurecraft to tie. But be warned about moorings at the docks of Tides Tavern of the Shoreline Restaurant. Both moorages dry at low tide.

The town of Gig Harbor is built immediately around the waterfront, having from the beginning been preoccupied with servicing and housing the large, local fishing fleet. So permanent moorage facilities and vessel repair operations abound. Art and gift shops, boutiques and chandleries cater to visiting boatmen and are all located within easy distance of the water. The name of the community derives from the fact that Captain John Wilkes, seeking shelter from a storm in 1852, would not enter the narrow access channel until his gig had made an exploration and taken soundings.

COUNTRY TOUCH, 3110 Harborview Dr., Gig Harbor, WA 98335. (206) 851-7722. Antiques, Collectables, furniture, etc. Owner: Sandra J. Pitt.

GIG HARBOR MARINA, Box 387, 3117 Harborview Drive, Gig Harbor, WA 98335. (206) 858 - 3535. Two marine railways: cap to 100 tons. Crane: to 9 tons. Slips. Dockside electricity. Hull and engine maintenance parts and repairs. Prop and shaft repairs. President: Walter Williamson.

GIG HARBOR YACHT SALES, 31119 Harborview Dr., Box 528, Gig Harbor, WA 98335. (206) 851 - 2674. All year. New and used boat and motor sales. Hull maintenance. Prop and shaft repairs. President: Ted H. Cooper.

HARBOR INN RESTAURANT (overlooking Gig Harbor Marina), 3111 Harbor Drive, Box 485, Gig Harbor, WA 98335. (206) 851 - 5454. Serving lunch and dinner daily. Opening at 11 AM. Sunday breakfast open at 9 AM. Owners: Bob and Gail Drohan.

M B COMMUNICATIONS, INC., 3219 Harborview Dr., Gig Harbor, WA 98335. (206) 851 - 9553. All year. 10 AM - 5:30 PM. Marine electronic sales and service. Owner: Max H. Bice.

MACINTOSH NAVIGATION AND BARGE CO, 3311 Harborview Dr., Gig Harbor, WA 98335. (206) 858 - 9395. All year. Boat and motor sales. Accommodations. Marine hardware. Slips. Boat storage, open. 100 foot Ketch Krestine for overnight lodging. Diving. Dinner and breakfast served. Small maritime weddings. Owner: Capt. Pete and Meghan Darrah.

MOSTLY BOOKS, Box 428, 3126 Harborview Drive, Gig Harbor,WA 98335. (206) 851 - 3219. Open Mon. - Sat.: 9:30 AM - 5:30 PM. Open Sun. in season 1 PM - 4 PM. New and used books. Marine books and cruising atlases. Guides and tide calendars. Charts. Paperbacks. Owners: Harry and Shirley Dearth.

MURPHY'S LANDING MARINA, 3901 Harborview Dr., Gig Harbor, WA 98335. (206) 851-3093. Condo slips. Security gates. Cable TV. Showers and laundry. Clubhouse. Dockside electricity. Manager: Marv Turner.

NAUTI-CAL'S INTERNATIONAL INC., 2905 Harborview Drive, Gig Harbor, WA 98335. (206) 851 - 8488. Open 9 AM - 6 PM. Yacht brokerage. Dealers for Com-Pac trailerable sailboats. Representatives for floats, docks and boat lifts. Sailboat rentals. President: Gary Loberg.

NEVILLE'S SHORELINE RESTAU-RANT, 8827 N Harborview Dr., Gig Harbor, WA 98335. (206) 851 - 9822. All year. Guest dock. Rental boats: sailboats, paddleboats, outboard motors. Waterfront dining, tow docks available for patron dining. Owner: N.J. Culy.

PENINSULA YACHT BASIN, 8913 N Harborview, Gig Harbor, WA 98335. (206) 858 - 2250. All year. Tue. - Sat.: 9 AM - 5 PM. Overnight guest dock with electricity. Slips. Moorage. Showers. Manager: Steve Luengen.

PLEASURECRAFT MARINA, 3215 Harborview, Gig Harbor, WA 98335. (206) 858 - 2350. All year. Winter: 9 AM - 4:30 PM. Summer: 9 AM - 5:30 PM. Fuel dock: gas and diesel. Charts. Marine hardware. Ice and beverages. Fishing: licenses, bait & tackle. Mgr: "Skip" Williams.

STUTZ FUEL SERVICE, 3003 Sound View Drive NW, Box 16, Gig Harbor, WA 98335. (206) 858 - 9131. All year. Fuel dock: gas and diesel, open Mon. - Fri.; 8 AM - 5:30 PM. Sat.; 8:30 AM - 2:30 PM. Kerosene. Lubricants. Vice President: Del Stutz.

TIDERUNNER INC, 8809 N Harborview Drive, Gig Harbor, WA 98335. (206) 851 - 9446. New and used boat and motor sales. Marine hardware. Electronic sales. Outboard parts and service.

MARINE PARKS

BURTON ACRES PARK (at Burton Peninsula on Vashon Island), 58 acres. Launching ramp. Picnic tables. Hiking trails. Restrooms. Anchorage only.

DOCKTON COUNTY PARK (in Quartermaster Harbor on Maury Island), P.O. Box 11, Vashon, WA 980070. (206) 463-9047. Ramp. Floats for 50 boats. Excellent anchorage. Picnic areas. Playground. Showers and restrooms. Cooking facilities.

Carr Inlet
SHELLFISH FOR HARVEST
Clams
Oysters
Crabs
Crabs (Pot Fishing)
Shrimp (Pot Fishing)
FACILITIES
Road Access
Boat Launch
Boat Access Only
Anchorage
NORTH
TO BREMERTON 13.5 MILES
TO BREMERTON 13 MILES
TO SHELTON 14 MILES
TO LONGBRANCH 3 MILES
COLVOS PASSAGE
Crescent Valley Rd
Gig Harbor
Sehmel Rd
Burley Lagoon
Henderson Bay
Sidney Rd
DEPT. OF NAT. RES. BEACH 35
DEPT. OF NAT. RES. BEACH 35A
Cramer Rd
Longbranch Rd
Gig Harbor
Wright - Bliss Rd
Cockrane Rd
Rocky Bay Pt. Rd
Rocky Bay
North Bay
ROCKY PT.
DEPT OF NAT. RES. BEACH 18
REACH ISL.
STRETCH ISLAND STATE PARK (undeveloped)
STRETCH ISL.
Grapeview Rd
DEPT. OF NAT. RES. BEACH 20
Vaughn Bay
S. Vaughn Rd
Lackey Rd
PAY
Glen Cove
ALLEN PT.
RAFT ISL.
CUTTS ISL. STATE PARK
KOPACHUCK ST. PK.
MAPLE HOLLOW DNR REC. AREA
Horsehead Bay
Dutcher Cove
Pickering Passage
DOUGALL PT.
CASE INLET
HARTSTENS ISL.
HERRON ISL.
FUDGE PT.
Van Geldern Cove
CARR INLET
Mayo Cove
PENROSE PT.
PENROSE PT. ST. PK.
Herron Rd
McKay Rd
GREEN PT.
NEARNS PT.
KETNERS PT.
FOX ISL.
Hale Passage
Hale Passage
Wollochet Bay
Wollochet Rd
Stone Rd
BEACH 1A
PT. FOSDICK
DEPT. OF NAT. RES. BEACH 1
DEPT. OF NAT. RES. BEACH 36
PT. DEFIANCE
TACOMA NARROWS BRIDGE
The Narrows
0 .5 1 2 Miles
302
16
3

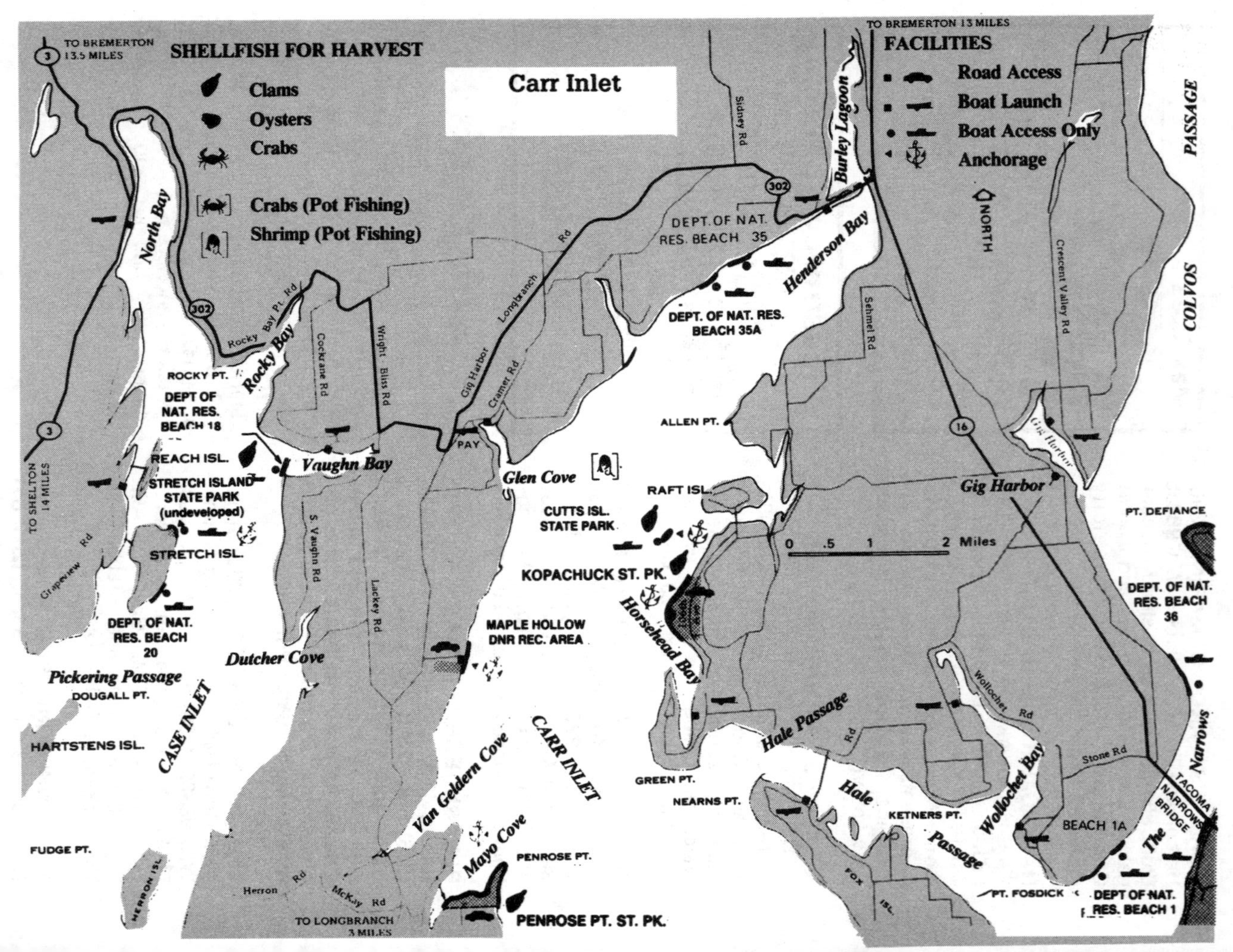

154

13

GIG HARBOR TO OLYMPIA

AIR TRANSPORTATION
Kenmore Air Harbor: (206) 486-1257
Lake Union Air: (800) 692-2993

CHAMBER OF COMMERCE
Olympia: (206) 357-3362
Olympia Visitor's Bureau:
(206) 357-3370
Shelton: (206) 426-2021
Tacoma Visitor's Bureau:
(206) 627-2175

COAST GUARD
VHF 16
Emergengies: (800) 592-9911
Seattle: (206) 442-7070

CUSTOMS
Tacoma/Olympia: (206) 593-6338

DECOMPRESSION CHAMBER
Keyport: (206) 396-5111
Virginia Mason, Seattle:
(206) 624-1144

FERRY INFORMATION
Washington State: (800) 542-0812

FISHING INFORMATION
(206) 753-6600

MARINE OPERATOR
VHF 85

POISON INFORMATION
(800) 732-6985

RED TIDE HOTLINE
(800) 562-5632

STATE PARK INFORMATION
(800) 562-0990

TAXI
Olympia: (206) 357-3700
Shelton: (206) 426-4446
Tacoma: (206) 627-2525
Vashon: (206) 463-3815

CHART 18448 † S of Point Defiance are numerous inlets, passages, and islands. At many of the villages the landing wharves have fallen into ruins, all transportation following the highways. These waters are navigated by log tows and by pleasure craft. Deep-draft vessels call at Olympia for lumber and other forest products. The depths are generally great, and the dangers are few. The shores are well wooded and moderately low. The beaches are sand and gravel, with boulders in places and are often backed by steep, bare sand and gravel bluffs. Olympia and Shelton are the only cities, but there are many smaller settlements. Strangers bound through these waters at night are advised to take a pilot.

CURRENTS † In the Narrows current velocities exceed 5 knots at times. At the N end of The Narrows the current sets N most of the time on the E side of the passage and S most of the time on the W side. (See Tidal Current Tables for daily current predictions for a midstream position near the N end of The Narrows and details of the current movement at other locations; these tables and the Tidal Current Charts, Puget Sound, Southern Part, should both be consulted for details of the complicated currents of this area. These are contained in this edition of the PACIFIC BOATING ALMANAC.

From Point Defiance to near Days Island, the E shore of THE NARROWS consists of high, bold bluffs. A tunnel is 1.7 miles SE of Point Defiance; from it a railroad track follows the shoreline to Nisqually River. The W shore is broken by inlets and passages which afford communication to small settlements devoted to lumbering or agriculture.

POINT EVANS, 2 miles S of Point Defiance on the W side of The Narrows, is marked by a light. Power cables with a clearance of 200 feet cross 200 yards S of the point. TACOMA NARROWS BRIDGE, a highway suspension bridge, crosses The Narrows a mile S of Point Evans. The clearance is 159 feet at the piers and 180 feet at the center. A private fog signal marks each of the two piers.

DAYS ISLAND is about 4.5 miles S of Point Defiance. The ferry slip and wharf here are in ruins. There are three marinas here, one on the E side of Days Island and two in the cove 150 yards E of the N end of the island. A total of about 200 berths are at the marina; electricity, gasoline, diesel fuel, water, ice, dry storage for over 500 craft and marine supplies are available. A 15 ton crane and hoists to 3 tons are available to handle craft for hull and engine repairs. A $2\frac{3}{4}$ fathom shoal lies 230 yards W of the former ferry slip.

A small boat channel, 1 foot deep, leads into DAYS ISLAND LAGOON. The channel favors the Days Island side and under the bridge is 30 yards from the island shore. Local boats anchor in 3 feet in the lagoon. The floats of a private yacht club are on the S and W sides of the lagoon. Anchorage for small-craft may be had E of the N end of Days Island.

Three miles S of Days Island, the shores consist of bare bluffs which are prominent from S. From here the route to Olympia continues SW and W through BALCH PASSAGE, Drayton Passage, and Dana Passage, then S into Budd Inlet. This route is deep and generally free of dangers.

CAUTION † The channel through BALCH PASSAGE is only about 100 yards wide between the 10-fathom curves, and the scale of the chart is small. Vessels should stay carefully in mid-channel, traffic permitting.

HALE PASSAGE, between FOX ISLAND and the mainland, enters on the W shore 5 miles S of Point Defiance. It is 4 miles to its junction with Carr Inlet. Near the W end the passage is crossed by a fixed highway bridge with a clearance of 31 feet. A shoal, marked on its NE side by a buoy, is 350 yards SE of the bridge and near the middle of the passage; the shoal is boulder strewn and bares. The channel is on the NE side of the buoy. A good small-craft anchorage is on either side of Tanglewood Island. The current in Hale Passage attains a velocity in excess of 3 knots at times. The E (ebb) current is stronger than the W (flood) current. (See Tidal Current Tables for current predictions contained in this edition of the PACIFIC BOATING ALMANAC.)

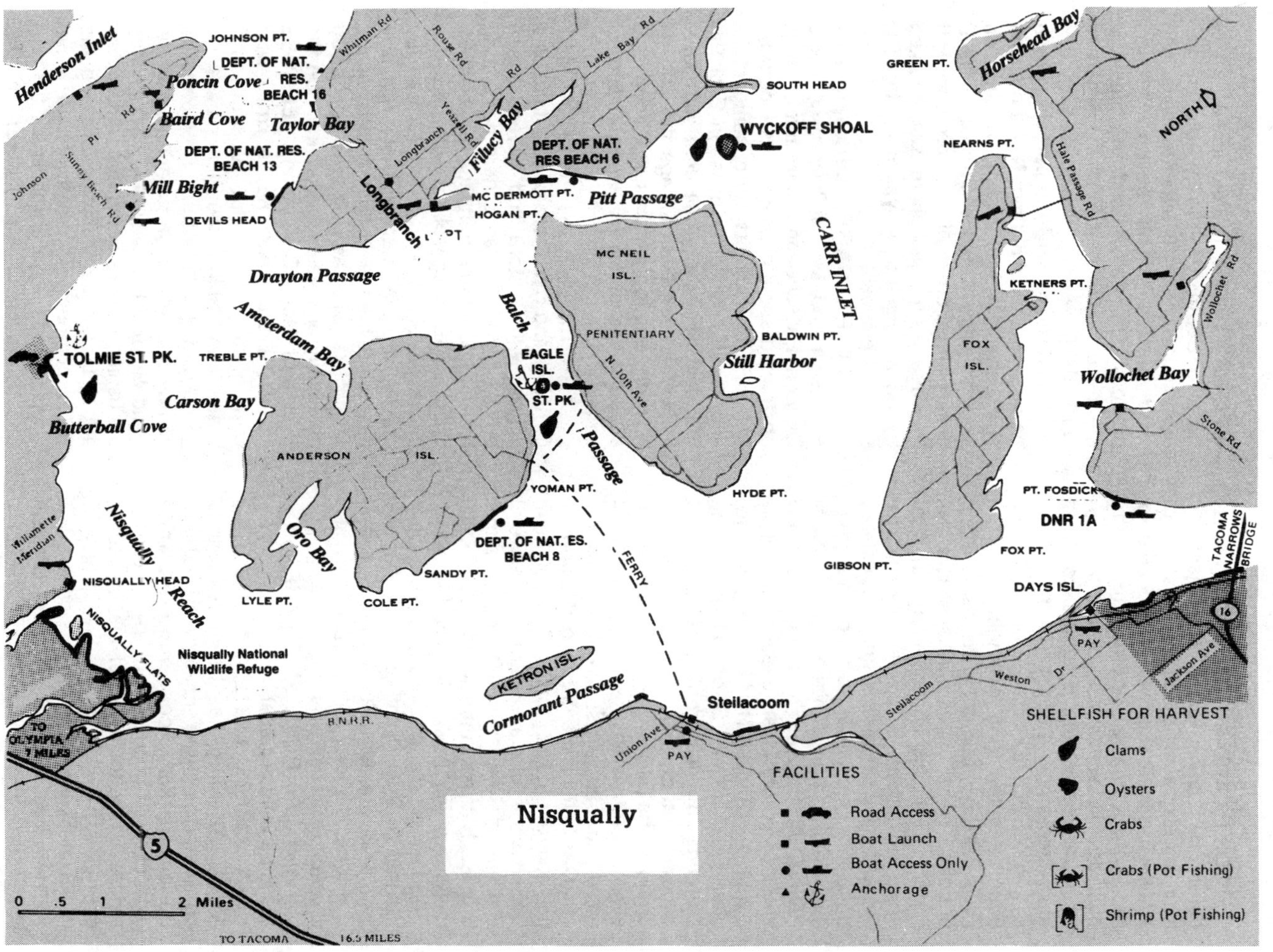

Henderson Inlet
JOHNSON PT.
DEPT. OF NAT. RES. BEACH 16
Poncin Cove
Baird Cove
Taylor Bay
DEPT. OF NAT. RES. BEACH 13
Mill Bight
DEVILS HEAD
Sunny Beach Rd
Johnson Pt.
Whitman Rd
Rouse Rd
Yeazell Rd
Longbranch
Filucy Bay
Lake Bay Rd
SOUTH HEAD
WYCKOFF SHOAL
DEPT. OF NAT. RES BEACH 6
MC DERMOTT PT.
HOGAN PT.
Pitt Passage
GREEN PT.
Horsehead Bay
NORTH
NEARNS PT.
Hale Passage Rd
KETNERS PT.
Wollochet Rd
CARR INLET
Drayton Passage
Amsterdam Bay
Balch
MC NEIL ISL.
PENITENTIARY
N 10th Ave
BALDWIN PT.
Still Harbor
FOX ISL.
Wollochet Bay
Stone Rd
TOLMIE ST. PK.
TREBLE PT.
EAGLE ISL. ST. PK.
Passage
Carson Bay
Butterball Cove
ANDERSON ISL.
YOMAN PT.
HYDE PT.
PT. FOSDICK
DNR 1A
Oro Bay
DEPT. OF NAT. ES. BEACH 8
SANDY PT.
FOX PT.
GIBSON PT.
DAYS ISL.
Nisqually Reach
Willamette Meridian
NISQUALLY HEAD
LYLE PT.
COLE PT.
FERRY
TACOMA NARROWS BRIDGE
16
NISQUALLY FLATS
Nisqually National Wildlife Refuge
KETRON ISL.
Cormorant Passage
Steilacoom
Steilacoom
Weston Dr.
Jackson Ave
PAY
TO OLYMPIA 7 MILES
B.N.R.R.
Union Ave
PAY
SHELLFISH FOR HARVEST
Clams
Oysters
Crabs
Crabs (Pot Fishing)
Shrimp (Pot Fishing)
FACILITIES
Road Access
Boat Launch
Boat Access Only
Anchorage
Nisqually
5
0 .5 1 2 Miles
TO TACOMA   16.5 MILES

FOX ISLAND is a village in the small cove near the NE end of Fox Island. It has a store and service station. TANGLEWOOD ISLAND, in the center of the cove, has a boys' camp, the buildings of which are prominent. A structure resembling a lighthouse is on the extreme N end of the island.

WOLLOCHET BAY is a small inlet about 2 miles long extending N from Hale Passage, about 1 mile inside the E entrance. The upper part is narrow and shoal. It affords an anchorage in mid-channel about 0.3 mile inside the entrance in 11 to 12 fathoms, sticky bottom. There are many private piers and mooring buoys in the bay. GIBSON POINT, the S tip of Fox Island and the N entrance point of Carr Inlet, is marked by a light. TOLIVA SHOAL, nearly in mid-channel 0.9 mile S of Gibson Point, consists of two rocks covered $1\frac{3}{4}$ fathoms and is marked by a lighted bell buoy. The shoal may be passed on either side, giving the buoy a berth of more than 500 yards.

CARR INLET enters the W shore of the sound about $7\frac{1}{2}$ miles SSW of Point Defiance. From the entrance, between Fox and McNeil Islands, it extends about 6 miles NW and then trends NNE for 8 miles terminating in flats at the head. Good anchorage is available in the upper reaches in 6 to 15 fathoms, soft bottom, and in several small coves on its S and E shores. From the entrance, a mid-channel course is safe.

A NAVAL RESTRICTED AREA is in the S part of Carr Inlet.

A 298°23'-118°23' MEASURED NAUTICAL MILE has been established on the NE shore of McNeil Island. Range markers, consisting of white diamond daymarks with red vertical stripes, mark the ends of the measured course.

The Washington State penitentiary, on the SE side of McNEIL ISLAND about 0.8 mile SW of HYDE POINT, is prominent when approaching. The wharf, built out to 16 feet, is lighted by a row of lights. Water is piped to the end of the wharf.

GERTRUDE is a village on the S side of Carr Inlet on the shore of STILL HARBOR, which is a bight on the N side of McNeil Island S of GERTRUDE

ISLAND. It has a landing in 10 feet of water. Depths in the middle of the harbor are $6\frac{3}{4}$ to 10 fathoms, sand and mud bottom. The bottom slopes gradually to a flat of sand and gravel at the head of the bay E of the wharf at Gertrude.

WYCKOFF SHOAL, part of which bares, extends 0.8 mile NW from the NW part of McNeil Island. A buoy on the NW edge of the shoal marks the E side of the channel leading into Pitt Passage. An aquaculture site, marked by private lighted buoys, is on the NE side of the shoal.

PITT PASSAGE, between Key Peninsula and McNeil Island, connects Drayton Passage and Carr Inlet. It is obstructed about midway of its length by PITT ISLAND and its surrounding rocks and shoals. Only the passage E of Pitt Island is used by small craft with local knowledge. In this passage the ebb (N current) is stronger than the flood and attains a velocity of 2.5 knots or more at times.

LAKEBAY, at the head of MAY COVE on the SW shore of Carr Inlet, is a village with a store and several small private piers. A marina here has a long pier and floats with berthage for about 35 craft; electricity, gasoline, water, and ice are available. About 7 feet can be carried to the marina pier, but the channel to the pier is difficult to navigate; strangers are advised to proceed cautiously or obtain local advice. On the E side of Mayo Cove, along PENROSE POINT, a State park has a small float with moorage for about 10 small-craft. Water is available at the State park.

(From Col. Robert E. Johnston comes this advice on entering Lakebay: "The channel has only one zig". Watch the fishing vessels going in or out, or use the chart and depth finder following the shore contour. The entrance to Mayo Cove provides one of the finest bottom-to-top views of Mt. Ranier in the Sound.")

HOME, a village on the W side of VON GELDERN COVE, has a store and service station. A bridge crosses the cove at its head. A shoal extends from the N shore at the entrance to the cove.

GLENCOVE is a small settlement in Glen Cove on the W side of Carr Inlet, about 5 miles N of South Head. It is a summer recreational area with a private wharf and float.

WAUNA is a village at the head of Carr Inlet, where the spit enclosing Burley Lagoon joins the mainland. A county road extends along the spit and across the entrance to the lagoon over a foxed highway bridge to Rosedale and Gig Harbor. The bridge has a clearance of 12 feet, (23 feet at center).

ROSEDALE is a residential community of the cove on the E side of Carr Inlet and 180 foot high RAFT ISLAND. There is an extensive shoal area around and between Raft Island and CUTTS ISLAND. The shores of these islands are strewn with boulders. A fixed highway bridge and overhead cable extend from the S side of Raft Island to the mainland. The bridge clearance is 17 feet, and the cable, 48 feet.

HORSEHEAD BAY, about 1 mile long, is directly N of Green Point, at the W extremity of Hale Passage. This is a residential area with several private wharves.

On the S side of McNeil Island, there is a ferry landing at BEE, a facility of the Federal penitentiary 1 mile E. The ferry connects with Steilacoom, Ketron Island, and ANDERSON ISLAND.

EAGLE ISLAND, small and wooded, is near the middle of Balch Passage, 0.2 mile from Anderson Island, and is marked on its N end by a light. Eagle Island is a State park with three state mooring buoys. On the shores of Anderson Island, S of Eagle Island, are private float landings.

EAGLE ISLAND REEF, 300 yards W of Eagle Island, bares 1 foot at its S part and has a depth of 3 feet at its N part. A lighted buoy is off the NW part of the reef.

DRAYTON PASSAGE, between Key Peninsula and Anderson Island, is about 3 miles long in a N direction; at its N end, it connects with Pitt Passage and Balch Passage, and its S end joins the W part of Nisqually Reach. With the exception of a spit extending 0.2 mile from the W shore, marked by a light, the waters are deep and free of dangers. Estimated current velocities of 1 to 2 knots occur at the SW end of the passage.

FILUCY BAY, on the W shore opposite Balch Passage, is about 1.5 miles long and irregular in shape; it is 0.4 mile wide at the entrance. Good anchorage in 7 to 8 fathoms, muddy bottom is available. There are numerous houses around the shores of this bay. LONGBRANCH, a village in the small cove opposite the entrance, has several stores and a service station. A pier and floats for about 30 fishing and pleasure craft are here. Ice, water, and limited marine supplies are available.

STEILACOOM is on the mainland about 9 miles SSW of Point Defiance. The town is of little commercial importance and has no waterfront facilities except for the ferry terminal which maintains service to Anderson, Ketron, and McNeil Islands. Limited berthage for small craft, gasoline, water, ice, and a hoist are available at the terminal. Limited engine repairs can be made. Indifferent anchorage may be had along the waterfront close inshore, but it is not recommended as the holding ground is poor and the currents have considerable velocity. Off Steilacoom there are tide rips which, with a wind opposing the current, are dangerous to small boats.

KETRON ISLAND, 10 miles SSW of Point Defiance and E of Anderson Island, is a small, narrow island which is privately owned. It is heavily wooded with bluff shores. CORMORANT PASSAGE, 0.5 mile wide, separates the island from the mainland S. The passage is clear, but is little used.

NISQUALLY REACH trends S and W around Anderson Island to Case Inlet. NISQUALLY FLATS, formed by NISQUALLY RIVER, bare at low water, occupying the S shore of the reach for nearly 1 mile offshore, is a fish and game refuge and used for commercial fish aquaculture. The flats are very soft mud and the edge is steep-to with deep water, sand bottom, close-to. The boat ramp at Nisqually Head is accessible only at high water. Lighted buoys mark the N edge of the flats and a light marks the S tip of Anderson Island at Lyle Point. THOMPSON COVE, on the W side of the Point, is a cable area and should not be used as an anchorage.

ORO BAY, in the SE part of Anderson Island, is an irregular bight between COLE POINT and LYLE POINT. Most of the bay is shallow; it affords an indifferent anchorage in about 10 fathoms, but is affected by the currents and affords little protection. A small shallow arm extends about 1 mile NW on the W side of the bay. An anchorage for small craft is here.

A wharf, built out from the mouth of SEQUALITCHEW CREEK, 13 miles SSW of Point Defiance, is 340 feet long, has 27 feet reported alongside, and a deck height of 19 feet. A powder plant wharf, currently unused, is about 1.5 mles NW of NISQUALLY HEAD, (47°07'N., 122°45'W.) there is a depth of about 24 feet alongside.

DEVILS HEAD, the S point of Key Peninsula, is 280 feet high and heavily wooded. A light is shown off the S tip of Devils Head.

JOHNSON POINT, 2 miles W of Devils Head, is 90 feet high. A light and fog signal are on the sandspit at the end of the point.

There are tow marinas on the W shore of Nisqually Reach, one 0.8 mile and one 1.9 miles SSE of Johnson Point. Gasoline, water, ice, and some marine supplies are available at each marina. The N marina has diesel fuel and a 5 ton hoist. The S marina has a 25 ton lift that can handle craft up to 20 feet long. Both marinas can make hull and engine repairs. Depths of 8 feet are off the floats at the N marina, but those at the S marina go dry at low tide.

LOCAL MAGNETIC DISTURBANCE † Differences of as much as 3° from normal variation have been observed along Henderson Inlet.

ITSAMI LEDGE, covered 1 fathom, lies 1 mile WSW of Johnson Point. It is surrounded by kelp and marked by a light. This is a danger in entering Henderson Inlet or Dana Passage. A fish haven, marked by private buoys, is close N of the light.

HENDERSON INLET, locally known as SOUTH BAY, immediately W of Johnson Point, extends about 4.5 miles in a S direction; the S part is an extensive flat. Good anchorage is inside the entrance in 5 to 6 fathoms, muddy bottom. A spit makes out about 0.2 mile N from the W point at the entrance; on the W shore, 0.8 mile S of the entrance point, is a long sandspit. There is a railroad log dump with booming grounds on the W side. Oyster beds abound in the S area of the bay.

CASE INLET, a popular sport fishing and resort area, extends some 14 miles N from Johnson Point. The flats at its head are only 2 miles from the head of Hood Canal. Depths are irregular, from 10 to 30 fathoms, but there are no off-lying danger.

HARTSTENE ISLAND forms the W side of the S part of the inlet. A marina in JARRELL COVE at the N end of the island has berths, gasoline, water, ice, and some groceries. The pier here has 10 feet reported alongside. The 200 foot Jarrell Cove State Park pier is directly across the cove from the marina. A State park float is farther up the cove.

HERRON ISLAND, about 4 miles N of the entrance and 0.3 miles W of the E side, is a popular summer resort, with moorings for small craft. A ferry connects with the mainland at the village of HERRON. The bar between the N end of Herron Island and the E shore has a least depth of about 13 feet, but with local knowledge a depth of 21 feet can be carried through by rounding the NE tip of Herron Island some 300 to 500 yards off.

McMICKEN ISLAND, 1.1 miles SW of Herron Island, is connected to Hartstene Island by a sandspit which bares at low water. Anchorage with a rocky bottom and protection from S winds is on the NW side of the island.

PICKERING PASSAGE indents the W shore of Case Inlet, about 2 miles N of Herron Island. The passage extends in a general S direction for 8 miles, connecting at its S end with Peale Passage and Totten Inlet. The shores are generally low and wooded, and the depths vary from $4\frac{1}{2}$ to 15 fathoms. Except for the shoals extending E from the mouth of Hammersley Inlet, the passage is free of outlying dangers and a mid-channel course is safe. In Pickering Passage the flood current sets from Case Inlet toward Hammersley Inlet and the ebb in the opposite direction. The strongest currents are near the S end where velocities reach 2.5 knots at

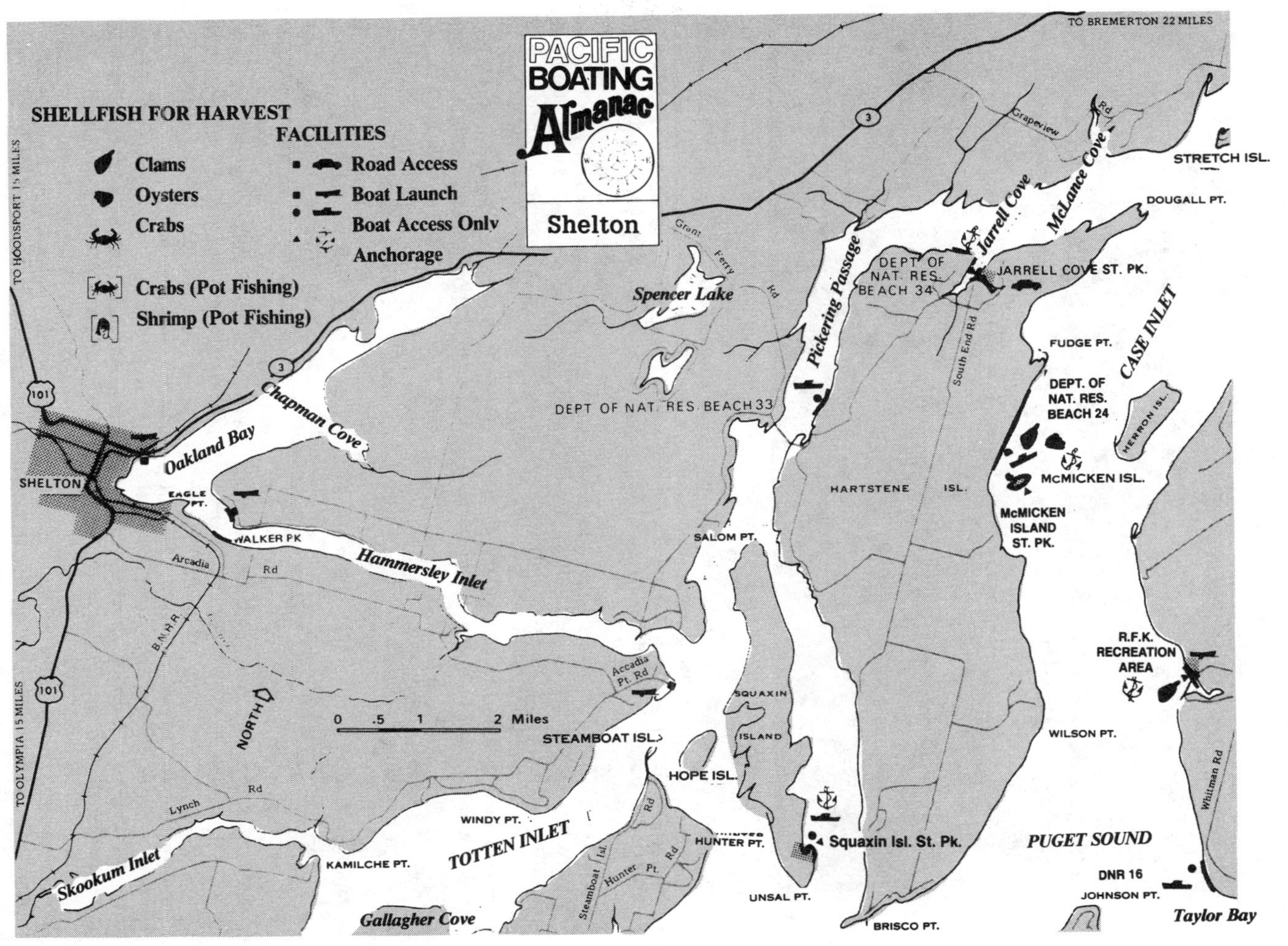
PACIFIC BOATING Almanac
Shelton
SHELLFISH FOR HARVEST
FACILITIES
Clams
Oysters
Crabs
Crabs (Pot Fishing)
Shrimp (Pot Fishing)
Road Access
Boat Launch
Boat Access Only
Anchorage
TO HOODSPORT 15 MILES
TO BREMERTON 22 MILES
Grapeview Rd
Jarrell Cove
McLance Cove
STRETCH ISL.
DOUGALL PT.
JARRELL COVE ST. PK.
DEPT. OF NAT. RES. BEACH 34
South End Rd
Pickering Passage
Grant Ferry Rd
Spencer Lake
FUDGE PT.
CASE INLET
DEPT. OF NAT. RES. BEACH 24
HERON ISL.
McMICKEN ISL.
McMICKEN ISLAND ST. PK.
Chapman Cove
DEPT OF NAT. RES. BEACH 33
Oakland Bay
SHELTON
EAGLE PT.
WALKER PK
HARTSTENE ISL.
SALOM PT.
Hammersley Inlet
Arcadia Rd
B.M.R.R.
Accadia Pt. Rd
NORTH
0 .5 1 2 Miles
SQUAXIN ISLAND
STEAMBOAT ISL.
HOPE ISL.
R.F.K. RECREATION AREA
WILSON PT.
Whitman Rd
TO OLYMPIA 15 MILES
101
Lynch Rd
Skookum Inlet
KAMILCHE PT.
WINDY PT.
TOTTEN INLET
Steamboat Isl.
Hunter Pt. Rd
HUNTER PT.
Squaxin Isl. St. Pk.
UNSAL PT.
BRISCO PT.
Gallagher Cove
PUGET SOUND
DNR 16
JOHNSON PT.
Taylor Bay

times. The settlements are served by highway. A fixed highway bridge with a clearance of 31 feet crosses the passage from Graham Point to Hartstene Island, about 2.6 miles N of the entrance to Hammersley Inlet.

STRETCH ISLAND is near the W shore of Case Inlet, just N of the entrance to Pickering Passage. There is no through channel W of this island. The N part of this island is partly cleared of trees and laid out in orchards; a winery and several grape juice factories, no longer operating, are here. There is a private landing wharf built out to 12 feet on the N end of the island. A fixed highway bridge with a clearance of 14 feet connects the mainland. GRAPE-VIEW is a village opposite Stretch Island.

REACH ISLAND, 0.2 mile N of Stretch Island, has been subdivided for homesites and is known as TREASURE ISLAND. It is separated from the W shore by a shallow channel known locally as FAIR HARBOR. The channel is spanned by a fixed bridge with a clearance of 16 feet. Favor the west shore. There is a marina on the mainland 0.3 mile south of the bridge. About 20 berths, gasoline, diesel, water, ice, store and Grapeview Port launching ramp are availalbe. The marina has navigable water at all times.

VAUGHN is a village on the N shore of VAUGHN BAY, which lies on the E side of Case Inlet about 4 miles from the head. There is a public launching ramp here. The combined civic center for all the small towns on the entire peninsula is at Vaughn. A channel 1½ feet deep leads to deeper water in the bay. Follow the N shore for 200 yards after entering in mid-channel off the end of the spit; then cross the bay parallel with the spit at a distance of 200 yards, heading toward the S shore; then follow the S shore at a distance of 200 yards, steering toward the head of the bay. Around the shores are numerous houses and orchards, and a little used log booming area.

ROCKY BAY is the shallow inlet N of Vaughn Bay. A float landing, in 10 feet of water N of WINDY BLUFF, is used at low tide when Vaughn Bay cannot be entered. A channel 3 feet deep leads to the lagoon back of the sandspit near WINDY BLUFF. It is necessary to come around the small sand island N of the spit. Oysterbeds are in the L side of the bay N of the spit.

ALLYN is a village on the W side of Case Inlet near the head about 0.5 mile N of SHERWOOD CREEK. A public pier and launching ramp are here. An oyster wharf is just N of Allyn.

Good anchorage may be had anywhere N of Hartstene Island, in 6 to 15 fathoms, muddy bottom.

There are numerous farms and several small settlements whose chief industries are oyster culture, farming, and some logging. The flats near the head of the inlet are largely covered with oysterbeds.

PEALE PASSAGE, about 4 miles long, extends NW between Hartstene and Squaxin Islands, and connects with Pickering Passage. It has a controlling depth of about 10 feet. Strangers should not attempt it. The current at times attains a velocity of 2.0 knots in the narrow part of the passage, and sets N on the flood.

CHART 18456 † DANA PASSAGE, between BRISCO POINT, the S point of Hartstene Island and the mainland, is about 2 miles long. It is the main route to Budd Inlet and Olympia, and also joins with three other bodies of water: Eld Inlet, Squaxin Passage, and Peale Passage. Squaxin Passage leads to Totten and Hammersley Inlets, and Peale Passage leads to Pickering Passage.

With the exception of Itsami Ledge near its E end, Dana Passage is clear and a midchannel course may be safely followed. The currents in Dana Passage frequently attain velocities of 3 knots or more.

BUDD INLET, 29 miles by water from Tacoma, is about 6 miles long, extending S from Dana Passage and temination in flats that bare at the head of EAST BAY and WEST BAY. The entrance is between COOPER POINT and DOFFLEMEYER POINT; the latter is marked by a light and fog signal. The entrance to Budd Inlet is deep except for the 28-foot shoal in the middle of the entrance. The shores are comparatively low and wooded, and the depths shoal less abruptly on the E than on the W side of the inlet. East Bay and West Bay are obstructed by flats and shoals that bare on about 0.8 mile, through which channels have been dredged to the Olympia waterfront.

OLYMPIA, (47°03'N, 122°54'W), the capital of the State of Washington, is a lumber port at the head of East and West bays at the S end of Budd Inlet. Over 90 percent of the waterborne traffic of the port concerns lumber and logs.

PROMINENT FEATURES † The capital dome and the radio tower on the N end of the port fill area are prominent landmarks from outside the entrance channel.

CHANNELS † A Federal project provides for a 30-foot channel from deepwater in Budd Inlet to a 30-foot turning basin off the W side of the port terminal near the head of West Bay. The channel is marked by a daybeacon, lights, buoys, and lighted ranges.

A dredged channel with a project depth of 13 feet leads SE from the 30-foot outer channel to a mooring basin on the E side of the peninsula at the head of Ast Bay. The channel is marked by a daybeacon and lights. (See Notice to Mariners and latest editions of charts for controlling depths.)

ANCHORAGE † Good anchorage may be had anywhere inside the entrance in muddy bottom.

DANGERS † OLYMPIA SHOAL, which bares, is about 0.4 mile off the W shore, 3 miles inside the entrance. A light is on the E side of the shoal and on its W side are lights marking the approach to the dredged channel. There are numerous shoals, piles, dolphins, and log booms on the E side of the harbor.

SE of Olympia Shoal is a 177°15'-357°15' MEASURED COURSE, 6,201 feet long. Olympia Shoal Light and Olympia Channel Light are markers.

TIDES † The mean range of the tide at Olympia is 10.5 feet, and the diurnal range of the tide is 14.4 feet.

SMALL-CRAFT FACILITIES † There are many marinas at Olympia. Berths, electricity, gasoline, diesel fuel, water, ice, launching ramps, storage and marine supplies are available. A 4½-ton hoist and a marine railway that can handle craft to 20 feet are at a marina just N of the port wharf. Hull and engine repairs can be made at a marina just S of the port wharf. A private yacht club has its moorings at the head of West Bay 0.3 mile S of the turning basin.

CHART 18448 † ELD INLET, locally known as MUD BAY, immediately W of Budd Inlet, is of little commercial importance. It affords good anchorage inside the entrance in 24 to 42 feet, soft bottom. A midchannel course is clear to the flats at its head. In entering, COOPER POINT, the E point at the entrance, should be given a berth of not less than 0.2 mile. Some logging and oystering are done here.

SQUAXIN PASSAGE (see also chart 18457), S of SQUAXIN ISLAND and HOPE ISLAND, is about 1 mile long and leads to Totten and Hammersley Inlets. A light on Hunter Point marks the SW entrance point of the passage. The N shore is foul; a shoal covered 19 feet is 150 yards off the W shore of Hope Island abreast Steamboat Island.

The passage is narrow, and strangers should proceed with caution. The S shore should be favored, and at the W end, the N point of Steamboat Island should be favored. The principal danger in the passage is a reef which bares at extreme low water, SE of Hope Island; a buoy is near its S end. This reef is easily avoided by keeping the N point of Steamboat Island well open of the S point of Hope Island. Tide rips are said to occur in Squaxin Passage. The usual velocity of the current is about 1.5 knots.

The passage between Hope and Squaxin Islands has a least depth of 9 feet in the middle; greater depths can be carried in the passage with local knowledge.

STEAMBOAT ISLAND, covered with private homes, is connected with CARLYON BEACH on the mainland by a roadway on piling. The island, practically a part of the mainland, has abrupt shores and is heavily wooded. The NW end of the island terminates in a long sandspit marked on the end by a daybeacon. A private pier is on the NW side of the island, and a pier and large building of a private yacht club are on Carlyon Beach just E of the roadway on piling.

TOTTEN INLET extends 9 miles SW from the W end of Squaxin Passage. A depth of 30 feet can be carried to a point off the entrance to Skookum inlet. A $3\frac{1}{2}$ fathom shoal is about in midchannel at the entrance, 620 yards SW of the S end of Steamboat Island. A spit exends W for about 100 yards from Steamboat Island. In entering, favor the W shore to avoid the spit and shoal. The inlet shoals gradually to near BURNS POINT, 100 feet high, on the S shore, where it bares at low tide.

OYSTER BAY, S of Burns Point, is an extensive mudflat; oysters are grown in this area, and there are log booms. S of the entrance to LITTLE SKOOKUM INLET, along the shores of Totten Inlet, are rock or concrete walls enclosing the oysterbeds. The walls are a danger to navigation, and the oyster industry discourages boatmen from entering these waters. Oyster processing wharves are on the N side of the inlet. Local knowledge is required to get to them. Good anchorage may be had anywhere inside the entrance of Skookum Inlet.

CHART 18457 † HAMMERSLEY INLET indents the W shore of the sound about a mile N of the W end of Squaxin Passage. It is about 6 miles long, expanding at it's head into OAKLAND BAY which is 3.5 miles long in a NE direction. The inlet is obstructed by shoals, particularly at its mouth, where there is an exensive bar. The rocky shoals have been partly removed. The channel, marked by some lights and buoys, has a controlling depth of about 8 feet to the town of Shelton on Oakland Bay. It is navigated only by small-craft, and by tugs with log rafts and railroad car floats; local knowledge is required. Tidal current velocities may reach 5 knots at times in the constricted parts of the inlet. (See Tidal Current Tables for current predictions contained in this edition of the PACIFIC BOATING ALMANAC.) Vessels enter on the flood, usually after half tide, and leave on the ebb, usually before maximum strength. Hammersley Inlet is considered dangerous for strangers.

Vessels with sharp rise of bilge should avoid the inlet as there is danger of capsizing in the strong current in case of grounding.

ARCADIA is a small settlement on the S point of the entrance of Hammersley Inlet. It has a public ramp for launching small pleasure craft. A light is on the point E of Arcadia.

SHELTON, at the head of the inlet, is a town of some commercial importance. Extensive logging, lumber and lumber product manufacturing interests are centered here. The W end of OAKLAND BAY is used primarily as a

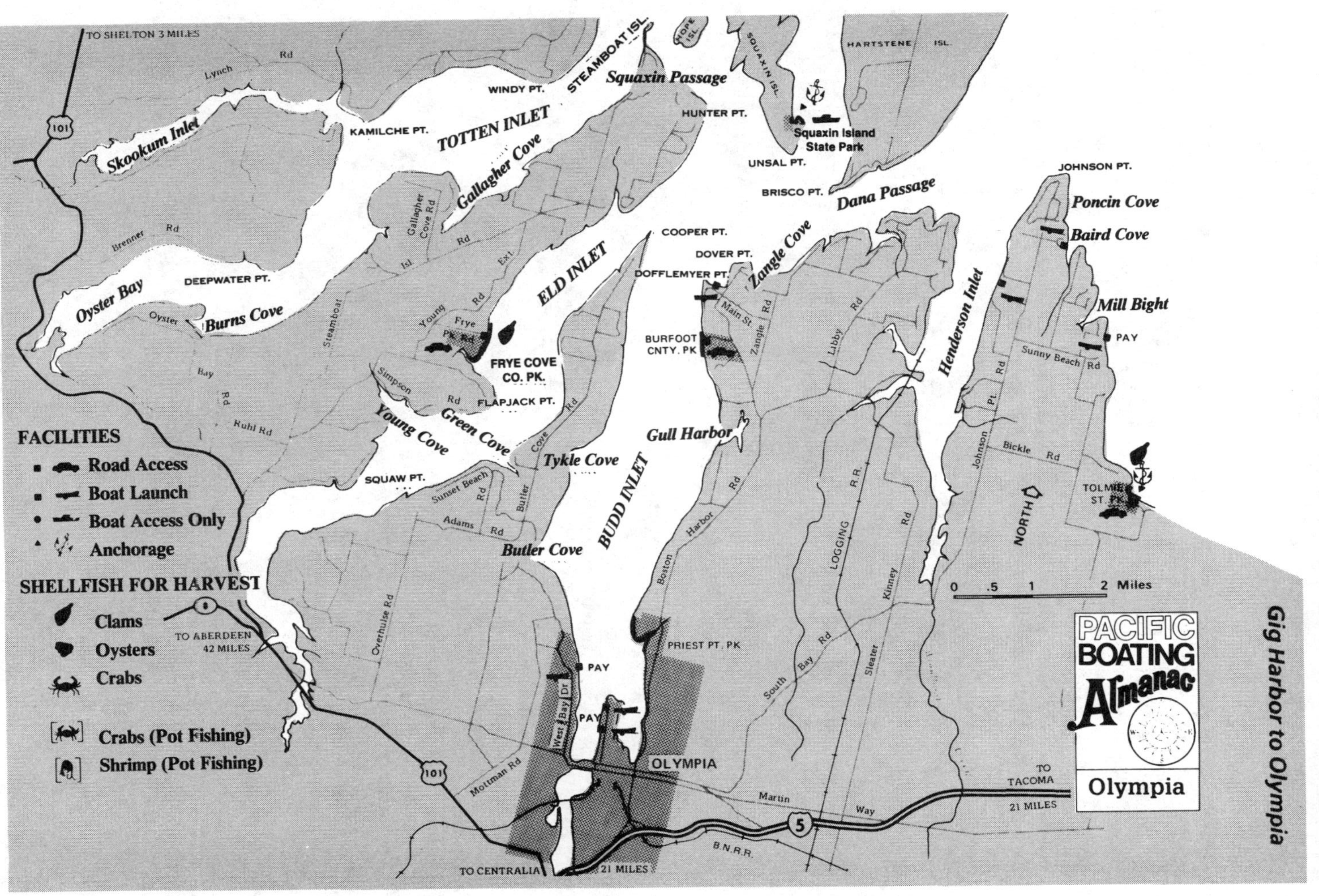
TO SHELTON 3 MILES
Lynch Rd
101
Skookum Inlet
WINDY PT.
KAMILCHE PT.
STEAMBOAT ISL.
Squaxin Passage
HOPE ISL.
SQUAXIN ISL.
HARTSTENE ISL.
TOTTEN INLET
HUNTER PT.
Squaxin Island State Park
UNSAL PT.
BRISCO PT.
Dana Passage
JOHNSON PT.
Poncin Cove
Baird Cove
Gallagher Cove
Gallagher Cove Rd
Brenner Rd
COOPER PT.
DOVER PT.
Zangle Cove
Zangle Rd
Henderson Inlet
Mill Bight
DEEPWATER PT.
Oyster Bay
Burns Cove
Oyster
Bay Rd
Steamboat
Isl
Rd
ELD INLET
DOFFLEMYER PT.
Main St.
Libby Rd
PAY
Young Rd
Ext.
Rd
Frye Pk.
BURFOOT CNTY. PK.
Sunny Beach Rd
Simpson Rd
FRYE COVE CO. PK.
FLAPJACK PT.
Ruhl Rd
Young Cove
Green Cove
Cove Rd
Gull Harbor
NORTH
Johnson Pt. Rd
Bickle Rd
FACILITIES
Road Access
Boat Launch
Boat Access Only
Anchorage
SHELLFISH FOR HARVEST
SQUAW PT.
Sunset Beach Rd
Adams Rd
Butler Rd
Tykle Cove
BUDD INLET
TOLMIE ST. PK.
Clams
Oysters
Crabs
TO ABERDEEN 42 MILES
Butler Cove
Overhulse Rd
Boston Harbor Rd
PRIEST PT. PK.
LOGGING R.R.
Kinney Rd
Sleater Rd
South Bay Rd
0 .5 1 2 Miles
Crabs (Pot Fishing)
Shrimp (Pot Fishing)
West Bay Dr
PAY
PAY
101
Mottman Rd
OLYMPIA
Martin Way
5
TO CENTRALIA 21 MILES
B.N.R.R.
TO TACOMA 21 MILES
PACIFIC BOATING Almanac
Olympia

storage area for logs trucked in from the Olympic Peninsula to be used by the mills at Shelton. Hammersley Inlet receives little commercial traffic. The mill stack is prominent from a considerable distance. Shelton is on a branch of the Burlington Northern Railroad; lumber is shipped largely by rail, however some railroad car ferrying is done. Railway trestles used as log dumps extend E across the flats from the Shelton waterfront. The Port of Shelton Marina, 0.3 mile from the head of the Shelton waterfront and on the N shore, has berths, electricity, gasoline, and water. A yacht club has its facilities at the marina. Some marine supplies are available in the town. There are no haulout or repair facilities at Shelton. Oysters are cultivated in the shoal portions of Oakland Bay.

-U.S. COAST PILOT 7
25th edition, August 1989
Corrected thru 10 22 90
Local Notice to Mariners

MARINE PARKS

BURFOOT COUNTY PARK (on east shore of Budd Inlet.) Moorings. Picnic areas.

SQUAXIN ISLAND STATE MARINE PARK (In Peale Passage, south end and east shore of Squaxin Island.) 31 acres. 10 mooring buoys, 405 feet of float space. Floats. Picnic areas. Campsties. Pit toilets. No water.

TOLMIE STATE PARK (on Sandy Point, northeast of Olympia), 12245 Tilley Road S., Olympia, WA 98502. (206) 456-6464. 105 acres. 12 mooring buoys. Underwater park. Picnic areas. Kitchen facilities. No showers, restrooms. Hiking trails. Public beach. Day use park, no overnight camping.

SHELTON

JARRELL'S COVE MARINA, E. 220 Wilson Rd., Shelton, WA 98584. (206) 426 - 8823. All year. 8 AM - 8 PM. Charts. Groceries. Ice. Laundry. LP gas refills. Marine hardware. Picnic area. RV campsites. Overnight guest dock with electricity. Fuel: gas and diesel. Fishing: licenses, bait and tackle. Water skiing. Owner: Gary Hink.

JARRELL COVE STATE PARK, E. 391 Wingert Rd., Shelton, WA 98584. (206) 426 - 9226. Open all year. Picnic area. RV campsites. Moorings. Park Manager: Thomas Snyder.

FACILITIES

GRAPEVIEW

9's FAIR HARBOR MARINA (on Case Inlet behind Reach Island-Treasure Island-just north of Hartstene Island. Between Bremerton & Shelton), E. 5050 Grapeview Loop Road, 3 mi. So. of Allyn, Box A, Grapeview, WA 98546. (206) 426 - 4028. All year. Open 7 AM - 7 PM. Two ramps: concrete. Closed Wed. Overnight accommodations. Fuel Dock: gas, diesel and mix. Groceries. Ice. Snack bar. Gift shop. Fishing: bait, tackle. Dockside electricity: (3). Managers: Ken & Phyllis Neyens.

OLYMPIA

BETTINE'S SOUTH SOUND MARINE, 6790 Martin Way, Olympia, WA 98506. (206) 491 - 1676. All year. New and used boat and motor sales. Marine hardware. Charts. Electronic sales. Hull and engine maintenance and repairs. Engine parts. Nautical gifts. Water skis. Owner: Ed Bettine.

BOSTON HARBOR MARINA (on Budd Inlet at Dofflemeyer Point), 312 - 73rd Avenue N.E., Olympia, WA 98506. (206) 357 - 5670. Ramp: concrete, open 24 hours. Fuel dock: gas and diesel, open 24 hours with security card. Overnight guest dock. Open Summer 8 AM - 8 PM; Winter 9 AM - 7 PM. Closed Monday. Gorceries. Ice. Wines. Fresh Seafood in season. Snack bar. Sanwiches. Fishing: bait, tackle. Owner: Barbara Cohen.

CANVAS WORKS, 401 N Columbia, Olympia, WA 98501. (206) 352 - 4481. Public docks. Marine canvas awnings. Owner: Gary Graybeal.

EAST BAY MARINA, 1022 Marine View Drive, Olympia, WA 98501. (206) 786-1256. Slips. Guest dock. Launching ramp. Showers, laundry and restrooms. Pumpout station. Boat sales. Dockside electricity. Manager: Mike Hendrickson..

OLYMPIA MARINA, (206) 352 - 0411. Moorage, gas, diesel and repairs.

PERCIVAL LANDING MARINE PARK, Guest dock for transients only in downtown Olympia. Maximum stay 3 days. Electrical hookups. Restrooms and showers. Picnic area. Operatored by Olympia Dept. of Parks & Recreation, 222 No. Columbia Olympia Center, Olympia, WA 98501. (206) 753 - 8380.

WEST BAY MARINA, 2100 West Bay Drive, Olympia, WA 98502. (206) 352-4863. All year. Daily: 9 AM - 5 PM. Summer: 9 AM - 8 PM. TUGS award winning resturant Hoist: 40 ton cap. Overnight guest dock with electricity. Slips to 40 feet. Hull and engine maintenance and repairs. Fuel dock: gas and diesel. Volvo Dealer Used boat sales. Electronic sales. LP gas refills. Marine hardware. Groceries and ice. Laundry. Chandlery, Clean Showers. Deli. Fishing: bait and tackle. Manager: Eileen Ribary

14

TACOMA
(47°17'N., 122°25'W.)

Tacoma is fast shaking off its traditional image as an industrial backwater devoid of interest for visitors. Recent completion of the Tacoma Dome sports center, and the ongoing program of rejuvenation in the city's historic downtown core, demonstrates the new vitality which has come to permeate Washington's third largest metropolis. It's now worth a skipper's time to put into Commencement Bay and head up City Waterway to one of the marinas located near the 11th Street Bridge. From there it is just a short uphill hike into the city center, with its Art Museum, period-piece Pantages Theatre, stores and Fireman's Park.

After visiting downtown Tacoma, a quick cruise westward along the south shore of Commencement Bay leads to beautiful Point Defiance Park, a 637-acre expanse of playgrounds, woodlands, sandy beaches and a boathouse which rents small day boats. Nearest moorage is at Warter Marina, unless you're lucky enough to have reciprocal priveleges with nearby Tacoma Yacht Club. On the way to Point Defiance are several shoreside restaurants with their own guest docks and probably the best food in Tacoma.

Tacoma's Daffodil Festival, held in April, is one of the earliest celebrations of spring to be held in the Northwest each year. For local boatmen, the Festival serves as kind of Opening Day.

CHART 18453 † DASH POINT, the E entrance of Commencement Bay, and the village of DASH POINT are a mile NE of Browns Point. There is a restaurant at the foot of the long pier which extends out from the N side of the point to a depth of 20 feet.

POINT DEFIANCE, the W entrance of Commencement Bay, terminates in a very prominent dirt bluff 160 feet high. A light and fog signal are just W of the point. POINT DEFIANCE PARK is wooded for a mile from the end of the point.

STORM WARNING SIGNALS ARE DISPLAYED . (See Chart.)

COMMENCEMENT BAY entrance lies 18 miles S of Alki Point and 56 miles S of Point Wilson. The bay is about 2.5 miles in length, easy of access and free of dangers. Log storage grounds are off the NE shore of the bay.

TACOMA, the second city in size and importance on the sound, occupies the S and SW shores of Commencement Bay and its residential area has grown N into Seattle's S suburbs and to Steilacoom on the SW.

The PORT OF TACOMA, (47°17'N., 122°25'W.) is a rapidly expanding major port, second only to Seattle in maritime importance on Puget Sound.

PROMINENT FEATURES † On entering Commencement Bay, either from the N via East Passage or Colvos Passage or from the S via The Narrows and Dalco Passage, Dash Point, Browns Point, and Point Defiance are prominent. BROWNS POINT LIGHT (47°18.4'N., 122°26.6'W.), 38 feet above the water, is shown from a 31 foot white tower on Browns point; a fog signal is at the station. The huge stack of an ore smelter at Ruston, 2 miles SE of Point Definance, is one of the most conspicuous landmarks in the approach to Commencement Bay; numerous stacks, tanks and towers for the navigator to use are visible once inside the bay.

A 132°05'-312°05' MEASURED NAUTICAL MILE is off the W shore of the bay just SE of Ruston. The front markers are orange squares, and the rear markers are orange rectangles. A range formed by two stacks E of City Waterway is paralled to the measured

mile course. A fishing reef, marked by private buoys is from 0.15 to 0.4 mile NW of the S measured mile course markers. A fish haven covered 21 feet, is just N of the public pier about 6 miles SE of the S measured mile course markers.

From the NE corner of Commencement Bay, the city waterfront extends NW to within 1.5 miles of Point Defiance. Along here are numerous industrial plants with wharves to accommodate vessels drawing 30 feet or more.

CITY WATERWAY is the westernmost of the channels at the head of the bay. A light and fog signal are on the E side of the entrance. A Federal project provides for depths of 29 feet in City Waterway to the South 11th Street Bridge, then 22 feet for 0.2 mile, then 19 feet to the head of the project.

There is one bridge over the waterway. The South 11th Street vertical lift bridge, 0.5 mile from the entrance to the waterway, has a clearance of 64 feet down and 139 feet up.

MIDDLE WATERWAY, NE of City Waterway, and ST. PAUL WATERWAY, NE of Middle Waterway are not Federal projects. Between the two waterways in an old lumber Wharf with deep water on all three sides, but the wharf is in poor condition and is not used. The inner parts of both waterways have shoaled and are not navigable. For about the outer 400 yards of each waterway, there are depths of 25 to 34 feet, but there is no deep-draft traffic. St. Paul Waterway is used for log storage by the large papermill which occupies the land on the NE side.

PUYALLUP WATERWAY, NE of St. Paul Waterway, discharges the water of PUYALLUP RIVER. A daybeacon is on a jetty on the E side of the entrance. The waterway has shoaled to such an extent that it cannot be used commercially. A light and fog signal mark a shoal area extending about 500 yards NW of the entrance. The fixed highway bridge, 0.8 mile above the mouth, has a clearance of 29 feet.

MILWAUKEE WATERWAY, NE of Puyallup Waterway, has depths of 25 feet at the entrance and 30 feet or more inside, but is not a Federal project.

SITCUM WATERWAY, NE of Milwaukee Waterway, has depths of 32 to 40 feet; it is not a Federal project. The Port of Tacoma's Pier 7 is on the E side. A private light is just off the NW end of Pier 7; it marks the NE side of the entrance to Sitcum Waterway.

The next two channels to the NE of Sitcum Waterway, BLAIR WATERWAY and HYLEBOS WATERWAY, are maintained as Federal projects. A light is off a shoal on the N side of the entrance, and a private light and fog signal are on the S side at the NW end of Pier 25; these aids mark the entrance to Hylebos Waterway. The entrance to Blair Waterway is marked by a private light on the SW side. The project depth in Hylebos Waterway has depths of 30 feet in the SW half and 35 feet in the NE half of the channel to East 11th Street; then to a lower turning basin extending to Lincoln Avenue, then a channel to a turning basin at the head of the project, all 35 feet deep.

The 11th Street bascule bridges over the Blair and Hylebos Waterways have clearances of 14 and 21 feet, respectively. The bridgetenders monitor VHF-FM channel 16 (156.80 MHz) and work on channel 13 (156.65 MHz). Call signal: Blair Bridgs, KZN-573; Hylebos Bridge, KZN-574. Power cables at both bridges have a clearance of 173 feet. A power cable across Blair Waterway just above Lincoln Avenue has a clearance of 170 feet.

(See Notice to mariners and the latest editions of charts for controlling depths in the various waterways in Tacoma Harbor.)

TIDES AND CURRENTS † The mean range of tide at Tacoma is 8.1 feet, and the diurnal range of tide is 11.8 feet. A range of about 19 feet may occur at the time of maximum tides. The tidal currents in the harbor have little velocity.

HARBOR REGULATIONS are administered by the harbormaster, whose headquarters are at the fire station at 901 South Fawcett Street. The general offices of the Port of Tacoma are in the Tacoma Building at the corner of 11th and A Streets; the Port of Tacoma terminal offices are at Pier 2.

SPEED † A city ordinance

prohibits speeds in excess of 5 knots on any of the waterways and within 200 yards of any shore or pier in the harbor.

SMALL-CRAFT FACILITIES † A public pier, owned by the city of Tacoma, is 0.6 mile SE of the S marker of the measured mile course on the SW side of Commencement Bay; small-craft moor here temporarily. There are numerous other small-craft facilities on Hylebos, Blair, and City Waterways, and on the SW shore of Commencement Bay.

-U.S. COAST PILOT 7
25th edition, August 1989
Corrected thru 10 22 90
Local Notice to Mariners

FACILITIES

TACOMA

ANDREASSEN BOAT WORKS, 5619 Marine View Dr., Tacoma, WA 98422. (206) 272 - 9513. All year. 8 AM - 5 PM. Wooden boat design. Construction and restoration. Wood and fiberglass repair. Hoist cap.: 9 tons. Owner: Dale Hoff.

CROW'S NEST MARINA, 5410 Marina View Dr., Tacoma, WA 98422. (206) 272 - 2827. All year. 10 AM - 6 PM. Closed Sun. and Mon. Ice. Laundry. Slips. Dockside electricity. Bait. Manager: Babe Whitish.

J & G MARINE SUPPLY, 1690 Marine View Drive, Tacoma, WA 98422. (206) 572 - 4217. Electronic sales and service. U.S. and Canadian charts. hardware. Morse controls. Paint. Owner: Harold Jacobson

PICK'S COVE MARINA, 2102 E "D" St., Tacoma, WA 98421. (206) 572-3625. Open daily, 8 AM - 5 PM. Full service boat yard. Travel lift cap.: 30 tons. Fuel dock: gas and diesel. Slips. Overnight guest dock. Boat storage. Hull and engine maintenance and repairs. Prop and shaft repairs. Manager: Rick Hamstreet.

TACOMA DIESEL & EQUIPMENT, 444 54th Ave. E, Tacoma, WA 98424. (206) 922 - 8171. All year. Mon. - Fri.; 8 AM - 5:30 PM. Sat.; 9 AM - 2 PM. Boat and motor sales. Electronic sales and repairs. Instrument repairs. Marine hardware. Manager: Jim Porter, Jr.

TACOMA YACHT CLUB (at north end of Point Defiance Park), 5401 N. Waterfront Drive, Tacoma, WA 98407. (206) 752 - 3555. Restaurant and bar. Guest moorage 48 hour limit (only to reciprocal clubs).

TIDERUNNER, INC., 9001 Pacific, Tacoma, WA 98444. (206) 537-7847. New and used boat and motor sales. Marine hardware. Electronic sales. Outboard part and service.

TOTEM MARINE SERVICES (under the 11th Bridge), 821 Dock Street, Tacoma, WA 98402. (206) 572 - 2666. Hoist cap.: 5 and 10 tons. New and used boat and motor sales. Boat and engine maintenance, parts and repairs. Prop and shaft repairs.

TYEE MARINA, 5618 Marine View Dr., Tacoma, WA 98422. (206) 383 - 5321. All year. Tues. - Sat.; 10 AM - 4:30 PM. Slips. Fuel dock: gas and 2 cycle oil. Office Manager: M. Wood.

DES MOINES

DES MOINES † Des Moines is situated on the eastern shore of East Passage, the heavily-traveled waterway between Seattle and the South Sound. The city-owned marina is modern and convenient, with space for transient pleasure vessels just inside the breakwater entrance, on the port hand. On the grounds of the marina are picnic tables, some with chessboard insets, and public restrooms with showers. A very popular public fishing pier immediately adjoins the marina.

The shopping center of Des Moines is within easy walking distance and is worth a visit for the variety of shops and stores. Very close to the marina is an excellent restaurant and about two miles south is Saltwater State Park with its beautiful shoreline, cliffs and woods.

BLOCK AND TACKLE BOATYARD, 22501 Dock St. S, Des Moines, WA 98188. (206) 878 - 4414. All year. Hoist: Stradlecraft, 37 ton. Boat storage. Hull and engine maintenance, parts and repair. Prop and shaft repair. Fuel dock: gas and diesel. Charts. LP gas refills. Marine hardware. Restaurant. Ice. Owner: Vernon E. Day.

CITY OF DES MOINES MARINA, 22307 Dock Ave. S, Des Moines, WA 98198. (206) 824-5700. All year. Winter: 8 AM - 5 PM. Summer: 6 AM - 9:30 PM. Hoist: 4 tons. Overnight guest dock. Slips up to 50 feet. Fuel dock: gas and diesel. LP gas refills. Waste disposal pumpout. Concrete fishing pier. Harbormaster: Jesse Cadena.

MARINE PARKS

CUTT'S ISLAND (Deadman) STATE MARINE PARK (1¼ mile west of Kopachuck), Access by boat only. Six acres. 9 mooring buoys. Underwater park. Pit toilets. No water.

EAGLE ISLAND STATE MARINE PARK (In Balch Passage between Anderson and McNeil Islands), Ten acres. Three mooring buoys. No facilities. No water. Watch depthsounder. Strong currents.

ROBERT F. KENNEDY RECREATION AREA (on Case Inlet near Whitman Cove), Launching ramp. Moorage float. Picnic tables. Hiking trails. Toilets.

KOPACHUCK STATE PARK (on Carr Inlet, 10 miles south of Rosedale), 109 acres. Ramp. Two mooring buoys. Underwater park. Picnic areas. Campsites. Showers.

MAPLE HOLLOW PICNIC AREA (1¼ miles north of Home, WA on west shore of Carr Inlet), Two mooring buoys. Picnic area. Warning: Approach from south. Avoid U.S. Naval Acoustic Range marked by a standing red triangle with a flashing light in center. Park operated by Dept. of Natural Resources.

McMICKEN ISLAND STATE MARINE PARK (on west shore of Case Inlet. Connected by sandbar with northeast side of Hartstene Island), 11 acres. Five mooring buoys. Campsites. Watch depthsounder.

PENROSE POINT STATE PARK (west side of Carr Inlet, 3 miles north of Longbranch), 321 158th KPS, Lakebay, WA 98349. (206) 884-2514. 146 acres. Eight mooring buoys, 130 feet of float space. Picnic areas. Campsites. Showers. Toilets. Playground. Hiking trails.

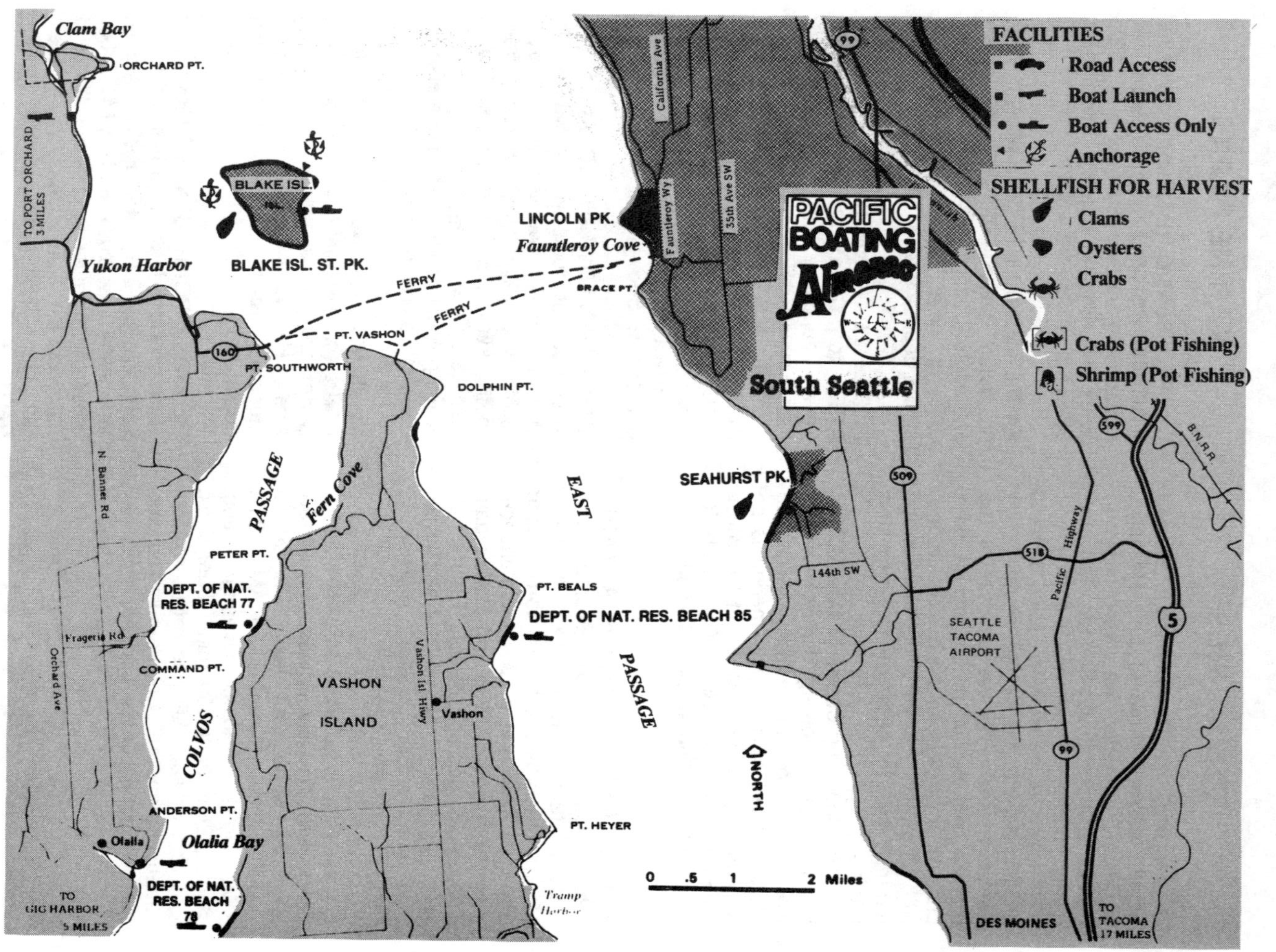
FACILITIES
Road Access
Boat Launch
Boat Access Only
Anchorage
SHELLFISH FOR HARVEST
Clams
Oysters
Crabs
Crabs (Pot Fishing)
Shrimp (Pot Fishing)
PACIFIC BOATING Almanac
South Seattle
NORTH
0 .5 1 2 Miles
Clam Bay
ORCHARD PT.
TO PORT ORCHARD 3 MILES
BLAKE ISL.
BLAKE ISL. ST. PK.
Yukon Harbor
LINCOLN PK.
Fauntleroy Cove
FERRY
FERRY
BRACE PT.
PT. VASHON
PT. SOUTHWORTH
DOLPHIN PT.
California Ave
Fauntleroy Wy
35th Ave SW
99
599
509
518
144th SW
Pacific Highway
5
99
SEATTLE TACOMA AIRPORT
B.N.R.R.
SEAHURST PK.
DES MOINES
TO TACOMA 17 MILES
PASSAGE
Fern Cove
EAST
PASSAGE
PETER PT.
DEPT. OF NAT. RES. BEACH 77
PT. BEALS
DEPT. OF NAT. RES. BEACH 85
COMMAND PT.
COLVOS
VASHON ISLAND
Vashon Isl. Hiwy
Vashon
N. Banner Rd
Fragaria Rd
Orchard Ave
ANDERSON PT.
Olalla
Olalia Bay
PT. HEYER
Tramp Harbor
DEPT. OF NAT. RES. BEACH 78
TO GIG HARBOR 5 MILES
160

15

SEATTLE AREA

SEATTLE † Attractions and accommodations for pleasure boatmen abound in Seattle. After fifteen years of trying we still haven't sampled all the restaurants, parks, private and public moorages that rim the city's two freshwater lakes, the Washington Ship Canal and Elliott Bay. But, like many other Puget Sound boating enthusiasts, we keep trying.

The most obvious Seattle stop, for those who don't want to go through the Chittenden Locks to Lake Union and Lake Washington, is the Port of Seattle's Shilshole Marina, located north of Elliott Bay at the Ship Canal's mouth. Until Everett enlarged its boat basin to over 2000-slip capacity, Shilshole was the largest marine facility in the Northwest. But today, filled with floats to the limits of its breakwater, Shilshole cannot enlarge further and holds only about 1600 boats. It handles a good many transients, however, and a bus runs regularly from the marina into downtown Shilshole, giving crews access to the entire range of urban activities.

There is little except temporary transient moorage on Elliott Bay (see Pier 49 Washington Street Moorage, for example), and most small craft avoid this big open bight because it is full of heavy shipping, ferries, tugs and similar industrial vessels; the wash from them all tosses boats badly, no matter how calm

the day. The rest of Seattle's facilities are reached by way of the Locks and the Ship Canal, entrance to which is just south of Shilshole marina. Ample extra line and close attention to both vocal and printed instructions will get you through the locks easily enough. Sometimes you'll be directed through the small lock, sometimes through the wide one. Directions will vary because continuous maintenance projects are necessary to keep the heavily-used gates and channels in good repair.

Lake Union has many marine services, private moorages that have some transient moorage, restaurants with docks and strips of shore built up with chandleries, yacht brokerages, charter offices. Our favorite spot is Franco's Hidden Harbor on the western shore, where you pass behind a bank of boathouses (white with turquoise trim, for identification) and tie up against the deck of the restaurant. You then step through a hinged gate two steps away from the nearest dining table. Half-tame Canada geese float below your elbow petitioning for bread crmubs---and the food in this restaurant is excellent, besides!

An easy curving channel, Montlake Cut, takes you through Portage Bay to the vast expanse of Lake Washington, on which face many separate municipalities, public and private docks and parks. Once there you are likely to stay awhile.

CHARTS 18449, 18446, 18447, 18474 † SHILSHOLE BAY is between Meadow Point and West Point. It is an open bight from which the Lake Washington Ship Canal is entered and is the site of the largest and most important single marina in the Seattle area. S of the canal entrance, clay cliffs extend for about 0.5 mile.

SHILSHOLE BAY MARINA, the small-craft basin just N of the canal entrance, is administered by the Port of Seattle. A long breakwater, marked at each end by a light, protects the basin on its W side. The basin has two entrances. In March 1974, the controlling depths were 14 feet in the N entrance and 15 feet in the S entrance; depths alongside the floats in the basin were about 15 feet in the S half, and about 10 feet in the N half of the basin.

There are berths at the concrete floats for 1,500 craft of up to 130 feet long, including a guest pier and transient berths. Electricity, gasoline, diesel fuel, water, ice, marine supplies and a pumpout station are available at the 600-foot pier at the midpoint of the basin. Propane is available at the S end of the basin. All berths have electricity and water. A 30-ton mobile crane, boat hoists, forklifts and a tidal grid are in the basin. A launching ramp is at the N end of the basin. A Coast Guard vessel is moored at the 600-foot pier.

STORM WARNING DISPLAY locations are listed on the NOS charts and shown on the Marine Weather Services Charts published by the National Weather Service.

WEST POINT, at the N entrance to Elliott Bay, is a low, sandy point which rises abruptly to an elevation of over 300 feet 0.5 mile from its tip. The edge of the shoal extending WSW from the point is marked by a lighted buoy. WEST POINT LIGHT (47°39.7'N., 122°26.1'W.), 27 feet above the water, is shown from a 23 foot white octagonal tower attached to a building on the end of the point; a fog signal is at the station. Prominent in the area are the pump tanks of a sewage treatment plant about 0.1 mile E of the light, a VTS antenna tower between the plant and the light, and a large white dome about 1 mile ESE of the light.

ALKI POINT, at the S entrance to Elliott Bay, is low with a small prominent wooded knoll about 80 feet high immediately back of it. E of the knoll lowland extends for nearly 0.4 mile before rising to the high land extending S from Duwamish Head. ALKI POINT LIGHT (47°34.6'N., 122°25.2'W.), 39 feet above the water, is shown from a 37 foot white octagonal tower attached to a building on the end of the point. A fog signal and a special radio direction finder calibration station are at the light.

ELLIOTT BAY indents the E shore of Puget Sound just N of Duwamish Head. The entrance is between West Point on the N and Alki Point 5 miles S. The bay proper, lying E of a line between Magnolia Bluff and Duwamish Head, has a width of about 2 miles and extends SE for nearly the same distance. The bay has deep depths throughout most of its area.

MAGNOLIA BLUFF, largely bare, light colored, and rising in places to nearly 300 feet, extends along the N shore from West Point to Smith Cove. FOURMILE ROCK is 60 yards offshore, 1.7 miles SSE of West Point Light. A light is on the rock.

DUWAMISH HEAD, 1.8 miles NE of Alki Point and rising to over 260 feet from the point, bounds Elliott Bay to the S. The bluff is tree covered, but is interspersed with houses. The lights of the houses along the beach and on the bluff are conspicuous at night. A shoal, extending over 0.2 mile N of the point, is marked by a light and fog signal.

CHART 18450 † SEATTLE, the largest and most important city in the Northwest and one of the major ports of the Pacific Coast, extends as a greater metropolitan area from Everett, the city on its N, almost to Tacoma, the major city to the S. This area is thickly populated, not only in that NS dimension but also E beyond the limits of Lake Washington and its shores.

The PORT OF SEATTLE 47°36'N., 122°20'W., includes an outer and inner harbor. The outer saltwater harbor includes Elliott Bay; East, West, and Duwamish Waterways; Shilshole Bay, and the portions of Puget Sound adjacent Ballard on the N and West

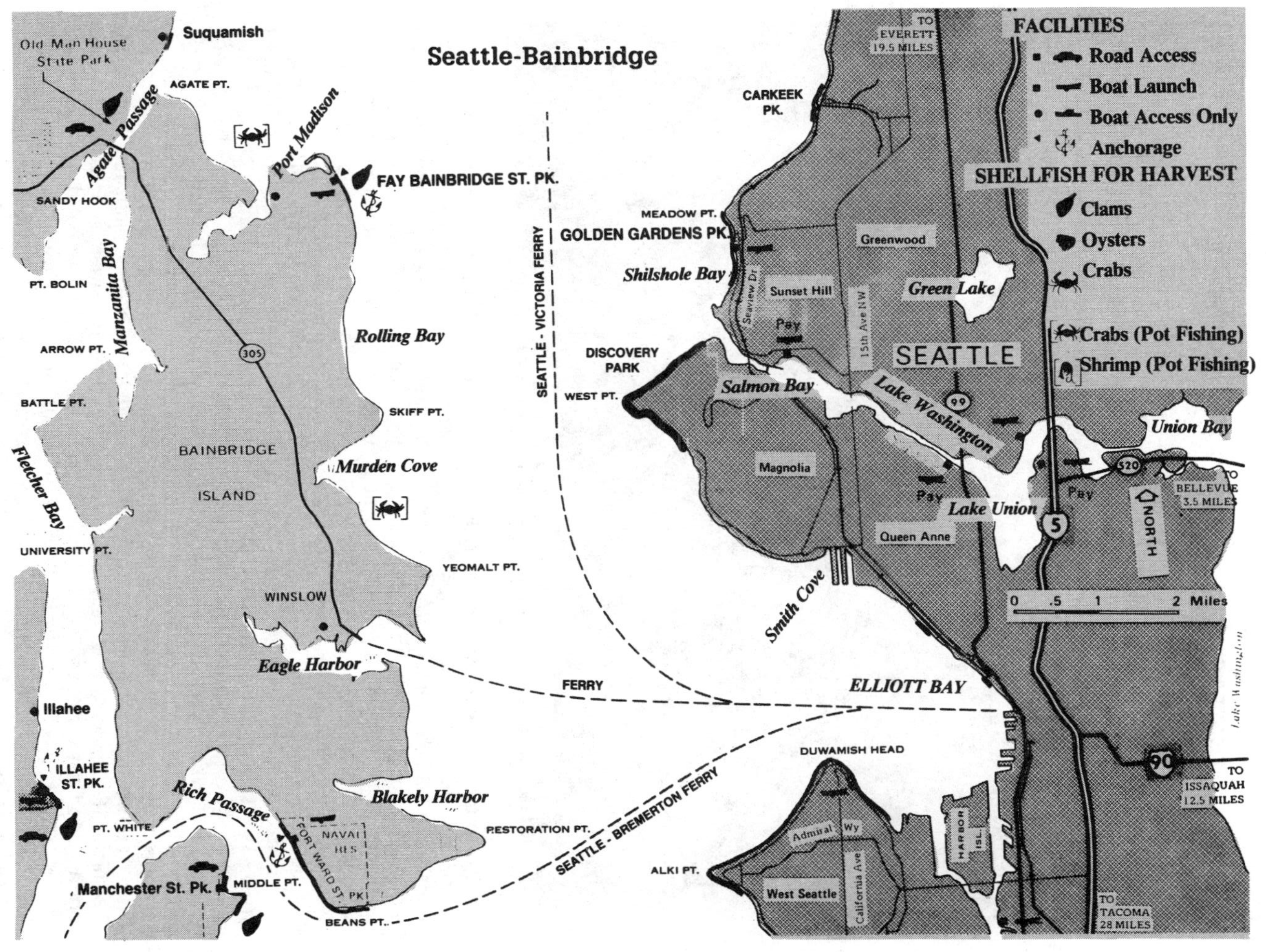
Seattle-Bainbridge
FACILITIES
Road Access
Boat Launch
Boat Access Only
Anchorage
SHELLFISH FOR HARVEST
Clams
Oysters
Crabs
Crabs (Pot Fishing)
Shrimp (Pot Fishing)
TO EVERETT 19.5 MILES
CARKEEK PK.
MEADOW PT.
GOLDEN GARDENS PK.
Shilshole Bay
Greenwood
Sunset Hill
Seaview Dr
15th Ave NW
Green Lake
SEATTLE
Pay
DISCOVERY PARK
WEST PT.
Salmon Bay
Lake Washington
Magnolia
Pay
Lake Union
Pay
Queen Anne
Union Bay
NORTH
5
99
520
TO BELLEVUE 3.5 MILES
0 .5 1 2 Miles
Smith Cove
ELLIOTT BAY
Lake Washington
TO ISSAQUAH 12.5 MILES
90
DUWAMISH HEAD
HARBOR ISL.
Admiral Wy
California Ave
West Seattle
ALKI PT.
TO TACOMA 28 MILES
Old Man House State Park
Suquamish
AGATE PT.
Agate Passage
SANDY HOOK
Port Madison
FAY BAINBRIDGE ST. PK.
Manzanita Bay
PT. BOLIN
ARROW PT.
Rolling Bay
BATTLE PT.
305
SKIFF PT.
BAINBRIDGE ISLAND
Murden Cove
SEATTLE - VICTORIA FERRY
Fletcher Bay
UNIVERSITY PT.
YEOMALT PT.
WINSLOW
Eagle Harbor
FERRY
Illahee
ILLAHEE ST. PK.
Rich Passage
PT. WHITE
NAVAL RES.
FORT WARD ST. PK.
Manchester St. Pk.
MIDDLE PT.
BEANS PT.
Blakely Harbor
RESTORATION PT.
SEATTLE - BREMERTON FERRY

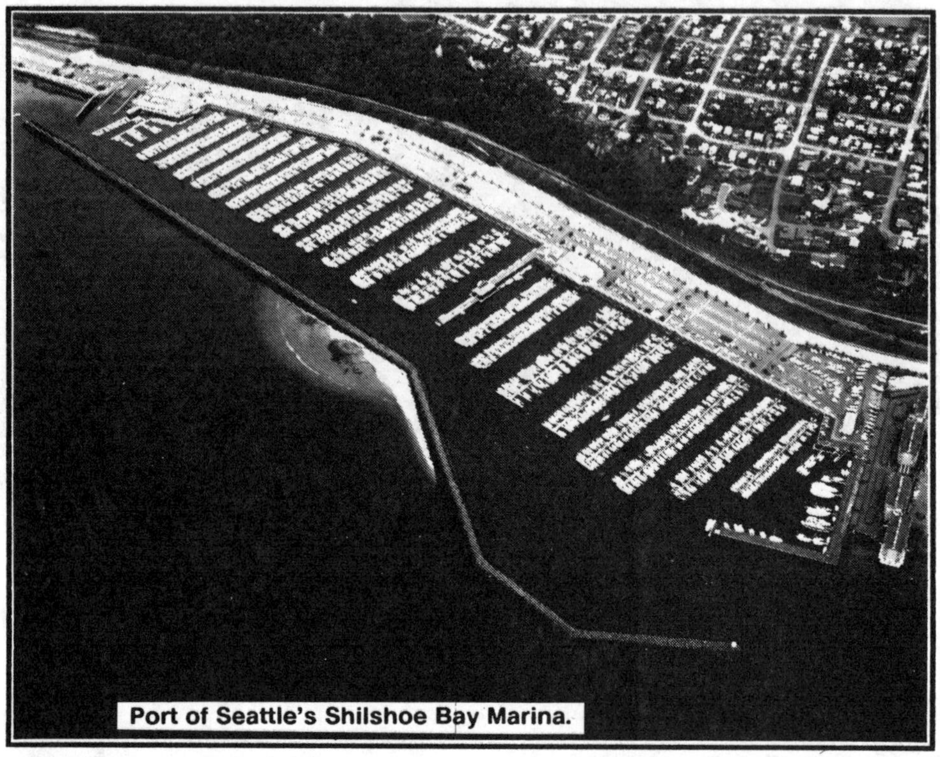

Port of Seattle's Shilshoe Bay Marina.

Seattle to the S of the entrance of Elliott Bay. Seattle's freshwater inner harbor consists of Lakes Union and Washington, which are connected with each other and with Puget Sound by the Lake Washington Ship Canal. Most of the waterfront facilities of the inner harbor are privately owned.

EAST WATERWAY is separated from West Waterway by HARBOR ISLAND. Several important terminals are on the waterway. Most of the N side of Harbor Island is occupied by the piers and drydocks of a shipyard. A private light, shown from the NE corner of Terminal 18, marks the W side of the entrance to East Waterway.

Most of the E side of WEST WATERWAY and the area W of the entrance are occupied by the facilities of two large shipyards. The SW side of the waterway is the site of the Port of Seattle's Terminal 5, which receive considerable deep-draft traffic. Several other wharves on the waterway also receive deep-draft vessels.

DUWAMISH WATERWAY, extending S from West Waterway, is fronted by factories and industrial plants for more than 4 miles. A number of log rafts are often anchored along the waterway around Kellogg Island and S of the 1st Avenue South Bridge.

PROMINENT FEATURES † In clear weather the skyline of Seattle itself is unmistakable. From N to S the conspicuous features are: the "Space Needle", a legacy from the 1962 World Fair; the red lighted "E" sign at pier 67; the Washington Building, of light sandstone, usually illuminated at night; The Seattle Tower; the square-topped Seattle First National Bank building, distinguished from two other skyscrapers by its slightly taller height and black color; the tower of the Smith Building and the 250 foot high King County Domed Stadium (Kingdome). From several miles off, the Space Needle and the Seattle First National Bank building are easily the most identifiable objects.

BRIDGES † There are no bridges over the Seattle waterfront in Elliott Bay, and none over East and West Waterways. The 4.5 mile Duwamish Waterway is crossed by four bascule bridges with clearances of 7 to 24 feet. The bridgetender of the Spokane Street bridge monitors VHF-FM channel 13 (156.65 MHz); call sign LSL-285. The bridgetender of the First Avenue South bridge monitors VHF-FM channel 13; call sign WHU-200. The power cables in this section have a least clearance of 90 feet.

TIDES AND CURRENTS † Tides at Seattle have a mean range of 7.7 feet and a diurnal range of 11.4 feet. A range of aobut 18 feet may occur at the time of maximum tides. (See Tide Tables for daily predictions contained in this edition of the PACIFIC BOATING ALMANAC.) As a rule, the tidal currents in the harbor have little velocity. At times however, with a falling tide, an appreciable current will be found setting NW along the waterfront. (See Tidal Current Charts for Page Sound, Northern Part, contained in this edition of the PACIFIC BOATING ALMANAC.)

WEATHER † Seattle is on a hilly stretch of land overlooking the saltwaters of Puget Sound to the W, and in an E direction, the waters of Lake Washington, an 18 mile long freshwater lake. The Lake Washington shoreline roughly parallels that of Puget Sound at distances varying from about 2.5 to 6 miles. Hills rise rather abruptly from both shorelines and reach elevations of more than 300 feet in the central sections and more than 500 feet in the extreme N and the SW sections. The general NS trend of the city is paralleled on the E by the Cascade Mountains, while to the W and NW, at somewhat greater distance, the Olympic Mountains rise abruptly. The main commercial section of the city lies along the E shore of Elliott Bay, an indentation in the Puget Sound shoreline.

The climate is mild and moderately moist due to the prevailing W air currents, which advance inland from the Pacific Ocean, and to the shielding

The Hiram M. Chittenden Locks.

effects of the Cascade Mountains, which serve to exclude and deflect the cold continental air toward the E. Although the city is 90 miles distant from the ocean at the nearest point, the marine air penetrates readily inland, an effect that is aided by the extensive water surface of Puget Sound. The prevailing W air currents cross vast reaches of ocean, acquiring much water vapor and a temperature near that of the sea. This effect is received from the general currents of the ocean rather than from the Japanese Current which curves far N into Alaskan waters. As a result of the rather steady influx of marine air, winters are comparatively warm and summers cool. Extremes of heat or cold are moderate and usually of short duration, and the daily range in temperature small.

The warmest summer and the coldest winter days come with N to E winds which have traveled under land influences from British Columbia or eastern Washington. In the summer, the numbers of days having maximum temperatures of 90°F or above averages less than 3, and only twice during the entire period of record has the temperature reached 100°F. Nighttime temperatures during the warmest months usually reach comfortable levels, and very seldom remain about 65°F. During the winter, daily maximum temperatures fail to rise above the freezing point on an average of only about 2 days per year, while the number of days having minimum temperatures of 32°F or below averages only 15 per year. An extreme low temperature of 3°F was recorded in January 1893, with 10°F the lowest recorded since that time. However, this circumstance may be attributed in part to the effects of urbanization. In general, temperatures may vary by several degrees at any one time throughout the city, depending on wind direction distance from shoreline, and elevation.

The normal precipitation of less than 34 inches is moderate compared with many points along the N Pacific Coast. Primarily this is due to the location of the city, which lies in the lee or dry side of the Olympic Mountains. The W or windward slopes of these mountains cause the moist marine winds to rise to cooler levels with heavy precipitation on the seaward slopes and diminished amounts E of the summits. A winter seasonal wet period along the Pacific Coast coincides with and is caused by the Aleutian Low. In summer this low pressure recedes N with higher pressures off the coast and results eventually in clear weather, rising temperatures, and decreased humidities. The area has, therefore, a pronounced but not sharply defined wet season extending usually from October through April, a period in which about 82 percent of the total precipitation occurs, and a dry season, May through September, with 18 percent. Excessive precipitation is rare, but in the wet season the continuance of light or moderate amounts is rather persistent. The average winter snowfall totals about 9 inches, and snow seldom remains on the ground for more than 1 or 2 days at a time. Maximum recorded snow depths have ranges from as little as a trace in several instances to over 21 inches. The occurence of light fog is most frequent during late fall and winter. Thunderstorms average about six per year, lightning damage is very infrequent, and tornadoes have never been reported in the city.

STORM WARNING DISPLAY locations are listed on the NOS charts and shown on the Marine Weather Services Charts published by the National Weather Service.

ROUTES † Vessels bound for the Strait of Georgia from Seattle can use the following routes: via ROSARIO STRAIT – an approximate mid-channel course using the vessel traffic system outbound lane (see beginning chapter 6 for Vessel Traffic Separation Scheme information), through Puget Sound and Admiralty Inlet to the precautionary are N of Point Wilson, then E of Partridge Bank, Smith Island, and Davidson Rock to the precautionary area at the S end of Rosario Strait, then N passing E of Belle Rock, Lydia Shoal, and Peapod Rocks, then leaving the vessel traffic system lanes at the precautionary area just N of Clark Island, and proceeding into the Strait of Georgia either N or S of Alden Bank; via HARO STRAIT – from Admiralty Inlet using the vessel traffic system outbound lane to the

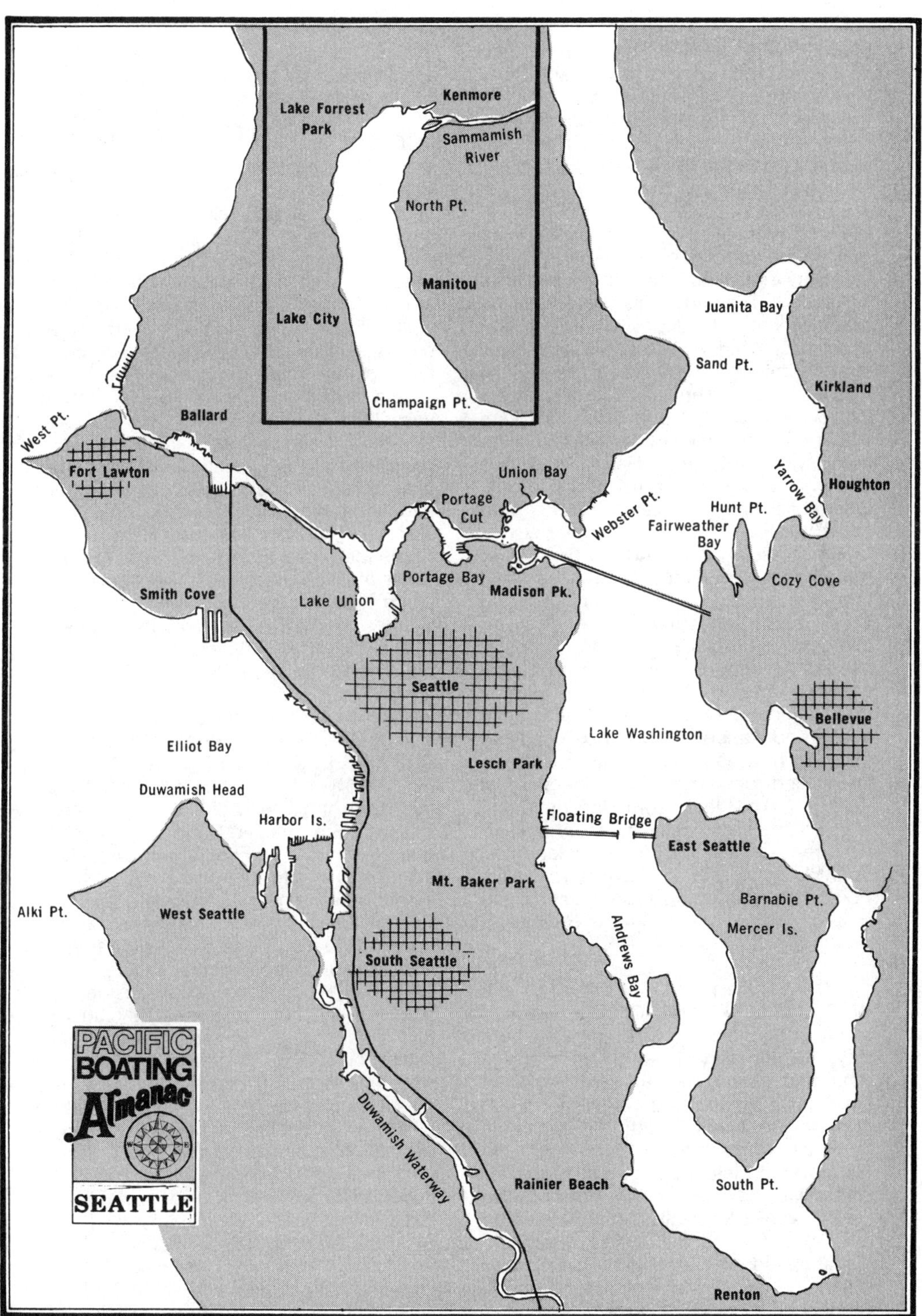

Lake Forrest Park
Kenmore
Sammamish River
North Pt.
Manitou
Lake City
Champaign Pt.
Juanita Bay
Sand Pt.
Kirkland
Yarrow Bay
Houghton
West Pt.
Ballard
Fort Lawton
Union Bay
Portage Cut
Hunt Pt.
Webster Pt.
Fairweather Bay
Cozy Cove
Smith Cove
Portage Bay
Lake Union
Madison Pk.
Seattle
Bellevue
Elliot Bay
Lesch Park
Lake Washington
Duwamish Head
Harbor Is.
Floating Bridge
East Seattle
Mt. Baker Park
Barnabie Pt.
Alki Pt.
West Seattle
Mercer Is.
South Seattle
Andrews Bay
Duwamish Waterway
PACIFIC BOATING Almanac
SEATTLE
Rainier Beach
South Pt.
Renton

precautionary are N of Point Wilson, then W of Partridge Banks and Hein Bank leaving the vessel traffic system lanes at the precautionary area just SE of Hein Bank, then through Haro Strait and Boundary Pass to the Strait of Georgia.

These routes are available for vessels of any draft. A range should be steered where available to ensure making the courses good.

Between Admiralty Inlet and the entrance to Rosario Strait, the current on the flood has a tendency to set a vessel E toward Whidbey Island; it also sets strongly through Deception Pass and up Rosario Strait. There is a strong W set in this area on the ebb tide. Through Rosario Strait the currents run with considerble velocity. Heavy tide rips and swirls are found off Black Rock, Obstruction Pass, Peapod Rocks, and Lawrence Point.

In crossing from Admiralty Inlet to the entrance of Haro Strait, the tidal currents setting to and from Rosario Strait and San Juan Channel, with estimated velocities of 2 to 3 knots, should be kept in mind. From Henry Island to around Turn Point, heavy tide rips are found on the ebb. Particularly heavy and dangerous tide rips occur on the ebb between East Point and Patos Island and for 2 miles N in the Strait of Georgia. The flood from Rosario Strait, which is felt as soon as the passage between Orcas and Sucia Islands is open, is apt to set a vessel toward East Point. The ebb in this vicinity sets to the E even before the Strait of Georgia is well open.

CHART 18447 † LAKE WASHINGTON SHIP CANAL extends from Puget Sound through Shilshole Bay, Salmon Bay, Lake Union, Portage Bay, and Union Bay to deep water in Lake Washington. Federal project depth through the canal is 30 feet, which is generally maintained. (See Notice to Mariners and latest editions of charts for controlling depths.) The entrance to Lake Washington Ship Canal is marked by a lighted range, lights, and buoys.

A speed limit of 4 knots is enforced within the guide piers of the Hiram M. Chittenden Locks. A speed limit of 7 knots is enforced elsewhere in the Lake Washington Ship Canal, except in an area marked by four private buoys in the N part of Lake Union.

The HIRAM M. CHITTENDEN LOCKS, a double lock, and a fixed dam are at the narrows of the entrance to Salmon Bay, 1.2 miles in from the sound. The large lock, a two-chamber structure, has a clear length of 760 feet, width of 80 feet, lift of 26 feet, and depth over the lower miter sill of 29 feet. The small lock has a clear length of 123 feet, width of 28 feet, lift of 26 feet, and depth over the lower sill of 16 feet. Passage time is less than 30 minutes for large vesels and 5 to 10 minutes for small vessels.

A saltwater barrier extends across the E end of the E chamber of the large lock to reduce the intrusion of slatwater into Lake Washington and to conserve water. Depths above Hiram M. Chittenden Locks are referred to low water of lakes which is 20 feet above the plane of mean lower low water of Puget Sound. Heights. Vertical clearance above Hiram M. Chittenden Locks are referred to the mean water level of the lakes, which is 21 feet above mean lower low water of Puget Sound.

STORM WARNING SIGNALS ARE DISPLAYED. (See chart.)

SALMON BAY extends for about 0.8 mile from the E end of the locks to the Ballard (15th Avenue) Bridge. There are numerous piers and floats with extensive small-craft facilities on the bay. Fishermen's Terminal, operated by the Port of Seattle, is immediately W of the Ballard Bridge. The terminal is the home port of a large commercial fishing fleet. Depths of 14 to 28 feet are alongside the piers. There are 700 berths for craft 27 to 176 feet long. Complete facilities for fishing boats are available at the 54 acre terminal, including electricity, gasoline, diesel fuel, water, net repair yards, and all types of marine supplies. Marine railways at the terminal can handle craft to 300 tons for complete repairs. A travel lift to 46 feet is also available at the terminal.

From Salmon Bay the canal leads E to LAKE UNION, which is about 1 mile long in a NS direction and about 0.5 mile wide. Depths in the lake range generally from 32 to 49 feet. There is a 10 foot shoal about 200 yards offshore from the SW end of the lake; it is marked by a buoy. Four private buoys in the N part of Lake Union mark an unrestricted speed zone, which is used by boat builders around the lake as a testing area. The buoys are frequently repositioned; caution is advised when transiting the area. There are numerous marinas and repair facilities, and several commercial wharves from which various commodities are shipped by barge.

PORTAGE BAY, E of Lake Union is the site of two major yacht clubs and many slips and finger piers for small craft.

STORM WARNING SIGNALS ARE DISPLAYED. (See chart.)

MONTLAKE CUT (Portage Cut) leads from Portage Bay past the conspicuous buildings and athletic stadium of UNIVERSITY OF WASHINGTON on the N side, then into UNION BAY, and thence into Lake Washington.

Lake Washington Ship Canal is crossed by five bascule bridges and two fixed bridges. Clearances of the drawspans are 17 to 43 feet. The bridgetenders of the drawbridges monitor VHF-FM channel 16 (156.80 MHz) and 13 (156.65 MHz) and work on channel 13. The call signs are as follows: Burlington Northern Railroad, KCE-201; Ballard, KJA-445; Fremont, KJA-442; University, KJA-441; Montlake, KJA-438. The fixed bridges have a least clearance of 127 feet. Cables crossing the canal have a least clearance of 155 feet.

LAKE WASHINGTON, the largest freshwater lake on Seattle's E side, provides deep and protected water over most of its length of nearly 16 miles. Its shores are studded with private piers and landings, and there are marinas and small-craft repair places at many locations.

There are few commercial installations. Except for a few oil wharves, commercial shipments are by barge.

The Evergreen Point (State Route 520) pontoon bridge crossing the lake

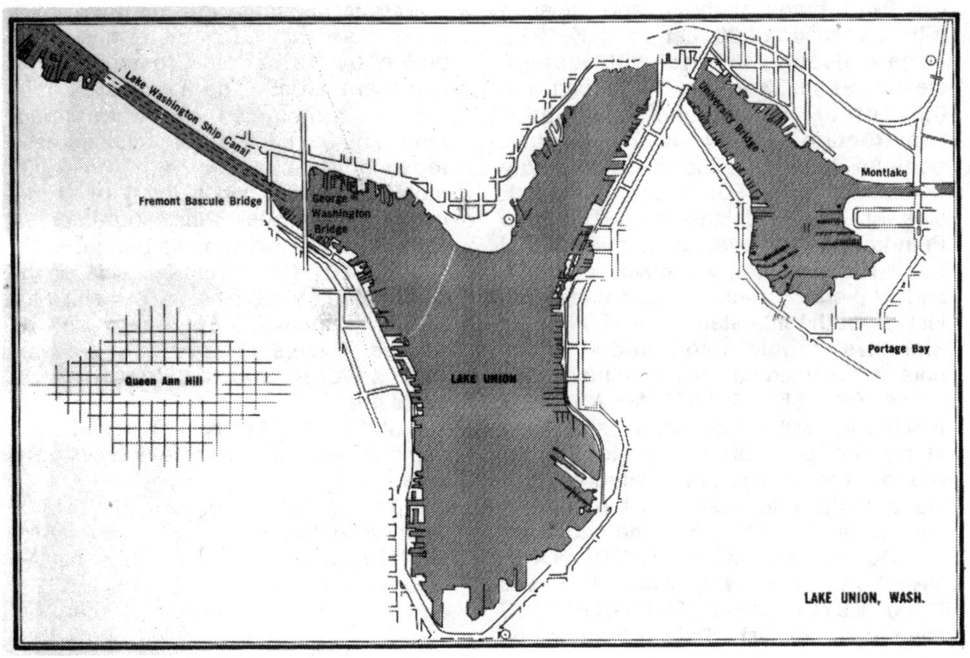

METEOROLOGICAL TABLE FOR COASTAL AREA OFF SEATTLE
Boundaries: Between 48°N., and 50°N., and from 129°W., eastward to coast

Weather elements	Jan.	Feb.	Mar.	Apr.	May	June	July	Aug.	Sept.	Oct.	Nov.	Dec.	Annual
Wind ≥ 34 knots (1)	4.3	3.3	2.3	1.6	1.1	*	*	*	1.0	2.2	3.3	2.9	1.9
Wave height ≥ 10 feet (1)	11.1	26.0	20.4	17.6	6.3	4.6	4.5	2.4	6.4	24.6	15.0	22.1	12.6
Visibility < 2 naut. mi (1)	5.6	4.7	3.7	1.9	2.7	3.7	6.2	8.0	6.2	6.4	6.5	4.0	5.1
Precipitation (1)	28.7	25.0	19.6	17.1	14.8	11.5	10.2	6.2	12.9	19.2	29.2	28.8	18.1
Temperature ≥ 85°F (1)	0	0	0	0	0	0	0	0	*	0	0	0	*
Mean Temperature (°F)	43.6	44.9	45.5	48.3	52.0	56.3	59.4	60.6	58.1	54.0	48.6	45.7	52.0
Temperature ≤ 32°F (1)	3.6	1.0	*	*	0	0	0	0	0	0	1.2	.8	.6
Mean relative humidity (%)	81	83	80	81	80	80	81	83	81	82	81	83	81
Sky overcast or obscured (1)	52.2	49.8	39.5	42.2	40.8	38.0	38.8	38.9	35.2	40.3	45.6	51.3	42.4
Mean cloud cover (eighths)	6.2	6.0	5.5	5.7	5.7	5.7	5.1	5.3	4.9	5.5	6.0	6.3	5.7
Mean sea-level pressure (2)	1,014	1,015	1,015	1,017	1,017	1,017	1,019	1,018	1,017	1,015	1,016	1,014	1,016
Extreme max. sea-level pressure (2)	1,041	1,041	1,039	1,033	1,035	1,031	1,034	1,030	1,037	1,038	1,041	1,042	1,042
Extreme min. sea-level pressure (2)	980	974	984	978	991	984	997	998	988	977	975	974	974
Prevailing wind direction	SE	S	W	NW	NW	NW	NW	NW	NW	NW	SE	S	NW
Thunder and lightning (1)	*	0	*	*	0	*	*	*	*	*	*	*	*

(1) Percentage frequency.
(2) Millibars.
* 0.0-0.5%

These data are based upon observations made by ships in passage. Such ships tend to avoid bad weather when possible, thus biasing the data toward good weather samples.

between East Seattle on the N end of MERCER ISLAND and the city proper has fixed spans at the E and W ends with clearances of 29 feet. In July 1985, a new floating bridge with design clearances of 33 feet at the E end and 35 feet at the W end was under construction just N of the existing pontoon bridge. The fixed highway (Interstate Route 90) bridge on the E side of Mercer Island from Barnabie Point to the mainland, has a clearance of 65'. The underwater remains of the E and W piers of a former fixed bridge are just SE of the Interstate Route 90 bridge. Mariners should use caution when outside the main navigation channel.

A 091°55'-271°55' MEASURED NAUTICAL MILE has been established along the pontoon bridge to Mercer Island. The targets are painted on both sides ot the bridge so that the courses can be run either N or S of the bridge.

Combined MEASURED HALF NAUTICAL MILE, NAUTICAL MILE, and 2,000 METER MEASURED COURSES have been esablished along the pontoon bridge from Foster Island to Evergreen Point on a bearing of 102°30'-282°30'. The half nautical and nautical mile courses are marked on the N side of the bridge by 18" circles resembling an engineers target. The half nautical mile markers have green and white quadrants, and the nautical mile markers have red and white quadrants. The 2,000 meter course is marked by 1 by 3 foot green markers with 3 inch white vertical stripes on both sides of the bridge.

HOUGHTON, at the NE side of the lake just S of Kirkland, is the site of a former shipyard. There are several unused oil piers in disrepair in this area and several marinas catering to yachtsmen.

JUANITA BAY, N of Kirkland, is a summer recreational area with several small piers.

The headquarters of the Naval Support Activity Seattle are at SAND POINT on the shore of the lake just NE of Union Bay.

-U.S. COAST PILOT 7
25th edition, August 1989
Corrected thru 10 22 90
Local Notice to Mariners

FACILITIES

SEATTLE AREA

ELLIOT BAY

CAPTAIN'S, 1914 Fourth Ave., Seattle, WA 98101-1107. (206) 448 - 2278. Nautical charts and books. Currently corrected British Admiralty charts. Instruments and instrument repairs. Manager: Jon Daniel.

CARLSEN NAVIGATION, INC, 1245 4th Ave S, Suite E, Seattle, WA 98134. (206) 622 - 3433. All year. Weekdays: 8 AM - 5:30 PM. Sat., 9AM - 1PM. Complete sales and service of clocks, barometers, binoculars, compasses, sextants and other navigational equipment. Complete world-wide coverage of navigation charts, maps and publications. Owner: George Carlsen.

DELTA MARINE INDUSTRIES, INC., (located on the Duwamish River) 1608 S. 96th Street, Seattle, WA 98108. (206) 763-2383. Complete repair facility for large or small vessels. Hull and engine rebuilding. 150 ton dry dock. 100 ton crane. 35 ton lift.

HARBOR ISLAND MARINA, (Freshwater moorage by West Seattle Bridge), 1041 S.W. Manning Street, Seattle, WA 98134. (206) 467-9400. Open Summer and Winter 9 AM - 5 PM; Fridays and Sundays: 9 AM - 7 PM. Fuel dock: gas and diesel. Slips. Guest dock. Laundry. Ice. Pumpout station. Dockside Electricity. Harbormaster: Chuck Richardson.

MASTER MARINE, 1411 S. Thistle, Seattle, WA 98108. (206) 762-0741. Engine & sterndrive sales & service.

OLE AND CHARLIES HIGH & DRY CO, 3568 W. Marginal Way SW, Seattle, WA 98106. (206) 937 - 3400. All year. May - Sept.: 8 AM - 6 PM, Oct. -- April: 9 AM - 5 PM. Monorail hoist cap.: 10,000 lbs. Dockside electricity. Slips to 26 feet. Moorings. Boat storage. Engine maintenance and repairs. Fuel: gas. Water skiing. Skin and scuba diving. Mgr: Kim Mickelsen.

RAINIER INSTRUMENTS INC., 8535 Perimeter Road South, Boeing Field, Seattle, WA 98108. (206) 763-8800. Sales and service of remote compass and tachometer systems. Instrument repairs. President: John Kroll.

SEACREST BOATHOUSE, 1660 Harbor Avenue S.W., Seattle, WA 98126. (206) 932-1050. Open daily 5 AM - 6 PM. Marine hardware. Ice. Fishing: bait, tackle. Rental boats, motors. Manager: Dave Nelson.

SEA WOLF BOAT SALES, 1661 Harbor Avenue S.W., Seattle, WA 98126. (206) 935-1661. Boat maintenance and repairs. Engine parts and repairs. Prop and shaft repair. Instrument repairs. Marine hardware. Fishing: bait, tackle. Skin diving equipment. Manager: Frank Wolff.

SOUTH PARK MARINA, (on Duwamish River in South Park area), 8604 Dallas Avenue S., Seattle, WA 98108. (206) 762-3880. Hoist cap.: 15 tons to 42 feet. Open Tuesday through Saturday 9 AM - 5 PM. Slips. Dry storage. Showers. Laundry. Do-it-yourself facilities only.

TIDERUNNER, INC., 1135 NW 46th Street, Seattle, WA 98107. (206) 782-7236. New and used boat and motor sales. Marine hardware. Electronic sales. Outboard parts and service.

WILSON MARINE SERVICE, 2930 Westlake N, Seattle, WA 98109. (206) 284 - 3630. All year. Mon - Sat.: 8 AM - 5 PM. Marine lift cap.: 25 tons and 50 ft. Hull and engine maintenance, repower and repairs. Engine parts. Prop and shaft repairs. OMC, Volvo, Merc factory authorized parts and service. Large repair yard. New and used boat and motor sales. Owners: Dennis Roehl and David Wilson.

YACHT RIGGERS INC, 4448 27th West, Seattle, WA 98199. (206) 282 - 7737. Masts and spars. Rigging. Lifelines. Halyards. Turnbuckles and backstay adjusters. Owner: Tom Hukle.

SHILSHOLE BAY

BOAT - IQUE LTD, 7001 Seaview Ave NW, Seattle, WA 98117. (206) 784 - 7273. All year. Winter: 10 AM - 6 PM. Summer: 10 AM - 8PM. Nautical books, gifts and clothing. Marine supplies. Owner: Rosa Lee Eacho.

CROW'S NEST, (6 blocks south of Shilshole Bay Marina), 6010 Seaview Avenue N.W., Seattle, WA 98117. (206) 783-6262. Marine hardware. Rigging. Charts and clothing. Safety equipment.

CRUISING EQUIPMENT CO, 6315 Seaview Ave NW, Seattle, WA 98107. (206) 782 - 8100. All year. Marine electrical system design and sales. Batteries, alternators, chargers, regulator/monitor, solar panels, inverters, refrigerators. Manager: Neal Fridley.

RAYS BOAT HOUSE FISHING RESORT, 6049 Seaview Avenue N.W., Seattle, WA 98107. (206) 789 - 3770. Waterfront restaurant. Dry storage. Fishing: rental boats and tackle. Under construction from fire damage. To be reopened by boating season.

SHILSHOLE BAY MARINA, 7001 Seaview Avenue NW, Seattle, WA 98117. (206) 728 3385. All year. 24 hours a day. Hoist cap.: 3 ton. Marine railway cap.: 30 ton. Overnight guest dock with electricity. Boat storage. Hull and engine maintenance, parts and repairs. Prop and shaft repair. Fuel: gas, diesel and mix. Groceries. Ice. Restaurant. Snack bar. Laundry. LP Gas refill. Waste disposal. Operated by the Port of Seattle. Manager: Ron Silkworth.

SHILSHOLE TEXACO MARINE, 7029 Seaview Avenue N.W., Seattle, WA 98117. (206) 783-7555. Gas, diesel and outboard mix. Groceries. Ice. Fishing: bait, tackle.

WEST MARINE PRODUCTS AT SHILSHOLE, 6317 Seaview Ave. NW, Seattle, WA 98107. (206) 789 - 4640. All year. Inflatable boat and motor sales. Charts. Electronic sales. Marine hardware, power and sail. Fishing: licenses, tackle. Manager: Wes Fridell.

BALLARD/SALMON BAY AREA

STIMSON MARINA (at Ballard inside locks on Ship Canal), 5265 Shilshole Avenue N.W., Seattle, WA 98107. (206) 784-1000. All year. Slips. Ice. Dockside Electricity: (7). Manager: Jack N. Hayes.

BALLARD OIL CO., 5300 26th N.W., Seattle, WA 98107. (206) 783-0241. Fuel dock: gas, diesel. Open daily 8 AM - 5 PM. Summer hours: 8 AM - 8 PM; Saturdays, 8 AM - 3 PM. Manager: Warren Aakervik, Jr.

BIRCHARD & AGEE MARINE SERVICE (in Ballard on south side of canal), 2100 W. Commodore Way, Seattle, WA 98199. (206) 282-3593. Open Monday - Friday 8 AM - 5 PM. Inboard, sterndrive sales and service. Engine parts. Prop and shaft repairs. Marine hardware. Owners: Ted Birchard and Doug Agee.

BOAT ELECTRIC CO, INC., 2834 NW Market St., Seattle, WA 98107. (206) 784 - 5908. All year. Mon - Fri.: 8:30 AM - 5:30 PM. Sat.: 9 AM - 12 NOON. Marine electrical supplies. Heating and refrigeration. President: Ray Bunn.

C - COMM, 6115 15th Ave NW, Seattle, WA 98107. (206) 783 - 0616. All year. 9 AM - 5:30 PM. Marine VHF and SSB sales and service. Commercial and amateur radio equipment. President: Dale L. Osterud.

CAPTAIN'S, Fisherman's Terminal, Seattle, WA 98119. (206) 283-7242. And 1914 - 4th Avenue, Seattle, WA 98101. (206) 448 - 2278. Nautical charts and books. Currently corrected British Admiralty charts. Instruments and instrument repairs. President: Leonard E. Shrock.

COVICH - WILLIAMS CO, 5219 Shilshole NW, Seattle, WA 98107. (206) 784 - 0171. All year. 8 AM - 5 PM. Fuel dock: gas and diesel. Owner: Mason Williams.

EWING STREET MOORINGS, 624 W Ewing St, Seattle, WA 98119. (206) 283 - 1075. All year. Hoist. 24 hours. Overnight guest dock. Moorings. Hull and engine maintenance and repair. Prop and shaft repairs. Owner: M. J. Wollaston.

HOUGH MARINE & MACHINE INC, 1111 NW Ballard Way, Seattle, WA 98107. (206) 789 - 1802 or (800) - 423 - 3509. Shaft and prop sales and service. Machine shop. Steering and cooling systems. Gauges. Couplings. Transmissions. Owner: Bruce Hough.

INFLATABLE BOATWORKS, INC, 2425 NW Market St, Seattle, WA 98107. (206) 789 - 7410. All year. Mon - Sat.: 10 AM - 5:30 PM. Winter hours: Tues. - Fri., 9 AM - 5:30 PM; Sat., 9 AM - 4 PM. Inflatable boat sales, repairs, life-raft sales, lifevests. Fishing. Waterskiing. Scuba diving. Cruising. Manager: Charles J. (Jim) Ingle.

STAN JONES INC., 3031 W. Commodore Way, Seattle, WA 98199. (206) 282-3738. Fiberglass repairs. Owner: Jack B. Clarke.

LE CLERCQ MARINE CONSTRUCTION INC., 1080 W. Ewing Street, Seattle, WA 98199. (206) 283-8555. Marine ways cap.: to 75 tons. Wood and fiberglass boat building and repairs. Engine installation. Manager: Bruce Ford.

LECO MARINE INC., (on south side of ship canal, 2 blocks southeast of Ballard Bridge), 1080 West Ewing Street, Seattle, WA 98119. (206) 285-0477. Moorage. President: William E. Logg.

LOCKHAVEN MARINA INC., (south side of canal, just inside the locks), 3030 W. Commodore Way, Seattle, WA 98199. (206) 283-6260. Hoist cap.: 5 tons and 30 feet. Slips. Boat repairs. Prop and shaft repairs. Dockside Electricity: (3) (6) (7). Owner: Ellis C. Hendrickson.

LUNDE ELECTRIC CO., 2401 N.W. Market Street, Seattle, WA 98107. (206) 783-6800. Electric sales and service.

MARINE ENGINE REPAIR CO, 338 W. Nickerson, Seattle, WA 98119. (206) 782 - 7670. All year. Mon - Fri.: 8 AM - 5 PM. Engine maintenance, parts and repairs. Prop and shaft repairs. New and used motor sales. Owner: Robert Allen.

MILLER & MILLER BOATYARD CO. (on south side of ship canal), 626 West Ewing Street, Seattle, WA 98199. (206) 285-5958. Open Monday - Friday: 8 AM - 5 PM. Saturday: 8 AM - 1 PM. Full service yard. Hull and engine maintenance and repairs. Haulouts to 12 tons and 40 feet. Prop and shaft repairs. Managers: Paul & Peg Miller.

NORTHWEST INSTRUMENT CO., 2525 W. Commodore Way, Seattle, WA 98199. (206) 284-8080. Electronic sales and service. Charts. President: John C. Rottler.

PUGET SOUND INSTRUMENT CO, 4611 11th NW, Seattle, WA 98107. (206) 789 - 1198. All year. Mon - Sat.: 8:30 AM - 5 PM. Marine electronic sales and service. Instrument repair. Marine Sales Manager: Tracy Prescott.

SALMON BAY BOATYARD INC., Fisherman's Terminal, (north end of west wall), 106 North 101st Street, Seattle, WA 98133. (206) 283-0593. Haulouts to 25 tons. Do-it-yourself shipyard facilities. Owner: Jack Hansen.

SALMON BAY MARINA, 2100 W. Commodore Way, Seattle, WA 98199. (206) 282-5555. Moorage. Manager: M. A. Merkley.

SEATTLE MARINE & FISHING SUPPLY CO., 2121 W. Commodore Way, Box 99098, Seattle, WA 98199. (206) 285-5010. Complete marine hardware. Commercial fishing gear and supplies.

SEATTLE SHIP SUPPLY CO., Fisherman's Terminal, Seattle, WA 98119. (206) 283 - 7000. Marine hardware. Gear for fishing boats and fishermen. Manager: Ted Hvatum.

SEAVIEW EAST, 4701 Shilshole N.W., Seattle, WA 98117. (Across from Fisherman's Terminal), (206) 789-3030. Open daily 8 AM - 5 PM. Closed Sunday. Hoist cap.: 70 tons. Crane cap.: 12,000 lbs. Full service or do-it-yourself. Engine work. Owner/operators: Phil Riise and Rick Hagaman.

STEWART'S MARINE ENGINE & MACHINE WORKS INC., 4600 Shilshole Avenue, N.W., Box 70301, Seattle WA 98107. (206) 789-4600. Engine maintenance and repairs. Mobile service.

SUNSET MARINE SUPPLY (two blocks west of the north end of Ballard Bridge), 4749 Ballard Avenue N.W., Seattle. WA 98107. (206) 527-8413. Marine hardware. Fasteners. Electronics. Fishing: Sport and commercial tackle.

WESBROOK MARINE CO., 5109 Shilshole Avenue, Ballard, WA 98107. (206) 789-3985. Open 8 AM - 4:30 PM, Monday - Friday. Crane cap.: 7-tons; elevator cap.: 100-tons. Full service yard. Hull repairs. Manager: Steve Helms.

LAKE UNION AREA

THE BOAT YARD, 3201 Fairview E, Seattle, WA 98102. (206) 323 - 3834. Full service shipyard. Two cranes: 100 tons and 90 feet. Boat building. Welding. Refrigeration. Hull and engine repairs. Prop and shaft repairs. Electronic repairs. President: R. Picot.

CROWS NEST 1900 North Northlake Way, Seattle, WA 98103 (206) 632-4462 Marine hardware. Rigging. Charts and Clothing. Safety equipment.

DUNATO AND SONS, INC, 115 N Northlake Way, Seatttle, WA 98103. (206) 633 - 1534. All year Vertical lift and railway: 100 tons Dockside electricity. Hull and engine maintenance. Owner: John Dunato.

FISHERIES SUPPLY CO, 1900 N Northlake Way, Seattle, WA 98103. (206) 632 - 4462. All year. Charts. Electronics. Inflatables, controls, marine hardware and safety gear.

VIC FRANCK'S BOAT COMPANY, INC. 1109 N. Northlake Way, Seattle, WA 98103. (206) 632 - 7000. All year. 8AM - 4.30PM. Electronic and instrument repairs. Vertical dry dock capacity. 100 feet and 100 tons. Hull and engine maintenance and repairs. Prop and shaft repairs. Vice President: Daniel V. Franck.

DOC FREEMAN'S INC, 999 N Northlake Way, Seattle, WA 98103. (206) 633 -1500. All year. Mon. - Fri.: , 8:30 AM - 5PM. Sat.: 8:30 AM - 3 PM. Marine hardware and equipment. Charts. Boating books. Foulweather gear. Engine parts. Boating accessories.

FREMONT BOAT CO, 1059 N Northlake Way, Seattle, WA 98103. (206) 632 - 0151. All year. 5 days a week. 8 AM - 5 PM. Open and covered slips up to 50 feet. Tugboat service. Owner: Mark H Freeman.

INDIGO MARINE 2520 Westlake Ave N Seattle, WA 98109. (206) 285 - 5744 All year 7:30 AM - 5 PM. Crane: 10 ton. Marine railway, 50 ton. Overnight guest dock with electricity. Slips up to 70 feet. Finger pier. Hull and engine maintenance and repairs. Engine parts. Prop and shaft repairs. Owner: Carrol W Brow.

LAKE UNION BOAT REPAIR, 3113 Fairview Avenue East, Seattle, WA 98102. (206) 323-5945. Hoist cap. 10 tons. Elevator cap.: 50 tons and 50 feet. Open 8 AM - 5 PM, Monday through Friday. Hull and engine maintenance parts and repairs. Wooden boat specialists. Prop and shaft repair. Boat and motor sales. Manager: Larry Lattin

LAKE UNION DRYDOCK CO., 1515 Fairview Avenue East, Seattle, WA 98102. (206) 323-6400. Major repairs of all types. 7 drydocks. Complete marine shops. Manager: Hobie Stebbins.

LAKE UNION LANDING (at southeast end of Lake Union), 1171 Fairview Avenue N., Seattle, WA 98109. (206) 625 - 9624. Slips. Guest dock.

LAKE UNION MARINA (on the west side of Lake Union), 2400 Westlake Avenue N., Seattle, WA 98109. (206) 283-3324. Open 9 AM - 6 PM. Hoist cap.: 13 tons and 40 feet. Boat maintenance and repairs. Electronics. Prop and shaft repairs. Do-it-yourself facilities. Manager: Dick Wright.

MARINE CENTER (on Lake Union) 1150 Fairview Avenue N., Box 9968, Seattle, WA 98109. (206) 682-1150. Marine hardware. Electronics. Nautical gifts, clothing. Charts.

MARINE PARTS NORTHWEST, 2940 Westlake Ave N., Seattle, WA 98109. (206) 283 - 5996. Distributors for gas and diesel engines, marine manifolds, parts and gears. Manager: Paul Shager.

MARINE SERVICENTER, 2370 Fairview AVE E, Seattle, WA 98102. (206) 323 - 2405. All year. 7 days a week, 8AM - 5PM. New and used boat sales. Instrument repairs. Crane cap.: 10 tons. Marine railway: 100 tons. Dockside electricity. Slips. Moorings. Hull and engine maintenance and repairs. Prop and shaft repairs. Rigging. Woodwork. Fiberglass repair. Welding. Owner: Jim and Jeanna Rard.

NORTHERN MARINE ELECTRONICS, INC, 1126 NW 45th, Seattle, WA 98107. (206) 782 - 3780. All year. Electronic sales and service. President: Charles Worst.

NORTHLAKE MARINA, 929 N. Northlake Way, Seattle, WA 98103. (206) 633-2114. Hoist cap.: 1 ton. Slips. Moorings. New and used boat and motor sales. Dockside Electricity: (4). Manager: Ed Stickland.

NORTHWEST MARINE CHARTERS, INC., 2400 Westlake Ave N,, Seattle, WA 98109. (206) 283 - 3040. All year. Bareboat charters. Power and sail to 60 feet. Skippered yachts to 100 feet. Cruise WA, B.C., & Alaska. Contact Robey Banks.

NORTHLAKE MARITIME CENTER, 2309 N Northlake Way, Seattle, WA 98103. (206) 547 - 7852. All year. Boat and motor sales. Electronic repairs. Travelift cap.: 60 tons. Slips and moorings. Boat storage. Hull and engine maintenance. Prop and shaft repairs. Owner: John Dunato.

NORTHWEST YACHT REPAIR (on Lake Union), 2400 Westlake North, Seattle, WA 98109. (206) 285-3460. Engine repairs. Sale and installation of heating systems. Marine electronics sales and repairs. Mast, sail, rigging sales and repairs.

PROFESSIONAL MARINE ENGINE REPAIR INC., 2046 Westlake Avenue N., Seattle, WA 98109. (206) 282-3399. Open daily. Marine ways cap.: 20 tons and 50 feet. Gas and diesel engine sales, parts and service. Engine repowering. I/O sales and service. Owner: Howard Taub.

SAILBOATS UNLIMITED INC., 2046 Westlake Avenue, N., Seattle, WA 98109. (206) 283-4664. Open 9:30 AM - 5:30 PM daily except Tuesday. Crane cap.: 10 tons. Hull and engine maintenance and repairs. Prop and shaft repairs. Electronic service. Do-it-yourself facilities. Marine hardware. Sailboat rentals and charters. Manager: Larry & Helen Ulm.

SEATTLE MARINA INC. (on Lake Union at the 45th Street exit from I-5), 2401 N. Northlake Way, Seattle, WA 98103. (206) 632-7311. Open daily 9 AM - 5 PM. Hoist cap.: 50 tons to 46 feet. Boat and engine maintenance and repairs. Prop and shaft repairs. Owner: T. R. Gillespie.

YOU CAN'T LEAVE PORT WITHOUT US

Bird-Johnson Company is your authorized MICHIGAN WHEEL distributor. We stock a wide range of recreational power and sailboat propellers in a variety of types and materials up to 3 feet in diameter. We also supply shafting and other marine propeller system accessories as well as operate a machine shop offering complete repair services. If you've been docked by a damaged propeller—call Bird-Johnson. We'll have you quickly on your way.

◤◢ BIRD-JOHNSON COMPANY

4451 14th Avenue NW • Seattle • WA 98107 • 206 782 9190 • US/AK: 800 426 6526

THUNDERBIRD MARINA, 2925 Fairview E., Seattle, WA 98102. (206) 322-3576. Slips.

TILLICUM MARINA, 1331 N. Northlake Way, Seattle, WA 98103. (206) 633-5454. Open and covered berths. Brokerage. New boat sales. Dockside Electricity: (3). Owner: John E. Nelson.

W. H. AUTOPILOTS INC, 655 NE Northlake Place, Seattle, WA 98105. (206) 633 - 1830. All year. Mon. - Fri.: 8 AM - 5 PM. Electronic sales and repair. Hydraulic steering systems. President: Wil Hamm.

WEST MARINE PRODUCTS, 2130 Westlake Avenue N., Seattle, WA 98109. (206) 282 - 2021. All year. Inflatable boat and motor sales. Charts. Electronic sales. Marine hardware, power and sail. Fishing: licenses, tackle. Manager: Brian Gallagher.

PORTAGE BAY AREA

BOB PICOT INC., 937 N.E. Boat Street, Seattle, WA 98105. (206) 632-6899. Boat tops, rails and cushions. Waterfront service dock. Owner: Bob Picot.

NORDIC BOAT YARD, 909 NE Boat Street, Seattle, WA 98105. (206) 547-4405. Machine shop, engine work, fiberglass & woodworking, upholstery.

TIMMERMAN MARINE SERVICE (on Portage Bay), 1101 N.E. Boat Street, Seattle, WA 98105. (206) 633-0044. Fuel dock: diesel, gas, mix and stove fuel. Diesel oil delivery. Line splicing. Ice. Groceries. Fishing: bait. Owner: Richard C. Timmerman.

LAKE WASHINGTON AREA

AQUA MARINA, 9520 Rainier Ave S, Seattle, WA 98118. (206) 722 - 6609. All year. Hoist cap.: 20 tons. Overnight guest dock with electricity. Slips: 16 to 60 feet. Gas. General Manager: Martin S. Luther.

CAREY'S MARINE SERVICE, 21518 1st Avenue W, Bothell WA 98021. (206) 481-5558. All year. Mobile marine service. Engine maintenance and repairs. Engine parts. Owner: Carey Gunter.

DAVIDSON'S UPLAKE MARINA INC. (at north end of Lake Washington, off Bothell Way between Hwy. 5 and 405), 6200 N.E. 175th Place, Box 100, Kenmore, WA 98155. (206) 486-7141. Open daily 8 AM - 6 PM. Hoist cap.: 12 tons and 40 feet. Fuel dock: gas and outboard mix, open 8 AM - dark. Dry storage. Marine hardware. Boat and engine maintenance and repairs. Prop and shaft repair. Do-it-yourself facilities. Dockside Electricity: (3). Manager: Ed Davidson.

HARBOR VILLAGE MARINA, 6155 Northeast 175th St, Seattle, WA 98155. (206) 485 - 7557. All year. Laundry. Waste pumpout. Guest moorage with electricity. Floats. Showers. Harbormaster: Bonita Davis.

LAKEWOOD MOORAGE, 4500 Lake Washington Blvd. S., Box 18403, Seattle, WA 98118. (206) 722-3887. Slips to 60 feet. Guest dock. Marine hardware. Groceries. Beer, wine and snacks. Ice. Picnic area. Owner: Kathie Schober.

LESCHI BOAT SERVICE INC. (at Leschi Yacht Basin. One mile north of Mercer Island Floating Bridge on west shore of Lake Washington), 130 Lakeside, Seattle, WA 98122. (206) 324-4100. Open seven days. Fuel dock: gas and outboard mix, open 9 AM - 5:30 PM. Hoist cap.: 4 tons and 26 feet. Ice. General Manager: John Arrigoni.

MERCER MARINE INC. (at Newport Yacht Basin, on east side of Lake Washington near East Channel Bridge), 3911 Lake Washington Blvd., S.E., Bellevue, WA 98006. (206) 641-2090. Open Monday - Friday 8 AM - 6 PM. Fuel dock: gas only, Mon. - Sat., 9 AM - 5 PM. Hoist cap.: 25 tons and 50 feet. Boat maintenance and repairs. Engine maintenance and repairs. Prop and shaft repairs. Owners: Doug & Margie Burbridge.

NEWPORT YACHT BASIN ASSN. (south of the East Mercer Island Bridge on the east shore of Lake Washington), 3911 Lake Washington Blvd. S.E., Bellevue, WA 98006. (206) 746-7225. Ramp adjacent: 2-lanes, concrete open 24 hours. Hoist cap.: 1½ tons open 9 AM - 7 PM; fall and spring 10 AM - 5 PM. Gas and oil. Slips. Manager: Mary Ann Currie.

SERVICE MARINE INC. (just NE of downtown Kirkland), 11837 N.E. 112th Street, Kirkland, WA 98033. (206) 822-2116. Open daily Monday - Friday 8:30 AM - 6 PM; Saturday 9 AM - 1 PM. Sterndrive and inboard repairs. Engine parts. Mobile dockside service. Marine hardware. Electronic sales and service. Owner: Tim Espeland.

YARROW BAY MARINA (one mile north of Evergreen Bridge), 5207 Lake Washington Blvd. N.E., Kirkland, WA 98033. (206) 822-6066. Open daily 8:30 AM - 6 PM. Hoist cap.: 1½ tons and 32 feet. Fuel dock: gas, diesel and oil. Slips. Dry storage. Boat maintenance and repairs. Engine repairs. Prop and shaft repairs. Do-it-yourself facilities. Owner: Donald Wilcox.

MARINE PARKS

GLEN COULON MEMORIAL PARK (in Renton at S end of Lake Washington), Moorings. Playground, picnic facilities, hiking trails. Swimming beach. Hot showers. Toilets. Concession stands. Boat rentals in summer. Fishing pier.

GOLDEN GARDENS PARK (adjacent to Shilshole Bay Marina) 210 Municipal Bldg., 600 4th Avenue, Seattle, WA 98104. (206) 684-8021. Andy Reynolds. Picnic areas. Ramp. Playground. Public beach. Fishing pier. Toilets.

KIRKLAND PARK (At city of Kirkland, east side of Lake Washington), Recreation slips. Commercial tour dock. Operated by Kirkland Parks Department, (206) 828 - 1213.

LESCHI PARK (west side of Lake Washington, lakeside S. off E. Alder), 210 Municipal Bldg., 600 4th Avenue, Seattle, WA 98104. (206) 684-8021, Andy Reynolds. Moorage. Fishing pier. Operated by Seattle Park Dept.

LUTHER BURBANK PARK (on Northeast shore of Mercer Island in Lake Washington), 2040 84th SE, Mercer Island, WA 98040. (206) 344-4232. Dock and floats. Picnic area. Hiking trails, restrooms. Store nearby. Daytime moorage.

MAGNUSON PARK (west side of Lake Washington at Sand Point), 210 Municipal Bldg., 600 4th Avenue, Seattle, WA 98104. (206) 684-8021, Andy Reynolds. Ramp. dock. Picnic area, playground. Swimming beach, toilets. Moorage limited.

SEWARD PARK (west side of Lake Washington at Andrews Bay), 210 Municipal Bldg., 600 4th Avenue, Seattle, WA 98104. (206) 684-8021, Andy Reynolds. Moorage at Lakewood Boat House. Ramp. Public beach. Picnic areas. Tennis courts. Trails. Restrooms.

STAN SAYRES MEMORIAL PARK (west side of Lake Washington south of the Leschi Park pier, Lake Washington Blvd. S and 46th S), 210 Municipal Bldg., 600 4th Avenue, Seattle, WA 98104. (206) 684-8021, Andy Reynolds. Floats with limited public moorage.

TRACY OWENS STATION PARK (near N end of Lake Washington), 16 acres. Picnic tables. Cooking facilities. Playground. Daytime moorage for small boats. CAUTION: Watch water depths. Fishing.

WASHINGTON STREET MOORAGE (at Pier 49, between the Washington State Ferry Terminal and the Alaskan Ferry Pier), This is a pocket park in downtown Seattle offering 600 feet of dock space with a time limit of 24 hours. Pioneer Square, the Kingdome and downtown Seattle are within walking distance. It is advisable to keep someone aboard for security. There is considerable surge.

AIR TRANSPORTATION
Kenmore Air Harbor: (206) 486-1257
Lake Union Air: (800) 692-2993

CHAMBER OF COMMERCE
Kirkland: (206) 822-7066
Seattle: (206) 447-7200

COAST GUARD
VHF 16
Emergencies: (800) 592-9911
Seattle: (206) 442-7070

DECOMPRESSION CHAMBER
Virginia Mason, Seattle:
(206) 624-1144

FERRY INFORMATION
Alaska: (800) 544-3352
British Columbia: (206) 682-6865
Princess Margerite: (206) 441-5560

MARINE OPERATOR
VHF 25

POISON INFORMATION
(800) 732-6985

POLICE
Seattle Harbor: (206) 583-2179

RED TIDE HOTLINE
(800) 562-5632

SPORTS FISHING HOTLINE
(800) 562-8988

STATE PARK INFORMATION
(800) 562-0990

WEATHER
VHF: WX1
(206) 526-6087

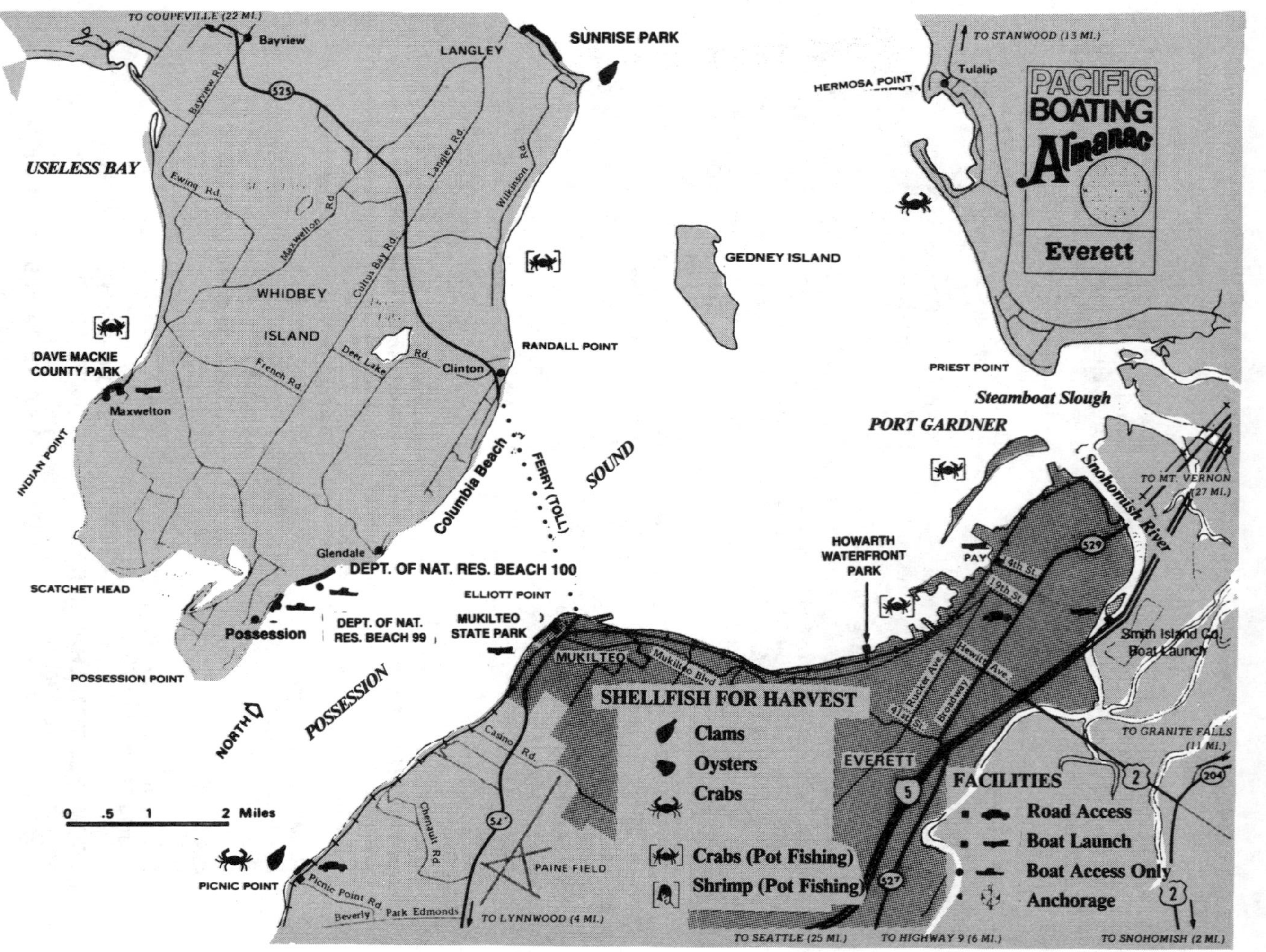

PACIFIC BOATING Almanac
Everett
TO COUPEVILLE (22 MI.)
Bayview
LANGLEY
SUNRISE PARK
TO STANWOOD (13 MI.)
HERMOSA POINT
Tulalip
USELESS BAY
Bayview Rd.
Ewing Rd.
Maxwelton Rd.
Langley Rd.
Wilkinson Rd.
Cultus Bay Rd.
WHIDBEY ISLAND
GEDNEY ISLAND
DAVE MACKIE COUNTY PARK
Maxwelton
French Rd.
Deer Lake
Clinton
RANDALL POINT
PRIEST POINT
Steamboat Slough
PORT GARDNER
Snohomish River
TO MT. VERNON (27 MI.)
INDIAN POINT
Columbia Beach
FERRY (TOLL)
SOUND
HOWARTH WATERFRONT PARK
PAY
4th St.
19th St.
529
Glendale
DEPT. OF NAT. RES. BEACH 100
SCATCHET HEAD
ELLIOTT POINT
Rucker Ave.
Hewitt Ave.
Broadway
Smith Island Co. Boat Launch
Possession
DEPT. OF NAT. RES. BEACH 99
MUKILTEO STATE PARK
MUKILTEO
Mukilteo Blvd
SHELLFISH FOR HARVEST
Clams
Oysters
Crabs
TO GRANITE FALLS (11 MI.)
POSSESSION POINT
NORTH
POSSESSION
Casino Rd.
EVERETT
5
FACILITIES
Road Access
Boat Launch
Boat Access Only
Anchorage
2
204
0 .5 1 2 Miles
Chenault Rd.
PAINE FIELD
Crabs (Pot Fishing)
Shrimp (Pot Fishing)
PICNIC POINT
Picnic Point Rd.
Beverly Park Edmonds
TO LYNNWOOD (4 MI.)
TO SEATTLE (25 MI.)
TO HIGHWAY 9 (6 MI.)
TO SNOHOMISH (2 MI.)
527
194

16

POSSESSION SOUND & EVERETT
(48°00'N., 122°13'W.)

AIR TRANSPORTATION
Kenmore Air Harbor: (206) 486-1257
Lake Union Air: (800) 692-2993

CHAMBER OF COMMERCE
Central Whidbey: (206) 678-5434
Edmonds: (206) 776-6711
Everett: (206) 252-5181
Freeland: (206) 321-4838
Langley: (206) 321-6765
North Whidbey: (206) 675-3535

COAST GUARD
VHF 16 or 22
Emergencies: (800) 592-9911
Snohomish County: (206) 252-5281
Seattle: (206) 442-7070

DECOMPRESSION CHAMBER
Virginia Mason, Seattle:
(206) 624-1144

FERRY TRANSPORTATION
Washington State: (800) 542-0812

FISHING INFORMATION
(206) 753-6600

MARINE OPERATOR
Bellingham: VHF 28, 85
Everett: VHF 24
Seattle: VHF 25

POISON INFORMATION
(800) 732-6985

RED TIDE HOTLINE
(800) 562-5632

STATE PARK INFORMATION
(800) 562-0990

CHART 18441 † POSSESSION SOUND joins Puget Sound at the S point of Whidbey Island and extends in a general N direction for 10 miles to its junction with Saratoga Passage and Port Susan. From the entrance it extends for 3.5 miles with an average width of 2 miles, and then expands into an irregular basin about 6 miles in diameter. (See the beginning of chapter 6 for regulations governing vessels transiting gill net fishing areas.)

The E part of this basin is filled with extensive flats, many of which uncover and rise abruptly from deep water. These flats are intersected by several shifting channels, forming the mouth of the Snohomish River. The waters of the sound are generally deep, and the only anchorage used by large vessels is off the town of Everett, close inshore, in 10 to 15 fathoms.

MEADOWDALE, a residential area on Browns Bay, is on the E side of the sound about 4 miles S of Possession Point. There is a large fishing wharf here with a hoist that can handle craft to 21 feet. Several floats are available during the summer months; gasoline, covered storage for about 40 craft and a restaurant are also available. Reported depths of 5 feet can be carried to the hoist at the end of the wharf.

GLENDALE is a village on the W side of the sound 2.2 miles N of Possession Point. A resort here, open during the summer months, has gasoline, water and ice. There is a marine railway here for launching small craft.

CHART 18443 † ELLIOT POINT, on the E side of Possession Sound 4 miles NE of Possession Point, is a low spit projecting some 200 yards from the high land. MUKILTEO LIGHT (47°56.9'N., 122°18.3'W), 33 feet above the water, is shown from a 30-foot white octagonal tower on the point; a fog signal is at the station.

MUKILTEO, (47°57'N., 122°18'W.) is a town E of Elliot Point. An automobile ferry runs between Mukilteo and Clinton on Whidbey Island. A light about 300 yards NNE of Mukilteo Light marks the approach to the ferry dock. A Government wharf for deep-draft vessels is at the Air Force fuel storage station 0.4 mile E of Mukilteo Light. The 10 tanks approximately in a line parallel to the beach are conspicuous.

There are several small-craft facilities at Mukilteo. Gasoline, water and a launching ramp are available. Limited outboard engine repairs can be made.

GEDNEY ISLAND, 3.5 miles N of Elliot Point is about 1.5 miles long in an E direction, high, wooded and prominent. From its E point a shoal extends E, the 5-fathom curve being at a distance of 0.8 mile. Foul ground extends 0.2 mile from the S side of the E half of the island. A buoy is on the N side of the shoal area. A fish haven, marked by private buoys, is about 0.5 mile S of Gedney Island in a bout 47°59'48"N., 122°18'30"W. A marina protected by a breakwater is on the NE side of the island. The breakwater is marked by a private light.

CLINTON, a village on RANDALL POINT, is the Whidbey Island terminus of the ferry from Mukilteo. The town has several stores; a restaurant is near the ferry slip. Gasoline is available.

CHART 18444 † EVERETT 48°00'N., 122°13'W., an important wood products shipping port is on the E side of Port Gardner, 4 miles NE of Elliot Point. The several tall pulpmill chimneys and the Port of Everett's large aluminum silo are prominent along the water.

CHANNELS † Depths of 22 feet or more are available to the main wharves in Port Gardner. A dredged channel with two settling basins extends inside a training dike and in the Snohomish River around the N half of the city to a lumbermill 6 miles above Port Gardner. The channel is marked by lights, buoys and lighted and unlighted ranges. In May - June 1985, the controlling depths were 15 feet to the first settling basin, with 9 to 16 feet in the middle of the basin, then 5 feet (6 feet at midchannel) to a point opposite 19th Street and NW end of the second settling basin (depths in the second settling basin are subject to continual change), then 2 feet for a midwidth of 75 feet from the second settling basin to a point opposite the lumbermill.

TIDES † The mean range of the tide at Everett is about 7.4 feet, and the diurnal range of the tide is 11.1 feet.

EVERETT YACHT HARBOR, oper-ated by the Port of Everett, is about a mile above the mouth of and on the E side of the Snohomish River Channel. The entrance to the harbor from the river channel is marked by two lighted markers. There are berths for more than 800 small-craft; transient mooring floats are maintained for visiting boats. A boatyard is on the E side of the harbor. A HARBORMASTER, whose office is on the N side of the harbor, assigns all berths. A Coast Guard vessel is berthed in the harbor.

SNOHOMISH RIVER, once heavily traveled by the light-draft river steamers and loggers, flows down through the dredged channel and settling basin near the yacht harbor and empties into Port Gardner just W of East Waterway. Traffic on the river above the the yacht harbor consists of log tows, tugs and barges and pleasure boats. Several pulp, plywood and lumber mills are along the river.

The Snohomish River is crossed by a railroad swing bridge with a least clearance of 9 feet about 0.6 mile E of Preston Point. U.S. Highway 529 crosses the river just above the railroad bridge and has a lift bridge with a least clearance of 38 feet. Interstate 5 crosses the river about 1.6 miles above the U.S. Highway 529 bridge; this fixed bridge has a clearance of 66 feet. The practical limit of navigation on the Snohomish River is 0.8 mile above the Interstate 5 highway bridge.

CHART 18443 † The flats N of Everett at the mouths of STEAMBOAT SLOUGH and EBEY SLOUGH are used for log storage. Steamboat Slough is crossed by a fixed bridge with a clearance of 41 feet and by three swing bridges with a least swing of 7 feet. Ebey Slough is crossed by two fixed bridges and two swing bridges. Clearances on the fixed bridges are 41 feet; clearances on the swing bridges are 5 feet. Overhead power cables with a least clearance of 53 feet cross Steamboat Slough. Navigation across the shallow flats should not be attempted without local knowledge. Local small-craft navigate Ebey Slough to MARYSVILLE. A marina and boatyard are just E of the railroad bridge in the town. Moorage is available and gasoline and diesel fuel are pumped. A marine railway can handle craft to 40 feet for hull and engine repairs. There is a public launching ramp just W of the Interstate 5 highway bridge at Marysville.

SANDY POINT, the S point at the entrance to Saratoga Passage is a low spit rising abruptly to 100 feet, with bluffs on each side; it is marked by a light.

CAMANO HEAD, 1.5 miles NNE of Sandy Point, is the SE point of Camano Island. A shoal, with a rock bare at low tide, extends nearly 0.2 mile SE from the point and is marked by a buoy.

TULALIP BAY, 4 miles NW of Everett, is a small cove on the mainland. On the N side are the village of Tulalip and the agency buildings of the Tulalip Indian Reservation. The bay is shoal, with rocks extending more than 300 yards S and W from the point on the N side of the entrance. A buoy marks the edge of the shoal water W of the point at the S side of the entrance. Several small wharves and landing floats, mostly dry at low water, are at Tulalip; however, it has no public facilities and log-booming grounds in the S of the bay. Mission Beach, immediately S of the bay, has several private boathouses and float landings.

-U.S. COAST PILOT 7
25th edition. August 1989
Corrected thru 10/22/90
Local Notice to Mariners

FACILITIES

MUKILTEO

MC CONNELL'S BOAT HOUSE, 718 Front St, Mukilteo, WA 98275. (206) 335 - 3411. Open March - Nov. Charts. Groceries. Ice. Snack bar. Dockside electricity. Dry land moorings. Private boat storage. Rental rowboats, skiffs and outboard motors. Fuel: gas and mix. Fishing: licenses, bait and tackle. Owner: George McConnell.

EVERETT

Everett † home of the second largest marina on the West Coast, is justifiably proud of its facilities. In addition to the Everett Marina Village, the marina has a full complement of marine-related businesses, including yacht brokerages, marine supplies, boat and engine repair, time share, canvas makers, fishing and pleasure charters, riverboat cruises with sea lion watches, and much more.

ACTION COMMUNICATIONS, 1402 W. Marine View Drive, Everett, WA 98201. (206) 259-9122. Loran, radar, marine radio sales and service. Richard Anderson.

CANVAS CRAFT, 1001½ - 14th Street, Everett, WA 98201. (206) 252 - 1069. Marine & industrial fabric application.

THE CORNER BOAT SHOP, 1402 West Marine View Drive, Everett, WA 98201, (206) 258 - 6700. Repairs. Retail & wholesale. Brad Tinius.

CROW'S NEST (near the Yacht Club), 14th Street Yacht Basin, Everett, WA 98201. (206) 258-9202. Marine hardware. Rigging. Charts and clothing. Safety equipment.

DAGMAR'S MARINA (north of Everett on the Snohomish River), 1871 Ross Avenue, Marysville, WA 98270. (206) 259-6124. Dry land marina. Open and covered moorage. Haulouts to 20 tons. Mechanical repairs. Canvas repairs. Bait and ice.

EVERETT BOAT HOUSE AND MARINA, 14th Street Yacht Basin, Everett, WA 98201. (206) 259-6053. Marine hardware. Engine Sales. Dry storage. Owner: Jim LaLone.

FISHERMAN'S BOAT SHOP, INC., 1016 - 14th Street, Everett, WA 98201. (206) 259 - 0137. Hoist cap.: 20 tons. Marine ways cap.: 300 tons. Dry storage. Machine shop. Wood and steel hull maintenance and repairs. Prop and shaft repairs. Dockside unlimited length. Manager: Richard Eitel.

GEDDES MARINA, 1326 First Street, Marysville, WA 98270. (206) 659 - 2575. All year. 2 marine railways cap.: to 42 feet. Tidal grid. Travelift cap.: to 40 feet; hoist cap.: to 25 feet. Slips. Dry storage. Boat maintenance and repairs. Boat and motor sales. Prop and shaft repair. Owner: William M. Geddes.

HARBOR MARINE, 1402 W. Marine View Drive, Everett, WA 98201. (206) 259-3285. Marine hardware, fiberglass repair and supply. Pressure washing and button.

McCONNELL'S BOAT HOUSE (adjacent Whidbey Island ferry terminal), 718 Front Street, Box 675, Mukilteo, WA 98275. (206) 355 - 3411. Open Feb. 25 - Oct. 31. Mukilteo State Park ramp nearby: 3 - lanes, concrete. Open 6 AM - 10 PM. Fuel dock: gas and outboard mix. Open during summer: 4:30 AM - 6 PM. Dry storage. Groceries. Ice. Fishing: bait and tackle. Rental boats, motors, tackle. Owner: George E. McConnell, Jr.

MEB MANUFACTURING CO. (1 block east of freeway), 3410 Everett AVenue, EVerett, Wa 98201. (206) 259 - 6074. Precision machining, fabrication. Welding and marine repairs. Prop and shaft repairs. Machine shop. Owners: Hank Johnson.

PERFORMANCE MARINE (next to Everett Public Launch), 930 W. Marineview Drive, Everett, WA 98201. (206) 258 - 9292. Open Mon. - Fri. 8:30 AM - 5 PM. Saturdays 9 AM -

12 PM. Inboard, outboard and sterndrive sales and service. Owners: Bill and Rick Hook.

PORT OF EVERETT MARINA, 1720 W Marine View Dr, Everett, WA 98201. (206) 259 - 6001. Ramp: 13-lanes, concrete. Hoist cap.: 5 tons, 27 feet. Two travelifts cap.: 30 and 35 tons. Fuel dock open 8 AM - 5 PM. Summer: 7AM - 7PM. Gas, diesel and outboard mix. Open and covered berths. Guest dock with electricity. Pumpout station. Marina Administrator: Connie Bennett.

SEACREST BOAT MOORAGE, 4020 Old Hwy. 99, Marysville, WA 98270. (206) 252 - 4823. All year. Open daily. Moorings. Haulouts to 38 feet. Boat and engine maintenance and repair. Do-it-yourself facilities. Manager: Archie Olson.

YACHTS WEST (at Everett Marina), 811 14th Street, Everett, WA 98201. (206) 259-3157. Hoist cap.: to 20 tons and 40 feet. Full service yard. Hull and engine maintenance, repairs and tune ups. Dry storage. New and used boat sales. Restaurants (4). Barber shop. Snack bar. Tackle and marine shop. Owners: Rick Gordon and Paul L. Dukich.

MARINE PARKS

MUKILTEO STATE PARK (at Elliot Point, Mukilteo, south of the ferry dock), 14 acre shoreline park. Mooring buoys. Picnic area. Ramp. Public beach, toilets.

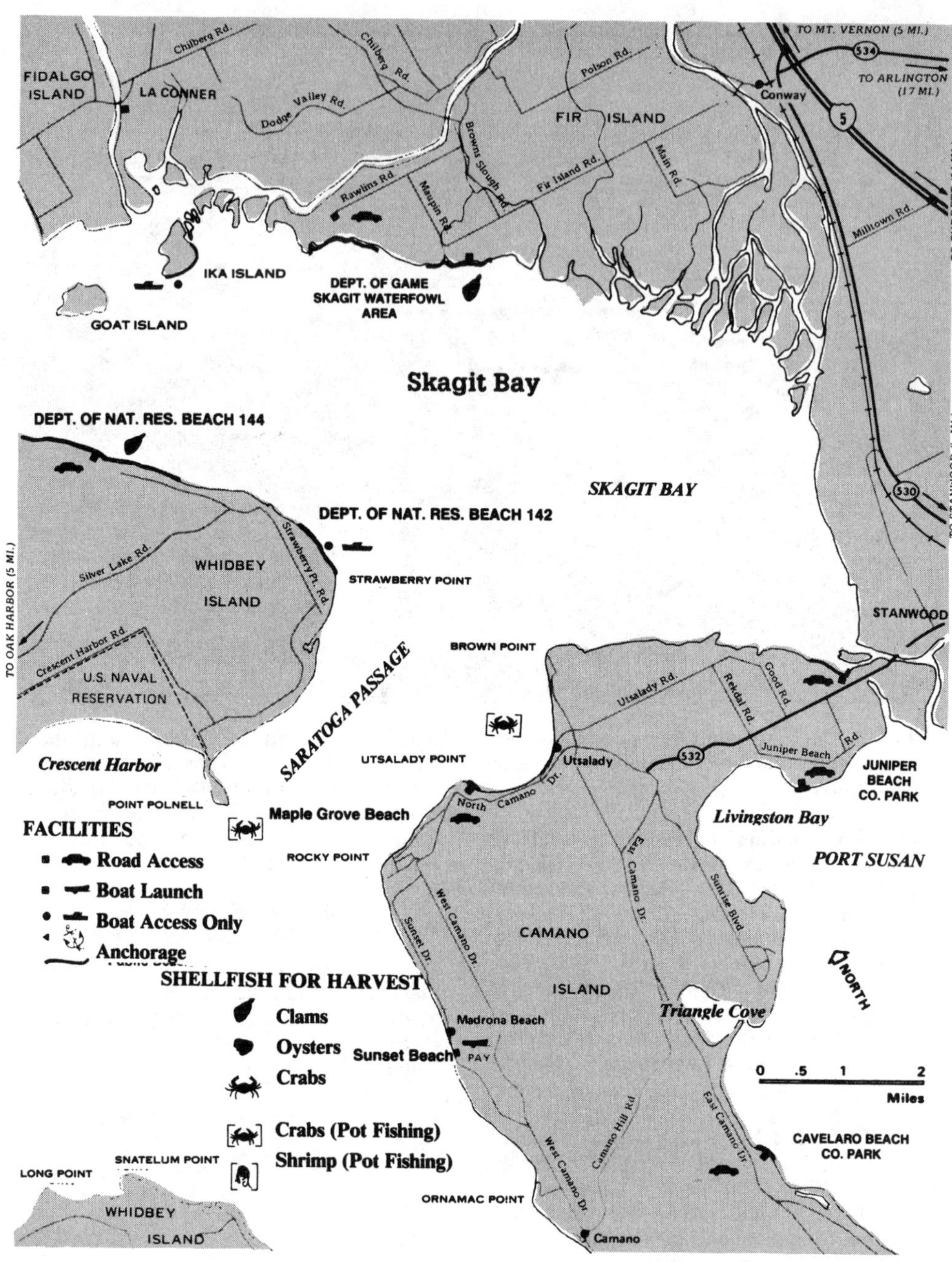

FACILITIES

- Road Access
- Boat Launch
- Boat Access Only
- Anchorage

SHELLFISH FOR HARVEST

- Clams
- Oysters
- Crabs
- Crabs (Pot Fishing)
- Shrimp (Pot Fishing)

17
CAMANO & WHIDBEY ISLANDS / DECEPTION PASS

AIR TRANSPORTATION
Kenmore Air Harbor: (206) 486-1257
Lake Union Air: (800) 692-2993

BUS TRANSPORTATION
Edmonds: (206) 778-2185
Everett/Mukilteo: (206) 259-8898
Greyhound: (206) 259-7294
Trailways: (800) 524-4411

CHAMBER OF COMMERCE
Central Whidbey: (206) 678-5434
Edmonds: (206) 776-6711
Everett: (206) 252-5181
Freeland: (206) 321-4838
Langley: (206) 321-6765
North Whidbey: (206) 675-3535

COAST GUARD
VHF 16 or 22
Emergencies: (800) 592-9911
Snohomish County: (206) 252-5281
Seattle: (206) 442-7070

DECOMPRESSION CHAMBER
Virginia Mason, Seattle:
(206) 624-1144

FERRY TRANSPORTATION
Washington State: (800) 542-0812

FISHING INFORMATION
(206) 753-6600

MARINE OPERATOR
Bellingham: VHF 28, 85
Everett: VHF 24
Seattle: VHF 25

POISON INFORMATION
(800) 732-6985

RED TIDE HOTLINE
(800) 562-5632

STATE PARK INFORMATION
(800) 562-0990

CHART 18441 † CAMANO ISLAND extends between Port Susan and Saratoga Passage. It is irregular in shape and 14 miles in length; the S portion consists of a long, narrow tongue that terminates in Camano Head, 340 feet high. At its N end it is separated from the mainland by DAVIS SLOUGH and South Pass and West Pass of the Stillaguamish River, all dry at low water. On the shores of the island are several resorts and unincorporated residential tracts.

PORT SUSAN, on the E side of Camano Island, extends about 11 miles in a NW direction, termination in flats which bare and extend over 3 miles wide at its head. There are several resort settlements. Deep water is throughout until nearing the head, where anchorage may be had off the extreme W edge of the flats in about 10 fathoms. Care should be used in approaching and anchoring, as the flats rise abruptly from deep water. A mussel raft marked by a private light, is in the N part in about 48°10'20"N., 122°26'30"W.

STANWOOD is in a dairy and farming district on the N side of the STILLAGUAMISH RIVER at the junction of SOUTH PASS and WEST PASS.

SARATOGA PASSAGE, on the W side of Camano Island, extends some 18 miles in a NW direction from its entrance between Sandy Point and Camano Head. At its N end it connects with Penn Cove and Crescent Harbor, and leads E into Skagit Bay. Depths in the passage are from 100 fathoms at the entrance to 15 fathoms at the Crescent Harbor entrance. There are few outlying dangers, and a midchannel course is clear.

There is considerable traffic in these waters, mostly pleasure and fishing craft with occasional tugs bound to or from Deception Pass. This is a resort area, along the shores of the islands are several small marinas which provide gasoline, limited berths, launching ramps, and lodgings. Principal commercial products are lumber and fish.

LANGLEY is a small town on Whidbey Island about 1.2 miles W of Sandy Point. Tugs often anchor off the beach between Langley and Sandy Point.

EAST POINT, 6 miles NW of Sandy Point, is a low sandspit about 300 yards long. It is marked by a light.

ELGER BAY, on the W shore of Camano Island across Saratoga Passage from East Point, is an open bight 1 mile wide. Tugs anchor here in W and NW winds.

HOLMES HARBOR, entered 8 miles NW of Sandy Point, indents Whidbey Island 5 miles in a S direction. Except for a sand and gravel wharf and a large private boathouse at the head of the harbor, only private pleasure piers are on the shores of Holmes Harbor. Depths range from 30 to 40 fathoms off the entrance to 17 fathoms near the head where good anchorage, except from N weather, may be had in mud bottom. A GENERAL ANCHORAGE is in Holmes Harbor. ROCKY POINT, at the E side of the entrance, is low but rises abruptly to 500 feet. BABY ISLAND is a small islet 0.2 mile off the point. Shoals, marked by a buoy extend NW from the island.

GREENBANK, a small farming settlement, is on the W side of Holmes Harbor at the entrance. It has a store and service station. Anchorage against W weather is available off Greenbank in 12 to 18 fathoms, muddy bottom. FREELAND, the business center for this area, is a small town at the head of Holmes Harbor.

CAMANO, a settlement on the E side of Saratoga Passage, is 3.5 miles NW of LOWELL POINT. A light is on ONAMAC POINT, 0.8 mile N of Camano. Private buoys mark a fish haven off the point. At Madrona Beach, about 2 miles N of Onamac Point, there are two summer resorts at which gasoline is available. Both have marine railways that can handle craft to 20 feet.

PENN COVE indents the W shore of the basin at the head of Saratoga Passage and extends W for about 3.5 miles. In mostweather, the cove affords good protection in 5 to 15 fathoms, good holding ground.

Off SNATELUM POINT, the S point at the entrance to Penn Cove, is a narrow spit extending N 0.5 mile, with $\frac{1}{2}$ fathom near its end. The spit is marked by a buoy.

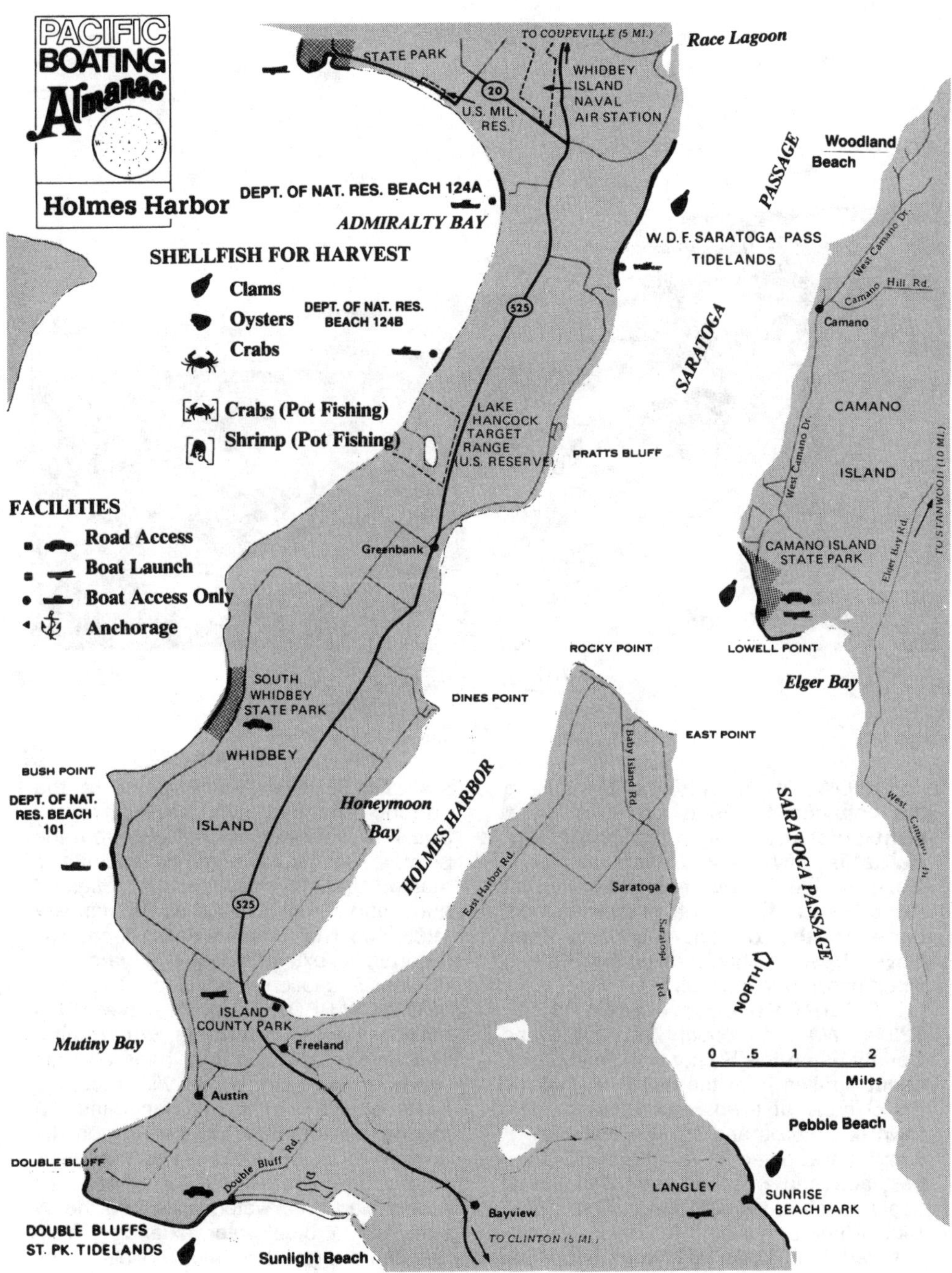
PACIFIC BOATING Almanac
Holmes Harbor
SHELLFISH FOR HARVEST
Clams
Oysters
Crabs
Crabs (Pot Fishing)
Shrimp (Pot Fishing)
FACILITIES
Road Access
Boat Launch
Boat Access Only
Anchorage
STATE PARK
TO COUPEVILLE (5 MI.)
Race Lagoon
20
U.S. MIL. RES.
WHIDBEY ISLAND NAVAL AIR STATION
PASSAGE
Woodland Beach
DEPT. OF NAT. RES. BEACH 124A
ADMIRALTY BAY
W. D. F. SARATOGA PASS TIDELANDS
West Camano Dr.
Camano Hill Rd.
Camano
525
DEPT. OF NAT. RES. BEACH 124B
SARATOGA
CAMANO ISLAND
TO STANWOOD (10 MI.)
LAKE HANCOCK TARGET RANGE (U.S. RESERVE)
PRATTS BLUFF
West Camano Dr.
CAMANO ISLAND STATE PARK
Elger Bay Rd.
Greenbank
ROCKY POINT
LOWELL POINT
Elger Bay
SOUTH WHIDBEY STATE PARK
DINES POINT
EAST POINT
Baby Island Rd.
West Camano Dr.
WHIDBEY
BUSH POINT
DEPT. OF NAT. RES. BEACH 101
ISLAND
Honeymoon Bay
HOLMES HARBOR
SARATOGA PASSAGE
East Harbor Rd.
Saratoga Rd.
Saratoga
525
NORTH
0 .5 1 2
Miles
ISLAND COUNTY PARK
Mutiny Bay
Freeland
Pebble Beach
Austin
DOUBLE BLUFF
Double Bluff Rd.
LANGLEY
SUNRISE BEACH PARK
DOUBLE BLUFFS ST. PK. TIDELANDS
Bayview
TO CLINTON (5 MI.)
Sunlight Beach

COUPEVILLE WHARF

BLOWERS BLUFF, the N point at the entrance to Penn Cove, is bare, light-colored, high and rounding. Rocks lie offshore 200 yards at places along the bluff. The shoal extending off the SW end of the bluff reaches almost one-third the distance across Penn Cove. Vessels should favor the S shore when passing this shoal.

COUPEVILLE, (48°14'N., 122°41'W.) the county seat of Island County, is on the S shore of Penn Cove, about 2 miles from the head. A tank on the S edge of town is prominent. The town has stores and service stations. A wharf here extends to about 12 feet; berthage and gasoline are available at floats attached to the E side of the wharf. Diesel fuel is available by truck. A rock covered 15 is about 300 yards NE of the wharf.

CHART 18428 † OAK HARBOR, which indents the N shore of Saratoga Passage W of Crescent Harbor, is a semicircular cove about 1 mile in diameter with depths of 20 to 9 feet.

MAYLOR POINT, the E point of the entrance, is foul with several rocks, awash at low water, 0.5 mile SE from the point. The natural entrance channel is marked by lights, daybeacons, a lighted buoy, and an unlighted buoy. In January 1985, shoaling to an unknown depth was reported to extend about 200 yards NE of Light 5; caution is advised. The town of OAK HARBOR on the N shore of the harbor serves a farming community. The long wharf here is in ruins and not used; however, small pier with moorage floats is just E of the pier in ruins. A marina, operated by the town, is on the E side of Oak Harbor. The marina is entered through the SW corner between a detached breakwater protecting the W side and a breakwater extending from the shore protecting the S side. The detached breakwater is marked by lights at both ends and a light at the outer end. A light is also at the end of the L-shaped pier just inside the entrance to the marina. Berthing, electricity, gasoline, diesel fuel, water, some marine supplies and a lift up to 4 tons are

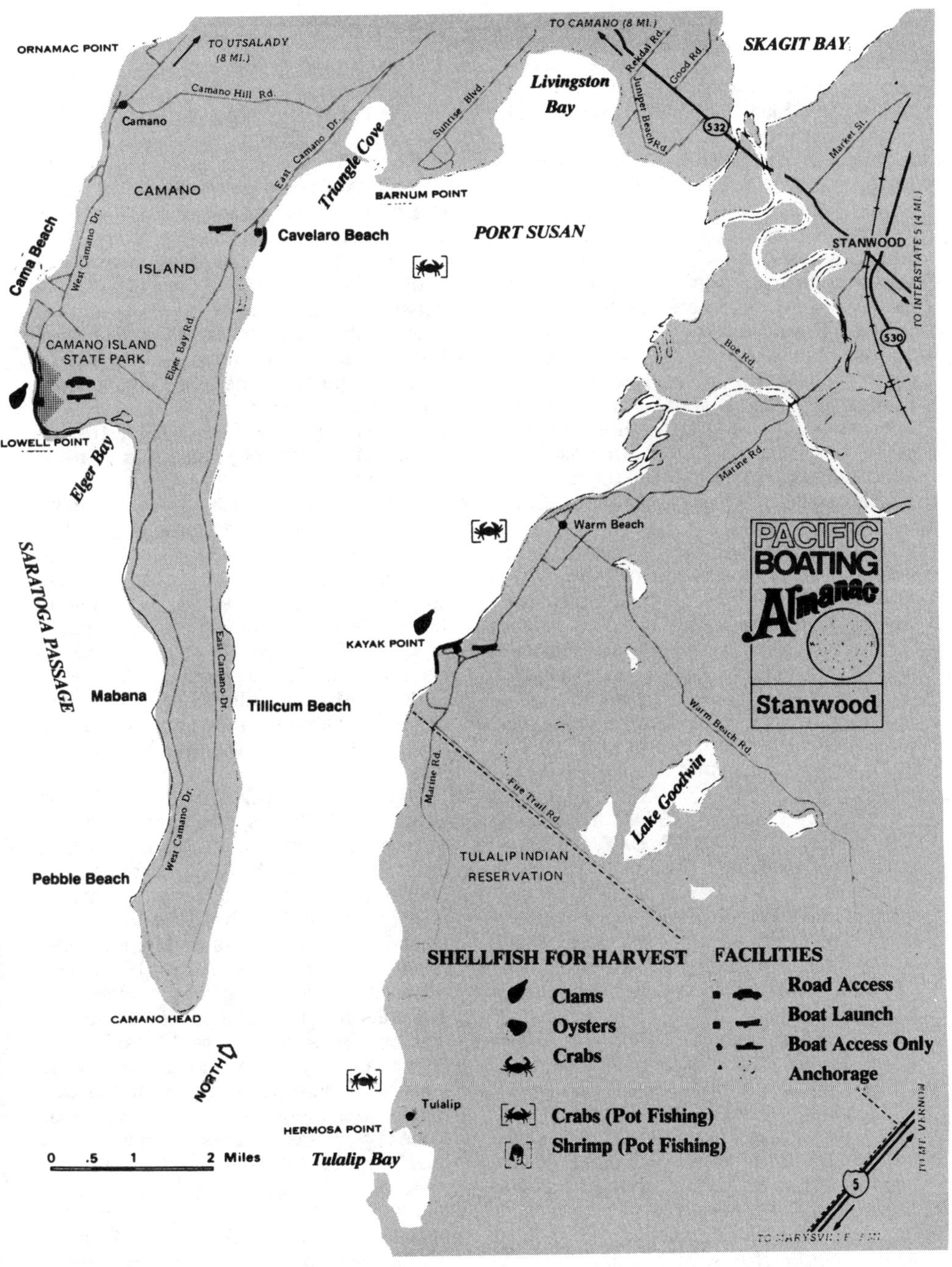
Camano and Whidbey Islands / Deception Pass
ORNAMAC POINT
TO UTSALADY (8 MI.)
TO CAMANO (8 MI.)
SKAGIT BAY
Camano Hill Rd.
Reddal Rd.
Good Rd.
Juniper Beach Rd.
Livingston Bay
Sunrise Blvd.
532
Market St.
Camano
East Camano Dr.
Triangle Cove
CAMANO
BARNUM POINT
STANWOOD
West Camano Dr.
Cama Beach
ISLAND
Cavelaro Beach
PORT SUSAN
TO INTERSTATE 5 (4 MI.)
530
Elger Bay Rd.
Boe Rd.
CAMANO ISLAND STATE PARK
LOWELL POINT
Elger Bay
Marine Rd.
SARATOGA PASSAGE
Warm Beach
PACIFIC BOATING Almanac
Mabana
East Camano Dr.
KAYAK POINT
Tillicum Beach
Warm Beach Rd.
Stanwood
Lake Goodwin
Marine Rd.
Fire Trail Rd.
West Camano Dr.
Pebble Beach
TULALIP INDIAN RESERVATION
CAMANO HEAD
SHELLFISH FOR HARVEST
FACILITIES
NORTH
Clams
Road Access
Oysters
Boat Launch
Crabs
Boat Access Only
Anchorage
Crabs (Pot Fishing)
Shrimp (Pot Fishing)
Tulalip
TO MT. VERNON
HERMOSA POINT
0 .5 1 2 Miles
Tulalip Bay
5
TO MARYSVILLE (7 MI.)

available. Hull, engine and electronic repairs can be made.

CRESCENT HARBOR, immediately E of Oak Harbor, is a semicircular bight 2 miles in diameter between FORBES POINT and POLNELL POINT. Polnell Point, marked by a light, is wooded and rather bold, and connected to the main island by low ground, giving the point the appearance of an island from a distance off. A shoal extends about 0.9 mile W of Polnell Point; another shoal extends about 0.2 mile S from this point. Shoals extend about 0.7 mile S and E from Forbes Point; the S shoal is marked by a lighted buoy. Foul ground surrounds this point, but otherwise the harbor is clear affording anchorage in 10 to 11 fathoms, muddy bottom. The harbor is exposed to the S. The large pier of the U.S. Naval Air Station Whidbey Island, extends from the W side of the harbor. Depths of 26 feet are alongside the outer two-thirds of the pier. This pier can be used only with permission. Services and/or provisions cannot be provided and ships' own power must be relied upon. A 183-foot T-pier used for fueling Naval vessels is on the N side of the main pier near the shoreward end.

CHARTS 18421, 18441, 18400 †
The entrance to SKAGIT BAY, southern part, lies between Polnell Point and Rocky Point. The bay is about 12 miles long in a WNW direction. The greater portion of it is filled with flats, bare at low water, and intersected by numerous channels discharging the waters of Skagit River.

A natural channel varying in width from 0.2 to 0.6 mile and marked by lights and buoys follows the E shoreline of Whidbey Island to the N end of the bay. Shoal water extends off for some 100 to 300 yards from the E shore of the island. The N part of Skagit Bay is described in chapter 18.

The controlling elevation of the flats at the mouth of South Fork is about 2.5 feet above mean lower low water, and the controlling depth at low tide depends on the river stage, probably not exceeding 1 foot during periods of minimum flow. The diurnal range at the mouth of the river is 11.3 feet. The

extreme range at this point is estimated to be 20 feet.

A fixed highway bridge with a clearance of 10 feet crosses the S Fork at CONWAY, 4.8 miles above the mouth.

UTSALADY, a small village on the N shore of Camano Island about 1.2 miles E of Rocky Point, has a store and service station. Vessels may anchor just E of UTSALADY POINT in a small inlet between shoal water of the flats and the shore in 3 to 6 fathoms, muddy bottom, with shelter from S winds. In the 1860's Utsalady became the first shipbuilding port in Puget Sound.

STRAWBERRY POINT, the E extremity of Whidbey Island, is marked by a light.

The SOUTH FORK channel leading into Skagit River winds through the flats N of Camano Island. Because of shoaling however, the channel has largely been abandoned by boat traffic to Mount Vernon except for local outboard boats; NORTH FORK is used instead. In December 1971, the mouth of the North Fork bared 2 feet at MLLW. There are several small-boat moorings along the banks of the river at MOUNT VERNON.

CHARTS 18427, 18429, 18421 †
DECEPTION PASS, the impressive 2-mile passage between Whidbey Island and FIDALGO ISLAND, provides a challenging route that connects the N end of Skagit Bay with the S end of Rosario Strait. Near its middle the width is reduced to 200 yards by PASS ISLAND. A fixed highway bridge over the pass has a clearance of 144 feet at the center and 104 feet elsewhere. Overhead teleiphone and power cables 100 yards and 0.2 mile E of the bridge have a minimum clearance of 150 feet. Deception Pass is used frequently by local boats bound from Seattle to Anacortes, Bellingham, and the San Juan Islands. The pass should be negotiated at the time of slack, since the velocity of the stream at other times makes it prohibitive to some craft. However, many fast boats run it at all stages of the tide. The pass is also used by log tows from the N bound to Everett or Seattle, which prefer this route to avoid the rough weather W of Whidbey Island.

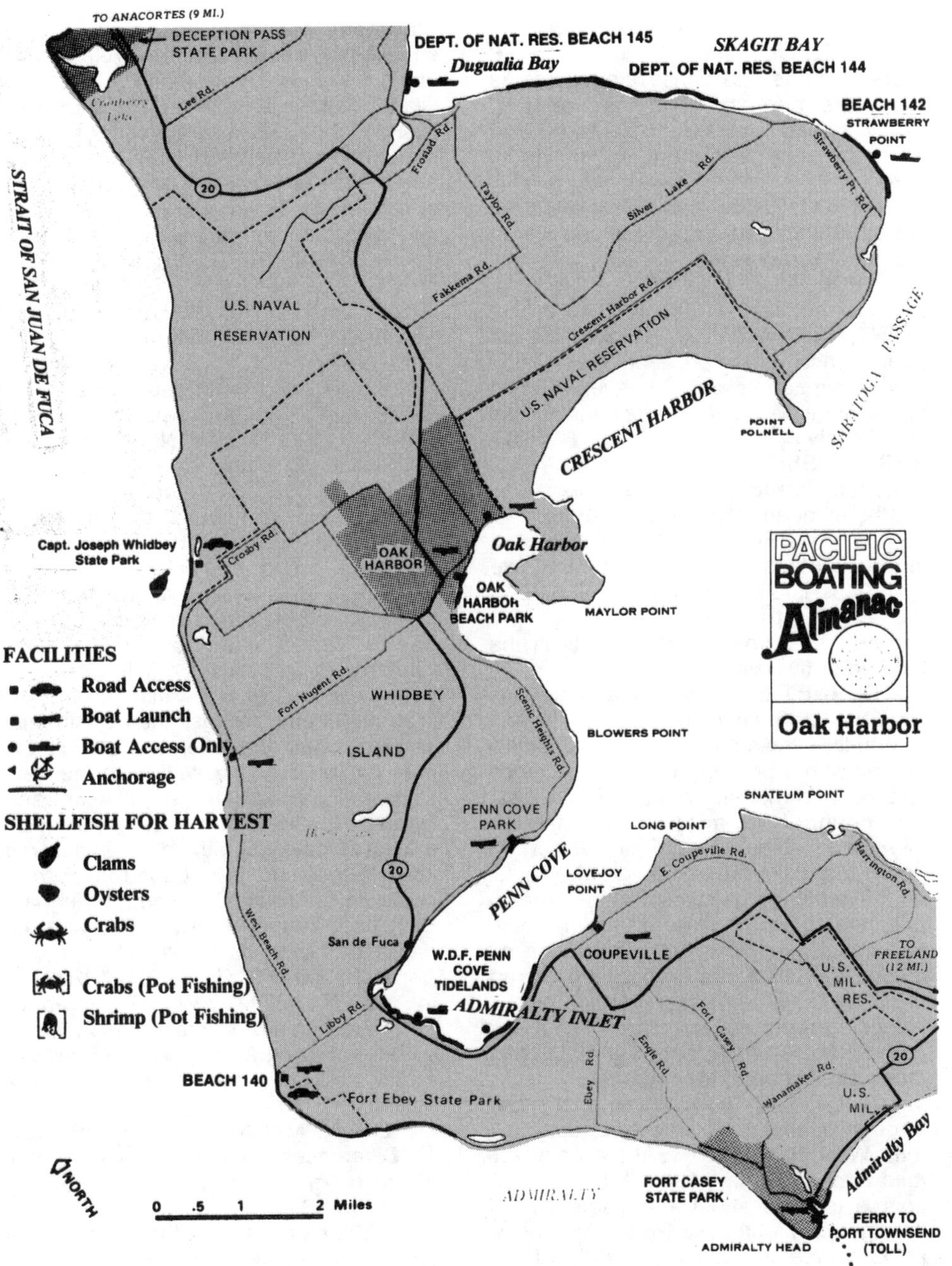
TO ANACORTES (9 MI.)
DECEPTION PASS STATE PARK
DEPT. OF NAT. RES. BEACH 145
Dugualia Bay
SKAGIT BAY
DEPT. OF NAT. RES. BEACH 144
BEACH 142
STRAWBERRY POINT
Cranberry Lake
Lee Rd.
Frosad Rd.
Taylor Rd.
Silver Lake Rd.
Strawberry Pt. Rd.
STRAIT OF SAN JUAN DE FUCA
U.S. NAVAL RESERVATION
Fakkema Rd.
Crescent Harbor Rd.
U.S. NAVAL RESERVATION
SARATOGA PASSAGE
CRESCENT HARBOR
POINT POLNELL
Capt. Joseph Whidbey State Park
Crosby Rd.
OAK HARBOR
Oak Harbor
OAK HARBOR BEACH PARK
MAYLOR POINT
PACIFIC BOATING Almanac
Oak Harbor
FACILITIES
Road Access
Boat Launch
Boat Access Only
Anchorage
Fort Nugent Rd.
WHIDBEY ISLAND
Scenic Heights Rd.
BLOWERS POINT
SNATEUM POINT
SHELLFISH FOR HARVEST
Clams
Oysters
Crabs
Crabs (Pot Fishing)
Shrimp (Pot Fishing)
PENN COVE PARK
LONG POINT
E. Coupeville Rd.
Harrington Rd.
PENN COVE
LOVEJOY POINT
West Beach Rd.
San de Fuca
W.D.F. PENN COVE TIDELANDS
COUPEVILLE
U.S. MIL. RES.
TO FREELAND (12 MI.)
ADMIRALTY INLET
Fort Casey Rd.
Libby Rd.
Ebey Rd.
Engle Rd.
Wanamaker Rd.
U.S. MIL.
BEACH 140
Fort Ebey State Park
NORTH
0   .5   1   2 Miles
ADMIRALTY
FORT CASEY STATE PARK
Admiralty Bay
ADMIRALTY HEAD
FERRY TO PORT TOWNSEND (TOLL)

Currents in the narrows of Deception Pass attain velocities in excess of 8 knots at times and cause strong eddies along the shores. With W weather, heavy swells and tide rips form and make passage dangerous to all small-craft.

CANOE PASS, N of Pass Island, is not recommended except for small craft with local knowledge.

DECEPTION ISLAND, 1 mile W of Pass Island, is 0.4 mile NW of WEST POINT, the NW end of Whidbey Island. Foul ground exists between West Point and Deception Island. Vessels should not attempt to pass between them, and should always stay in NORTHWEST PASS. Shoals also extend N of Deception Island with depths of less than 2 fathoms nearly 200 yards offshore.

STRAWBERRY ISLAND lies almost in the middle of Deception Pass, 0.4 mile E of Pass Island. BEN URE ISLAND is 0.2 S of Strawberry Island at the entrance to Cornet Bay; a light is at the NE end of the island.

CORNET BAY, shallow and suitable for small-craft only, indents the N end of Whidbey Island, in Deception Pass. A marina with a privately dredged entrance channel and mooring basin is in the bay; the channel is marked by private daymarks. The marina has about 85 open and covered berths at the floats, and electricity, gasoline, water, diesel fuel, ice, launching ramp, 4-ton hoist, and marine supplies; hull repairs can be made. A State maintained small-craft facility is E of the marina; berthing and a launching ramp are available. Overhead power cables with clearance of 56 feet cross the W end of the bay.

ROUTES † from W the best water through Deception Pass will be found 0.3 mile W of ROSARIO HEAD, a point 0.5 mile N of Deception Island. Steer a SE course to pass about 100 yards SW of the light on Lighthouse Point; then follow an E course through the middle of the pass, being careful to guard against sets from the current when running partly across it. After passing under the bridge, favor slightly the N shore so as to avoid the pinnacle rocks and ledges making out from the S shore. After leaving Pass Island, steer to pass about midway between Ben Ure and Strawberry Islands. Strawberry Island should not be approached within 125 yards because a reef extends S of the island. From a position off Ben Ure Island Light 2, steer a NE course to pass about midway between HOYPUS POINT and YOKEKO POINT. The flood current N and W of Strawberry Island sets NE and should be guarded against.

BOWMAN (RESERVATION) BAY, a small bight between RESERVATION HEAD and Rosario Head, offers anchorage for small craft in $2\frac{1}{4}$ fathoms, mud bottom. NORTH WEST ISLAND between Rosario Head and Sares Head, is 28 feet high and grass-covered. SARES HEAD, 1 mile N of Deception Island is steep to and 480 feet high.

BURROWS BAY indents the W shore of Fidalgo Island between BIZ POINT and FIDALGO HEAD. Burrows Bay is a broad open bight affording anchorage in the N part, in 15 to 16 fathoms, soft bottom. Protection from W and N is afforded by BURROWS ISLAND and ALLAN ISLAND, but the bay is exposed to S weather. In the SE part, the depths are less than 6 fathoms, and in places shoals extend almost 0.4 mile off the E and S shores of the bay. E of the passage between Allan and Burrows Islands is a middle ground with a least depth of 5 fathoms. Small craft using Deception Pass, bound to or from points in the islands or from Bellingham Bay, pass through Burrows Bay and the passage of Burrows Island.

BURROWS ISLAND LIGHT (48°28.6'N., 122°42.7'W), 57 feet above the water, is shown from a 34-foot white square tower on a building at the W end of the island; a fog signal is at the station.

LOCAL MAGNETIC DISTURBANCE † Differences from normal variation of 4° have been observed on the E shore of Burrows Bay.

WILLIAMSON ROCKS, a group of small, grass-covered islets and rocks, lie 0.5 mile S of Allan Island and are marked on the S side by a lighted gong buoy. DENNIS SHOAL, 500 yards off the S shore of Allan Island and 0.6 mile NW of Williamson Rocks, bares and is marked on is W side by a buoy.

-U.S. COAST PILOT 7
25th edition, August 1989
Corrected thru 10.22.90
Local Notice to Mariners

FACILITIES

COUPEVILLE

COUPEVILLE † Located on the south side of Penn Cove on Whidbey Island, Coupeville is small, historic and eager for visitors. Sea captains of the mid-19th Century turned farmer and settled here. A string of small shops made up a waterfront village on the bluff above the water. Today these structures are ice cream parlors, restaurants, gift shops, antique shops. Fishing vessels shelter by the town's tall timber pier, and small craft tie up to its set of mismatched floats. The community occupies a pleasantly rising hill on which a number of fine old frame homes recall a way of life now over a century old.

An artists' colony has grown up in this picturesque backwater and every summer an open-air Arts Festival takes place near the big fixed wharf that is the town's landmark. This small docking facility makes a highly desirable waystop for a summer cruise.

COUPEVILLE HARBOR STORE, on the wharf, Box 869, Coupeville, WA 98239. (206) 678 - 3625. Open daily 8 AM - 6 PM. Fuel dock: gas, diesel and mix. Guest dock. Nautical books and charts. Deli-snacks. Ice. Owner: Mike Williams.

PORT OF COUPEVILLE (Penn Cove on Whidbey Island), Box 577, Coupeville, WA 98239. (206) 678 - 5020. All year. Fuel dock: gas, diesel and outboard mix. Open Summer: 8 AM - 10 PM; Winter: 9 AM - 8 PM. Moorings. Showers. Deli in wharf building.

THE CAPTAIN WHIDBEY INN (at head end of Penn Cove on east side of Whidbey Island), 2072 W. Captain Whidbey Inn Road, Coupeville, WA 98239. (206) 678 - 4097. All year. Waterfront restaurant with guest dock and moorage. Dock limited to vessels with draft 6 feet or less. Breakfast, lunch, dinner. Overnight accommodations. Sailboat and bike rentals. Innkeeper: Capt. John C. Stone.

STANWOOD

BRYANT HARDWARE & IMPLEMENT CO, 27030 102nd NW, Stanwood, WA 98292. (206) 629-2511. All year. 8 AM - 5 PM. Boat and motor sales. Charts. Electronic sales and repairs. Instrument repairs. Marine hardware. Prop and shaft repairs. Fishing: licenses & tackle. Manager: Ed Bryant.

Port of Coupeville guest and fuel dock. Marine store and deli.

OAK HARBOR

OAK HARBOR † The public, municipal boat basin on Oak Harbor changes little from year to year, a fact that delights most yachtsmen in the area. It is a fine waystop between the populous centers of Puget Sound and the San Juan Islands. Its tricky approach through shallow waters at the neck of the harbor is very well marked and the numbered navigational aids lead you directly into the guest moorage of the marina. Winds from south and west are deflected by high ground and a tall bluff.

You must walk about two miles from the boat basin to reach the small town of Oak Harbor, but it's a pleasant stroll and the town is attractive.

Across Penn Cove from Oak Harbor is the Captain Whidbey Inn, its main building made entirely out of small madrona logs and its lounge graced by a huge stone hearth. Dinners are good and reservations are necessary, especially on weekends.

CORNET BAY MARINE CO, 5191 N. Cornet Bay Rd., Oak Harbor, WA 98277. (206) 675 - 5411. All year. Public ramp adjacent: 2-lanes, concrete. Hoist cap: to 28'. Summer hours: 7 AM - 7 PM. After Sept 8: 8 AM - 5 PM. Winter: 9 AM - 4 PM. Gas, diesel and outboard mix. LP refills. Moorings. Overnight guest dock with electricity. Beer, wine, ice, groceries. Complete service repair at EQ Harbor Service ½ block west. Fishing: bait, tackle. Managers: E. Nelson and K. Kranig.

E.Q. HARBOR SERVICE, (adjacent Cornet Bay Marine Co.), 265 W Cornet Bay Rd., Oak Harbor, WA 98277. (206) 679 - 4783. Hull and engine repairs. Marine supplies, Shamrock "New" boat sales, brokerage boats. Operated by Earl Nelson & Kathleen Kranig.

OAK HARBOR MARINA, 3075 - 300 Avenue West, Oak Harbor, WA 98277. (206) 679 - 2628. Ramp: 6 - lanes, concrete. Open 24 hours with parking. Fuel dock: gas and diesel. Open Summer; 8 AM - 5 PM daily. Open and covered moorage for boats up to 60'.

Guest dock. Dry storage. Hoist cap.: 4 tons. Open 8 AM - 5 PM. Tidal grid. Showers. LP refills. Ice. Pumpout station. toilets. Playground. Dockside electricity. Operated by City of Oak Harbor. Harbormstr.: Roger Leonhardi.

MARINE SERVICES, 181 W. Whitehall Place, Oak Harbor, WA 98277. (206) 675 - 7900. Emergency: 675 - 8896. Haulouts. Wood and fiberglass repairs. Welding. Diving and salvage. Boat building, outfitting and repair. Sterndrive sales and service. Vessel assist small boat tower. Dry storage. Owner: John Aydelotte.

WHIDBEY MARINE DESIGN & CONSTRUCTION, 221 W. Cornet Bay Road, Oak Harbor, WA 98277. (206) 675-1445. Boat design, construction & repair.

LANGLEY

LANGLEY MARINA LTD. (in Langley Harbor, Whidbey Island), Box 353, 202 Wharf Street, Langley, WA 98260. (206) 353 - 1771. All year. Hoist cap.: 4 tons. Open 9 AM - 6 PM Labor Day to Memorial Day. Sundays 9 AM - 5 PM. Fuel dock: gas and outboard mix. Open daily 8 AM. Boat maintenance and repairs. Engine parts and repairs. Marine hardware. Brokerage. Ice. Groceries. Beer. Fishing: bait and tackle. Manager: Barney Hein.

LANGLEY SMALL BOAT HARBOR, (in Langley Harbor, Whidbey Island, Saratoga Passage), Ramp. Transient moorage. Adjacent park with picnic area, restrooms. Restaurant and groceries nearby. Replaces the former city harbor facilities destroyed by storm in 1982. Operated by the City of Langley, Box 366, Langley, WA 98260. (206) 321 - 4246.

FREELAND

BUSH POINT MARINA, 326 S. Main Street, Freeland, WA 98249. (206) 321 - 1824. Ramp and marine ways. Hoist cap.: to 22 feet and 6000 pounds. Fuel. Ice. Fishing: bait and tackle. Rental boats and motors.

MUTINY BAY RESORT, (South Whidbey Island), Box 249, Freeland, WA 98249. (206) 321 - 4500. All year. Fuel dock: gas. Guest dock and moorings. Covered dry storage. RV sites. Private fishing dock. Hot showers. Fishing: bait and tackle. Water skiing. Skin and scuba diving. Manager: R. M. Frank.

NICHOLS BROS. BOATYARD, 5400 S. Cameron Road, on Whidbey Island, Box 580, Freeland, WA 98249. (206) 321 - 5500. Custom boatbuilding in aluminum and steel. President: Matthey Nichols.

WHIDBEY MARINE & AUTO SUPPLY, Box 248, Freeland, WA 98249. (206) 321 - 5262. Marine hardware.

MARINE PARKS

BOWMAN BAY STATE PARK (just W of Deception Pass on N shore), Moorage float. Picnic area. Trail to Pass Lake.

CAMANO ISLAND STATE PARK (on Camano Island SW of Stanwood beyond Hwy. 532), 134 acres. 2669 South Park Road, Camano Island, WA 98292. (206) 387 - 3031 or 387 - 2575. Ramp. Picnic areas. Campsites. Showers. Toilets.

DECEPTION PASS STATE PARK ($\frac{1}{4}$ mile E of Cornet Bay Marina at Cornet Bay), 5258 N. Cornet Road, Oak Harbor, WA 98277. 2339 acres. Ramp: 4 - lanes concrete, open 24 hours. Seven mooring buoys, 640 feet of float space. Guest dock. Picnic areas. Showers. Toilets.

FORT CASEY STATE PARK (3 miles south of Coupeville in Keystone Harbor), 137 acres. Ramp and dock. Campsites. Picnic area. Hiking trails. Underwater park nearby. Pit toilets.

HOPE ISLAND STATE PARK (in Skagit Bay 3 miles E of Deception Pass), Mooring buoys. Picnic area. Beach walks. No drinking water.

SKAGIT ISLAND STATE PARK (on Skagit Bay just E of Deception Pass), Mooring buoys. Picnic area. Campsites. Trails. No drinking water.

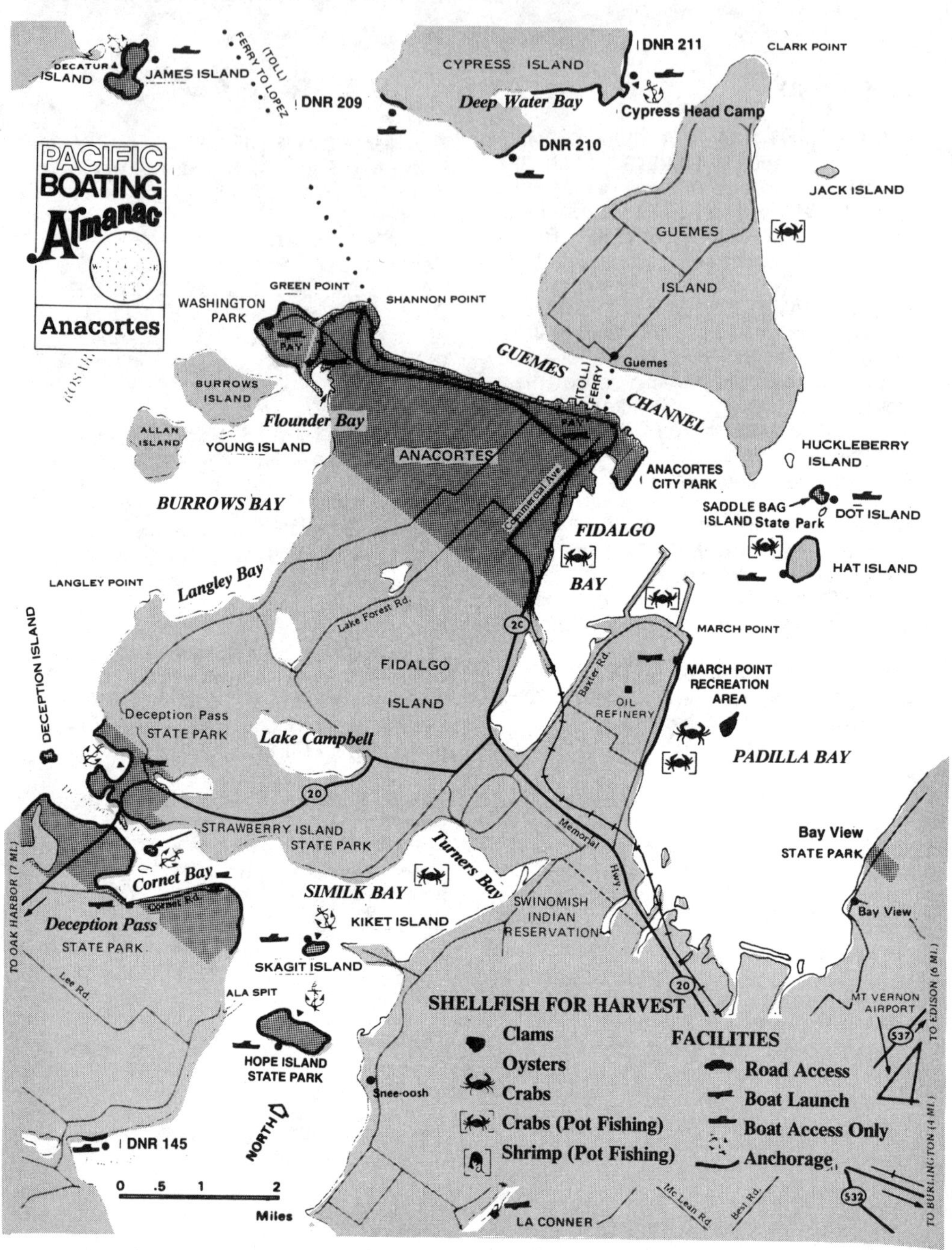

PACIFIC BOATING Almanac
Anacortes

DECATUR ISLAND
JAMES ISLAND
(TOLL) FERRY TO LOPEZ
DNR 209
CYPRESS ISLAND
Deep Water Bay
DNR 210
DNR 211
CLARK POINT
Cypress Head Camp
JACK ISLAND
GUEMES ISLAND
GREEN POINT
SHANNON POINT
WASHINGTON PARK
GUEMES
Guemes
(TOLL) FERRY
CHANNEL
HUCKLEBERRY ISLAND
BURROWS ISLAND
Flounder Bay
ALLAN ISLAND
YOUNG ISLAND
ANACORTES
Commercial Ave.
ANACORTES CITY PARK
SADDLE BAG ISLAND State Park
DOT ISLAND
HAT ISLAND
BURROWS BAY
FIDALGO BAY
LANGLEY POINT
Langley Bay
Lake Forest Rd.
MARCH POINT
MARCH POINT RECREATION AREA
2c
DECEPTION ISLAND
FIDALGO ISLAND
Baxter Rd.
OIL REFINERY
PADILLA BAY
Deception Pass STATE PARK
Lake Campbell
Bay View STATE PARK
20
Bay View
TO OAK HARBOR (7 MI.)
STRAWBERRY ISLAND STATE PARK
Memorial Hwy.
Cornet Bay
Cornet Rd.
Turners Bay
SIMILK BAY
SWINOMISH INDIAN RESERVATION
Deception Pass STATE PARK
Lee Rd.
KIKET ISLAND
SKAGIT ISLAND
ALA SPIT
HOPE ISLAND STATE PARK
Snee-oosh
20
MT VERNON AIRPORT
537
TO EDISON (6 MI.)
NORTH
DNR 145
0   .5   1   2
Miles
La Conner
Mc Lean Rd.
Best Rd.
532
TO BURLINGTON (4 MI.)

SHELLFISH FOR HARVEST
Clams
Oysters
Crabs
Crabs (Pot Fishing)
Shrimp (Pot Fishing)

FACILITIES
Road Access
Boat Launch
Boat Access Only
Anchorage

18

SKAGIT BAY TO ANACORTES
LaCONNER, ANACORTES

AIR TRANSPORTATION
Kenmore Air Harbor: (206) 486-1257
Lake Union Air: (800) 692-2993

CHAMBER OF COMMERCE
Anacortes: (206) 293-3832
Bellingham: (206) 734-1330
Blaine: (206) 332-5037
Mount Vernon: (206) 336-9555

COAST GUARD
VHF 16 or 22
Emergencies: (800) 592-9911
Anacortes: (206) 293-9555
Bellingham: 9206) 734-1692
Seattle: (206) 442-7070

CUSTOMS
Anacortes: (206) 293-2331
Bellingham: (206) 734-5463
Blaine: (206) 332-6318
Cap Sante: (206) 293-2331
The Basin at Point Roberts:
    (206) 945-2314
Point Roberts: (206) 945-2314
Skyline Marina: (206) 293-2331
White Rock: (206) 536-7671
After Hours: (800) 562-5943

DECOMPRESSION CHAMBER
Virginia Mason, Seattle:
    (206) 624-1144

FERRY TRANSPORTATION
Washington State: (800) 542-0812

FISHING INFORMATION
(206) 753-6600

MARINE OPERATOR
Bellingham: VHF 28, 85
Victoria: VHF 27, 85

POISON INFORMATION
(800) 732-6985

PROPANE
Cornet Bay Marina
LaConner Landing
Skyline Marina

RED TIDE HOTLINE
(800) 562-5632

STATE PARK INFORMATION
(800) 562-0990

TOURIST INFORMATION
Bellingham: (206) 671-3990
White Rock: (206) 536-6844

TOWING AND ASSISTANCE
(Non-Emergency)
Anacortes Diesel/Marine:
    (206) 293-3000
Marine Services: (206) 675-7900
Tim's Mobile: (206) 376-2332/VHF 16

CHART 18427 † SKAGIT BAY, N part between the N part of Whidbey Island and the mainland, is entered from the N through Deception Pass and from the S through Saratoga Passage, Skagit River, described in chapter 11, empties into the SE part of the bay.

The greater portion of Skagit Bay is filled with flats, bare at low water. Shoals extend 100 to 300 yards off the Whidbey Island shore.

Along the shore of Whidbey Island, between it and the edge of the flats, is a natural channel varying in width from 0.2 to 0.5 mile, except at Hope Island, where it narrows to 150 yards. The channel is marked with lights and buoys from Deception Pass to the N entrance of Saratoga Passage. The main channel from Deception Pass, S through Skagit Bay has depths of 6 fathoms or more.

Velocity and direction of the current vary throughout this channel. The flood current enters through Deception Pass and sets in a generally S direction. The ebb flows in a general N direction. SW of Hope Island, the velocity is 2.3 knots on the flood and 2.0 knots on the ebb. S of Goat Island the velocity is 1.8 knots on the flood and 1.4 knots on the ebb. N of Rocky Point the velocity is 0.6 knot on the flood and 1.0 knot on the ebb.

SIMILK BAY, at the N end of Skagit Bay, is used for log rafting operations and is unsafe for navigation. SKAGIT ISLAND and KIKET ISLAND, 111 feet and 194 feet high, respectively, are just S of Similk Bay opposite the E entrance to Deception Pass. HOPE ISLAND, 1 mile S of Skagit Island, is fringed with rocks off its E side, and marked by a light on its W point. BEN URE SPIT, across the channel from Hope Island, is a low projecting point within a shoal extending about 350 yards E.

Good anchorage may be had N of Hope Island, and vessels at times make use of this anchorage area while waiting for slack water in Deception Pass.

The narrow channel W of Hope Island is used by small craft with local knowledge. This channel, with a controlling depth of 5 fathoms, passes 130 yards off the Hope Island shore. The bottom is rocky and very irregular, and numerous dangers marked by havey kelp are between the channel and the Fidalgo Island shore. A summer anchorage for pleasure craft is S of SNEE-OOSH (HUNOT) POINT.

SEAL ROCKS, 1.4 miles S of Hope Island, lie on the E side of the main channel. They are marked by a light.

SWINOMISH CHANNEL is a dredged channel that connects the waters of Skagit Bay with those of Padilla Bay, about 10 miles to the N. The entrance channel from Skagit Bay leads ENE between two jetties, then N of GOAT ISLAND, which is rocky, steep and timber covered, thence through HOLE IN THE WALL, in the S part of Fidalgo Island and then N to Padilla Bay. The S jetty, submerged except for a small section near Goat Island, extends about 0.6 mile W of Goat Island and is marked by a light off its W end, extends W about 1.1 miles from the S end of Fidalgo Island. A 072°-252° LIGHTED RANGE marks the entrance channel from Skagit Bay and other navigational aids mark the channel to Padilla Bay. In July-August 1985, the centerline controlling depth was 8 feet from Skagit Bay to deep water in Padilla Bay.

Several bridges and overhead power and telephone cables cross Swinomish Channel; minimum clearance of the power cables is 72 feet. Just S of La Conner, the highway fixed bridge has a clearance of 45 feet or 75 feet for a center width of 310 feet. At the Padilla Bay entrance, the railroad swing bridge has a clearance of 5 feet, the span is left in the open position until a train approaches. Twin fixed highway bridges 0.2 mile S of the swingbridge have a clearance of 75 feet.

Most of the yachts going between Bellingham and Seattle prefer Swinomish Channel to Deception Pass because of the calmer water and shorter run. The channel is used extensively for towing logs.

LA CONNER, near the S end of Swinomish Channel, is the center of a rich agricultural district, and has several fish canneries. Many commercial fishing boats operate from here. Piers, wharves, and mooring floats are along the entire waterfront, much of which is bulkheaded. There are several marinas along the channel at La Conner. The largest marinas are operated by Skagit County

CYPRESS ISLAND
GUENEZ ISLAND
ANACORTES
CAP SANTE MARINA

in the county basins on the E side of the channel about 0.6 mile and 0.8 mile N of the highway fixed bridge. The entrance to the S basin is constricted by pilings that extend from the N side. The S basin has about 180 covered and uncovered berths with electricity and water, and a 40 ton mobile hoist at its N end. The hoist is used jointly by the marina and a machine shop on the N side of the S basin. Complete hull and engine repair facilities are available at the machine shop. Gasoline, diesel fuel, and marina supplies are available at several marinas in the area. A firm, on the E side of the channel at the S end of town, builds fiberglass boats and does limited hull repair work. A tug company, N of the basin, has tugs up to 2,400 hp available. An extensive log storage and sorting yard is on the W side of the channel opposite the tug company. Logs are moored along both sides of the channel near the storage yard.

GUEMES CHANNEL, between Guemes Island on the N and Fidalgo Island on the S, leads E from Rosario Strait to Padilla Bay. The channel, which is about 3 miles long and 0.5 mile wide at its narrowest point, has depths of 8 to 18 fathoms; the main part of the channel has been wire-dragged to depths of more than 33 feet. Lighted buoys mark the channel at the W end.

LOCAL MAGNETIC DISTURBANCE † Differences from normal variation of as much as 14° have been observed off the SE point of Guemes Island.

SHANNON POINT, the S point at the W entrance of Guenes Channel, is low and rounding, and marked by a light and fog signal. A shoal extends 200 yards N from the point. The current velocity in Guemes Channel exceeds 5 knots at times. It is reported that the flood (E current) is accompanied by an eddy between the E end of Guemes Island and Cap Sante with the W counter-current extending about 200 yards from the shore along the N side of Fidalgo Island.

SHIP HARBOR is a bight close E of Shannon Point, at the W entrance to Guemes Channel. The inter-island ferry slips and headquarters are here. Vessels anchoring here in heavy weather should be caution of dragging anchor because the bottom is not good holding ground.

CITY OF SEATTLE ROCK, covered 1½ fathoms, is 200 yards offshore on the S side of the channel, 2 miles E of Shannon Point.

ANACORTES, on the S shore of Guemes Channel, is a fishing and lumber center with two salmon canneries, and a pulpmill and a plywood plant. The port is incorporated as the PORT OF ANACORTES, (48°31'N., 122°37'W.) Commerce includes logs and lumber products seafood (including salmon), petroleum products, and farm produce. The most prominent charted landmark in the area is a tall, abandoned stack standing on bare ground about 0.5 mile NW of the entrance to Cap Sante Waterway.

CAP SANTE (CAPSANTE) WATER-WAY, a dredged channel leading to the E waterfront of Anacortes, is marked by daybeacons and lights. The ends of the breakwaters forming the boat haven are marked by lights. In March 1986, the centerline controlling depth from deep water in Fidalgo Bay to the mooring basin was 11 feet with depths of 6½ to 12 feet in the middle of the basin and lesser depths along the sides. The Port of Anacortes controls the boat haven. There are berths, with electricity and water, for about 960 craft; transient berths are available. A HARBOR MASTER assigns berths. A marina at the basin operates a fuel dock at which gasoline and diesel fuel are available. Water, ice, supplies, a 4-ton lift, and a 30-ton lift that can handle vessels to 55 feet long, are available at the marina. Hull, engine and electronic repairs can be made at the marina. A Coast Guard vessel is stationed at Cap Sante Boat Haven.

A dredged channel, marked by lights and buoys, extends about 0.7 mile SW from the entrance to Cap Sante Waterway to the marina. In March 1986, the midchannel controlling depth was 16 feet. In 1982, a marina was under construction at the N end of the industrial waterfront area. Berthing with water, electricity, storage boxes, and telephone connections are available. In April 1982, a reported depth of 11 feet was in the marina and alongside the

Skyline Marina, Flounder Bay, Anacortes.

berths. Gasoline, diesel fuel and repair facilities are at the marina; a 60-ton lift is available.

TIDES † The mean range of tide at Anacortes is 4.8 feet and the diurnal range of the tide is 8.2 feet.

HARBOR REGULATIONS † The port is controlled by a port commission and a manager whose office is on the port wharf at the foot of Commercial Avenue.

FIDALGO BAY, a shallow arm of Padilla Bay, extends S from the E end of Guemes Channel.

PADILLA BAY, between the mainland and the N part of Fidalgo Island, is largely occupied by drying flats, but deep water lies E of Anacortes and Guemes Island. Entrance to the bay may be had from Rosario Strait through Guemes Channel; a passage E of Guemes Island leads into Padilla Bay from the N.

MARCH POINT, low and wooded, is the peninsula between Fidalgo and Padilla Bays.

LOCAL MAGNETIC DISTURBANCE † Differences from normal variation of 2° have been observed in the vicinity of March Point.

BAY VIEW, a village across the flats of Padilla Bay ESE from March Point, has no facilities except for a small boat repair shop.

FLOUNDER BAY, a well-sheltered basin and popular yachting harbor at the N end of Burrows Bay, is the site of a large marina with an airstrip. The entrance channel is protected by jetties, and is marked by private lights and daybeacons. In 1980, 13 feet was reported in the entrance. Gasoline, diesel fuel, water, ice, about 250 berths with electricity, transient berths, dry storage facilities, launching ramp, two 1½ ton hoists, 24 ton lift, and marine supplies are available at the marina. Hull, engine, and electronic repairs can be made. A highway connects the bay with the State ferry terminal in Ship Harbor and with Anacortes.

-U.S COAST PILOT 7
25th edition, August 1989
Corrected thru 10 22 90
Local Notice to Mariners

ANACORTES

ANACORTES † A small but burgeoning city, Anacortes, on the northern rim of Fidaldo Island, is growing faster than any other boating-oriented community in the Northwest. Within a very few years, the shores of Fidalgo Island have been built up to include two big new condo marinas (Anacortes Marina and Skyline Marina), a huge new depot for trans-shipment for goods to Alaska, and many smaller marine enterprises. Together they sturdily support Anacortes' claim to be the "Gateway to the San Juan and Gulf Islands," focal point of pleasure boating in the North Sound.

Boat chartering is a big part of Anacortes' commerical activity, and the town has several marine parks, seamen's commemmorative plaques and a maritime museum. Two proud ethnic groups, Serbs and Croatians, have helped build this city, and their descendants make their traditional costumes, ceremonial dances and cuisine a part of Anacortes' community life. An annual Arts and Crafts Festival highlights each summer, and increasing numbers of good restaurants have sprung up to serve the large influx of summer visitors as well as the year around population of Anacortes. Guemes Island, Cypress Island, Sinclair Island and a cluster of small landfalls between them offer excellent gunkholding opportunities just north of Anacortes.

FACILITIES

ANACORTES

ABC YACHT CHARTERS INC, 1905 Skyline Way, Anacortes, WA 98221 (at Flounder Bay), (206) 293 - 9533. WA toll free: (800) 562 - 2686; out of state; (800) 426 - 2313. (Since 1947). All year. Charter fleet of over 100 yachts, both sail and power cruisers. From 26 to 65 feet. Bare boat and skippered. Total service to fleet includes search and rescue plus float plane service. Local airport pickup. Used boat and motor sales. Charts. Electronic sales and service. Groceries and ice. Hull and engine maintenance, parts and repairs. Prop and shaft repairs. Fishing: licenses, bait and tackle. Owners: Gene and Carolyn Jordeth.

ANACORTES DIESEL AND MARINE, (at Anacortes Marina) Box 130, Anacortes, WA 98211. (206) 293 - 3000. Open 24 hours, 6 days. Monitor VHF channels 16 & 9. Authorized sales and service for Detroit, Westerbeke and Perkins Marine Diesel engines. Also, Ford and other makes. Parts inventory. VDO Marine Instruments. Marine batteries. Owner: Ian Bannerman.

ANACORTES DIVING & SUPPLY, 2502 Commercial Avenue, Anacortes, WA 98221. (206) 293 - 2070. Diving equipment, sales and service. Rentals. Air refills. Salvage.

ANACORTES MARINA (on Fridalgo Bay, between 22nd and 26th Streets and T Avenue), Box 846, Anacortes, WA 98221. (206) 293 - 4543. Condo slips. Guest moorage. Mobile hoist cap.: 60 tons and 60 feet. Engine repair, welding and painting. Outfitting. Rigging. Gas and diesel.

ANACORTES MARINE ELECTRONICS INC., 919 Commercial Avenue, Anacortes, WA 98221. (206) 293 - 6100. Electronic sales and service.

ANACORTES YACHT CHARTERS, Box 69, Anacortes, WA 98221. (206) 293 - 4555. Toll free, (800) 842 - 4002 or in WA (800) 233 - 3004. Charter boats, sail and power from 28 to 58 feet. Bareboat or skippered.

ANCHOR COVE MARINA, 1600 Fifth Street, Anacortes, WA 98221. (206) 293 - 7033. Open and covered slips available on minimum one month rental basis. Laundry. Developer: Irene C. Nelson. Dockside Electricity.

BAY MARINE, 1302 Commercial Avenue, Anacorets, WA 98221. (206) 293 - 6819. Stern drive sales and service.

BLAKE'S SKAGIT RESORT & MARINA, 1171-A Rawlings Road, Mount Vernon, WA 98273. (206) 445 - 6533. Ramp: 1 - lane, concrete. Fuel dock: gas and mix. Open 7 AM - 5 PM. LP refills. Slips. Guest dock. New and used boats and motors. Ice. Marine hardware. RV sites. Picnic area. Restaurant. Fishing: bait and tackle. Rental tackle and boats. Manager: Paul D. Blake.

CAP SANTE BOAT HAVEN, PORT OF ANACORTES, P.O. Box 297, Anacortes, WA 98221. (206) 293 - 0694. All year. Daily. Winter: 8 AM - 5 PM, Summer: 7 AM - 9 PM. Hoist cap.: 25 ton. Overnight guest dock with electricity. Slips. Boat storage. 1030 berths. Fuel dock: gas, diesel and mix. Hull and engine maintenance, parts and repairs. Prop and shaft repairs. Laundry. Restaurants. Waste disposal pumpout. RV campsites. Picnic and park areas. Harbormaster: Dale Fowler.

HANDI GALS (at Anacortes Marina.) Box 1034, Anacortes, WA 98221. (206) 293-6810. Boat cleaning and maintenance. Specialists in teak and fiberglass. Marine discount store. Owners: Dana Bower and Emily Hoch.

J.D.'S MARINA (end of U Avenue), 202 U Avenue, Anacortes, Wa 98221. (206) 293 - 2410. HOist cap.: 35 tons to 40 feet; marine ways: 50 tons to 60 feet. Open Mon. - Fri.: 8 AM - 5 PM; Sat.: 7 AM - 3 PM. Open Sunday. Fuel dock: gas, diesel and propane. Open same hours. Dry storage. Marine hardware and supplies. Ice. Restaurant adjacent. Owner: Jack Dixon.

LAE AUTO PARTS, 103 E. Kincaid, Mount Vernon, WA 98273. (206) 336 - 6101. Marine electrical. Engine parts. Meters and instrumants. Cable systems. Batteris.

LOVRIC'S SEA-CRAFT, 3022 Oakes Avenue, Anacorets, WA 98221. (206) 293-2042. Three marine ways cap. to 2,000 tons. Crane cap.: 10 tons. Boat building. Boat maintenance and repair. Engine repairs. Owner: Anton Lovric.

MARINE DISCOUNT STORE, P.O. Box 366, Anacortes, WA 98221. (206) 293 - 3621. All year. Marine hardware. Charts. Electronic sales. Ice. Fishing: licenses and tackle. Owners: Ernie Taber and Mark Norgard.

MARINE SUPPLY & HARDWARE CO., 202 Commercial Avenue, Anacortes, Wa 98221. (206) 293 - 3014. Chandlery with rope, chain, cable and blocks. hardwrae. Paint, boots, foul weather gear. Fishing: tackle.

SKYLINE MARINA, INC. (one-half mile west of the Anacortes Ferry landing), Flounder Bay, Anacortes, WA 98221. (206) 293 - 5134. All year. Two self-service monorails, cap.: 5.000 lbs. to 24 feet. Travelift cap.: 35 tons. Fuel dock: gas and diesel. Open 8 AM - 6:30 PM. Slips. Dry storage. Boat repairs and maintenance. Engine sales and repairs. Charter boats, power and sail. Mairne hardware. Brokerage. Electronic sales and service. Groceries. Ice. Restaurant. showers. Fishing: bait, tackle. Rental boats. Dockside electricity: (7). Manager: George Wasilewski.

THE CANVAS HOUSE, 501 Commercial Avenue, Box 274 and 30th and "T", Anacortes, WA 98221. (206) 293 - 5485. Marine canvas. Sailboat hardware. Owners: Sam and Barb.

LA CONNER

La Conner itself is a picturesque (sometimes quaint) little town, compact and very diverse. You can walk the length of its waterfront street in ten minutes and explore an astonishing number of small shops and eateries. An artists' colony, La Conner has colorful historic roots and many ties with the Swinomish Indian tribe whose reservation forms the west shore of the Cut.

BESELIN MARINA, North Basin, LaConner Marina. La Conner, WA 98257. (206) 466 - 3913. Hoist cap.: 100 tons. Engine maintenance and repairs. Machine shops. Prop and shaft repairs. Painting. Floating boat shop.

BOATERS DISCOUNT CENTER, (between the marina's on the channel), 601 Dunlap Street, La Conner, WA 98257. (206) 466 - 3540. Open year round, 100' dock by spring of 1990. Friendly people to serve your needs. U.S. Marine Achilles inflatables, authorized force outboard dealer and service shop. Complete range of supplies, electronics, bait tackle plus clothing and giftware.

LA CONNER LANDING, (on Swinomish Channel), 101 N 1st St, La Conner, WA 98257. (206) 466 - 4478. All year. Mon - Sat: 8 AM - 7 PM. Sun: 8 AM - 6 PM. Boat and motor sales. Charts. Electronics marine equipment and hardware. Engine maintenance and repairs. Fuel dock: gas, diesel, mix and propane. Fishing: licenses, bait and tackle. Owners: Tom and Jack Hohmann.

LA CONNER MACHINE & DRYDOCK INC., Box 1, La Conner, WA 98257. (206) 466 - 3629. Full service shipyard. Owner: Lee Johnson.

LA CONNER MARINA (on the Swinomish Channel), 3rd Street, La Conner, WA 98257. (206) 466-3118. Two hoists. Slips. Guest dock. Fuel dock: gas and diesel. Showers. Laundry. Tilets. Pumpout station. Shipyard, marine supplies and services adjacent. Dockside electricity: (7). Operated by Port of Skagit County. Harbormaster: Jack Blanchard.

MARINE CHANDLERS, 109 N. First Street, Box 777, La Conner, WA 98257. (206) 466 - 3161. Marine hardware and supplies. Sailboat equipment. Foul weather gear. Charts. Wine shop and bookstore. Owners: Rich Machen and Katie Berg.

GUEMES ISLAND

GUEMES ISLAND FISHING RESORT (at northeast end of Guemes Island), 325 Guemes Island Road, Anacortes, WA 98221. (206) 293 - 6643. Open May 1 - Sept. 15. Ramp: 1 - lane, concrete. Open sunrise to sunset. Marine railway cap.: to 18 feet. Gas and outboard mix. Overnight accommodations. Camping. Trailer park. Showers. Groceries. Pool. Fishing: bait. Boat and motor rentals. Owners: Charlie and Mimi Townsend.

MARINE PARKS

CYPRESS HEAD MARINE RECREATION AREA (east side of Cypress Island, 4½ miles from Anacortes), Mailing address: Dept. of Natural Resources, Attn: Tim Boyd, Public Affairs, Room 206, John A. Cherberg Bldg. Olympia, WA 98504. (206) 753-5330. Four mooring buoys. Dinghy float. Campsites. Picnic areas. Trails. Operated by Dept. of Natural Resources.

PELICAN BEACH MARINE RECREATION AREA (north side of Cypress Island, 7 miles from Anacortes), Mailing address: Dept. of Natural Resources, Attn: Tim Boyd, Public Affairs, Room 206, John A. Cherberg Bldg. Olympia, WA 98504. (206) 753-5330. Four mooring buoys. Campsites. Picnic areas. Pit toilets. Trails. Operated by Dept. of Natural Resources.

SADDLEBAG ISLAND STATE MARINE PARK (2 miles ENE of Anacortes), 23 acres. Good anchorage in both north and south coves of island. Campsites. Pit toilets.

STRAWBERRY ISLAND PARK (in Strawverry Bay on west side of Cypress Island), Mailing address: Dept. of Natural Resources, Attn: Tim Boyd, Public Affairs, Room 206, John A. Cherberg Bldg. Olympia, WA 98504. (206) 753-5330. Picnic area. Toilet. No water. Anchorage in the bay. Operated by Washington Department of Natural Resources.

SUNSET BEACH – WASHINGTON PARK PUBLIC RAMP (turn west on 12th Street, 4 miles from city center), P.O. Box 547, Anacortes, WA 98221. (206) 293 - 5171. All year. Fee. Ramp: 2 - lanes, concrete. Park open sunrise to sunset. Camping. Trailer sites. Picnic areas. Playground. Operated by City of Anacortes.

Outstanding marine books
distributed by:

ROYCE'S *SAILING ILLUSTRATED* HOMESTUDY GUIDE, the challenging new book by Pat Royce, is based on a lifetime of sailing instruction. Whether you're a new dinghy sailor or the skipper of a "maxi," you'll find much of interest. Designed to accompany SAILING ILLUSTRATED, the all-time boating best seller, the new SAILING ILLUSTRATED HOMESTUDY GUIDE takes a fresh look at the world of sail and is ideal for sailing schools to be combined with "hands-on" experiences.

This will make you a better sailor. If not, return it within 10 days for a full refund.

ROYCE'S SAILING ILLUSTRATED HOMESTUDY GUIDE. 8½ x 11. Trade paperback. 164 pages. $10.95.

WESTERN MARINE ENTERPRISES INC.

Post Office Box 341668
Los Angeles, CA 90034

**Please include $2.75 shipping per order.
California residents add 6.5% sales tax.**

223

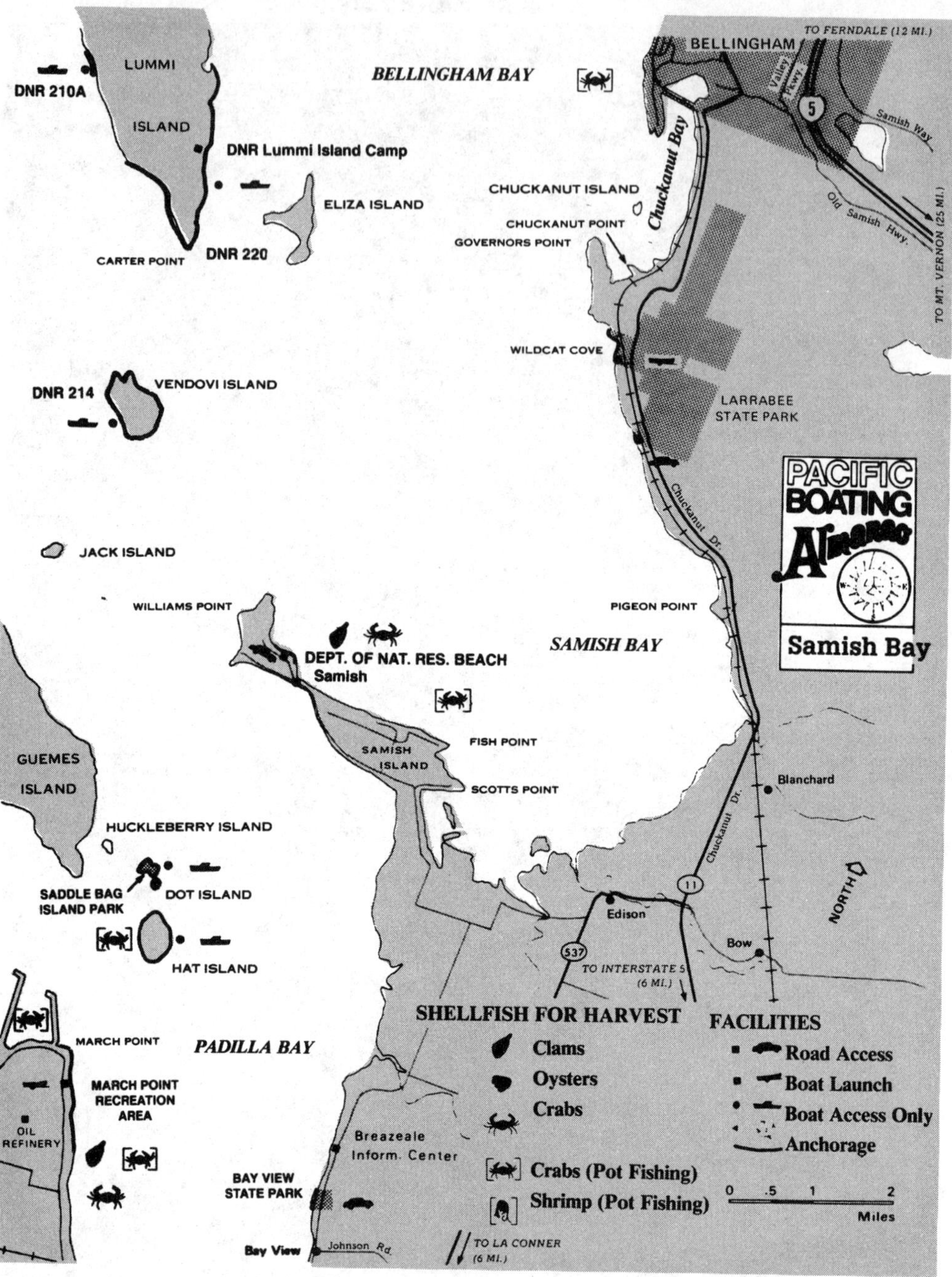

BELLINGHAM BAY
TO FERNDALE (12 MI.)
BELLINGHAM
Valley Pkwy.
5
Samish Way
Old Samish Hwy.
TO MT. VERNON (25 MI.)
Chuckanut Bay
LUMMI
ISLAND
DNR 210A
DNR Lummi Island Camp
ELIZA ISLAND
CHUCKANUT ISLAND
CHUCKANUT POINT
GOVERNORS POINT
CARTER POINT
DNR 220
WILDCAT COVE
LARRABEE
STATE PARK
DNR 214
VENDOVI ISLAND
Chuckanut Dr.
PACIFIC
BOATING
Almanac
N W E S K
Samish Bay
JACK ISLAND
WILLIAMS POINT
PIGEON POINT
DEPT. OF NAT. RES. BEACH
Samish
SAMISH BAY
SAMISH
ISLAND
FISH POINT
SCOTTS POINT
GUEMES
ISLAND
Blanchard
HUCKLEBERRY ISLAND
SADDLE BAG
ISLAND PARK
DOT ISLAND
Chuckanut Dr.
NORTH
11
HAT ISLAND
Edison
Bow
537
TO INTERSTATE 5
(6 MI.)
MARCH POINT
PADILLA BAY
MARCH POINT
RECREATION
AREA
SHELLFISH FOR HARVEST
FACILITIES
OIL
REFINERY
Clams
Road Access
Oysters
Boat Launch
Crabs
Boat Access Only
Breazeale
Inform. Center
Crabs (Pot Fishing)
Anchorage
BAY VIEW
STATE PARK
Shrimp (Pot Fishing)
0 .5 1 2
Miles
Bay View
Johnson Rd.
TO LA CONNER
(6 MI.)

19
BELLINGHAM, BLAINE & POINT ROBERTS

AIR TRANSPORTATION
Kenmore Air Harbor: (206) 486-1257
Lake Union Air: (800) 692-2993

CHAMBER OF COMMERCE
Anacortes: (206) 293-3832
Bellingham: (206) 734-1330
Blaine: (206) 332-5037
Mount Vernon: (206) 336-9555

COAST GUARD
VHF 16 or 22
Emergencies: (800) 592-9911
Anacortes: (206) 293-9555
Bellingham: 9206) 734-1692
Seattle: (206) 442-7070

CUSTOMS
Anacortes: (206) 293-2331
Bellingham: (206) 734-5463
Blaine: (206) 332-6318
Cap Sante: (206) 293-2331
The Basin at Point Roberts:
  (206) 945-2314
Point Roberts: (206) 945-2314
Skyline Marina: (206) 293-2331
White Rock: (206) 536-7671
After Hours: (800) 562-5943

DECOMPRESSION CHAMBER
Virginia Mason, Seattle:
  (206) 624-1144

FERRY TRANSPORTATION
Washington State: (800) 542-0812

FISHING INFORMATION
(206) 753-6600

MARINE OPERATOR
Bellingham: VHF 28, 85
Victoria: VHF 27, 85

POISON INFORMATION
(800) 732-6985

PROPANE
Cornet Bay Marina
LaConner Landing
Skyline Marina

RED TIDE HOTLINE
(800) 562-5632

STATE PARK INFORMATION
(800) 562-0990

TOURIST INFORMATION
Bellingham: (206) 671-3990
White Rock: (206) 536-6844

TOWING AND ASSISTANCE
(Non-Emergency)
Anacortes Diesel/Marine:
  (206) 293-3000
Marine Services: (206) 675-7900
Tim's Mobile: (206) 376-2332/VHF 16

CHART 18424 † WILLIAM POINT, 100 feet high, is the W point of SAMISH ISLAND which forms the N side of Padilla Bay. The point is wooded and, because of the low land E of it, appears as an island although it is connected with the mainland. It is marked by a light.

BELLINGHAM CHANNEL, deep between Cypress and Guemes Island, is the most direct route to Bellingham Bay from S. Between Cypress, Guemes and Sinclair Islands the tidal currents have considerable velocity, but between Sinclair and Vendovi islands the velocities are considerably less.

In July 1983, Bellingham Channel Lighted Bell Buoy 6, about 300 yards NW of Clark Point, was reported to submerge during periods of strong currents.

Lighted buoys marked the E side of Bellingham Channel.

A light is on the W side of Bellingham Channel off the E side of Cypress Island. CONE ISLANDS, a group of five islets on the W side of Bellingham Channel, lie 0.4 mile E of the NE side of Cypress Island.

CLARK POINT, on the E side off Bellingham Channel, is a steep bluff forming the N point of Guemes Island. A reef extends 300 yards N from the point. A marina, about 1.6 miles SE of Clark Point, has gasoline. A launching ramp and a hoist that can handle small craft to 18 feet is available. VENDOVI ISLAND is 1.8 miles NE of Clark Point. Shoaling to 4 fathoms, 0.4 mile SW of Vendovi Island, is marked by a buoy. A light marks the E side of the island. A private light is in a small cove on the NW side of Vendovi Island.

Deep-draft vessels approaching Bellingham Bay from N use the channel between Lummi and Sinclair Islands. With the exception of Viti Rocks and the dangers N of Sinclair Islands, this channel is free of danger. The fairway is deep and has a width of 0.6 mile at its narrowest part, between VITI ROCKS and CARTER POINT, the S tip of Lummi Island. The northwesternmost Viti Rock is 35 feet high, 200 yards long and marked by a light. A lighted bell buoy marks the shoal extending SSE from the southernmost rock.

HALE PASSAGE, 6 miles long, separates Lummi Island from the mainland to the NE. Depths in the passage vary from 2 fathoms on the bar near the NW end to 20 fathoms in the SE end of the channel.

LUMMI POINT, on the W side of Hale Passage 1.5 miles SE of Point Migley, is marked by a lighted buoy. A light is on the E side of Lummi Island 3 miles SE of Lummi Point.

LUMMI ISLAND, a village on the W side of Hale Passage, is 1 mile S of Lummi Point. The village and island are linked to the mainland at GOOSEBERRY POINT by an automobile ferry. The ferry dock at Lummi Island is marked by a private light and fog signal. A pier, adjacent to the ferry slip at Gooseberry Point has a 6 ton hoist that can handle craft 28 feet long; gasoline, water, ice, marine supplies and hull and engine repairs are available. Depths of 4 feet are reported off the end of the pier at the hoist.

From POINT FRANCIS, the rounded high bluff at the SE entrance of Hale Passage, a shoal and broken ground extend SSE to Eliza Island. The depths range from 5 to less than $1\frac{1}{2}$ fathoms about midway between the point and the island. A lighted buoy is about 300 yards S of the $1\frac{1}{2}$ fathom spot.

BELLINGHAM BAY, from William Point to the head, is about 12 miles long and 3 miles wide. Anchorage may be obtained almost anywhere in the bay S of the flats; the depths, over the greater portion, range form 6 to 15 fathoms. Because of the mud bottom, vessels are apt to drag anchor in heavy weather.

SAMISH BAY, separated from Padilla Bay by Samish Island, with flats bare for a considerable distance at low water, forms the SE part of Bellingham Bay. Extensive oyster culture is carried on in the E portion of the bay.

ELIZA ISLAND, low and partly wooded, lies 1 mile NE of Carter Point. Shoals fringe most of the island, which should not be approached closer than about 400 yards. A rock covered 1 fathom lies some 500 yards N of the W tip of the island.

Vessels anchoring between Lummi Island and Eliza Island during heavy weather should be cautious of dragging

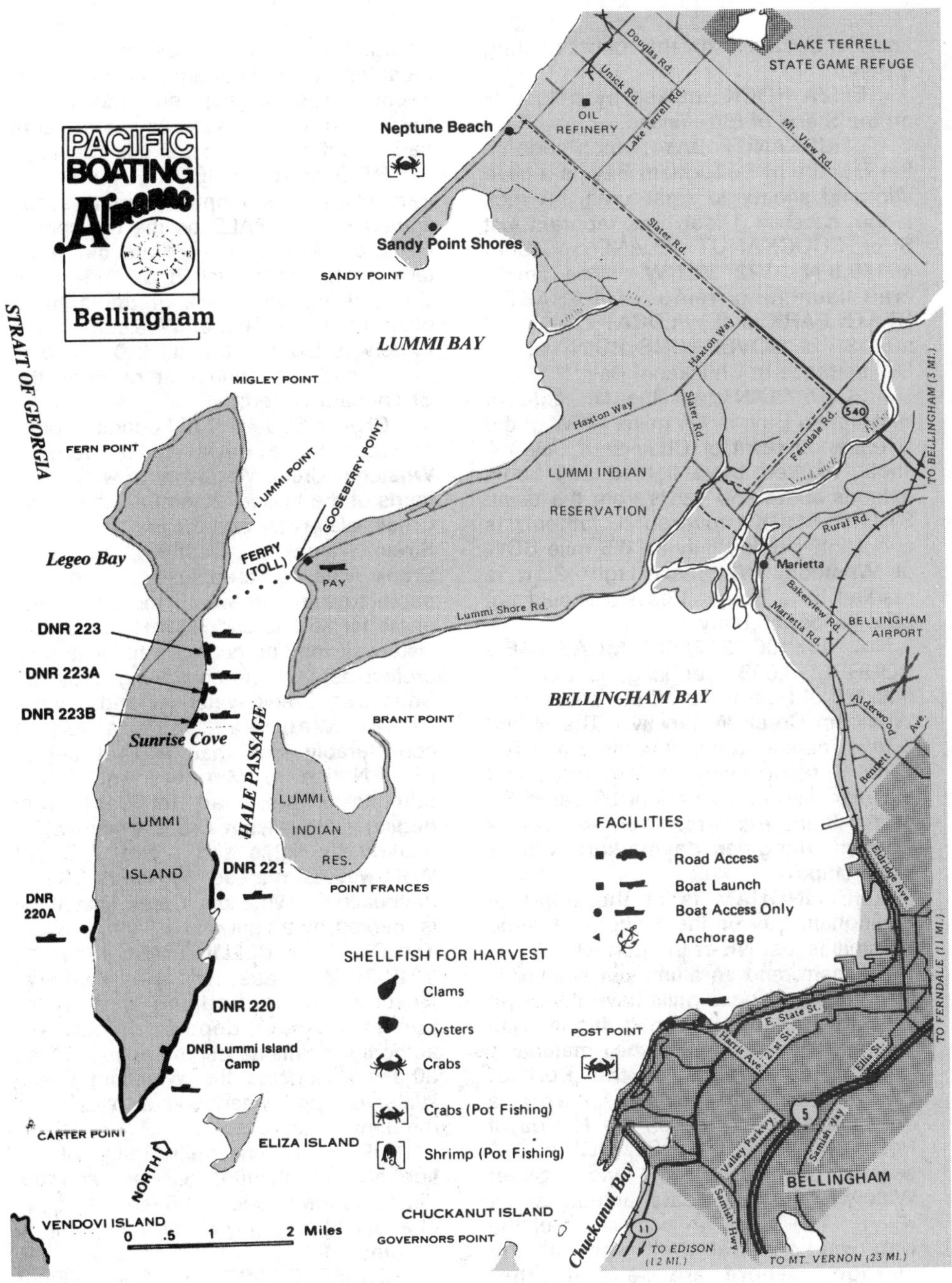
PACIFIC BOATING Almanac
Bellingham
STRAIT OF GEORGIA
LAKE TERRELL STATE GAME REFUGE
Douglas Rd
Unick Rd.
OIL REFINERY
Lake Terrell Rd.
Mt. View Rd.
Neptune Beach
Slater Rd.
Sandy Point Shores
SANDY POINT
LUMMI BAY
Haxton Way
Haxton Way
Slater Rd.
Ferndale Rd.
540
TO BELLINGHAM (3 MI.)
MIGLEY POINT
FERN POINT
LUMMI POINT
GOOSEBERRY POINT
LUMMI INDIAN RESERVATION
Rural Rd.
Legeo Bay
FERRY (TOLL)
PAY
Marietta
Bakerview Rd.
Marietta Rd.
BELLINGHAM AIRPORT
DNR 223
Lummi Shore Rd.
DNR 223A
BELLINGHAM BAY
DNR 223B
Sunrise Cove
HALE PASSAGE
BRANT POINT
Alderwood Ave.
Bennett Ave.
LUMMI ISLAND
LUMMI INDIAN RES.
DNR 221
POINT FRANCES
DNR 220A
Eldridge Ave.
TO FERNDALE (11 MI.)
FACILITIES
Road Access
Boat Launch
Boat Access Only
Anchorage
DNR 220
SHELLFISH FOR HARVEST
Clams
Oysters
Crabs
Crabs (Pot Fishing)
Shrimp (Pot Fishing)
POST POINT
E. State St.
DNR Lummi Island Camp
Harris Ave.
21st St.
Ellis St.
5
CARTER POINT
NORTH
ELIZA ISLAND
Valley Parkway
Samish Way
BELLINGHAM
VENDOVI ISLAND
0 .5 1 2 Miles
CHUCKANUT ISLAND
GOVERNORS POINT
Chuckanut Bay
11
TO EDISON (12 MI.)
Samish Hwy.
TO MT. VERNON (23 MI.)

anchor because of the poor holding ground.

ELIZA ROCK, marked by a light, is off the S end of Eliza Island.

CHUCKANUT BAY, which indents the E shore of Bellingham Bay, is a cove affording shelter to small craft. A rock ledge, covered 3 feet, was reported just S of CHUCKANUT ISLAND in about 48°40.5'N., 122°30.1'W. The small-craft launching ramp of LARABEE STATE PARK is at WILDCAT COVE, 0.6 mile SE of GOVERNORS POINT at the SW entrance to Chuckanut Bay.

POST POINT, on the NE side of Bellingham Bay, is 1.5 miles NNW of the N entrance point of Chuckanut Bay. A shoal, marked by a lighted bell buoy, extends about 450 yards from the point. STARR ROCK, covered 1 fathom, is about 200 yards offshore, 0.5 mile SSW of Whatcom Waterway Light 2; it is marked by a buoy. Vessels should not pass inside the buoy.

A 037°06'-217°06' MEASURED COURSE, 3,038 feet long, is about 1 mile NE of Post Point off the entrance to Whatcom Creek Waterway. The N and S front markers are 500 yards E and 700 yards S, respectively, of Starr Rock, and the rear markers are about 20 yards SE of the front markers. All are yellow wooden triangular daymarkers with a black stripe.

BELLINGHAM is at the head of Bellingham Bay on the E shore. A large Pulpmill is just NE of the port wharves at Bellingham, and an aluminum smelter is at Ferndale. These mills have their own wharves, but use the port facilities to ship and receive some of their material.

The S terminal of the Port of Bellingham, a cannery, and a boatbuilding plant are on the N side of Post Point at SOUTH BELLINGHAM. A seafood plant is on the I and J Street Waterway; fishing boats unload at its wharf. The areas on both sides of the waterway channel are used for log storage. There are several other seafood wharves, oil docks, and other commercial facilities around the harbor.

WHATCOM CREEK WATERWAY at the SE end of Bellingham Harbor, SQUALICUM CREEK WATERWAY at the NW end of the harbor, and I AND J STREET WATERWAY between, provide dredged channel access to the port facilities at Bellingham. Bellingham Yacht Harbor is adjacent and SE of Squalicum Creek Waterway; the yacht harbor is described later in this chapter.

PROMINENT FEATURES † Particularly prominent at night is the lighted sign HERALD on the newspaper building. Also prominent are the water tank on top of the tall B & B Furniture Co. building, the stack at the cement plant 1.9 miles NW of Whatcom Creek Waterway Light 2, the stack 0.3 mile to the E and the church spire near the Bellingham Waterfront.

CHANNELS † A Federal project provides for a depth of 30 feet in Whatcom Creek Waterway to within 250 yards of the bridge, 26 feet in Squalicum Creek Waterway and 18 feet in I and J Street Waterway. Depths in Whatcom Creek Waterway are usually near project depth to the Port wharf; the controlling depth for Middle and Inner Reach of this waterway may be considerably less than project depth. The controlling depth for Squalicum Creek Waterway and I and J Street Waterway may also be considerably less than Project depth. (See Notice to Mariners and latest editions of the chart for controlling depths.) Squalicum Creek Waterway is marked by lights and I and J Street Waterway is marked by lights and a daybeacon. Whatcom Creek Waterway is marked by a light and a lighted range. The PORT OF BELLINGHAM, 48°45'N., 122°30'W., assists the Federal Government in dredging and main-taining channel depths. The port authority maintains depths of more than 30 feet alongside the Whatcom Creek Waterway port wharf and also dredges the small-craft basin.

TIDES † The mean range of the tide at Bellingham is 5.2 feet and the diurnal range of tide is 8.6 feet. A range of aobut 14 feet may occur at the time of maximum tides.

COAST GUARD † Coast Guard station is at Squalicum small boat harbor.

REPAIRS † Complete repair facilities are available for small craft. A propeller works, several machine shops, engine and deck gear suppliers and an electronic repair company are along the Bellingham waterfront. The larger of two repair yards is just W of the Port of Bellingham South Terminal. This yard has a machine shop and a marine railway that can handle vessels up to 200 tons, 120 feet long or 32 feet wide for hull repairs. Another repair yard, at Squalicum Boat Harbor, has a marine railway that can handle vessels up to 150 tons, 86 feet long, or 26 feet wide for hull repairs. Several local machine shops in the area do engine repair work for the two repair yards.

SQUALICUM BOAT HARBOR, adjacent to and SE of the Squalicum Creek Waterway, is protected by breakwaters on its SE and SW sides. The harbor can be entered from the SE between the two breakwaters, or from the NW from the Squalicum Creek Waterway. The channelward ends of the breakwaters at the SE entrance are marked by lights; a fog signal is sounded from the southernmost light. The entrance from the Squalicum Creek Waterway is also marked by two lights. Depths inside the harbor are 10 to 15 feet.

Berths for about 2,200 pleasure craft and fishing boats are in the harbor. A guest float is maintained near the harbormaster's office on the NE side of the harbor. Gasoline, diesel fuel, electricity, water, ice, and marine supplies are available. Several marine equipment repair and fishing supply firms are in the area N of the SE entrance to the harbor.

A small-craft basin, protected by a breakwater on its S side, is N of I & J Street Waterway. The basin can be entered from I & J Street Waterway. A light on the outer end of the breakwater and a daybeacon to the N displaying the words "DANGER LOG BOOM," mark the entrance. Depths of 9 to 12 feet are in the basin.

STORM WARNING SIGNALS ARE DISPLAYED. (See chart.)

CHART 18400 † THE STRAIT OF GEORGIA extends some 115 miles NW from its S end, in the vicinity of Alden Bank, and is bordered on the W by Vancouver Island, B.C., and on the E by the mainland of Canada. General depths are great and in many places exceed 200 fathoms.

Vessels bound to the Strait of Georgia from Puget Sound should give the SW shore, between Boundary and Active Passes, a berth of at least 2 miles because it is fringed with dangers. Point Roberts, on the N shore, affords an excellent landmark.

(See chapter 6 for regulations governing vessels transiting gill net fishing areas.)

A VESSEL TRAFFIC SERVICE has been established in the Strait of Juan de Fuca, E of Port Angeles, and in the adjacent waters.

CURRENTS † The tidal currents in the Strait of Georgia are not nearly as strong as those in the channels leading to it from the Strait of Juan de Fuca. The currents in the Strait of Georgia attain a velocity of 3 knots at times, particularly during the freshets of the summer, when the Fraser River discharges a large volume of freshwater. This fresh water, which has a peculiar milky color, flows across the banks at the mouth of the river and almost directly toward Active Pass. Frequently this water extends entirely across the strait and at times reaches into the inner channels along the shore of Vancouver Island; at other times, it reaches only to the middle of the strait and forms a striking contrast with the deep blue water of the Strait of Georgia.

In the middle of the strait N of Patos and Saturna Islands, the velocity of the current varies from 1 to 3 knots, seldom exceeding the latter. The velocity is still less NW of the mouth of the Fraser River, where the strait is about 15 miles wide. The tidal currents SE of the mouth of Fraser River are slightly stronger off the S shore than off the N shore. The currents within a line joining Point Roberts and Sandy Point are scarcely felt, and good anchorage can be obtained in this vicinity.

The tidal currents are stronger close to the S shore which is swept by the rapid currents out of Active, Porlier and Bagriola Passes. The south-going tidal current in the Strait of Georgia sets strongly SW into Active Pass.

WINDS AND VISIBILITY † In the open waters of the Georgia Strait, winds are usually either northwesterlies or southeasterlies. Southeasterlies are more frequent from October through March. Close to the British Columbia coast, they are often deflected and become easterlies. While the Georgia Strait is somewhat sheltered from the sea by the mountains of Vancouver Island, gales still occur three or four times per month. While some are associated with the intense storms of winter, particularly dangerous gales occur in clear weather. These are locally known as SQUAMISH WINDS. They occur periodically in most of the main inlets in winter. They come up suddenly and may exceed 50 knots. Squamishes occur when a vast pool of very cold air accumulates on the interior plateau of British Columbia. A pressure fall at sea will trigger a movement of this air toward the coast. This flow is intensified by the direction and narrowness of the inlets. As the air reaches the mouths of these inlets, it spreads out over the strait and wind speed diminish. Winds rarely remain strong 15 to 20 miles away. Howe Sound, Jervis, Toba, and Bute Inlets all experience squamishes each winter.

In summer, winds in the Rosario and Haro Straits are usually southwesterlies. Summer breezes are variable and baffling in the San Juan Islands. N of Point Roberts, in the middle of the Georgia Strait, the prevailing winds are northwesterlies. Gales are uncommon, particularly in midsummer, when storm activity reaches a lull.

Georgia Strait is more affected by land fogs than sea fogs. These fogs form on cool nights under clear skies and light winds and usually dissipate early afternoon. These conditions are most prevalent from September through February. During prolonged periods of cold, clear, calm weather, these fogs may persist for several days at a time. Land fog is more local than sea fog. Visibilities fall below 0.75 mile on about 20 days annually, but this can increase to 60 days in preferred locations like the flat land in the delta of the Fraser River where the low water temperatures of the river help produce the fog.

CHARTS 18421, 18424, 18431 †
SANDY POINT, about 2.5 miles N of LUMMI BAY, is the site of an extensive housing development fronting a privately dredged basin. A marina with fuel dock is in the basin. A light and daybeacon are off the entrance to the basin. In 1973, it was reported that a depth of about 6 feet could be carried to the fuel dock. Gasoline, water, and a 1½ ton hoist are available at the marina.

Between Sandy Point and CHERRY POINT, (48°52'N., 122°45'W.) about 4.5 miles NW, the shore of the mainland forms a bight in which there are no off-lying dangers. The piers of two large oil refineries and an aluminum smelter are in the bight. A general anchorage is off Cherry Point.

The 1,800 foot pier of the Mobil Oil Co. refinery is at FERNDALE, 2.4 miles N of Sandy Point.

POINT WHITEHORN, about 2.8 miles NW of Cherry Point, is a conspicuous, bold bluff about 150 feet high; its seaward face is a steep cliff of white clay.

BIRCH BAY, on the E side of the Strait of Georgia between Point Whitehorn and BIRCH POINT, is an open bight. It affords some protection, in 4 to 5 fathoms, from N, but is open to the SW. Flats that bare occupy a considerable area at the head of the bay. A number of resorts are along the shore; however, there are no facilities for small craft.

The INTERNATIONAL BOUNDARY between the United States and Canada is marked by three sets of range lights where it crosses Semiahmoo and Boundary Bays. One set is in the E part of Semiahmoo Bay, and the other two sets are N of Point Roberts on the W side of Boundary Bay.

The PEACE MONUMENT on the boundary is a white masonry arch, facing N and S, about 28 feet above the ground. It is a distinctive landmark as it stands alone and shows offshore against a background of dark trees.

POINT ROBERTS is the prominent feature in approaching from either N or S. The E face is about 180 feet high and is composed of white, vertical bluffs. The point is well wooded and because of the low land behind it, is usually made as an island, especially from S. The SW extremity of the point is marked by a light. Extensive night drift fishing in the

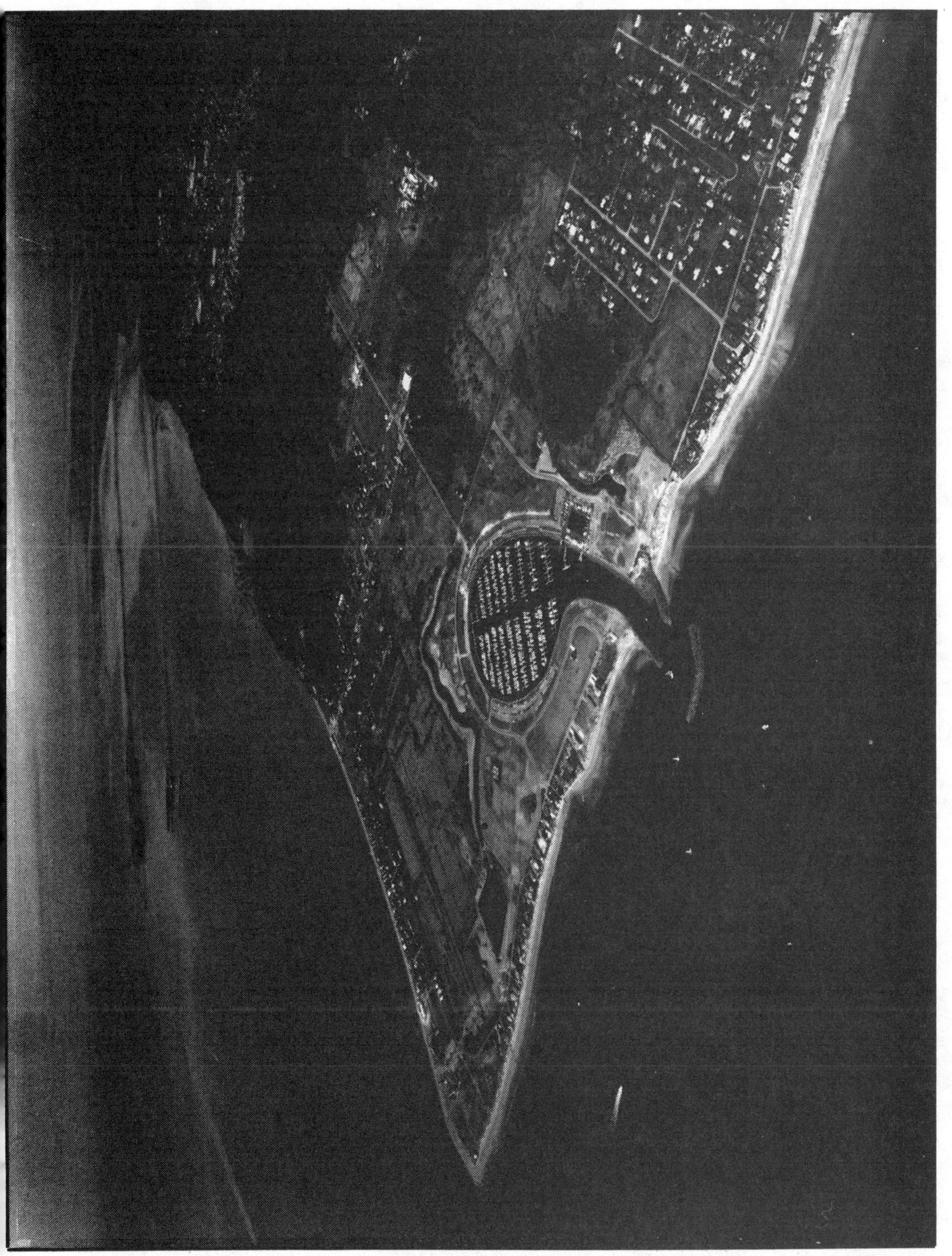

Point Roberts

area from Point Roberts to Blaine makes night navigation difficult.

Point Roberts is a CUSTOMS PORT OF ENTRY.

Temporary anchorage may be obtained W of Point Roberts in 8 fathoms, good holding ground, about 1 mile 321° from Point Roberts Light. The position is about 0.3 mile from the edge of Roberts Bank; vessels should not anchor any farther N.

SEMIAHMOO BAY has its entrance between Birch Point and Kwomais Point, about 5 miles NNW. It is connected with Drayton Harbor by a narrow channel. The E part of the bay is shoal with extensive sand flats in the SE part. Anchorage may be had in the bay in 3½ to 9 fathoms on the NW side of Semiahmoo Spit, affording protection from S and SE storms.

DRAYTON HARBOR is a small cove formed by SEMIAHMOO SPIT, the extension of a sandspit N of Birch Point. It is about 2 miles long, but flats that bare at low water occupy a large area in the E and S parts of the harbor.

A light with fog signal and a buoy about 700 yards to the WSW are near the N end of the extensive sand flats off the NW side of Semiahmoo Spit.

The channel from Semiahmoo Bay to the cannery wharf on Semiahmoo Spit and to Blaine Harbor, E of the cannery wharf, has a controlling depth of about 21 feet; greater depths are possible with local knowledge. The 15 foot spot about 130 yards N of the cannery wharf, and the 9 foot spot about 300 yards E of the E end of the wharf should be avoided.

BLAINE HARBOR, 49°00'N., 122°45'W., at Blaine, is a large and well equipped small-boat basin near the entrance on the N shore of Drayton Harbor. The harbor is an active fishing center operated by the Port of Bellingham. A light marks the outer end of the breakwater that protects the basin on the S side. In September 1981, depths through the entrance and in the basin were 11 feet except for shoaling along the edges. The harbor has berths for about 300 boats; 200 additional berths are being planned by the Port of Bellingham. A harbormaster is on duty in the harbor. Fish processing plants and a fish reduction plant are in operation. Gasoline, diesel fuel, electricity, water, ice, launching ramp, dry storage facilities, and marine supplies are available in the harbor. A repair yard with a marine railway that can handle vessels to 200 tons, 80 feet long, or 21 feet wide is also available; hull repairs can be made. A depth of 2 feet has been reported at the entrance to the marine railway.

STORM WARNING SIGNALS ARE DISPLAYED. (See chart.)

BLAINE, a small town on the NE shore of Drayton harbor, is a customs port of entry.

QUARANTINE, CUSTOMS, IMMI- GRATION AND AGRICULTURAL QUARANTINE. The United States Canadian boundary line passes through the N edge of town. Interstate Highway 5 and the Burlington Northern Railroad serve the town.

The mean range of tide at Blaine is 5.9 feet and the diurnal range of tide is 9.5 feet.

The average velocity of the CURRENT in Drayton Harbor entrance is 1.0 knot. The flood sets SE and the ebb NW.

Several buildings, an elevated tank, and a cannery constituting the town of SEMIAHMOO, 48°59'N., 122°46'W., are at the N end of the sandspit. Adjacent to the cannery is a marine railway for exclusive use of the cannery boats.

To enter Drayton Harbor and Blaine Harbor from Semiahmoo Bay, pass about 300 yards N of Semiahmoo Bay Light, and steer a course about midway between the cannery wharf and the Blaine Harbor boat basin taking care to avoid the 15 foot spot about 130 yards N of the cannery wharf. After passing the cannery wharf, favor the N side of the channel to avoid the 9-foot spot E of the E end of the cannery, and make Blaine Harbor or anchor as convenient in Drayton Harbor. Anchoring in the shoal water of Drayton Harbor is not recommended beacuse the floating debris and vegetation may clog a vessel's underwater intakes.

The depths in Drayton Harbor and its entrance are subject to change.

-U.S COAST PILOT 7
25th edition, August 1989
Corrected thru 10.22.90
Local Notice to Mariners

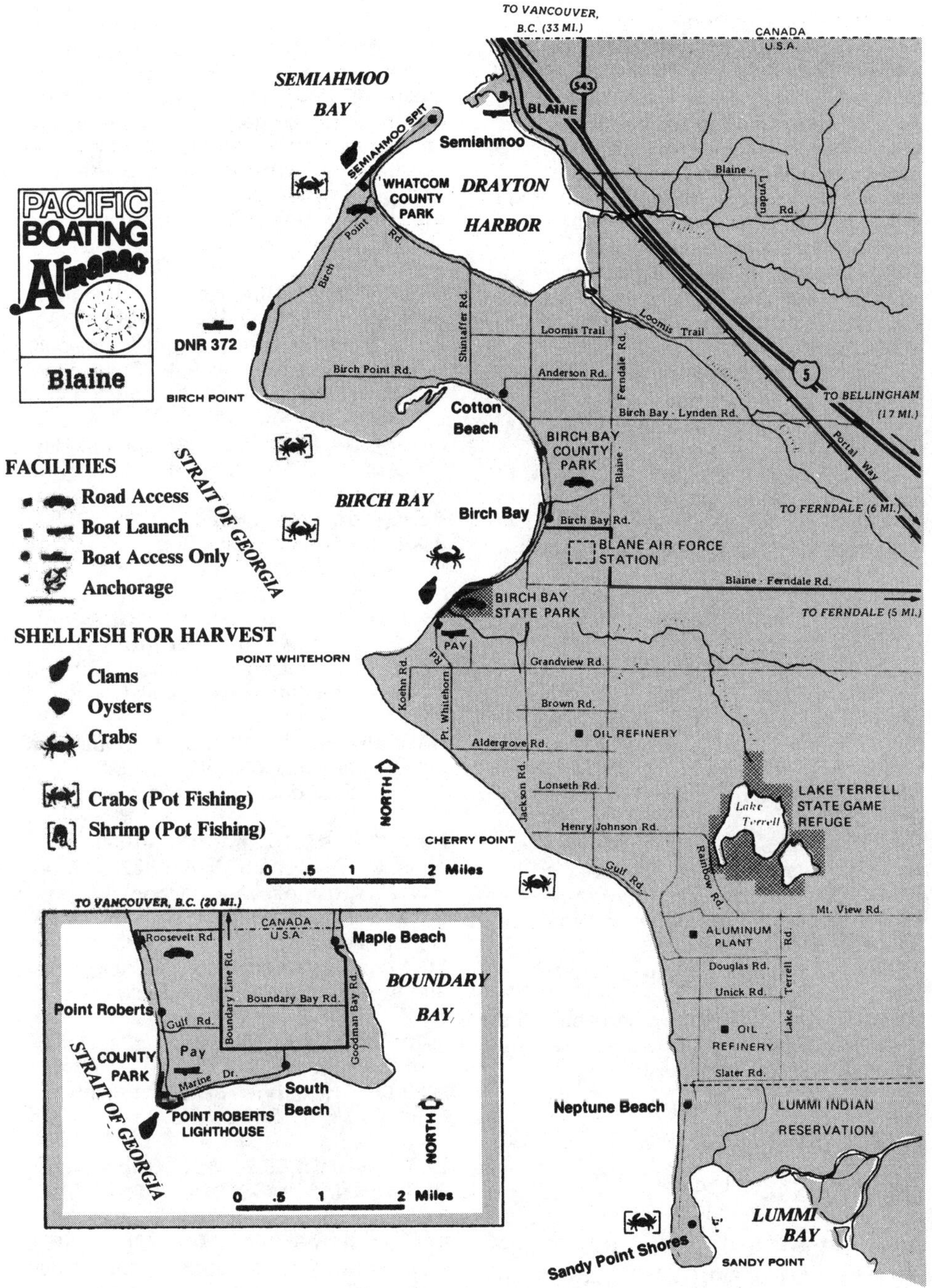
PACIFIC BOATING Almanac
Blaine
SEMIAHMOO BAY
SEMIAHMOO SPIT
Semiahmoo
WHATCOM COUNTY PARK
DRAYTON HARBOR
BLAINE
TO VANCOUVER, B.C. (33 MI.)
CANADA
U.S.A.
543
Blaine
Lynden
Rd.
Birch Point Rd.
Shintaffer Rd.
Loomis Trail
Loomis Trail
Anderson Rd.
Ferndale Rd.
5
DNR 372
BIRCH POINT
Birch Point Rd.
Birch Point
Cotton Beach
Birch Bay - Lynden Rd.
TO BELLINGHAM (17 MI.)
Portal Way
TO FERNDALE (6 MI.)
BIRCH BAY COUNTY PARK
STRAIT OF GEORGIA
BIRCH BAY
Birch Bay
Birch Bay Rd.
Blaine
BLANE AIR FORCE STATION
FACILITIES
Road Access
Boat Launch
Boat Access Only
Anchorage
POINT WHITEHORN
BIRCH BAY STATE PARK
PAY
Blaine - Ferndale Rd.
TO FERNDALE (5 MI.)
SHELLFISH FOR HARVEST
Clams
Oysters
Crabs
Crabs (Pot Fishing)
Shrimp (Pot Fishing)
Koehn Rd.
Pt. Whitehorn Rd.
Grandview Rd.
Brown Rd.
Aldergrove Rd.
OIL REFINERY
Jackson Rd.
Lonseth Rd.
Henry Johnson Rd.
NORTH
CHERRY POINT
LAKE TERRELL STATE GAME REFUGE
Lake Terrell
Rainbow Rd.
Gulf Rd.
Mt. View Rd.
ALUMINUM PLANT
Douglas Rd.
Unick Rd.
Lake Terrell Rd.
OIL REFINERY
Slater Rd.
0 .5 1 2 Miles
TO VANCOUVER, B.C. (20 MI.)
CANADA
U.S.A.
Roosevelt Rd.
Maple Beach
BOUNDARY BAY
Point Roberts
Boundary Line Rd.
Boundary Bay Rd.
Goodman Bay Rd.
Gulf Rd.
COUNTY PARK
Pay
STRAIT OF GEORGIA
Marine Dr.
South Beach
POINT ROBERTS LIGHTHOUSE
NORTH
0 .5 1 2 Miles
Neptune Beach
LUMMI INDIAN RESERVATION
Sandy Point Shores
SANDY POINT
LUMMI BAY

BELLINGHAM

BELLINGHAM † Squalicum Harbor, the Port of Bellingham's smallcraft facility, has changed so fast in the past few years that it is a constant surprise. A big second basin was dredged, then filled with enough new floats to more than double the total moorage capacity. For the first time a set of good concrete launch ramps has been built inside the harbor. Two long loading docks add to their convenience.

Because of environmental concerns the port was not allowed to link the old and new basins with a connecting channel.

Grounds around the new part of Squalicum Harbor are still in a state of construction, but shops and services at the new Harbor Center Building are rapidly coming on line. One result of the new space is a mushrooming new boat-charter business. Several charter firms are now challenging the long time lead of Anacortes in this field and seem destined to make Bellingham a principal base for Northwestern boat charterins.

A municipal bus runs frequently from the marina into downtown Bellingham, which has itself undergone a remarkable rejuvenation to become an attractive place to visit. Within easy walking distance of the harbor is the Maritime Heritage Center, a unique facility located at the mouth of Whatcom Creek. Its salmon-rearing ponds, spawning grounds and open-air fish ladders let you follow the fish life cycle in detail. During the rainy season there is a spectacular waterfall where the Creek enters the Heritage Center.

FACILITIES

BELLINGHAM

B & J FIBERGLASS INC, 4905 Guide Meridan, Bellingham, WA 98226. (206) 398 - 9342. All year. Daily, 8 AM - 5:30 PM. Closed Sun. Custom fiberglass shop. Fiberglass construction, repairs and sales. Hull repairs on premises or in water. President: Jerry Sundean.

CAPTAIN'S CABIN, 2 Harbor Mall, Bellingham, WA 98225. (206) 647 - 2628. All year. Marine hardware. New and used marine gear. Charts. New and used boat and motor sales. Inflatable repairs. Outboard maintenance. Complete sailboat supplies. Stove repairs. Yamaha outboards and aluminum boats. Owner: Steve Guyer.

DOCKSIDE MARINE, 1001 "C" Street, Bellingham, WA 98225. (206) 733 - 2805. Custom boat building and repair. Specialty fine teak work. Build steel sailboats. Owner: Paul R. Sorenson.

FISHERMAN'S COVE MARINA (on Hale Pasage between Lumni Island and mainland), Gooseberry Point, Bellingham, WA 98226. (206) 758 - 2444. All year. Open Summer: 6 AM - 12 AM; Winter & Am - 10 PM. Fuel dock: gas. Dry storage. Hoist cap.: to 28 feet. Engine repairs. Groceries. Marine hardware. Liquor store. Restaurant adjacent. Fishing: bait and tackle. Lumni Indian Business Council.

HARBOR MARINE FUEL, 21 Squalicum Fill, Bellingham, WA 98227. (206) 734 - 1710. Fuel dock: gas and diesel.

HILTON HARBOR MARINA, 1000 Hilton Avenue, Bellingham, WA 98225. (206) 733 - 1110. All year. Open Summer: 8 AM - 7 PM; Winter: daylight hours. Dry storage only. Hoist cap.: to 32 feet. Fuel dock: gas and mix. Fishing: bait and tackle. Manager: Jon Rick.

ISLANDER ELECTRONICS, #24 Harbor Mall, Bellingham, WA 98225. (206) 676 - 1990. Electronic sales and service. Manager: Gary Sutherland.

LFS CHANDLERY, 851 Coho Way, Bellingham, WA 98225. (206) 734 - 3336. Toll free in WA (800) 562 - 8819; outside WA (800) 426 - 8860. Complete marine supplies for power and sail. Fishing: Commercial fishing gear. Nautical charts and books. Owner: Gary Nelson.

MARINE SALES AND EQUIPMENT CO, 1000 "C" Street, Bellingham, WA 98225. (206) 733 - 2340. All year. Mon - Fri: 8:30 AM - 5:30 PM. Sat: 9 AM - 12 Noon. Hull and engine repairs. Prop and shaft repair. Hoist cap.: 30,000 lbs. Boat storage yard. Railway cap.: 30,000 lbs. Instrument repair. Bronze and aluminum prop repairs. Marine hardware. Owner: Terry Peterson.

MARINE SERVICES NORTHWEST, 2551 Roeder Ave, Bellingham, WA 98225. (206) 671 - 3820. Complete marine hardware. New and used boat and motor sales. Hull and engine maintenance, parts and repairs. Prop and shaft repairs. Haulouts for 50,000 lbs. Owner: Chuck Lindhout.

NEDDER HYDRAULICS, 1411 Roeder Ave, Bellingham, WA 98225. (206) 734 - 9829. All year. 7 AM - 6 PM. Hydraulic sales and service. Fabrication and welding of aluminum and steel products. Manager: Jim Armstrong.

RADAR MARINE ELECTRONICS, 17 Squalicum Mall, Bellingham, WA 98225. (206) 733 - 2102. Electronic sales and service. Manager: W.E. Pulse.

RASMUSSEN'S MARINE ELECTRIC, 2 - 4 Squalicum Mall, Bellingham, WA, 98225. (206) 671 - 2992. All year. Mon - Fri; 8 AM - 5 PM. Marine hardware. Electrical sales. All electrical generators and alternators, installations, repairs and parts. Owner: Donald Rasmussen.

REDDEN NET COMPANY, INC., 2626 Harbor Loop, Bellingham, WA 98225. (206) 733 - 0250. All year. Marine hardware. Commercial fishing gear. Charts.

SQUALICUM HARBOR, #6 Esplanade, Squalicum Harbor, Bellingham, WA 98227 -1737. (206) 676 - 2500. All year. Mon - Fri: 8 AM - 5 PM. Sat: 10 AM - 4 PM. Boat and motor sales. Charts. Electronic sales and repairs. Groceries. Accommodations. Laundry.

Restaurant. Instrument repairs. LP gas refills. Marine hardware. Waste disposal pumpout. Ramp: 4 - lane concrete. Hoist. Slips. Overnight guest dock with electricity. Moorings. Boat storage yard. Boat rentals. Fuel dock: gas and diesel. Fishing: licenses, bait and tackle. Harbor Manager: Art Choat.

SQUALICUM MARINE UPHOLSTERY, Squalicum Mall #15, Bellingham, WA 98225. (206) 733 - 4353. All year. Canvas and upholstery repair. Any type of custom canvas covers, cushions, etc. Boat interiors. Owner: Robert Gilmore.

STAFF SAILS, 1000 Hilton Avenue, Bellingham, WA 98225. (206) 734 - 8559. Sailmaking and repairs.

TRI-COUNTY ENGINE, 2696 Roeder Avenue, Bellingham, WA 98225. (206) 733 - 8880. Diesel engine maintenance, parts and repairs. Reverse gear service. Cummins and Detroit diesel engine sales. Perkins, Catapillar.

WEB LOCKER, 21 Squalicum Mall, Bellingham, WA 98225. (206) 676 - 0512. Grocery and diner.

WELDCRAFT STEEL AND MARINE INC., 9 Squalicum Way, Bellingham, WA 98225. (206) 734 - 2280. Marine railway and two cranes up to 250 tons. Fuel dock open daylight hours. Moorings. Boat maintenance and repairs. Dry storage. Engine repairs. Propeller repairs. Marine hardware. Brokerage. Owner: Owen J.E. Wilson.

WIGHT MARINE SERVICE, 2124 E. Bakerview Road, Bellingham, WA 98226. (206) 733 - 8987. Complete machine shop. Metal fabrication, welding, repair.

BLAINE

BLAINE BOAT HARBOR, Box 1245, Blaine,WA 98230. (206) 332 - 8037. All year. Ramp: 2 - lanes concrete, open 24 hours. Fuel dock: gas and diesel. Open 8 AM - 5 PM. Boat maintenance and repairs. Engine parts and repairs. Prop and shaft repair. Marine hardware. Restaurant. Groceries. Ice. Overnight

accommodations. Laundry. Pumpout Station. Fishing: bait and tackle. Charter boats. Dockside electricity. Operated by Port of Bellingham. Dockmaster: Victor McCaleb.

BLAINE MARINE SERVICE (the harbor), Box 2130, Blaine, WA 98230. (206) 332 - 4964. Haulouts to 40 feet. Dry storage. Hull repairs. Engine and sterndrive repairs on boats to 30 feet. Welding. Stainless steel fabrication and repair.

SEMIAHMOO MARINA, 9540 Semiahmoo Parkway, Blaine, WA 98230. (206) 371 - 5700. Full service marina. Fuel dock: gas, diesel and propane. Repair yard with 35 ton Travelift. Engine and hull repair. Chandlerly. Groceries. Fishing: tackle. Resort (The Inn at Semiahmoo) now open. Boutique. Golf course. Laundry. Showers. Transient moorage. Marina Manager: Mike Rehmke.

WESTMAN INDUSTRIAL CO., Blaine Boat Harbor, Box 1698, Blaine, WA 98230. (206) 332 - 5051. Open Mon. - Fri.: 8 AM - 5 PM. Full service shipyard. Travelift cap.: 35 tons. Marine ways cap.: 300 tons. Hull and engine maintenance and repairs. Prop and shaft repairs. Do-it-yourself facilities. Owner: Carl Westman.

POINT ROBERTS, WASHINGTON

POINT ROBERTS MARINA RESORT, 713 Simundson Drive, Point Roberts, WA 98281. (206) 945 - 2255. Travelift cap.: 30 tons. Monorail hoist cap.: 2 tons. Fuel dock: gas and diesel. Open Summer: Mon - Thurs. 8 AM - 9 PM, Fri. - Sun. 7 AM - 10 PM. Winter: Fri. - Sun 8 AM - 5 PM. Guest dock. Sips to 120 feet. Hull and engine maintenance, parts and repairs. Groceries. Ice. U.S. Customs Port of Entry. Fishing: licenses and bait. Dockside electricity: (7) (10).

MARINE PARKS

BOULEVARD PARK (at waterfront on E side of Bellingham Bay), Mailing address: Bellingham Parks Dept., 210 Lotti, Bellingham, WA 98225. (206) 676 - 6985. Dock. Picnic area. Playground. Observation tower. Toilets. Operated by Bellingham Parks Dept. (206) 676 - 6985. Caution: use care in approaching dock at low water.

LARRABEE STATE PARK (seven miles south of Bellingham), 245 Chuckanut Drive, Bellingham, WA 98226. (206) 676 - 2093 or 676 - 2094. Ramp: 2 - lanes, concrete. Open 6:30 AM - Dusk, April 1 - Sept. 30; 8 AM - Dusk, Oct. 1 - Mar. 31. 1886 acres. Picnic areas. Toilets. Showers. Camp and trailer sites. Manager: Jim Farmer.

LIGHTHOUSE COUNTY PARK, Point Roberts. Dock. Ramp: concrete. Picnic area. Camping. Playground. Toilets. Public phone. Operated by Whatcom County Parks Department (206) 945 - 4911. Manager: Carl Prince.

SEMIAHMOO COUNTY PARK (on Semiahmoo Spit at Drayton Harbor, near Blaine), Picnic area. Historical museum. Rental canoes. Clamming. Toilets. Operated by Whatcom County Parks Department (206) 722 - 2900. Moorage at nearby Semiahmoo Marina. Manager: Mike Grasser.

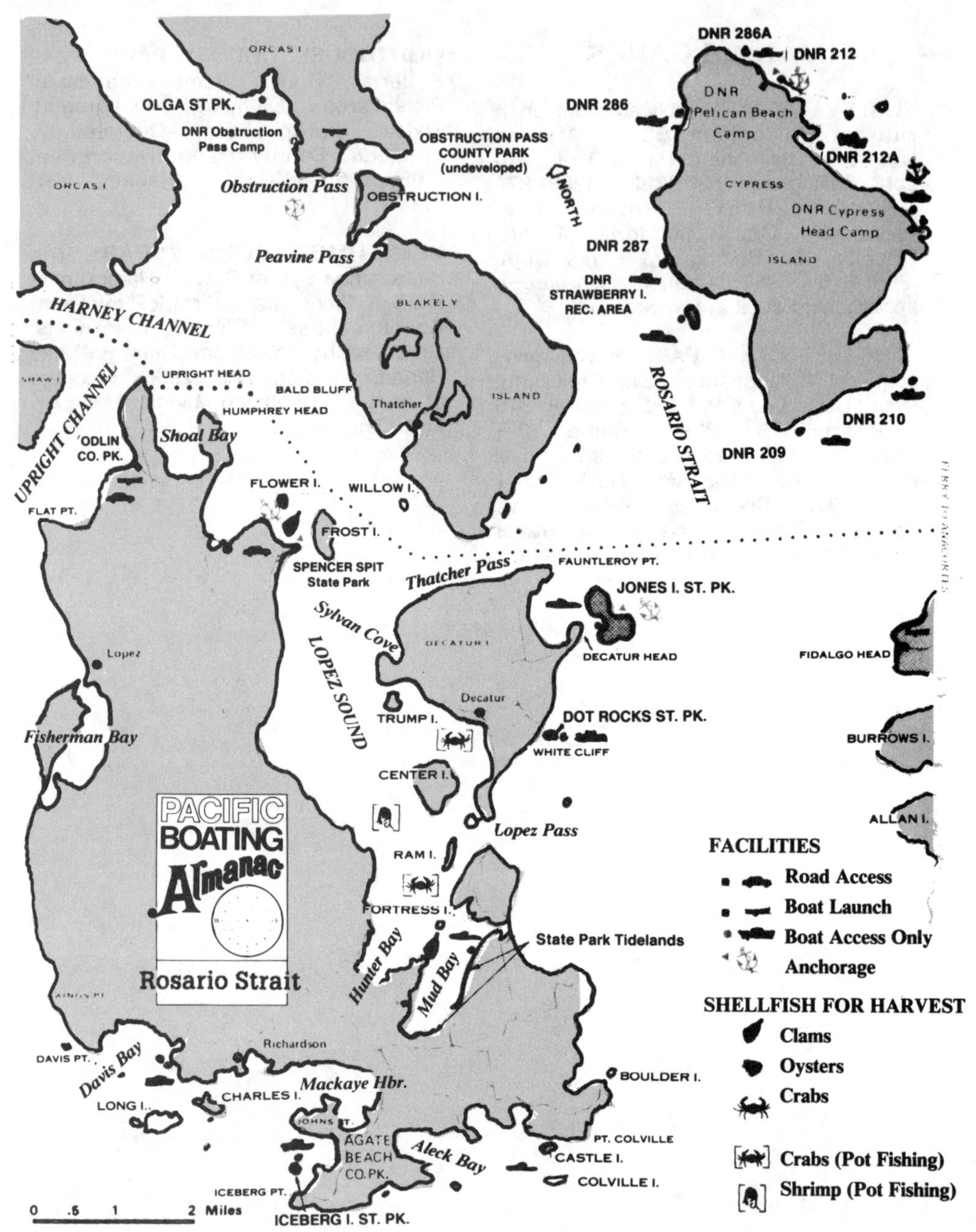

ORCAS I.
OLGA ST PK.
DNR Obstruction Pass Camp
Obstruction Pass
ORCAS I.
OBSTRUCTION I.
OBSTRUCTION PASS COUNTY PARK (undeveloped)
NORTH
Peavine Pass
DNR 286A
DNR 212
DNR 286
DNR Pelican Beach Camp
DNR 212A
CYPRESS
DNR Cypress Head Camp
ISLAND
DNR 287
DNR STRAWBERRY I. REC. AREA
HARNEY CHANNEL
BLAKELY
ROSARIO STRAIT
SHAW I.
UPRIGHT CHANNEL
UPRIGHT HEAD
BALD BLUFF
HUMPHREY HEAD
Thatcher
ISLAND
ODLIN CO. PK.
Shoal Bay
FLAT PT.
FLOWER I.
WILLOW I.
FROST I.
DNR 210
DNR 209
SPENCER SPIT State Park
Thatcher Pass
FAUNTLEROY PT.
JONES I. ST. PK.
Lopez
Sylvan Cove
DECATUR I.
DECATUR HEAD
FIDALGO HEAD
LOPEZ SOUND
Decatur
Fisherman Bay
TRUMP I.
DOT ROCKS ST. PK.
WHITE CLIFF
BURROWS I.
CENTER I.
PACIFIC BOATING Almanac
Rosario Strait
RAM I.
Lopez Pass
ALLAN I.
FORTRESS I.
State Park Tidelands
Hunter Bay
Mud Bay
FACILITIES
Road Access
Boat Launch
Boat Access Only
Anchorage
SHELLFISH FOR HARVEST
Clams
Oysters
Crabs
Crabs (Pot Fishing)
Shrimp (Pot Fishing)
Richardson
BOULDER I.
DAVIS PT.
Davis Bay
Mackaye Hbr.
LONG I.
CHARLES I.
JOHNS PT.
AGATE BEACH CO. PK.
Aleck Bay
PT. COLVILLE
CASTLE I.
COLVILLE I.
ICEBERG PT.
ICEBERG I. ST. PK.
0   .5   1   2 Miles
FERRY TO ANACORTES

20
SAN JUAN ISLANDS AND SURROUNDING AREAS

AIR TRANSPORTATION
Kenmore Air Harbor: (206) 486-1257
Lake Union Air: (800) 692-2993

COAST GUARD
Emergencies: (800) 592-9911
VHF 16 or 22
Anacortes: (206) 293-9555
Seattle: (206) 442-7070

CUSTOMS
Anacortes: (206) 293-2331
Friday Harbor: (206) 378-2080
After Hours/Holidays: (800) 562-5943

DECOMPRESSION CHAMBER
Keyport: (206) 396-5111
Virginia Mason, Seattle:
(206) 624-1144

FERRY TRANSPORTATION
Friday Harbor: (206) 378-4777
Lopez: (206) 468-2252
Orcas: (206) 376-2134
Washington State: (800) 542-0812

MARINE OPERATOR
Bellingham: VHF 28, 85
Victoria: VHF 27, 85

RED TIDE HOTLINE
(800) 562-5632

STATE PARK INFORMATION
(800) 562-0990

TAXI
Lopez Island: (206) 468-3397
San Juan Island: (206) 378-4711

TOURIST INFORMATION
Lopez Island: (206) 468-3377
Orcas Island: (206) 376-2273
San Juan Island: (206) 378-5420

WEATHER
VHF WX-1
CKDA: 1200 AM
CFMS: 98.5 FM
CHQM: 1320 AM

REFUGE COVE, Desertion Sound, B.C.

CHARTS 18421, 18432, 18433, 18434 † The waters of the SAN JUAN ISLANDS embrace the passages and bays N of the E end of the Strait of Juan de Fuca. These passages are used extensively by pleasure craft, especially in July, August and September. Some tugs and barges use the larger passes. Automobile ferries, operated by the State of Washington, are on regular roundtrip runs from Anacortes through Thatcher Pass, Harney Channel, Wasp Passage, San Juan Channel, Spieden Channel, and across Haro Strait to Sidney, B.C. The island ferry landings are at Upright Head, Lopez Island; on the E side of the entrance to Blind Bay, Shaw Island; Orcas, Orcas Island; and Friday Harbor, San Juan Island. Oceangoing vessels normally use Haro and Rosario Straits and do not run the channels and passes in the San Juan Islands. Many resorts and communities have supplies and moorage available for the numerous pleasure craft cruising in these waters. Well sheltered anchorages are numerous.

(Regulations governing vessels transiting gill net fishing areas are given in chapter 6.)

The directions which follow are intended for use only in clear weather; in thick weather or at night strangers should take a pilot for large vessels. Small craft should not attempt navigation under these conditions without local knowledge. Sailing craft should not attempt the passages against the current unless the wind is fair and fresh. A reliable auxiliary engine for sailboats is an absloute necessity. The tidal currents have great velocity in places, causing heavy tide rips that are dangerous. Beacuse of the variable direction and velocity of the currents, compass courses are of little value, and where followed, allowance must be made for the set of the current.

HARO STRAIT and BOUNDARY PASS form the westermnost of the three main channels leading from the Strait of Juan de Fuca to the SE end of the Strait of Georgia; it is the one most generally used. Vessels bound from the W to ports in Alaska or British Columbia should use Haro Strait and Boundary Pass, as it is the widest channel and is well marked. Vessels bound N from Puget Sound may use Rosario Strait or Haro Strait; the use of San Juan Channel by deep-draft vessels is not recommended.

A VESSEL TRAFFIC SERVICE has been established in the Strait of Juan de Fuca, E of Port Angeles, and in the adjacent waters.

From off the S part of San Juan Island, Haro Strait extends N for about 16 miles to Turn Point Light on Stuart Island, then Boundary Pass leads NE for 11 miles to its junction with the Strait of Georgia between East Point, the E end of Saturna Island, B.C., and Patos Island, the small United States island; both of which are marked by lights. These waterways have widths from 2 to 6 miles, and the depths are generally great.

No difficulty will be experienced in navigating Haro Strait and Boundary Pass in clear weather.

The International Boundary between the United States and Canada passes through Haro Strait and Boundary Pass.

TIDAL CURRENTS † In Haro Strait and Boundary Pass the flood current sets N, and the ebb current sets in the opposite direction. The ebb usually runs longer and has a greater velocity than the flood. E of the N entrance, the flood sets E on both sides of Sucia Islands and E across Alden Bank; the velocity is 1 to 2 knots. Off Turn Point, the ebb may attain a velocity of 6 knots during large tides. The current has moderate velocity between Sucia Islands and Orcas Island. There is a large daily inequality in the current. (See Tidal Current Tables for predicted times and velocities contained in this edition of the PACIFIC BOATING ALMANAC.) Heavy tide rips occur on MIDDLE BANK and N of it and around Discovery Island. Tide rips also occur between Henry Island and Turn Point on the ebb and around Turn Point. Heavy dangerous tide rips occur between East Point and Patos Island and for 2 miles N in the Strait of Georgia. The flood current sets E from Discovery Island across the S end of Haro Strait until close to San Juan Island. This E set is especially noticeable during the first half of the flood.

Rocky MIDDLE BANK, with a least depth of 11 fathoms, is in the S

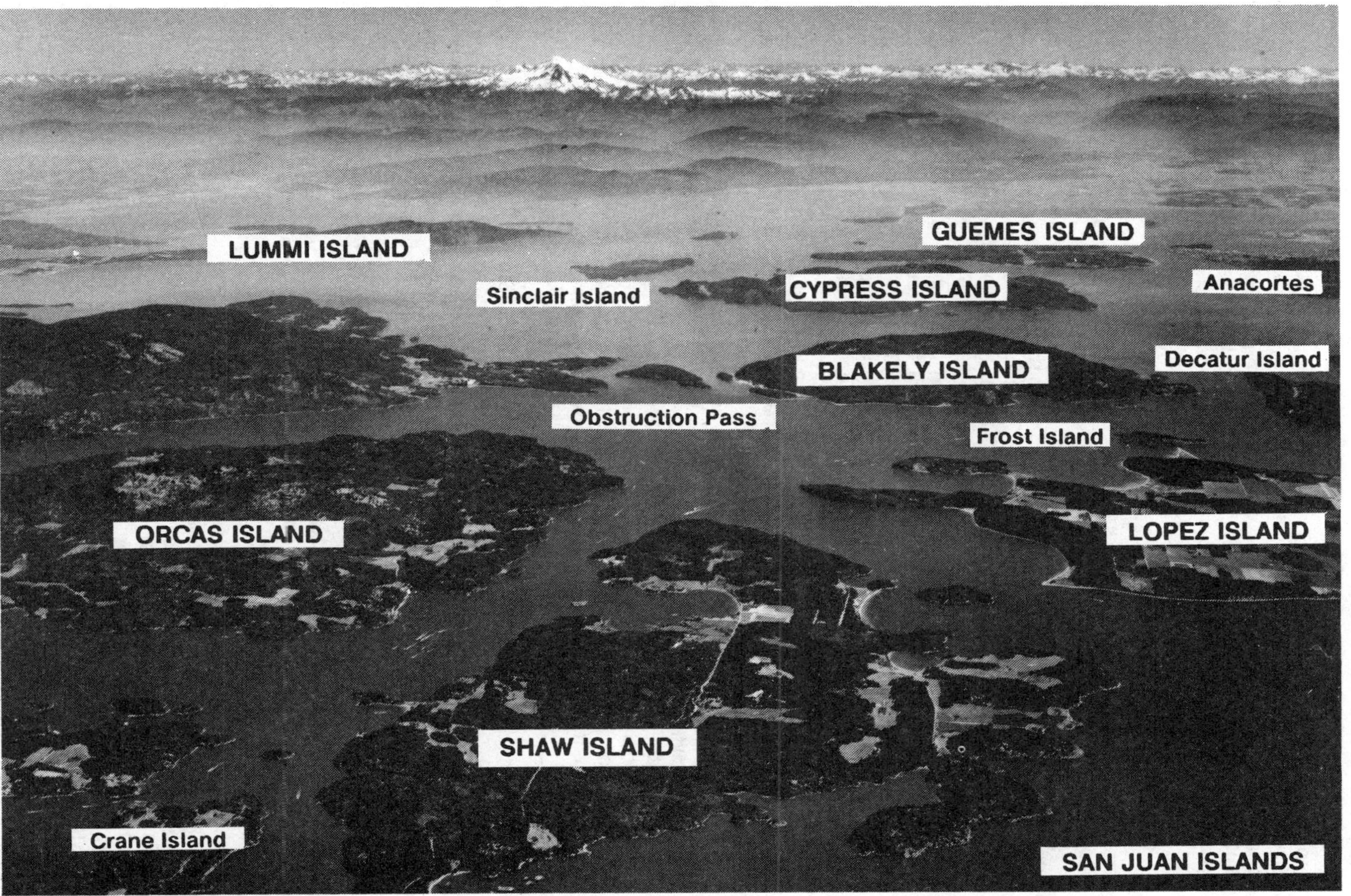

San Juan Islands and their surrounding neighbors.

approach to Haro Strait. The bank is about 3.5 miles long and the least depth is in its NE part and 5.5 miles SW of Cattle Point Light on the southernmost tip of San Juan Islands. In the vicinity of this bank heavy tide rips, dangerous to small-craft, form in bad weather.

Two small banks, covered 7 and 9 fathoms, lie about 3.5 miles NW of Middle Bank. The S bank is marked by a lighted buoy. In bad weather, heavy tide rips form over these banks.

CHARTS 18421, 18431, 18432, 18433, 18434 † STUART ISLAND, NW of Spieden Island, two prominent hills 640 feet high near the middle. TURN POINT, the W extremity, is bold, steep-to and marked by a light and fog signal.

REID HARBOR indents to SE shore of Stuart Island and trends NW about 1.5 miles. The harbor, which is landlocked and 400 yards wide, affords good anchorage in 4 to 5 fathoms, soft bottom. The State Parks and Recreation Commission maintains a small-craft pier and facilities here. The harbor is free of danger, but from the E entrance point foul ground extends about halfway across the entrance. Enter in midchannel and anchor anywhere in the middle of the wider portion of the harbor.

PREVOST HARBOR, on the N shore of Stuart Island about 1.5 miles E of Turn Point, affords good shelter and anchorage. The village of PREVOST, with 7 feet at the wharf, is on the W shore. Mail is delivered to the island by air. The State Parks and Recreation Commission maintains a float landing for small boats.

SATELLITE ISLAND lies within Prevost Harbor with reefs and shoals extending off its SE extremity. Vessels should not pass E of the island. Enter in midchannel W of Satellite Island and anchor in 6 to 7 fathoms, muddy bottom, in the middle of the wider portion just within the entrance keeping clear of a rock that uncovers 6 feet, 200 yards off the S shore.

JOHNS PASS, between Stuart Island and JOHNS ISLAND close E, is much used by fishing vessels and small boats. At the S end of the pass foul ground extends about 0.6 mile SE from Stuart Island.

WALDRON ISLAND, 6.5 miles E of Turn Point is steep and rocky on the E side, but flat with sandy beaches on the N and W sides. It is irregular in shape and 3 miles long. The highest point, 612 feet, is near POINT DISNEY, its S end. On the N and E sides of the island is a high yellow sand bluff, terminating abruptly in POINT HAMMOND.

COWLITZ BAY, which indents the SW shore of Waldron Island, is a broad, open bight affording anchorage in fair weather. Shoal water extends 0.5 mile S of SANDY POINT, the W end of the island. MOUATT REEF, with a least depth of ½ fathom and marked by kelp, lies 0.4 mile offshore and 0.5 mile N of Point Disney. The village of WALDRON, with a wharf built out to a depth of 7 feet, is on the shore NE of Mouatt Reef. Waldron has a small general store.

BARE ISLAND, small, grassy, and bare of trees, is 0.5 mile NNW of Point Hammond, and SKIPJACK ISLAND, 120 feet high and wooded, is about 1.2 miles NW of Point Hammond. The passage between them should be avoided because of its high current velocity. A small, bare rock is off the E end of Skipjack Island, and a group of rocks awash, are about midway between it and Bare Island. A light is on the NW side of Skipjack Island.

PATOS ISLAND, 4.3 miles NNE of Point Hammond, is 60 feet high and wooded except at its W end toward which it gradually decreases in height. ACTIVE COVE, at the SW extremity of the island, is reported to be a good anchorage for small vessels with local knowledge. PATOS ISLAND LIGHT, 48°47.3'N., 122°58.2'W., 52 feet above the water, is shown from a 38 foot white square frame tower on ALDEN POINT, the W point of the island; a fog signal is at the light.

SUCIA ISLANDS, consisting of one large and several smaller islands, lie SE of Patos Island and 2.5 miles N of Orcas Island. The large island, 200 feet high and heavily wooded, is horseshoe-shaped; its W side is a series of steep, wooded cliffs. ECHO BAY indents the E side of the island. In W weather small vessels with local knowledge can find good anchorage in 4 to 5 fathoms near the head of the bay. At the head of

FOSSIL BAY, on the S side of SUCIA ISLAND, there is a State Parks and Recreation Commission small-craft anchorage and float pier; water is available.

Reefs extend about 1.5 miles W of Sucia Islands to WEST BANK, which has a minimum depth of $1\frac{1}{4}$ fathoms. It is unwise to pass between the bank and the islands.

CLEMENTS REEF, 0.5 mile N of Sucia Islands, is about 1.2 miles long and 0.3 mile wide. It is marked at the NW end by a buoy and at the SE end by a daybeacon. The channel between this reef and Sucia Islands should not be attempted without local knowledge.

The tidal currents are particularly heavy and dangerous between Patos Island and East Point on Saturna Island, B.C., and for 2 miles N in the Strait of Georgia. The passage between Patos Island and Sucia Islands is almost free of tide rips, and the tidal currents set more fairly through it and are less strong and more regular than in Boundary Pass.

HARO STRAIT, SW APPROACH (CANADA) † The several channels and passages leading between the islands and dangers off the coast of British Columbia from Gonzales Point to CADBORO POINT, 2.8 miles NNE, constitute the SW approach to Haro Strait. These passages and channels should be used only by vessels with local knowledge.

The side of Haro Strait W of the international line is bordered by several islands and reefs, the most important of which are, from S to N; KELP REEFS, marked by a light, about 7 miles N of Discovery Island; SIDNEY ISLAND with a radiobeacon on the NW part, about 3 miles NW of the light on Kelp Reefs; MORESBY ISLAND, marked by a light, about 16 miles N of Baynes Channel and Discovery Island, and the smaller islands and reefs in between.

SWANSON CHANNEL, used sometimes as an alternate route by vessels bound for Alaska points, extends NW between Moresby Island and the PENDER ISLANDS, and connects ultimately with Active Pass to reach the Strait of Georgia in 48°53'N.

ACTIVE PASS is deep but tortuous and in its narrowest part is about 600 yards wide. The dangers do not extend over 200 yards from shore. Vessels should enter the pass at slack water, if possible, but a vessel with a speed of 10 knots can always get through. A vessel with local knowledge can take advantage of the eddies and variations of the tidal currents, but others should keep in midchannel. Great care should be taken to avoid the shoals on either side of the N entrance to the pass.

ENTERPRISE REEF, in the S approach to Active Pass, consists of two rocky heads about 400 yards apart. The W head uncovers 3 feet, and the E head is awash. Foul ground extends between the heads and 200 yards W of the W head. A light is on the W head, and a buoy marks the E head.

SOUTH PENDER ISLAND, 3 miles N of Stuart Island, is marked by a light on GOWLLAND POINT, its SE extremity. The last of the Canadian lights in this stretch is on EAST POINT, the E point of SATURNA ISLAND, 6.2 miles ENE of Gowlland Point.

ROSENFELD ROCK, 1.2 miles NNE of East Point, is marked by a lighted buoy. The rock is covered by $1\frac{1}{4}$ fathoms, and rocks that bare are within 900 yards of it. Close E of the rock. overfalls and dangerous tide rips are formed.

SAN JUAN CHANNEL, the middle one of three principal channels leading from the Strait of Juan de Fuca to the Strait of Georgia, separates San Juan Island from the islands E. It is 13 miles long from its S end to its junction with president Channel at the N end. San Juan Channel is deep throughout and, except near its S entrance, has few offlying dangers.

CURRENTS † In the S end of San Juan Channel, between Goose Island and Deadman Island, the average current velocity is 2.6 knots on the flood and ebb, however, maximum flood currents of 5 knots or more cause severe rips and eddies. Daily current predictions for this location may be obtained from the Tidal Current Tables contained in this editon of the PACIFIC BOATING ALMANAC.

CATTLE POINT, marked by a light and a seasonal fog signal, is the SE extremity of San Juan Island and forms

the W point at the S entrance to San Juan Channel. Cattle were once loaded here for shipment to and from Victoria.

SALMON BANK, S of Cattle Point and on the W side of MIDDLE CHANNEL, is an extensive shoal covered $1\frac{1}{2}$ to 3 fathoms; it is marked by a lighted gong buoy. Kelp grows on the rocks. WHALE ROCKS, two dark rocks about 5 feet hight, are on the E side of Middle Channel 0.6 mile W of Long Island. There are $2\frac{1}{4}$ fathom spots nearby.

LONG ISLAND, 1.5 miles NW of Iceberg Point, is the largest of a group of islands on the E side of the entrance to San Juan Channel.

LOPEZ ISLAND, is the southeasternmost one of the San Juan Islands; LOPEZ HILL, 488 feet high, is near the S midsection of the island. ICEBERG POINT, 3.3 miles SE of Cattle Point, is at the W extremity of the S Part of Lopez Island. A light and seasonal fog signal are on the point.

RICHARDSON, 48°27'N., 122°54'W. is a village on the N shore of the cove N of Iceberg Point, and close N of CHARLES ISLAND. Five fuel tanks are prominent from seaward. A wharf directly below the fuel tanks has a face 120 feet long and extends over rocks to a depth of 17 feet. Gasoline, diesel fuel, water, and ice, are available. Outboard engine repairs can be made. Fishing boats operate from here when fishing the Strait of Juan de Fuca. Overhead power with clearances of 54 feet are between on a ledge extending from the shore off Richardson.

MACKAYE HARBOR, N of Iceberg Point, has several private piers used by seafood company vessels. The harbor affords good shelter in 5 to 6 fathoms, soft mud; small craft with local knowledge can obtain excellent shelter in BARLOW BAY on the S side of the harbor. Vessels approaching Mackaye Harbor or Richardson should pass at least 0.3 mile S and E of the off-lying islands and islets. Local vessels, by keeping close to the N shore to avoid rocks near midchannel, use a small passage between Lopez and Charles Islands, but this should not be attempted without local knowledge. TWIN ROCKS,

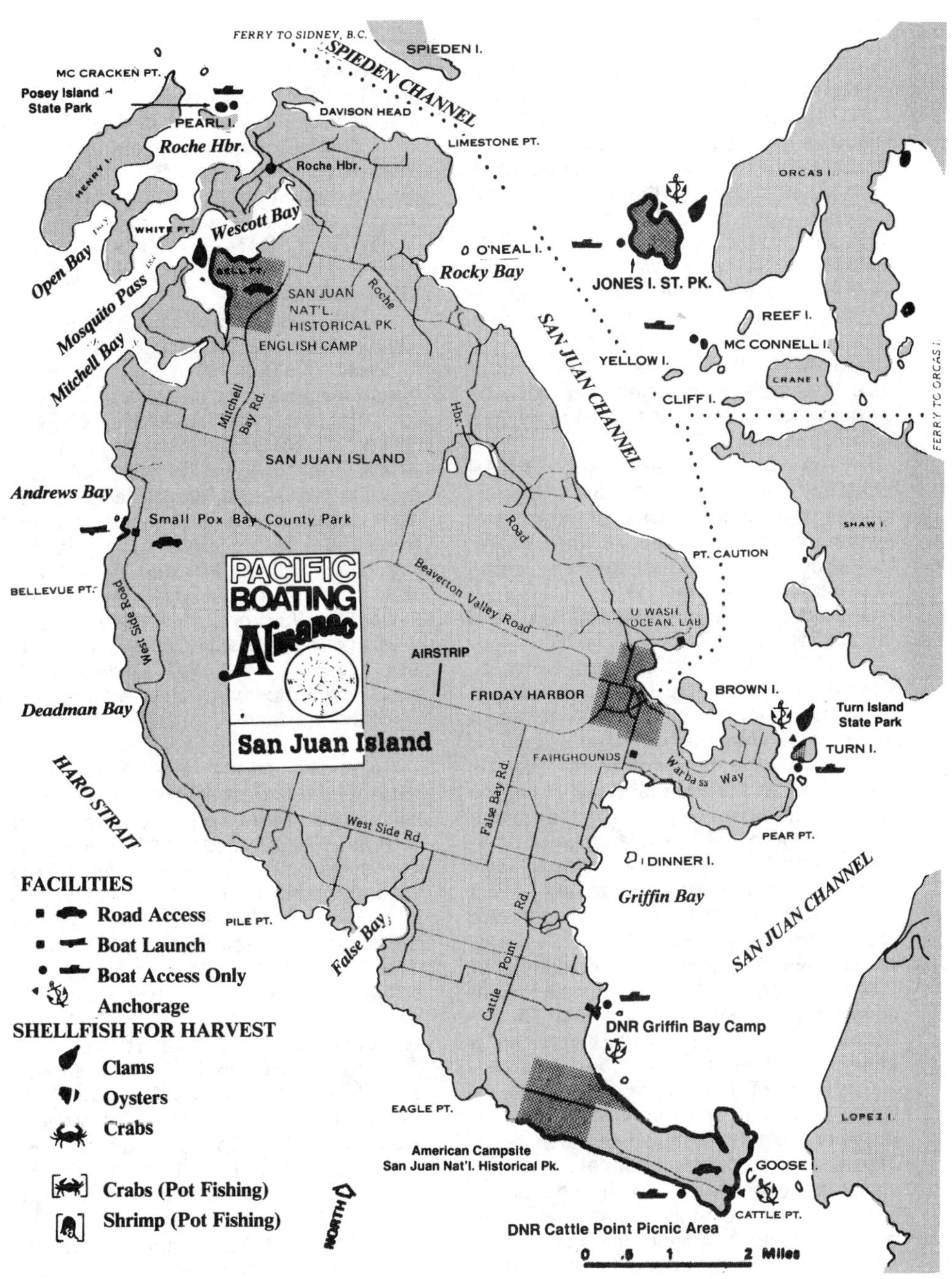
FERRY TO SIDNEY, B.C.
SPIEDEN I.
SPIEDEN CHANNEL
MC CRACKEN PT.
Posey Island State Park
DAVISON HEAD
PEARL I.
Roche Hbr.
LIMESTONE PT.
ORCAS I.
HENRY I.
Roche Hbr.
WHITE PT.
Wescott Bay
O'NEAL I.
Rocky Bay
JONES I. ST. PK.
Open Bay
BELL PT.
Roche
SAN JUAN NAT'L. HISTORICAL PK.
ENGLISH CAMP
REEF I.
MC CONNELL I.
Mosquito Pass
YELLOW I.
SAN JUAN CHANNEL
Mitchell Bay
CLIFF I.
CRANE I.
Mitchell Bay Rd.
SAN JUAN ISLAND
Hbr.
FERRY TO ORCAS I.
Andrews Bay
Small Pox Bay County Park
Road
SHAW I.
PT. CAUTION
BELLEVUE PT.
West Side Road
PACIFIC BOATING Almanac
San Juan Island
Beaverton Valley Road
U. WASH OCEAN. LAB
AIRSTRIP
Deadman Bay
FRIDAY HARBOR
BROWN I.
Turn Island State Park
TURN I.
HARO STRAIT
FAIRGROUNDS
Warbass Way
FACILITIES
Road Access
Boat Launch
Boat Access Only
Anchorage
PILE PT.
False Bay Rd.
PEAR PT.
DINNER I.
Griffin Bay
SHELLFISH FOR HARVEST
Clams
Oysters
Crabs
West Side Rd.
False Bay
Cattle Point Rd.
SAN JUAN CHANNEL
DNR Griffin Bay Camp
Crabs (Pot Fishing)
Shrimp (Pot Fishing)
NORTH
EAGLE PT.
LOPEZ I.
American Campsite
San Juan Nat'l. Historical Pk.
GOOSE I.
CATTLE PT.
DNR Cattle Point Picnic Area
0   .5   1   2 Miles

in midchannel of this small passage, is marked by a daybeacon.

DAVIS POINT, the SW end of Lopez Island, is on the E side of the S entrance to San Juan Channel. DEADMAN ISLAND is close off the E side of the entrance, and several rocks lie within 600 yards N of the Island. GOOSE ISLAND, small and low, lies about 0.5 mile N of Cattle Point and close off the W side of the entrance to San Juan Channel.

SHARK REEF, awash, lies over a mile N of Deadman Island and close off some white cliffs on the E side of San Juan Channel.

From Goose Island N to PEAR POINT, the W side of San Juan Channel is foul with many rocks covered and awash within 0.7 mile of the shore. However, good anchorage for small vessels can be had W of HARBOR ROCK, at the S end, between the 10 and 20 fathom curves.

NORTH BAY is entered between Pear Point and DINNER ISLAND. Gravel is barged from pits on the NW shore of the bay to Vancouver Island. LITTLE ISLAND, at the head of North Bay, is connected to the mainland by a narrow spit. A small cannery is on Little Island, and the shores of the island have been bulkheaded. The bay affords fair anchorage in 7 to 10 fathoms, about 800 yards N of Dinner Island. Two dangers are in the approaches to the bay; a rocky shoal covered $\frac{3}{4}$ fathom 0.7 mile E of Dinner Island, and another rock shoal covered $\frac{3}{4}$ fathom 0.4 mile SE of Dinner Island. The passage W of Dinner Island should not attempted.

FISHERMAN BAY, on the E side of San Juan Channel abreast North Bay, is a shallow lagoon entered by a marked, narrow, and tortuous channel. A rock awash is on the E side of the channel at the mouth of the bay. Good anchorage with shelter from all winds may be had in 10 to 12 feet, soft bottom, for small craft with local knowledge. The tidal currents have considerable velocity. LOPEZ is a small village at the entrance. A resort in the bay has a pier and floats with berths for about 45 craft. Electricity, gasoline, water, ice, restaurant, and overnight facilities are available. Outboard engine repairs can be made.

CHARTS 18421, 18431, 18432 †
WHITE ROCK, 35 feet high, is about 2.7 miles N of the junction of Spieden and San Juan Channels and about midway between Flattop and Waldron Islands. Rocks bare and covered, marked by kelp, extend nearly 0.3 mile NW from White Rock. DANGER ROCK, covered 3 feet and marked by kelp, lies 0.3 mile SE of White Rock.

The NW approach to San Juan Channel from Boundary Pass extends between Waldron Island on the E and Stuart Island and its dangers on the W.

PRESIDENT CHANNEL, between Waldron and Orcas Islands, is about 5 miles long. Depths are generally great and the passage is free of dangers. The tidal currents have a velocity of 2 to 5 knots, and heavy swirls and tide rips, especially with an adverse wind, are off the N point of Waldron Island and between Waldron and Patos Islands. The rips are generally heaviest with the ebb current. Rips and swirls are also heavy off Limestone Point and the E end of Spieden Island.

CHART 18421 † SAN JUAN ISLAND the largest of the group, is about 13 miles long, rugged, and partly wooded. MOUNT DALLAS, the highest of several hills on the island, rises abruptly from the middle of the W side to a height of 1,036 feet. In most places the shores are free of outlying dangers. The N end of the island is indented by several small bays that, with the exception of Roche Harbor, are shoal and of no commercial importance.

From EAGLE POINT, the W shore of San Juan Island trends NW and forms the E side of Haro Strait. This shore is steep-to and rocky, and beyond 400 yards offshore it is free of danger; however, the depths off this shore are too great for anchoring.

KANAKA BAY, a small cove used by fishing boats, is 2.5 miles NW of Eagle Point.

LIME KILN LIGHT 48°31.0'N., 123°09.1'W., 55 feet above water, is shown from a 38-foot white octagonal tower attached to a building on the W side of San Juan Isalnd; a fog signal is at the light. Two dwellings are about 150 yards SE of the light. Rocks awash lie

close inshore about 1 mile SE of the light.

LOCAL MAGNETIC DISTURBANCE † Differences from the normal variation of as much as 4° have been observed in the vicinity of BELLEVUE POINT, 1 mile N of Lime Kiln Light.

During the June-October fishing season, many purse seiners operate in this area. At night these vessels anchor close inshore, generally between Cattle Point and Pile Point.

HANBURY POINT 48°34.7'N., 123°10.3'W., 3.8 miles N of Lime Kiln Light, is the N entrance point to MITCHELL BAY, one of a series of well-sheltered bays on the NW coast of the island. A small islet 3 feet high is in the center of the bay about 350 yards SE of the entrance. A rock about 100 yards W of the islet uncovers 6 feet. The only safe passage into the bay is N of the islet. SNUG HARBOR, a resort and yacht haven on the S side of Nitchell Bay, has about 90 berths with electricity, gasoline, water, ice, and limited marine supplies. A launching ramp is available; engine repairs can be made to small-craft. MOSQUITO PASS, available only to small-craft with local knowledge, leads N from Hanbury Point to GARRISON BAY, WESTCOTT BAY and ROCHE HARBOR.

A large aquaculture facility, covered 3 feet and consisting of clam beds and suspended oyster racks, is in the middle of Westcott Bay about 1 mile above the entrance. Mariners should use caution in the area.

HENRY ISLAND is close W of the N point of San Juan Island, from which it is separated by Mosquito Pass and Roche Harbor.

KELLETT BLUFF, at the S end of Henry Island, is steep and rocky and prominent from either S or N. It is marked by a light. OPEN BAY, E of Kellett Bluff, offers good holding ground and protection for small boats from N and E weather.

ROCHE HARBOR, 48°37'N., 123°10'W., has its main entrance between the N end of Henry Island and the W end of PEARL ISLAND, which is marked by a light. Sandspits covered 17 and 18 feet extend into the channel from the islands on each side of the entrance. The landlocked harbor has depths of 4 to 9 fathoms. It affords good anchorage and in the summer is used extensively by yachts.

A large resort is on the E side of Roche Harbor. The resort operates a wharf with shed, floats with berths for about 250 craft, a hotel, cabins, a general store, and a restaurant. Electricity, gasoline, diesel fuel, water, ice, a launching ramp, and marine supplies are available. A CUSTOMS OFFICE is on the W side of the wharf. A customs officer is here full time in the summer and on call from Friday Harbor in the winter to inspect visiting Canadian yachts. The customs officer also performs IMMIGRATION and AGRI-CULTURAL QUARANTINE inspections. A mail plane uses the landing strip at Harbor. A paved road leads to Friday Harbor.

The resort here was the largest lime works W of the Mississippi for many years. A fleet of company-owned sailing ships hauled barreled lime from the works. The company had its own barrel-stove mill on the point E of Pearl Island, The present resort's hotel was in the harbor. The quarry tunnels and the ruins of the old mill are still prominent.

BATTLESHIP ISLAND, small and 30 feet high, is about 0.2 mile WNW of McCracken Point, the N extremity of Henry Island, and is the W point in the approaches to the Roche Harbor.

DANGER SHOAL, with a least depth of 1 fathom, is in the fairway to Spieden Channel about midway between Battleship Island and Spieden Bluff. A lighted horn buoy is close SW of the shoal, which is marked by kelp.

A rock, marked by kelp with $1\frac{3}{4}$ fathoms over it, is about 200 yards NW of BARREN ISLAND, 0.7 mile E of McCracken Point; it is marked by a buoy. Another rock, marked by kelp and covered 1 fathom, is about 350 yards E.

SPIEDEN CHANNEL leads E between Spieden Island on the N and Battleship, Henry, and San Juan Islands on the S; the channel leads from Haro Strait to President Channel and San Juan

ROCHE HARBOR RESORT, SAN JUAN ISLAND. Situated on the site of the former Roche Harbor Lime and Cement Company Town, the resort has sixteen of its buildings listed on the National Registry of Historic Places. The resort was restored in the 1950's, but maintains the unique charm of its heritage.

Channel. The E entrance, the narrowest part, is 0.6 mile wide, and for 2 miles W of it the channel is free of danger. However, in the W entrance, which has an irregular bottom, are several dangers but the fairway is deep throughout. The meeting of the flood currents, which flow E from Haro Strait and W from San Juan Channel, cause heavy tide rips and eddies. This channel is not recommended for sailing craft.

SPIEDEN ISLAND lies with SPIEDEN BLUFF, its NW end, 1.6 miles NNE of Battleship Island. The island is 2.5 miles long in an E direction with an extreme width of 0.5 mile. GREEN POINT, the E end of which is marked by a light, is low and grassy. The S side of the island has few trees, but the N face is well wooded.

There are several dangers SE of Spieden Bluff. CENTER REEF, which bares, is 0.7 mile S of the bluff; it is marked off its SW side by a buoy. SENTINELL ROCK and SENTINEL ISLAND are closer inshore; a rock midway between them is covered $\frac{3}{4}$ fathom.

CHARTS 18433, 18434 † At TURN ISLAND, off the E side of San Juan Island, San Juan Channel turns NW for about 7.5 miles and connects at its N end with Spieden Channel and President Channel.

TURN ROCK, about 0.2 mile E of Turn Island, is a ledge bare at half tide; it should be given a berth of at least 100 yards; A light is on the rock. REID ROCK, 1.4 miles NW of TURN ROCK, lies in midchannel off the entrance to Friday Harbor. The rock, covered $2\frac{1}{4}$ fathoms, rises abruptly from deep water. It is marked by a lighted bell buoy.

FRIDAY HARBOR, 1.4 miles W of Turn Island, is a small cove about 1 mile long and nearly as wide. BROWN ISLAND, locally known as Friday Island because of the housing development here, occupies the middle of the harbor, with shoals nearly 200 yards wide off both its E and S shores. A shoal, covered $3\frac{1}{4}$ fathoms and marked by a buoy, extends nearly into midchannel from the W shore of the island. Shoals off the SE end of the island are marked by a daybeacon. The harbor may be entered either E or W of Brown Island. Anchorage may be had off the wharves in 6 to 7 fathoms, and city floats provide berthing space for pleasure craft.

FRIDAY HARBOR, 48°32'N., 123°01''W., the town on the W shore of the cove, is the county seat and the population center of San Juan Island, which has some farming and cattle and sheep raising. It is headquarters for the gill net fishing fleet operating through the W part of the islands.

The University of Washington maintains a marine biological laboratory 0.4 mile NNW of the N end of Brown Island. The E pier, a high structure cantilevered about 35 feet out from shore, makes a prominent landmark in entering Friday Harbor. Near the main building is the landing wharf with a 32 foot face and depths of 11 to 13 feet alongside. The wharf is exposed to winds from the NE, but is easily approached. It is marked by private lights.

Friday Harbor is a CUSTOMS PORT OF ENTRY. The customs office is adjacent the harbormaster's office at the port's small-craft harbor. The customs officer also performs IMMIGRATION and AGRICULTURAL QUARANTINE inspections.

The inter-island medical clinic at Friday Harbor is the only complete medical facility in the San Juan Islands. In addition, Orcas and Lopez Islands have small clinics with resident physicians and paramedics. Air ambulance service to Seattle, Anacortes, or Bellingham is available on all the large islands.

Friday Harbor has three wharves. Two are oil wharves with 11 feet reported at their face; they receive petroleum products for the island. Diesel fuel and gasoline are available for small-craft at these wharves. The SE oil pier has floats with electricity for about 50 small-craft in reported depths of 4 to 9 feet on the S side of the pier. Water and ice are available. Hull repairs can be made. The ferry slip is just SE of these wharves. SE of the ferry slip are condominiums with private docks. The Port of Friday Harbor small-craft harbor, protected on the S and E sides by a long floating breakwater marked at

Entrance to FISHERMAN BAY, Lopez Island at an extreme low tide showing the channel which is well marked. Use Chart 18421.

the N end by a light, is just NW of the oil wharves. Berths with electrictiy for about 464 craft and water are available. About 150 of this total capacity are used for transient berthing. NOTE: Vessels should not anchor within 100 yards of the floating breakwater because of the danger of fouling with the breakwater's anchor cables. Gasoline is available at a float NW of the port's small-craft harbor. A seaplane float is near the customs float at the port's small-craft harbor. Water, ice and some marine supplies are available at Friday Harbor.

Two shipyards are at the S end of Friday Harbor. The SE shipyard has a marine railway that can handle boats up to 65 feet long. A 25 ton lift is at the SE yard, and a 50 ton lift is at the NW yard. Complete hull and engine repairs can be made.

Freight and passengers reach Friday Harbor by airplane or by State ferry. The town has an airport with surfaced runways; twin-engined aircraft can be accommodated. Mail is transported by air.

POINT GEORGE, the W point at the entrance to PARKS BAY, is across the channel from Friday Harbor. Good anchorage for small-craft in 6 to 8 fathoms, soft bottom, can be had in this bay. The head of the bay, however, is foul.

WASP ISLANDS lie in the W approach to West Sound between NECK POINT, the SW extremity of Orcas Island. Several narrow channels lead between the islands; the channels in general use are the North and Pole Passes, close under the Orcas Island shore. The tidal currents have considerable velocity in the channels, which should be attempted only by vessels with local knowledge.

WASP PASSAGE leads from San Juan Channel to West Sound and separates Crane Island from the N shore of Shaw Island. The passage should not be attempted without local knowledge. A light is on the rock 300 yards W of Bell Island and SHIRT TAIL REEF, at the W end of the pass.

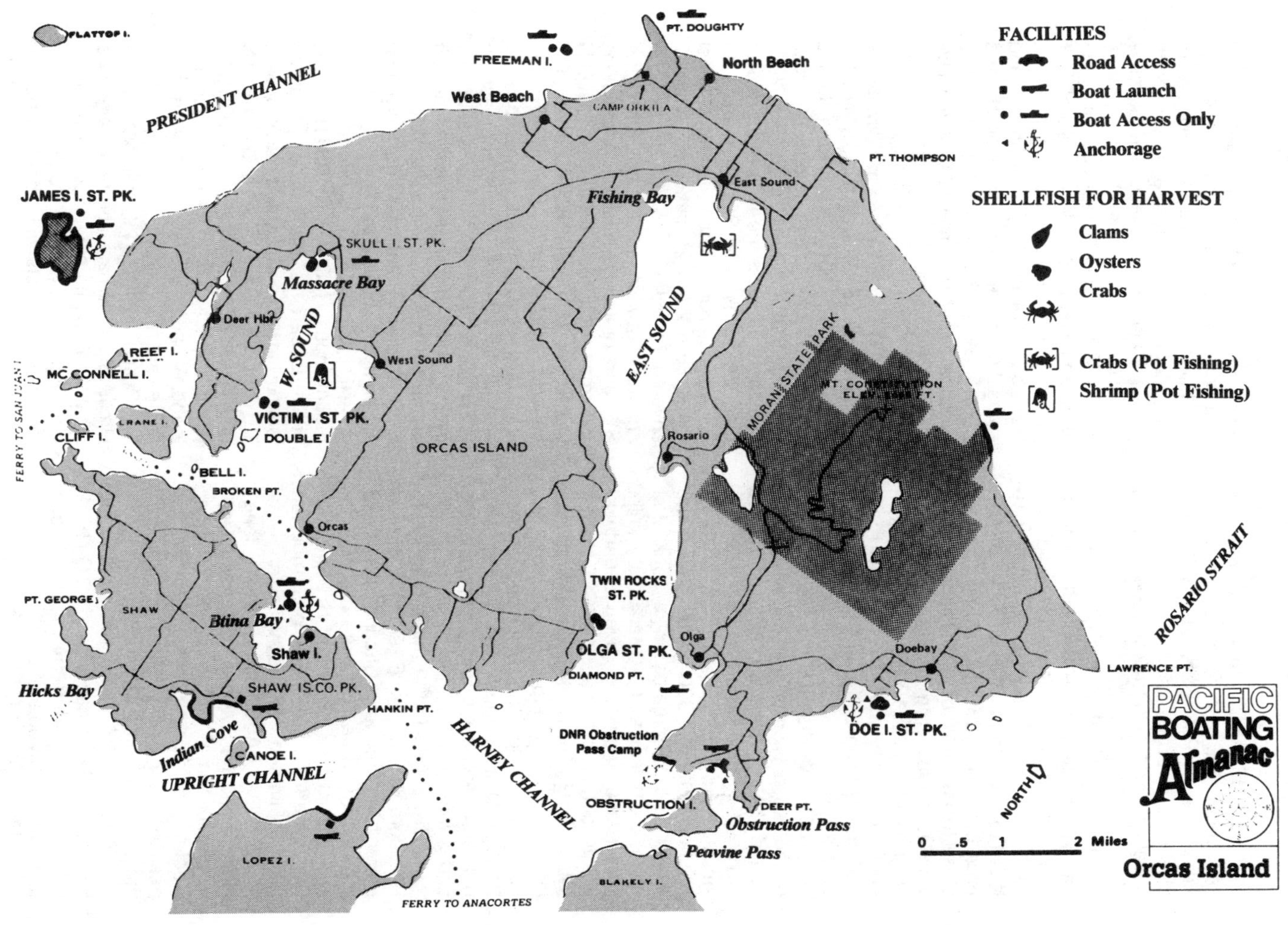

PRESIDENT CHANNEL
FLATTOP I.
FREEMAN I.
PT. DOUGHTY
North Beach
West Beach
CAMP ORKILA
PT. THOMPSON
East Sound
Fishing Bay
JAMES I. ST. PK.
SKULL I. ST. PK.
Massacre Bay
EAST SOUND
MORAN STATE PARK
MT. CONSTITUTION ELEV. 2454 FT.
Deer Hbr.
REEF I.
W. SOUND
West Sound
MC CONNELL I.
CLIFF I.
CRANE I.
VICTIM I. ST. PK.
DOUBLE I.
ORCAS ISLAND
Rosario
FERRY TO SAN JUAN I.
BELL I.
BROKEN PT.
Orcas
TWIN ROCKS ST. PK.
PT. GEORGE
SHAW
Btina Bay
Shaw I.
OLGA ST. PK.
Olga
DIAMOND PT.
Doebay
LAWRENCE PT.
Hicks Bay
SHAW IS.CO. PK.
HANKIN PT.
DNR Obstruction Pass Camp
DOE I. ST. PK.
Indian Cove
CANOE I.
UPRIGHT CHANNEL
HARNEY CHANNEL
OBSTRUCTION I.
DEER PT.
Obstruction Pass
LOPEZ I.
Peavine Pass
BLAKELY I.
FERRY TO ANACORTES
ROSARIO STRAIT

FACILITIES
Road Access
Boat Launch
Boat Access Only
Anchorage

SHELLFISH FOR HARVEST
Clams
Oysters
Crabs
Crabs (Pot Fishing)
Shrimp (Pot Fishing)

NORTH
0 .5 1 2 Miles

PACIFIC BOATING Almanac
Orcas Island

BELL ISLAND, small and wooded, lies about 0.3 mile E of Crane Island. Vessels using Pole Pass pass Bell Island close-to in order to avoid reefs and shoals extending from the Orcas Island shore.

CLIFF ISLAND, the southernmost of the Wasp Islands, is 0.4 mile SW of Crane Island, and is marked by a light on its S side. LOW ISLAND, small and 10 feet high, is about 700 yards W of Cliff Island, and NOB ISLAND, 40 feet high, is close-to and NW of Cliff Island. Local vessels bound from Friday Harbor to Deer Harbor use a clear deep channel about 70 yards wide through the rocks and shoals lying between Cliff Island and Low Island.

YELLOW ISLAND, the westernmost of the Wasp Islands, lies about 0.8 mile WNW of Neck Point and about 3.5 miles NNW of Friday Harbor. The island is small, grassy, and nearly bare of trees. A shoal extends 300 yards W of the island and terminates in a rock that uncovers 3 feet and is marked by kelp. This island should be given a berth of not less than 0.5 mile. MCCONNELL ISLAND, NE of Yellow Island, is the largest of the group. COON ISLAND, lies close to and SE of McConnell Island. BIRD ROCK, which uncovers, lies between McConnell and Crane Islands, and is marked by a light.

JONES ISLAND, 2 miles N of Wasp Passage, is on the E side of the N entrance to San Juan Channel; the island is wooded. Small pleasure craft anchor in the bights on the N and S shores. A State marine park here has mooring facilities; limited water is available.

SPRING PASSAGE separates Jones Island from the SW part of Orcas Island. A daybeacon with the words "Danger Rocks" is on the NW side of the passage near Jones Island. In general, the passage is free of danger.

ROCKY BAY is an open bight in the E side of San Juan Island. O'NEAL ISLAND, surrounded by a shoal, lies almost in the middle of the bay.

LIMESTONE POINT, about 1.2 miles NNW of O'Neal Island, forms the W point of the N entrance ot San Juan Channel, and is the NE portion of San Juan Island. Heavy tide rips and eddies form off Limestone Point and Green Point on Spieden Island, 0.7 mile N.

LONESOME COVE, 0.2 mile W of Limestone Point, has a resort with cabins. Limited berthage and gasoline are available.

FLATTOP ISLAND, prominent in the N approaches to San Juan Channel, is 1 mile NE of the E end of Spieden Island. It is about 174 feet high, flat on top, and sparsely covered with underbrush and trees. GULL ROCK, 33 feet high and bare, is about 0.3 mile NW of the NW shore of the island.

CHART 18434 † MINOR PASSAGES, SAN JUAN ISLANDS - UPRIGHT CHANNEL, between Lopez Island and Shaw Island, is about 3 miles long. CANOE ISLAND, off FLAT POINT, constricts the passage to a width of less than 400 yards. Flat Point is marked by a light. General depths in the channel range from 20 to 25 fathoms. A shoal, covered $7\frac{1}{2}$ fathoms, is 700 yards SSW and a rock awash is 250 yards SW of the SW end of Canoe Island. Anchorages for small craft may be had in INDIAN COVE, W of Canoe Island, in 4 to 7 fathoms, soft bottom.

HARNEY CHANNEL, between Shaw and Orcas Islands, is the approach to West Sound from the E. General depths in the channel range from 11 to 30 fathoms with a 9 fathom shoal 700 yards E of Borken Point, the northernmost extremity of Shaw Island.

ORCAS ISLAND is wooded and mountainous. MOUNT CONSTITUTION, in its E part, is marked by a stone lookout tower and lighted radio tower. TURTLEBACK MOUNTAIN (TURTLEBACK RANGE) and ORCAS KNOB, conical, and bare on the summit, in the W part of the island, are prominent and easily recognized.

POINT DOUGHTY, the NW tip of Orcas Island, is bare and terminates in a small knob on its outer end. A resort in the bight, 1.5 miles SSW of Point Doughty, has floats with about 40 berths, gasoline, water, ice, a concrete launching ramp, and some marine supplies. In 1973, a depth of 4 feet was reported at the floats.

LOCAL MAGNETIC DISTURB-ANCES † Differences from the normal variation of 2° or more have been observed in the vicinity of Point Doughty.

PARKER REEF, marked by a light, is about 0.7 mile off the N shore of Orcas Island and uncovers. The rocky reef extends about 110 yards in all directions from the light, except on the E side, where it extends about 160 yards from the light. Kelp covers the reef and the area between it and the shore. There are several shoal spots of $1\frac{3}{4}$ to $2\frac{3}{4}$ fathoms in the area within the 10 fathom curve SSW and W of Parker Reef.

A passsage between Sucia Islands on the N and Orcas Island on the S connects the N end of President Channel with the junction of the Strait of Georgia and Rosario Strait.

ORCAS, 48°36'N., 122°56'W., the settlement on the N shore in a cove at the W end of Harney Channel, is a summer resort. Several stores are here. An oil company distributor has a wharf with about 10 feet at its face; gasoline and diesel fuel are available. The ferry slip just E of the wharf serves the inter-island ferry that operates from Anacortes. A rock, covered $2\frac{1}{2}$ fathoms, is about 125 yards S of the wharf, deep water is between the rock and the shore.

BLIND BAY, a small cove indenting Shaw Island just opposite Orcas, is shoal and in it there are several reefs. BLIND ISLAND is in the entrance. A private daybeacon marks a rock that uncovers 3 feet on the E side of the entrance. SHAW ISLAND, a village at the E entrance, is served by the ferry. It has a store, warehouse, and a float landing with berths for about 25 craft. Gasoline, diesel fuel, water, and ice are available. BROKEN POINT, 1.6 miles W of the Shaw Island landing, projects some 0.3 mile N from the N side of the island. It is quite prominent.

WEST SOUND indents the W part of the S shore of Orcas Island for about 2.8 miles. MASSACRE BAY is in the N part. The depths range from 7 to 20 fathoms. Anchorage in 7 to 12 fathoms may be had anywhere N of DOUBLE ISLAND which consists of two small islands connected at low water; it is close to the W shore near the entrance.

WEST SOUND, a settlement on the E shore about 2 miles inside the entrance, has a wharf with 10 feet off its end. Only a few piling remain of an old sawmill wharf. Care should be taken when leaving the wharf to avoid some submerged piling about 100 feet SW of it. Gasoline, water, and marine supplies are available at West Sound.

PICNIC ISLAND, is a low islet in the S part of the cove, close S from West Sound settlement. A shoal extends about 150 yards W from the island. In the bight W of the island is a marina with berths for about 80 small craft. An 11 ton hoist here can handle craft to 36 feet for hull and engine repairs. Marine supplies and a salvage and retrieval tug are available. In 1969, a channel with a depth of $1\frac{1}{2}$ feet was reported to exist between Picnic Island and Orcas Island; local knowledge is advised.

HARBOR ROCK, 4 feet high, lies in midchannel about 1.9 miles above the entrance to the sound; it is just inside Massacre Bay. The rocky patch marked by a daybeacon, is of small extent and is surrounded by depths of $1\frac{3}{4}$ to 10 fathoms.

NORTH PASS, between Steep Point on Orcas Island and the Wasp Islands, leads E from San Juan Channel to Deer Harbor and into Pole Pass. The pass is about 0.2 mile wide between Steep Point and REEF ISLAND, and is free of outlying dangers, except for a rock covered by $1\frac{3}{4}$ fathoms 0.3 mile E of the N end of Reef Island.

DEER HARBOR, E of Steep Point, has good anchorage in 6 to 7 fathoms about 0.2 mile from the head. FAWN ISLAND lies near the entrance of the harbor and about 200 yards from the W shore; vessels may pass on either side. The E shore of Deer Harbor should be given a berth of at least 300 yards because of a shoal which in some places extends more than 200 yards off.

DEER HARBOR, on the E side of the harbor, is a village with stores, a marina, and an inn. Pleasure boats call here frequently in the summer. Berths, electricity, gasoline, diesel fuel, water, and some marine supplies are available.

WEST SOUND MARINA, Orcas Island has a fuel dock, guest berths and provides engine repairs. Use Chart 18425.

A private light is on the end of a pier about 0.8 mile SSE of the town of Deer Harbor.

CRANE ISLAND is off the entrance to Deer Harbor and about 1 mile SE of Steep Point. The N shore of the island is foul with bare and covered rocks within 250 yards of it. A shoal covered ½ fathom is 350 yards N of the center of the N side of the island, and a rock that uncovers 5 feet is 200 yards off the E point, with foul ground between it and the shore.

POLE PASS leads from North Pass to West Sound and separates Crane Island from Orcas Island; the fairway is 75 yards wide in its narrowest part. Pole Pass should not be attempted without local knowledge. A light is on the NE side of the pass at its narrowest part.

CHARTS 18421, 18429, 18430 † EAST SOUND indents Orcas Island NNW for about 6 miles. Depths very from 15 fathoms at the entrance to 9 fathoms less than 0.2 mile from the head. There are no outlying dangers, and the shores may be approached to within 0.2 mile; however, a shoal covered less than 5 fathoms extends some 700 yards off the W shore, 0.8 mile inside the entrance. Anchorage may be had anywhere in the sound.

LOCAL MAGNETIC DISTURBANCE † Differences from the normal variation of more than 2° have been reported in the upper end of East Sound.

OLGA is a summer resort on the W shore of BUCK BAY, a small cove on the E shore of the sound just inside the entrance. Gasoline, water, and ice may be obtained. A State-owned pier here has reported depths of 10 feet at its face.

CASCADE BAY, a small cove on the E side of the sound, about 3 miles N is the entrance, is the site of a large resort with floats having berths with electricity for about 60 craft. Gasoline, diesel fuel, water, ice, a launching ramp, and a restaurant are available. Depths of 8 feet are reported alongside the floats. The large white resort hotel on ROSARIO POINT, the W point of the bay, is conspicuous.

EASTSOUND, a summer resort in the W of two small adjoining coves at the head of the sound, is the second largest village in the islands. The wharf is built out to a depth of 7½ feet; gasoline and water are available. A medical clinic, is at Eastsound; air ambulance service to Anacortes, Bellingham, or Seattle is available.

OBSTRUCTION PASS, with a least width of 350 yards, separates OBSTRUCTION ISLAND from Orcas Island, and leads W from Rosario Strait to the inner passages and sounds of the San Juan Islands. A launching ramp and float are on the N side of the pass about 0.6 mile NW of Deer Point; depths alongside the float are about 4 feet. Caution is advised because of the numerous private pilings and moorings in the area. Obstruction Pass is marked by lights on the N side of Obstruction Island.

PEAVINE PASS, safer and straighter than Obstruction Pass, separates Blakely Island from Obstruction Island. The pass is a little over 200 yards wide at its narrowest part, and in midchannel the least depth is 6 fathoms. Peavine Pass Light 1, on the SW point of Obstruction Island, marks the W entrance to the pass. In 1973, two submerged rocks were reported in the pass about 0.4 mile E of Peavine Pass Light 1. A group of bare rocks, marked by a daybeacon, lie about 0.2 mile offshore from Blakely Island at the E entrance to Peavine Pass and a rock, covered 1¾ fathoms and marked on its S side by a lighted buoy, is 1.3 miles SW of Peavine Pass Light 1.

The currents through Obstruction and Peavine Passes have estimated velocities of 5.5 to 6.5 knots at times. Heavy tide rips occur E of Obstruction Island.

BLAKELY ISLAND, E of Lopez and Shaw Islands, is privately owned and maintained but open to the public. At its N end, bordering on Peavine Pass, is a small-craft basin and channel. About 65 berths are at the cove dock and inside the basin. An airplane landing strip and lodging are nearby. Gasoline, diesel fuel, water, ice, and some marine supplies are available.

THATCHERS PASS, between Blakely Island and DECATUR ISLAND, is about 0.5 mile wide in its narrowest part. The pass is deep and free of danger, except for LAWSON ROCK, marked by a daybeacon, in midchannel 700 yards N of Fauntleroy Point. The S point of Blakely Island is marked by a light.

FAUNTLEROY POINT, the NE end of Deactur Island, is marked by a light. With a S wind and ebb current, heavy rips will be encountered off the E entrance to Thatcher Pass.

LEO REEF in the entrance to SWIFTS BAY, on the NE end of Lopez Island, uncovers and is marked by a light.

In 1981, a rock covered 3 feet was reported about 350 yards WNW of Leo Reef Light. PORT STANLEY is a small village on the shores of Swifts Bay.

UPRIGHT HEAD, the northernmost point of Lopez Island, is a narrow peninsula that attains an elevation of 260 feet. A ferry slip is in the small cove at the tip of this peninsula. A private light is 50 yards out from the slip. There is daily ferry service with the other islands and the mainland.

LOPEZ SOUND, on the E side of Lopez Island, may be entered from Rosario Strait by Thatcher Pass. The depths in the greater part of the sound are 3 to 5 fathoms, muddy bottom, but a narrow and deeper channel is along the E shore.

Fair Protection in SE weather can be had in the area W of DECATUR ISLAND and N of CENTER ISLAND in 3 to 5 fathoms, mud bottom. Strong winds blow across the low neck at the S end of Decatur Island and may make the area W uncomfortable for small-craft. Good anchorage in W weather can be had in the large bight on the W side of the sound.

DECATUR is a small village on the W side of Decatur Island. A wharf with depths of 8 feet at its end is here.

LOPEZ PASS, S of Decatur Island, leads from Rosario Strait into Lopez Sound, the pass has depths of 9 to 12 fathoms but is very narrow and little used. A light is at the S end of Decatur Island.

ROSARIO STRAIT, the easternmost of the three main channels leading from the Strait of Juan de Fuca to the Strait of Georgia, is 20 miles long and from 1.5 to

5 miles wide. The water is deep, and the most important dangers are marked.

The strait is in constant use by vessels bound to Bellingham, Anacortes, and the San Juan Islands. Vessels bound for British Columbia or Alaska also frequentluy use it in preference to the passages farther W, when greater advantage can be taken of the tidal currents.

A VESSEL TRAFFIC SERVICE has since been established in the Strait of Juan de Fuca, E of Port Angeles, and in the adjacent waters.

CURRENTS † For times and velocities of current in Rosario Strait and vicinity, the Tidal Current Tables should be consulted. They are contained in this edition of the PACIFIC BOATING ALMANAC. The currents in Lopez, Thatcher, and Obstruction Passes are reported to attain velocities of 3 to 7 knots. This should be kept in mind when proceeding through Rosario Strait, particularly at night or in thick weather. On the ebb of a large tide off the enterance to the passes a S wind causes tide rips that are dangerous to small-craft.

Small-craft can get good protection from W and S weather by anchoring near the end of WATMOUGH BAY, at the extreme end of the Lopez Island.

COLVILLE ISLAND, 64 feet high, small and bare of trees, is off the SE end of Lopez Island. Heavy kelp extends W of Colville Island DAVIDSON ROCK, 0.3 mile E of Colville Island, bares and is marked by a light. Mariners should give Colville Island and Davidson Rock a good berth. The southbound lane of the Traffic Seperation Scheme is close S and E of Davidson Rock.

ALECK BAY, the W and largest of three small bays in the S shore of Lopez Island, affords good anchorage except in SE winds for small vessels in 4 to 7 fathoms, mud bottom. Rocks, awash in these waters, and caution is essential.

A bank covered 10 to 20 fathoms extends across the S enterance to Rosario Strait. A shoal covered $3\frac{1}{2}$ fathoms and marked by a lighted bell buoy is in the W part of the bank, 1.6 miles E of Davidson Rock Light. LAWSON REEF, small in extent with a least depth of $1\frac{3}{4}$ fathoms and marked

by a lighted bell buoy, is in the E part of the bank, 1.7 miles W of Deception Island.

CHARTS 18421, 18424, 18429, 18430, 18431. BIRD ROCKS, consisting of three rocks close together, are near the middle of Rosario Strait, about 2 miles WNW of Burrows Island Light. The southernmost and largest is 37 feet high. There is deep water close-to, and passage may be made on either side of the rocks.

BELLE ROCK, bare at extreme low water and marked by a light, is about 0.5 mile NE of Bird Rocks. Belle Rock can be passed about 0.6 mile to the E by keeping TIDE POINT, the W extremity of Cypress Island, and LAWRENCE POINT, the E end of Orcas Island, in range on a bearing of about 359°.

Rosario Strait is generally clear, with great depths, except for the following principal offshore dangers:

KELLETT LEDGE, 2 miles N of Point Colbille, extends 700 yards off CAPE ST. MARY, on the SE part of Lopez Island. The ledge is marked by kelp and a buoy and uncovers at the lowest tides.

JAMES ISLAND is close off DECATUR HEAD, the E end of Decatur Island, and between the two is a deep but narrow passage; on the island are two hills with heights of 260 and 219 feet.

POINTER ISLAND, 16 feet high, is 0.3 mile off the SE shore of Blakely Island, and BLACK ROCK, 4 feet high and marked by a light, is 0.5 mile off the E shore of the island. In July 1983, Rosario Strait Lighted Bell Buoy 11, marking the NE side of a 7 fathom spot in about 48° 33'22"N., 122°45'24"W., was reported to submerge during periods of strong currents.

CYPRESS ISLAND, 1,530 feet high, steep on the lower slopes and gently rounding at the top, is on the E side of Rosario Strait and opposite Blakely Island. From S the island appears to lie in the middle of Rosario Strait.

A shoal extends about 0.4 mile S from REEF POINT, the SW tip of Cypress Island. A lighted buoy is about 0.7 mile S of Reef Point. Vessels rounding the point should not attempt to pass between the buoy and the point as submerged piles and heavy kelp may exist in that area.

STRAWBERRY ISLAND, small, low and wooded, is about 400 yards off the W shore of Cypress Island. Pasasage E of it is not recommended. An indifferent anchorage may be had in STRAWBERRY BAY in 7 fathoms; it is seldom used.

LYDIA SHOAL, a patch covered $3\frac{3}{4}$ fathoms and marked on its S side by a lighted gong buoy, lies 1 mile E of Obstruction Pass Light. PEAPOD ROCKS, marked by a light on the largest rock of the group at the N end, are mile 1 S of Lawrence Point on Orcas Island. This group of island extends about 1 mile in a NE direction, some 0.5 mile from the Orcas Island shore, which is fringed with rocks and reefs.

BUCKEYE SHOAL, with a least depth of $3\frac{1}{2}$ fathoms, lies 1.2 miles SSE from NORTH PEA POD and is marked by a lighted bell buoy. Between this and the N end of Cypress Island are CYPRESS REEF, a dangerous rocky patch marked by a daybeacon, and TOWHEAD ISLAND, 0.3 mile to the SE and abut 400 yards N of the N end of Cypress Island. The passage between the two is used by local vessels, especially those plying between Obstruction Pass and Bellingham Bay.

DOE BAY indents the SE shore of Orcas Island abreast Peapos Rocks. DOE BAY (Doebay), a village on the bay has a wharf with 12 feet at its end; during strong S winds the wharf should not be approached. Doe Island, 0.6 mile SSW of Doe Bay, is a State Park.

SINCLAIR ISLAND, N of Cypress Island is wooded and comparatively low in places; dangerous reefs extend 0.8 mile off the N shore. Portions of BOULDER REEF, the outermost danger, uncover at half tide; kelp marking the reef is frequently drawn under by the current. The outter end of the reef is marked by a lighted bell buoy. URBAN, a village at the SW end of the island, has a pier with depths of 12 feet at the end.

LUMMI ISLAND, wooded and about 8 miles long, forms the E side of the N end of Rosario Strait, opposite Orcas Island. The N part is low, but in the S part LUMMI PEAK attains an elevation of 1,600 feet.

LUMMI ROCKS are off the SW shore of Lunni Island about 3 miles W of CARTER POINT, the S tip. They are marked by a light.

Shoals extend over 0.5 mile from POINT MIGLEY, the NW extremity of LUMMI Island; the NW edge of the shoals is marked by a lighted buoy. VILLAGE POINT on the NW side of Lummi Island is marked by a light. A marina in LEGOE BAY, the open bight SE of Village Point, has gasoline, diesel fuel, water, ice and a 2 ton hoist; repairs to outboard engines can be made.

CLARK ISLAND and BARNES ISLAND, and the several adjacent rocks and islets lie almost in the middle of Rosario Strait, about 2.5 miles NNW of Lawrence Point on Orcas Island. These island may be passed on either side, giving them a berth of 0.5 mile.

MATIA ISLAND, a wildlife refuge about 4 miles W of Point Migley, is 120 feet high and wooded. The mooring float of a State marine park is in the small cove on the NW side of the island; water is available. PUFFIN ISLAND, 40 feet high is about 0.2 mile E of Maria Island. A reef, marked at its SE extremety by a light, extends E from the SE end of Matia Island to a point about 0.2 E of Puffin Island. Mariners should not attempt to pass between the islands

ALDEN BANK, 3 miles N of Matia Island, with the 10 fathom curve is about 3 miles long in a SE direction. The shoalest part, on which are patched of $2\frac{3}{4}$ and 3 fathoms, covering a considerable area, is near the SE part of the bank. The bank is marked by lighted gong buoys off its NW and SE extremities and by a buoy on its E edge.

-U.S. COAST PILOT 7
25th edition, August 1989
Corrected thru 10 22 90
Local Notice to Mariners

FACILITIES

LOPEZ

ISLANDS MARINE CENTER, INC., Box 153, Fisherman Bay Road, Lopez, WA 98261. (206) 468 - 3377. All year. Boat and motor sales. Charts. Electronic sales. Beverages. Ice. LP gas refills. Marine hardware. Picnic area. Ramp: 1 - lane, concrete. Hoist: 15 ton. Guest dock. Slips. Boat storage. Hull and engine maintenance and parts. Prop and shaft repairs. Fishing: salmon tags, bait and tackle. Owner: Ronald Meng.

RICHARDSON GENERAL STORE, Rt 1, Box 2140, Lopez Island, WA 98261. (206) 468 - 2275. All year. Summer: 9 AM - 7 PM. Winter: 10 AM - 6 PM. Sunday: 11 AM - 4 PM. Gas and diesel. Groceries. Hardware. Ice. Fishing: bait and tackle. Owners: Sue and Ken Shaw.

THE ISLANDER LOPEZ (on Fisherman Bay, Lopez Island, 5 miles from ferry landing), Lopez, WA 98261. (206) 468 - 2233. All year. Fuel dock. Slips. Laundry. Groceries. Restaurant and Lounge. Ice. Overnight accommodations. Swimming pool. Fishing: bait. charter boats. Dockside electricity. Owner: Bill Burke.

ROCHE HARBOR

ROCHE HARBOR RESORT Box 1, Roche Harbor, WA 98250. (206) 378 - 2155. All year. Monitor VHF 16 and 68. Buoys for rent. Boat and motor sales. Charts. Groceries. Accommodations. Ice. Laundry. LP gas refills. Marine hardware. Picnic area. Restaurant. Pool. Ramp. Slips. Moorings. Storage. Rental rowboats, canoes, skiffs, sailboats and outboard motors. Fuel: gas and diesel. Fishing: licenses, bait and tackle. Water skiing. President: Neil Tarte.

ROCHE HARBOR INN, SAN JUAN ISLAND. Formerly the home of Roche Harbor's founder, John S. McMillin, the restaurant is noted for its excellent dining and unsurpassed atmosphere.

FRIDAY HARBOR

CUSTOMS CLEARANCE AT FRIDAY HARBOR AND ROCHE HARBOR †
Since July 1, 1980, pleasure vessels entering the U.S. from Canada may obtain Customs clearance by phone. The returning yachtsman must travel to a Customs Port of Entry in the Seattle District after leaving Canada without intermediate landings ashore. The skipper may only then walk to the nearest telephone and call a number that is posted at the head of each float. There are two numbers, one is the local number of the officer in charge of that port. The other number is a toll-free number available after hours and on Sundays and holidays. The toll-free number must be reached through the local telephone operator. Direct dialing from public telephone at Friday Harbor and Roche Harbor for 800 numbers is not possible. For complete information see Chapter 21 in this edition of the PACIFIC BOATING ALMANAC.

ALBERT JENSEN & SON SHIPYARD, Box 666, Friday Harobr, WA 98250. (206) 378 - 4343. All year. Travelift cap.: 25 tons. Open 8 AM - 5 PM. Dry storage. Full service shipyard. Boat maintenance and repairs. Engine parts and repairs. Marine railway: 65 feet. Marine hardware. Manager: Nourdine Jensen.

FRIDAY HARBOR DRUG CO., 210 Spring Street, Friday Harbor, WA 98250. (206) 378 - 4421. Charts and cruising guides. Nautical instruments. Land maps. Full service pharmacy.

FRIDAY HARBOR ELECTRONICS, 271 Front Street, Friday Harbor, WA 98250. (206) 378 - 4915. Installation and repair of marine electronic equipment, including VHF, CB, radar, depth sounders. Owner: Kim Smith and Tami Oldham.

FRIDAY HARBOR HARDWARE & MARINE, Upper Spring Street, Friday Harbor, WA 98250. (206) 378 - 4622. Open daily. Marine hardware. Air refills. Fishing: tackle.

LONESOME COVE RESORT (Speiden Channel), 5810 Lonesome Cove Road, Friday Harbor, WA 98250. (206) 378 - 4477. Slips. Moorings. Cabins. Rental boats and motors. Manager: Larry Penquite.

PORT OF FRIDAY HARBOR MARINA & SEAPLANE HARBOR (just E of the ferry dock), Box 889, Friday Harbor, WA 98250. (206) 378 - 2688. Complete services available nearby. Slips. Guest dock. Showers. Dockside electricity: (5), (10). Pumpout station. Operated by Port of Friday Harbor. U.S. Customs Port of Entry. Harbormaster: Bart Mathews.

SAN JUAN CANVAS COMPANY, 271 Front Street, Friday Harbor, WA 98250. (206) 378 - 4119. Sailmaking and repair; marine canvas work.

SAN JUAN MARINA, (adjacent ferry terminal), 2 Spring St. W, Box 340, Friday Harbor, WA 98250. (206) 378 - 2841. All year. May - Sept: 8 AM - 6 PM. 7 Days. Oct. - April: 8:30 AM - 5:30 PM. Closed Sun. New and used boat and motor sales. Charts. Marine hardware. Hoist cap.: 22,000 lbs. Hull and engine maintenance, parts and repairs. Fuel dock: gas and diesel. Fishing: bait, tackle. Charter and rental boats.

SHIPYARD COVE MARINA (adjacent Albert Jensen & Son shipyard), 740 Turn Point Road, Friday Harbor, WA 98250. (206) 378 - 5101. Limited moorage permanent and transient. Dockside electricity. Ramp: 1 - lane concrete. Laundromat. Showers. Manager: Arne Bentzen.

SNUG HARBOR MARINA RESORT (on Mitchell Bay, 9 miles from ferry landing on Beaverton Valley Road), 2371 Mitchell Bay Road, Friday Harbor, WA 98250. (206) 378 - 4762. All year. Ramp. Haulout. Gas and outboard mix. Slips. Guest dock. Groceries. Charter boats. Tidal grid. Fishing: rental boats and motors. Dockside electricity. Scuba air. Owners: Dick and Jeanne Barnes.

UNION OIL DOCK, 4009 Roche Harbor, Friday Harbor, WA 98250. (206) 378 - 2464. Fuel dock: gas and diesel. Manager: Robert Boyce.

WIND 'N SAILS SAILBOAT CHARTERS, (at San Juan Marina), Box 337, Friday Harbor, WA 98250. (206) 378 - 5343 collect. Year round charters, daily and weekly. Owners: Ray and Paula Rutledge.

BLAKELY ISLAND

BLAKELY ISLAND GENERAL STORE AND MARINA, Blakely Island, WA 98222. (206) 375 - 6121. All year. Overnight dock with electricity. Slips. Moorings. Fuel: gas and diesel. Groceries. Ice. Laundry. Picnic area. Fishing: bait and tackle. Managers: Chuck and Pam Read.

LUMMI ISLAND

VILLAGE POINT MARINA, 4232 Legoe Bay Drive, Lummi Island WA, 98262. (206) 758 - 2565. Ramp and storage with limited moorage for the full service restaurant including beer and wine. Open year-round except Mon., Tues. and Wed. during the winter months.

ORCAS ISLAND

AQUATIC DIVERS (on Orcas Island), P.O. Box 565, Eastsound, WA 98245. (206) 376 - 4918. Marine rescue and salvage operations. Diving for maintenance, inspection and repair of boats. On 24-hour call.

B & E ORCAS ISLAND MARINE, Rt. 1, Box 97A, North Beach Road, Eastsound, WA 98245. (206) 376 - 2644. Complete engine, equipment and boat repair. Mobile service available. Monitor VHF Channel 16.

CAPTAIN COOK'S RESORT (on N shore of Orcas Island), Rt. 1, Box 1040, Eastsound, WA 98245. (206) 376-2242. Ramp, mooring buoys for transient boats, grocery, restaurant, lounge. Fishing: bait and tackle. Tennis courts.

DEER HARBOR RESORT & MARINA (Orcas Island) Box 176, Deer Harbor, WA 98243. (206) 376 - 4420. Fuel dock: gas, diesel and LP refills. Open 9 AM - 7 PM. Guest dock and slips. Charts. Restaurant. Groceries. Ice. Picnic area. Indoor swimming pool. Cabins and motel accommodations. Gift shop. Showers. Fishing: bait, tackle. Dockside electricity: (3) (5). Owners: David and Jean McIntyre.

ORCAS STORE, Box 11, Orcas, WA 98280. (206) 376 - 4384. All year. Groceries and ice. Will deliver to boat at Orcas Landing. Charts. Picnic area. Guest dock. Fuel: gas and diesel. Full service grocery store. Freshness is guaranteed! Fishing: bait and tackle. Owner: G. Peterson.

ROSARIO RESORT (Ferry from Anacortes), Orcas Island, Eastsound, WA 98245. (206) 376 - 2222. All year. Ramp: cement, open daylight hours. Fuel dock: gas, diesel and outboard mix. Open 8 AM - 8 PM in summer. Mooring buoys. Snack bar, restaurant. Groceries. Ice. Overnight accommodations. Pool. Showers. Laundry. Dockmaster: Bill Mason. Note: From July 1 through Labor Day weekend, visiting yachts must purchase daily script good for marina and resort purchases. Dockside electricity: (7). General Manager: Sarah Geiser.

RUSSELL'S LANDING, Box 196, Orcas, WA 98280. (206) 376 - 4389. All year. Summer: 8 AM - 6 PM. Winter: 9 AM - 6 PM. Fuel: gas and diesel. Moorings. Charts. Groceries. Accommodations. Snack bar. Guest dock. Slips. Fishing. Owner/Jobber: F.C. Russell.

SMUGGLERS VILLA, P.O. Box 79, Eastsound, WA 98245. (206) 376 - 2297. Condo Units with individual moorage. Pool, tennis courts. Rented by day or longer. Manager: Jena and Scott Sticklin.

TIM'S MOBILE MARINE REPAIR (at Orcas ferry landing), Box 63, Orcas, WA 98280. (206) 376 - 2332. Engine and mechanical repairs. Will come to your boat. Towing. Monitors VHF 16; and CB 9, day and night. BMW marine sales and service. Owners: Tim and Joyce Jones.

WEST BEACH RESORT ORCAS ISLAND (Westside) Rt 1, Box 510, Eastsound, WA 98245. (206) 376 - 2240. All year. Fuel dock: gas and propane. Moorage. Groceries. Ice. Housekeeping cabins. RV campsites. Camping. Showers. Scuba air refills. Laundry. Fishing: bait and tackle. Rental boats and motors.

WEST SOUND MARINA INC, Box 19, Orcas, WA 98280. (206) 376 - 2314. All year. Travelift cap.: 30 tons to 65 feet. Fuel dock: gas and diesel; Summer: 8 AM - 5 PM. Winter: 9 AM - 5 PM. Closed Sun. Slips. Guest docks with electricity. Charts. Dry storage. Boat and engine maintenance and repair. Hull repair. Prop and shaft repair. Electronic sales and service. LP gas refills. Marine hardware. Salvage and retrieval tug. Groceries and ice. Owner: Mike Wareham.

WEST SOUND STORE (on West Sound, Orcas Island), Eastsound, WA 98245. (206) 376 - 4440. Open Mon. - Sat.: 9 AM - 6 PM; Sun. 12 PM - 5 PM. Fuel: gas and mix. Groceries. Deli. Ice. Wines and beer. Owners: Craig and Lynda Sanders.

SHAW ISLAND

SHAW ISLAND FRANCISCAN SERVICE AND LITTLE PORTION STORE, Box 455, Shaw Island, WA 98286. (206) 468 - 2288. All year. 9:30 AM - 5 PM. Groceries and ice. RV campsites (no hook-ups). Ramp. Overnight guest dock. Moorings. Fuel: gas only. Fishing: licenses and tackle. Manager: Sister Kateri Visocky.

MARINE PARKS

BLIND ISLAND BAY STATE MARINE PARK (behind Blind Island N of Shaw Island), 6 acres. 4 mooring buoys. Picnic facilities. Pit toilets.

CLARK ISLAND STATE MARINE PARK (¾ miles NE of Orcas Island). 56 acres. 9 mooring buoys. Campsites. Pit toilets. No water.

DOE ISLAND STATE MARINE PARK (E of Orcas Island). Six acres. No mooring buoys, 60 feet of float space. Campsites. Picnic area. Pit toilets. No water.

GRIFFIN BAY PARK (just N of the American Camp section of the San Juan Naitonal Historical Park), access by boat only. 19 acres. Mooring buoys. Campsites. Picnic areas. Operated by the Dept. of Natural Resources.

JAMES ISLAND STATE MARINE PARK (E of Decatur Island on Rosario Strait), 114 acres. Dock. Picnic facilities. Hiking trails. 5 mooring buoys, 90 feet of float space. Campsites. Pit toilets. No water.

JONES ISLAND STATE MARINE PARK (¾ mile off SW shore of Orcas Island). 188 acres. Three mooring buoys, 275 feet of float space. Picnic area. Camping, hiking trails, toilets. A wildlife reserve.

MATIA ISLAND STATE MARINE PARK (NE of Orcas Island). 145 acres. Two mooring buoys, 90 feet of float space. Picnic facilities. Pit toilets. Hiking trails.

OBSTRUCITON PASS BOATING AREA, Orcas Island. Access by boat only. 80 acres. Two mooring buoys. Campsites. Picnic area. Hiking trails. Pit toilets. No water. Operated by Department of Nautral Resources.

ODLIN COUNTY PARK (NW side of Lopez Island), (206) 468 - 2496. 80 acres. Dock. Campsites. Picnic areas. Playground. Toilets.

PATOS ISLAND STATE MARINE PARK (4 miles NW of Sucia Island). Access by boat only. 207 acres. 2 mooring buoys. Picnic area. Campsites. No water.

POSEY ISLAND MARINE PARK (off NW end of San Juan Island), at entrance to Roche Harbor. 1 acre. Picnic tables. No water. Pit toilet.

SAN JUAN NATIONAL HISTORICAL PARK, Box 429, Friday Harbor, WA 98250. (206) 378 - 2240. Open daylight hours. Park is divided into two sections: English Camp (529 acres), located at Garrison Bay on NW side of the island, and American Camp (122 acres), located on SE side at Griffin Bay. Facilities at English Camp: anchorage, dinghy float, picnic area. Toilets. Restored historical buildings. Hiking trail. Facilities at American Camp: mooring buoys at adjacent Griffin Bay Park. Picnic areas. Historical Walk. No water at either location. Operated by National Park Service.

SPENCER SPIT STATE PARK (on E side of Lopez Island), 130 acres. (206) 468 - 2251. 12 mooring buoys. Picnic area. Campsites. Overnight shelter. Hiking trails. Water available. Modern restroom.

STUART ISLAND STATE MARINE PARKS, Reid Harbor: - 44 acres. 15 mooring buoys, 478 feet on float space, dock. Picnic facilities. Hiking trails. Prevost Harbor: 40 acres. 7 mooring buoys, 380 feet of float space, dock. Picnic facilities. Hiking trails. Campsites. Fresh water well.

SUCIA ISLAND STATE MARINE PARK (N of Orcas Island), Property donated by an association of yacht clubs. 562 acres. Moorings and dock. Picnic facilities. Hiking trails. Campsites. Pit toilets. Mooring buoys as follows: Echo Bay - 14; Fox Cove - 4; Shallow Bay - 8; Ewing Cove - 4; Shoring Bay - 2; Fossil Bay - 16.

TURN ISLAND STATE MARINA PARK (E of San Juan Island), 35 acres. Picnic facilities. 3 mooring buoys. Pit toilets. No water. Campsites. Hiking trail.

Rosario Resort Hotel, Eastsound, WA.

21

CROSSING THE BORDER

U.S. BOATS ENTERING CANADA † Pleasure craft may enter Canada by trailer or under their own power for a period up to 12 months under permit obtainable from Customs at port of entry. There are no special restrictions on small craft entering the waters of British Columbia. Small craft may cruise B.C. waters subject only to the usual requirements of the Customs and Immigration Service.

The first landing of a pleasure craft arriving in Canada from a foreign country shall be made at a Customs port. Where due to stress of weather or other unforseen emergency, a pleasure craft lands at a place which is not a Custom port the operator shall report the circumstances to the nearest Customs office or the Royal Canadian Mounted Police.

TELEPHONE REPORTING † Only the master of each vessel may go ashore to report, and it must be done immediately upon arrival. After reporting, the master then returns to his vessel. Passengers may not go ashore until Customs inspection is completed.

In the Vancouver and Victoria areas, a telephone reporting system is available. Verbal clearance may be extended if you report from any marina accessible by road in the Vancouver area, or from designated marinas in the Victoria area. 24-hour Customs clearance numbers are: **Vancouver,** (604) 666 - 0272; **Victoria,** (604) 388 - 3339; **Sidney,** (604) 356 - 6644 or 356 - 6645.

Designated marinas in the Victoria area are: **Victoria,** Customs dock, Royal Victoria Yacht Club, Oak Bay Marina;

Brentwood Bay, Angler's Anchorage; **Esquimalt,** Armed Forces Yacht Club; **Sidney,** Government Dock, Van Isle Marina, Canoe Cove, Tseum Harbour.

Other Canadian Ports of Entry are: Bamfield, Bedwell Harbor, Campbell River, Courtenay, Kitimat, Nanaimo, Port Alberni, Powell River, Prince Rupert, Stewart, Ucluelet and White Rock. Hours and days of service vary widely at these ports, so it would be wise to check beforehand if planning entry there.

It is not necessary to report to Customs if you are sportfishing or cruising only, do not anchor, land or contact a "hovering vessel." If fishing, though, be sure you have obtained a Canadian license.

Where a combined inward / outward report has been filed by a non-resident further reporting at Customs will not be necessary either prior to or at time of departure unless articles were documented on a temporary permit at time of arrival in Canada or unless other goods which require documentary control are being carried on the outward journey. In this event the report outward must be filed with Customs at actual time of departure from Canada.

ENTRY FROM THE UNITED STATES OF AMERICA † Citizens or permanent residents of the U.S.A. can cross the U.S.A. – Canadian border either way without difficulty or delay. They do not require passports or visas. However, to assist officers of both countries to speed the crossing, native-born U.S. citizens should carry some identifying paper like a birth, baptismal or voter's certificate that shows their citizenship. Naturalized U.S. citizens should carry a naturalization certificate or some other evidence of citizenship, just in case they are asked for it. Permanent residents of the U.S.A. who are not American citizens are advised to have their Alien Registration Receipt Card (U.S. Form 1-151).

Visitors to the U.S.A. who have a single entry visa to that country should check with an office of the United States Immigration and Naturalization Service to make sure that they have all the papers they need to get back into the U.S.A.

Temporary visitors in the U.S.A. who wish to visit Canada do not need visas. This, however, does not apply to persons who are simply in continuous transit through the U.S.A.

Persons under 18 years of age who are not accompanied by an adult should bring a letter with them from a parent or guardian giving them permission to travel to Canada.

RE-ENTRY INTO U.S.A. † It is, of course, the responsibility of the traveller to satisfy U.S. Immigration authorities of his right to re-enter the United States.

Normally, Canadian immigration officers will caution persons entering from the United States if it is considered they may have difficulty in returning.

TOURISTS' BAGGAGE † The necessary wearing-apparel and personal effects in use by the visitors are admitted free of duty. Up to 50 cigars, 200 cigarettes, 2 pounds of tobacco, and 40 ounces of alcoholic beverages per adult person may be included. This does not apply to merchandise or articles intended for other persons or for sale. All goods must be declared.

GIFTS † Gifts, excluding tobacco, alcoholic beverages, and advertising matter, brought into or mailed to Canada by nonresidents for relatives or friends may be allowed free entry if the total value of the gift or gifts for any one recipient from any one donor does not exceed $40.

SPORTING OUTFITS, EQUIPMENT, ETC. † Visitors may also bring in sporting outfits and other equipment for their own use by declaring them at entry. These can include fishing-tackle, portable boats, outboard motors, equipment for camping, golf, tennis and other games, radios and portable or table-model television sets used for the reception of sound broadcasting and television programs, musical instruments, typewriters, cameras (with a reasonable amount of film and flash bulbs) in their possession on arrival. Although not a requirement, it may facilitate entry if visitors have a list (in triplicate) of all removable items carried, such as radio, television, electrical appliances, outboard motors, guns, etc., with a description of each item, including serial numbers where possible. A deposit equal to duties and taxes may be required for any such articles which are documented.

All such articles must be identified and reported outward within six months after entry.

FIREARMS, FISHING-TACKLE † A visitor does not require a Federal permit to possess rifles, shotguns, or fishing-tackle in Canada. He must provide Canadian customs with a description of such equipment and serial numbers of guns so that the articles may be readily cleared upon their return. Admission of equipment, however, does not give the right to hunt or fish. Hunting and fishing is governed by Provincial laws (comparable to State laws in the United States). Nonresident licenses are required for each Province, where the visitor should ensure that he is familiar with the laws of the Provinces in which he is traveling. Regulations may be obtained from the Canadian Government Travel Bureau, Ottawa, Canada.

Two hundred rounds of ammunition per person are admitted duty free. *Revolvers, pistols and fully automatic firearms are prohibited.* Canada customs will not store any prohibited weapons. So leave them at home. If prohibited firearms are not declared and are found individuals will be arrested and prosecuted.

VEHICLES † The entry of automobiles and trailers into Canada for touring purposes is a quick routine matter without payment of any duty or fee. Temporary admission permits, good for the duration of a visit (up to six months), will be issued for campers and trailers. The permits are issued at ports of entry and are good for any port of exit. Motor-vehicle registration forms must be carried and if the vehicle is leased from a U-drive company a copy of the rental contract is required.

Vehicles from all countries other than the United States, except the State of Hawaii, transported direct to Canada by air or sea, must be thoroughly washed or otherwise treated to remove all soil and an affidavit or declaration to that effect must accompany the vehicle. (Vehicles arriving in the United States must meet the same requirement and are similarly inspected on arrival by U.S. officials).

Drivers' licenses, whether from any State of the United States or from other countries and international drivers' licenses, are valid in Canada.

Motorcycles – Persons riding motorcycles in British Columbia and Alberta are required by law to wear safety helmets.

OPERATION OR RADIO COMMUNI-CATION EQUIPMENT † The operation in Canada of certain types of two-way mobile radio equipment installed in vehicles, pleasure boats, etc., or personally carried, as well as certain classes of amateur radio equipment, may be authorized by licenses or otherwise permitted. U.S. citizens visiting Canada may be issued a tourist radio service license for citizens' radio service stations licensed in the United States as Class D stations. Also, radiotelephone equipment having a power input of 100 milliwatts or less operating in the 26.97 - 27.27 mcs. band, may be operated in Canada without formal licensing. Application forms, regulatory information, etc., may be obtained on request by writing to the Regional Superintendent, Radio Regulations, Department of Transport, nearest the proposed port of entry. These officials are at 739 West Hastings Street, Vancouver 1, British Columbia.

DOGS † Hunting and pet dogs may be brought in free of duty under the following regulation:

Dogs from the United States of America, over 3 months of age, must be accompanied by a certificate signed by a licensed veterinarian of Canada or the United States certifying that the dog has been vaccinated against rabies during the preceding 3 years; such certificate shall carry an adequate and legible description of the dog and date of vaccination and shall be initialled by the inspecting official at the customs port of entry and returned to the owner. The type of vaccine used, tissue culture of chick embryo, does not affect the certificates required.

CATS † Rabies certificates are required for cats under the same conditions as for dogs.

U.S.A. RESIDENTS VISITING CANADA FOR MORE THAN 48 HOURS † United States residents returning from Canada may take back, once every 31 days, merchandise for household use to the value of $400 free of United States duty and tax, provided they have remained in Canada 48 hours. The exemption will be based on the fair retail value of the article acquired and goods must accompany the resident upon arrival in the United States. Members of a family household traveling together may combine their personal exemptions – thus a family of five could be entitled to a total exemption of $2000. Up to 100 cigars per person may be imported into the U.S. by U.S. residents, and also one liter (33 oz. U.S.) of alcoholic beverages if the resident has attained the age of twenty-one years. Cigarettes may be imported by persons sixteen years of age and over. If, however, the State laws of residence prohibit importation of any such goods, Unites States Customs will not clear.

U.S.A. RESIDENTS VISITING CANADA FOR LESS THAN 48 HOURS † Residents of the United States visiting Canada for less than 48 hours may take back for personal or household use merchandise to the fair retail value of $25 free of United States duty and tax. Any or all of the following may be included so long as the total value does not exceed $25.

If any article brought back is subject to duty or tax, or if the total value of all articles exceeds $25, no article may be exempted from duty or tax. Members of a family household are not permitted to combine their purchases under this exemption.

Persons crossing the International Boundary at one point and swinging back in to the United States in order to travel to another part of Canada should inquire at United States Customs regarding special exemption requirements.

U.S. CUSTOMS REPORTING REQUIREMENTS

CUSTOMS USER FEE † Effective July 7, 1986, a Customs user Fee for private boats, 30' and over in length, will be collected on first arrival in the U.S. The fee is good for the calendar year (Jan-Dec) and the receipt must be shown on each arrival. Individuals wishing to use the telephone reporting system may pay the fee in advance and will be asked for the serialized number on the receipt. The fee for 1987 is $25.00. This fee is in addition to any overtime charges that may be collected. It is advisable to check with your local U.S. Customs office for possible changes in the law or its applicability before your trip.

GOOD NEWS FOR PLEASURE BOATS † Since July 1, 1980, boaters save both time and money under a new system that allows operators of pleasure boats and yachts to report to Customs by telephone when they arrive at port of entry within the Seattle District form a foreign port or place

Previously, boaters could only report their arrival in person and had to pay overtime charges for reporting during off-duty hours; those hours being between 5:00 PM and 8:00 AM, Monday through Saturday and on Sundays and holidays.

The new arrival system enables boaters to report their arrival by dialing the number listed for the port at which they arrive, or the toll-free number for off-duty hours. If, in the judgment of the Customs officer receiving the report, it would be in the best interest of the Government, the pleasure vessel will be boarded and inspected in the normal manner. This inspection will normally be performed by a local Customs inspector at the port of arrival. Customs enforcement officers will monitor the new system to detect and prosecute any violations of the law. If such on-board Customs examinations are performed during off-duty hours, there will be an overtime charge.

DEFINITIONS AND EXPLANATIONS

BOAT † A boat or vessel not engaged in trade (not carrying merchandise or passengers for hire) such as pleasure boats and yachts regardless of size.

WHEN REPORT IS REQUIRED † Operators of boats arriving in U.S. Territorial waters after having been within any foreign jurisdiction or having had any contact with any hovering vessel or boat are required to report their arrival to Customs.

WHO REPORTS TO CUSTOMS † The person in charge of the boat or his designated representative must report to Customs in person or by telephone. Vessels reporting must be tied up to a dock within port limits.

TIME OF REPORTING † This report must be made no later than 24 hours after the boat has come to rest. Leaving the boat for any purpose other than reporting to Customs is a violation.

REPORTING LOCATION † The first place within a Customs Port of Entry at which the boat comes to rest.

REPORTING PROCEDURE † A person acting for the boat may go ashore only to report arrival to Customs either in person or by telephone. (See telephone numbers below). No other person may leave the boat or no baggage or merchandise may be removed until the report of arrival is made to and release granted by a Customs officer.

FAILURE TO REPORT † If, after first coming to rest within U.S. Territorial waters, any person leaves the boat for any purpose other than to report arrival to Customs, such action will constitute failure to report arrival of a boat and /or unloading passengers, baggage or merchandise without Customs permission and the boat may become subject to seizure and forfeiture (19 USC 1436, 1453, 1545, 1560).

INFORMATION TO BE GIVEN IN REPORT
1. Name and registration, documentation, or other government assigned boat number.
2. Name of owner/operator.
3. Names, nationalities and dates of birth of all persons on board.
4. Itemized list of all articles acquired aboard, whether by purchase, gift or otherwise and the foreign value of each item.
5. Itemized list of stores and supplies acquired aboard whether dutiable or not.

OTHER AGENCIES REPORTING REQUIREMENTS † Reporting your arrival to Customs does not relieve you of your responsibility for complying with requirements of other Federal Agencies. The Customs Officer accepting your report will advise you of these requirements.

U.S. CUSTOMS PORTS OF ENTRY †
If you plan to arrive on a Sunday or holiday or other than normal business hours, contact your intended Port of Entry for information. Pleasure vessels arriving at other than normal business hours will incure overtime charges of $25.00 maximum.

CUSTOMS TELEPHONE NUMBERS †
To report your arrival, call the telephone numbers listed. Call the toll free number after 5:00 PM / before 8:00 AM on weekdays or any time on holidays or Sundays.

Aberdeen	(206) 532 - 2030
Anacortes	(206) 293 - 2331
Bellingham	(206) 734 - 5463
Blaine	(206) 332 - 6318
Everett	(206) 257 - 0246
Friday/Roche Harbor	(206) 378 - 2080
Neah Bay	*(206) 645 - 2312
Olympia	(206) 593 - 6338
Point Roberts	(206) 945 - 2314
Port Angeles	(206) 457 - 4311
Port Townsend	(206) 385 - 3777
Seattle	(206) 442 - 4678
Tacoma	(206) 593 - 6336

(Services Olympia)
* (If no answer, call U.S. Coast Guard at (206) 645 - 2236)

After 5 PM / before 8 AM on Weekdays, or on SUNDAYS and HOLIDAYS.

TOLL FREE: 1 - 800 - 562 - 5943**

**If difficulties are experienced in reaching the toll free number, contact local telephone operator for appropriate local access code.

NOTE: Vessels licensed for fisheries and trade may not use the 1 - 800 number. Call the local number.

> *Anyone with questions concerning U.S. Customs regulations and procedures is encouraged to contact their local Customs office, or the District office in Seattle at (206) 442 - 4678. Questions concerning entry into and travel within Canada should be directed to the Canadian Government Travel Bureau in Seattle, (206) 223 - 1777.*

CANADIAN CUSTOMS / PORTS OF ENTRY

PORT	AREA	TIME	TEL. NO.
BEDWELL HARBOUR	Customs Float	Clsd. Oct. 1 - Apr. 30 May 1 - May 20 9am to 5pm May 21 - Sept. 9 8am to 8pm Sept. 10 - Sept. 30 9am to 5pm	629-3363
CAMPBELL RIVER	Harbour	8:30am to 4:30pm Monday - Friday	287-3761
COURTENAY (COMOX)	Gov't Wharf	8:30am to 4:30 pm Monday - Friday	334-3424
KITIMAT	Harbour	8:30am - 4:30 pm Monday - Friday	632-7611
NANAIMO	Harbour Commission Small Boat Float Brenchin Point	24 Hour Service 24 Hour Service	754-0341
PORT ALBERNI	Harbour	8:30am - 4:30pm Monday - Friday	723-6612
POWELL RIVER	Harbour	8:30am - 4:30 pm Monday - Friday	485-2243
PRINCE RUPERT	Harbour	7am to 10pm	624-3313
SIDNEY	Customs Float	24 Hour Service	356-6644 356-6645
TRAIL	Trail Dock Columbia River	8:15am to 4:30pm 4:30pm to 8:15am Weekends & Holidays	364-2534 364-2545
BAMFIELD	Harbour	24 Hour Service	728-3388
UCLUELET	Harbour	24 Hour Service (evening)	726-4472 726-7034
VICTORIA	Inner Harbour	24 Hour Service	388-3339
VANCOUVER	Harbour	24 Hour Service	666-0272 666-0273 666-0274
WHITE ROCK	Gov't Wharf	24 Hour Service	531-7581

PLEASE NOTE

After the hours indicated there is a charge for Customs Service of $54.00 for the first 2 hours, or portion thereof, and $27.00 for each hour, or portion thereof, in excess of 2 hours. The ports designated by an asterisk (*) have extended hours of service for boaters convenience.

In addition to the Special Service Charge, a charge for transportation may also be applicable.

IF DRINK YOU MUST

WASHINGTON † Liquor is sold by package in state liquor stores and by the drink. Beer, wine and liquor sold by the drink from noon to midnight on Sunday; no package sales Sunday. Legal age 21. None may be imported from another state.

OREGON † Liquor is sold by package in state liquor stores and by the drink. Legal age 21. Interstate import limit one quart.

BRITISH COLUMBIA † In B.C., liquor of any type can be purchased only through the Liquor Control Board or premises licensed by the board.

The LCB is a body of the provincial government.

No liquor – including wine and beer – is sold through any private retail business.

Licensed premises are outlets which serve liquor under license of the LCB, which operates under the Liquor Act. For more detailed information contact the Licensing Board at (604) 660-7323.

MAIN OUTLETS † These outlets consist mainly of the following:

"A" Public Houses which serve any alcoholic drink and are licensed by the Liquor Control and Licensing Branch.

"A" lounges, where all types of mixed drinks are sold, are always incorporated with hotels, motels, lodges or private facilities.

Lounge atmosphere is considerably more formal than it is in the "A" Public Houses. Often they provide live entertainment such as a honky-tonk pianist or a jazz combo.

Restaurants – standard or specialty – are often licensed to dispense mixed drinks. Others may be licensed only to serve wine or beer. In all cases liquor is served in dining places with meals only.

OTHER POINTS † Beer may be bought for take-out in "A" or "D" Public Houses.

Liquor is served or sold on Sundays between 11 AM and 12 midnight at pubs, lounges or LCB outlets.

Liquor cannot be consumed in public – such as on beaches, in parks or in open view anywhere.

The legal drinking age is 19 years old.

The amount of liquor a U.S. visitor may take back is based on state laws at the point of his re-entry not the state of which he is a resident.

For Washington State the maximum amount of duty-free liquor that can be taken back by one adult persons after a 48-hour visit is 32 ounces. Anything before 48 hours or more than 32 ounces is dutiable.

Persons crossing the International Boundary at one point and swinging back into the U.S. in order to travel to another part of Canada should inquire at U.S. customs regarding special exemption requirements. Phone (206) 332-5771 for more information regarding customs.

BRITISH COLUMBIA COASTAL LIQUOR STORES

Beverage alcohol products are available at Government liquor stores – retail outlets which are open daily, with some exceptions in small communities.

The liquor stores operated by the Liquor Distribution Branch are either self-serve or conventional type. The agency stores are located in remote and isolated areas and operated by proprietors of "general stores" under contract to the branch to provide service where it is not practical for the branch to establish and operate government retail stores.

Purchase and consumption of liquor may not be made by persons under the age of 19 years.

The following is a list of government and agency stores in the coastal areas.

For detailed information regarding the locations listed below, contact Liquor Distribution Branch, Store Operations, 3200 E. Broadway, Vancouver, B.C. V5M 1Z6 or phone (604) 254-5711.

Alert Bay, Maple Street

Bella Coola
Blind Channel, Blind Channel Store
Bowen Island, Snug Cove Gen. Store

Campbell River, 1301 Tyee Plaza
Chemainus, Legion Street
Comox, 206 Port Augusta Street
Courtenay, 300 Eighth Avenue

Dawson Landing, General Store
Duncan, 490 Robertson Street

Esquimalt, 1310 Esquimalt

Galiano Island, Galiano Delicatessen
Ganges, Saltspring Island
Garden Bay, John Henry's Marinas
Gibsons, Sunnycrest Shopping Centre
Gold River

Kitimat, 602 Enterprise Avenue

Ladner, 5194 Trunk Road
Ladysmith, High Street
Lund, General Store

Madiera Park, Pender Harbour
Mayne Island, Miners Bay Trading Post
Masset

Mission, Mission Shopping Plaza

Namu, B.C. Packers Ltd.
Nanaimo, 25 Cavan Street
Nanaimo, Terminal Park Shop. Centre
New Westminster, Eighth & McBride
New Westminster, 56 Tenth Street
North Vancouver-Capilano
North Vancouver, 175 West Second St.
North Vancouver, Lynn Valley

Ocean Falls
Ocean Park, 12881 - 16th Avenue

Parksville, 139 S. Alberni Hwy.
Port Alberni, 745 Tenth Avenue
Port Alberni, North Port Shop. Centre
Port Coquitlam, 2332 Marpole Street
Port Hardy
Port McNeill, 218 Campbell Way
Port Moody, 50 Queen Street
Port Renfrew, General Store
Powell River, 4284 Joyce Avenue
Prince Rupert, 100 West Second Ave.

Quadra Island, Heriot Bay Store
Qualicum, 691 Memorial Avenue
Queen Charlotte City

Refuge Cove, General Store
Richmond, Brighouse, 811-B Park Rd
Richmond, Seafair, 877 No. 1 Road

Saanich, 1087 McKenzie Avenue
Sandspit, Ed's Meats & Groceries
Saturna Island, General Store
Sayward, Sayward Foods Ltd.
Sechelt, Inlet Avenue
Sidney, 2343 Beacon Avenue
Sooke, 6713 Sooke Road
Squamish, 38129 Second Avenue
Squirrel Cove, General Store
Stewart

Tsawwassen, 1217 - 56th Street

Vananda, Texada Food Market

Ucluelet, Main Street

West Vancouver, 242 - 16th Street
West Vancouver, Park Royal Shop. Ctr.
White Rock, 1499 Johnston Road
Winter Harbour, Lynn Sales, Ltd.

Zeballos, Village Liquor Store

BRITISH COLUMBIA FISHING & RECREATIONAL HARBOURS

In this combined list of facilities administered by several federal agencies, the location and services available are listed below. Fees are payable at all locations. Contact the Harbour Manager on arrival to arrange a berth space, power, etc. Berthing priorities are in the following order: (1) Canadian Fishing Vessels. (2) Commercial Vessels. (3) Recreational Vessels.

Recreational vessels are encouraged to make use of the many full service marinas in certain areas and use the public harbours for coastal or transient purposes. Rafting up at floats during busy periods is a requirement and no obstructions are to be placed hindering vessels from coming alongside. The figures opposite each entry indicate the amount of berth space in meters. Data supplied by Small Craft Harbours Branch, Department of Fisheries and Oceans, Vancouver.

Ahousat 75, 63. Mooring Log.
Albion 116. Ramp. Lights. Power.
Alert Bay 1098, 630. Breakwater.
    Garbage. Derrick. Freshwater.
    Lights Power.
Alice Arm 33. Derrick.
Alliford Bay 40.
Armentieres Channel 3-Buoys.

Bamfield: East 310.
            Port Desire 45. Ramp.
            West 427, 60. Garbage.
Beal Cove 3-Buoys.
Beattie Anchorage 3-Buoys.
Bedwell Harbour (South Pender) 60.
    Breakwater. Lights. Phone.
    Customs.
Bella Bella 675, 72. Breakwater.
    3-Buoys. Phone.
Bella Coola 978, 755. Ramp.
    Breakwater.
    Garbage. Derrick & Grid. Lights.
    Phone.
Big Bay (Yaculta Landing) 214.
    Breakwater.
Billings Bay 45.

Blind Channel 37. Fender Log
Blubber Bay (Texada Is.) 31.
Brentwood Bay: Marchant Rd. 45.
                Verdier Ave. 75
Brooks Peninsula 3-Buoys.
Browning Harbour (N. Pender Is.) 67.
    Breakwater
Bull Harbour 75.
Burgoyne Bay 26.
Butler Cove 3-Buoys.

Campbell River 2526. Breakwater.
    Garbage. Freshwater. Lights.
    Power.
Cape Mudge 209. Breakwater. Power.
    Marine Ways.
Carew Bay (Kano Inlet) 3-Buoys.
Caulfield 30. Power.
Chemainus 430.
Christie Passage 2-Buoys.
Coal Harbour 230.
Comox 667. Breakwater.
    Derrick & Grid.
    Freshwater. Lights. Power.
Cortes Bay 196. Garbage. Phone.
Courtenay Slough 536. Derrick.
    Freshwater. Lights.
Cowichan Bay 727. Breakwater.
    Garbage. Derrick. Freshwater.
    Lights.
Cracroft 52. Fender Log.
Crescent Beach 53. Power.
Crofton 423. Ramp. Breakwater.
    Garbage. Derrick. Lights.

Dawson Harbour 1-Buoy.
Deep Bay (Baynes Sound) 862.
    Breakwater. Garbage. Derrick &
    Grid. Freshwater. Lights. Power.
Deep Cove (Burrard Inlet) 30.
Degnen Bay 120. Garbage. Derrick.
    Lights. Power.
Denman Island 75. Ramp. Breakwater.

Eastbourne (Keats Is.) 37. Mooring Log.
Edith Harbour 4-Buoys.
Egmont 397. Garbage. Derrick.
Esperanza 37.
Evans Bay (Read Is.) 45.

Fair Harbour 70.
False Bay 90.
Fanny Bay 135. Breakwater.
Fernwood (Walker Hook) 30.
Finn Bay (Lund) 120.
Ford Cove 334. Breakwater. Garbage.
    Derrick.

Frederick Island 2-Buoys.
Freeman Passage 4-Buoys.
Friendly Cove 30. Breakwater.
Fulford Harbour 15, 90. Garbage.
    Lights.

Gambier Harbour 75.
Ganges 60, 847. Breakwater. Garbage.
    Freshwater. Lights. Power. Slip.
Gibsons 700, 1031. Breakwater.
    Derrick. Fixed Slip.
Gold River 183. Derrick.
Goose Cove (Athlow Bay) 3-Buoys.
Gordon Cove 1-Buoy.
Gorge Harbour (Cortex Is.) 56. Garbage.
Granite Bay 49.
Greenville 102.

Halfmoon Bay 64.
Halkett Bay (Gambier Is.) 43.
Haney 56.
Hartley Bay 45.
Haysport 52.
Heater Harbour 1-Buoy.
Heriot Bay 397. Garbage. Derrick.
    Lights. Power.
Hope Bay 217. Lights. Phone.
Horseshoe Bay 159.
Horton Bay (Mayne Is.) 157. Garbage.
Hospital Bay 367. Garbage.
Hot Springs Cove 247. Fender Logs.
Hoya Passage 2-Buoys.
Hunts Inlet (Porcher Is.) 64.

Irvines Landing 212. Garbage.

Jedway Bay 1-Buoy.
Jeune Landing 31.

Kanaka Landing (Haney) 274. Lights.
Keats Island 30.
Kelsey Bay 401, 115. Breakwater.
Kincolith 30. Derrick.
Kingcome Inlet 64. Boomsticks.
Kiokathli Inlet 2-Buoys.
Kitimat 409, 33. Breakwater.
Kitkatla 240. Breakwater.
Klaskino Anchorage 4-Buoys.
Klaskish Anchorage 4-Buoys.
Klaskish Inlet 8-Buoys.
Klemtu 195.
Kuper Island 57. Slip.
Kyuquot 64.

Ladner 36.
Ladysmith 622, 56. Ramp. Breakwater.

Garbage. Derrick. Freshwater.
    Lights.
Larsen Harbour 6-Buoys.
Louscoone Inlet 1-Buoy.
Lund 510. Ramp. Breakwater.
    Garbage. Freshwater. Lights.
    Power.
Lyall Harbour 154.

Madiera Park 480. Garbage. Derrick.
    Freshwater. Lights. Power.
Mansons Landing 169. Garbage.
    Phone.
Maple Bay 150. Garbage. Lights.
Marktosis (Ahousat) 596.
Masset (Delkatla Slough) 825. Garbage.
    Derrick & Grid. Freshwater. Lights.
    Power.
Mayne Island 58.
McIvors Landing (Fraser River) 176.
    Derrick (Private). Lights.
    Power (Private).
Mazzarredo Islands 2-Buoys.
McMillan Island 79. Shear Boom.
Mill Bay 52. Garbage.
Minstrel Island 345. Lights.
Mitchell Bay 34.
Montague Harbour 120.
Mount Gardner (Bowen Is.) 45.
Murchison Island 3-Buoys.
Musgrave (Saltspring Is.) 41.

Naden Harbour 3-Buoys.
Nanaimo 750. Breakwater. Garbage.
    Freshwater. Lights. Power.
    Washrooms. Winch. Showers.
Nesto Inlet 2-Buoys.
New Brighton 164.
New Westminster (Brunette River) 56.
North Galiano 34.
Northwest Bay. Breakwater.

Ocean Falls 1608. Ramp. Lights.
    Power (Private).
Okeover Arm (Okeover Inlet) 90.
    Breakwater. Derrick.
Oona River 304. Breakwater. 2-Buoys.
Opisat 206. Derrick.
Owen Bay 90.

Piers Island 78.
Pillar Bay 2-Buoys.
Pitt Meadows (Bonson Road) 45.
Porpoise Bay 360. Garbage. Derrick.
    Freshwater. Lights. Power.
Port Alberni: China Creek 1500. Ramp.
    Breakwater. Garbage. Freshwater.

Lights. Power. Washrooms.
Showers. Dump Station. Clutesi
Haven 1500. Ramp. Breakwater.
Garbage. Freshwater. Lights.
Power. Washrooms. Showers.
Fishermans Harbour 1100.
Port Clements 176, 45. Breakwater.
Lights.
Port Graves (Gambier Is.) 58.
Port Hardy 1435, 165. Breakwater.
Garbage. Derrick. Freshwater.
Lights. Power.
Port McNeill 510, 69. Breakwater.
Garbage. Freshwater. Lights.
Power.
Port Neville 63. Lights. Power. Fender.
Port Renfrew 73.
Port Simpson 870. Breakwater.
Port Washington 140. Slip.
Powell Lake 109.
Powell River 1046. Breakwater.
Garbage. Derrick. Freshwater.
Lights. Power.
Prince Rupert: Cow Bay 170.
Breakwater. Garbage.
Dodge Cove 220. Derrick.
Lights.
Fairview Bay 1160. Breakwater.
Garbage. Derrick. Lights.
Metlakatla 73. Lights.
Port Edward 320. Ramp.
Garbage. Derrick. Power Shear
Boom.
Fender Logs.
Rushbrooke 1320. Ramp.
Breakwater. Garbage. Derrick.
Lights.

Qualicum Beach (French Creek) 997.
Ramp. Breakwater. Garbage.
Derrick. Lights. Power.
Quathiaski Cove 510. Ramp. Garbage.
Derrick. Lights. Power.
Quatsino 76. Derrick.
Queen Charlotte City 900. Breakwater.
Lights. Power.

Ramsay Island 2-Buoys.
Redonda Bay 150.
Refuge Cove 120.
Retreat Cove 60.
Rivers Inlet (Owikeno) 30.
Rock Bay 45.
Rose Harbour 3-Buoys.

Saanichton 16.
Saltery Bay 332. Garbage. Lights.

Sandspit 93. Ramp.
Savary Island 29. Breakwater.
Sea Otter Cove 8-Buoys.
Seechelt. Breakwater.
Secret Cove 221.
Section Cove 3-Buoys.
Shearwater 7-Buoys.
Shoal Bay 194.
Sidney (Beacon Ave.) 555. Breakwater.
Garbage. Lights. Customs.
Silverdale. Shear Boom.
Skidegate 112.
Skidegate Channel 1-Buoy.
Snug Cove 253.
Sointula 870. Breakwater. Garbage.
Derrick. Lights. Power.
Sooke 540. Garbage. Derrick. Lights.
Power.
Squamish 330. Lights.
Squirrel Cove (Cortes Is.) 163. Derrick.
Squitty Bay 120. Garbage.
Steveston (2nd Ave.) 232. Breakwater.
Garbage. Derrick & Grid. Lights.
Stewart 103, 124.
Stuart Island 191. Garbage. Derrick.
Sturdies Bay 111, 71. Derrick.
Sullivan Bay 60.
Surge Narrows (Read Is.) 75.
Surrey (Gundersen Slough) 88.
Swartz Bay 30.

Tahsis 154. Ramp. Breakwater.
Tartu Inlet 2-Buoys.
Thetis Island 43. Slip.
Thurston Harbour 5-Buoys.
Tofino: Armitage Point 326. Garbage.
Derrick. Lights. 8-Buoys.
4th Street 1083. Breakwater.
Garbage. Freshwater. Lights.
Power.
Wingen Lane 105. Breakwater.
1st Street. Wharf. Lights.
Tsehum Harbor 836. Ramp.
Breakwater. Garbage. Derrick.
Freshwater. Lights. Power. Phone.

Ucluelet: Boat Harbour 1106.
Breakwater. Garbage. Freshwater.
Lights. Power.
East 120.
Ittatsoo 206.
Main Street 90.
Otter Street 367. Garbage.
Lights. Phone.
Union Bay 67. Ramp. Breakwater.

Vanada (Texada Is.) 37. Ramp.

An Invitation to **The Marina at BridgePoint**

Down by the riverside… a market of marvelous foods, specialty retail, and unique maritime experiences.

It's the North Fraser River that gives BridgePoint both it's character and diversions.
Located 6 nautical miles on the North Arm of the Fraser River,
The Marina at BridgePoint offers the highest service available in boat moorage.

FEATURING:
- Permanent & transient moorage
- Showers & Laundry
- Marina Centre
- Concrete docks
- Fuel & services close by

- Fresh foods market
- Restaurants & pub
- Specialty retail
- Charters
- Tours
- International airport only 3 miles

The Marina at Bridgepoint
8811 River Road
Richmond, B.C. V6X 1Y6

For reservations call: (604) 273-8560
Marine: VHF Channel 68 #CHE672

22

GULF ISLANDS (CANADA)

SOUTH PENDER ISLAND

BEDWELL HARBOUR RESORT, South Pender Island, B.C. V0N 2M0. (604) 629 - 3212. Fuel dock: gas, diesel and mix. Open 8 AM - 8 PM. Guest slips. Groceries. Ice. Charts. Overnight accommodations. Showers. Pool. Laundry. Restaurant. Pub and snack bar. Boat and bike rentals. Canadian Customs Port of Entry, May to September. Fishing: licenses, bait and tackle. Dockside electricity. Owner/ Managers: Larry and Betty Hildreth.

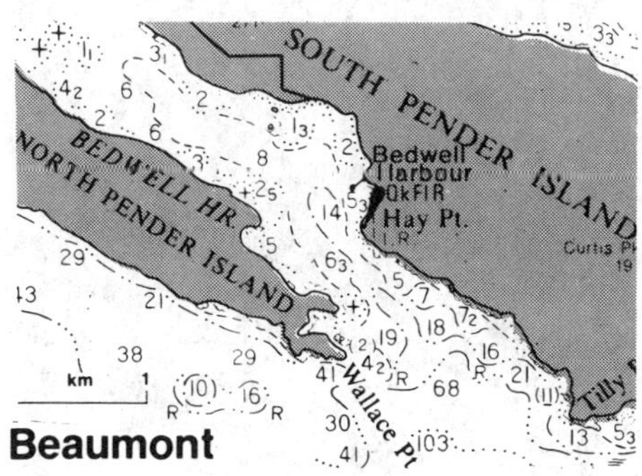

Beaumont

NORTH PENDER ISLAND

OTTER BAY MARINA, Pender Island, B.C. V0N 2M0. (604) 629 - 3579. Groceries and beverages. Ice. Laundry. Picnic area, recreational vehicle campsites. April - Oct. 7 AM - 11 PM. Ramp: 1 - lane, concrete. Overnight guest dock. Dockside electricity. Rental rowboats, canoes and skiffs. Fuel dock: mix. Fishing: licenses, bait and tackle. Owner: Robert Melville.

PORT BROWNING MARINA RESORT, General Delivery, North Pender Island, B.C., Canada V0N 2M0. (604) 629 - 3493. Old and new friends meet at the remodeled Port Browning Marina Resort, located at the head of Port Browning on North Pender Island. Customs check-in at Bedwell Harbour. Proceed through Pender Canal. Restaurant, entertainment. Fishing: licenses and tackle. Tennis, swimming pool. Rooms available nearby. Campsites. Store. Reser-vations recommended July / Aug.

SALTSPRING ISLAND

SALTSPRING ISLAND † 18 miles long with widths varying from 2 - 10 miles. Ganges is the main center of commerce for the Gulf Islands. The Island was first settled in the 1850's where the name derives from the many pools of springs that contain a large percentage of salt water. Of interest, the pastoral scenery of Ruckle Provincial Park, a pioneer Gulf Islands farm located at Beaver Point, 5 miles by road from Fulford Harbour; the

BEDWELL HARBOUR RESORT on S Pender Island, is a Canadian Customs Port of Entry with ample guest docks. Fuel, food and lodging are available.

Protected moorings and slips are found on the E side of Gabriola Island in SILVA BAY between Tugboat and Sear Islands. Use Chart 3310.

picturesque village of Ganges; the view of the Gulf Islands from Mount Maxwell Provincial Park.

GANGES GOVERNMENT BOAT BASIN, R.R. Box 308, Ganges, B.C. V0S 1E0. (604) 537 - 5711. Behind breakwater S of peninsula in Ganges Harbour. Enter by marked channel. Docks. Transient moorage. Ramp: 1 - lane, concrete, open 24 hours. Dockside electricity. Harbourmaster: R. Stuart.

GANGES MARINA, moorage, power, fuels. (604) 537 - 5242.

HARBOURS END MARINE & EQUIP-MENT, Box 1440, Ganges, B.C. V0S 1E0. (604) 537-4202. All year. Boat and motor sales. Ice. Marine hardware. Picnic area. Marine railway cap.: 30', 20,000 lbs. Hours: 8:30 AM - 5:30 PM. Guest dock and electricity. Slips and moorings. Boat storage. Hull maintenance and repairs. Engine repairs and parts. Prop and shaft repairs.

Fishing boat rentals. Charter fishing boats. Vice President: Murray Rourke.

PRINCESS MARGARET MARINE PARK, (Portland Island, at the junction of Swanson Channel and Satellite Channel, SE of Saltspring Island, is the park). 485 acres. Sandy beaches on the NW and SW shores. Fair weather anchorages at North Bay behind Chads Island and near Tortoise Island on the S side of the park. The island should be approached with caution since there are numerous reefs and shoals around it. Limited development includes trails that circle and cross the island and a well for water. Small islands lying offshore are private property and should be respected. The center of the island is an abandoned sheep ranch and wild sheep and deer may be observed from the trails that crisscross the park and follow the shoreline.

GABRIOLA ISLAND

GABRIOLA ISLAND -- SILVA BAY †
The main port for Vancouver based
yachts entering or leaving the Gulf
Islands. It is also an alternate jumping
off point to Nanaimo for those heading
upcoast from the Gulf Islands. The main
entrance is from Commodore Passage,
but access from the south may be made
west of Sear Island and from the north
west of Carlos Island. Note the buoy
west of Carlos Island is a port hand buoy
in observance that the upstream
direction for buoyage on the B.C. coast
is northerly.

PAGES RESORT & MARINA, Site 30,
R.R. 2, Gabriola Island, B.C. V0R 1X0.
(604) 247 - 8931. All year. Fuel dock.
Moorings. Showers. Laundry.
Cottages. Campground. Ice. Sailboard
rentals. Paperback books. Gabriola
Reefs Dive Shop. Owners: Ted and
Phyllis Reeve.

SILVA BAY MARINA & SHIPYARD LTD.,
RR 2, Gabriola Island, B.C. V0R 1X0.
(604) 247-9317/247-8044. All year.
Travelift cap.: 12 tons. Marine railways
cap.: 200 tons. Full ship service yard.
Hull maintenance and repairs. Engine
sales, parts and repairs. Sterndrive
repairs. Prop and shaft repairs.
Electronic and instrument repairs.
Woodwork, fiberglass repairs. Painting.
Emergency towing and salvage service.
Marine hardware store. Brokerage.
Marine surveys. All weather harbor.
Excellent year round fishing and diving.
Fully staffed year round shipyards.
Restaurant and pub year round. Charts.
Owner: Roger Mundell.

DeCOURCY ISLAND

PIRATES COVE MARINA PARK, (On SE
side of DeCourcy Island). 78 acres. A
sheltered anchorage with dinghy dock on
Pylades Channel is connected with a
beach area on Ruxton Passage.
Entering anchorage from Pylades

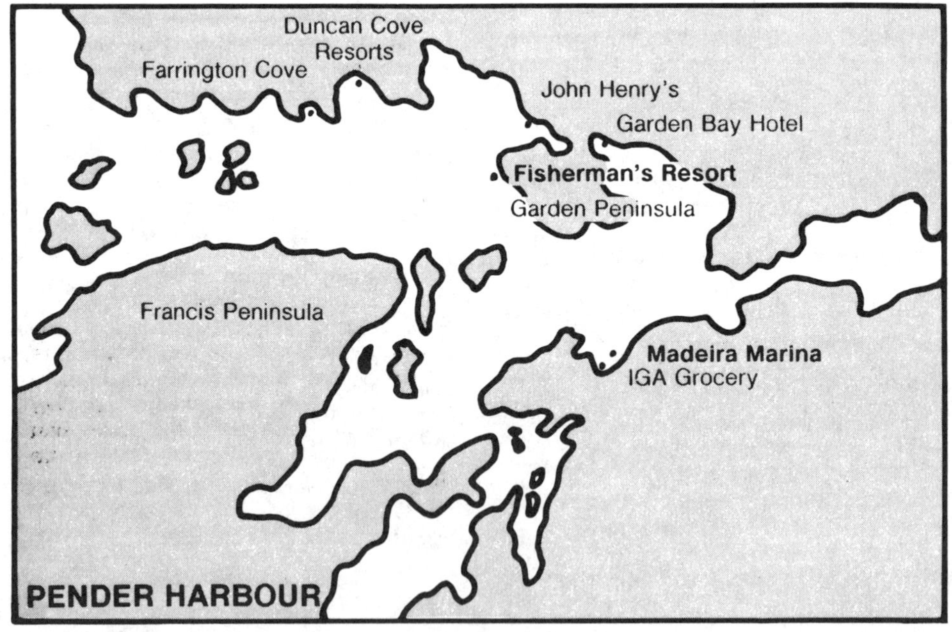

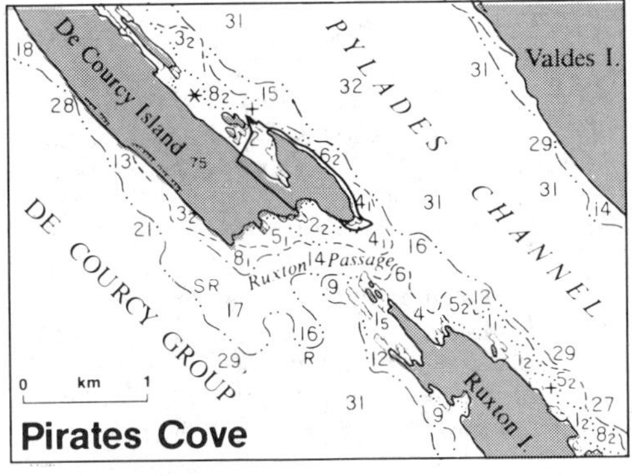

Pirates Cove

Channel, keep clear of kelp-covered reef extending N from the point at the entrance to the channel leading to the cove. The best course is just east of center channel. At low tide the channel must be negotiated with care. Dock to starboard upon entry is private. Care should be exercised in setting anchor. Hiking trails. Picnic area. Camping. Toilets. Additional anchorage at Whaleboat Island Provinicial Marine Park. The depth at the entrance is less than a fathom at extreme low tide. Although the cove is landlocked, it is subject to gusty winds and care must be taken when anchoring. The bay in Ruxton Passage provides good anchorage in northwesterly winds. Strategically located for boaters waiting for slack water in either Dodd Narrows or Gabriola Pass.

ECHO BAY

ECHO BAY RESORT, Simoom Sound P.O. Echo Bay, B.C. V0P 1S0. (604) 949-4911. All year. Charts. Groceries and beverages. Ice. Accommodations. Laundry. Guest dock. Moorings. Rental outboard motors. Showers. Post office. Lounge. Incinerator. Shore power 15 & 30 AMP. Scheduled air service from Seattle, Campbell River. Fuel dock: gas and diesel. Fishing: licenses, bait and tackle. Boat rentals. Owners: Bob & Nancy Richter.

GALIANO ISLAND

THE MARINA AT MONTAGUE, R.R. 1, Montague Road, Galiano, B.C. V0N 1P0. (604) 539 - 5733. Open Easter through Thanksgiving. Moorage. Overnight. Fuel dock: gas, diesel and mix. Groceries. Ice. Fishing: licenses, bait and tackle. Rental boats. Dockside electricity. Owner/Operators: Rick, Shirley & T.J. Coulter.

MONTAGUE HARBOUR MARINE PARK, (a land-locked bay on the SW side of Galiano Island providing protected anchorage). 243 acres. Enter from Trincomali Channel from the S through the passage between Phillimore Point and Julia Island or from the N between Parker Island and Galiano Island. Gray Peninsula, a fairly heavy forrested promontory, is connected to Galiano Island and the main park area by a narrow neck of land. Sandy beaches in Montague Harbour and on the N side of Gray Peninsula. Wharf, dinghy floats and mooring buoys. Tent and RV camping. Toilets. Picnic area and a launching ramp. Hiking trails. Fuel, store, supplies, some repairs at nearby marina. Accessible by road and car ferry from Swartz Bay via Montague Harbour or from Tswassen via Sturdies Bay. Because of its location, good anchorage, variety of facilities and accessibility by road to other attractions on Galiano Island, this is the most popular marine park in the Gulf Islands S of Nanaimo.

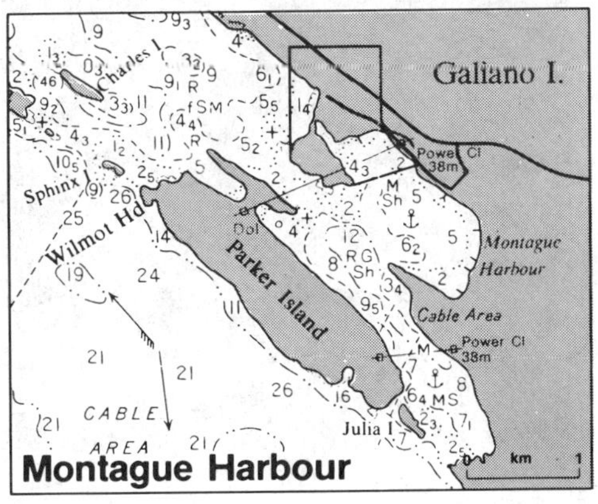

Montague Harbour

SALISHAN RESORT, R.R. 2, Galiano Island, B.C. V0N 1P0. (604)539 - 2689. Open May to October. Mooring. Housekeeping units. Fishing. Owners: The Stafford's.

MAYNE ISLAND

ACTIVE PASS AUTO & MARINE LTD., (Miners Bay), Box 90, Mayne Island, B.C. V0N 2J0. (604) 539-5411. Fuel dock: gas, diesel and mix. Open 7 AM - 7 PM. LP refills. Charts. Ice. Groceries. Bike rentals. Freezer. Service. Fishing: licenses, bait and tackle. Owner: Trueman Norcross.

ESSO MARINE SERVICE, (604) 539 - 2411. Gas, diesel, moorage.

SPRINGWATER LODGE, (on Active Pass) Box 39, Mayne Island, B.C. V0N 2J0. (604) 539 - 5521. All year. Guest dock. Overnight accommodations. Restaurant.

SATURNA ISLAND

CABBAGE ISLAND MARINE PARK, (off the NE coast of Tumbo Island, E of Saturna Island). 10 acres. Enter from the Strait of Georgia and Tumbo Channel through Reef Harbour. Approach with caution. Sheltered anchorage on W side. Sandy beach. Undeveloped. This was donated for a park by the Nature Conservancy of Canada and is left in its natural state as an example of a Gulf Island ecology.

ESSO MARINE STATION, Saturna Point Marina. (604) 539 - 5725. Gas, diesel, ice, groceries, moorage.

LYALL HARBOUR, Saturna Island, B.C. V0N 2Y0. (604) 539-5725. All year. Charts. Groceries. Ice. Snack bar. Pub. Fuel: gas, diesel and oil. Fishing: licenses, bait and tackle. Owner: Dick Silverberg.

WINTER COVE MARINE PARK, (at the N tip of Saturna Island). 228 acres. Normally entered from Plumper Sound and Navy Channel from the W and SW.

TELEGRAPH HARBOUR at the NE end of Kuper Island, has 2 marinas: Telegraph Harbour Marina and Thetis Island Marina. Use Chart 3310.

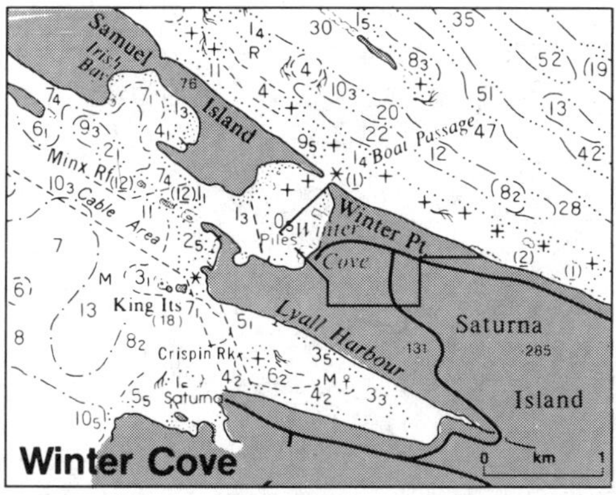

Entry can be made from the Strait of Georgia to the NE through Boat Passage but care must be exercised in the passage where currents can run to 7 knots. Minx Reef can pose a hazard on the way in from Plumper Sound. Anchorage is sheltered except from NW winds. There is only about 6½ feet of water at low tide. Limited day-use facilities ashore. Accessible by car ferry from Swartz Bay. This park, along with Cabbage Island, is of particular interest to nature-lovers. The cove is frequented by seals and other marine life while the upland is mainly undeveloped except for an abandoned quarry. Groceries are available in Lyall Harbor.

THETIS ISLAND

TELEGRAPH HARBOUR MARINA, Thetis Island, B.C. V0R 2Y0. (604) 246 - 9511. Open: April-Oct. Charts, groceries. Ice. Laundry. Snack bar. Ramp: 1-lane, blacktop. Guest dock. Dockside electricity. Slips. Engine maintenance and repairs. Fuel dock: gas, diesel. Fishing: licenses, bait and tackle. Owner: Peter Lazensy.

THETIS ISLAND MARINA, Thetis Island, B.C. V0R 2Y0. (604) 246-3464. Groceries and beverages. Ice. Laundry. Picnic area. Overnight guest dock. Dockside electricity. Slips and moorings. Fuel dock: gas and diesel. Fishing: licenses, bait and tackle. Water skiing. Pub. Pool Room. Owner: Peter and Tooner Quinn.

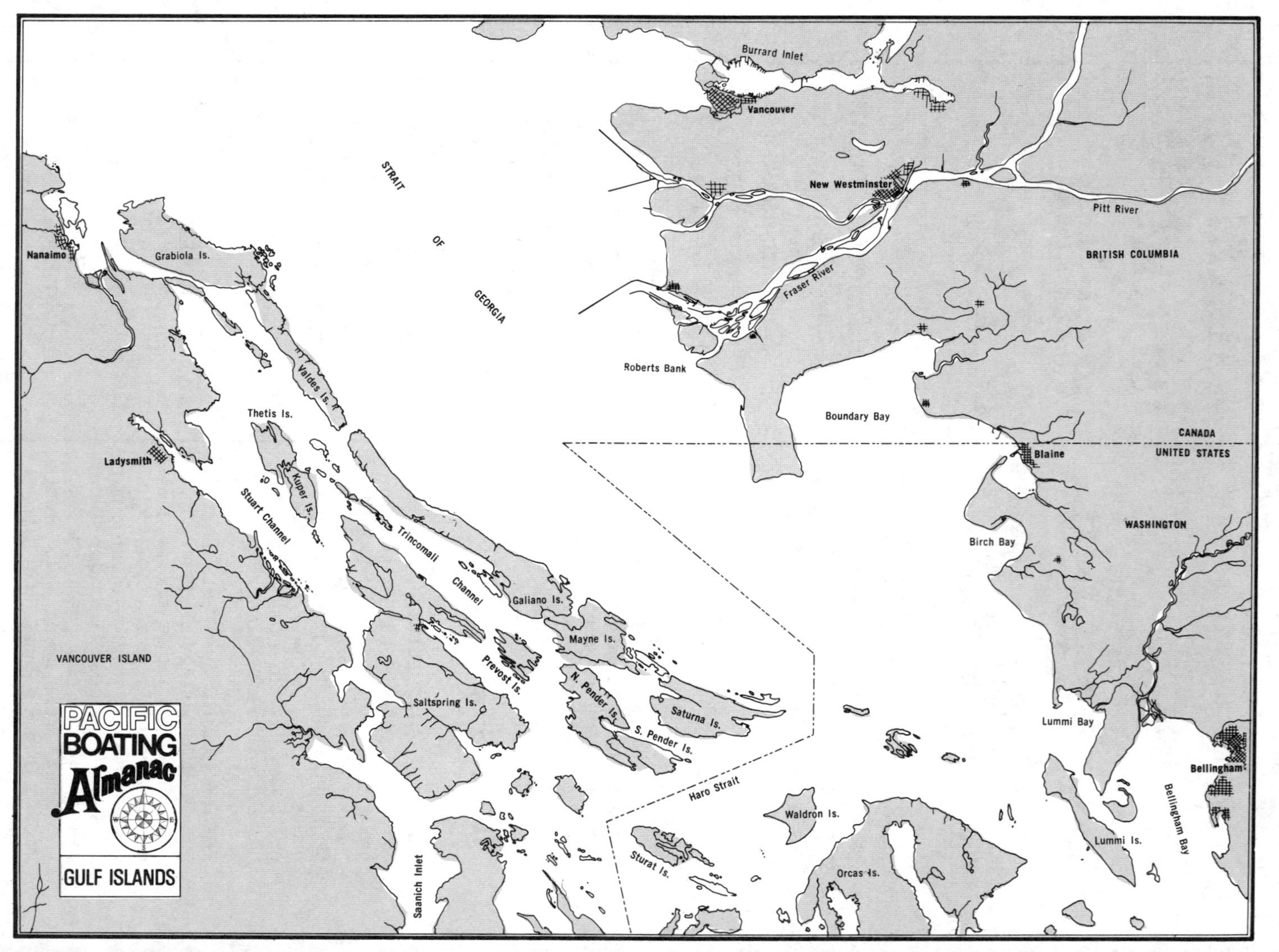
Burrard Inlet
Vancouver
New Westminster
Pitt River
BRITISH COLUMBIA
Fraser River
Roberts Bank
Boundary Bay
CANADA
UNITED STATES
Blaine
WASHINGTON
Birch Bay
STRAIT
OF
GEORGIA
Nanaimo
Grabiola Is.
Valdes Is.
Thetis Is.
Ladysmith
Kuper Is.
Stuart Channel
Trincomali
Channel
Galiano Is.
Mayne Is.
Prevost Is.
VANCOUVER ISLAND
Saltspring Is.
N. Pender Is.
S. Pender Is.
Saturna Is.
Lummi Bay
Haro Strait
Waldron Is.
Bellingham
Saanich Inlet
Sturat Is.
Orcas Is.
Lummi Is.
Bellingham Bay
PACIFIC BOATING Almanac
GULF ISLANDS

23

BRITISH COLUMBIA, CANADA
SOUTHEAST VANCOUVER ISLAND

FACILITIES

MAPLE BAY

BIRD'S EYE COVE MARINA, 6271 Genoa Bay Road, Duncan, B.C. V9L 1M3. (604) 748 - 3142. All year. Fuel dock: gas, diesel and mix. Open daily 7 AM - 9 PM. Gift shop. Pub and restaurant adjoining. Fishing: licenses, bait and tackle. Manager: Doug Lait.

COVE YACHTS LTD./COVE MARINA, (at Bird's Eye Cove) 6261 Genoa Bay Road, R.R. 1, Duncan, B.C. V9L 1M3. (604) 748 - 8136. All year. Marine ways cap.: 100 tons. Crane cap.: 4 tons. Boat building and repair. Moorage. Chandlery. Pressure wash. Ice. Owner/Manager: Phil and Sandra Pidcock.

GENOA BAY MARINA LTD., RR 1, Duncan, B.C. V9L 1M3. (604) 746 - 7621. (9 miles E of Duncan of Genoa Bay Road). Ramp: 1 - lane, concrete. Fuel dock: gas, diesel and propane. Open daylight hours. Moorage all year. Tidal grid Cafe licensed open weekends March, April, May, September and October. Open daily 8 AM - 8 PM from May 19 - September 5. Groceries, gifts, ice, showers, laundry. Fishing: licenses, bait and tackle. dockside electricity: (3) and some (4a). Owners: Mike and Kay Muenzler, Jim Kiedaisch.

MAI TAI RESTAURANT, 6161 Genoa Bay Road, RR 1, Duncan, B.C., V9L 1M3. (604) 746 - 7796. Steaks, seafoods, ribs and the islands most unique salad boat. "Super Sunday Brunches" served smorgasbord style. Dinner from 5:30 PM daily, Sunday brunch 10 AM - 2 PM.

MAPLE BAY MARINA AND SHIPYARD, (SW corner Bird's Eye Cove). R.R. 1, 6145 Genoa Bay Road, Duncan, B.C. V9L 1M3. (604) 746 - 4131. All year. Fuel dock: gas, diesel and outboard mix. Open 8 AM - 8 PM in July & August. Guest moorage. Covered berths. Marine hardware. Groceries.

MAPLE BAY on the W side of Sansum Narrows is the home of Cove Yachts and Maple Bay Marina, both full service marinas in Birds Eye Cove.

MANANA LODGE on Ladysmith Harbour offers many features including fuel, groceries, guest facilities, waterfront dining, showers and laundry.

Ice. Laundry. Showers. Charts. Brokerage. Marine lift and repair facilities. Fishing: Live bait, tackle. Dockside electricity: (3). Wheelhouse Lounge and Galley Family Restaurant. New dining lounge "The Shipyard". Owned and operated by Anchor Ventures, Inc., Joseph M. Silva.

COWICHAN BAY

ANCHOR MARINA, 1721 Cowichan Bay, Cowichan Bay, B.C. V0R 1N0. (604) 746 - 5424. All year. Overnight moorings. Engine parts and repairs. Marine hardware. Coffee shop. Fishing: bait and tackle. Boat and tackle rentals.

Dockside electricity: (3). Manager: Ken and Linda Gardiner.

BLUENOSE MARINA, 1765 Cowichan Bay Road, Cowichan Bay, B.C. V0R 1N0. (604) 748 - 2222. All year. Open daylight hours. Ramp: 2 - lanes, concrete, adjacent. Slips and guest dock. Ice. Restaurant. Grocery. Laundromat and showers. Fishing: bait and tackle. Rental boats and motors. Manager: Keith Sandilands.

CHERRY POINT MARINA, 1241 Cherry Pt. Road, Cobble Hill, B.C. V0R 1L0. (604) 748 - 0453. Ramp: 3 - lanes, concrete. Hoist cap.: 6 tons. Marine ways cap.: 12 tons. Slips. Dry storage. Hull and engine maintenance and repair.

CANOE COVE MARINA lies within short walking distance from the ferry terminal at Swartz Bay. A fuel dock, hoist and repair services are available.

Between Sidney and Swartz Bay, TSEHUM HARBOUR provides small-craft facilities for Victoria and the Saanich Peninsula. Use Chart 3455.

RV sites. Picnic area. Ice. Fishing: bait and tackle. Rental boats. Owner: Mary K. Blades.

COWICHAN SHIPYARD LTD., (2 miles E of Hwy. 1). 1719 Cowichan Bay Road, Cowichan Bay, B.C. V0R 1N0. (604) 743 - 2233. Two marine ways cap.: to 50 feet. Open daylight hours. Hull maintenance and repairs. Owners: Les and Grant Blundell.

PIER 66 MARINA LTD., 1745 Cowichan Bay Rd., Cowichan Bay, B.C. V0R 1N0. (604) 748 - 8444. Open all year. Boat and motor sales. Charts. Ice. Marine hardware. Overnight guest dock. Rental boats. Engine maintenance and parts. Fuel: gas, diesel and mix. Fishing: licenses, bait and tackle. Charter boats. Water skiing. Pres: Bob Parmenter.

WILCUMA LODGE & RESORT, (off Island Hwy. at Cowichan Bay) R.R. 3, Cobble Hill, B.C. V0R 1L0. (604) 746 - 6348. Open May 15 to Oct. 15. Slips. Guest dock. Overnight accommodations. Cabins. Swimming pool. Rental boats, motors and tackle. Owner: Bernie and Eleanor Gilding.

DAWSONS LANDING

DAWSONS LANDING GENERAL STORE, Dawsons Landing, B.C. V0N 1M0. All Year. Fuel dock: gas, diesel and mix. Open 9 AM - 6 PM. Marine hardware. Groceries. Liquor. Ice. Fishing: bait, tackle. Owner: T. Bachen.

LADYSMITH

DOLBY'S SERVICE LTD., P.O. Box 9, Ladysmith, B.C. V0R 2E0. (604) 245 - 2246. Marine sales and service. Dealers for Mercury and Campion.

INN OF THE SEA RESORT, 3600 Yellowpoint Road, RR 3, Ladysmith, B.C. V0R 2E0. (604) 245-2211. Restaurant, lounge, concrete floating wharf. Shore power, fresh water, laundry facilities. Playground. Heated outdoor pool. Ice.

IVY GREEN PROVINCIAL PARK, located along a stream with some saltwater beach, this park has campsites, picnic sites, fresh water, restrooms and a pump-out for RV's.

MANANA LODGE AND MARINA, RR 1, 4760 Brenton Page Rd., Ladysmith, B.C. V0R 2E0. (604) 245- 2312. All year. Moorings. Fuel dock: gas and diesel, open 8 AM - 8 PM. Guest rooms. Licensed waterfront dining. Limited hours Sept to May. Picnic area. Groceries. Ice. Showers. Dockside electricity. Laundry. Fishing: bait and tackle. Gift Shop. A Bed & Breakfast Inn.

PRICE'S MARINE, located at Ivy Green Marina. (604) 245 - 8233. Complete repair facility. gas, diesel, inboards, outboards. Volvo, Mercury, OMC.

ZUIDERZEE CAMPSITES, RR#3, Lady Smith, B.C. V0R 2E0. (604) 722-2334. Ice. Picnic Area. Recreational vehicle campsites. Ramp. Rental boats. Water skiing. Owner: Gus Schuyt.

SIDNEY
(49°39'N., 123°23'W.)

ALL BAY MARINE LTD, 2204 Harbour Rd., Sidney, B.C. V8L 2P6. (604) 656 - 0513. All year. Boat and motor sales. Charts. Electronic sales and repairs. Groceries. Ice. Instrument repairs. Marine hardware. Prop and shaft repairs. Fishing: licenses, bait and tackle. President: Al Storey.

THE BOATER'S EXCHANGE, (take Sandowne Park turnoff on Hwy 17) 10221 Mcdonald Park Road, RR 3, Sidney, B.C. V8L 3X9. (604) 655 - 3101. Good used marine equipment. Vire Engines. Mon. - Sat., 9:30 AM 5 PM.

BOSUN'S CHARTERS at "Bosun's Landing", 2240 Harbour Rd., Box 2464, Sidney, B.C. V8L 3Y3. (604) 656-6644. All year. Guest dock with electricity. Moorage slips. Power and sailboats to 40'. Fishing charters. Small boat rentals. Owners: Tim and Vicki Melville.

CANOE COVE MARINA, 2300 Canoe Cove Road, P.O. Box 2099, Sidney, B.C. V8L 3S6. (604) 656-5566. All year. Marine ways cap.: 40 tons. Travelift cap.: 12 tons. Fuel dock: gas, diesel and mix. Hours: 8 AM - 6 PM. Office hours: 8 AM - 4:30 PM. Open and covered moorings. Dry storage. Marine hardware. Charts. Boat and engine maintenance and repairs. Engine parts. Restaurant. Showers. Ice. Fishing: bait and tackle. Comptroller: K.M. Bryan.

CHARTHOUSE MARINA, (Deep Cove) 10992 Madrona Drive, R.R. 1, Sidney, B.C. V8L 3R9. (604) 656 - 8185. Fuel dock: gas and mix. Slips. Ice. Manager: Lawrence Lambert.

GULF ISLANDS CRUISING SCHOOL LTD., located at Canoe Cove Marina in Sidney, B.C. Mailing address: P.O. Box 2532, Sidney, B.C. V8L 4B9. (604) 656-2628. Offering Canadian Yachting Association basic, intermediate and advanced cruising courses. Also bareboat charters from 26' - 40'. Owners/operators: Bruce and Fran Stott.

HALL'S BOATHOUSE, (Finlayson Arm, S end of Saanich Inlet on Hwy. 1, 12 miles N of Victoria.) #14-2892 Trans Canada Hwy., R.R. 6, Victoria, B.C. V8X 3X2. (604) 478 - 4407. Ramp: concrete. Fuel dock: gas and outboard mix. Open: 8 AM - dark. Fishing: bait and tackle. Owners: Art and May Hall.

MENZIES OUTBOARD STERNDRIVE, 2071 Malaview Avenue, Sidney, B.C. V8L 3X9. (604) 656-3221. All year. New and used boats and motors. Outboard - sterndrive repairs. Haul-out to 28 ft. Powerboats. Emergency service.

MILL BAY MARINA, Box 137, Mill Bay, B.C. V0R 2P0. (604) 743 - 4112. Concrete ramp. Fuel dock: gas, diesel and LP refills. Open: 8 AM - 8 PM. Slips. guest dock. Ice. Laundry. Fishing: licenses, bait and tackle. Rental boats. RV Park. Owner/Manager.: Edward Albury.

NORTH SAANICH MARINA, Box 2000, Sidney, B.C. V8L 3S3. (604) 656-5558. Winter: 8:30 AM - 5 PM; Summer: 7:30 AM - 8 PM. Charts. Ice. Ramp. Guest dock. Slips. Fuel dock: gas, diesel and mix. Fishing: licenses, bait. Owner: Oak Bay Group of Companies.

PHILBROOK'S BOATYARD, 2324 Harbour Road, Sidney, B.C. V8L 2P6. (604) 656 - 1157. Complete yacht service center. A covered work yard and haulouts on two ways to 100 feet provide emergency, annual and refit repairs for both sail and power vessels.

SIDNEY PROPELLOR AND MARINE POWER LTD, Box 2146, Sidney, B.C. V8L 3S6. (604) 656 - 3421. Mon - Fri: 8 AM - 5 PM. New and used motor sales. Engine maintenance. Prop and shaft repairs. Engine parts. President: Willi Fahning.

TSEHUM STERNDRIVE LTD, 2075 Tryon Rd, Sidney, B.C. V8L 3X9. (604) 656 - 1221. Hoist. Marine ways. Slips. Guest dock. Marine hardware. Electronic repairs. New and used boat and motor sales. Hull and engine maintenance and repairs. Instrument repairs. Boat storage. Picnic area. Fishing tackle. President: Lesley Fekete.

VAN ISLE MARINA, 2320 Harbour Road, Tsehum Harbour, Sidney, B.C. V8L 2P6. (604) 656-1138. All year. Customs entry dock. Ramp: 1-lane, concrete. Open daylight hours: 8 AM to 9 PM, 7 days. Hoist cap.: 4 tons. Marine ways cap.: 60 tons. Fuel dock: gas, diesel and outboard mix. Open daylight hours. LPG and CNG refills. Slips. Guest dock. Dry storage. Boat maintenance and repairs. Engine parts and repairs. Prop and shaft repair. Electrical shop. Marine store. Brokerage. Laundry. Ice. Restaurant. Overnight moorage. Showers. Dockside electricity. Fishing: bait and tackle. Manager: Mark Dickinson.

SOOKE
(48°22'N., 123°43'W.)

CHEANUH MARINA, East Sooke Road, Becher Bay, RR 1, Sooke, B.C. V0S 1N0. (604) 478 - 4880. All year. Open daily during daylight hours. Ramp: 3 - lanes, concrete. Slips and guest dock. Fuel dock: gas only. Boat and motor maintenance and repairs. Fishing: bait and tackle. Rental boats and motors.

SUNNY SHORES RESORT & MARINA, (18 miles W of Victoria on Hwy. 14; 3 miles before Sooke) 5621 Sooke Road RR 1, Sooke, B.C. V0S 1N0. (604) 642 - 5731. Modern housekeeping units with color cable TV, tent & trailer sites, firepits, picnic tables, clean washrooms, laundromat, large pool, mini golf, giant slide, horseshoes, shuffleboard, children's playground. Full marina facilities, ramp, moorage, gas, diesel, bait, tackle shop. Pets on leash. Open all year.

SOOKE HARBOUR MARINA, 6971 W. Coast Rd., RR 4, Sooke, B.C. V0S 1N0. (604) 642 - 3236. All year. Ramp: 2-lane, concrete. Rental boats. Moorings. Camping. Showers. Fishing: licenses, bait and tackle. Charters. All Sooke Day 3rd Sat in July: logging shows and competitions. "Sooke Harbour House" gourmet restaurant, will pick up boaters. Manager: Marc Van Hasselt.

SQUIRREL COVE

SQUIRREL COVE GENERAL STORE, Box 1, Squirrel Cove, B.C. V0P 1T0. (604) 935-6327. All year. Charts. Groceries and beverages. Ice. LP gas refills. Marine Hardware. Fishing: licenses, bait and tackle. Water skiing. Owners: Irv & Doreen Reedel.

STUART ISLAND

BIG BAY MARINA, Stuart Island, B.C. V0P 1V0. Radiotelephone (604) N628700. Open May - Sept. New and used motor sales. Charts. Groceries. Accommodations. Ice. Laundry. Restaurant. Guest dock. Dockside electricity. Slips. Fuel dock: gas and diesel. Fishing: licenses, bait and tackle. Charter boats with guides. Salt water rapids. Owners: Bruce & Kay Knierim.

STUART ISLAND RESORT, Stuart Island, B.C. V0P 1V0. (604) 859-5499, radiotelephone. Open May - Sept.

Charts. Groceries. Accommodations. Ice. Laundry. Restaurant. Ramp. Hoist. Guest dock. Moorings. Fuel: gas and diesel. Fishing: licenses, bait and tackle. Manager: Jamie Yauis.

VICTORIA
(48°25'N., 123°24'W.)

BOSUN'S LOCKER LTD., 580 Johnson Street, Victoria, B.C. V8W 1M3. (604) 386 - 1308. All year. Charts. Electronic sales. Marine hardware. Yacht supplies. Charter sailboats, skippered or bareboat. Rigging, splicing and stove repairs. President: Wayne Dusmuir.

ESSO MARINE FUEL STATION, 22 Huron Street, Victoria, B.C. V8V 4R1. (604) 384-8712. All year. Fuel dock: gas and diesel. Ice. Laundry. Fishing: licenses, bait. Agent: W.R. Lindner.

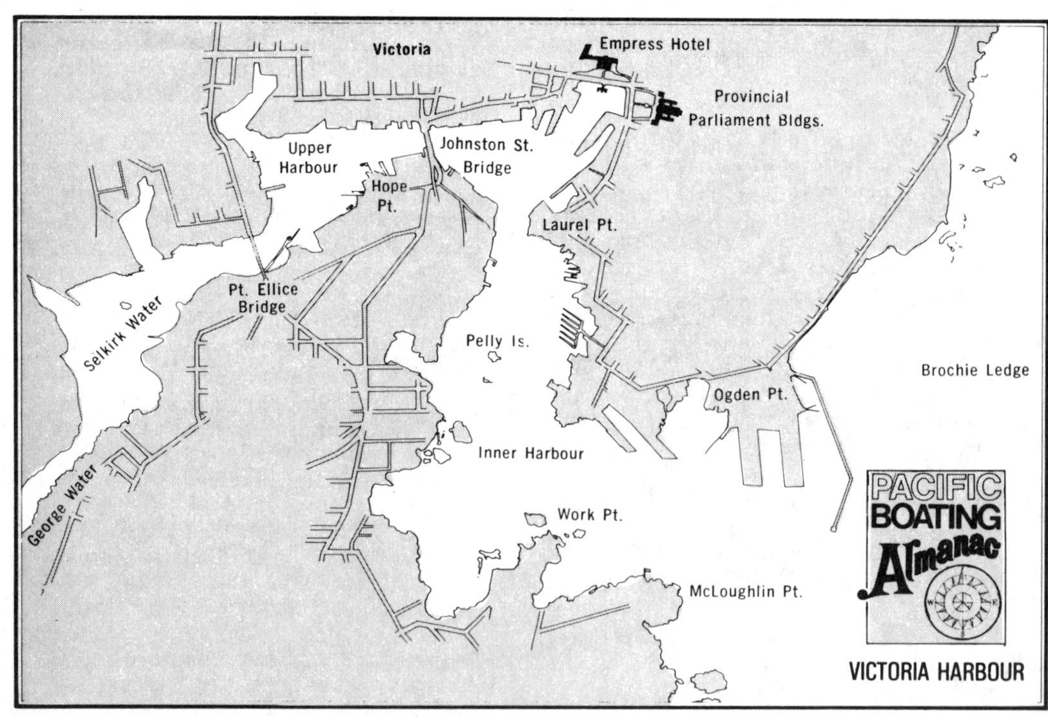

FREDERICK GOERTZ LTD., 507 Yates Street, Victoria, B.C. V8W 1K7. (604) 386-8375. Open all year. Charts. Electronic sales and repairs. Instrument repairs. Open: 9 AM - 5 PM Mon. - Sat. Manager: E.C. Redding.

OCEAN WEST MARINE FUELS AND SUPPLIES LTD., 122 Kingston Street, Victoria, B.C. V8V 1V4. (604) 388-7224. All year. 6 AM - 6 PM. Charts. Groceries. Ice. Laundry. Marine hardware. Snack bar. Waste disposal pumpout. Fuel dock: gas, diesel and mix. Fishing: licenses, bait and tackle. Showers. Owner: M. and L. Barry.

MARITIME MUSEUM, 28 Bastion Square, Victoria, B.C. V8W 1H9. (604) 385-4222. All year. Ships models. Marine artifacts illustrating the history of the Pacific Northwest. Nautical bookstore. Director: John MacFarlane.

SAILTREND ENTERPRISES LTD, 1327 Beach Dr, Victoria, B.C. V8S 2N4. (604) 592 - 2711. Closed first two weeks in January. Charts. Electronic sales. Marine hardware. Mast Hoist. Fuel: CNG, kerosene, alcohol. Instruments. Wet-weather gear. Shoes. Paint. Plumbing supplies. Complete rigging service with swaging and splicing. Owner: Kaspar Schibli.

VICTORIA MARINE ELECTRIC LTD, 31 Erie St, Victoria, B.C. V8V 1P8. (604) 383 - 9731. All year. Electrical sales and repairs. Instrument repairs. Hydraulic steering and engine controls and boat wiring. Owner: Brian Stilling.

MARINE PARKS

D'ARCY ISLAND MARINE PARK, (a small island in Haro Strait) 210 acres. Numerous reefs and shoals in the vicinity. Approach with caution. Enter from the W to S of the lighthouse. No sheltered anchorages. Undeveloped. Little D'Arcy Island to the E is private property. Please respect it and refrain from landing there.

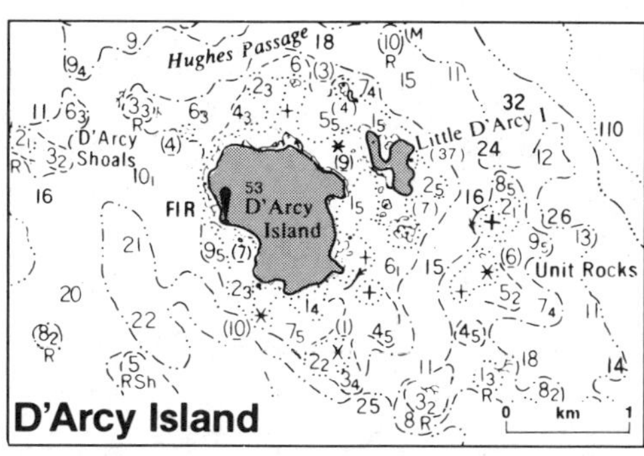

D'Arcy Island

DISCOVERY ISLAND MARINE PARK, (S half of Discovery Island 2 miles E of Victoria). 153 acres. Lighthouse at Seabird Point. Enter from Plumper Passage or Hecate Passage from the W or into Rudlin Bay from the S. No sheltered anchorage. Undeveloped. N portion of Discovery Island, adjacent Chatham Island and some of the smaller islands nearby are Indian Reserve lands. Please respect this area.

ISLE-de-LIS MARINE PARK, (Rum Island at the E end of Gooch Island where Prevost Passage meets Haro Strait is the park). 13 acres. A small natural area with hiking trail and beaches. No other developments.

SIDNEY SPIT MARINE PARK, (at the N end of Sidney Island). 1000 acres. Anchor on W side of spit. Wharf and landing-float for small boats. Sandy beach and shallow bottom. Camping and picnicking. Toilets. Hiking trails. Drinking water. Enter from Haro Strait via Miners Channel or Sidney Channel. Of interest is the herd of European fallow deer in the fields and turkeys that were introduced to Sidney Island, also the large heronry to the SE of the lagoon which in itself is noted as a resting area for fowl.

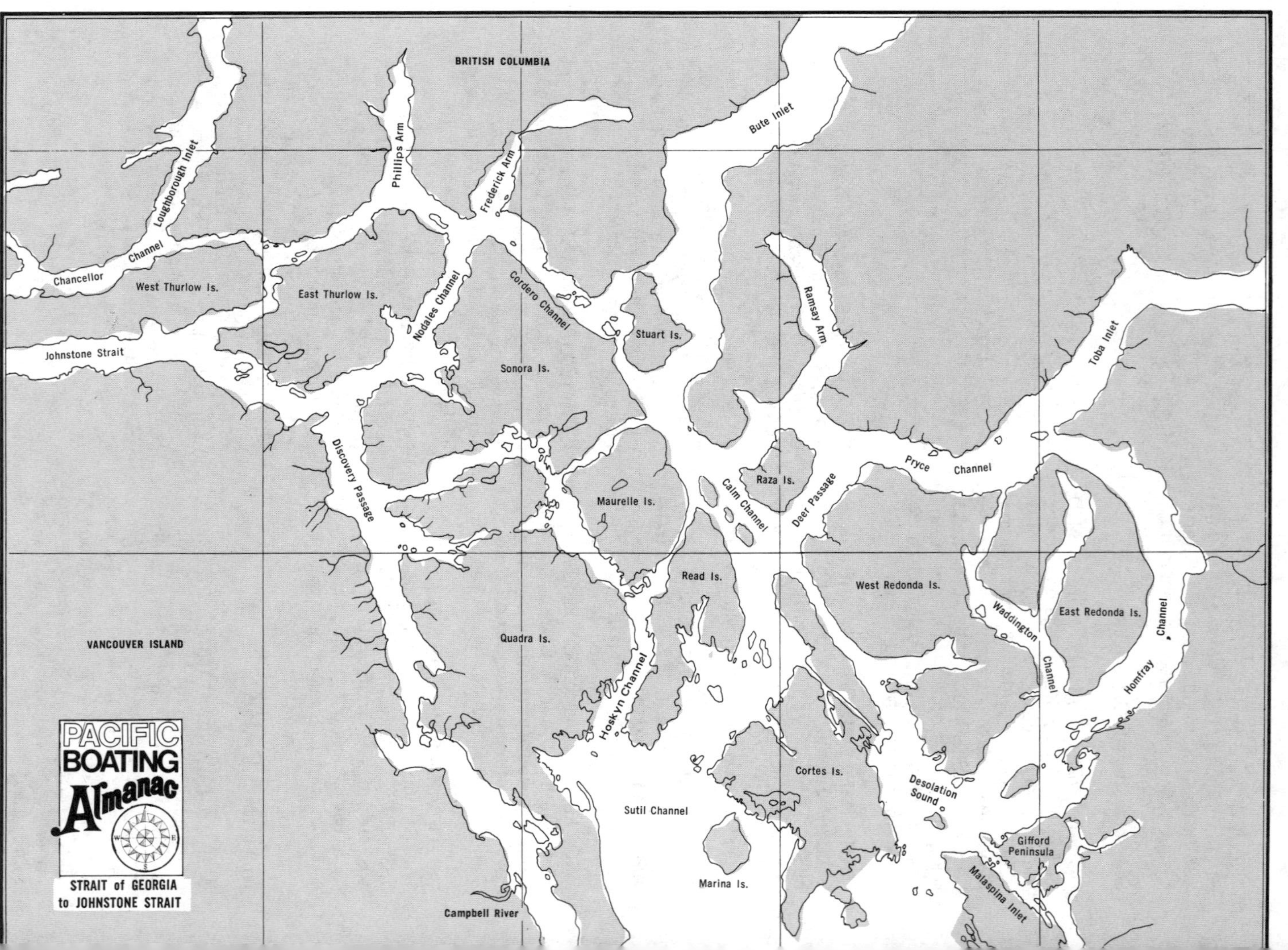

BRITISH COLUMBIA
Loughborough Inlet
Phillips Arm
Frederick Arm
Bute Inlet
Chancellor Channel
West Thurlow Is.
East Thurlow Is.
Nodales Channel
Cordero Channel
Stuart Is.
Ramsay Arm
Toba Inlet
Johnstone Strait
Sonora Is.
Discovery Passage
Pryce Channel
Raza Is.
Deer Passage
Maurelle Is.
Calm Channel
Read Is.
West Redonda Is.
Waddington Channel
East Redonda Is.
Homfray Channel
Quadra Is.
Hoskyn Channel
VANCOUVER ISLAND
Cortes Is.
Desolation Sound
Sutil Channel
Gifford Peninsula
Marina Is.
Malaspina Inlet
Campbell River
PACIFIC BOATING Almanac
STRAIT of GEORGIA to JOHNSTONE STRAIT

24

VANCOUVER AREA

FACILITIES

SURREY

CRESCENT BEACH MARINA, 12555 Crescent Rd, Surrey, B.C. V4A 2V4. (604) 531-7551. All year. Ramp: 2 - lanes, cement. Fuel dock: gas, diesel and mix. New and used motor sales. Charts. Electronic sales. Ice. Marine hardware. Guest dock with electricity. Slips and moorings. Boat storage. Boat hauling to 42' and 25 tons. Hoist: 10 tons. Fishing: licenses, bait and tackle. Charter boats. Engine maintenance and repairs. Prop and shaft repairs. Manager: Dal Young.

FRASER RIVER

CAPTAIN'S COVE MARINA, 6100 Ferry Road, Delta, B.C. V4K 3M9. (604) 946-1244.

DEAS HARBOUR MARINA, 5825 60th Avenue, Delta, B.C. V4K 4E2. (604) 946-1251. All year. Boat and motor sales. Charts. Electronic sales and repairs. Ice. Instrument repairs. Marine hardware. Restaurant. Ramp: 1-lane, cement. Guest dock with electricity. Slips and mooring. Boat and engine maintenance and repairs. Fuel dock: gas and mix. Fishing: licenses, bait and tackle. Owner: Stuart David.

DELTA CHARTERS INC., 3500 Cessna Drive, Richmond, B.C. V7B 1C7. (604) 273 - 4211. Bareboat and skippered charters. Power and sail. Sailing lessons, fishing charters, river tours.

Located at Delta's River Inn, near the Vancouver Airport.

FITZWRIGHT SURVIVAL SYSTEMS, 5811B Cedarbridge Way, Richmond, B.C. V6X 2A8. (604) 270-2313. Life rafts and survival suits.

GALLEON MARINE, 8211 River Road, Richmond, B.C. V6X 1X8. (604) 273-7544. Open all year. 9 AM - 6 PM. New and used boat and motor sales. Electronic Sales. Marine hardware. Engine maintenance, boat moving, boat trailer rentals and parts. Owners: Hank Zacharias and Dennis Binstead.

KWIK BOAT REPAIR, 8191 River Road, Richmond, B.C. V6X 1X8. (604) 273-6568.

LANDMARK YACHT SERVICE, 8051 River Road, Richmond, B.C. V6X 1X8. (604) 278-7718.

MARINELAND, 340 Lysander Lane, Richmond, B.C. V7B 1C3. (604) 273-3955.

MASSEY'S MACHINE & MARINE SHOP LTD., 4926 Delta Street, Delta, B.C. V4K 2V2. (604) 946 - 4488. Paints, marine supplies and hardware. Haulouts. All coastal charts.

NEW WESTMINSTER MARINE FUEL, (604) 521 - 2324. Gas, diesel water, repairs and moorage.

PITT MEADOWS MARINA, 14179 Reichenbach, Pitt Meadows, B.C. V3Y 1Z1. (604) 465-6969. Showers, ramps, guest dock moorage. Dry and covered storage. Fuel: Gas and diesel.

R Y M PROPELLER, 8060D Capstan Way, Richmond, B.C. V6X 1R5. (604) 278-7833. Propeller repairs. Aluminum gas tanks.

RICHMOND MARINA, 8191 River Road, Richmond, B.C. (604) 278-8612. Haulouts: 26'. Titlegrid up to 50'. Boat repairs and sales. Laundromat. Moorage for 100 boats.

RICHMOND MARINE FUEL, (604) 278 - 2181. Gas, diesel and water.

RIVER CITY MARINA, 23080 Dyke Road, Richmond, B.C. (604) 526-4154.

RIVER MARINE SUPPLIES, 8060 Capstan Way, Richmond, B.C. V6X 1X7. (604) 270-9455. Open year round. New and used boat and motor sales. Electronic sales. Ice. Stores and heaters. Fishing: licenses, bait and tackle. Boat rentals. Galley equipment. Manager: Peter Johnston.

SHELTER ISLAND MARINA, #115-6911 Graybar Road, Richmond, B.C. V6R 1R3. (604) 270-6272. All year. Boat and motor sales. Charts. Electronic sales. Groceries. Ice. Laundry. Marine hardware. Picnic area. Restaurant. Waste disposal pumpout. Ramp. Hoist: 60 ton. Guest dock with electricity. Slips and moorings. Boat storage. Boat maintenance and repairs and parts. RV hookups. Manager: Terry McPhail.

SKIPPER'S LOCKER INC., 8151 Capstan Way, Richmond, B.C. V6Y 1R3. (604) 273-4739. Open all year. New and used boat and motor sales. Marine hardware and supplies. Engine maintenance and repairs. Engine parts. Manager: Verne Taylor.

SKYLINE MARINA, 8031 River Road, Richmond, B.C. V6X 1X8. (604) 273-3977. Moorage, service, repairs and modifications to all sizes.

STEVESTON MARINE, 3560 Moncton Street, Richmond, B.C. V6X 1X8. (604) 277-7031.

TOM-MAC SHIPYARDS, 17011 River Road, Richmond, B.C. V6V 1L8. (604) 278-1516.

TRITES MARINE SERVICES, 12820 Trites Road, Richmond, B.C. V7E 3R8. (604) 277-2520. Boat repairs.

VANCOUVER MARINA, 8331 River Road, Richmond, B.C. V6X 1Y1. (604) 278-9787.

WES-DEL MARINA, 3473 River Road W., Ladner, B.C. (604) 946-4544.

WEST COAST FIBERGLASS, LTD, 2315 Simpson Rd., Richmond, B.C. V6X 2R2. (604) 270 - 2635. Marine hardware. Boat storage yard. Hull maintenance and repairs. President: W. Mills.

FALSE CREEK, in the SE part of English Bay, close to downtown Vancouver, is a busy yachting center. Use Chart 3482.

VANCOUVER

ALEXANDER MARINE LTD., 570 Davie Street, Vancouver, B.C. V6B 2G4. (604) 689-5972. Open all year. Mon. - Fri. 9:30 AM - 5 PM, Sat. 10 AM - 4 PM. Canadian and U.S. Charts. Nautical books. Navigational instruments. President: Alex Wong.

AUSTEN MARINE LTD., 560 Cardero Street, Vancouver, B.C. V6G 2W6. (604) 681 - 1822. All year. Complete marine engine repairs and installations. Owner: Gus Olsten.

BEACH AVENUE MARINA, 1008 Beach, Vancouver, B.C. (604) 682-0221.

BOATHOUSE MARINE SUPPLIES, 29-566 Cardero, Vancouver, B.C. (604) 685-4341.

BOVEY MARINE / THE QUARTER-DECK, 375 Water Street, Vancouver, B.C. (604) 685-8216.

BURRARD MARINE ESSO, fuel barge at Burrard Bridge, Vancouver, B.C. (604) 733-6731. Ice, gas, diesel, oils, CNG and convenience items.

C R C MARINE ELECTRONICS, 1161 Commercial, Vancouver, B.C. (604) 251-1334.

CALIFORNIA MARINE, P.O. Box 35054, Station E, Vancouver, B.C. V6M 4G1. New and used boat and motor sales. Marine hardware. Open year-round, 9:30 AM - 5 PM. Owner. Dave Hutchison.

CHARTERS MARINE PUB, at Vancouver Yacht Hotel, Vancouver, B.C. (604) 681-2366.

CHEVRON MARINE, Coal Harbour fuel barge, Vancouver, B.C. Mailing address: Chevron Canada, 1500 1050 W. Pender Street., Vancouver, B.C. V6E 3T4. Attn: Jack Monk coded 200. (604) 681-7725.

COAL HARBOR MARINA, 566 Cardero Street, Vancouver, B.C. (604) 682-6841. Moorage.

CRAMER ENGINEERING, 1495 Frances, Vancouver, B.C. V5L 1Z1. (604) 225-0115.

CUSTOM MARINE ELECTRIC LTD, 570 Cardero St, Vancouver, B.C. V6G 2W6. (604) 681 - 5836. All year. Marine electrical and corrosion control specialists. President: Bryan Holgate.

ESSO MARINE STATION-BARGE IN COAL HARBOUR, (604) 689 - 7371. Gas, diesel, stove, shower and ice.

FREDERICK GOERTZ LTD., 1256 W. Pender Street, Vancouver, B.C V6E 2S8. (604) 684-7541. Victoria Branch: 507 Yates Street, Victoria B.C. V8W 1K7. (604) 386-8375 Fax (604) 386-2325. Open all year. Charts. Electronic sales and repairs. Instrument repairs. Open: 8 AM - 5 PM Mon. - Fri. President: R.S. Wells.

GRANVILLE ISLAND BOAT LIFT, 1650 Duranleau, Vancouver, B.C. (604) 685-6924.

GRANVILLE ISLAND MARINA, (604) 681 - 3474. Pump-out.

PELICAN BAY YACHT CHARTERS LTD., at the Granville Island Hotel Marina (overlooking False Creek) 1253 Johnson St., Vancouver, B.C. V6H 3R9. (604) 683 - 3232. Transient slips by reservation. Overnight accommodations. Waterfront restaurant. Showers. Dockside electricity. Full service marina and hotel.

FALSE CREEK YACHT CLUB, 1650 Granville Street, Vancouver, B.C. V6Z 1N3. (604) 687-6874. Full facilities: power, water, ice, laundry, waste disposal pumpout. Two marine elevators (up to 18 tons), boat brokers, sales and service. Guest moorage, parking, security gates. Within walking distance to city center. Open all year 8 AM - 4:30 PM. Manager: Carole Schindler.

HARUNA UPHOLSTERY, 6544 Victoria Drive, Vancouver, B.C. (604) 324-3726. Sales and repairs. Hardware and supplies.

HEATHER CIVIC MARINA, 600 Stamps Landing, Vancouver, B.C. (604) 874-2814. Power lift: 10 ton capacity. Moorage.

HY-SEAS MARINE ELECTRONICS, 1628 Duranleau, Granville Island, Vancouver, B.C. V6H 3S4. (604) 669-1740. Electronic sales and repairs.

JIB SET CRUISING CLUB, 1020 Beach Avenue, Vancouver, B.C. (604) 689-1477. Sailing school. Charter boats. Membership sailing club.

K & D MARINE, 1815 Boatlift Lane, Vancouver, B.C. (604) 681-5511.

KITS BOAT SALES, 1616 Duranleau, Vancouver, B.C. V6G 2W6. (604) 687-3293.

KITSILANO MARINE SUPPLY, 1530 W. 2nd, Vancouver, B.C. V6J 1H2. (604) 736-8891. Marine hardware.

ISLAND MARINE, 1648 Duranleau Street, Vancouver, B.C. V6H 3S4. (604) 681-6318. All year. 9 AM - 5:30 PM. Charts. Marine hardware. Fishing: licenses, tackle. President: Len Collett.

MARINE MAIL ORDER SUPPLY, 1368 W. Broadway Street, Vancouver, B.C. V6H 1H2. (604) 736-3565. All year. Charts. Electronic sales and repairs. Instrument repairs. Marine hardware. Marine clothing. Navigation gear. Owner: Maynard Martin.

MARINELAND CRUISING CLUB, at Vancouver Yacht Hotel, Vancouver, B.C. (604) 681-2366.

MARITIME SERVICES LTD., Div. of Triton Holdings, 3440 Bridgeway Street, Vancouver, B.C. V5K 1B6. (604) 294-4444. All year. Charts. Electronic sales and repairs. 24-hour service. Inflatable sales. Owner: Padam Misri.

MENCHIONS SHIPYARD, 562 Cardero, Vancouver, B.C. V6G 2W6 (604) 685-6839. Boat haulouts 20' - 90', repairs, woodwork.

P R MARINE SERVICES, 1650 Duranleau, Vancouver, B.C. (604) 687-8807.

PACIFIC SPAR LTD, 1528 Duranleau St, Granville Island, Vancouver, B.C. V6H 3S4. (604) 687 - 3010. All year. Marine hardware. Mast tower. 65 foot dock. Manager: Tim Doyle.

PETRO-CANADA, Coal Harbour fuel barge, Vancouver, B.C. Mailing address: 3281 W. 34th Avenue, Vancouver, B.C. V6N 2K3, Attn: Bill Black. (604) 681-6020.

THE QUARTERDECK, 1660 Duranleau, Vancouver, Granville Island, B.C. V6H 3S4. (604) 683-8232. Nautical accessories. Books, charts and net gear.

ROBISON BROS. MARINE STATION, P.O. Box 2250, Vancouver, B.C. V6B 3W2. (604) 681-3841. Ice. Snack bar. Fuel: gas, diesel and mix. Open 24 hours. Fishing: licenses, bait and tackle. Owner: Norm Robison.

ROTON INDUSTRIES, 1518 Duranleau, Vancouver, B.C. (604) 688-2325.

SPRUCE HARBOUR MARINA, 1015 Ironworks Passage, Vancouver, B.C. V6H 3R4. (604) 733-3512. Casual moorage. Electrical hook-ups.

THE VANCOUVER YACHT HOTEL / MARINELAND YACHT SALES, 552 Cardero Street, Vancouver, B.C. (604) 681-2366. All year. Boat and motor sales. Electronic sales and repairs. Accommodations. Instrument repairs. Marine hardware. Restaurant. Waste disposal pumpout. Guest dock with electricity. Boat and engine maintenance and parts. Owner: David Wiens.

TRILIGHT YACHT SERVICES, 1782 Alberni Street, Vancouver, B.C. (604) 681-1417.

WESTERN MARINE, 1494 Powell Street, Vancouver B.C. V5L 5B5. (604) 253-7721. Marine hardware distributor.

WESTIN BAYSHORE MARINA, 1601 W. Georgia Street, Vancouver, B.C V6G 2V4. (604) 682-3377. Yacht Charters. Hotel moorage, slips. Restaurants, pool, health club.

NORTH VANCOUVER

ALLIED SHIPBUILDERS, 1870 Harbour Road, North Vancouver, B.C. V7H 1A1. (604) 929-2365. Boat repairs.

ALVIS MARINE LTD., 1681 Columbia Street, North Vancouver, B.C. V7J 1A5. (604) 985-3905. Wood and fiberglass hull maintenance and repairs. Spray painting. New construction. New boat sales. President: John Evetts.

ANCHOR MARINE CANVAS, 1335 Fernwood Avenue, North Vancouver, B.C. V7P 1K3. (604) 986-6669. Crescent Hardware. Marine canvas repairs. Manager: Demitri Dragonas.

BOOMERANG ANCHOR LIFT, 7234 209 A Street, Langley, B.C. (604) 530-1156. Anchor lift. Supervac and buoys.

CREATIVE CANVAS, 2207 Whitman, North Vancouver, B.C. V7A 2C6. (604) 929-5044. Canvas. Convertible tops.

DOMCOM SERVICES, 1776 Deep Cove Road, North Vancouver, B.C. V7G 1S5. (604) 929-1432. Refrigeration and air conditioning design and repair.

FINDLAY IMPORTS LTD., 101-1429 Dominion Street, North Vancouver, B.C. (604) 985-8747. Sailboat hardware specialists.

THE FOAM SHOP, 1323 Marine, North Vancouver, B.C. (604) 980-8813. Cushion repairs. Upholstery for boat interiors.

FRASER FIBREGLASS, Lynnwood Marina, North Vancouver, B.C. (604) 985-1098.

GIBSON'S LANDING on the W side of Shoal Channel has a public wharf. This is a good source of supplies for visitors to the nearby Plumper Cover Marine Park. Use Charts 3508, 3586.

GAR & WOOD YACHT RESTORATIONS, 1681 Columbia, Lynnwood Marina, North Vancouver, B.C. (604) 980-9172. Refurnishing to new and classic boats. Some engine repairs.

GENERAL BOAT WORKS, 1460 Columbia Street, North Vancouver, B.C. V7J 1A2. (604) 986-6211. Open daily: 7:30 AM - 4 PM. Engine and stern drive rebuilding and servicing. Wood and fiberglass hull repairs. Spray painting. Riveted and wiring aluminum boats repaired. Covered dry storage. Haulouts. Manager: Rod Baker.

HARDY'S MARINE, Lynnwood Marina, North Vancouver, B.C. (604) 988-4840.

J & J PROPELLER, 338 East Esplanade, North Vancouver, B.C. V7L 1A4. (604) 985-2413. Manufacturing and repairing marine propellers.

JACK MURRAY MARINE, 1538 Columbia Street, North Vancouver, B.C. (604) 980-0189. Marine repairs.

LYNNWOOD MARINA, (directly W of Second Narrows Bridge on N shore) 1681 Columbia Street, North Vancouver, B.C. V7J 1A5. (604) 985-1533. Open: 8 AM - 4:30 PM. Two mobile hoists cap.: 60 tons. Covered and open slips. Moorings and laundry. Dry storage. Do-it-yourself facilities. Shipwright available. Restaurant. Owner: Harry J. Powell.

MARISOL MARINE CENTER, 1637 Columbia Street, North Vancouver, B.C. V7J 1A5. (604) 986-5291. Yacht sales, power and sail. Marine diesel and gas engines, transmissions and replacement parts. Sales and service. Located at the Lynnwood Marina.

MARTIN MARINE, 121 W. 1st Street, North Vancouver, B.C. V7M 1B1. (604) 985-0911. Chandlery. Marine store.

MOSQUITO CREEK MARINA, 415 West Esplanade, North Vancouver, B.C. V7L 4J5. (604) 987-4113. New and used boat and motor sales. Ice. Restaurant. Hoist cap.: 35 tons, open 8 AM - 4:30 Mon. - Sat. Overnight guest dock. Hull maintenance and repairs. Engine maintenance and repairs. Prop and shaft repairs. Fuel: gas, diesel and mix, open 8 AM - 4:30 Mon. - Sat.

NOR-CO FIBERGLASS, 604-105 W. Keith, North Vancouver, B.C. (604) 986-5132.

NORTH SHORE CANVAS, 342 E. Esplanade #1, North Vancouver, B.C. V7L 1A4. (604) 988-1810. Boat tops and awnings.

NORTH SHORE DIESEL, 1538 Bay, North Vancouver, B.C. (604) 984-0247.

NORTH SHORE MARINE SERVICE / SPEEDY MARINE SERVICE, Mosquito Creek Marina, North Vancouver, B.C. (604) 980-2441. Electronic sales and repairs. Marine hardware. Hull and engine maintenance and repairs. Engine parts. Prop and shaft repairs.

OBAN MARINE, 10324A 12th, Surrey, B.C. V3V 4G1. (604) 987-9633. New and used boat and motor sales. Electronic sales. Marine hardware. Hull and engine maintenance and repairs. Engine parts. Prop and shaft repairs.

OSBORNE PROPELLERS, 1865 Spicer, North Vancouver, B.C. V7H 1A1. (604) 929-8407. Manufacture and repair propellers.

THE OUTBOARD CENTRE, 755 Marine Drive, North Vancouver, B.C. V7M 1H4. (604) 988-8564. New and used boat and motor sales. Marine hardware. hull and engine maintenance and repairs. Engine parts. Prop and shaft repairs.

PROPELLER ADJUSTERS, 20 Bewicke, North Vancouver, B.C. V7M 3B5. (604) 980-7903. Propeller manufacturing and repairs.

HORSHOE BAY. In addition to a public wharf and a ferry terminal, there are numerous small-craft floats. Use Chart 3508.

BOATING FUEL CONSERVATION TIPS

1. **BALANCE YOUR LOAD:** This enables your boat to get on plane quickly and reach the desired speed without plowing or porpoising.

2. **USE YOUR WEATHER EYE:** Avoid false starts if prevailing air and sea conditions are questionable. Brisk winds and heavy chop siphon fuel tanks.

3. **CHECK YOUR PROPELLER:** A damaged prop will waste fuel. Keep propeller blades clean and in good condition. Also adjust diameter and pitch for the level of activity you use most.

4. **AVOID EXCESSIVE IDLING:** Whenever you have to stop, turn off the ignition. A warm engine restarts easily without choking.

5. **SLOW DOWN:** High speed runs can be exhilarating, but a wide open throttle can increase fuel consumption by 50% or more over mid-range speeds.

6. **WATCH YOUR WEIGHT:** The lighter your boat, the less horsepower required to propel it.

7. **PLAN YOUR TRIP:** A true course is the shortest and any reduction in running time is fuel saved.

8. **TAKE SHORTER CRUISES:** You don't have to travel a hundred miles to enjoy the water. Visit those spots closer to home. Once you are there, enjoy water related activities such as fishing, sunning and exploring.

9. **TUNE-UP YOUR ENGINE:** Proper ignition timing and clean spark plugs assure extra mileage. Inspect the carburetor for proper float level, correct jetting and smooth choke operation.

10. **CHECK YOUR TRAILER:** Keep car and trailer tires properly inflated. Don't overload or use too small a trailer. Lubricate wheel bearings. Try to get in and out of the launching ramp area with a minimum of fuss and idling.

11. **CHECK THE TIDES:** Boating against the tide is like running against the wind -- it takes more effort. Make the tides work to your advantage. It can save your fuel.

12. **CLEAN YOUR HULL:** Keep a slick bottom. A clean hull means reduced underwater drag.

RAUER-ELECTRONICS, 1329 Pemberton, North Vancouver, B.C. V7P 2R6. (604) 985-3355. Sales and service for marine electronics.

ROTOR ELECTRIC, 1385 Main, North Vancouver, B.C. (604) 985-3401.

SALTY DOG GENERAL STORE, #206 - 80 Orwell St, North Vancouver, B.C. V73 3RS. (604) 980 - 0690. New and used marine hardware. Snack bar. Groceries and beverages. Ice. Closed December. President: Bev Powell.

SEA SCANNER MARINE, 1331 Pemberton, North Vancouver, B.C. (604) 985-5773. Wholesale marine equipment distributor.

SEYCOVE MARINA LTD., 2890 Panorama Drive, North Vanocuver, B.C. V7G 1V6. (604) 929-1251. Open year round. 9 AM - 6 PM. Launching facility. Fuel dock: gas, diesel and mix. Moorings. Engine maintenance and repairs. Marine hardware. Ice. Groceries. New and used boats and motors. Electronic sales and repairs. Fishing: licenses, bait and tackle. Charter boats. Pres.: A.C. George.

VANCOUVER SHIPYARDS CO. LTD., 50 Pemberton Avenue, North Vancouver, B.C. V7P 2R2. (604) 988-6361.

WAKE SAILS INTERNATIONAL INC., 246 E. First, North Vancouver, B.C. V7J 1B3. (604) 985 - 8031.

WEST VANCOUVER AREA

HORSESHOE BAY

THE BOAT CENTRE, 6695 Nelson Avenue, Horseshoe Bay, B.C. V7W 2B2. (604) 921-7438.

THE BOATHOUSE RESTAURANT, Horseshoe Bay, B.C.

FRASER'S MARINE SERVICE, 5729 Bluebell Drive, West Vancouver, B.C. V7W 1T2. (604) 921 - 7331. Engine sales and service.

HORSESHOE BAY MARINE SERVICES, 6705 Nelson Avenue, Horseshoe Bay, B.C. V7W 2B2. (604) 921-9558. Diving and towing service. Marineways cap.: 30'. Salvage work.

LIONS BAY MARINA LTD., 60 Lions Bay Avenue, Lions Bay, B.C. Y0N 2E0. (604) 921-7510. Ice. LP Gas refills. Open Jan 15 - Dec 15. Hours: Summer, 8 AM - 8 PM; Winter, 8 AM - 5 PM. Ramp: 1 - lane, asphalt. Open: daylight. Hoist: Forklift, cap.: to 27 feet. Open 8 AM - 8 PM. Overnight guest dock. Boat storage yard, open and covered. Hull and engine maintenance. Repairs and parts. Prop and shaft repairs. Fuel dock: gas and mix. Hours: 8 AM - 8 PM. Fishing: licenses and bait. President: E. Wolder.

NEWMAN CREEK MARINA, #6 Strachan Creek, West Vancouver, B.C. V7W 1C6. (604) 921-9636. Ice, laundry, marine hardware, snack bar. Open year round. & AM - 8 PM. fuel barge. Ramp: 1 - lane, concrete. Manager: M. Neitzel.

NORTH WEST PROPELLER & REPAIR LTD., Sunset Marina, West Vancouver, B.C. V7W 2T7. (604) 921-7479.

SEWELL'S LIMITED, 6695 Nelson Avenue, West Vancouver, B.C. V7W 2B2. (604) 921-7461. New and used boat and motor sales. Charts. Electronic sales. Ice. Picnic area. Restaurant. Ramp: 2-lane. Hoist cap.: 4 tons. Guest dock. Dockside electricity. Boat maintenance and repairs. Fuel dock: gas, diesel and mix. Fishing: licenses, bait and tackle. Boat rentals. Owner: D. Sewell.

SUNSET MARINA, 34 Sunset Beach, West Vancouver, B.C. V7W 2T7. (604) 921-7476. Full service marina with restaurant, wet and dry moorage, launch ramp, fuel, repairs and charters.

VANCOUVER FISH-ON GUIDING SERVICES LTD., 7120 Marine Drive, West Vancouver, B.C. V7W 2T3. (604) 921-3474. Picnic area. Snack bar. Fishing: licenses, bait and tackle. Charter boats. Diving. Owner: Warren McIntyre.

FISHERMAN'S COVE

A-1 CANVAS, LTD., Fisherman's Cove Marina, West Vancouver, B.C. V7W 2S2. (604) 921-7017.

FISHERMAN'S COVE, 5908 Marine Drive, West Vancouver, B.C. (604) 921-7333. Rental boats. Fuel: gas, diesel and mix. Open weekdays 7 AM - 8 PM; weekends 5 AM - 9 PM. Fishing: licenses, bait and tackle. Charter rentals. Ice. Snacks.

FISHERMAN'S COVER SERVICE CENTER, Fisherman's Cove Marina, West Vancouver, B.C. (604) 921-8811.

RACE ROCK YACHT SERVICES LTD., 5908 Marine Drive, West Vancouver, B.C. V7W 2S2. (604) 921-7007. Fuel dock: gas, diesel and mix. LP refills. Travelift cap.: 40 tons. Hull maintenance and repairs. Dry storage. Prop and shaft repairs. Fishing: licenses, bait and tackle. Narrow access channel. Inbound traffic to keep marker on the starboard beam. Light to medium traffic. Administrator: K.W. Diener.

THUNDERBIRD MARINA, 5776 Marine Drive, West Vancouver, B.C. V7W2S2. (604) 921-7434. Lift cap.: 26'. Marine railway cap.: 18,000 lbs. Moorings.

THUNDERBIRD MARINE SUPPLIES, Thunderbird Marina, West Vancouver, B.C. (604) 921-9011. Electronic sales. Ice. Marine hardware. Snack bar. Fishing: licenses, bait and tackle.

VANCOUVER OUTBOARD CENTRE, 5776 Marine Drive, Thunderbird Marina, West Vancouver, B.C. V7W 2S2. (604) 921-9527. Engine sales, service and parts.

25

STRAIT OF GEORGIA

FACILITIES

BELLA BELLA

SHEARWATER MARINE CENTRE, Shearwater, Bella Bella, B.C. V0T 1B0. (604) 957-2305. All year. Blacktop ramp. Marine railway cap.: 150 tons. Moorings, storage, rental boats. Hull and engine maintenance and repairs. Engine parts. Fuel dock: gas and diesel. New and used boats and motors. Electronic sales and repairs. Accommodations. Laundry. Ice. Marine hardware. Restaurant. Groceries. Waste disposal pumpout. Full service hotel. Landing strip.

SHEARWATER MARINE LTD AND FISHERMEN'S INN, P.O. Box 94447, Richmond, B.C. V6Y 1A8. (800) 663 - 2370. Located at Shearwater, Denny Island in the heart of the central coast, B.C.'s finest slamon fishing waters. Open year round. Deluxe accommodations. Souvenirs, gifts, groceries, bait tackle, ice, fishing licenses, guides and information, laundry, propane, water and dockside electricity. Marine repairs. Moorage is free.

BLIND CHANNEL

BLIND CHANNEL RESORT, Blind Channel, B.C. V0P 1B0. (604) 286-2178. Restaurant. Charts. Guest dock and dockside electricity. Fuel dock: gas and diesel. Liquor store. Post office. Groceries. Ice. Laundry. Showers. Cabins. Fishing: bait, licenses. Building lots available. Owners: The Richters.

CAMP CORDERO, General Delivery, Blind Channel, B.C. V0P 1B0. Phone: N693620. Open all year. Accommodations. Restaurant. Guest dock. Rental: outboard motor rentals. Fishing: licenses, bait. Package rates. Director: Reinhardt Kuppers.

MINSTREL ISLAND

LAGOON COVE MARINA, Lagoon Cove, East Cracroft Island, Box 42, Minstrel Island, B.C. V0P 1L0. VHF Channel 16. Charts. Ice. General store; home-baked bread, souvenirs. LP gas refills. Marine hardware. Marine railway, 15 tons. Overnight dock. Dockside electricity. Moorings. Rentals. Engine main-tenance, repairs. Fuel dock: gas, diesel, mix. 8 AM - 8 PM. Fishing: licenses. Owners: J. & M. Laan.

MINSTREL ISLAND RESORT Pub & Resturant, Minstrel Island, B.C. V0P 1L0. Phone: N-666899YG. Open all year. Fuel dock: gas, diesel and aviation gas. LP refills. Moorage. Groceries. Ice. Liquor. Showers. Laundry Lodging. Fishing bait and tackle. Rental Boats. Managers: Grant & Sylvia Douglas

BOWEN ISLAND - SNUG COVE

BOWEN ISLAND MARINA, 19 Cardena Drive, Bowen Island, B.C. V0N 1G0. (604) 974-9710. All year. Open: 7 AM - 10 PM. On call - 24 hours. Fuel dock. Pump 'n Tackle shop. Ice. Fishing: bait, tackle. Rental boats. Nearby: General store with liquor outlet,

The fuel dock at **BROWN's BAY MARINA**, in Discovery Passage N of Seymour Narrows, is open all year.

CAMPBELL RIVER on the W side of Discovery Passage, noted for sportfishing, has several launching ramps and a marina. This is the last major source of supplies and repairs on Vancouver Island for those heading N. Use Chart 3565.

bakery, boutique clothing, bike rentals, garden and gift store, deli, real estate, notory, post office and restaurant with pub. Snug Cove, Bowen Island is located approximately five miles from Vancouver. Crippin Park, a Vancouver regional park, is located in Snug Cove, as is our marina. Owners/operators: Norma, Dennis and Darran Dallas.

UNION STEAMSHIP MARINA, P.O. 250, Snug Cove, Bowen Island B.C. V0N 1G0. (604) 947-0707. All year. Groceries and beverages. Hotel/Motel accommodations. Ice. Picnic Area. Restaurant. Snack bar. Ramp: 1-lane, concrete. Guest dock. Dockside electricity. Slips 70'. Fuel dock: gas, diesel, mix. Fishing: licenses, bait and tackle. Complete new Harbour facility planned for 1989. Charter boats. Owner: Rondy Dike.

BOWSER

BOWSER BILL'S FAMILY FISHING RESORT, Box 104, Bowser, B.C. V0R 1G0. (604) 757-8363. Open April 15 - Oct. 15. Groceries. Accommodations. Ice. Laundry. RV campsites. Waste disposal pumpout. Ramp: 1 - lane, cement. Marine railway. Dry storage. Rental boats. Fuel dock: gas and mix. Fishing: licenses, bait and tackle. Charter boats. Water skiing. President: J. Leinweber.

DEEP BAY FISHING RESORT, RR #1 Site 160 C-26, Bowser, B.C. (604) 757-8424. Ramp: 1-lane, concrete. 7 AM to dark. Accommodations. Ice. Laundry. LP gas refills. RV campsites. Rental boats. Fishing: licenses, bait, tackle. Charters. Water skiing, skin and scuba diving. Managers: G. & D. Webb.

SHADY SHORES FISHING RESORT, Box 18, Site 118, Bowser, B.C. V0R 1G0. (604) 757-8595. Open April to Oct. Accommodations. Ramp. Rental boats. Fuel dock: gas. Fishing: licenses, bait and tackle. Charter Boats. Owners: John and Jean Stevenson.
SHIP AND SHORE MARINE, RR #1 Site 160 C-69, Bowser, B.C. V0R 1G0. (604) 757-8750. Location next to

Government wharf (on waterfront), Deep Bay, B.C. Open April 15 to Oct. 15. Facilities: good fishing area, R.V. camping, boat launch ramp, fishing tackle and licences, boat rentals, fuel, ice, grocery store, cafe, games room, Marine repairs and supplies, diver, fiberglass fabrication.

BRENTWOOD BAY

ANGLERS ANCHORAGE MARINA, 933 Marchant Road, RR 1, Brentwood Bay, B.C. V0S 1A0. (604) 652 - 3531. Located at the head of Brentwood Bay next to Butchart Gardens. Protected moorage for over 200 boats on daily or annual basis. Water, 15 and 30 amp power available. Fuel dock: gas, diesel. Ice. Chandlery. Fishing: licenses, bait.

BRENTWOOD BOAT RENTALS, Box 88, Brentwood Bay, Vancouver Island, B.C. V0S 1A0. (604) 652-1014. All year. Fuel dock: gas. Marine ways to 22' Bed & Breakfast. Coffee bar. Fishing: bait, tackle. Guide service. Owners: Don and Marion Turner.

BRENTWOOD INN RESORT, 7172 Brentwood Drive, Brentwood Bay, B.C. V0S 1A0. (604) 652 - 2413. 65 berth marina, power and water, showers, laundry and store open 7 days a week all year.

BUTCHART GARDENS, Mailing address: Box 4010, Postal Station A, Victoria, B.C. V8X 3X4. (604) 652 - 5256. Visitors can experience a new dimension to these world-class gardens by arriving in their own boats or dinghies via the waterside entrance. The entrance is located in a lovely, secluded cove, just to port when entering Tod Inlet. Day floats, with about 150 feet of moorage and four Topper buoys are located in the cove. dock facilities may be restricted at times. Overnight moorage is permitted on the buoys, but not at the floats.

ESSO MARINE STATION-ANGLERS ANCHORAGE MARINA, gas, diesel, moorage. (604) 652 - 3531.

GILBERT MARINE & GUIDE SERVICE, 789 Saunders Lane, Brentwood Bay, B.C. V0S 1A0. (604) 652-2211. All year. Fuel dock: gas. Moorings. Boat maintenance and repairs. Ice. Fishing: bait and tackle. Rental motor boats. Charter boats, guide service. Dockside electricity. Skin and scuba diving. Groceries. Marine railway. Owner: Harold Lacy.

HANSEN'S BOATWORKS, 900 Marchant Rd., RR#1, Brentwood Bay, B.C. V0S 1A0. (604) 652 - 0252. All year. 8 AM - 6 PM. Marine ways cap.: 25 tons. Hull maintenance and repairs. Guest dock. Marine hardware. Owners: John and Janet Hansen.

CAMPBELL RIVER AREA
(50°02'N., 125°14'W.)

BIG BAY MARINA RESORT, Big Bay Post Office, Stuart Island, B.C. V0P 1V0. (604) 286 - 2003 or 335 - 2931. Radiophone via Campbell River Marine Operator. Identify number: N628700 on Campbell River channel J L. Restaurant and lounge. Game room. Laundry and shower facilities. Moorage, sea plane moorage, gas, diesel, cabins, water, provision store and fishing guide service.

BOATLAND LTD, 2625 N. Island Highway, Campbell River, B.C. V9W 2H4. (604) 286 - 0752. All Mercury products. Mercury engines and drives, sales and service. Factory certified master mechanics. KMV Boats. All Speed and Road Runner Galvanized trailers.

CAMPBELL RIVER LODGE AND FISHING RESORT, 1760 Island Hwy, Campbell River, B.C. V9W 2E7. (604) 287 - 7446 or (800) 663 - 7212, Feb. 18 - Aug 18. All year. 7 AM - 1 AM. Accommodations. Dining Room. Pub. Picnic area. Laundry. Guided whaler charters. Fishing: licenses and bait. Skin and scuba diving. Campbell River's oldest fishing lodge. Manager: Ted Arbour.

CARMAC DIESEL, 1790 Perkins Road, Campbell River, B.C. V9W 4R9. (604) 923 - 6298 or 286 - 9688. Sales, parts and service. Company owned float plane service.

CHEVRON MARINE, P.O. Box 968, Campbell River, B.C. V9W GY4. (604) 287 - 3319. All year. Fuel dock: gas, diesel, mix and CNG refills. Full line of marine lubricants. Ice. Showers, laundry. Rental cars and trucks. Agent: Dave Facey

ESSO MARINE STATION-SEAWAY MARINE SALES, located behind the S rip-rap breakwater. (604) 287 - 3456. Gas, diesel, stove, ice, showers.

KILLARNEY RESORT, Saratoga Beach, Vancouver Island, B.C.. Mailing address: Site 110, Unit 1, RR #1, Campbell River, B.C. V9W 3S4. (604) 337-5459. Open: late May- mid-Sept. Accommodations: beach cottage housekeeping units. Rental boats and tackle, tractor launching and storage for small boats. Salt water fishing licences. Excellent clam beds in non-polluted environment. Hiking trails nearby for all fitness levels. Bird sanctuary on Mitlenatch Island - 7 miles away by sea. Manager: Joy Johnston.

EGMONT, near the junction of Agamemnon Channel, is a point of departure to visit the turbulent Skookumchuck Narrows. Use Chart 3589.

NORTH ISLAND PROPELLER, 2635 N. Island Highway, Campbell River, B.C. V9W 2H4. (604) 286 - 3271. Sales and expert repair service to all types of propellers.

OCEAN PACIFIC MARINE SUPPLY, 871 A Island Hwy., Campbell River, B.C. V0W 2C2. (604) 286-1011. All year. Charts. Electronic sales and repairs. Marine hardware. Marine railway 50'. Dockside electricity. Slips and moorings. Hull maintenance and repairs. Owners: L. Hansen and B. Kempling.

PACIFIC PLAYGROUNDS RESORT & MARINA, (15 miles S of Campbell River directly across from Desolation Sound) RR #1, Campbell River, B.C. V9W 3S4. (604) 337-5600. 280 boat slips to 45': electricity, water. Fuel dock, launch ramp. Marine hardware. Charts. Fishing: licenses, bait and tackle. Large covered dry storage. Bare boat charters. Three mechanics on call. Guides for fishing and/or cruising. 210 RV sites: electricity, water and fuel. 20 Bungalows. Groceries. Picnic sites. Showers. Swimming pool. Tennis courts. Golf course. Driving range. Miniature golf.

SALMON POINT RESORT TRAILER PARK AND MARINA, 2176 Salmon Point Rd., Campbell River, B.C. V9W 3S4. Open: April - Oct. Groceries and beverages. Ice. Laundry. Picnic area. Restaurant. Snack bar. RV campsites. Ramp: 2 - lanes, cement. Overnight guest dock. Slips. Storage. Fuel dock: gas and mix. Fishing: licenses, bait and tackle. Boat rentals and charters. Owner: F. Copithorne.

SEASIDE MOTEL, 87 South Island Highway, Campbell River, B.C. V9W 1A2. (604) 287-3343. Year round. Picnic area. Accommodations. Ice. Marine railway cap.: 2000 lbs. (1 ton). Rental skiffs and outboard motors. Fishing: licenses, bait and tackle. Charter boats. Owner: Roy Grant.

SEAWAY MARINE SERVICES, Box 137, Campbell River, B.C. V9W 5A7. (604) 287-3456. Open all year. Fuel dock: gas and diesel. Moorings. Prop and shaft repairs. Ice. Electronic sales. Fishing: bait and tackle. Manager: Stan Palmer.

SPORTFISH CENTRE, 975 Tyee Plaza, Campbell River, B.C. V9W 1A2. (604) 287-4911. All year, during daylight hours. New and used boat and motor sales. Electronic sales. Groceries and beverages. Accommodations. Ice. Laundry. Marine hardware. Picnic area. Restaurant. Overnight guest dock. Slips and moorings. Fuel dock: gas, diesel and mix. Fishing: licenses, bait and tackle. Charter boats. Owner: Paul Mackay.

QUADRA ISLAND

COMOX

APRIL POINT LODGE, FISHING RESORT AND MARINA, Post Office Box 1, Campbell River, B.C.. (604) 285 - 2222. This world-renowned resort complex serves the needs of yachtsmen, fishing parties and other vacationers. Boaters pass the lodge, located on the point, and proceed to the well protected moorage floats in the inner harbor. 7,000 feet of moorage is available on a daily, weekly, monthly or yearly basis. The Cannery Row Store, an OMC repair facility with factory trained mechanics and fibergalss repairs, showers, laundromat, and garbage drop are located at the moorage site. A full time mechanic in on duty. Water, 20, 30 and 50 ampere power, both 110 and 220 volts are provided on the floats. Gas, diesel, propane and dry storage are available.

BLACK FIN PUB MARINA LTD., P.O. 1381, Comox, B.C. V9N 7Z9. (604) 339-4664. Marine Pub. Moorage. Showers and laundry service. Fuel dock: diesel, gas 50:1. Ice. Fishing: tackle, licenses and rod rentals. Shopping centre one block away. Gateway to world famous Desolation Sound. Owner: Greg Ward.

GORDON GREER LTD, 201 - 1797 Comox Ave, Comox, B.C. V9N 4A1. (604) 339 - 4914. All year. Fuel dock: gas, diesel and mix. Ramp: 3-lanes, cement. Overnight guest dock with electricity. New and used boat and motor sales. Electronic and instrument repairs. Marine hardware. Picnic area. Fishing: licenses and tackle. Rental and charter boats. Hull and engine maintenance and repairs. Owners: John Myers and Bob Stevenson.

QUATHIASKI COVE-PETRO CANADA, Mailing address: Box 340, Quadra Island, B.C. V0P 1N0. (604) 285 - 3212. Gas, diesel, mix, kerosene, oils ice, fishing tackle, ice cream bars, confections and good water are available at this fuel facility. Owned and operated by Lloyd and Noreen Gray.

SECRET COVE

BUCCANEER MARINA, RR 1, Halfmoon Bay, B.C. V0N 1Y0. (604) 885 - 7888. This facility is located in the NE arm. The fuel dock dispenses Chevron marine products. A Daiwa Derby weigh-in station, this marina also carries propane, CNG, live and frozen bait, tackle, ice, groceries and fishing licenses. Three mechanics are on duty specializing in Mercury, OMC, and Volvo engines. Marine parts and hardware. Haulouts to 35'. Hull repairs, steam cleaning and bottom painting can be provided. Moorage is on a yearly basis with many spots available for boats with breakdowns. Open 7 days a week, year round.

ESSO MARINE STATION-SECRET COVE MARINA, Box 1118, Sechelt, B.C. V0N 3A0. (604) 885 - 3533. Gas, diesel, water, power, ice, live bait, store, laundry, showers and moorage.

HEROIT BAY INN & MARINA, Box 100, Heroit Bay, B.C. V0P 1H0. (604) 285-3322. Open all year. Charts. Accommodations. Ice. Laundry. Picnic area. RV campsites. Restaurant. LP gas refills. Guest dock. Dockside electricity. Slips. Engine parts. Fuel dock: gas and diesel. Fishing: licenses, boat rentals, bait and tackle. Owners: Lyle Acton and Angela Plasterer.

JOLLY ROGER INN, Secret Cove, B.C. V0N 1V0. (604) 885 - 7184. Resort hotel with moorage, town houses,

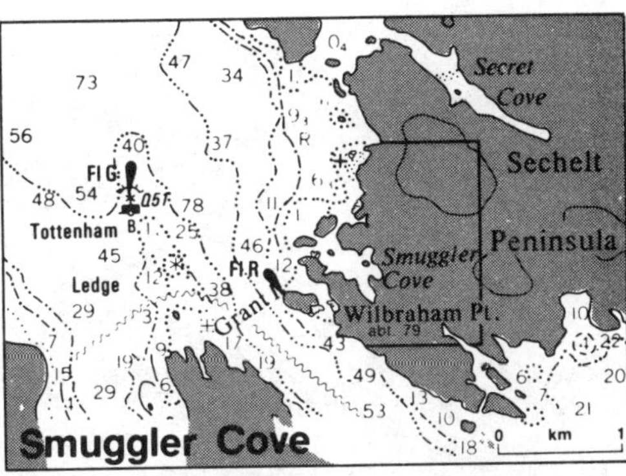

restaurant and lounge on the middle arm of Secret Cove.

SECRET COVE MARINA, Box 1118, Sechelt, B.C. V0N 3A0. (604) 885 - 3533 for fishing or moorage information. To reach Secret Cove Marina, bear to port upon entering Secret Cove. Fuel dock: gas, diesel and water. Fishing: bait and tackle. Power, water, fish cleaning tables and garbage deposit. Showers and laundry facilities. Nominal daytime tie-up charge allows use of all facilities. Grocery store.

GARDEN BAY

A B HADDOCK MARINE LTD., Box 38, Garden Bay, B.C. V0N 1S0. (604) 883 - 2811. Sales and service. Complete mechanical repairs. Marine ways and boat moving. Located at Hospital Bay, Pender Harbour.

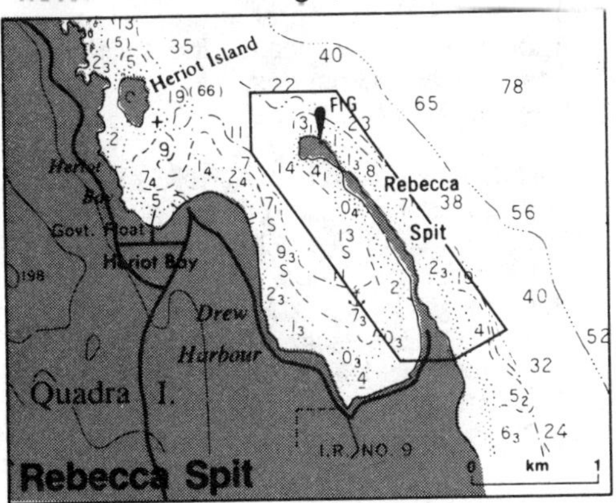

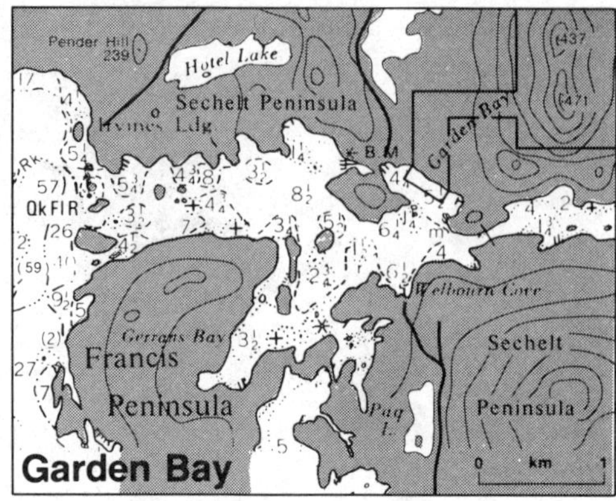

DUNCAN COVE RESORT, Mailing address: P.O. Box 18, Garden Bay, B.C. V0N 1S0. (604) 883 - 2424. Moorage for boats to 80'. Cottages. RV and trailer sites to 32' with full hook-ups provided. Campsites. Sani-dump station, showers, washrooms and laundry facilities. Propane bottles can be filled. Boat rentals. Launching for boats up to 30'. Fishing: bait and tackle.

THE FISHERMAN'S RESORT & MARINA, Box 1, Garden Bay, B.C. V0N 1S0. (604) 883-2336. All year. Hours: 7 AM - 10 PM. Ramp: 1 - lane, asphalt. Guest dock. Waterfront cottages and RV sites. Ice. Charts. Showers and laundry. Fishing: licenses, bait and tackle. Rental boats. Hiking trails. Lake swimming. Golf. Tennis. Dockside electricity. Owner: Peter Benjafield.

GARDEN BAY HOTEL, P.O. Box 90, Garden Bay, B.C. V0N 1S0. (604) 883 - 2674. Moorage is available directly in front of this full-licensed restaurant and pub.

GARDEN BAY MARINE PARK, road access from Hwy 101. Anchorage is possible off undeveloped marine park land. The park land includes Mount Daniel, of historical importance to the local Sechelt Indians.

IRVINES LANDING, RR1, Irvines Landing Road, Garden Bay, B.C. V0N 1S0. (604) 883 - 2296. Gas, diesel, oils, power, water, ice, lodging, restaurant, launching, moorage.

JOHN HENRY'S MARINAS, P.O. Box 40, Garden Bay, B.C. V0N 1S0. (604) 883 - 2253. Gas, diesel, propane, post office, liquor agency, canned and frozen goods, fresh meats.

CORTES ISLAND

CORTES BAY MARINE RESORT, Box 12, Cortes Bay, Cortes Island, B.C. V0P 1K0. (604) 935-6361. Open: April - Oct. Fuel dock: gas, diesel and mix. Open: 9 AM - 9 PM. Ramp. Guest dock. Marine hardware. Charts. Groceries. Ice. Cabins. Showers. Laundry. Licensed teahouse. Fresh bakery. Fishing: bait and tackle. Rental boats. Dockside electricity. Wonderful family resort, adjacent excellent boating and fishing areas. Manager: Rankin B. Smith.

GORGE HARBOUR MARINA & RESORT, Box 89, Whaletown, B.C. V0P 1Z0. (604) 935 - 6433. New boat and motor sales . Charts. Electronic sales and repairs. Groceries. Propane. Accommodations. Ice. Laundry. Marine hardware. Picnic area. Restaurant. Ramp. Overnight guest dock. Moorings. Engine parts. Fuel dock: gas, diesel and mix. Fishing: licenses, bait and tackle. Charter boats. Boat rentals. RV Park. Owner: Gay and I. Whitey Brayer.

DENMAN ISLAND

DENMAN GENERAL STORE, (near government wharf) 1069 N.W. Road, Denman Island, B.C. V0R 1T0. (604) 335 - 2293. General store. Liquor. Agency store. Propane and bulk fuel. Post office. Groceries. Ice. Fishing: licenses, bait and tackle.

SANDY ISLAND MARINE PARK, (includes Sandy Island, locally known as Tree Island and Seal Islets off the NW tip of Denman Island near the N entrance to Baynes Sound). 83 acres. Sandy beaches. The spit connecting islands with Denman Island dries at low tide. Fairly sheltered anchorage on the S side of Sandy Island. Toilets.

GIBSONS

GIBSONS MARINA, Box 1520, Gibsons, B.C. V0N 1V0. (604) 886 - 8686. All year. Charts. Elecronic sales. Ice. Laundry. Marine hardware. RV campsites. Waste disposal pumpout. Ramp: 2-lane, concrete. Guest docks with dockside electricity. Slips. Fishing: licenses, bait and tackle. Charter boats. Boat rentals. Water skiing. Scuba diving. Manager: A. McGinnis.

GRAMMA'S MARINE INN LTD., Box 425, Gibsons, B.C. V0N 1V0. (604) 886-8215. All year. Mon. - Thur.: 10 AM - 1 PM. Fri. - Sun.: 11 AM - 1 PM. Restaurant. Laundry. Ice. Overnight guest dock. Pub: Cold beer and wine store. Owner: Christopher Danroth.

HARBOURVIEW MARINE, 706 Hwy 101, Gibsons, B.C. V0N 1V0. (604) 886 - 2233. Complete line of marine hardware, pressure washing, boat moving.

HYAK MARINE SERVICES LTD., P.O. Box 948, Gibsons, B.C. V0N 1V0. (604) 886-9011. Open daily sunrise to sunset. Groceries and beverages. Ice. Overnight guest dock. Marine railway cap.: 100 tons. Hull maintenance and repairs. Engine maintenance and repairs. Fuel dock: gas, diesel, mix and stove oil. Fishing: licenses, bait and tackle. Charter boats. Owner: Bruce Gravelle.

MARINER'S RESTAURANT, Mailing Address: P.O. Box 399, Gibsons, B.C. V0N 1V0. (604) 886 - 2334. Fresh and live seafoods served with a waterfront view, just within Molly's Reach. Take-out foods.

SUNSHINE COAST YACHTS, (604) 886 - 2628. Located on the water at Gibsons Marina. Brokers for new and used, power and sail.

TIDELINE MARINA, 5637 Wharf Road, P.O. Box 978, Sechelt, B.C. V0N 3A0. (604) 885 - 4141. Supplies, sales, repairs, dockside service.

HORNBY ISLAND
(40°30'N., 124°41'W.)

FORD'S COVE MARINE LTD., Hornby Island, B.C. V0R 1Z0. (604) 335 - 2169. All year. Fuel dock: gas, diesel and outboard mix. Moorings at government wharf. Waterfront self-contained cottages. Campsites. Groceries. Ice. Fishing: bait and tackle. Owner: Jennifer Fredbeck.

TRIBUNE BAY PROVINCIAL PARK, Excellent sandy beach for swimming and sunbathing. Picnicking and hiking. Nearby Helliwell Park provides miles of shoreline trails. Fairweather anchorage in bay, government floats in Ford Cove.

JERVIS INLET

EGMONT MARINA RESORT, (just E of Earl's Cove). Egmont, B.C. V0N 1N0. (604) 883-2298. Concrete ramp open all year. Fuel dock: gas, diesel and mix, open 7 AM to 9 PM. Last fuel stop on route to Princess Louisa Inlet. Slips to 50 feet. Dry storage. Campsites. Restaurant. Store. Charts. Pub. Laundry and showers Divers Air Station. open 24 hours. Ice. Fishing: licenses, bait and tackle. Chevron Marine Products. Rental boats and tackle. Charter boats. Fish freezing.

PRINCESS LOUISA MARINA PARK, 110 acres. Enter Jervis Inlet from Malaspina Strait directly or via Agamemnon Channel. Entrance to Princess Louisa Inlet through Malibu Rapids is narrow and subject to strong tidal currents. Access by charter boats from Pender Harbour or Egmont. Focal point of the park is the spectacular 150 foot Chatterbox Falls. Floats and secure anchorage. Picnic area. Campsites. Toilets. Hiking trails to Chatterbox Falls. The park is supported in part by the non-profit Princess Louisa International Society. Annual membership $10., Life membership $100. Secretary, 18005 - 113th Avenue SE, Renton, WA 98055.

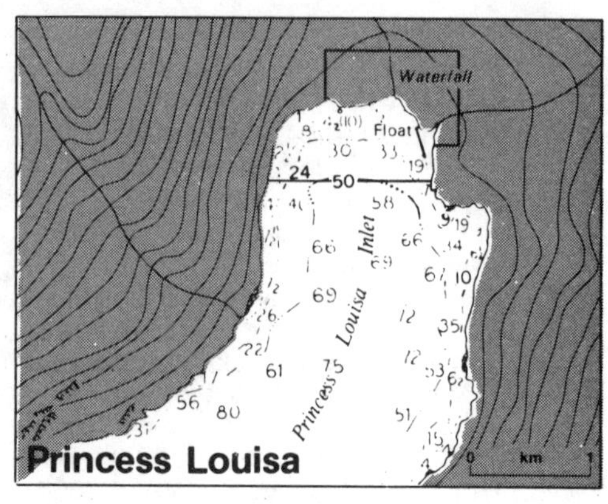

MACDONALD ISLAND, (2½ miles down the Inlet from the Marine Park) Facilities include island and 1500 feet of waterfront on the mainland adjacent. There are no charges for mooring here or at Princess Louisa Marine Park.

One of the most spectacular gunkholes in the NW lies at the foot of Chatterbox Falls in Princess Louisa Inlet.

LASQUETI ISLAND
(40°29'N., 124°22'W.)

LASQUETI ISLAND STORE & MARINA, Weldon Rd., Lasqueti Island, B.C. V0R 2J0. (604) 333 - 8846. All year. Hours open: 7 AM daily - 10 AM Sunday, June - Sept. Closed Tues. after summer season. Fuel dock: gas and diesel. Licensed restaurant. Bed and breakfast. Ice. Groceries. Excellent fishing and scuba diving. Managers: Gil and Anita Vossler.

MADEIRA PARK

COHO MARINA RESORT, P.O. Box 160, Madeira Park, B.C. V0N 2H0. (604) 883 - 2248. Moorage, marine hardware, ice and tackle. Campsites and trailer sites, showers and launch ramp.

ESSOR MARINE STATION, (604) 883 - 2663. Gas, diesel, stove, propane, ice, moorage, laundry. Located on Francis Peninsula at Donnely Landing, W of Gerrans's Bay.

HEADWATER MARINA, P.O. Box 71, Madeira Park, B.C. V0N 2H0. (604) 883 - 2406. Located atentrance to Gunboat Bay. Launch ramp, moorage, power, water, repairs, showers and campsites.

MADEIRA MARINA, (in Welbourn Cove on E side of Government dock. Protected anchorage and moorage in Pender Harbour.) Box 189, Madeira Park, B.C. V0N 2H0. (604) 883-2266. All year. Ramp: 1 - lane, concrete. Open 24 hours. Boat repairs. Engine parts, repairs. Marine hardware. Brokerage. Ice. (4) 2 bedroom motel units. Laundromat. Water taxi's. RV campsites. Fishing: salt water licenses, bait and tackle. Golf Course nearby. MC/Visa Accepted Owners: Bob and Ruth King.

MANSON'S LANDING

MANSON'S LANDING STORE, Box 68, Manson's Landing, B.C. V0P 1K0. (604) 935-6364. Open all year. Fuel dock: gas and diesel. Groceries and beverages. Ice. Picnic area. Fishing: licenses, bait and tackle. Water skiing. Owners: Irv and Doreen Reedel.

NANAIMO

AIR RAINBOW, 1956 Zorkin Road, Nanaimo, B.C. V9R 5K4. (604) 753 - 2020. Seaplane charter air service.

ANCHORAGE MARINA, (604) 754-5585. Gas, diesel, water, repairs and moorage.

THE BOAT BASIN, Box 131, Nanaimo, B.C. V9R 5K4 (604) 754 - 5053. FAX (604) 753 - 4899. Moorage, ice, power, water, showers, laundromat. Adjacent Harbour Park Mall.

DINGHY DOCK PUB & RESTURANT P.O. Box 771, Nanaimo, B.C. V9R5M2 (604) 753-2373 Covenient Store, Laundry, Showers. Limited tie-up space. Nanaimo's only floating Pub. Proprieter: Capt. Bob

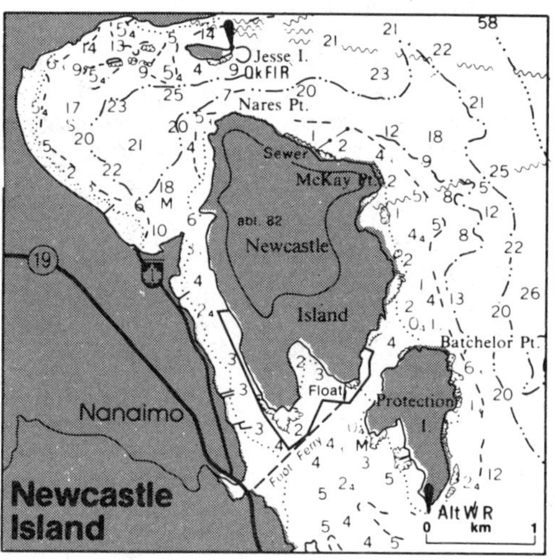

Farmer's Market at Nanaimo with moorage for 40 guest boats.

BRECHIN POINT MARINA. LTD., P.O. Box 178, Nanaimo, B.C. V9R 5K9. (604) 753-6122. Open: 6 AM - 9 PM Summer, 8 AM - 4:30 PM Winter. (N end of Newcastle Channel on Zorkin Rd.) Fuel dock: gas, diesel and mix. Aviation, turbo and jet fuel available. LP refills. Ice. Fishing: licenses, bait and tackle. Port of entry for Canada Customs for vessels and seaplanes. Owners: Larry and Joan Hume.

DOGWOOD MARINE SUPPLY, 1740 Stewart Avenue, Nanaimo, B.C. V9S 4E6. (604) 754 - 3261. Mercury headquarters, sales and service. Marine parts and accessories.

NANAIMO MARINA, (604) 754 - 2732. Moorage, power, water and repairs.

NANAIMO SHIPYARD (1985) LTD., 1040 Stewart Avenue, Nanaimo, B.C. V9S 4C9. (604) 753 - 1151.

NANAIMO SMALL-CRAFT HARBOUR, (Commercial Inlet Basin at City Center), 104 Front Street, Box 131, Nanaimo, B.C. V9R 5K4. (604) 753- **4146. Radio watch VHF Channel 16. Fuel available in the harbor. Crane cap.: 1000 lbs. Showers. Ice. Laundromat. 6000 ft. guest moorage in July and August. Complete seaplane terminal with pub and restaurant. Charters and schedules to Vancouver and Washington State. Dockside electricity and water. Shopping center across the street. Operated by Nanaimo Harbour Commission.**

NEWCASTLE MARINA LTD., 1300 Stewart Avenue, Nanaimo, B.C. V9S 4E1. (604) 753-1431. Travelift cap.: 60 tons. Dockside electricity. Hull and engine repairs. Prop and shaft repairs. Laundry. Showers. Ice. Boat Brokerage. Welder. Manager: Gerald Chow.

ST. JEAN'S, (604) 754 - 2185. Moorage, gas and diesel.

STONE'S MOORAGE, (604) 753 - 4388. Repairs.

NANOOSE
(49°16'N., 124°09'W.)

SCHOONER COVE RESORT HOTEL AND MARINA (on Vancouver Island between Nanaimo and Parksville) Schooner House, Box 12, Nanoose Bay, B.C. V0R 2R0. (604) 468-7691. All year. Ramp. Fuel dock. Slips. Guest dock. Hotel. Pub and restaurant. Condominiums. Convenience store. Laundry. Showers. Pool. Tennis Courts. Golf. Fishing and diving charters.

QUALICUM

FRENCH CREEK MARINA STORE, RR1, Site 132, C-10, Qualicum, B.C. V0R 2T0. (604) 248 - 8912. Conveniently located for the boater. Groceries, camping supplies. Fishing and sailing charters.

PARKSVILLE

FEDERAL BOAT BASIN, (at French Creek). Rt. 2, Parksville, B.C. V0R 2S0. All year. Ramp: 4 - lanes, concrete. Open 24 hours. Fuel dock: gas, diesel and outboard mix. Fuel dock in the basin. Government dock. Dockside electricity. Harbor Manager: George Rose.

LO COST MARINE, (604) 248 - 4363. Just a 10 minute walk from The Dock Is. Hwy and Wembley Road. Charts and publications. Hardware and accessories.

PORT ALBERNI

CHEVRON CANADA LTD. FUEL DOCK, Box 4, Port Alberni, B.C. V9Y 7M6. (604) 723-7351. All year. 8 AM - 5 PM. Fuel: gas, diesel and mix. Manager: Cecil Hopps.

VALLEY HEATING OIL, 1966 LTD., 5433 Argyle Street, Port Alberni, B.C. V9Y 1T6. (604) 723-8411. All year. Fuel dock: gas, diesel, mix. Charts. Electronic sales, repairs. Groceries. Accommodations. Ice. Instrument repairs. Laundry. Marine hardware. Restaurant. Ramp: 3-lane, cement. Hoist. Guest dock, electricity. Slips, moorings. Boat maintenance, repairs, parts. Fishing: licenses, bait, tackle. Charter boats. Water skiing. Skin, scuba diving. Mgrs: L. Berg, C. McPherson.

N of Powell River, LUND is the terminus of Hwy 101, and is the gateway for Desolation Sound. The Breakwater Inn Resort has provisions, moorage, fuel dock and boat repair along with hotel accommodations and meals.

POWELL RIVER

BEACH GARDENS RESORT HOTEL & MARINA, 7074 Westminster Ave, Powell River, B.C. V8A 1C5. (604) 485-6267. Fax (604) 485-2343 All year. Accom - modations. Waterfront rooms, Coffee shop, Dining Room, Pub, Beer & Wine store, fitness Centre. Pool, Guest dock. Marine fuel, Ice, live bait, fishing licenses. Air station. Fishing charters & tours. small boat rentals.

CHARTER ASSOCIATES, 1733 West 4th Avenue, Vancouver, B.C. V6J 1M2. (604) 736 - 3738. Sail or power, bareboat or skippered. Located in Vancouver and at Beach Gardens Marina.

LES KOLESZAR SERVICES LTD, 4462 Willingdon Avenue, Powell River, B.C. V8A 2M6. (604) 485-5616. Year round: 8:30 AM - 5:30 PM. Marine hardware. New and used boats and motors. Electronic sales. Engine maintenance and repairs. Engine parts. President: Les Koleszar.

OKEOVER RESORT, RR #2 Craig Road, Powell River, B.C. V8A 4Z3. (604) 483-4602. Ramp. Moorings at Government wharf. General store. Restaurant. Ice. Dockside electricity. Special Diving feature: shipwrecks and underwater caves. Fully liscensed dining room with unique atmosphere, oyster picking and clam digging (when open). Government wharf in front of Resort with Hoist and approx. 250 ft. dockspace. Director: Manfred Heins.

SOUTH BOAT HARBOUR FISHERMAN'S FLOATS, 6910 Duncan Street, Powell River, B.C. V8A 1V4. (604) 485-5244. Open year round. Ramp: 2 - lanes, concrete. Guest dock. Dockside electricity. Publicly operated. Leaseholder: Corp. of the Dist. of Powell River.

LUND

BREAKWATER INN RESORT, Lund, B.C. (604) 483 - 3187. All year. Fuel dock: gas, diesel and mix. Groceries. Ice. Marine hardware. Ramp. Moorage at government wharf adjacent. Boat repairs. Charts. Sailing charters. Laundry and showers. Hotel, motel, air conditioned dining lounge and coffee shop. Pub. Liquor store. Post Office. Fishing: bait and tackle. Rental boats. Owner: Ewald Werner.

RAGGED ISLANDS MARINE, (3 miles N of Lund, B.C.) Box 22, Lund, B.C. V0N 2G0. Petro-Canada fuel dock: gas, diesel and water. Open all year, 7 AM - 10 PM. Managers: Derek and Wendy Cox.

REFUGE COVE

REFUGE COVE GENERAL STORE, Refuge Cove, B.C. V0P 1P0. Radio telephone N678982. Open: May - Oct. Fuel dock: gas, diesel, propane and oils. Moorings. Charts. Groceries. Ice. Laundry. Marine hardware. Deli. LP gas refills. Fishing: bait and tackle. Liquor store. Hamburger stand. Managers: Pat Lovell and Colin Robertson.

2 miles S of Powell River, Westview has facilities for fishing boats and yachts. Supplies of all kinds are available here or at Powell River. Use Chart 3508.

Hunter Is.
Queens Sound
Fitz Hugh Sound
Hakai Pass
Calvert Is.
Rivers Inlet
PACIFIC BOATING Almanac
LOWER B.C. COAST
BRITISH COLUMBIA
Smith Sound
Smith Inlet
QUEEN CHARLOTTE SOUND
Belize Inlet
Seymour Inlet
Gordon Channel
Nigel Is.
Coletas Channel
Broughton Is.
Cape Scott
Queen Charlotte Strait
Malcolm Is.
Broughton Strait
Forward Inlet
Johnstone Strait
Vancouver Island
Quatsino Sound

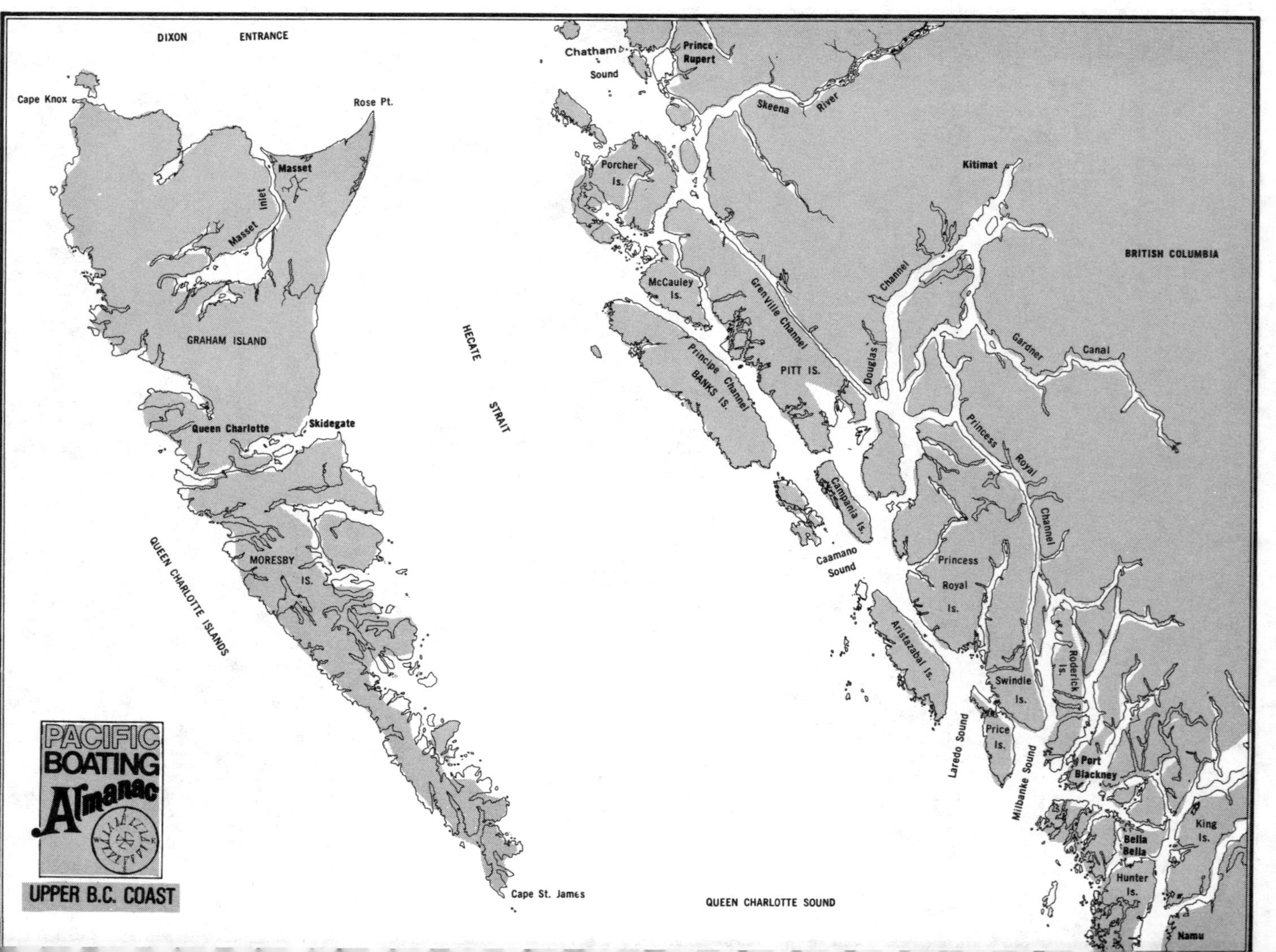

DIXON ENTRANCE
Cape Knox
Rose Pt.
Masset
Masset Inlet
GRAHAM ISLAND
Queen Charlotte
Skidegate
MORESBY IS.
QUEEN CHARLOTTE ISLANDS
Cape St. James
HECATE STRAIT
Chatham Sound
Prince Rupert
Skeena River
Porcher Is.
McCauley Is.
Grenville Channel
Principe Channel
BANKS IS.
PITT IS.
Douglas Channel
Kitimat
Gardner Canal
BRITISH COLUMBIA
Campania Is.
Caamano Sound
Princess Royal Channel
Princess Royal Is.
Aristazabal Is.
Swindle Is.
Roderick Is.
Laredo Sound
Price Is.
Milbanke Sound
Port Blackney
Bella Bella
King Is.
Hunter Is.
Namu
QUEEN CHARLOTTE SOUND
PACIFIC BOATING Almanac
UPPER B.C. COAST

26

NORTHERN BRITISH COLUMBIA

FACILITIES

PORT HARDY

PORT HARDY MARINE HARDWARE, 6465 Hardy Bay Road, Port Hardy, B.C. VON 2P0. (604) 949-6461. Marine hardware. Electronic sales. Charts. Fishing: licenses, bait and tackle. Charter boats. Owner: George Corkum.

PORT HARDY MARINE SERVICE, 6555 Hardy Bay Road, P.O. Box 2508, Port Hardy, B.C. VON 2P0. (604) 949 - 9611. Parts, sales and service Mercury outboards, MerCruiser and Volvo stern drives.

QUARTERDECK MARINE INDUSTRIES, P.O. Box 910, Port Hardy, B.C. VON 2P0. (604) 949-6551. Open Summer 6 AM - 10 PM; Winter: 9 AM - 5:30 PM. Ramp: 2 - lanes, concrete. Open 24 hours. Fuel dock: gas, diesel and mix. Slips. Guest dock. Engine parts, maintenance and repairs. Marine hardware. Charts. Ice. New and used boats and motors. Dive Shop. Fishing: licenses, bait and tackle. Rental tackle with rental boats and motors. Owner: Vern Logan.

ALERT BAY

ALERT BAY, P.O. Box 28, Alert Bay, B.C. VON 1A0. (604) 974-5213. New and used boat and motor sales. Charts. Electronic sales and repairs. Groceries. Accommodations. Ice. Instrument repairs. Laundry. Marine hardware. Picnic area. Restaurant. RV campsites. Cement ramp. Fuel dock: gas and

diesel. Hull and engine maintenance and repairs. Fishing: licenses, bait and tackle. Charter boats.

SHELL MARINA, P.O. Box 488, Port McNeill, B.C. VON 2R0. (604) 956 - 3336. Marine fuels, ICG, aviation gas, propane, repairs, parts, float plane base.

TELEGRAPH COVE

FAREWELL HARBOUR YACHT CLUB, Telegraph Cove, B.C. VON 3J0. Radio-telephone, N486324. Channel JPALERT BAY. June - Oct. Accommodations. Restaurant. Hot tub. Guiding fishing. Licenses available. Owners: Paul and Mark Weaver.

TOFINO

WEIGH WEST MARINA, Box 553, Tofino, B.C. V0R 2Z0. (604) 725-3277. Accommodations. Ice. Laundry. Restaurant. Ramp: 1 - lane, concrete. Overnight guest dock. Dockside electricity. Outboard motor rentals.

PRINCE RUPERT

JOHNNY'S MACHINE SHOP, No. 8 Cow Bay Road, Prince Rupert, B.C. V8J 1A5. (604) 624-3003. All year. Engine maintenance and repairs. Engine parts. Prop and shaft repairs. Motor sales. New and used marine hardware. Instrument repairs. Owner: John Basso.

KHATADA MARINE LTD., P.O. Box 864, Prince Rupert, B.C. V8I 3Y1. (604) 624-6666. Open all year. 8 AM - 8

PM. Marine hardware. Overnight guest dock. Dockside electricity. Fuel dock: gas, diesel and mix. Owner: Robert Mitchell.

PORT EDWARD MARINE SERVICES LTD (at Port Edward near the S approach to Prince Rupert) Bayview Dr., Box 220, Prince Rupert, B.C. V8J 3P8. (604) 628 - 3245. Open daily: 8 AM - 4:30 PM. Fuel dock: gas, diesel and mix. Guest dock. Dry storage. Full service boatyard. Haulouts to 40 feet. Fiberglass repairs. Hull and engine maintenance and repairs. Engine parts. Prop and shaft repairs. Volvo Penta dealer sales and service. Electronic sales and service. Marine hardware. Fishing gear. Dockside electricity. Owner: Allan Sheppard.

SIMOOM SOUND

ECHO BAY RESORT, Simoom Sound Post Office, B.C. V0P 1S0. (604) 949 - 4911. Store, laundry and shower facilities. Moorage floats in sheltered locations. 15 and 30 amp shore power. New water system. Ice. Rental boats. Fishing.

SULLIVAN BAY

SULLIVAN BAY MARINA RESORT, Sullivan Bay, B.C. V0N 3H0. (604) 949-4905. Open year round. Charts. Groceries and beverages. Accommodations. Ice. Laundry. LP gas refills. Guest dock. Dockside electricity. Engine repairs and parts. Fuel dock: gas and diesel. Rental: skiffs and outboard motor. Slips. Fishing: licenses, bait and tackle. Pres: J.P. Finnerty.

UCLUELET

ERIK LARSEN DIESEL CO. LTD., 1351 Eber Road, Box 245, Ucluelet, B.C. V0R 3A0. (604) 726-7011. Open all year. 8 AM - 5 PM. New and used engine sales, service and parts. Prop and shaft repair. General welding and repairs. Pres: Erik Larsen.

RUSSELL MARINE LTD, Box 14, Ucluelet, B.C. V0R 3A0. (604) 726-4368. Fuel dock: gas and diesel. Marine ways. Boat maintenance and repairs. Marine hardware. Manager: William Russell.

WHALEBOAT ISLAND

WHALEBOAT ISLAND MARINE PARK, (at the S end of Tuxton Island N of Whaleboat Passage that connects Pylades Channel and Stuart Channel and separates Ruxton and Pylades Islands). 25 acres. Limited anchorage. An alternative to nearby Pirates Cove Marine Park. Undeveloped.

27

SOUTHEASTERN ALASKA

KETCHIKAN
(55°20'N., 131°39'W.)

A complete array of services are available to the visiting yachtsman. Included are marine repairs and supplies, engine parts, divers, haulouts, marine fuel, laundry and showers. U.S. Customs does not accept phone-in reporting. Upon arrival, phone the Customs and arrange to meet a representative. There may be a charge for services after normal business hours. For tourist information, visit the Ketchikan Visitors Bureau, (on the cruise ship dock), 131 Front Street. (907) 225 - 6166.

AIR MARINE HARBOR, (8 miles N of Ketchikan). Box 8944, Ketchikan 99901. (907) 247 - 2282. All year. Open daily Tues. thru Sat.: 9:00 AM - 5:30 PM. Ramp usable on half to full tide. Travelift cap.: to 30 tons. Fuel dock: gas. Dry storage open and covered. Owner: Stan A. Oaksmith III.

ALASKA OUTBOARD SERVICE, 1405 Tongass Avenue, Ketchikan, AK 99901. (907) 225 - 4980. All year. Motors. Outboard engine repairs. Limited marine hardware. Owner: Oral Freeman.

ANDERES OIL CO, P.O. Box 5858, Ketchikan, AK 99901. (907) 225 - 2163. All year. 8 AM - 5 PM. Fuel dock: gas, diesel and mix. Partner: Ernie Anderes.

AURORA COMMUNICATIONS, 1900 Tongass Ave, Box 5412, Ketchikan, AK 99901. (907) 225 - 4164. All year. Electronic sales and service. Marine hardware and electrical. Instrument repair. Owner: Don Cunning.

BAR HARBOR BOAT BASIN (1.5 miles N of City Center) Mailing address: City of Ketchikan, Port & Harbors Dept., 334 Front Street, Ketchikan, AK 99901. (907) 335 - 3111 ext. 332. All year. 54 reserved stalls, 300 feet transient moorage. Harbormaster monitors VHF 16. Hours: 8 AM - 5 PM Oct. - April; 8 AM to Midnight, May - Sept.

CITY FLOAT (4 blocks N of City Center) Mailing address: City of Ketchikan, Port and Harbors Dept., 334 Front Street, Ketchikan, AK 99901. (907) 225 - 3111 ext. 332. All year. 1200 foot transient moorage. Groceries. Banking. Repairs. Supplies. Harbormaster monitors VHF 16. Hours: 8 AM - 5 PM Oct. - April; 8 AM to Midnight, May - Sept.

HOLE-IN-THE-WALL FLOAT (8 miles S of City Center) Mailing address: City of Ketchikan, Port and Harbors Dept., 334 Front Street, Ketchikan, AK 99901. (907) 225 3111 ext. 332. All year. 25 reserved stalls, 40 foot transient float. Harbormaster monitors VHF 16. Hours: 8 AM - 5 PM Oct. - April; 8 AM to Midnight, May - Sept.

LIGHTHOUSE MARINE REPAIR, Mile 11, North Tongass Hwy. Rt. 1, Box 751, Ketchikan, AK 99901. (907) 247 - 8330. Marine engines, parts and service. Dry storage. Owner: Stan Rhodes.

Thomas Boat Basin, Ketchikan, first port of entry in SE Alaska.

MANZANITA BAY FLOAT (on Behm Canal 9.5 miles from Ketchikan) Detached float for layover and weather refuge. No facilities. Operated by the State.

MOUNTAIN POINT RAMP (4½ miles from City Center on South Tongass Hwy.) All year. Ramp: 1 - lane concrete. Open 24 hours. Parking. No facilities. Operated by City of Ketchikan.

RYUS FLOAT (at city center, foot of Dock Street, midway between Thomas Basin and City Float.) All year. Loading zone. Limited to four hours. Operated by the City of Ketchikan. Harbormaster monitors VHF Channel 16. Groceries and restrooms nearby.

THOMAS BOAT BASIN (2 blocks S of City Center) Mailing Address: City of Ketchikan, Port & Harbors Dept., 334 Front Street, Ketchikan, AK 99901. (907) 225 - 3111 ext. 332. All year. 173 reserved stalls, 400 foot transient float. Groceries. Machine shop. Electronics repair. Harbormaster monitors VHF 16. 8 AM - 5 PM Oct. - April; 8 AM to Minight, May - Sept.

TIMBER AND MARINE SUPPLY, 2547 Tongass Ave., Ketchikan, AK 99901. (907) 225 - 6644. All year. Outboard sales and service. Boat sales. Marine hardware. Chainsaws and accessories. Honda products. Owner: Lyle Simpson.

UNION FUEL DOCK, Box 7660, Ketchikan, AK 99901. (907) 225 - 4176. All year. Fuel dock: gas and diesel. Open 8 AM - 5 PM. Mon. through Fri.: 8 AM - 4 PM on Saturdays in summer.

WHITE PASS FUEL DOCK, Box 7398, Ketchikan, AK 99901. (907) 225 - 2106. All year. Fuel dock: gas, diesel and mix. Open 7 days a week 8 AM - 5 PM, May 1 - Sept. 30. Mon. - Fri. rest of the year. Custom clearance available. Oil changing facility. Showers. Manager: Richard W. Bevens.

HYDER
(55°55'N., 130°00'W,)

HYDER FLOATS (on W side of Portland Canal near mouth of Salmon River) Public floats. Launching ramp. Fuel and supplies at Steward, 7 miles N in B. C. Canadian customs at border. Operated by the community of Hyder.

CLOVER PASS
(55°28'N., 131°48'W.)

CLOVER PASS RESORT (15 Mile North Tongass Hwy.) Box 7322, Ketchikan, AK 99901. (907) 247 - 2234. Slips. Fuel dock: gas and mix only. Overnight accommodations. RV sites. Restaurant. Cocktail lounge. Laundry. Showers. Fishing: bait and tackle. Rental boats. Charters. Travel agency. Liquor store. Owner: Jerry Engleman.

KNUDSON COVE (14 miles N of City Center) Mailing Address: City of Ketchikan, Port & Harbors Dept., 334 Front Street, Ketchikan, AK 99901. (907) 225 - 3111 ext. 332. All year. 54 reserved stalls, 300 feet transient moorage. Harbormaster monitors VHF 16. 8 AM - 5 PM Oct. - April; 8 AM to Midnight, May - Sept.

KNUDSON COVE MARINA, R#1, Box 965, Ketchikan, AK 99901. (907) 247 8500. All year. Groceries. Accommodations. Ice. Marine hardware. Restaurant. Ramp: 2 - lane, concrete. Slips. Some off-season boat storage. Fuel dock: gas, diesel and mix. Fishing: licenses, bait and tackle. Boat rental and charter boats. Manager: Horbert Laughlin.

NAHA BAY

LORING FLOAT (about 20 miles N of Ketchikan at NE corner of Naha Bay on the E side of the Behm Canal) Public float, about 2 blocks from Loring. No facilities. Operated by State. Trail for the Forest Service float leads to Roosevelt Lagoon, past Orton Ranch and up to Heckman Lake. Bear observation post is at small falls just up from Orton Ranch.

HELM BAY

HELM BAY (on Cleveland Peninsula, 20 miles from Ketchikan on northwestern side of bay) Detached float for layover only. No facilities. Operated by State. Forest Service cabin on beach $\frac{1}{4}$ mile from float located behind Forss Island.

YES BAY
(55°55'N., 131°48'W.)

YES BAY LODGE (on the Behm Canal, 41 miles from Ketchikan) Mailing address: Yes Bay, AK 99950. (907) 247-1575. Open May 15 to Oct. 1. Fuel dock: gas and mix. Open daylight hours. Overnight accommodations. Reservations required. Restaurant. Fishing: licenses, bait, guide service. Caution: large rocks across from fuel dock are covered at high tide. Owners: The Hack Family.

KASAAN
(55°32'N., 132°42'W.)

KASAAN FLOATS (on Prince of Wales Island) Public floats and dock. No facilities. Operated by State.

HOLLIS

HOLLIS RAMP & FLOATS (off Twelvemile Arm, N of Cat Island, about 30 miles from Craig and Klawock) Ramp, dock and floats only. No facilities.

THORNE BAY

JERRY'S OUTBOARD SERVICE (Prince of Wales Island) Thorne Bay.,AK 99950. Outboard and stern drive sales and service. Owner: Jerry Manier.

McFARLAND'S FLOATEL, P.O. Box 159, Thorne Bay, AK 99919. (907) 828 - 3335. Moored in Thorne Bay on the E side of Prince of Wales Island off Clarence Strait, just 45 miles N of Ketchikan. Bed & Breakfast style accommodations. Self-guided or chartered expeditions. Fishing, sightseeing, beachcombing, crabbing, shrimping and hunting.

MEYER'S CHUCK

MEYER'S TRADING CO. (Cleveland Peninsula off Clarence Strait) Meyers Chuck, AK 99903. Call VHF channel 16 or CB channel 11. All year. Fuel available: gas and diesel, 10 AM - 5 PM. Public floats. Tidal grid. Groceries and liquor. Post office. Fishing: licenses and tackle. Owners: Bob and Donna Meyer.

WRANGELL
(56°28'N., 132°23'W.)

ANGERMAN'S INC., P.O. Box 928, Wrangell, AK 99929. (907) 874 - 3640. Fishing: licenses, bait and tackle. Clothing and sporting goods. Owner: J.R. Angerman.

BAY COMPANY, Box 797, Wrangell, AK 99929. (907) 874 - 3340. Outboard motor sales and service. Marine supplies. Fishing: bait and tackle. Owner: Chet Powell, Jr.

BENJAMIN'S SUPERMARKET (downtown) Box 21, Outer Drive, Wrangell, AK 99929. (907) 874 - 2341. Open 8 AM - 6 PM, closed Sundays. Groceries. Meat and produce. Liquor. Deli. Bakery. Owner: Bryant Benjamin.

BUNESS BROS., Box 681, Wrangell, AK 99929. (907) 874 - 3811. New and used boat and motor sales and service. Manager: Ole Buness.

CHEVRON USA FUEL DOCK, Box 50, Wrangell, AK 99929. (907) 874 - 3522. All year. Fuel dock: gas, diesel and mix. Open 8:30 AM - 5 PM, Mon. through Fri.; Sat. 8:30 AM - 11:30 AM (Summer only). Showers. Manager: Earl Kloster.

FREEMAN-BELL, Box 1021, Wrangell, AK 99929. (907) 874 - 3427. Welding. Machine shop. Mechanical and hydraulic repairs. Owner: Mike Bell. Harbormaster: (907) 874 - 3736. Monitors VHF channel 16.

HANSEN BOAT SHOP, P.O. Box 225, Wrangell, AK 99929. (907) 874 - 3586. All year. Marine railways cap.: 50 and 80 tons. Hull maintenance and repairs. Slips. Owner: Olaf B. Hansen.

ISLAND MARINE (at small boat harbor) Box 122, Wrangell, AK 99929. (907) 874 - 2314. Open Monday through Saturday: 8 AM - 5 PM. Complete engine maintenance and repairs. Machine shop. Welding. Owner: Harold Conine.

OTTESEN'S INC., Box 81, Wrangell, AK 99929. (907) 874 - 3377. Marine hardware. Charts. Fishing: licenses and tackle. Manager: Eric Ottesen.

PORT OF WRANGELL, Box 531, Wrangell, AK 99929. (907) 874 - 3736. All year. Ramp: 2-lanes, asphalt. Hoist: 2000 lbs. Overnight guest dock. Hull and engine maintenance, parts and repair. Fuel: gas, diesel and mix. Fishing: licenses, bait and tackle. Water skiing. Wrangell Museum. Petroglyph Beach. Harbormaster: Ronald Phillips.

SHOEMAKER BAY HARBOR (on Wrangell Island 4 miles SE of the city center near Wrangell Institute.) Annual moorge. Dockside electricity. Potable water on floats. Operated by the City of Wrangell.

UNION FUEL DOCK, Wrangell, AK 99929. (907) 874 - 3276. All year. Fuel dock: gas and diesel. Open Monday through Friday: 8:30 AM - 5 PM; Saturday: 8:30 AM - 1 PM summer only. Closed Sunday. Showers. Laundry. Distributor: S.R. Privett.

METLAKATLA
(55°08'N., 131°34'W.)

METLAKATLA BOAT HARBOR (Nichols Passage, S side of cannery ½ mile from village center) All year. Ramp. Transient moorage. Public floats. Operated by Village of Metlakatla. Harbormaster monitors VHF channel 16. Tidal grid nearby. Dockside electricity.

TAMGAS

TAMGAS HARBOR FLOATS (SW side of Tamgas Harbor, 3 miles W of Annette Airport.) Operated by Annette Outboard Club for pleasure craft. Guest dock. Groceries at village, 7 miles away. Nearest launching ramp, ¼ mile at Coast Guard Station.

HYDABURG
(55°12'N., 132°50'W.)

HYDABURG FLOATS (½ mile N of town) Public floats. Tidal grid. Fuel available at cannery. Groceries available in town. Harbormaster monitors CB channel 11. Dockside electricity.

ULLOA CHANNEL
(55°18'N., 133°14'W.)

WATERFALL RESORT (On Ulloa Channel, on the W coast of Prince of Wales Island. Plane service from Ketchikan) Mailing address: Box 6440, Ketchikan, AK 99901. (800) 544 - 5125. Former cannery converted to a sport fishing resort. Lodge (by reservation). Groceries. Liquor. Fuel dock – emergency basis only.

CRAIG
(55°28'N., 133°09'W.)

J. T. BROWN STORE, Box 40, Craig, AK 99921. (907) 826 - 3290. All year. Groceries. Charts. Electronics. Fishing: bait and tackle. Commercial fishing gear. Diving service available. Owners: Charles and Lynn Fischhaber.

CRAIG CITY FLOAT AND DOCK (at city center) Craig, AK 99921. All year. Public dock and floats. Loading zone only. Tidal grid. Dockside electricity. Operated by City of Craig. Harbormaster: Pam Miller.

JONESES MARINA INC. (across from City Float) Box 206, Craig, AK 99921. (907) 826 - 3468. Outboard engine sales and service.

NORTH COVE FLOAT (N side of peninsula, ¼ mile from city center) Craig, AK 99921. All year. Launching ramp. Assigned and transient moorage. Operated by City of Craig. Dockside electricity: (8). Harbormaster monitors VHf channel 16 and CB channels 11 and 12. Harbormaster: Pam Miller.

SOUTH COVE FLOAT (S side of peninsula, ¼ mile from city center) Craig, AK 99921. All year. Assigned moorings with a few transient berths. Tidal grid. Operated by City of Craig. Dockside electricity: (8). Harbormaster monitors VHF channel 16 and CB channels 11 and 12. Harbormaster: Pam Miller.

WHITE PASS ALASKA, Box 9, Craig, AK 99921. (907) 826 - 3296. All year. Fuel dock: gas and diesel. Open Summer: 7 AM - 5 PM, Monday through Saturday; Winter: 8 AM - 5 PM, Monday through Friday.

YATES HARDWARE, Box 208, Craig, AK 99921. (907) 826-3285. Open Monday through Saturday, 8 AM - 6 PM. Marine hardware and supplies. Owner: Leslie Yates.

NOTE: Fishing and hunting licenses are available at the Ketchikan First Bank, Prince of Whales Branch. Open Tuesday - Saturday, 10 AM - 3 PM.

KLAWOK
(55°33'N., 133°06'W.)

KLAWOCK DOCK (¼ mile N of village center, 9 miles from Craig, adjacent cannery) Public dock. Tidal grid. Repair facilities and fuel available at cannery in season. Groceries. Dockside electrcity.

KLAWOCK FLOAT (at village center, 9 miles from Craig) Public floats. Tidal grid. Repair facilities and fuel at cannery in season. Dockside electricity.

KELLY COVE

KELLY COVE (on SE end of Noyes Island) Fish buying scow anchored in cove in season. Limited moorage. Good anchorage near entrance to cove. Laundry and showers. Monitor VHF channel 16.

STEAMBOAT BAY
(55°32'N., 133°38'W.)

STEAMBOAT BAY INC., Box 132, Craig, AK 99921. Fuel dock: gas and diesel. Open daily in season: 8 AM - 10 PM. Mechanic and carpenter available for emergency repairs. Groceries. Hardware. Ice. Showers and laundry. Limited moorage. Good anchorage at head of bay near cannery. Monitor VHF channel 16. Fishing: bait and tackle.

PORT PROTECTION

PORT PROTECTION FLOAT (in Wooden Wheel Cove) Detached public float for transient mooring. No facilities.

POINT BAKER

POINT BAKER FLOATS (off Sumner Strait, on W side of False Island) Public floats. Tidal grid. Water on float except in winter. Post office and telephone on float. Restrooms. Dockside electricity. Operated by State.

POINT BAKER TRADING POST (NW tip of Prince of Whales Island) Box 130, Pt. Baker, AK 99927. (907) 559 - 2204. Fuel dock: gas and diesel. Guest dock. Groceries. Meat. Liquor. Bar and

Petersburg, the "Little Norway" of Alaska, at the N end of Wrangell Narrows.

restaurant. Laundry. Ice. Showers. Dockside electricity. Radio watch on VHF channel 16. Owners: Judy wright, Herb Hoyt and Bud Elliott.

PETERSBURG
(56°49'N., 132°57'W.)

BEACHCOMBER INN, located 4 miles S of town on Mitkof Hwy. Moorage, lodging, breakfast and dinner.

HAMMER & WIKAN INC., Box 249, Petersburg, AK 99833. (907) 772 - 4246. All year. Marine hardware. Groceries. Meats. Produce. Fishing: Commercial and sport outfitters.

MIDDLE HARBOR (S of Whitney-Fidalgo pier at city center.) (907) 772 - 4688. All year. Guest moorage only by arrangement with harbormaster. Laundry, groceries. Post office nearby. Operated by Port Authority City of Petersburg. Harbormaster monitors VHF channel 16 and CB channel 9. Dockside electricity.

NORTH HARBOR (N of Whitney-Fidalgo pier at city center.) (907) 772 - 4688. All year. Ramp: 1 - lane, concrete. Open 24 hours. Public floats transient moorage up to 8 hours. Tidal grid. Restrooms and showers. Nearby laundry, groceries and post office. Operated by Port Authority City of Petersburg. Harbormaster monitors VHF channel 16 and CB channel 9. Dockside electricity.

PAPKES LANDING FLOAT (on Wrangell Narrows, 13 miles S of Petersburg) Public float. Guest dock. No facilities. Maintained by State.

PETERSBURG SHIPWRIGHTS, 916 S Nordic Drive, Box 378, Petersburg, AK 99833. (907) 772 - 3596. Full marine facility. Aluminum and steel refrigeration repairs. Marine railway to 500 tons. Two cradles to 120 feet. Wood and fiberglass hull repair. Manager: Fred Paulsen.

PORT OF PETERSBURG, (907) 772 - 4688. Moorage, power, water at the head of each ramp. VHF channel 16.

SOUTH HARBOR, New addition to accommodate 240 boats 40 - 100 feet. Moorage assigned by harbormaster. Contact harbormaster by VHF channel 16 or CB channel 9 for availability. Dockside electricity.

UNION FUEL DOCK, Box 749, Petersburg, AK 99833. (907) 772 - 4219. All year. Fuel dock: gas and diesel. Open 8 AM - 5 PM, Monday - Saturday. Distributor: T. M. Smith.

WEST PETERSBURG FLOAT ($\frac{1}{4}$ mile from Petersburg on N shore of Wrangell Narrows) Public float. Guest dock. Note: Dry at low tide. No facilities. Maintained by State.

WHITE PASS ALAKSA, Box 769, Petersburg, AK 99833. (907) 772 - 4251. All year. Fuel dock: gas, diesel and mix. Open 8 AM - 5 PM. Manager: Oscar Jones.

ENTRANCE ISLAND

ENTRANCE ISLAND FLOAT (in Hobart Bay on SE side of island.) Detached float. No facilities. Primarily for layover or harbor of refuge.

TAKU HARBOR

TAKU HARBOR (off Stephens Passage, eE side of harbor) All year. Public float. No facilities. Well protected harbor of refuge. Operated by State.

DOUGLAS

DOUGLAS BOAT HARBOR (inside Juneau Island on S side of Gastineau Channel 2$\frac{1}{2}$ miles SE of Juneau-Douglas Bridge, $\frac{1}{4}$ mile from city center) Ramp: 1 - lane, concrete. Open 24 hours. Public floats. Guest dock. Transient mooring. Tidal grid. Groceries and laundry nearby at city center. Operated by City of Juneau.

Juneau offers the visitor two boat harbors; Harris Harbor just N of the bridge, and Aurora Harbor in the right foreground.

Harbormaster monitors VHF channel 16. Dockside electricity.

NORTH DOUGLAS LAUNCHING RAMP (on Douglas Island about 9 miles N of Juneau off the North Douglas Hwy.) Ramp: 2 - lanes, concrete. No facilities. Anchorage is possible between the ramp and Hut Point but is exposed to both northerly and westerly winds. Parking area for autos and boat trailers.

TANNER'S SERVICE CENTER, INC., Box 329, Douglas, AK 99824. (907) 364 - 2434. New and used boat and motor sales. Marine hardware. Engine repairs, parts and service. Manager: William D League.

JUNEAU
(59°18'N., 134°25'W.)

ALASKA SHIP CHANDLERS, 1050 Harbor Avenue, Juneau, AK 99801. (907) 586 - 1402. Open 9 AM - 5 PM. Marine hardware. Charts. Electronic sales. New and used boats and motors. Engine parts and service. Prop and shaft repair.

AURORA FUEL DOCK INC., 2 Aurora Basin, Juneau, AK 99801. (907) 586 - 2402. All year. May - Sept.: daily, 9:30 AM - 5:30 PM. Oct - April: Mon. - Fri., 2:30 PM - 5:30 PM; Sat., 11 AM - 5:30 PM. Fuel dock: gas, diesel, mix and lube oils. LP gas refills. Fishing: licenses and bait. Manager: Tom Krehbiel.

CHANNEL MARINA INC., 2591 Channel Drive, Juneau, AK 99801. (907) 586 - 3347. Ramp: 1 - lane, dirt. Engine parts, repairs and service. New and used boat and motor sales. Marine hardware. Electronics. Owner: Henry D. Bryson.

HARRIS COMMERCIAL MARINE, 809 W. 12th Street, Juneau, AK 99801. (907) 586 - 3190. Marine hardware. Vice President: Richard M. Allen.

HARRIS HARBOR (first harbor N of bridge, 1 mile from city center) All year. Launching ramp. Public floats. Guest dock. Transient moorage. Groceries and laundry nearby. Tidal grid. Operated by City of Juneau. Harbormaster monitors VHF channel 16; nights call (907) 586 - 3300. Dockside electricity.

JUNEAU HARBORMASTER, located at head of fuel dock in Aurora Harbor Contact on VHF channel 16 or by landline (907) 586 - 5255. Emergencies: Juneau Police call 911. Office hours 0800 - 1630, Monday through Saturday. Mailing Address: 155 S. Seward Street, Juneau, AK 99801.

TAKU OIL SALES, INC, Box 769, Juneau, AK 99802. (907) 586 - 1276. All year. 8 AM - 5 PM daily. Closed Sun. Petroleum sales: gas, diesel, mix and lubricants. Director: Robert Peterson.

WILLIE'S MARINE SERVICE, 10010 Camden Place, Juneau, AK 99801. (907) 789 - 4831. All year. Boat hauling. Inboard/ outboard engine repair. New and used boat and motor sales. Instrument repairs. Marine hardware. Owners: William and Tara Harris.

AUKE BAY

AUKE BAY FLOATS (12 miles from Juneau via Glacier Hwy. at head of Auke Bay, 2 miles S of ferry terminal) All year. 2 - Ramps: 2 - lanes each, concrete. Open 24 hours. Parking. Public floats. Transient moorage. Tidal grid. Groceries. Operated by City of Juneau. Harbormaster monitors VHF channel 16.

FISHERMEN'S BEND (at head of Auke Bay, adjacent public floats) Box 210627, Auke Bay, AK 99821. (907) 789 - 7312. All year. Fuel dock: gas, diesel and mix. Liquor store. Marine hardware. Fishing: bait and tackle. President: Troy Andrew.

PORT ALEXANDER
(56°15'N., 134°39'W.)

PORT ALEXANDER, Two public floats; the first is in the outer harbor, the second is 500 yards northward on the E side of the inner harbor. Tidal grid. Maintained by State.

KAKE
(56°58'N., 133°56'W.)

KAKE DOCK (2 blocks from village) Kake, AK 99830. All year. Public floats. Tidal grid. Groceries nearby. Dockside electricity. Operated by Village of Kake.

PORTAGE COVE (Keku Strait, 2 miles E of Kake) All year. Public floats. Grocery nearby. Operated by Village of Kake.

BARANOF

BARANOF FLOATS (Well protected harbor of refuge at head of Warm Springs Bay, NE of waterfall) All year. Public floats. Groceries available. Maintained by State Division of Water and Harbors. Harbormaster: (907) 747 - 3439. VHF channel 16, CB channel 11.

WARM SPRINGS ENTERPRISES at Baranof Warm Springs, 9720 Trappers Lane, Juneau, AK 99801. Groceries, cabins, hot mineral baths, emergency fuel.

ANGOON

ANGOON BOAT HARBOR (one mile SE of village on Kootznahoo side) Angoon, AK 99820. Public floats. Guest dock. Transient moorage. Tidal grid. Groceries and supplies three blocks away. Harbormaster monitors CB channel 5.

STANDARD FUEL DOCK (at Angoon Dock on Chatham Strait side) Angoon, AK 99820. Fuel service on call. Gas and diesel.

TENAKEE SPRINGS
(57°47'N., 135°12'W.)

R. NOYER, Box 511, Tenakee Springs, AK 99841. General mechanic and boat builder. Wood, fiberglass. Electrical and mechanical repairs.

SNYDER MERCANTILE COMPANY, P.O. Box 505, Tenakee Springs, AK 99841. (907) 736 - 2205. All year. Daily: 9 AM - 5 PM. Closed Sun. Marine hardware. Fuel: gas, diesel and 2-cycle oil. Accommodations. Groceries. Fishing: licenses, bait and tackle. Mineral hot springs. Good hiking. Whale watching. General Manager: Don Pegues.

TENAKEE FLOATS (on Tenakee Inlet, ½ mile E of Tenakee Springs) All year. Public floats. Tidal grid. Maintained by State.

TENAKEE TAVERN, Box 54, Tenakee Springs, AK 99841. (907) 736 - 9238. Victorian Inn, bar, laundry, showers, overnight accommodations and meals. Owner: Bettye Adams.

SWANSONS HARBOR

SWANSON HARBOR REFUGE FLOAT (on W side of Chatham Strait and NW tip of Couverden Island.) Detached float. Open moorage. No facilities. Harbor of refuge only.

FUNTER BAY
(58°15'N., 134°54'W.)

FUNTER BAY DOCK (in N portion of bay) Public dock. No facilities.

FUNTER BAY FLOAT (in SE corner of bay) A detached float for layover or harbor of refuge. No facilities.

LETNIKOF COVE
(59°11'N., 135°24'W.)

LETNIKOF COVE (on Chilkat Peninsula, 5 miles E of Haines on Mud Bay Road) Public floats. Facilities available at Haines. Good shelter from SE winds. Floats removed during winter months. Four day limit at the guest dock. Harbormaster monitors VHF channel 16 and CB channel 9.

HAINES
(59°14'N., 135°26'W.)

HAINES SMALL BOAT HARBOR (inside breakwater 1 block from city center) Box 1049, Haines, AK 99827. (907) 766 - 2448 or 766 - 2760. All year. Ramp: concrete. Open 24 hours. Guest dock. Slips. Tidal grid. Fuel dock: gas, diesel and stove oil. LP refills. Groceries, liquor, supplies, boat parts and engine repairs in City of Haines. Harbormaster monitors VHF channel 16 and CB channel 9. Dockside electricity: (3). Operated by City of Haines, Bob Stokley, Harbormaster.

SKAGWAY
(59°27'N., 135°20'W.)

CHEVRON USA FUEL DOCK (WHITE PASS ALASKA) Box 396, Skagway, AK 99840. (907) 983 - 2259. All year. Fuel dock: gas and diesel. Open 9 AM - 5 PM, Monday through Friday. Agent: Gil A. Meroney.

SKAGWAY BOAT HARBOR (E of ferry terminal, ¼ mile from city center) All year. Port office monitors VHF channel 16. Ramp at N end. Public floats. Groceries nearby. Tidal grid. Dockside electricity. Operated by City of Skagway. (907) 983 - 2542. Harbormaster: John Mielke.

SITKA
(57°03'N., 135°20'W.)

ALASKA PROPELLER CO., 1511-3 Sawmill Creek Road, Sitka, AK 99835. (907) 747 - 8989. Dry dock cap.: 400 tons. Travelift cap.: 65 tons. Open and covered dry storage. Prop and shaft repair. Props for all vessels including I/O and outboards. Hull and engine maintenance and repairs.

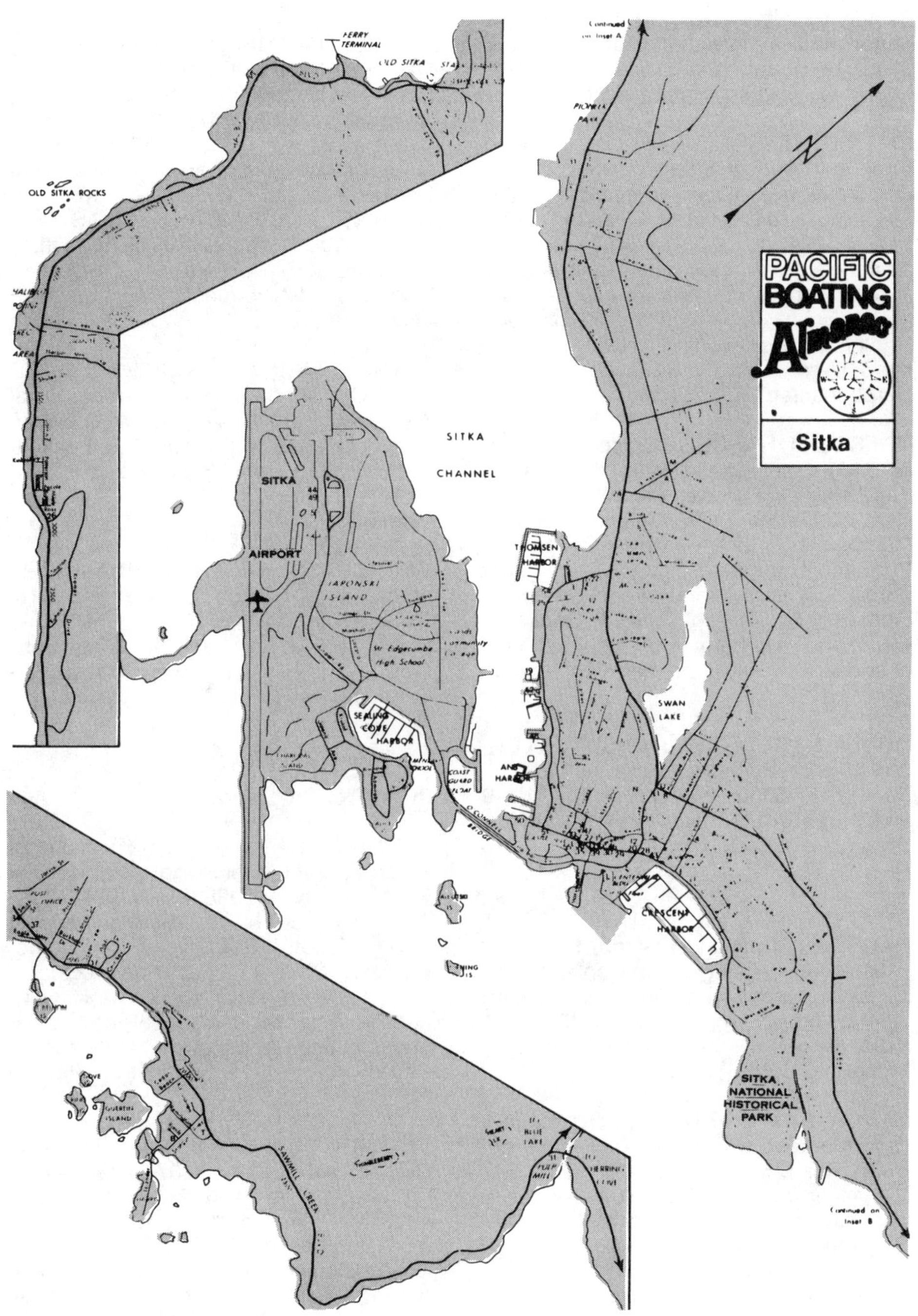

FERRY TERMINAL
OLD SITKA STATE
Continued on Inset A
PICNIC PARK
OLD SITKA ROCKS
HALIBUT POINT
PACIFIC BOATING ALMANAC
Sitka
SITKA CHANNEL
SITKA
AIRPORT
JAPONSKI ISLAND
THOMSEN HARBOR
Mt. Edgecumbe High School
SEALING COVE HARBOR
COAST GUARD FLOAT
SWAN LAKE
ANB HARBOR
O'CONNELL BRIDGE
CRESCENT HARBOR
SITKA NATIONAL HISTORICAL PARK
SAWMILL CREEK
BLUE LAKE
HERRING COVE
Continued on Inset B

ALLEN MARINE WAYS, Box 1049, Sitka, AK 99835. (907) 747 - 8100. All year. 60 ton travelift. Open 8 AM - 5 PM. Minor hull maintenance and repairs. Minor prop and shaft repairs. Marine hardware. Owner: Robert Allen.

CITY FLOAT (Alaska Native Brotherhood Dock at S end of Sitka Narrows, just W of bridge, two blocks from city center) 304 Lake #104, Sitka, AK 99835. (907) 747 - 3294 or 747 - 3439. All year. Assigned moorings. Guest mooring by arrangement with harbormaster. Tidal grid adjacent. Operated by City of Sitka. Dockside electricity. Harbormaster monitors VHF channel 16. Harbormaster: R. J. Guhl.

CRESCENT HARBOR (Crescent Bay, E of bridge, two blocks from city center) 304 Lake #104, Sitka, AK 99835. (907) 747 - 3294 or 747 - 3439. All year. Ramp: 1 - lane. Open 24 hours. Permanent moorings only. No guest dock. Tidal grid and grocery nearby. Operated by City of Sitka. Dockside electricity. Harbormaster monitors VHF channel 16. Harbormaster: Richard J. Guhl.

DUDS 'N SUDS LAUNDROCENTER, 904 Halibut Point Rd, Sitka, AK 99835. (907) 747- 5050. All year. 7 AM - 9 PM. Laundry and dry cleaning. Showers. Snack bar. Owner: Fred Reeder.

SEALING COVE SMALL BOAT HARBOR (on Japonski Island) Ramp: 2 - lanes with parking. Transient mooring by arrangement with the Harbormaster. Operated by City of Sitka. 304 Lake #104, Sitka, AK 99835. Harbormaster: Richard J. Guhl.

SILVER BAY ENGINE & EQUIPMENT CO. (Jamestown Bay) 1305 Sawmill Creek Road, Sitka, AK 99835. (907) 747 - 8644 or 747 - 8645. New and used boat and motor sales. Marine hardware. Electronics. Engine repairs, parts and service. Covered and open dry storage. Hull maintenance and repairs.

SITKA FUELS INC., Box 1947, Sitka, AK 99835. (907) 747 - 8460. Fuel dock: gas, diesel, mix and LP refills. Open 8 AM - 5 PM. Closed Sundays.

THOMSEN HARBOR (N side of Sitka Narrows, ¾ mile NW of bridge, ½ mile from city center) 304 Lake #104, Sitka, AK 99835. (907) 747 - 3294 or 747 - 3439. All year. Assigned moorings. Guest mooring by arrangement with harbormaster. Groceries nearby. Operated by City of Sitka. Harbormaster: Richard J. Guhl. Office at head of gangway. Dockside electricity. Harbormaster monitors VHF channel 16.

UNOCAL FUEL DOCK/SITKA SOUND OIL CO., 329-333 Katlian Street, Sitka, AK 99835. (907) 747 - 3224. All year. Fuel dock: gas and diesel. Open daily 8 AM - 6 PM. Open Sunday in summer. Marine batteries, filters. Manager: Lynne Grant.

WHITE PASS ALASKA MARINA (next to bridge at 1 Lincoln Street) Box 418, Sitka, AK 99835. (907) 747 - 3414. All year. Fuel dock: gas, diesel and mix. Open 8 AM - 6 PM, Monday - Saturday. Manager: Warren Pellett, Jr.

PELICAN
(57°58'N., 136°14'W.)

PELICAN BOAT HARBOR (E shore of Lisianski Inlet, Chichagof Island) Box 757, Pelican Ak 99832. (907) 735 - 2202. All year. Major fishing and supply port. Public floats. Tidal grids. Grocery. Showers. Dockside electricity: (7). Upon arrival check with harbormaster at harbor office. Use phone at head of gangway. Operated by City of Pelican. Harbormaster: Patricia Phillips.

PELICAN SEAFOODS INC, Box 110, Pelican, AK 99832. (907) 735 - 2204. All year. 8 AM - 5 PM. Hoist cap.: 4000 lbs. Fuel dock: gas, diesel and mix. LP gas refills. Marine hardware. Groceries and ice. Fishing: bait and tackle. Skin and scuba diving. Only accessible by water. Manager: Eric Norman.

ELFIN COVE
(58°12'N., 136°21'W.)

This is a beautiful settlement, population of 35, with a picturesque inner harbor. Consult the COAST PILOT before entering the harbor. The chart is not very clear and the channel is very narrow.

ELFIN COVE (on Chichagof Island off Cross Sound, at village center) Elfin Cove, AK 99825. Sheltered harbor in all weather. Inner harbor dredged to 8 feet MLLW. Public floats. Tidal grids. Fuel dock. General store and fuel dock operate minimum hours in winter. Cafe, rooms to rent. Laundry. Showers, gift shop, rental houses. Open May 1 - Sept. 15.

ELFIN COVE CHEVRON FUEL DOCK (last fuel stop before heading north across Gulf of Alaska) P.O. Box 4, Elfin Cove, AK 99825. (907) 239 - 2208. Open 8 AM - 9 PM, 7 days. Fuel dock: gas, diesel and LP refills. Fishing: licenses and tackle.

ELFIN GENERAL SUPPLY (store on Elfin Inn Way) Elfin Cove, AK 99825. Open daily 8 AM - 9 PM May 1 to Sept. 15. Groceries. Fresh produce. Limited hardware. Showers. Laundry. Hot tub. Liquor store adjacent. Ice. Fishing: bait and tackle.

RADAR MARINE, Elfin Cove, AK 99825. April through Sept. Open 9 AM - 9 PM, closed Sundays. Electronic sales and service. Marine hardware. Owner: David Walton.

TERRY'S MARINE REPAIR, Box 775, Pelican AK 99832. (907) 735 - 4382. Outboard, inboard, I/O engine repairs. Owner: Terry Wirta.

GLACIER BAY
NATIONAL MONUMENT

GLACIER BAY NATIONAL PARK (Bartlett Cove) Mailing address: Gustavus, AK 99826. Open May 15 - Sept. 15. Fuel dock: gas and diesel. Open 8 AM - 3 PM. Limited guest dock. Anchor off and use dinghy. No supplies. Lodge. Restaurant. Daily glacier cruises and flights. Evening naturalist programs. Campsites. Fishing: charter boats. The Park Service monitors VHF channel 16.

SPECIAL NOTE - Regulations are now in effect June 1 through August 31 to protect Humpback whales in Glacier Bay National Park. All vessels, except for commercial fishing vessels actively engaged in fishing, must have a valid permit to enter Glacier Bay during the whale season. Application for permits may be directed to the Superintendent, Glacier Bay National Park, Gustavus, AK 99826. (907) 697 - 2230. Application via VHF radio, channel 16, may be made to KWM-20, Bartlett Cove, between 8 AM - 4 PM. Permits are limited. Additional regulations control vessel course and speed in certain areas.

GUSTAVUS

GUSTAVUS DOCK (1 mile from Gustavus Inn) Dock and float on outboard end. No facilities. Fuel available 12 miles away in Glacier Bay at Bartlett cove. Float removed in winter. Operated by State.

EXCURSION INLET
(59°33'N., 139°44'W.)

HOONAH HARBOR (Port Frederick Bay, Chichagof Island, at village center) Hoonah, AK 99829. (907) 945 - 3670. All year. New harbor facilities. Inner harbor protected all winds, transit float immediate left of entrance. Public floats, two tidal grids. Laundry. Showers. Operated by the city of Hoonah. Harbormaster monitors VHF channel 16. Working channel 9 or 14. Dockside electricity. Harbormaster: Paul Dybdahl.

HOONAH SEAFOODS, P.O. Box 117, Hoonah, AK 99829. (907) 945 - 3211. All year. Fuel dock: gas, diesel and mix. Open 9 AM - 6 PM, Monday - Saturday. Marine hardware. Charts. Groceries. Fishing: bait, tackle, supplies.

L. KANE STORE (S of public floats) Box 116, Hoonah, AK 99829. (907) 945 - 3311. All year. Fuel dock: gas, diesel and mix. Open 9 AM - 6 PM. Marine hardware. Groceries. Ice. Guest dock. Fishing: bait and tackle.

YAKUTAT

(59°33'N., 139°44'W.)

YAKUTAT HARBOR, Box 6, Yakutat, AK 99689. (907) 784 - 3323. All year. Ramp: gravel. Slips. Overnight guest dock with electricity. Moorings. Fuel: gas, diesel. Fishing: licenses and tackle. Harbormaster: Margie Thomason.

INDEX

SPECIAL FEATURES

WE NEED YOUR HELP

The ALMANAC has always relied on its Regional Reporters for accurate, mile-by-mile information on travel throughout the West Coast -- but we don't rely only on staffers for information. Each year (for 27 years now) we've found that some of our best travel information has come from readers - you and your fellow travelers.

If, during your travels, you find changes such as the opening of a new facility, the closure of a fuel dock or other changes that will be helpful to fellow travelers, please give us the details on the form that follows (or on a separate sheet of paper) and mail it to The Editor, The Pacific Boating Almanac, P.O. Box 341668, Los Angeles, CA 90034 We'll take note of your report when we prepare the 1992 ALMANAC.

Please feel free to elaborate -- we're always anxious to hear about your travel experiences on the West Coast (favorite attractions, routes traveled, areas that might deserve more editorial coverage next year or whatever).

Have a fantastic trip . . . and let us know how it goes!

– The Editor

On Page _______ of the 1991 ALMANAC, So. Cal No. Cal PNW Edition, in column _______ (1 or 2) we suggest that you make the following change(s):

____
____
____
____
____
____

On Page _______ of the 1991 ALMANAC, So. Cal No. Cal PNW Edition, in column _______ (1 or 2) we suggest that you make the following change(s):

____
____
____
____
____
____

On Page _______ of the 1991 ALMANAC, So. Cal No. Cal PNW Edition, in column _______ (1 or 2) we suggest that you make the following change(s):

____
____
____
____
____
____

On Page _______ of the 1991 ALMANAC, So. Cal No. Cal PNW Edition, in column _______ (1 or 2) we suggest that you make the following change(s):

____
____
____
____
____
____

On Page _______ of the 1991 ALMANAC, So. Cal No. Cal PNW Edition, in column _______ (1 or 2) we suggest that you make the following change(s):

____
____
____
____
____

First Aid

Much of first aid is common sense. Many possible problems arising when boating are more easily prevented than treated. Being prepared saves much time in the long run. CPR courses should be taken. Personal Flotation Devices (PFD's) should be handy as well as First Aid Kits and sunscreen. It is important to know how to seek medical assistance should the need arise.

INDEX

HOW TO CALL FOR HELP

Call the Coast Guard on Channel 16 (156.80 MHz) or Bay Watch (in Southern California).

BASIC FIRST AID KIT

The cost of an adequate medical kit is $500 - $750. All prescription medications should be carefully labeled with name of drug, both brand and generic, as well as specific indications for use and recommended doseage.

DRESSING AND BANDAGES
Bandaids
    Small
    Large - 2 inch
Large bulky dressings, e.g. "Surgepads"
Gauze sponges
Tape - waterproof
Ace Bandages (2) - 3 or 4 inch
Rib belt
Eye patches
Butterfly bandaids or Steristrips for lacerations
Aluminum finger splints
Q-tips
Telfa dressing (burns)

GASTRO INTESTINAL
Maalox or Mylanta - antacid
Lomotil and/or Pepto-Bismol - diarrhea*
Dulcolax tablets - constipation
Combid Spansules - nausea/vomiting/seasickness*

SEASICKNESS
Compazine - 5 - 10 mg tablets*
    Suppositories 25 mg (adult)
    Liquid
Dramamine
Phenergan - suppositories or liquid*
Transderm V (Scopolamine)

Combinations
    Scopolamine/Dexedrine*
    Phenergan/Ephedrine*

CARDIAC
Nitroglycerine - 0.4 mg*
Nitrostat 4x25 - <u>leave in original package</u>*

COLDS/ALLERGIES
Naldecon - one tablet 3 times daily*

INFECTIONS/ANTIBIOTICS
Tegopen - oral penicillin 250 mg, (1) four times daily*
Keflex or other cephalosporin*
Flagyl (Metronidazole - special purposes)*
Bactrim - or Septra (Sulfa Trimethoprim)*
Vibramycin (Doxycycline - may cause photosensitivity)*
Ampicillin/Amoxicillin) broad spectrum penicillin*

SEDATIVES/TRANQUILIZER
Ativan 1 mg (short action) for sleep/tranquilizer*
    (very few only for emergency use)
Compazine tablets 10 mg, 1 or 2 every 3-4 hours*
    (doubles for seasickness)

STIMULANTS
Dexedrine 5 mg*

ANALEGESICS
Percodan or Empirin w/ Codeine for more servere pain* (1-2 tablets every 4 hrs.)
Aspirin
Tylenol
Nonsteroid Anti-inflammatory, e.g. Naprosyn, etc.*

MUSCLE RLAXANTS
Soma 350 mg - for sprains, etc., (1) every four hours*

EAR/NOSE/THROAT
Auralgan for ear pain
Neosporin ophthalmic drops for eye infections*
Visine, etc., for minor irritation
Cortisporin ear drops for ear canal infection*

SKIN
Synalar .025% cortisone cream for skin allergies/insect bites*
Silvadene Cream for burns - use with Telfa dressings (non-sticking) or
Neosporin Ointment or Betadine Ointment*

MISCELLANEOUS
Resuscitube - airway
Zephiran antiseptic - aerosol
Thermometer
    Oral or rectal if children aboard; "Stubby" may be used for either oral/rectal
Tweezers
First Aid Manual
Phisohex*

RESUSCITATION

Life depends on oxygen reaching the brain. For this to happen air must be able to get from the mouth to the lungs via the airway. Blood must be able to flow from the lungs to the brain and back. Lack of spontaneous respiration for as short a time as two minutes can be fatal and for ten minutes will almost certainly be fatal. The following will help guide you in case of this emergency.

WHEN BREATHING STOPS, WHATEVER THE CAUSE, START ARTIFICIAL RESPIRATION AT ONCE.

DROWNING
Start artificial respiration by mouth to mouth method with patient flat if possible.
There is no time to remove dentures, loosen clothing to try to decide if the heart is still beating.

MOUTH TO MOUTH ARTIFICIAL RESPIRATION
- Lay the patient on his back on a firm surface.
- Clear the mouth with the finger.
- Extend the head by supporting the nape of the neck and pressing the forehead backwards.
- Press the angle of the lower jaw forward from behind or pull the jaw forward with the thumb in the mouth.
- Place the heel of one hand on the forehead, keep the head extended and pinch the nostrils with finger and thumb.
- Take a deep breath.
- Open your mouth wide and seal your lips around the patient's mouth.
- Blow into his lungs until they are filled.
- Remove your mouth.
- Watch the patient's chest fall.
- Repeat every five or six seconds.
- If due to injury it is impossible to seal the patient's mouth, then close his mouth and blow through his nose.
- In small children it may be necessary to seal your lips around the mouth and nose.

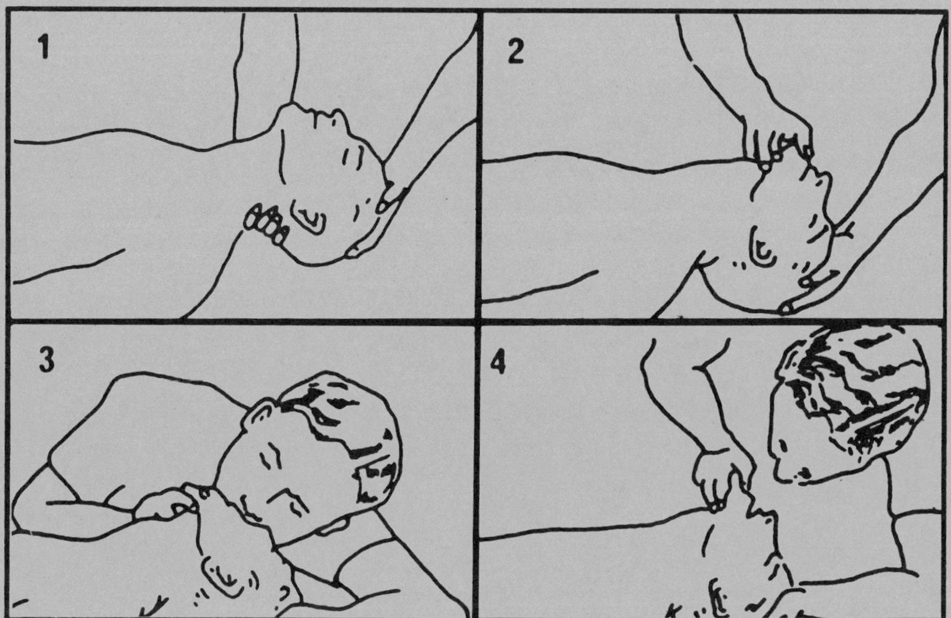

1 Neck is lifted
2 Head is fully tilted back
3 Lungs are inflated via nose or mouth
4 Victim exhales by himself, if necessary, through his mouth

Most people using this head-tilt oral method find in the excitement of the moment that it is not distasteful, but the few who are repulsed by the thought of physical contact with the patient can use a special mask, or a simple device such as a Cross Venti-Breather.

A brisk blow should be administered on the breast bone after the first inflation if there is no obvious pulse or heart-beat. (Do NOT waste time looking for a pulse.)

IF AFTER TEN INFLATIONS THE PATIENT'S COLOR REMAINS BLUE-GREY:

Strike the breastbone sharply once with the fist (this will sometimes start the heart beating).

Clear airway (removing dentures if loose).

Loosen clothing.

Start external cardiac massage.

EXTERNAL CARDIAC MASSAGE

Raise the legs to the vertical to run blood back to the heart.

With the heel of one hand on the lower half of the breastbone, sternum, (not the ribs) and the other hand on top, press vertically downwards using your whole weight. Press down and release once a second (in an unconscious adult the breastbone may be pressed down one and a half inches, more than this may fracture ribs).

Continue artificial respiration – two breaths after every fifteen compressions.

Resuscitation should be continued as long as possible following the slightest suggestion of improvement, i.e. Change of color, pupils contracting, pulse felt in the neck or sign of breathing.

Pause every few minutes to see if the heart is beating.

AFTER TREATMENT

When a steady pulse can be felt − stop cardiac massage.

When spontaneous breathing has been restored, continue to keep patient warm. Remove wet clothing when consciousness returns.

Massage limbs under the coverings to promote circulation.

When power of swallowing returns, give warm drinks − not alcohol.

Keep the patient quiet and under observation for twenty four hours as delayed effects may occur.

FIRST AID FOR CHOKING

1. Ask: Are you choking? If the victim cannot beath, cough, or speak. . .
2. Give the Heimlich Maneuver. Stand behind the victim. Wrap your arms around the victim's waist. Make a fist with one hand. Place your fist (thumbside) against the victim's stomach in the midline just above the navel and well below the rib margin. Grasp your fist with your other hand. Press into stomach with a quick upward thrust.
3. Repeat thrust if necessary.

If a victim has become unconscious:

4. Sweep the mouth.
5. Attempt rescue breathing.
6. Give 6-10 abdominal thrusts.

Repeat steps 4,5, and 6 as necessary.

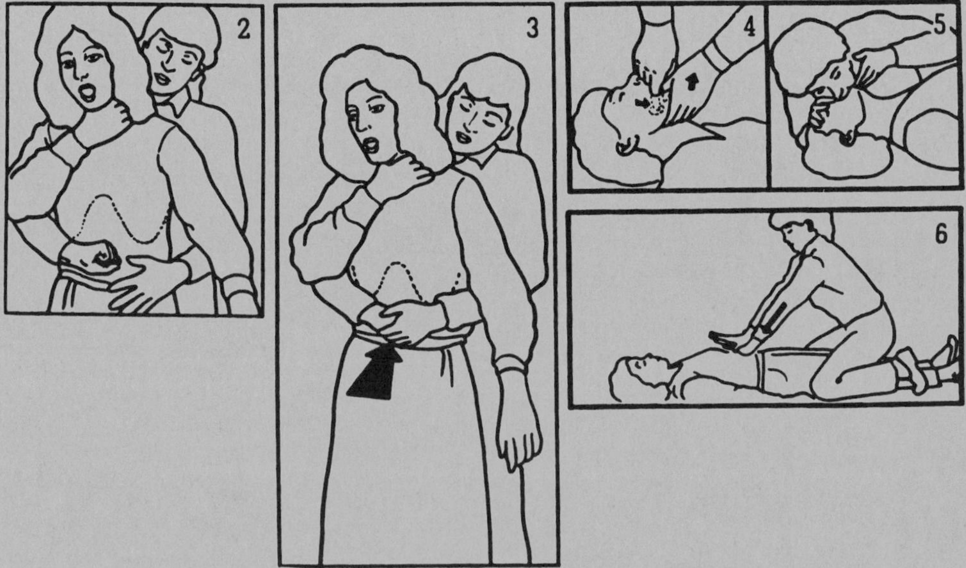

HYPOTHERMIA

Hypothermia is a below normal temperature in the core or central part of the body. When this temperature falls below 90°F serious complications begin to develop. Survival time in cold water depends on the water temperature, body size, fat and activity in the water. One should not immerse his head in the water because much heat is lost that way. An "average" person wearing light clothing and a personal flotation device (PFD), who is not moving in approximate 50°F water, could survive between 2 and 3 hours. If there is anything to hold on to such as a plank or part of a boat, one should bring as much of his body out of the water as possible. Water conducts heat much faster than air. It is <u>most important</u> to wear a PFD. Huddling with other people in the water or assuming the fetal position (with head out of water) may help. If in huddle position place children in the middle of the circle.

Once the victim is rescued (on boat or land) make sure he has an open airway and is able to breathe. Then check for respiration and pulse. If none is evident, immediately begin CPR. Preventing further heat loss is also essential. Carefully remove all wet clothing. Wrap him in blankets or a sleeping bag. Warm water bottles or other gentle warming devices should be placed under his neck, by his groin and on the sides of his chest. Transport to a hospital as soon as possible.

DO NOT:
- Place an unconscious victim in a bath tub.
- Give a victim anything to drink, including hot liquids and especially alcohol.
- Rub the victim's skin, BUT especially do **NOT** rub it with snow.

AVOID HYPOTHERMIA
Since most boaters who die in water related accidents had no intention of going in the water, the obvious answer is to avoid those behaviors that cause accidental immersion. Therefore, **DO NOT**:
- Stand or move around in a small boat.
- Overload your boat or distribute the load unevenly.
- Decelerate suddenly, allowing the sternwake to overtake and swamp the boat by washing over the transom.
- Let alcohol inpair good judgement.

Always wear a Personal Flotation Device (PFD) when on the water.

Do not swim to keep warm. Extra heat is lost to the arms, legs and skin. Swimming and treading water increase the cooling rate by about 35%.

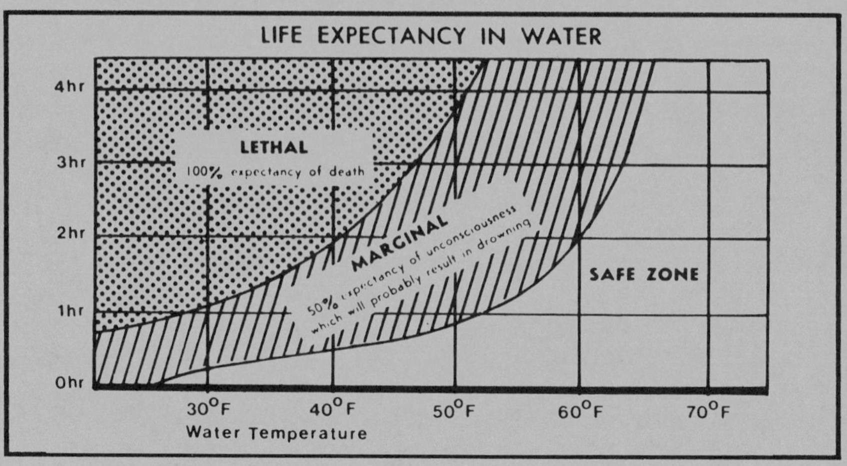

For more information on hypothermia write or call the Department of Boating and Waterways, 1629 "S" Street, Sacramento, CA 95814-7291 (916) 445-2616.

CRITICAL AREAS OF HEAT LOSS

In addition to the head, other areas of high heat loss in cold water are the side of the chest and the groin area. Special attention should be given to these areas to reduce body heat loss.

H.E.L.P. (Heat Escape Lessening Posture)

Hold your arms tight against the sides of your chest. Also raise your thighs to close off the groin region. This simple practice results in increasing predicted survival time by almost 50%. It is impossible to assume the H.E.L.P. position while wearing some Personal Flotation Devices (PFD's). However, even a partial H.E.L.P position gives some protection.

Huddle

Studies show that if a huddle is formed so that the sides of the chest are held closely together, a 50% increase in predicted survival time is obtained. Placing children in the middle of the circle will lend them some of the adult body heat and extend their survival time.

Hypothermia information compiled from *The Seattle Times Boater's Guide*.

INJURY	SIGNS	TREATMENT
Broken Bones	Pain, tenderness, deformity and possible bleeding.	Keep broken bone ends and adjacent joints from moving; control bleeding, treat for shock.
Burns	DEGREE: 1st—Skin is red. 2nd—Skin is blistered. 3rd—Skin is charred.	Pain of 1st degree and small 2nd degree burns can be relieved by excluding air. Three ways to exclude air from 1st or 2nd degree burns are: 1.) Submerge in cold water; 2.) Apply a cold pack; 3.) Cover with a thick dressing or unused plastic. For a 3rd degree burn, cover with dry clean cloth and call for medical help. If the victim's face is burned, he may stop breathing. Be ready to give artificial respiration.
Heart Failure Epilepsy	Victim is ill with no apparent external injury. Clutching chest, extreme shortness of breath, convulsions.	Place the victim in a comfortable position, usually sitting up. Call for medical help and give prescribed heart medicine if available. If not breathing, give artificial respiration. Victims with convulsions should be laid down in a cleared, open area. Never place anything in the person's mouth.
Objects in eyes, ears and nose	Local irritation, tearing and wetting	Eye: Don't rub. Lift particles out with corner of clean handkerchief. If unsuccessful or if the particle is embedded, cover both eyes and get medical attention. Ear and nose: get medical attention, don't try to remove.
Poisoning	Blurred vision, stomach cramps, vomiting, headaches, convulsions or deep sleep.	Save label of poison container for I.D. and call emergency help. If victim is conscious, dilute the poison with milk or water. Do not neutralize with counteragents or give oils. If victim is unconscious, do not give fluids.
Shock	Pale, clammy skin, irregular breathing, fast weak pulse.	Keep person lying down and maintain normal body temperature (98.6). Do not give fluids if victim is unconscious.
Sunburn	Red, painful skin and chills. Fever and shock occasionally accompany severe sunburns.	Apply cold water. Do not re-expose burned area to sun until completely healed. Get medical attention.
Unconsciousness	Victim is not awake, does not respond to external stimuli.	Treat for shock. Turn head to side in case of vomiting. Get medical attention. Stand by to give artificial respiration if breathing stops. Never give liquids or foods to an unconscious person.

EPILEPSY WITH CONVULSIONS

Put victim on back. Make sure surrounding area is clear so victim will not injure himself. If easily done, put tightly rolled cloth between jaws (to the side) so victim won't bite his tongue. Keep victim calm and quiet for several hours afterward. Get medical attention.

EYE INJURY

a) Chemicals in the eye. Lie victim down. Pour copious amount of water into corner of eye letting it run to other side to completely remove chemicals. Seek immediate medical attention. Cover eye with sterile compress.

b) <u>Foreign Body in eye</u>. If foreign body can be seen beneath the lower eyelid it can be removed with the corner of a damp handkerchief. (Do not remove it if it is on the clear part of the eye). If you cannot see it, it might be under the top lid. If this is so, pull the top lid over the bottom lid. The bottom lashes may then sweep it clear. The victim may also try immersing his face in clean water while blinking several times.

FRACTURES

Some of the symptoms of a fracture are pain, swelling, deformity and abnormal movement. Excessive swelling means there is bleeding into the surrounding tissues. In this case, do not bandage too tightly because this may stop circulation to the rest of the limb. If bone pierces the skin, cover with sterile dressing. Immobilize extremity by splinting. Loosen surrounding clothing and keep limb elevated with pillows. Administer pain killers. Seek medical attention.

HEART ATTACK

Heart attack is suspected when a person complains of chest pain or persistant indigestion accompanied by shortness of breath, sweating, nausea or vomiting. Chest pain may radiate to the arm, neck or jaw. Reassure person, keep him at rest, keep warm with blanket and seek immediate medical attention. Pain killers and/or nitroglycerine may be given.

CARDIAC ARREST

If a person is unconcsious and unresponsive, is not breathing and has no pulse; it is likely that cardiac arrest exists. CPR (pages F-4 and F-5 should be initiated and immediate medical help sought.

SHOCK (Resulting from Injury)

Keep victim lying down. Control bleeding. Maintain normal body temperature. Keep legs elevated on pillows. Seek immediate medical attention.

HEATSTROKE

The victim may suddenly collapse and appear confused and dizzy. He might have a high temperature of around 105° or more. Remove his clothing. Cool him immediately by using cold compresses over his body. Open windows or vents. Keep him cool.

SNAKEBITE

If pain or swelling occurs, apply tourniquet above bite. Immoblilize bitten extremity. (For severe pain or swelling) use sterile blade to make cut over bite and suction out venom for ½ hour. Transport to hospital immediately. (If snake is killed, bring along for identification).

BLEEDING

Direct and firm pressure applied to the wound will usually stop bleeding within 5-10 minutes. (If available, use a sterile gauze or dressing, if not, use a clean piece of material). Victim should be lying down and affected part should be elevated above the heart. If the above is unsuccessful, a tourniquet may be applied above the wound on the limb but should not be left on longer than 15 minutes.

MINOR CUTS

Wash with cold water; apply antiseptic; apply clean bandage. (observe for swelling, discoloration, numbness, foul odor, drainage).

BURNS

To cool the area of the burn use clean fresh water for at least 15 minutes. (Ice cubes in a baggie may be used for cooling purposes only). Carefully remove victim's clothing. Lightly cover with sterile bandage, if available. (Do not attempt to clean out wound or apply ointments if skin is broken.) If skin is not broken, a mild burn ointment or petroleum jelly may be applied.

HEAD INJURY

Keep patient lying down and quiet. Observe for breathing difficulties or vomiting. If bleeding from scalp, wash with plenty of water and apply pressure with gauze for a prolonged period of time.

CONCUSION: defined as a head injury which results in temporary loss of consciousness.

1. Keep airways open. Use the semiprone position face down for the tongue to naturally fall forward. If patient has vomited, clear from the mouth to prevent aspiration of vomitus into lungs.
2. Handle patient as if the neck has been broken until proven otherwise. Immobilize head and neck.
3. Perform a quick neurological examination starting with a written log every 5-10 minutes until consciousness reappears. The main elements of this examination include:

A. Look for alertness or excessive sleepiness. What does it take to make the patient respond? Is there reaction to pain?

B. Are the pupils equal in size? Do they respond to light (constriciton of pupil is the usual response).

C. Is there weakness or paralysis of limbs on one or both sides of the body?

Recovery is usually complete with some headache or dizziness which will gradually lessen over a few days. Irritability, forgetfulness or insomnia may also occur. For any other lasting or unusual symptoms seek IMMEDIATE MEDICAL ADVICE.

SEASICKNESS

PREVENTION

To prevent seasickness, avoid large meals and alcohol before sailing. Keep warm. Anti-seasickness medication such as scopolomine patches or anti-seasickness pills should be taken early as directed on package. Some people feel better without food when under way for short periods of time. Others may want dry bread or crackers, hot soup or tea. Prolonged sickness is dangerous. If a person is vomiting, it is preferable to have him use a bucket for this purpose than to be leaning over the side of a moving vessel.

At the first suggestion of seasickness one should get up on deck or in the cockpit and perhaps lie down. Staying below at this time is quite incorrect. Medication is important both prophylactically (preventative) and as treatment. It is false heroics for a person with a known tendency toward seasickness not to take medication prophylactically.

MEDICATION

There are many medications available. Most fall into one or more of three drug classes: **antihistamines, anticholinergics,** or **phenothiazines**. **Dramamine, Marazene**, and **Bonine** are available without prescription, while **Compazine, Combid, Tigan** are available only on prescription. **Transderm V** is a new therapeutic system of sustained release of a long established medication, **Scopolamine**. A small patch is applied behind the ear and releases medication in a sustained and even fashion over 72 hours.

Scopolamine belongs to a group of drugs called **anticholinergics** and must be used with care, particularly in the elderly who have a greater incidence of glaucoma, prostate obstruction, etc. The most common side effect is drowsiness. The Transderm V - Scopolamine system is said to be 75% effective. It is very important for the skipper or some other responsible person to gain as much experience as possible with a single medication in all its forms and to be knowledgeable of its side effects. For those anticipating a lengthy passage, it is recommended that they try the drug chosen while day-sailing or cruising locally. This gives information regarding tolerance to medication, that is, excess drowsiness and other side effects and also efficiency of medication.

TREATMENT

After a great deal of first hand experience (fortunately, none of it personal), I have come to favor the use of "Compazine". This is an excellent anti-nauseant and has a mild tranquilizer effect which may be beneficial in controlling the accompanying anxiety. It is available in several forms: A rapid-acting tablet of 3-4 hours duration, a long acting capsule or spansule of 8-10 hours duration, syrup, suppository and injectable form. Compazine is a phenothiazine and is contraindicated in children. NASA is currently using combination drugs. We have used these in refractive cases of seasickness with good success. Combinations include **Phenergan** (promethazine) 25 mg. and ephedrine 25-50 mg or **dextroamphetamine** 5 mg and scopolamine 0.4 - 0.6 mg. These combinations include a **sympathomimetic** drug, e.g., ephhedrine or dextroamphetamine, with either Phenergan (promethazine) a phenothiazine with antihistamine properties or scopolamine, an anticholinergic drug.

The preventive treatment of seasickness must begin two or more hours prior to boarding. A long acting or spansule type capsule of 8-10 hours duration may be taken or shorter duration, 3-4 hour tablets. As the day progresses, short-acting tablets or another capsule may be taken. Once the illness has taken hold, oral tablets often do not stay down a sufficiently long period to be absorbed and, therefore, another form of administration is necessary. If a physician is aboard, then the route of choice is injection. Lay people, however, are often too quick to want to give injections and if not fully knowledgeable may well do more harm than good. Two often overlooked modes of administration are rectal suppository and oral syrup. Even if the patient throws up, some of the syrup must remain in the stomach and be absorbed, and thus far I have never seen anyone throw up a suppository.

- Seasick information written by Robert Kahn, M.D.

AVOIDING PARALYTIC SHELLFISH POISONING

Reproduced through the courtesy of University of Washington Sea Grant Program. Information written by Louisa Nishitani and Kenneth K. Chew.

Fond of shellfish? Washington waters offer a delectable variety of clams, oysters, mussels, and scallops readily available to be gathered and enjoyed. At certain times, however, some shellfish become unsafe to eat because they contain a poison harmful to human beings. Paralytic shellfish poisoning, commonly known as PSP, is a danger that you as a shellfish consumer can avoid by being well informed and observing certain basic precautions.

PSP

Paralytic shellfish poisoning (PSP) is a serious illness caused by eating shellfish that have consumed large amounts of a poisoning-produing microscopic organism called *Gonyaulax catenella*. (This scientific name if pronounced gone-ee-al'-ax cat-a-nell's, and the organism has no common name.) The *Gonyaulax* toxins are extremely potent nerve poisons; in fact, as little as one milligram (0.000035 ounce) is enough to kill an adult. The poisons themselves, as well as the illness they cause, are referred to as PSP. The poison acts very rapidly, and no antidote has as yet been discovered.

PSP Occurrences

The accumulation of PSP toxins in shellfish is not a new phenomenon, nor is it one confined to just Washington. It has been occurring for hundreds of years in many parts of the world, primarily in temperate waters. Along the Pacific Coast, poisonous shellfish have been found all the way from Alaska to California. The first recorded death in this region occurred in 1793 when one of Captain Vancouver's men died after eating toxic shellfish in British Columbia. Indian tribes were undoubtedly aware of the problem long before that.

PSP Seasons

In general, shellfish are more likely to become poisonous in late spring, summer, and fall then in winter. However, you should be aware that some species -- particularly butter clams and scallops -- tend to be toxic for longer periods extending into winter or even throughout the year in some areas. In spring, longer days and warmer waters encourage faster growth of the swimming stage of *G. catenella.*

Symptoms

Early symptoms of PSP are a tingling of the lips and tongue, which may begin within minutes of eating poisonous shellfish or may take an hour or two to develop. Depending on the amount of toxin a person has taken in, symptoms may progress to tingling of fingers and toes and then loss of control of arms and legs, followed by difficulty in breathing. Some individuals have a sense of floating, while others are nauseated. If a person consumes enough poison, death can result from paralysis of the breathing mechanism, in as little as two hours. Approximately 15 percent of the reported cases of PSP have resulted in death.

You should be careful to distinguish these symptoms of PSP from two other types of illness sometimes caused by eating shellfish -- allergic reactions and gastrointestinal problems or hepatitis resulting from sewage pollution.

Treatment

It is essential to begin treating PSP immediately -- as soon as the lips or tongue begin to tingle, because the poisons can take effect rapidly and, as indicated, there is no known antidote for them. Induce vomiting and give a brisk laxative to remove the toxic shellfish from the digestive tract. **Get the patient to a doctor at once**. If this is not possible, prepare to administer artificial respiraiton, which may be required for many hours.

Shellfish Subject to PSP

Unfortunately, all species of bivalve shellfish (clams, oysters, mussels, and scallops) commonly eaten in Washington have been found to contain poisons at some time. Different species vary considerably, however, in the rates at which they become toxic, on the total amounts of toxin they take up, and in the speed with which they get rid of it.

PSP and Red Tides

No doubt you have heard a great deal about red tides over the years. Unfortunately, there is much misunderstanding about the relationship between red tides and poisonous shellfish, including a widespread tendency to equate the two. This misconception has led to the dangerous false assumption that shellfish are safe to eat if no red tide is visible. On the other hand, some people in Puget Sound believe that because they have eaten clams safely for years even when red tides were present, they can continue to do so.

Keep in mind that although a red tide may indiate that shellfish are toxic, it is dangerous to assume that lack of a red tide means that shellfish are safe to eat. Determining what shellfish gathering areas in Washington are safe or unsafe is the responsibility of the state and/or counties.

PSP Hotline

The State of Washington maintains a hotline with current information on closures for recreational gathering of shellfish as set by counties. The recordings are updated whenever changes in closures are made. You are urged to take advantage of this service and call a hotline number each time before gathering shellfish. The hotline numbers for Washington and British Columbia are listed below. If you are heading north, you can also find out about PSP closures by checking with the local fishery officers in British Columbia or with health officers in Alaska, or anywhere else along the Pacific Coast that you may be heading.

Washington -- (800) 562-5632

British Columbia -- (604) 666-1284

In California, consult your local Fish & Game Department

The following is a medical history form we have used with excellent success in numerous offshore long distance races. Quite quickly and briefly past medical problems and future potential ones are brought to the fore. If there are any questions or the skipper wishes a professional review his family physician or yacht club Fleet Surgeon could quite quickly review the forms. We feel very strongly that a form of this nature should be a mandatory requirement for each crew member of a long distance racing or cruising yacht.

MEDICAL HISTORY FORM FOR OFFSHORE PASSAGES

RACE_______________________________________

YACHT______________________________________

NAME:____ AGE:______

ADDRESS:____

______________________________________ PHONE:____________

PREVIOUS SERIOUS ILLNESS:_______________________________________

____

PREVIOUS OPERATIONS and/or SERIOUS ACCIDENTS:__________________

____

CURRENT ILLNESS (e.g. DIABETES/CARDIAC/ULCERS):________________

____

DRUG ALLERGIES:____

____

CURRENT MEDICATIONS:____

____

It is strongly advised if you wear glasses, dentures, contact lenses, prescription sunglasses, that you bring an extra pair. If you are taking any mediaciton bring twice the amount you think you will need in two separate containers. Don't forget sunglasses, suntan lotion, etc.

Please fill in the above and return to me as soon as possible.

____
Yacht's Surgeon

Table of Contents

NON-EMERGENCY ASSISTANCE - POLICY

The Thirteenth Coast Guard District is updating a list of commercial operators available for response to non-emergency vessel incidents within this region. It is the Coast Guard's policy to not interfere with private industry when there is no threat to life of property. When we receive a call for assistance and determine that it is clearly a non-emergency, we will normally attempt to notify commercial towing companies of the situation. It is up to the towing company to both respond within a reasonable period of time and negotiate a satisfactory contract with the operator of the vessel. The operator is under no obligation to utilize the commercial assistance·and the Coast Guard will not accept any obligation for costs incurred by the towing company. If the troubled vessel refuses commercial assistance, the case will be reviewed for possible Coast Guard or other resource response using reasonable time criteria. The Coast Guard will continue to handle some non-emergency cases so that our boat crews can retain their skills. In order to be placed on our notification list, commercial operators must apply in writing to the Commander (osr), Thirteenth Coast Guard District, 915 Second Avenue, Seattle, WA 98174 - 1067 and indicate their ability to comply with the following requirements:

a. *Possess vessel documentation or registration appropriate for the vessel size and area of operations.*

b. *Be equipped with a VHF-FM marine radio capable of operating on at least channels 16 and 22. If the operator anticipates operating more than 25 miles offshore, a marine HF SSB radio will also be required.*

c. *Carry a portable dewatering pump of 50 gallons per minute capacity or greater.*

d. *Carry appropriate towing equipment - lines, hawsers, fenders, bridles, emergency breakaway gear - and also be equipped with adequate bitts.*

e. *Provide the Coast Guard with a chart, or description, depicting your service area and giving approximate response times for your vessels to selected spots within the service area.*

❦ Coastal Storm Warnings ❦

SMALL CRAFT ADVISORIES

DAYTIME SIGNAL   NIGHT SIGNAL

One RED pennant displayed by day and a RED light over a WHITE light at night to indicate winds as high as 33 knots (38 m.p.h.) and/or sea conditions considered dangerous to small craft operations are forecast for the area, (see note on last page).

GALE

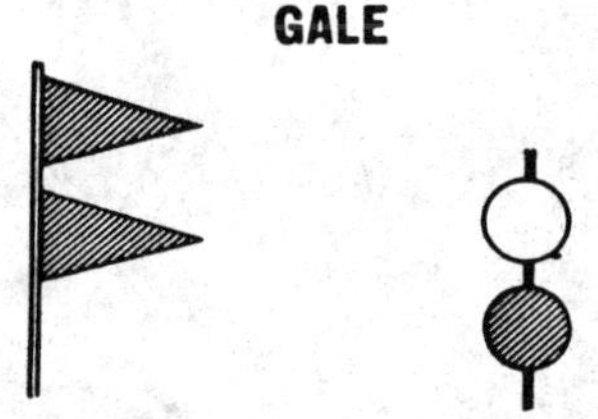

DAYTIME SIGNAL   NIGHT SIGNAL

Two RED pennants displayed by day and a WHITE light above a RED light at night to indicate winds within the range 34 to 47 knots (39 to 54 m.p.h.) are forecast for the area.

STORM

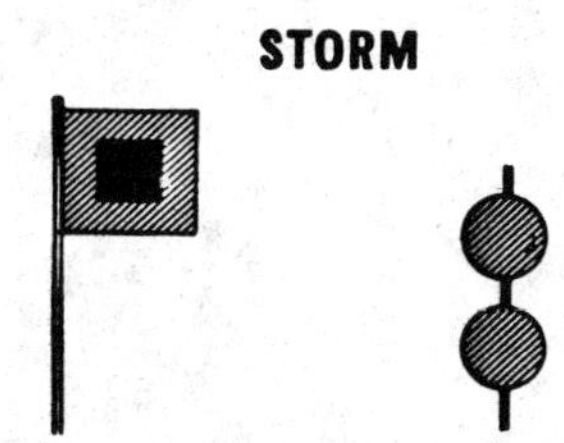

DAYTIME SIGNAL   NIGHT SIGNAL

A single square RED flag with a BLACK center displayed during daytime and two RED lights at night to indicate that winds 48 knots (55 m.p.h.) and above are forecast for the area. If the winds are associated with a tropical cyclone (hurricane), the "Storm Warning" display indicates winds 48 to 63 knots (55 to 73 m.p.h.) are forecast.

HURRICANE

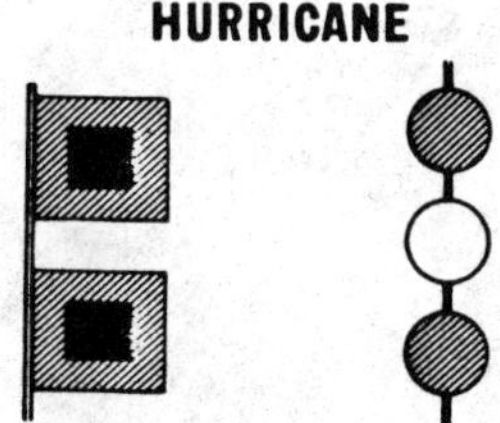

DAYTIME SIGNAL   NIGHT SIGNAL

Displayed only in connection with a tropical cyclone (hurricane). Two square RED flags with BLACK centers displayed by day and a WHITE light between two RED lights at night to indicate that winds 64 knots (74 m.p.h.) and above are forecast for the area.

COASTAL STORM WARNING DISPLAY STATIONS

Chetco River CG Station (Day only) • Roque River CG Patrol (Day only - Seasonal) • Coquille River CG Patrol (Day only - Seasonal) • Coos Bay CG Station (Day only) • Coos Head Lookout (Day only) • Umpqua River CG Lookout (Day only) • Umpqua River CG Station (Day only) • Siuslaw River CG Station (Day only) • Yaquina Bay CG Station (Day only) • Depoe Bay CG Station (Day only) • Tillamook Bay CG Station (Day only) • Tillamook Bay CG Lookout (Day only - Seasonal) • Cape Disappointment (Day only) • Bellingham (Day only) • Nahcotta (Day only) • Grays Harbor CG Satation (Day only) • Oceran Shores Marina (Day only) • Tacoma-Point Defiance (Day only) • Des Moines Small Boat Harbor (Day only) • Seattle-Lake Union (Day only) • Seattle Yacht Club • Seattle-U.S. Gov't Locks (Day only) • Seattle-Shilshole Bay Marina (Day only) • Quillayute River CG Station (Day only) • Neah Bay CG Station • Blaine.

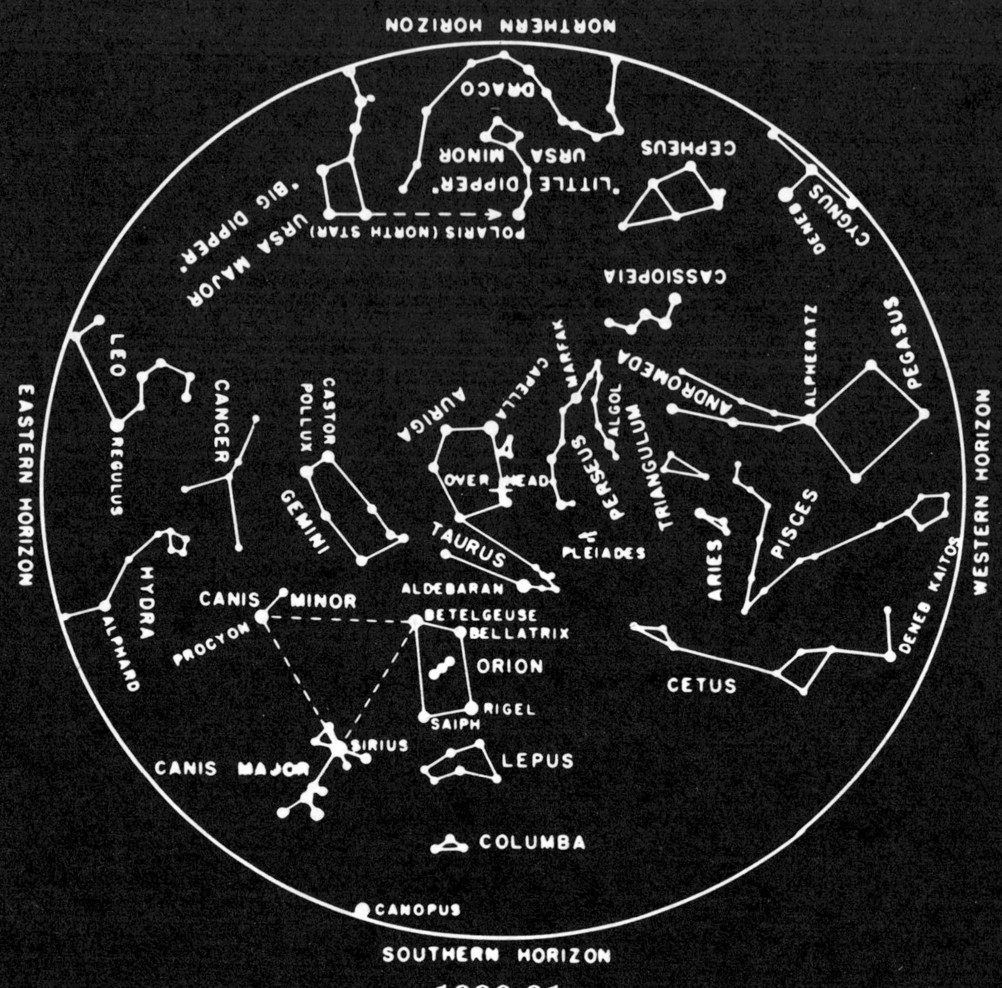

1990-91
THE NIGHT SKY—WINTER

This chart shows the principal navigational stars above the horizon at about the following local standard times: 11 P.M., December 15; 9 P.M., January 15; 7 P.M., February 15. It is for the latitude of 34° North, but it is practical within ten degrees of this. Hold the ALMANAC vertically and turn the page so that the direction you are facing shows on the bottom of the chart.

Venus is behind the sun in December, and returns to the evening sky in late January. It remains visible until mid-summer. Mars shines bright and red in Taurus in December, and fades during the winter. It is not far from the red star Aldebaran. Jupiter lies opposite the sun in Cancer. Saturn is in the morning sky in Capricornus from mid-February.

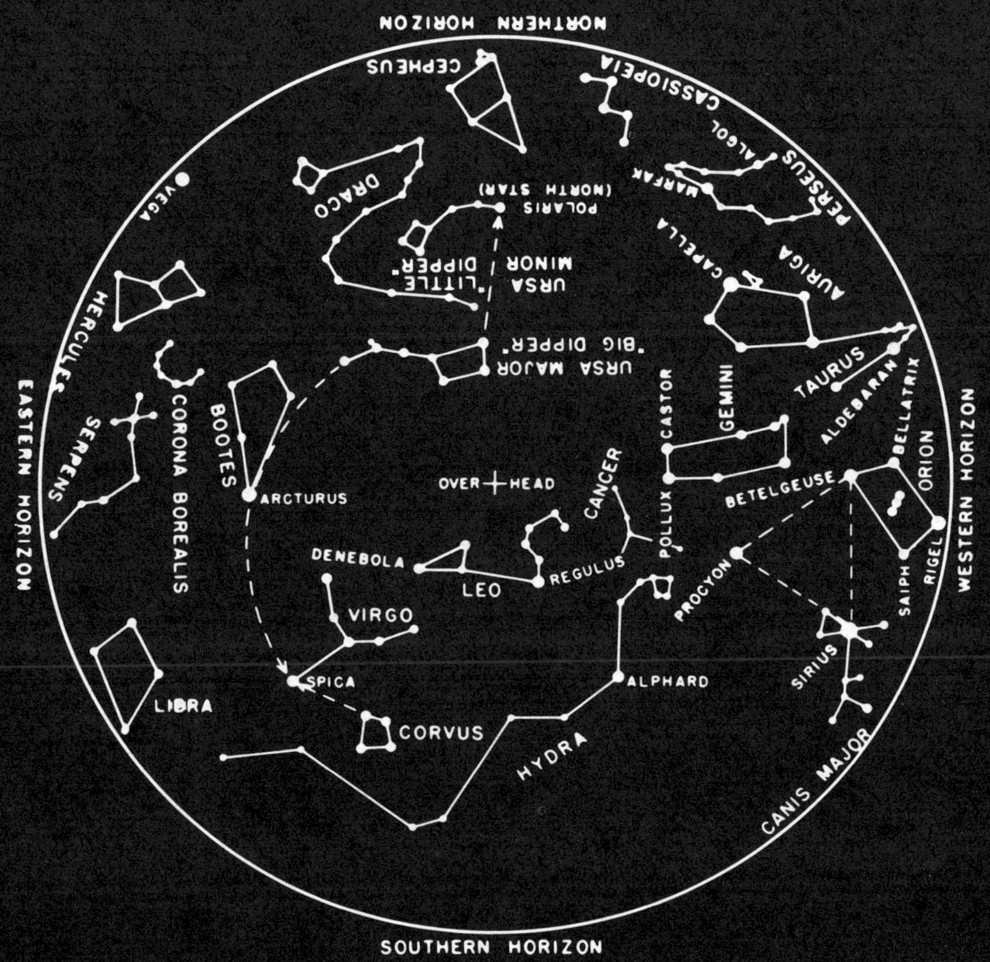

1991
THE NIGHT SKY—SPRING

This chart shows the principal navigational stars above the horizon at about the following local standard times: 11 P.M., March 15; 9 P.M., April 15; 7 P.M., May 15. It is for the latitude of 34° North, but it is practical within ten degrees of this. Hold the ALMANAC vertically and turn the page so that the direction you are facing shows on the bottom of the chart.

Venus is the brilliant "evening star" through August. Mars is above Venus, and it moves from Taurus into Gemini. Mars, which is fainter than Venus, is midway between Venus and Jupiter in April. Jupiter is to the east of Mars in Cancer. Saturn is in the morning sky in Capricornus. The distance between Venus, Mars, and Jupiter narrows steadily; they are within a few degrees of each other in mid-June.

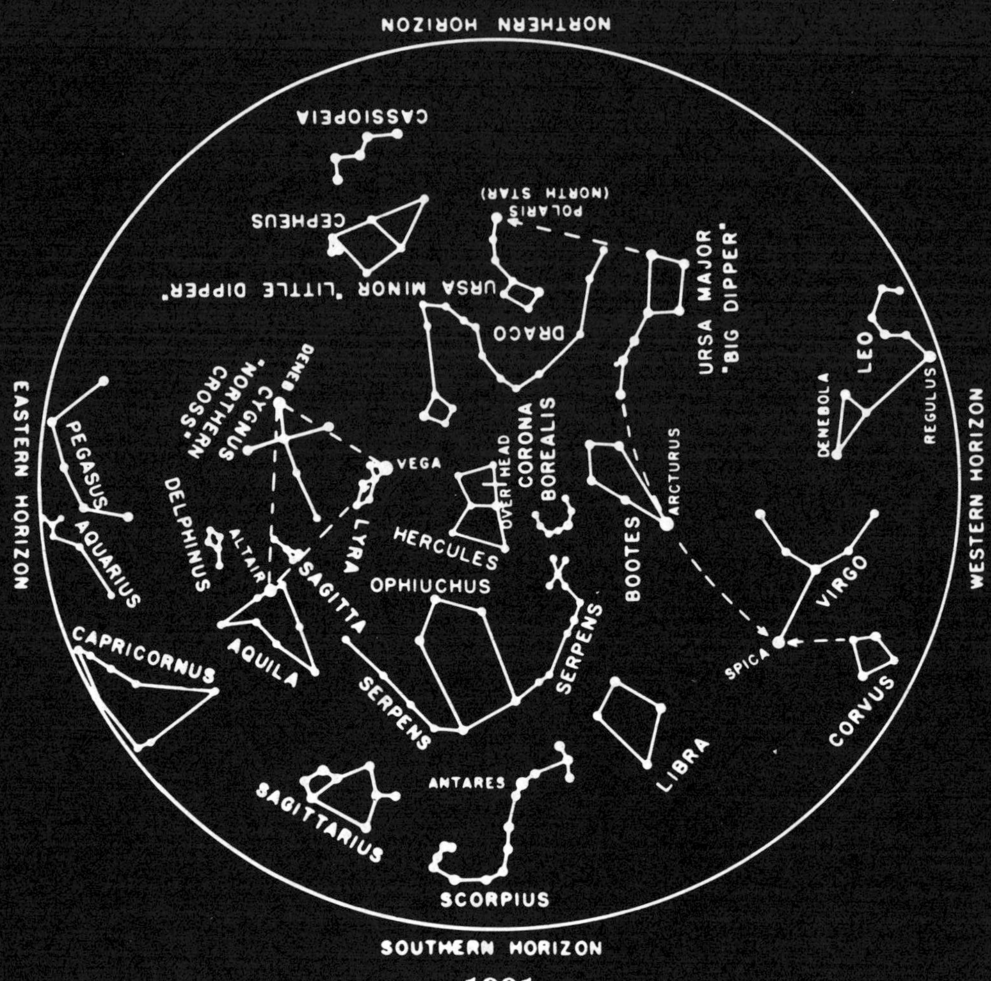

1991
THE NIGHT SKY—SUMMER

This chart shows the principal navigational stars above the horizon at about the following local standard times: 11 P.M., June 15; 9 P.M., July 15; 7 P.M., August 15. It is for the latitude of 34° North, but it is practical within ten degrees of this. Hold the ALMANAC vertically and turn the page so that the direction you are facing shows on the bottom of the chart.

Venus, Mars, and Jupiter are grouped tightly in Cancer in the evening sky in early June. Venus is the brightest, followed by Jupiter and then Mars. They reverse positions from (bottom to top) V-M-J to J-M-V after June 15. Mercury joins the trio briefly in mid-July, passing a scant 0.1° from Jupiter on July 14. Venus and Jupiter then align with the sun. Saturn is opposite the sun in the evening sky in Capricornus.

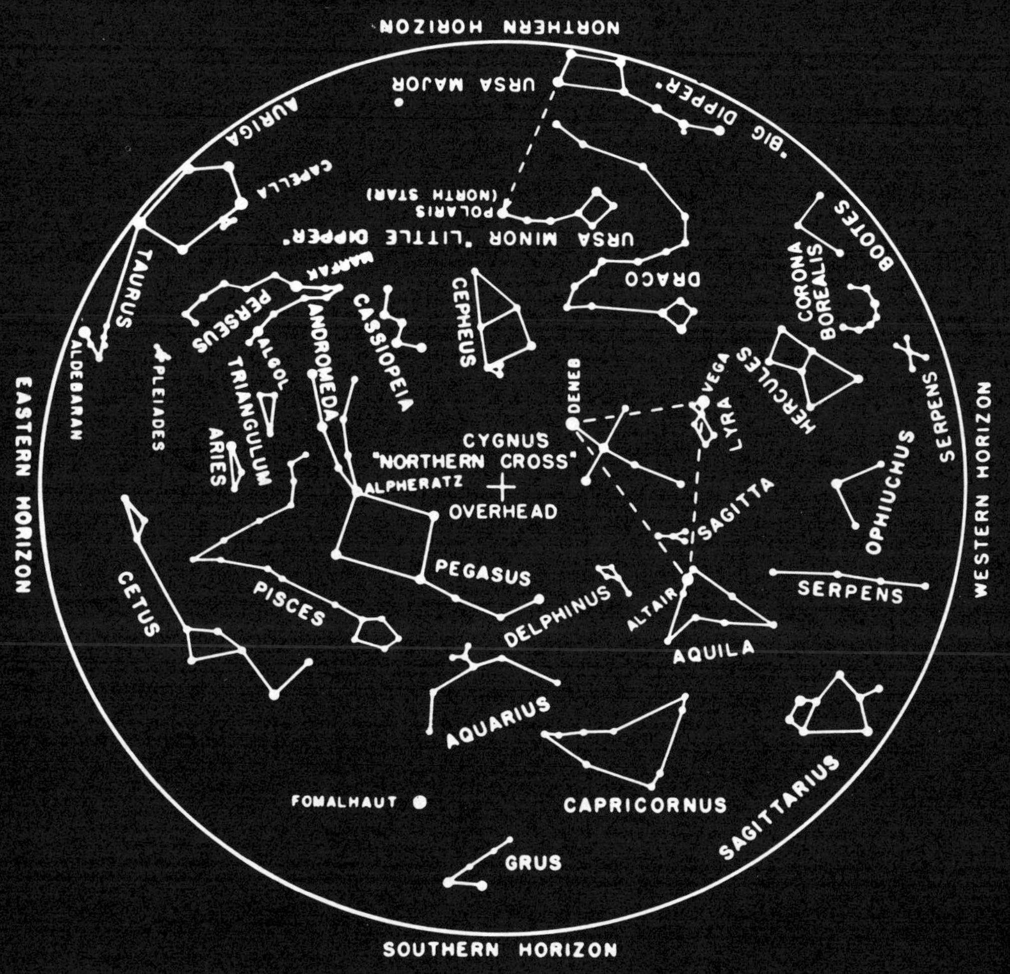

1991
THE NIGHT SKY—FALL

This chart shows the principal navigational stars above the horizon at about the following local standard times: 11 P.M., September 15; 9 P.M., October 15; 7 P.M,. November 15. It is for the latitude of 34° North, but it is practical within ten degrees of this. Hold the ALMANAC vertically and turn the page so that the direction you are facing shows on the bottom of the chart.

Venus and Jupiter reappear in the morning sky in September. Venus is brighter and rises first until October 14, when Venus passes 3° from Jupiter; Jupiter then rises first. Mars slowly moves behind the sun in September and cannot be seen from then until January. Saturn is in the evening sky through the end of the year.

Helmsmanship is the ability of a seaman to steer a vessel well. Some knowledge can be learned in a classroom or from a book . . . but the ability comes from actual experience. And any helmsmanship "rules" are only general statements because boats, like seamen, have individual characteristics: specific strengths and weaknesses. Obviously a boat with a shallow draft will handle differently than a deep-draft boat. Outboards and inboard-outboards are steered by changing their thrust direction and react differently than rudder-steered boats. Likewise, heavy, displacement hulls will react differently than light, planing hulls.

"Feel" of the Craft is Essential in Becoming a Good Helmsman:

When you take the helm of any boat for the first time, relax and get to know her. Don't force large corrections. As much as possible let her find her own way through the waves. Don't try to steer an exact compass course—few can. Be content to let the swings through two or three degrees average out. Remember even though it looks like the compass card swings by the lubberline, it's the other way around—steer accordingly.

Compensating at the Helm:

When a craft swings and changes course, the inexperienced helmsman tends to allow her to overswing because of the lag between the turning of the wheel and the craft's actual response. The experienced helmsman will return the rudder to midships before the boat actually reaches the new heading. In some cases he may use some opposite rudder action to check the craft's swinging motion.

Yawing:

Yawing from side to side on an embarrassingly crooked course is a sure sign of a novice "at the helm." To keep your craft on a straight course . . . you must "anticipate". Only by constantly observing the boat's swing can you quickly correct her course . . . with just a little rudder. Use of too much rudder means you are not anticipating . . . but allowing her to get too far off course before making your correction.

Turn the wheel slowly, deliberately sudden movements are the exception . . . not the rule of a good helmsman.

Pick a Point to Steer By:

Choose some obvious landmark; a rock formation, a distant church steeple (but don't steer by a cloud formation. Not only do they move . . . they also change shape!) At night, of course, use a star. You can conveniently use a reference point for general direction and drop your eyes occasionally to check your course on the compass.

Let the Sea Dictate to You:

If you are driving into a head sea, your craft will undoubtedly be slowed down in order to prevent any more pounding than necessary. The swing of the bow can be corrected with slight rudder changes.

Your stern is apt to be thrown about by overtaking waves in a following sea . . . so you must anticipate and check the yawing as much as you can.

If your stern is tossed high by an overtaking sea and tends to be thrown to starboard, you must apply right rudder (and often a great amount of rudder) in order to meet her.

AIDS TO NAVIGATION

These include both floating and fixed objects and range from a small buoy to a manned lightship or a lighthouse complete with audible, visible and electronic signals. Navigational aids help a boatowner know his location and the safe course on which he should proceed.

Buoy:

A floating marker anchored to the bottom and sometimes equipped with audible, visual and/or electronic signals. It marks out navigable channels as shown on the chart.

Daybeacon:

An unlighted fixed structure with a pointer, sign or "daymarker".

Light:

A fixed aid (floating or on land) with an identification number and a light at the top.

Ranges:

Pairs of lighted or unlighted fixed aids which indicate the centerline of a channel. One marker is closer to you than the other. When you line them up your craft is in the channel.

Radiobeacon:

A transmitter which broadcasts a characteristic signal to aid navigating at night, in fog or between distant points beyond the range of normal visibility.

Electronic Navigation System:

One or more radio transmitters emitting special signals to aid in navigating in fog or when out of sight of land.

Easily Memorized Reminder: RRR

Red Right Returning

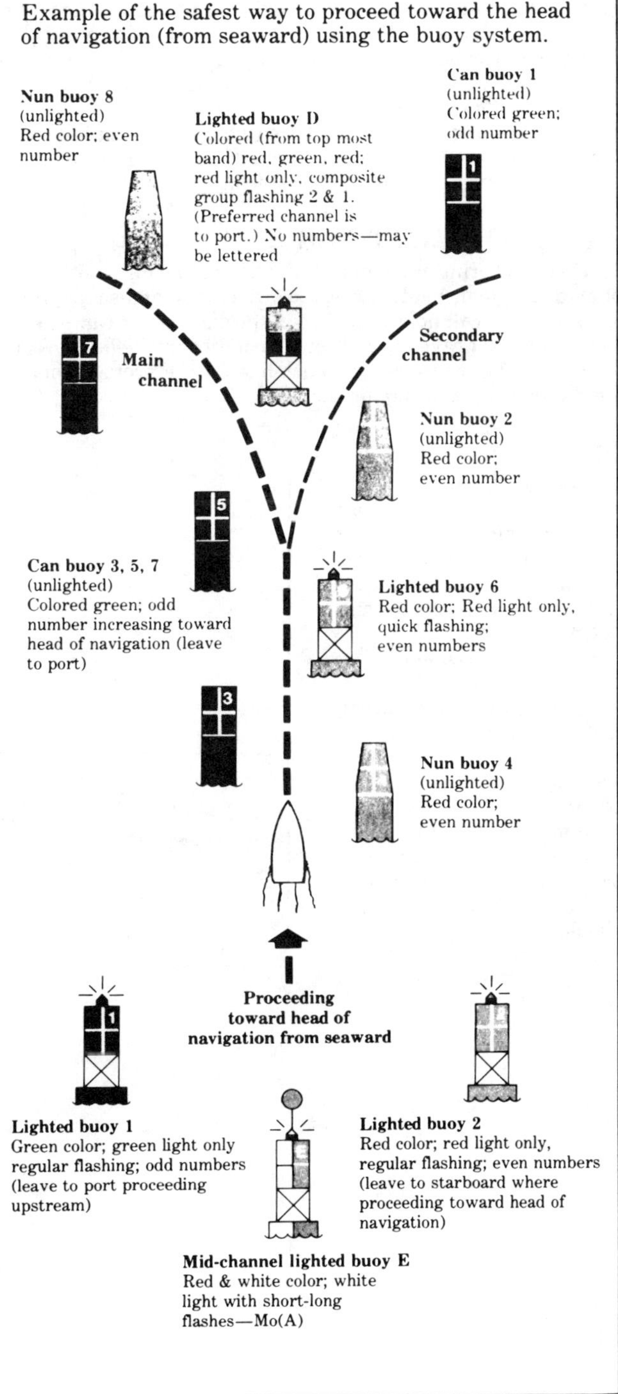

ANCHORING

The best anchorage offers a good holding bottom, water of suitable depth, and protection from wind and passing craft. Anchorages are often indicated on charts by the anchor symbol and desirable anchorage areas are shown by solid magenta lines. If you can't find a suitable harbor, select a cove with protection from the direction of the wind, or the quarter from which it's expected.

Under a windward bank or shore (where the wind blows from the bank toward your boat) is an alternative, although you must be wary of wind shifts which might expose you to storms.

TYPES OF BOTTOMS

When anchoring remember that the best holding bottoms are mixtures of mud and sand, mud and clay and firm mud and sand. Gravel or hard sand bottoms will hold well if your specific anchor can penetrate them. Loose sand or gravel or soft mud should be avoided. Don't anchor in deep water; you'll have to use too much line for the proper scope . . . which allows too wide a swing for the boat.

SCOPE

Adequate "scope" is necessary if your boat is to be anchored safely. Scope is the ratio of the length of the anchor line to the distance from the bow chocks to the bottom.

Satisfactory scope is generally considered to be a ratio of 7 to 1. If you anchor in 10 feet of water (from the bow chocks to the bottom)... you should pay out 70 feet of rode.

Remember also that a rising tide will change the scope. If the distance becomes 15 feet to the bottom, you should pay out another 35 feet of rode.

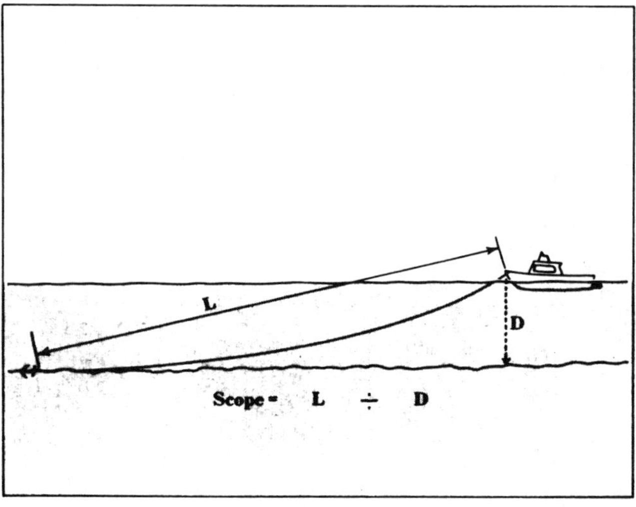

ANCHORING

ANCHORING IN SPECIAL SITUATIONS

2 Techniques to Reducing Wave Effects:

a. To reduce wave effects use 2 anchors; place a small anchor ahead of your main anchor and double the scope.

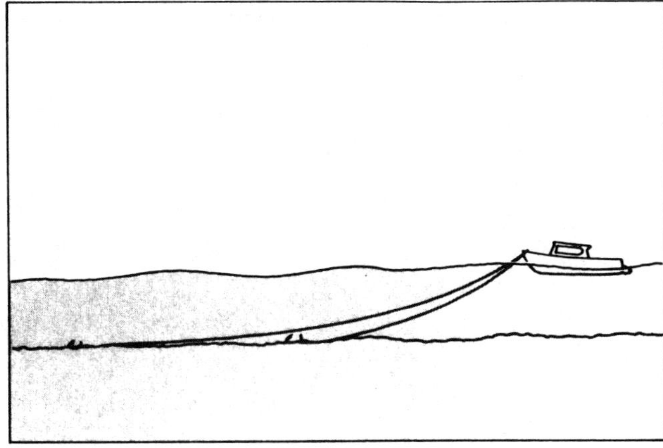

b. Weights or heavy chain on the rode will effectively reduce wave shocks.

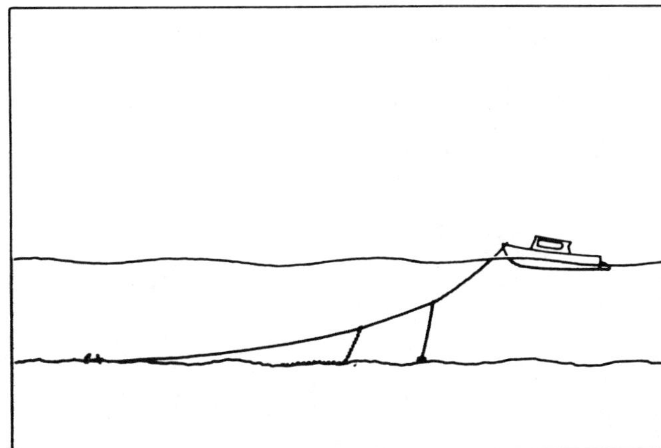

Reducing Boat-Swing:

To reduce boat-swing use two anchors, with or without weights. They will reduce the diameter of the swing by about 50%.

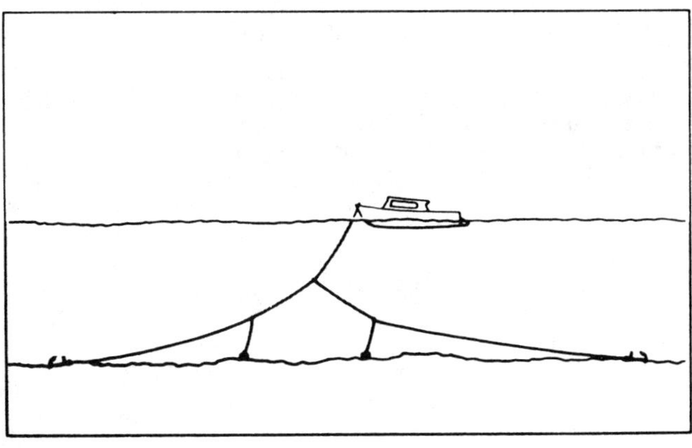

PERMANENT MOORINGS
A. The Standard Approach:

A buoy removes the weight of the chain or other rode and gives the bow more buoyancy.

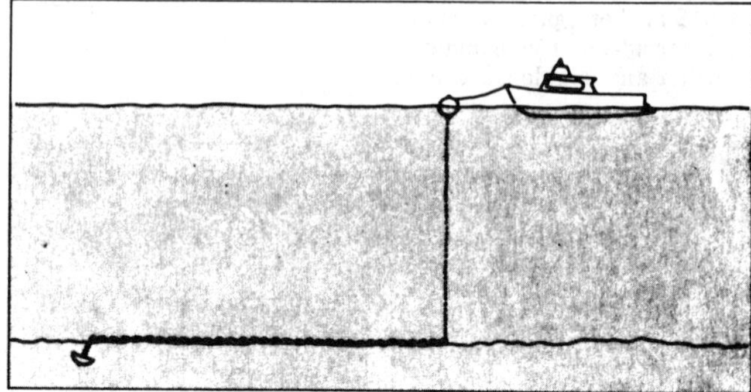

B. An Alternate Method:

An excellent mooring arrangement consists of three or more anchors set in a circle. Weights may also be added.

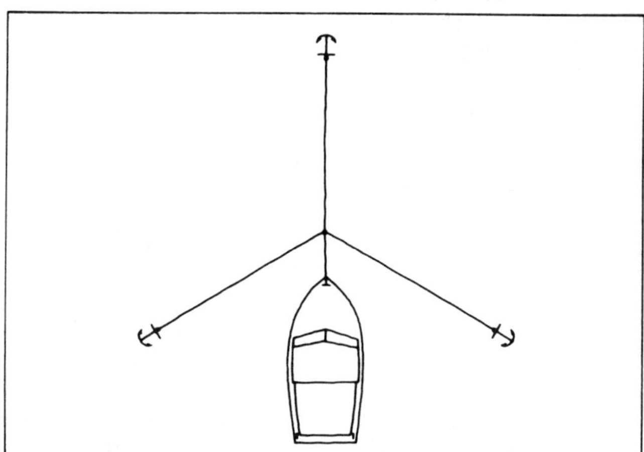

TEMPORARY ANCHORING

Approach the anchorage by running directly into the wind or current, whichever is stronger. Choose a naturally-sheltered spot and be sure there is ample depth to remain clear of hazards at ebb tide, such as sand bars or reefs. Be sure of a good holding bottom.

In crowded areas use a stern anchor to prevent your boat from swinging into another craft. Be aware of any cross currents or winds which may cause anchors to drag. If you notice drag, reset the anchor and increase the scope.

Consider that your boat (and all other boats in the anchorage area) are in the middle of "circles" . . . don't anchor too close to anyone and let your "circles" overlap.

When anchoring overnight, always display a strong, bright anchor light.

COASTAL NAVIGATION

When cruising the shore line, keep a lookout for points that will be easy to identify. A good practice is to try to determine your position every fifteen minutes and plot it on your chart. Then by travelling at a constant speed and on a known course you can estimate the distance from your last known position.

Two basic methods of using charts with compass bearings to find your approximate position:

The Cross Bearing Method:

Used whenever two or more charted or land objects . . . buoys, lighthouses, light vessels, church steeples . . . are visible to you. These references should not be less than 30° apart: preferably, they should be closer to 90° apart. To obtain a cross bearing, take a bearing on each object, draw the lines on the chart, and ascertain your position at their intersection. If more than two bearings are taken, they will not usually intersect at a point, but rather in a triangle, and the size of this triangle is proportionate to the accuracy of your bearings. The smaller the triangle, the more accurate your plotting. Be sure to use the inner (magnetic) compass rose in drawing a bearing line on your chart, and also to correct for deviation of your compass.

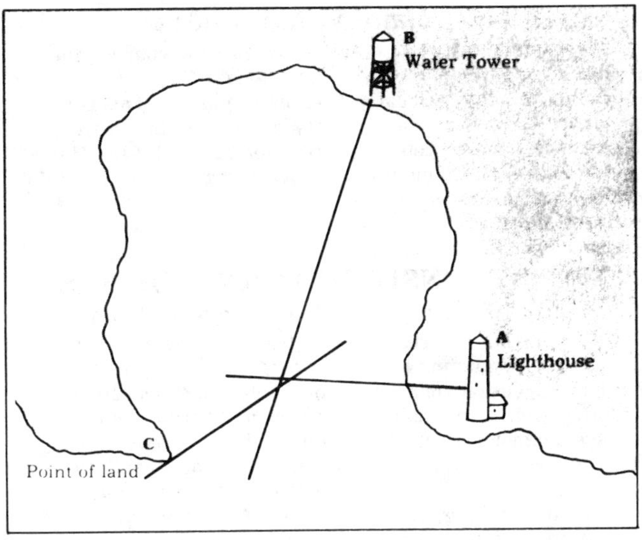

The Bow and Beam Method:

Keep dead on your course, and when the charted landmark (lighthouse, church steeple, etc.) is exactly 45°, or "Four Points", off your bow, note your time and speed. When the landmark is exactly abeam, note your time and speed again. The distance that you run between these two bearings is your distance off the object on the Beam Bearing. You've formed a 90° triangle (two equal sides) and, so, if you have traveled 3 miles between the two bearings, your distance off the charted landmark is 3 miles.

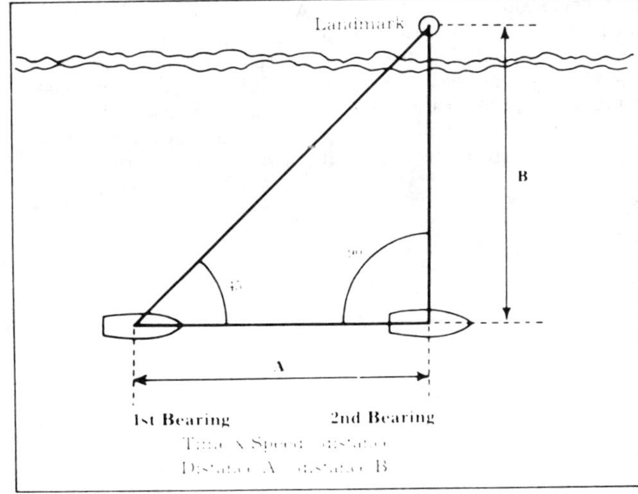

One of the unwritten laws of the sea is that you should give help to fellow seamen when it is needed. In most cases, the Coast Guard "saves the day," but there are situations when some timely help on your part may save some boatowner hours of labor later when the tide has fallen or the wind and the sea have changed.

Assistance usually means passing him a tow-line so he can get out of some unfortunate position; or towing him to the Coast Guard station or back to port.

STRANDING (Running Aground)

Stranding, in most situations, is more an incovenience than an actual danger. If you know what to do and work quickly, you might lose only a few minutes from your otherwise enjoyable cruise.

Don't throw your engine into reverse and gun it in an effort to pull off. This is the typical, almost instinctive, reaction . . . and it may be exactly what you shouldn't do!

STOP AND CONSIDER THREE THINGS:

The Stage of the Tide

If it's rising and the sea is quiet (and not pounding on your hull) time is on your side. Whatever efforts you make will be even more effective after time has passed and the tide has risen.

If the tide is falling, you must act immediately or you may spend considerable time aground and possibly damage your boat.

The Shape of Your Hull

What is its point of greatest draft? This should tell you what part is most likely to be touching. If the hull has any tendency to swing because of wind or waves, the spot above which it pivots is probably the part that is grounded.

The Type of Bottom

If you're in sand, don't reverse hard . . . you'll probably wash sand from astern and throw it directly under the keel bedding the boat even more firmly to the bottom. *At all times while aground caution should be used in reversing; you may pump sand or mud into the engine.* If you reverse on rocky bottom you may actually drag the hull and cause more damage than occurred with the original grounding.

And, if grounded forward, given the tendency of the stern to swing to port, reversing a single-screw boat which has a right-hand propeller may swing the hull broadside to even greater contact with a soft bottom.

USING A KEDGE

If your boat is solidly aground, the first action to take immediately is to take out an anchor (kedge) and set it firmly; this is called kedging.

Make a line fast to the stern bitts or something solid; then, if you have a dinghy, row out as far as possible and set the anchor.

If you don't have a dinghy and the water is not hazardous, you may swim out (supporting the anchor on a life preserver or cushion) and drop the anchor. Also wear a life preserver or jacket to save your energy.

Although the basic rule is that an anchor should never be thrown . . . this may be one situation in which you may have to throw it. Getting a kedge anchor set is that important. And it may prove necessary to pull the anchor in and throw it several times to get it set firmly.

Where to Set Out the Kedge

First, remember the sideways-turning effect of a reversing single screw; unless the boat has twin screws, set the kedge at a compensating angle from the boat's stern. Most propellers are right hand. So, set the anchor slightly to starboard of the stern for two definite advantages. When pulling together with the kedge line and reverse, the craft will have almost a straight pull on it; and when used alternately; first by pulling on the line and then by giving a short "jolt" with reverse . . . the "wiggling" to the stern and keel may help to start the boat moving.

At all times while aground, keep the kedge-line as taut as the pulling strength of you and your crew permits. Such constant pull, combined with the wake of a passing vessel of some size, may help lift the keel from the bottom.

Two kedges placed at an acute angle from either side of your craft may also be pulled upon alternately for that important stern "wiggle" that could set you free.

Where the bottom is sandy, you may also have the propeller going ahead while you pull; this may wash some sand away from under the keel (but your kedge line must be kept absolutely taut.)

If you have several bodies aboard, have them move quickly from side to side in an effort to roll the boat, making the keel "work" in the bottom. Shift any heavy objects from over the grounded portion so as to lighten that section and make it more maneuverable. If you have a dinghy, consider loading it with people and such ballast and taking it ashore.

And if you have spars, swing the boom outboard with crew on it to heave the boat down and raise the keel.

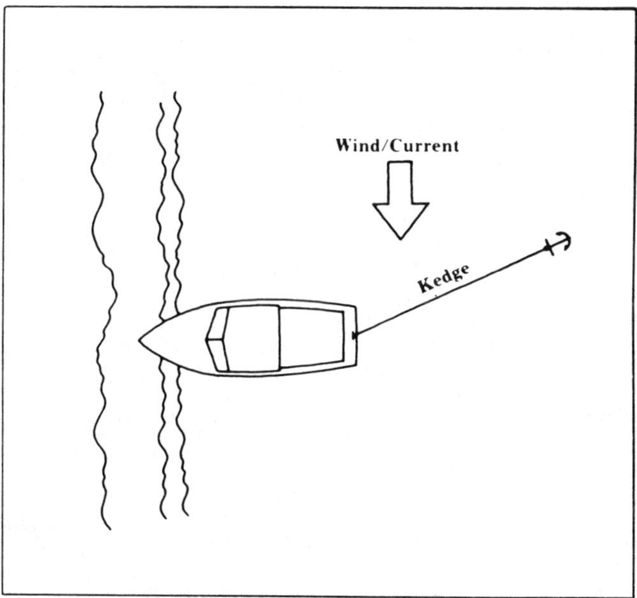

Obviously, if the boat has been strained open or stove in, you are better off where you are than back in the water. Consider taking an anchor ashore and securing her if she is seriously damaged.

Get out a kedge. This is the first thing to do when you go aground. It stops you from being driven further aground and may be used to pull yourself free as waves from passing craft lift your boat.

ASSISTING

More often than you may think, the assisting boat joins the troubled boat . . . and also needs assistance. Assisting someone takes more than good intentions. It takes nautical "horse sense" not to attempt an impossible rescue job; and it takes good judgment in deciding exactly what you should do.

Consider the Stranded Craft

Observe its size and its approximate weight in comparison to your own boat. Then, only after discussing the procedure with the stranded skipper, should you take action.

Get a Line to the Stranded Boat . . . Safely.

Before you go in to pass a line, be aware of the shoal area. Remember that wind and current and the effect of reversing your propeller may cause your boat to swing broadside in the shallows as she backs. In that case you'd better figure some other way of passing the line. Perhaps you should back in. The wind or current may compensate for the reversed screw . . . keeping her straight . . . with the bow headed out for best maneuverability. You, in assisting, should then pull straight ahead with full power.

If there is no way to make a reasonably safe approach, you may have to move off a fair distance, drop anchor and get a line over by dinghy, by buoying the line and floating it over, or by swimming over with it.

Don't Just Sit There Waiting For the Coast Guard or the Tide!

You should be gathering valuable information: take soundings around the entire position of the boat. There may be some bottom contour changes you can take advantage of (or, at least you can better inform the Coast Guard when they arrive). You may discover, through soundings, that straight backward pulling with kedges and engine is not necessary; swinging the stern to starboard or port may be just the thing to set you free or put the boat in a more maneuverable position.

Lastly, hail a passing boat. Explain the situation and ask the skipper to run his craft back and forth making as big a wake as possible. Then "work" with your pulling muscles and your engine.

And, if you're "high and dry" . . . brace your boat so she is as upright as possible. When the tide comes in, she'll refloat much easier.

Straining With Success

When the wind or current (or both) is broadside to the direction of the pull, it is best for the assisting boat to remain anchored while pulling. If not, when she takes the strain she will lose her own maneuverability and will gradually make leeway . . . and even put her aground broadside! Remember that most recreational boats were not created equal with tug boats! Cleats and bitts are probably not strong enough nor are they properly placed for such work. It is best to run a bridle arund the whole hull of the stranded vessel. And the assisting boat should also be bridled if there is any question of her ability to withstand concentrated strains.

In case the stranded boat should come off . . . she should have a kedge out for control. And, since she may be without power, she should have another anchor handy to keep her from going back aground.

All the while, of course, the assisting boat captain must make sure all lines are kept clear of propellers and that no sudden surge "snap" is put on a slack line.

Small craft must generally make the pull with a line made fast near the stern. Maneuverability is thus restricted and so a bow anchor should be put out for safe control. As soon as the stranded boat comes free, slack of the anchor line should be taken up to prevent the assisting (pulling) boat from being carried into shoal water.

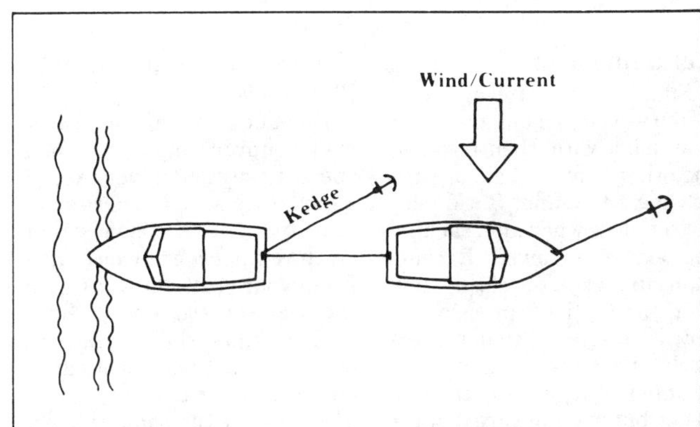

To increase maneuverability in case a bow anchor cannot be set, the tow-line should be secured to a cleat located forward of the stern (and on the up-wind or up-current side). Be sure this cleat has the capacity to take a heavy strain.

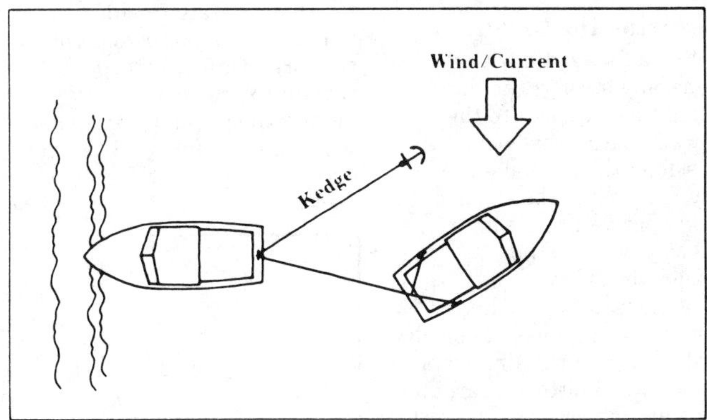

Since the strains set up are greater than the capacity of most bitts and cleats on small craft, a bridle is the best insurance. Be sure to pad any pressure points to protect both craft against any chafing or scarring.

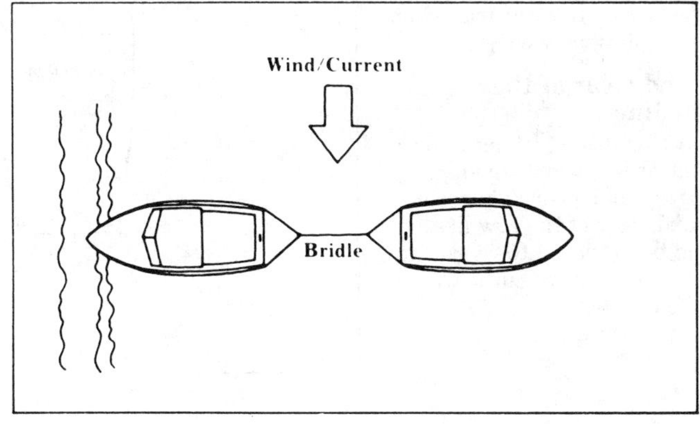

STRANDING, ASSISTING & TOWING

TOWING

Towing, as with assisting a stranded boat, requires careful attention to the physical capabilities of your craft, while considering the other vessel, its location, the wind and the current.

In fine weather with a small sea, towing is a relatively simple chore. Under foul weather conditions or with improper methods, towing can prove both dangerous and expensive to both parties. Better to wait for the Coast Guard rather than make conditions worse.

Get a line over

Simply stated, towing requires you to maneuver your boat in line with, then ahead of, the other boat . . . along with passing a tow-line. But don't get too close when approaching the boat to be towed. Rather than running in too close, buoy a long line with life preservers. Tow it astern and then make a circle under the stern of the disabled craft, getting the line to her but making sure it stays clear of her propeller.

Securing the tow-line

Since forward bitts are generally strong, the line should be fastened to the towed boat at that point. If possible, do not make the tow-line fast to the stern of the lead boat because it interferes greatly with the boat's maneuverability.

Make fast the tow-line as far forward as permissible or else make a bridle running from the forward bitts . . . around the superstructure . . . to the forward part of the cockpit (and be sure to wrap gear when any chafing may occur).

Stand clear of the tow-line

A tow-line which parts or a cleat or bitt which suddenly lets go can be very dangerous. Stand clear of the tow-line! And be prepared to release it quickly . . . or to cut it with a knife or a hatchet.

Use easy motion . . . not just muscle

Don't begin towing with a lot of power or in a big hurry. Gain speed slowly and never exceed a moderate speed. There's no reason to put excessive strain on the skipper, crew or craft. Keep your craft "in step" with the boat you are towing. Be sure to adjust the tow-line length so that both boats are on the crest or in the trough of the sea at the same time. This cruising "rhythm" makes for smooth, safe towing.

If your boat is towing and is the larger craft, be especially careful to cruise at a very moderate speed; a fast speed will make the smaller boat yaw and possibly capsize.

When towing a larger boat alongside, spring lines should take the strain. Place fenders at points of contact; springs should be made up with no slack. When the skipper of the smaller towing boat puts her rudder to port or to starboard for a turn, both boats will respond simultaneously as one unit.

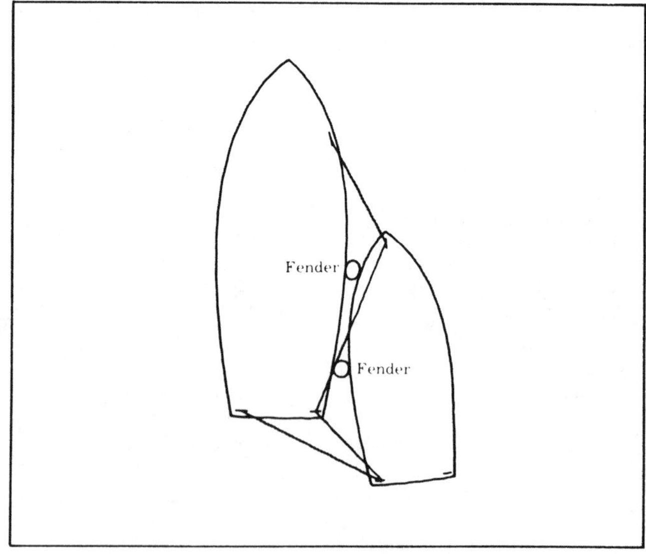

"THICK" WEATHER PILOTING

"Thick" weather includes fog, haze, heavy rain or snow . . . anything which creates conditions of reduced visibility on the water. Fog is probably the most common, as well as the most severe.

When Piloting in Fog, You Have One Objective: The Safety of Your Boat and Crew

The most common form of fog is created when a humid mass of air is cooled by passing over a cold area of water (or land). So, when caught in a fog, you may escape it by searching out the warmer areas of water. On the East Coast, these can be found in shallow water or off river and stream mouths, along with inlets or bays where tidal currents aren't strong.

Operate Your Boat at a Moderate Speed

Consider moderate speed to be that speed which will allow you to stop your boat in half the limit of visibility, i. e., to fully stop in 50 feet if you can only see 100 feet.

Stop, Listen and Look

Stop your boat every few minutes and listen for fog signals, other boats and any other navigational aids. Look and keep looking. Post crew members to keep a "sharp eye" about them. And, to prevent another craft from creeping up on you, use a tow spear: tow a dinghy on plenty of line . . . or an oar, cushion, floorboard . . . any object that floats . . . so anyone coming up astern will see or bump it long before they get to your craft.

Give a Fog Signal

If a power boat: a prolonged blast of 4 to 6 seconds . . . at intervals of not more than 1 minute.

If a sail boat: 1 if close hauled on starboard tack.

2 if close hauled on port tack.

3 if you are running with the wind abaft the beam.

If at anchor: ring a bell for about 5 seconds at intervals of not more than 1 minute.

CLEATING

Everyone should know how to quickly and correctly make fast to a cleat. Tied in the right way, the line exerts the greatest strain next to the deck. Improperly making fast to a cleat may create one of two problems: the line can suddenly, unexpectedly come loose . . . or you can't free the line quickly when you need to. Incorrect cleating can result in a good-natured ribbing or a serious accident.

Make sure every crew member can cleat properly.

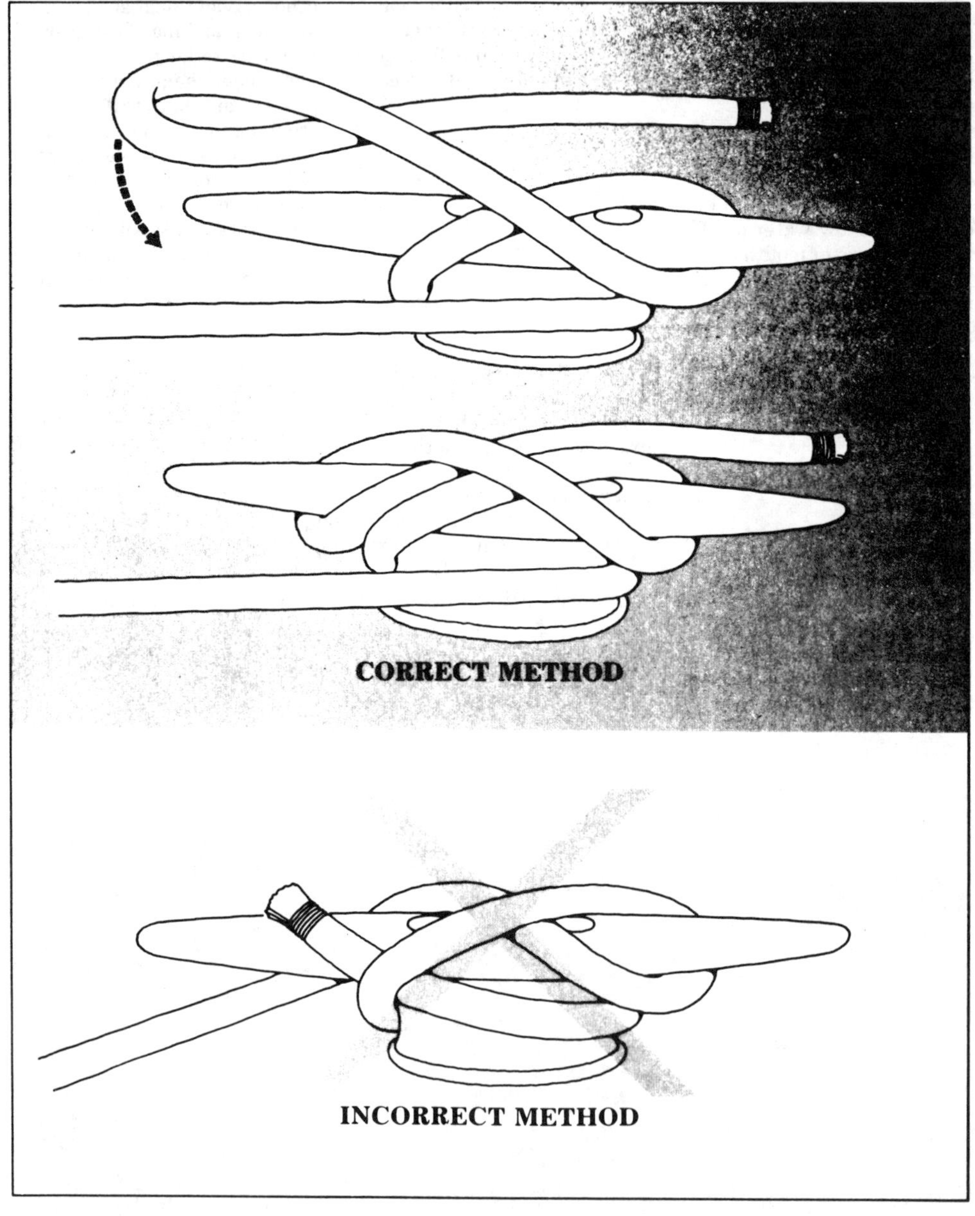

Basic Knots

CLOVE HITCH

USE: to fasten a rope around an object. When tied at the end of a rope, a half hitch should be added around the standing part.

OVERHAND KNOT

USE: mostly with string and twine, to keep it from pulling through a hole, pulley or loop of another knot.

FIGURE EIGHT KNOT

USE: primarily, to keep the end of a rope from running through a block.

SQUARE KNOT

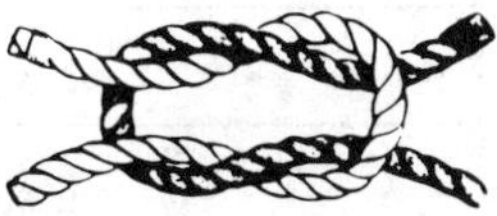

USE: largely for package tying, or wherever a simple knot is needed to join two ropes of equal size.

NOT THIS—a granny knot

BOWLINE

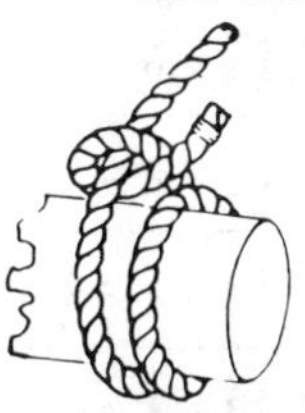

USE: anywhere a loop is needed which will not slip, as for mooring a boat.

ROUND TURN AND TWO HALF HITCHES

USE: wherever the end of a rope is to be fastened around a spar, or ring.

SHEET BEND

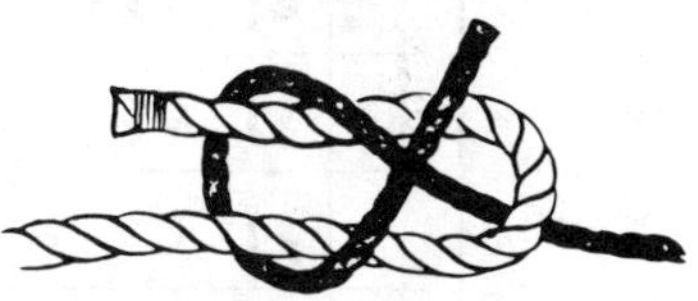

USE: to join two light ropes or two ropes of unequal size.

FISHERMAN'S KNOT

USE: to join two fishlines, pieces of twine, or light rope.

TABLE FOR ESTIMATING TIME OF TRANSIT

Distance	Speed in knots																		
	8	9	10	11	12	13	14	15	16	17	18	19	20	21	22	23	24	25	30
Nautical miles	Days-hours	Days-hours	Days-hours	Days-hours	Days-hours	Days-hours	Days-hours	Days-hours	Days-hours	Days-hours	Days-hours	Days-hours	Days-hours	Days-hours	Days-hours	Days-hours	Days-hours	Days-hours	Days-hours
10	0-1	0-1	0-1	0-1	0-1	0-1	0-1	0-1	0-1	0-1	0-1	0-1	0-1						
20	0-3	0-2	0-2	0-2	0-2	0-2	0-1	0-1	0-1	0-1	0-1	0-1	0-1	0-1	0-1	0-1	0-1	0-1	0-1
30	0-4	0-3	0-3	0-3	0-3	0-2	0-2	0-2	0-2	0-2	0-2	0-2	0-2	0-1	0-1	0-1	0-1	0-1	0-1
40	0-5	0-4	0-4	0-4	0-3	0-3	0-3	0-3	0-3	0-2	0-2	0-2	0-2	0-2	0-2	0-2	0-2	0-2	0-1
50	0-6	0-6	0-5	0-5	0-4	0-4	0-4	0-3	0-3	0-3	0-3	0-3	0-3	0-2	0-2	0-2	0-2	0-2	0-2
60	0-8	0-7	0-6	0-5	0-5	0-5	0-4	0-4	0-4	0-4	0-3	0-3	0-3	0-3	0-3	0-3	0-3	0-2	0-2
70	0-9	0-8	0-7	0-6	0-6	0-5	0-5	0-5	0-4	0-4	0-4	0-4	0-4	0-3	0-3	0-3	0-3	0-3	0-2
80	0-10	0-9	0-8	0-7	0-7	0-6	0-6	0-5	0-5	0-5	0-4	0-4	0-4	0-4	0-4	0-3	0-3	0-3	0-3
90	0-11	0-10	0-9	0-8	0-8	0-7	0-6	0-6	0-6	0-5	0-5	0-5	0-5	0-4	0-4	0-4	0-4	0-4	0-3
100	0-13	0-11	0-10	0-9	0-8	0-8	0-7	0-7	0-6	0-6	0-6	0-5	0-5	0-5	0-5	0-4	0-4	0-4	0-3
200	1-1	0-22	0-20	0-18	0-17	0-15	0-14	0-13	0-13	0-12	0-11	0-11	0-10	0-10	0-9	0-9	0-8	0-8	0-7
300	1-14	1-9	1-6	1-3	1-1	0-23	0-21	0-20	0-19	0-18	0-17	0-16	0-15	0-14	0-14	0-13	0-13	0-12	0-10
400	2-2	1-20	1-16	1-12	1-9	1-7	1-5	1-3	1-1	1-0	0-22	0-21	0-20	0-19	0-18	0-17	0-17	0-16	0-13
500	2-15	2-8	2-2	1-21	1-18	1-14	1-12	1-9	1-7	1-5	1-4	1-2	1-1	1-0	0-23	0-22	0-21	0-20	0-17
600	3-3	2-19	2-12	2-7	2-2	1-22	1-19	1-16	1-14	1-11	1-9	1-8	1-6	1-5	1-3	1-2	1-1	1-0	0-20
700	3-16	3-6	2-22	2-16	2-10	2-6	2-2	1-23	1-20	1-17	1-15	1-13	1-11	1-9	1-8	1-6	1-5	1-4	0-23
800	4-4	3-17	3-8	3-1	2-19	2-14	2-9	2-5	2-2	1-23	1-20	1-18	1-16	1-14	1-12	1-11	1-9	1-8	1-3
900	4-17	4-4	3-18	3-10	3-3	2-21	2-16	2-12	2-8	2-5	2-2	1-23	1-21	1-19	1-17	1-15	1-14	1-12	1-6
1,000	5-5	4-15	4-4	3-19	3-11	3-5	2-23	2-19	2-15	2-11	2-8	2-5	2-2	2-0	1-21	1-19	1-18	1-16	1-9
2,000	10-10	9-6	8-8	7-14	6-23	6-10	5-23	5-13	5-5	4-22	4-15	4-9	4-4	3-23	3-19	3-15	3-11	3-8	2-19
3,000	15-15	13-21	12-12	11-9	10-10	9-15	8-22	8-8	7-20	7-8	6-23	6-14	6-6	5-23	5-16	5-10	5-5	5-0	4-4
4,000	20-20	18-12	16-16	15-4	13-21	12-20	11-22	11-8	10-10	9-19	9-6	8-19	8-8	7-22	7-14	7-6	6-23	6-16	5-13
5,000	26-1	23-4	20-20	18-23	17-9	16-1	14-21	13-21	13-1	12-6	11-14	10-23	10-10	9-22	9-11	9-1	8-16	8-8	6-23
6,000	31-6	27-19	25-0	22-17	20-20	19-6	17-21	16-16	15-15	14-17	13-21	13-4	12-12	11-22	11-9	10-21	10-10	10-0	8-8

DETERMINATION OF WIND SPEED BY SEA CONDITION

Miles per hour	Knots	Descriptive	Sea Conditions	Wind force (Beaufort)	Probable wave height (in ft.)
0-1	0-1	Calm	Sea smooth and mirror-like.	0	
1-3	1-3	Light air	Scale-like ripples without foam crests.	1	1/4
4-7	4-6	Light breeze	Small, short wavelets; crests have a glassy appearance and do not break.	2	1/2
8-12	7-10	Gentle breeze	Large wavelets; some crests begin to break, foam of glassy appearance. Occasional white foam crests.	3	2
13-18	11-16	Moderate breeze	Small waves, become longer; fairly frequent white foam crests.	4	4
19-24	17-21	Fresh breeze	Moderate waves, taking a more pronounced long form; many white foam crests, there may be some spray.	5	6
25-31	22-27	Strong breeze	Large waves begin to form; white foam crests are more extensive everywhere, there may be some spray.	6	10
32-38	28-33	Near gale	Sea heaps up and white foam from breaking waves begins to be blown in streaks along the direction of the wind; spindrift begins.	7	14
39-46	34-40	Gale	Moderately high waves of greater length, edges of crests break into spindrift, foam is blown in well-marked streaks along the direction of the wind.	8	18
47-54	41-47	Strong gale	High waves; dense streaks of foam along the direction of the wind; crests of waves begin to topple, tumble, and roll over; spray may reduce visibility.	9	23
55-63	48-55	Storm	Very high waves with long overhanging crests. The resulting foam in great patches is blown in dense white streaks along the direction of the wind. On the whole, the surface of the sea is white in appearance. The tumbling of the sea becomes heavy and shocklike. Visibility is reduced.	10	29
64-72	56-63	Violent storm	Exceptionally high waves that may obscure small and medium-sized ships. The sea is completely covered with long white patches of foam lying along the direction of the wind. Everywhere the edges of the wave crests are blown into froth. Visibility is reduced.	11	37
73 or more	64 or more	Hurricane	The air is filled with foam and spray. Sea completely white with driving spray; visibility very much reduced.	12	45

ATMOSPHERIC PRESSURE CONVERSION TABLE

Inches	Millibars	Inches	Millibars	Inches	Millibars
28.44	963	29.32	993	30.21	1023
28.53	966	29.41	996	30.30	1026
28.62	969	29.50	999	30.39	1029
28.70	972	29.59	1002	30.48	1032
28.79	975	29.68	1005	30.56	1035
28.88	978	29.77	1008	30.65	1038
28.97	981	29.86	1011	30.74	1041
29.06	984	29.94	1014	30.83	1044
29.15	987	30.03	1017	30.92	1047
29.24	990	30.12	1020	31.01	1050

Distance of Visibility of Objects at Sea

The following table gives the approximate geographic range of visibility for an object which may be seen by an observer whose eye is at sea level; in practice, therefore, it is necessary to add to these a distance of visibility corresponding to the height of the observer's eye above sea level.

Height, feet	Nautical miles	Height, feet	Nautical miles	Height, feet	Nautical miles	Height, feet	Nautical miles	Height, feet	Nautical miles
6	2.8	48	7.9	220	17.0	660	29.4	2,000	51.2
8	3.1	50	8.1	240	17.7	680	29.9	2,200	53.8
10	3.6	55	8.5	260	18.5	700	30.3	2,400	56.2
12	4.0	60	8.9	280	19.2	720	30.7	2,600	58.5
14	4.3	65	9.2	300	19.9	740	31.1	2,800	60.6
15	4.4	70	9.6	320	20.5	760	31.6	3,000	62.8
16	4.6	75	9.9	340	21.1	780	32.0	3,200	64.9
18	4.9	80	10.3	360	21.7	800	32.4	3,400	66.9
20	5.1	85	10.6	380	22.3	820	32.8	3,600	68.6
22	5.4	90	10.9	400	22.9	840	33.2	3,800	70.7
24	5.6	95	11.2	420	23.5	860	33.6	4,000	72.5
26	5.8	100	11.5	440	24.1	880	34.0	4,200	74.3
28	6.1	110	12.0	460	24.6	900	34.4	4,400	76.1
30	6.3	120	12.6	480	25.1	920	34.7	4,600	77.7
32	6.5	130	13.1	500	25.6	940	35.2	4,800	79.4
34	6.7	140	13.6	520	26.1	960	35.5	5,000	81.0
36	6.9	150	14.1	540	26.7	980	35.9	6,000	88.8
38	7.0	160	14.5	560	27.1	1,000	36.2	7,000	96.0
40	7.2	170	14.9	580	27.6	1,200	39.6	8,000	102.6
42	7.4	180	15.4	600	28.0	1,400	42.9	9,000	108.7
44	7.6	190	15.8	620	28.6	1,600	45.8	10,000	114.6
46	7.8	200	16.2	640	29.0	1,800	48.6		

Conversion Table, Degrees to Points and Vice Versa

° '	Points	° '	Points	° '	Points	° '	Points
0 00	N	90 00	E	180 00	S	270 00	W
2 49		92 49		182 49		272 49	
5 38	N ½ E	95 38	E ½ S	185 38	S ½ W	275 38	W ½ N
8 26		98 26		188 26		278 26	
11 15	N x E	101 15	E x S	191 15	S x W	281 15	W x N
14 04		104 04		194 04		284 04	
16 53	N x E ½ E	106 53	ESE ½ E	196 53	S x W ½ W	286 53	WNW ½ W
19 41		109 41		199 41		289 41	
22 30	NNE	112 30	ESE	202 30	SSW	292 30	WNW
25 19		115 19		205 19		295 19	
28 08	NNE ½ E	118 08	SE x E ½ E	208 08	SSW ½ W	298 08	NW x W ½ W
30 56		120 56		210 56		300 56	
33 45	NE x N	123 45	SE x E	213 45	SW x S	303 45	NW x W
36 34		126 34		216 34		306 34	
39 23	NE ½ N	129 23	SE ½ E	219 23	SW ½ S	309 23	NW ½ W
42 11		132 11		222 11		312 11	
45 00	NE	135 00	SE	225 00	SW	315 00	NW
47 49		137 49		227 49		317 49	
50 38	NE ½ E	140 38	SE ½ S	230 38	SW ½ W	320 38	NW ½ N
53 26		143 26		233 26		323 26	
56 15	NE x E	146 15	SE x S	236 15	SW x W	326 15	NW x N
59 04		149 04		239 04		329 04	
61 53	NE x E ½ E	151 53	SSE ½ E	241 53	SW x W ½ W	331 53	NNW ½ W
64 41		154 41		244 41		334 41	
67 30	ENE	157 30	SSE	247 30	WSW	337 30	NNW
70 19		160 19		250 19		340 19	
73 08	ENE ½ E	163 08	S x E ½ E	253 08	WSW ½ W	343 08	N x W ½ W
75 56		165 56		255 56		345 56	
78 45	E x N	168 45	S x E	258 45	W x S	348 45	N x W
81 34		171 34		261 34		351 34	
84 23	E ½ N	174 23	S ½ E	264 23	W ½ S	354 23	N ½ W
87 11		177 11		267 11		357 11	

Conversion Tables

INTERNATIONAL NAUTICAL MILES TO STATUTE MILES

1 nautical mile   6,076.10 feet or 1,852 meters   1 statute mile = 5,280 feet or 1,609.35 meters

Nautical miles	0	1	2	3	4	5	6	7	8	9
0	0.000	1.151	2.302	3.452	4.603	5.754	6.905	8.055	9.206	10.357
10	11.508	12.659	13.809	14.960	16.111	17.262	18.412	19.563	20.714	21.865
20	23.016	24.166	25.317	26.468	27.619	28.769	29.920	31.071	32.222	33.373
30	34.523	35.674	36.825	37.976	39.126	40.277	41.428	42.579	43.730	44.880
40	46.031	47.182	48.333	49.483	50.634	51.785	52.936	54.087	55.237	56.388
50	57.539	58.690	59.840	60.991	62.142	63.293	64.444	65.594	66.745	67.896
60	69.047	70.197	71.348	72.499	73.650	74.801	75.951	77.102	78.253	79.404
70	80.554	81.705	82.856	84.007	85.158	86.308	87.459	88.610	89.761	90.911
80	92.062	93.213	94.364	95.515	96.665	97.816	98.967	100.118	101.268	102.419
90	103.570	104.721	105.871	107.022	108.173	109.324	110.475	111.625	112.776	113.927

STATUTE MILES TO INTERNATONAL NAUTICAL MILES

Statute miles	0	1	2	3	4	5	6	7	8	9
0	0.000	0.869	1.738	2.607	3.476	4.345	5.214	6.083	6.952	7.821
10	8.690	9.559	10.428	11.297	12.166	13.035	13.904	14.773	15.642	16.511
20	17.380	18.249	19.118	19.986	20.855	21.724	22.593	23.462	24.331	25.200
30	26.069	26.938	27.807	28.676	29.545	30.414	31.283	32.152	33.021	33.890
40	34.759	35.628	36.497	37.366	38.235	39.104	39.973	40.842	41.711	42.580
50	43.449	44.318	45.187	46.056	46.925	47.794	48.663	49.532	50.401	51.270
60	52.139	53.008	53.877	54.746	55.615	56.484	57.353	58.222	59.091	59.959
70	60.828	61.697	62.566	63.435	64.304	65.173	66.042	66.911	67.780	68.649
80	69.518	70.387	71.256	72.125	72.994	73.863	74.732	75.601	76.470	77.339
90	78.208	79.077	79.946	80.815	81.684	82.553	83.422	84.291	85.160	86.029

FEET TO METERS

Feet	0	1	2	3	4	5	6	7	8	9
0	0.00	0.30	0.61	0.91	1.22	1.52	1.83	2.13	2.44	2.74
10	3.05	3.35	3.66	3.96	4.27	4.57	4.88	5.18	5.49	5.79
20	6.10	6.40	6.71	7.01	7.32	7.62	7.92	8.23	8.53	8.84
30	9.14	9.45	9.75	10.06	10.36	10.67	10.97	11.28	11.58	11.89
40	12.19	12.50	12.80	13.11	13.41	13.72	14.02	14.33	14.63	14.93
50	15.24	15.54	15.85	16.15	16.46	16.76	17.07	17.37	17.68	17.98
60	18.29	18.59	18.90	19.20	19.51	19.81	20.12	20.42	20.73	21.03
70	21.34	21.64	21.95	22.25	22.55	22.86	23.16	23.47	23.77	24.08
80	24.38	24.69	24.99	25.30	25.60	25.91	26.21	26.52	26.82	27.13
90	27.43	27.74	28.04	28.35	28.65	28.96	29.26	29.57	29.87	30.17

METERS TO FEET

Meters	0	1	2	3	4	5	6	7	8	9
0	0.00	3.28	6.56	9.84	13.12	16.40	19.68	22.97	26.25	29.53
10	32.81	36.09	39.37	42.65	45.93	49.21	52.49	55.77	59.06	62.34
20	65.62	68.90	72.18	75.46	78.74	82.02	85.30	88.58	91.86	95.14
30	98.42	101.71	104.99	108.27	111.55	114.83	118.11	121.39	124.67	127.95
40	131.23	134.51	137.80	141.08	144.36	147.64	150.92	154.20	157.48	160.76
50	164.04	167.32	170.60	173.88	177.16	180.45	183.73	187.01	190.29	193.57
60	196.85	200.13	203.41	206.69	209.97	213.25	216.54	219.82	223.10	226.38
70	229.66	232.94	236.22	239.50	242.78	246.06	249.34	252.62	255.90	259.19
80	262.47	265.75	269.03	272.31	275.59	278.87	282.15	285.43	288.71	291.99
90	295.28	298.56	301.84	305.12	308.40	311.68	314.96	318.24	321.52	324.80

Radio Bearing Conversion Table

Table of corrections, in minutes

[DIFFERENCE OF LONGITUTE IN DEGREES]

Mid. L.	½°	1°	1½°	2°	2½°	3°	3½°	4°	4½°	5°	5½°	6°	6½°	7°	7½°	8°	8½°	9°	9½°	10°
15°	4	8	12	16	19	23	27	31	35	40	43	47	50	54	58	62	66	70	74	78
16°	4	8	12	17	21	25	29	33	37	41	45	50	54	58	62	66	70	74	79	83
17°	4	9	13	18	22	26	31	35	39	44	48	53	57	61	66	70	75	79	83	88
18°	5	9	13	19	23	28	32	37	42	46	51	56	60	65	70	74	79	83	88	93
19°	5	10	15	20	24	29	34	39	44	49	54	59	63	68	73	78	83	88	93	98
20°	5	10	15	21	26	31	36	41	46	51	56	62	67	72	77	82	87	92	98	103
21°	5	11	16	21	27	32	38	43	48	54	59	64	70	75	81	86	91	97	102	108
22°	6	11	17	22	28	34	39	45	51	56	62	67	73	79	84	90	96	101	107	112
23°	6	12	18	23	29	35	41	47	53	59	64	70	76	82	88	94	100	105	111	117
24°	6	12	18	24	31	37	43	49	55	61	67	73	79	85	92	98	104	110	116	122
25°	6	13	19	25	32	38	44	51	57	63	70	76	82	89	95	101	108	114	120	127
26°	7	13	20	26	33	39	46	53	59	66	72	79	85	92	99	105	112	118	125	131
27°	7	14	20	27	34	41	48	54	61	68	75	82	89	95	102	109	116	123	129	136
28°	7	14	21	28	35	42	49	56	63	70	77	84	92	99	106	113	120	127	134	141
29°	7	15	21	29	36	44	51	58	65	73	80	87	95	102	109	116	124	131	138	145
30°	7	15	22	30	38	45	53	60	68	75	83	90	98	105	113	120	127	135	143	150
31°	8	15	23	31	39	46	54	62	70	77	85	93	100	108	116	124	131	139	146	155
32°	8	16	24	32	40	48	56	64	72	79	87	95	103	111	119	127	135	143	151	159
33°	8	16	25	33	41	49	57	65	74	82	90	98	106	114	123	131	139	147	155	163
34°	8	17	25	34	42	50	59	67	75	84	92	101	109	117	126	134	143	151	159	168
35°	9	17	26	34	43	52	60	69	77	86	95	103	112	120	129	138	146	155	163	172
36°	9	18	26	35	44	53	62	71	79	88	97	106	115	123	132	141	150	159	168	176
37°	9	18	27	36	45	54	63	72	81	90	99	108	117	126	135	144	153	163	172	181
38°	9	18	28	37	46	55	65	74	83	92	102	111	120	129	139	148	157	166	175	185
39°	9	19	28	38	47	57	66	75	85	94	104	113	123	132	142	151	160	170	179	189
40°	10	19	29	39	48	58	68	77	87	96	106	116	125	135	145	154	164	174	183	193
41°	10	20	30	39	49	59	69	79	89	98	108	118	128	138	148	157	167	177	187	197
42°	10	20	30	40	50	60	70	80	90	100	110	120	130	140	151	161	171	181	191	201
43°	10	20	31	41	51	61	72	82	92	102	113	123	133	143	153	164	174	184	194	205
44°	10	21	31	42	52	63	73	83	94	104	115	125	135	146	156	167	177	188	198	208
45°	11	21	32	42	53	64	74	85	95	106	117	127	138	149	159	170	180	191	201	212
46°	11	22	32	43	54	65	76	86	97	108	119	129	140	151	162	173	183	194	205	216
47°	11	22	33	44	55	66	77	88	99	110	121	132	143	154	165	176	186	197	208	219
48°	11	22	33	45	56	67	78	89	100	111	123	134	145	156	167	178	190	201	212	223
49°	11	23	34	45	57	68	79	91	102	113	125	136	147	158	170	181	192	204	215	226
50°	11	23	34	46	57	69	80	92	103	115	126	138	149	161	172	184	195	207	218	230
51°	12	23	35	47	58	70	82	93	105	117	128	140	152	163	175	186	198	210	221	233
52°	12	24	35	47	59	71	83	95	106	118	130	142	154	165	177	189	201	213	225	236
53°	12	24	36	48	60	72	84	96	108	120	132	144	156	168	180	192	204	216	228	240
54°	12	24	36	49	61	73	85	97	109	121	133	146	158	170	182	194	206	218	231	243
55°	12	25	37	49	61	74	86	98	111	123	135	147	160	172	184	197	209	221	233	246
56°	12	25	37	50	62	75	87	100	112	124	137	149	162	174	187	199	211	224	236	249
57°	13	25	38	50	63	75	88	101	113	126	138	151	164	176	189	201	214	226	239	252
58°	13	25	38	51	64	76	89	102	115	127	140	153	165	178	191	204	216	229	242	254
59°	13	26	39	51	64	77	90	103	116	129	141	154	167	180	193	206	219	231	244	257
60°	13	26	39	52	65	78	91	104	117	130	143	156	169	182	195	208	221	234	247	260

Example.   A ship in latitude 39°51'. N., longitude 67°35' W., by dead reckoning, obtains a radio bearing of 299° true on the radiobeacon located in latitude 40°37'. N., longitude 69°37' W.

Radiobeacon station	Latitute	40°37' N.
Dead-reckoning position of ship	Latitute	39°51'
Middle latitude		40°14'
Radiobeacon station	Longitute	69°37' W.
Dead-reckoning position of ship	Longitute	67°35'
Longitude difference		2°02'

Entering the table with a difference of longitude of 2°, which is the nearest tabulated value and opposite 40° middle latitude, the correction of 39' is read.

As the ship is east of the radiobeacon, a minus correction is applied. The Mercator bearing then will be 299° – 000°39' = 298°21'. To facilitate plotting, subtract 180° and plot from the position of the radiobeacon the bearing 298°21' – 180°, or 118°21' (Mercator bearing reckoned clockwise from true north).

MEAN SURFACE WATER TEMPERATURES (T) AND DENSITIES (D)

Stations	Years	Jan (T) °C	Jan (D) σ_{15}	Feb (T) °C	Feb (D) σ_{15}	Mar (T) °C	Mar (D) σ_{15}	Apr (T) °C	Apr (D) σ_{15}	May (T) °C	May (D) σ_{15}	June (T) °C	June (D) σ_{15}	July (T) °C	July (D) σ_{15}	Aug (T) °C	Aug (D) σ_{15}	Sept (T) °C	Sept (D) σ_{15}	Oct (T) °C	Oct (D) σ_{15}	Nov (T) °C	Nov (D) σ_{15}	Dec (T) °C	Dec (D) σ_{15}	Mean (T) °C	Mean (D) σ_{15}
La Jolla, Calif. 32°52'N., 117°15'W	56	13.9	24.9	13.9	24.8	14.4	24.8	15.4	24.9	16.9	25.0	18.4	25.0	19.9	25.0	20.8	25.0	19.3	24.9	18.0	24.9	16.3	24.9	14.9	24.9	16.8	24.9
Newport Bay, Calif. 33°36'N., 117°53'W	17	14.0	24.4	14.5	24.4	15.4	24.5	16.6	24.5	17.7	24.9	19.0	25.0	20.3	25.0	21.2	25.0	19.9	25.0	18.7	24.9	16.4	24.6	14.7	24.5	17.4	24.7
Los Angeles (Outer Harbor), Calif. 33°43'N., 118°16'W	49	13.9	24.7	14.2	24.6	14.7	24.8	15.4	24.9	16.2	25.1	17.7	25.1	18.9	25.1	19.7	25.1	19.0	25.1	18.1	25.0	16.5	24.9	14.8	24.8	16.6	24.9
Santa Monica, Calif. 34°00'N., 118°30'W	27	13.5	24.9	13.7	24.9	13.9	25.0	14.7	25.0	15.7	25.2	17.5	25.2	19.2	25.2	19.9	25.2	19.0	25.1	17.6	25.0	15.7	25.0	14.3	24.9	16.2	25.0
Avila Beach, Calif. 35°10'N., 120°44'W	27	12.4	24.5	12.5	24.4	12.3	24.7	12.5	24.9	13.1	25.2	14.1	25.4	15.4	25.4	15.9	25.3	15.7	25.2	15.0	25.1	13.9	24.9	12.8	24.8	13.8	25.0
Pacific Grove, Calif. 36°37'N., 121°54'W	51	11.8	24.7	12.0	24.6	12.2	24.6	12.4	24.7	12.8	24.9	13.4	25.0	13.8	25.0	13.9	25.0	14.2	25.0	13.7	24.9	12.9	24.8	12.4	24.8	13.0	24.8
San Francisco (Ft. Point), Calif. 37°48'N., 122°28'W	51	10.4	21.1	10.9	20.0	11.6	19.9	12.4	20.0	13.1	20.7	13.9	21.5	14.7	22.9	15.2	23.7	15.5	23.8	14.8	23.8	13.0	23.2	11.2	22.4	13.1	21.9
Alameda, Calif. 37°47'N., 122°18'W	33	10.3	17.3	11.9	15.6	13.9	15.7	16.1	16.5	17.8	17.6	19.4	18.7	20.5	20.5	20.5	21.8	20.2	22.4	17.7	21.9	14.4	21.1	11.4	19.5	16.2	19.0
Crescent City, Calif. 41°45'N., 124°12'W	37	9.6	20.8	9.9	20.7	10.2	21.1	10.7	21.8	11.5	22.6	12.5	23.3	13.6	24.0	14.3	24.1	13.5	24.2	12.1	24.0	11.2	22.8	10.2	21.8	11.7	22.6
Astoria (Tongue Pt.), Oreg. 46°13'N., 123°46'W	48	4.7	0.1	5.4	-0.2	7.4	-0.5	10.5	-0.7	13.4	-0.7	15.8	-0.6	18.6	-0.5	19.3	-0.2	17.5	0.4	14.0	1.0	9.4	0.9	6.2	0.5	11.8	0.0
Neah Bay, Wash. 48°22'N., 124°37'W	37	7.3	22.4	7.4	22.2	7.9	22.5	9.1	22.7	10.6	23.2	11.6	23.2	11.8	23.7	11.6	23.9	11.3	23.8	10.6	23.4	9.4	22.9	8.2	22.5	9.7	23.0
Seattle (Elliott Bay), Wash. 47°36'N., 122°20'W	50	8.6	20.4	8.2	20.0	8.2	19.9	8.9	19.5	10.3	19.5	11.9	19.9	13.1	20.7	13.4	21.4	13.0	21.8	12.2	21.8	10.8	21.5	9.6	20.9	10.7	20.6
Hilo, Hawaii 19°44'N., 155°03'W	26	22.3	19.6	22.2	19.2	22.1	19.0	22.2	17.6	22.7	18.2	23.3	18.9	23.7	18.5	23.9	18.6	24.2	19.2	24.1	19.5	23.5	19.3	22.7	18.9	23.1	18.9
Honolulu, Hawaii 21°18'N., 157°52'W	28	24.4	25.4	24.3	25.6	24.3	25.6	24.7	25.8	25.4	25.8	26.0	25.8	26.4	25.9	26.8	25.9	26.9	25.9	26.9	25.9	26.1	25.8	25.0	25.7	25.6	25.8
Kaneohe Bay, Hawaii 21°26'N., 157°48'W	16	22.7	25.3	22.7	25.4	23.3	25.1	23.8	25.3	25.1	25.4	26.2	25.9	26.3	25.9	26.6	26.0	26.7	26.0	26.2	25.9	24.7	25.6	23.1	25.4	24.8	25.6
Midway Islands 28°13'N., 177°22'W	28	19.7	26.4	19.5	26.4	20.1	26.5	21.0	26.5	22.7	26.6	25.1	26.7	26.4	26.7	26.9	26.6	26.9	26.6	25.1	26.5	23.2	26.5	21.3	26.4	23.2	26.5

F (Fahrenheit) = 1.8C (Celsius) + 32

Density as used in this table is the specific gravity of the sea water or the ratio between the weight of a sea-water sample and the weight of an equal volume of distilled water at 15°C (59°F). These figures representing density at 15°C (ρ_{15}) are expressed in terms of sigma-t (σ_t) where t = 15°C and $\sigma_{15} = (\rho_{15} - 1)$ 1000. Thus, for ρ_{15} = 1.0238, σ_{15} = 23.8. Obtain the pamphlet, "Surface Water Temperature and Density, Pacific Coast, North and South America and Pacific Ocean Islands. NOS Publication 31-3," for greater detail: for sale by Superintendent of Documents. U.S. Government Printing Office, Washington, D.C. 20402, price $1.00.

These tables were prepared by the National Environmental Satellite, Data, and Information Service. Station level pressure refers to the actual pressure taken at the elevation of the station. Where it has been reduced to sea level, the term sea level pressure is used. Time given is local standard time.

* means less than 0.5 percent.
** means less than 0.5 day.
t means trace (not measurable) of precipitation.

SAN DIEGO, CALIFORNIA (32°44'N., 117°10'W.) Elevation 13 ft. (4.0m)

WEATHER ELEMENTS	JAN.	FEB.	MAR.	APR.	MAY	JUNE	JULY	AUG.	SEPT.	OCT.	NOV.	DEC.	YEAR	YEARS OF RECORD
SEA LEVEL PRESSURE														
Mean (Millibars)	1018.7	1017.9	1016.7	1015.8	1014.7	1013.1	1013.2	1012.9	1011.9	1014.2	1016.9	1018.0	1015.3	28
TEMPERATURE (DEGREES F)														
Mean	55.2	56.7	58.1	60.7	63.3	65.5	69.6	71.4	69.9	66.1	60.8	56.7	62.9	30
Mean Daily Maximum	64.6	65.6	66.0	67.6	69.4	71.1	75.3	77.3	76.5	73.8	70.1	66.1	70.3	30
Mean Daily Minimum	45.8	47.8	50.1	53.8	57.2	59.9	63.9	65.4	63.2	58.4	51.5	47.2	55.4	30
Extreme Highest	86	85	85	91	91	90	92	90	111	107	97	88	111	15
Extreme Lowest	31	38	39	44	48	51	57	58	56	43	38	36	31	15
RELATIVE HUMIDITY														
Average Percentage (1000 l.s.t.)	54	56	59	58	64	69	69	67	65	58	57	55	61	15
Average Percentage (1600 l.s.t.)	55	57	59	58	63	67	66	66	64	61	63	57	61	15
CLOUD COVER														
Average Amount (Tenths)	4.9	5.0	5.2	5.2	5.7	5.6	4.5	4.1	4.0	4.3	4.1	4.7	4.8	35
Mean Number of Days with Clear Skies	13	11	11	10	9	9	13	15	16	15	15	14	151	35
Mean Number of Days with Cloudy Skies	11	10	10	10	11	9	5	4	5	7	7	9	98	35
PRECIPITATION														
Mean Amount (Inches)	1.88	1.48	1.55	0.81	0.15	0.05	0.01	0.07	0.13	0.34	1.25	1.73	9.45	30
Greatest Amount (Inches)	6.26	5.31	5.89	3.58	0.95	0.38	0.13	0.87	1.90	2.90	5.82	7.60	24.93	35
Least Amount (Inches)	t	0.00	t	t	0.00	0.00	0.00	0.00	0.00	0.00	0.00	0.03	3.41	35
Maximum in 24 hrs. (Inches)	2.65	1.71	2.40	1.40	0.42	0.28	0.10	0.83	0.90	1.20	2.44	3.07	3.07	35
Mean Amount of Snow (Inches)	t	0.0	0.0	0.0	0.0	0.0	0.0	0.0	0.0	0.0	0.0	t	t	35
Maximum Snowfall in 24 hrs. (Inches)	t	0.0	0.0	0.0	0.0	0.0	0.0	0.0	0.0	0.0	0.0	t	.t	35
Mean Number of Days with Snow (One Inch or More)	0	0	0	0	0	0	0	0	0	0	0	0	0	35
0.01 Inch or More, Mean Number of Days	6	6	7	5	2	1	**	**	1	2	5	6	41	35
WIND														
Mean Wind Speed (Knots) (0700 l.s.t.)	2.8	3.0	3.6	4.2	4.4	4.5	3.7	3.5	3.4	2.8	2.6	2.7		28
Mean Wind Speed (Knots) (1300 l.s.t.)	7.4	8.5	9.6	10.3	10.1	9.6	9.0	9.2	9.5	9.0	8.2	7.4		28
Direction (Percentage of Obs.): at 0700 l.s.t.														
North	7.0	7.8	6.6	6.9	6.0	6.7	9.4	9.6	14.8	11.0	8.8	8.2		28
North Northeast	3.7	3.5	2.9	2.7	2.1	2.7	2.4	3.9	4.8	4.5	3.9	4.1		28
Northeast	2.6	2.9	2.4	1.6	1.1	0.9	1.0	1.3	1.5	3.0	2.9	3.1		28
East Northeast	2.1	2.0	1.6	1.2	0.5	0.7	0.5	0.2	0.7	1.4	1.7	2.4		28
East	10.3	8.8	8.0	3.9	1.5	0.8	0.4	0.8	1.5	4.2	8.4	9.8		28
East Southeast	11.5	9.3	8.7	4.9	2.4	1.1	0.2	0.9	1.8	5.1	8.3	9.0		28
Southeast	8.6	8.8	10.3	6.8	4.3	3.4	1.5	2.2	3.1	8.0	8.2	9.2		28
South Southeast	3.8	4.5	5.8	7.8	7.7	6.5	4.4	4.5	4.7	5.0	4.3	3.3		28
South	3.0	3.5	4.3	8.4	12.0	14.9	10.2	9.9	7.3	4.7	3.3	2.3		28
South Southwest	1.4	1.3	2.2	3.9	8.9	9.4	9.1	6.2	4.3	2.0	1.3	1.0		28
Southwest	1.2	1.1	2.8	4.7	7.6	9.0	6.4	4.6	3.6	2.6	1.3	1.4		28
West Southwest	1.0	1.5	1.8	3.2	5.3	4.5	2.9	3.4	2.5	1.5	0.9	1.3		28
West	2.2	3.5	4.5	7.7	9.8	6.4	6.3	6.5	4.9	2.8	2.6	2.3		28
West Northwest	2.0	2.8	3.8	6.4	6.8	5.8	7.6	7.4	5.1	3.3	2.5	1.5		28
Northwest	3.2	3.4	4.8	6.5	6.9	9.7	14.9	12.6	9.7	5.4	3.0	2.8		28
North Northwest	2.8	2.1	3.0	5.0	5.0	6.7	9.7	10.2	12.0	6.5	3.3	2.4		28
Calm	33.5	33.1	26.5	18.5	12.1	10.9	13.0	15.7	17.5	29.0	35.2	35.8		28
Direction (Percentage of Obs.): at 1300 l.s.t.														
North	3.0	1.5	0.8	0.2	0.3	0.2	0.4	0.4	0.8	1.1	1.9	3.7		28
North Northeast	0.5	0.2	0.1	0.2	0.1	0.0	0.2	0.0	0.1	0.2	0.2	0.6		28
Northeast	0.6	0.1	0.1	*	0.0	0.0	0.1	0.0	*	0.3	0.2	0.7		28
East Northeast	0.2	0.1	0.1	*	0.1	0.0	0.0	0.0	0.0	0.1	0.4	0.5		28
East	0.4	0.1	0.1	0.0	0.0	0.0	0.0	0.0	0.2	0.4	0.5	0.4		28
East Southeast	0.4	0.1	0.1	*	0.1	0.0	0.0	0.0	0.0	0.2	0.3	0.6		28
Southeast	1.2	0.4	0.2	*	0.1	0.0	0.2	*	*	0.2	0.6	1.2		28
South Southeast	3.3	1.9	1.6	0.9	0.4	0.2	0.1	0.2	0.6	0.6	2.2	2.1		28
South	8.6	8.1	6.4	5.1	4.5	5.2	3.5	3.0	4.0	4.1	7.1	7.5		28
South Southwest	8.1	6.6	7.9	9.2	10.6	14.0	12.9	9.6	7.2	6.5	6.9	6.9		28
Southwest	6.3	7.1	6.1	8.5	10.4	13.0	8.7	8.5	7.0	6.6	6.1	6.9		28
West Southwest	4.2	4.1	7.8	8.1	10.6	8.9	6.7	6.7	4.4	5.5	4.1	3.7		28
West	12.0	13.8	20.9	21.7	25.0	22.5	20.1	21.9	15.6	16.8	13.0	11.7		28
West Northwest	16.1	18.9	22.0	24.9	20.9	22.1	25.1	27.9	26.5	22.3	19.2	13.2		28
Northwest	24.2	28.9	19.2	18.3	14.8	12.5	19.4	19.2	27.9	26.3	28.0	25.3		28
North Northwest	8.5	7.0	4.4	2.8	2.3	1.5	2.6	2.6	5.4	8.7	8.2	11.9		28
Calm	2.3	1.1	0.2	*	*	*	0.1	*	0.2	0.3	1.1	3.2		28
VISIBILITY														
Days with Visibility equal to or less than 1/4 mile	4	3	2	1	1	1	1	1	3	4	4	4	28	35

Nautical & Statute Miles

CONVERSION TABLE

Nautical miles to statute miles				Statute miles to nautical miles			
Nautical miles	Statute miles	Nautical miles	Statute miles	Statute miles	Nautical miles	Statute miles	Nautical miles
1	1. 151	51	58. 690	1	0. 869	51	44. 318
2	2. 302	52	59. 841	2	1. 738	52	45. 187
3	3. 452	53	60. 991	3	2. 607	53	46. 056
4	4. 603	54	62. 142	4	3. 476	54	46. 925
5	5. 754	55	63. 293	5	4. 345	55	47. 794
6	6. 905	56	64. 444	6	5. 214	56	48. 663
7	8. 055	57	65. 594	7	6. 083	57	49. 532
8	9. 206	58	66. 745	8	6. 952	58	50. 401
9	10. 357	59	67. 896	9	7. 821	59	51. 270
10	11. 508	60	69. 047	10	8. 690	60	52. 139
11	12. 659	61	70. 198	11	9. 559	61	53. 008
12	13. 809	62	71. 348	12	10. 428	62	53. 877
13	14. 960	63	72. 499	13	11. 297	63	54. 746
14	16. 111	64	73. 650	14	12. 166	64	55. 614
15	17. 262	65	74. 801	15	13. 035	65	56. 483
16	18. 412	66	75. 951	16	13. 904	66	57. 352
17	19. 563	67	77. 102	17	14. 773	67	58. 221
18	20. 714	68	78. 253	18	15. 642	68	59. 090
19	21. 865	69	79. 404	19	16. 511	69	59. 959
20	23. 016	70	80. 555	20	17. 380	70	60. 828
21	24. 166	71	81. 705	21	18. 249	71	61. 697
22	25. 317	72	82. 856	22	19. 117	72	62. 566
23	26. 468	73	84. 007	23	19. 986	73	63. 435
24	27. 619	74	85. 158	24	20. 855	74	64. 304
25	28. 769	75	86. 308	25	21. 724	75	65. 173
26	29. 920	76	87. 459	26	22. 593	76	66. 042
27	31. 071	77	88. 610	27	23. 462	77	66. 911
28	32. 222	78	89. 761	28	24. 331	78	67. 780
29	33. 373	79	90. 912	29	25. 200	79	68. 649
30	34. 523	80	92. 062	30	26. 069	80	69. 518
31	35. 674	81	93. 213	31	26. 938	81	70. 387
32	36. 825	82	94. 364	32	27. 807	82	71. 256
33	37. 976	83	95. 515	33	28. 676	83	72. 125
34	39. 127	84	96. 665	34	29. 545	84	72. 994
35	40. 277	85	97. 816	35	30. 414	85	73. 863
36	41. 428	86	98. 967	36	31. 283	86	74. 732
37	42. 579	87	100. 118	37	32. 152	87	75. 601
38	43. 730	88	101. 269	38	33. 021	88	76. 470
39	44. 880	89	102. 419	39	33. 890	89	77. 339
40	46. 031	90	103. 570	40	34. 759	90	78. 208
41	47. 182	91	104. 721	41	35. 628	91	79. 077
42	48. 333	92	105. 872	42	36. 497	92	79. 946
43	49. 484	93	107. 022	43	37. 366	93	80. 815
44	50. 634	94	108. 173	44	38. 235	94	81. 684
45	51. 785	95	109. 324	45	39. 104	95	82. 553
46	52. 936	96	110. 475	46	39. 973	96	83. 422
47	54. 087	97	111. 626	47	40. 842	97	84. 291
48	55. 237	98	112. 776	48	41. 711	98	85. 160
49	56. 388	99	113. 927	49	42. 580	99	86. 029
50	57. 539	100	115. 078	50	43. 449	100	86. 898

Speed-Time-Distance

Min-utes	Speed in knots																Min-utes
	0.5	1.0	1.5	2.0	2.5	3.0	3.5	4.0	4.5	5.0	5.5	6.0	6.5	7.0	7.5	8.0	
	Miles	Miles	Miles	Miles	Miles	Miles	Miles	Miles	Miles	Miles	Miles	Miles	Miles	Miles	Miles	Miles	
1	0.0	0.0	0.0	0.0	0.0	0.0	0.1	0.1	0.1	0.1	0.1	0.1	0.1	0.1	0.1	0.1	1
2	0.0	0.0	0.0	0.1	0.1	0.1	0.1	0.1	0.2	0.2	0.2	0.2	0.2	0.2	0.2	0.3	2
3	0.0	0.0	0.1	0.1	0.1	0.2	0.2	0.2	0.2	0.2	0.3	0.3	0.3	0.4	0.4	0.4	3
4	0.0	0.1	0.1	0.1	0.2	0.2	0.2	0.3	0.3	0.3	0.4	0.4	0.4	0.5	0.5	0.5	4
5	0.0	0.1	0.1	0.2	0.2	0.2	0.3	0.3	0.4	0.4	0.5	0.5	0.5	0.6	0.6	0.7	5
6	0.0	0.1	0.2	0.2	0.2	0.3	0.4	0.4	0.4	0.5	0.6	0.6	0.6	0.7	0.8	0.8	6
7	0.1	0.1	0.2	0.2	0.3	0.4	0.4	0.5	0.5	0.6	0.6	0.7	0.8	0.8	0.9	0.9	7
8	0.1	0.1	0.2	0.3	0.3	0.4	0.5	0.5	0.6	0.7	0.7	0.8	0.9	0.9	1.0	1.1	8
9	0.1	0.2	0.2	0.3	0.4	0.4	0.5	0.6	0.7	0.8	0.8	0.9	1.0	1.0	1.1	1.2	9
10	0.1	0.2	0.2	0.3	0.4	0.5	0.6	0.7	0.8	0.8	0.9	1.0	1.1	1.2	1.2	1.3	10
11	0.1	0.2	0.3	0.4	0.5	0.6	0.6	0.7	0.8	0.9	1.0	1.1	1.2	1.3	1.4	1.5	11
12	0.1	0.2	0.3	0.4	0.5	0.6	0.7	0.8	0.9	1.0	1.1	1.2	1.3	1.4	1.5	1.6	12
13	0.1	0.2	0.3	0.4	0.5	0.6	0.8	0.9	1.0	1.1	1.2	1.3	1.4	1.5	1.6	1.7	13
14	0.1	0.2	0.4	0.5	0.6	0.7	0.8	0.9	1.0	1.2	1.3	1.4	1.5	1.6	1.8	1.9	14
15	0.1	0.2	0.4	0.5	0.6	0.8	0.9	1.0	1.1	1.2	1.4	1.5	1.6	1.8	1.9	2.0	15
16	0.1	0.3	0.4	0.5	0.7	0.8	0.9	1.1	1.2	1.3	1.5	1.6	1.7	1.9	2.0	2.1	16
17	0.1	0.3	0.4	0.6	0.7	0.8	1.0	1.1	1.3	1.4	1.6	1.7	1.8	2.0	2.1	2.3	17
18	0.2	0.3	0.4	0.6	0.8	0.9	1.0	1.2	1.4	1.5	1.6	1.8	2.0	2.1	2.2	2.4	18
19	0.2	0.3	0.5	0.6	0.8	1.0	1.1	1.3	1.4	1.6	1.7	1.9	2.1	2.2	2.4	2.5	19
20	0.2	0.3	0.5	0.7	0.8	1.0	1.2	1.3	1.5	1.7	1.8	2.0	2.2	2.3	2.5	2.7	20
21	0.2	0.4	0.5	0.7	0.9	1.0	1.2	1.4	1.6	1.8	1.9	2.1	2.3	2.4	2.6	2.8	21
22	0.2	0.4	0.6	0.7	0.9	1.1	1.3	1.5	1.6	1.8	2.0	2.2	2.4	2.6	2.8	2.9	22
23	0.2	0.4	0.6	0.8	1.0	1.2	1.3	1.5	1.7	1.9	2.1	2.3	2.5	2.7	2.9	3.1	23
24	0.2	0.4	0.6	0.8	1.0	1.2	1.4	1.6	1.8	2.0	2.2	2.4	2.6	2.8	3.0	3.2	24
25	0.2	0.4	0.6	0.8	1.0	1.2	1.5	1.7	1.9	2.1	2.3	2.5	2.7	2.9	3.1	3.3	25
26	0.2	0.4	0.6	0.9	1.1	1.3	1.5	1.7	2.0	2.2	2.4	2.6	2.8	3.0	3.2	3.5	26
27	0.2	0.4	0.7	0.9	1.1	1.4	1.6	1.8	2.0	2.2	2.5	2.7	2.9	3.2	3.4	3.6	27
28	0.2	0.5	0.7	0.9	1.2	1.4	1.6	1.9	2.1	2.3	2.6	2.8	3.0	3.3	3.5	3.7	28
29	0.2	0.5	0.7	1.0	1.2	1.4	1.7	1.9	2.2	2.4	2.7	2.9	3.1	3.4	3.6	3.9	29
30	0.2	0.5	0.8	1.0	1.2	1.5	1.8	2.0	2.2	2.5	2.8	3.0	3.2	3.5	3.8	4.0	30
31	0.3	0.5	0.8	1.0	1.3	1.6	1.8	2.1	2.3	2.6	2.8	3.1	3.4	3.6	3.9	4.1	31
32	0.3	0.5	0.8	1.1	1.3	1.6	1.9	2.1	2.4	2.7	2.9	3.2	3.5	3.7	4.0	4.3	32
33	0.3	0.6	0.8	1.1	1.4	1.6	1.9	2.2	2.5	2.8	3.0	3.3	3.6	3.8	4.1	4.4	33
34	0.3	0.6	0.8	1.1	1.4	1.7	2.0	2.3	2.6	2.8	3.1	3.4	3.7	4.0	4.2	4.5	34
35	0.3	0.6	0.9	1.2	1.5	1.8	2.0	2.3	2.6	2.9	3.2	3.5	3.8	4.1	4.4	4.7	35
36	0.3	0.6	0.9	1.2	1.5	1.8	2.1	2.4	2.7	3.0	3.3	3.6	3.9	4.2	4.5	4.8	36
37	0.3	0.6	0.9	1.2	1.5	1.8	2.2	2.5	2.8	3.1	3.4	3.7	4.0	4.3	4.6	4.9	37
38	0.3	0.6	1.0	1.3	1.6	1.9	2.2	2.5	2.8	3.2	3.5	3.8	4.1	4.4	4.8	5.1	38
39	0.3	0.6	1.0	1.3	1.6	2.0	2.3	2.6	2.9	3.2	3.6	3.9	4.2	4.6	4.9	5.2	39
40	0.3	0.7	1.0	1.3	1.7	2.0	2.3	2.7	3.0	3.3	3.7	4.0	4.3	4.7	5.0	5.3	40
41	0.3	0.7	1.0	1.4	1.7	2.0	2.4	2.7	3.1	3.4	3.8	4.1	4.4	4.8	5.1	5.5	41
42	0.4	0.7	1.0	1.4	1.8	2.1	2.4	2.8	3.2	3.5	3.8	4.2	4.6	4.9	5.2	5.6	42
43	0.4	0.7	1.1	1.4	1.8	2.2	2.5	2.9	3.2	3.6	3.9	4.3	4.7	5.0	5.4	5.7	43
44	0.4	0.7	1.1	1.5	1.8	2.2	2.6	2.9	3.3	3.7	4.0	4.4	4.8	5.1	5.5	5.9	44
45	0.4	0.8	1.1	1.5	1.9	2.2	2.6	3.0	3.4	3.8	4.1	4.5	4.9	5.2	5.6	6.0	45
46	0.4	0.8	1.2	1.5	1.9	2.3	2.7	3.1	3.4	3.8	4.2	4.6	5.0	5.4	5.8	6.1	46
47	0.4	0.8	1.2	1.6	2.0	2.4	2.7	3.1	3.5	3.9	4.3	4.7	5.1	5.5	5.9	6.3	47
48	0.4	0.8	1.2	1.6	2.0	2.4	2.8	3.2	3.6	4.0	4.4	4.8	5.2	5.6	6.0	6.4	48
49	0.4	0.8	1.2	1.6	2.0	2.4	2.9	3.3	3.7	4.1	4.5	4.9	5.3	5.7	6.1	6.5	49
50	0.4	0.8	1.2	1.7	2.1	2.5	2.9	3.3	3.8	4.2	4.6	5.0	5.4	5.8	6.2	6.7	50
51	0.4	0.8	1.3	1.7	2.1	2.6	3.0	3.4	3.8	4.2	4.7	5.1	5.5	6.0	6.4	6.8	51
52	0.4	0.9	1.3	1.7	2.2	2.6	3.0	3.5	3.9	4.3	4.8	5.2	5.6	6.1	6.5	6.9	52
53	0.4	0.9	1.3	1.8	2.2	2.6	3.1	3.5	4.0	4.4	4.9	5.3	5.7	6.2	6.6	7.1	53
54	0.4	0.9	1.4	1.8	2.2	2.7	3.2	3.6	4.0	4.5	5.0	5.4	5.8	6.3	6.8	7.2	54
55	0.5	0.9	1.4	1.8	2.3	2.8	3.2	3.7	4.1	4.6	5.0	5.5	6.0	6.4	6.9	7.3	55
56	0.5	0.9	1.4	1.9	2.3	2.8	3.3	3.7	4.2	4.7	5.1	5.6	6.1	6.5	7.0	7.5	56
57	0.5	1.0	1.4	1.9	2.4	2.8	3.3	3.8	4.3	4.8	5.2	5.7	6.2	6.6	7.1	7.6	57
58	0.5	1.0	1.4	1.9	2.4	2.9	3.4	3.9	4.4	4.8	5.3	5.8	6.3	6.8	7.2	7.7	58
59	0.5	1.0	1.5	2.0	2.5	3.0	3.4	3.9	4.4	4.9	5.4	5.9	6.4	6.9	7.4	7.9	59
60	0.5	1.0	1.5	2.0	2.5	3.0	3.5	4.0	4.5	5.0	5.5	6.0	6.5	7.0	7.5	8.0	60

Speed-Time-Distance

Min-utes	Speed in knots																Min-utes
	8.5	9.0	9.5	10.0	10.5	11.0	11.5	12.0	12.5	13.0	13.5	14.0	14.5	15.0	15.5	16.0	
	Miles	Miles	Miles	Miles	Miles	Miles	Miles	Miles	Miles	Miles	Miles	Miles	Miles	Miles	Miles	Miles	
1	0.1	0.2	0.2	0.2	0.2	0.2	0.2	0.2	0.2	0.2	0.2	0.2	0.2	0.2	0.3	0.3	1
2	0.3	0.3	0.3	0.3	0.4	0.4	0.4	0.4	0.4	0.4	0.4	0.5	0.5	0.5	0.5	0.5	2
3	0.4	0.4	0.5	0.5	0.5	0.6	0.6	0.6	0.6	0.6	0.7	0.7	0.7	0.8	0.8	0.8	3
4	0.6	0.6	0.6	0.7	0.7	0.7	0.8	0.8	0.8	0.9	0.9	0.9	1.0	1.0	1.0	1.1	4
5	0.7	0.8	0.8	0.8	0.9	0.9	1.0	1.0	1.0	1.1	1.1	1.2	1.2	1.2	1.3	1.3	5
6	0.8	0.9	1.0	1.0	1.0	1.1	1.2	1.2	1.2	1.3	1.4	1.4	1.4	1.5	1.6	1.6	6
7	1.0	1.0	1.1	1.2	1.2	1.3	1.3	1.4	1.5	1.5	1.6	1.6	1.7	1.8	1.8	1.9	7
8	1.1	1.2	1.3	1.3	1.4	1.5	1.5	1.6	1.7	1.7	1.8	1.9	1.9	2.0	2.1	2.1	8
9	1.3	1.4	1.4	1.5	1.6	1.6	1.7	1.8	1.9	2.0	2.0	2.1	2.2	2.2	2.3	2.4	9
10	1.4	1.5	1.6	1.7	1.8	1.8	1.9	2.0	2.1	2.2	2.2	2.3	2.4	2.5	2.6	2.7	10
11	1.6	1.6	1.7	1.8	1.9	2.0	2.1	2.2	2.3	2.4	2.5	2.6	2.7	2.8	2.8	2.9	11
12	1.7	1.8	1.9	2.0	2.1	2.2	2.3	2.4	2.5	2.6	2.7	2.8	2.9	3.0	3.1	3.2	12
13	1.8	2.0	2.1	2.2	2.3	2.4	2.5	2.6	2.7	2.8	2.9	3.0	3.1	3.2	3.4	3.5	13
14	2.0	2.1	2.2	2.3	2.4	2.6	2.7	2.8	2.9	3.0	3.2	3.3	3.4	3.5	3.6	3.7	14
15	2.1	2.2	2.4	2.5	2.6	2.8	2.9	3.0	3.1	3.2	3.4	3.5	3.6	3.8	3.9	4.0	15
16	2.3	2.4	2.5	2.7	2.8	2.9	3.1	3.2	3.3	3.5	3.6	3.7	3.9	4.0	4.1	4.3	16
17	2.4	2.6	2.7	2.8	3.0	3.1	3.3	3.4	3.5	3.7	3.8	4.0	4.1	4.2	4.4	4.5	17
18	2.6	2.7	2.8	3.0	3.2	3.3	3.4	3.6	3.8	3.9	4.0	4.2	4.4	4.5	4.6	4.8	18
19	2.7	2.8	3.0	3.2	3.3	3.5	3.6	3.8	4.0	4.1	4.3	4.4	4.6	4.8	4.9	5.1	19
20	2.8	3.0	3.2	3.3	3.5	3.7	3.8	4.0	4.2	4.3	4.5	4.7	4.8	5.0	5.2	5.3	20
21	3.0	3.2	3.3	3.5	3.7	3.8	4.0	4.2	4.4	4.6	4.7	4.9	5.1	5.2	5.4	5.6	21
22	3.1	3.3	3.5	3.7	3.8	4.0	4.2	4.4	4.6	4.8	5.0	5.1	5.3	5.5	5.7	5.9	22
23	3.3	3.4	3.6	3.8	4.0	4.2	4.4	4.6	4.8	5.0	5.2	5.4	5.6	5.8	5.9	6.1	23
24	3.4	3.6	3.8	4.0	4.2	4.4	4.6	4.8	5.0	5.2	5.4	5.6	5.8	6.0	6.2	6.4	24
25	3.5	3.8	4.0	4.2	4.4	4.6	4.8	5.0	5.2	5.4	5.6	5.8	6.0	6.2	6.5	6.7	25
26	3.7	3.9	4.1	4.3	4.6	4.8	5.0	5.2	5.4	5.6	5.8	6.1	6.3	6.5	6.7	6.9	26
27	3.8	4.0	4.3	4.5	4.7	5.0	5.2	5.4	5.6	5.8	6.1	6.3	6.5	6.8	7.0	7.2	27
28	4.0	4.2	4.4	4.7	4.9	5.1	5.4	5.6	5.8	6.1	6.3	6.5	6.8	7.0	7.2	7.5	28
29	4.1	4.4	4.6	4.8	5.1	5.3	5.6	5.8	6.0	6.3	6.5	6.8	7.0	7.2	7.5	7.7	29
30	4.2	4.5	4.8	5.0	5.2	5.5	5.8	6.0	6.2	6.5	6.8	7.0	7.2	7.5	7.8	8.0	30
31	4.4	4.6	4.9	5.2	5.4	5.7	5.9	6.2	6.5	6.7	7.0	7.2	7.5	7.8	8.0	8.3	31
32	4.5	4.8	5.1	5.3	5.6	5.9	6.1	6.4	6.7	6.9	7.2	7.5	7.7	8.0	8.3	8.5	32
33	4.7	5.0	5.2	5.5	5.8	6.0	6.3	6.6	6.9	7.2	7.4	7.7	8.0	8.2	8.5	8.8	33
34	4.8	5.1	5.4	5.7	6.0	6.2	6.5	6.8	7.1	7.4	7.6	7.9	8.2	8.5	8.8	9.1	34
35	5.0	5.2	5.5	5.8	6.1	6.4	6.7	7.0	7.3	7.6	7.9	8.2	8.5	8.8	9.0	9.3	35
36	5.1	5.4	5.7	6.0	6.3	6.6	6.9	7.2	7.5	7.8	8.1	8.4	8.7	9.0	9.3	9.6	36
37	5.2	5.6	5.9	6.2	6.5	6.8	7.1	7.4	7.7	8.0	8.3	8.6	8.9	9.2	9.6	9.9	37
38	5.4	5.7	6.0	6.3	6.6	7.0	7.3	7.6	7.9	8.2	8.6	8.9	9.2	9.5	9.8	10.1	38
39	5.5	5.8	6.2	6.5	6.8	7.2	7.5	7.8	8.1	8.4	8.8	9.1	9.4	9.8	10.1	10.4	39
40	5.7	6.0	6.3	6.7	7.0	7.3	7.7	8.0	8.3	8.7	9.0	9.3	9.7	10.0	10.3	10.7	40
41	5.8	6.2	6.5	6.8	7.2	7.5	7.9	8.2	8.5	8.9	9.2	9.6	9.9	10.2	10.6	10.9	41
42	6.0	6.3	6.6	7.0	7.4	7.7	8.0	8.4	8.8	9.1	9.4	9.8	10.2	10.5	10.8	11.2	42
43	6.1	6.4	6.8	7.2	7.5	7.9	8.2	8.6	9.0	9.3	9.7	10.0	10.4	10.8	11.1	11.5	43
44	6.2	6.6	7.0	7.3	7.7	8.1	8.4	8.8	9.2	9.5	9.9	10.3	10.6	11.0	11.4	11.7	44
45	6.4	6.8	7.1	7.5	7.9	8.2	8.6	9.0	9.4	9.8	10.1	10.5	10.9	11.2	11.6	12.0	45
46	6.5	6.9	7.3	7.7	8.0	8.4	8.8	9.2	9.6	10.0	10.4	10.7	11.1	11.5	11.9	12.3	46
47	6.7	7.0	7.4	7.8	8.2	8.6	9.0	9.4	9.8	10.2	10.6	11.0	11.4	11.8	12.1	12.5	47
48	6.8	7.2	7.6	8.0	8.4	8.8	9.2	9.6	10.0	10.4	10.8	11.2	11.6	12.0	12.4	12.8	48
49	6.9	7.4	7.8	8.2	8.6	9.0	9.4	9.8	10.2	10.6	11.0	11.4	11.8	12.2	12.7	13.1	49
50	7.1	7.5	7.9	8.3	8.8	9.2	9.6	10.0	10.4	10.8	11.2	11.7	12.1	12.5	12.9	13.3	50
51	7.2	7.6	8.1	8.5	8.9	9.4	9.8	10.2	10.6	11.0	11.5	11.9	12.3	12.8	13.2	13.6	51
52	7.4	7.8	8.2	8.7	9.1	9.5	10.0	10.4	10.8	11.3	11.7	12.1	12.6	13.0	13.4	13.9	52
53	7.5	8.0	8.4	8.8	9.3	9.7	10.2	10.6	11.0	11.5	11.9	12.4	12.8	13.2	13.7	14.1	53
54	7.6	8.1	8.6	9.0	9.4	9.9	10.4	10.8	11.2	11.7	12.2	12.6	13.0	13.5	14.0	14.4	54
55	7.8	8.2	8.7	9.2	9.6	10.1	10.5	11.0	11.5	11.9	12.4	12.8	13.3	13.8	14.2	14.7	55
56	7.9	8.4	8.9	9.3	9.8	10.3	10.7	11.2	11.7	12.1	12.6	13.1	13.5	14.0	14.5	14.9	56
57	8.1	8.6	9.0	9.5	10.0	10.4	11.0	11.4	11.9	12.4	12.8	13.3	13.8	14.2	14.7	15.2	57
58	8.2	8.7	9.2	9.7	10.2	10.6	11.1	11.6	12.1	12.6	13.0	13.5	14.0	14.5	15.0	15.5	58
59	8.4	8.8	9.3	9.8	10.3	10.8	11.3	11.8	12.3	12.8	13.3	13.8	14.3	14.8	15.2	15.7	59
60	8.5	9.0	9.5	10.0	10.5	11.0	11.5	12.0	12.5	13.0	13.5	14.0	14.5	15.0	15.5	16.0	60

Speed-Time-Distance

Min-utes	Speed in knots																Min-utes
	16.5	17.0	17.5	18.0	18.5	19.0	19.5	20.0	20.5	21.0	21.5	22.0	22.5	23.0	23.5	24.0	
	Miles	Miles	Miles	Miles	Miles	Miles	Miles	Miles	Miles	Miles	Miles	Miles	Miles	Miles	Miles	Miles	
1	0.3	0.3	0.3	0.3	0.3	0.3	0.3	0.3	0.3	0.4	0.4	0.4	0.4	0.4	0.4	0.4	1
2	0.6	0.6	0.6	0.6	0.6	0.6	0.6	0.6	0.7	0.7	0.7	0.7	0.8	0.8	0.8	0.8	2
3	0.8	0.8	0.9	0.9	0.9	1.0	1.0	1.0	1.0	1.0	1.1	1.1	1.1	1.2	1.2	1.2	3
4	1.1	1.1	1.2	1.2	1.2	1.3	1.3	1.3	1.4	1.4	1.4	1.5	1.5	1.5	1.6	1.6	4
5	1.4	1.4	1.5	1.5	1.5	1.6	1.6	1.7	1.7	1.8	1.8	1.8	1.9	1.9	2.0	2.0	5
6	1.6	1.7	1.8	1.8	1.8	1.9	2.0	2.0	2.0	2.1	2.2	2.2	2.2	2.3	2.4	2.4	6
7	1.9	2.0	2.0	2.1	2.2	2.2	2.3	2.3	2.4	2.4	2.5	2.6	2.6	2.7	2.7	2.8	7
8	2.2	2.3	2.3	2.4	2.5	2.5	2.6	2.7	2.7	2.8	2.9	2.9	3.0	3.1	3.1	3.2	8
9	2.5	2.6	2.6	2.7	2.8	2.8	2.9	3.0	3.1	3.2	3.2	3.3	3.4	3.4	3.5	3.6	9
10	2.8	2.8	2.9	3.0	3.1	3.2	3.2	3.3	3.4	3.5	3.6	3.7	3.8	3.8	3.9	4.0	10
11	3.0	3.1	3.2	3.3	3.4	3.5	3.6	3.7	3.8	3.8	3.9	4.0	4.1	4.2	4.3	4.4	11
12	3.3	3.4	3.5	3.6	3.7	3.8	3.9	4.0	4.1	4.2	4.3	4.4	4.5	4.6	4.7	4.8	12
13	3.6	3.7	3.8	3.9	4.0	4.1	4.2	4.3	4.4	4.6	4.7	4.8	4.9	5.0	5.1	5.2	13
14	3.8	4.0	4.1	4.2	4.3	4.4	4.6	4.7	4.8	4.9	5.0	5.1	5.2	5.4	5.5	5.6	14
15	4.1	4.2	4.4	4.5	4.6	4.8	4.9	5.0	5.1	5.2	5.4	5.5	5.6	5.8	5.9	6.0	15
16	4.4	4.5	4.7	4.8	4.9	5.1	5.2	5.3	5.5	5.6	5.7	5.9	6.0	6.1	6.3	6.4	16
17	4.7	4.8	5.0	5.1	5.2	5.4	5.5	5.7	5.8	6.0	6.1	6.2	6.4	6.5	6.7	6.8	17
18	5.0	5.1	5.2	5.4	5.6	5.7	5.8	6.0	6.2	6.3	6.4	6.6	6.8	6.9	7.0	7.2	18
19	5.2	5.4	5.5	5.7	5.9	6.0	6.2	6.3	6.5	6.6	6.8	7.0	7.1	7.3	7.4	7.6	19
20	5.5	5.7	5.8	6.0	6.2	6.3	6.5	6.7	6.8	7.0	7.2	7.3	7.5	7.7	7.8	8.0	20
21	5.8	6.0	6.1	6.3	6.5	6.6	6.8	7.0	7.2	7.4	7.5	7.7	7.9	8.0	8.2	8.4	21
22	6.0	6.2	6.4	6.6	6.8	7.0	7.2	7.3	7.5	7.7	7.9	8.1	8.2	8.4	8.6	8.8	22
23	6.3	6.5	6.7	6.9	7.1	7.3	7.5	7.7	7.9	8.0	8.2	8.4	8.6	8.8	9.0	9.2	23
24	6.6	6.8	7.0	7.2	7.4	7.6	7.8	8.0	8.2	8.4	8.6	8.8	9.0	9.2	9.4	9.6	24
25	6.9	7.1	7.3	7.5	7.7	7.9	8.1	8.3	8.5	8.8	9.0	9.2	9.4	9.6	9.8	10.0	25
26	7.2	7.4	7.6	7.8	8.0	8.2	8.4	8.7	8.9	9.1	9.3	9.5	9.8	10.0	10.2	10.4	26
27	7.4	7.6	7.9	8.1	8.3	8.6	8.8	9.0	9.2	9.4	9.7	9.9	10.1	10.4	10.6	10.8	27
28	7.7	7.9	8.2	8.4	8.6	8.9	9.1	9.3	9.6	9.8	10.0	10.3	10.5	10.7	11.0	11.2	28
29	8.0	8.2	8.5	8.7	8.9	9.2	9.4	9.7	9.9	10.2	10.4	10.6	10.9	11.1	11.4	11.6	29
30	8.2	8.5	8.8	9.0	9.2	9.5	9.8	10.0	10.2	10.5	10.8	11.0	11.2	11.5	11.8	12.0	30
31	8.5	8.8	9.0	9.3	9.6	9.8	10.1	10.3	10.6	10.8	11.1	11.4	11.6	11.9	12.1	12.4	31
32	8.8	9.1	9.3	9.6	9.9	10.1	10.4	10.7	10.9	11.2	11.5	11.7	12.0	12.3	12.5	12.8	32
33	9.1	9.4	9.6	9.9	10.2	10.4	10.7	11.0	11.3	11.6	11.8	12.1	12.4	12.6	12.9	13.2	33
34	9.4	9.6	9.9	10.2	10.5	10.8	11.0	11.3	11.6	11.9	12.2	12.5	12.8	13.0	13.3	13.6	34
35	9.6	9.9	10.2	10.5	10.8	11.1	11.4	11.7	12.0	12.2	12.5	12.8	13.1	13.4	13.7	14.0	35
36	9.9	10.2	10.5	10.8	11.1	11.4	11.7	12.0	12.3	12.6	12.9	13.2	13.5	13.8	14.1	14.4	36
37	10.2	10.5	10.8	11.1	11.4	11.7	12.0	12.3	12.6	13.0	13.3	13.6	13.9	14.2	14.5	14.8	37
38	10.4	10.8	11.1	11.4	11.7	12.0	12.4	12.7	13.0	13.3	13.6	13.9	14.2	14.6	14.9	15.2	38
39	10.7	11.0	11.4	11.7	12.0	12.4	12.7	13.0	13.3	13.6	14.0	14.3	14.6	15.0	15.3	15.6	39
40	11.0	11.3	11.7	12.0	12.3	12.7	13.0	13.3	13.7	14.0	14.3	14.7	15.0	15.3	15.7	16.0	40
41	11.3	11.6	12.0	12.3	12.6	13.0	13.3	13.7	14.0	14.4	14.7	15.0	15.4	15.7	16.1	16.4	41
42	11.6	11.9	12.2	12.6	13.0	13.3	13.6	14.0	14.4	14.7	15.0	15.4	15.8	16.1	16.4	16.8	42
43	11.8	12.2	12.5	12.9	13.3	13.6	14.0	14.3	14.7	15.0	15.4	15.8	16.1	16.5	16.8	17.2	43
44	12.1	12.5	12.8	13.2	13.6	13.9	14.3	14.7	15.0	15.4	15.8	16.1	16.5	16.9	17.2	17.6	44
45	12.4	12.8	13.1	13.5	13.9	14.2	14.6	15.0	15.4	15.8	16.1	16.5	16.9	17.2	17.6	18.0	45
46	12.6	13.0	13.4	13.8	14.2	14.6	15.0	15.3	15.7	16.1	16.5	16.9	17.2	17.6	18.0	18.4	46
47	12.9	13.3	13.7	14.1	14.5	14.9	15.3	15.7	16.1	16.4	16.8	17.2	17.6	18.0	18.4	18.8	47
48	13.2	13.6	14.0	14.4	14.8	15.2	15.6	16.0	16.4	16.8	17.2	17.6	18.0	18.4	18.8	19.2	48
49	13.5	13.9	14.3	14.7	15.1	15.5	15.9	16.3	16.7	17.2	17.6	18.0	18.4	18.8	19.2	19.6	49
50	13.8	14.2	14.6	15.0	15.4	15.8	16.2	16.7	17.1	17.5	17.9	18.3	18.8	19.2	19.6	20.0	50
51	14.0	14.4	14.9	15.3	15.7	16.2	16.6	17.0	17.4	17.8	18.3	18.7	19.1	19.6	20.0	20.4	51
52	14.3	14.7	15.2	15.6	16.0	16.5	16.9	17.3	17.8	18.2	18.6	19.1	19.5	19.9	20.4	20.8	52
53	14.6	15.0	15.5	15.9	16.3	16.8	17.2	17.7	18.1	18.6	19.0	19.4	19.9	20.3	20.8	21.2	53
54	14.8	15.3	15.8	16.2	16.6	17.1	17.6	18.0	18.4	18.9	19.4	19.8	20.2	20.7	21.2	21.6	54
55	15.1	15.6	16.0	16.5	17.0	17.4	17.9	18.3	18.8	19.2	19.7	20.2	20.6	21.1	21.5	22.0	55
56	15.4	15.9	16.3	16.8	17.3	17.7	18.2	18.7	19.1	19.6	20.1	20.5	21.0	21.5	21.9	22.4	56
57	15.7	16.2	16.6	17.1	17.6	18.0	18.5	19.0	19.5	20.0	20.4	20.9	21.4	21.8	22.3	22.8	57
58	16.0	16.4	16.9	17.4	17.9	18.4	18.8	19.3	19.8	20.3	20.8	21.3	21.8	22.2	22.7	23.2	58
59	16.2	16.7	17.2	17.7	18.2	18.7	19.2	19.7	20.2	20.6	21.1	21.6	22.1	22.6	23.1	23.6	59
60	16.5	17.0	17.5	18.0	18.5	19.0	19.5	20.0	20.5	21.0	21.5	22.0	22.5	23.0	23.5	24.0	60

CURRENT AND TIDE TABLES

Velocity of Current at any Time

TABLE A

Interval between slack and maximum current

Interval between slack and desired time (h. m.)	1 20	1 40	2 00	2 20	2 40	3 00	3 20	3 40	4 00	4 20	4 40	5 00	5 20	5 40
0 20	0.4	0.3	0.3	0.2	0.2	0.2	0.2	0.1	0.1	0.1	0.1	0.1	0.1	0.1
0 40	0.7	0.6	0.5	0.4	0.4	0.3	0.3	0.3	0.3	0.2	0.2	0.2	0.2	0.2
1 00	0.9	0.8	0.7	0.6	0.6	0.5	0.5	0.4	0.4	0.4	0.3	0.3	0.3	0.3
1 20	1.0	1.0	0.9	0.8	0.7	0.6	0.6	0.5	0.5	0.5	0.4	0.4	0.4	0.4
1 40	-----	1.0	1.0	0.9	0.8	0.8	0.7	0.7	0.6	0.6	0.5	0.5	0.5	0.4
2 00	-----	-----	1.0	1.0	0.9	0.9	0.8	0.8	0.7	0.7	0.6	0.6	0.6	0.5
2 20	-----	-----	-----	1.0	1.0	0.9	0.9	0.8	0.8	0.7	0.7	0.7	0.6	0.6
2 40	-----	-----	-----	-----	1.0	1.0	1.0	0.9	0.9	0.8	0.8	0.7	0.7	0.7
3 00	-----	-----	-----	-----	-----	1.0	1.0	1.0	0.9	0.9	0.8	0.8	0.8	0.7
3 20	-----	-----	-----	-----	-----	-----	1.0	1.0	1.0	0.9	0.9	0.9	0.8	0.8
3 40	-----	-----	-----	-----	-----	-----	-----	1.0	1.0	1.0	0.9	0.9	0.9	0.9
4 00	-----	-----	-----	-----	-----	-----	-----	-----	1.0	1.0	1.0	1.0	0.9	0.9
4 20	-----	-----	-----	-----	-----	-----	-----	-----	-----	1.0	1.0	1.0	1.0	0.9
4 40	-----	-----	-----	-----	-----	-----	-----	-----	-----	-----	1.0	1.0	1.0	1.0
5 00	-----	-----	-----	-----	-----	-----	-----	-----	-----	-----	-----	1.0	1.0	1.0
5 20	-----	-----	-----	-----	-----	-----	-----	-----	-----	-----	-----	-----	1.0	1.0
5 40	-----	-----	-----	-----	-----	-----	-----	-----	-----	-----	-----	-----	-----	1.0

TABLE B

Interval between slack and maximum current

Interval between slack and desired time (h. m.)	1 20	1 40	2 00	2 20	2 40	3 00	3 20	3 40	4 00	4 20	4 40	5 00	5 20	5 40
0 20	0.5	0.4	0.4	0.3	0.3	0.3	0.3	0.3	0.2	0.2	0.2	0.2	0.2	0.2
0 40	0.8	0.7	0.6	0.5	0.5	0.5	0.4	0.4	0.4	0.4	0.3	0.3	0.3	0.3
1 00	0.9	0.8	0.8	0.7	0.7	0.6	0.6	0.5	0.5	0.5	0.4	0.4	0.4	0.4
1 20	1.0	1.0	0.9	0.8	0.8	0.7	0.7	0.6	0.6	0.6	0.5	0.5	0.5	0.5
1 40	-----	1.0	1.0	0.9	0.9	0.8	0.8	0.7	0.7	0.7	0.6	0.6	0.6	0.6
2 00	-----	-----	1.0	1.0	0.9	0.9	0.9	0.8	0.8	0.7	0.7	0.7	0.7	0.6
2 20	-----	-----	-----	1.0	1.0	1.0	0.9	0.9	0.8	0.8	0.8	0.7	0.7	0.7
2 40	-----	-----	-----	-----	1.0	1.0	1.0	0.9	0.9	0.9	0.8	0.8	0.8	0.7
3 00	-----	-----	-----	-----	-----	1.0	1.0	1.0	0.9	0.9	0.9	0.9	0.8	0.8
3 20	-----	-----	-----	-----	-----	-----	1.0	1.0	1.0	1.0	0.9	0.9	0.9	0.8
3 40	-----	-----	-----	-----	-----	-----	-----	1.0	1.0	1.0	1.0	0.9	0.9	0.9
4 00	-----	-----	-----	-----	-----	-----	-----	-----	1.0	1.0	1.0	1.0	0.9	0.9
4 20	-----	-----	-----	-----	-----	-----	-----	-----	-----	1.0	1.0	1.0	1.0	0.9
4 40	-----	-----	-----	-----	-----	-----	-----	-----	-----	-----	1.0	1.0	1.0	1.0
5 00	-----	-----	-----	-----	-----	-----	-----	-----	-----	-----	-----	1.0	1.0	1.0
5 20	-----	-----	-----	-----	-----	-----	-----	-----	-----	-----	-----	-----	1.0	1.0
5 40	-----	-----	-----	-----	-----	-----	-----	-----	-----	-----	-----	-----	-----	1.0

Use table A for all places except those listed below for table B.

Use table B for Deception Pass, Seymour Narrows, Sergius Narrows, Isanotski Strait, and all stations in table 2 which are referred to these points.

1. From predictions find the time of slack water and the time and velocity of maximum current (flood or ebb), one of which is immediately before and the other after the time for which the velocity is desired.

2. Find the interval of time between the above slack and maximum current, and enter the top of table A or B with the interval which most nearly agrees with this value.

3. Find the interval of time between the above slack and the time desired, and enter the side of table A or B with the interval which most nearly agrees with this value.

4. Find, in the table, the factor corresponding to the above two intervals, and multiply the maximum velocity by this factor. The result will be the approximate velocity at the time desired.

1991 CURRENT TABLES

For Daylight Savings Time, add one hour.

GRAYS HARBOR (Entrance)

F-Flood, Dir. 060° True   E-Ebb, Dir. 240° True

JANUARY

Day	Slack Water Time h.m.	Maximum Current Time h.m.	Vel. knots
1 Tu	0148	0439	2.5E
	0714	1011	2.4F
	1306	1648	4.6E
	2015	2333	3.1F
2 W	0234	0526	2.7E
	0809	1104	2.3F
	1357	1737	4.4E
	2058		
3 Th		0017	3.1F
	0318	0615	2.8E
	0903	1155	2.2F
	1447	1821	4.0E
	2140		
4 F		0057	2.9F
	0401	0703	2.8E
	1000	1247	1.9F
	1537	1909	3.5E
	2221		
5 Sa		0135	2.6F
	0443	0754	2.8E
	1059	1341	1.6F
	1630	1957	2.9E
	2301		
6 Su		0218	2.3F
	0526	0847	2.7E
	1202	1452	1.3F
	1727	2045	2.3E
	2343		
7 M		0255	2.0F
	0611	0941	2.7E
	1312	1619	1.0F
	1830	2145	1.8E
8 Tu	0028	0340	1.7F
	0657	1037	2.7E
	1428	1742	1.0F
	1941	2250	1.4E
9 W	0118	0436	1.4F
	0746	1134	2.7E
	1540	1846	1.1F
	2057	2354	1.2E
10 Th	0215	0558	1.2F
	0837	1232	2.8E
	1639	1947	1.4F
	2210		
11 F		0055	1.2E
	0317	0714	1.2F
	0929	1323	3.0E
	1726	2038	1.6F
	2312		
12 Sa		0153	1.3E
	0418	0803	1.2F
	1018	1412	3.1E
	1805	2125	1.8F
13 Su	0001	0242	1.4E
	0512	0842	1.3F
	1104	1457	3.3E
	1839	2202	2.0F
14 M	0042	0327	1.6E
	0559	0913	1.4F
	1146	1536	3.5E
	1910	2238	2.2F
15 Tu	0119	0409	1.8E
	0642	0938	1.5F
	1226	1615	3.6E
	1939	2305	2.3F

Day	Slack Water Time h.m.	Maximum Current Time h.m.	Vel. knots
16 W	0153	0447	2.0E
	0722	1007	1.6F
	1303	1647	3.6E
	2009	2321	2.3F
17 Th	0226	0522	2.2E
	0802	1040	1.7F
	1340	1719	3.5E
	2039	2339	2.4F
18 F	0258	0555	2.3E
	0843	1115	1.8F
	1418	1748	3.4E
	2110		
19 Sa		0002	2.5F
	0329	0624	2.5E
	0927	1154	1.8F
	1457	1821	3.2E
	2143		
20 Su		0031	2.5F
	0401	0704	2.7E
	1014	1237	1.8F
	1542	1858	2.9E
	2219		
21 M		0103	2.4F
	0436	0739	2.8E
	1107	1328	1.6F
	1634	1943	2.5E
	2259		
22 Tu		0142	2.3F
	0514	0833	2.9E
	1206	1423	1.5F
	1739	2036	2.1E
	2344		
23 W		0231	2.1F
	0600	0930	3.0E
	1313	1537	1.3F
	1858	2139	1.7E
24 Th	0038	0324	1.9F
	0655	1041	3.1E
	1426	1706	1.3F
	2023	2307	1.4E
25 F	0141	0431	1.7F
	0759	1157	3.3E
	1540	1909	1.6F
	2144		
26 Sa		0033	1.4E
	0254	0551	1.6F
	0907	1305	3.6E
	1645	2012	2.0F
	2255		
27 Su		0143	1.7E
	0407	0717	1.8F
	1012	1403	3.9E
	1741	2107	2.5F
	2353		
28 M		0242	2.0E
	0515	0829	2.0F
	1112	1500	4.2E
	1831	2155	2.8F
29 Tu	0043	0335	2.4E
	0615	0928	2.2F
	1207	1549	4.3E
	1915	2238	3.0F
30 W	0127	0424	2.8E
	0710	1018	2.4F
	1259	1636	4.3E
	1956	2317	3.1F
31 Th	0207	0509	3.0E
	0801	1106	2.4F
	1348	1720	4.1E
	2034	2352	3.0F

FEBRUARY

Day	Slack Water Time h.m.	Maximum Current Time h.m.	Vel. knots
1 F	0246	0553	3.2E
	0850	1149	2.3F
	1436	1801	3.8E
	2111		
2 Sa		0021	2.8F
	0323	0634	3.2E
	0939	1231	2.1F
	1522	1842	3.3E
	2146		
3 Su		0053	2.6F
	0400	0719	3.2E
	1029	1316	1.8F
	1609	1925	2.7E
	2221		
4 M		0122	2.3F
	0438	0801	3.0E
	1121	1400	1.5F
	1659	2007	2.2E
	2258		
5 Tu		0151	1.9F
	0518	0850	2.8E
	1219	1459	1.1F
	1754	2055	1.7E
	2340		
6 W		0228	1.6F
	0601	0946	2.6E
	1326	1648	0.9F
	1859	2157	1.2E
7 Th	0028	0311	1.2F
	0651	1048	2.5E
	1442	1813	0.9F
	2014	2313	1.0E
8 F	0129	0415	1.0F
	0748	1151	2.5E
	1556	1916	1.1F
	2133		
9 Sa		0027	1.0E
	0241	0617	0.9F
	0849	1252	2.6E
	1653	2012	1.4F
	2240		
10 Su		0124	1.2E
	0355	0745	1.0F
	0948	1346	2.8E
	1735	2057	1.7F
	2331		
11 M		0219	1.4E
	0457	0832	1.2F
	1041	1431	3.1E
	1810	2136	2.0F
12 Tu	0012	0304	1.8E
	0546	0907	1.4F
	1128	1514	3.3E
	1841	2209	2.2F
13 W	0046	0343	2.1E
	0628	0936	1.6F
	1211	1551	3.4E
	1910	2232	2.3F
14 Th	0118	0419	2.4E
	0707	0959	1.8F
	1252	1625	3.5E
	1939	2247	2.4F
15 F	0149	0454	2.7E
	0746	1029	2.0F
	1332	1659	3.4E
	2009	2305	2.5F

Day	Slack Water Time h.m.	Maximum Current Time h.m.	Vel. knots
16 Sa	0218	0526	2.9E
	0825	1104	2.2F
	1412	1729	3.3E
	2040	2328	2.6F
17 Su	0249	0555	3.2E
	0907	1143	2.2F
	1454	1803	3.1E
	2113	2359	2.6F
18 M	0320	0632	3.3E
	0952	1224	2.2F
	1540	1841	2.8E
	2149		
19 Tu		0034	2.5F
	0354	0713	3.4E
	1042	1314	2.0F
	1632	1922	2.4E
	2230		
20 W		0113	2.3F
	0434	0802	3.3E
	1140	1407	1.7F
	1733	2016	1.9E
	2317		
21 Th		0158	2.1F
	0522	0859	3.2E
	1246	1512	1.5F
	1847	2125	1.5E
22 F	0015	0257	1.7F
	0623	1017	3.1E
	1401	1705	1.3F
	2010	2300	1.3E
23 Sa	0127	0413	1.4F
	0736	1137	3.1E
	1519	1856	1.6F
	2130		
24 Su		0023	1.5E
	0250	0551	1.4F
	0853	1249	3.3E
	1628	2000	2.0F
	2237		
25 M		0130	1.8E
	0411	0739	1.6F
	1003	1350	3.6E
	1724	2051	2.4F
	2331		
26 Tu		0227	2.3E
	0519	0842	2.0F
	1106	1445	3.8E
	1811	2136	2.7F
27 W	0016	0317	2.8E
	0615	0936	2.3F
	1202	1532	3.9E
	1852	2215	2.9F
28 Th	0056	0402	3.2E
	0704	1019	2.5F
	1252	1618	3.8E
	1930	2250	2.9F

Time meridian 120° W.   0000 is midnight.   1200 is noon.

GRAYS HARBOR (Entrance)

1991 CURRENT TABLES

For Daylight Saving Time, add one hour.

F-Flood, Dir. 060° True   E-Ebb, Dir. 240° True

MARCH

Day	Slack Water Time h.m.	Maximum Current Time h.m.	Vel. knots	Day	Slack Water Time h.m.	Maximum Current Time h.m.	Vel. knots
1 F	0133	0445	3.4E	16 Sa	0105	0422	3.3E
	0750	1100	2.5F		0726	1018	2.3F
	1339	1700	3.6E		1322	1635	3.2E
	2004	2319	2.8F		1935	2226	2.5F
2 Sa	0208	0523	3.6E	17 Su	0136	0455	3.6E
	0832	1139	2.4F		0806	1052	2.5F
	1423	1738	3.3E		1405	1709	3.1E
	2038	2344	2.6F		2009	2257	2.6F
3 Su	0242	0603	3.5E	18 M	0208	0530	3.8E
	0914	1212	2.2F		0848	1131	2.6F
	1506	1818	2.9E		1450	1746	2.9E
	2110				2045	2330	2.6F
4 M		0009	2.4F	19 Tu	0243	0607	3.8E
	0316	0640	3.4E		0933	1216	2.5F
	0957	1245	2.0F		1538	1825	2.6E
	1549	1853	2.5E		2125		
	2144						
5 Tu		0031	2.1F	20 W		0009	2.5F
	0349	0719	3.2E		0321	0650	3.8E
	1041	1321	1.7F		1024	1303	2.3F
	1634	1930	2.0E		1631	1914	2.2E
	2220				2210		
6 W		0100	1.8F	21 Th		0050	2.2F
	0425	0801	2.9E		0404	0742	3.6E
	1130	1402	1.3F		1120	1358	2.0F
	1724	2011	1.6E		1732	2011	1.8E
	2301				2303		
7 Th		0135	1.5F	22 F		0142	1.8F
	0504	0849	2.6E		0457	0843	3.3E
	1227	1457	1.0F		1225	1511	1.7F
	1823	2112	1.2E		1842	2131	1.5E
	2351						
8 F		0219	1.1F	23 Sa	0009	0245	1.4F
	0552	0953	2.3E		0604	1000	3.0E
	1335	1722	0.9F		1338	1710	1.6F
	1934	2233	1.0E		1958	2257	1.5E
9 Sa	0055	0320	0.8F	24 Su	0130	0414	1.2F
	0655	1106	2.2E		0724	1121	2.9E
	1451	1842	1.0F		1453	1836	1.8F
	2050	2354	1.0E		2110		
10 Su	0215	0449	0.7F	25 M		0010	1.8E
	0807	1214	2.3E		0301	0627	1.3F
	1556	1937	1.3F		0843	1230	3.0E
	2156				1601	1933	2.1F
					2210		
11 M		0055	1.3E	26 Tu		0112	2.2E
	0336	0718	0.8F		0420	0743	1.6F
	0915	1311	2.5E		0956	1333	3.1E
	1646	2020	1.6F		1656	2022	2.4F
	2246				2259		
12 Tu		0147	1.6E	27 W		0209	2.7E
	0439	0809	1.1F		0521	0840	2.0F
	1015	1400	2.8E		1059	1425	3.2E
	1725	2057	1.9F		1742	2110	2.6F
	2327				2342		
13 W		0234	2.1E	28 Th		0254	3.1E
	0528	0847	1.5F		0611	0927	2.3F
	1107	1442	3.0E		1154	1512	3.2E
	1759	2130	2.1F		1822	2143	2.6F
14 Th	0002	0311	2.5E	29 F	0019	0339	3.5E
	0609	0917	1.8F		0655	1012	2.5F
	1154	1523	3.1E		1243	1555	3.2E
	1831	2145	2.2F		1857	2218	2.6F
15 F	0034	0346	2.9E	30 Sa	0054	0418	3.7E
	0647	0945	2.1F		0735	1049	2.5F
	1239	1559	3.2E		1328	1636	3.0E
	1902	2203	2.4F		1931	2239	2.4F
				31 Su	0128	0456	3.8E
					0812	1123	2.4F
					1410	1715	2.7E
					2003	2302	2.3F

APRIL

Day	Slack Water Time h.m.	Maximum Current Time h.m.	Vel. knots	Day	Slack Water Time h.m.	Maximum Current Time h.m.	Vel. knots
1 M	0200	0530	3.7E	16 Tu	0133	0504	4.2E
	0849	1153	2.3F		0831	1126	2.8F
	1451	1751	2.4E		1445	1733	2.6E
	2036	2326	2.1F		2021	2304	2.5F
2 Tu	0232	0605	3.5E	17 W	0213	0547	4.2E
	0927	1221	2.1F		0918	1211	2.7F
	1531	1826	2.1E		1536	1818	2.3E
	2111	2351	1.9F		2107	2349	2.3F
3 W	0304	0638	3.3E	18 Th	0257	0634	4.0E
	1007	1250	1.8F		1009	1303	2.5F
	1614	1901	1.8E		1630	1914	2.1E
	2149				2159		
4 Th		0022	1.6F	19 F		0038	2.0F
	0336	0713	3.0E		0346	0729	3.7E
	1051	1330	1.5F		1105	1358	2.2F
	1701	1942	1.5E		1729	2017	1.9E
	2233				2300		
5 F		0059	1.4F	20 Sa		0135	1.6F
	0412	0754	2.7E		0444	0830	3.3E
	1141	1417	1.3F		1206	1515	2.0F
	1756	2036	1.3E		1833	2131	1.8E
	2326						
6 Sa		0144	1.0F	21 Su	0013	0249	1.3F
	0455	0855	2.4E		0554	0947	3.0E
	1238	1522	1.1F		1312	1651	1.9F
	1900	2200	1.1E		1939	2247	1.9E
7 Su	0032	0243	0.8F	22 M	0141	0443	1.1F
	0558	1006	2.2E		0713	1100	2.7E
	1342	1741	1.1F		1419	1803	2.0F
	2005	2315	1.2E		2040	2352	2.2E
8 M	0152	0403	0.6F	23 Tu	0308	0627	1.3F
	0719	1122	2.1E		0832	1207	2.6E
	1445	1842	1.3F		1521	1901	2.1F
	2104				2134		
9 Tu		0019	1.5E	24 W		0051	2.6E
	0311	0619	0.7F		0420	0730	1.7F
	0836	1226	2.2E		0945	1307	2.6E
	1540	1927	1.5F		1616	1950	2.2F
	2153				2221		
10 W		0110	1.9E	25 Th		0144	3.0E
	0413	0731	1.1F		0515	0825	2.0F
	0943	1320	2.4E		1049	1402	2.6E
	1626	2000	1.7F		1703	2035	2.3F
	2234				2302		
11 Th		0156	2.4E	26 F		0232	3.4E
	0501	0816	1.5F		0601	0917	2.2F
	1042	1409	2.6E		1144	1447	2.5E
	1707	2025	1.9F		1744	2110	2.2F
	2311				2340		
12 F		0234	2.9E	27 Sa		0313	3.6E
	0544	0851	1.9F		0641	0958	2.4F
	1134	1451	2.7E		1233	1533	2.5E
	1745	2048	2.2F		1821	2141	2.2F
	2346						
13 Sa		0314	3.4E	28 Su	0015	0352	3.8E
	0624	0929	2.2F		0718	1037	2.4F
	1223	1533	2.8E		1316	1615	2.3E
	1822	2116	2.4F		1856	2203	2.0F
14 Su	0020	0349	3.8E	29 M	0049	0427	3.8E
	0705	1002	2.5F		0753	1110	2.3F
	1311	1611	2.8E		1357	1654	2.2E
	1900	2149	2.5F		1930	2223	1.9F
15 M	0056	0424	4.1E	30 Tu	0122	0502	3.7E
	0747	1043	2.7F		0827	1143	2.2F
	1357	1652	2.7E		1437	1728	2.0E
	1939	2225	2.5F		2006	2251	1.8F

Time meridian 120° W. 0000 is midnight. 1200 is noon.

1991 CURRENT TABLES

For Daylight Savings Time, add one hour.

GRAYS HARBOR (Entrance)

F-Flood, Dir. 060° True   E-Ebb, Dir. 240° True

MAY

Day	Slack Water Time h.m.	Maximum Current Time h.m.	Vel. knots	Day	Slack Water Time h.m.	Maximum Current Time h.m.	Vel. knots
1 W	0154	0536	3.5E	16 Th	0153	0534	4.4E
	0902	1208	2.1F		0906	1209	2.8F
	1516	1807	1.9E		1530	1818	2.3E
	2043	2320	1.6F		2055	2338	2.2F
2 Th	0225	0609	3.3E	17 F	0242	0625	4.2E
	0940	1230	1.9F		0956	1303	2.7F
	1558	1844	1.7E		1623	1913	2.2E
	2124	2351	1.5F		2154		
3 F	0257	0640	3.1E	18 Sa		0034	1.9F
	1020	1305	1.7F		0336	0719	3.8E
	1644	1929	1.5E		1049	1401	2.5F
	2211				1718	2017	2.2E
					2300		
4 Sa		0032	1.3F	19 Su		0135	1.5F
	0331	0725	2.8E		0436	0820	3.4E
	1104	1348	1.6F		1143	1506	2.3F
	1733	2017	1.4E		1814	2121	2.2E
	2306						
5 Su		0119	1.0F	20 M	0015	0256	1.2F
	0412	0810	2.5E		0544	0927	2.9E
	1153	1439	1.5F		1240	1617	2.2F
	1826	2122	1.4E		1909	2224	2.4E
6 M	0011	0215	0.8F	21 Tu	0139	0445	1.2F
	0510	0912	2.3E		0658	1032	2.5E
	1245	1537	1.4F		1337	1723	2.1F
	1919	2231	1.5E		2003	2325	2.6E
7 Tu	0124	0324	0.7F	22 W	0259	0610	1.3F
	0630	1017	2.1E		0814	1138	2.3E
	1339	1637	1.4F		1434	1820	2.0F
	2009	2332	1.8E		2053		
8 W	0236	0453	0.7F	23 Th		0021	2.9E
	0754	1132	2.0E		0407	0714	1.6F
	1432	1735	1.5F		0928	1238	2.1E
	2056				1528	1913	2.0F
					2139		
9 Th		0025	2.3E	24 F		0112	3.2E
	0338	0630	1.0F		0501	0809	1.8F
	0908	1230	2.1E		1034	1333	2.0E
	1523	1827	1.7F		1618	1958	1.9F
	2138				2222		
10 F		0111	2.8E	25 Sa		0159	3.4E
	0430	0737	1.5F		0547	0858	2.1F
	1014	1324	2.1E		1131	1421	1.9E
	1611	1911	1.9F		1703	2035	1.9F
	2219				2302		
11 Sa		0157	3.3E	26 Su		0244	3.6E
	0516	0824	1.9F		0626	0941	2.2F
	1113	1418	2.2E		1220	1510	1.9E
	1657	1953	2.1F		1745	2106	1.8F
	2300				2340		
12 Su		0238	3.8E	27 M		0325	3.7E
	0601	0908	2.3F		0702	1022	2.2F
	1207	1501	2.3E		1304	1551	1.9E
	1742	2034	2.3F		1824	2129	1.7F
	2341						
13 M		0321	4.1E	28 Tu	0016	0404	3.7E
	0646	0951	2.6F		0736	1059	2.2F
	1259	1549	2.4E		1344	1634	1.8E
	1827	2117	2.4F		1903	2157	1.6F
14 Tu	0023	0404	4.4E	29 W	0051	0439	3.6E
	0731	1036	2.8F		0809	1133	2.2F
	1349	1636	2.4E		1423	1712	1.8E
	1914	2203	2.4F		1942	2222	1.6F
15 W	0107	0449	4.5E	30 Th	0125	0515	3.5E
	0818	1120	2.9F		0842	1202	2.1F
	1439	1724	2.4E		1502	1752	1.7E
	2003	2249	2.4F		2022	2253	1.5F
				31 F	0158	0547	3.4E
					0917	1218	2.0F
					1542	1828	1.7E
					2106	2331	1.4F

JUNE

Day	Slack Water Time h.m.	Maximum Current Time h.m.	Vel. knots	Day	Slack Water Time h.m.	Maximum Current Time h.m.	Vel. knots
1 Sa	0232	0618	3.2E	16 Su		0031	1.9F
	0953	1247	2.0F		0328	0707	3.8E
	1622	1909	1.7E		1027	1346	2.7F
	2153				1654	1957	2.6E
					2253		
2 Su		0012	1.3F	17 M		0135	1.7F
	0307	0657	3.0E		0426	0801	3.3E
	1032	1320	1.9F		1114	1437	2.5F
	1704	1954	1.7E		1742	2056	2.7E
	2246						
3 M		0057	1.1F	18 Tu	0003	0249	1.4F
	0348	0738	2.7E		0528	0859	2.8E
	1113	1401	1.9F		1202	1531	2.3F
	1747	2046	1.8E		1831	2151	2.7E
	2345						
4 Tu		0148	1.0F	19 W	0118	0422	1.2F
	0441	0823	2.4E		0636	1001	2.3E
	1156	1444	1.8F		1252	1630	2.0F
	1830	2141	1.9E		1920	2251	2.8E
5 W	0049	0255	0.9F	20 Th	0233	0542	1.3F
	0552	0924	2.2E		0749	1102	1.9E
	1243	1531	1.8F		1344	1729	1.8F
	1914	2238	2.2E		2009	2348	3.0E
6 Th	0156	0409	0.9F	21 F	0343	0649	1.4F
	0714	1023	1.9E		0903	1203	1.6E
	1333	1622	1.8F		1438	1827	1.7F
	1959	2334	2.6E		2056		
7 F	0259	0528	1.1F	22 Sa		0043	3.1E
	0834	1137	1.8E		0441	0748	1.6F
	1426	1719	1.8F		1013	1305	1.5E
	2045				1533	1920	1.6F
					2143		
8 Sa		0027	3.0E	23 Su		0132	3.3E
	0357	0651	1.4F		0529	0840	1.8F
	0947	1243	1.8E		1114	1357	1.5E
	1520	1815	1.9F		1626	2005	1.5F
	2133				2228		
9 Su		0118	3.5E	24 M		0218	3.4E
	0450	0800	1.9F		0611	0927	2.0F
	1052	1344	1.8E		1205	1445	1.5E
	1614	1912	2.0F		1715	2048	1.5F
	2221				2311		
10 M		0209	3.9E	25 Tu		0301	3.5E
	0541	0856	2.3F		0647	1008	2.1F
	1152	1442	2.0E		1249	1532	1.6E
	1708	2003	2.2F		1801	2117	1.5F
	2310				2351		
11 Tu		0258	4.3E	26 W		0342	3.5E
	0630	0944	2.6F		0720	1047	2.1F
	1246	1533	2.1E		1329	1615	1.7E
	1802	2056	2.3F		1844	2139	1.5F
12 W	0000	0346	4.5E	27 Th	0029	0421	3.5E
	0718	1033	2.9F		0751	1120	2.2F
	1338	1625	2.3E		1406	1654	1.8E
	1856	2146	2.4F		1925	2208	1.5F
13 Th	0050	0437	4.6E	28 F	0106	0454	3.5E
	0806	1121	3.0F		0822	1147	2.2F
	1428	1717	2.4E		1441	1734	1.8E
	1951	2241	2.3F		2006	2241	1.5F
14 F	0142	0526	4.5E	29 Sa	0142	0528	3.4E
	0853	1208	3.0F		0853	1202	2.2F
	1517	1809	2.5E		1517	1811	1.9E
	2048	2336	2.2F		2049	2316	1.5F
15 Sa	0234	0615	4.2E	30 Su	0217	0557	3.3E
	0940	1256	2.9F		0926	1222	2.2F
	1605	1903	2.5E		1552	1845	2.0E
	2148				2134	2355	1.4F

Time meridian 120° W.   0000 is midnight.   1200 is noon.

GRAYS HARBOR (Entrance)

1991 CURRENT TABLES

For Daylight Saving Time, add one hour.

F-Flood, Dir. 060° True   E-Ebb, Dir. 240° True

JULY

Days 1–15:

Day	Slack Water Time h.m.	Max Current Time h.m.	Vel. knots
1 M	0254	0632	3.1E
	0959	1249	2.2F
	1627	1920	2.1E
	2222		
2 Tu		0040	1.4F
	0335	0707	2.8E
	1035	1322	2.2F
	1702	2001	2.2E
	2314		
3 W		0127	1.3F
	0425	0748	2.5E
	1114	1359	2.1F
	1739	2050	2.4E
4 Th	0012	0223	1.2F
	0527	0840	2.2E
	1157	1444	2.0F
	1820	2141	2.6E
5 F	0115	0328	1.1F
	0643	0939	1.8E
	1245	1531	1.9F
	1906	2241	2.8E
6 Sa	0221	0445	1.2F
	0804	1050	1.6E
	1340	1629	1.9F
	1958	2346	3.2E
7 Su	0327	0618	1.4F
	0923	1212	1.5E
	1440	1732	1.8F
	2055		
8 M		0049	3.5E
	0428	0747	1.8F
	1034	1321	1.6E
	1544	1839	1.9F
	2154		
9 Tu		0147	3.9E
	0524	0847	2.2F
	1137	1422	1.8E
	1648	1947	2.0F
	2251		
10 W		0242	4.2E
	0616	0938	2.6F
	1232	1520	2.1E
	1749	2048	2.2F
	2347		
11 Th		0336	4.5E
	0705	1025	2.9F
	1322	1612	2.4E
	1847	2146	2.3F
12 F	0041	0425	4.5E
	0750	1110	3.1F
	1408	1701	2.7E
	1944	2241	2.4F
13 Sa	0134	0514	4.4E
	0835	1151	3.1F
	1453	1752	2.9E
	2040	2332	2.3F
14 Su	0226	0600	4.1E
	0917	1234	3.0F
	1536	1841	3.0E
	2136		
15 M		0026	2.1F
	0318	0647	3.7E
	0959	1312	2.8F
	1619	1932	3.0E
	2234		

Days 16–31:

Day	Slack Water Time h.m.	Max Current Time h.m.	Vel. knots
16 Tu		0125	1.9F
	0412	0735	3.2E
	1040	1354	2.5F
	1702	2022	3.0E
	2336		
17 W		0226	1.6F
	0509	0830	2.6E
	1123	1434	2.2F
	1746	2113	2.9E
18 Th	0042	0345	1.3F
	0610	0921	2.0E
	1207	1518	1.8F
	1833	2212	2.9E
19 F	0154	0509	1.2F
	0718	1025	1.6E
	1256	1614	1.5F
	1922	2309	2.8E
20 Sa	0307	0623	1.2F
	0832	1131	1.3E
	1352	1728	1.3F
	2014		
21 Su		0007	2.9E
	0413	0724	1.4F
	0946	1236	1.2E
	1455	1849	1.2F
	2107		
22 M		0104	2.9E
	[illegible]	0819	1.6F
	1051	1331	1.2E
	1559	1950	1.2F
	2159		
23 Tu		0153	3.1E
	0550	0904	1.8F
	1143	1425	1.4E
	1657	2035	1.3F
	2247		
24 W		0240	3.2E
	0626	0945	2.0F
	1226	1510	1.6E
	1747	2112	1.4F
	2332		
25 Th		0323	3.4E
	0658	1026	2.1F
	1303	1553	1.8E
	1831	2139	1.5F
26 F	0013	0400	3.4E
	0727	1057	2.2F
	1338	1633	2.0E
	1911	2204	1.6F
27 Sa	0052	0434	3.5E
	0756	1118	2.3F
	1410	1709	2.2E
	1951	2228	1.6F
28 Su	0130	0509	3.4E
	0825	1129	2.3F
	1441	1743	2.3E
	2030	2304	1.7F
29 M	0207	0537	3.3E
	0854	1147	2.3F
	1512	1812	2.5E
	2111	2341	1.7F
30 Tu	0245	0606	3.1E
	0926	1212	2.4F
	1542	1841	2.6E
	2155		
31 W		0020	1.7F
	0327	0641	2.8E
	1000	1245	2.3F
	1613	1918	2.8E
	2244		

AUGUST

Days 1–15:

Day	Slack Water Time h.m.	Max Current Time h.m.	Vel. knots
1 Th		0109	1.7F
	0414	0722	2.5E
	1037	1320	2.3F
	1648	2005	2.9E
	2338		
2 F		0156	1.5F
	0512	0811	2.1E
	1119	1402	2.1F
	1729	2059	2.9E
3 Sa	0040	0259	1.4F
	0623	0908	1.7E
	1209	1453	1.9F
	1820	2202	3.0E
4 Su	0149	0417	1.3F
	0744	1024	1.4E
	1308	1556	1.7F
	1922	2315	3.1E
5 M	0301	0607	1.4F
	0906	1153	1.4E
	1418	1707	1.6F
	2030		
6 Tu		0030	3.4E
	0409	0739	1.8F
	1018	1309	1.6E
	1531	1833	1.7F
	2138		
7 W		0133	3.7E
	0508	0838	2.2F
	1120	1413	1.9E
	1642	1950	1.9F
	2242		
8 Th		0229	4.0E
	0600	0925	2.6F
	1211	1504	2.4E
	1745	2054	2.2F
	2340		
9 F		0323	4.2E
	0646	1009	2.9F
	1257	1557	2.8E
	1842	2149	2.4F
10 Sa	0035	0409	4.3E
	0729	1048	3.1F
	1340	1642	3.1E
	1936	2241	2.5F
11 Su	0127	0456	4.1E
	0810	1123	3.1F
	1420	1729	3.3E
	2027	2327	2.5F
12 M	0216	0539	3.8E
	0848	1200	2.9F
	1459	1813	3.4E
	2117		
13 Tu		0015	2.3F
	0305	0624	3.4E
	0926	1233	2.7F
	1537	1856	3.4E
	2208		
14 W		0101	2.1F
	0355	0708	2.9E
	1004	1303	2.4F
	1617	1942	3.2E
	2301		
15 Th		0150	1.7F
	0446	0751	2.3E
	1043	1338	2.0F
	1657	2033	3.0E
	2359		

Days 16–31:

Day	Slack Water Time h.m.	Max Current Time h.m.	Vel. knots
16 F		0252	1.3F
	0542	0845	1.8E
	1125	1417	1.6F
	1742	2126	2.8E
17 Sa	0104	0428	1.1F
	0645	0947	1.3E
	1215	1502	1.3F
	1832	2225	2.6E
18 Su	0218	0550	1.1F
	0757	1057	1.1E
	1315	1608	1.0F
	1930	2332	2.5E
19 M	0332	0653	1.2F
	0913	1204	1.1E
	1428	1820	0.9F
	2032		
20 Tu		0033	2.6E
	0432	0750	1.4F
	1019	1307	1.2E
	1544	1928	1.0F
	2132		
21 W		0126	2.8E
	0517	0838	1.7F
	1110	1400	1.5E
	1646	2023	1.2F
	2226		
22 Th		0214	3.0E
	0554	0917	1.9F
	1151	1445	1.8E
	1735	2100	1.4F
	2314		
23 F		0257	3.1E
	0625	0952	2.1F
	1226	1527	2.1E
	1817	2133	1.6F
	2358		
24 Sa		0336	3.3E
	0654	1017	2.2F
	1259	1605	2.4E
	1855	2154	1.8F
25 Su	0038	0409	3.3E
	0722	1034	2.3F
	1329	1638	2.7E
	1931	2219	1.9F
26 M	0118	0443	3.3E
	0750	1046	2.4F
	1358	1709	2.9E
	2008	2249	2.1F
27 Tu	0157	0512	3.1E
	0820	1107	2.4F
	1427	1735	3.1E
	2048	2326	2.1F
28 W	0237	0543	2.9E
	0852	1136	2.4F
	1456	1809	3.2E
	2130		
29 Th		0003	2.1F
	0320	0618	2.7E
	0927	1209	2.4F
	1527	1848	3.3E
	2217		
30 F		0048	2.0F
	0408	0657	2.3E
	1006	1246	2.3F
	1603	1933	3.3E
	2310		
31 Sa		0138	1.8F
	0505	0748	1.9E
	1051	1329	2.0F
	1648	2026	3.1E

Time meridian 120° W. 0000 is midnight. 1200 is noon.

GRAYS HARBOR
(Entrance)

For Daylight Savings Time, add one hour.

F-Flood, Dir. 060° True   E-Ebb, Dir. 240° True

SEPTEMBER

Day	Slack Water Time h.m.	Maximum Current Time h.m.	Vel. knots	Day	Slack Water Time h.m.	Maximum Current Time h.m.	Vel. knots
1 Su	0011	0239	1.5F	16 M	0118	0505	1.0F
	0614	0848	1.6E		0722	1024	1.1E
	1145	1424	1.7F		1248	1511	0.8F
	1745	2135	3.0E		1841	2249	2.3E
2 M	0122	0400	1.4F	17 Tu	0232	0619	1.1F
	0733	1015	1.3E		0834	1135	1.1E
	1254	1529	1.5F		1410	1754	0.6F
	1857	2257	3.0E		1953	2357	2.3E
3 Tu	0238	0607	1.5F	18 W	0337	0714	1.4F
	0852	1150	1.4E		0937	1238	1.4E
	1414	1701	1.3F		1532	1911	0.9F
	2016				2101		
4 W		0013	3.2E	19 Th		0054	2.5E
	0348	0724	1.9F		0426	0759	1.6F
	1000	1259	1.8E		1026	1331	1.7E
	1535	1848	1.5F		1633	2000	1.2F
	2130				2201		
5 Th		0121	3.4E	20 F		0143	2.7E
	0447	0816	2.3F		0506	0840	1.9F
	1056	1357	2.3E		1106	1413	2.1E
	1646	2005	1.9F		1719	2041	1.5F
	2236				2253		
6 F		0214	3.7E	21 Sa		0225	2.8E
	0538	0901	2.6F		0540	0909	2.0F
	1144	1447	2.8E		1141	1454	2.5E
	1746	2102	2.3F		1757	2113	1.7F
	2335				2340		
7 Sa		0307	3.8E	22 Su		0307	3.0E
	0622	0942	2.9F		0612	0930	2.1F
	1226	1535	3.3E		1213	1529	2.9E
	1838	2151	2.5F		1833	2136	2.0F
8 Su	0028	0352	3.8E	23 M	0023	0342	3.0E
	0702	1021	2.9F		0642	0943	2.3F
	1305	1620	3.6E		1243	1604	3.2E
	1925	2235	2.7F		1909	2203	2.2F
9 M	0118	0436	3.6E	24 Tu	0105	0417	3.0E
	0740	1052	2.9F		0713	1003	2.4F
	1342	1659	3.8E		1313	1634	3.5E
	2010	2318	2.6F		1946	2233	2.4F
10 Tu	0205	0518	3.3E	25 W	0147	0447	2.9E
	0816	1121	2.7F		0746	1032	2.4F
	1418	1740	3.8E		1343	1707	3.7E
	2054	2357	2.5F		2026	2310	2.5F
11 W	0251	0559	2.9E	26 Th	0229	0524	2.7E
	0851	1149	2.4F		0821	1103	2.4F
	1454	1821	3.6E		1415	1742	3.8E
	2139				2109	2349	2.4F
12 Th		0035	2.2F	27 F	0315	0602	2.4E
	0336	0637	2.5E		0859	1140	2.4F
	0927	1218	2.1F		1450	1821	3.7E
	1529	1900	3.4E		2156		
	2225						
13 F		0116	1.8F	28 Sa		0034	2.3F
	0423	0720	2.0E		0405	0645	2.1E
	1005	1249	1.8F		0942	1221	2.1F
	1607	1945	3.0E		1530	1906	3.5E
	2315				2249		
14 Sa		0159	1.5F	29 Su		0125	2.0F
	0514	0808	1.6E		0503	0740	1.8E
	1049	1324	1.4F		1033	1306	1.8F
	1648	2036	2.7E		1619	2004	3.3E
					2350		
15 Su	0012	0316	1.1F	30 M		0230	1.7F
	0613	0912	1.2E		0610	0849	1.5E
	1141	1407	1.1F		1137	1410	1.5F
	1738	2138	2.4E		1723	2115	3.0E

OCTOBER

Day	Slack Water Time h.m.	Maximum Current Time h.m.	Vel. knots	Day	Slack Water Time h.m.	Maximum Current Time h.m.	Vel. knots
1 Tu	0059	0406	1.6F	16 W	0124	0522	1.2F
	0723	1020	1.5E		0750	1100	1.3E
	1255	1527	1.2F		1348	1600	0.5F
	1844	2241	2.9E		1905	2308	2.1E
2 W	0211	0553	1.7F	17 Th	0225	0623	1.3F
	0834	1139	1.8E		0846	1202	1.6E
	1424	1728	1.2F		1508	1833	0.7F
	2007	2357	2.9E		2021		
3 Th	0320	0658	2.0F	18 F		0009	2.1E
	0935	1242	2.2E		0319	0712	1.5F
	1546	1911	1.5F		0934	1255	2.0E
	2123				1608	1928	1.0F
					2129		
4 F		0102	3.0E	19 Sa		0102	2.3E
	0418	0749	2.3F		0406	0745	1.7F
	1026	1338	2.7E		1015	1336	2.5E
	1650	2009	2.0F		1653	2013	1.4F
	2230				2227		
5 Sa		0155	3.2E	20 Su		0149	2.4E
	0508	0834	2.5F		0446	0812	1.9F
	1111	1429	3.3E		1051	1419	2.9E
	1743	2100	2.3F		1732	2048	1.8F
	2329				2318		
6 Su		0246	3.2E	21 M		0232	2.5E
	0551	0913	2.6F		0524	0828	2.0F
	1151	1512	3.7E		1125	1457	3.3E
	1830	2145	2.6F		1809	2117	2.1F
7 M	0021	0330	3.2E	22 Tu	0006	0312	2.6E
	0630	0948	2.6F		0600	0854	2.2F
	1228	1555	3.9E		1158	1530	3.7E
	1912	2228	2.7F		1847	2145	2.4F
8 Tu	0109	0415	3.0E	23 W	0052	0351	2.6E
	0707	1017	2.5F		0636	0926	2.3F
	1304	1634	4.0E		1232	1604	4.0E
	1953	2305	2.6F		1927	2220	2.6F
9 W	0153	0454	2.8E	24 Th	0137	0427	2.5E
	0742	1042	2.3F		0714	0959	2.4F
	1338	1711	3.9E		1307	1640	4.1E
	2032	2342	2.5F		2008	2301	2.7F
10 Th	0237	0534	2.5E	25 F	0223	0508	2.4E
	0817	1106	2.1F		0755	1038	2.4F
	1412	1748	3.7E		1344	1719	4.2E
	2111				2053	2342	2.6F
11 F		0015	2.2F	26 Sa	0311	0551	2.3E
	0319	0611	2.1E		0839	1118	2.3F
	0854	1135	1.9F		1425	1805	4.0E
	1446	1824	3.4E		2141		
	2152						
12 Sa		0047	1.9F	27 Su		0032	2.5F
	0403	0654	1.8E		0402	0640	2.1E
	0933	1205	1.6F		0928	1205	2.0F
	1520	1900	3.1E		1511	1854	3.8E
	2236				2233		
13 Su		0121	1.6F	28 M		0122	2.3F
	0451	0739	1.5E		0459	0741	1.9E
	1019	1246	1.3F		1027	1300	1.7F
	1557	1945	2.7E		1606	1955	3.4E
	2326				2331		
14 M		0210	1.3F	29 Tu		0230	2.0F
	0545	0839	1.3E		0601	0855	1.8E
	1114	1329	1.0F		1138	1407	1.3F
	1642	2040	2.4E		1714	2104	3.0E
15 Tu	0022	0338	1.1F	30 W	0033	0357	1.9F
	0647	0951	1.2E		0705	1013	1.9E
	1223	1430	0.7F		1302	1539	1.1F
	1746	2156	2.2E		1834	2221	2.7E
				31 Th	0139	0522	2.0F
					0806	1121	2.2E
					1431	1748	1.2F
					1956	2334	2.6E

Time meridian 120° W. 0000 is midnight. 1200 is noon.

GRAYS HARBOR (Entrance)

1991 CURRENT TABLES

For Daylight Saving Time, add one hour.

F-Flood, Dir. 060° True   E-Ebb, Dir. 240° True

NOVEMBER

Day	Slack Water Time h.m.	Maximum Current Time h.m.	Vel. knots
1 F	0242	0627	2.1F
	0902	1222	2.6E
	1548	1859	1.6F
	2113		
2 Sa		0037	2.6E
	0340	0721	2.2F
	0951	1315	3.1E
	1648	2000	2.0F
	2222		
3 Su		0133	2.6E
	0431	0806	2.3F
	1035	1406	3.5E
	1737	2051	2.3F
	2321		
4 M		0224	2.5E
	0516	0845	2.3F
	1115	1450	3.8E
	1820	2137	2.5F
5 Tu	0013	0313	2.5E
	0557	0916	2.2F
	1153	1531	4.0E
	1900	2218	2.6F
6 W	0100	0354	2.4E
	0635	0945	2.1F
	1229	1610	4.0E
	1937	2257	2.5F
7 Th	0143	0437	2.2E
	0712	1012	2.0F
	1304	1645	3.9E
	2013	2330	2.4F
8 F	0223	0516	2.1E
	0749	1036	1.8F
	1338	1721	3.7E
	2049		
9 Sa		0003	2.2F
	0304	0555	1.9E
	0827	1105	1.7F
	1411	1755	3.5E
	2126		
10 Su		0027	2.0F
	0345	0634	1.7E
	0909	1140	1.5F
	1444	1831	3.2E
	2205		
11 M		0100	1.8F
	0430	0719	1.5E
	0956	1215	1.2F
	1519	1906	2.9E
	2248		
12 Tu		0137	1.6F
	0517	0810	1.4E
	1051	1302	1.0F
	1559	1955	2.5E
	2334		
13 W		0226	1.5F
	0608	0911	1.4E
	1157	1357	0.7F
	1653	2052	2.2E
14 Th	0023	0321	1.4F
	0700	1016	1.6E
	1311	1509	0.6F
	1810	2200	2.0E
15 F	0116	0422	1.4F
	0750	1115	1.8E
	1426	1644	0.6F
	1934	2309	1.9E
16 Sa	0209	0519	1.5F
	0836	1206	2.2E
	1529	1839	0.9F
	2050		
17 Su		0012	1.9E
	0300	0607	1.6F
	0919	1255	2.7E
	1619	1934	1.3F
	2156		
18 M		0107	1.9E
	0348	0648	1.8F
	0959	1337	3.1E
	1703	2019	1.7F
	2256		
19 Tu		0158	2.0E
	0434	0731	1.9F
	1039	1419	3.6E
	1745	2056	2.1F
	2349		
20 W		0244	2.1E
	0519	0811	2.1F
	1118	1501	4.0E
	1827	2136	2.4F
21 Th	0039	0327	2.2E
	0603	0854	2.3F
	1159	1543	4.3E
	1910	2214	2.7F
22 F	0127	0412	2.3E
	0618	0935	2.4F
	1241	1624	4.4E
	1954	2257	2.8F
23 Sa	0215	0459	2.3E
	0736	1022	2.4F
	1326	1707	4.4E
	2040	2339	2.8F
24 Su	0303	0549	2.3E
	0826	1111	2.2F
	1413	1756	4.3E
	2128		
25 M		0028	2.8F
	0354	0640	2.2E
	0922	1200	2.0F
	1504	1847	4.0E
	2217		
26 Tu		0122	2.6F
	0446	0741	2.2E
	1025	1258	1.7F
	1601	1941	3.5E
	2309		
27 W		0218	2.4F
	0540	0843	2.2E
	1136	1407	1.4F
	1707	2046	3.0E
28 Th	0003	0324	2.2F
	0635	0947	2.4E
	1257	1545	1.2F
	1821	2156	2.6E
29 F	0100	0437	2.1F
	0730	1052	2.6E
	1421	1731	1.2F
	1939	2304	2.3E
30 Sa	0158	0543	2.0F
	0822	1151	2.9E
	1536	1844	1.5F
	2058		

DECEMBER

Day	Slack Water Time h.m.	Maximum Current Time h.m.	Vel. knots
1 Su		0007	2.0E
	0256	0643	2.0F
	0912	1249	3.2E
	1637	1944	1.8F
	2210		
2 M		0108	1.9E
	0351	0733	2.0F
	0958	1338	3.5E
	1727	2035	2.1F
	2312		
3 Tu		0203	1.9E
	0441	0816	1.9F
	1041	1425	3.7E
	1810	2126	2.3F
4 W	0005	0251	1.9E
	0527	0857	1.8F
	1122	1507	3.8E
	1849	2207	2.4F
5 Th	0051	0336	1.9E
	0609	0926	1.8F
	1201	1549	3.8E
	1924	2248	2.4F
6 F	0132	0419	1.9E
	0649	0947	1.7F
	1238	1626	3.8E
	1957	2323	2.3F
7 Sa	0210	0500	1.9E
	0729	1015	1.6F
	1314	1702	3.7E
	2030	2352	2.2F
8 Su	0248	0538	1.8E
	0809	1050	1.6F
	1348	1736	3.5E
	2103		
9 M		0015	2.1F
	0326	0618	1.8E
	0851	1121	1.4F
	1422	1808	3.3E
	2138		
10 Tu		0035	2.1F
	0405	0654	1.8E
	0937	1159	1.3F
	1457	1840	3.0E
	2214		
11 W		0106	2.0F
	0444	0735	1.8E
	1028	1240	1.2F
	1535	1917	2.8E
	2252		
12 Th		0140	1.9F
	0525	0826	1.8E
	1124	1329	1.0F
	1621	2002	2.4E
	2333		
13 F		0221	1.8F
	0607	0915	1.9E
	1227	1430	0.8F
	1723	2053	2.1E
14 Sa	0017	0304	1.7F
	0650	1013	2.1E
	1334	1537	0.8F
	1844	2156	1.8E
15 Su	0106	0353	1.7F
	0735	1109	2.4E
	1439	1659	0.9F
	2007	2306	1.6E
16 M	0158	0450	1.7F
	0821	1207	2.8E
	1539	1839	1.2F
	2124		
17 Tu		0020	1.5E
	0254	0545	1.7F
	0909	1259	3.2E
	1633	1947	1.6F
	2231		
18 W		0124	1.6E
	0349	0643	1.8F
	0958	1350	3.7E
	1723	2042	2.0F
	2331		
19 Th		0219	1.8E
	0445	0737	2.0F
	1047	1438	4.1E
	1810	2127	2.4F
20 F	0025	0310	2.0E
	0538	0832	2.2F
	1137	1527	4.4E
	1857	2210	2.7F
21 Sa	0115	0402	2.2E
	0632	0922	2.3F
	1227	1612	4.6E
	1942	2257	2.9F
22 Su	0203	0451	2.4E
	0725	1018	2.4F
	1317	1701	4.6E
	2027	2339	3.0F
23 M	0249	0539	2.6E
	0820	1107	2.3F
	1408	1746	4.4E
	2112		
24 Tu		0022	3.0F
	0335	0632	2.7E
	0917	1202	2.2F
	1501	1837	4.0E
	2157		
25 W		0109	2.9F
	0422	0724	2.7E
	1018	1257	1.9F
	1556	1929	3.5E
	2243		
26 Th		0154	2.7F
	0509	0820	2.8E
	1124	1402	1.6F
	1656	2026	3.0E
	2330		
27 F		0243	2.4F
	0558	0918	2.8E
	1237	1527	1.3F
	1803	2122	2.4E
28 Sa	0019	0340	2.1F
	0647	1017	2.9E
	1354	1705	1.3F
	1917	2231	1.9E
29 Su	0112	0448	1.8F
	0738	1119	3.0E
	1511	1822	1.4F
	2035	2338	1.6E
30 M	0209	0557	1.6F
	0830	1216	3.1E
	1619	1927	1.6F
	2152		
31 Tu		0042	1.4E
	0310	0700	1.5F
	0922	1311	3.3E
	1714	2022	1.8F
	2300		

Time meridian 120° W. 0000 is midnight. 1200 is noon.

STRAIT OF JUAN de FUCA (ENTRANCE)

1991 CURRENT TABLES

For Daylight Saving Time, add one hour.

JANUARY

Day	Slack Water Time h.m.	Maximum Current Time h.m.	Vel. knots	Day	Slack Water Time h.m.	Maximum Current Time h.m.	Vel. knots
1 Tu		0211	1.6F	16 W		0225	1.1F
	0524	0838	1.5E		0525	0854	1.3E
		1355	*			1408	*
		2003	2.3E			2006	1.8E
	2356						
2 W		0255	1.6F	17 Th	0005	0254	1.1F
	0605	0925	1.6E		0552	0922	1.3E
		1452	*			1446	*
		2052	2.2E			2041	1.8E
3 Th	0043	0341	1.5F	18 F	0039	0326	1.0F
	0643	1010	1.7E		0617	0951	1.4E
	1425	1546	0.3F			1527	*
	1709	2143	2.0E			2115	1.7E
4 F	0131	0423	1.3F	19 Sa	0114	0355	0.9F
	0719	1057	1.7E		0639	1025	1.5E
	1519	1644	0.3F			1609	*
	1810	2233	1.7E			2156	1.5E
5 Sa	0221	0507	1.1F	20 Su	0152	0427	0.8F
	0752	1145	1.7E		0701	1054	1.6E
	1617	1745	0.3F			1656	*
	1915	2329	1.4E			2241	1.4E
6 Su	0315	0551	0.8F	21 M	0234	0458	0.7F
	0823	1230	1.7E		0723	1136	1.6E
	1716	1847	0.3F		1615	1749	0.3F
	2027				1930	2336	1.1E
7 M		0028	1.1E	22 Tu	0324	0537	0.5F
	0416	0634	0.6F		0747	1218	1.7E
	0851	1322	1.7E		1703	1851	0.4F
	1814	1958	0.3F		2052		
	2150						
8 Tu		0139	0.9E	23 W		0037	0.9E
	0528	0725	0.3F		0427	0624	0.3F
	0915	1413	1.7E		0811	1305	1.8E
	1908	2107	0.4F		1756	2007	0.5F
	2321				2228		
9 W		0256	0.8E	24 Th		0157	0.8E
		0819	*			0719	*
		1505	1.7E			1406	1.9E
	1956	2215	0.5F		1850	2116	0.6F
10 Th	0049	0417	0.7E	25 F	0007	0322	0.8E
		0920	*			0822	*
		1557	1.8E			1507	2.0E
	2039	2310	0.7F		1944	2230	0.9F
11 F	0201	0525	0.8E	26 Sa	0132	0443	0.9E
		1016	*			0938	*
		1648	1.8E			1611	2.0E
	2117	2359	0.8F		2035	2328	1.1F
12 Sa	0258	0622	0.9E	27 Su	0238	0554	1.0E
		1112	*			1053	*
		1732	1.8E			1712	2.1E
	2153				2125		
13 Su		0042	0.9F	28 M		0022	1.3F
	0344	0707	1.0E		0331	0649	1.2E
		1200	*			1200	*
		1812	1.9E			1810	2.2E
	2227				2213		
14 M		0117	1.0F	29 Tu	0416	0109	1.4F
	0422	0750	1.1E			0736	1.4E
		1247	*		1137	1258	0.3F
		1849	1.9E		1417	1905	2.2E
	2300				2300		
15 Tu		0152	1.1F	30 W	0455	0155	1.4F
	0455	0819	1.2E			0820	1.6E
		1330	*		1216	1352	0.4F
		1930	1.9E		1526	1954	2.2E
	2332				2345		
				31 Th		0234	1.4F
					0531	0901	1.7E
					1258	1444	0.5F
					1629	2043	2.0E

FEBRUARY

Day	Slack Water Time h.m.	Maximum Current Time h.m.	Vel. knots	Day	Slack Water Time h.m.	Maximum Current Time h.m.	Vel. knots
1 F	0031	0315	1.3F	16 Sa	0020	0252	0.9F
	0604	0940	1.8E		0526	0912	1.6E
	1342	1535	0.5F		1318	1508	0.4F
	1726	2131	1.8E		1658	2104	1.6E
2 Sa	0116	0356	1.1F	17 Su	0057	0323	0.8F
	0634	1019	1.8E		0548	0940	1.7E
	1429	1624	0.5F		1349	1549	0.5F
	1821	2219	1.6E		1751	2145	1.5E
3 Su	0202	0431	0.9F	18 M	0136	0352	0.7F
	0701	1100	1.8E		0609	1015	1.8E
	1520	1717	0.5F		1428	1635	0.6F
	1916	2308	1.3E		1847	2228	1.3E
4 M	0252	0513	0.6F	19 Tu	0220	0427	0.5F
	0725	1142	1.8E		0631	1054	1.8E
	1615	1809	0.4F		1514	1729	0.6F
	2014	2359	1.1E		1948	2326	1.1E
5 Tu	0350	0550	0.4F	20 W	0315	0508	0.4F
	0746	1227	1.7E		0653	1137	1.9E
	1715	1912	0.4F		1608	1826	0.6F
	2121				2100		
6 W		0103	0.9E	21 Th		0027	0.9E
		0637	*			0553	*
		1317	1.7E			1230	1.9E
	1816	2021	0.4F		1709	1935	0.6F
	2239				2223		
7 Th		0219	0.7E	22 F		0145	0.8E
		0727	*			0653	*
		1414	1.6E			1334	1.8E
	1913	2130	0.4F		1815	2051	0.7F
					2350		
8 F	0003	0341	0.7E	23 Sa		0317	0.8E
		0834	*			0812	*
		1513	1.6E			1448	1.8E
	2003	2233	0.5F		1919	2205	0.8F
9 Sa	0118	0458	0.8E	24 Su	0107	0436	1.0E
		0945	*			0939	*
		1609	1.6E			1558	1.9E
	2047	2324	0.7F		2018	2306	1.0F
10 Su	0216	0557	0.9E	25 M	0207	0539	1.2E
		1053	*			1057	*
		1706	1.6E			1706	1.9E
	2126				2113		
11 M		0006	0.8F	26 Tu		0000	1.1F
	0302	0639	1.1E		0256	0627	1.4E
		1147	*		1036	1200	0.3F
		1748	1.7E		1323	1808	2.0E
	2202				2203		
12 Tu		0049	0.9F	27 W		0049	1.1F
	0340	0716	1.2E		0337	0710	1.6E
		1233	*		1108	1257	0.5F
		1835	1.8E		1441	1857	2.0E
	2237				2250		
13 W		0122	1.0F	28 Th		0132	1.1F
	0412	0745	1.3E		0413	0747	1.8E
		1311	*		1144	1344	0.6F
		1911	1.8E		1546	1948	1.9E
	2311				2336		
14 Th		0153	1.0F				
	0439	0815	1.4E				
		1351	*				
		1948	1.8E				
	2346						
15 F		0222	1.0F				
	0504	0843	1.5E				
	1252	1427	0.3F				
	1605	2027	1.7E				

Time meridian 120° W. 0000 is midnight. 1200 is noon.
If three consecutive entries are marked (E) the middle one is not a true maximum but an intermediate value to show the current pattern.
* Current weak and variable.

STRAIT OF JUAN de FUCA
(Entrance)

1991 CURRENT TABLES

For Daylight Saving Time, add one hour.

MARCH

Days 1–15

Day	Slack Water Time (h.m.)	Maximum Current Time (h.m.)	Vel. (knots)
1 F		0210	1.1F
	0445	0828	1.9E
	1222	1433	0.7F
	1642	2035	1.8E
2 Sa	0020	0247	0.9F
	0514	0905	1.9E
	1302	1516	0.8F
	1734	2118	1.7E
3 Su	0104	0322	0.8F
	0539	0940	1.9E
	1344	1559	0.8F
	1822	2203	1.5E
4 M	0149	0357	0.6F
	0602	1016	1.9E
	1429	1648	0.7F
	1910	2248	1.3E
5 Tu	0240	0430	0.4F
	0620	1057	1.8E
	1518	1734	0.6F
	1959	2335	1.1E
6 W		0510	*
		1136	1.7E
	1613	1825	0.5F
	2053		
7 Th		0032	0.9E
		0551	*
		1224	1.6E
	1713	1928	0.4F
	2156		
8 F		0143	0.8E
		0646	*
		1319	1.5E
	1815	2035	0.4F
	2308		
9 Sa		0308	0.8E
		0802	0.3E
		1421	1.4E
	1914	2140	0.5F
10 Su	0017	0424	0.9E
		0924	0.3E
		1532	1.4E
	2006	2236	0.6F
11 M	0116	0512	1.0E
		1033	*
		1632	1.4E
	2051	2325	0.7F
12 Tu	0202	0556	1.2E
		1124	*
		1721	1.5E
	2132		
13 W		0004	0.7F
	0240	0629	1.3E
		1210	*
		1810	1.6E
	2211		
14 Th		0039	0.8F
	0312	0700	1.5E
	1112	1252	0.3F
	1432	1852	1.6E
	2248		
15 F		0114	0.8F
	0339	0729	1.6E
	1131	1328	0.5F
	1530	1933	1.7E
	2325		

Days 16–31

Day	Slack Water Time (h.m.)	Maximum Current Time (h.m.)	Vel. (knots)
16 Sa		0146	0.8F
	0404	0757	1.7E
	1156	1409	0.7F
	1623	2013	1.6E
17 Su	0004	0215	0.7F
	0427	0830	1.9E
	1226	1449	0.8F
	1714	2056	1.6E
18 M	0044	0250	0.6F
	0451	0901	2.0E
	1302	1530	0.9F
	1806	2137	1.4E
19 Tu	0129	0325	0.5F
	0514	0940	2.0E
	1343	1615	0.9F
	1900	2225	1.3E
20 W	0221	0402	0.3F
	0538	1019	2.0E
	1432	1708	0.9F
	1959	2323	1.1E
21 Th		0446	*
		1106	1.9E
	1528	1806	0.9F
	2103		
22 F		0026	1.0E
		0539	*
		1206	1.8E
	1632	1915	0.8F
	2214		
23 Sa		0147	1.0E
		0654	*
		1313	1.7E
	1742	2029	0.8F
	2325		
24 Su		0304	1.1E
		0824	*
		1432	1.6E
	1853	2135	0.8F
25 M	0029	0418	1.2E
		0949	*
		1552	1.6E
	1959	2240	0.9F
26 Tu	0123	0509	1.4E
		1100	*
		1702	1.6E
	2058	2333	0.9F
27 W	0208	0558	1.6E
	1006	1157	0.5F
	1351	1759	1.7E
	2152		
28 Th		0018	0.9F
	0246	0639	1.8E
	1039	1250	0.7F
	1500	1853	1.7E
	2241		
29 F		0101	0.8F
	0319	0718	1.9E
	1113	1333	0.8F
	1558	1942	1.6E
	2328		
30 Sa		0139	0.7F
	0348	0753	2.0E
	1150	1416	0.9F
	1650	2023	1.6E
31 Su	0013	0215	0.6F
	0414	0826	2.0E
	1227	1458	1.0F
	1736	2108	1.4E

APRIL

Days 1–15

Day	Slack Water Time (h.m.)	Maximum Current Time (h.m.)	Vel. (knots)
1 M	0059	0250	0.4F
	0435	0900	2.0E
	1305	1539	0.9F
	1820	2146	1.3E
2 Tu	0149	0321	0.3F
	0453	0935	1.9E
	1345	1619	0.9F
	1903	2231	1.2E
3 W		0354	*
		1009	1.8E
	1428	1700	0.8F
	1946	2317	1.0E
4 Th		0436	*
		1048	1.6E
	1516	1746	0.7F
	2032		
5 F		0012	1.0E
		0520	*
		1133	1.5E
	1609	1840	0.6F
	2122		
6 Sa		0115	0.9E
		0621	0.3E
		1228	1.4E
	1709	1939	0.5F
	2217		
7 Su		0224	0.9E
		0739	0.3E
		1335	1.3E
	1812	2042	0.5F
	2313		
8 M		0333	1.0E
		0857	0.3E
		1445	1.2E
	1912	2139	0.5F
9 Tu	0004	0420	1.2E
		1007	*
		1553	1.2E
	2006	2228	0.5F
10 W	0048	0503	1.3E
		1102	*
		1655	1.3E
	2055	2311	0.6F
11 Th	0126	0538	1.5E
	1001	1145	0.3F
	1332	1744	1.4E
	2140	2350	0.6F
12 F	0159	0612	1.7E
	1019	1227	0.6F
	1439	1830	1.4E
	2223		
13 Sa		0028	0.5F
	0229	0642	1.8E
	1044	1309	0.8F
	1537	1916	1.5E
	2306		
14 Su		0101	0.5F
	0257	0716	2.0E
	1114	1350	1.0F
	1630	1959	1.5E
	2350		
15 M		0139	0.5F
	0325	0751	2.1E
	1148	1431	1.2F
	1722	2045	1.4E

Days 16–30

Day	Slack Water Time (h.m.)	Maximum Current Time (h.m.)	Vel. (knots)
16 Tu	0038	0218	0.4F
	0353	0828	2.2E
	1228	1514	1.2F
	1814	2133	1.4E
17 W	0132	0257	0.3F
	0421	0910	2.2E
	1312	1603	1.3F
	1907	2222	1.3E
18 Th		0342	*
		0955	2.1E
	1402	1654	1.2F
	2002	2323	1.2E
19 F		0439	*
		1046	2.0E
	1458	1752	1.1F
	2058		
20 Sa		0027	1.2E
		0542	*
		1145	1.8E
	1602	1853	1.0F
	2155		
21 Su		0136	1.2E
		0702	*
		1301	1.6E
	1712	1958	0.9F
	2251		
22 M		0244	1.3E
		0829	*
		1420	1.4E
	1825	2104	0.8F
	2343		
23 Tu		0347	1.5E
		0946	*
		1540	1.4E
	1935	2205	0.7F
24 W	0029	0436	1.7E
	0902	1053	0.4F
	1247	1650	1.4E
	2040	2255	0.6F
25 Th	0110	0525	1.8E
	0936	1148	0.6F
	1406	1751	1.4E
	2140	2346	0.5F
26 F	0145	0607	1.9E
	1011	1238	0.8F
	1510	1842	1.4E
	2234		
27 Sa		0026	0.5F
	0216	0642	2.0E
	1046	1321	1.0F
	1605	1931	1.3E
	2326		
28 Su		0107	0.3F
	0241	0717	2.0E
	1121	1358	1.0F
	1652	2017	1.3E
29 M		0143	*
		0752	2.0E
	1157	1439	1.1F
	1735	2058	1.2E
30 Tu		0218	*
		0826	2.0E
	1232	1518	1.0F
	1816	2139	1.2E

Time meridian 120° W. 0000 is midnight. 1200 is noon.
If three consecutive entries are marked (E) the middle one is not a true maximum but an intermediate
value to show the current pattern.
* Current weak and variable.

STRAIT OF JUAN de FUCA (ENTRANCE)

1991 CURRENT TABLES

For Daylight Saving Time, add one hour.

MAY

Day	Slack Water Time (h.m.)	Maximum Current Time (h.m.)	Vel. (knots)
1 W		0250	*
		0859	1.9E
	1309	1556	1.0F
	1854	2220	1.1E
2 Th		0328	*
		0932	1.8E
	1348	1635	0.9F
	1932	2304	1.1E
3 F		0410	*
		1009	1.6E
	1429	1714	0.8F
	2011	2354	1.1E
4 Sa		0500	0.3E
		1054	1.5E
	1516	1759	0.7F
	2051		
5 Su		0048	1.1E
		0601	0.3E
		1143	1.3E
	1609	1846	0.6F
	2132		
6 M		0145	1.1E
		0709	0.3E
		1245	1.2E
	1707	1940	0.5F
	2213		
7 Tu		0234	1.2E
		0822	*
		1356	1.1E
	1809	2032	0.5F
	2253		
8 W		0320	1.4E
		0928	*
		1507	1.1E
	1911	2126	0.4F
	2331		
9 Th		0403	1.5E
		1027	*
		1616	1.1E
	2011	2211	0.4F
10 F	0007	0442	1.7E
	0909	1118	0.5F
	1328	1712	1.1E
	2106	2257	0.4F
11 Sa	0041	0521	1.9E
	0935	1200	0.8F
	1438	1806	1.2E
	2159	2339	0.3F
12 Su	0115	0557	2.0E
	1006	1248	1.0F
	1537	1858	1.3E
	2251		
13 M		0023	0.3F
	0150	0639	2.2E
	1041	1331	1.2F
	1632	1948	1.3E
	2343		
14 Tu		0104	0.3F
	0225	0719	2.3E
	1121	1414	1.4F
	1725	2039	1.3E
15 W		0153	*
		0804	2.3E
	1204	1503	1.5F
	1815	2128	1.4E
16 Th		0242	*
		0849	2.3E
	1250	1550	1.5F
	1904	2222	1.4E
17 F		0336	*
		0940	2.1E
	1341	1641	1.4F
	1953	2317	1.4E
18 Sa		0435	*
		1035	1.9E
	1436	1733	1.2F
	2040		
19 Su		0015	1.4E
		0544	*
		1136	1.7E
	1536	1830	1.1F
	2126		
20 M		0116	1.5E
		0703	*
		1249	1.5E
	1642	1927	0.9F
	2210		
21 Tu		0213	1.6E
		0818	*
		1405	1.3E
	1754	2027	0.7F
	2252		
22 W		0310	1.7E
	0751	0935	0.3F
	1121	1522	1.2E
	1908	2121	0.5F
	2331		
23 Th		0358	1.8E
	0830	1037	0.5F
	1255	1633	1.1E
	2021	2216	0.4F
24 F	0005	0447	1.9E
	0908	1132	0.7F
	1410	1735	1.1E
	2131	2305	0.3F
25 Sa	0036	0528	2.0E
	0946	1221	0.9F
	1512	1834	1.1E
		2348	*
26 Su		0609	2.0E
	1022	1306	1.0F
	1604	1921	1.1E
27 M		0033	*
		0648	2.0E
	1057	1345	1.1F
	1649	2008	1.1E
28 Tu		0111	*
		0720	2.0E
	1132	1424	1.1F
	1729	2047	1.1E
29 W		0147	*
		0755	1.9E
	1206	1501	1.1F
	1806	2128	1.1E
30 Th		0228	*
		0830	1.8E
	1240	1533	1.1F
	1840	2209	1.1E
31 F		0309	*
		0905	1.7E
	1316	1607	1.0F
	1913	2246	1.2E

JUNE

Day	Slack Water Time (h.m.)	Maximum Current Time (h.m.)	Vel. (knots)
1 Sa		0354	*
		0943	1.6E
	1354	1645	0.9F
	1945	2328	1.2E
2 Su		0441	0.3E
		1026	1.5E
	1435	1723	0.8F
	2016		
3 M		0010	1.2E
		0534	*
		1115	1.3E
	1521	1806	0.7F
	2047		
4 Tu		0056	1.3E
		0637	*
		1206	1.2E
	1613	1847	0.6F
	2118		
5 W		0138	1.4E
		0744	*
		1313	1.0E
	1711	1932	0.5F
	2148		
6 Th		0223	1.5E
		0849	*
		1421	0.9E
	1817	2021	0.4F
	2218		
7 F		0307	1.7E
	0757	0949	0.4F
	1151	1536	0.9E
	1927	2111	0.3F
	2251		
8 Sa		0352	1.8E
	0825	1045	0.6F
	1320	1644	0.9E
	2204		*
9 Su		0439	2.0E
	0859	1135	0.9F
	1432	1747	1.0E
	2253		*
10 M		0522	2.2E
	0936	1224	1.2F
	1533	1842	1.1E
	2349		*
11 Tu		0609	2.3E
	1017	1313	1.4F
	1628	1936	1.2E
12 W		0039	*
		0657	2.4E
	1101	1400	1.5F
	1717	2028	1.3E
13 Th		0135	*
		0747	2.4E
	1146	1449	1.6F
	1804	2117	1.4E
14 F		0232	*
		0835	2.3E
	1234	1535	1.5F
	1848	2210	1.5E
15 Sa		0331	*
		0930	2.1E
	1324	1622	1.4F
	1930	2300	1.6E
16 Su		0432	*
		1025	1.9E
	1416	1710	1.3F
	2010	2349	1.7E
17 M		0535	*
		1123	1.6E
	1513	1801	1.0F
	2048		
18 Tu		0043	1.7E
		0648	*
		1230	1.4E
	1615	1853	0.8F
	2124		
19 W		0135	1.8E
	0622	0759	0.3F
	0941	1340	1.1E
	1724	1945	0.6F
	2158		
20 Th		0230	1.8E
	0712	0909	0.4F
	1118	1457	1.0E
	1842	2036	0.4F
	2228		
21 F		0319	1.9E
	0758	1018	0.6F
	1247	1611	0.9E
		2136	*
22 Sa		0411	1.9E
	0842	1113	0.7F
	1402	1718	0.9E
		2228	*
23 Su		0457	1.9E
	0922	1207	0.9F
	1503	1821	0.9E
		2320	*
24 M		0540	1.9E
	1000	1248	1.0F
	1553	1913	1.0E
25 Tu		0004	*
		0620	1.9E
	1036	1327	1.0F
	1635	1956	1.1E
26 W		0051	*
		0658	1.9E
	1110	1404	1.1F
	1712	2034	1.1E
27 Th		0133	*
		0733	1.9E
	1144	1439	1.1F
	1744	2110	1.2E
28 F		0211	*
		0810	1.8E
	1217	1511	1.1F
	1814	2145	1.2E
29 Sa		0252	*
		0845	1.7E
	1251	1543	1.0F
	1842	2220	1.3E
30 Su		0335	*
		0922	1.6E
	1326	1615	0.9F
	1908	2254	1.3E

Time meridian 120° W. 0000 is midnight. 1200 is noon.
If three consecutive entries are marked (E) the middle one is not a true maximum but an intermediate value to show the current pattern.
* Current weak and variable.

STRAIT OF JUAN de FUCA (Entrance)

1991 CURRENT TABLES

For Daylight Saving Time, add one hour.

JULY

Day	Slack Water Time h.m.	Max Current Time h.m.	Vel. knots
1 M		0419	*
		1003	1.5E
	1404	1646	0.8F
	1933	2324	1.4E
2 Tu		0507	*
		1046	1.3E
	1446	1723	0.7F
	1957		
3 W		0005	1.5E
		0601	*
		1137	1.2E
	1533	1758	0.6F
	2021		
4 Th		0043	1.6E
		0700	*
		1237	1.0E
	1628	1839	0.4F
	2045		
5 F		0126	1.7E
	0628	0808	0.3F
	0955	1348	0.9E
	1736	1927	0.3F
	2112		
6 Sa		0216	1.8E
	0706	0912	0.5F
	1138	1505	0.8E
		2024	*
7 Su		0309	1.9E
	0747	1018	0.7F
	1307	1622	0.8E
		2125	*
8 M		0402	2.1E
	0830	1115	1.0F
	1421	1728	0.9E
		2228	*
9 Tu		0455	2.2E
	0914	1208	1.2F
	1521	1830	1.1E
		2332	*
10 W		0551	2.3E
	1000	1257	1.4F
	1612	1924	1.2E
11 Th		0032	*
		0645	2.3E
	1046	1346	1.5F
	1658	2009	1.4E
12 F		0130	*
		0735	2.3E
	1133	1429	1.5F
	1739	2058	1.6E
13 Sa	0102	0227	0.3F
	0348	0829	2.2E
	1220	1515	1.5F
	1818	2143	1.7E
14 Su	0150	0321	0.3F
	0453	0919	2.0E
	1308	1559	1.3F
	1854	2228	1.8E
15 M	0241	0419	0.4F
	0557	1013	1.8E
	1358	1642	1.1F
	1929	2317	1.8E

Day	Slack Water Time h.m.	Max Current Time h.m.	Vel. knots
16 Tu	0336	0516	0.4F
	0703	1109	1.5E
	1452	1728	0.9F
	2001		
17 W		0003	1.8E
	0433	0618	0.4F
	0813	1208	1.3E
	1551	1814	0.6F
	2030		
18 Th		0054	1.8E
	0532	0727	0.4F
	0931	1314	1.0E
	1700	1900	0.4F
	2057		
19 F		0145	1.8E
	0630	0836	0.5F
	1057	1431	0.8E
		1954	*
20 Sa		0240	1.8E
	0724	0945	0.6F
	1223	1550	0.8E
		2052	*
21 Su		0332	1.8E
	0813	1047	0.7F
	1338	1706	0.8E
		2152	*
22 M		0426	1.8E
	0858	1138	0.8F
	1438	1803	0.9E
		2255	*
23 Tu		0514	1.8E
	0937	1223	0.9F
	1525	1851	1.0E
		2348	*
24 W		0557	1.8E
	1014	1302	1.0F
	1605	1933	1.1E
25 Th		0033	*
		0638	1.8E
	1049	1337	1.0F
	1638	2008	1.2E
26 F		0119	*
		0716	1.8E
	1122	1410	1.0F
	1708	2037	1.3E
27 Sa		0159	*
		0755	1.8E
	1155	1442	1.0F
	1734	2106	1.3E
28 Su		0237	*
		0830	1.7E
	1229	1512	1.0F
	1758	2138	1.4E
29 M		0314	*
		0907	1.6E
	1303	1540	0.9F
	1820	2209	1.5E
30 Tu		0355	*
		0945	1.5E
	1340	1609	0.8F
	1841	2238	1.5E
31 W		0439	*
		1030	1.3E
	1421	1641	0.6F
	1901	2313	1.6E

AUGUST

Day	Slack Water Time h.m.	Max Current Time h.m.	Vel. knots
1 Th	0351	0530	0.3F
	0711	1113	1.2E
	1507	1718	0.5F
	1922	2355	1.7E
2 F	0436	0626	0.4F
	0824	1214	1.0E
	1605	1759	0.3F
	1943		
3 Sa		0040	1.8E
	0526	0729	0.4F
	0950	1323	0.8E
		1848	*
4 Su		0131	1.8E
	0619	0840	0.6F
	1124	1445	0.8E
		1951	*
5 M		0232	1.9E
	0713	0955	0.8F
	1251	1608	0.8E
		2101	*
6 Tu		0336	2.0E
	0806	1056	1.0F
	1400	1717	1.0E
		2218	*
7 W		0443	2.1E
	0857	1151	1.1F
	1456	1812	1.2E
		2327	*
8 Th		0540	2.1E
	0946	1238	1.3F
	1543	1901	1.4E
	2305		
9 F		0029	0.3F
	0149	0639	2.2E
	1034	1324	1.3F
	1624	1950	1.6E
	2344		
10 Sa		0126	0.4F
	0303	0729	2.2E
	1121	1407	1.3F
	1701	2031	1.7E
11 Su	0025	0218	0.5F
	0409	0820	2.1E
	1207	1450	1.2F
	1736	2113	1.9E
12 M	0109	0307	0.6F
	0510	0908	1.9E
	1255	1531	1.1F
	1808	2154	1.9E
13 Tu	0156	0401	0.7F
	0608	0957	1.7E
	1343	1611	0.9F
	1837	2235	1.9E
14 W	0246	0454	0.6F
	0706	1051	1.4E
	1435	1651	0.7F
	1904	2320	1.9E
15 Th	0341	0550	0.6F
	0806	1145	1.2E
	1535	1733	0.4F
	1927		

Day	Slack Water Time h.m.	Max Current Time h.m.	Vel. knots
16 F		0005	1.8E
	0440	0648	0.5F
	0911	1246	1.0E
		1821	*
17 Sa		0056	1.7E
	0542	0757	0.5F
	1025	1402	0.8E
		1915	*
18 Su		0155	1.6E
	0643	0907	0.5F
	1144	1526	0.8E
		2021	*
19 M		0255	1.6E
	0739	1010	0.6F
	1255	1639	0.8E
		2135	*
20 Tu		0354	1.6E
	0827	1103	0.7F
	1353	1734	1.0E
		2239	*
21 W		0449	1.6E
	0910	1150	0.8F
	1439	1819	1.1E
		2334	*
22 Th		0537	1.6E
	0948	1230	0.8F
	1517	1854	1.2E
23 F		0019	*
		0620	1.7E
	1024	1305	0.9F
	1549	1930	1.3E
24 Sa		0100	*
		0701	1.7E
	1059	1334	0.9F
	1616	1957	1.4E
25 Su	0012	0142	0.3F
	0305	0737	1.7E
	1134	1405	0.9F
	1641	2026	1.5E
26 M	0034	0215	0.4F
	0356	0814	1.7E
	1209	1435	0.8F
	1702	2052	1.6E
27 Tu	0059	0252	0.5F
	0445	0849	1.6E
	1245	1506	0.7F
	1722	2122	1.7E
28 W	0129	0329	0.5F
	0535	0930	1.5E
	1323	1534	0.6F
	1741	2151	1.7E
29 Th	0205	0415	0.6F
	0628	1011	1.3E
	1407	1604	0.5F
	1801	2225	1.8E
30 F	0247	0500	0.6F
	0725	1100	1.1E
	1459	1639	0.3F
	1820	2310	1.8E
31 Sa	0337	0555	0.6F
	0831	1200	1.0E
		1724	*

Time meridian 120° W. 0000 is midnight. 1200 is noon.
If three consecutive entries are marked (E) the middle one is not a true maximum but an intermediate value to show the current pattern.
* Current weak and variable.

T-12

STRAIT OF JUAN de FUCA (ENTRANCE)

1991 CURRENT TABLES

For Daylight Saving Time, add one hour.

SEPTEMBER

Day	Slack Water Time h.m.	Maximum Current Time h.m.	Vel. knots
1 Su	0435	0001	1.8E
	0947	0703	0.6F
		1315	0.8E
		1823	*
2 M	0539	0058	1.8E
	1109	0814	0.7F
		1439	0.8E
		1939	*
3 Tu	0643	0212	1.8E
	1225	0929	0.8F
		1555	1.0E
		2104	*
4 W	0745	0323	1.8E
	1327	1029	0.9F
		1702	1.2E
		2224	*
5 Th	0841	0436	1.8E
	1418	1126	1.0F
	2203	1753	1.4E
		2332	0.3F
6 F	0054	0535	1.9E
	0933	1216	1.1F
	1501	1836	1.6E
	2235		
7 Sa	0216	0026	0.5F
	1022	0632	1.9E
	1539	1301	1.1F
	2311	1918	1.8E
8 Su	0324	0118	0.7F
	1110	0723	1.9E
	1613	1342	1.0F
	2350	1959	1.9E
9 M	0424	0205	0.8F
	1157	0812	1.8E
	1644	1421	0.9F
		2035	2.0E
10 Tu	0031	0253	0.9F
	0519	0900	1.7E
	1244	1459	0.8F
	1712	2115	2.0E
11 W	0114	0340	0.9F
	0611	0943	1.5E
	1333	1535	0.6F
	1737	2154	2.0E
12 Th	0201	0425	0.8F
	0701	1032	1.3E
	1428	1615	0.4F
	1758	2232	1.9E
13 F	0251	0516	0.7F
	0753	1126	1.1E
		1652	*
		2315	1.7E
14 Sa	0346	0609	0.6F
	0848	1222	0.9E
		1742	*
15 Su	0447	0007	1.6E
	0949	0711	0.5F
		1336	0.9E
		1837	*

Day	Slack Water Time h.m.	Maximum Current Time h.m.	Vel. knots
16 M	0550	0103	1.5E
	1054	0818	0.5F
		1453	0.9E
		1952	0.3E
17 Tu	0652	0211	1.4E
	1158	0921	0.5F
		1602	1.0E
		2113	*
18 W	0747	0315	1.4E
	1252	1015	0.6F
		1654	1.1E
		2224	*
19 Th	0834	0417	1.4E
	1337	1106	0.6F
		1735	1.2E
		2317	*
20 F	0917	0511	1.4E
	1415	1145	0.7F
		1809	1.4E
21 Sa	0956	0000	*
	1446	0557	1.5E
	2254	1222	0.7F
		1841	1.5E
22 Su	0225	0039	0.4F
	1034	0638	1.6E
	1513	1254	0.7F
	2314	1910	1.6E
23 M	0320	0117	0.5F
	1112	0718	1.6E
	1537	1323	0.7F
	2339	1938	1.7E
24 Tu	0410	0153	0.7F
	1150	0757	1.5E
	1559	1356	0.6F
		2007	1.8E
25 W	0007	0232	0.8F
	0458	0836	1.5E
	1230	1427	0.5F
	1620	2036	1.9E
26 Th	0040	0310	0.9F
	0547	0920	1.4E
	1314	1458	0.4F
	1640	2111	2.0E
27 F	0118	0353	0.9F
	0639	1003	1.3E
	1406	1537	0.3F
	1700	2152	2.0E
28 Sa	0203	0441	0.9F
	0734	1054	1.1E
		1616	*
		2235	1.9E
29 Su	0255	0536	0.9F
	0834	1201	1.0E
		1710	*
		2328	1.8E
30 M	0355	0639	0.8F
	0939	1311	1.0E
		1819	*

OCTOBER

Day	Slack Water Time h.m.	Maximum Current Time h.m.	Vel. knots
1 Tu	0504	0036	1.7E
	1046	0747	0.8F
		1428	1.1E
		1944	*
2 W	0614	0152	1.6E
	1149	0901	0.8F
		1536	1.2E
		2113	*
3 Th	0722	0315	1.6E
	1244	1001	0.8F
		1636	1.4E
		2226	*
4 F	0824	0427	1.6E
	1330	1058	0.8F
	2134	1721	1.6E
		2327	0.5F
5 Sa	0123	0528	1.6E
	0920	1147	0.8F
	1411	1808	1.8E
	2207		
6 Su	0237	0021	0.7F
	1012	0625	1.7E
	1446	1230	0.8F
	2243	1845	2.0E
7 M	0339	0110	0.9F
	1102	0715	1.6E
	1518	1311	0.7F
	2321	1926	2.1E
8 Tu	0433	0153	1.0F
	1151	0804	1.6E
	1545	1351	0.6F
		2003	2.1E
9 W	0000	0235	1.1F
	0523	0849	1.5E
	1240	1427	0.4F
	1610	2037	2.1E
10 Th	0040	0321	1.1F
	0609	0932	1.3E
	1335	1503	0.3F
	1629	2112	2.0E
11 F	0122	0359	1.0F
	0654	1018	1.2E
		1539	*
		2150	1.8E
12 Sa	0206	0445	0.9F
	0738	1107	1.1E
		1620	*
		2231	1.7E
13 Su	0254	0530	0.7F
	0824	1203	1.0E
		1711	*
		2316	1.5E
14 M	0348	0625	0.6F
	0912	1309	1.0E
		1812	0.3E
15 Tu	0448	0011	1.3E
	1003	0721	0.6F
		1414	1.0E
		1931	0.3E

Day	Slack Water Time h.m.	Maximum Current Time h.m.	Vel. knots
16 W	0551	0118	1.2E
	1055	0825	0.5F
		1514	1.1E
		2050	*
17 Th	0652	0230	1.2E
	1143	0917	0.5F
		1605	1.2E
		2157	*
18 F	0748	0339	1.2E
	1225	1009	0.5F
		1644	1.4E
		2250	*
19 Sa	0839	0439	1.2E
	1302	1051	0.5F
	2147	1719	1.5E
		2334	0.4F
20 Su	0124	0528	1.3E
	0925	1132	0.5F
	1334	1751	1.7E
	2205		
21 M	0228	0015	0.6F
	1009	0617	1.3E
	1402	1209	0.5F
	2228	1824	1.8E
22 Tu	0324	0052	0.8F
	1052	0701	1.4E
	1428	1244	0.4F
	2256	1853	2.0E
23 W	0415	0132	1.0F
	1136	0741	1.4E
	1453	1315	0.4F
	2328	1928	2.1E
24 Th	0505	0210	1.1F
	1223	0825	1.4E
	1519	1350	0.3F
		2003	2.1E
25 F	0005	0252	1.2F
	0554	0911	1.3E
		1430	*
		2040	2.2E
26 Sa	0046	0338	1.2F
	0644	0959	1.3E
		1513	*
		2124	2.1E
27 Su	0132	0423	1.2F
	0735	1054	1.2E
		1604	*
		2215	2.0E
28 M	0225	0518	1.1F
	0828	1157	1.2E
		1707	*
		2310	1.8E
29 Tu	0325	0618	1.0F
	0922	1300	1.2E
		1825	*
30 W	0432	0021	1.6E
	1015	0721	0.9F
		1409	1.3E
		1949	*
31 Th	0544	0141	1.4E
	1106	0826	0.8F
		1510	1.5E
		2113	*

Time meridian 120° W. 0000 is midnight. 1200 is noon.
If three consecutive entries are marked (E) the middle one is not a true maximum but an intermediate value to show the current pattern.
* Current weak and variable.

STRAIT OF JUAN de FUCA (Entrance)

1991 CURRENT TABLES

For Daylight Saving Time, add one hour.

NOVEMBER

Day	Slack Water Time h.m.	Maximum Current Time h.m.	Vel. knots
1 F	0657 1153 2034	0303 0929 1605 2224	1.3E 0.7F 1.7E 0.4F
2 Sa	0015 0806 1236 2107	0419 1024 1653 2321	1.3E 0.6F 1.9E 0.7F
3 Su	0141 0908 1313 2143	0522 1113 1737	1.3E 0.5F 2.0E
4 M	0250 1007 1347 2220	0010 0619 1159 1816	0.9F 1.4E 0.5F 2.1E
5 Tu	0348 1102 1416 2257	0059 0710 1239 1854	1.1F 1.3E 0.4F 2.1E
6 W	0438 2334	0141 0757 1320 1929	1.2F 1.3E * 2.1E
7 Th	0524	0222 0841 1356 2005	1.2F 1.3E * 2.1E
8 F	0012 0605	0301 0924 1437 2042	1.2F 1.2E * 2.0E
9 Sa	0050 0644	0341 1006 1514 2117	1.1F 1.2E * 1.8E
10 Su	0129 0722	0419 1054 1557 2156	1.0F 1.1E * 1.7E
11 M	0211 0759	0457 1142 1648 2235	0.9F 1.1E 0.3E 1.5E
12 Tu	0257 0836	0542 1230 1746 2330	0.8F 1.1E 0.3E 1.3E
13 W	0348 0915	0629 1322 1857	0.6F 1.2E 0.3E
14 Th	0446 0953	0028 0719 1417 2011	1.2E 0.5F 1.3E *
15 F	0549 1031	0135 0812 1506 2117	1.0E 0.5F 1.4E *
16 Sa	0653 1108	0252 0903 1547 2218	1.0E 0.4F 1.5E *
17 Su	0755 1142 2100	0401 0952 1627 2303	1.0E 0.3F 1.7E 0.5F
18 M	0115 0853 1214 2123	0458 1035 1704 2350	1.0E 0.3F 1.8E 0.7F
19 Tu	0223 0947 1247 2151	0553 1119 1741	1.1E 0.3F 2.0E
20 W	0322 2224	0033 0642 1200 1817	1.0F 1.2E * 2.1E
21 Th	0415 2300	0114 0728 1241 1857	1.2F 1.2E * 2.2E
22 F	0505 2340	0155 0817 1324 1937	1.3F 1.3E * 2.3E
23 Sa	0552	0238 0905 1413 2024	1.4F 1.3E * 2.3E
24 Su	0024 0639	0324 0953 1506 2109	1.5F 1.3E * 2.2E
25 M	0111 0724	0410 1046 1602 2202	1.4F 1.4E * 2.0E
26 Tu	0203 0809	0501 1139 1707 2301	1.3F 1.4E * 1.8E
27 W	0300 0853	0555 1239 1821	1.1F 1.5E *
28 Th	0404 0936	0005 0650 1337 1941	1.5E 0.9F 1.6E *
29 F	0514 1018 1921 2243	0122 0747 1435 2058	1.3E 0.7F 1.7E 0.3F
30 Sa	0630 1058 2002	0245 0849 1528 2207	1.1E 0.5F 1.8E 0.5F

DECEMBER

Day	Slack Water Time h.m.	Maximum Current Time h.m.	Vel. knots
1 Su	0025 0748 1135 2042	0402 0945 1618 2309	1.1E 0.4F 2.0E 0.8F
2 M	0148 0903 1209 2122	0511 1036 1705 2358	1.1E 0.3F 2.0E 0.9F
3 Tu	0255 2201	0613 1130 1748	1.1E * 2.1E
4 W	0350 2238	0047 0706 1213 1829	1.1F 1.1E * 2.1E
5 Th	0437 2315	0128 0751 1255 1906	1.2F 1.1E * 2.1E
6 F	0518 2350	0209 0836 1337 1941	1.2F 1.2E * 2.0E
7 Sa	0554	0244 0915 1418 2017	1.2F 1.2E * 1.9E
8 Su	0025 0627	0319 0954 1454 2052	1.1F 1.2E * 1.8E
9 M	0101 0658	0354 1033 1537 2127	1.1F 1.2E * 1.7E
10 Tu	0138 0728	0428 1110 1626 2209	1.0F 1.2E * 1.5E
11 W	0217 0757	0504 1152 1717 2254	0.9F 1.3E * 1.3E
12 Th	0301 0826	0544 1234 1818 2347	0.7F 1.3E * 1.2E
13 F	0350 0854	0624 1315 1923	0.6F 1.4E *
14 Sa	0448 0922	0044 0709 1400 2032	1.0E 0.5F 1.5E *
15 Su	0555 0950 1950 2324	0159 0757 1447 2133	0.9E 0.3F 1.6E 0.3F
16 M	2015	0315 0847 1530 2230	0.8E * 1.8E 0.5F
17 Tu	0058 2046	0427 0941 1616 2319	0.8E * 1.9E 0.8F
18 W	0213 2121	0530 1030 1703	0.9E * 2.1E
19 Th	0315 2200	0007 0626 1127 1748	1.1F 1.0E * 2.2E
20 F	0408 2240	0055 0716 1218 1833	1.3F 1.1E * 2.3E
21 Sa	0455 2323	0139 0804 1311 1922	1.4F 1.3E * 2.3E
22 Su	0539	0224 0851 1407 2011	1.5F 1.4E * 2.3E
23 M	0008 0621	0307 0940 1501 2101	1.5F 1.5E * 2.2E
24 Tu	0056 0701	0353 1026 1559 2156	1.5F 1.6E * 2.0E
25 W	0146 0739	0439 1113 1701 2251	1.3F 1.7E * 1.7E
26 Th	0239 0816 1642 1936	0527 1208 1807 2354	1.1F 1.7E 0.3F 1.4E
27 F	0339 0852 1740 2104	0619 1257 1916	0.9F 1.8E 0.3F
28 Sa	0447 0925 1837 2241	0103 0709 1356 2035	1.2E 0.6F 1.8E 0.4F
29 Su	0607 0957 2032	0222 0805 1448 2147	1.0E 0.4F 1.9E 0.6F
30 M	0018 2018	0345 0907 1545 2250	0.9E * 1.9E 0.7F
31 Tu	0141 2102	0459 1005 1634 2345	0.9E * 1.9E 0.9F

Time meridian 120° W. 0000 is midnight. 1200 is noon.
If three consecutive entries are marked (E) the middle one is not a true maximum but an intermediate value to show the current pattern.
* Current weak and variable.

1991 CURRENT TABLES

For Daylight Saving Time, add one hour.

RACE ROCKS
(Strait of Juan de Fuca)

Times and Heights of High and Low Waters

JANUARY

Day	Slack Water Time h.m.	Maximum Current Time h.m.	Vel. knots
1 Tu		0305	3.4F
	0725	0945	1.3E
	1315	1440	0.4F
	1600	2100	3.0E
2 W	0025	0350	3.4F
	0800	1020	1.4E
	1400	1530	0.4F
	1700	2150	2.8E
3 Th	0115	0430	3.2F
	0830	1100	1.5E
	1500	1625	0.4F
	1755	2245	2.4E
4 F	0200	0510	2.8F
	0900	1145	1.6E
	1605	1730	0.4F
	1905	2335	1.9E
5 Sa	0250	0550	2.4F
	0925	1230	1.7E
	1715	1850	0.3F
	2040		
6 Su		0040	1.4E
	0335	0630	1.9F
	0945	1330	1.8E
	1825	2030	0.4F
	2255		
7 M		0150	0.9E
	0425	0710	1.4F
	1005	1430	1.9E
	1920	2205	0.7F
8 Tu	0105	0310	0.6E
	0525	0750	0.8F
	1015	1525	2.0E
	2005	2315	1.1F
9 W	0240	0430	0.4E
	0645	0830	0.3F
	1010	1615	2.1E
	2045		
10 Th		0010	1.4F
	0355	0555	0.4E
		0920	0.1E
		1700	2.1E
	2120		
11 F		0050	1.7F
	0455	0745	0.6E
		1040	0.4E
		1745	2.1E
	2155		
12 Sa		0125	1.9F
	0535	0850	0.8E
		1155	0.5E
		1835	2.1E
	2225		
13 Su		0155	2.1F
	0610	0910	0.9E
		1255	0.5E
		1920	2.2E
	2300		
14 M		0220	2.3F
	0635	0910	0.9E
		1335	0.4E
		2000	2.3E
	2330		
15 Tu		0250	2.4F
	0700	0930	1.0E
		1415	0.3E
		2035	2.3E

Day	Slack Water Time h.m.	Maximum Current Time h.m.	Vel. knots
16 W	0005	0320	2.5F
	0715	0955	1.1E
		1450	0.2F
		2110	2.3E
17 Th	0035	0350	2.5F
	0735	1015	1.2E
		1520	0.1E
		2140	2.3E
18 F	0105	0420	2.5F
	0750	1035	1.4E
		1555	0.1E
		2215	2.1E
19 Sa	0140	0450	2.3F
	0805	1100	1.6E
		1640	0.0
		2250	1.8E
20 Su	0210	0525	2.2F
	0825	1135	1.8E
	1705	1730	0.0
	1755	2340	1.4E
21 M	0245	0555	1.9F
	0840	1215	2.0E
	1725	1830	0.2F
	1940		
22 Tu		0040	1.0E
	0325	0630	1.5F
	0905	1300	2.2E
	1800	1950	0.4F
	2210		
23 W		0155	0.7E
	0415	0705	1.2F
	0925	1355	2.4E
	1840	2120	0.8F
24 Th	0115	0305	0.5E
	0515	0750	0.8F
	0955	1450	2.6E
	1925	2235	1.4F
25 F	0245	0420	0.4E
	0640	0845	0.4F
	1025	1550	2.7E
	2010	2335	2.0F
26 Sa	0355	0545	0.5E
	0830	0955	0.2F
	1110	1650	2.9E
	2100		
27 Su		0025	2.5F
	0445	0655	0.7E
	0955	1110	0.2F
	1220	1755	3.0E
	2150		
28 M		0115	2.9F
	0530	0745	0.9E
	1050	1220	0.3F
	1340	1855	3.1E
	2235		
29 Tu		0200	3.1F
	0605	0825	1.2E
	1135	1325	0.5F
	1500	1950	3.2E
	2325		
30 W		0240	3.3F
	0640	0900	1.4E
	1220	1420	0.7F
	1610	2040	3.1E
31 Th	0010	0325	3.2F
	0705	0935	1.6E
	1310	1515	0.9F
	1715	2130	2.8E

FEBRUARY

Day	Slack Water Time h.m.	Maximum Current Time h.m.	Vel. knots
1 F	0055	0400	3.0F
	0730	1015	1.9E
	1400	1610	0.9F
	1820	2225	2.4E
2 Sa	0135	0440	2.7F
	0750	1055	2.1E
	1455	1705	0.9F
	1925	2315	1.9E
3 Su	0220	0515	2.3F
	0810	1140	2.2E
	1555	1805	0.9F
	2040		
4 M		0015	1.4E
	0305	0550	1.8F
	0830	1225	2.2E
	1655	1910	0.9F
	2225		
5 Tu		0115	1.0E
	0350	0625	1.3F
	0850	1315	2.2E
	1750	2030	0.9F
6 W	0015	0220	0.7E
	0450	0705	0.8F
	0905	1405	2.2E
	1850	2155	1.0F
7 Th	0140	0330	0.5E
	0610	0745	0.3F
	0910	1455	2.1E
	1940	2310	1.3F
8 F	0250	0455	0.5E
		0830	0.1E
		1555	2.0E
	2030	2355	1.5F
9 Sa	0345	0615	0.6E
		0940	0.3E
		1705	2.0E
	2110		
10 Su		0040	1.7F
	0430	0710	0.8E
		1105	0.4E
		1805	2.2E
	2155		
11 M		0115	1.9F
	0500	0740	0.9E
		1215	0.3E
		1850	2.3E
	2230		
12 Tu		0150	2.1F
	0530	0810	1.1E
		1305	0.1E
		1935	2.5E
	2305		
13 W		0220	2.3F
	0550	0836	1.3E
	1255	1350	0.1F
	1440	2010	2.6E
	2340		
14 Th		0250	2.4F
	0610	0900	1.5E
	1300	1430	0.3E
	1545	2045	2.5E
15 F	0015	0320	2.5F
	0630	0925	1.8E
	1320	1510	0.4F
	1640	2120	2.4E

Day	Slack Water Time h.m.	Maximum Current Time h.m.	Vel. knots
16 Sa	0050	0350	2.4F
	0645	0950	2.0E
	1350	1550	0.6F
	1730	2200	2.2E
17 Su	0125	0425	2.2F
	0705	1025	2.3E
	1430	1635	0.7F
	1830	2250	1.9E
18 M	0200	0455	2.0F
	0725	1100	2.5E
	1510	1725	0.8F
	1930	2345	1.5E
19 Tu	0240	0530	1.6F
	0745	1145	2.7E
	1600	1820	1.0F
	2055		
20 W		0045	1.3E
	0330	0605	1.3F
	0810	1235	2.8E
	1650	1925	1.1F
	2300		
21 Th		0145	1.0E
	0430	0645	0.9F
	0840	1330	2.8E
	1745	2035	1.4F
22 F	0040	0250	0.9E
	0545	0735	0.6F
	0915	1425	2.8E
	1845	2150	1.7F
23 Sa	0155	0355	0.9E
	0710	0835	0.3F
	0955	1530	2.9E
	1940	2255	2.0F
24 Su	0255	0510	0.9E
	0830	0945	0.2F
	1055	1635	2.9E
	2035	2350	2.3F
25 M	0350	0615	1.1E
	0935	1100	0.3F
	1220	1740	3.0E
	2130		
26 Tu		0045	2.5F
	0430	0700	1.3E
	1025	1215	0.5F
	1355	1840	3.0E
	2220		
27 W		0130	2.7F
	0505	0740	1.6E
	1105	1315	0.8F
	1515	1935	3.0E
	2305		
28 Th		0215	2.8F
	0535	0820	1.9E
	1150	1415	1.1F
	1625	2025	2.8E
	2350		

Time meridian 120° W. 0000 is midnight. 1200 is noon.
If three consecutive entries are marked (E) the middle one is not a true maximum but an intermediate value to show the current pattern.

RACE ROCKS
(Strait of Juan de Fuca)

1991 CURRENT TABLES

For Daylight Saving Time, add one hour.

Times and Heights of High and Low Waters

MARCH

Days 1–15

Day	Slack Water Time (h.m.)	Maximum Current Time (h.m.)	Vel. (knots)
1 F		0255	2.7F
	0555	0855	2.2E
	1230	1505	1.4F
	1730	2115	2.5E
2 Sa	0035	0330	2.5F
	0620	0935	2.5E
	1315	1555	1.5F
	1830	2210	2.2E
3 Su	0120	0405	2.3F
	0640	1010	2.6E
	1400	1640	1.6F
	1930	2300	1.9E
4 M	0200	0440	1.9F
	0700	1055	2.7E
	1450	1725	1.6F
	2035	2355	1.5E
5 Tu	0250	0515	1.4F
	0725	1135	2.6E
	1535	1815	1.5F
	2155		
6 W		0050	1.2E
	0345	0550	0.9F
	0745	1220	2.5E
	1630	1910	1.3F
	2310		
7 Th		0145	1.0E
	0455	0630	0.5F
	0800	1310	2.3E
	1730	2015	1.2F
8 F	0020	0240	0.9E
	0630	0715	0.1F
	0800	1400	2.1E
	1830	2130	1.2F
9 Sa	0120	0355	0.8E
		0810	0.2E
		1500	2.0E
	1930	2245	1.3F
10 Su	0210	0515	0.9E
		0915	0.3E
		1610	2.0E
	2020	2340	1.4F
11 M	0300	0610	1.1E
		1040	0.3E
		1720	2.1E
	2110		
12 Tu		0020	1.6F
	0335	0645	1.3E
		1155	0.1E
		1815	2.3E
	2155		
13 W		0100	1.8F
	0410	0715	1.5E
	1130	1250	0.2E
	1400	1900	2.4E
	2235		
14 Th		0140	2.0F
	0435	0745	1.8E
	1140	1335	0.5F
	1520	1945	2.4E
	2315		
15 F		0210	2.0F
	0500	0810	2.1E
	1200	1420	0.8F
	1620	2025	2.4E
	2355		

Days 16–31

Day	Slack Water Time (h.m.)	Maximum Current Time (h.m.)	Vel. (knots)
16 Sa		0245	2.0F
	0520	0835	2.5E
	1230	1500	1.1F
	1715	2110	2.2E
17 Su	0035	0320	1.9F
	0540	0910	2.8E
	1305	1545	1.4F
	1810	2205	2.0E
18 M	0115	0350	1.7F
	0600	0945	3.0E
	1345	1625	1.6F
	1910	2255	1.9E
19 Tu	0205	0425	1.4F
	0625	1030	3.1E
	1425	1715	1.7F
	2015	2350	1.7E
20 W	0255	0505	1.0F
	0650	1120	3.2E
	1515	1805	1.8F
	2135		
21 Th		0040	1.5E
	0355	0545	0.7F
	0715	1210	3.1E
	1610	1900	1.8F
	2255		
22 F		0135	1.4E
	0510	0630	0.4F
	0745	1305	3.0E
	1710	2000	1.8F
23 Sa	0000	0235	1.3E
	0635	0725	0.2F
	0815	1405	2.8E
	1810	2110	1.8F
24 Su	0105	0340	1.3E
	0810	0830	0.0
	0850	1505	2.7E
	1910	2215	1.9F
25 M	0155	0450	1.4E
	0915	0950	0.0
	1020	1615	2.6E
	2010	2315	1.9F
26 Tu	0245	0545	1.6E
	0950	1110	0.3F
	1230	1725	2.5E
	2110		
27 W		0010	2.0F
	0325	0630	1.9E
	1025	1220	0.6F
	1415	1825	2.5E
	2200		
28 Th		0100	2.0F
	0355	0705	2.2E
	1100	1320	1.0F
	1535	1925	2.4E
	2255		
29 F		0140	1.9F
	0420	0740	2.5E
	1135	1410	1.4F
	1645	2015	2.2E
	2340		
30 Sa		0220	1.8F
	0440	0815	2.8E
	1210	1455	1.8F
	1740	2110	2.0E
31 Su	0030	0255	1.6F
	0505	0855	3.0E
	1245	1535	2.0F
	1835	2200	1.9E

APRIL

Days 1–15

Day	Slack Water Time (h.m.)	Maximum Current Time (h.m.)	Vel. (knots)
1 M	0115	0330	1.3F
	0525	0930	3.0E
	1320	1615	2.1F
	1930	2250	1.7E
2 Tu	0205	0405	1.0F
	0550	1010	3.0E
	1400	1655	2.0F
	2025	2340	1.6E
3 W	0300	0440	0.7F
	0610	1055	2.8E
	1440	1735	1.9F
	2120		
4 Th		0025	1.4E
	0410	0520	0.3F
	0625	1140	2.5E
	1530	1825	1.6F
	2215		
5 F		0110	1.3E
		0600	0.0
		1225	2.3E
	1625	1915	1.4F
	2310		
6 Sa		0200	1.2E
		0650	0.3E
		1315	2.0E
	1725	2015	1.3F
	2355		
7 Su		0305	1.2E
		0745	0.4E
		1410	1.9E
	1830	2115	1.2F
8 M	0045	0425	1.3E
		0850	0.5E
		1515	1.8E
	1925	2220	1.2F
9 Tu	0130	0520	1.4E
		1025	0.3E
		1625	1.8E
	2020	2315	1.3F
10 W	0210	0555	1.7E
		1140	0.1E
		1730	1.9E
	2110		
11 Th		0005	1.3F
	0245	0620	2.0E
	1055	1235	0.3F
	1410	1825	2.0E
	2200		
12 F		0045	1.3F
	0315	0645	2.3E
	1105	1325	0.8F
	1535	1920	2.0E
	2250		
13 Sa		0130	1.3F
	0340	0720	2.7E
	1125	1405	1.3F
	1640	2015	1.9E
	2345		
14 Su		0205	1.2F
	0405	0755	3.1E
	1200	1450	1.8F
	1735	2115	1.9E
15 M	0035	0245	1.1F
	0430	0835	3.3E
	1235	1530	2.1F
	1835	2205	1.8E

Days 16–30

Day	Slack Water Time (h.m.)	Maximum Current Time (h.m.)	Vel. (knots)
16 Tu	0125	0320	0.9F
	0455	0920	3.5E
	1315	1610	2.3F
	1935	2255	1.8E
17 W	0220	0400	0.6F
	0520	1005	3.5E
	1355	1655	2.4F
	2035	2345	1.8E
18 Th	0325	0440	0.4F
	0545	1100	3.4E
	1445	1745	2.3F
	2135		
19 F		0030	1.7E
	0445	0525	0.1F
	0605	1150	3.2E
	1540	1835	2.2F
	2230		
20 Sa		0120	1.7E
		0615	0.1E
		1245	2.9E
	1640	1930	2.0F
	2325		
21 Su		0215	1.6E
		0715	0.3E
		1345	2.6E
	1745	2035	1.7F
22 M	0010	0330	1.7E
		0835	0.3E
		1450	2.3E
	1845	2135	1.5F
23 Tu	0055	0440	1.9E
		1020	0.2E
		1605	2.0E
	1950	2235	1.4F
24 W	0135	0525	2.1E
	1020	1135	0.2F
	1255	1720	1.9E
	2050	2330	1.2F
25 Th	0205	0605	2.4E
	1035	1235	0.7F
	1445	1820	1.8E
	2155		
26 F		0020	1.0F
	0230	0635	2.7E
	1100	1325	1.2F
	1605	1920	1.7E
	2300		
27 Sa		0105	0.9F
	0255	0710	2.9E
	1125	1405	1.6F
	1705	2015	1.6E
	2355		
28 Su		0145	0.7F
	0315	0745	3.0E
	1150	1440	1.9F
	1755	2110	1.6E
29 M	0050	0220	0.5F
	0340	0820	3.1E
	1220	1515	2.1F
	1845	2155	1.5E
30 Tu	0145	0300	0.3F
	0400	0855	3.0E
	1250	1550	2.2F
	1930	2240	1.5E

Time meridian 120° W. 0000 is midnight. 1200 is noon.
If three consecutive entries are marked (E) the middle one is not a true maximum but an intermediate value to show the current pattern.

1991 CURRENT TABLES

For Daylight Saving Time, add one hour.

RACE ROCKS
(Strait of Juan de Fuca)

Times and Heights of High and Low Waters

MAY

Day	Slack Water Time h.m.	Maximum Current Time h.m.	Maximum Current Vel. knots
1	0245	0335	0.2F
W	0415	0940	2.9E
	1325	1630	2.1F
	2010	2320	1.5E
2		0410	0.1E
Th		1020	2.7E
	1405	1705	2.0F
	2050	2355	1.5E
3		0445	0.3E
F		1105	2.5E
	1450	1750	1.7F
	2130		
4		0035	1.4E
Sa		0525	0.5E
		1145	2.2E
	1540	1835	1.5F
	2210		
5		0115	1.3E
Su		0610	0.6E
		1230	2.0E
	1635	1920	1.3F
	2250		
6		0205	1.3E
M		0705	0.7E
		1320	1.8E
	1735	2010	1.2F
	2325		
7		0305	1.4E
Tu		0810	0.7E
		1420	1.6E
	1830	2100	1.0F
8	0000	0405	1.6E
W		1000	0.5E
		1530	1.5E
	1925	2155	0.9F
9	0035	0445	2.0E
Th		1125	0.1E
		1645	1.4E
	2025	2250	0.8F
10	0105	0520	2.3E
F	1025	1220	0.4F
	1415	1755	1.4E
	2130	2345	0.6F
11	0135	0555	2.7E
Sa	1035	1310	1.1F
	1545	1905	1.4E
	2240		
12		0035	0.5F
Su	0210	0635	3.1E
	1100	1350	1.7F
	1655	2015	1.5E
	2350		
13		0126	0.4F
M	0240	0720	3.4E
	1130	1435	2.2F
	1755	2110	1.5E
14	0050	0210	0.3F
Tu	0315	0805	3.6E
	1210	1515	2.5F
	1850	2200	1.6E
15	0145	0250	0.3F
W	0345	0855	3.6E
	1255	1555	2.7F
	1945	2245	1.7E
16	0245	0335	0.2F
Th	0415	0950	3.6E
	1340	1640	2.7F
	2035	2325	1.7E
17		0410	0.0
F		1040	3.4E
	1430	1725	2.5F
	2120		
18		0005	1.7E
Sa		0505	0.2E
		1135	3.1E
	1525	1815	2.2F
	2200		
19		0055	1.7E
Su		0605	0.4E
		1230	2.7E
	1620	1905	1.9F
	2240		
20		0155	1.8E
M		0715	0.5E
		1330	2.2E
	1720	2000	1.5F
	2315		
21		0325	1.9E
Tu		0915	0.4E
		1440	1.8E
	1825	2055	1.2F
	2345		
22		0425	2.2E
W		1050	0.1E
		1605	1.5E
	1930	2150	0.8F
23	0010	0505	2.4E
Th	1020	1155	0.4F
	1345	1720	1.3E
	2050	2245	0.5F
24	0025	0540	2.6E
F	1030	1245	0.8F
	1525	1825	1.2E
	2230	2340	0.2F
25	0035	0610	2.8E
Sa	1050	1325	1.2F
	1630	1925	1.2E
26		0025	0.0
Su		0645	2.8E
	1115	1355	1.6F
	1725	2020	1.2E
27		0110	0.2E
M		0720	2.9E
	1140	1430	1.8F
	1810	2110	1.3E
28		0150	0.3E
Tu		0800	2.9E
	1205	1500	2.0F
	1850	2145	1.3E
29		0230	0.3E
W		0840	2.8E
	1240	1535	2.0F
	1920	2220	1.4E
30		0305	0.4E
Th		0920	2.7E
	1310	1610	2.0F
	1950	2255	1.4E
31		0340	0.4E
F		1000	2.6E
	1350	1645	1.9F
	2015	2325	1.4E

JUNE

Day	Slack Water Time h.m.	Maximum Current Time h.m.	Maximum Current Vel. knots
1		0415	0.5E
Sa		1040	2.4E
	1430	1720	1.7F
	2045	2355	1.4E
2		0450	0.6E
Su		1115	2.3E
	1510	1800	1.6F
	2115		
3		0030	1.4E
M		0530	0.7E
		1155	2.0E
	1555	1840	1.4F
	2140		
4		0105	1.5E
Tu		0620	0.8E
		1240	1.8E
	1645	1920	1.2F
	2205		
5		0150	1.6E
W		0730	0.7E
		1340	1.5E
	1730	1955	1.0F
	2230		
6		0245	1.9E
Th		0925	0.5E
		1450	1.2E
	1830	2040	0.8F
	2300		
7		0335	2.2E
F		1110	0.0
		1610	1.0E
	1935	2130	0.5F
	2325		
8		0425	2.5E
Sa	0940	1200	0.6F
	1435	1730	1.0E
	2105	2230	0.2F
	2350		
9		0515	2.9E
Su	1000	1250	1.3F
	1600	1855	1.0E
	2250	2340	0.1F
10	0020	0600	3.2E
M	1030	1335	2.0F
	1705	2005	1.2E
11	0015	0040	0.0
Tu	0105	0655	3.4E
	1110	1415	2.4F
	1805	2055	1.3E
12	0100	0135	0.1F
W	0205	0750	3.6E
	1155	1500	2.8F
	1850	2140	1.5E
13	0140	0225	0.1F
Th	0305	0845	3.7E
	1240	1540	2.9F
	1935	2215	1.6E
14	0230	0310	0.1F
F	0350	0940	3.6E
	1325	1625	2.8F
	2015	2255	1.7E
15	0335	0400	0.1F
Sa	0425	1030	3.3E
	1415	1710	2.6F
	2050	2340	1.8E
16		0455	0.1E
Su		1120	2.9E
	1505	1755	2.2F
	2125		
17		0025	1.8E
M		0600	0.3E
		1215	2.4E
	1600	1840	1.8F
	2150		
18		0125	1.9E
Tu		0730	0.3E
		1320	1.9E
	1655	1925	1.4F
	2215		
19		0240	2.1E
W		0925	0.1E
		1435	1.4E
	1800	2010	0.9F
	2235		
20		0345	2.3E
Th	0920	1050	0.2F
	1230	1600	1.1E
	1915	2100	0.4F
	2240		
21		0430	2.5E
F	0940	1150	0.6F
	1425	1715	1.0E
		2155	0.0
22		0510	2.5E
Sa	1005	1240	1.0F
	1545	1825	0.9E
		2255	0.3E
23		0550	2.6E
Su	1030	1315	1.3F
	1645	1940	1.0E
		2355	0.5E
24		0630	2.6E
M	1100	1350	1.6F
	1730	2035	1.1E
25		0045	0.6E
Tu		0710	2.7E
	1125	1420	1.7F
	1805	2100	1.1E
26		0130	0.5E
W		0755	2.7E
	1200	1450	1.9F
	1835	2130	1.2E
27		0210	0.5E
Th		0835	2.7E
	1230	1520	1.9F
	1900	2155	1.3E
28		0245	0.4E
F		0915	2.7E
	1305	1555	1.9F
	1925	2225	1.3E
29		0320	0.4E
Sa		0950	2.6E
	1335	1625	1.9F
	1945	2250	1.4E
30		0350	0.4E
Su		1020	2.5E
	1410	1700	1.8F
	2005	2315	1.5E

Time meridian 120° W. 0000 is midnight. 1200 is noon.
If three consecutive entries are marked (E) the middle one is not a true maximum but an intermediate value to show the current pattern.

RACE ROCKS
(Strait of Juan de Fuca)

1991 CURRENT TABLES

For Daylight Saving Time, add one hour.

Times and Heights of High and Low Waters

JULY

Day	Slack Water Time (h.m.)	Maximum Current Time (h.m.)	Vel. (knots)
1 M		0425	0.5E
		1055	2.2E
	1445	1735	1.7F
	2025	2345	1.6E
2 Tu		0510	0.5E
		1130	2.0E
	1525	1805	1.5F
	2050		
3 W		0020	1.8E
		0605	0.5E
		1220	1.6E
	1605	1840	1.3F
	2110		
4 Th		0105	2.0E
		0715	0.4E
		1325	1.3E
	1650	1915	1.0F
	2130		
5 F		0155	2.2E
		0855	0.1E
		1440	1.0E
	1750	1955	0.7F
	2155		
6 Sa		0250	2.4E
	0825	1025	0.4F
	1305	1555	0.8E
	1905	2045	0.4F
	2220		
7 Su		0350	2.7E
	0845	1130	1.0F
	1455	1715	0.8E
	2050	2145	0.1F
	2240		
8 M		0445	2.9E
	0920	1225	1.7F
	1605	1840	0.9E
		2300	0.0
9 Tu		0545	3.2E
	1005	1310	2.2F
	1705	1940	1.1E
	2340		
10 W		0010	0.0
	0040	0640	3.4E
	1050	1400	2.7F
	1750	2025	1.3E
11 Th	0010	0110	0.2F
	0210	0740	3.5E
	1135	1440	2.9F
	1830	2105	1.5E
12 F	0045	0205	0.3F
	0320	0835	3.6E
	1220	1525	3.0F
	1910	2145	1.6E
13 Sa	0130	0300	0.4F
	0420	0925	3.4E
	1310	1605	2.9F
	1940	2225	1.8E
14 Su	0225	0355	0.4F
	0520	1020	3.1E
	1355	1645	2.7F
	2010	2305	2.0E
15 M	0330	0455	0.4F
	0615	1110	2.7E
	1445	1730	2.3F
	2035	2355	2.1E

Day	Slack Water Time (h.m.)	Maximum Current Time (h.m.)	Vel. (knots)
16 Tu	0440	0600	0.3F
	0725	1210	2.1E
	1535	1810	1.8F
	2100		
17 W		0045	2.2E
	0550	0720	0.3F
	0900	1315	1.6E
	1630	1850	1.3F
	2120		
18 Th		0140	2.3E
	0655	0850	0.4F
	1110	1425	1.2E
	1730	1930	0.8F
	2135		
19 F		0240	2.3E
	0750	1015	0.7F
	1305	1540	1.0E
	1855	2015	0.3F
	2135		
20 Sa		0335	2.4E
	0835	1125	1.0F
	1425	1700	0.9E
		2110	0.2E
21 Su		0435	2.4E
	0915	1215	1.3F
	1530	1820	0.9E
		2220	0.4E
22 M		0530	2.4E
	0955	1255	1.5F
	1625	1930	1.0E
		2335	0.6E
23 Tu		0620	2.4E
	1030	1330	1.7F
	1710	2010	1.1E
24 W		0035	0.5E
		0710	2.5E
	1105	1405	1.8F
	1740	2035	1.2E
25 Th		0125	0.4E
		0750	2.6E
	1140	1435	2.0F
	1810	2100	1.3E
26 F		0205	0.2E
		0830	2.7E
	1210	1505	2.1F
	1830	2125	1.4E
27 Sa		0240	0.1E
		0905	2.6E
	1245	1535	2.1F
	1850	2150	1.5E
28 Su		0315	0.1E
		0935	2.5E
	1315	1610	2.1F
	1910	2215	1.7E
29 M		0350	0.0
		1010	2.3E
	1345	1640	2.0F
	1930	2240	1.8E
30 Tu		0430	0.0
		1045	2.0E
	1420	1710	1.8F
	1945	2315	2.0E
31 W	0445	0515	0.0
	0545	1135	1.7E
	1455	1740	1.5F
	2005	2350	2.2E

AUGUST

Day	Slack Water Time (h.m.)	Maximum Current Time (h.m.)	Vel. (knots)
1 Th	0510	0610	0.1F
	0710	1230	1.4E
	1540	1815	1.2F
	2025		
2 F		0035	2.3E
	0545	0715	0.3F
	0855	1335	1.1E
	1630	1850	0.9F
	2050		
3 Sa		0130	2.5E
	0625	0835	0.6F
	1145	1440	0.9E
	1740	1935	0.6F
	2115		
4 Su		0225	2.6E
	0710	0955	1.0F
	1335	1550	0.8E
	1905	2025	0.3F
	2145		
5 M		0325	2.8E
	0755	1100	1.6F
	1450	1710	0.8E
	2040	2135	0.1F
	2225		
6 Tu		0425	2.9E
	0845	1200	2.0F
	1550	1820	1.0E
	2155	2250	0.1F
	2340		
7 W		0530	3.1E
	0935	1250	2.5F
	1640	1915	1.2E
	2240		
8 Th		0000	0.3F
	0110	0635	3.3E
	1025	1340	2.8F
	1725	1955	1.4E
	2320		
9 F		0105	0.5F
	0240	0730	3.3E
	1115	1420	3.0F
	1800	2035	1.7E
10 Sa	0005	0205	0.8F
	0355	0825	3.3E
	1200	1505	3.0F
	1830	2115	1.9E
11 Su	0050	0300	1.0F
	0500	0915	3.1E
	1245	1545	2.9F
	1900	2155	2.2E
12 M	0140	0355	1.1F
	0605	1010	2.7E
	1330	1620	2.6F
	1920	2235	2.4E
13 Tu	0235	0450	1.2F
	0715	1105	2.3E
	1420	1700	2.2F
	1945	2320	2.5E
14 W	0330	0545	1.2F
	0830	1205	1.8E
	1510	1740	1.7F
	2010		
15 Th		0005	2.5E
	0425	0645	1.1F
	1000	1305	1.4E
	1605	1820	1.2F
	2030		

Day	Slack Water Time (h.m.)	Maximum Current Time (h.m.)	Vel. (knots)
16 F		0100	2.5E
	0525	0800	1.1F
	1135	1410	1.1E
	1715	1900	0.7F
	2045		
17 Sa		0150	2.3E
	0625	0925	1.2F
	1255	1520	1.0E
	1845	1950	0.2F
	2050		
18 Su		0250	2.2E
	0725	1040	1.3F
	1400	1645	0.9E
		2050	0.2E
19 M		0355	2.1E
	0820	1140	1.5F
	1500	1800	1.0E
		2210	0.4E
20 Tu		0510	2.1E
	0910	1225	1.6F
	1550	1855	1.1E
		2340	0.3E
21 W		0605	2.2E
	0950	1305	1.8F
	1630	1930	1.3E
22 Th		0040	0.2E
		0655	2.4E
	1030	1340	2.0F
	1700	2000	1.4E
23 F	0100	0125	0.0
	0155	0735	2.5E
	1110	1410	2.1F
	1725	2025	1.5E
24 Sa	0050	0205	0.2F
	0315	0815	2.5E
	1145	1445	2.2F
	1750	2055	1.7E
25 Su	0105	0240	0.4F
	0410	0855	2.5E
	1220	1515	2.2F
	1810	2120	1.9E
26 M	0125	0315	0.6F
	0500	0930	2.3E
	1250	1545	2.1F
	1825	2145	2.1E
27 Tu	0150	0355	0.7F
	0545	1010	2.0E
	1325	1615	1.9F
	1845	2215	2.3E
28 W	0225	0435	0.8F
	0635	1055	1.8E
	1405	1645	1.6F
	1900	2250	2.4E
29 Th	0300	0520	0.9F
	0735	1150	1.5E
	1445	1715	1.3F
	1920	2330	2.5E
30 F	0340	0610	1.0F
	0900	1240	1.3E
	1540	1750	0.9F
	1945		
31 Sa		0015	2.6E
	0430	0705	1.2F
	1050	1340	1.1E
	1640	1835	0.6F
	2010		

Time meridian 120° W. 0000 is midnight. 1200 is noon.
If three consecutive entries are marked (E) the middle one is not a true maximum but an intermediate value to show the current pattern.

1991 CURRENT TABLES

For Daylight Saving Time, add one hour.

RACE ROCKS
(Strait of Juan de Fuca)

Times and Heights of High and Low Waters

SEPTEMBER

Day	Slack Water Time h.m.	Maximum Current Time h.m.	Vel. knots
1 Su		0110	2.6E
	0525	0815	1.4F
	1220	1435	1.0E
	1800	1925	0.3F
	2040		
2 M		0205	2.6E
	0620	0925	1.6F
	1330	1545	0.9E
	1925	2020	0.2F
	2120		
3 Tu		0310	2.6E
	0720	1035	1.9F
	1430	1705	1.0E
	2040	2135	0.1F
	2225		
4 W		0415	2.7E
	0815	1135	2.2F
	1525	1805	1.2E
	2135	2255	0.2F
5 Th	0010	0520	2.8E
	0910	1230	2.5F
	1610	1850	1.5E
	2215		
6 F		0005	0.5F
	0155	0625	2.8E
	1000	1315	2.7F
	1650	1930	1.7E
	2255		
7 Sa		0110	0.9F
	0320	0720	2.8E
	1050	1400	2.7F
	1720	2005	2.0E
	2340		
8 Su		0210	1.3F
	0435	0815	2.7E
	1140	1440	2.7F
	1745	2045	2.3E
9 M	0020	0300	1.6F
	0540	0910	2.5E
	1225	1520	2.5F
	1810	2125	2.5E
10 Tu	0100	0345	1.9F
	0640	1005	2.2E
	1315	1555	2.2F
	1830	2205	2.7E
11 W	0145	0435	2.0F
	0750	1100	1.9E
	1400	1630	1.8F
	1855	2245	2.7E
12 Th	0235	0520	2.0F
	0900	1155	1.6E
	1455	1710	1.4F
	1920	2335	2.6E
13 F	0325	0610	1.8F
	1015	1250	1.4E
	1555	1750	0.9F
	1940		
14 Sa		0020	2.4E
	0420	0710	1.6F
	1125	1345	1.1E
	1710	1835	0.4F
	2000		
15 Su		0110	2.1E
	0520	0820	1.5F
	1225	1455	1.0E
	1900	1930	0.0
	1955		
16 M		0210	1.9E
	0620	0950	1.5F
	1325	1630	1.0E
		2040	0.2E
17 Tu		0325	1.7E
	0725	1055	1.5F
	1420	1735	1.1E
		2235	0.2E
18 W		0445	1.8E
	0820	1145	1.6F
	1505	1820	1.3E
		2355	0.0
19 Th		0545	1.9E
	0910	1230	1.7F
	1545	1855	1.4E
	2325		
20 F		0045	0.2F
	0200	0635	2.0E
	0955	1305	1.8F
	1615	1925	1.6E
	2330		
21 Sa		0125	0.4F
	0305	0720	2.1E
	1035	1340	1.9F
	1640	1950	1.8E
	2345		
22 Su		0200	0.7F
	0400	0800	2.1E
	1115	1410	1.9F
	1700	2020	2.0E
23 M	0005	0235	1.0F
	0455	0845	2.0E
	1155	1445	1.8F
	1720	2045	2.2E
24 Tu	0030	0310	1.3F
	0545	0930	1.9E
	1235	1515	1.7F
	1735	2110	2.4E
25 W	0100	0345	1.5F
	0635	1020	1.7E
	1320	1550	1.4F
	1755	2145	2.5E
26 Th	0130	0425	1.7F
	0735	1105	1.6E
	1405	1620	1.1F
	1815	2225	2.6E
27 F	0210	0505	1.8F
	0845	1155	1.4E
	1455	1655	0.8F
	1835	2310	2.6E
28 Sa	0255	0555	1.9F
	1000	1240	1.3E
	1600	1735	0.5F
	1900		
29 Su		0000	2.6E
	0345	0645	1.9F
	1105	1330	1.2E
	1710	1820	0.3F
	1930		
30 M		0055	2.5E
	0445	0750	1.9F
	1205	1430	1.1E
	1835	1915	0.1F

OCTOBER

Day	Slack Water Time h.m.	Maximum Current Time h.m.	Vel. knots
1 Tu		0150	2.4E
	0545	0855	1.9F
	1305	1550	1.1E
	2005	2025	0.0
	2045		
2 W		0255	2.3E
	0650	1005	2.0F
	1400	1700	1.3E
	2055	2155	0.1F
	2255		
3 Th		0410	2.2E
	0750	1105	2.0F
	1445	1750	1.5E
	2130	2320	0.4F
4 F	0110	0520	2.2E
	0850	1200	2.1F
	1530	1830	1.8E
	2205		
5 Sa		0025	0.9F
	0245	0625	2.2E
	0945	1250	2.1F
	1600	1905	2.0E
	2240		
6 Su		0120	1.3F
	0405	0720	2.1E
	1040	1335	2.0F
	1625	1940	2.3E
	2315		
7 M		0210	1.8F
	0510	0820	2.0E
	1130	1415	1.9F
	1650	2015	2.5E
	2350		
8 Tu		0255	2.2F
	0610	0915	1.9E
	1220	1450	1.7F
	1710	2055	2.7E
9 W	0030	0335	2.5F
	0710	1005	1.7E
	1310	1530	1.4F
	1735	2135	2.7E
10 Th	0105	0415	2.5F
	0810	1055	1.6E
	1405	1605	1.1F
	1800	2215	2.5E
11 F	0145	0455	2.4F
	0910	1140	1.5E
	1500	1645	0.8F
	1825	2300	2.3E
12 Sa	0230	0535	2.2F
	1005	1230	1.3E
	1605	1725	0.4F
	1845	2350	2.0E
13 Su	0320	0625	1.9F
	1055	1320	1.1E
	1735	1815	0.1F
	1850		
14 M		0040	1.7E
	0420	0725	1.6F
	1145	1430	1.0E
		1910	0.2E
15 Tu		0135	1.5E
	0525	0835	1.4F
	1235	1620	1.1E
		2050	0.3E
16 W		0245	1.3E
	0625	0955	1.3F
	1325	1710	1.2E
		2310	0.1E
17 Th		0415	1.3E
	0725	1050	1.3F
	1405	1745	1.3E
	2235	2355	0.2F
18 F	0105	0520	1.4E
	0820	1140	1.3F
	1440	1815	1.5E
	2235		
19 Sa		0040	0.5F
	0225	0615	1.5E
	0915	1220	1.3F
	1510	1845	1.7E
	2245		
20 Su		0115	0.8F
	0330	0700	1.5E
	1010	1300	1.3F
	1530	1910	1.9E
	2300		
21 M		0150	1.2F
	0430	0755	1.5E
	1100	1335	1.2F
	1555	1935	2.1E
	2320		
22 Tu		0220	1.6F
	0525	0845	1.5E
	1150	1410	1.1F
	1615	2000	2.3E
	2345		
23 W		0255	2.0F
	0620	0935	1.5E
	1240	1445	0.9F
	1635	2035	2.5E
24 Th	0015	0330	2.3F
	0715	1020	1.5E
	1330	1520	0.8F
	1655	2115	2.6E
25 F	0050	0410	2.5F
	0810	1105	1.5E
	1425	1600	0.6F
	1720	2200	2.7E
26 Sa	0135	0450	2.5F
	0905	1145	1.5E
	1520	1635	0.4F
	1745	2250	2.6E
27 Su	0220	0535	2.4F
	0955	1225	1.4E
	1625	1720	0.2F
	1810	2340	2.5E
28 M	0315	0625	2.3F
	1045	1315	1.3E
	1755	1810	0.0
	1830		
29 Tu		0035	2.3E
	0410	0720	2.1F
	1135	1420	1.3E
		1915	0.1E
30 W		0135	2.0E
	0515	0820	1.9F
	1225	1555	1.4E
		2055	0.1E
31 Th		0245	1.7E
	0620	0930	1.7F
	1310	1650	1.6E
	2100	2235	0.3F

Time meridian 120° W. 0000 is midnight. 1200 is noon.
If three consecutive entries are marked (E) the middle one is not a true maximum but an intermediate
value to show the current pattern.

RACE ROCKS
(Strait of Juan de Fuca)

1991 CURRENT TABLES

For Daylight Saving Time, add one hour.

Times and Heights of High and Low Waters

NOVEMBER

Days 1–15

Day	Slack Water Time (h.m.)	Max Current Time (h.m.)	Vel. (knots)
1 F	0020	0410	1.6E
	0725	1030	1.5F
	1355	1730	1.8E
	2125	2345	0.7F
2 Sa	0215	0525	1.5E
	0830	1125	1.4F
	1430	1805	2.0E
	2155		
3 Su		0040	1.3F
	0335	0630	1.5E
	0940	1220	1.2F
	1455	1835	2.2E
	2225		
4 M		0125	1.8F
	0445	0730	1.4E
	1045	1305	1.0F
	1515	1910	2.4E
	2255		
5 Tu		0205	2.2F
	0545	0830	1.4E
	1150	1345	0.8F
	1540	1945	2.5E
	2325		
6 W		0240	2.5F
	0640	0920	1.4E
	1245	1425	0.7F
	1600	2025	2.5E
	2355		
7 Th		0315	2.7F
	0730	1005	1.4E
	1335	1505	0.5F
	1625	2105	2.4E
8 F	0030	0350	2.7F
	0815	1045	1.4E
	1430	1540	0.4F
	1650	2150	2.2E
9 Sa	0105	0425	2.5F
	0855	1125	1.3E
	1530	1620	0.2F
	1710	2235	2.0E
10 Su	0145	0505	2.3F
	0935	1205	1.2E
		1700	0.0
		2320	1.7E
11 M	0230	0550	2.0F
	1015	1245	1.1E
		1750	0.2E
12 Tu		0005	1.4E
	0320	0635	1.7F
	1055	1340	1.0E
		1845	0.4E
13 W		0055	1.2E
	0420	0725	1.4F
	1130	1555	1.0E
		2210	0.3E
14 Th		0150	0.9E
	0515	0815	1.2F
	1205	1635	1.2E
		2305	0.1E
15 F		0315	0.8E
	0615	0910	1.0F
	1235	1700	1.3E
	2215	2350	0.2F

Days 16–30

Day	Slack Water Time (h.m.)	Max Current Time (h.m.)	Vel. (knots)
16 Sa	0110	0445	0.8E
	0715	1005	0.8F
	1305	1725	1.5E
	2155		
17 Su		0030	0.6F
	0245	0545	0.8E
	0820	1105	0.6F
	1325	1745	1.7E
	2155		
18 M		0100	1.0F
	0355	0645	0.9E
	0940	1155	0.5F
	1350	1810	1.9E
	2210		
19 Tu		0130	1.5F
	0455	0745	1.0E
	1100	1245	0.4F
	1415	1835	2.2E
	2235		
20 W		0200	2.0F
	0550	0840	1.1E
	1205	1330	0.3F
	1440	1915	2.4E
	2305		
21 Th		0235	2.5F
	0640	0930	1.3E
	1300	1410	0.3F
	1515	2000	2.6E
	2345		
22 F		0310	2.8F
	0725	1010	1.4E
	1345	1450	0.3F
	1550	2050	2.7E
23 Sa	0025	0350	3.0F
	0810	1045	1.4E
	1430	1530	0.2F
	1625	2140	2.7E
24 Su	0105	0430	3.0F
	0850	1125	1.4E
	1525	1615	0.2F
	1705	2230	2.6E
25 M	0155	0510	2.8F
	0935	1200	1.4E
	1630	1705	0.1F
	1735	2325	2.4E
26 Tu	0245	0600	2.5F
	1015	1250	1.4E
		1800	0.1E
27 W		0015	2.0E
	0345	0650	2.2F
	1055	1355	1.5E
		1925	0.1E
28 Th		0120	1.6E
	0440	0740	1.8F
	1130	1525	1.6E
	2010	2135	0.1F
	2255		
29 F		0240	1.2E
	0545	0835	1.4F
	1205	1620	1.9E
	2035	2255	0.6F
30 Sa	0120	0410	1.0E
	0650	0935	1.0F
	1230	1700	2.0E
	2105	2355	1.1F

DECEMBER

Days 1–15

Day	Slack Water Time (h.m.)	Max Current Time (h.m.)	Vel. (knots)
1 Su	0255	0525	0.9E
	0810	1035	0.7F
	1250	1730	2.2E
	2135		
2 M		0045	1.6F
	0410	0635	0.9E
	0955	1135	0.4F
	1310	1805	2.3E
	2205		
3 Tu		0125	2.0F
	0515	0750	1.0E
	1135	1230	0.1F
	1325	1845	2.3E
	2235		
4 W		0155	2.3F
	0605	0850	1.1E
	1300	1315	0.0
	1330	1920	2.3E
	2305		
5 Th		0225	2.5F
	0650	0935	1.1E
		1400	C.0
		2005	2.3E
	2335		
6 F		0300	2.6F
	0725	1000	1.2E
		1440	0.1E
		2045	2.2E
7 Sa	0010	0330	2.6F
	0800	1025	1.2E
		1515	0.1E
		2130	2.1E
8 Su	0045	0405	2.5F
	0830	1055	1.2E
		1555	0.1E
		2210	1.9E
9 M	0120	0440	2.3F
	0855	1130	1.1E
		1630	0.2E
		2250	1.7E
10 Tu	0155	0515	2.1F
	0920	1200	1.1E
		1715	0.3E
		2325	1.4E
11 W	0235	0555	1.9F
	0945	1235	1.1E
		1800	0.4E
12 Th		0005	1.1E
	0315	0630	1.6F
	1005	1310	1.1E
		1905	0.5E
13 F		0050	0.8E
	0355	0705	1.4F
	1025	1355	1.2E
		2240	0.2E
14 Sa		0155	0.6E
	0440	0740	1.1F
	1040	1440	1.4E
	2135	2330	0.1F
15 Su	0055	0320	0.4E
	0535	0820	0.8F
	1055	1525	1.6E
	2055		

Days 16–31

Day	Slack Water Time (h.m.)	Max Current Time (h.m.)	Vel. (knots)
16 M		0005	0.6F
	0255	0455	0.3E
	0650	0900	0.4F
	1110	1610	1.9E
	2100		
17 Tu		0030	1.2F
	0410	0615	0.4E
	0840	1005	0.2F
	1125	1700	2.2E
	2125		
18 W		0100	1.8F
	0505	0725	0.6E
		1130	0.0
		1745	2.4E
	2155		
19 Th		0130	2.3F
	0550	0820	0.8E
		1235	0.0
		1840	2.7E
	2235		
20 F		0210	2.8F
	0630	0905	1.0E
	1250	1330	0.1F
	1405	1935	2.8E
	2320		
21 Sa		0245	3.1F
	0710	0940	1.2E
	1315	1415	0.2F
	1510	2030	3.0E
22 Su	0000	0325	3.3F
	0745	1015	1.3E
	1350	1505	0.3F
	1610	2120	2.9E
23 M	0050	0410	3.2F
	0820	1045	1.4E
	1440	1555	0.3F
	1700	2210	2.7E
24 Tu	0135	0450	3.1F
	0855	1125	1.5E
	1540	1645	0.3F
	1755	2305	2.4E
25 W	0225	0535	2.8F
	0925	1210	1.6E
	1650	1750	0.2F
	1900	2355	1.9E
26 Th	0315	0615	2.3F
	0955	1305	1.8E
	1800	1920	0.2F
	2050		
27 F		0105	1.4E
	0405	0700	1.9F
	1015	1405	1.9E
	1900	2110	0.4F
	2335		
28 Sa		0220	1.0E
	0505	0745	1.3F
	1040	1510	2.1E
	1950	2235	0.9F
29 Su	0135	0345	0.7E
	0610	0835	0.8F
	1055	1605	2.2E
	2030	2340	1.3F
30 M	0305	0510	0.6E
	0745	0930	0.3F
	1100	1650	2.3E
	2105		
31 Tu	0415	0030	1.7F
		0635	0.6E
		1035	0.1E
		1730	2.3E
		2140	0.0

Time meridian 120° W. 0000 is midnight. 1200 is noon.
If three consecutive entries are marked (E) the middle one is not a true maximum but an intermediate
value to show the current pattern.

1991 CURRENT TABLES

For Daylight Saving Time, add one hour.

ADMIRALTY INLET
(off Bush Point)

Times and Heights of High and Low Waters

F-Flood, Dir. 130° True   E-Ebb, Dir. 005° True

JANUARY

Days 1–15:

Day	Slack Water Time (h.m.)	Maximum Current Time (h.m.)	Vel. (knots)
1 Tu		0241	3.6F
	0615	0908	2.4E
	1234	1424	0.9F
	1611	2030	4.2E
2 W	0010	0326	3.6F
	0656	0957	2.6E
	1326	1519	1.0F
	1711	2124	3.9E
3 Th	0056	0410	3.4F
	0735	1041	2.8E
	1419	1616	1.0F
	1811	2213	3.5E
4 F	0142	0452	3.1F
	0811	1128	2.9E
	1514	1714	1.0F
	1915	2305	2.9E
5 Sa	0229	0537	2.6F
	0846	1212	3.0E
	1611	1816	1.0F
	2024	2359	2.3E
6 Su	0318	0619	2.1F
	0918	1300	3.0E
	1708	1921	1.0F
	2142		
7 M		0100	1.8E
	0411	0705	1.6F
	0950	1349	3.0E
	1806	2028	1.1F
	2311		
8 Tu		0211	1.3E
	0513	0754	1.1F
	1021	1442	3.0E
	1901	2142	1.3F
9 W	0045	0330	1.0E
	0629	0849	0.7F
	1053	1534	3.0E
	1952	2247	1.6F
10 Th	0208	0448	1.0E
	0757	0947	0.5F
	1128	1627	3.0E
	2038	2342	1.8F
11 F	0313	0555	1.1E
	0921	1048	0.3F
	1209	1720	3.1E
	2120		
12 Sa		0031	2.1F
	0404	0654	1.3E
	1028	1144	0.3F
	1255	1803	3.1E
	2159		
13 Su		0112	2.3F
	0445	0737	1.5E
	1119	1234	0.3F
	1344	1844	3.2E
	2235		
14 M		0150	2.5F
	0521	0814	1.7E
	1200	1319	0.3F
	1433	1922	3.2E
	2309		
15 Tu		0225	2.6F
	0552	0854	1.9E
	1235	1359	0.4F
	1519	1957	3.2E
	2341		

Days 16–31:

Day	Slack Water Time (h.m.)	Maximum Current Time (h.m.)	Vel. (knots)
16 W		0254	2.7F
	0622	0925	2.0E
	1309	1437	0.5F
	1604	2036	3.2E
17 Th	0013	0325	2.7F
	0648	0954	2.2E
	1340	1515	0.6F
	1650	2112	3.1E
18 F	0045	0354	2.6F
	0713	1022	2.3E
	1412	1554	0.7F
	1739	2147	2.8E
19 Sa	0118	0426	2.4F
	0736	1055	2.5E
	1446	1639	0.8F
	1833	2228	2.6E
20 Su	0154	0455	2.2F
	0758	1127	2.7E
	1524	1728	0.9F
	1934	2311	2.2E
21 M	0233	0530	1.9F
	0822	1205	2.8E
	1607	1822	1.1F
	2044		
22 Tu		0008	1.8E
	0318	0607	1.5F
	0848	1248	3.0E
	1656	1923	1.2F
	2207		
23 W		0110	1.4E
	0413	0654	1.2F
	0918	1337	3.1E
	1751	2034	1.5F
	2341		
24 Th		0229	1.1E
	0525	0745	0.8F
	0955	1434	3.2E
	1848	2147	1.8F
25 F	0116	0353	1.1E
	0656	0853	0.6F
	1042	1538	3.4E
	1946	2254	2.2F
26 Sa	0234	0516	1.2E
	0829	1010	0.5F
	1143	1641	3.6E
	2042	2357	2.6F
27 Su	0335	0622	1.6E
	0943	1124	0.5F
	1256	1744	3.8E
	2134		
28 M		0050	3.0F
	0425	0719	2.0E
	1040	1227	0.7F
	1410	1840	3.9E
	2224		
29 Tu		0138	3.2F
	0508	0603	2.3E
	1129	1327	1.0F
	1519	1934	4.0E
	2312		
30 W		0223	3.3F
	0547	0848	2.7E
	1214	1421	1.2F
	1623	2023	3.8E
	2357		
31 Th		0304	3.3F
	0622	0931	2.9E
	1300	1513	1.4F
	1723	2112	3.6E

FEBRUARY

Days 1–15:

Day	Slack Water Time (h.m.)	Maximum Current Time (h.m.)	Vel. (knots)
1 F	0041	0344	3.0F
	0655	1009	3.1E
	1345	1601	1.5F
	1821	2201	3.2E
2 Sa	0124	0426	2.7F
	0725	1049	3.2E
	1432	1656	1.5F
	1920	2249	2.7E
3 Su	0208	0502	2.2F
	0754	1130	3.2E
	1520	1745	1.5F
	2020	2338	2.2E
4 M	0252	0539	1.7F
	0821	1211	3.1E
	1612	1840	1.4F
	2125		
5 Tu		0032	1.6E
	0342	0620	1.3F
	0847	1257	3.0E
	1707	1943	1.3F
	2239		
6 W		0135	1.2E
	0443	0704	0.8F
	0914	1346	2.8E
	1806	2051	1.3F
7 Th	0003	0251	1.0E
	0604	0757	0.4F
	0942	1444	2.7E
	1905	2200	1.4F
8 F	0127	0413	0.9E
		0906	*
		1545	2.6E
	1959	2303	1.6F
9 Sa	0235	0530	1.1E
		1015	*
		1641	2.7E
	2048	2357	1.8F
10 Su	0326	0524	1.3E
		1124	*
		1736	2.8E
	2131		
11 M		0040	2.1F
	0407	0709	1.6E
	1057	1217	0.3F
	1332	1821	2.9E
	2209		
12 Tu		0119	2.3F
	0440	0742	1.9E
	1127	1302	0.5F
	1434	1903	3.0E
	2245		
13 W		0154	2.4F
	0510	0817	2.1E
	1154	1343	0.7F
	1529	1944	3.1E
	2319		
14 Th		0223	2.5F
	0536	0846	2.4E
	1221	1423	0.9F
	1620	2020	3.1E
	2352		
15 F		0252	2.5F
	0559	0915	2.6E
	1249	1500	1.2F
	1710	2057	3.0E

Days 16–28:

Day	Slack Water Time (h.m.)	Maximum Current Time (h.m.)	Vel. (knots)
16 Sa		0026	2.3F
	0621	0941	2.8E
	1319	1542	1.4F
	1800	2136	2.8E
17 Su	0101	0355	2.1F
	0542	1010	3.0E
	1352	1621	1.6F
	1852	2217	2.5E
18 M	0138	0424	1.9F
	0705	1045	3.1E
	1431	1706	1.7F
	1949	2301	2.2E
19 Tu	0219	0459	1.6F
	0730	1124	3.2E
	1516	1759	1.7F
	2052	2356	1.8E
20 W	0307	0534	1.2F
	0758	1207	3.2E
	1608	1857	1.8F
	2206		
21 Th		0100	1.4E
	0408	0622	0.9F
	0831	1300	3.2E
	1709	2006	1.8F
	2330		
22 F		0217	1.2E
	0531	0725	0.5F
	0912	1404	3.1E
	1815	2122	1.9F
23 Sa	0056	0345	1.2E
	0713	0844	0.3F
	1010	1519	3.1E
	1921	2235	2.2F
24 Su	0208	0502	1.5E
	0840	1010	0.4F
	1134	1628	3.2E
	2024	2335	2.5F
25 M	0305	0604	1.9E
	0940	1126	0.6F
	1306	1738	3.3E
	2120		
26 Tu		0032	2.7F
	0351	0555	2.3E
	1027	1229	1.0F
	1427	1834	3.5E
	2211		
27 W		0119	2.8F
	0430	0740	2.7E
	1109	1325	1.4F
	1537	1929	3.5E
	2259		
28 Th		0201	2.8F
	0505	0819	3.0E
	1149	1415	1.7F
	1639	2018	3.4E
	2344		

ADMIRALTY INLET (off Bush Point)

1991 CURRENT TABLES

For Daylight Saving Time, add one hour.

Times and Heights of High and Low Waters

F-Flood, Dir. 180° True   E-Ebb, Dir. 005° True

MARCH

Day	Slack Water Time h.m.	Maximum Current Time h.m.	Vel. knots	Day	Slack Water Time h.m.	Maximum Current Time h.m.	Vel. knots
1 F		0239	2.7F	16 Sa		0213	2.0F
	0536	0858	3.2E		0458	0829	3.0E
	1229	1501	1.9F		1202	1441	1.9F
	1735	2106	3.1E		1721	2045	2.7E
2 Sa	0026	0315	2.4F	17 Su	0007	0246	1.9F
	0605	0934	3.4E		0522	0900	3.3E
	1309	1548	2.0F		1234	1519	2.2F
	1328	2148	2.8E		1812	2125	2.6E
3 Su	0109	0354	2.1F	18 M	0047	0316	1.7F
	0532	1010	3.4E		0546	0931	3.4E
	1349	1629	2.0F		1310	1602	2.3F
	1919	2231	2.4E		1903	2209	2.4E
4 M	0151	0424	1.7F	19 Tu	0128	0352	1.5F
	0657	1043	3.3E		0612	1008	3.5E
	1431	1713	1.9F		1351	1647	2.4F
	2011	2318	2.0E		1958	2258	2.1E
5 Tu	0236	0501	1.2F	20 W	0216	0433	1.2F
	0721	1124	3.1E		0642	1047	3.5E
	1517	1801	1.7F		1439	1737	2.4F
	2105				2057	2353	1.8E
6 W		0007	1.6E	21 Th	0313	0516	0.9F
	0327	0536	0.8F		0715	1137	3.4E
	0744	1203	2.8E		1533	1838	2.3F
	1607	1857	1.5F		2204		
	2205						
7 Th		0101	1.3E	22 F		0057	1.6E
	0431	0523	0.5F		0426	0613	0.6F
	0806	1248	2.6E		0754	1236	3.1E
	1704	1958	1.4F		1636	1944	2.1F
	2315				2316		
8 F		0215	1.1E	23 Sa		0213	1.5E
		0718	*		0600	0726	0.3F
		1347	2.4E		0846	1345	2.9E
	1806	2107	1.3F		1745	2058	2.1F
9 Sa	0029	0334	1.1E	24 Su	0027	0336	1.6E
		0829	*		0733	0852	0.3F
		1453	2.3E		1008	1503	2.8E
	1908	2211	1.4F		1856	2209	2.1F
10 Su	0136	0450	1.2E	25 M	0129	0448	1.9E
		0953	*		0837	1018	0.5F
		1603	2.3E		1154	1519	2.8E
	2003	2310	1.6F		2002	2310	2.2F
11 M	0228	0545	1.5E	26 Tu	0221	0541	2.3E
		1059	*		0925	1129	0.9F
		1704	2.4E		1331	1732	2.8E
	2052	2357	1.8F		2101		
12 Tu	0309	0626	1.8E	27 W		0001	2.3F
	1019	1156	0.5F		0303	0630	2.7E
	1330	1755	2.6E		1006	1227	1.4F
	2135				1449	1830	2.9E
					2155		
13 W		0034	2.0F	28 Th		0049	2.3F
	0342	0703	2.1E		0340	0709	3.1E
	1043	1242	0.8F		1044	1318	1.8F
	1439	1841	2.7E		1555	1921	2.9E
	2215				2244		
14 Th		0109	2.1F	29 F		0130	2.1F
	0410	0732	2.5E		0413	0746	3.3E
	1107	1324	1.2F		1121	1405	2.2F
	1538	1923	2.8E		1652	2010	2.8E
	2253				2330		
15 F		0142	2.1F	30 Sa		0205	1.9F
	0435	0800	2.7E		0442	0822	3.5E
	1134	1400	1.6F		1158	1447	2.4F
	1631	2004	2.6E		1743	2053	2.6E
	2330						
				31 Su	0014	0242	1.7F
					0509	0857	3.5E
					1234	1528	2.4F
					1830	2136	2.4E

APRIL

Day	Slack Water Time h.m.	Maximum Current Time h.m.	Vel. knots	Day	Slack Water Time h.m.	Maximum Current Time h.m.	Vel. knots
1 M	0058	0317	1.4F	16 Tu	0037	0250	1.2F
	0533	0929	3.4E		0452	0857	3.8E
	1310	1605	2.4F		1239	1546	3.0F
	1916	2217	2.1E		1908	2203	2.3E
2 Tu	0142	0351	1.0F	17 W	0126	0331	1.0F
	0556	1002	3.2E		0525	0940	3.8E
	1348	1646	2.2F		1323	1633	3.0F
	2001	2301	1.9E		2001	2254	2.1E
3 W	0230	0426	0.7F	18 Th	0222	0416	0.8F
	0618	1039	3.0E		0603	1027	3.7E
	1429	1728	2.0F		1413	1724	2.9F
	2047	2347	1.6E		2057	2353	2.0E
4 Th	0327	0503	0.5F	19 F	0328	0509	0.6F
	0639	1116	2.8E		0645	1118	3.4E
	1514	1815	1.8F		1508	1823	2.7F
	2138				2155		
5 F		0041	1.4E	20 Sa		0057	1.9E
		0551	*		0449	0613	0.4F
		1203	2.5E		0736	1219	3.0E
	1604	1910	1.6F		1609	1926	2.4F
	2234				2254		
6 Sa		0144	1.3E	21 Su		0208	2.0E
		0646	*		0615	0733	0.3F
		1257	2.2E		0849	1333	2.7E
	1702	2009	1.5F		1716	2030	2.2F
	2333				2351		
7 Su		0255	1.3E	22 M		0316	2.2E
		0803	*		0724	0858	0.4F
		1406	2.0E		1032	1450	2.4E
	1803	2111	1.5F		1826	2134	2.1F
8 M	0028	0401	1.5E	23 Tu	0042	0417	2.5E
		0925	*		0216	1018	0.8F
		1517	2.0E		1220	1609	2.3E
	1904	2209	1.5F		1934	2233	1.9F
9 Tu	0116	0453	1.8E	24 W	0127	0508	2.8E
	0915	1035	0.3F		0900	1123	1.3F
	1154	1621	2.0E		1352	1720	2.2E
	2000	2300	1.6F		2038	2326	1.8F
10 W	0156	0535	2.1E	25 Th	0207	0554	3.2E
	0932	1128	0.7F		0940	1221	1.8F
	1328	1723	2.1E		1506	1821	2.2E
	2051	2339	1.6F		2136		
11 Th	0229	0608	2.5E	26 F		0010	1.6F
	0955	1217	1.2F		0242	0633	3.4E
	1440	1811	2.2E		1018	1308	2.2F
	2139				1607	1912	2.2E
					2230		
12 F		0021	1.6F	27 Sa		0053	1.4F
	0258	0639	2.8E		0314	0712	3.5E
	1021	1258	1.7F		1054	1353	2.5F
	1541	1859	2.3E		1700	2000	2.2E
	2223				2320		
13 Sa		0058	1.6F	28 Su		0134	1.2F
	0326	0714	3.2E		0342	0746	3.6E
	1050	1339	2.2F		1129	1428	2.6F
	1635	1948	2.4E		1747	2045	2.1E
	2307						
14 Su		0132	1.5F	29 M		0210	1.0F
	0353	0745	3.5E		0409	0821	3.5E
	1122	1421	2.6F		1204	1509	2.6F
	1727	2031	2.4E		1830	2128	2.0E
	2351						
15 M		0209	1.4F	30 Tu		0249	0.8F
	0421	0620	3.7E		0433	0855	3.4E
	1159	1503	2.8F		1238	1546	2.6F
	1817	2117	2.4E		1911	2209	1.9E

1991 CURRENT TABLES

For Daylight Saving Time, add one hour.

ADMIRALTY INLET (off Bush Point)

Times and Heights of High and Low Waters

F-Flood, Dir. 180° True   E-Ebb, Dir. 005° True

MAY

Day	Slack Water Time h.m.	Max. Current Time h.m.	Vel. knots
1 W	0144	0320	0.5F
	0456	0927	3.2E
	1313	1621	2.5F
	1950	2247	1.8E
2 Th	0237	0357	0.3F
	0518	1000	3.0E
	1351	1702	2.3F
	2031	2330	1.7E
3 F		0443	*
		1041	2.7E
	1431	1743	2.1F
	2114		
4 Sa		0022	1.6E
		0526	*
		1124	2.5E
	1515	1828	1.9F
	2157		
5 Su		0120	1.6E
		0626	*
		1212	2.2E
	1604	1918	1.8F
	2242		
6 M		0210	1.7E
		0738	*
		1315	1.9E
	1658	2012	1.6F
	2324		
7 Tu		0304	1.9E
		0854	*
		1424	1.7E
	1758	2104	1.5F
8 W	0003	0353	2.2E
	0558	0958	0.4F
	1144	1539	1.6E
	1859	2152	1.4F
9 Th	0038	0435	2.5E
	0640	1055	1.0F
	1320	1641	1.7E
	2000	2241	1.3F
10 F	0111	0513	2.9E
	0608	1148	1.5F
	1435	1744	1.8E
	2058	2323	1.2F
11 Sa	0143	0549	3.2E
	0939	1233	2.1F
	1539	1839	1.9E
	2153		
12 Su		0008	1.1F
	0216	0627	3.6E
	1013	1315	2.6F
	1635	1931	2.0E
	2246		
13 M		0053	1.0F
	0250	0706	3.9E
	1051	1401	3.0F
	1727	2017	2.1E
	2337		
14 Tu		0135	1.0F
	0328	0749	4.1E
	1132	1444	3.3F
	1818	2108	2.2E
15 W	0030	0221	0.9F
	0408	0832	4.1E
	1216	1533	3.4F
	1907	2200	2.2E
16 Th	0125	0312	0.8F
	0452	0919	4.0E
	1303	1620	3.4F
	1957	2249	2.2E
17 F	0226	0404	0.6F
	0541	1010	3.8E
	1353	1712	3.2F
	2046	2345	2.3E
18 Sa	0334	0505	0.5F
	0636	1104	3.4E
	1447	1806	2.9F
	2135		
19 Su		0045	2.3E
	0446	0614	0.5F
	0743	1207	2.9E
	1544	1901	2.6F
	2222		
20 M		0143	2.5E
	0555	0733	0.5F
	0910	1316	2.4E
	1646	2000	2.3F
	2308		
21 Tu		0245	2.7E
	0655	0850	0.8F
	1052	1436	2.0E
	1752	2055	1.9F
	2350		
22 W		0339	3.0E
	0746	1005	1.2F
	1234	1552	1.8E
	1901	2151	1.6F
23 Th	0030	0428	3.2E
	0831	1109	1.6F
	1402	1703	1.7E
	2011	2247	1.3F
24 F	0107	0517	3.4E
	0913	1204	2.0F
	1513	1805	1.7E
	2117	2336	1.1F
25 Sa	0141	0558	3.5E
	0952	1253	2.3F
	1612	1904	1.7E
	2218		
26 Su		0018	0.8F
	0214	0637	3.5E
	1029	1334	2.5F
	1702	1951	1.7E
	2314		
27 M		0106	0.7F
	0244	0715	3.5E
	1104	1415	2.7F
	1745	2036	1.8E
28 Tu	0007	0142	0.5F
	0312	0751	3.4E
	1139	1452	2.7F
	1824	2117	1.8E
29 W	0058	0222	0.4F
	0340	0823	3.3E
	1213	1526	2.7F
	1901	2157	1.8E
30 Th	0150	0259	0.3F
	0406	0859	3.2E
	1247	1602	2.6F
	1936	2234	1.8E
31 F		0337	*
		0934	3.0E
	1321	1637	2.5F
	2011	2318	1.8E

JUNE

Day	Slack Water Time h.m.	Max. Current Time h.m.	Vel. knots
1 Sa		0420	*
		1015	2.8E
	1357	1714	2.4F
	2046		
2 Su		0000	1.9E
	0509		*
		1052	2.5E
	1436	1753	2.2F
	2119		
3 M		0042	2.0E
	0606		*
		1139	2.2E
	1518	1834	2.0F
	2152		
4 Tu		0123	2.1E
	0706		*
		1238	1.9E
	1605	1917	1.7F
	2223		
5 W		0206	2.3E
	0647	0811	0.3F
	0941	1339	1.6E
	1659	2003	1.5F
	2253		
6 Tn		0253	2.5E
	0716	0918	0.7F
	1130	1453	1.4E
	1801	2048	1.2F
	2325		
7 F		0336	2.8E
	0748	1021	1.2F
	1307	1606	1.3E
	1909	2140	1.0F
	2358		
8 Sa		0419	3.2E
	0824	1117	1.8F
	1427	1716	1.4E
	2019	2234	0.9F
9 Su	0035	0505	3.5E
	0903	1205	2.3F
	1533	1818	1.5E
	2126	2325	0.8F
10 M	0116	0552	3.8E
	0944	1256	2.8F
	1630	1913	1.7E
	2228		
11 Tu		0020	0.7F
	0202	0640	4.1E
	1028	1345	3.2F
	1722	2004	1.9E
	2326		
12 W		0110	0.7F
	0252	0728	4.2E
	1113	1431	3.5F
	1810	2059	2.1E
13 Th	0021	0205	0.8F
	0345	0818	4.2E
	1200	1518	3.6F
	1856	2148	2.3E
14 F	0117	0302	0.8F
	0441	0907	4.1E
	1248	1607	3.5F
	1940	2236	2.5E
15 Sa	0215	0359	0.8F
	0540	1001	3.7E
	1337	1653	3.3F
	2022	2330	2.6E
16 Su	0315	0501	0.8F
	0645	1057	3.3E
	1427	1743	3.0F
	2103		
17 M		0020	2.8E
	0417	0606	0.8F
	0758	1156	2.7E
	1520	1831	2.6F
	2142		
18 Tu		0113	2.9E
	0518	0716	0.9F
	0922	1302	2.2E
	1616	1921	2.1F
	2220		
19 W		0205	3.1E
	0615	0830	1.1F
	1056	1411	1.7E
	1719	2011	1.6F
	2256		
20 Th		0258	3.2E
	0709	0941	1.4F
	1232	1528	1.4E
	1829	2105	1.2F
	2332		
21 F		0349	3.3E
	0758	1048	1.7F
	1359	1645	1.3E
	1945	2203	0.9F
22 Sa		0440	3.4E
	0844	1145	2.0F
	1509	1754	1.3E
	2102	2257	0.6F
23 Su	0043	0526	3.4E
	0927	1233	2.3F
	1506	1852	1.4E
	2212	2348	0.5F
24 M	0119	0611	3.4E
	1006	1318	2.5F
	1653	1941	1.5E
	2313		
25 Tu		0034	0.4F
	0156	0649	3.4E
	1043	1357	2.6F
	1733	2022	1.6E
26 W	0005	0120	0.3F
	0233	0728	3.3E
	1118	1434	2.6F
	1808	2103	1.7E
27 Th	0052	0202	0.3F
	0310	0805	3.2E
	1152	1507	2.7F
	1841	2140	1.8E
28 F		0243	*
		0840	3.1E
	1224	1540	2.6F
	1911	2215	1.9E
29 Sa		0322	*
		0915	3.0E
	1257	1612	2.6F
	1940	2245	2.0E
30 Su		0404	*
		0956	2.8E
	1330	1645	2.4F
	2007	2324	2.2E

ADMIRALTY INLET
(off Bush Point)

1991 CURRENT TABLES

For Daylight Saving Time, add one hour.

Times and Heights of High and Low Waters

F-Flood, Dir. 180° True   E-Ebb, Dir. 005° True

JULY

Day	Slack Water Time h.m.	Maximum Current Time h.m.	Vel. knots
1 M	0337	0449	0.3F
	0600	1031	2.5E
	1405	1718	2.2F
	2033	2358	2.3E
2 Tu	0415	0538	0.4F
	0701	1116	2.2E
	1443	1753	2.0F
	2058		
3 W		0036	2.4E
	0452	0633	0.5F
	0814	1206	1.8E
	1525	1828	1.7F
	2123		
4 Th		0113	2.6E
	0532	0732	0.7F
	0941	1305	1.5E
	1616	1908	1.4F
	2150		
5 F		0155	2.8E
	0614	0838	1.0F
	1116	1416	1.2E
	1717	1959	1.1F
	2220		
6 Sa		0244	3.1E
	0659	0944	1.5F
	1252	1534	1.1E
	1831	2048	0.8F
	2256		
7 Su		0337	3.3E
	0746	1045	1.9F
	1414	1654	1.1E
	1953	2151	0.6F
	2341		
8 M		0432	3.6E
	0834	1145	2.4F
	1522	1800	1.3E
	2110	2259	0.6F
9 Tu	0035	0525	3.8E
	0922	1237	2.9F
	1518	1859	1.6E
	2215		
10 W		0002	0.6F
	0137	0621	4.0E
	1011	1328	3.2F
	1706	1952	2.0E
	2313		
11 Th		0101	0.7F
	0241	0712	4.2E
	1059	1415	3.5F
	1750	2040	2.3E
12 F	0005	0158	0.9F
	0345	0805	4.1E
	1146	1501	3.5F
	1831	2128	2.6E
13 Sa	0057	0254	1.0F
	0448	0858	3.9E
	1233	1547	3.4F
	1909	2215	2.8E
14 Su	0148	0351	1.2F
	0552	0949	3.6E
	1320	1630	3.2F
	1945	2300	3.0E
15 M	0241	0449	1.2F
	0657	1045	3.1E
	1408	1714	2.8F
	2020	2346	3.1E

Day	Slack Water Time h.m.	Maximum Current Time h.m.	Vel. knots
16 Tu	0335	0547	1.3F
	0806	1137	2.6E
	1457	1800	2.3F
	2054		
17 W		0031	3.2E
	0432	0654	1.3F
	0922	1238	2.0E
	1550	1842	1.8F
	2127		
18 Th		0123	3.2E
	0529	0759	1.4F
	1045	1345	1.5E
	1650	1930	1.3F
	2159		
19 F		0214	3.1E
	0626	0908	1.5F
	1214	1503	1.2E
	1803	2026	0.8F
	2232		
20 Sa		0306	3.1E
	0722	1016	1.6F
	1339	1522	1.1E
	1930	2122	0.5F
	2308		
21 Su		0406	3.1E
	0814	1117	1.9F
	1449	1736	1.1E
	2057	2225	0.3F
	2350		
22 M		0457	3.1E
	0901	1208	2.1F
	1544	1833	1.3E
	2209	2326	0.3F
23 Tu	0038	0545	3.1E
	0943	1253	2.2F
	1627	1920	1.5E
	2303		
24 W		0020	0.3F
	0131	0627	3.1E
	1022	1334	2.4F
	1704	2003	1.7E
	2345		
25 Th		0106	0.3F
	0223	0709	3.2E
	1057	1409	2.5F
	1736	2034	1.9E
26 F	0021	0148	0.4F
	0312	0751	3.1E
	1130	1441	2.6F
	1805	2109	2.1E
27 Sa	0054	0229	0.5F
	0359	0823	3.1E
	1202	1514	2.5F
	1831	2142	2.2E
28 Su	0125	0306	0.6F
	0445	0902	2.9E
	1234	1541	2.5F
	1855	2209	2.4E
29 M	0157	0346	0.7F
	0533	0937	2.7E
	1306	1610	2.3F
	1917	2239	2.5E
30 Tu	0229	0424	0.8F
	0624	1013	2.5E
	1341	1540	2.1F
	1939	2209	2.6E
31 W	0304	0511	1.0F
	0720	1056	2.2E
	1418	1711	1.8F
	2000	2342	2.8E

AUGUST

Day	Slack Water Time h.m.	Maximum Current Time h.m.	Vel. knots
1 Th	0343	0600	1.1F
	0824	1145	1.8E
	1500	1746	1.5F
	2024		
2 F		0023	2.9E
	0428	0558	1.2F
	0938	1244	1.5E
	1551	1825	1.1F
	2051		
3 Sa		0106	3.0E
	0519	0801	1.4F
	1104	1352	1.2E
	1656	1916	0.8F
	2124		
4 Su		0203	3.1E
	0615	0910	1.7F
	1235	1514	1.0E
	1819	2019	0.6F
	2207		
5 M		0302	3.2E
	0713	1019	2.0F
	1356	1638	1.2E
	1951	2133	0.4F
	2306		
6 Tu		0406	3.4E
	0810	1123	2.4F
	1501	1747	1.4E
	2108	2248	0.5F
7 W	0020	0513	3.6E
	0905	1218	2.8F
	1552	1843	1.8E
	2207	2355	0.7F
8 Th	0138	0610	3.8E
	0956	1309	3.0F
	1637	1933	2.2E
	2256		
9 F		0055	1.0F
	0251	0706	3.9E
	1045	1354	3.2F
	1716	2020	2.6E
	2343		
10 Sa		0153	1.3F
	0359	0800	3.8E
	1132	1439	3.2F
	1752	2102	2.9E
11 Su	0028	0247	1.6F
	0503	0849	3.6E
	1218	1521	3.0F
	1826	2143	3.2E
12 M	0114	0338	1.7F
	0604	0939	3.3E
	1303	1600	2.7F
	1858	2224	3.3E
13 Tu	0201	0430	1.8F
	0704	1029	2.8E
	1349	1640	2.3F
	1929	2303	3.3E
14 W	0250	0522	1.8F
	0806	1121	2.3E
	1437	1721	1.8F
	1959	2346	3.3E
15 Th	0341	0617	1.7F
	0911	1215	1.8E
	1530	1803	1.3F
	2028		

Day	Slack Water Time h.m.	Maximum Current Time h.m.	Vel. knots
16 F		0035	3.1E
	0437	0720	1.5F
	1023	1317	1.4E
	1633	1851	0.8F
	2057		
17 Sa		0126	2.9E
	0537	0827	1.5F
	1142	1434	1.1E
	1753	1942	0.5F
	2128		
18 Su		0221	2.7E
	0638	0937	1.5F
	1302	1556	1.0E
		2051	*
19 M		0324	2.7E
	0736	1040	1.5F
	1409	1709	1.2E
		2205	*
20 Tu		0424	2.7E
	0829	1135	1.8F
	1502	1808	1.4E
		2307	*
21 W		0521	2.7E
	0914	1221	2.0F
	1543	1850	1.7E
	2237		
22 Th		0005	0.4F
	0128	0609	2.8E
	0954	1302	2.2F
	1618	1925	1.9E
	2308		
23 F		0051	0.6F
	0229	0652	2.9E
	1031	1337	2.3F
	1647	2000	2.2E
	2337		
24 Sa		0132	0.8F
	0323	0728	2.9E
	1105	1406	2.3F
	1713	2029	2.4E
25 Su	0004	0207	1.0F
	0413	0808	2.9E
	1139	1435	2.3F
	1737	2056	2.6E
26 M	0032	0247	1.2F
	0500	0844	2.8E
	1212	1504	2.1F
	1758	2124	2.7E
27 Tu	0100	0324	1.4F
	0548	0919	2.6E
	1247	1532	1.9F
	1819	2151	2.9E
28 W	0132	0401	1.6F
	0637	1000	2.4E
	1323	1601	1.7F
	1839	2223	3.0E
29 Th	0207	0443	1.7F
	0730	1043	2.1E
	1403	1636	1.4F
	1902	2257	3.1E
30 F	0248	0532	1.7F
	0829	1131	1.8E
	1449	1711	1.1F
	1928	2338	3.1E
31 Sa	0337	0627	1.8F
	0936	1232	1.5E
	1546	1800	0.8F
	1958		

1991 CURRENT TABLES

For Daylight Saving Time, add one hour.

ADMIRALTY INLET
(off Bush Point)

Times and Heights of High and Low Waters

SEPTEMBER

Days 1–15

Day	Slack Water Time h.m.	Maximum Current Time h.m.	Vel. knots
1 Su		0029	3.1E
	0434	0730	1.8F
	1054	1341	1.2E
	1703	1854	0.5F
	2037		
2 M		0127	3.0E
	0538	0844	1.9F
	1215	1505	1.2E
	1840	2011	0.3F
	2133		
3 Tu		0238	3.0E
	0645	0955	2.1F
	1328	1627	1.4E
	2006	2134	0.3F
	2256		
4 W		0352	3.1E
	0749	1101	2.3F
	1427	1730	1.8E
	2106	2252	0.6F
5 Th	0032	0503	3.2E
	0847	1155	2.5F
	1514	1824	2.3E
	2153	2358	1.0F
6 F	0158	0604	3.3E
	0941	1244	2.7F
	1555	1907	2.7E
	2236		
7 Sa		0055	1.4F
	0312	0659	3.4E
	1030	1331	2.7F
	1631	1948	3.1E
	2317		
8 Su		0147	1.8F
	0417	0751	3.3E
	1118	1410	2.6F
	1704	2029	3.4E
	2358		
9 M		0236	2.1F
	0516	0640	3.2E
	1204	1450	2.4F
	1735	2106	3.5E
10 Tu	0039	0323	2.3F
	0612	0929	2.9E
	1249	1528	2.0F
	1904	2142	3.5E
11 W	0121	0408	2.3F
	0706	1015	2.5E
	1335	1607	1.6F
	1832	2223	3.4E
12 Th	0205	0455	2.2F
	0800	1104	2.1E
	1424	1642	1.2F
	1858	2301	3.2E
13 F	0252	0544	2.0F
	0855	1157	1.7E
	1520	1723	0.8F
	1923	2343	2.9E
14 Sa	0344	0641	1.8F
	0956	1252	1.4E
	1630	1812	0.4F
	1948		
15 Su		0033	2.7E
	0441	0743	1.6F
	1102	1406	1.2E
		1911	*

Days 16–30

Day	Slack Water Time h.m.	Maximum Current Time h.m.	Vel. knots
16 M		0130	2.4E
	0544	0846	1.5F
	1211	1521	1.2E
		2024	*
17 Tu		0239	2.2E
	0647	0956	1.5F
	1313	1633	1.4E
		2143	*
18 W		0347	2.2E
	0744	1051	1.6F
	1403	1726	1.7E
		2254	*
19 Th		0447	2.3E
	0834	1136	1.8F
	1444	1805	2.0E
	2201	2345	0.5F
20 F	0129	0544	2.4E
	0918	1217	1.9F
	1517	1840	2.3E
	2226		
21 Sa		0031	0.9F
	0234	0627	2.5E
	0959	1252	1.9F
	1545	1909	2.5E
	2251		
22 Su		0112	1.2F
	0330	0709	2.6E
	1037	1326	1.9F
	1610	1941	2.8E
	2317		
23 M		0149	1.6F
	0421	0750	2.6E
	1114	1355	1.8F
	1633	2009	3.0E
	2344		
24 Tu		0225	1.9F
	0509	0828	2.6E
	1152	1426	1.7F
	1655	2037	3.2E
25 W	0014	0300	2.1F
	0557	0908	2.4E
	1230	1455	1.5F
	1717	2108	3.4E
26 Th	0047	0342	2.3F
	0645	0949	2.3E
	1311	1528	1.3F
	1741	2143	3.4E
27 F	0125	0424	2.4F
	0736	1035	2.0E
	1357	1605	1.0F
	1808	2220	3.4E
28 Sa	0209	0512	2.4F
	0832	1128	1.8E
	1452	1645	0.7F
	1839	2305	3.3E
29 Su	0300	0607	2.3F
	0934	1228	1.6E
	1602	1740	0.5F
	1915	2359	3.1E
30 M	0359	0708	2.1F
	1041	1343	1.5E
	1733	1851	0.3F
	2004		

OCTOBER

Days 1–15

Day	Slack Water Time h.m.	Maximum Current Time h.m.	Vel. knots
1 Tu		0108	2.9E
	0506	0813	2.1F
	1149	1459	1.6E
		2019	*
2 W		0225	2.7E
	0616	0930	2.1F
	1250	1608	1.9E
	2007	2141	0.4F
	2315		
3 Th		0343	2.6E
	0724	1033	2.2F
	1342	1704	2.4E
	2054	2256	0.9F
4 F	0058	0457	2.7E
	0826	1126	2.2F
	1426	1755	2.8E
	2135	2358	1.4F
5 Sa	0222	0558	2.8E
	0923	1217	2.2F
	1505	1838	3.2E
	2214		
6 Su		0053	1.9F
	0331	0656	2.8E
	1015	1259	2.1F
	1539	1917	3.5E
	2252		
7 M		0136	2.3F
	0422	0743	2.8E
	1105	1341	1.9F
	1611	1954	3.7E
	2330		
8 Tu		0225	2.6F
	0526	0832	2.6E
	1152	1417	1.6F
	1640	2030	3.7E
9 W	0008	0306	2.7F
	0616	0918	2.4E
	1240	1454	1.3F
	1707	2106	3.6E
10 Th	0047	0348	2.6F
	0704	1001	2.2E
	1328	1530	1.0F
	1732	2141	3.4E
11 F	0127	0431	2.5F
	0750	1050	1.9E
	1420	1611	0.7F
	1756	2220	3.2E
12 Sa	0209	0512	2.2F
	0838	1137	1.7E
	1522	1652	0.4F
	1817	2259	2.8E
13 Su	0254	0559	2.0F
	0928	1232	1.5E
		1740	*
		2346	2.5E
14 M	0345	0654	1.7F
	1022	1337	1.4E
		1842	*
15 Tu		0041	2.2E
	0442	0753	1.6F
	1117	1445	1.5E
		1958	*

Days 16–31

Day	Slack Water Time h.m.	Maximum Current Time h.m.	Vel. knots
16 W		0146	2.0E
	0543	0853	1.5F
	1209	1546	1.7E
		2119	*
17 Th		0300	1.8E
	0644	0948	1.5F
	1254	1637	2.0E
	2102	2222	0.3F
	2352		
18 F		0409	1.9E
	0741	1041	1.5F
	1333	1716	2.3E
	2120	2317	0.7F
19 Sa	0123	0507	1.9E
	0834	1123	1.5F
	1405	1749	2.6E
	2142		
20 Su		0006	1.2F
	0233	0601	2.1E
	0922	1201	1.5F
	1434	1821	2.9E
	2207		
21 M		0047	1.7F
	0331	0647	2.2E
	1007	1237	1.4F
	1501	1853	3.2E
	2234		
22 Tu		0124	2.1F
	0423	0731	2.2E
	1051	1311	1.3F
	1526	1925	3.4E
	2304		
23 W		0204	2.5F
	0512	0813	2.2E
	1134	1346	1.2F
	1553	1958	3.7E
	2338		
24 Th		0241	2.8F
	0600	0857	2.2E
	1218	1421	1.1F
	1621	2033	3.8E
25 F	0015	0323	2.9F
	0648	0941	2.1E
	1305	1502	0.9F
	1653	2115	3.8E
26 Sa	0057	0407	3.0F
	0738	1029	2.0E
	1358	1545	0.7F
	1727	2156	3.7E
27 Su	0143	0453	2.9F
	0830	1125	1.9E
	1502	1636	0.5F
	1807	2245	3.4E
28 M	0234	0550	2.7F
	0924	1226	1.9E
	1519	1737	0.3F
	1855	2344	3.1E
29 Tu	0332	0649	2.5F
	1020	1331	2.0E
		1853	*
30 W		0051	2.7E
	0436	0752	2.3F
	1115	1439	2.2E
	1855	2018	0.4F
	2147		
31 Th		0212	2.4E
	0545	0856	2.1F
	1206	1542	2.5E
	1947	2141	0.7F
	2342		

ADMIRALTY INLET (off Bush Point)

1991 CURRENT TABLES

For Daylight Saving Time, add one hour.

Times and Heights of High and Low Waters

NOVEMBER

Day	Slack Water Time h.m.	Maximum Current Time h.m.	Vel. knots
1 F		0331	2.2E
	0655	0956	1.9F
	1252	1635	2.9E
	2031	2254	1.3F
2 Sa	0121	0447	2.1E
	0802	1051	1.8F
	1333	1723	3.2E
	2112	2352	1.8F
3 Su	0241	0554	2.2E
	0905	1145	1.6F
	1410	1800	3.5E
	2151		
4 M		0042	2.3F
	0346	0647	2.2E
	1002	1228	1.4F
	1445	1847	3.7E
	2229		
5 Tu		0130	2.6F
	0442	0740	2.2E
	1056	1309	1.2F
	1516	1923	3.8E
	2306		
6 W		0213	2.8F
	0532	0826	2.1E
	1148	1351	1.0F
	1545	2001	3.7E
	2343		
7 Th		0248	2.9F
	0617	0911	2.1E
	1238	1428	0.8F
	1612	2035	3.6E
8 F	0019	0329	2.8F
	0659	0954	1.9E
	1329	1505	0.5F
	1638	2110	3.4E
9 Sa	0056	0408	2.6F
	0739	1037	1.8E
	1424	1544	0.3F
	1700	2145	3.1E
10 Su	0134	0446	2.5F
	0820	1124	1.7E
	1626		*
	2226		2.8E
11 M	0214	0529	2.2F
	0900	1209	1.7E
		1715	*
	2307		2.5E
12 Tu	0257	0615	2.0F
	0942	1302	1.7E
	1812		*
	2356		2.2E
13 W	0344	0658	1.8F
	1023	1358	1.8E
		1923	*
14 Th		0054	1.8E
	0437	0752	1.6F
	1103	1449	2.0E
		2040	*
15 F		0207	1.6E
	0535	0844	1.4F
	1141	1536	2.2E
	2010	2149	0.4F
	2331		
16 Sa		0319	1.5E
	0638	0933	1.3F
	1215	1619	2.5E
	2031	2245	0.9F
17 Su	0110	0431	1.5E
	0741	1019	1.2F
	1248	1654	2.8E
	2057	2333	1.4F
18 M	0225	0528	1.6E
	0841	1107	1.1F
	1319	1733	3.2E
	2126		
19 Tu		0021	2.0F
	0327	0623	1.7E
	0937	1149	1.0F
	1351	1810	3.5E
	2158		
20 W		0102	2.5F
	0421	0714	1.8E
	1029	1230	0.9F
	1424	1849	3.8E
	2233		
21 Th		0143	2.9F
	0511	0759	2.0E
	1118	1313	0.8F
	1500	1926	4.0E
	2312		
22 F		0227	3.2F
	0558	0846	2.0E
	1208	1354	0.8F
	1540	2007	4.1E
	2353		
23 Sa		0309	3.3F
	0545	0934	2.1E
	1300	1445	0.7F
	1622	2056	4.0E
24 Su	0037	0353	3.4F
	0731	1023	2.2E
	1357	1536	0.6F
	1709	2141	3.8E
25 M	0124	0442	3.3F
	0818	1115	2.2E
	1459	1630	0.5F
	1803	2234	3.5E
26 Tu	0215	0532	3.0F
	0904	1210	2.3E
	1608	1737	0.5F
	1907	2330	3.0E
27 W	0309	0625	2.7F
	0949	1309	2.5E
	1718	1851	0.5F
	2028		
28 Th		0039	2.5E
	0408	0723	2.3F
	1033	1408	2.7E
	1820	2013	0.7F
	2210		
29 F		0153	2.1E
	0513	0819	2.0F
	1116	1503	3.0E
	1914	2128	1.1F
	2357		
30 Sa		0313	1.7E
	0623	0916	1.6F
	1157	1559	3.2E
	2002	2239	1.6F

DECEMBER

Day	Slack Water Time h.m.	Maximum Current Time h.m.	Vel. knots
1 Su	0133	0434	1.6E
	0737	1013	1.3F
	1237	1648	3.5E
	2047	2339	2.0F
2 M	0251	0542	1.6E
	0849	1107	1.1F
	1314	1735	3.6E
	2129		
3 Tu		0030	2.4F
	0354	0641	1.7E
	0955	1155	0.8F
	1351	1818	3.7E
	2209		
4 W		0119	2.7F
	0446	0734	1.8E
	1055	1243	0.7F
	1425	1859	3.7E
	2247		
5 Th		0200	2.8F
	0531	0819	1.8E
	1150	1325	0.5F
	1458	1938	3.6E
	2323		
6 F		0235	2.9F
	0611	0904	1.8E
	1241	1407	0.4F
	1530	2013	3.5E
	2358		
7 Sa		0315	2.8F
	0648	0943	1.9E
	1330	1445	0.3F
	1600	2049	3.3E
8 Su	0033	0351	2.7F
	0723	1023	1.9E
	1526		*
	2124		3.1E
9 M	0107	0423	2.6F
	0756	1101	1.9E
	1607		*
	2200		2.8E
10 Tu	0142	0458	2.4F
	0828	1143	2.0E
	1652		*
	2237		2.5E
11 W	0218	0534	2.2F
	0859	1218	2.0E
	1747		*
	2324		2.2E
12 Th	0258	0615	2.0F
	0930	1300	2.1E
	1844		*
13 F		0011	1.8E
	0342	0654	1.7F
	0959	1347	2.3E
	1831	1950	0.3F
	2115		
14 Sa		0116	1.5E
	0434	0735	1.4F
	1029	1430	2.5E
	1902	2057	0.6F
	2305		
15 Su		0230	1.2E
	0535	0824	1.1F
	1058	1516	2.7E
	1935	2206	1.0F
16 M	0048	0347	1.1E
	0646	0917	0.9F
	1130	1559	3.0E
	2010	2301	1.6F
17 Tu	0211	0457	1.2E
	0800	1007	0.7F
	1206	1648	3.3E
	2048	2350	2.1F
18 W	0318	0602	1.3E
	0909	1104	0.6F
	1247	1731	3.6E
	2128		
19 Th		0039	2.6F
	0414	0656	1.6E
	1011	1158	0.6F
	1334	1818	3.9E
	2209		
20 F		0125	3.0F
	0503	0747	1.8E
	1105	1247	0.7F
	1426	1906	4.1E
	2253		
21 Sa		0210	3.4F
	0548	0836	2.0E
	1157	1342	0.7F
	1520	1954	4.2E
	2337		
22 Su		0255	3.5F
	0631	0923	2.3E
	1248	1433	0.8F
	1617	2044	4.1E
23 M	0023	0339	3.5F
	0712	1007	2.5E
	1341	1530	0.9F
	1715	2131	3.9E
24 Tu	0109	0426	3.4F
	0752	1056	2.7E
	1436	1629	0.9F
	1818	2227	3.5E
25 W	0157	0511	3.1F
	0831	1145	2.8E
	1535	1730	0.9F
	1927	2323	2.9E
26 Th	0248	0557	2.7F
	0909	1238	3.0E
	1635	1839	1.0F
	2047		
27 F		0025	2.4E
	0342	0645	2.2F
	0946	1329	3.1E
	1736	1953	1.1F
	2217		
28 Sa		0134	1.8E
	0443	0740	1.7F
	1023	1425	3.2E
	1834	2104	1.4F
	2356		
29 Su		0252	1.4E
	0554	0835	1.2F
	1101	1520	3.3E
	1929	2219	1.7F
30 M	0130	0418	1.2E
	0716	0933	0.9F
	1139	1615	3.4E
	2020	2320	2.0F
31 Tu	0248	0533	1.3E
	0841	1035	0.6F
	1219	1706	3.4E
	2107		

1991 CURRENT TABLES

THE NARROWS

For Daylight Saving Time, add one hour.

Times and Heights of High and Low Waters

F-Flood, Dir. 135° True   E-Ebb, Dir. 335° True

JANUARY

Day	Slack Water Time h.m.	Maximum Current Time h.m.	Vel. knots	Day	Slack Water Time h.m.	Maximum Current Time h.m.	Vel. knots
1		0246	5.7F	16		0304	4.3F
Tu	0649	0936	2.6E	W	0706	1004	2.1E
	1222	1437	2.5F		1244	1453	1.9F
	1702	2048	5.0E		1719	2102	3.6E
2	0022	0334	5.7F	17	0032	0339	4.4F
W	0731	1021	2.8E	Th	0733	1027	2.2E
	1312	1530	2.7F		1322	1536	2.1F
	1801	2143	4.8E		1802	2135	3.6E
3	0111	0420	5.6F	18	0107	0414	4.4F
Th	0811	1104	3.0E	F	0758	1048	2.4E
	1402	1624	2.8F		1358	1620	2.3F
	1901	2232	4.4E		1846	2208	3.5E
4	0159	0504	5.2F	19	0140	0449	4.3F
F	0849	1149	3.2E	Sa	0823	1110	2.6E
	1453	1718	2.8F		1434	1701	2.5F
	2002	2321	3.8E		1934	2249	3.2E
5	0246	0550	4.7F	20	0215	0526	4.1F
Sa	0925	1231	3.2E	Su	0847	1139	2.8E
	1545	1812	2.8F		1511	1746	2.6F
	2107				2027	2333	2.8E
6		0017	3.0E	21	0251	0604	3.7F
Su	0333	0635	4.0F	M	0912	1212	3.0E
	1000	1316	3.2E		1551	1835	2.8F
	1638	1910	2.8F		2128		
	2218						
7		0113	2.3E	22		0019	2.4E
M	0423	0719	3.4F	Tu	0332	0647	3.2F
	1036	1402	3.2E		0940	1251	3.2E
	1733	2007	2.7F		1637	1929	3.0F
	2338				2239		
8		0222	1.6E	23		0115	1.9E
Tu	0518	0806	2.7F	W	0420	0732	2.7F
	1112	1453	3.1E		1012	1339	3.3E
	1828	2110	2.7F		1730	2030	3.2F
9	0106	0356	1.2E	24	0002	0220	1.4E
W	0621	0857	2.1F	Th	0523	0825	2.2F
	1151	1549	3.0E		1051	1430	3.5E
	1923	2218	2.8F		1829	2133	3.4F
10	0235	0523	1.1E	25	0134	0345	1.1E
Th	0730	0952	1.7F	F	0643	0922	1.8F
	1234	1648	3.0E		1139	1531	3.6E
	2016	2319	3.0F		1932	2240	3.8F
11	0349	0635	1.2E	26	0300	0532	1.1E
F	0839	1047	1.4F	Sa	0807	1027	1.6F
	1321	1742	3.1E		1238	1640	3.8E
	2107				2035	2345	4.2F
12		0017	3.3F	27	0409	0656	1.5E
Sa	0446	0730	1.4E	Su	0921	1131	1.7F
	0942	1148	1.3F		1346	1751	4.1E
	1412	1833	3.2E		2134		
	2154						
13		0108	3.6F	28		0046	4.7F
Su	0529	0819	1.6E	M	0502	0753	1.9E
	1036	1239	1.4F		1022	1234	2.0F
	1502	1918	3.4E		1457	1856	4.4E
	2238				2230		
14		0149	3.9F	29		0143	5.0F
M	0605	0900	1.8E	Tu	0547	0836	2.4E
	1123	1327	1.5F		1116	1334	2.4F
	1550	1952	3.5E		1605	1954	4.6E
	2318				2322		
15		0228	4.2F	30		0232	5.2F
Tu	0637	0933	2.0E	W	0626	0921	2.8E
	1205	1410	1.7F		1205	1429	2.8F
	1635	2027	3.6E		1708	2049	4.6E
	2356						
				31	0011	0317	5.3F
				Th	0702	1000	3.2E
					1251	1520	3.1F
					1807	2138	4.4E

FEBRUARY

Day	Slack Water Time h.m.	Maximum Current Time h.m.	Vel. knots	Day	Slack Water Time h.m.	Maximum Current Time h.m.	Vel. knots
1	0057	0358	5.1F	16	0047	0345	4.2F
F	0735	1035	3.4E	Sa	0711	1003	2.9E
	1337	1610	3.4F		1320	1557	3.1F
	1905	2222	4.0E		1849	2158	3.4E
2	0141	0439	4.7F	17	0122	0420	4.0F
Sa	0807	1115	3.6E	Su	0733	1030	3.2E
	1422	1658	3.5F		1353	1640	3.4F
	2002	2311	3.5E		1937	2236	3.2E
3	0225	0519	4.2F	18	0158	0455	3.7F
Su	0838	1146	3.6E	M	0756	1059	3.5E
	1508	1747	3.4F		1429	1725	3.6F
	2059	2357	2.8E		2029	2318	2.8E
4	0308	0559	3.6F	19	0237	0533	3.3F
M	0909	1225	3.4E	Tu	0822	1136	3.6E
	1555	1837	3.3F		1510	1811	3.8F
	2200				2127		
5		0047	2.2E	20		0005	2.4E
Tu	0354	0641	3.0F	W	0319	0616	2.9F
	0940	1303	3.2E		0853	1215	3.7E
	1645	1929	3.1F		1557	1903	3.8F
	2308				2234		
6		0143	1.5E	21		0058	1.8E
W	0445	0727	2.3F	Th	0409	0703	2.4F
	1013	1346	3.0E		0929	1300	3.7E
	1738	2024	2.9F		1653	2001	3.7F
					2352		
7	0027	0257	1.0E	22		0208	1.4E
Th	0545	0814	1.8F	F	0515	0758	1.9F
	1051	1440	2.8E		1013	1401	3.5E
	1835	2127	2.8F		1758	2106	3.7F
8	0156	0453	0.9E	23	0120	0339	1.1E
F	0655	0911	1.4F	Sa	0637	0900	1.6F
	1137	1544	2.6E		1111	1506	3.4E
	1935	2235	2.8F		1909	2217	3.8F
9	0318	0610	1.0E	24	0242	0530	1.2E
Sa	0809	1010	1.2F	Su	0759	1009	1.5F
	1234	1700	2.6E		1224	1628	3.5E
	2032	2342	3.0F		2017	2328	4.0F
10	0416	0705	1.3E	25	0345	0643	1.7E
Su	0914	1113	1.2F	M	0909	1120	1.7F
	1339	1804	2.8E		1348	1750	3.6E
	2125				2120		
11		0035	3.3F	26		0029	4.2F
M	0458	0754	1.6E	Tu	0433	0733	2.2E
	1009	1213	1.4F		1007	1227	2.2F
	1442	1855	3.1E		1507	1859	3.9E
	2212				2217		
12		0124	3.6F	27		0125	4.5F
Tu	0531	0832	1.9E	W	0513	0816	2.8E
	1055	1304	1.7F		1057	1326	2.7F
	1539	1937	3.3E		1617	1957	4.1E
	2255				2309		
13		0159	3.9F	28		0210	4.6F
W	0559	0903	2.1E	Th	0548	0857	3.2E
	1135	1353	2.0F		1143	1420	3.3F
	1630	2015	3.4E		1719	2046	4.1E
	2334				2356		
14		0236	4.1F				
Th	0624	0926	2.4E				
	1212	1434	2.4F				
	1717	2046	3.5E				
15	0011	0310	4.2F				
F	0648	0945	2.6E				
	1247	1517	2.8F				
	1803	2121	3.5E				

THE NARROWS

1991 CURRENT TABLES

For Daylight Saving Time, add one hour.

Times and Heights of High and Low Waters

F-Flood, Dir. 135° True   E-Ebb, Dir. 335° True

MARCH

Day	Slack Water Time h.m.	Max Current Time h.m.	Vel. knots	Day	Slack Water Time h.m.	Max Current Time h.m.	Vel. knots
1 F		0251	4.5F	16 Sa		0234	3.7F
	0621	0930	3.6E		0551	0855	3.1E
	1226	1506	3.7F		1208	1454	3.6F
	1815	2133	3.9E		1803	2108	3.3E
2 Sa	0041	0331	4.3F	17 Su	0026	0312	3.7F
	0651	1003	3.7E		0615	0921	3.5E
	1308	1552	4.0F		1241	1535	4.1F
	1907	2216	3.6E		1850	2144	3.2E
3 Su	0123	0407	3.9F	18 M	0105	0348	3.5F
	0720	1034	3.8E		0640	0951	3.8E
	1348	1637	4.0F		1316	1618	4.4F
	1958	2257	3.1E		1939	2225	3.0E
4 M	0205	0448	3.5F	19 Tu	0145	0427	3.2F
	0748	1104	3.7E		0707	1026	4.0E
	1429	1719	4.0F		1355	1701	4.6F
	2048	2337	2.6E		2031	2311	2.7E
5 Tu	0247	0524	3.0F	20 W	0228	0508	2.8F
	0817	1137	3.5E		0738	1105	4.1E
	1511	1805	3.7F		1438	1749	4.6F
	2140				2127	2359	2.3E
6 W		0019	2.0E	21 Th	0315	0552	2.4F
	0331	0607	2.5F		0814	1148	4.0E
	0846	1212	3.2E		1529	1843	4.4F
	1556	1851	3.4F		2231		
	2238						
7 Th		0106	1.5E	22 F		0054	1.8E
	0419	0649	2.0F		0411	0643	2.0F
	0919	1255	2.9E		0858	1237	3.8E
	1647	1944	3.1F		1628	1943	4.1F
	2345				2342		
8 F		0211	1.1E	23 Sa		0205	1.5E
	0518	0739	1.5F		0520	0740	1.7F
	0958	1342	2.6E		0952	1339	3.4E
	1744	2041	2.8F		1735	2046	3.9F
9 Sa	0103	0400	0.8E	24 Su	0058	0342	1.4E
	0628	0833	1.2F		0638	0847	1.5F
	1048	1444	2.4E		1103	1454	3.1E
	1848	2147	2.7F		1848	2155	3.7F
10 Su	0221	0535	1.0E	25 M	0208	0518	1.7E
	0741	0936	1.1F		0752	1003	1.6F
	1154	1601	2.3E		1232	1625	3.0E
	1951	2253	2.8F		1958	2303	3.7F
11 M	0321	0631	1.3E	26 Tu	0304	0619	2.2E
	0845	1044	1.2F		0855	1115	2.0F
	1313	1723	2.4E		1405	1754	3.1E
	2048	2352	3.0F		2102		
12 Tu	0403	0714	1.6E	27 W		0003	3.8F
	0938	1148	1.5F		0349	0708	2.7E
	1427	1825	2.7E		0948	1224	2.6F
	2139				1524	1901	3.3E
					2159		
13 W		0040	3.3F	28 Th		0056	3.8F
	0435	0749	2.0E		0427	0747	3.2E
	1021	1239	2.0F		1036	1320	3.2F
	1530	1914	2.9E		1631	1957	3.4E
	2224				2251		
14 Th		0121	3.5F	29 F		0141	3.8F
	0503	0816	2.4E		0501	0824	3.6E
	1059	1328	2.5F		1119	1409	3.8F
	1625	1953	3.1E		1728	2046	3.4E
	2307				2339		
15 F		0200	3.7F	30 Sa		0223	3.6F
	0528	0835	2.7E		0532	0855	3.8E
	1134	1411	3.1F		1159	1452	4.2F
	1715	2032	3.2E		1819	2127	3.3E
	2347						
				31 Su	0023	0301	3.4F
					0602	0926	3.9E
					1238	1535	4.4F
					1907	2208	3.0E

APRIL

Day	Slack Water Time h.m.	Max Current Time h.m.	Vel. knots	Day	Slack Water Time h.m.	Max Current Time h.m.	Vel. knots
1 M	0106	0336	3.1F	16 Tu	0048	0316	2.9F
	0630	0952	3.9E		0549	0916	4.4E
	1315	1611	4.4F		1246	1557	5.2F
	1952	2248	2.7E		1939	2218	2.8E
2 Tu	0148	0414	2.7F	17 W	0134	0359	2.7F
	0658	1023	3.7E		0624	0957	4.5E
	1353	1652	4.3F		1329	1646	5.3F
	2036	2324	2.3E		2031	2307	2.6E
3 W	0230	0452	2.4F	18 Th	0221	0446	2.4F
	0727	1052	3.5E		0703	1040	4.4E
	1431	1735	4.0F		1417	1734	5.1F
	2122				2126	2356	2.3E
4 Th		0000	1.9E	19 F	0313	0533	2.2F
	0314	0533	2.0F		0748	1128	4.2E
	0757	1127	3.2E		1510	1828	4.8F
	1513	1821	3.7F		2225		
	2212						
5 F		0046	1.5E	20 Sa		0057	2.0E
	0403	0616	1.6F		0413	0630	1.9F
	0833	1209	2.9E		0842	1225	3.8E
	1600	1906	3.4F		1610	1926	4.4F
	2309				2326		
6 Sa		0142	1.2E	21 Su		0211	1.9E
	0500	0707	1.3F		0521	0732	1.7F
	0915	1258	2.6E		0948	1332	3.3E
	1655	2002	3.1F		1715	2024	4.0F
7 Su	0012	0306	1.1E	22 M	0027	0330	2.0E
	0606	0804	1.1F		0631	0841	1.7F
	1010	1355	2.2E		1113	1450	2.8E
	1756	2102	2.9F		1824	2129	3.7F
8 M	0114	0443	1.2E	23 Tu	0122	0445	2.3E
	0713	0908	1.1F		0737	0955	2.0F
	1123	1508	2.0E		1250	1624	2.6E
	1900	2202	2.8F		1932	2231	3.4F
9 Tu	0207	0538	1.5E	24 W	0212	0542	2.8E
	0811	1013	1.3F		0834	1109	2.5F
	1250	1630	2.0E		1421	1748	2.6E
	2001	2257	2.8F		2037	2332	3.2F
10 W	0250	0617	1.8E	25 Th	0255	0629	3.2E
	0900	1116	1.7F		0925	1214	3.1F
	1412	1742	2.2E		1537	1855	2.7E
	2056	2348	3.0F		2136		
11 Th	0324	0646	2.3E	26 F		0021	3.1F
	0942	1214	2.4F		0333	0712	3.6E
	1520	1839	2.4E		1011	1309	3.6F
	2147				1640	1952	2.7E
					2230		
12 F		0034	3.1F	27 Sa		0109	2.9F
	0354	0712	2.7E		0408	0746	3.8E
	1019	1302	3.1F		1052	1352	4.1F
	1618	1925	2.6E		1734	2041	2.7E
	2235				2320		
13 Sa		0116	3.1F	28 Su		0150	2.7F
	0422	0738	3.2E		0441	0819	3.9E
	1054	1346	3.8F		1131	1435	4.4F
	1710	2009	2.8E		1821	2122	2.6E
	2320						
14 Su		0155	3.1F	29 M	0006	0228	2.5F
	0449	0806	3.6E		0512	0848	3.9E
	1130	1428	4.4F		1209	1514	4.5F
	1800	2052	2.9E		1904	2204	2.5E
15 M	0004	0236	3.0F	30 Tu	0050	0308	2.3F
	0518	0839	4.1E		0542	0917	3.8E
	1207	1514	4.9F		1246	1551	4.5F
	1849	2133	2.9E		1945	2239	2.3E

1991 CURRENT TABLES

THE NARROWS

For Daylight Saving Time, add one hour.

Times and Heights of High and Low Waters

F-Flood, Dir. 135° True   E-Ebb, Dir. 335° True

MAY

Day	Slack Water Time h.m.	Max Current Time h.m.	Vel. knots	Day	Slack Water Time h.m.	Max Current Time h.m.	Vel. knots
1 W	0133	0345	2.1F	16 Th	0121	0338	2.3F
	0612	0949	3.7E		0552	0935	4.8E
	1322	1627	4.4F		1312	1629	5.7F
	2026	2312	2.1E		2027	2304	2.5E
2 Th	0215	0427	1.9F	17 F	0212	0427	2.3F
	0643	1020	3.5E		0641	1026	4.6E
	1400	1709	4.2F		1403	1721	5.5F
	2108	2349	1.8E		2117	2357	2.4E
3 F	0300	0508	1.6F	18 Sa	0307	0518	2.1F
	0718	1101	3.2E		0736	1117	4.3E
	1440	1752	4.0F		1456	1812	5.1F
	2151				2208		
4 Sa		0031	1.6E	19 Su		0057	2.4E
	0348	0551	1.4F		0406	0618	2.1F
	0757	1136	2.9E		0840	1218	3.7E
	1522	1837	3.7F		1553	1906	4.6F
	2237				2258		
5 Su		0119	1.5E	20 M		0200	2.5E
	0443	0645	1.3F		0509	0721	2.0F
	0844	1225	2.6E		0955	1322	3.1E
	1610	1926	3.4F		1653	2001	4.1F
	2324				2346		
6 M		0214	1.5E	21 Tu		0303	2.7E
	0541	0740	1.2F		0612	0829	2.1F
	0944	1320	2.2E		1124	1442	2.5E
	1704	2019	3.1F		1756	2056	3.6F
7 Tu	0011	0316	1.6E	22 W	0033	0406	2.9E
	0639	0840	1.3F		0712	0943	2.4F
	1059	1424	1.9E		1259	1612	2.1E
	1803	2111	2.9F		1902	2153	3.1F
8 W	0053	0405	1.8E	23 Th	0116	0501	3.2E
	0731	0942	1.6F		0807	1052	2.8F
	1228	1535	1.8E		1427	1735	2.0E
	1905	2206	2.8F		2007	2247	2.7F
9 Th	0131	0454	2.2E	24 F	0158	0551	3.5E
	0817	1044	2.1F		0857	1155	3.3F
	1353	1654	1.8E		1542	1844	2.0E
	2006	2255	2.7F		2109	2342	2.4F
10 F	0207	0529	2.7E	25 Sa	0238	0636	3.7E
	0858	1139	2.8F		0943	1249	3.8F
	1506	1803	1.9E		1643	1940	2.1E
	2105	2348	2.6F		2207		
11 Sa	0240	0607	3.1E	26 Su		0030	2.2F
	0937	1230	3.6F		0316	0713	3.8E
	1609	1901	2.1E		1026	1334	4.1F
	2201				1735	2033	2.2E
					2300		
12 Su		0030	2.5F	27 M		0114	2.0F
	0314	0644	3.6E		0352	0748	3.8E
	1016	1320	4.3F		1106	1415	4.3F
	1704	1953	2.3E		1819	2116	2.2E
	2253				2348		
13 M		0119	2.5F	28 Tu		0157	1.9F
	0349	0725	4.1E		0427	0821	3.8E
	1057	1406	4.9F		1145	1454	4.4F
	1756	2039	2.5E		1900	2157	2.1E
	2343						
14 Tu		0204	2.4F	29 W	0033	0238	1.8F
	0426	0806	4.5E		0501	0849	3.7E
	1139	1454	5.4F		1222	1531	4.5F
	1846	2130	2.5E		1938	2236	2.0E
15 W	0032	0251	2.4F	30 Th	0117	0319	1.7F
	0507	0848	4.7E		0536	0924	3.6E
	1225	1539	5.6F		1259	1609	4.4F
	1936	2213	2.5E		2014	2307	1.9E
				31 F	0159	0400	1.6F
					0612	0955	3.5E
					1336	1648	4.3F
					2051	2336	1.9E

JUNE

Day	Slack Water Time h.m.	Max Current Time h.m.	Vel. knots	Day	Slack Water Time h.m.	Max Current Time h.m.	Vel. knots
1 Sa	0243	0442	1.5F	16 Su	0251	0508	2.5F
	0651	1034	3.3E		0736	1109	4.2E
	1414	1728	4.2F		1441	1752	5.1F
	2127				2139		
2 Su		0012	1.8E	17 M		0034	2.9E
	0328	0531	1.5F		0346	0605	2.5F
	0735	1111	3.0E		0844	1206	3.6E
	1452	1809	3.9F		1534	1841	4.6F
	2202				2220		
3 M		0047	1.8E	18 Tu		0129	3.1E
	0417	0618	1.4F		0444	0707	2.6F
	0826	1159	2.7E		1000	1310	2.8E
	1532	1854	3.7F		1628	1930	3.9F
	2237				2300		
4 Tu		0123	1.9E	19 W		0224	3.2E
	0506	0711	1.5F		0542	0809	2.6F
	0927	1248	2.3E		1125	1424	2.2E
	1617	1937	3.4F		1726	2022	3.3F
	2311				2340		
5 W		0205	2.1E	20 Th		0319	3.3E
	0555	0808	1.7F		0639	0918	2.8F
	1041	1345	1.9E		1255	1553	1.7E
	1708	2024	3.0F		1829	2113	2.7F
	2345						
6 Th		0253	2.4E	21 F	0021	0413	3.4E
	0643	0906	2.0F		0734	1026	3.0F
	1206	1448	1.6E		1422	1719	1.5E
	1808	2115	2.7F		1935	2207	2.2F
7 F	0019	0336	2.7E	22 Sa	0103	0506	3.5E
	0729	1006	2.5F		0826	1129	3.3F
	1332	1605	1.4E		1538	1830	1.5E
	1915	2206	2.4F		2041	2303	1.9F
8 Sa	0054	0425	3.1E	23 Su	0146	0557	3.5E
	0814	1104	3.2F		0914	1224	3.6F
	1451	1723	1.5E		1640	1929	1.7E
	2023	2300	2.2F		2143	2354	1.7F
9 Su	0133	0513	3.5E	24 M	0229	0642	3.6E
	0859	1201	3.9F		1000	1315	3.9F
	1558	1833	1.6E		1730	2020	1.8E
	2128	2351	2.1F		2239		
10 M	0215	0600	4.0E	25 Tu		0045	1.6F
	0945	1253	4.6F		0312	0725	3.6E
	1657	1936	1.9E		1043	1356	4.1F
	2227				1811	2104	1.9E
					2328		
11 Tu		0042	2.1F	26 W		0131	1.5F
	0300	0651	4.4E		0354	0800	3.6E
	1032	1347	5.1F		1124	1435	4.2F
	1751	2030	2.1E		1848	2145	1.9E
	2322						
12 W		0135	2.1F	27 Th	0014	0216	1.6F
	0349	0742	4.7E		0435	0833	3.6E
	1121	1436	5.6F		1203	1513	4.3F
	1840	2119	2.3E		1922	2220	2.0E
13 Th	0014	0226	2.2F	28 F	0056	0259	1.6F
	0441	0831	4.9E		0516	0905	3.6E
	1210	1526	5.8F		1240	1550	4.4F
	1928	2210	2.5E		1954	2249	2.0E
14 F	0105	0320	2.3F	29 Sa	0137	0342	1.7F
	0536	0922	4.9E		0557	0941	3.5E
	1300	1615	5.7F		1316	1625	4.4F
	2013	2255	2.7E		2024	2318	2.1E
15 Sa	0157	0413	2.4F	30 Su	0217	0423	1.8F
	0634	1016	4.7E		0640	1016	3.3E
	1350	1704	5.5F		1351	1702	4.2F
	2057	2345	2.8E		2052	2339	2.1E

THE NARROWS

1991 CURRENT TABLES

For Daylight Saving Time, add one hour.

Times and Heights of High and Low Waters

F-Flood, Dir. 135° True   E-Ebb, Dir. 335° True

JULY

Day	Slack Water Time h.m.	Max Current Time h.m.	Vel. knots
1 M	0257	0508	1.8F
	0726	1053	3.1E
	1426	1740	4.0F
	2119		
2 Tu		0007	2.3E
	0338	0553	1.9F
	0818	1136	2.7E
	1502	1821	3.7F
	2146		
3 W		0042	2.4E
	0420	0641	2.1F
	0917	1219	2.4E
	1541	1902	3.4F
	2214		
4 Th		0116	2.6E
	0504	0736	2.3F
	1026	1314	1.9E
	1626	1945	2.9F
	2243		
5 F		0156	2.9E
	0551	0833	2.6F
	1145	1416	1.5E
	1722	2034	2.5F
	2316		
6 Sa		0245	3.1E
	0640	0932	3.0F
	1312	1531	1.2E
	1832	2127	2.1F
	2355		
7 Su		0336	3.4E
	0733	1034	3.5F
	1436	1653	1.1E
	1949	2223	1.9F
8 M	0040	0432	3.7E
	0827	1134	4.0F
	1548	1824	1.3E
	2101	2320	1.8F
9 Tu	0133	0531	4.1E
	0921	1233	4.6F
	1648	1928	1.6E
	2206		
10 W		0017	1.9F
	0231	0630	4.4E
	1015	1328	5.1F
	1739	2023	2.0E
	2303		
11 Th		0117	2.1F
	0332	0729	4.7E
	1107	1420	5.4F
	1825	2113	2.4E
	2355		
12 F		0212	2.4F
	0434	0825	4.9E
	1158	1509	5.6F
	1907	2154	2.7E
13 Sa	0045	0307	2.7F
	0536	0916	4.8E
	1247	1555	5.5F
	1946	2237	3.0E
14 Su	0135	0401	2.9F
	0638	1009	4.5E
	1336	1641	5.3F
	2023	2319	3.3E
15 M	0226	0455	3.1F
	0741	1101	4.0E
	1424	1727	4.8F
	2059		
16 Tu		0005	3.4E
	0317	0547	3.2F
	0846	1156	3.3E
	1512	1812	4.2F
	2135		
17 W		0050	3.5E
	0410	0644	3.1F
	0956	1251	2.6E
	1603	1856	3.6F
	2210		
18 Th		0133	3.5E
	0504	0744	3.1F
	1113	1402	1.9E
	1657	1943	2.9F
	2247		
19 F		0225	3.4E
	0559	0844	3.0F
	1236	1525	1.4E
	1758	2034	2.3F
	2327		
20 Sa		0319	3.2E
	0656	0949	3.0F
	1403	1656	1.2E
	1905	2127	1.8F
21 Su	0011	0420	3.1E
	0751	1054	3.1F
	1522	1811	1.2E
	2014	2224	1.5F
22 M	0100	0522	3.1E
	0745	1155	3.3F
	1624	1913	1.4E
	2119	2325	1.3F
23 Tu	0153	0620	3.2E
	0935	1249	3.5F
	1712	2002	1.6E
	2216		
24 W		0019	1.4F
	0246	0703	3.3E
	1021	1338	3.8F
	1750	2045	1.8E
	2305		
25 Th		0110	1.5F
	0337	0744	3.4E
	1104	1413	4.0F
	1823	2120	2.0E
	2348		
26 F		0156	1.7F
	0425	0818	3.5E
	1143	1450	4.2F
	1851	2151	2.1E
27 Sa	0028	0239	1.9F
	0509	0853	3.5E
	1220	1525	4.2F
	1918	2216	2.2E
28 Su	0106	0319	2.1F
	0553	0924	3.4E
	1255	1557	4.2F
	1942	2237	2.4E
29 M	0142	0403	2.3F
	0638	0957	3.3E
	1329	1632	4.1F
	2006	2254	2.6E
30 Tu	0217	0444	2.5F
	0724	1036	3.1E
	1402	1709	3.9F
	2029	2322	2.8E
31 W	0253	0527	2.7F
	0814	1115	2.8E
	1437	1746	3.5F
	2052	2353	3.0E

AUGUST

Day	Slack Water Time h.m.	Max Current Time h.m.	Vel. knots
1 Th	0330	0615	2.8F
	0910	1159	2.4E
	1515	1825	3.1F
	2118		
2 F		0028	3.1E
	0412	0705	3.0F
	1014	1250	1.9E
	1559	1909	2.6F
	2148		
3 Sa		0111	3.3E
	0501	0800	3.1F
	1129	1351	1.5E
	1654	2000	2.2F
	2224		
4 Su		0201	3.4E
	0557	0902	3.3F
	1255	1502	1.1E
	1807	2055	1.8F
	2309		
5 M		0300	3.5E
	0659	1005	3.6F
	1421	1638	1.0E
	1930	2152	1.6F
6 Tu	0005	0403	3.6E
	0802	1113	4.0F
	1534	1814	1.3E
	2046	2300	1.6F
7 W	0111	0514	3.9E
	0903	1214	4.4F
	1630	1916	1.7E
	2150		
8 Th		0003	1.9F
	0223	0622	4.2E
	1001	1312	4.8F
	1716	2005	2.2E
	2245		
9 F		0105	2.3F
	0334	0723	4.4E
	1055	1403	5.1F
	1756	2048	2.7E
	2335		
10 Sa		0159	2.8F
	0441	0819	4.6E
	1145	1448	5.1F
	1833	2129	3.1E
11 Su	0022	0255	3.3F
	0544	0914	4.5E
	1233	1533	5.0F
	1907	2208	3.5E
12 M	0109	0347	3.6F
	0644	1003	4.1E
	1320	1616	4.7F
	1940	2245	3.7E
13 Tu	0155	0435	3.8F
	0743	1051	3.7E
	1405	1656	4.2F
	2012	2322	3.8E
14 W	0242	0527	3.8F
	0842	1141	3.0E
	1451	1737	3.6F
	2045		
15 Th		0002	3.7E
	0330	0616	3.7F
	0944	1231	2.4E
	1539	1821	3.0F
	2118		
16 F		0045	3.5E
	0420	0710	3.4F
	1051	1329	1.7E
	1631	1906	2.4F
	2153		
17 Sa		0129	3.2E
	0514	0805	3.2F
	1207	1454	1.2E
	1731	1959	1.9F
	2234		
18 Su		0224	2.9E
	0612	0906	3.0F
	1330	1634	1.0E
	1840	2052	1.4F
	2322		
19 M		0329	2.7E
	0713	1015	2.9F
	1450	1745	1.1E
	1951	2152	1.2F
20 Tu	0021	0446	2.7E
	0812	1119	3.0F
	1551	1844	1.4E
	2056	2257	1.2F
21 W	0128	0553	2.8E
	0906	1220	3.2F
	1635	1931	1.6E
	2150	2358	1.4F
22 Th	0232	0648	3.0E
	0955	1307	3.5F
	1710	2012	1.9E
	2236		
23 F		0048	1.7F
	0330	0730	3.2E
	1039	1342	3.7F
	1738	2045	2.2E
	2317		
24 Sa		0136	2.1F
	0421	0805	3.3E
	1119	1419	3.9F
	1804	2110	2.4E
	2354		
25 Su		0219	2.5F
	0508	0835	3.3E
	1156	1454	3.9F
	1827	2129	2.6E
26 M	0028	0300	2.8F
	0553	0909	3.3E
	1232	1526	3.9F
	1850	2146	2.9E
27 Tu	0101	0340	3.1F
	0637	0945	3.2E
	1307	1558	3.7F
	1911	2212	3.1E
28 W	0134	0419	3.4F
	0723	1020	3.0E
	1343	1635	3.5F
	1934	2239	3.3E
29 Th	0208	0502	3.6F
	0812	1059	2.7E
	1420	1714	3.1F
	1958	2312	3.5E
30 F	0245	0549	3.7F
	0905	1144	2.3E
	1500	1753	2.7F
	2027	2348	3.6E
31 Sa	0328	0637	3.7F
	1007	1237	1.9E
	1547	1838	2.2F
	2101		

1991 CURRENT TABLES

THE NARROWS

For Daylight Saving Time, add one hour.

Times and Heights of High and Low Waters

F—Flood, Dir. 135° True   E—Ebb, Dir. 335° True

SEPTEMBER

Day	Slack Water Time h.m.	Maximum Current Time h.m.	Vel. knots	Day	Slack Water Time h.m.	Maximum Current Time h.m.	Vel. knots
1 Su		0035	3.5E	16 M		0127	2.6E
	0421	0734	3.7F		0525	0824	3.0F
	1119	1335	1.4E		1246	1557	1.1E
	1647	1929	1.8F		1818	2020	1.2F
	2144				2236		
2 M		0128	3.4E	17 Tu		0235	2.3E
	0523	0837	3.6F		0628	0927	2.8F
	1240	1454	1.1E		1358	1714	1.2E
	1805	2029	1.6F		1928	2125	1.1F
	2238				2346		
3 Tu		0233	3.3E	18 W		0357	2.2E
	0632	0943	3.7F		0731	1033	2.8F
	1401	1639	1.2E		1456	1814	1.5E
	1926	2138	1.5F		2030	2231	1.2F
	2349						
4 W		0351	3.3E	19 Th	0107	0521	2.3E
	0742	1052	3.9F		0829	1133	3.0F
	1506	1802	1.6E		1538	1851	1.8E
	2036	2249	1.7F		2121	2333	1.6F
5 Th	0112	0508	3.5E	20 F	0221	0616	2.6E
	0847	1155	4.1F		0921	1222	3.2F
	1557	1859	2.1E		1611	1928	2.1E
	2135	2355	2.2F		2204		
6 F	0235	0622	3.7E	21 Sa		0030	2.0F
	0946	1249	4.3F		0324	0705	2.8E
	1638	1944	2.7E		1007	1302	3.3F
	2226				1639	1955	2.5E
					2242		
7 Sa		0056	2.8F	22 Su		0112	2.6F
	0349	0725	4.0E		0417	0744	2.9E
	1040	1341	4.5F		1050	1340	3.4F
	1715	2022	3.2E		1705	2016	2.8E
	2313				2316		
8 Su		0152	3.4F	23 M		0154	3.1F
	0454	0821	4.0E		0505	0819	3.0E
	1130	1423	4.4F		1130	1415	3.5F
	1748	2057	3.6E		1728	2038	3.1E
	2357				2349		
9 M		0241	3.9F	24 Tu		0235	3.6F
	0553	0908	3.9E		0551	0853	3.0E
	1217	1504	4.2F		1209	1449	3.4F
	1821	2133	3.9E		1751	2101	3.4E
10 Tu	0040	0330	4.3F	25 W	0022	0315	4.0F
	0648	0954	3.6E		0636	0930	3.0E
	1302	1545	3.9F		1247	1527	3.2F
	1852	2206	4.0E		1815	2128	3.7E
11 W	0123	0416	4.4F	26 Th	0055	0355	4.3F
	0741	1040	3.2E		0721	1007	2.8E
	1347	1625	3.5F		1326	1606	3.0F
	1922	2242	3.9E		1841	2159	3.9E
12 Th	0205	0502	4.3F	27 F	0130	0442	4.5F
	0834	1125	2.7E		0810	1048	2.6E
	1431	1707	3.0F		1407	1643	2.6F
	1953	2317	3.7E		1910	2238	4.0E
13 F	0249	0547	4.1F	28 Sa	0211	0525	4.5F
	0928	1209	2.2E		0903	1134	2.2E
	1518	1749	2.4F		1452	1726	2.3F
	2025	2353	3.4E		1945	2317	3.9E
14 Sa	0336	0633	3.7F	29 Su	0258	0618	4.4F
	1026	1306	1.6E		1002	1229	1.9E
	1610	1831	1.9F		1545	1815	1.9F
	2101				2026		
15 Su		0038	3.0E	30 M		0006	3.7E
	0427	0726	3.3F		0353	0713	4.1F
	1132	1414	1.2E		1109	1329	1.5E
	1710	1922	1.5F		1652	1913	1.6F
	2143				2118		

OCTOBER

Day	Slack Water Time h.m.	Maximum Current Time h.m.	Vel. knots	Day	Slack Water Time h.m.	Maximum Current Time h.m.	Vel. knots
1 Tu		0107	3.4E	16 W		0142	2.2E
	0458	0815	3.9F		0537	0842	2.9F
	1221	1457	1.4E		1255	1628	1.4E
	1807	2018	1.5F		1901	2056	1.1F
	2226				2314		
2 W		0217	3.1E	17 Th		0259	1.9E
	0609	0921	3.7F		0641	0941	2.8F
	1329	1628	1.6E		1346	1721	1.6E
	1921	2129	1.6F		1957	2159	1.3F
	2354						
3 Th		0340	2.9E	18 F	0044	0421	1.9E
	0721	1026	3.7F		0742	1037	2.8F
	1425	1744	2.1E		1427	1758	2.0E
	2024	2243	2.0F		2045	2303	1.8F
4 F	0130	0509	3.0E	19 Sa	0206	0539	2.0E
	0827	1129	3.7F		0838	1128	2.8F
	1511	1829	2.7E		1501	1833	2.4E
	2118	2349	2.6F		2126	2359	2.4F
5 Sa	0254	0624	3.2E	20 Su	0313	0636	2.2E
	0928	1223	3.8F		0929	1214	2.9F
	1551	1912	3.3E		1531	1856	2.8E
	2206				2203		
6 Su		0049	3.3F	21 M		0046	3.0F
	0404	0727	3.3E		0409	0715	2.4E
	1022	1312	3.7F		1017	1255	2.9F
	1627	1949	3.7E		1559	1918	3.2E
	2250				2238		
7 M		0141	4.0F	22 Tu		0129	3.7F
	0505	0819	3.4E		0500	0759	2.6E
	1113	1353	3.6F		1102	1335	2.9F
	1700	2025	4.0E		1626	1947	3.6E
	2332				2312		
8 Tu		0229	4.4F	23 W		0212	4.3F
	0559	0906	3.3E		0546	0836	2.7E
	1200	1436	3.3F		1146	1413	2.8F
	1732	2059	4.1E		1653	2016	4.0E
					2347		
9 W	0013	0311	4.7F	24 Th		0254	4.8F
	0649	0951	3.1E		0632	0918	2.7E
	1246	1513	3.0F		1228	1454	2.7F
	1803	2129	4.1E		1723	2051	4.2E
10 Th	0053	0354	4.7F	25 F	0024	0336	5.1F
	0737	1031	2.8E		0719	0954	2.6E
	1330	1554	2.7F		1312	1535	2.5F
	1834	2200	4.0E		1756	2128	4.4E
11 F	0132	0437	4.6F	26 Sa	0104	0420	5.2F
	0823	1111	2.4E		0808	1042	2.4E
	1415	1635	2.3F		1357	1619	2.3F
	1905	2235	3.7E		1834	2209	4.4E
12 Sa	0213	0518	4.3F	27 Su	0149	0507	5.1F
	0911	1152	2.0E		0900	1131	2.2E
	1501	1718	1.9F		1447	1706	2.1F
	1938	2314	3.3E		1917	2258	4.2E
13 Su	0256	0605	3.9F	28 M	0239	0600	4.9F
	1001	1241	1.6E		0955	1226	2.0E
	1552	1759	1.6F		1544	1759	1.8F
	2015	2353	3.0E		2008	2352	3.8E
14 M	0343	0651	3.5F	29 Tu	0335	0655	4.5F
	1057	1342	1.3E		1053	1329	1.9E
	1651	1852	1.3F		1650	1858	1.7F
	2059				2111		
15 Tu		0041	2.5E	30 W		0055	3.3E
	0437	0745	3.2F		0437	0752	4.1F
	1157	1512	1.2E		1151	1446	2.0E
	1756	1951	1.1F		1759	2009	1.7F
	2157				2232		
				31 Th		0204	2.8E
					0546	0853	3.8F
					1246	1602	2.3E
					1905	2121	1.9F

THE NARROWS

1991 CURRENT TABLES

For Daylight Saving Time, add one hour.

Times and Heights of High and Low Waters

F-Flood, Dir. 135° True   E-Ebb, Dir. 335° True

NOVEMBER

Day	Slack Water Time h.m.	Maximum Current Time h.m.	Vel. knots
1 F	0010	0334	2.5E
	0656	0955	3.5F
	1335	1703	2.8E
	2004	2235	2.4F
2 Sa	0147	0510	2.4E
	0803	1055	3.3F
	1419	1754	3.2E
	2056	2343	3.1F
3 Su	0309	0626	2.5E
	0906	1150	3.1F
	1459	1839	3.7E
	2143		
4 M		0040	3.8F
	0417	0725	2.6E
	1003	1239	2.9F
	1537	1918	4.0E
	2227		
5 Tu		0129	4.3F
	0514	0816	2.7E
	1056	1322	2.7F
	1612	1953	4.1E
	2309		
6 W		0212	4.6F
	0604	0905	2.7E
	1145	1406	2.5F
	1646	2028	4.2E
	2349		
7 Th		0254	4.8F
	0649	0946	2.6E
	1231	1445	2.3F
	1719	2058	4.1E
8 F	0027	0335	4.8F
	0732	1028	2.4E
	1315	1527	2.1F
	1752	2132	3.9E
9 Sa	0105	0413	4.7F
	0813	1103	2.1E
	1359	1608	1.9F
	1825	2207	3.6E
10 Su	0144	0452	4.4F
	0855	1144	1.9E
	1445	1651	1.7F
	1901	2244	3.3E
11 M	0224	0535	4.1F
	0938	1221	1.7E
	1534	1736	1.4F
	1941	2321	3.0E
12 Tu	0306	0621	3.8F
	1022	1308	1.6E
	1627	1825	1.3F
	2028		
13 W		0008	2.6E
	0353	0706	3.5F
	1107	1404	1.6E
	1725	1921	1.2F
	2128		
14 Th		0103	2.2E
	0444	0758	3.2F
	1150	1500	1.7E
	1823	2021	1.3F
	2245		
15 F		0206	1.8E
	0542	0851	2.9F
	1231	1556	1.9E
	1915	2125	1.5F
16 Sa	0016	0316	1.6E
	0644	0943	2.7F
	1309	1639	2.2E
	2001	2227	2.0F
17 Su	0144	0441	1.5E
	0746	1034	2.5F
	1345	1712	2.6E
	2043	2326	2.7F
18 M	0257	0548	1.6E
	0846	1125	2.4F
	1418	1748	3.1E
	2122		
19 Tu		0014	3.4F
	0358	0649	1.9E
	0942	1210	2.3F
	1451	1827	3.5E
	2201		
20 W		0102	4.1F
	0452	0740	2.1E
	1034	1256	2.3F
	1526	1904	4.0E
	2239		
21 Th		0146	4.7F
	0541	0823	2.2E
	1123	1341	2.3F
	1603	1943	4.3E
	2320		
22 F		0232	5.2F
	0628	0907	2.4E
	1210	1426	2.3F
	1642	2026	4.6E
23 Sa	0002	0317	5.5F
	0715	0951	2.4E
	1257	1513	2.3F
	1725	2110	4.8E
24 Su	0047	0406	5.6F
	0802	1037	2.4E
	1345	1602	2.2F
	1813	2157	4.7E
25 M	0135	0452	5.5F
	0850	1127	2.4E
	1437	1653	2.2F
	1906	2248	4.4E
26 Tu	0226	0543	5.2F
	0937	1221	2.4E
	1534	1749	2.1F
	2006	2343	3.9E
27 W	0319	0634	4.8F
	1025	1316	2.5E
	1635	1850	2.1F
	2118		
28 Th		0044	3.2E
	0417	0727	4.2F
	1111	1420	2.7E
	1737	1955	2.2F
	2244		
29 F		0159	2.6E
	0519	0824	3.7F
	1156	1521	2.9E
	1839	2107	2.4F
30 Sa	0021	0325	2.1E
	0626	0920	3.2F
	1241	1624	3.2E
	1937	2221	2.9F

DECEMBER

Day	Slack Water Time h.m.	Maximum Current Time h.m.	Vel. knots
1 Su	0155	0500	1.9E
	0735	1016	2.7F
	1325	1719	3.5E
	2030	2326	3.4F
2 M	0317	0617	1.9E
	0841	1113	2.4F
	1408	1807	3.8E
	2119		
3 Tu		0027	3.9F
	0424	0721	2.0E
	0943	1208	2.2F
	1449	1848	3.9E
	2205		
4 W		0115	4.2F
	0518	0810	2.2E
	1039	1256	2.0F
	1530	1928	4.0E
	2247		
5 Th		0200	4.5F
	0605	0859	2.2E
	1130	1339	1.9F
	1609	2006	4.0E
	2328		
6 F		0241	4.6F
	0647	0940	2.2E
	1217	1421	1.8F
	1646	2039	3.9E
7 Sa	0007	0316	4.6F
	0725	1021	2.2E
	1300	1504	1.8F
	1723	2115	3.8E
8 Su	0045	0355	4.6F
	0801	1052	2.1E
	1343	1545	1.7F
	1801	2144	3.6E
9 M	0123	0433	4.5F
	0836	1127	2.0E
	1425	1629	1.6F
	1840	2221	3.4E
10 Tu	0159	0511	4.3F
	0910	1202	1.9E
	1509	1714	1.6F
	1923	2300	3.1E
11 W	0237	0551	4.0F
	0943	1231	2.0E
	1556	1759	1.6F
	2012	2343	2.7E
12 Th	0315	0632	3.7F
	1016	1306	2.0E
	1644	1852	1.6F
	2110		
13 F		0025	2.3E
	0357	0718	3.4F
	1048	1345	2.1E
	1733	1946	1.7F
	2220		
14 Sa		0122	1.8E
	0444	0804	3.0F
	1120	1430	2.3E
	1822	2042	1.9F
	2344		
15 Su		0225	1.5E
	0541	0852	2.6F
	1153	1513	2.6E
	1909	2144	2.3F
16 M	0113	0340	1.2E
	0649	0943	2.2F
	1229	1602	2.9E
	1956	2244	2.9F
17 Tu	0236	0503	1.2E
	0800	1034	2.0F
	1308	1653	3.3E
	2041	2342	3.5F
18 W	0345	0624	1.3E
	0907	1128	1.9F
	1350	1742	3.7E
	2127		
19 Th		0036	4.2F
	0443	0724	1.6E
	1007	1223	1.9F
	1437	1830	4.1E
	2213		
20 F		0125	4.8F
	0534	0813	1.9E
	1101	1312	2.0F
	1526	1917	4.5E
	2300		
21 Sa		0214	5.3F
	0621	0902	2.2E
	1152	1403	2.1F
	1618	2008	4.8E
	2348		
22 Su		0303	5.6F
	0705	0944	2.4E
	1240	1456	2.3F
	1712	2059	4.9E
23 M	0036	0351	5.7F
	0747	1030	2.6E
	1329	1546	2.5F
	1808	2148	4.8E
24 Tu	0124	0437	5.6F
	0828	1114	2.8E
	1419	1641	2.6F
	1908	2240	4.4E
25 W	0213	0524	5.3F
	0908	1202	3.0E
	1512	1736	2.7F
	2013	2335	3.8E
26 Th	0303	0610	4.8F
	0947	1250	3.2E
	1608	1835	2.8F
	2126		
27 F		0034	3.1E
	0356	0659	4.1F
	1026	1339	3.3E
	1706	1938	2.8F
	2247		
28 Sa		0143	2.3E
	0453	0748	3.4F
	1105	1436	3.4E
	1805	2041	2.9F
29 Su	0017	0305	1.7E
	0556	0841	2.8F
	1147	1533	3.4E
	1903	2152	3.1F
30 M	0151	0441	1.4E
	0705	0937	2.2F
	1231	1634	3.5E
	1959	2300	3.4F
31 Tu	0316	0607	1.5E
	0816	1035	1.8F
	1318	1734	3.5E
	2052		

1991 CURRENT TABLES

DECEPTION PASS

For Daylight Saving Time, add one hour.

Times and Heights of High and Low Waters

JANUARY

Day	Slack Water Time (h.m.)	Maximum Current Time (h.m.)	Vel. (knots)	Day	Slack Water Time (h.m.)	Maximum Current Time (h.m.)	Vel. (knots)
1 Tu		0015	7.2F	16 W		0044	6.4F
	0359	0634	7.1E		0424	0702	6.7E
	1012	1233	4.8F		1043	1301	4.5F
	1506	1826	7.8E		1543	1847	7.0E
	2141				2203		
2 W		0104	7.3F	17 Th		0120	6.5F
	0444	0726	7.4E		0456	0737	6.9E
	1100	1324	5.1F		1116	1337	4.7F
	1604	1918	7.7E		1622	1929	7.1E
	2230				2237		
3 Th		0153	7.2F	18 F		0155	6.5F
	0528	0811	7.5E		0527	0811	7.1E
	1147	1417	5.3F		1146	1418	4.9F
	1701	2010	7.6E		1700	2011	7.1E
	2319				2310		
4 F		0239	7.0F	19 Sa		0233	6.4F
	0610	0858	7.6E		0555	0849	7.2E
	1234	1505	5.4F		1214	1456	5.1F
	1759	2059	7.3E		1740	2050	7.0E
					2344		
5 Sa	0008	0325	6.7F	20 Su		0312	6.2F
	0651	0944	7.5E		0622	0925	7.2E
	1320	1557	5.4F		1243	1535	5.2F
	1858	2151	6.9E		1823	2131	6.7E
6 Su	0058	0413	6.2F	21 M	0020	0348	5.9F
	0732	1029	7.4E		0649	1003	7.2E
	1408	1648	5.3F		1314	1620	5.2F
	2001	2245	6.4E		1911	2216	6.4E
7 M	0151	0502	5.7F	22 Tu	0059	0429	5.4F
	0813	1117	7.2E		0718	1042	7.0E
	1459	1743	5.2F		1351	1705	5.2F
	2109	2340	5.9E		2008	2308	6.0E
8 Tu	0249	0551	5.0F	23 W	0145	0516	4.9F
	0855	1205	6.9E		0752	1127	6.9E
	1551	1841	5.2F		1436	1802	5.2F
	2220				2118		
9 W		0040	5.4E	24 Th		0006	5.5E
	0358	0646	4.4F		0243	0608	4.2F
	0941	1258	6.7E		0832	1220	6.7E
	1646	1943	5.2F		1532	1903	5.3F
	2333				2242		
10 Th		0144	5.0E	25 F		0112	5.2E
	0517	0743	3.9F		0405	0711	3.6F
	1032	1352	6.5E		0923	1320	6.6E
	1742	2042	5.2F		1638	2009	5.5F
11 F	0040	0255	5.0E	26 Sa	0006	0226	5.2E
	0635	0845	3.5F		0559	0822	3.4F
	1129	1448	6.4E		1031	1425	6.6E
	1835	2143	5.4F		1750	2116	5.8F
12 Sa	0138	0406	5.2E	27 Su	0116	0340	5.6E
	0743	0946	3.4F		0726	0933	3.5F
	1229	1543	6.4E		1154	1530	6.8E
	1925	2236	5.7F		1858	2221	6.3F
13 Su	0228	0503	5.5E	28 M	0213	0444	6.2E
	0840	1044	3.6F		0827	1038	4.1F
	1325	1634	6.5E		1314	1634	7.2E
	2010	2323	5.0F		1958	2316	6.7F
14 M	0310	0548	6.0E	29 Tu	0302	0539	6.8E
	0927	1135	3.6F		0917	1135	4.7F
	1416	1723	6.7E		1420	1731	7.5E
	2051				2052		
15 Tu		0005	6.2F	30 W		0007	7.0F
	0349	0627	6.4E		0345	0626	7.3E
	1007	1216	4.2F		1000	1227	5.3F
	1502	1808	6.9E		1513	1821	7.8E
	2128				2141		
				31 Th		0052	7.2F
					0424	0709	7.7E
					1040	1313	5.8F
					1610	1909	7.9E
					2227		

FEBRUARY

Day	Slack Water Time (h.m.)	Maximum Current Time (h.m.)	Vel. (knots)	Day	Slack Water Time (h.m.)	Maximum Current Time (h.m.)	Vel. (knots)
1 F		0135	7.2F	16 Sa		0130	6.6F
	0502	0750	7.9E		0448	0739	7.6E
	1118	1358	6.0F		1101	1350	5.9F
	1659	1956	7.8E		1646	1948	7.5E
	2310				2253		
2 Sa		0217	7.0F	17 Su		0204	6.5F
	0537	0827	7.9E		0513	0812	7.6E
	1156	1440	6.1F		1125	1427	6.0F
	1746	2040	7.6E		1722	2024	7.4E
	2351				2324		
3 Su		0256	6.6F	18 M		0238	6.2F
	0611	0909	7.8E		0536	0847	7.6E
	1234	1525	6.1F		1152	1502	6.1F
	1834	2125	7.2E		1801	2105	7.2E
					2358		
4 M	0032	0337	6.1F	19 Tu		0315	5.8F
	0643	0948	7.6E		0602	0922	7.5E
	1313	1610	5.9F		1223	1545	6.0F
	1925	2210	6.6E		1846	2150	6.7E
5 Tu	0113	0419	5.5F	20 W	0036	0351	5.2F
	0716	1029	7.2E		0630	1003	7.2E
	1355	1658	5.5F		1300	1632	5.8F
	2022	2258	5.9E		1939	2239	6.2E
6 W	0200	0506	4.7F	21 Th	0121	0440	4.5F
	0749	1115	6.7E		0704	1046	6.9E
	1443	1751	5.1F		1346	1725	5.5F
	2130	2353	5.2E		2048	2338	5.5E
7 Th	0302	0557	3.8F	22 F	0222	0537	3.7F
	0828	1206	6.2E		0746	1142	6.5E
	1542	1851	4.8F		1446	1831	5.3F
	2252				2220		
8 F		0102	4.6E	23 Sa		0050	5.1E
	0443	0700	3.0F		0412	0648	3.0F
	0922	1308	5.8E		0847	1253	6.1E
	1654	2003	4.7F		1607	1947	5.3F
					2352		
9 Sa	0012	0218	4.4E	24 Su		0212	5.1E
	0625	0813	2.6F		0516	0813	2.9F
	1048	1413	5.6E		1026	1412	6.1E
	1806	2114	4.9F		1741	2104	5.6F
10 Su	0116	0353	4.8E	25 M	0102	0336	5.7E
	0738	0930	2.8F		0727	0932	3.6F
	1219	1521	5.8E		1216	1524	6.4E
	1906	2218	5.3F		1857	2212	6.1F
11 M	0206	0503	5.5E	26 Tu	0155	0439	6.4E
	0828	1037	3.5F		0816	1038	4.5F
	1326	1622	6.1E		1332	1530	7.0E
	1956	2307	5.7F		1957	2307	6.5F
12 Tu	0247	0536	6.1E	27 W	0239	0526	7.1E
	0907	1126	4.1F		0857	1129	5.3F
	1417	1711	6.6E		1429	1726	7.4E
	2038	2345	6.1F		2048	2352	5.8F
13 W	0322	0605	6.6E	28 Th	0318	0607	7.6E
	0941	1204	4.7F		0934	1214	6.0F
	1500	1753	6.9E		1518	1811	7.8E
	2116				2133		
14 Th		0021	6.4F				
	0353	0636	7.1E				
	1010	1240	5.2F				
	1537	1832	7.3E				
	2150						
15 F		0056	6.6F				
	0422	0709	7.4E				
	1037	1315	5.6F				
	1612	1910	7.4E				
	2222						

DECEPTION PASS

1991 CURRENT TABLES

For Daylight Saving Time, add one hour.

Times and Heights of High and Low Waters

MARCH

Day	Slack Water Time h.m.	Maximum Current Time h.m.	Vel. knots
1		0033	6.9F
F	0354	0642	7.9E
	1009	1255	6.4F
	1603	1854	7.9E
	2214		
2		0111	6.9F
Sa	0427	0718	8.1E
	1043	1336	6.6F
	1646	1935	7.9E
	2253		
3		0148	6.6F
Su	0457	0755	8.1E
	1115	1414	6.7F
	1727	2015	7.6E
	2329		
4		0227	6.2F
M	0526	0830	7.9E
	1147	1450	6.5F
	1808	2054	7.2E
5	0005	0303	5.7F
Tu	0554	0906	7.5E
	1220	1532	6.1F
	1851	2135	6.6E
6	0042	0344	5.0F
W	0621	0947	7.1E
	1255	1616	5.7F
	1941	2223	5.9E
7	0124	0427	4.1F
Th	0651	1032	6.4E
	1336	1708	5.1F
	2044	2320	5.1E
8	0228	0520	3.2F
F	0728	1121	5.8E
	1430	1809	4.6F
	2208		
9		0023	4.5E
Sa	0435	0628	2.4F
	0826	1230	5.2E
	1556	1923	4.4F
	2334		
10		0147	4.4E
Su	0617	0754	2.2F
	1036	1345	5.0E
	1732	2042	4.6F
11	0040	0327	5.0E
M	0718	0924	2.9F
	1218	1501	5.3E
	1841	2149	5.0F
12	0128	0424	5.7E
Tu	0759	1021	3.8F
	1318	1603	5.9E
	1932	2236	5.5F
13	0207	0457	6.4E
W	0831	1100	4.7F
	1404	1651	6.5E
	2015	2313	6.0F
14	0241	0526	6.9E
Th	0900	1135	5.3F
	1443	1731	7.0E
	2052	2348	6.2F
15	0310	0557	7.4E
F	0926	1210	5.9F
	1518	1808	7.4E
	2126		

Day	Slack Water Time h.m.	Maximum Current Time h.m.	Vel. knots
16		0024	6.4F
Sa	0337	0630	7.7E
	0951	1244	6.3F
	1552	1845	7.6E
	2159		
17		0057	6.4F
Su	0402	0702	7.9E
	1014	1319	6.6F
	1627	1923	7.7E
	2231		
18		0133	6.2F
M	0426	0735	7.9E
	1040	1354	6.7F
	1703	2001	7.6E
	2304		
19		0208	5.9F
Tu	0451	0809	7.8E
	1109	1433	6.7F
	1743	2042	7.3E
	2341		
20		0245	5.4F
W	0519	0846	7.6E
	1143	1515	6.5F
	1830	2127	6.8E
21	0023	0328	4.8F
Th	0551	0931	7.2E
	1224	1602	6.1F
	1925	2219	6.2E
22	0116	0419	4.0F
F	0630	1020	6.7E
	1314	1701	5.7F
	2038	2322	5.6E
23	0241	0525	3.2F
Sa	0723	1121	6.1E
	1420	1812	5.3F
	2207		
24		0039	5.3E
Su	0447	0646	2.8F
	0852	1241	5.7E
	1556	1933	5.3F
	2330		
25		0206	5.5E
M	0611	0813	3.3F
	1104	1407	5.8E
	1736	2048	5.5F
26	0033	0321	6.2E
Tu	0706	0930	4.3F
	1232	1520	6.3E
	1848	2155	5.9F
27	0123	0414	6.9E
W	0749	1025	5.2F
	1334	1622	6.9E
	1945	2244	6.2F
28	0205	0457	7.4E
Th	0826	1112	6.0F
	1424	1713	7.3E
	2034	2326	6.4F
29	0242	0534	7.8E
F	0901	1153	6.5F
	1508	1752	7.6E
	2117		
30		0004	6.4F
Sa	0316	0610	8.0E
	0934	1230	6.8F
	1550	1833	7.7E
	2156		
31		0043	6.3F
Su	0346	0643	8.1E
	1006	1305	6.9F
	1629	1911	7.6E
	2233		

APRIL

Day	Slack Water Time h.m.	Maximum Current Time h.m.	Vel. knots
1		0120	6.0F
M	0414	0719	8.0E
	1036	1342	6.8F
	1707	1950	7.3E
	2309		
2		0155	5.6F
Tu	0441	0754	7.7E
	1105	1420	6.6F
	1746	2029	6.9E
	2345		
3		0230	5.0F
W	0507	0830	7.3E
	1135	1459	6.2F
	1827	2111	6.4E
4	0023	0312	4.3F
Th	0534	0910	6.7E
	1207	1541	5.7F
	1913	2157	5.8E
5	0113	0400	3.5F
F	0607	0955	6.1E
	1246	1634	5.2F
	2012	2253	5.2E
6	0237	0456	2.7F
Sa	0651	1048	5.4E
	1336	1733	4.7F
	2128	2358	4.9E
7	0429	0609	2.2F
Su	0808	1158	4.8E
	1457	1845	4.4F
	2245		
8		0115	5.0E
M	0547	0734	2.5F
	1033	1315	4.7E
	1645	1959	4.5F
	2347		
9		0228	5.5E
Tu	0636	0849	3.4F
	1158	1429	5.2E
	1800	2101	4.9F
10	0035	0323	6.1E
W	0713	0942	4.3F
	1254	1527	5.8E
	1854	2150	5.3F
11	0114	0405	6.7E
Th	0744	1021	5.1F
	1338	1615	6.4E
	1939	2232	5.6F
12	0148	0438	7.2E
F	0812	1100	5.8F
	1416	1657	6.9E
	2019	2310	5.9F
13	0217	0513	7.5E
Sa	0838	1135	6.3F
	1453	1738	7.3E
	2057	2347	6.0F
14	0245	0548	7.8E
Su	0904	1211	6.7F
	1530	1817	7.5E
	2133		
15		0024	5.9F
M	0312	0624	8.0E
	0931	1248	7.0F
	1608	1857	7.6E
	2210		

Day	Slack Water Time h.m.	Maximum Current Time h.m.	Vel. knots
16		0100	5.7F
Tu	0340	0659	8.0E
	1002	1327	7.1F
	1648	1941	7.4E
	2249		
17		0139	5.4F
W	0411	0738	7.8E
	1037	1411	7.0F
	1733	2024	7.2E
	2334		
18		0224	4.9F
Th	0445	0821	7.5E
	1116	1456	6.7F
	1823	2115	6.8E
19	0027	0314	4.3F
F	0526	0906	7.1E
	1203	1547	6.4F
	1923	2210	6.3E
20	0140	0413	3.7F
Sa	0618	1007	6.5E
	1259	1648	5.9F
	2032	2317	6.0E
21	0314	0524	3.3F
Su	0735	1117	6.0E
	1414	1759	5.6F
	2147		
22		0027	6.0E
M	0438	0644	3.4F
	0933	1234	5.7E
	1550	1912	5.4F
	2255		
23		0143	6.3E
Tu	0541	0806	4.1F
	1113	1351	5.8E
	1718	2022	5.5F
	2352		
24		0248	6.7E
W	0631	0911	5.0F
	1225	1504	6.3E
	1827	2123	5.7F
25	0040	0337	7.2E
Th	0713	1002	5.8F
	1321	1559	6.7E
	1924	2212	5.8F
26	0122	0421	7.5E
F	0751	1046	6.3F
	1409	1650	7.0E
	2013	2254	5.8F
27	0159	0500	7.8E
Sa	0826	1123	6.7F
	1453	1734	7.2E
	2057	2336	5.7F
28	0233	0535	7.8E
Su	0900	1203	6.9F
	1534	1811	7.2E
	2138		
29		0011	5.5F
M	0304	0611	7.8E
	0931	1239	6.9F
	1614	1850	7.1E
	2218		
30		0049	5.2F
Tu	0332	0646	7.6E
	1002	1315	6.8F
	1653	1929	6.9E
	2257		

1991 CURRENT TABLES

DECEPTION PASS

For Daylight Saving Time, add one hour.

Times and Heights of High and Low Waters

F-Flood, Dir. 090° True   E-Ebb, Dir. 270° True

MAY

Day	Slack Water Time h.m.	Maximum Current Time h.m.	Vel. knots	Day	Slack Water Time h.m.	Maximum Current Time h.m.	Vel. knots
1 W		0129	4.8F	16 Th		0121	4.8F
	0400	0723	7.3E		0342	0717	7.7E
	1031	1355	6.5F		1017	1352	7.1F
	1732	2009	6.6E		1729	2015	7.1E
	2338				2340		
2 Th		0208	4.3F	17 F		0212	4.5F
	0430	0802	6.9E		0428	0805	7.4E
	1102	1437	6.2F		1103	1444	6.9F
	1813	2053	6.2E		1821	2106	6.9E
3 F	0026	0253	3.7F	18 Sa	0042	0305	4.2F
	0503	0845	6.4E		0523	0900	7.0E
	1136	1518	5.8F		1156	1539	6.6F
	1858	2141	5.9E		1917	2203	6.7E
4 Sa	0127	0344	3.2F	19 Su	0151	0408	4.0F
	0545	0931	5.9E		0633	0957	6.6E
	1216	1610	5.3F		1257	1636	6.2F
	1951	2236	5.6E		2016	2304	6.7E
5 Su	0243	0443	2.8F	20 M	0301	0517	4.1F
	0643	1029	5.3E		0801	1104	6.2E
	1307	1708	5.0F		1410	1740	5.9F
	2050	2333	5.5E		2115		
6 M	0357	0549	2.7F	21 Tu		0006	6.7E
	0814	1133	5.0E		0404	0627	4.4F
	1416	1807	4.8F		0935	1216	5.9E
	2150				1531	1842	5.6F
					2212		
7 Tu		0036	5.7E	22 W		0108	6.9E
	0455	0659	3.2F		0500	0733	4.9F
	1002	1240	4.9E		1056	1328	5.9E
	1543	1909	4.8F		1648	1944	5.4F
	2243				2304		
8 W		0134	6.0E	23 Th		0203	7.1E
	0540	0800	3.9F		0549	0836	5.4F
	1119	1346	5.2E		1203	1435	6.1E
	1701	2007	4.9F		1756	2042	5.3F
	2329				2351		
9 Th		0226	6.4E	24 F		0255	7.3E
	0616	0852	4.7F		0634	0927	5.9F
	1215	1445	5.7E		1300	1533	5.3E
	1803	2058	5.0F		1856	2133	5.1F
10 F	0009	0308	6.9E	25 Sa	0035	0338	7.4E
	0649	0937	5.4F		0715	1015	6.3F
	1303	1537	6.2E		1351	1622	6.4E
	1855	2143	5.2F		1949	2218	5.0F
11 Sa	0044	0349	7.2E	26 Su	0114	0421	7.5E
	0719	1018	5.0F		0753	1058	6.5F
	1346	1622	6.6E		1438	1709	6.5E
	1942	2225	5.3F		2039	2303	4.0F
12 Su	0118	0431	7.6E	27 M	0151	0500	7.5E
	0750	1100	6.5F		0830	1139	6.6F
	1428	1707	6.9E		1521	1752	6.5E
	2026	2307	5.3F		2125	2345	4.6F
13 M	0150	0510	7.8E	28 Tu	0226	0539	7.4E
	0822	1139	6.9F		0905	1218	6.6F
	1511	1752	7.1E		1603	1833	6.5E
	2111	2352	5.2F		2211		
14 Tu	0224	0549	7.9E	29 W		0027	4.4F
	0857	1222	7.1F		0300	0620	7.2E
	1554	1837	7.2E		0938	1258	5.5F
	2156				1643	1915	6.4E
					2256		
15 W		0035	5.1F	30 Th		0109	4.1F
	0301	0632	7.9E		0335	0702	7.0E
	0935	1307	7.2F		1011	1339	6.4F
	1640	1923	7.2E		1723	1956	6.4E
	2245				2342		
				31 F		0153	3.8F
					0413	0744	5.7E
					1045	1420	6.2F
					1803	2040	6.3E

JUNE

Day	Slack Water Time h.m.	Maximum Current Time h.m.	Vel. knots	Day	Slack Water Time h.m.	Maximum Current Time h.m.	Vel. knots
1 Sa	0031	0240	3.6F	16 Su	0035	0259	4.7F
	0456	0827	6.4E		0535	0851	7.2E
	1122	1505	5.9F		1155	1525	6.8F
	1844	2125	6.2E		1858	2147	7.3E
2 Su	0122	0329	3.5F	17 M	0130	0357	4.8F
	0546	0916	6.0E		0643	0950	6.9E
	1203	1550	5.7F		1253	1617	6.5F
	1925	2213	6.2E		1946	2239	7.3E
3 M	0213	0423	3.5F	18 Tu	0224	0456	5.0F
	0646	1007	5.7E		0757	1048	6.6E
	1250	1639	5.4F		1354	1711	6.0F
	2008	2304	6.2E		2034	2333	7.2E
4 Tu	0303	0517	3.6F	19 W	0318	0554	5.1F
	0757	1105	5.5E		0912	1149	6.2E
	1344	1731	5.2F		1500	1807	5.6F
	2051	2354	6.3E		2122		
5 W	0349	0615	4.0F	20 Th		0023	7.2E
	0914	1202	5.3E		0411	0655	5.3F
	1446	1821	5.0F		1025	1251	5.9E
	2134				1610	1902	5.1F
					2210		
6 Th		0041	6.5E	21 F		0117	7.1E
	0431	0709	4.4F		0503	0756	5.5F
	1025	1301	5.4E		1133	1355	5.7E
	1553	1912	4.8F		1720	1959	4.7F
	2215				2258		
7 F		0131	6.7E	22 Sa		0208	7.1E
	0510	0801	5.0F		0553	0851	5.7F
	1129	1400	5.6E		1236	1458	5.7E
	1701	2005	4.7F		1828	2055	4.4F
	2256				2346		
8 Sa		0218	6.9E	23 Su		0258	7.0E
	0549	0852	5.5F		0641	0943	5.9F
	1226	1454	5.8E		1333	1559	5.7E
	1806	2055	4.6F		1931	2146	4.1F
	2337						
9 Su		0303	7.2E	24 M	0033	0345	7.0E
	0627	0940	6.0F		0726	1034	6.1F
	1318	1549	6.1E		1424	1651	5.8E
	1906	2146	4.6F		2028	2238	4.0F
10 M	0019	0349	7.4E	25 Tu	0119	0434	6.9E
	0708	1028	6.5F		0809	1121	6.2F
	1409	1640	6.4E		1510	1740	5.0E
	2004	2237	4.6F		2120	2326	3.9F
11 Tu	0103	0437	7.6E	26 W	0205	0519	6.9E
	0750	1115	6.8F		0849	1204	6.3F
	1458	1732	6.7E		1553	1821	6.2E
	2059	2326	4.6F		2208		
12 W	0149	0524	7.7E	27 Th		0014	3.9F
	0834	1203	7.1F		0250	0603	6.9E
	1546	1822	6.9E		0927	1243	6.3F
	2153				1632	1904	6.3E
					2251		
13 Th		0017	4.6F	28 F		0100	4.0F
	0239	0614	7.7E		0333	0649	6.9E
	0921	1252	7.2F		1004	1324	6.3F
	1534	1915	7.1E		1709	1945	5.5E
	2247				2332		
14 F		0110	4.6F	29 Sa		0143	4.1F
	0333	0703	7.7E		0416	0731	5.7E
	1010	1342	7.2F		1039	1404	6.3F
	1722	2004	7.2E		1744	2022	5.6E
	2341						
15 Sa		0204	4.7F	30 Su	0011	0227	4.2F
	0431	0756	7.5E		0500	0814	6.5E
	1101	1433	7.0F		1115	1445	6.2F
	1810	2056	7.2E		1817	2105	5.7E

DECEPTION PASS

1991 CURRENT TABLES

For Daylight Saving Time, add one hour.

Times and Heights of High and Low Waters

F-Flood, Dir. 090° True   E-Ebb, Dir. 270° True

JULY

Day	Slack Water Time h.m.	Maximum Current Time h.m.	Vel. knots
1 M	0047	0309	4.3F
	0545	0858	6.5E
	1151	1525	6.0F
	1850	2144	6.8E
2 Tu	0122	0354	4.4F
	0633	0944	6.3E
	1230	1607	5.8F
	1921	2226	6.8E
3 W	0158	0439	4.5F
	0726	1030	6.0E
	1313	1649	5.4F
	1953	2308	6.8E
4 Th	0234	0527	4.7F
	0824	1121	5.8E
	1400	1734	5.0F
	2027	2351	6.8E
5 F	0314	0618	4.9F
	0930	1216	5.5E
	1456	1825	4.6F
	2104		
6 Sa		0038	6.8E
	0359	0713	5.1F
	1041	1316	5.4E
	1603	1920	4.2F
	2146		
7 Su		0129	6.8E
	0449	0810	5.4F
	1152	1417	5.4E
	1724	2016	3.9F
	2236		
8 M		0222	6.9E
	0543	0907	5.8F
	1258	1521	5.6E
	1848	2117	3.8F
	2333		
9 Tu		0320	7.0E
	0638	1006	6.2F
	1356	1622	6.0E
	1958	2215	4.0F
10 W	0035	0415	7.2E
	0733	1100	6.6F
	1449	1720	6.4E
	2058	2313	4.3F
11 Th	0139	0510	7.5E
	0827	1152	6.9F
	1537	1814	6.9E
	2150		
12 F		0010	4.7F
	0242	0604	7.6E
	0919	1241	7.1F
	1522	1902	7.3E
	2237		
13 Sa		0102	5.0F
	0341	0656	7.7E
	1009	1330	7.2F
	1705	1948	7.5E
	2322		
14 Su		0153	5.4F
	0439	0748	7.7E
	1059	1417	7.1F
	1746	2035	7.7E
15 M	0007	0242	5.6F
	0536	0837	7.5E
	1148	1502	6.9F
	1827	2119	7.7E

Day	Slack Water Time h.m.	Maximum Current Time h.m.	Vel. knots
16 Tu	0052	0331	5.7F
	0634	0931	7.3E
	1237	1550	6.5F
	1907	2204	7.6E
17 W	0138	0423	5.7F
	0733	1020	6.8E
	1328	1635	6.0F
	1947	2249	7.4E
18 Th	0226	0515	5.6F
	0837	1114	6.3E
	1423	1727	5.3F
	2028	2338	7.2E
19 F	0318	0611	5.5F
	0947	1212	5.7E
	1528	1818	4.6F
	2112		
20 Sa		0030	6.9E
	0413	0712	5.3F
	1100	1316	5.2E
	1646	1917	4.0F
	2202		
21 Su		0124	6.6E
	0512	0813	5.3F
	1212	1427	5.0E
	1809	2019	3.5F
	2302		
22 M		0222	6.4E
	0611	0920	5.4F
	1316	1537	5.1E
	1923	2124	3.3F
23 Tu	0007	0321	6.3E
	0706	1017	5.6F
	1410	1652	5.5E
	2023	2225	3.4F
24 W	0110	0418	6.4E
	0755	1107	5.9F
	1455	1739	5.9E
	2112	2318	3.8F
25 Th	0206	0507	6.6E
	0839	1151	6.1F
	1534	1814	6.3E
	2153		
26 F		0007	4.2F
	0253	0555	6.8E
	0919	1231	6.3F
	1609	1849	6.6E
	2229		
27 Sa		0048	4.5F
	0336	0637	6.9E
	0955	1306	6.4F
	1642	1921	6.9E
	2301		
28 Su		0123	4.8F
	0415	0715	7.0E
	1028	1342	6.5F
	1712	1956	7.1E
	2330		
29 M		0202	5.1F
	0452	0755	7.1E
	1101	1417	6.4F
	1739	2030	7.2E
	2358		
30 Tu		0240	5.2F
	0530	0833	7.0E
	1133	1456	6.2F
	1805	2105	7.2E
31 W	0025	0319	5.3F
	0609	0915	6.8E
	1206	1531	5.9F
	1830	2141	7.2E

AUGUST

Day	Slack Water Time h.m.	Maximum Current Time h.m.	Vel. knots
1 Th	0053	0400	5.3F
	0652	0957	6.5E
	1242	1608	5.4F
	1857	2221	7.0E
2 F	0126	0442	5.3F
	0743	1044	6.1E
	1324	1649	4.9F
	1928	2304	6.8E
3 Sa	0207	0537	5.2F
	0845	1138	5.6E
	1415	1740	4.2F
	2004	2351	6.6E
4 Su	0257	0632	5.2F
	1003	1239	5.2E
	1525	1840	3.6F
	2050		
5 M		0050	6.5E
	0359	0736	5.3F
	1130	1352	5.1E
	1716	1951	3.2F
	2153		
6 Tu		0156	6.4E
	0512	0845	5.6F
	1245	1504	5.3E
	1855	2101	3.3F
	2316		
7 W		0301	6.6E
	0625	0949	6.0F
	1345	1612	5.9E
	2000	2209	3.9F
8 Th	0042	0406	6.9E
	0730	1050	6.5F
	1434	1709	6.6E
	2049	2307	4.6F
9 F	0153	0503	7.3E
	0826	1140	6.8F
	1513	1758	7.2E
	2133		
10 Sa		0001	5.3F
	0252	0557	7.7E
	0915	1227	7.1F
	1558	1844	7.6E
	2212		
11 Su		0050	5.8F
	0346	0646	7.9E
	1003	1311	7.1F
	1636	1924	7.9E
	2251		
12 M		0135	6.2F
	0435	0733	7.9E
	1148	1353	7.0F
	1712	2004	8.0E
	2329		
13 Tu		0217	6.4F
	0524	0818	7.8E
	1131	1433	6.7F
	1747	2043	8.0E
14 W	0007	0302	6.4F
	0612	0903	7.4E
	1213	1518	6.2F
	1820	2125	7.8E
15 Th	0047	0347	6.2F
	0703	0951	5.9E
	1257	1500	5.6F
	1854	2207	7.4E

Day	Slack Water Time h.m.	Maximum Current Time h.m.	Vel. knots
16 F	0130	0435	5.8F
	0800	1039	6.2E
	1346	1645	4.8F
	1930	2255	6.9E
17 Sa	0218	0527	5.4F
	0907	1133	5.5E
	1450	1738	3.9F
	2011	2345	6.4E
18 Su	0316	0628	5.0F
	1026	1239	4.8E
	1626	1841	3.1F
	2106		
19 M		0045	5.9E
	0429	0740	4.8F
	1147	1356	4.6E
	1805	1957	2.7F
	2235		
20 Tu		0154	5.6E
	0545	0853	4.9F
	1254	1546	4.9E
	1918	2117	2.9F
21 W	0007	0304	5.7E
	0649	1005	5.3F
	1345	1652	5.6E
	2009	2222	3.5F
22 Th	0114	0406	6.1E
	0741	1052	5.7F
	1427	1723	6.2E
	2048	2313	4.2F
23 F	0205	0454	6.5E
	0824	1129	6.0F
	1502	1748	6.6E
	2121	2348	4.8F
24 Sa	0248	0539	6.9E
	0902	1204	6.3F
	1534	1817	7.0E
	2151		
25 Su		0023	5.3F
	0325	0618	7.2E
	0937	1238	6.4F
	1503	1849	7.3E
	2218		
26 M		0058	5.7F
	0359	0654	7.4E
	1008	1313	6.5F
	1529	1920	7.5E
	2242		
27 Tu		0132	5.9F
	0433	0729	7.4E
	1039	1345	6.3F
	1653	1953	7.6E
	2306		
28 W		0204	6.1F
	0507	0808	7.3E
	1109	1417	6.1F
	1716	2026	7.5E
	2330		
29 Th		0243	6.1F
	0543	0846	7.1E
	1141	1454	5.7F
	1739	2059	7.4E
	2359		
30 F		0320	6.0F
	0624	0927	6.7E
	1215	1531	5.1F
	1806	2138	7.1E
31 Sa	0033	0403	5.8F
	0714	1013	6.2E
	1258	1613	4.4F
	1837	2219	6.8E

1991 CURRENT TABLES

DECEPTION PASS

For Daylight Saving Time, add one hour.

Times and Heights of High and Low Waters

F-Flood, Dir. 090° True   E-Ebb, Dir. 270° True

SEPTEMBER

Day	Slack Water Time h.m.	Maximum Current Time h.m.	Vel. knots	Day	Slack Water Time h.m.	Maximum Current Time h.m.	Vel. knots
1 Su	0115	0458	5.5F	16 M	0214	0549	4.8F
	0816	1111	5.6E		0951	1206	4.7E
	1354	1708	3.6F		1627	1815	2.4F
	1917	2312	6.3E		2022		
2 M	0210	0602	5.2F	17 Tu		0013	5.2E
	0942	1220	5.1E		0341	0703	4.5F
	1531	1819	2.9F		1113	1336	4.6E
	2013				1759	1941	2.3F
					2236		
3 Tu		0022	6.0E	18 W		0128	5.0E
	0325	0715	5.2F		0515	0825	4.6F
	1115	1337	5.1E		1217	1524	5.2E
	1743	1941	2.8F		1857	2110	3.1F
	2146						
4 W		0139	5.9E	19 Th	0007	0247	5.3E
	0500	0832	5.4F		0624	0930	5.0F
	1228	1458	5.6E		1306	1609	5.9E
	1857	2101	3.4F		1938	2206	4.0F
	2342						
5 Th		0255	6.3E	20 F	0106	0348	5.9E
	0623	0937	5.9F		0716	1015	5.5F
	1323	1606	6.3E		1345	1638	6.5E
	1946	2206	4.4F		2011	2243	4.8F
6 F	0102	0401	6.8E	21 Sa	0151	0436	6.5E
	0727	1034	6.3F		0758	1054	5.9F
	1408	1651	7.0E		1419	1707	7.0E
	2027	2300	5.3F		2040	2318	5.4F
7 Sa	0202	0456	7.4E	22 Su	0229	0513	6.9E
	0819	1122	6.7F		0836	1131	6.1F
	1448	1736	7.6E		1449	1736	7.4E
	2105	2345	6.0F		2107	2351	5.9F
8 Su	0253	0545	7.8E	23 M	0304	0550	7.3E
	0906	1204	6.9F		0910	1205	6.2F
	1525	1815	8.0E		1516	1808	7.6E
	2140				2131		
9 M		0027	6.5F	24 Tu		0024	6.3F
	0339	0630	8.0E		0337	0627	7.5E
	0950	1246	6.9F		0942	1236	6.2F
	1559	1852	8.2E		1540	1840	7.8E
	2215				2154		
10 Tu		0108	6.8F	25 W		0057	6.6F
	0423	0712	8.0E		0410	0703	7.5E
	1030	1324	6.7F		1014	1310	6.0F
	1631	1930	8.2E		1603	1914	7.8E
	2249				2218		
11 W		0149	6.9F	26 Th		0135	6.7F
	0506	0753	7.7E		0445	0742	7.4E
	1110	1403	6.3F		1046	1345	5.7F
	1702	2008	8.0E		1627	1947	7.7F
	2323				2245		
12 Th		0230	6.7F	27 F		0211	6.6F
	0549	0837	7.3E		0523	0820	7.2E
	1149	1440	5.7F		1120	1424	5.2F
	1731	2046	7.7E		1653	2024	7.5E
	2358				2317		
13 F		0312	6.4F	28 Sa		0249	6.4F
	0635	0920	6.7E		0606	0906	6.7E
	1230	1521	5.0F		1200	1503	4.5F
	1801	2125	7.1E		1723	2102	7.1E
					2355		
14 Sa	0035	0357	5.9F	29 Su		0338	6.1F
	0726	1008	6.0E		0658	0957	6.2E
	1318	1610	4.1F		1251	1550	3.9F
	1834	2211	6.5E		1900	2151	6.6E
15 Su	0117	0448	5.3F	30 M	0041	0434	5.7F
	0830	1102	5.3E		0805	1058	5.5E
	1432	1705	3.2F		1410	1655	3.1F
	1914	2304	5.8E		1950	2252	6.0E

OCTOBER

Day	Slack Water Time h.m.	Maximum Current Time h.m.	Vel. knots	Day	Slack Water Time h.m.	Maximum Current Time h.m.	Vel. knots
1 Tu	0142	0543	5.3F	16 W	0246	0629	4.5F
	0931	1209	5.4E		1026	1302	5.1E
	1616	1815	2.7F		1729	1920	2.6F
	2012				2227		
2 W		0009	5.6E	17 Th		0100	4.7E
	0311	0658	5.2F		0429	0742	4.6F
	1054	1329	5.6E		1126	1413	5.6E
	1741	1941	3.2F		1817	2036	3.5F
	2226				2346		
3 Th		0131	5.7E	18 F		0212	5.1E
	0455	0813	5.4F		0542	0839	4.9F
	1159	1442	6.2E		1213	1504	6.2E
	1836	2057	4.2F		1854	2127	4.4F
4 F	0001	0248	6.2E	19 Sa	0040	0314	5.7E
	0614	0920	5.8F		0637	0930	5.2F
	1250	1541	6.8E		1252	1543	6.7E
	1919	2156	5.2F		1925	2206	5.2F
5 Sa	0105	0349	6.8E	20 Su	0124	0359	6.3E
	0714	1011	6.1F		0722	1012	5.5F
	1333	1624	7.4E		1326	1618	7.2E
	1957	2241	6.0F		1953	2241	5.8F
6 Su	0157	0444	7.3E	21 M	0202	0441	6.8E
	0805	1056	6.3F		0802	1051	5.7F
	1411	1705	7.8E		1356	1654	7.5E
	2032	2326	6.6F		2020	2316	6.3F
7 M	0243	0529	7.6E	22 Tu	0238	0519	7.1E
	0850	1138	6.4F		0840	1126	5.8F
	1446	1742	8.1E		1424	1729	7.8E
	2107				2045	2352	6.7F
8 Tu		0005	7.0F	23 W	0314	0558	7.3E
	0326	0610	7.7E		0915	1202	5.7F
	0932	1217	6.3F		1450	1801	7.9E
	1519	1820	8.2E		2111		
	2140						
9 W		0043	7.1F	24 Th		0027	6.9F
	0408	0651	7.7E		0350	0637	7.4E
	1012	1255	6.0F		0951	1239	5.5F
	1549	1856	8.1E		1516	1838	7.9E
	2212				2140		
10 Th		0121	7.0F	25 F		0105	7.0F
	0448	0730	7.4E		0429	0718	7.3E
	1051	1332	5.6F		1029	1316	5.2F
	1617	1933	7.8E		1545	1915	7.7E
	2243				2212		
11 F		0201	6.8F	26 Sa		0146	6.9F
	0529	0812	7.0E		0511	0801	7.1E
	1130	1411	5.0F		1112	1359	4.7F
	1646	2010	7.4E		1618	1954	7.5E
	2316				2250		
12 Sa		0243	5.4F	27 Su		0231	6.7F
	0613	0854	6.5E		0559	0850	6.7E
	1214	1456	4.3F		1203	1446	4.2F
	1716	2049	6.8E		1657	2043	7.1E
	2350				2333		
13 Su		0325	5.9F	28 M		0320	6.4F
	0702	0941	5.9E		0654	0945	6.3E
	1311	1541	3.5F		1310	1544	3.6F
	1750	2138	6.1E		1746	2138	6.5E
14 M	0030	0417	5.3F	29 Tu	0026	0419	6.0F
	0801	1039	5.4E		0759	1048	6.1E
	1438	1643	2.7F		1440	1653	3.2F
	1938	2233	5.4E		1857	2242	5.0E
15 Tu	0123	0518	4.8F	30 W	0133	0527	5.6F
	0914	1142	5.0E		0911	1156	5.0E
	1617	1756	2.3F		1605	1810	3.4F
	2008	2343	4.3E		2047	2359	5.7E
				31 Th	0304	0638	5.4F
					1019	1306	6.3E
					1710	1929	4.0F
					2237		

DECEPTION PASS

1991 CURRENT TABLES

For Daylight Saving Time, add one hour.

Times and Heights of High and Low Waters

F-Flood, Dir. 090° True   E-Ebb, Dir. 270° True

NOVEMBER

Day	Slack Water Time h.m.	Max Current Time h.m.	Vel. knots	Day	Slack Water Time h.m.	Max Current Time h.m.	Vel. knots
1		0118	5.8E	16		0126	5.1E
F	0438	0747	5.5F	Sa	0441	0745	4.8F
	1118	1413	6.7E		1107	1403	6.4E
	1800	2038	4.9F		1758	2036	4.6F
	2354						
2		0229	6.2E	17	0001	0226	5.5E
Sa	0553	0848	5.6F	Su	0544	0836	4.9F
	1208	1504	7.2E		1148	1448	6.8E
	1844	2133	5.7F		1832	2121	5.3F
3	0053	0330	6.6E	18	0049	0316	6.0E
Su	0653	0939	5.7F	M	0638	0924	5.0F
	1251	1549	7.6E		1224	1530	7.1E
	1923	2218	6.3F		1903	2159	5.9F
4	0144	0422	7.0E	19	0132	0405	6.4E
M	0746	1025	5.8F	Tu	0726	1006	5.1F
	1330	1631	7.8E		1258	1611	7.4E
	2000	2300	6.8F		1934	2241	6.4F
5	0231	0508	7.2E	20	0214	0449	6.7E
Tu	0833	1107	5.7F	W	0810	1048	5.1F
	1406	1709	8.0E		1330	1651	7.6E
	2036	2341	7.0F		2005	2322	6.7F
6	0314	0551	7.2E	21	0255	0535	6.9E
W	0917	1148	5.5F	Th	0854	1131	5.0F
	1439	1747	7.9E		1403	1730	7.8E
	2110				2038		
7		0018	7.0F	22		0003	7.0F
Th	0356	0630	7.1E	F	0337	0618	7.0E
	0959	1227	5.2F		0938	1214	4.9F
	1511	1827	7.8E		1439	1811	7.8E
	2143				2114		
8		0059	6.9F	23		0047	7.1F
F	0437	0711	6.9E	Sa	0421	0703	7.1E
	1042	1307	4.8F		1025	1257	4.7F
	1541	1904	7.5E		1518	1854	7.7E
	2215				2154		
9		0138	6.7F	24		0129	7.1F
Sa	0517	0754	6.6E	Su	0507	0749	7.0E
	1126	1348	4.3F		1116	1347	4.5F
	1613	1943	7.1E		1602	1941	7.5E
	2248				2238		
10		0220	6.3F	25		0218	6.9F
Su	0600	0837	6.3E	M	0555	0843	6.9E
	1216	1434	3.8F		1213	1440	4.2F
	1649	2026	6.6E		1655	2033	7.1E
	2323				2328		
11		0305	5.9F	26		0312	6.7F
M	0645	0925	6.0E	Tu	0647	0936	6.8E
	1316	1525	3.3F		1316	1539	4.1F
	1732	2115	6.0E		1758	2132	6.7E
12	0003	0354	5.5F	27	0024	0407	6.3F
Tu	0736	1019	5.7E	W	0742	1033	6.7E
	1427	1626	2.9F		1423	1642	4.1F
	1832	2213	5.4E		1919	2235	6.3E
13	0053	0448	5.1F	28	0130	0508	6.0F
W	0831	1117	5.7E	Th	0839	1131	6.8E
	1536	1730	2.9F		1527	1750	4.4F
	2003	2314	5.0E		2052	2340	6.0E
14	0159	0547	4.8F	29	0247	0609	5.7F
Th	0928	1216	5.8E	F	0935	1231	6.9E
	1634	1838	3.2F		1625	1859	4.8F
	2147				2218		
15		0019	4.9E	30		0052	5.9E
F	0322	0650	4.7F	Sa	0408	0711	5.4F
	1020	1312	6.0E		1029	1328	7.1E
	1720	1940	3.9F		1717	2002	5.4F
	2303				2331		

DECEMBER

Day	Slack Water Time h.m.	Max Current Time h.m.	Vel. knots	Day	Slack Water Time h.m.	Max Current Time h.m.	Vel. knots
1		0200	6.0E	16		0134	5.3E
Su	0522	0807	5.2F	M	0434	0741	4.5F
	1119	1422	7.3E		1030	1355	6.7E
	1805	2101	5.9F		1730	2032	5.2F
2	0034	0303	6.2E	17	0009	0232	5.5E
M	0628	0904	5.1F	Tu	0545	0835	4.3F
	1205	1511	7.4E		1113	1442	6.9E
	1849	2148	6.3F		1810	2121	5.7F
3	0129	0401	6.4E	18	0104	0329	5.8E
Tu	0726	0953	4.9F	W	0651	0927	4.3F
	1249	1556	7.5E		1157	1529	7.1E
	1931	2237	6.5F		1851	2209	6.2F
4	0219	0451	6.5E	19	0155	0422	6.1E
W	0820	1041	4.8F	Th	0750	1017	4.3F
	1330	1641	7.5E		1243	1618	7.3E
	2011	2322	6.7F		1933	2257	6.6F
5	0305	0535	6.5E	20	0243	0513	6.5E
Th	0909	1127	4.6F	F	0845	1107	4.4F
	1409	1723	7.5E		1330	1706	7.5E
	2049				2017	2345	6.9F
6		0001	6.7F	21	0329	0604	6.8E
F	0348	0620	6.6E	Sa	0937	1158	4.5F
	0957	1211	4.4F		1420	1755	7.6E
	1447	1804	7.3E		2102		
	2126						
7		0043	6.7F	22		0032	7.1F
Sa	0430	0702	6.5E	Su	0414	0652	7.0E
	1042	1254	4.2F		1026	1249	4.6F
	1525	1846	7.1E		1513	1842	7.7E
	2201				2149		
8		0124	6.5F	23		0119	7.2F
Su	0509	0742	6.5E	M	0459	0742	7.2E
	1128	1339	4.0F		1115	1340	4.8F
	1604	1929	6.9E		1608	1935	7.6E
	2236				2238		
9		0205	6.3F	24		0208	7.1F
M	0548	0824	6.4E	Tu	0543	0830	7.4E
	1213	1424	3.9F		1204	1431	5.0F
	1647	2012	6.5E		1707	2024	7.5E
	2313				2328		
10		0249	6.1F	25		0257	7.0F
Tu	0627	0906	6.4E	W	0628	0918	7.4E
	1300	1512	3.8F		1254	1525	5.1F
	1736	2059	6.2E		1810	2119	7.2E
	2351						
11		0332	5.8F	26	0021	0347	6.6F
W	0706	0954	6.4E	Th	0713	1007	7.4E
	1348	1601	3.7F		1345	1622	5.2F
	1831	2150	5.9E		1917	2215	6.8E
12	0034	0419	5.5F	27	0118	0439	6.2F
Th	0745	1042	6.3E	F	0758	1058	7.4E
	1435	1555	3.8F		1438	1718	5.3F
	1936	2242	5.6E		2030	2314	6.4E
13	0123	0508	5.2F	28	0220	0531	5.7F
F	0826	1127	6.4E	Sa	0845	1149	7.2E
	1522	1749	4.0F		1533	1818	5.4F
	2048	2337	5.3E		2146		
14	0219	0557	4.9F	29		0018	6.0E
Sa	0907	1218	6.4E	Su	0329	0628	5.2F
	1506	1845	4.3F		0933	1244	7.1E
	2201				1628	1921	5.5F
					2301		
15		0034	5.2E	30		0121	5.7E
Su	0323	0647	4.7F	M	0446	0726	4.5F
	0948	1305	5.5E		1024	1338	7.0E
	1649	1936	4.7F		1724	2022	5.6F
	2308						
				31	0011	0229	5.5E
				Tu	0603	0826	4.2F
					1118	1434	6.9E
					1817	2123	5.8F

1991 CURRENT TABLES

ROSARIO STRAIT

For Daylight Saving Time, add one hour.

Times and Heights of High and Low Waters

F-Flood, Dir. 335° True   E-Ebb, Dir. 175° True

JANUARY

Day	Slack Water Time h.m.	Maximum Current Time h.m.	Vel. knots	Day	Slack Water Time h.m.	Maximum Current Time h.m.	Vel. knots
1 Tu	0001	0254	2.7F	16 W	0022	0315	2.1F
	0716	0945	1.4E		0728	1009	1.4E
	1251	1418	0.6F			1434	*
	1548	2105	3.4E			2120	2.6E
2 W	0043	0338	2.7F	17 Th	0052	0340	2.1F
	0747	1022	1.6E		0747	1036	1.5E
	1346	1511	0.6F		1421	1520	0.3F
	1650	2148	3.2E		1629	2149	2.5E
3 Th	0125	0420	2.7F	18 F	0122	0411	2.1F
	0816	1104	1.9E		0803	1106	1.7E
	1444	1610	0.6F		1501	1609	0.4F
	1754	2231	2.9E		1727	2218	2.3E
4 F	0206	0502	2.5F	19 Sa	0150	0447	2.1F
	0844	1150	2.1E		0818	1138	1.8E
	1542	1707	0.6F		1541	1659	0.5F
	1859	2319	2.3E		1826	2245	2.0E
5 Sa	0248	0539	2.3F	20 Su	0219	0524	1.9F
	0910	1240	2.2E		0831	1210	1.9E
	1640	1807	0.6F		1621	1747	0.6F
	2005				1927	2314	1.6E
6 Su		0008	1.8E	21 M	0248	0600	1.7F
	0329	0619	2.0F		0844	1245	2.1E
	0936	1330	2.3E		1703	1836	0.7F
	1737	1902	0.6F		2031	2351	1.1E
	2119						
7 M		0115	1.2E	22 Tu	0319	0636	1.5F
	0411	0658	1.6F		0859	1327	2.2E
	1001	1419	2.4E		1749	1932	0.8F
	1834	2002	0.6F		2153		
	2305						
8 Tu		0231	0.7E	23 W		0058	0.7E
	0456	0737	1.2F		0355	0717	1.2F
	1023	1512	2.5E		0921	1416	2.4E
	1931	2218	0.6F		1840	2031	0.9F
9 W	0139	0337	0.4E	24 Th	0014	0300	0.3E
	0550	0825	0.9F		0437	0800	0.8F
	1044	1602	2.6E		0949	1511	2.6E
	2027	2356	0.9F		1936	2143	1.0F
10 Th	0323	0454	0.3E	25 F		0419	*
	0718	0915	0.5F			0855	0.5F
	1107	1648	2.6E		1026	1608	2.7E
	2117				2034	2327	1.3F
11 F		0051	1.2F	26 Sa	0414	0539	0.3E
	0434	0644	0.3E		0815	0959	0.3F
	0903	1016	0.3F		1114	1706	2.9E
	1136	1740	2.6E		2129		
	2201						
12 Sa		0128	1.5F	27 Su		0042	1.7F
	0525	0821	0.6E		0503	0701	0.5E
		1118	*		1002	1113	0.3F
		1531	2.6E		1221	1812	3.0E
	2240				2218		
13 Su		0203	1.7F	28 M		0125	2.0F
	0605	0901	0.8E		0540	0804	0.9E
		1214	*		1103	1215	0.4F
		1920	2.7E		1339	1910	3.1E
	2316				2304		
14 M		0238	1.9F	29 Tu		0200	2.3F
	0637	0930	1.0E		0611	0845	1.3E
		1303	*		1152	1316	0.6F
		2004	2.7E		1456	2007	3.1E
	2350				2347		
15 Tu		0253	2.0F	30 W		0240	2.4F
	0705	0940	1.2E		0640	0927	1.7E
		1348	*		1239	1410	0.7F
		2044	2.7E		1611	2056	3.1E
				31 Th	0028	0315	2.4F
					0706	1002	2.0E
					1326	1505	0.9F
					1722	2142	2.9E

FEBRUARY

Day	Slack Water Time h.m.	Maximum Current Time h.m.	Vel. knots	Day	Slack Water Time h.m.	Maximum Current Time h.m.	Vel. knots
1 F	0108	0353	2.4F	16 Sa	0101	0335	1.9F
	0731	1039	2.3E		0701	1026	2.1E
	1414	1602	1.0F		1404	1552	0.9F
	1828	2224	2.5E		1815	2213	2.1E
2 Sa	0147	0430	2.2F	17 Su	0130	0410	1.8F
	0755	1118	2.5E		0715	1053	2.3E
	1504	1656	1.0F		1439	1639	1.1F
	1928	2306	2.1E		1910	2242	1.8E
3 Su	0225	0505	2.0F	18 M	0159	0449	1.6F
	0818	1156	2.5E		0728	1116	2.4E
	1555	1747	1.0F		1518	1729	1.2F
	2026	2355	1.6E		2005	2317	1.4E
4 M	0303	0546	1.7F	19 Tu	0229	0527	1.4F
	0839	1242	2.5E		0744	1145	2.5E
	1646	1836	1.0F		1603	1816	1.3F
	2127				2104	2358	1.0E
5 Tu		0049	1.1E	20 W	0302	0603	1.2F
	0343	0623	1.4F		0806	1226	2.6E
	0857	1327	2.4E		1653	1907	1.3F
	1740	1925	0.9F		2218		
	2246						
6 W		0155	0.7E	21 Th		0112	0.6E
	0426	0703	1.0F		0343	0646	0.9F
	0914	1420	2.4E		0833	1317	2.5E
	1836	2021	0.8F		1750	2002	1.3F
7 Th	0057	0306	0.4E	22 F	0011	0248	0.4E
	0523	0746	0.7F		0440	0733	0.6F
	0932	1517	2.3E		0905	1429	2.5E
	1936	2311	0.7F		1853	2109	1.2F
8 F	0249	0420	0.3E	23 Sa	0220	0404	0.4E
	0703	0834	0.3F		0632	0831	0.3F
	0952	1610	2.2E		0943	1542	2.5E
	2035				2000	2246	1.3F
9 Sa		0021	1.0F	24 Su	0327	0527	0.5E
	0357	0658	0.4E			0945	*
		0940	*			1651	2.5E
		1704	2.2E		2103		
	2127						
10 Su		0106	1.3F	25 M		0020	1.6F
	0445	0801	0.6E		0411	0643	0.8E
		1048	*			1104	*
		1759	2.3E			1800	2.5E
	2211				2159		
11 M		0139	1.5F	26 Tu		0103	1.8F
	0521	0838	0.9E		0446	0742	1.3E
		1155	*		1057	1218	0.4F
		1855	2.3E		1408	1903	2.6E
	2250				2247		
12 Tu		0204	1.7F	27 W		0138	2.0F
	0550	0859	1.2E		0517	0823	1.7E
		1251	*		1138	1316	0.8F
		1944	2.4E		1537	1958	2.6E
	2326				2331		
13 W		0221	1.8F	28 Th		0211	2.0F
	0614	0912	1.4E		0544	0858	2.1E
	1227	1335	0.4F		1219	1411	1.0F
	1511	2026	2.4E		1650	2049	2.6E
	2359						
14 Th		0237	1.9F				
	0632	0935	1.7E				
	1259	1420	0.6F				
	1616	2104	2.4E				
15 F	0031	0306	1.9F				
	0647	0958	1.9E				
	1331	1507	0.8F				
	1717	2138	2.3E				

ROSARIO STRAIT

1991 CURRENT TABLES

For Daylight Saving Time, add one hour.

Times and Heights of High and Low Waters

F-Flood, Dir. 335° True   E-Ebb, Dir. 175° True

MARCH

Day	Slack Water Time h.m.	Maximum Current Time h.m.	Vel. knots	Day	Slack Water Time h.m.	Maximum Current Time h.m.	Vel. knots
1 F	0012	0242	2.0F	16 Sa	0006	0221	1.6F
	0610	0931	2.5E		0529	0915	2.3E
	1259	1502	1.3F		1246	1450	1.3F
	1755	2136	2.4E		1753	2127	2.0E
2 Sa	0051	0317	1.9F	17 Su	0039	0258	1.5F
	0634	1006	2.7E		0545	0944	2.6E
	1341	1551	1.4F		1317	1534	1.6F
	1853	2217	2.1E		1846	2205	1.8E
3 Su	0129	0356	1.7F	18 M	0112	0333	1.4F
	0657	1040	2.8E		0602	1011	2.8E
	1424	1639	1.5F		1351	1621	1.8F
	1945	2256	1.8E		1937	2242	1.6E
4 M	0208	0432	1.5F	19 Tu	0145	0414	1.2F
	0717	1114	2.7E		0622	1037	2.9E
	1508	1722	1.4F		1431	1708	1.9F
	2035	2339	1.4E		2028	2323	1.3E
5 Tu	0248	0509	1.2F	20 W	0222	0455	1.0F
	0735	1152	2.6E		0648	1106	2.9E
	1555	1804	1.4F		1517	1757	1.9F
	2126				2124		
6 W		0029	1.0E	21 Th		0011	1.0E
	0332	0550	1.0F		0308	0539	0.8F
	0752	1229	2.4E		0718	1141	2.8E
	1645	1850	1.2F		1609	1848	1.8F
	2226				2230		
7 Th		0127	0.7E	22 F		0127	0.7E
	0427	0632	0.7F		[illegible]	0626	0.6F
	0810	1321	2.2E		0752	1232	2.6E
	1739	1940	1.0F		1709	1937	1.6F
	2357				2356		
8 F		0246	0.5E	23 Sa		0244	0.6E
	0542	0717	0.4F		0550	0721	0.4F
	0830	1426	2.0E		0827	1402	2.3E
	1837	2037	0.9F		1814	2038	1.4F
9 Sa	0146	0357	0.5E	24 Su	0123	0357	0.8E
		0806	*			0824	*
		1529	1.9E			1525	2.1E
	1939	2207	0.8F		1922	2155	1.3F
10 Su	0252	0512	0.6E	25 M	0221	0507	1.0E
		0911	*			0940	*
		1632	1.8E			1639	2.0E
	2039				2030	2329	1.4F
11 M		0021	1.1F	26 Tu	0303	0608	1.4E
	0337	0710	0.8E		1001	1113	0.3F
		1028	*		1310	1749	2.0E
		1727	1.9E		2131		
	2131						
12 Tu		0054	1.2F	27 W		0022	1.5F
	0410	0737	1.1E		0338	0659	1.8E
		1142	*		1041	1238	0.7F
		1822	1.9E		1458	1851	2.0E
	2216				2224		
13 W		0109	1.4F	28 Th		0057	1.5F
	0435	0758	1.4E		0408	0746	2.2E
	1124	1240	0.4F		1118	1333	1.1F
	1437	1919	2.0E		1617	1954	2.0E
	2255				2310		
14 Th		0123	1.5F	29 F		0132	1.5F
	0455	0821	1.7E		0437	0821	2.6E
	1149	1326	0.7F		1155	1415	1.4F
	1551	2008	2.0E		1724	2043	2.0E
	2332				2354		
15 F		0151	1.6F	30 Sa		0203	1.4F
	0513	0850	2.1E		0503	0858	2.8E
	1217	1408	1.0F		1232	1457	1.6F
	1655	2049	2.0E		1822	2126	1.9E
				31 Su	0035	0237	1.3F
					0527	0931	2.9E
					1309	1537	1.8F
					1912	2206	1.7E

APRIL

Day	Slack Water Time h.m.	Maximum Current Time h.m.	Vel. knots	Day	Slack Water Time h.m.	Maximum Current Time h.m.	Vel. knots
1 M	0116	0317	1.1F	16 Tu	0057	0259	1.0F
	0548	1006	2.9E		0451	0934	3.2E
	1347	1615	1.8F		1317	1602	2.3F
	1957	2246	1.5E		1954	2237	1.3E
2 Tu	0159	0354	0.9F	17 W	0139	0342	0.8F
	0607	1035	2.8E		0523	1003	3.2E
	1426	1657	1.8F		1358	1650	2.3F
	2040	2329	1.2E		2042	2322	1.2E
3 W	0246	0437	0.7F	18 Th	0232	0429	0.7F
	0625	1106	2.6E		0600	1040	3.1E
	1508	1739	1.7F		1445	1738	2.3F
	2123				2133		
4 Th		0015	1.0E	19 F		0017	1.0E
	0343	0518	0.5F		0340	0518	0.5F
	0646	1133	2.4E		0638	1119	2.9E
	1553	1821	1.5F		1537	1829	2.1F
	2213				2227		
5 F		0114	0.8E	20 Sa		0122	1.0E
	0452	0603	0.3F		0500	0613	0.3F
	0708	1210	2.1E		0719	1214	2.5E
	1642	1905	1.4F		1634	1917	1.9F
	2315				2327		
6 Sa		0223	0.7E	21 Su		0237	1.1E
		0654	*			0711	*
		1301	1.8E			1343	2.1E
	1735	1956	1.2F		1735	2012	1.7F
7 Su	0029	0338	0.8E	22 M	0025	0339	1.3E
		0746	*			0820	*
		1436	1.6E			1511	1.8E
	1832	2051	1.1F		1840	2110	1.5F
8 M	0129	0434	1.0E	23 Tu	0113	0436	1.7E
		0847	*			0944	*
		1546	1.5E			1621	1.6E
	1934	2154	1.0F		1948	2219	1.3F
9 Tu	0210	0527	1.2E	24 W	0153	0530	2.0E
		1006	*		0939	1206	0.5F
		1654	1.4E		1405	1730	1.4E
	2034	2300	1.1F		2054	2321	1.2F
10 W	0240	0612	1.5E	25 Th	0227	0618	2.4E
		1130	*		1018	1303	1.0F
		1752	1.4E		1538	1840	1.3E
	2129	2349	1.1F		2154		
11 Th	0303	0647	1.8E	26 F		0010	1.1F
	1044	1231	0.6F		0258	0706	2.7E
	1504	1853	1.4E		1055	1345	1.4F
	2217				1651	1945	1.4E
					2248		
12 F		0024	1.2F	27 Sa		0047	1.0F
	0324	0726	2.1E		0325	0745	2.9E
	1110	1313	1.1F		1131	1422	1.7F
	1616	1948	1.5E		1752	2036	1.4E
	2300				2336		
13 Sa		0103	1.2F	28 Su		0123	0.9F
	0343	0758	2.5E		0349	0824	3.0E
	1138	1352	1.5F		1206	1455	1.9F
	1718	2033	1.5E		1843	2118	1.4E
	2340						
14 Su		0141	1.2F	29 M	0022	0203	0.8F
	0402	0833	2.8E		0410	0859	3.0E
	1208	1432	1.9F		1241	1526	2.0F
	1814	2116	1.5E		1927	2200	1.3E
15 M	0019	0217	1.1F	30 Tu	0109	0240	0.7F
	0424	0904	3.0E		0429	0933	3.0E
	1240	1518	2.1F		1316	1559	2.0F
	1905	2156	1.5E		2006	2235	1.2E

1991 CURRENT TABLES

ROSARIO STRAIT

For Daylight Saving Time, add one hour.

Times and Heights of High and Low Waters

F-Flood, Dir. 335° True   E-Ebb, Dir. 175° True

MAY

Day	Slack Water Time h.m.	Maximum Current Time h.m.	Vel. knots
1 W	0159	0321	0.5F
	0450	1004	2.8E
	1352	1638	2.0F
	2043	2317	1.1E
2 Th	0257	0405	0.3F
	0514	1031	2.6E
	1429	1716	1.9F
	2121		
3 F		0004	1.0E
		0451	*
		1056	2.4E
	1508	1755	1.8F
	2200		
4 Sa		0101	1.0E
		0540	*
		1119	2.1E
	1550	1836	1.7F
	2242		
5 Su		0203	1.0E
		0632	*
		1154	1.8E
	1635	1921	1.6F
	2325		
6 M		0304	1.1E
		0727	*
		1303	1.4E
	1723	2009	1.4F
7 Tu	0005	0353	1.4E
		0828	*
		1501	1.2E
	1817	2058	1.2F
8 W	0039	0436	1.6E
		0940	*
		1610	1.0E
	1918	2153	1.1F
9 Th	0106	0511	1.9E
	0938	1104	0.3F
	1346	1713	0.9E
	2025	2244	1.0F
10 F	0130	0549	2.2E
	1003	1211	0.9F
	1522	1820	0.9E
	2129	2333	0.9F
11 Sa	0152	0630	2.5E
	1032	1254	1.4F
	1635	1921	1.0E
	2225		
12 Su		0015	0.8F
	0216	0710	2.8E
	1103	1335	1.9F
	1738	2017	1.0E
	2314		
13 M		0102	0.8F
	0245	0751	3.1E
	1137	1413	2.2F
	1831	2104	1.1E
	2359		
14 Tu		0145	0.8F
	0319	0828	3.3E
	1214	1459	2.5F
	1919	2147	1.2E
15 W	0046	0226	0.7F
	0357	0908	3.4E
	1253	1548	2.6F
	2003	2230	1.2E

Day	Slack Water Time h.m.	Maximum Current Time h.m.	Vel. knots
16 Th	0140	0315	0.6F
	0439	0946	3.4E
	1336	1635	2.6F
	2044	2319	1.3E
17 F	0243	0408	0.5F
	0525	1025	3.2E
	1423	1721	2.6F
	2126		
18 Sa		0010	1.3E
	0355	0506	0.4F
	0613	1112	2.8E
	1512	1810	2.4F
	2207		
19 Su		0110	1.4E
	0508	0603	0.3F
	0705	1208	2.3E
	1604	1856	2.2F
	2248		
20 M		0212	1.6E
		0708	*
		1330	1.8E
	1658	1944	1.9F
	2329		
21 Tu		0314	1.9E
		0815	*
		1447	1.4E
	1755	2031	1.5F
22 W	0008	0403	2.2E
	0821	1009	0.3F
	1235	1602	1.1E
	1858	2126	1.2F
23 Th	0045	0451	2.5E
	0909	1204	0.8F
	1440	1711	0.9E
	2009	2223	1.0F
24 F	0118	0539	2.7E
	0951	1257	1.3F
	1606	1825	0.8E
	2120	2319	0.8F
25 Sa	0148	0625	2.9E
	1031	1340	1.6F
	1714	1939	0.8E
	2225		
26 Su		0006	0.7F
	0213	0709	3.0E
	1108	1417	1.8F
	1809	2042	0.9E
	2321		
27 M		0048	0.5F
	0235	0751	3.0E
	1143	1450	2.0F
	1854	2125	1.0E
28 Tu	0014	0128	0.4F
	0257	0830	3.0E
	1218	1515	2.0F
	1933	2200	1.1E
29 W	0106	0209	0.3F
	0321	0906	2.9E
	1252	1548	2.1F
	2007	2229	1.1E
30 Th		0255	*
		0941	2.8E
	1325	1619	2.1F
	2039	2312	1.1E
31 F		0340	*
		1009	2.6E
	1359	1653	2.1F
	2108	2352	1.2E

JUNE

Day	Slack Water Time h.m.	Maximum Current Time h.m.	Vel. knots
1 Sa		0429	*
		1031	2.4E
	1433	1732	2.0F
	2136		
2 Su		0035	1.2E
		0520	*
		1054	2.1E
	1508	1810	2.0F
	2203		
3 M		0130	1.3E
		0613	*
		1123	1.7E
	1544	1849	1.8F
	2228		
4 Tu		0219	1.5E
		0706	*
		1211	1.3E
	1623	1930	1.6F
	2252		
5 W		0302	1.7E
		0805	*
		1354	1.0E
	1705	2013	1.4F
	2312		
6 Th		0344	2.0E
		0909	*
		1530	0.7E
	1753	2058	1.1F
	2333		
7 F		0419	2.2E
	0846	1025	0.5F
	1356	1639	0.6E
	1854	2150	0.8F
	2358		
8 Sa		0501	2.5E
	0921	1145	1.0F
	1539	1746	0.5E
	2020	2245	0.7F
9 Su	0030	0540	2.8E
	0957	1237	1.6F
	1655	1859	0.5E
	2146	2336	0.6F
10 M	0108	0625	3.1E
	1035	1319	2.0F
	1753	1958	0.7E
	2250		
11 Tu		0025	0.6F
	0151	0713	3.3E
	1114	1400	2.3F
	1839	2053	0.9E
	2345		
12 W		0114	0.6F
	0236	0803	3.4E
	1155	1443	2.6F
	1919	2136	1.1E
13 Th	0038	0207	0.5F
	0325	0849	3.5E
	1236	1532	2.7F
	1954	2221	1.3E
14 F	0135	0257	0.5F
	0418	0936	3.4E
	1319	1618	2.7F
	2028	2305	1.5E
15 Sa	0237	0354	0.5F
	0514	1017	3.1E
	1403	1703	2.6F
	2100	2354	1.7E

Day	Slack Water Time h.m.	Maximum Current Time h.m.	Vel. knots
16 Su	0342	0456	0.4F
	0616	1106	2.7E
	1449	1747	2.5F
	2132		
17 M		0043	1.9E
	0445	0556	0.4F
	0723	1203	2.1E
	1535	1830	2.2F
	2203		
18 Tu		0140	2.1E
	0545	0658	0.4F
	0839	1311	1.6E
	1623	1911	1.9F
	2234		
19 W		0235	2.4E
	0643	0805	0.5F
	1029	1428	1.1E
	1712	1954	1.5F
	2305		
20 Th		0327	2.6E
	0740	0950	0.6F
	1258	1536	0.8E
	1808	2041	1.1F
	2336		
21 F		0412	2.7E
	0834	1146	0.9F
	1455	1648	0.5E
	1921	2131	0.8F
22 Sa	0005	0501	2.8E
	0922	1245	1.3F
	1616	1805	0.5E
	2047	2232	0.5F
23 Su	0034	0548	2.9E
	1006	1328	1.6F
	1720	1957	0.6E
	2207	2327	0.4F
24 M	0103	0637	2.9E
	1046	1409	1.8F
	1809	2052	0.7E
	2313		
25 Tu		0016	0.3F
	0133	0723	2.9E
	1123	1440	1.9F
	1848	2133	0.9E
26 W		0059	*
		0807	2.8E
	1158	1509	2.0F
	1922	2156	1.1E
27 Th		0147	*
		0848	2.8E
	1231	1530	2.0F
	1951	2223	1.2E
28 F		0232	*
		0923	2.7E
	1303	1557	2.1F
	2015	2252	1.3E
29 Sa		0321	*
		0952	2.5E
	1334	1629	2.1F
	2037	2327	1.4E
30 Su		0412	*
		1021	2.3E
	1404	1703	2.1F
	2056		

ROSARIO STRAIT

1991 CURRENT TABLES

For Daylight Saving Time, add one hour.

Times and Heights of High and Low Waters

F-Flood, Dir. 335° True   E-Ebb, Dir. 175° True

JULY

Day	Slack Water Time (h.m.)	Max Current Time (h.m.)	Vel. (knots)
1 M		0003	1.5E
		0503	*
		1048	2.0E
	1435	1741	2.0F
	2114		
2 Tu		0043	1.6E
		0555	*
		1109	1.7E
	1506	1816	1.8F
	2129		
3 W		0127	1.8E
		0645	*
		1146	1.3E
	1538	1853	1.6F
	2143		
4 Th		0207	1.9E
	0629	0735	0.4F
	0902	1249	0.8E
	1614	1930	1.3F
	2158		
5 F		0250	2.2E
	0710	0836	0.5F
	1114	1451	0.5E
	1654	2015	1.0F
	2220		
6 Sa		0330	2.4E
	0755	0944	0.8F
	1405	1608	0.3E
	1743	2101	0.7F
	2250		
7 Su		0414	2.7E
	0841	1108	1.1F
		1721	*
		2200	0.5F
	2329		
8 M		0501	2.9E
	0927	1217	1.6F
	1701	1836	0.3E
	2120	2303	0.4F
9 Tu	0019	0555	3.1E
	1012	1307	2.0F
	1747	1945	0.6E
	2238	2358	0.4F
10 W	0117	0651	3.2E
	1056	1348	2.3F
	1824	2041	0.9E
	2335		
11 Th		0056	0.5F
	0218	0747	3.3E
	1139	1430	2.5F
	1855	2122	1.2E
12 F	0027	0151	0.6F
	0320	0841	3.3E
	1221	1512	2.6F
	1924	2205	1.6E
13 Sa	0119	0246	0.6F
	0426	0930	3.2E
	1303	1556	2.6F
	1952	2240	1.9E
14 Su	0214	0345	0.7F
	0536	1014	2.9E
	1345	1638	2.5F
	2019	2323	2.1E
15 M	0310	0447	0.8F
	0647	1101	2.5E
	1427	1718	2.3F
	2046		
16 Tu		0010	2.3E
	0407	0542	0.8F
	0757	1151	1.9E
	1509	1757	2.1F
	2112		
17 W		0100	2.5E
	0502	0639	0.8F
	0910	1248	1.4E
	1553	1839	1.7F
	2137		
18 Th		0151	2.6E
	0558	0739	0.8F
	1042	1402	0.9E
	1638	1920	1.3F
	2201		
19 F		0245	2.6E
	0655	0850	0.8F
	1254	1514	0.6E
	1732	2001	1.0F
	2224		
20 Sa		0335	2.6E
	0753	1121	0.9F
	1447	1623	0.4E
	1848	2051	0.6F
	2248		
21 Su		0426	2.6E
	0849	1222	1.2F
	1604	1748	0.3E
	2030	2147	0.3F
	2316		
22 M		0520	2.6E
	0939	1311	1.5F
	1700	1956	0.5E
		2255	*
23 Tu		0609	2.6E
	1022	1348	1.6F
	1743	2039	0.8E
		2352	*
24 W		0700	2.6E
	1101	1421	1.8F
	1818	2118	1.0E
25 Th		0046	*
		0747	2.6E
	1136	1446	1.9F
	1846	2137	1.2E
26 F		0134	*
		0828	2.6E
	1209	1459	1.9F
	1910	2152	1.4E
27 Sa	0123	0217	0.3F
	0328	0906	2.5E
	1240	1526	2.0F
	1929	2221	1.6E
28 Su	0202	0304	0.3F
	0423	0940	2.4E
	1310	1555	2.0F
	1946	2249	1.7E
29 M	0241	0352	0.4F
	0521	1014	2.2E
	1339	1627	1.9F
	2000	2318	1.9E
30 Tu	0320	0441	0.5F
	0620	1042	1.9E
	1408	1704	1.8F
	2013	2351	2.0E
31 W	0359	0531	0.6F
	0719	1109	1.6E
	1436	1740	1.6F
	2024		

AUGUST

Day	Slack Water Time (h.m.)	Max Current Time (h.m.)	Vel. (knots)
1 Th		0027	2.1E
	0439	0619	0.8F
	0820	1140	1.2E
	1507	1819	1.4F
	2038		
2 F		0102	2.2E
	0522	0709	0.9F
	0933	1235	0.7E
	1541	1854	1.1F
	2057		
3 Sa		0145	2.3E
	0611	0804	0.9F
	1125	1426	0.4E
	1621	1937	0.8F
	2124		
4 Su		0238	2.4E
	0704	0907	1.0F
		1551	*
		2026	0.5F
	2157		
5 M		0337	2.6E
	0802	1029	1.2F
	1538	1708	0.3E
	1910	2127	0.3F
	2242		
6 Tu		0434	2.7E
	0859	1205	1.5F
	1630	1818	0.4E
	2129	2243	0.3F
	2346		
7 W		0537	2.8E
	0951	1252	1.8F
	1708	1927	0.8E
	2235	2348	0.4F
8 Th	0107	0640	2.9E
	1039	1329	2.1F
	1740	2016	1.2E
	2325		
9 F		0050	0.6F
	0229	0741	3.0E
	1123	1408	2.3F
	1808	2057	1.6E
10 Sa	0010	0144	0.8F
	0348	0831	3.0E
	1205	1446	2.3F
	1835	2136	2.0E
11 Su	0056	0240	1.0F
	0503	0920	2.8E
	1245	1525	2.3F
	1901	2214	2.4E
12 M	0143	0336	1.1F
	0612	1007	2.6E
	1326	1604	2.1F
	1926	2251	2.6E
13 Tu	0232	0433	1.2F
	0716	1049	2.2E
	1406	1643	1.9F
	1951	2331	2.7E
14 W	0323	0525	1.3F
	0817	1138	1.7E
	1447	1723	1.7F
	2014		
15 Th		0014	2.7E
	0415	0619	1.2F
	0920	1229	1.2E
	1531	1805	1.4F
	2036		
16 F		0101	2.6E
	0510	0708	1.1F
	1034	1337	0.8E
	1621	1845	1.0F
	2055		
17 Sa		0157	2.4E
	0606	0802	1.0F
	1226	1451	0.5E
	1724	1930	0.7F
	2115		
18 Su		0257	2.3E
	0706	0919	0.8F
	1414	1600	0.4E
	1853	2018	0.3F
	2137		
19 M		0351	2.3E
	0807	1151	1.0F
	1523	1734	0.5E
	2120		*
20 Tu		0447	2.2E
	0904	1241	1.2F
	1612	1926	0.7E
	2232		*
21 W		0542	2.2E
	0952	1318	1.4F
	1651	2013	1.0E
	2345		*
22 Th		0638	2.2E
	1033	1347	1.6F
	1721	2036	1.2E
23 F		0040	*
		0727	2.3E
	1109	1404	1.7F
	1746	2051	1.5E
24 Sa	0009	0126	0.4F
	0315	0810	2.3E
	1144	1417	1.7F
	1806	2112	1.7E
25 Su	0040	0206	0.6F
	0416	0852	2.3E
	1216	1443	1.8F
	1822	2141	2.0E
26 M	0112	0249	0.8F
	0514	0927	2.2E
	1247	1518	1.7F
	1837	2209	2.1E
27 Tu	0144	0335	1.0F
	0608	1002	2.0E
	1317	1549	1.6F
	1850	2234	2.3E
28 W	0218	0421	1.1F
	0701	1033	1.7E
	1346	1624	1.5F
	1902	2259	2.4E
29 Th	0254	0506	1.3F
	0753	1106	1.4E
	1416	1705	1.3F
	1917	2322	2.5E
30 F	0336	0555	1.3F
	0848	1147	1.0E
	1449	1744	1.0F
	1938	2351	2.5E
31 Sa	0423	0643	1.4F
	0954	1245	0.7E
	1530	1823	0.8F
	2004		

1991 CURRENT TABLES

ROSARIO STRAIT

For Daylight Saving Time, add one hour.

Times and Heights of High and Low Waters

F-Flood, Dir. 335° True   E-Ebb, Dir. 175° True

SEPTEMBER

Day	Slack Water Time h.m.	Maximum Current Time h.m.	Vel. knots	Day	Slack Water Time h.m.	Maximum Current Time h.m.	Vel. knots
1		0036	2.4E	16		0205	2.0E
Su	0517	0737	1.3F	M	0612	0819	1.0F
	1127	1418	0.4E		1319	1548	0.6E
	1627	1910	0.5F			1953	*
	2035						
2		0143	2.4E	17		0312	1.8E
M	0618	0834	1.2F	Tu	0713	0930	0.9F
	1333	1540	0.4E		1422	1703	0.7E
	1813	2003	0.3F			2055	*
	2112						
3		0307	2.3E	18		0415	1.8E
Tu	0724	0950	1.3F	W	0814	1152	1.0F
	1447	1654	0.5E		1506	1819	1.0E
		2115	*			2211	*
4		0418	2.4E	19		0511	1.8E
W	0828	1121	1.4F	Th	0908	1231	1.2F
	1532	1805	0.8E		1538	1906	1.3E
		2234	*			2340	*
5		0524	2.4E	20		0606	1.8E
Th	0926	1221	1.7F	F	0955	1252	1.3F
	1606	1900	1.2E		1604	1929	1.5E
	2229	2348	0.4F		2308		
6	0138	0633	2.4E	21		0037	0.4F
F	1018	1303	1.8F	Sa	0243	0703	1.8E
	1637	1948	1.7E		1037	1307	1.4F
	2310				1625	1958	1.8E
					2332		
7		0051	0.8F	22		0116	0.7F
Sa	0313	0731	2.5E	Su	0351	0751	1.9E
	1104	1336	1.9F		1115	1329	1.4F
	1705	2025	2.1E		1644	2027	2.1E
	2350						
8		0148	1.1F	23	0000	0152	1.1F
Su	0429	0824	2.5E	M	0450	0833	1.9E
	1147	1411	1.9F		1150	1400	1.4F
	1733	2104	2.5E		1701	2055	2.4E
9	0030	0237	1.4F	24	0028	0233	1.4F
M	0537	0913	2.3E	Tu	0545	0914	1.8E
	1228	1451	1.8F		1224	1433	1.4F
	1759	2139	2.8E		1716	2124	2.6E
10	0112	0326	1.6F	25	0058	0315	1.6F
Tu	0639	0957	2.1E	W	0636	0950	1.7E
	1308	1528	1.6F		1257	1510	1.2F
	1825	2215	2.9E		1731	2151	2.7E
11	0155	0414	1.7F	26	0129	0358	1.8F
W	0734	1040	1.8E	Th	0725	1027	1.5E
	1350	1609	1.4F		1331	1550	1.1F
	1848	2252	2.9E		1750	2214	2.0E
12	0240	0505	1.7F	27	0206	0446	1.9F
Th	0826	1125	1.5E	F	0813	1106	1.2E
	1434	1646	1.2F		1407	1632	0.9F
	1909	2329	2.7E		1815	2237	2.8E
13	0328	0548	1.6F	28	0248	0534	1.9F
F	0920	1212	1.1E	Sa	0905	1151	1.0E
	1524	1733	0.9F		1452	1715	0.7F
	1929				1845	2312	2.7E
14		0010	2.5E	29	0337	0621	1.8F
Sa	0419	0635	1.4F	Su	1004	1255	0.7E
	1020	1315	0.8E		1601	1803	0.5F
	1626	1815	0.6F		1918	2351	2.5E
	1949						
15		0101	2.2E	30	0433	0712	1.7F
Su	0514	0725	1.2F	M	1119	1419	0.7E
	1143	1431	0.6E		1737	1852	0.3F
	1743	1858	0.3F		1953		
	2009						

OCTOBER

Day	Slack Water Time h.m.	Maximum Current Time h.m.	Vel. knots	Day	Slack Water Time h.m.	Maximum Current Time h.m.	Vel. knots
1		0056	2.3E	16		0220	1.5E
Tu	0536	0809	1.5F	W	0609	0831	1.1F
	1241	1534	0.8E		1304	1623	1.1E
		1957	*			2036	0.3E
2		0247	2.0E	17		0335	1.4E
W	0642	0913	1.4F	Th	0708	0929	1.0F
	1341	1635	1.1E		1344	1706	1.3E
		2110	*			2154	*
3		0403	1.9E	18		0438	1.3E
Th	0751	1027	1.4F	F	0809	1035	1.0F
	1424	1733	1.4E		1414	1749	1.6E
		2238	*				
4		0514	1.9E	19		0008	*
F	0855	1137	1.4F	Sa		0533	1.3E
	1459	1822	1.9E		0906	1126	1.1F
	2214				1438	1828	1.9E
					2231		
5		0012	0.7F	20		0039	0.6F
Sa	0232	0621	1.9E	Su	0304	0636	1.3E
	0952	1222	1.5F		0957	1207	1.1F
	1530	1910	2.3E		1459	1903	2.2E
	2251				2255		
6		0109	1.1F	21		0105	1.1F
Su	0355	0723	1.9E	M	0412	0727	1.3E
	1042	1302	1.5F		1042	1244	1.1F
	1559	1952	2.7E		1517	1938	2.5E
	2328				2322		
7		0152	1.5F	22		0139	1.5F
M	0505	0820	1.9E	Tu	0511	0816	1.4E
	1128	1337	1.4F		1124	1319	1.0F
	1626	2029	2.9E		1535	2010	2.8E
					2351		
8		0234	1.8F	23		0215	1.9F
Tu	0605	0905	1.8E	W	0605	0901	1.4E
	1212	1413	1.3F		1203	1354	1.0F
	1652	2108	3.1E		1555	2043	3.0E
9	0043	0316	2.0F	24	0022	0257	2.1F
W	0659	0946	1.7E	Th	0654	0942	1.4E
	1255	1454	1.1F		1241	1435	0.9F
	1716	2143	3.1E		1620	2112	3.1E
10	0122	0358	2.0F	25	0056	0339	2.3F
Th	0747	1031	1.5E	F	0740	1020	1.3E
	1341	1530	0.9F		1322	1518	0.7F
	1737	2215	3.0E		1650	2143	3.2E
11	0202	0440	2.0F	26	0134	0427	2.3F
F	0832	1112	1.3E	Sa	0825	1103	1.1E
	1431	1611	0.7F		1412	1602	0.6F
	1758	2248	2.8E		1725	2212	3.1E
12	0245	0522	1.8F	27	0216	0515	2.3F
Sa	0917	1201	1.0E	Su	0912	1154	1.0E
	1533	1700	0.4F		1519	1651	0.4F
	1820	2318	2.5E		1803	2247	2.9E
13	0331	0604	1.7F	28	0305	0603	2.2F
Su	1006	1301	0.9E	M	1001	1252	1.0E
		1746	*		1641	1748	0.3F
	2355		2.1E		1843	2333	2.5E
14	0420	0650	1.5F	29	0358	0650	2.0F
M	1103	1412	0.8E	Tu	1053	1406	1.1E
		1835	*			1845	*
15		0050	1.8E	30		0040	2.1E
Tu	0513	0737	1.3F	W	0456	0743	1.8F
	1209	1521	0.9E		1146	1510	1.3E
		1930	*			1949	*
				31		0228	1.7E
				Th	0559	0836	1.6F
					1234	1605	1.7E
						2107	*

ROSARIO STRAIT

1991 CURRENT TABLES

For Daylight Saving Time, add one hour.

Times and Heights of High and Low Waters

F-Flood, Dir. 335° True   E-Ebb, Dir. 175° True

NOVEMBER

Day	Slack Water Time h.m.	Maximum Current Time h.m.	Vel. knots
1 F		0350	1.5E
	0705	0936	1.4F
	1316	1658	2.1E
	2112	2327	0.4F
2 Sa	0131	0501	1.3E
	0814	1039	1.2F
	1352	1747	2.4E
	2152		
3 Su		0036	1.0F
	0314	0609	1.2E
	0920	1134	1.1F
	1424	1831	2.8E
	2230		
4 M		0123	1.5F
	0432	0716	1.2E
	1019	1218	1.0F
	1453	1919	3.0E
	2307		
5 Tu		0200	1.8F
	0535	0813	1.3E
	1112	1258	0.9F
	1520	1957	3.2E
	2344		
6 W		0240	2.0F
	0629	0902	1.3E
	1200	1340	0.8F
	1544	2037	3.2E
7 Th	0020	0311	2.1F
	0715	0943	1.3E
	1248	1417	0.7F
	1606	2112	3.1E
8 F	0056	0344	2.2F
	0756	1025	1.2E
	1339	1459	0.5F
	1628	2147	3.0E
9 Sa	0133	0421	2.1F
	0834	1106	1.2E
	1438	1546	0.3F
	1652	2218	2.7E
10 Su	0211	0457	2.0F
	0911	1149	1.1E
	1630		*
	2243		2.5E
11 M	0249	0539	1.9F
	0947	1242	1.0E
	1723		*
	2309		2.1E
12 Tu	0330	0619	1.8F
	1025	1341	1.1E
	1813		*
	2337		1.8E
13 W	0413	0701	1.6F
	1104	1443	1.2E
	1909		*
14 Th		0028	1.4E
	0459	0747	1.4F
	1141	1538	1.4E
	2009		*
15 F		0236	1.1E
	0550	0835	1.2F
	1214	1617	1.7E
	2124		*

Day	Slack Water Time h.m.	Maximum Current Time h.m.	Vel. knots
16 Sa		0353	0.9E
	0649	0924	1.1F
	1242	1655	2.0E
	2129	2342	0.3F
17 Su	0141	0456	0.8E
	0758	1019	0.9F
	1306	1733	2.2E
	2151		
18 M		0024	0.8F
	0319	0559	0.8E
	0907	1110	0.8F
	1328	1812	2.5E
	2219		
19 Tu		0053	1.3F
	0431	0706	0.8E
	1007	1157	0.7F
	1351	1850	2.8E
	2249		
20 W		0121	1.8F
	0531	0801	0.9E
	1058	1239	0.7F
	1419	1929	3.0E
	2322		
21 Th		0201	2.1F
	0622	0849	1.0E
	1145	1322	0.7F
	1452	2007	3.3E
	1356		
22 F	[illegible]	0241	2.4F
	[illegible]	0931	1.1E
	1229	1404	0.6F
	1530	2044	3.4E
23 Sa	0033	0323	2.6F
	0747	1013	1.2E
	1318	1450	0.5F
	1611	2121	3.4E
24 Su	0113	0409	2.6F
	0825	1054	1.2E
	1417	1541	0.4F
	1655	2200	3.2E
25 M	0155	0456	2.6F
	0902	1144	1.3E
	1526	1636	0.4F
	1744	2243	2.9E
26 Tu	0241	0542	2.5F
	0938	1239	1.4E
	1637	1736	0.3F
	1836	2330	2.5E
27 W	0329	0629	2.3F
	1015	1340	1.6E
	1839		*
28 Th		0034	1.9E
	0420	0714	2.0F
	1053	1438	1.9E
		1942	*
29 F		0209	1.4E
	0515	0802	1.7F
	1130	1532	2.2E
	1948	2100	0.3F
	2337		
30 Sa		0327	1.0E
	0616	0851	1.3F
	1207	1622	2.5E
	2040	2335	0.7F

DECEMBER

Day	Slack Water Time h.m.	Maximum Current Time h.m.	Vel. knots
1 Su	0210	0441	0.8E
	0727	0946	1.0F
	1243	1711	2.8E
	2126		
2 M		0038	1.2F
	0345	0556	0.7E
	0846	1045	0.8F
	1317	1759	3.0E
	2208		
3 Tu		0119	1.7F
	0457	0716	0.8E
	0959	1139	0.6F
	1348	1845	3.1E
	2248		
4 W		0202	1.9F
	0553	0827	0.9E
	1101	1227	0.5F
	1416	1932	3.1E
	2325		
5 Th		0237	2.1F
	0640	0914	1.0E
	1155	1309	0.4F
	1442	2015	3.1E
6 F	0001	0312	2.2F
	0720	0945	1.1E
	1247	1352	0.3F
	1509	2052	3.0E
7 Sa	0037	0339	2.2F
	0754	1020	1.2E
	1437		*
		2127	2.9E
8 Su	0111	0408	2.2F
	0825	1055	1.2E
	1523		*
		2200	2.7E
9 M	0144	0437	2.1F
	0852	1130	1.3E
	1612		*
		2226	2.4E
10 Tu	0217	0512	2.1F
	0918	1216	1.3E
	1703		*
		2251	2.1E
11 W	0250	0551	2.0F
	0942	1304	1.4E
	1754		*
		2312	1.8E
12 Th	0324	0629	1.8F
	1005	1356	1.5E
	1847		*
		2347	1.4E
13 F	0359	0707	1.6F
	1027	1439	1.7E
	1944		*
14 Sa		0043	0.9E
	0439	0750	1.4F
	1046	1521	1.9E
	2044		*
15 Su		0307	0.6E
	0523	0833	1.1F
	1104	1601	2.2E
	2032	2202	0.4F

Day	Slack Water Time h.m.	Maximum Current Time h.m.	Vel. knots
16 M	0140	0419	0.4E
	0619	0922	0.8F
	1128	1642	2.4E
	2107	2345	0.9F
17 Tu	0336	0530	0.4E
	0748	1015	0.6F
	1159	1721	2.7E
	2144		
18 W		0031	1.4F
	0451	0639	0.4E
	0930	1111	0.5F
	1238	1806	2.9E
	2221		
19 Th		0109	1.8F
	0545	0742	0.6E
	1038	1206	0.5F
	1323	1853	3.1E
	2259		
20 F		0144	2.2F
	0628	0836	0.8E
	1131	1255	0.5F
	1411	1944	3.3E
	2337		
21 Sa		0226	2.5F
	0703	0919	1.0E
	1220	1344	0.5F
	1502	2030	3.4E
22 Su	0017	0308	2.6F
	0735	0959	1.3E
	1310	1433	0.5F
	1556	2112	3.4E
23 M	0057	0353	2.7F
	0804	1041	1.5E
	1406	1530	0.5F
	1654	2156	3.2E
24 Tu	0138	0436	2.7F
	0833	1125	1.7E
	1505	1628	0.5F
	1756	2243	2.8E
25 W	0220	0519	2.6F
	0902	1213	1.9E
	1607	1728	0.6F
	1902	2332	2.3E
26 Th	0304	0601	2.3F
	0931	1303	2.1E
	1707	1828	0.6F
	2014		
27 F		0029	1.7E
	0349	0642	2.0F
	1000	1359	2.4E
	1805	1930	0.6F
	2145		
28 Sa		0146	1.2E
	0436	0725	1.6F
	1029	1451	2.6E
	1904	2039	0.6F
29 Su	0004	0303	0.8E
	0530	0812	1.2F
	1059	1543	2.7E
	2002	2310	0.9F
30 M	0226	0420	0.5E
	0640	0901	0.8F
	1129	1634	2.8E
	2056		
31 Tu		0023	1.3F
	0357	0537	0.4E
	0816	1003	0.5F
	1201	1724	2.9E
	2145		

1991 CURRENT TABLES — SAN JUAN CHANNEL

For Daylight Saving Time, add one hour.

Times and Heights of High and Low Waters

JANUARY

Days 1–15

Day	Slack Water Time h.m.	Maximum Current Time h.m.	Vel. knots
1 Tu		0203	5.2F
	0603	0844	2.9E
	1158	1400	1.6F
	1616	2003	4.2E
	2322		
2 W		0251	5.0F
	0645	0927	3.0E
	1250	1457	1.6F
	1717	2048	3.8E
3 Th	0009	0338	4.7F
	0725	1015	3.0E
	1343	1554	1.6F
	1819	2141	3.3E
4 F	0056	0426	4.2F
	0803	1102	2.9E
	1437	1652	1.7F
	1925	2230	2.6E
5 Sa	0145	0507	3.6F
	0840	1153	2.9E
	1530	1750	1.7F
	2042	2335	1.9E
6 Su	0237	0551	2.9F
	0917	1242	2.9E
	1621	1852	1.8F
	2215		
7 M		0048	1.3E
	0334	0635	2.2F
	0954	1331	2.9E
	1713	2004	1.9F
	2352		
8 Tu		0213	1.0E
	0439	0728	1.6F
	1033	1422	2.9E
	1803	2128	2.3F
9 W	0114	0332	0.9E
	0557	0826	1.1F
	1114	1508	2.9E
	1852	2229	2.7F
10 Th	0218	0448	1.0E
	0720	0936	0.9F
	1156	1553	2.9E
	1938	2314	3.1F
11 F	0309	0555	1.2E
	0832	1035	0.8F
	1239	1641	3.0E
	2020	2351	3.4F
12 Sa	0352	0644	1.5E
	0926	1117	0.9F
	1321	1723	3.1E
	2059		
13 Su		0026	3.6F
	0429	0721	1.7E
	1009	1159	0.9F
	1403	1805	3.2E
	2135		
14 M		0059	3.8F
	0503	0754	1.9E
	1048	1238	1.0F
	1444	1844	3.2E
	2208		
15 Tu		0130	3.9F
	0534	0817	2.1E
	1124	1319	1.1F
	1525	1922	3.3E
	2240		

Days 16–31

Day	Slack Water Time h.m.	Maximum Current Time h.m.	Vel. knots
16 W		0202	4.0F
	0602	0840	2.2E
	1159	1400	1.2F
	1609	1957	3.2E
	2311		
17 Th		0237	3.9F
	0630	0907	2.4E
	1236	1441	1.3F
	1654	2032	3.1E
	2342		
18 F		0313	3.8F
	0656	0935	2.5E
	1313	1526	1.4F
	1743	2109	2.8E
19 Sa	0016	0348	3.6F
	0721	1011	2.6E
	1352	1611	1.6F
	1838	2152	2.5E
20 Su	0054	0429	3.3F
	0747	1052	2.7E
	1433	1700	1.8F
	1941	2239	2.0E
21 M	0139	0508	2.9F
	0815	1135	2.8E
	1518	1755	2.0F
	2100	2348	1.6E
22 Tu	0234	0555	2.3F
	0847	1226	2.9E
	1607	1855	2.3F
	2239		
23 W		0104	1.2E
	0343	0642	1.8F
	0926	1323	3.1E
	1701	2007	2.6F
24 Th	0014	0224	1.2E
	0510	0746	1.3F
	1015	1419	3.2E
	1759	2123	3.1F
25 F	0129	0347	1.3E
	0648	0903	1.1F
	1115	1516	3.5E
	1858	2232	3.8F
26 Sa	0231	0504	1.6E
	0811	1012	1.1F
	1219	1616	3.7E
	1955	2325	4.3F
27 Su	0325	0612	2.1E
	0913	1114	1.3F
	1323	1719	3.9E
	2049		
28 M		0014	4.7F
	0412	0704	2.5E
	1003	1208	1.6F
	1425	1815	4.1E
	2138		
29 Tu		0100	4.9F
	0455	0747	2.9E
	1049	1300	1.8F
	1526	1909	4.1E
	2225		
30 W		0146	4.9F
	0535	0824	3.1E
	1132	1351	2.0F
	1625	1954	4.0E
	2309		
31 Th		0228	4.6F
	0611	0901	3.2E
	1216	1440	2.2F
	1724	2040	3.6E
	2353		

FEBRUARY

Days 1–15

Day	Slack Water Time h.m.	Maximum Current Time h.m.	Vel. knots
1 F		0312	4.2F
	0644	0936	3.2E
	1301	1535	2.3F
	1822	2123	3.1E
2 Sa	0036	0351	3.6F
	0716	1012	3.2E
	1348	1624	2.3F
	1921	2210	2.4E
3 Su	0121	0430	3.0F
	0746	1053	3.0E
	1435	1712	2.3F
	2026	2305	1.8E
4 M	0209	0511	2.4F
	0815	1136	2.8E
	1524	1808	2.2F
	2145		
5 Tu		0012	1.2E
	0304	0554	1.8F
	0845	1229	2.6E
	1615	1904	2.1F
	2316		
6 W		0136	0.9E
	0412	0642	1.2F
	0920	1323	2.5E
	1708	2023	2.2F
7 Th	0040	0304	0.8E
	0534	0739	0.8F
	1006	1417	2.5E
	1804	2142	2.4F
8 F	0145	0421	0.9E
	0705	0854	0.6F
	1107	1515	2.5E
	1858	2244	2.8F
9 Sa	0235	0529	1.2E
	0817	1013	0.6F
	1211	1608	2.6E
	1948	2323	3.1F
10 Su	0316	0616	1.5E
	0906	1101	0.8F
	1307	1658	2.8E
	2032	2358	3.4F
11 M	0352	0649	1.8E
	0944	1143	1.1F
	1357	1746	2.9E
	2111		
12 Tu		0030	3.6F
	0423	0716	2.1E
	1017	1221	1.4F
	1445	1820	3.1E
	2146		
13 W		0102	3.8F
	0452	0745	2.4E
	1048	1300	1.6F
	1531	1905	3.2E
	2219		
14 Th		0133	3.8F
	0518	0806	2.6E
	1119	1339	1.8F
	1617	1940	3.2E
	2252		
15 F		0206	3.7F
	0543	0831	2.8E
	1150	1420	2.1F
	1704	2021	3.1E
	2326		

Days 16–28

Day	Slack Water Time h.m.	Maximum Current Time h.m.	Vel. knots
16 Sa		0240	3.5F
	0607	0901	3.0E
	1222	1503	2.3F
	1753	2058	2.9E
17 Su	0003	0317	3.2F
	0631	0932	3.1E
	1258	1549	2.5F
	1847	2141	2.5E
18 M	0044	0358	2.8F
	0656	1007	3.1E
	1339	1639	2.7F
	1947	2233	2.1E
19 Tu	0134	0439	2.4F
	0725	1052	3.1E
	1426	1730	2.8F
	2100	2334	1.6E
20 W	0235	0524	1.8F
	0758	1145	3.0E
	1521	1832	2.9F
	2230		
21 Th		0056	1.3E
	0353	0624	1.3F
	0839	1249	2.9E
	1623	1941	3.0F
	2359		
22 F		0223	1.3E
	0526	0733	0.9F
	0938	1354	3.0E
	1729	2102	3.2F
23 Sa	0111	0343	1.5E
	0658	0855	0.8F
	1059	1502	3.1E
	1837	2214	3.7F
24 Su	0209	0457	1.9E
	0808	1013	1.1F
	1222	1606	3.3E
	1940	2311	4.1F
25 M	0258	0554	2.3E
	0900	1114	1.5F
	1334	1713	3.5E
	2036	2358	4.3F
26 Tu	0341	0643	2.8E
	0944	1205	2.0F
	1439	1810	3.6E
	2126		
27 W		0040	4.3F
	0420	0718	3.1E
	1024	1251	2.4F
	1539	1903	3.6E
	2212		
28 Th		0120	4.2F
	0454	0753	3.3E
	1102	1338	2.7F
	1636	1946	3.5E
	2255		

SAN JUAN CHANNEL — 1991 CURRENT TABLES

For Daylight Saving Time, add one hour.

Times and Heights of High and Low Waters

MARCH

Day	Slack Water Time h.m.	Maximum Current Time h.m.	Vel. knots	Day	Slack Water Time h.m.	Maximum Current Time h.m.	Vel. knots
1 F		0158	3.8F	16 Sa		0132	3.2F
	0526	0826	3.4E		0448	0752	3.3E
	1140	1421	2.8F		1106	1400	3.0F
	1729	2029	3.2E		1710	2007	3.0E
	2337				2313		
2 Sa		0238	3.4F	17 Su		0209	3.0F
	0556	0857	3.4E		0513	0824	3.5E
	1218	1509	2.9F		1139	1441	3.3F
	1821	2110	2.8E		1801	2050	2.8E
					2356		
3 Su	0019	0315	2.9F	18 M		0249	2.6F
	0623	0929	3.3E		0540	0857	3.5E
	1257	1552	2.9F		1215	1530	3.5F
	1914	2151	2.2E		1854	2135	2.5E
4 M	0103	0354	2.3F	19 Tu	0045	0332	2.2F
	0648	1002	3.0E		0608	0936	3.5E
	1338	1639	2.8F		1258	1619	3.6F
	2009	2239	1.7E		1953	2228	2.1E
5 Tu	0152	0433	1.8F	20 W	0144	0421	1.8F
	0713	1039	2.7E		0641	1020	3.3E
	1423	1727	2.6F		1349	1711	3.6F
	2113	2340	1.2E		2101	2335	1.8E
6 W	0250	0516	1.3F	21 Th	0255	0512	1.3F
	0739	1127	2.4E		0719	1115	3.0E
	1512	1816	2.4F		1448	1812	3.4F
	2230				2220		
7 Th		0057	1.0E	22 F		0058	1.6E
	0401	0603	0.8F		0417	0611	0.9F
	0810	1226	2.2E		0809	1224	2.8E
	1608	1921	2.3F		1554	1920	3.3F
	2350				2338		
8 F		0227	0.9E	23 Sa		0221	1.7E
	0524	0706	0.5F		0542	0727	0.7F
	0857	1332	2.1E		0926	1340	2.7E
	1707	2035	2.3F		1704	2036	3.3F
9 Sa	0054	0343	1.1E	24 Su	0042	0331	1.9E
	0649	0822	0.4F		0656	0855	0.9F
	1020	1435	2.1E		1111	1451	2.7E
	1808	2149	2.5F		1815	2150	3.5F
10 Su	0144	0444	1.4E	25 M	0135	0438	2.3E
	0752	0944	0.6F		0754	1013	1.4F
	1151	1530	2.2E		1240	1559	2.8E
	1905	2240	2.8F		1921	2248	3.6F
11 M	0224	0527	1.7E	26 Tu	0219	0525	2.7E
	0835	1041	1.0F		0839	1114	2.0F
	1258	1627	2.4E		1351	1707	2.9E
	1955	2319	3.1F		2019	2333	3.7F
12 Tu	0258	0602	2.0E	27 W	0258	0608	3.1E
	0909	1126	1.4F		0919	1159	2.5F
	1354	1720	2.6E		1453	1805	3.0E
	2039	2353	3.3F		2111		
13 W	0328	0631	2.4E	28 Th		0015	3.5F
	0939	1202	1.8F		0333	0645	3.3E
	1445	1805	2.8E		0955	1243	2.9F
	2119				1550	1855	3.0E
					2157		
14 Th		0024	3.4F	29 F		0050	3.2F
	0356	0658	2.7E		0404	0718	3.5E
	1008	1237	2.3F		1030	1323	3.2F
	1533	1847	2.9E		1643	1940	2.9E
	2156				2241		
15 F		0057	3.4F	30 Sa		0126	2.9F
	0423	0724	3.0E		0434	0747	3.5E
	1037	1317	2.7F		1104	1406	3.4F
	1622	1927	3.0E		1733	2019	2.7E
	2234				2324		
				31 Su		0204	2.4F
					0500	0816	3.5E
					1137	1442	3.4F
					1819	2057	2.4E

APRIL

Day	Slack Water Time h.m.	Maximum Current Time h.m.	Vel. knots	Day	Slack Water Time h.m.	Maximum Current Time h.m.	Vel. knots
1 M	0007	0240	2.0F	16 Tu		0224	2.0F
	0525	0847	3.3E		0451	0827	3.9E
	1211	1526	3.3F		1145	1512	4.3F
	1905	2137	2.0E		1858	2133	2.5E
2 Tu	0053	0319	1.6F	17 W	0053	0313	1.6F
	0549	0920	3.0E		0527	0912	3.8E
	1247	1607	3.2F		1231	1603	4.3F
	1953	2220	1.7E		1955	2228	2.2E
3 W	0147	0400	1.2F	18 Th	0200	0404	1.3F
	0614	0955	2.7E		0608	0957	3.5E
	1328	1650	3.0F		1324	1659	4.2F
	2047	2315	1.4E		2057	2338	2.0E
4 Th	0249	0445	0.9F	19 F	0313	0504	1.0F
	0642	1036	2.4E		0657	1056	3.0E
	1414	1737	2.8F		1424	1757	3.9F
	2148				2203		
5 F		0025	1.2E	20 Sa		0059	2.0E
	0400	0538	0.6F		0428	0609	0.8F
	0716	1131	2.0E		0802	1206	2.6E
	1507	1832	2.6F		1529	1857	3.6F
	2255				2307		
6 Sa		0148	1.2E	21 Su		0209	2.2E
	0515	0634	0.4F		0537	0723	0.8F
	0806	1240	1.8E		0941	1325	2.4E
	1606	1930	2.4F		1638	2009	3.3F
	2354						
7 Su		0250	1.4E	22 M	0003	0310	2.5E
	0623	0747	0.4F		0638	0857	1.2F
	0939	1348	1.8E		1130	1443	2.3E
	1707	2042	2.5F		1748	2117	3.2F
8 M	0041	0339	1.7E	23 Tu	0050	0401	2.8E
	0715	0911	0.7F		0728	1012	1.8F
	1131	1452	1.8E		1254	1553	2.2E
	1809	2139	2.6F		1856	2212	3.0F
9 Tu	0120	0420	2.0E	24 W	0131	0447	3.1E
	0754	1013	1.2F		0812	1105	2.4F
	1247	1550	2.0E		1404	1658	2.3E
	1907	2225	2.7F		1958	2303	2.9F
10 W	0154	0457	2.4E	25 Th	0207	0530	3.3E
	0827	1054	1.7F		0850	1151	3.0F
	1347	1645	2.2E		1504	1759	2.3E
	.1959	2307	2.9F		2054	2343	2.6F
11 Th	0224	0530	2.7E	26 F	0239	0607	3.5E
	0857	1136	2.4F		0926	1231	3.4F
	1441	1738	2.4E		1559	1853	2.3E
	2047	2343	2.9F		2143		
12 F	0252	0604	3.1E	27 Sa		0018	2.3F
	0926	1215	3.0F		0309	0640	3.5E
	1532	1827	2.6E		1000	1307	3.6F
	2133				1648	1936	2.3E
					2230		
13 Sa		0018	2.8F	28 Su		0053	2.0F
	0320	0639	3.4E		0336	0711	3.5E
	0957	1254	3.5F		1032	1343	3.7F
	1623	1915	2.7E		1733	2015	2.2E
	2218				2315		
14 Su		0100	2.6F	29 M		0128	1.6F
	0348	0713	3.7E		0402	0740	3.4E
	1029	1337	3.9F		1103	1419	3.7F
	1713	1958	2.8E		1816	2050	2.1E
	2305						
15 M		0137	2.3F	30 Tu	0001	0207	1.3F
	0418	0750	3.9E		0427	0812	3.3E
	1105	1419	4.2F		1135	1500	3.6F
	1805	2044	2.7E		1857	2126	1.9E
	2355						

1991 CURRENT TABLES   SAN JUAN CHANNEL

For Daylight Saving Time, add one hour.

Times and Heights of High and Low Waters

MAY

Day	Slack Water Time h.m.	Maximum Current Time h.m.	Vel. knots
1 W	0051	0248	1.0F
	0454	0845	3.0E
	1209	1541	3.5F
	1939	2209	1.7E
2 Th	0147	0334	0.8F
	0523	0920	2.8E
	1246	1623	3.4F
	2023	2255	1.6E
3 F	0248	0423	0.6F
	0557	0959	2.4E
	1327	1708	3.2F
	2111		
4 Sa		0000	1.5E
	0352	0514	0.5F
	0639	1050	2.1E
	1414	1754	3.0F
	2202		
5 Su		0102	1.6E
	0452	0609	0.4F
	0737	1154	1.8E
	1507	1843	2.8F
	2251		
6 M		0157	1.8E
	0544	0714	0.5F
	0910	1303	1.6E
	1603	1937	2.6F
	2334		
7 Tu		0240	2.1E
	0628	0830	0.8F
	1106	1411	1.5E
	1704	2033	2.5F
8 W	0011	0315	2.4E
	0705	0934	1.4F
	1231	1510	1.6E
	1809	2128	2.4F
9 Th	0045	0356	2.8E
	0740	1029	2.1F
	1336	1609	1.7E
	1914	2215	2.4F
10 F	0116	0435	3.1E
	0813	1110	2.8F
	1434	1710	1.9E
	2015	2303	2.3F
11 Sa	0147	0514	3.5E
	0847	1152	3.5F
	1528	1808	2.2E
	2112	2345	2.2F
12 Su	0219	0555	3.8E
	0922	1234	4.1F
	1621	1902	2.4E
	2206		
13 M		0027	2.0F
	0253	0636	4.0E
	0959	1318	4.6F
	1713	1950	2.6E
	2300		
14 Tu		0112	1.8F
	0330	0722	4.2E
	1040	1407	4.8F
	1805	2039	2.6E
	2356		
15 W		0201	1.5F
	0412	0806	4.2E
	1125	1457	4.9F
	1856	2132	2.6E
16 Th	0057	0257	1.3F
	0458	0853	4.0E
	1213	1551	4.8F
	1948	2224	2.5E
17 F	0203	0357	1.1F
	0551	0942	3.6E
	1307	1643	4.5F
	2042	2332	2.4E
18 Sa	0310	0457	1.0F
	0653	1040	3.0E
	1405	1737	4.2F
	2136		
19 Su		0041	2.5E
	0414	0603	1.0F
	0813	1153	2.5E
	1506	1833	3.7F
	2228		
20 M		0142	2.7E
	0512	0715	1.2F
	0955	1310	2.1E
	1610	1932	3.2F
	2317		
21 Tu		0236	2.9E
	0606	0842	1.6F
	1138	1425	1.8E
	1717	2033	2.7F
22 W	0000	0321	3.2E
	0656	0954	2.2F
	1301	1538	1.7E
	1826	2134	2.4F
23 Th	0038	0406	3.3E
	0740	1051	2.8F
	1410	1650	1.7E
	1934	2224	2.1F
24 F	0113	0447	3.4E
	0820	1136	3.2F
	1510	1755	1.7E
	2037	2307	1.8F
25 Sa	0145	0526	3.5E
	0857	1213	3.6F
	1602	1850	1.8E
	2132	2345	1.5F
26 Su	0215	0605	3.5E
	0932	1248	3.8F
	1648	1935	1.9E
	2222		
27 M		0027	1.3F
	0243	0640	3.4E
	1005	1325	3.8F
	1730	2010	1.9E
	2309		
28 Tu		0103	1.1F
	0311	0712	3.3E
	1037	1400	3.9F
	1808	2045	1.9E
	2356		
29 W		0141	0.9F
	0340	0747	3.2E
	1109	1438	3.8F
	1845	2120	1.9E
30 Th	0044	0224	0.7F
	0413	0820	3.1E
	1141	1516	3.7F
	1921	2154	1.8E
31 F	0136	0313	0.6F
	0450	0856	2.8E
	1215	1557	3.6F
	1958	2236	1.8E

JUNE

Day	Slack Water Time h.m.	Maximum Current Time h.m.	Vel. knots
1 Sa	0230	0402	0.6F
	0532	0933	2.5E
	1252	1636	3.5F
	2034	2321	1.8E
2 Su	0322	0449	0.6F
	0623	1018	2.2E
	1333	1718	3.3F
	2111		
3 M		0009	2.0E
	0409	0541	0.6F
	0726	1115	1.8E
	1418	1800	3.0F
	2148		
4 Tu		0058	2.2E
	0452	0642	0.8F
	0851	1216	1.5E
	1509	1845	2.7F
	2225		
5 W		0140	2.4E
	0532	0743	1.2F
	1040	1332	1.4E
	1607	1938	2.4F
	2301		
6 Th		0226	2.7E
	0611	0848	1.7F
	1212	1435	1.3E
	1715	2034	2.1F
	2337		
7 F		0304	3.1E
	0651	0951	2.4F
	1323	1540	1.4E
	1832	2131	1.9F
8 Sa	0013	0350	3.4E
	0731	1045	3.2F
	1425	1648	1.6E
	1949	2224	1.8F
9 Su	0050	0433	3.7E
	0812	1128	3.9F
	1522	1752	1.9E
	2057	2313	1.7F
10 M	0130	0522	4.0E
	0854	1215	4.5F
	1616	1853	2.2E
	2157		
11 Tu		0002	1.6F
	0212	0611	4.2E
	0938	1303	4.9F
	1708	1947	2.4E
	2253		
12 W		0052	1.5F
	0259	0700	4.3E
	1024	1353	5.1F
	1757	2034	2.6E
	2349		
13 Th		0147	1.4F
	0351	0748	4.3E
	1111	1443	5.2F
	1844	2122	2.7E
14 F	0047	0244	1.3F
	0449	0840	4.1E
	1200	1535	5.0F
	1930	2212	2.8E
15 Sa	0146	0345	1.3F
	0552	0930	3.6E
	1252	1626	4.6F
	2015	2307	2.8E
16 Su	0244	0446	1.4F
	0701	1027	3.0E
	1346	1715	4.2F
	2059		
17 M		0006	2.9E
	0341	0547	1.5F
	0821	1135	2.3F
	1442	1803	3.5F
	2142		
18 Tu		0102	3.0E
	0435	0655	1.7F
	0956	1250	1.8E
	1541	1853	2.9F
	2224		
19 W		0153	3.1E
	0527	0812	1.9F
	1134	1406	1.4E
	1646	1947	2.3F
	2305		
20 Th		0241	3.2E
	0617	0929	2.4F
	1259	1524	1.3E
	1757	2047	1.7F
	2345		
21 F		0327	3.3E
	0705	1032	2.8F
	1408	1637	1.2E
	1913	2144	1.4F
22 Sa	0022	0408	3.3E
	0749	1120	3.2F
	1507	1746	1.3E
	2024	2238	1.2F
23 Su	0057	0451	3.3E
	0830	1159	3.5F
	1556	1846	1.5E
	2123	2323	1.0F
24 M	0132	0532	3.3E
	0907	1230	3.7F
	1639	1927	1.7E
	2213		
25 Tu		0002	0.9F
	0206	0614	3.2E
	0943	1305	3.8F
	1717	2004	1.8E
	2258		
26 W		0040	0.9F
	0241	0649	3.2E
	1016	1341	3.9F
	1751	2033	1.9E
	2340		
27 Th		0122	0.8F
	0318	0727	3.2E
	1048	1416	3.9F
	1823	2100	2.0E
28 F	0022	0205	0.8F
	0358	0800	3.1E
	1120	1453	3.8F
	1854	2129	2.0E
29 Sa	0105	0248	0.8F
	0441	0835	2.9E
	1152	1528	3.7F
	1923	2204	2.1E
30 Su	0148	0338	0.9F
	0529	0914	2.7E
	1225	1605	3.6F
	1952	2235	2.2E

SAN JUAN CHANNEL — 1991 CURRENT TABLES

For Daylight Saving Time, add one hour.

Times and Heights of High and Low Waters

JULY

Day	Slack Water Time h.m.	Maximum Current Time h.m.	Vel. knots
1 M	0231	0423	1.0F
	0622	0955	2.3E
	1301	1642	3.4F
	2020	2316	2.3E
2 Tu	0312	0512	1.1F
	0723	1042	1.9E
	1342	1721	3.0F
	2049		
3 W		0002	2.5E
	0352	0603	1.4F
	0839	1144	1.5E
	1430	1803	2.6F
	2120		
4 Th		0048	2.7E
	0433	0700	1.7F
	1016	1255	1.3E
	1528	1852	2.2F
	2154		
5 F		0133	2.9E
	0517	0806	2.1F
	1152	1407	1.2E
	1640	1947	1.8F
	2234		
6 Sa		0222	3.2E
	0604	0915	2.7F
	1309	1516	1.2E
	1807	2052	1.5F
	2318		
7 Su		0311	3.4E
	0654	1016	3.4F
	1414	1632	1.4E
	1935	2156	1.3F
8 M	0007	0404	3.7E
	0744	1109	4.1F
	1511	1741	1.7E
	2048	2254	1.3F
9 Tu	0059	0500	4.0E
	0834	1158	4.6F
	1604	1844	2.1E
	2148	2348	1.4F
10 W	0153	0555	4.2E
	0923	1249	5.0F
	1653	1936	2.5E
	2240		
11 Th		0040	1.5F
	0251	0651	4.3E
	1012	1337	5.1F
	1738	2021	2.8E
	2330		
12 F		0135	1.6F
	0351	0741	4.3E
	1059	1426	5.1F
	1820	2104	3.0E
13 Sa	0020	0232	1.7F
	0454	0828	4.0E
	1147	1515	4.8F
	1900	2145	3.1E
14 Su	0112	0329	1.9F
	0559	0919	3.5E
	1235	1601	4.3F
	1938	2233	3.1E
15 M	0204	0426	2.0F
	0706	1011	2.9E
	1326	1645	3.8F
	2014	2319	3.1E
16 Tu	0257	0526	2.1F
	0819	1111	2.2E
	1418	1727	3.1F
	2050		
17 W		0010	3.1E
	0349	0624	2.1F
	0944	1225	1.6E
	1515	1812	2.4F
	2127		
18 Th		0104	3.0E
	0441	0733	2.2F
	1119	1344	1.2E
	1620	1905	1.7F
	2207		
19 F		0157	3.0E
	0534	0850	2.4F
	1244	1507	1.0E
	1734	2002	1.2F
	2249		
20 Sa		0243	2.9E
	0626	1006	2.7F
	1353	1625	1.0E
	1858	2110	0.9F
	2335		
21 Su		0331	2.9E
	0716	1057	3.0F
	1448	1732	1.2E
	2013	2214	0.8F
22 M	0022	0420	2.9E
	0712	1136	3.3F
	1534	1827	1.5E
	2111	2303	0.8F
23 Tu	0108	0506	3.0E
	0844	1211	3.6F
	1613	1908	1.7E
	2156	2346	0.9F
24 W	0152	0555	3.1E
	0921	1246	3.7F
	1648	1939	1.9E
	2234		
25 Th		0027	1.0F
	0235	0632	3.1E
	0956	1315	3.8F
	1719	2008	2.1E
	2309		
26 F		0104	1.1F
	0318	0710	3.1E
	1029	1350	3.8F
	1747	2029	2.2E
	2344		
27 Sa		0145	1.2F
	0402	0745	3.1E
	1100	1422	3.7F
	1814	2056	2.4E
28 Su	0019	0228	1.3F
	0448	0818	3.0E
	1131	1456	3.6F
	1839	2122	2.5E
29 M	0054	0311	1.5F
	0535	0858	2.7E
	1203	1532	3.4F
	1902	2154	2.6E
30 Tu	0130	0354	1.6F
	0626	0935	2.4E
	1238	1608	3.1F
	1926	2226	2.7E
31 W	0208	0443	1.8F
	0724	1024	2.0E
	1320	1649	2.7F
	1952	2308	2.7E

AUGUST

Day	Slack Water Time h.m.	Maximum Current Time h.m.	Vel. knots
1 Th	0250	0532	2.0F
	0833	1121	1.6E
	1410	1730	2.3F
	2020	2353	2.8E
2 F	0336	0626	2.3F
	1001	1232	1.3E
	1514	1819	1.8F
	2056		
3 Sa		0050	2.9E
	0427	0729	2.5F
	1135	1348	1.2E
	1633	1916	1.4F
	2140		
4 Su		0147	3.1E
	0524	0845	2.9F
	1254	1505	1.2E
	1808	2024	1.1F
	2238		
5 M		0245	3.3E
	0624	0955	3.5F
	1358	1624	1.5E
	1935	2140	1.1F
	2345		
6 Tu		0345	3.5E
	0723	1056	4.1F
	1453	1733	1.9E
	2041	2245	1.3F
7 W	0052	0445	3.8E
	0819	1145	4.5F
	1541	1830	2.3E
	2133	2342	1.6F
8 Th	0156	0545	4.0E
	0911	1231	4.8F
	1625	1917	2.8E
	2219		
9 F		0032	1.9F
	0300	0640	4.1E
	1000	1318	4.8F
	1706	1955	3.1E
	2303		
10 Sa		0124	2.2F
	0402	0731	4.0E
	1046	1401	4.6F
	1743	2034	3.3E
	2346		
11 Su		0216	2.4F
	0503	0818	3.8E
	1132	1447	4.2F
	1818	2113	3.4E
12 M	0031	0309	2.6F
	0604	0906	3.3E
	1219	1530	3.7F
	1851	2149	3.4E
13 Tu	0118	0401	2.6F
	0705	0954	2.7E
	1306	1613	3.1F
	1923	2230	3.2E
14 W	0206	0455	2.6F
	0810	1050	2.0E
	1358	1655	2.4F
	1954	2313	3.0E
15 Th	0257	0546	2.5F
	0925	1157	1.4E
	1457	1737	1.8F
	2026		
16 F		0006	2.7E
	0349	0646	2.4F
	1051	1319	1.1E
	1605	1826	1.2F
	2102		
17 Sa		0105	2.6E
	0444	0756	2.4F
	1214	1443	1.0E
	1724	1922	0.8F
	2150		
18 Su		0201	2.5E
	0540	0919	2.5F
	1320	1606	1.1E
	1849	2039	0.6F
	2254		
19 M		0258	2.5E
	0637	1022	2.8F
	1412	1707	1.3E
	2000	2200	0.6F
20 Tu	0002	0352	2.5E
	0729	1110	3.1F
	1454	1755	1.6E
	2049	2251	0.9F
21 W	0100	0441	2.7E
	0815	1143	3.3F
	1530	1832	1.9E
	2128	2332	1.1F
22 Th	0151	0530	2.8E
	0856	1215	3.5F
	1602	1903	2.1E
	2200		
23 F		0011	1.4F
	0238	0613	2.9E
	0932	1245	3.6F
	1631	1926	2.4E
	2231		
24 Sa		0047	1.7F
	0324	0654	3.0E
	1006	1316	3.6F
	1658	1950	2.6E
	2301		
25 Su		0122	1.9F
	0409	0729	3.0E
	1039	1348	3.5F
	1722	2013	2.8E
	2330		
26 M		0203	2.1F
	0454	0806	2.9E
	1111	1420	3.3F
	1745	2041	2.9E
27 Tu	0000	0244	2.3F
	0541	0841	2.7E
	1146	1458	3.0F
	1807	2110	3.0E
28 W	0033	0329	2.5F
	0631	0922	2.4E
	1225	1535	2.6F
	1831	2142	3.0E
29 Th	0111	0415	2.7F
	0726	1011	2.1E
	1312	1616	2.2F
	1857	2223	3.0E
30 F	0155	0506	2.8F
	0831	1105	1.7E
	1411	1705	1.7F
	1928	2312	2.9E
31 Sa	0247	0601	2.9F
	0952	1222	1.4E
	1525	1755	1.3F
	2007		

1991 CURRENT TABLES — SAN JUAN CHANNEL

For Daylight Saving Time, add one hour.

Times and Heights of High and Low Waters

SEPTEMBER

Day	Slack Water Time h.m.	Maximum Current Time h.m.	Vel. knots	Day	Slack Water Time h.m.	Maximum Current Time h.m.	Vel. knots
1 Su		0013	2.8E	16 M		0115	2.0E
	0346	0704	3.0F		0448	0820	2.4F
	1120	1348	1.3E		1233	1533	1.3E
	1653	1858	0.9F		1839	2012	0.4F
	2101				2216		
2 M		0117	2.8E	17 Tu		0224	2.0E
	0451	0819	3.1F		0548	0932	2.5F
	1234	1504	1.5E		1321	1621	1.5E
	1822	2015	0.8F		1937	2139	0.6F
	2219				2347		
3 Tu		0228	3.0E	18 W		0320	2.1E
	0559	0934	3.5F		0646	1021	2.8F
	1333	1615	1.8E		1401	1704	1.8E
	1934	2137	1.0F		2019	2235	1.0F
	2348						
4 W		0334	3.2E	19 Th	0054	0415	2.3E
	0704	1038	3.9F		0738	1101	3.0F
	1423	1717	2.3E		1435	1743	2.1E
	2028	2245	1.5F		2052	2317	1.5F
5 Th	0105	0435	3.4E	20 F	0149	0504	2.4E
	0804	1128	4.2F		0823	1133	3.1F
	1507	1806	2.7E		1505	1810	2.4E
	2113	2336	2.0F		2122	2350	1.9F
6 F	0212	0539	3.5E	21 Sa	0238	0549	2.6E
	0857	1212	4.3F		0903	1205	3.2F
	1546	1847	3.1E		1532	1837	2.7E
	2154				2151		
7 Sa		0026	2.5F	22 Su		0027	2.3F
	0314	0634	3.6E		0325	0633	2.7E
	0946	1252	4.1F		0941	1237	3.1F
	1623	1924	3.4E		1558	1903	3.0E
	2233				2218		
8 Su		0112	2.9F	23 M		0100	2.7F
	0414	0723	3.5E		0411	0711	2.8E
	1033	1332	3.8F		1018	1309	3.0F
	1657	1959	3.6E		1622	1932	3.2E
	2312				2246		
9 M		0158	3.1F	24 Tu		0138	3.0F
	0511	0811	3.3E		0457	0750	2.7E
	1118	1413	3.3F		1056	1346	2.7F
	1728	2032	3.6E		1646	2001	3.4E
	2351				2316		
10 Tu		0247	3.2F	25 W		0220	3.3F
	0606	0853	2.9E		0545	0830	2.6E
	1203	1453	2.8F		1136	1427	2.4F
	1758	2106	3.5E		1711	2032	3.4E
					2349		
11 W	0031	0334	3.2F	26 Th		0303	3.5F
	0700	0938	2.4E		0634	0914	2.4E
	1251	1534	2.2F		1223	1508	2.0F
	1826	2141	3.2E		1738	2109	3.4E
12 Th	0114	0423	3.1F	27 F	0028	0352	3.5F
	0757	1029	1.9E		0729	1001	2.1E
	1345	1620	1.7F		1319	1554	1.6F
	1853	2222	2.9E		1809	2148	3.2E
13 F	0201	0511	2.9F	28 Sa	0115	0443	3.5F
	0900	1131	1.4E		0831	1100	1.8E
	1448	1705	1.2F		1429	1643	1.2F
	1922	2309	2.5E		1846	2239	3.0E
14 Sa	0252	0602	2.7F	29 Su	0210	0541	3.5F
	1014	1254	1.1E		0944	1220	1.6E
	1601	1754	0.8F		1549	1744	0.9F
	1955				1933	2347	2.7E
15 Su		0009	2.2E	30 M	0314	0642	3.4F
	0348	0703	2.5F		1100	1345	1.7E
	1130	1424	1.1E		1711	1851	0.7F
	1721	1851	0.5F		2043		
	2046						

OCTOBER

Day	Slack Water Time h.m.	Maximum Current Time h.m.	Vel. knots	Day	Slack Water Time h.m.	Maximum Current Time h.m.	Vel. knots
1 Tu		0103	2.6E	16 W		0138	1.7E
	0424	0755	3.3F		0448	0819	2.5F
	1205	1459	2.0E		1221	1528	1.8E
	1824	2014	0.8F		1903	2101	0.7F
	2229				2327		
2 W		0214	2.6E	17 Th		0240	1.7E
	0535	0908	3.4F		0549	0921	2.5F
	1259	1557	2.4E		1259	1605	2.1E
	1922	2140	1.3F		1940	2206	1.2F
3 Th	0007	0325	2.7E	18 F	0043	0337	1.8E
	0643	1009	3.5F		0648	1009	2.6F
	1344	1648	2.8E		1332	1640	2.5E
	2008	2243	2.0F		2012	2251	1.8F
4 F	0123	0431	2.8E	19 Sa	0141	0432	2.0E
	0746	1103	3.6F		0741	1048	2.7F
	1424	1733	3.1E		1401	1713	2.8E
	2049	2332	2.6F		2041	2326	2.4F
5 Sa	0228	0533	2.9E	20 Su	0233	0523	2.1E
	0842	1145	3.5F		0830	1126	2.7F
	1500	1814	3.5E		1428	1743	3.1E
	2127				2110		
6 Su		0015	3.2F	21 M		0002	2.9F
	0328	0628	3.0E		0322	0612	2.3E
	0933	1227	3.2F		0916	1201	2.6F
	1533	1849	3.7E		1454	1818	3.4E
	2204				2139		
7 M		0058	3.5F	22 Tu		0037	3.4F
	0423	0719	2.9E		0410	0655	2.5E
	1020	1303	2.9F		1000	1234	2.4F
	1604	1922	3.7E		1520	1850	3.6E
	2239				2209		
8 Tu		0139	3.7F	23 W		0118	3.8F
	0516	0802	2.7E		0458	0739	2.5E
	1106	1339	2.4F		1044	1312	2.1F
	1633	1956	3.7E		1548	1926	3.8E
	2315				2242		
9 W		0221	3.7F	24 Th		0159	4.1F
	0605	0844	2.5E		0546	0822	2.5E
	1153	1419	1.9F		1132	1355	1.8F
	1700	2029	3.5E		1619	2003	3.8E
	2350				2319		
10 Th		0307	3.6F	25 F		0244	4.3F
	0654	0926	2.1E		0636	0909	2.4E
	1243	1502	1.5F		1227	1444	1.5F
	1727	2100	3.2E		1653	2041	3.7E
11 F	0028	0352	3.5F	26 Sa	0001	0335	4.3F
	0743	1011	1.8E		0729	0959	2.2E
	1340	1545	1.1F		1331	1535	1.2F
	1753	2138	2.8E		1733	2126	3.5E
12 Sa	0109	0437	3.2F	27 Su	0050	0429	4.2F
	0836	1106	1.5E		0826	1100	2.0E
	1446	1633	0.7F		1444	1634	0.9F
	1822	2221	2.4E		1820	2219	3.1E
13 Su	0156	0524	3.0F	28 M	0146	0524	4.0F
	0935	1222	1.3E		0928	1216	2.0E
	1559	1725	0.5F		1558	1736	0.8F
	1858	2314	2.0E		1922	2324	2.7E
14 M	0249	0616	2.7F	29 Tu	0250	0623	3.7F
	1038	1348	1.4E		1031	1333	2.2E
	1711	1825	0.3F		1706	1849	0.8F
	1951				2052		
15 Tu		0023	1.7E	30 W		0046	2.3E
	0347	0713	2.5F		0359	0729	3.4F
	1134	1443	1.6E		1128	1435	2.5E
	1815	1936	0.4F		1806	2013	1.1F
	2133				2249		
				31 Th		0207	2.2E
					0509	0835	3.2F
					1216	1524	2.9E
					1858	2135	1.7F

SAN JUAN CHANNEL

1991 CURRENT TABLES

For Daylight Saving Time, add one hour.

Times and Heights of High and Low Waters

NOVEMBER

Day	Slack Water Time h.m.	Maximum Current Time h.m.	Vel. knots	Day	Slack Water Time h.m.	Maximum Current Time h.m.	Vel. knots
1 F	0024	0317	2.2E	16 Sa	0024	0257	1.4E
	0619	0940	3.0F		0547	0909	2.2F
	1258	1613	3.2E		1224	1540	2.7E
	1943	2238	2.4F		1926	2213	2.0F
2 Sa	0138	0425	2.2E	17 Su	0129	0356	1.5E
	0726	1032	2.8F		0653	0958	2.2F
	1336	1654	3.5E		1255	1616	3.1E
	2023	2325	3.1F		1958	2255	2.7F
3 Su	0241	0530	2.3E	18 M	0224	0454	1.7E
	0827	1113	2.6F		0756	1041	2.1F
	1410	1736	3.7E		1325	1655	3.4E
	2101				2031	2337	3.4F
4 M		0008	3.6F	19 Tu	0316	0551	1.9E
	0338	0631	2.3E		0853	1123	2.0F
	0921	1154	2.3F		1355	1733	3.7E
	1441	1815	3.7E		2104		
	2137						
5 Tu		0045	3.9F	20 W		0015	4.0F
	0430	0719	2.3E		0406	0644	2.2E
	1011	1232	2.0F		0946	1204	1.9F
	1511	1849	3.7E		1427	1816	3.9E
	2212				2140		
6 W		0125	4.0F	21 Th		0058	4.4F
	0518	0800	2.3E		0455	0733	2.4E
	1059	1312	1.6F		1037	1247	1.7F
	1539	1924	3.6E		1502	1858	4.1E
	2245				2218		
7 Th		0206	4.0F	22 F		0142	4.7F
	0603	0841	2.1E		0743	0816	2.5E
	1147	1348	1.3F		1130	1336	1.5F
	1606	1957	3.4E		1542	1941	4.1E
	2319				2259		
8 F		0244	3.9F	23 Sa		0232	4.9F
	0645	0916	2.0E		0632	0905	2.5E
	1238	1431	1.0F		1227	1427	1.3F
	1634	2028	3.2E		1627	2024	4.0E
	2353				2345		
9 Sa		0325	3.7F	24 Su		0321	4.8F
	0727	0957	1.8E		0721	0954	2.5E
	1335	1518	0.7F		1330	1523	1.1F
	1704	2103	2.9E		1718	2113	3.7E
10 Su	0030	0407	3.5F	25 M	0035	0414	4.6F
	0810	1046	1.6E		0811	1052	2.4E
	1438	1607	0.5F		1435	1626	1.0F
	1738	2145	2.5E		1818	2208	3.2E
11 M	0110	0451	3.3F	26 Tu	0129	0506	4.3F
	0856	1143	1.6E		0902	1158	2.5E
	1541	1659	0.4F		1539	1729	1.1F
	1821	2231	2.1E		1931	2310	2.7E
12 Tu	0156	0534	3.0F	27 W	0229	0600	3.9F
	0944	1251	1.6E		0953	1305	2.7E
	1640	1756	0.4F		1638	1838	1.2F
	1920	2331	1.7E		2108		
13 W	0247	0622	2.8F	28 Th		0027	2.1E
	1030	1346	1.8E		0333	0655	3.3F
	1731	1859	0.5F		1042	1402	2.9E
	2054				1734	1955	1.5F
					2259		
14 Th		0045	1.4E	29 F		0149	1.8E
	0343	0715	2.6F		0441	0753	2.8F
	1113	1429	2.1E		1127	1451	3.2E
	1814	2014	0.8F		1825	2118	2.1F
	2256						
15 F		0155	1.4E	30 Sa	0032	0305	1.7E
	0443	0809	2.4F		0553	0858	2.4F
	1151	1505	2.4E		1209	1537	3.4E
	1851	2118	1.3F		1913	2226	2.8F

DECEMBER

Day	Slack Water Time h.m.	Maximum Current Time h.m.	Vel. knots	Day	Slack Water Time h.m.	Maximum Current Time h.m.	Vel. knots
1 Su	0147	0420	1.6E	16 M	0111	0321	1.2E
	0706	0958	2.0F		0605	0906	1.7F
	1247	1622	3.5E		1148	1527	3.2E
	1956	2315	3.3F		1913	2227	2.9F
2 M	0250	0530	1.7E	17 Tu	0212	0427	1.3E
	0815	1047	1.8F		0726	1001	1.5F
	1322	1703	3.6E		1226	1613	3.5E
	2037	2358	3.7F		1954	2312	3.6F
3 Tu	0345	0629	1.8E	18 W	0307	0533	1.6E
	0915	1130	1.5F		0837	1054	1.5F
	1355	1742	3.6E		1306	1659	3.8E
	2114				2036	2354	4.3F
4 W		0033	4.0F	19 Th	0358	0633	2.0E
	0433	0718	1.9E		0936	1141	1.5F
	1007	1211	1.3F		1349	1748	4.0E
	1426	1823	3.6E		2118		
	2149						
5 Th		0112	4.1F	20 F		0042	4.8F
	0516	0801	2.0E		0446	0722	2.3E
	1055	1246	1.1F		1030	1229	1.5F
	1457	1900	3.5E		1435	1837	4.3E
	2223				2202		
6 F		0147	4.1F	21 Sa		0128	5.1F
	0555	0834	2.0E		0533	0810	2.6E
	1141	1328	0.9F		1121	1320	1.4F
	1528	1934	3.4E		1526	1926	4.3E
	2256				2247		
7 Sa		0224	4.0F	22 Su		0217	5.2F
	0631	0909	2.0E		0618	0856	2.7E
	1228	1411	0.8F		1214	1415	1.4F
	1602	2009	3.2E		1622	2014	4.2E
	2329				2333		
8 Su		0301	3.9F	23 M		0306	5.1F
	0707	0940	1.9E		0702	0941	2.8E
	1317	1456	0.7F		1309	1512	1.5F
	1639	2044	3.0E		1723	2103	3.9E
9 M	0002	0342	3.7F	24 Tu	0022	0354	4.8F
	0741	1015	1.9E		0744	1030	2.9E
	1408	1545	0.6F		1406	1615	1.5F
	1721	2120	2.6E		1829	2156	3.3E
10 Tu	0037	0420	3.5F	25 W	0114	0443	4.3F
	0816	1057	1.9E		0826	1125	2.9E
	1459	1632	0.6F		1502	1715	1.7F
	1810	2203	2.3E		1944	2257	2.6E
11 W	0115	0500	3.3F	26 Th	0209	0532	3.7F
	0850	1145	2.0E		0908	1220	3.0E
	1547	1725	0.7F		1558	1819	1.8F
	1909	2252	1.8E		2113		
12 Th	0157	0539	3.0F	27 F		0009	2.0E
	0925	1235	2.1E		0309	0621	3.0F
	1632	1820	0.8F		0950	1317	3.1E
	2029	2353	1.4E		1652	1929	2.0F
					2256		
13 F	0244	0622	2.6F	28 Sa		0130	1.5E
	1000	1323	2.3E		0414	0715	2.3F
	1714	1920	1.1F		1033	1409	3.2E
	2217				1746	2052	2.3F
14 Sa		0104	1.2E	29 Su	0030	0255	1.3E
	0340	0711	2.3F		0528	0817	1.7F
	1036	1403	2.6E		1115	1459	3.3E
	1754	2025	1.5F		1838	2207	2.8F
	2357						
15 Su		0216	1.1E	30 M	0147	0416	1.2E
	0447	0804	1.9F		0650	0921	1.3F
	1111	1445	2.9E		1158	1545	3.3E
	1834	2131	2.2F		1927	2300	3.3F
				31 Tu	0249	0529	1.4E
					0807	1022	1.1F
					1240	1634	3.3E
					2012	2344	3.6F

1991 CURRENT TABLES

ACTIVE PASS

For Daylight Saving Time, add one hour.

Times and Heights of High and Low Waters

JANUARY

Day	Slack Water Time (h.m.)	Maximum Current Time (h.m.)	Vel. (knots)
1 Tu		0150	6.9F
	0530	0825	4.7E
	1150	1400	2.2F
	1610	1955	5.7E
	2305		
2 W		0240	6.8F
	0615	0915	5.0E
	1240	1455	2.5F
	1710	2045	5.3E
	2355		
3 Th		0325	6.4F
	0655	1000	5.1E
	1330	1550	2.7F
	1815	2140	4.8E
4 F	0045	0410	5.7F
	0730	1040	5.0E
	1415	1640	2.7F
	1915	2230	4.0E
5 Sa	0130	0450	4.8F
	0805	1125	4.8E
	1500	1735	2.7F
	2020	2320	3.2E
6 Su	0215	0535	3.9F
	0840	1210	4.5E
	1550	1830	2.6F
	2125		
7 M		0015	2.4E
	0305	0615	3.0F
	0915	1255	4.2E
	1640	1930	2.5F
	2240		
8 Tu		0120	1.8E
	0405	0705	2.1F
	0950	1340	3.8E
	1730	2030	2.6F
9 W	0000	0235	1.5E
	0525	0805	1.4F
	1030	1435	3.5E
	1815	2135	2.8F
10 Th	0115	0400	1.6E
	0705	0910	0.9F
	1105	1525	3.4E
	1900	2230	3.3F
11 F	0215	0510	2.0E
	0845	1020	0.6F
	1150	1615	3.4E
	1940	2320	4.0F
12 Sa	0310	0605	2.5E
	1000	1120	0.4F
	1235	1705	3.6E
	2025		
13 Su		0005	4.5F
	0355	0655	2.9E
	1050	1210	0.5F
	1325	1750	3.8E
	2105		
14 M		0045	5.0F
	0435	0735	3.3E
	1130	1255	0.6F
	1420	1830	4.1E
	2145		
15 Tu		0125	5.3F
	0510	0810	3.5E
	1155	1335	0.9F
	1510	1915	4.2E
	2230		
16 W		0205	5.3F
	0545	0845	3.6E
	1220	1415	1.3F
	1605	1955	4.3E
	2310		
17 Th		0240	5.1F
	0615	0915	3.7E
	1245	1450	1.6F
	1655	2035	4.2E
	2350		
18 F		0315	4.8F
	0640	0945	3.8E
	1310	1530	2.0F
	1745	2115	3.9E
19 Sa	0025	0345	4.3F
	0700	1010	3.9E
	1335	1605	2.3F
	1840	2155	3.6E
20 Su	0100	0415	3.9F
	0725	1040	4.1E
	1410	1645	2.5F
	1930	2235	3.1E
21 M	0135	0445	3.5F
	0750	1115	4.2E
	1450	1735	2.7F
	2030	2325	2.6E
22 Tu	0220	0525	3.0F
	0815	1155	4.3E
	1535	1825	2.8F
	2140		
23 W		0025	2.1E
	0310	0610	2.4F
	0850	1240	4.3E
	1625	1930	3.1F
	2300		
24 Th		0135	1.8E
	0425	0710	1.8F
	0935	1340	4.3E
	1725	2045	3.5F
25 F	0025	0305	1.9E
	0600	0820	1.3F
	1030	1445	4.4E
	1825	2155	4.2F
26 Sa	0140	0425	2.4E
	0740	0945	1.1F
	1135	1555	4.6E
	1920	2255	5.1F
27 Su	0245	0535	3.1E
	0900	1100	1.3F
	1250	1655	4.9E
	2020	2355	5.8F
28 M	0335	0630	3.8E
	0955	1205	1.7F
	1405	1755	5.2E
	2110		
29 Tu		0045	6.3F
	0420	0720	4.5E
	1045	1300	2.3F
	1510	1850	5.4E
	2205		
30 W		0135	6.4F
	0505	0805	4.9E
	1130	1350	2.8F
	1615	1945	5.4E
	2255		
31 Th		0220	6.3F
	0545	0850	5.2E
	1210	1440	3.2F
	1715	2035	5.2E
	2345		

FEBRUARY

Day	Slack Water Time (h.m.)	Maximum Current Time (h.m.)	Vel. (knots)
1 F		0300	5.8F
	0620	0930	5.2E
	1250	1530	3:5F
	1810	2125	4.7E
2 Sa	0030	0340	5.1F
	0655	1005	5.1E
	1330	1615	3.5F
	1905	2210	4.1E
3 Su	0115	0420	4.2F
	0725	1045	4.8E
	1410	1700	3.4F
	2000	2255	3.3E
4 M	0155	0500	3.3F
	0750	1120	4.5E
	1455	1745	3.1F
	2055	2345	2.5E
5 Tu	0245	0535	2.5F
	0820	1200	4.0E
	1540	1840	2.8F
	2200		
6 W		0045	1.9E
	0340	0620	1.6F
	0845	1240	3.5E
	1625	1935	2.7F
	2315		
7 Th		0155	1.5E
	0500	0710	0.9F
	0915	1335	3.1E
	1715	2045	2.7F
8 F	0035	0325	1.5E
	0705	0825	0.3F
	0945	1435	2.8E
	1810	2150	3.1F
9 Sa	0145	0445	1.9E
	0905	0950	0.1F
	1035	1540	2.9E
	1905	2250	3.6F
10 Su	0235	0545	2.4E
	0955	1100	0.3F
	1205	1635	3.1E
	1955	2335	4.2F
11 M	0320	0625	2.9E
	1020	1150	0.6F
	1320	1730	3.5E
	2040		
12 Tu		0020	4.6F
	0400	0705	3.3E
	1045	1235	1.1F
	1420	1815	4.0E
	2130		
13 W		0100	4.9F
	0435	0735	3.6E
	1105	1310	1.7F
	1520	1900	4.3E
	2215		
14 Th		0140	4.9F
	0505	0805	3.8E
	1125	1350	2.3F
	1610	1945	4.5E
	2255		
15 F		0215	4.7F
	0530	0835	4.0E
	1150	1425	2.8F
	1700	2025	4.4E
	2335		
16 Sa		0245	4.4F
	0555	0900	4.2E
	1215	1500	3.3F
	1750	2105	4.2E
17 Su	0015	0315	4.0F
	0615	0930	4.5E
	1250	1540	3.5F
	1835	2145	3.8E
18 M	0050	0345	3.6F
	0640	1000	4.6E
	1325	1620	3.7F
	1930	2225	3.3E
19 Tu	0125	0420	3.1F
	0705	1040	4.7E
	1405	1710	3.7F
	2025	2310	2.8E
20 W	0210	0500	2.6F
	0735	1120	4.6E
	1455	1800	3.6F
	2130		
21 Th		0010	2.3E
	0305	0545	2.0F
	0815	1210	4.3E
	1550	1905	3.5F
	2245		
22 F		0125	2.0E
	0425	0650	1.3F
	0900	1310	4.0E
	1650	2020	3.7F
23 Sa	0005	0255	2.1E
	0615	0815	0.9F
	1005	1425	3.8E
	1755	2135	4.1F
24 Su	0120	0415	2.6E
	0750	0945	1.0F
	1130	1540	4.0E
	1900	2240	4.7F
25 M	0215	0520	3.4E
	0850	1100	1.5F
	1300	1650	4.3E
	2005	2335	5.2F
26 Tu	0305	0610	4.1E
	0940	1200	2.2F
	1415	1750	4.7E
	2100		
27 W		0025	5.5F
	0350	0655	4.7E
	1020	1250	2.9F
	1520	1845	5.0E
	2155		
28 Th		0115	5.5F
	0430	0735	5.0E
	1055	1335	3.5F
	1615	1935	5.1E
	2245		

ACTIVE PASS

1991 CURRENT TABLES

For DaylFor Daylight Saving Time, add one hour.

Times and Heights of High and Low Waters

MARCH

Day	Slack Water Time h.m.	Maximum Current Time h.m.	Vel. knots	Day	Slack Water Time h.m.	Maximum Current Time h.m.	Vel. knots
1 F		0155	5.2F	16 Sa		0140	4.0F
	0505	0815	5.1E		0440	0750	4.4E
	1130	1420	4.0F		1100	1355	4.0F
	17.10	2025	4.9E		1655	2010	4.5E
	2335				2320		
2 Sa		0235	4.7F	17 Su		0215	3.8F
	0540	0850	5.1E		0505	0820	4.7E
	1205	1500	4.2F		1130	1435	4.5F
	1800	2110	4.6E		1745	2050	4.3E
3 Su	0020	0315	4.1F	18 M	0000	0245	3.4F
	0610	0925	4.9E		0530	0855	5.0E
	1245	1545	4.2F		1210	1520	4.7F
	1850	2150	4.0E		1835	2135	4.0E
4 M	0100	0350	3.3F	19 Tu	0040	0320	3.0F
	0635	1000	4.7E		0600	0930	5.1E
	1320	1625	4.0F		1250	1605	4.8F
	1940	2235	3.3E		1925	2220	3.5E
5 Tu	0145	0425	2.6F	20 W	0125	0400	2.6F
	0700	1035	4.3E		0630	1010	5.0E
	1400	1705	3.7F		1335	1650	4.6F
	2030	2320	2.7E		2020	2310	3.0E
6 W	0230	0500	1.8F	21 Th	0215	0445	2.1F
	0725	1110	3.8E		0705	1055	4.6E
	1440	1750	3.3F		1425	1745	4.3F
	2125				2120		
7 Th		0015	2.1E	22 F		0010	2.7E
	0330	0540	1.1F		0325	0540	1.5F
	0745	1150	3.2E		0750	1150	4.1E
	1520	1845	2.9F		1520	1845	4.0F
	2230				2230		
8 F		0120	1.7E	23 Sa		0125	2.5E
	0455	0635	0.5F		0450	0655	1.0F
	0805	1235	2.8E		0850	1255	3.6E
	1615	1950	2.8F		1620	1955	3.9F
	2345				2340		
9 Sa		0245	1.7E	24 Su		0245	2.7E
	0725	0755	0.0		0630	0825	0.9F
	0825	1340	2.4E		1015	1415	3.2E
	1715	2100	2.9F		1735	2110	4.0F
10 Su	0050	0405	2.0E	25 M	0045	0355	3.3E
	0850	0925	0.1F		0740	0945	1.3F
	1000	1500	2.4E		1155	1535	3.3E
	1820	2205	3.2F		1845	2215	4.2F
11 M	0145	0500	2.5E	26 Tu	0140	0455	3.9E
	0905	1035	0.5F		0830	1055	2.0F
	1200	1610	2.7E		1320	1645	3.7E
	1920	2300	3.7F		1950	2310	4.4F
12 Tu	0230	0545	3.0E	27 W	0225	0545	4.4E
	0925	1125	1.1F		0910	1145	2.8F
	1320	1705	3.3E		1425	1745	4.1E
	2015	2345	4.0F		2050		
13 W	0310	0615	3.4E	28 Th		0000	4.5F
	0945	1205	1.8F		0310	0625	4.7E
	1420	1755	3.8E		0945	1235	3.6F
	2105				1520	1835	4.4E
					2145		
14 Th		0025	4.2F	29 F		0045	4.3F
	0345	0650	3.7E		0350	0705	4.9E
	1005	1240	2.6F		1020	1315	4.2F
	1515	1840	4.3E		1615	1925	4.6E
	2155				2235		
15		0105	4.2F	30 Sa		0130	4.0F
	0410	0720	4.1E		0420	0740	4.9E
	0	1320	3.4E		1050	1355	4.6F
		1925	4.5E		1705	2010	4.5E
					2325		
				31 Su		0210	3.4F
					0450	0815	4.8E
					1125	1435	4.8F
					1750	2055	4.2E

APRIL

Day	Slack Water Time h.m.	Maximum Current Time h.m.	Vel. knots	Day	Slack Water Time h.m.	Maximum Current Time h.m.	Vel. knots
1 M	0010	0245	2.9F	16 Tu		0220	2.7F
	0520	0845	4.6E		0445	0820	5.4E
	1200	1515	4.7F		1140	1500	5.7F
	1840	2135	3.8E		1830	2125	4.1E
2 Tu	0055	0320	2.3F	17 W	0040	0305	2.4F
	0545	0920	4.4E		0520	0905	5.4E
	1235	1555	4.5F		1225	1545	5.7F
	1925	2220	3.3E		1920	2215	3.8E
3 W	0140	0355	1.7F	18 Th	0135	0350	2.1F
	0605	0950	4.0E		0605	0950	5.1E
	1310	1635	4.2F		1310	1635	5.4F
	2010	2305	2.8E		2015	2310	3.5E
4 Th	0230	0435	1.1F	19 F	0235	0445	1.7F
	0630	1025	3.5E		0650	1040	4.5E
	1350	1715	3.7F		1400	1730	4.9F
	2055	2355	2.4E		2110		
5 F	0335	0515	0.6F	20 Sa		0010	3.4F
	0655	1105	3.0E		0345	0545	1.4F
	1430	1805	3.3F		0750	1140	3.8E
	2150				1455	1830	4.4F
					2205		
6 Sa		0055	2.2E	21 Su		0115	3.4F
	0505	0610	0.3F		0500	0705	1.2F
	0720	1155	2.5E		0905	1250	3.2E
	1515	1900	3.0F		1600	1930	4.0F
	2245				2300		
7 Su		0200	2.1E	22 M		0225	3.6F
	0645	0730	0.1F		0615	0825	1.4F
	0815	1300	2.2E		1040	1405	2.8E
	1620	2005	2.8F		1710	2040	3.7F
	2345				2355		
8 M		0310	2.4E	23 Tu		0325	3.9E
	0730	0850	0.3F		0710	0940	2.0F
	1010	1420	2.1E		1215	1525	2.8E
	1730	2110	2.9F		1820	2145	3.6F
9 Tu	0040	0400	2.7E	24 W	0050	0420	4.2E
	0755	0955	0.9F		0755	1040	2.7F
	1155	1535	2.4E		1330	1635	3.1E
	1840	2205	3.1F		1930	2240	3.5F
10 W	0125	0445	3.1E	25 Th	0140	0505	4.4E
	0820	1045	1.7F		0835	1130	3.4F
	1310	1635	3.0E		1430	1730	3.5E
	1940	2255	3.3F		2035	2330	3.3F
11 Th	0205	0520	3.6E	26 F	0220	0550	4.6E
	0840	1125	2.6F		0905	1210	4.1F
	1410	1730	3.5E		1520	1825	3.8E
	2040	2340	3.4F		2135		
12 F	0240	0555	4.0E	27 Sa		0020	3.0F
	0910	1205	3.5F		0300	0625	4.6E
	1505	1820	4.0E		0940	1255	4.6F
	2130				1610	1910	4.0E
					2230		
13 Sa		0020	3.3F	28 Su		0100	2.6F
	0310	0630	4.4E		0330	0700	4.6E
	0940	1250	4.4F		1015	1330	4.9F
	1555	1905	4.3E		1655	2000	3.9E
	2220				2320		
14 Su		0100	3.2F	29 M		0140	2.2F
	0340	0705	4.9E		0400	0735	4.5E
	1015	1330	5.1F		1045	1410	5.1F
	1650	1950	4.4E		1745	2045	3.8E
	2305						
15 M		0140	3.0F	30 Tu	0010	0220	1.7F
	0410	0740	5.2E		0425	0810	4.3E
	1055	1415	5.5F		1120	1450	5.1F
	1740	2040	4.3E		1830	2125	3.5E
	2350						

1991 CURRENT TABLES

ACTIVE PASS

For Daylight Saving Time, add one hour.

Times and Heights of High and Low Waters

SEPTEMBER

Day	Slack Water Time h.m.	Maximum Current Time h.m.	Vel. knots
1 Su	0315	0635	3.6F
	1015	1255	2.0E
	1600	1815	1.3F
	2025		
2 M		0035	4.0E
	0415	0740	3.7F
	1130	1415	2.1E
	1740	1935	0.9F
	2130		
3 Tu		0145	3.8E
	0520	0855	4.0F
	1240	1540	2.6E
	1910	2105	1.0F
	2300		
4 W		0305	3.8E
	0625	1000	4.5F
	1340	1645	3.3E
	2015	2225	1.5F
5 Th	0030	0415	4.1E
	0730	1100	5.0F
	1430	1735	4.1E
	2100	2325	2.3F
6 F	0145	0520	4.6E
	0830	1155	5.3F
	1515	1820	4.7E
	2145		
7 Sa		0020	3.1F
	0255	0615	5.0E
	0925	1240	5.4F
	1555	1905	5.1E
	2220		
8 Su		0105	3.8F
	0350	0710	5.1E
	1020	1325	5.2F
	1635	1945	5.3E
	2300		
9 M		0155	4.4F
	0450	0800	5.1E
	1110	1410	4.7F
	1710	2025	5.4E
	2340		
10 Tu		0240	4.7F
	0540	0850	4.8E
	1200	1450	4.1F
	1745	2100	5.2E
11 W	0020	0325	4.7F
	0635	0935	4.2E
	1245	1530	3.3F
	1815	2140	4.9E
12 Th	0100	0405	4.5F
	0725	1020	3.6E
	1335	1610	2.6F
	1840	2215	4.5E
13 F	0140	0450	4.1F
	0820	1110	2.9E
	1425	1650	1.8F
	1910	2255	3.9E
14 Sa	0220	0540	3.7F
	0915	1205	2.4E
	1530	1735	1.1F
	1935	2335	3.3E
15 Su	0305	0630	3.2F
	1015	1310	2.0E
	1700	1830	0.5F
	2000		
16 M		0025	2.8E
	0355	0730	3.0F
	1120	1430	2.0E
	1900	1950	0.1F
	2040		
17 Tu		0130	2.3E
	0455	0840	3.0F
	1225	1545	2.3E
	2015	2115	0.2F
	2220		
18 W		0245	2.3E
	0600	0940	3.2F
	1320	1640	2.8E
	2045	2225	0.6F
19 Th	0005	0355	2.5E
	0700	1035	3.5F
	1405	1720	3.2E
	2105	2310	1.3F
20 F	0115	0450	3.0E
	0755	1125	3.8F
	1445	1755	3.5E
	2125	2350	2.0F
21 Sa	0215	0540	3.5E
	0850	1205	3.9F
	1515	1825	3.8E
	2145		
22 Su		0025	2.7F
	0305	0625	4.0E
	0935	1240	3.9F
	1545	1855	4.1E
	2210		
23 M		0100	3.4F
	0355	0710	4.2E
	1020	1320	3.7F
	1615	1925	4.3E
	2235		
24 Tu		0140	4.0F
	0440	0750	4.2E
	1105	1350	3.3F
	1635	1955	4.6E
	2310		
25 W		0215	4.4F
	0530	0830	4.0E
	1145	1425	3.0F
	1700	2030	4.8E
	2345		
26 Th		0255	4.7F
	0615	0915	3.7E
	1225	1500	2.6F
	1725	2105	4.9E
27 F	0025	0340	4.7F
	0705	1000	3.3E
	1305	1535	2.3F
	1755	2140	4.8E
28 Sa	0105	0425	4.6F
	0800	1045	3.0E
	1355	1615	1.8F
	1830	2225	4.6E
29 Su	0150	0515	4.4F
	0855	1145	2.7E
	1500	1710	1.4F
	1915	2315	4.1E
30 M	0245	0610	4.1F
	0955	1250	2.6E
	1620	1820	1.0F
	2015		

OCTOBER

Day	Slack Water Time h.m.	Maximum Current Time h.m.	Vel. knots
1 Tu		0020	3.6E
	0345	0720	3.9F
	1100	1405	2.8E
	1750	1945	0.9F
	2140		
2 W		0135	3.2E
	0455	0830	3.9F
	1205	1520	3.3E
	1900	2110	1.4F
	2320		
3 Th		0300	3.2E
	0605	0935	4.1F
	1300	1615	3.9E
	1950	2220	2.1F
4 F	0050	0410	3.5E
	0715	1035	4.3F
	1350	1705	4.5E
	2035	2315	3.0F
5 Sa	0200	0515	4.0E
	0820	1130	4.4F
	1435	1750	4.9E
	2110		
6 Su		0005	3.8F
	0300	0610	4.4E
	0915	1215	4.3F
	1515	1830	5.1E
	2150		
7 M		0050	4.5F
	0350	0700	4.6E
	1010	1300	4.0F
	1550	1910	5.2E
	2225		
8 Tu		0130	5.0F
	0445	0745	4.6E
	1100	1345	3.5F
	1625	1945	5.2E
	2300		
9 W		0215	5.2F
	0535	0835	4.3E
	1150	1425	2.9F
	1655	2025	4.9E
	2340		
10 Th		0255	5.2F
	0620	0920	3.9E
	1240	1505	2.3F
	1725	2100	4.6E
11 F	0015	0340	4.9F
	0710	1005	3.5E
	1330	1540	1.6F
	1750	2135	4.2E
12 Sa	0055	0420	4.5F
	0755	1055	3.0E
	1425	1620	1.1F
	1815	2210	3.7E
13 Su	0130	0500	4.0F
	0845	1145	2.6E
	1535	1710	0.6F
	1845	2250	3.0E
14 M	0215	0550	3.5F
	0935	1245	2.4E
	1700	1810	0.3F
	1920	2340	2.5E
15 Tu	0300	0640	3.1F
	1025	1345	2.4E
	1825	1925	0.2F
	2025		
16 W		0045	2.0E
	0355	0745	2.9F
	1120	1450	2.6E
	1915	2045	0.4F
	2215		
17 Th		0205	1.9E
	0505	0845	2.8F
	1215	1540	2.9E
	1940	2145	1.0F
	2355		
18 F		0320	2.2E
	0620	0945	2.9F
	1300	1625	3.3E
	2005	2235	1.8F
19 Sa	0105	0420	2.7E
	0725	1035	3.0F
	1340	1700	3.6E
	2025	2315	2.6F
20 Su	0200	0515	3.2E
	0820	1120	3.1F
	1415	1735	4.0E
	2055	2350	3.5F
21 M	0255	0600	3.7E
	0910	1200	3.0F
	1445	1810	4.4E
	2120		
22 Tu		0030	4.3F
	0345	0645	3.9E
	1000	1240	2.9F
	1515	1840	4.8E
	2155		
23 W		0110	4.9F
	0435	0735	4.0E
	1050	1315	2.6F
	1540	1915	5.1E
	2235		
24 Th		0155	5.4F
	0520	0820	4.0E
	1135	1355	2.4F
	1615	1955	5.3E
	2315		
25 F		0235	5.7F
	0610	0905	3.8E
	1220	1435	2.1F
	1650	2035	5.3E
	2355		
26 Sa		0325	5.7F
	0700	0950	3.6E
	1310	1520	1.9F
	1730	2120	5.1E
27 Su	0040	0410	5.4F
	0750	1045	3.5E
	1405	1615	1.6F
	1815	2210	4.6E
28 M	0130	0500	5.0F
	0840	1140	3.4E
	1515	1715	1.4F
	1915	2305	3.9E
29 Tu	0220	0555	4.6F
	0930	1240	3.4E
	1625	1825	1.2F
	2030		
30 W		0010	3.3E
	0320	0655	4.1F
	1025	1345	3.6F
	1735	1945	1.7
	2200		
31 Th		0130	
	0430	0800	
	1120	1450	
	1835	210	
	2340		

ACTIVE PASS

1991 CURRENT TABLES

For DaylFor Daylight Saving Time, add one hour.

Times and Heights of High and Low Waters

NOVEMBER

Day	Slack Water Time h.m.	Maximum Current Time h.m.	Vel. knots
1		0250	2.7E
F	0545	0905	3.6F
	1215	1545	4.3E
	1920	2205	2.7F
2	0100	0400	3.0E
Sa	0655	1005	3.5F
	1305	1635	4.6E
	2005	2300	3.5F
3	0205	0505	3.4E
Su	0805	1100	3.3F
	1350	1720	4.8E
	2040	2345	4.3F
4	0300	0600	3.7E
M	0905	1150	3.0F
	1430	1800	4.9E
	2115		
5		0030	4.8F
Tu	0350	0650	4.0E
	1005	1235	2.7F
	1505	1835	4.9E
	2150		
6		0110	5.3F
W	0440	0740	4.0E
	1100	1320	2.2F
	1535	1915	4.8E
	2225		
7		0155	5.5F
Th	0525	0825	3.9E
	1150	1400	1.8F
	1605	1950	4.7E
	2305		
8		0235	5.4F
F	0610	0910	3.7E
	1245	1440	1.4F
	1635	2025	4.4E
	2340		
9		0315	5.2F
Sa	0655	0955	3.5E
	1335	1520	1.0F
	1705	2100	4.0E
10	0020	0355	4.8F
Su	0735	1040	3.2E
	1430	1605	0.7F
	1740	2140	3.5E
11	0055	0435	4.4F
M	0815	1120	3.0E
	1525	1650	0.6F
	1820	2220	3.0E
12	0135	0515	3.9F
Tu	0855	1210	2.9E
	1620	1745	0.5F
	1910	2310	2.4E
13	0215	0555	3.4F
W	0935	1255	2.9E
	1715	1845	0.5F
	2025		
14		0005	2.0E
Th	0310	0645	2.9F
	1015	1345	2.9E
	1755	1955	0.8F
	2155		
15		0120	1.8E
F	0410	0745	2.6F
	1100	1435	3.1E
	1830	2055	1.4F
	2330		

Day	Slack Water Time h.m.	Maximum Current Time h.m.	Vel. knots
16		0235	1.8E
Sa	0525	0845	2.4F
	1145	1520	3.4E
	1900	2150	2.1F
17	0045	0340	2.2E
Su	0640	0940	2.3F
	1225	1605	3.8E
	1935	2235	3.0F
18	0145	0440	2.7E
M	0745	1030	2.3F
	1305	1645	4.2E
	2005	2320	4.0F
19	0240	0535	3.1E
Tu	0845	1115	2.2F
	1340	1725	4.7E
	2040		
20		0005	4.9F
W	0335	0630	3.5E
	0940	1200	2.1F
	1415	1805	5.1E
	2120		
21		0050	5.6F
Th	0425	0715	3.8E
	1035	1250	2.0F
	1455	1845	5.5E
	2205		
22		0135	6.2F
F	0515	0805	4.0E
	1125	1335	2.0F
	1540	1930	5.6E
	2250		
23		0220	6.4F
Sa	0600	0855	4.1E
	1215	1425	1.9F
	1625	2020	5.6E
	2335		
24		0310	6.3F
Su	0650	0945	4.2E
	1310	1515	1.9F
	1720	2110	5.2E
25	0025	0355	6.0F
M	0735	1035	4.2E
	1405	1615	1.9F
	1820	2200	4.6E
26	0115	0445	5.5F
Tu	0815	1125	4.3E
	1500	1715	1.9F
	1930	2300	3.9E
27	0205	0535	4.9F
W	0900	1220	4.3E
	1600	1820	1.9F
	2045		
28		0000	3.2E
Th	0300	0630	4.2F
	0950	1315	4.3E
	1700	1930	2.1F
	2210		
29		0115	2.6E
F	0405	0725	3.5F
	1035	1410	4.4E
	1755	2040	2.5F
	2340		
30		0230	2.4E
Sa	0520	0830	3.0F
	1125	1505	4.4E
	1845	2145	3.1F

DECEMBER

Day	Slack Water Time h.m.	Maximum Current Time h.m.	Vel. knots
1	0055	0345	2.4E
Su	0635	0935	2.5F
	1215	1600	4.5E
	1930	2240	3.7F
2	0200	0450	2.7E
M	0755	1030	2.2F
	1300	1645	4.5E
	2010	2330	4.3F
3	0255	0550	3.1E
Tu	0905	1125	1.9F
	1340	1730	4.5E
	2045		
4		0015	4.9F
W	0345	0645	3.4E
	1005	1215	1.6F
	1415	1805	4.5E
	2125		
5		0055	5.3F
Th	0435	0730	3.6E
	1105	1300	1.3F
	1450	1845	4.5E
	2200		
6		0135	5.5F
F	0520	0820	3.7E
	1200	1345	1.1F
	1525	1925	4.4E
	2235		
7		0215	5.5F
Sa	0600	0900	3.6E
	1245	1425	0.9F
	1600	2000	4.2E
	2315		
8		0255	5.4F
Su	0640	0940	3.6E
	1330	1505	0.9F
	1640	2040	3.9E
	2355		
9		0330	5.0F
M	0715	1015	3.5E
	1405	1545	0.9F
	1730	2120	3.5E
10	0030	0405	4.6F
Tu	0745	1055	3.4E
	1445	1630	0.9F
	1820	2200	3.1E
11	0110	0440	4.0F
W	0815	1125	3.3E
	1520	1715	1.0F
	1910	2245	2.6E
12	0145	0520	3.5F
Th	0840	1205	3.3E
	1600	1805	1.1F
	2015	2335	2.2E
13	0230	0555	3.0F
F	0915	1245	3.3E
	1640	1900	1.4F
	2130		
14		0030	1.8E
Sa	0320	0640	2.5F
	0945	1325	3.4E
	1720	1955	1.8F
	2250		
15		0140	1.7E
Su	0430	0735	2.1F
	1025	1415	3.6E
	1800	2100	2.4F

Day	Slack Water Time h.m.	Maximum Current Time h.m.	Vel. knot
16	0015	0255	1.8
M	0545	0835	1.8
	1110	1505	3.9
	1840	2155	3.3
17	0125	0410	2.1
Tu	0705	0935	1.6
	1155	1555	4.3
	1925	2250	4.2
18	0225	0515	2.6
W	0820	1035	1.6
	1240	1645	4.8
	2010	2340	5.2
19	0320	0610	3.2
Th	0925	1130	1.6
	1330	1735	5.3
	2055		
20		0030	5.9F
F	0410	0705	3.7E
	1020	1225	1.7F
	1425	1825	5.7E
	2145		
21		0120	6.5F
Sa	0500	0755	4.1E
	1115	1320	2.0F
	1525	1915	5.8E
	2235		
22		0205	6.8F
Su	0545	0840	4.5E
	1205	1415	2.2F
	1625	2010	5.7E
	2325		
23		0255	6.7F
M	0630	0930	4.8E
	1250	1510	2.5F
	1725	2100	5.4E
24	0010	0340	6.3F
Tu	0710	1015	5.0E
	1340	1605	2.7F
	1830	2155	4.8E
25	0100	0425	5.7F
W	0750	1100	5.0E
	1430	1700	2.8F
	1935	2250	4.1E
26	0150	0510	4.9F
Th	0830	1145	4.9E
	1525	1800	2.8F
	2045	2345	3.3E
27	0240	0600	4.0F
F	0910	1235	4.8E
	1620	1900	2.8F
	2200		
28		0050	2.6E
Sa	0340	0650	3.2F
	0950	1330	4.5E
	1715	2010	2.9F
	2320		
29		0205	2.1E
Su	0450	0750	2.3F
	1035	1425	4.2E
	1805	2115	3.1F
30	0040	0325	2.0E
M	0620	0855	1.7F
	1120	1520	4.0E
	1855	2215	3.6F
31	0150	0440	2.2E
Tu	0750	1005	1.3F
	1205	1610	4.0E
	1940	2310	4.1F

1991 CURRENT TABLES

For Daylight Saving Time, add one hour.

BURRARD INLET
(First Narrows)

Times and Heights of High and Low Waters

JANUARY

Day	Slack Water Time h.m.	Maximum Current Time h.m.	Vel. knots
1 Tu	0005	0340	6.1F
	0745	1010	2.5E
	1300	1510	1.6F
	1710	2125	5.8E
2 W	0055	0425	6.0F
	0820	1055	2.9E
	1400	1610	1.7F
	1815	2215	5.3E
3 Th	0140	0510	5.7F
	0855	1140	3.2E
	1455	1710	1.8F
	1920	2305	4.6E
4 F	0220	0550	5.1F
	0930	1225	3.5E
	1550	1805	1.8F
	2020	2355	3.7E
5 Sa	0300	0630	4.5F
	1000	1310	3.6E
	1645	1905	1.7F
	2130		
6 Su		0045	2.7E
	0340	0710	3.8F
	1035	1355	3.6E
	1745	2005	1.6F
	2245		
7 M		0135	1.8E
	0415	0750	3.0F
	1105	1440	3.5E
	1840	2115	1.6F
8 Tu	0015	0240	1.1E
	0455	0830	2.3F
	1135	1530	3.4E
	1930	2225	1.8F
9 W	0205	0355	0.6E
	0550	0920	1.6F
	1205	1615	3.4E
	2020	2335	2.3F
10 Th	0345	0530	0.5E
	0720	1015	1.0F
	1235	1705	3.5E
	2100		
11 F		0030	2.9F
	0455	0650	0.7E
	0910	1115	0.6F
	1300	1750	3.7E
	2135		
12 Sa		0120	3.6F
	0545	0755	1.0E
	1050	1210	0.3F
	1325	1835	4.0E
	2215		
13 Su		0205	4.2F
	0630	0845	1.3E
	1155	1305	0.3F
	1405	1920	4.3E
	2255		
14 M		0245	4.7F
	0705	0925	1.5E
	1235	1350	0.3F
	1500	2000	4.5E
	2340		
15 Tu		0320	4.9F
	0740	1000	1.6E
	1300	1435	0.6F
	1600	2045	4.6E

Day	Slack Water Time h.m.	Maximum Current Time h.m.	Vel. knots
16 W	0020	0355	4.8F
	0805	1030	1.8E
	1325	1520	0.9F
	1700	2125	4.5E
17 Th	0100	0430	4.6F
	0825	1055	2.0E
	1355	1600	1.2F
	1800	2205	4.2E
18 F	0135	0500	4.2F
	0845	1125	2.3E
	1425	1645	1.5F
	1855	2245	3.7E
19 Sa	0205	0525	3.9F
	0855	1150	2.7E
	1505	1730	1.7F
	1950	2320	3.2E
20 Su	0230	0550	3.6F
	0915	1220	3.0E
	1545	1815	1.8F
	2050		
21 M		0000	2.6E
	0255	0620	3.3F
	0935	1255	3.4E
	1635	1910	1.8F
	2155		
22 Tu		0045	1.9E
	0325	0650	3.0F
	1000	1340	3.7E
	1730	2010	1.9F
	2315		
23 W		0140	1.3E
	0400	0730	2.5F
	1035	1425	3.9E
	1825	2125	2.2F
24 Th	0100	0255	0.7E
	0450	0820	2.0F
	1115	1525	4.2E
	1925	2240	2.8F
25 F	0255	0430	0.5E
	0610	0925	1.6F
	1200	1625	4.5E
	2025	2355	3.5F
26 Sa	0415	0605	0.7E
	0800	1045	1.2F
	1255	1730	4.8E
	2120		
27 Su		0055	4.4F
	0510	0715	1.3E
	0945	1200	1.2F
	1400	1830	5.2E
	2210		
28 M		0145	5.1F
	0555	0815	1.9E
	1100	1310	1.4F
	1505	1930	5.4E
	2300		
29 Tu		0235	5.5F
	0635	0905	2.5E
	1155	1410	1.7F
	1615	2025	5.5E
	2350		
30 W		0320	5.7F
	0710	0945	3.0E
	1245	1510	2.1F
	1725	2115	5.3E
31 Th	0040	0405	5.5F
	0740	1030	3.4E
	1335	1605	2.4F
	1825	2205	4.8E

FEBRUARY

Day	Slack Water Time h.m.	Maximum Current Time h.m.	Vel. knots
1 F	0120	0445	5.1F
	0810	1105	3.7E
	1420	1655	2.6F
	1930	2250	4.1E
2 Sa	0200	0520	4.5F
	0840	1145	3.8E
	1505	1745	2.6F
	2025	2335	3.3E
3 Su	0240	0555	3.8F
	0905	1225	3.9E
	1555	1835	2.5F
	2130		
4 M		0020	2.5E
	0310	0625	3.1F
	0935	1300	3.8E
	1640	1930	2.2F
	2235		
5 Tu		0110	1.6E
	0345	0700	2.4F
	1000	1340	3.5E
	1735	2025	2.1F
	2355		
6 W		0205	0.9E
	0420	0735	1.7F
	1025	1425	3.3E
	1825	2135	2.0F
7 Th	0140	0325	0.4E
	0510	0820	1.1F
	1045	1515	3.1E
	1920	2250	2.3F
8 F	0330	0505	0.3E
	0700	0920	0.5F
	1105	1610	3.1E
	2010	2355	2.8F
9 Sa	0435	0640	0.6E
	0935	1035	0.1F
	1130	1710	3.2E
	2100		
10 Su		0050	3.4F
	0515	0740	1.1E
	1110	1150	0.1F
	1230	1805	3.5E
	2145		
11 M		0135	3.9F
	0550	0820	1.4E
	1135	1250	0.3F
	1400	1855	3.9E
	2230		
12 Tu		0215	4.3F
	0620	0850	1.7E
	1150	1340	0.7F
	1515	1945	4.2E
	2315		
13 W		0250	4.4F
	0645	0915	2.0E
	1210	1425	1.3F
	1625	2030	4.3E
	2355		
14 Th		0325	4.3F
	0705	0945	2.3E
	1235	1505	1.8F
	1725	2115	4.3E
15 F	0040	0355	4.1F
	0725	1010	2.7E
	1305	1545	2.3F
	1820	2155	4.0E

Day	Slack Water Time h.m.	Maximum Current Time h.m.	Vel. knots
16 Sa	0115	0425	3.8F
	0740	1035	3.1E
	1340	1630	2.6F
	1915	2235	3.5E
17 Su	0145	0450	3.5F
	0755	1105	3.5E
	1420	1715	2.8F
	2010	2310	3.0E
18 M	0210	0515	3.2F
	0815	1140	3.9E
	1505	1800	2.8F
	2105	2350	2.3E
19 Tu	0235	0545	2.9F
	0840	1215	4.1E
	1555	1850	2.7F
	2210		
20 W		0035	1.7E
	0305	0620	2.6F
	0910	1300	4.2E
	1650	1950	2.7F
	2325		
21 Th		0135	1.1E
	0345	0700	2.1F
	0945	1350	4.1E
	1750	2100	2.7F
22 F	0105	0255	0.6E
	0445	0755	1.5F
	1030	1450	4.0E
	1850	2220	3.1F
23 Sa	0245	0430	0.6E
	0635	0915	1.0F
	1125	1600	4.0E
	1955	2330	3.6F
24 Su	0350	0600	1.1E
	0840	1045	0.8F
	1235	1715	4.1E
	2055		
25 M		0030	4.2F
	0435	0705	1.8E
	1000	1210	1.1F
	1400	1820	4.4E
	2150		
26 Tu		0125	4.7F
	0515	0755	2.5E
	1055	1315	1.6F
	1520	1920	4.6E
	2245		
27 W		0210	4.9F
	0550	0835	3.0E
	1140	1410	2.2F
	1635	2015	4.6E
	2335		
28 Th		0255	4.8F
	0620	0915	3.5E
	1220	1500	2.8F
	1740	2105	4.5E

BURRARD INLET
(First Narrows)

1991 CURRENT TABLES

For Daylight Saving Time, add one hour.

Times and Heights of High and Low Waters

MARCH

Day	Slack Water Time h.m.	Maximum Current Time h.m.	Vel. knots
1 F	0020	0335	4.5F
	0650	0950	3.8E
	1300	1550	3.2F
	1840	2155	4.1E
2 Sa	0105	0410	4.0F
	0720	1025	4.0E
	1340	1635	3.4F
	1935	2240	3.5E
3 Su	0145	0445	3.5F
	0745	1100	4.1E
	1420	1720	3.4F
	2030	2325	2.8E
4 M	0220	0515	2.9F
	0805	1135	4.1E
	1505	1805	3.2F
	2125		
5 Tu		0005	2.1E
	0250	0545	2.3F
	0830	1210	3.9E
	1545	1855	2.9F
	2225		
6 W		0050	1.5E
	0325	0615	1.7F
	0850	1245	3.6E
	1630	1945	2.6F
	2340		
7 Th		0145	0.9E
	0405	0650	1.1F
	0910	1325	3.2E
	1720	2045	2.5F
8 F	0105	0300	0.6E
	0515	0730	0.5F
	0925	1415	2.9E
	1810	2155	2.5F
9 Sa	0235	0440	0.6E
	0750	0840	0.1F
	0925	1515	2.7E
	1910	2300	2.8F
10 Su	0335	0605	0.9E
		1015	0.1E
		1625	2.7E
	2010		
11 M		0000	3.1F
	0415	0655	1.3E
	1040	1135	0.2F
	1230	1735	3.0E
	2105		
12 Tu		0050	3.5F
	0445	0730	1.7E
	1045	1235	0.7F
	1415	1835	3.3E
	2200		
13 W	0130		3.7F
	0515	0755	2.1E
	1100	1320	1.4F
	1535	1925	3.7E
	2245		
14 Th	0205		3.7F
	0535	0825	2.5E
	1120	1405	2.2F
	1635	2010	3.8E
	2330		
15 F	0240		3.5F
	0555	0850	3.0E
	1150	1445	2.9F
	1735	2055	3.8E

Day	Slack Water Time h.m.	Maximum Current Time h.m.	Vel. knots
16 Sa	0010	0310	3.3E
	0615	0920	3.5E
	1225	1530	3.4F
	1835	2140	3.5E
17 Su	0050	0340	3.1F
	0635	0950	4.0E
	1305	1615	3.8F
	1930	2220	3.1E
18 M	0120	0410	2.9F
	0655	1025	4.4E
	1350	1700	3.9F
	2025	2305	2.6E
19 Tu	0150	0445	2.7F
	0720	1105	4.7E
	1435	1745	3.8F
	2120	2350	2.0E
20 W	0225	0520	2.4F
	0755	1145	4.7E
	1525	1840	3.7F
	2225		
21 Th		0040	1.5E
	0305	0600	2.0F
	0830	1230	4.5E
	1615	1935	3.5F
	2335		
22 F		0145	1.2E
	0405	0650	1.4F
	0910	1325	4.1E
	1715	2040	3.4F
23 Sa	0050	0305	1.1E
	0540	0755	0.9F
	1000	1430	3.7E
	1815	2150	3.4F
24 Su	0200	0430	1.4E
	0740	0930	0.6F
	1110	1545	3.3E
	1920	2300	3.6F
25 M	0255	0545	1.9E
	0905	1100	0.8F
	1250	1700	3.3E
	2025		
26 Tu		0000	3.9F
	0345	0640	2.6E
	1000	1215	1.4F
	1425	1810	3.4E
	2125		
27 W		0055	4.0F
	0420	0725	3.1E
	1040	1315	2.1F
	1545	1910	3.6E
	2220		
28 Th		0140	4.0F
	0455	0800	3.6E
	1115	1405	2.8F
	1650	2005	3.7E
	2315		
29 F		0220	3.7F
	0525	0835	3.9E
	1150	1450	3.4F
	1750	2055	3.5E
30 Sa	0000	0300	3.3F
	0555	0910	4.1E
	1225	1535	3.9F
	1845	2145	3.2E
31 Su	0045	0335	2.8F
	0615	0945	4.3E
	1305	1615	4.1F
	1940	2230	2.8E

APRIL

Day	Slack Water Time h.m.	Maximum Current Time h.m.	Vel. knots
1 M	0130	0405	2.3F
	0640	1015	4.3E
	1340	1700	4.1F
	2035	2315	2.3E
2 Tu	0205	0440	1.8F
	0700	1050	4.2E
	1420	1740	3.9F
	2130	2355	1.8E
3 W	0245	0510	1.4F
	0720	1125	4.0E
	1500	1825	3.6F
	2225		
4 Th		0045	1.3E
	0330	0540	0.9F
	0740	1200	3.6E
	1540	1910	3.3F
	2325		
5 F		0140	1.0E
	0425	0615	0.5F
	0755	1235	3.2E
	1620	2000	3.0F
6 Sa	0025	0245	0.9E
	0610	0705	0.1F
	0800	1325	2.8E
	1710	2055	2.8F
7 Su	0120	0400	1.0E
		0820	0.1E
		1425	2.4E
	1805	2200	2.8F
8 M	0210	0505	1.3E
		0955	0.0
		1540	2.3E
	1910	2300	2.9F
9 Tu	0255	0550	1.7E
	0935	1110	0.5F
	1245	1655	2.4E
	2015	2350	2.9F
10 W	0325	0625	2.2E
	0950	1210	1.2F
	1425	1800	2.7E
	2115		
11 Th		0035	3.0F
	0350	0655	2.7E
	1010	1255	2.1F
	1540	1900	2.9E
	2210		
12 F		0115	2.9F
	0415	0730	3.2E
	1040	1340	3.0F
	1645	1950	3.1E
	2255		
13 Sa		0150	2.8F
	0440	0800	3.8E
	1115	1425	3.8F
	1745	2040	3.0E
	2340		
14 Su		0225	2.6F
	0500	0835	4.4E
	1155	1510	4.4F
	1840	2125	2.8E
15 M	0020	0300	2.5F
	0530	0915	5.0E
	1240	1600	4.7F
	1940	2210	2.5E

Day	Slack Water Time h.m.	Maximum Current Time h.m.	Vel. knots
16 Tu	0100	0335	2.
	0600	0955	5.
	1325	1645	4.
	2035	2300	2.
17 W	0140	0415	2.
	0635	1035	5.
	1415	1735	4.
	2130	2350	1.
18 Th	0230	0500	1.
	0715	1120	5
	1500	1825	4
	2230		
19 F		0050	1
	0330	0550	1
	0800	1210	4
	1550	1920	4
	2325		
20 Sa		0155	1
	0455	0655	0
	0850	1305	3
	1640	2020	4
21 Su	0020	0305	2
	0630	0815	0
	0955	1415	3
	1740	2120	3
22 M	0110	0415	2
	0755	0945	0
	1130	1530	2
	1840	2220	3
23 Tu	0200	0515	2
	0855	1105	1
	1320	1645	2
	1945	2320	3
24 W	0245	0605	3
	0940	1210	1
	1450	1800	2
	2050		
25 Th		0015	3
	0325	0645	3
	1015	1305	2
	1605	1900	2
	2155		
26 F		0100	2
	0355	0725	4
	1045	1350	3
	1705	1955	2
	2250		
27 Sa		0145	2
	0425	0800	4
	1120	1435	3
	1805	2045	2
	2345		
28 Su		0220	2
	0445	0830	4
	1155	1520	4
	1900	2135	2
29 M	0035	0255	[illegible]
	0505	0905	[illegible]
	1230	1600	[illegible]
	1955	2225	[illegible]
30 Tu	0120	0330	[illegible]
	0525	0940	[illegible]
	1310	1640	[illegible]
	2045	2310	[illegible]

1991 CURRENT TABLES

For Daylight Saving Time, add one hour.

BURRARD INLET
(First Narrows)

Times and Heights of High and Low Waters

MAY

Days 1–15

Day	Slack Water Time (h.m.)	Maximum Current Time (h.m.)	Vel. (knots)
1 W	0210	0405	0.9F
	0550	1010	4.3E
	1345	1720	4.4F
	2135	2355	1.6E
2 Th	0255	0435	0.6F
	0610	1045	4.1E
	1425	1800	4.1F
	2220		
3 F		0040	1.4E
	0350	0515	0.4F
	0635	1120	3.7E
	1500	1840	3.8F
	2300		
4 Sa		0130	1.4E
	0500	0600	0.2F
	0655	1200	3.2E
	1540	1925	3.5F
	2340		
5 Su		0220	1.4E
	0645	0655	0.0
	0710	1245	2.7E
	1620	2010	3.2F
6 M	0015	0310	1.6E
	0800	0810	0.0
	0815	1345	2.2E
	1705	2055	2.9F
7 Tu	0050	0400	1.9E
	0810	0925	0.3F
	1045	1455	1.9E
	1805	2150	2.7F
8 W	0125	0440	2.3E
	0830	1035	0.9F
	1245	1610	1.8E
	1910	2240	2.6F
9 Th	0200	0520	2.8E
	0855	1135	1.7F
	1420	1725	1.9E
	2015	2330	2.5F
10 F	0225	0600	3.3E
	0930	1230	2.6F
	1540	1825	2.1E
	2115		
11 Sa		0015	2.3F
	0255	0635	4.0E
	1005	1320	3.5F
	1650	1925	2.2E
	2210		
12 Su		0055	2.2F
	0325	0715	4.7E
	1045	1410	4.4F
	1750	2020	2.2E
	2305		
13 M		0140	2.0F
	0400	0800	5.3E
	1130	1455	5.0F
	1850	2115	2.2E
	2355		
14 Tu		0225	1.9F
	0435	0845	5.7E
	1220	1545	5.4F
	1945	2205	2.1E
15 W		0310	1.8F
	0515	0930	5.8E
	1305	1635	5.6F
	2040	2300	2.1E

Days 16–31

Day	Slack Water Time (h.m.)	Maximum Current Time (h.m.)	Vel. (knots)
16 Th	0140	0400	1.6F
	0600	1015	5.6E
	1355	1725	5.5F
	2125	2355	2.2E
17 F	0245	0455	1.4F
	0655	1105	5.1E
	1440	1815	5.2F
	2215		
18 Sa		0050	2.4E
	0355	0555	1.2F
	0750	1200	4.4E
	1525	1900	4.8F
	2255		
19 Su		0145	2.6E
	0510	0705	1.0F
	0855	1255	3.6E
	1615	1955	4.3F
	2340		
20 M		0245	2.9E
	0630	0820	0.9F
	1015	1400	2.7E
	1705	2045	3.9F
21 Tu	0020	0340	3.2E
	0735	0940	1.1F
	1155	1510	2.1E
	1800	2140	3.4F
22 W	0105	0435	3.5E
	0825	1055	1.6F
	1335	1625	1.7E
	1905	2235	2.9F
23 Th	0145	0525	3.7E
	0910	1155	2.2F
	1505	1740	1.6E
	2010	2330	2.5F
24 F	0220	0605	3.9E
	0945	1250	2.9F
	1615	1845	1.6E
	2125		
25 Sa		0015	2.0F
	0250	0645	4.1E
	1020	1335	3.6F
	1720	1945	1.7E
	2230		
26 Su		0100	1.5F
	0315	0720	4.3E
	1050	1420	4.2F
	1815	2045	1.8E
	2335		
27 M		0140	1.1F
	0335	0755	4.4E
	1125	1505	4.6F
	1910	2135	1.8E
28 Tu	0035	0220	0.8F
	0355	0830	4.5E
	1205	1545	4.8F
	2000	2225	1.7E
29 W	0130	0300	0.5F
	0420	0905	4.5E
	1245	1625	4.9F
	2045	2310	1.6E
30 Th	0220	0335	0.3F
	0445	0945	4.4E
	1320	1705	4.7F
	2125	2350	1.6E
31 F	0310	0420	0.3F
	0520	1020	4.1E
	1400	1740	4.4F
	2155		

JUNE

Days 1–15

Day	Slack Water Time (h.m.)	Maximum Current Time (h.m.)	Vel. (knots)
1 Sa		0025	1.6E
	0355	0500	0.3F
	0605	1100	3.7E
	1435	1815	4.1F
	2225		
2 Su		0100	1.8E
	0440	0550	0.3F
	0655	1140	3.2E
	1505	1850	3.7F
	2250		
3 M		0140	1.9E
	0530	0645	0.3F
	0800	1220	2.6E
	1540	1925	3.3F
	2310		
4 Tu		0215	2.2E
	0610	0745	0.4F
	0915	1310	2.1E
	1620	2000	3.0F
	2340		
5 W		0255	2.5E
	0655	0850	0.8F
	1050	1415	1.7E
	1705	2045	2.7F
6 Th	0005	0340	2.9E
	0730	1000	1.3F
	1235	1525	1.4E
	1800	2130	2.4F
7 F	0040	0420	3.4E
	0810	1100	2.0F
	1415	1640	1.2E
	1905	2225	2.2F
8 Sa	0110	0505	4.0E
	0850	1200	2.9F
	1540	1755	1.3E
	2015	2315	2.0F
9 Su	0145	0555	4.6E
	0935	1300	3.9F
	1655	1905	1.4E
	2125		
10 M		0010	1.8F
	0225	0640	5.3E
	1025	1350	4.7F
	1755	2005	1.6E
	2230		
11 Tu		0100	1.6F
	0310	0730	5.8E
	1110	1445	5.4F
	1850	2105	1.8E
	2335		
12 W		0155	1.6F
	0400	0820	6.0E
	1200	1535	5.8F
	1940	2200	2.1E
13 Th	0040	0255	1.5F
	0450	0910	6.0E
	1245	1620	6.0F
	2025	2250	2.4E
14 F	0140	0350	1.5F
	0550	1005	5.7E
	1335	1710	5.8F
	2105	2340	2.7E
15 Sa	0245	0450	1.5F
	0650	1055	5.0E
	1420	1755	5.5F
	2140		

Days 16–30

Day	Slack Water Time (h.m.)	Maximum Current Time (h.m.)	Vel. (knots)
16 Su		0030	3.1E
	0345	0555	1.5F
	0800	1150	4.2E
	1505	1840	5.0F
	2220		
17 M		0120	3.4E
	0450	0700	1.5F
	0910	1240	3.3E
	1545	1920	4.4F
	2255		
18 Tu		0210	3.6E
	0555	0810	1.5F
	1030	1340	2.4E
	1630	2005	3.7F
	2330		
19 W		0300	3.7E
	0655	0920	1.6F
	1200	1445	1.6E
	1720	2055	3.0F
20 Th	0010	0350	3.8E
	0745	1030	1.9F
	1340	1600	1.1E
	1815	2145	2.3F
21 F	0045	0440	3.8E
	0830	1135	2.4F
	1515	1720	0.9E
	1930	2240	1.7F
22 Sa	0115	0525	3.9E
	0910	1230	3.0F
	1630	1835	1.0E
	2055	2330	1.2F
23 Su	0145	0605	4.0E
	0950	1320	3.6F
	1730	1945	1.2E
	2220		
24 M		0020	0.8F
	0210	0645	4.2E
	1025	1405	4.2F
	1820	2040	1.4E
	2340		
25 Tu		0110	0.5F
	0230	0725	4.3E
	1105	1445	4.7F
	1910	2130	1.5E
26 W	0045	0155	0.3F
	0300	0805	4.5E
	1140	1530	4.9F
	1950	2215	1.6E
27 Th	0135	0240	0.3F
	0340	0845	4.5E
	1220	1605	4.9F
	2025	2250	1.7E
28 F	0210	0320	0.4F
	0430	0925	4.4E
	1300	1640	4.7F
	2055	2325	1.8E
29 Sa	0235	0405	0.5F
	0530	1005	4.1E
	1335	1715	4.4F
	2115	2355	2.0E
30 Su	0310	0450	0.7F
	0625	1045	3.6E
	1410	1745	4.0F
	2135		

BURRARD INLET (First Narrows)

1991 CURRENT TABLES

For Daylight Saving Time, add one hour.

Times and Heights of High and Low Waters

JULY

Day	Slack Water Time (h.m.)	Maximum Current Time (h.m.)	Vel. (knots)
1 M		0020	2.2E
	0345	0535	0.9F
	0725	1125	3.1E
	1440	1815	3.6F
	2150		
2 Tu		0050	2.5E
	0420	0625	1.0F
	0825	1205	2.6E
	1510	1840	3.3F
	2210		
3 W		0120	2.8E
	0505	0715	1.1F
	0930	1245	2.0E
	1540	1910	3.0F
	2235		
4 Th		0200	3.1E
	0550	0815	1.3F
	1050	1340	1.5E
	1615	1950	2.7F
	2300		
5 F		0240	3.4E
	0640	0920	1.7F
	1230	1445	1.0E
	1700	2035	2.3F
	2335		
6 Sa		0330	3.8E
	0730	1030	2.3F
	1415	1610	0.7E
	1800	2130	1.9F
7 Su	0010	0425	4.3E
	0820	1140	3.1F
	1550	1735	0.7E
	1925	2230	1.6F
8 M	0055	0520	4.8E
	0910	1240	4.0F
	1655	1850	1.0E
	2055	2335	1.4F
9 Tu	0145	0615	5.3E
	1000	1335	4.9F
	1750	1955	1.4E
	2220		
10 W		0040	1.4F
	0240	0710	5.7E
	1050	1425	5.5F
	1835	2050	1.9E
	2330		
11 Th		0145	1.5F
	0345	0805	5.9E
	1140	1515	5.8F
	1915	2140	2.4E
12 F	0030	0245	1.7F
	0450	0900	5.8E
	1230	1600	5.9F
	1955	2230	2.9E
13 Sa	0125	0345	1.9F
	0555	0950	5.4E
	1315	1645	5.7F
	2025	2315	3.3E
14 Su	0220	0445	2.1F
	0705	1045	4.7E
	1400	1725	5.2F
	2100	2355	3.7E
15 M	0315	0545	2.2F
	0810	1135	3.9E
	1445	1805	4.6F
	2135		

Day	Slack Water Time (h.m.)	Maximum Current Time (h.m.)	Vel. (knots)
16 Tu		0040	3.9E
	0410	0640	2.2F
	0915	1225	3.0E
	1520	1845	3.9F
	2205		
17 W		0125	4.0E
	0505	0740	2.1F
	1030	1320	2.1E
	1600	1925	3.2F
	2235		
18 Th		0210	3.9E
	0605	0845	2.0F
	1150	1420	1.3E
	1640	2010	2.5F
	2310		
19 F		0300	3.7E
	0700	0955	2.1F
	1330	1530	0.8E
	1735	2055	1.7F
	2340		
20 Sa		0350	3.6E
	0750	1105	2.5F
	1515	1700	0.6E
	1900	2150	1.1F
21 Su	0010	0440	3.5E
	0835	1205	3.0F
	1630	1830	0.7E
	2050	2255	0.6F
22 M	0035	0530	3.6E
	0915	1255	3.5F
	1720	1935	1.0E
	2235	2355	0.3F
23 Tu	0105	0615	3.8E
	0955	1340	4.1F
	1805	2030	1.4E
	2350		
24 W		0050	0.2F
	0150	0700	4.0E
	1040	1425	4.5F
	1840	2110	1.6E
25 Th	0030	0140	0.3F
	0250	0745	4.2E
	1120	1505	4.7F
	1915	2145	1.8E
26 F	0050	0225	0.6F
	0355	0830	4.3E
	1200	1540	4.6F
	1940	2210	2.0E
27 Sa	0115	0310	0.9F
	0455	0910	4.2E
	1240	1615	4.4F
	2005	2240	2.2E
28 Su	0140	0350	1.3F
	0555	0955	4.0E
	1320	1640	4.0F
	2020	2305	2.4E
29 M	0210	0435	1.6F
	0650	1030	3.5E
	1350	1710	3.7F
	2035	2330	2.7E
30 Tu	0245	0515	1.8F
	0745	1110	3.0E
	1415	1735	3.3F
	2050		
31 W		0000	3.1E
	0325	0600	1.9F
	0840	1145	2.4E
	1440	1800	3.0F
	2110		

AUGUST

Day	Slack Water Time (h.m.)	Maximum Current Time (h.m.)	Vel. (knots)
1 Th		0035	3.4E
	0410	0650	1.9F
	0940	1225	1.8E
	1505	1830	2.8F
	2135		
2 F		0110	3.6E
	0500	0745	2.0F
	1055	1315	1.2E
	1535	1905	2.4F
	2200		
3 Sa		0155	3.8E
	0555	0850	2.2F
	1230	1425	0.7E
	1620	1950	2.0F
	2240		
4 Su		0250	4.1E
	0650	1005	2.6F
	1420	1550	0.5E
	1730	2050	1.5F
	2325		
5 M		0350	4.3E
	0750	1115	3.3F
	1540	1725	0.6E
	1920	2205	1.2F
6 Tu	0020	0455	4.6E
	0845	1220	4.1F
	1635	1840	1.1E
	2105	2325	1.1F
7 W	0125	0600	4.9E
	0940	1315	4.8F
	1720	1940	1.8E
	2220		
8 Th		0040	1.4F
	0240	0700	5.2E
	1030	1405	5.3F
	1800	2030	2.4E
	2320		
9 F		0145	1.8F
	0355	0755	5.3E
	1125	1450	5.4F
	1835	2115	3.0E
10 Sa	0015	0240	2.3F
	0500	0850	5.2E
	1210	1535	5.4F
	1910	2155	3.5E
11 Su	0100	0340	2.7F
	0610	0940	4.9E
	1300	1615	5.0F
	1940	2240	3.9E
12 M	0150	0430	3.0F
	0710	1030	4.3E
	1340	1655	4.5F
	2010	2320	4.1E
13 Tu	0235	0525	3.1F
	0815	1120	3.5E
	1420	1735	3.9F
	2040	2355	4.2E
14 W	0325	0615	3.0F
	0915	1210	2.7E
	1500	1810	3.2F
	2110		
15 Th		0040	4.1E
	0415	0710	2.7F
	1025	1300	1.8E
	1535	1845	2.5F
	2135		

Day	Slack Water Time (h.m.)	Maximum Current Time (h.m.)	Vel. (knot)
16 F		0120	3.8E
	0505	0805	2.5F
	1140	1355	1.1E
	1620	1925	1.8F
	2205		
17 Sa		0205	3.5E
	0600	0910	2.4F
	1315	1510	0.7E
	1720	2010	1.1F
	2230		
18 Su		0255	3.2E
	0655	1020	2.5F
	1450	1645	0.6E
	1905	2110	0.5F
	2255		
19 M		0350	3.1E
	0745	1130	2.9F
	1555	1815	0.9E
	2130	2230	0.1F
	2320		
20 Tu		0450	3.1E
	0835	1225	3.4F
	1640	1915	1.3E
	2255	2340	0.1F
21 W	0025	0550	3.3E
	0925	1310	3.8F
	1720	1955	1.6E
	2320		
22 Th		0040	0.3F
	0155	0640	3.6E
	1010	1350	4.1F
	1750	2030	1.9E
	2340		
23 F		0130	0.8F
	0310	0730	3.8E
	1055	1430	4.2F
	1820	2055	2.2E
	2355		
24 Sa		0210	1.3F
	0415	0815	4.0E
	1140	1505	4.1F
	1840	2120	2.4E
25 Su	0020	0255	1.9F
	0515	0900	3.9E
	1220	1535	3.8F
	1900	2150	2.7E
26 M	0050	0335	2.3F
	0610	0940	3.7E
	1255	1605	3.4F
	1915	2215	3.1E
27 Tu	0120	0415	2.7F
	0705	1020	3.2E
	1325	1630	3.1F
	1930	2245	3.5E
28 W	0200	0455	2.9F
	0800	1055	2.7E
	1355	1655	2.8F
	1945	2315	3.8E
29 Th	0245	0540	2.9F
	0855	1135	2.1E
	1420	1720	2.6F
	2010	2350	4.1E
30 F	0330	0630	2.8F
	0955	1215	1.5E
	1445	1750	2.3F
	2040		
31 Sa		0030	4.1E
	0420	0725	2.8F
	1105	1310	1.0E
	1520	1830	1.9F
	2110		

1991 CURRENT TABLES

For Daylight Saving Time, add one hour.

BURRARD INLET (First Narrows)

Times and Heights of High and Low Waters

SEPTEMBER

Day	Slack Water Time h.m.	Maximum Current Time h.m.	Vel. knots
1 Su		0120	4.1E
	0515	0825	2.8F
	1235	1425	0.7E
	1620	1925	1.4F
	2155		
2 M		0215	4.0E
	0615	0940	3.0F
	1400	1555	0.7E
	1800	2040	1.0F
	2250		
3 Tu		0325	3.9E
	0715	1050	3.5F
	1505	1720	1.1E
	2000	2210	0.8F
4 W	0005	0440	4.0E
	0820	1155	4.0F
	1555	1825	1.8E
	2125	2335	1.1F
5 Th	0135	0545	4.2E
	0915	1250	4.4F
	1635	1920	2.5E
	2220		
6 F		0045	1.7F
	0255	0650	4.4E
	1010	1335	4.7F
	1710	2000	3.2E
	2305		
7 Sa		0140	2.4F
	0410	0745	4.5E
	1105	1420	4.7F
	1745	2040	3.7E
	2350		
8 Su		0235	3.0F
	0515	0840	4.4E
	1155	1505	4.4F
	1815	2120	4.1E
9 M	0030	0325	3.5F
	0620	0930	4.1E
	1240	1545	4.0F
	1845	2200	4.3E
10 Tu	0115	0415	3.8F
	0720	1020	3.6E
	1325	1620	3.4F
	1915	2235	4.4E
11 W	0155	0500	3.8F
	0820	1105	2.9E
	1405	1655	2.8F
	1940	2315	4.4E
12 Th	0240	0550	3.7F
	0915	1155	2.2E
	1440	1730	2.2F
	2005	2350	4.1E
13 F	0325	0640	3.4F
	1020	1245	1.6E
	1525	1805	1.6F
	2030		
14 Sa		0030	3.8E
	0410	0730	3.0F
	1130	1340	1.1E
	1615	1840	1.0F
	2050		
15 Su		0110	3.3E
	0500	0830	2.8F
	1245	1455	0.8E
	1740	1930	0.4F
	2105		

Day	Slack Water Time h.m.	Maximum Current Time h.m.	Vel. knots
16 M		0200	2.9E
	0550	0930	2.7F
	1400	1625	0.9E
		2045	0.0
17 Tu		0300	2.6E
	0645	1040	2.9F
	1455	1745	1.2E
		2215	0.1E
18 W		0410	2.5E
	0745	1135	3.1F
	1540	1830	1.6E
	2225	2330	0.2F
19 Th	0030	0520	2.7E
	0840	1225	3.4F
	1615	1905	2.0E
	2235		
20 F		0025	0.7F
	0210	0615	3.0E
	0935	1305	3.5F
	1645	1935	2.3E
	2250		
21 Sa		0110	1.4F
	0325	0710	3.3E
	1025	1345	3.5F
	1710	2005	2.7E
	2310		
22 Su		0150	2.2F
	0430	0755	3.5E
	1110	1420	3.3F
	1730	2030	3.1E
	2335		
23 M		0230	2.8F
	0525	0840	3.4E
	1150	1450	3.0F
	1745	2100	3.5E
24 Tu	0010	0315	3.4F
	0620	0925	3.2E
	1230	1520	2.8F
	1805	2130	4.0E
25 W	0045	0355	3.8F
	0715	1005	2.8E
	1300	1545	2.5F
	1825	2200	4.4E
26 Th	0125	0440	3.9F
	0810	1045	2.3E
	1330	1615	2.3F
	1850	2235	4.6E
27 F	0210	0525	3.9F
	0905	1130	1.8E
	1405	1650	2.1F
	1920	2315	4.7E
28 Sa	0255	0615	3.8F
	1005	1220	1.4E
	1445	1730	1.8F
	1955		
29 Su		0000	4.5E
	0345	0705	3.6F
	1110	1320	1.1E
	1540	1815	1.3F
	2030		
30 M		0050	4.1E
	0440	0805	3.5F
	1220	1430	1.1E
	1710	1925	0.9F
	2120		

OCTOBER

Day	Slack Water Time h.m.	Maximum Current Time h.m.	Vel. knots
1 Tu		0150	3.7E
	0535	0915	3.5F
	1320	1555	1.4E
	1900	2055	0.6F
	2235		
2 W		0305	3.3E
	0640	1020	3.6F
	1415	1705	2.0E
	2030	2225	0.8F
3 Th	0020	0425	3.2E
	0745	1120	3.8F
	1500	1800	2.7E
	2125	2345	1.4F
4 F	0200	0535	3.3E
	0850	1215	3.9F
	1540	1850	3.3E
	2210		
5 Sa		0045	2.2F
	0320	0640	3.4E
	0945	1305	3.9F
	1620	1930	3.8E
	2245		
6 Su		0135	3.0F
	0430	0740	3.5E
	1040	1350	3.7F
	1650	2005	4.2E
	2325		
7 M		0225	3.7F
	0530	0830	3.5E
	1135	1430	3.3F
	1720	2045	4.5E
8 Tu	0000	0310	4.2F
	0630	0920	3.2E
	1220	1510	2.8F
	1745	2120	4.7E
9 W	0040	0355	4.4F
	0725	1010	2.8E
	1305	1545	2.3F
	1810	2155	4.7E
10 Th	0120	0440	4.4F
	0825	1100	2.3E
	1350	1620	1.8F
	1835	2230	4.5E
11 F	0200	0525	4.3F
	0920	1145	1.9E
	1435	1650	1.3F
	1855	2305	4.2E
12 Sa	0240	0610	3.9F
	1015	1235	1.5E
	1525	1730	0.9F
	1920	2340	3.8E
13 Su	0320	0655	3.6F
	1110	1330	1.2E
	1635	1810	0.4F
	1935		
14 M		0020	3.2E
	0405	0745	3.3F
	1205	1440	1.2E
	1845	1905	0.0
	1925		
15 Tu		0110	2.7E
	0450	0840	3.0F
	1300	1550	1.3E
		2025	0.2E

Day	Slack Water Time h.m.	Maximum Current Time h.m.	Vel. knots
16 W		0210	2.3E
	0540	0935	2.9F
	1345	1650	1.6E
		2155	0.1E
17 Th		0325	2.0E
	0640	1035	2.9F
	1425	1735	2.0E
	2130	2305	0.4F
18 F	0040	0440	2.1E
	0745	1125	2.9F
	1500	1810	2.4E
	2140		
19 Sa		0000	1.2F
	0220	0545	2.3E
	0850	1210	2.8F
	1525	1840	2.8E
	2200		
20 Su		0045	2.0F
	0330	0640	2.5E
	0945	1250	2.7F
	1550	1910	3.3E
	2225		
21 M		0130	2.9F
	0435	0735	2.7E
	1035	1325	2.6F
	1610	1940	3.9E
	2300		
22 Tu		0210	3.6F
	0530	0820	2.7E
	1120	1400	2.4F
	1635	2015	4.4E
	2335		
23 W		0255	4.3F
	0630	0905	2.5E
	1200	1435	2.2F
	1700	2050	4.9E
24 Th	0020	0340	4.7F
	0725	0955	2.2E
	1235	1510	2.0F
	1725	2130	5.2E
25 F	0100	0425	4.8F
	0820	1040	2.0E
	1315	1550	1.8F
	1800	2210	5.3E
26 Sa	0145	0515	4.8F
	0915	1130	1.8E
	1405	1630	1.6F
	1840	2255	5.1E
27 Su	0235	0600	4.6F
	1005	1225	1.7E
	1505	1720	1.3F
	1925	2340	4.7E
28 M	0320	0650	4.4F
	1055	1325	1.7E
	1620	1820	0.9F
	2015		
29 Tu		0035	4.0E
	0410	0745	4.1F
	1145	1430	2.0E
	1750	1940	0.7F
	2120		
30 W		0135	3.3E
	0500	0845	3.8F
	1235	1535	2.4E
	1920	2105	0.7F
	2255		
31 Th		0250	2.7E
	0600	0945	3.6F
	1325	1635	2.9E
	2020	2230	1.1F

BURRARD INLET (First Narrows)

1991 CURRENT TABLES

For Daylight Saving Time, add one hour.

Times and Heights of High and Low Waters

NOVEMBER

Day	Slack Water Time h.m.	Maximum Current Time h.m.	Vel. knots	Day	Slack Water Time h.m.	Maximum Current Time h.m.	Vel. knots
1 F	0045	0410	2.4E	16 Sa	0030	0350	1.5E
	0705	1045	3.5F		0640	1015	2.5F
	1405	1730	3.4E		1335	1705	2.8E
	2110	2340	1.9F		2050	2325	1.5F
2 Sa	0220	0525	2.3E	17 Su	0210	0505	1.6E
	0815	1140	3.3F		0745	1105	2.3F
	1445	1815	3.9E		1405	1740	3.3E
	2150				2120		
3 Su		0040	2.7F	18 M		0015	2.4F
	0340	0630	2.4E		0330	0610	1.7E
	0920	1230	3.0F		0850	1150	2.1F
	1525	1855	4.2E		1430	1820	3.9E
	2225				2150		
4 M		0130	3.4F	19 Tu		0105	3.3F
	0445	0730	2.5E		0440	0710	1.8E
	1020	1315	2.6F		0945	1235	2.0F
	1555	1935	4.5E		1500	1855	4.6E
	2300				2230		
5 Tu		0215	4.1F	20 W		0150	4.2F
	0545	0825	2.5E		0540	0800	1.9E
	1115	1355	2.2F		1040	1315	1.9F
	1620	2010	4.7E		1530	1935	5.2E
	2335				2310		
6 W		0300	4.6F	21 Th		0240	4.8F
	0640	0915	2.3E		0635	0855	1.9E
	1210	1435	1.8F		1130	1355	1.8F
	1645	2045	4.8E		1605	2020	5.6E
					2355		
7 Th	0015	0340	4.8F	22 F		0325	5.3F
	0735	1005	2.1E		0730	0945	1.9E
	1300	1510	1.3F		1220	1440	1.7F
	1710	2120	4.8E		1645	2105	5.8E
8 F	0050	0425	4.9F	23 Sa	0040	0415	5.5F
	0830	1055	1.9E		0820	1035	1.9E
	1350	1545	0.9F		1315	1530	1.6F
	1730	2155	4.6E		1735	2150	5.7E
9 Sa	0130	0505	4.7F	24 Su	0130	0500	5.5F
	0920	1140	1.7E		0905	1125	2.1E
	1445	1625	0.6F		1410	1625	1.5F
	1755	2230	4.3E		1825	2240	5.3E
10 Su	0210	0545	4.4F	25 M	0215	0545	5.3F
	1000	1230	1.6E		0945	1215	2.3E
	1545	1705	0.4F		1515	1725	1.3F
	1820	2310	3.8E		1920	2330	4.7E
11 M	0245	0625	4.0F	26 Tu	0300	0630	5.0F
	1040	1315	1.5E		1025	1310	2.6E
	1655	1750	0.2F		1630	1830	1.1F
	1845	2345	3.2E		2025		
12 Tu	0320	0705	3.6F	27 W		0025	3.8E
	1120	1405	1.6E		0345	0720	4.5F
	1745	1850	0.0		1105	1405	2.9E
	2000				1745	1940	1.0F
					2140		
13 W		0030	2.7E	28 Th		0125	3.0E
	0400	0750	3.3F		0430	0810	4.0F
	1155	1455	1.8E		1150	1505	3.2E
		1955	0.0		1855	2100	1.2F
					2315		
14 Th		0125	2.1E	29 F		0230	2.2E
	0445	0835	3.0F		0525	0905	3.5F
	1230	1540	2.0E		1230	1600	3.5E
	2005	2115	0.2F		1955	2220	1.5F
	2225						
15 F		0230	1.7E	30 Sa	0100	0350	1.7E
	0535	0925	2.7F		0625	1000	3.0F
	1305	1625	2.3E		1310	1650	3.8E
	2025	2225	0.7F		2040	2330	2.2F

DECEMBER

Day	Slack Water Time h.m.	Maximum Current Time h.m.	Vel. knots	Day	Slack Water Time h.m.	Maximum Current Time h.m.	Vel. knots
1 Su	0235	0505	1.5E	16 M	0200	0415	0.9E
	0735	1055	2.5F		0630	0955	2.0F
	1350	1740	4.1E		1245	1645	3.7E
	2125				2040	2345	2.5F
2 M		0025	2.9F	17 Tu	0335	0535	0.9E
	0355	0620	1.5E		0740	1050	1.7F
	0850	1150	2.1F		1320	1735	4.3E
	1425	1820	4.3E		2120		
	2200						
3 Tu		0115	3.6F	18 W		0040	3.5F
	0500	0725	1.6E		0445	0645	1.0E
	1000	1240	1.7F		0855	1140	1.6F
	1455	1900	4.5E		1400	1820	5.0E
	2235				2205		
4 W		0205	4.2F	19 Th		0135	4.4F
	0600	0825	1.7E		0545	0745	1.3E
	1110	1320	1.3F		1005	1235	1.5F
	1520	1940	4.7E		1445	1910	5.5E
	2315				2250		
5 Th		0245	4.7F	20 F		0225	5.1F
	0655	0915	1.8E		0635	0840	1.6E
	1210	1405	0.9F		1110	1330	1.5F
	1545	2015	4.8E		1535	2000	5.9E
	2350				2340		
6 F		0330	5.0F	21 Sa		0310	5.7F
	0740	1005	1.8E		0720	0935	1.9E
	1305	1445	0.7F		1210	1425	1.6F
	1615	2055	4.8E		1630	2050	6.0E
7 Sa	0030	0410	5.1F	22 Su	0025	0355	5.9F
	0825	1050	1.8E		0800	1020	2.3E
	1400	1525	0.5F		1310	1525	1.7F
	1645	2130	4.6E		1730	2140	5.8E
8 Su	0105	0450	4.9F	23 M	0110	0440	5.8F
	0905	1130	1.8E		0835	1110	2.7E
	1445	1605	0.4F		1405	1625	1.8F
	1725	2210	4.3E		1830	2230	5.3E
9 M	0145	0525	4.6F	24 Tu	0155	0525	5.6F
	0935	1205	1.8E		0910	1155	3.1E
	1530	1650	0.4F		1505	1720	1.8F
	1805	2245	3.8E		1935	2320	4.6E
10 Tu	0220	0600	4.2F	25 W	0240	0610	5.1F
	1000	1240	1.9E		0945	1245	3.4E
	1615	1735	0.4F		1605	1825	1.8F
	1855	2325	3.3E		2040		
11 W	0250	0630	3.8F	26 Th		0015	3.7E
	1025	1315	2.0E		0320	0650	4.6F
	1705	1825	0.4F		1020	1330	3.7E
	1950				1710	1930	1.7F
					2155		
12 Th		0005	2.7E	27 F		0110	2.8E
	0320	0705	3.4F		0405	0735	3.9F
	1050	1355	2.2E		1100	1425	3.8E
	1750	1925	0.5F		1810	2040	1.7F
	2055				2320		
13 F		0050	2.1E	28 Sa		0210	1.9E
	0355	0740	3.0F		0450	0820	3.2F
	1115	1435	2.5E		1135	1515	3.8E
	1835	2025	0.7F		1915	2155	1.9F
	2225						
14 Sa		0145	1.6E	29 Su	0100	0325	1.2E
	0435	0820	2.6F		0540	0915	2.5F
	1145	1515	2.8E		1215	1610	3.9E
	1920	2135	1.1F		2005	2305	2.3F
15 Su	0010	0255	1.2E	30 M	0245	0445	0.9E
	0525	0905	2.3F		0655	1010	1.8F
	1215	1600	3.2E		1255	1700	3.9E
	2000	2245	1.7F		2050		
				31 Tu		0010	2.9F
					0410	0610	0.9E
					0825	1110	1.3F
					1325	1750	4.0E
						2135	0.0

Current Differences and Other Constants

NO.	PLACE	METER DEPTH	POSITION Lat.	Long.	TIME DIFFERENCES Min. before Flood	Flood	Min. before Ebb	Ebb	SPEED RATIOS Flood	Ebb	Minimum before Flood	Maximum Flood	Minimum before Ebb	Maximum Ebb
		ft	° ' N	° ' W	h. m.	h. m.	h. m.	h. m.			knots deg.	knots deg.	knots deg.	knots deg.
	COLUMBIA RIVER and APPROACHES <15> Time meridian, 120°W				on GRAYS HARBOR ENT.									
719	Walker Island Channel <17>...............	20	46 09.17	123 02.57	- - -	- - -	- - -	-1 29	- -	0.1	- - - -	- - - -	- - - -	0.2 319
720	Walker Island, south of..................	12	46 08.47	123 02 75	+5 46	+4 15	+2 41	+5 09	0.2	0.4	0.0 - -	0.4 148	0.0 - -	1.2 330
721	Slaughters Channel <17>..................	18	46 07.42	122 59.22	- - -	- - -	- - -	-1 15	- -	0.2	- - - -	- - - -	- - - -	0.6 306
								+5 51		0.7				2.0 306
722	Cottonwood Island, west of <17>.........	34	46 04.28	122 53.45	- - -	- - -	- - -	-1 02	- -	0.1	- - - -	- - - -	- - - -	0.4 325
								+5 58		0.6				1.5 328
723	Kalma Upper Range <17>...................	13	46 00.17	122 51.08	- - -	- - -	- - -	-0 35	- -	0.3	- - - -	- - - -	- - - -	0.8 343
								+5 58		0.7				2.0 342
	WASHINGTON COAST													
745	South Bend, Willapa River................		46 40	123 48	+0 19	+0 20	+0 24	-0 06	0.6	0.5	0.0 - -	1.2 090	0.0 - -	1.4 270
	GRAYS HARBOR													
750	Entrance, 0.2 mile south of north jetty.		46 56	124 10	-0 28	+0 16	+0 10	-0 47	1.3	0.6	0.0 - -	2.5 070	0.0 - -	1.7 243
755	Entrance, Point Chehalis Range...........		46 55	124 09	+0 08	-0 11	-0 22	-0 21	0.9	1.1	0.0 - -	1.7 092	0.0 - -	3.1 268
760	Entrance, 0.6 mile WNW of Westport.......		46 55	124 07	0 00	0 00	+0 06	0 00	1.2	0.7	0.0 - -	2.2 044	0.0 - -	1.9 238
765	GRAYS HARBOR ENTRANCE....................		46 55	124 08	Daily Predictions						0.0 - -	1.9 061	0.0 - -	2.8 242
770	Entrance, 1.1 miles NW of Westport.......		46 55	124 08	+0 04	-0 06	-0 05	-0 23	0.9	0.9	0.0 - -	1.8 078	0.0 - -	2.5 233
775	Channel, 1.5 miles north of Westport....		46 56	124 06	-0 22	-0 04	-0 04	-0 25	0.7	0.6	0.0 - -	1.4 036	0.0 - -	1.8 226
780	Channel, 2.1 miles NNE of Westport......		46 56	124 05	-0 02	0 00	-0 02	+0 02	0.6	0.5	0.0 - -	1.2 021	0.0 - -	1.3 249
785	Aberdeen, Chehalis River <18>...........		46 58	123 49	- - -	+0 35	- - -	+0 28	- -	- -	0.0 - -	- - 042	0.0 - -	- - 230
790	Westport, channel 0.4 mile NE of........		46 55	124 06	-0 41	-0 04	-0 19	-0 36	1.0	0.7	0.0 - -	1.9 113	0.0 - -	1.9 310
	WASHINGTON-BRITISH COLUMBIA COAST				on SAN FRANCISCO BAY ENT.									
795	Quillayute River entrance...............		47 55	124 38	-0 18	-0 18	-0 18	-0 18	0.1	0.4	0.0 - -	0.3 015	0.0 - -	1.3 195
800	Cape Alava, 4.4 miles west of <14>......		48 10	124 50	- - -	- - -	- - -	- - -	- -	- -	- - - -	- - - -	- - - -	- - - -
805	Swiftsure Bank <14>.....................		48 33	125 00	- - -	- - -	- - -	- - -	- -	- -	- - - -	- - - -	- - - -	- - - -
810	Vancouver Island, west coast <19>.......		- - -	- - -	- - -	- - -	- - -	- - -	- -	- -	- - - -	- - - -	- - - -	- - - -
	STRAIT of JUAN DE FUCA				on STRAIT of JUAN DE FUCA ENT.									
815	STRAIT OF JUAN DE FUCA ENTRANCE.........		48 27	124 35	Daily Predictions						0.0 - -	0.6 115	0.0 - -	1.5 290
820	Pillar Point............................		48 16	124 04	-0 35	+0 06	+1 27	+0 52	1.2	1.2	0.0 - -	1.4 100	0.0 - -	0.9 280
					on RACE ROCKS									
825	Angeles Point, 2.3 miles north of.......		48 12	123 33	+1 22	+0 21	-0 32	+0 13	0.8	1.1	0.0 - -	1.0 078	0.0 - -	2.2 260
830	RACE ROCKS, 4 miles south of............		48 14	123 32	Daily Predictions						0.0 - -	1.2 091	0.0 - -	2.0 271
835	Race Rocks, 0.5 mile southeast of.......		48 17	123 31	-1 10	- - -	-1 23	- - -	- -	- -	- - - -	- - - -	- - - -	- - - -
840	Race Passage............................		48 18	123 32	-1 21	- - -	-1 53	- - -	- -	- -	- - - -	- - - -	- - - -	- - - -
845	Port Angeles............................		48 08	123 25	Current weak and variable									
850	Ediz Hook Light, 1.4 miles southeast of.		48 07	123 24	Current weak and variable									

Endnotes can be found at the end of Table 2.

Current Differences and Other Constants

NO.	PLACE	METER DEPTH	POSITION Lat.	POSITION Long.	TIME DIFFERENCES Min. before Flood	TIME DIFFERENCES Flood	TIME DIFFERENCES Min. before Ebb	TIME DIFFERENCES Ebb	SPEED RATIOS Flood	SPEED RATIOS Ebb	Minimum before Flood	Maximum Flood	Minimum before Ebb	Maximum Ebb
		ft	° ' N	° ' W	h. m.	h. m.	h. m.	h. m.			knots deg.	knots deg.	knots deg.	knots deg.
	STRAIT of JUAN DE FUCA Time meridian, 120°W				on ADMIRALTY INLET									
855	Ediz Hook Light, 1.2 miles north of.....		48 10	123 25	-0 32	-0 19	-0 05	-0 05	0.5	0.4	0.0 - -	0.8 080	0.0 - -	1.1 295
860	Ediz Hook Light, 5.3 miles ENE of.......		48 11	123 17	+0 39	+0 12	-0 07	-0 14	0.6	0.8	0.0 - -	1.0 055	0.0 - -	2.0 215
865	Trial Island, 5.2 miles SSW of..........		48 19	123 22	-0 08	+0 39	+1 22	+0 55	0.7	0.5	0.0 - -	1.1 045	0.0 - -	1.4 235
870	New Dungeness Light, 2.8 miles NNW of...		48 14	123 08	+0 57	+0 27	-0 13	+0 16	0.3	0.5	0.0 - -	0.5 075	0.0 - -	1.2 255
875	New Dungeness Light, 6 miles NNE of.....		48 16	123 03	+0 51	+0 55	+0 27	+0 36	0.3	0.4	0.0 - -	0.5 050	0.0 - -	1.1 255
880	Discovery Island, 7.6 miles SSE of......		48 18	123 10	+0 27	+0 15	+0 51	+0 30	0.4	0.4	0.0 - -	0.7 035	0.0 - -	1.0 260
885	Discovery Island, 3 miles SSE of........		48 23	123 12	+0 23	+0 15	+0 02	+0 40	0.6	0.9	0.0 - -	0.9 025	0.0 - -	2.3 250
890	Cattle Point, 2.8 miles SSW of <21>.....		48 24	123 00	-1 17	+0 52	+1 04	-0 42	0.4	0.2	0.0 - -	0.6 046	0.2 126	0.4 187
895	Cattle Point, 5 miles SSW of............		48 23	123 01	+1 14	+1 11	+1 20	+0 44	0.6	0.3	0.0 - -	0.9 120	0.0 - -	0.9 210
900	Violet Point, 3.7 miles north of <22>...		48 11	122 55	- - -	+0 22	-0 36	+0 09	0.2	0.5	0.0 - -	0.4 100	0.0 - -	1.2 270
905	Violet Point, 3.2 miles northwest of....		48 10	122 58	-0 05	-0 32	-0 08	-0 17	0.3	0.4	0.0 - -	0.6 120	0.0 - -	1.0 325
910	Kamen Point, 1.3 miles southwest of.....		48 06	122 58	-1 10	-0 52	-1 06	-0 34	0.2	0.4	0.0 - -	0.3 125	0.0 - -	1.0 265
915	Discovery Bay entrance <23>.............		48 06	122 54	- - -	- - -	- - -	- - -	- -	- -	- - -	- - - -	- - -	- - - -
920	Smith Island, 2 miles east of <24>......		48 19	122 48	+1 22	+0 51	- - -	+0 19	0.2	0.2	0.0 - -	0.4 - -	0.0 - -	0.5 220
925	Smith Island, 1.4 miles SSW of..........		48 18	122 51	-0 06	+0 03	+0 29	+0 25	0.4	0.4	0.0 - -	0.7 090	0.0 - -	1.0 280
930	Smith Island, 3.7 miles ESE of <25>.....		48 18	122 45	- - -	+1 11	- - -	+1 35	- -	0.3	- - -	- - - -	0.0 - -	0.9 225
935	Point Partridge, 1.6 miles NW of <26>...		48 15	122 48	- - -	- - -	- - -	- - -	- -	0.4	- - -	- - - -	- - -	1.1 175
940	Point Partridge, 3.7 miles west of......		48 14	122 52	+1 27	+0 17	-0 24	+0 42	0.2	0.8	0.0 - -	0.4 140	0.0 - -	2.1 250
	ADMIRALTY INLET													
945	Point Wilson, 1.1 miles WNW of..........		48 10	122 46	-1 53	-0 58	-0 08	-0 54	1.5	1.1	0.0 - -	2.4 085	0.0 - -	2.8 285
950	Point Wilson, 0.5 mi., northeast of <27>		48 09	122 45	-1 08	-1 27	-0 47	-0 48	1.4	1.0	0.0 - -	2.2 114	0.0 - -	2.6 298
955	Point Wilson, 1.4 miles northeast of <2>		48 10	122 44	-0 28	-0 17	+0 41	+0 07	2.0	1.3	0.0 - -	3.4 112	0.0 - -	3.5 297
960	Point Wilson, 2.3 miles NE of <27>......		48 10	122 42	-1 29	-0 07	+0 33	-0 07	1.0	1.0	0.0 - -	2.0 143	0.0 - -	2.3 323
965	Admiralty Head, 0.5 mile west of........		48 09	122 42	-0 31	-0 03	+0 01	-0 07	1.3	1.2	0.0 - -	2.1 145	0.0 - -	3.1 025
970	Point Wilson, 0.8 mile east of..........		48 09	122 44	-0 53	-0 20	+0 27	-0 54	1.5	1.0	0.0 - -	2.5 165	0.0 - -	2.6 280
975	Port Townsend, 0.5 mile S of Pt. Hudson.		48 07	122 45	Current weak and variable						0.0 - -	0.3 238	0.0 - -	0.5 048
980	Point Hudson, 0.5 mile east of..........		48 07	122 44	-3 21	-2 36	-2 42	-2 26	0.8	0.2	0.0 - -	1.2 115	0.0 - -	0.6 010
	Marrowstone Point													
985	1.1 miles northwest of..............		48 07	122 42	-3 31	-2 20	-1 02	-1 42	0.8	0.5	0.0 - -	1.3 100	0.0 - -	1.3 275
990	0.4 mile northeast of <27>...........		48 06	122 41	-1 20	-1 03	-0 04	-1 03	1.1	1.1	0.0 - -	2.4 122	0.0 - -	3.1 338
995	0.3 mile northeast of...............		48 06	122 41	-0 53	-1 36	-1 13	-0 13	1.2	1.1	0.0 - -	2.0 170	0.0 - -	2.8 015
1000	1.6 miles northeast of <27>.........		48 07	122 40	-0 16	+0 07	-0 03	-0 17	1.2	1.2	0.0 - -	2.3 152	0.0 - -	2.6 344
1005	2.5 miles northeast of <28>.........		48 08	122 38	- - -	- - -	- - -	- - -	- -	- -	- - -	- - - -	- - -	- - - -
1010	Nodule Point, 0.5 mile southeast of.....		48 02	122 40	-1 27	-0 47	-0 59	-0 24	1.2	1.0	0.0 - -	2.0 160	0.0 - -	2.5 339
1015	ADMIRALTY INLET (off Bush Point)........		48 02	122 38	Daily Predictions						0.0 - -	1.6 179	0.0 - -	2.6 003
1020	Bush Point Light, 0.5 mile NW of........		48 02	122 37	-0 32	-0 21	-0 09	-0 35	1.1	1.1	0.0 - -	1.7 141	0.0 - -	2.9 309
1025	Mutiny Bay, 3.3 miles SE of Bush Point..		47 59	122 33	- - -	-2 11	- - -	-2 25	0.6	0.4	0.0 - -	1.0 133	0.0 - -	1.1 354
1030	Olele Point, 1.8 miles ENE of <9>.......		47 59	122 38	-0 34	-0 31	-0 34	-0 37	0.5	0.5	0.0 - -	0.8 167	0.0 - -	1.3 352
					on DECEPTION PASS									
1035	Port Townsend Canal....................		48 02	122 44	+0 06	-0 40	-0 46	-0 31	0.5	0.4	0.0 - -	2.6 150	0.0 - -	2.9 330

Endnotes can be found at the end of Table 2.

Current Differences and Other Constants

NO.	PLACE	METER DEPTH (ft)	POSITION Lat. (° ′ N)	POSITION Long. (° ′ W)	TIME DIFF. Min. before Flood (h. m.)	TIME DIFF. Flood (h. m.)	TIME DIFF. Min. before Ebb (h. m.)	TIME DIFF. Ebb (h. m.)	SPEED RATIOS Flood	SPEED RATIOS Ebb	Minimum before Flood (knots deg.)	Maximum Flood (knots deg.)	Minimum before Ebb (knots deg.)	Maximum Ebb (knots deg.)
	HOOD CANAL Time meridian, 120°W					on ADMIRALTY INLET								
1040	Foulweather Bluff		47 56	122 38	0 00	-0 24	-0 15	-0 25	0.4	0.4	0.0 --	0.7 140	0.0 --	0.9 325
1045	Port Gamble Bay, 0.5 mile N of entrance.		47 52	122 35	Current weak and variable									
1050	Port Gamble Bay entrance		47 51	122 35	-1 03	-0 39	+0 04	-0 14	0.6	0.3	0.0 --	0.9 185	0.0 --	0.7 000
1055	Port Gamble Bay		47 50	122 34	Current weak and variable									
1060	South Point		47 49	122 41	- - -	-0 44	- - -	-0 29	0.4	0.4	0.0 --	0.6 218	0.0 --	1.0 040
1065	Hazel Point		47 42	122 46	- - -	-0 54	- - -	-0 52	0.3	0.3	0.0 --	0.4 183	0.0 --	0.8 005
1070	Chinom Point		47 32	123 02	Current weak and variable									
1075	The Great Bend		47 21	123 02	- - -	-1 06	- - -	-0 50	0.3	0.2	0.0 --	0.4 049	0.0 --	0.5 251
	PUGET SOUND													
1080	Useless Bay		47 59	122 30	Current weak and variable									
1085	Foulweather Bluff		47 57	122 35	+0 09	+0 01	+0 14	-0 18	0.9	0.7	0.0 --	1.5 115	0.0 --	1.8 335
1090	Edmonds, 2.7 miles WSW of		47 48	122 27	+0 44	+0 06	+0 13	+0 19	0.1	0.2	0.0 --	0.2 170	0.0 --	0.5 000
1095	Apple Cove Point, 0.5 mile east of		47 49	122 28	- - -	-0 11	- - -	-0 29	0.3	0.3	0.0 --	0.5 168	0.0 --	0.8 008
1100	President Point, 1.5 miles east of		47 46	122 26	- - -	-0 38	- - -	-0 41	0.2	0.2	0.0 --	0.3 203	0.0 --	0.5 024
1105	Port Madison entrance		47 44	122 30	Current weak and variable									
1110	Agate Passage, north end		47 43	122 33	-1 28	-1 00	-0 18	-0 59	0.8	0.7	0.0 --	1.2 230	0.0 --	1.8 032
1115	Agate Passage, south end <27>		47 43	122 34	-1 25	-0 53	0 00	-0 47	2.0	1.4	0.0 --	3.3 216	0.0 --	3.6 037
1120	Port Orchard		47 38	122 35	Current weak and variable									
1125	Port Orchard, off Keyport		47 42	122 36	Current weak and variable									
1130	Liberty Bay entrance, Port Orchard		47 42	122 38	- - -	-0 06	- - -	+0 22	0.4	0.3	0.0 --	0.7 280	0.0 --	0.8 113
1135	Shilshole Bay		47 41	122 25	Current weak and variable									
1140	West Point, 0.3 mile west of		47 40	122 26	-0 44	-0 43	-0 16	-0 47	0.4	0.3	0.0 --	0.7 225	0.0 --	0.7 015
1145	West Point, 1.2 miles west of		47 40	122 28	Current weak and variable									
1150	Elliott Bay entrance		47 37	122 24	Current weak and variable									
1155	Alki Point, 0.3 mile west of		47 35	122 26	-0 36	-0 44	-0 13	-0 39	0.3	0.2	0.0 --	0.5 160	0.0 --	0.5 330
1160	Restoration Point, 0.6 mile ESE of		47 35	122 28	- - -	-0 38	- - -	-0 06	0.3	0.3	0.0 --	0.5 135	0.0 --	0.7 034
	Rich Passage													
1165	Approach, north of Blake Island		47 34	122 30	- - -	-0 17	- - -	+0 44	0.1	0.3	0.0 --	0.2 301	0.0 --	0.9 071
1170	East end		47 34	122 32	- - -	+0 37	- - -	+0 51	0.5	0.4	0.0 --	0.8 321	0.0 --	1.1 143
1175	Off Pleasant Beach		47 35	122 32	-0 14	-0 15	+0 36	+0 43	0.8	1.1	0.0 --	1.3 330	0.0 --	2.8 132
1180	West end		47 35	122 34	-0 44	-0 08	+0 46	+0 22	1.5	1.2	0.0 --	2.4 238	0.0 --	3.1 055
1185	Port Orchard, southwest of Waterman		47 34	122 36	Current weak and variable									
1190	Sinclair Inlet		- - -	- - -	Current weak and variable									
1195	Port Washington Narrows, south ent		47 34	122 37	-0 09	+0 13	+0 55	+1 08	0.6	0.7	0.0 --	1.0 326	0.0 --	1.7 154
1200	Port Washington Narrows, north ent <27>		47 36	122 40	-0 25	+0 19	+1 08	+1 15	1.4	0.8	0.0 --	2.2 330	0.0 --	2.2 156
1205	Blake Island, southwest of		47 32	122 30	-2 58	-2 37	-1 06	-0 25	0.2	0.2	0.0 --	0.3 131	0.0 --	0.5 326
						on THE NARROWS								
1210	Colvos Passage <29>		- - -	- - -	- - -	- - -	- - -	+0 49	--	0.4	-- --	-- --	-- --	1.1 016
1215	East Passage		- - -	- - -	Current weak and variable									
1220	Quartermaster Harbor entrance		47 21	122 29	- - -	-0 31	- - -	-0 09	0.1	0.1	0.0 --	0.4 349	0.0 --	0.4 167
1225	Commencement Bay		- - -	- - -	Current weak and variable									
1230	Dalco Passage <30>		47 20	122 31	- - -	-0 11	- - -	- - -	0.4	--	0.0 --	1.3 290	0.0 --	-- --
1235	Gig Harbor entrance		47 20	122 34	-0 39	-0 57	-0 46	+0 11	0.3	0.4	0.0 --	0.9 016	0.0 --	1.2 176

Endnotes can be found at the end of Table 2.

Current Differences and Other Constants

NO.	PLACE	METER DEPTH	POSITION — Lat.	POSITION — Long.	TIME DIFF. — Min. before Flood	TIME DIFF. — Flood	TIME DIFF. — Min. before Ebb	TIME DIFF. — Ebb	SPEED RATIOS — Flood	SPEED RATIOS — Ebb	AVG — Minimum before Flood	AVG — Maximum Flood	AVG — Minimum before Ebb	AVG — Maximum Ebb
		ft	° ′ N	° ′ W	h. m.	h. m.	h. m.	h. m.			knots deg.	knots deg.	knots deg.	knots deg.
	PUGET SOUND. Time meridian, 120°W				on THE NARROWS									
	The Narrows													
1240	THE NARROWS, north end (midstream)...		47 18	122 33	Daily Predictions						0.0 - -	3.2 136	0.0 - -	2.8 334
1245	North End (east side) <31>..........		47 18	122 32	- - -	- - -	- - -	+0 23	- -	1.4	0.0 - -	- - - -	0.0 - -	3.8 340
1250	North End (west side) <32>..........		47 18	122 33	- - -	+0 08	+0 05	-1 28	0.9	0.4	0.0 - -	3.0 143	0.0 - -	1.1 324
1255	0.1 mile east of Point Evans <33>....		47 17	122 33	-0 06	-0 06	-0 28	+0 02	1.3	1.2	0.0 - -	4.3 201	0.0 - -	3.4 023
1260	South end (midstream) <34>..........		47 16	122 33	-0 05	+0 04	-0 16	-0 05	1.2	1.1	0.0 - -	3.8 218	0.0 - -	3.1 022
1265	Hale Passage, east end <31>.........		47 15	122 35	- - -	- - -	- - -	-2 44	- -	0.3	0.0 - -	- - - -	0.0 - -	0.7 093
1270	Hale Passage, west end.............		47 17	122 39	0 00	-1 12	-2 20	-1 00	0.4	0.6	0.0 - -	1.4 299	0.0 - -	1.8 119
1275	Carr Inlet........................		- - -	- - -	Current weak and variable									
1280	Gibson Point, 0.8 mile east of..........		47 13	122 35	+0 28	+0 43	+0 08	+0 15	0.7	0.6	0.0 - -	2.1 203	0.0 - -	1.8 029
1285	Cormorant Passage <35>............		47 09	122 37	- - -	- - -	- - -	+2 06	- -	0.3	0.0 - -	- - - -	0.0 - -	0.7 026
1290	Nisqually Reach, E of Sandy Point <36>..		47 09	122 39	- - -	- - -	- - -	+1 17	- -	0.3	0.0 - -	- - - -	0.0 - -	0.8 036
1295	Nisqually Reach....................		47 07	122 42	+0 26	+0 24	+0 20	+0 31	0.3	0.4	0.0 - -	1.1 259	0.0 - -	1.1 044
1300	Balch Passage.....................		47 11	122 41	-0 09	-1 07	-0 40	-0 40	0.4	0.8	0.0 - -	1.1 296	0.0 - -	2.2 107
1305	Pitt Passage, east of Pitt Island........		47 13	122 43	-0 55	-1 16	-1 43	-1 24	0.3	0.5	0.0 - -	0.9 204	0.0 - -	1.4 028
1310	Drayton Passage <37>..............		47 10	122 44	- - -	- - -	- - -	-1 44	- -	0.1	0.0 - -	- - - -	0.0 - -	0.4 030
1315	Devils Head, west of <38>...........		47 10	122 47	- - -	- - -	- - -	+0 22	- -	0.2	0.0 - -	- - - -	0.0 - -	0.6 158
1320	Dana Passage.....................		47 10	122 52	+0 17	-0 09	-0 06	-0 12	0.5	0.8	0.0 - -	1.5 249	0.0 - -	2.2 076
1325	Budd Inlet entrance.................		47 08	122 55	- - -	-0 42	- - -	-0 19	0.2	0.1	0.0 - -	0.7 236	0.0 - -	0.4 031
1330	Olympia, Budd Inlet.................		47 05	122 55	Current weak and variable									
1335	Eld Inlet entrance..................		47 09	122 56	-0 04	+0 09	-0 36	-0 10	0.3	0.2	0.0 - -	0.9 224	0.0 - -	0.6 028
1340	Unsal Point, 0.3 mile south of <39>.....		47 10	122 54	- - -	- - -	- - -	-1 04	- -	0.4	0.0 - -	- - - -	0.0 - -	1.2 137
1345	Peale Passage, south end............		47 11	122 53	- - -	-0 09	- - -	-0 28	0.1	0.1	0.0 - -	0.4 341	0.0 - -	0.4 173
1350	Peale Passage, north end............		47 13	122 55	-0 14	-0 23	-0 56	-0 30	0.2	0.4	0.0 - -	0.5 319	0.0 - -	1.2 145
1355	Squaxin Passage, north of Hunter Point..		47 11	122 55	-0 42	-0 32	-0 33	-0 45	0.4	0.4	0.0 - -	1.4 286	0.0 - -	1.2 121
1360	Totten Inlet entrance................		47 11	122 57	-0 19	+0 02	-0 25	-0 09	0.5	0.4	0.0 - -	1.7 243	0.0 - -	1.0 054
	Hammersley Inlet													
1365	0.8 mile east of Libby Point..........		47 12	122 58	+1 00	+0 37	+0 05	+1 06	0.7	0.9	0.0 - -	2.3 283	0.0 - -	2.4 102
1370	west of Skookum Point.............		47 12	123 02	+1 14	+1 29	+0 57	+1 04	0.5	0.6	0.0 - -	1.7 287	0.0 - -	1.6 101
1375	Pickering Passage, south end.........		47 13	122 56	+1 05	+1 06	+0 21	+0 53	0.4	0.5	0.0 - -	1.3 190	0.0 - -	1.3 013
1380	Pickering Passage, off Graham Point.....		47 15	122 56	+1 17	+1 03	+0 24	+1 20	0.3	0.5	0.0 - -	1.1 199	0.0 - -	1.3 034
1385	Pickering Passage, north end..........		47 18	122 51	+1 24	+1 03	+1 11	+1 33	0.2	0.2	0.0 - -	0.6 250	0.0 - -	0.6 067
1390	Case Inlet, 1 mile SE of McMicken Island		47 14	122 51	Current weak and variable									
	POSSESSION SOUND–SKAGIT BAY				on ADMIRALTY INLET									
1395	Possession Sound..................		- - -	- - -	Current weak and variable									
1400	Port Susan.......................		48 06	122 22	Current weak and variable									
1405	Saratoga Passage..................		- - -	- - -	Current weak and variable									
1410	Skagit Bay, 1 mile north of Rocky Point.		48 16	122 32	- - -	+0 56	- - -	+1 47	0.4	0.4	0.0 - -	0.6 060	0.0 - -	1.0 236
					on DECEPTION PASS									
1415	Skagit Bay, 1 mi. S of Goat Island <41>.		48 21	122 32	-1 07	-1 26	-0 53	-0 53	0.3	0.2	0.0 - -	1.8 139	0.0 - -	1.4 312
1420	Skagit Bay, channel SW of Hope Island..		48 24	122 35	-0 20	-0 40	-0 08	-0 15	0.4	0.3	0.0 - -	2.3 165	0.0 - -	2.0 344

Endnotes can be found at the end of Table 2.

Current Differences and Other Constants

NO.	PLACE	METER DEPTH (ft)	POSITION Lat. (° ' N)	POSITION Long. (° ' W)	TIME DIFF. Min. before Flood (h.m.)	TIME DIFF. Flood (h.m.)	TIME DIFF. Min. before Ebb (h.m.)	TIME DIFF. Ebb (h.m.)	SPEED RATIOS Flood	SPEED RATIOS Ebb	Minimum before Flood (knots)	(deg.)	Maximum Flood (knots)	(deg.)	Minimum before Ebb (knots)	(deg.)	Maximum Ebb (knots)	(deg.)
	ROSARIO STRAIT <40> Time meridian, 120°W																	
					on DECEPTION PASS													
1425	Yokeko Point, Deception Pass		48 25	122 37	+0 04	-0 24	-0 25	+0 17	0.4	0.4	0.0	- -	2.1	064	0.0	- -	2.7	222
1430	DECEPTION PASS, (Narrows)		48 24	122 38	Daily Predictions						0.0	- -	5.2	090	0.0	- -	6.6	270
					on ROSARIO STRAIT													
1435	Deception Island, 1.0 mile west of		48 24	122 42	- - -	+1 14	- - -	-1 23	0.6	0.5	0.0	- -	0.6	035	0.0	- -	1.0	210
1440	Iceberg Point, 2.1 miles SSW of		48 23	122 55	-0 34	-0 05	+1 21	-0 10	1.0	0.4	0.0	- -	1.1	010	0.0	- -	0.8	260
1445	Colville Island, 1 mile SSE of		48 24	122 49	+0 19	+0 31	+0 46	+0 07	1.0	1.2	0.0	- -	1.1	055	0.0	- -	2.3	235
1450	Colville Island, 1.4 miles east of		48 25	122 47	+0 03	+0 14	+0 17	-0 14	1.4	1.0	0.0	- -	1.6	055	0.0	- -	1.9	215
1455	Deception Island, 2.7 miles west of		48 25	122 44	+1 08	+0 50	+0 38	-0 34	0.8	0.7	0.0	- -	0.9	015	0.0	- -	1.3	190
1460	W Point, Whidbey I., 1.8 mi. SW of <9>		48 23	122 42	- - -	+0 46	- - -	-2 23	0.6	0.5	0.0	- -	0.6	005	0.0	- -	1.0	207
1465	Deception Island, 1.3 miles NW of		48 25	122 42	- - -	+0 04	- - -	-2 29	1.2	0.6	0.0	- -	1.3	017	0.0	- -	1.1	161
1470	ROSARIO STRAIT		48 28	122 47	Daily Predictions						0.0	- -	1.1	335	0.0	- -	1.9	175
1475	Lopez Pass		48 29	122 49	-1 13	-1 33	-0 39	-1 16	1.4	1.0	0.0	- -	1.6	275	0.0	- -	1.9	085
1480	Burrows Bay, 0.5 mile east of Allan I.		48 28	122 41	-3 01	-0 48	+0 22	-0 43	0.9	0.2	0.0	- -	1.0	022	0.0	- -	0.4	209
1485	Burrows I.-Allan I., Passage between		48 28	122 42	-2 05	-0 34	+0 09	-0 57	2.0	0.7	0.0	- -	2.2	304	0.0	- -	1.4	096
1490	Burrows Island Light, 0.8 miles WNW of		48 29	122 44	+0 29	+0 30	+0 13	+0 16	1.0	1.1	0.0	- -	1.1	015	0.0	- -	2.1	200
1495	Fidalgo Head-Burrows Island, between		48 29	122 42	- - -	-1 03	-0 32	-1 57	1.6	0.5	0.0	- -	1.8	270	0.0	- -	0.9	090
1500	Green Point, 0.8 mile northwest of		48 30	122 42	-0 55	-0 30	-0 08	-1 02	1.8	1.0	0.0	- -	2.0	020	0.0	- -	1.9	190
1505	Shannon Point, 2.0 miles west of		48 31	122 44	-0 19	+0 49	+0 50	-0 16	1.2	1.0	0.0	- -	1.4	005	0.0	- -	1.8	190
1510	Fauntleroy Point Light, 0.8 mile ESE of		48 31	122 46	+0 08	+0 16	-1 10	-0 33	1.1	0.7	0.0	- -	1.2	310	0.0	- -	1.4	125
1515	Thatcher Pass		48 32	122 48	+0 43	+1 01	+1 26	+0 51	0.4	0.5	0.0	- -	0.4	300	0.0	- -	0.9	075
1520	Frost-Willow Island, between		48 32	122 50	+0 46	+1 14	+0 19	+0 29	0.6	0.4	0.0	- -	0.6	010	0.0	- -	0.8	126
1525	Strawberry Island, 0.8 mile west of		48 34	122 45	+0 43	+0 46	+0 37	+0 30	1.4	1.4	0.0	- -	1.5	020	0.0	- -	2.6	190
1530	Peavine Pass, west entrance		48 35	122 49	-0 42	-0 41	-0 26	-0 52	1.6	1.2	0.0	- -	1.7	055	0.0	- -	2.2	285
1535	Obstruction Pass Light, 0.4 mile NW of		48 36	122 49	-0 59	-0 44	-0 38	-0 49	1.2	0.5	0.0	- -	1.3	100	0.0	- -	1.0	270
1540	Peapod Rocks Light, 1.2 miles south of		48 38	122 45	+0 08	+1 12	+0 49	-0 15	1.2	1.0	0.0	- -	1.3	030	0.0	- -	1.9	215
1545	Barnes Island, 0.8 mile southwest of		48 41	122 47	+0 37	+1 20	-0 07	+0 08	0.6	0.5	0.0	- -	0.6	315	0.0	- -	0.9	140
1550	Raccoon Point, 0.6 mile NNE of		48 42	122 50	-0 36	-0 45	-1 41	-0 20	0.6	0.4	0.0	- -	0.6	286	0.0	- -	0.8	101
1555	Parker Reef Light, 0.5 mile north of		48 44	122 54	+1 31	+1 02	+1 14	+1 02	1.0	0.8	0.0	- -	1.1	067	0.0	- -	1.5	278
1560	Matia Island, 0.8 mile west of		48 45	122 52	+0 22	+0 26	-0 26	+0 14	1.1	0.8	0.0	- -	1.2	350	0.0	- -	1.5	206
1565	Bound. Pass, 2 mi. NNE of Skipjack I.		48 46	123 01	+0 26	+0 34	+0 49	-0 02	1.6	1.4	0.5	295	1.7	041	0.2	120	2.7	203
1570	Guemes Channel, west entrance		48 31	122 39	-0 21	-0 33	-1 24	-0 36	0.8	1.1	0.0	- -	0.9	095	0.0	- -	2.1	255
1575	Padilla Bay, 0.8 mi. NW of March Pt <42>		48 31	122 35	- -	- -	- -	- -	- -	- -	- -	- -	- -	- -	- -	- -	- -	- -
1580	Guemes Island, 0.5 mile east of		48 32	122 34	Current weak and variable													
1585	Huckleberry Island, 0.5 mile north of		48 33	122 34	-3 17	+0 18	+0 36	-1 10	0.7	0.3	0.0	- -	0.8	006	0.0	- -	0.6	253
1590	William Point Light, 0.8 mile W of		48 35	122 35	- - -	+0 36	- - -	+0 23	0.1	0.2	0.0	- -	0.1	- -	0.0	- -	0.3	230
1595	Eliza Island, 0.5 mile southeast of		48 39	122 34	Current weak and variable													
1600	Bellingham Channel, off Cypress I. Light		48 34	122 40	-0 48	+0 08	-0 49	-0 51	1.1	1.2	0.0	- -	1.2	045	0.0	- -	2.2	185
1605	Towhead Island, 0.4 mile east of		48 37	122 42	-1 55	+1 13	+2 43	+0 01	0.7	0.2	0.0	- -	0.8	315	0.0	- -	0.4	125
1610	Sinclair Island Light, 0.6 mile SE of		48 36	122 39	+0 16	+0 48	+0 22	+0 18	1.3	0.8	0.0	- -	1.4	045	0.0	- -	1.6	210
1615	Sinclair Island, 1 mile northeast of		48 38	122 39	+0 51	+1 04	-0 29	+0 58	0.1	0.4	0.0	- -	0.1	307	0.0	- -	0.8	112
1620	Sinclair Island, 1 mile NE of <43>		48 39	122 39	- - -	- - -	- - -	+1 23	- -	0.4	- -	- -	- -	- -	- -	- -	0.8	110
1625	Lawrence Point, Orcas I., 1.3 mi. NE of		48 41	122 43	+0 56	+0 58	+0 59	+0 55	1.2	0.8	0.0	- -	1.4	345	0.0	- -	1.4	145
1630	Hale Passage, 0.5 mile SE of Lummi Point		48 44	122 41	-0 43	+0 05	+0 20	-0 11	1.0	0.5	0.0	- -	1.1	350	0.0	- -	1.0	145
1635	Clark Island, 1.6 miles north of		48 44	122 46	+0 47	+1 14	+0 44	-0 02	0.6	0.6	0.0	- -	0.7	335	0.0	- -	1.1	150
1640	Matia Island, 1.4 miles north of		48 46	122 51	+0 02	+0 57	+0 59	+0 08	0.6	0.3	0.0	- -	0.6	330	0.0	- -	0.6	190
1645	Parker Reef Light, 1 mile north of		48 45	122 54	- - -	+1 38	- - -	-0 52	0.9	0.4	0.0	- -	1.0	065	0.0	- -	0.7	265

Endnotes can be found at the end of Table 2.

Current Differences and Other Constants

NO.	PLACE	METER DEPTH	POSITION		TIME DIFFERENCES				SPEED RATIOS		AVERAGE SPEEDS AND DIRECTIONS							
			Lat.	Long.	Min. before Flood	Flood	Min. before Ebb	Ebb	Flood	Ebb	Minimum before Flood		Maximum Flood		Minimum before Ebb		Maximum Ebb	
		ft	° ' N	° ' W	h. m.	h. m.	h. m.	h. m.			knots deg.		knots deg.		knots deg.		knots deg.	
	ROSARIO STRAIT <40> Time meridian, 120°W				on ROSARIO STRAIT													
1650	Puffin Island Light, 4.8 miles north of.		48 49	122 48	+0 18	+1 30	+0 55	+0 11	0.4	0.4	0.0	- -	0.5	325	0.0	- -	0.8	210
1652	Neptune Beach, 1.2 miles NW of <44>.....		48 49	122 44	- - -	+1 43	- - -	- - -	0.4	- -	0.0	- -	0.4	359	0.0	- -	- -	- -
1653	Cherry Point, 1.5 miles SE of...........		48 51	122 43	- - -	+1 04	- - -	+0 13	0.3	0.2	0.0	- -	0.3	326	0.0	- -	0.3	116
	SAN JUAN CHANNEL				on SAN JUAN CHANNEL													
1655	Cattle Point, 1.2 miles southeast of....		48 26	122 57	+0 11	-0 20	+0 34	-0 01	0.3	0.9	0.0	- -	0.8	340	0.0	- -	2.4	195
1660	SAN JUAN CHANNEL (south entrance).......		48 28	122 57	Daily Predictions						0.0	- -	2.6	010	0.0	- -	2.6	180
1665	Kings Point, Lopez Island, 1 mile NNW of		48 29	122 57	+0 51	-0 07	+0 27	+0 36	0.6	0.5	0.0	- -	1.6	020	0.0	- -	1.3	185
1670	Pear Point, 1.1 miles east of...........		48 31	122 57	+0 40	+1 09	-0 10	+1 01	0.4	0.5	0.0	- -	1.0	359	0.0	- -	1.4	203
1675	Turn Rock Light, 1.9 miles northwest of.		48 33	123 00	+1 19	+1 22	+0 20	-0 01	0.4	0.5	0.0	- -	0.9	330	0.0	- -	1.3	135
1680	Crane Island, south of, Wasp Passage....		48 35	123 00	-0 10	+0 35	+0 29	+0 07	0.2	0.1	0.0	- -	0.4	288	0.0	- -	0.3	075
1685	Wasp Passage Light, 0.5 mile WSW of.....		48 36	122 59	+0 19	+0 28	+0 15	-0 15	0.5	0.4	0.0	- -	1.2	300	0.0	- -	1.1	110
1690	Spring Passage, south entrance..........		48 37	123 02	+0 04	-1 09	-0 43	-0 13	0.4	0.4	0.0	- -	0.9	010	0.0	- -	1.0	150
1695	Limestone Point, Spieden Channel........		48 38	123 07	+0 23	-0 12	-1 00	+0 26	0.7	1.2	0.0	- -	1.8	085	0.0	- -	3.2	283
1700	Point Disney, 1.6 miles east of.........		48 40	123 00	+2 36	+1 31	+0 48	+1 51	0.2	0.8	0.0	- -	0.5	020	0.0	- -	2.2	230
1705	Harney Channel..........................		48 35	122 55	+0 15	+0 21	+0 11	+0 05	0.2	0.3	0.0	- -	0.6	250	0.0	- -	0.7	120
1710	East Sound entrance.....................		48 35	122 51	Current weak and variable													
1715	East Sound, 0.2 mile SW of Rosario Point		48 39	122 53	Current weak and variable													
	HARO STRAIT and BOUNDARY PASS				on ADMIRALTY INLET													
1720	Discovery Island, 3.3 miles northeast of		48 27	123 09	+1 16	+1 03	+0 59	+0 59	0.8	0.6	0.0	- -	1.3	345	0.0	- -	1.6	170
1725	Kellett Bluff, west of..................		48 35	123 14	+0 01	+0 20	+0 36	+0 20	1.0	0.8	0.0	- -	1.6	000	0.0	- -	2.1	170
1730	Turn Point, Boundary Pass...............		48 41	123 15	+0 26	+0 51	+1 18	+0 26	0.4	0.6	0.0	- -	0.7	080	0.0	- -	1.6	260
1735	Skipjack Island, 2 miles NNE of.........		48 46	123 01	See station No. 1565						0.0	- -	1.7	040	0.0	- -	2.7	205
					on SAN JUAN CHANNEL													
1740	Johns Island, 0.8 mile north of.........		48 41	123 09	-0 15	-0 31	+0 06	+0 49	0.2	0.2	0.0	- -	0.6	090	0.0	- -	0.6	350
1745	Waldron Island, 1.7 miles west of.......		48 42	123 07	+0 37	+0 36	+1 10	+1 05	0.5	0.4	0.0	- -	1.4	040	0.0	- -	1.2	260
1750	Skipjack Island, 1.5 miles northwest of.		48 45	123 04	+1 17	+1 19	+1 08	+1 12	0.3	0.5	0.0	- -	0.8	035	0.0	- -	1.4	290
1755	Point Hammond, 1.1 miles northwest of...		48 44	123 02	+1 11	+1 05	+0 27	+1 13	0.2	0.9	0.0	- -	0.6	055	0.0	- -	2.4	255
					on ROSARIO STRAIT													
1760	Alden Point, Patos Island, 2 miles S of.		48 45	122 59	+0 09	-0 26	+0 15	-0 53	0.9	1.1	0.0	- -	1.0	025	0.0	- -	2.1	185
1765	Patos Island Light, 1.4 miles west of...		48 47	123 00	+0 19	+0 30	+0 40	-0 02	0.8	1.0	0.0	- -	0.8	065	0.0	- -	2.0	180
1770	Toe Point, Patos Island, 0.5 mile S of..		48 47	122 56	-2 31	+0 49	+0 51	-0 47	1.4	0.8	0.0	- -	1.6	045	0.0	- -	1.6	270
	GEORGIA STRAIT				on ADMIRALTY INLET													
1775	Drayton Harbor Entrance.................		48 59	122 46	-0 27	-0 11	+0 48	+0 13	0.6	0.4	0.0	- -	1.0	133	0.0	- -	1.0	313

Endnotes can be found at the end of Table 2.

Tidal Differences and Other Constants

NO.	PLACE	POSITION		DIFFERENCES				RANGES		Mean Tide Level
		Lat.	Long.	Time		Height		Mean	Diurnal	
				High water	Low water	High water	Low water			
		° ′ N	° ′ .W	h. m.	h. m.	ft	ft	ft	ft	ft
	OREGON–Continued Time meridian, 120°W									
	Siuslaw River									
827	Entrance	44 01	124 08	+0 03	+0 19	+0.5	0.0	5.5	7.3	4.0
829	Florence	43 58	124 06	+0 53	+1 14	-0.2	-0.2	5.0	6.6	3.5
831	Waldport, Alsea Bay	44 26	124 04	+0 30	+0 47	+0.8	0.0	5.8	7.7	4.1
	Yaquina Bay and River									
833	Bar at entrance	44 37	124 05	+0 08	+0 25	+1.0	+0.1	5.9	7.9	4.2
835	Newport	44 38	124 03	+0 18	+0 28	+1.1	+0.1	6.0	8.0	4.3
837	Southbeach	44 38	124 03	+0 07	+0 17	+1.4	+0.1	6.3	8.3	4.5
839	Yaquina	44 36	124 01	+0 29	+0 41	+1.3	+0.1	6.2	8.2	4.4
841	Winant	44 35	124 00	+0 37	+1 02	+1.3	0.0	6.3	8.2	4.3
843	Toledo	44 37	123 56	+1 03	+1 25	+1.2	-0.1	6.3	8.1	4.2
845	Taft, Siletz Bay	44 56	124 01	+0 22	+0 59	-0.3	-0.3	5.0	6.6	3.4
847	Kernville, Siletz River	44 54	124 00	+0 58	+1 39	-0.8	-0.4	4.6	6.1	3.1
849	Nestucca Bay entrance	45 10	123 58	+0 29	+0 58	+0.7	-0.1	5.8	7.6	4.0
	Tillamook Bay									
851	Barview	45 34	123 57	+0 16	+0 42	+0.6	-0.1	5.7	7.5	3.9
853	Garibaldi	45 34	123 55	+0 48	+1 02	+0.9	0.0	5.9	7.8	4.2
855	Miami Cove	45 33	123 54	+0 49	+1 12	+0.5	-0.1	5.6	7.4	3.9
857	Bay City	45 31	123 54	+1 07	+1 46	+0.2	-0.2	5.4	7.1	3.7
859	Tillamook, Hoquarten Slough	45 28	123 51	+1 26	+3 01	-0.3	-0.5	5.2	6.6	3.3
	Nehalem River									
861	Brighton	45 40	123 56	+0 25	+0 40	+0.9	0.0	5.9	7.8	4.1
863	Nehalem	45 43	123 53	+0 51	+1 42	+0.3	-0.3	5.6	7.2	3.7
	OREGON and WASHINGTON Columbia River ⟨5⟩									
865	Columbia River entrance (N. Jetty)	46 16	124 04	-0 44	-1 00	-1.0	+0.1	5.6	7.5	4.0
867	Ilwaco, Baker Bay, Wash.	46 18	124 02	-0 13	+0 01	-0.8	-0.1	6.0	7.6	4.0
869	Chinook, Baker Bay, Wash.	46 16	123 57	-0 13	-0 34	-0.5	0.0	6.2	7.9	4.2
871	Hungry Harbor, Wash.	46 16	123 51	+0 04	-0 09	-0.2	+0.1	6.4	8.2	4.4
873	Point Adams, Oreg.	46 12	123 57	-0 25	-0 38	-0.2	+0.1	6.4	8.3	4.4
875	Warrenton, Skipanon River, Oreg.	46 10	123 55	-0 13	-0 19	-0.1	+0.1	6.5	8.3	4.4
877	Astoria (Youngs Bay), Oreg.	46 10	123 50	-0 13	-0 14	+0.1	+0.1	6.7	8.6	4.5
879	Astoria (Port Docks), Oreg.	46 11	123 52	-0 08	-0 03	-0.5	0.0	6.2	8.0	4.2
881	ASTORIA (Tongue Point), Oreg.	46 12	123 46	Daily predictions				6.6	8.4	4.4
883	Settlers Point, Oreg.	46 10	123 41	+0 22	+0 53	-0.5	-0.1	6.3	8.0	4.1
885	Harrington Point, Wash.	46 16	123 39	+0 21	+0 52	-0.8	-0.2	6.1	7.7	3.9
887	Skamokawa, Steamboat Slough, Wash.	46 16	123 27	+0 56	+1 45	- -	- -	5.6	6.9	- -
889	Cathlamet, Wash.	46 12	123 23	+1 15	+2 15	- -	- -	5.2	6.4	- -
891	Wauna, Oreg.	46 10	123 24	+1 17	+2 19	- -	- -	5.2	6.3	- -
893	Eagle Cliff, Wash.	46 10	123 14	+1 43	+3 01	- -	- -	4.5	5.5	- -
895	Stella, Wash.	46 11	123 07	+2 01	+3 30	- -	- -	4.0	4.9	- -
897	Longview, Wash.	46 06	122 57	+2 27	+4 14	- -	- -	3.3	4.0	- -
899	Kalama, Wash.	46 00	122 51	+2 54	+4 55	- -	- -	2.6	3.2	- -
901	Saint Helens, Oreg.	45 52	122 48	+3 31	+5 44	- -	- -	2.0	2.5	- -
903	Knapp Landing, Wash.	45 44	122 45	+4 26	+6 28	- -	- -	1.5	2.0	- -
905	Kelley Point, Oreg.	45 39	122 46	+5 26	+7 16	- -	- -	1.4	2.0	- -
907	St. Johns, Willamette River, Oreg.	45 35	122 46	+5 08	+7 26	- -	- -	1.7	2.2	- -
909	Portland, Willamette River, Oreg.	45 31	122 40	+5 05	+7 37	- -	- -	1.8	2.4	- -
911	Vancouver, Wash.	45 37	122 40	+5 45	+7 38	- -	- -	1.3	1.8	- -
913	Ellsworth, Wash.	45 36	122 33	+6 11	+8 03	- -	- -	1.0	1.4	- -
915	Washougal, Wash.	45 35	122 23	- - -	- - -	- -	- -	0.5	0.9	- -
917	Warrendale, Oreg.	45 37	122 00	- - -	- -	- -	- -	0.4	0.6	- -
	WASHINGTON									
919	Long Beach	46 21	124 03	-1 05	-0 59	*0.80	*0.80	6.2	8.1	4.4
	Willapa Bay and River									
921	Willapa Bay entrance	46 43	124 04	-0 37	-0 43	*0.80	*0.80	6.2	8.1	4.4
923	Nahcotta, Willapa Bay	46 30	124 01	+0 20	+0 16	0.0	-0.1	8.0	10.2	5.4
925	Tarlatt Slough, Willapa Bay	46 22	124 00	+0 21	+0 54	*0.91	*0.47	7.9	9.4	4.6
927	Bay Center, Palix River	46 38	123 57	-0 09	+0 04	-1.3	-0.2	6.8	8.9	4.7
929	Toke Point, Willapa Bay	46 42	123 58	-0 36	-0 19	-1.6	-0.2	6.5	8.5	4.5
931	South Bend, Willapa River	46 40	123 48	-0 04	-0 08	-0.3	-0.2	7.8	9.8	5.2
933	Raymond, Willapa River	46 41	123 45	+0 02	-0 03	-0.2	-0.1	7.8	9.9	5.3
935	Grayland	46 49	124 06	-1 05	-0 59	*0.80	*0.80	6.2	8.1	4.4
937	Westport (ocean)	46 53	124 07	-1 05	-0 56	*0.84	*0.84	6.4	8.5	4.6
	Grays Harbor									
939	Point Chehalis	46 55	124 07	-0 32	-0 43	-1.1	-0.1	6.9	9.0	4.8
941	Bay City	46 52	124 04	-0 15	-0 32	-0.9	-0.1	7.1	9.2	4.9
943	Markham	46 54	124 00	-0 19	-0 12	-0.9	-0.2	7.2	9.2	4.9
945	North Channel	46 58	123 57	-0 06	-0 01	-0.4	-0.1	7.6	9.7	5.2
947	ABERDEEN	46 58	123 51	Daily predictions				7.9	10.1	5.4
949	Montesano, Chehalis River	46 58	123 36	+1 21	+1 48	*0.80	*0.53	6.7	8.1	4.1
951	Pacific Beach	47 13	124 12	-1 02	-0 59	*0.85	*0.85	6.5	8.6	4.6
953	Point Grenville	47 18	124 16	-1 02	-0 59	*0.85	*0.85	6.5	8.6	4.6
955	Destruction Island	47 40	124 29	-1 01	-1 03	*0.87	*0.87	6.6	8.7	4.7
957	La Push, Quillayute River	47 55	124 38	-1 00	-0 47	*0.84	*0.84	6.5	8.5	4.6
959	Cape Alava (Flattery Rocks)	48 10	124 44	-0 53	-0 39	*0.81	*0.81	6.0	8.2	4.4

Endnotes can be found at the end of table 2.

Tidal Differences and Other Constants

NO.	PLACE	POSITION Lat.	Long.	DIFFERENCES Time High water	Low water	Height High water	Low water	RANGES Mean	Diurnal	Mean Tide level
		° ' N	° ' W	h. m.	h. m.	ft	ft	ft	ft	ft
	Strait of Juan de Fuca ⟨6⟩ Time meridian, 120°W									
961	Cape Flattery, Tatoosh Island...........	48 23	124 44	-0 46	-0 46	*0.80	*0.80	5.8	8.0	4.2
963	Neah Bay................................	48 22	124 37	-0 37	-0 35	*0.78	*0.78	5.5	7.9	4.2
965	Clallam Bay.............................	48 16	124 18	-0 11	-0 08	*0.76	*0.76	5.0	7.7	4.3
967	Twin Rivers.............................	48 10	123 57	+0 09	+0 11	*0.71	*0.71	4.4	7.0	4.1
969	Crescent Bay............................	48 10	123 44	-2 41	-2 02	*0.80	*0.80	4.1	6.7	4.1
971	Port Angeles............................	48 07	123 26	-1 33	-1 23	*0.86	*0.86	4.2	7.2	4.4
973	Dungeness...............................	48 10	123 07	-0 54	-0 38	*0.90	*0.90	4.4	7.6	4.2
975	Sequim Bay entrance.....................	48 05	123 03	-0 39	-0 07	*0.94	*0.94	4.8	7.9	4.8
977	Gardiner, Discovery Bay.................	48 04	122 55	-0 47	-0 17	*0.94	*0.94	4.8	7.9	4.8
979	Smith Island...........................	48 19	122 50	-0 13	-0 25	*0.83	*0.83	4.2	7.0	4.5
981	Point Partridge........................	48 14	122 46	-0 11	-0 15	*0.92	*0.92	4.5	7.7	4.7
	Admiralty Inlet									
983	Admiralty Head.........................	48 10	122 40	-0 11	+0 20	0.0	-0.1	5.2	8.4	5.1
985	PORT TOWNSEND..........................	48 07	122 45	Daily predictions				5.2	8.4	5.1
987	Port Townsend (Point Hudson)...........	48 07	122 45	-0 11	-0 06	+0.2	0.0	5.3	8.6	5.2
989	Marrowstone Point......................	48 06	122 41	+0 02	+0 05	+0.4	-0.1	5.6	8.8	5.3
991	Mystery Bay, Marrowstone Island........	48 03	122 41	+0 13	+0 48	-0.2	-0.1	5.0	8.2	5.0
993	Bush Point.............................	48 02	122 36	+0 32	+1 11	+0.4	-0.1	5.6	8.8	5.2
995	Oak Bay................................	48 01	122 43	+0 08	+0 27	+0.9	0.0	6.0	9.4	5.6
	Hood Canal									
997	Port Ludlow............................	47 55	122 41	-0 28	-0 17	*0.87	*0.87	6.4	9.9	5.9
999	Port Gamble............................	47 51	122 35	-0 11	-0 04	*0.90	*0.90	6.7	10.3	6.1
1001	Bangor Wharf...........................	47 45	122 44	-0 15	+0 08	-0.4	0.0	7.3	10.9	6.4
1003	Zelatched Point, Dabob Bay.............	47 43	122 49	-0 04	-0 01	0.0	+0.1	7.6	11.5	6.7
1005	Seabeck................................	47 38	122 50	+0 02	+0 07	+0.2	+0.1	7.8	11.6	6.8
1007	Pleasant Harbor........................	47 40	122 55	-0 09	+0 05	+0.1	+0.1	7.7	11.6	6.8
1009	Union..................................	47 21	123 06	+0 01	+0 14	+0.3	+0.1	7.9	11.8	6.9
	Puget Sound									
1011	Hansville..............................	47 55	122 33	-0 02	+0 08	-1.1	-0.1	6.7	10.3	6.1
1013	Point No Point.........................	47 55	122 32	-0 11	-0 12	*0.91	*0.91	6.7	10.4	6.1
1015	Edmonds................................	47 49	122 23	0 00	+0 06	-0.5	0.0	7.2	10.9	6.4
1017	Port Madison...........................	47 42	122 32	-0 03	-0 04	0.0	0.0	7.7	11.4	6.6
1019	Poulsbo, Liberty Bay...................	47 44	122 39	+0 07	+0 12	+0.5	+0.1	8.1	11.9	6.9
1021	Brownsville, Port Orchard..............	47 39	122 37	+0 07	+0 12	+0.3	0.0	8.0	11.7	6.8
1023	SEATTLE (Madison St.), Elliott Bay.....	47 36	122 20	Daily predictions				7.7	11.4	6.7
1025	Eighth Ave. S., Duwamish Waterway......	47 32	122 19	+0 10	+0 11	-0.2	0.0	7.5	11.1	6.5
1027	Port Blakely...........................	47 36	122 30	+0 07	+0 07	+0.1	0.0	7.8	11.5	6.7
1029	Pleasant Beach, Rich Passage...........	47 36	122 32	+0 06	+0 11	+0.1	0.0	7.8	11.5	6.7
1031	Bremerton, Port Orchard................	47 33	122 38	+0 12	+0 16	+0.3	0.0	8.0	11.7	6.8
1033	Tracyton, Dyes Inlet...................	47 37	122 40	+0 35	+1 00	+0.9	0.0	8.6	12.3	7.1
1035	South Colby, Yukon Harbor..............	47 31	122 32	+0 06	+0 11	+0.2	0.0	7.9	11.6	6.7
1037	Des Moines.............................	47 24	122 20	+0 08	+0 13	+0.3	0.0	8.0	11.7	6.8
1039	Burton, Quartermaster Harbor...........	47 23	122 28	+0 12	+0 17	+0.5	0.0	8.2	11.9	6.9
1041	Gig Harbor.............................	47 20	122 35	+0 05	+0 15	+0.5	0.0	8.2	11.8	6.9
1043	Tacoma, Commencement Bay...............	47 17	122 25	+0 12	+0 10	+0.4	0.0	8.1	11.8	6.8
1045	Arletta, Hale Passage..................	47 17	122 39	+0 22	+0 37	+1.6	0.0	9.3	13.0	7.4
1047	Home, Von Geldern Cove, Carr Inlet.....	47 16	122 45	+0 32	+0 43	+2.2	+0.2	9.7	13.6	7.8
1049	Wauna, Carr Inlet......................	47 23	122 38	+0 19	+0 37	+1.7	0.0	9.4	13.1	7.5
1051	Steilacoom.............................	47 10	122 36	+0 21	+0 36	+1.7	0.0	9.4	13.1	7.5
1053	Hyde Point, McNeil Island..............	47 12	122 39	+0 28	+0 45	+2.0	+0.2	9.5	13.4	7.7
1055	Sequalitchew Creek, Nisqually Reach....	47 07	122 40	+0 29	+0 46	+2.0	+0.1	9.6	13.4	7.7
1057	Longbranch, Filucy Bay.................	47 13	122 45	+0 25	+0 40	+2.1	+0.1	9.7	13.5	7.7
1059	Henderson Inlet........................	47 09	122 50	+0 32	+0 49	+2.5	+0.2	10.0	14.0	8.0
1061	Vaughn, Case Inlet.....................	47 20	122 46	+0 40	+0 51	+2.7	+0.2	10.2	14.1	8.1
1063	Allyn, Case Inlet......................	47 23	122 49	+0 26	+0 47	+2.7	0.0	10.2	14.1	8.1
1065	Walkers Landing, Pickering Passage.....	47 17	122 56	+0 40	+0 51	+2.8	+0.2	10.3	14.3	8.1
1067	Arcadia, Pickering Passage.............	47 12	122 56	+0 34	+0 55	+2.9	+0.2	10.4	14.4	8.2
1069	Shelton, Oakland Bay...................	47 13	123 05	+1 11	+1 55	+2.7	-0.2	10.6	14.2	7.9
1071	Burns Point, Totten Inlet..............	47 07	123 03	+0 41	+0 58	+3.5	+0.2	11.0	15.0	8.5
1073	Rocky Point, Eld Inlet.................	47 04	123 01	+0 39	+0 56	+3.2	+0.3	10.6	14.7	8.4
1075	Dofflemeyer Point, Boston Harbor.......	47 08	122 54	+0 44	+0 57	+3.0	+0.3	10.4	14.4	8.3
1077	Olympia, Budd Inlet....................	47 03	122 54	+0 30	+0 47	+3.0	+0.2	10.5	14.4	8.2
	Possession Sound and Port Susan									
1079	Mukilteo...............................	47 57	122 18	+0 13	+0 08	-0.4	-0.1	7.4	11.0	6.4
1081	Everett................................	47 59	122 13	-0 10	-0 10	-0.3	0.0	7.4	11.1	6.5
1083	Tulalip................................	48 04	122 17	+0 07	+0 02	-0.1	0.0	7.6	11.2	6.6
1085	Kayak Point............................	48 08	122 22	-0 05	+0 03	-0.5	-0.1	7.3	10.9	6.3
1087	Stanwood, Stillaguamish River ⟨7⟩......	48 14	122 22	+0 23	+2 14	*0.62	*0.29	5.7	7.4	3.6

Endnotes can be found at the end of table 2.

Tidal Differances and Other Contants

	DIFFERENCES				
PLACE	**Time**		**Height**		**Mean**
	High water	Low water	High water	Low water	Tide level
	h. m.	h. m.	ft	ft	ft
Rosario Strait, etc.		on PORT TOWNSEND			
Reservation Bay, Fidalgo Island	-0 15	-0 05	*0.90	*0.90	4.7
Aleck Bay, Lopez Island	-0 18	-0 08	*0.88	*0.88	4.6
Burrows Bay (Allan Island)	+0 09	+0 03	*0.95	*0.88	4.8
Anacortes, Guemes Channel	+0 22	+0 33	*0.96	*1.00	5.0
Swinomish Channel ent., Padilla Bay	+0 36	+1 17	0.0	0.0	5.1
Thatcher Pass	+0 31	+0 18	*0.96	*0.92	4.9
Strawberry Bay, Cypress Island	+0 34	+0 52	*0.95	*0.95	4.9
Peavine Pass	+0 34	+0 18	*0.98	*0.92	4.9
Eagle Harbor, Cypress Island	+0 36	+0 48	*0.98	*0.92	4.9
Bellingham Bay					
Chuckanut Bay	+0 33	+0 53	*0.0	-0.1	5.1
Bellingham	+0 39	+1 08	+0.1	0.0	5.2
Hale Passage					
Point Migley	+0 56	+0 51	+0.1	0.0	5.2
Rosario, East Sound, Orcas Island	+0 27	+1 04	*0.96	*0.96	4.9
Upright Head, Lopez Island	+0 26	+0 44	*0.93	*0.93	4.8
Orcas, Orcas Island	+0 33	+0 56	*0.90	*0.90	4.7
San Juan Channel					
Richardson, Lopez Island	-0 21	-0 11	*0.87	*0.87	4.5
Friday Harbor, San Juan Island	+0 35	+0 56	*0.92	*0.92	4.8
Strait of Georgia					
Echo Bay, Sucia Islands	+1 01	+1 34	+0.1	0.0	5.2
Ferndale	+0 49	+1 20	+0.5	0.0	5.4
Blaine, Semiahmoo Bay	+0 59	+1 27	+0.9	+0.1	5.6
Haro Strait					
Kanaka Bay, San Juan Island	-0 11	-0 02	*0.86	*0.86	4.5
Roche Harbor, San Juan Island	+0 29	+0 52	*0.90	*0.90	4.7
Turn Point, Stuart Island	+0 24	+0 47	*0.90	*0.90	4.7
Boundary Pass					
Patos Island Wharf	+1 03	+1 30	0.2	*0.0	5.2
BRITISH COLUMBIA					
Passages inside Vancouver Island**		on VICTORIA			
Sooke, Vancouver Island	-0 11	-0 33	+0.8	+0.5	6.6
Esquimalt, Vancouver Island	+0 12	+0 17	0.0	-0.1	6.3
VICTORIA, Vancouver Island		Daily predictions			6.3
		on VANCOUVER			
Sidney, Haro Strait	-1 01	-1 12	*0.71	*0.61	7.1
Fulford Harbor, Saltspring Island	-0 55	-1 08	-3.5	-1.0	7.6
Active Pass, Mayne Island	-0 16	-0 30	-1.5	-0.8	8.6
Cowichan Bay	-0 53	-1 09	-3.0	-0.6	8.1
Chemainus, Stuart Channel	-0 51	-1 03	-2.2	-1.0	8.3
Ladysmith	-0 53	-1 02	-2.3	-0.8	8.4
Sand Heads, Fraser River	-0 25	-0 27	-1.2	-1.1	8.7
Atkinson Point, Burrard Inlet	-0 25	-0 27	-1.2	-1.1	8.7
VANCOUVER, Burrard Inlet		Daily predictions			9.9
Squamish, Howe Sound	-0 24	-0 24	-0.8	-1.2	8.9
Nanaimo	-0 20	-0 20	0.0	+0.1	10.0
Pender Harbor, Malaspina Strait	-0 22	-0 22	-1.1	-1.2	8.8
Comox, Baynes Sound	-0 18	-0 20	-0.4	-1.5	9.0
Whaletown, Cortes Island	-0 15	-0 17	+0.5	-0.2	10.0
Duncan Bay, Discovery Passage	-1 03	-1 16	-3.7	-1.5	7.4
Redonda Bay, Deer Passage	-0 07	-0 08	+1.2	+0.5	10.8
Yuculta, Cordero Channel	-0 59	-0 36	-0.2	+1.0	10.4
Waddington Harbor, Bute Inlet	-0 12	-0 08	+0.6	-0.4	10.1
Gowlland Harbor, Discovery Passage	-1 09	-1 18	-3.0	-0.9	8.0
Seymour Narrows (Canoe Pass)	-2 30	-3 30	-0.0	+0.5	10.0
Owen Bay, Okisollo Channel	-3 01	-3 02	-1.4	-0.2	8.9

(vertical note in center of table:) ALL TIMES ARE STANDARD. FOR DAYLIGHT SAVINGS TIME, ADD ONE HOUR.

*Ratio — Heights of high or low waters may be obtained by multiplying the heights at the reference station by the respective high or low water ratio.

**For the passages inside Vancouver Island the height differences apply only to the higher high and lower low waters at the indicated reference station.

ASTORIA (Tongue Point)

1991 TIDE TABLES

For Daylight Saving Time, add one hour.

Times and Heights of High and Low Waters

JANUARY

Day	h m	ft	cm	Day	h m	ft	cm
1 Tu	0200	8.1	247	16 W	0207	7.7	235
	0719	3.1	94		0729	3.3	101
	1308	10.2	311		1309	9.0	274
	2019	-1.5	-46		2012	-0.2	-6
2 W	0245	8.4	256	17 Th	0239	7.9	241
	0813	2.8	85		0811	3.1	94
	1400	10.0	305		1348	8.9	271
	2103	-1.2	-37		2043	-0.1	-3
3 Th	0330	8.6	262	18 F	0309	8.1	247
	0906	2.5	76		0847	2.8	85
	1452	9.5	290		1426	8.7	265
	2145	-0.8	-24		2109	0.1	3
4 F	0413	8.8	268	19 Sa	0337	8.3	253
	1001	2.3	70		0926	2.6	79
	1544	8.8	268		1505	8.4	256
	2227	-0.1	-3		2138	0.4	12
5 Sa	0454	8.9	271	20 Su	0404	8.6	262
	1057	2.2	67		1008	2.3	70
	1636	8.0	244		1551	7.9	241
	2306	0.7	21		2207	0.9	27
6 Su	0537	8.9	271	21 M	0436	8.8	268
	1155	2.1	64		1057	2.0	61
	1739	7.2	219		1646	7.3	223
	2348	1.5	46		2245	1.5	46
7 M	0619	8.9	271	22 Tu	0512	9.0	274
	1258	2.0	61		1152	1.8	55
	1848	6.5	198		1750	6.6	201
					2324	2.2	67
8 Tu	0034	2.3	70	23 W	0554	9.0	274
	0704	8.8	268		1301	1.5	46
	1404	1.7	52		1914	6.1	186
	2003	6.2	189				
9 W	0125	3.0	91	24 Th	0019	2.9	88
	0755	8.7	265		0647	9.1	277
	1510	1.4	43		1417	1.1	34
	2119	6.1	186		2043	6.0	183
10 Th	0225	3.5	107	25 F	0129	3.5	107
	0844	8.6	262		0751	9.1	277
	1610	0.9	27		1536	0.5	15
	2224	6.4	195		2206	6.3	192
11 F	0327	3.8	116	26 Sa	0251	3.8	116
	0933	8.7	265		0903	9.3	283
	1704	0.5	15		1642	-0.1	-3
	2322	6.7	204		2311	6.8	207
12 Sa	0426	3.9	119	27 Su	0408	3.8	116
	1021	8.7	265		1010	9.5	290
	1749	0.2	6		1740	-0.7	-21
13 Su	0010	7.0	213	28 M	0007	7.3	223
	0519	3.9	119		0517	3.4	104
	1106	8.8	268		1111	9.7	296
	1831	-0.1	-3		1831	-1.1	-34
14 M	0053	7.3	223	29 Tu	0055	7.9	241
	0604	3.7	113		0617	2.9	88
	1148	8.9	271		1210	9.9	302
	1908	-0.2	-6		1916	-1.2	-37
15 Tu	0132	7.5	229	30 W	0138	8.3	253
	0649	3.5	107		0713	2.4	73
	1230	9.0	274		1302	9.8	299
	1942	-0.2	-6		1959	-1.1	-34
				31 Th	0220	8.7	265
					0805	1.9	58
					1353	9.6	293
					2037	-0.8	-24

FEBRUARY

Day	h m	ft	cm	Day	h m	ft	cm
1 F	0258	9.0	274	16 Sa	0228	8.5	259
	0853	1.6	49		0830	1.6	49
	1443	9.1	277		1418	8.5	259
	2116	-0.3	-9		2040	0.4	12
2 Sa	0334	9.1	277	17 Su	0254	8.8	268
	0942	1.4	43		0909	1.2	37
	1530	8.5	259		1501	8.1	247
	2151	0.3	9		2109	0.8	24
3 Su	0409	9.1	277	18 M	0322	9.0	274
	1028	1.3	40		0948	0.9	27
	1620	7.8	238		1548	7.6	232
	2225	1.1	34		2141	1.3	40
4 M	0444	9.0	274	19 Tu	0354	9.2	280
	1120	1.3	40		1034	0.7	21
	1713	7.0	213		1640	7.0	213
	2302	1.9	58		2217	1.9	58
5 Tu	0520	8.8	268	20 W	0430	9.2	280
	1213	1.4	43		1129	0.7	21
	1815	6.4	195		1747	6.4	195
	2342	2.7	82		2301	2.6	79
6 W	0601	8.5	259	21 Th	0516	9.1	277
	1315	1.5	46		1236	0.8	24
	1926	5.9	180		1907	6.0	183
					2358	3.2	98
7 Th	0030	3.4	104	22 F	0613	8.8	268
	0648	8.2	250		1357	0.7	21
	1424	1.5	46		2034	5.9	180
	2043	5.8	177				
8 F	0138	3.9	119	23 Sa	0117	3.7	113
	0747	8.0	244		0728	8.6	262
	1533	1.2	37		1518	0.4	12
	2157	6.0	183		2152	6.3	192
9 Sa	0248	4.1	125	24 Su	0249	3.7	113
	0850	7.9	241		0851	8.6	262
	1632	0.9	27		1626	-0.1	-3
	2257	6.4	195		2253	6.9	210
10 Su	0357	4.0	122	25 M	0408	3.3	101
	0952	8.1	247		1005	8.8	268
	1722	0.5	15		1723	-0.5	-15
	2343	6.8	207		2345	7.5	229
11 M	0456	3.7	113	26 Tu	0514	2.7	82
	1045	8.3	253		1109	9.0	274
	1804	0.2	6		1812	-0.7	-21
12 Tu	0025	7.2	219	27 W	0027	8.1	247
	0547	3.3	101		0610	1.9	58
	1133	8.5	259		1205	9.1	277
	1840	0.0	0		1851	-0.7	-21
13 W	0057	7.5	229	28 Th	0108	8.5	259
	0631	2.9	88		0701	1.3	40
	1215	8.7	265		1257	9.1	277
	1913	-0.1	-3		1931	-0.5	-15
14 Th	0132	7.8	238				
	0713	2.5	76				
	1257	8.7	265				
	1943	0.0	0				
15 F	0200	8.2	250				
	0751	2.0	61				
	1339	8.7	265				
	2013	0.1	3				

MARCH

Day	h m	ft	cm	Day	h m	ft	cm
1 F	0144	8.9	271	16 Sa	0115	8.4	256
	0749	0.8	24		0730	0.7	21
	1344	8.8	268		1329	8.2	250
	2008	-0.1	-3		1939	0.7	21
2 Sa	0219	9.1	277	17 Su	0144	8.8	268
	0835	0.5	15		0809	0.2	6
	1431	8.5	259		1412	8.0	244
	2042	0.4	12		2011	1.0	30
3 Su	0251	9.1	277	18 M	0212	9.1	277
	0917	0.3	9		0848	-0.2	-6
	1517	8.0	244		1458	7.8	238
	2115	1.0	30		2043	1.4	43
4 M	0321	9.0	274	19 Tu	0244	9.3	283
	0959	0.4	12		0930	-0.4	-12
	1602	7.4	226		1548	7.3	223
	2148	1.6	49		2119	1.9	58
5 Tu	0351	8.8	268	20 W	0319	9.3	283
	1041	0.6	18		1019	-0.3	-9
	1649	6.8	207		1644	6.8	207
	2223	2.3	70		2201	2.4	73
6 W	0425	8.5	259	21 Th	0402	9.2	280
	1127	0.8	24		1115	-0.1	-3
	1745	6.3	192		1747	6.4	195
	2259	2.9	88		2253	2.9	88
7 Th	0500	8.1	247	22 F	0452	8.8	268
	1222	1.2	37		1221	0.2	6
	1851	5.9	180		1903	6.1	186
	2350	3.5	107		2358	3.3	101
8 F	0545	7.7	235	23 Sa	0558	8.3	253
	1328	1.4	43		1338	0.4	12
	2006	5.7	174		2021	6.2	189
9 Sa	0056	3.9	119	24 Su	0125	3.5	107
	0651	7.4	226		0723	7.9	241
	1443	1.4	43		1456	0.3	9
	2120	5.9	180		2128	6.7	204
10 Su	0215	3.9	119	25 M	0252	3.2	98
	0807	7.2	219		0847	7.8	238
	1547	1.1	34		1559	0.1	3
	2219	6.3	192		2226	7.3	223
11 M	0330	3.7	113	26 Tu	0407	2.5	76
	0920	7.4	226		1000	8.0	244
	1640	0.8	24		1655	0.0	0
	2304	6.7	204		2312	7.9	241
12 Tu	0432	3.2	98	27 W	0507	1.7	52
	1021	7.6	232		1104	8.2	250
	1725	0.6	18		1740	0.0	0
	2341	7.2	219		2354	8.4	256
13 W	0525	2.6	79	28 Th	0600	0.9	27
	1114	7.9	241		1159	8.2	250
	1802	0.4	12		1820	0.2	6
14 Th	0015	7.6	232	29 F	0031	8.8	268
	0609	1.9	58		0649	0.3	9
	1200	8.1	247		1248	8.2	250
	1833	0.4	12		1857	0.5	15
15 F	0046	8.1	247	30 Sa	0103	9.0	274
	0649	1.3	40		0731	-0.2	-6
	1245	8.2	250		1334	8.0	244
	1907	0.5	15		1933	0.9	27
				31 Su	0135	9.1	277
					0813	-0.4	-12
					1420	7.8	238
					2008	1.3	40

Time meridian 120° W. 0000 is midnight. 1200 is noon.
Heights are referred to mean lower low water which is the chart datum of soundings.

1991 TIDE TABLES

For Daylight Saving Time, add one hour.

ASTORIA
(Tongue Point)

Times and Heights of High and Low Waters

APRIL

Day	Time h m	Height ft	Height cm	Day	Time h m	Height ft	Height cm
1 M	0207	9.0	274	16 Tu	0134	9.4	287
	0853	-0.4	-12		0833	-1.2	-37
	1502	7.5	229		1455	7.5	229
	2043	1.8	55		2021	2.1	64
2 Tu	0235	8.8	268	17 W	0213	9.5	290
	0930	-0.3	-9		0918	-1.3	-40
	1546	7.1	216		1547	7.2	219
	2116	2.3	70		2106	2.4	73
3 W	0304	8.6	262	18 Th	0255	9.4	287
	1009	0.0	0		1010	-1.1	-34
	1631	6.7	204		1644	6.9	210
	2151	2.7	82		2155	2.8	85
4 Th	0335	8.3	253	19 F	0344	9.0	274
	1048	0.3	9		1105	-0.7	-21
	1721	6.3	192		1745	6.7	204
	2232	3.2	98		2257	3.0	91
5 F	0412	7.9	241	20 Sa	0439	8.5	259
	1136	0.7	21		1208	-0.3	-9
	1819	6.0	183		1851	6.7	204
	2318	3.5	107				
6 Sa	0500	7.5	229	21 Su	0008	3.2	98
	1235	1.1	34		0555	7.8	238
	1925	5.9	180		1315	0.1	3
					1959	6.9	210
7 Su	0024	3.7	113	22 M	0129	3.0	91
	0603	7.0	213		0718	7.4	226
	1341	1.3	40		1421	0.4	12
	2030	6.1	186		2058	7.3	223
8 M	0142	3.7	113	23 Tu	0248	2.4	73
	0722	6.8	207		0840	7.2	219
	1448	1.3	40		1523	0.5	15
	2125	6.4	195		2148	7.9	241
9 Tu	0259	3.3	101	24 W	0357	1.6	49
	0844	6.8	207		0953	7.2	219
	1541	1.2	37		1615	0.7	21
	2210	6.9	210		2233	8.4	256
10 W	0400	2.6	79	25 Th	0456	0.8	24
	0951	7.0	213		1055	7.3	223
	1629	1.1	34		1701	0.9	27
	2248	7.4	226		2314	8.7	265
11 Th	0455	1.8	55	26 F	0546	0.1	3
	1049	7.3	223		1148	7.4	226
	1709	1.0	30		1743	1.2	37
	2322	7.9	241		2349	9.0	274
12 F	0541	1.0	30	27 Sa	0632	-0.4	-12
	1140	7.5	229		1238	7.4	226
	1746	1.1	34		1822	1.6	49
	2355	8.4	256				
13 Sa	0626	0.3	9	28 Su	0024	9.0	274
	1229	7.6	232		0715	-0.7	-21
	1825	1.3	40		1324	7.4	226
					1901	1.9	58
14 Su	0026	8.8	268	29 M	0055	8.9	271
	0709	-0.4	-12		0751	-0.8	-24
	1319	7.7	235		1406	7.3	223
	1900	1.5	46		1936	2.3	70
15 M	0100	9.2	280	30 Tu	0126	8.8	268
	0751	-0.9	-27		0829	-0.8	-24
	1406	7.6	232		1450	7.1	216
	1942	1.8	55		2014	2.6	79

MAY

Day	Time h m	Height ft	Height cm	Day	Time h m	Height ft	Height cm
1 W	0153	8.6	262	16 Th	0151	9.6	293
	0905	-0.6	-18		0909	-1.8	-55
	1532	6.9	210		1545	7.3	223
	2050	2.9	88		2058	2.7	82
2 Th	0226	8.4	256	17 F	0243	9.3	283
	0943	-0.3	-9		1001	-1.5	-46
	1615	6.7	204		1638	7.3	223
	2128	3.1	94		2155	2.8	85
3 F	0301	8.1	247	18 Sa	0338	8.9	271
	1020	0.0	0		1054	-1.0	-30
	1700	6.5	198		1733	7.3	223
	2210	3.3	101		2259	2.8	85
4 Sa	0342	7.8	238	19 Su	0439	8.2	250
	1100	0.3	9		1147	-0.5	-15
	1750	6.4	195		1829	7.4	226
	2257	3.5	107				
5 Su	0427	7.4	226	20 M	0009	2.6	79
	1145	0.7	21		0550	7.5	229
	1842	6.4	195		1246	0.1	3
					1924	7.7	235
6 M	0001	3.5	107	21 Tu	0122	2.3	70
	0526	6.9	210		0707	6.9	210
	1239	1.0	30		1343	0.6	18
	1934	6.5	198		2017	8.0	244
7 Tu	0111	3.3	101	22 W	0235	1.7	52
	0642	6.5	198		0825	6.6	201
	1335	1.2	37		1437	1.1	34
	2023	6.9	210		2107	8.4	256
8 W	0221	2.8	85	23 Th	0341	1.0	30
	0803	6.4	195		0936	6.5	198
	1431	1.4	43		1529	1.5	46
	2109	7.3	223		2152	8.7	265
9 Th	0327	2.1	64	24 F	0437	0.3	9
	0917	6.4	195		1039	6.6	201
	1523	1.6	49		1619	1.9	58
	2149	7.9	241		2232	8.9	271
10 F	0421	1.2	37	25 Sa	0529	-0.3	-9
	1023	6.6	201		1135	6.8	207
	1611	1.8	55		1707	2.2	67
	2226	8.4	256		2311	8.9	271
11 Sa	0512	0.3	9	26 Su	0613	-0.7	-21
	1119	6.9	210		1225	6.9	210
	1658	2.0	61		1749	2.5	76
	2303	8.9	271		2345	8.9	271
12 Su	0600	-0.5	-15	27 M	0655	-0.9	-27
	1217	7.1	216		1312	7.0	213
	1743	2.2	67		1831	2.8	85
	2342	9.3	283				
13 M	0646	-1.2	-37	28 Tu	0020	8.7	265
	1309	7.3	223		0735	-0.9	-27
	1831	2.4	73		1354	7.0	213
					1913	3.0	91
14 Tu	0023	9.5	290	29 W	0055	8.6	262
	0735	-1.6	-49		0810	-0.9	-27
	1401	7.3	223		1436	7.0	213
	1917	2.5	76		1952	3.1	94
15 W	0107	9.7	296	30 Th	0127	8.5	259
	0821	-1.8	-55		0845	-0.7	-21
	1452	7.3	223		1518	6.9	210
	2006	2.7	82		2031	3.2	98
				31 F	0202	8.3	253
					0921	-0.5	-15
					1554	6.9	210
					2111	3.2	98

JUNE

Day	Time h m	Height ft	Height cm	Day	Time h m	Height ft	Height cm
1 Sa	0241	8.1	247	16 Su	0333	8.7	265
	0954	-0.3	-9		1033	-1.1	-34
	1636	6.8	207		1707	7.9	241
	2151	3.2	98		2251	2.1	64
2 Su	0320	7.8	238	17 M	0432	8.0	244
	1028	0.0	0		1119	-0.5	-15
	1713	6.9	210		1753	8.1	247
	2239	3.2	98		2355	1.9	58
3 M	0405	7.4	226	18 Tu	0538	7.2	219
	1105	0.3	9		1207	0.2	6
	1753	7.0	213		1842	8.2	250
	2332	3.0	91				
4 Tu	0459	6.9	210	19 W	0101	1.6	49
	1147	0.7	21		0650	6.5	198
	1835	7.2	219		1259	1.0	30
					1931	8.4	256
5 W	0034	2.8	85	20 Th	0209	1.1	34
	0606	6.4	195		0804	6.1	186
	1232	1.2	37		1351	1.6	49
	1920	7.5	229		2019	8.5	259
6 Th	0143	2.3	70	21 F	0315	0.6	18
	0724	6.0	183		0918	6.0	183
	1324	1.6	49		1447	2.2	67
	2003	7.8	238		2107	8.5	259
7 F	0249	1.5	46	22 Sa	0415	0.1	3
	0845	5.9	180		1022	6.1	186
	1420	2.0	61		1539	2.6	79
	2049	8.3	253		2151	8.6	262
8 Sa	0350	0.7	21	23 Su	0507	-0.4	-12
	0957	6.1	186		1119	6.3	192
	1515	2.4	73		1632	2.9	88
	2134	8.7	265		2234	8.5	259
9 Su	0447	-0.2	-6	24 M	0552	-0.7	-21
	1103	6.4	195		1211	6.5	198
	1614	2.6	79		1722	3.0	91
	2221	9.1	277		2315	8.5	259
10 M	0539	-0.9	-27	25 Tu	0636	-0.8	-24
	1203	6.7	204		1257	6.7	204
	1710	2.8	85		1809	3.1	94
	2309	9.5	290		2354	8.4	256
11 Tu	0631	-1.5	-46	26 W	0716	-0.9	-27
	1257	6.9	210		1339	6.8	207
	1806	2.8	85		1852	3.1	94
	2357	9.7	296				
12 W	0721	-1.9	-58	27 Th	0033	8.4	256
	1351	7.2	219		0753	-0.9	-27
	1901	2.8	85		1421	6.9	210
					1933	3.0	91
13 Th	0050	9.7	296	28 F	0111	8.3	253
	0811	-2.0	-61		0826	-0.8	-24
	1441	7.4	226		1453	7.0	213
	1956	2.7	82		2015	3.0	91
14 F	0142	9.6	293	29 Sa	0147	8.2	250
	0858	-2.0	-61		0858	-0.6	-18
	1530	7.6	232		1528	7.0	213
	2052	2.5	76		2054	2.8	85
15 Sa	0237	9.2	280	30 Su	0225	8.0	244
	0947	-1.6	-49		0929	-0.4	-12
	1619	7.7	235		1600	7.2	219
	2151	2.3	70		2135	2.7	82

Time meridian 120° W. 0000 is midnight. 1200 is noon.
Heights are referred to mean lower low water which is the chart datum of soundings.

ASTORIA
(Tongue Point)

1991 TIDE TABLES

For Daylight Saving Time, add one hour.

Times and Heights of High and Low Waters

JULY

Day	h m	ft	cm	Day	h m	ft	cm
1 M	0307	7.7	235	16 Tu	0420	7.6	232
	0957	-0.2	-6		1044	-0.2	-6
	1631	7.3	223		1710	8.4	256
	2216	2.5	76		2331	1.0	30
2 Tu	0350	7.3	223	17 W	0520	6.8	207
	1027	0.2	6		1126	0.6	18
	1702	7.5	229		1753	8.4	256
	2305	2.2	67				
3 W	0439	6.8	207	18 Th	0031	0.9	27
	1102	0.6	18		0626	6.1	186
	1739	7.7	235		1213	1.4	43
	2358	1.9	58		1838	8.2	250
4 Th	0541	6.2	189	19 F	0134	0.7	21
	1139	1.2	37		0736	5.7	174
	1817	7.9	241		1303	2.1	64
					1927	8.1	247
5 F	0100	1.5	46	20 Sa	0243	0.5	15
	0657	5.7	174		0854	5.5	168
	1228	1.8	55		1403	2.7	82
	1903	8.2	250		2020	8.0	244
6 Sa	0209	1.0	30	21 Su	0346	0.1	3
	0821	5.5	168		1000	5.7	174
	1327	2.4	73		1504	3.0	91
	1954	8.4	256		2113	7.9	241
7 Su	0319	0.3	9	22 M	0442	-0.2	-6
	0941	5.6	171		1100	6.0	183
	1433	2.8	85		1606	3.1	94
	2051	8.7	265		2204	7.9	241
8 M	0424	-0.4	-12	23 Tu	0533	-0.5	-15
	1050	6.0	183		1151	6.3	192
	1542	3.0	91		1701	3.0	91
	2151	9.0	274		2253	8.0	244
9 Tu	0523	-1.1	-34	24 W	0615	-0.7	-21
	1149	6.4	195		1236	6.5	198
	1651	3.0	91		1751	2.9	88
	2250	9.3	283		2335	8.0	244
10 W	0618	-1.6	-49	25 Th	0653	-0.8	-24
	1245	6.8	207		1313	6.7	204
	1751	2.8	85		1836	2.7	82
	2346	9.5	290				
11 Th	0709	-2.0	-61	26 F	0017	8.1	247
	1333	7.2	219		0728	-0.8	-24
	1852	2.4	73		1348	6.9	210
					1916	2.4	73
12 F	0041	9.5	290	27 Sa	0059	8.1	247
	0755	-2.0	-61		0801	-0.7	-21
	1421	7.5	229		1423	7.1	216
	1949	2.0	61		1955	2.2	67
13 Sa	0137	9.3	283	28 Su	0138	8.0	244
	0841	-1.9	-58		0829	-0.6	-18
	1506	7.9	241		1449	7.3	223
	2042	1.7	52		2034	1.9	58
14 Su	0232	8.9	271	29 M	0215	7.8	238
	0923	-1.5	-46		0856	-0.4	-12
	1548	8.1	247		1517	7.5	229
	2138	1.4	43		2113	1.7	52
15 M	0324	8.4	256	30 Tu	0255	7.5	229
	1004	-0.9	-27		0923	-0.1	-3
	1628	8.3	253		1543	7.7	235
	2233	1.1	34		2151	1.4	43
				31 W	0337	7.1	216
					0951	0.3	9
					1612	7.9	241
					2233	1.1	34

AUGUST

Day	h m	ft	cm	Day	h m	ft	cm
1 Th	0423	6.6	201	16 F	0601	5.9	180
	1023	0.8	24		1129	1.9	58
	1644	8.1	247		1742	7.8	238
	2324	0.9	27				
2 F	0524	6.0	183	17 Sa	0055	0.5	15
	1100	1.4	43		0711	5.4	165
	1724	8.2	250		1221	2.6	79
					1832	7.5	229
3 Sa	0024	0.7	21	18 Su	0201	0.5	15
	0640	5.5	168		0827	5.3	162
	1150	2.1	64		1325	3.0	91
	1813	8.2	250		1932	7.2	219
4 Su	0137	0.4	12	19 M	0312	0.4	12
	0806	5.2	158		0936	5.5	168
	1251	2.7	82		1438	3.2	98
	1915	8.2	250		2037	7.1	216
5 M	0256	0.0	0	20 Tu	0411	0.1	3
	0929	5.4	165		1034	5.8	177
	1411	3.0	91		1544	3.1	94
	2025	8.3	253		2139	7.2	219
6 Tu	0405	-0.5	-15	21 W	0503	-0.2	-6
	1035	5.8	177		1123	6.2	189
	1533	3.0	91		1642	2.7	82
	2136	8.5	259		2231	7.4	226
7 W	0507	-1.1	-34	22 Th	0546	-0.4	-12
	1134	6.4	195		1205	6.6	201
	1643	2.6	79		1733	2.3	70
	2242	8.8	268		2320	7.6	232
8 Th	0602	-1.5	-46	23 F	0623	-0.5	-15
	1225	6.9	210		1237	6.9	210
	1746	2.1	64		1816	1.9	58
	2340	9.0	274				
9 F	0648	-1.7	-52	24 Sa	0005	7.8	238
	1308	7.4	226		0655	-0.5	-15
	1844	1.5	46		1309	7.2	219
					1857	1.5	46
10 Sa	0036	9.0	274	25 Su	0044	7.8	238
	0732	-1.7	-52		0726	-0.4	-12
	1350	7.9	241		1338	7.4	226
	1938	1.0	30		1936	1.2	37
11 Su	0131	8.9	271	26 M	0126	7.7	235
	0814	-1.4	-43		0755	-0.2	-6
	1429	8.2	250		1405	7.7	235
	2028	0.5	15		2012	0.8	24
12 M	0221	8.5	259	27 Tu	0205	7.6	232
	0853	-1.0	-30		0821	0.0	0
	1509	8.4	256		1431	7.9	241
	2118	0.2	6		2049	0.4	12
13 Tu	0313	7.9	241	28 W	0245	7.3	223
	0931	-0.4	-12		0849	0.4	12
	1545	8.5	259		1457	8.2	250
	2207	0.1	3		2126	0.2	6
14 W	0404	7.2	219	29 Th	0330	6.9	210
	1007	0.4	12		0917	0.8	24
	1623	8.4	256		1527	8.3	253
	2300	0.2	6		2208	0.0	0
15 Th	0459	6.5	198	30 F	0419	6.4	195
	1046	1.1	34		0953	1.4	43
	1700	8.2	250		1602	8.4	256
	2353	0.3	9		2257	0.0	0
				31 Sa	0517	5.8	177
					1035	2.0	61
					1644	8.3	253
					2359	0.1	3

SEPTEMBER

Day	h m	ft	cm	Day	h m	ft	cm
1 Su	0633	5.4	165	16 M	0114	0.7	21
	1127	2.5	76		0751	5.4	165
	1739	8.0	244		1253	3.3	101
					1841	6.7	204
2 M	0115	0.1	3	17 Tu	0223	0.7	21
	0757	5.3	162		0900	5.6	171
	1243	3.0	91		1409	3.3	101
	1848	7.8	238		1957	6.6	201
3 Tu	0236	-0.1	-3	18 W	0328	0.6	18
	0915	5.6	171		0958	6.0	183
	1412	3.1	94		1523	3.0	91
	2014	7.7	235		2107	6.7	204
4 W	0349	-0.4	-12	19 Th	0421	0.4	12
	1019	6.1	186		1041	6.5	198
	1533	2.7	82		1619	2.4	73
	2130	7.9	241		2210	7.0	213
5 Th	0448	-0.8	-24	20 F	0503	0.2	6
	1111	6.8	207		1120	6.9	210
	1642	2.0	61		1711	1.8	55
	2239	8.2	250		2301	7.2	219
6 F	0538	-1.1	-34	21 Sa	0540	0.1	3
	1156	7.4	226		1152	7.3	223
	1743	1.2	37		1754	1.2	37
	2338	8.4	256		2346	7.4	226
7 Sa	0624	-1.1	-34	22 Su	0613	0.2	6
	1235	7.9	241		1223	7.7	235
	1836	0.5	15		1834	0.6	18
8 Su	0031	8.4	256	23 M	0030	7.5	229
	0703	-0.9	-27		0645	0.3	9
	1314	8.4	256		1249	8.0	244
	1923	-0.1	-3		1911	0.1	3
9 M	0122	8.3	253	24 Tu	0112	7.5	229
	0742	-0.5	-15		0716	0.6	18
	1349	8.6	262		1317	8.3	253
	2011	-0.5	-15		1949	-0.3	-9
10 Tu	0213	7.9	241	25 W	0155	7.4	226
	0820	0.0	0		0745	0.9	27
	1425	8.7	265		1345	8.6	262
	2054	-0.7	-21		2025	-0.6	-18
11 W	0259	7.5	229	26 Th	0238	7.2	219
	0853	0.6	18		0816	1.3	40
	1457	8.6	262		1414	8.7	265
	2139	-0.6	-18		2106	-0.6	-24
12 Th	0348	6.9	210	27 F	0324	6.8	207
	0931	1.2	37		0852	1.7	52
	1530	8.3	253		1450	8.8	268
	2225	-0.4	-12		2149	-0.8	-24
13 F	0439	6.4	195	28 Sa	0417	6.4	195
	1007	1.9	58		0930	2.2	67
	1605	8.0	244		1529	8.7	265
	2313	0.0	0		2241	-0.6	-18
14 Sa	0536	5.9	180	29 Su	0516	6.0	183
	1052	2.5	76		1023	2.6	79
	1647	7.5	229		1615	8.3	253
					2344	-0.3	-9
15 Su	0009	0.4	12	30 M	0630	5.8	177
	0641	5.5	168		1126	3.0	91
	1145	3.0	91		1718	7.9	241
	1733	7.1	216				

Time meridian 120° W. 0000 is midnight. 1200 is noon.
Heights are referred to mean lower low water which is the chart datum of soundings.

1991 TIDE TABLES

For Daylight Saving Time, add one hour.

ASTORIA
(Tongue Point)

Times and Heights of High and Low Waters

OCTOBER

Day	h m	ft	cm	Day	h m	ft	cm
1 Tu	0057	0.0	0	16 W	0127	1.0	30
	0748	5.9	180		0814	6.1	186
	1248	3.2	98		1339	3.5	107
	1840	7.4	226		1911	6.4	195
2 W	0214	0.0	0	17 Th	0228	1.1	34
	0855	6.3	192		0906	6.5	198
	1419	2.9	88		1451	3.0	91
	2009	7.3	223		2031	6.4	195
3 Th	0322	-0.1	-3	18 F	0324	1.1	34
	0954	6.9	210		0951	7.0	213
	1536	2.2	67		1552	2.3	70
	2128	7.5	229		2137	6.6	201
4 F	0421	-0.2	-6	19 Sa	0406	1.1	34
	1042	7.6	232		1029	7.5	229
	1640	1.3	40		1642	1.5	46
	2237	7.7	235		2235	6.9	210
5 Sa	0507	-0.2	-6	20 Su	0448	1.1	34
	1121	8.2	250		1101	7.9	241
	1733	0.4	12		1727	0.8	24
	2333	7.9	241		2327	7.1	216
6 Su	0551	0.0	0	21 M	0526	1.2	37
	1200	8.7	265		1131	8.4	256
	1822	-0.3	-9		1807	0.1	3
7 M	0025	7.9	241	22 Tu	0013	7.3	223
	0631	0.3	9		0602	1.5	46
	1236	8.9	271		1203	8.8	268
	1908	-0.8	-24		1849	-0.5	-15
8 Tu	0114	7.8	238	23 W	0059	7.4	226
	0709	0.7	21		0637	1.7	52
	1310	9.0	274		1233	9.1	277
	1953	-1.1	-34		1927	-1.0	-30
9 W	0200	7.6	232	24 Th	0146	7.4	226
	0745	1.2	37		0713	2.0	61
	1343	8.9	271		1308	9.3	283
	2032	-1.1	-34		2009	-1.2	-37
10 Th	0247	7.3	223	25 F	0234	7.3	223
	0823	1.7	52		0754	2.3	70
	1415	8.7	265		1343	9.4	287
	2114	-0.9	-27		2052	-1.3	-40
11 F	0333	6.9	210	26 Sa	0324	7.1	216
	0859	2.2	67		0837	2.6	79
	1447	8.4	256		1425	9.3	283
	2156	-0.5	-15		2140	-1.1	-34
12 Sa	0421	6.6	201	27 Su	0416	6.9	210
	0938	2.7	82		0925	2.9	88
	1519	8.0	244		1511	9.0	274
	2238	-0.1	-3		2233	-0.8	-24
13 Su	0510	6.2	189	28 M	0515	6.7	204
	1023	3.1	94		1023	3.1	94
	1555	7.6	232		1606	8.5	259
	2325	0.4	12		2332	-0.4	-12
14 M	0609	6.0	183	29 Tu	0618	6.7	204
	1115	3.4	104		1131	3.3	101
	1647	7.1	216		1712	7.9	241
15 Tu	0022	0.8	24	30 W	0037	0.1	3
	0712	5.9	180		0723	6.9	210
	1222	3.6	110		1255	3.1	94
	1750	6.7	204		1838	7.3	223
				31 Th	0144	0.4	12
					0826	7.3	223
					1416	2.6	79
					2004	7.0	213

NOVEMBER

Day	h m	ft	cm	Day	h m	ft	cm
1 F	0247	0.6	18	16 Sa	0211	1.8	55
	0918	7.9	241		0849	7.6	232
	1530	1.7	52		1514	2.3	70
	2123	7.1	216		2102	6.3	192
2 Sa	0342	0.8	24	17 Su	0301	2.0	61
	1003	8.5	259		0928	8.1	247
	1629	0.8	24		1607	1.5	46
	2229	7.3	223		2206	6.6	201
3 Su	0431	1.1	34	18 M	0348	2.2	67
	1045	9.0	274		1006	8.6	262
	1721	-0.1	-3		1659	0.6	18
	2327	7.4	226		2306	6.9	210
4 M	0516	1.4	43	19 Tu	0434	2.4	73
	1122	9.3	283		1043	9.1	277
	1810	-0.7	-21		1744	-0.2	-6
					2357	7.1	216
5 Tu	0018	7.5	229	20 W	0520	2.6	79
	0558	1.7	52		1120	9.5	290
	1200	9.4	287		1827	-0.8	-24
	1852	-1.0	-30				
6 W	0105	7.5	229	21 Th	0049	7.4	226
	0637	2.1	64		0605	2.8	85
	1233	9.3	283		1157	9.8	299
	1934	-1.1	-34		1912	-1.2	-37
7 Th	0153	7.5	229	22 F	0138	7.5	229
	0718	2.5	76		0653	3.0	91
	1305	9.2	280		1239	9.9	302
	2013	-1.0	-30		1957	-1.5	-46
8 F	0235	7.4	226	23 Sa	0227	7.6	232
	0755	2.8	85		0739	3.1	94
	1339	8.9	271		1324	9.9	302
	2052	-0.8	-24		2044	-1.5	-46
9 Sa	0319	7.2	219	24 Su	0319	7.6	232
	0836	3.1	94		0831	3.1	94
	1412	8.6	262		1413	9.7	296
	2130	-0.4	-12		2130	-1.3	-40
10 Su	0402	7.0	213	25 M	0408	7.6	232
	0915	3.4	104		0924	3.2	98
	1447	8.3	253		1505	9.3	283
	2207	0.0	0		2223	-0.9	-27
11 M	0447	6.8	207	26 Tu	0500	7.7	235
	0958	3.6	110		1024	3.1	94
	1526	7.9	241		1604	8.7	265
	2247	0.4	12		2313	-0.3	-9
12 Tu	0534	6.7	204	27 W	0555	7.8	238
	1047	3.7	113		1133	3.0	91
	1614	7.5	229		1710	8.0	244
	2332	0.8	24				
13 W	0626	6.7	204	28 Th	0006	0.3	9
	1150	3.7	113		0650	8.0	244
	1708	7.0	213		1245	2.7	82
					1829	7.3	223
14 Th	0019	1.2	37	29 F	0105	0.9	27
	0715	6.9	210		0743	8.4	256
	1301	3.5	107		1405	2.2	67
	1822	6.5	198		1950	6.9	210
15 F	0115	1.5	46	30 Sa	0202	1.5	46
	0803	7.2	219		0835	8.8	268
	1409	3.0	91		1515	1.4	43
	1945	6.3	192		2110	6.7	204

DECEMBER

Day	h m	ft	cm	Day	h m	ft	cm
1 Su	0259	2.0	61	16 M	0150	2.7	82
	0923	9.1	277		0822	8.6	262
	1614	0.6	18		1528	1.5	46
	2218	6.9	210		2139	6.3	192
2 M	0352	2.4	73	17 Tu	0249	3.1	94
	1008	9.4	287		0910	9.0	274
	1709	-0.1	-3		1627	0.6	18
	2317	7.1	216		2245	6.6	201
3 Tu	0444	2.7	82	18 W	0349	3.4	104
	1048	9.5	290		0957	9.4	287
	1755	-0.5	-15		1719	-0.1	-3
					2345	7.0	213
4 W	0010	7.3	223	19 Th	0445	3.5	107
	0530	3.0	91		1045	9.8	299
	1127	9.5	290		1810	-0.8	-24
	1839	-0.8	-24				
5 Th	0058	7.4	226	20 F	0037	7.3	223
	0615	3.2	98		0542	3.5	107
	1204	9.4	287		1135	10.1	308
	1919	-0.8	-24		1900	-1.2	-37
6 F	0140	7.5	229	21 Sa	0129	7.6	232
	0657	3.4	104		0636	3.4	104
	1239	9.2	280		1226	10.2	311
	1957	-0.7	-21		1946	-1.5	-46
7 Sa	0223	7.6	232	22 Su	0217	7.9	241
	0739	3.5	107		0732	3.2	98
	1317	9.0	274		1316	10.2	311
	2033	-0.5	-15		2032	-1.5	-46
8 Su	0303	7.5	229	23 M	0303	8.2	250
	0818	3.6	110		0825	3.0	91
	1351	8.8	268		1411	10.0	305
	2107	-0.3	-9		2117	-1.2	-37
9 M	0340	7.5	229	24 Tu	0349	8.4	256
	0858	3.6	110		0921	2.8	85
	1428	8.6	262		1503	9.5	290
	2140	0.0	0		2203	-0.8	-24
10 Tu	0419	7.5	229	25 W	0433	8.6	262
	0940	3.6	110		1018	2.5	76
	1506	8.3	253		1602	8.8	268
	2212	0.4	12		2248	-0.1	-3
11 W	0454	7.5	229	26 Th	0520	8.8	268
	1023	3.6	110		1121	2.3	70
	1550	7.9	241		1704	8.0	244
	2247	0.8	24		2332	0.7	21
12 Th	0532	7.6	232	27 F	0608	8.9	271
	1116	3.5	107		1227	2.1	64
	1641	7.3	223		1814	7.2	219
	2323	1.2	37				
13 F	0611	7.7	235	28 Sa	0022	1.5	46
	1214	3.3	101		0657	9.0	274
	1743	6.7	204		1337	1.7	52
					1931	6.6	201
14 Sa	0005	1.7	52	29 Su	0115	2.3	70
	0654	8.0	244		0748	9.1	277
	1319	2.9	88		1446	1.2	37
	1859	6.3	192		2051	6.4	195
15 Su	0054	2.2	67	30 M	0214	2.9	88
	0736	8.3	253		0840	9.2	280
	1429	2.2	67		1555	0.7	21
	2022	6.1	186		2203	6.5	198
				31 Tu	0316	3.3	101
					0928	9.2	280
					1650	0.2	6
					2306	6.8	207

Time meridian 120° W.   0000 is midnight.   1200 is noon.
Heights are referred to mean lower low water which is the chart datum of soundings.

ABERDEEN

1991 TIDE TABLES

For Daylight Saving Time, add one hour.

Times and Heights of High and Low Waters

JANUARY

Day	Time (h m)	Height (ft)	Height (cm)	Day	Time (h m)	Height (ft)	Height (cm)
1 Tu	0152	10.1	308	16 W	0156	9.4	287
	0726	3.7	113		0738	4.3	131
	1309	12.6	384		1312	11.0	335
	2008	-1.4	-43		2009	0.2	6
2 W	0240	10.4	317	17 Th	0225	9.6	293
	0818	3.4	104		0820	4.0	122
	1402	12.2	372		1350	10.9	332
	2053	-1.1	-34		2045	0.4	12
3 Th	0325	10.7	326	18 F	0256	9.9	302
	0908	3.2	98		0900	3.8	116
	1452	11.6	354		1427	10.6	323
	2137	-0.4	-12		2120	0.7	21
4 F	0408	10.9	332	19 Sa	0326	10.2	311
	0958	3.0	91		0939	3.6	110
	1544	10.8	329		1507	10.2	311
	2219	0.4	12		2153	1.2	37
5 Sa	0450	10.9	332	20 Su	0357	10.4	317
	1049	2.9	88		1020	3.3	101
	1639	9.9	302		1550	9.7	296
	2304	1.4	43		2228	1.9	58
6 Su	0532	11.0	335	21 M	0432	10.7	326
	1144	2.9	88		1107	2.9	88
	1736	9.1	277		1643	9.1	277
	2349	2.4	73		2300	2.6	79
7 M	0617	10.9	332	22 Tu	0511	10.9	332
	1240	2.8	85		1200	2.6	79
	1837	8.4	256		1743	8.5	259
					2342	3.4	104
8 Tu	0036	3.3	101	23 W	0600	11.1	338
	0703	10.8	329		1300	2.3	70
	1339	2.7	82		1855	8.0	244
	1945	7.9	241				
9 W	0129	4.1	125	24 Th	0034	4.2	128
	0749	10.8	329		0655	11.2	341
	1438	2.4	73		1409	1.9	58
	2052	7.7	235		2016	7.8	238
10 Th	0229	4.7	143	25 F	0150	4.8	146
	0839	10.7	326		0759	11.3	344
	1536	2.0	61		1517	1.3	40
	2202	7.8	238		2133	7.9	241
11 F	0328	5.0	152	26 Sa	0309	5.0	152
	0931	10.8	329		0903	11.5	351
	1633	1.6	49		1623	0.5	15
	2305	8.0	244		2249	8.4	256
12 Sa	0425	5.1	155	27 Su	0420	4.8	146
	1020	10.9	332		1007	11.8	360
	1723	1.1	34		1723	-0.2	-6
					2352	9.0	274
13 Su	0001	8.4	256	28 M	0523	4.3	131
	0521	4.9	149		1108	12.0	366
	1108	11.0	335		1814	-0.7	-21
	1809	0.6	18				
14 M	0046	8.7	265	29 Tu	0047	9.7	296
	0610	4.7	143		0619	3.6	110
	1151	11.1	338		1206	12.1	369
	1851	0.3	9		1902	-1.0	-30
15 Tu	0121	9.1	277	30 W	0133	10.3	314
	0656	4.5	137		0714	3.0	91
	1233	11.1	338		1301	12.0	366
	1931	0.2	6		1947	-0.9	-27
				31 Th	0215	10.8	329
					0803	2.4	73
					1351	11.7	357
					2029	-0.6	-18

FEBRUARY

Day	Time (h m)	Height (ft)	Height (cm)	Day	Time (h m)	Height (ft)	Height (cm)
1 F	0253	11.1	338	16 Sa	0218	10.3	314
	0849	2.0	61		0839	2.3	70
	1439	11.2	341		1417	10.3	314
	2111	0.1	3		2053	1.0	30
2 Sa	0329	11.2	341	17 Su	0248	10.6	323
	0937	1.8	55		0918	1.9	58
	1527	10.4	317		1458	9.9	302
	2150	0.9	27		2127	1.6	49
3 Su	0406	11.2	341	18 M	0318	10.9	332
	1022	1.8	55		0958	1.6	49
	1614	9.6	293		1542	9.4	287
	2230	1.8	55		2159	2.2	67
4 M	0442	11.0	335	19 Tu	0354	11.0	335
	1109	2.0	61		1043	1.4	43
	1704	8.9	271		1635	8.9	271
	2310	2.8	85		2235	2.9	88
5 Tu	0522	10.8	329	20 W	0435	11.1	338
	1200	2.1	64		1135	1.3	40
	1800	8.1	247		1735	8.2	250
	2352	3.6	110		2320	3.7	113
6 W	0605	10.5	320	21 Th	0525	11.0	335
	1255	2.3	70		1237	1.4	43
	1858	7.6	232		1845	7.7	235
7 Th	0045	4.4	134	22 F	0019	4.4	134
	0656	10.2	311		0626	10.8	329
	1352	2.4	73		1345	1.3	40
	2008	7.3	223		2006	7.5	229
8 F	0144	5.0	152	23 Sa	0135	4.8	146
	0751	10.0	305		0736	10.6	323
	1457	2.2	67		1455	1.0	30
	2124	7.3	223		2124	7.8	238
9 Sa	0251	5.2	158	24 Su	0255	4.8	146
	0851	10.0	305		0918	10.6	323
	1557	1.9	58		1601	0.6	18
	2233	7.6	232		2234	8.4	256
10 Su	0356	5.1	155	25 M	0409	4.2	128
	0950	10.1	308		0959	10.8	329
	1652	1.4	43		1702	0.1	3
	2325	8.1	247		2333	9.1	277
11 M	0456	4.8	146	26 Tu	0513	3.4	104
	1043	10.3	314		1105	11.0	335
	1742	0.9	27		1754	-0.2	-6
12 Tu	0014	8.6	262	27 W	0019	9.8	299
	0547	4.3	131		0608	2.5	76
	1131	10.5	320		1200	11.1	338
	1824	0.5	15		1840	-0.4	-12
13 W	0049	9.1	277	28 Th	0101	10.4	317
	0634	3.7	113		0658	1.7	52
	1217	10.6	323		1253	11.0	335
	1903	0.3	9		1922	-0.2	-6
14 Th	0121	9.5	290				
	0717	3.2	98				
	1259	10.6	323				
	1942	0.3	9				
15 F	0149	9.9	302				
	0758	2.7	82				
	1338	10.5	320				
	2017	0.6	18				

MARCH

Day	Time (h m)	Height (ft)	Height (cm)	Day	Time (h m)	Height (ft)	Height (cm)
1 F	0139	10.9	332	16 Sa	0105	10.2	311
	0744	1.1	34		0733	1.0	30
	1341	10.8	329		1324	9.9	302
	2003	0.2	6		1948	1.0	30
2 Sa	0214	11.1	338	17 Su	0138	10.6	323
	0827	0.7	21		0815	0.5	15
	1426	10.3	314		1407	9.8	299
	2042	0.8	24		2025	1.5	46
3 Su	0247	11.1	338	18 M	0210	10.9	332
	0909	0.6	18		0857	0.1	3
	1508	9.8	299		1451	9.4	287
	2121	1.5	46		2102	2.0	61
4 M	0320	10.9	332	19 Tu	0244	11.0	335
	0952	0.7	21		0939	-0.1	-3
	1550	9.1	277		1537	9.0	274
	2157	2.3	70		2142	2.6	79
5 Tu	0352	10.6	323	20 W	0323	11.0	335
	1035	0.9	27		1027	-0.1	-3
	1635	8.5	259		1630	8.5	259
	2235	3.1	94		2224	3.2	98
6 W	0430	10.3	314	21 Th	0408	10.8	329
	1121	1.3	40		1120	0.1	3
	1722	7.9	241		1732	7.9	241
	2317	3.8	116		2315	3.8	116
7 Th	0512	9.9	302	22 F	0501	10.4	317
	1211	1.7	52		1218	0.4	12
	1819	7.4	226		1845	7.6	232
8 F	0003	4.4	134	23 Sa	0018	4.2	128
	0602	9.5	290		0610	10.0	305
	1310	2.0	61		1323	0.7	21
	1922	7.1	216		1957	7.6	232
9 Sa	0105	4.8	146	24 Su	0133	4.3	131
	0703	9.2	280		0726	9.6	293
	1412	2.1	64		1431	0.8	24
	2038	7.1	216		2109	8.0	244
10 Su	0217	5.0	152	25 M	0249	4.0	122
	0812	9.1	277		0841	9.5	290
	1516	1.9	58		1537	0.7	21
	2143	7.4	226		2209	8.7	265
11 M	0325	4.7	143	26 Tu	0359	3.2	98
	0915	9.2	280		0953	9.6	293
	1614	1.5	46		1633	0.5	15
	2239	7.9	241		2301	9.4	287
12 Tu	0428	4.1	125	27 W	0459	2.2	67
	1015	9.4	287		1056	9.8	299
	1705	1.1	34		1726	0.4	12
	2321	8.5	259		2345	10.0	305
13 W	0521	3.4	104	28 Th	0552	1.2	37
	1108	9.6	293		1155	9.9	302
	1749	0.8	24		1812	0.5	15
	2359	9.1	277				
14 Th	0609	2.6	79	29 F	0024	10.5	320
	1155	9.9	302		0640	0.4	12
	1832	0.7	21		1243	9.8	299
					1852	0.7	21
15 F	0032	9.7	296	30 Sa	0100	10.8	329
	0653	1.8	55		0723	-0.2	-6
	1240	10.0	305		1329	9.7	296
	1910	0.8	24		1934	1.1	34
				31 Su	0133	10.8	329
					0805	-0.5	-15
					1410	9.4	287
					2013	1.6	49

Time meridian 120° W. 0000 is midnight. 1200 is noon.
Heights are referred to mean lower low water which is the chart datum of soundings.

1991 TIDE TABLES

ABERDEEN

For Daylight Saving Time, add one hour.

Times and Heights of High and Low Waters

APRIL

Day	h m	ft	cm	Day	h m	ft	cm
1 M	0205	10.7	326	16 Tu	0136	11.1	338
	0843	-0.5	-15		0835	-1.5	-46
	1451	9.0	274		1443	8.9	271
	2050	2.2	67		2041	2.5	76
2 Tu	0238	10.5	320	17 W	0216	11.1	338
	0924	-0.3	-9		0922	-1.5	-46
	1531	8.5	259		1536	8.6	262
	2128	2.8	85		2126	2.9	88
3 W	0310	10.1	308	18 Th	0301	10.9	332
	1004	0.1	3		1011	-1.3	-40
	1609	8.1	247		1632	8.3	253
	2206	3.3	101		2215	3.3	101
4 Th	0345	9.8	299	19 F	0352	10.4	317
	1048	0.5	15		1104	-0.8	-24
	1655	7.6	232		1733	8.0	244
	2245	3.8	116		2311	3.6	110
5 F	0424	9.3	283	20 Sa	0451	9.8	299
	1135	1.0	30		1200	-0.3	-9
	1749	7.3	223		1839	8.0	244
	2333	4.3	131				
6 Sa	0515	8.9	271	21 Su	0017	3.7	113
	1229	1.4	43		0600	9.2	280
	1849	7.1	216		1300	0.2	6
					1942	8.2	250
7 Su	0034	4.5	137	22 M	0126	3.5	107
	0618	8.5	259		0716	8.7	265
	1327	1.6	49		1403	0.6	18
	1952	7.2	219		2044	8.6	262
8 M	0144	4.5	137	23 Tu	0238	2.9	88
	0730	8.3	253		0833	8.5	259
	1429	1.7	52		1503	0.9	27
	2051	7.6	232		2136	9.2	280
9 Tu	0254	4.1	125	24 W	0344	2.0	61
	0839	8.2	250		0943	8.5	259
	1525	1.6	49		1601	1.1	34
	2140	8.1	247		2225	9.7	296
10 W	0356	3.3	101	25 Th	0441	1.0	30
	0941	8.4	256		1046	8.5	259
	1621	1.5	46		1652	1.2	37
	2225	8.7	265		2305	10.2	311
11 Th	0451	2.3	70	26 F	0531	0.2	6
	1038	8.7	265		1142	8.6	262
	1708	1.3	40		1739	1.4	43
	2308	9.4	287		2345	10.4	317
12 F	0540	1.3	40	27 Sa	0618	-0.5	-15
	1132	8.9	271		1232	8.7	265
	1755	1.4	43		1824	1.7	52
	2345	10.0	305				
13 Sa	0625	0.3	9	28 Su	0020	10.5	320
	1221	9.1	277		0700	-1.0	-30
	1837	1.5	46		1316	8.6	262
					1905	2.0	61
14 Su	0021	10.5	320	29 M	0054	10.4	317
	0709	-0.5	-15		0741	-1.1	-34
	1309	9.2	280		1355	8.5	259
	1919	1.7	52		1945	2.4	73
15 M	0058	10.8	329	30 Tu	0128	10.3	314
	0752	-1.1	-34		0820	-1.1	-34
	1355	9.1	277		1437	8.2	250
	1959	2.1	64		2026	2.8	85

MAY

Day	h m	ft	cm	Day	h m	ft	cm
1 W	0202	10.0	305	16 Th	0157	11.1	338
	0859	-0.9	-27		0907	-2.4	-73
	1513	8.0	244		1534	8.5	259
	2104	3.2	98		2113	2.9	88
2 Th	0234	9.7	296	17 F	0248	10.7	326
	0939	-0.6	-18		0956	-2.0	-61
	1554	7.7	235		1629	8.4	256
	2143	3.5	107		2206	3.0	91
3 F	0308	9.4	287	18 Sa	0344	10.1	308
	1019	-0.2	-6		1047	-1.5	-46
	1635	7.5	229		1725	8.5	259
	2224	3.8	116		2304	3.0	91
4 Sa	0347	9.0	274	19 Su	0446	9.4	287
	1105	0.3	9		1139	-0.8	-24
	1721	7.4	226		1820	8.6	262
	2312	4.0	122				
5 Su	0436	8.5	259	20 M	0007	2.9	88
	1151	0.7	21		0552	8.6	262
	1814	7.4	226		1235	0.0	0
					1916	8.9	271
6 M	0009	4.1	125	21 Tu	0111	2.5	76
	0538	8.0	244		0704	8.0	244
	1242	1.1	34		1330	0.7	21
	1906	7.7	235		2008	9.3	283
7 Tu	0113	3.9	119	22 W	0217	1.9	58
	0647	7.7	235		0817	7.6	232
	1337	1.4	43		1426	1.3	40
	1957	8.0	244		2056	9.6	293
8 W	0219	3.3	101	23 Th	0319	1.1	34
	0757	7.5	229		0927	7.5	229
	1433	1.7	52		1522	1.8	55
	2047	8.6	262		2142	9.9	302
9 Th	0319	2.4	73	24 F	0418	0.4	12
	0906	7.6	232		1029	7.5	229
	1528	1.9	58		1617	2.1	64
	2132	9.2	280		2225	10.1	308
10 F	0418	1.4	43	25 Sa	0507	-0.3	-9
	1008	7.8	238		1129	7.6	232
	1623	2.0	61		1707	2.4	73
	2215	9.8	299		2305	10.2	311
11 Sa	0509	0.3	9	26 Su	0553	-0.9	-27
	1106	8.1	247		1219	7.7	235
	1713	2.2	67		1754	2.6	79
	2258	10.3	314		2345	10.2	311
12 Su	0558	-0.8	-24	27 M	0638	-1.2	-37
	1201	8.3	253		1304	7.8	238
	1801	2.3	70		1838	2.8	85
	2340	10.8	329				
13 M	0645	-1.6	-49	28 Tu	0022	10.1	308
	1254	8.5	259		0719	-1.3	-40
	1848	2.5	76		1346	7.8	238
					1920	3.0	91
14 Tu	0025	11.1	338	29 W	0057	9.9	302
	0732	-2.2	-67		0759	-1.3	-40
	1346	8.6	262		1424	7.8	238
	1935	2.6	79		2002	3.2	98
15 W	0110	11.2	341	30 Th	0133	9.7	296
	0819	-2.4	-73		0838	-1.2	-37
	1438	8.6	262		1500	7.7	235
	2024	2.7	82		2043	3.4	104
				31 F	0211	9.5	290
					0917	-0.9	-27
					1539	7.7	235
					2124	3.5	107

JUNE

Day	h m	ft	cm	Day	h m	ft	cm
1 Sa	0244	9.1	277	16 Su	0335	9.9	302
	0955	-0.6	-18		1025	-1.6	-49
	1614	7.7	235		1701	9.1	277
	2206	3.6	110		2251	2.1	64
2 Su	0321	8.8	268	17 M	0435	9.1	277
	1035	-0.2	-6		1112	-0.8	-24
	1656	7.8	238		1749	9.3	283
	2251	3.6	110		2347	1.9	58
3 M	0407	8.3	253	18 Tu	0538	8.2	250
	1117	0.3	9		1202	0.1	3
	1735	8.0	244		1837	9.5	290
	2344	3.4	104				
4 Tu	0503	7.8	238	19 W	0047	1.6	49
	1159	0.8	24		0645	7.5	229
	1820	8.3	253		1254	1.1	34
					1925	9.7	296
5 W	0039	3.1	94	20 Th	0150	1.2	37
	0606	7.4	226		0753	7.0	213
	1245	1.3	40		1347	1.9	58
	1905	8.7	265		2013	9.8	299
6 Th	0141	2.5	76	21 F	0250	0.8	24
	0717	7.1	216		0903	6.8	207
	1336	1.9	58		1442	2.5	76
	1954	9.1	277		2059	9.8	299
7 F	0242	1.7	52	22 Sa	0349	0.2	6
	0830	7.0	213		1009	6.8	207
	1435	2.3	70		1541	2.9	88
	2040	9.6	293		2146	9.9	302
8 Sa	0343	0.7	21	23 Su	0442	-0.2	-6
	0937	7.1	216		1109	6.9	210
	1535	2.7	82		1633	3.2	98
	2131	10.1	308		2232	9.9	302
9 Su	0438	-0.3	-9	24 M	0531	-0.7	-21
	1041	7.3	223		1203	7.2	219
	1633	2.9	88		1726	3.2	98
	2220	10.6	323		2315	9.8	299
10 M	0532	-1.3	-40	25 Tu	0614	-1.0	-30
	1143	7.7	235		1251	7.4	226
	1731	3.0	91		1814	3.3	101
	2310	11.0	335		2356	9.8	299
11 Tu	0623	-2.1	-64	26 W	0658	-1.2	-37
	1241	8.0	244		1333	7.5	229
	1824	2.9	88		1900	3.2	98
	2359	11.2	341				
12 W	0714	-2.6	-79	27 Th	0038	9.7	296
	1337	8.3	253		0737	-1.3	-40
	1917	2.8	85		1409	7.7	235
					1942	3.2	98
13 Th	0052	11.2	341	28 F	0114	9.6	293
	0802	-2.8	-85		0817	-1.2	-37
	1429	8.5	259		1441	7.8	238
	2009	2.6	79		2025	3.2	98
14 F	0144	11.0	335	29 Sa	0152	9.4	287
	0850	-2.7	-82		0854	-1.0	-30
	1522	8.7	265		1513	7.9	241
	2101	2.4	73		2105	3.1	94
15 Sa	0239	10.6	323	30 Su	0228	9.1	277
	0939	-2.3	-70		0931	-0.7	-21
	1614	8.9	271		1545	8.1	247
	2154	2.3	70		2146	3.0	91

Time meridian 120° W. 0000 is midnight. 1200 is noon.
Heights are referred to mean lower low water which is the chart datum of soundings.

ABERDEEN

1991 TIDE TABLES

For Daylight Saving Time, add one hour.

Times and Heights of High and Low Waters

JULY

Day	h m	ft	cm	Day	h m	ft	cm
1 M	0306	8.7	265	16 Tu	0419	8.8	268
	1006	-0.3	-9		1044	-0.3	-9
	1619	8.4	256		1709	9.8	299
	2229	2.8	85		2321	1.0	30
2 Tu	0349	8.3	253	17 W	0515	8.0	244
	1042	0.2	6		1128	0.7	21
	1652	8.6	262		1752	9.8	299
	2315	2.6	79				
3 W	0437	7.8	238	18 Th	0016	0.9	27
	1119	0.8	24		0618	7.2	219
	1733	8.9	271		1215	1.7	52
					1837	9.7	296
4 Th	0007	2.2	67	19 F	0115	0.9	27
	0538	7.3	223		0723	6.7	204
	1157	1.5	46		1306	2.5	76
	1815	9.2	280		1927	9.5	290
5 F	0103	1.7	52	20 Sa	0215	0.8	24
	0645	6.9	210		0829	6.4	195
	1242	2.2	67		1403	3.2	98
	1903	9.6	293		2018	9.4	287
6 Sa	0205	1.1	34	21 Su	0314	0.5	15
	0759	6.6	201		0939	6.4	195
	1343	2.8	85		1506	3.5	107
	1957	9.9	302		2111	9.4	287
7 Su	0309	0.3	9	22 M	0412	0.2	6
	0911	6.6	201		1049	6.6	201
	1455	3.3	101		1604	3.6	110
	2053	10.2	311		2201	9.4	287
8 M	0412	-0.5	-15	23 Tu	0503	-0.2	-6
	1021	6.9	210		1142	6.9	210
	1604	3.4	104		1700	3.5	107
	2153	10.6	323		2250	9.5	290
9 Tu	0511	-1.4	-43	24 W	0550	-0.6	-18
	1131	7.3	223		1230	7.3	223
	1708	3.3	101		1753	3.3	101
	2249	10.9	332		2337	9.6	293
10 W	0604	-2.1	-64	25 Th	0635	-0.9	-27
	1230	7.9	241		1308	7.6	232
	1806	2.9	88		1839	3.0	91
	2347	11.1	338				
11 Th	0656	-2.5	-76	26 F	0019	9.6	293
	1322	8.4	256		0715	-1.0	-30
	1902	2.4	73		1340	7.9	241
					1923	2.8	85
12 F	0040	11.1	338	27 Sa	0101	9.5	290
	0744	-2.7	-82		0752	-1.0	-30
	1412	8.9	271		1412	8.2	250
	1954	2.0	61		2004	2.5	76
13 Sa	0135	10.9	332	28 Su	0137	9.3	283
	0831	-2.5	-76		0829	-0.8	-24
	1459	9.3	283		1440	8.5	259
	2046	1.6	49		2043	2.3	70
14 Su	0231	10.4	317	29 M	0215	9.1	277
	0915	-2.0	-61		0905	-0.5	-15
	1545	9.6	293		1509	8.7	265
	2137	1.2	37		2124	2.0	61
15 M	0323	9.7	296	30 Tu	0254	8.7	265
	0959	-1.2	-37		0937	0.1	3
	1626	9.7	296		1537	9.0	274
	2229	1.1	34		2203	1.8	55
				31 W	0333	8.3	253
					1009	0.7	21
					1610	9.3	283
					2245	1.5	46

AUGUST

Day	h m	ft	cm	Day	h m	ft	cm
1 Th	0421	7.8	238	16 F	0546	7.2	219
	1040	1.3	40		1136	2.4	73
	1645	9.5	290		1748	9.4	287
	2333	1.3	40				
2 F	0515	7.3	223	17 Sa	0033	0.8	24
	1112	2.0	61		0645	6.6	201
	1728	9.6	293		1228	3.2	98
					1838	9.1	277
3 Sa	0029	1.0	30	18 Su	0132	1.0	30
	0622	6.8	207		0755	6.3	192
	1158	2.7	82		1327	3.7	113
	1821	9.7	296		1936	8.9	271
4 Su	0136	0.7	21	19 M	0235	1.0	30
	0738	6.5	198		0907	6.4	195
	1303	3.4	104		1433	4.0	122
	1922	9.8	299		2035	8.8	268
5 M	0241	0.2	6	20 Tu	0336	0.8	24
	0854	6.5	198		1013	6.6	201
	1429	3.7	113		1536	3.9	119
	2028	10.0	305		2134	8.9	271
6 Tu	0349	-0.4	-12	21 W	0433	0.4	12
	1009	6.9	210		1110	7.1	216
	1546	3.6	110		1638	3.5	107
	2134	10.3	314		2228	9.1	277
7 W	0449	-1.1	-34	22 Th	0521	0.0	0
	1115	7.5	229		1153	7.6	232
	1652	3.1	94		1729	3.0	91
	2236	10.5	320		2318	9.3	283
8 Th	0547	-1.6	-49	23 F	0604	-0.3	-9
	1211	8.2	250		1229	8.1	247
	1752	2.4	73		1817	2.5	76
	2339	10.8	329				
9 F	0635	-2.0	-61	24 Sa	0001	9.4	287
	1259	8.9	271		0646	-0.5	-15
	1848	1.7	52		1301	8.5	259
					1900	2.0	61
10 Sa	0034	10.8	329	25 Su	0043	9.4	287
	0723	-2.0	-61		0725	-0.4	-12
	1345	9.5	290		1329	8.9	271
	1938	1.0	30		1941	1.6	49
11 Su	0127	10.6	323	26 M	0121	9.3	283
	0806	-1.7	-52		0800	-0.1	-3
	1424	9.9	302		1357	9.2	280
	2027	0.5	15		2020	1.2	37
12 M	0219	10.1	308	27 Tu	0201	9.1	277
	0848	-1.1	-34		0836	0.3	9
	1505	10.1	308		1426	9.5	290
	2115	0.2	6		2059	0.9	27
13 Tu	0309	9.4	287	28 W	0239	8.8	268
	0930	-0.4	-12		0908	0.9	27
	1544	10.2	311		1454	9.7	296
	2203	0.1	3		2138	0.6	18
14 W	0358	8.7	265	29 Th	0321	8.4	256
	1012	0.6	18		0939	1.5	46
	1622	10.0	305		1529	9.9	302
	2249	0.3	9		2220	0.5	15
15 Th	0451	7.9	241	30 F	0408	7.9	241
	1054	1.5	46		1011	2.2	67
	1704	9.8	299		1603	10.0	305
	2341	0.5	15		2309	0.5	15
				31 Sa	0504	7.4	226
					1050	2.8	85
					1648	9.9	302

SEPTEMBER

Day	h m	ft	cm	Day	h m	ft	cm
1 Su	0004	0.5	15	16 M	0052	1.2	37
	0612	6.9	210		0719	6.7	204
	1143	3.5	107		1255	4.3	131
	1748	9.7	296		1850	8.5	259
2 M	0110	0.5	15	17 Tu	0152	1.4	43
	0728	6.7	204		0825	6.8	207
	1258	3.9	119		1402	4.3	131
	1858	9.6	293		1959	8.4	256
3 Tu	0219	0.3	9	18 W	0254	1.4	43
	0845	6.9	210		0930	7.1	216
	1421	4.0	122		1509	4.1	125
	2014	9.6	293		2102	8.5	259
4 W	0327	0.0	0	19 Th	0353	1.1	34
	0956	7.5	229		1019	7.6	232
	1535	3.5	107		1611	3.5	107
	2125	9.8	299		2201	8.7	265
5 Th	0428	-0.4	-12	20 F	0443	0.8	24
	1056	8.2	250		1101	8.2	250
	1642	2.7	82		1705	2.7	82
	2231	10.1	308		2253	9.0	274
6 F	0523	-0.8	-24	21 Sa	0529	0.6	18
	1145	9.0	274		1139	8.8	268
	1740	1.7	52		1751	1.9	58
	2333	10.3	314		2342	9.2	280
7 Sa	0613	-0.9	-27	22 Su	0611	0.6	18
	1227	9.7	296		1211	9.4	287
	1832	0.7	21		1834	1.2	37
8 Su	0029	10.3	314	23 M	0025	9.3	283
	0656	-0.8	-24		0650	0.7	21
	1309	10.2	311		1243	9.8	299
	1920	0.0	0		1915	0.6	18
9 M	0118	10.1	308	24 Tu	0107	9.3	283
	0740	-0.4	-12		0728	1.0	30
	1347	10.6	323		1314	10.2	311
	2006	-0.5	-15		1955	0.1	3
10 Tu	0207	9.7	296	25 W	0147	9.2	280
	0820	0.2	6		0805	1.5	46
	1423	10.6	323		1346	10.4	317
	2049	-0.6	-18		2034	-0.2	-6
11 W	0252	9.2	280	26 Th	0229	8.9	271
	0900	0.9	27		0842	2.0	61
	1459	10.5	320		1418	10.6	323
	2134	-0.5	-15		2116	-0.4	-12
12 Th	0337	8.6	262	27 F	0313	8.6	262
	0939	1.7	52		0918	2.6	79
	1534	10.2	311		1452	10.6	323
	2219	-0.1	-3		2200	-0.3	-9
13 F	0424	8.0	244	28 Sa	0404	8.1	247
	1019	2.5	76		0957	3.1	94
	1614	9.8	299		1534	10.4	317
	2304	0.3	9		2250	-0.1	-3
14 Sa	0514	7.4	226	29 Su	0501	7.7	235
	1104	3.2	98		1043	3.7	113
	1659	9.3	283		1624	10.1	308
	2354	0.8	24		2346	0.2	6
15 Su	0612	6.9	210	30 M	0608	7.4	226
	1152	3.8	116		1144	4.1	125
	1749	8.9	271		1730	9.7	296

Time meridian 120° W. 0000 is midnight. 1200 is noon.
Heights are referred to mean lower low water which is the chart datum of soundings.

1991 TIDE TABLES

ABERDEEN

For Daylight Saving Time, add one hour.

Times and Heights of High and Low Waters

OCTOBER

Day	Time h m	Height ft	Height cm	Day	Time h m	Height ft	Height cm
1 Tu	0049	0.5	15	16 W	0109	1.7	52
	0724	7.5	229		0739	7.6	232
	1300	4.2	128		1331	4.6	140
	1848	9.3	283		1914	8.3	253
2 W	0156	0.6	18	17 Th	0206	1.9	58
	0833	7.9	241		0834	8.0	244
	1417	3.9	119		1438	4.2	128
	2007	9.2	280		2023	8.3	253
3 Th	0301	0.6	18	18 F	0305	1.9	58
	0935	8.5	259		0923	8.5	259
	1527	3.1	94		1540	3.4	104
	2120	9.3	283		2127	8.4	256
4 F	0403	0.5	15	19 Sa	0358	1.9	58
	1027	9.3	283		1008	9.1	277
	1631	2.1	64		1634	2.5	76
	2226	9.5	290		2225	8.7	265
5 Sa	0455	0.5	15	20 Su	0447	1.9	58
	1113	10.0	305		1046	9.8	299
	1725	1.0	30		1723	1.6	49
	2326	9.7	296		2316	9.0	274
6 Su	0545	0.5	15	21 M	0532	2.0	61
	1155	10.6	323		1123	10.3	314
	1814	0.0	0		1808	0.7	21
7 M	0019	9.8	299	22 Tu	0004	9.2	280
	0629	0.8	24		0614	2.1	64
	1232	11.0	335		1158	10.8	329
	1900	-0.6	-18		1851	-0.1	-3
8 Tu	0109	9.7	296	23 W	0050	9.3	283
	0711	1.2	37		0656	2.4	73
	1309	11.1	338		1234	11.1	338
	1945	-0.9	-27		1931	-0.6	-18
9 W	0154	9.4	287	24 Th	0135	9.3	283
	0753	1.7	52		0736	2.8	85
	1342	11.0	335		1310	11.3	344
	2026	-0.9	-27		2015	-0.9	-27
10 Th	0236	9.1	277	25 F	0222	9.2	280
	0832	2.3	70		0817	3.1	94
	1418	10.8	329		1349	11.4	347
	2105	-0.6	-18		2057	-1.0	-30
11 F	0318	8.7	265	26 Sa	0309	8.9	271
	0911	2.9	88		0859	3.5	107
	1452	10.4	317		1430	11.3	344
	2147	-0.2	-6		2145	-0.8	-24
12 Sa	0400	8.2	250	27 Su	0401	8.7	265
	0951	3.5	107		0947	3.9	119
	1529	9.9	302		1517	10.9	332
	2232	0.3	9		2234	-0.4	-12
13 Su	0448	7.8	238	28 M	0459	8.5	259
	1035	4.0	122		1040	4.2	128
	1608	9.4	287		1614	10.4	317
	2319	0.9	27		2329	0.1	3
14 M	0541	7.5	229	29 Tu	0603	8.5	259
	1123	4.5	137		1144	4.3	131
	1659	8.9	271		1721	9.7	296
15 Tu	0012	1.4	43	30 W	0028	0.6	18
	0639	7.4	226		0708	8.7	265
	1223	4.7	143		1254	4.1	125
	1804	8.5	259		1840	9.2	280
				31 Th	0129	1.1	34
					0807	9.2	280
					1406	3.6	110
					1959	8.9	271

NOVEMBER

Day	Time h m	Height ft	Height cm	Day	Time h m	Height ft	Height cm
1 F	0232	1.5	46	16 Sa	0210	2.7	82
	0903	9.8	299		0827	9.5	290
	1514	2.7	82		1500	3.4	104
	2111	8.9	271		2046	8.2	250
2 Sa	0330	1.8	55	17 Su	0306	3.0	91
	0952	10.4	317		0911	10.0	305
	1614	1.6	49		1559	2.5	76
	2220	9.0	274		2151	8.4	256
3 Su	0423	2.0	61	18 M	0400	3.2	98
	1038	11.0	335		0955	10.6	323
	1709	0.6	18		1651	1.4	43
	2318	9.2	280		2247	8.7	265
4 M	0513	2.2	67	19 Tu	0449	3.4	104
	1118	11.3	344		1038	11.1	338
	1755	-0.1	-3		1739	0.5	15
					2342	9.0	274
5 Tu	0011	9.3	283	20 W	0539	3.6	110
	0600	2.5	76		1118	11.6	354
	1158	11.5	351		1825	-0.4	-12
	1840	-0.6	-18				
6 W	0059	9.3	283	21 Th	0033	9.2	280
	0643	2.8	85		0627	3.7	113
	1235	11.5	351		1202	12.0	366
	1923	-0.8	-24		1910	-0.9	-27
7 Th	0141	9.3	283	22 F	0123	9.4	287
	0726	3.2	98		0712	3.8	116
	1310	11.3	344		1244	12.1	369
	2003	-0.7	-21		1956	-1.3	-40
8 F	0224	9.1	277	23 Sa	0215	9.5	290
	0806	3.6	110		0801	3.9	119
	1343	11.0	335		1330	12.1	369
	2043	-0.5	-15		2043	-1.3	-40
9 Sa	0303	8.9	271	24 Su	0305	9.5	290
	0848	3.9	119		0848	4.0	122
	1420	10.7	326		1418	11.9	363
	2123	-0.1	-3		2129	-1.0	-30
10 Su	0342	8.6	262	25 M	0356	9.5	290
	0928	4.3	131		0939	4.1	125
	1455	10.3	314		1509	11.4	347
	2203	0.4	12		2219	-0.5	-15
11 M	0424	8.4	256	26 Tu	0451	9.6	293
	1010	4.6	140		1034	4.1	125
	1534	9.8	299		1610	10.7	326
	2248	0.9	27		2309	0.1	3
12 Tu	0512	8.3	253	27 W	0547	9.8	299
	1059	4.8	146		1136	4.0	122
	1623	9.3	283		1715	9.9	302
	2333	1.4	43				
13 W	0557	8.4	256	28 Th	0001	0.9	27
	1152	4.9	149		0639	10.0	305
	1719	8.8	268		1239	3.6	110
					1829	9.2	280
14 Th	0021	1.9	58	29 F	0057	1.7	52
	0649	8.6	262		0735	10.4	317
	1255	4.7	143		1347	3.1	94
	1828	8.4	256		1943	8.7	265
15 F	0117	2.4	73	30 Sa	0154	2.4	73
	0741	9.0	274		0825	10.8	329
	1400	4.2	128		1453	2.3	70
	1937	8.2	250		2059	8.5	259

DECEMBER

Day	Time h m	Height ft	Height cm	Day	Time h m	Height ft	Height cm
1 Su	0251	3.0	91	16 M	0207	3.9	119
	0914	11.2	341		0816	10.7	326
	1552	1.5	46		1519	2.4	73
	2207	8.6	262		2114	8.1	247
2 M	0350	3.4	104	17 Tu	0311	4.3	131
	1001	11.4	347		0907	11.2	341
	1647	0.8	24		1617	1.5	46
	2306	8.7	265		2220	8.3	253
3 Tu	0442	3.7	113	18 W	0410	4.6	140
	1044	11.6	354		0956	11.6	354
	1736	0.2	6		1711	0.5	15
					2323	8.7	265
4 W	0004	8.9	271	19 Th	0507	4.6	140
	0533	3.9	119		1046	12.0	366
	1127	11.6	354		1803	-0.3	-9
	1820	-0.2	-6				
5 Th	0051	9.1	277	20 F	0019	9.1	277
	0620	4.1	125		0601	4.5	137
	1206	11.6	354		1137	12.4	378
	1903	-0.3	-9		1851	-1.0	-30
6 F	0133	9.2	280	21 Sa	0113	9.5	290
	0705	4.2	128		0654	4.3	131
	1244	11.4	347		1228	12.6	384
	1942	-0.3	-9		1940	-1.3	-40
7 Sa	0215	9.2	280	22 Su	0203	9.9	302
	0747	4.3	131		0745	4.0	122
	1323	11.2	341		1321	12.5	381
	2023	-0.2	-6		2026	-1.3	-40
8 Su	0250	9.2	280	23 M	0252	10.2	311
	0828	4.5	137		0836	3.7	113
	1358	10.9	332		1413	12.2	372
	2101	0.1	3		2113	-1.0	-30
9 M	0325	9.1	277	24 Tu	0342	10.4	317
	0909	4.6	140		0927	3.5	107
	1433	10.6	323		1505	11.6	354
	2139	0.5	15		2158	-0.4	-12
10 Tu	0400	9.2	280	25 W	0429	10.7	326
	0950	4.7	143		1021	3.3	101
	1512	10.2	311		1604	10.8	329
	2218	0.9	27		2244	0.4	12
11 W	0436	9.2	280	26 Th	0515	10.9	332
	1035	4.7	143		1117	3.1	94
	1554	9.7	296		1706	9.9	302
	2257	1.5	46		2333	1.4	43
12 Th	0515	9.4	287	27 F	0602	11.0	335
	1125	4.6	140		1216	2.8	85
	1643	9.1	277		1812	9.1	277
	2336	2.1	64				
13 F	0557	9.7	296	28 Sa	0021	2.4	73
	1218	4.4	134		0652	11.2	341
	1743	8.6	262		1318	2.5	76
					1922	8.5	259
14 Sa	0021	2.7	82	29 Su	0116	3.3	101
	0642	10.0	305		0744	11.2	341
	1318	3.9	119		1422	2.2	67
	1852	8.2	250		2035	8.1	247
15 Su	0108	3.3	101	30 M	0215	4.0	122
	0728	10.3	314		0835	11.3	344
	1417	3.3	101		1523	1.7	52
	2003	8.0	244		2149	8.1	247
				31 Tu	0314	4.5	137
					0925	11.3	344
					1622	1.2	37
					2254	8.3	253

Time meridian 120° W. 0000 is midnight. 1200 is noon.
Heights are referred to mean lower low water which is the chart datum of soundings.

PORT TOWNSEND

1991 TIDE TABLES

For Daylight Saving Time, add one hour.

Times and Heights of High and Low Waters

JANUARY

Day	h m	ft	cm	Day	h m	ft	cm
1	0549	10.1	308	16	0557	9.1	277
Tu	1013	7.4	226	W	1052	6.6	201
	1502	9.1	277		1503	7.6	232
	2220	-2.8	-85		2216	-1.0	-30
2	0626	10.1	308	17	0618	9.1	277
W	1112	6.7	204	Th	1126	6.2	189
	1605	8.6	262		1552	7.3	223
	2307	-2.1	-64		2248	-0.7	-21
3	0702	10.0	305	18	0641	9.1	277
Th	1215	5.9	180	F	1203	5.5	168
	1711	7.9	241		1646	6.9	210
	2349	-1.0	-30		2324	0.0	0
4	0737	9.9	302	19	0706	9.2	280
F	1323	5.0	152	Sa	1245	4.8	146
	1820	7.0	213		1743	6.5	198
					2356	0.9	27
5	0035	0.3	9	20	0730	9.2	280
Sa	0809	9.8	299	Su	1330	4.0	122
	1429	4.1	125		1850	6.1	186
	1935	6.3	192				
6	0120	1.8	55	21	0027	2.1	64
Su	0844	9.6	293	M	0754	9.2	280
	1532	3.1	94		1419	3.1	94
	2107	5.7	174		2011	5.7	174
7	0203	3.4	104	22	0059	3.5	107
M	0915	9.4	287	Tu	0819	9.2	280
	1626	2.2	67		1508	2.1	64
	2310	5.7	174		2157	5.7	174
8	0254	4.9	149	23	0135	4.9	149
Tu	0944	9.1	277	W	0844	9.3	283
	1715	1.4	43		1603	1.1	34
9	0120	6.5	198	24	0024	6.4	195
W	0400	6.2	189	Th	0217	6.3	192
	1012	8.8	268		0913	9.4	287
	1758	0.8	24		1658	0.1	3
10	0243	7.5	229	25	0948	9.4	287
Th	0530	7.1	216	F	1754	-0.7	-21
	1041	8.5	259				
	1840	0.3	9				
11	0332	8.2	250	26	0303	8.4	256
F	0656	7.5	229	Sa	0539	8.1	247
	1106	8.3	253		1031	9.4	287
	1920	-0.2	-6		1851	-1.4	-43
12	0407	8.7	265	27	0338	9.1	277
Sa	0810	7.7	235	Su	0707	8.1	247
	1145	8.2	250		1139	9.3	283
	1957	-0.5	-15		1943	-1.9	-58
13	0439	9.0	274	28	0413	9.5	290
Su	0904	7.6	232	M	0817	7.7	235
	1233	8.0	244		1302	9.1	277
	2034	-0.8	-24		2035	-2.1	-64
14	0506	9.1	277	29	0445	9.7	296
M	0945	7.4	226	Tu	0912	7.1	216
	1323	7.9	241		1411	8.9	271
	2109	-1.1	-34		2121	-2.0	-61
15	0534	9.1	277	30	0517	9.7	296
Tu	1017	7.1	216	W	1005	6.2	189
	1418	7.8	238		1520	8.6	262
	2143	-1.1	-34		2206	-1.5	-46
				31	0548	9.7	296
				Th	1056	5.2	158
					1623	8.2	250
					2249	-0.6	-18

FEBRUARY

Day	h m	ft	cm	Day	h m	ft	cm
1	0617	9.6	293	16	0545	8.8	268
F	1146	4.3	131	Sa	1120	3.7	113
	1725	7.6	232		1709	7.0	213
	2328	0.5	15		2259	1.3	40
2	0646	9.5	290	17	0608	8.9	271
Sa	1238	3.4	104	Su	1155	2.8	85
	1829	7.0	213		1806	6.8	207
					2333	2.4	73
3	0010	1.8	55	18	0631	8.9	271
Su	0715	9.4	287	M	1237	1.9	58
	1327	2.6	79		1913	6.7	204
	1939	6.5	198				
4	0049	3.2	98	19	0005	3.6	110
M	0741	9.1	277	Tu	0655	9.0	274
	1419	2.0	61		1323	1.2	37
	2102	6.2	189		2028	6.6	201
5	0133	4.5	137	20	0044	4.9	149
Tu	0806	8.9	271	W	0720	9.0	274
	1514	1.6	49		1417	0.5	15
	2255	6.3	192		2209	6.7	204
6	0219	5.8	177	21	0126	6.1	186
W	0834	8.6	262	Th	0748	9.0	274
	1606	1.2	37		1517	0.1	3
7	0105	7.0	213	22	0012	7.3	223
Th	0338	6.8	207	F	0220	7.1	216
	0900	8.3	253		0824	8.9	271
	1702	0.9	27		1623	-0.3	-9
8	0221	7.7	235	23	0138	8.0	244
F	0524	7.3	223	Sa	0421	7.7	235
	0935	8.0	244		0913	8.8	268
	1755	0.6	18		1729	-0.6	-18
9	0303	8.2	250	24	0227	8.6	262
Sa	0701	7.4	226	Su	0609	7.7	235
	1020	7.8	238		1028	8.5	259
	1845	0.3	9		1832	-0.8	-24
10	0338	8.5	259	25	0305	8.9	271
Su	0805	7.2	219	M	0723	7.1	216
	1122	7.6	232		1205	8.3	253
	1930	0.1	3		1928	-0.9	-27
11	0403	8.7	265	26	0334	9.1	277
M	0847	6.9	210	Tu	0818	6.3	192
	1235	7.5	229		1327	8.2	250
	2012	-0.2	-6		2020	-0.7	-21
12	0425	8.7	265	27	0403	9.1	277
Tu	0916	6.5	198	W	0907	5.3	162
	1337	7.5	229		1437	8.1	247
	2050	-0.3	-9		2106	-0.3	-9
13	0447	8.7	265	28	0431	9.1	277
W	0947	6.0	183	Th	0946	4.2	128
	1431	7.4	226		1540	8.0	244
	2122	-0.3	-9		2149	0.4	12
14	0505	8.7	265				
Th	1013	5.3	162				
	1522	7.4	226				
	2154	0.0	0				
15	0526	8.7	265				
F	1045	4.5	137				
	1614	7.2	219				
	2227	0.5	15				

MARCH

Day	h m	ft	cm	Day	h m	ft	cm
1	0459	9.0	274	16	0421	8.3	253
F	1031	3.1	94	Sa	1006	2.2	67
	1640	7.8	238		1633	7.3	223
	2227	1.3	40		2204	2.3	70
2	0523	8.9	271	17	0443	8.4	256
Sa	1110	2.2	67	Su	1038	1.2	37
	1739	7.6	232		1727	7.4	226
	2308	2.3	70		2239	3.2	98
3	0549	8.8	268	18	0506	8.5	259
Su	1149	1.5	46	M	1116	0.3	9
	1837	7.3	223		1826	7.5	229
	2347	3.4	104		2315	4.1	125
4	0613	8.6	262	19	0530	8.6	262
M	1231	1.0	30	Tu	1158	-0.4	-12
	1937	7.1	216		1932	7.6	232
					2357	5.2	158
5	0029	4.5	137	20	0559	8.6	262
Tu	0636	8.3	253	W	1247	-0.8	-24
	1316	0.8	24		2041	7.6	232
	2049	7.0	213				
6	0111	5.5	168	21	0042	6.1	186
W	0700	8.1	247	Th	0627	8.5	259
	1401	0.7	21		1343	-0.9	-27
	2219	7.0	213		2203	7.7	235
7	0214	6.3	192	22	0145	6.8	207
Th	0726	7.8	238	F	0706	8.4	256
	1457	0.8	24		1442	-0.7	-21
					2336	8.0	244
8	0009	7.3	223	23	0326	7.2	219
F	0356	6.8	207	Sa	0758	8.0	244
	0800	7.5	229		1553	-0.4	-12
	1559	0.9	27				
9	0125	7.7	235	24	0045	8.3	253
Sa	0542	6.9	210	Su	0519	7.0	213
	0843	7.2	219		0917	7.6	232
	1703	0.9	27		1704	-0.2	-6
10	0210	7.9	241	25	0131	8.5	259
Su	0701	6.6	201	M	0639	6.3	192
	0951	6.9	210		1100	7.2	219
	1805	0.8	24		1810	0.2	6
11	0242	8.1	247	26	0208	8.6	262
M	0746	6.2	189	Tu	0731	5.3	162
	1121	6.8	207		1236	7.1	216
	1854	0.7	21		1909	0.6	18
12	0307	8.1	247	27	0242	8.6	262
Tu	0818	5.7	174	W	0813	4.2	128
	1236	6.8	207		1357	7.3	223
	1939	0.7	21		1958	1.1	34
13	0325	8.1	247	28	0310	8.6	262
W	0843	5.0	152	Th	0850	3.0	91
	1349	6.8	207		1505	7.4	226
	2021	0.8	24		2043	1.8	55
14	0344	8.1	247	29	0336	8.5	259
Th	0909	4.2	128	F	0927	1.9	58
	1445	7.0	213		1603	7.6	232
	2053	1.1	34		2125	2.6	79
15	0402	8.2	250	30	0401	8.4	256
F	0934	3.3	101	Sa	1001	1.0	30
	1539	7.1	216		1658	7.7	235
	2129	1.6	49		2207	3.4	104
				31	0423	8.2	250
				Su	1033	0.2	6
					1751	7.8	238
					2246	4.2	128

Time meridian 120° W. 0000 is midnight. 1200 is noon.
Heights are referred to mean lower low water which is the chart datum of soundings.

1991 TIDE TABLES

PORT TOWNSEND

For Daylight Saving Time, add one hour.

Times and Heights of High and Low Waters

APRIL

Day	h m	ft	cm	Day	h m	ft	cm
1 M	0443	8.0	244	16 Tu	0402	8.3	253
	1108	-0.2	-6		1046	-1.9	-58
	1843	7.8	238		1838	8.4	256
	2328	5.0	152		2303	5.8	177
2 Tu	0506	7.8	238	17 W	0434	8.4	256
	1145	-0.5	-15		1133	-2.3	-70
	1935	7.7	235		1937	8.5	259
					2355	6.3	192
3 W	0018	5.6	171	18 Th	0506	8.3	253
	0528	7.6	232		1221	-2.2	-67
	1226	-0.4	-12		2039	8.5	259
	2034	7.7	235				
4 Th	0111	6.1	186	19 F	0058	6.7	204
	0554	7.3	223		0551	8.0	244
	1309	-0.2	-6		1317	-1.8	-55
	2140	7.6	232		2148	8.5	259
5 F	0235	6.4	195	20 Sa	0229	6.8	207
	0625	7.0	213		0647	7.6	232
	1400	0.2	6		1417	-1.1	-34
	2256	7.6	232		2249	8.5	259
6 Sa	0421	6.4	195	21 Su	0419	6.4	195
	0707	6.7	204		0803	6.9	210
	1459	0.6	18		1526	-0.3	-9
					2343	8.6	262
7 Su	0008	7.6	232	22 M	0545	5.5	168
	0550	6.1	186		0942	6.3	192
	0806	6.3	192		1633	0.6	18
	1603	0.9	27				
8 M	0054	7.7	235	23 Tu	0032	8.6	262
	0645	5.6	171		0637	4.4	134
	0936	5.9	180		1133	6.1	186
	1709	1.2	37		1739	1.4	43
9 Tu	0122	7.7	235	24 W	0109	8.5	259
	0717	5.0	152		0719	3.2	98
	1115	5.8	177		1312	6.3	192
	1806	1.5	46		1837	2.3	70
10 W	0148	7.8	238	25 Th	0141	8.4	256
	0743	4.2	128		0757	2.0	61
	1245	5.9	180		1427	6.7	204
	1855	1.8	55		1932	3.2	98
11 Th	0209	7.8	238	26 F	0210	8.3	253
	0808	3.3	101		0829	0.9	27
	1357	6.2	189		1532	7.2	219
	1936	2.3	70		2018	4.0	122
12 F	0229	7.8	238	27 Sa	0233	8.1	247
	0828	2.2	67		0901	0.0	0
	1500	6.7	204		1625	7.6	232
	2018	2.8	85		2106	4.7	143
13 Sa	0250	7.9	241	28 Su	0255	7.9	241
	0858	1.0	30		0930	-0.7	-21
	1557	7.2	219		1717	7.9	241
	2057	3.5	107		2150	5.3	162
14 Su	0312	8.1	247	29 M	0314	7.7	235
	0930	-0.2	-6		1002	-1.2	-37
	1650	7.7	235		1805	8.1	247
	2138	4.3	131		2237	5.8	177
15 M	0335	8.2	250	30 Tu	0335	7.5	229
	1007	-1.2	-37		1034	-1.4	-43
	1742	8.1	247		1848	8.2	250
	2217	5.0	152		2323	6.1	186

MAY

Day	h m	ft	cm	Day	h m	ft	cm
1 W	0357	7.3	223	16 Th	0348	8.4	256
	1109	-1.5	-46		1113	-3.3	-101
	1930	8.2	250		1933	9.1	277
					2359	6.8	207
2 Th	0017	6.3	192	17 F	0440	8.1	247
	0423	7.1	216		1204	-2.9	-88
	1147	-1.3	-40		2023	9.1	277
	2019	8.2	250				
3 F	0126	6.4	195	18 Sa	0118	6.6	201
	0455	6.8	207		0539	7.6	232
	1229	-0.9	-27		1259	-2.1	-64
	2106	8.0	244		2115	9.1	277
4 Sa	0256	6.3	192	19 Su	0251	6.0	183
	0539	6.4	195		0652	6.8	207
	1316	-0.4	-12		1355	-1.0	-30
	2159	7.9	241		2204	9.0	274
5 Su	0436	5.9	180	20 M	0417	5.1	155
	0621	6.0	183		0818	6.0	183
	1407	0.2	6		1454	0.2	6
	2242	7.9	241		2247	8.9	271
6 M	0528	5.4	165	21 Tu	0519	3.9	119
	0744	5.5	168		1005	5.5	168
	1504	0.9	27		1556	1.6	49
	2324	7.9	241		2329	8.8	268
7 Tu	0609	4.6	140	22 W	0615	2.6	79
	0920	5.0	152		1158	5.5	168
	1600	1.6	49		1659	2.9	88
	2352	7.8	238				
8 W	0638	3.8	116	23 Th	0003	8.6	262
	1110	4.9	149		0657	1.4	43
	1700	2.3	70		1336	6.0	183
					1754	4.0	122
9 Th	0021	7.9	241	24 F	0035	8.4	256
	0659	2.8	85		0729	0.4	12
	1253	5.3	162		1454	6.7	204
	1754	3.1	94		1901	5.0	152
10 F	0044	7.9	241	25 Sa	0101	8.2	250
	0721	1.6	49		0801	-0.4	-12
	1414	5.9	180		1551	7.4	226
	1843	3.9	119		1955	5.8	177
11 Sa	0107	8.0	244	26 Su	0125	7.9	241
	0753	0.3	9		0833	-1.0	-30
	1517	6.7	204		1640	8.0	244
	1935	4.7	143		2051	6.3	192
12 Su	0131	8.1	247	27 M	0145	7.7	235
	0822	-1.0	-30		0901	-1.5	-46
	1613	7.5	229		1725	8.3	253
	2021	5.4	165		2140	6.5	198
13 M	0157	8.3	253	28 Tu	0205	7.5	229
	0901	-2.1	-64		0933	-1.8	-55
	1701	8.2	250		1804	8.5	259
	2111	6.0	183		2231	6.6	201
14 Tu	0229	8.5	259	29 W	0229	7.4	226
	0940	-2.9	-88		1008	-1.9	-58
	1754	8.7	265		1839	8.5	259
	2202	6.5	198		2322	6.6	201
15 W	0306	8.5	259	30 Th	0257	7.2	219
	1025	-3.4	-104		1043	-1.9	-58
	1842	9.0	274		1918	8.5	259
	2257	6.8	207				
				31 F	0015	6.5	198
					0336	6.9	210
					1122	-1.7	-52
					1952	8.4	256

JUNE

Day	h m	ft	cm	Day	h m	ft	cm
1 Sa	0118	6.3	192	16 Su	0106	5.7	174
	0418	6.6	201		0548	7.2	219
	1202	-1.3	-40		1238	-1.7	-52
	2025	8.3	253		2034	9.3	283
2 Su	0230	5.9	180	17 M	0228	4.8	146
	0514	6.1	186		0704	6.3	192
	1244	-0.7	-21		1329	-0.3	-9
	2103	8.3	253		2113	9.2	280
3 M	0343	5.4	165	18 Tu	0341	3.7	113
	0616	5.6	171		0833	5.5	168
	1326	0.1	3		1421	1.2	37
	2135	8.2	250		2150	9.0	274
4 Tu	0431	4.6	140	19 W	0440	2.5	76
	0735	5.0	152		1021	5.2	158
	1405	1.0	30		1517	2.8	85
	2205	8.2	250		2227	8.8	268
5 W	0507	3.7	113	20 Th	0536	1.4	43
	0913	4.6	140		1218	5.5	168
	1454	2.1	64		1619	4.3	131
	2232	8.2	250		2300	8.6	262
6 Th	0539	2.7	82	21 F	0618	0.4	12
	1109	4.6	140		1358	6.3	192
	1542	3.3	101		1725	5.5	168
	2257	8.2	250		2327	8.3	253
7 F	0607	1.5	46	22 Sa	0658	-0.3	-9
	1310	5.2	158		1507	7.2	219
	1645	4.5	137		1838	6.3	192
	2324	8.3	253		2356	8.1	247
8 Sa	0639	0.2	6	23 Su	0733	-0.8	-24
	1430	6.2	189		1602	7.8	238
	1747	5.5	168		1947	6.8	207
	2350	8.4	256				
9 Su	0715	-1.0	-30	24 M	0021	7.8	238
	1532	7.2	219		0806	-1.2	-37
	1853	6.3	192		1644	8.3	253
					2047	6.9	210
10 M	0019	8.6	262	25 Tu	0046	7.6	232
	0757	-2.2	-67		0839	-1.5	-46
	1621	8.1	247		1716	8.5	259
	1955	6.8	207		2140	6.9	210
11 Tu	0056	8.8	268	26 W	0118	7.4	226
	0839	-3.1	-94		0914	-1.7	-52
	1703	8.7	265		1748	8.5	259
	2051	7.1	216		2226	6.8	207
12 W	0142	8.8	268	27 Th	0203	7.3	223
	0924	-3.6	-110		0950	-1.8	-55
	1748	9.1	277		1817	8.5	259
	2149	7.1	216		2304	6.5	198
13 Th	0230	8.7	265	28 F	0245	7.1	216
	1010	-3.8	-116		1026	-1.8	-55
	1830	9.3	283		1844	8.4	256
	2251	6.9	210		2347	6.2	189
14 F	0333	8.4	256	29 Sa	0334	6.8	207
	1059	-3.5	-107		1101	-1.6	-49
	1912	9.4	287		1914	8.4	256
	2356	6.4	195				
15 Sa	0439	7.9	241	30 Su	0035	5.8	177
	1148	-2.8	-85		0428	6.4	195
	1951	9.3	283		1137	-1.1	-34
					1939	8.4	256

Time meridian 120° W. 0000 is midnight. 1200 is noon.
Heights are referred to mean lower low water which is the chart datum of soundings.

PORT TOWNSEND

1991 TIDE TABLES

For Daylight Saving Time, add one hour.

Times and Heights of High and Low Waters

JULY

Day	Time (h m)	ft	cm	Day	Time (h m)	ft	cm
1 M	0124	5.2	158	16 Tu	0142	3.3	101
	0525	5.9	180		0715	6.2	189
	1212	-0.4	-12		1300	1.0	30
	2008	8.4	256		2017	9.0	274
2 Tu	0212	4.6	140	17 W	0245	2.3	70
	0625	5.4	165		0840	5.6	171
	1248	0.5	15		1349	2.6	79
	2033	8.4	256		2049	8.8	268
3 W	0301	3.7	113	18 Th	0344	1.5	46
	0740	4.9	149		1027	5.5	168
	1322	1.7	52		1441	4.1	125
	2059	8.4	256		2124	8.5	259
4 Th	0351	2.8	85	19 F	0441	0.8	24
	0912	4.7	143		1230	6.0	183
	1357	3.0	91		1547	5.4	165
	2123	8.4	256		2153	8.2	250
5 F	0433	1.7	52	20 Sa	0531	0.2	6
	1119	4.9	149		1403	6.8	207
	1439	4.4	134		1706	6.3	192
	2148	8.5	259		2225	7.9	241
6 Sa	0514	0.6	18	21 Su	0617	-0.2	-6
	1336	5.7	174		1502	7.5	229
	1539	5.6	171		1836	6.8	207
	2216	8.6	262		2257	7.7	235
7 Su	0557	-0.6	-18	22 M	0702	-0.5	-15
	1448	6.8	207		1544	8.0	244
	1704	6.6	201		1948	6.9	210
	2246	8.7	265		2339	7.5	229
8 M	0644	-1.6	-49	23 Tu	0742	-0.8	-24
	1536	7.7	235		1621	8.2	250
	1827	7.2	219		2045	6.8	207
	2328	8.9	271				
9 Tu	0731	-2.5	-76	24 W	0027	7.3	223
	1615	8.4	256		0821	-1.0	-30
	1936	7.4	226		1651	8.3	253
					2122	6.5	198
10 W	0024	8.9	271	25 Th	0119	7.2	219
	0821	-3.1	-94		0857	-1.2	-37
	1651	8.8	268		1716	8.2	250
	2039	7.2	219		2157	6.2	189
11 Th	0130	8.8	268	26 F	0215	7.1	216
	0910	-3.4	-104		0933	-1.3	-40
	1726	9.1	277		1739	8.2	250
	2139	6.7	204		2229	5.7	174
12 F	0235	8.6	262	27 Sa	0300	6.9	210
	0959	-3.3	-101		1007	-1.2	-37
	1801	9.2	280		1802	8.1	247
	2239	6.0	183		2304	5.2	158
13 Sa	0345	8.2	250	28 Su	0353	6.7	204
	1045	-2.7	-82		1042	-0.8	-24
	1336	9.2	280		1822	8.2	250
	2338	5.2	158		2343	4.6	140
14 Su	0451	7.6	232	29 M	0445	6.4	195
	1129	-1.8	-55		1114	-0.2	-6
	1911	9.2	280		1844	8.2	250
15 M	0040	4.3	131	30 Tu	0020	3.9	119
	0559	6.9	210		0537	6.0	183
	1218	-0.5	-15		1142	0.6	18
	1945	9.1	277		1906	8.2	250
				31 W	0100	3.1	94
					0639	5.7	174
					1218	1.7	52
					1932	8.3	253

AUGUST

Day	Time (h m)	ft	cm	Day	Time (h m)	ft	cm
1 Th	0145	2.3	70	16 F	0241	0.7	21
	0751	5.4	165		1018	6.3	192
	1246	2.9	88		1423	5.2	158
	1955	8.3	253		2018	7.9	241
2 F	0234	1.5	46	17 Sa	0336	0.5	15
	0923	5.4	165		1211	6.6	201
	1318	4.2	128		1542	6.1	186
	2019	8.3	253		2053	7.5	229
3 Sa	0327	0.7	21	18 Su	0435	0.4	12
	1127	5.7	174		1334	7.2	219
	1400	5.5	168		1724	6.5	198
	2048	8.4	256		2129	7.2	219
4 Su	0424	-0.1	-3	19 M	0532	0.3	9
	2120	8.5	259		1426	7.6	232
					1848	6.5	198
					2221	7.0	213
5 M	0524	-0.9	-27	20 Tu	0624	0.1	3
	1433	7.4	226		1508	7.9	241
	1700	7.2	219		1949	6.3	192
	2207	8.5	259		2333	6.8	207
6 Tu	0620	-1.5	-46	21 W	0715	-0.1	-3
	1513	8.0	244		1536	7.9	241
	1830	7.3	223		2024	5.9	180
	2313	8.5	259				
7 W	0715	-2.0	-61	22 Th	0035	6.8	207
	1546	8.4	256		0759	-0.2	-6
	1939	6.9	210		1602	7.9	241
					2056	5.5	168
8 Th	0032	8.5	259	23 F	0134	6.8	207
	0805	-2.3	-70		0837	-0.3	-9
	1617	8.6	262		1623	7.8	238
	2036	6.3	192		2127	4.9	149
9 F	0145	8.4	256	24 Sa	0230	6.8	207
	0856	-2.3	-70		0909	-0.2	-6
	1648	8.7	265		1640	7.8	238
	2127	5.4	165		2153	4.3	131
10 Sa	0258	8.2	250	25 Su	0319	6.8	207
	0943	-1.8	-55		0941	0.1	3
	1717	8.8	268		1700	7.8	238
	2217	4.4	134		2224	3.5	107
11 Su	0404	7.9	241	26 M	0411	6.7	204
	1029	-1.1	-34		1017	0.6	18
	1749	8.8	268		1720	7.9	241
	2309	3.3	101		2256	2.7	82
12 M	0509	7.5	229	27 Tu	0502	6.6	201
	1111	0.0	0		1045	1.4	43
	1818	8.7	265		1741	7.9	241
					2328	1.9	58
13 Tu	0001	2.4	73	28 W	0554	6.5	198
	0613	7.0	213		1117	2.3	70
	1153	1.3	40		1806	7.9	241
	1847	8.6	262				
14 W	0053	1.6	49	29 Th	0007	1.2	37
	0722	6.5	198		0656	6.4	195
	1236	2.7	82		1152	3.4	104
	1917	8.4	256		1828	8.0	244
15 Th	0146	1.0	30	30 F	0053	0.5	15
	0841	6.3	192		0806	6.4	195
	1322	4.0	122		1227	4.5	137
	1949	8.2	250		1849	8.0	244
				31 Sa	0142	0.1	3
					0929	6.5	198
					1306	5.6	171
					1918	8.0	244

SEPTEMBER

Day	Time (h m)	ft	cm	Day	Time (h m)	ft	cm
1 Su	0237	-0.3	-9	16 M	0333	0.6	18
	1118	6.8	207		1240	7.5	229
	1405	6.5	198		1746	6.2	189
	1954	8.0	244		2039	6.4	195
2 M	0343	-0.5	-15	17 Tu	0439	0.7	21
	1255	7.3	223		1333	7.6	232
	1555	7.0	213		1848	5.8	177
	2042	7.9	241		2158	6.2	189
3 Tu	0452	-0.8	-24	18 W	0542	0.8	24
	1352	7.8	238		1409	7.7	235
	1739	7.0	213		1930	5.4	165
	2158	7.8	238		2324	6.1	186
4 W	0557	-0.9	-27	19 Th	0638	0.8	24
	1427	8.1	247		1436	7.7	235
	1849	6.4	195		2002	4.8	146
	2331	7.7	235				
5 Th	0655	-1.0	-30	20 F	0045	6.2	189
	1500	8.3	253		0723	0.9	27
	1942	5.6	171		1458	7.6	232
					2027	4.1	125
6 F	0101	7.7	235	21 Sa	0149	6.4	195
	0750	-0.8	-24		0805	1.1	34
	1528	8.4	256		1516	7.6	232
	2029	4.5	137		2052	3.3	101
7 Sa	0216	7.8	238	22 Su	0243	6.6	201
	0839	-0.4	-12		0841	1.5	46
	1600	8.4	256		1535	7.6	232
	2116	3.3	101		2117	2.4	73
8 Su	0322	7.8	238	23 M	0335	6.8	207
	0924	0.3	9		0913	2.0	61
	1626	8.4	256		1552	7.7	235
	2157	2.2	67		2145	1.5	46
9 M	0423	7.7	235	24 Tu	0425	7.0	213
	1006	1.2	37		0948	2.6	79
	1653	8.3	253		1613	7.8	238
	2240	1.2	37		2218	0.5	15
10 Tu	0525	7.6	232	25 W	0517	7.2	219
	1048	2.3	70		1023	3.4	104
	1721	8.2	250		1635	7.8	238
	2322	0.5	15		2250	-0.3	-9
11 W	0625	7.4	226	26 Th	0613	7.4	226
	1130	3.4	104		1058	4.3	131
	1746	8.0	244		1657	7.9	241
					2328	-0.8	-24
12 Th	0004	0.0	0	27 F	0712	7.5	229
	0727	7.3	223		1137	5.2	158
	1216	4.4	134		1722	7.9	241
	1811	7.8	238				
13 F	0049	-0.1	-3	28 Sa	0014	-1.2	-37
	0836	7.2	219		0816	7.6	232
	1311	5.3	162		1222	6.0	183
	1837	7.5	229		1751	7.9	241
14 Sa	0135	0.0	0	29 Su	0106	-1.2	-37
	0956	7.1	216		0930	7.7	235
	1425	6.0	183		1322	6.6	201
	1909	7.1	216		1829	7.8	238
15 Su	0230	0.3	9	30 M	0204	-1.0	-30
	1122	7.3	223		1046	7.8	238
	1609	6.3	192		1505	6.9	210
	1945	6.8	207		1915	7.5	229

Time meridian 120° W. 0000 is midnight. 1200 is noon.
Heights are referred to mean lower low water which is the chart datum of soundings.

1991 TIDE TABLES

PORT TOWNSEND

For Daylight Saving Time, add one hour.

Times and Heights of High and Low Waters

OCTOBER

Day	Time (h m)	Height (ft)	Height (cm)
1 Tu	0312	-0.6	-18
	1202	8.1	247
	1700	6.6	201
	2037	7.1	216
2 W	0422	-0.3	-9
	1251	8.2	250
	1812	5.9	180
	2224	6.8	207
3 Th	0533	0.2	6
	1332	8.4	256
	1901	4.9	149
4 F	0008	6.8	207
	0633	0.7	21
	1404	8.4	256
	1940	3.7	113
5 Sa	0134	7.0	213
	0726	1.3	40
	1434	8.4	256
	2021	2.4	73
6 Su	0246	7.3	223
	0818	2.0	61
	1501	8.3	253
	2057	1.2	37
7 M	0346	7.7	235
	0902	2.9	88
	1527	8.2	250
	2136	0.2	6
8 Tu	0445	7.9	241
	0948	3.7	113
	1551	8.1	247
	2211	-0.6	-18
9 W	0538	8.1	247
	1033	4.6	140
	1615	7.9	241
	2246	-1.0	-30
10 Th	0630	8.2	250
	1115	5.3	162
	1637	7.7	235
	2322	-1.1	-34
11 F	0725	8.1	247
	1209	5.8	177
	1705	7.4	226
12 Sa	0003	-0.9	-27
	0821	8.0	244
	1315	6.2	189
	1727	7.0	213
13 Su	0046	-0.6	-18
	0923	7.9	241
	1448	6.3	192
	1759	6.7	204
14 M	0135	0.0	0
	1031	7.9	241
	1638	6.1	186
	1844	6.2	189
15 Tu	0235	0.5	15
	1131	7.8	238
	1754	5.7	174
	1957	5.8	177
16 W	0340	1.1	34
	1216	7.8	238
	1836	5.1	155
	2136	5.5	168
17 Th	0443	1.5	46
	1248	7.8	238
	1908	4.4	134
	2323	5.4	165
18 F	0545	1.9	58
	1317	7.8	238
	1930	3.6	110
19 Sa	0053	5.6	171
	0635	2.4	73
	1340	7.8	238
	1955	2.7	82
20 Su	0200	6.1	186
	0719	2.9	88
	1400	7.8	238
	2016	1.7	52
21 M	0259	6.6	201
	0801	3.5	107
	1417	7.9	241
	2042	0.6	18
22 Tu	0351	7.2	219
	0840	4.2	128
	1439	8.0	244
	2110	-0.5	-15
23 W	0440	7.7	235
	0919	4.9	149
	1501	8.1	247
	2145	-1.4	-43
24 Th	0532	8.2	250
	1001	5.5	168
	1526	8.2	250
	2221	-2.0	-61
25 F	0623	8.5	259
	1043	6.1	186
	1554	8.2	250
	2303	-2.4	-73
26 Sa	0713	8.7	265
	1133	6.6	201
	1627	8.1	247
	2349	-2.3	-70
27 Su	0812	8.8	268
	1234	6.9	210
	1705	7.9	241
28 M	0041	-1.9	-58
	0915	8.8	268
	1359	7.0	213
	1757	7.5	229
29 Tu	0138	-1.3	-40
	1014	8.8	268
	1552	6.5	198
	1909	6.9	210
30 W	0241	-0.4	-12
	1105	8.8	268
	1715	5.6	171
	2102	6.3	192
31 Th	0348	0.6	18
	1151	8.8	268
	1807	4.4	134
	2259	6.0	183

NOVEMBER

Day	Time (h m)	Height (ft)	Height (cm)
1 F	0455	1.7	52
	1230	8.8	268
	1851	3.1	94
2 Sa	0045	6.2	189
	0603	2.7	82
	1304	8.7	265
	1930	1.8	55
3 Su	0205	6.8	207
	0659	3.7	113
	1333	8.6	262
	2005	0.6	18
4 M	0315	7.5	229
	0754	4.6	140
	1400	8.5	259
	2037	-0.3	-9
5 Tu	0412	8.1	247
	0844	5.3	162
	1425	8.3	253
	2109	-1.1	-34
6 W	0503	8.5	259
	0932	5.9	180
	1445	8.1	247
	2141	-1.5	-46
7 Th	0549	8.8	268
	1021	6.4	195
	1506	7.9	241
	2217	-1.7	-52
8 F	0635	8.9	271
	1113	6.6	201
	1530	7.6	232
	2250	-1.6	-49
9 Sa	0717	8.9	271
	1213	6.7	204
	1559	7.3	223
	2328	-1.4	-43
10 Su	0806	8.7	265
	1323	6.7	204
	1627	7.0	213
11 M	0010	-0.9	-27
	0847	8.6	262
	1500	6.4	195
	1706	6.5	198
12 Tu	0054	-0.3	-9
	0931	8.5	259
13 W	0145	0.5	15
	1015	8.4	256
	1721	5.3	162
	1924	5.4	165
14 Th	0237	1.3	40
	1053	8.3	253
	1757	4.5	137
	2114	5.0	152
15 F	0333	2.2	67
	1125	8.3	253
	1824	3.6	110
	2310	4.9	149
16 Sa	0433	3.1	94
	1150	8.2	250
	1349	2.6	79
17 Su	0059	5.4	165
	0531	4.0	122
	1216	8.3	253
	1912	1.5	46
18 M	0218	6.2	189
	0626	4.8	146
	1239	8.3	253
	1939	0.4	12
19 Tu	0317	7.0	213
	0715	5.6	171
	1301	8.4	256
	2006	-0.8	-24
20 W	0406	7.9	241
	0804	6.2	189
	1329	8.6	262
	2041	-1.8	-55
21 Th	0452	8.6	262
	0853	6.8	207
	1355	8.7	265
	2119	-2.6	-79
22 F	0537	9.1	277
	0945	7.1	216
	1431	8.8	268
	2201	-3.1	-94
23 Sa	0623	9.4	287
	1034	7.3	223
	1511	8.7	265
	2245	-3.1	-94
24 Su	0705	9.6	293
	1132	7.3	223
	1557	8.5	259
	2333	-2.8	-85
25 M	0756	9.6	293
	1241	7.1	216
	1652	8.0	244
26 Tu	0024	-2.0	-61
	0841	9.6	293
	1406	6.5	198
	1809	7.2	219
27 W	0118	-1.0	-30
	0927	9.5	290
	1537	5.6	171
	1935	6.4	195
28 Th	0214	0.4	12
	1010	9.4	287
	1649	4.3	131
	2124	5.8	177
29 F	0313	1.9	58
	1050	9.4	287
	1745	3.0	91
	2324	5.7	174
30 Sa	0418	3.4	104
	1129	9.3	283
	1830	1.7	52

DECEMBER

Day	Time (h m)	Height (ft)	Height (cm)
1 Su	0113	6.3	192
	0524	4.7	143
	1201	9.1	277
	1909	0.6	18
2 M	0235	7.2	219
	0630	5.8	177
	1232	8.9	271
	1941	-0.3	-9
3 Tu	0338	8.1	247
	0734	6.6	201
	1257	8.6	262
	2013	-1.0	-30
4 W	0427	8.7	265
	0838	7.1	216
	1323	8.4	256
	2048	-1.4	-43
5 Th	0512	9.1	277
	0930	7.3	223
	1344	8.2	250
	2120	-1.6	-49
6 F	0554	9.3	283
	1024	7.3	223
	1409	7.9	241
	2152	-1.7	-52
7 Sa	0626	9.3	283
	1112	7.2	219
	1441	7.7	235
	2228	-1.6	-49
8 Su	0658	9.2	280
	1206	7.0	213
	1526	7.4	226
	2305	-1.3	-40
9 M	0732	9.1	277
	1258	6.7	204
	1612	7.0	213
	2344	-0.9	-27
10 Tu	0804	9.0	274
	1404	6.3	192
	1657	6.5	198
11 W	0021	-0.2	-6
	0836	8.9	271
	1506	5.7	174
	1803	5.9	180
12 Th	0059	0.6	18
	0906	8.9	271
	1611	4.9	149
	1919	5.3	162
13 F	0141	1.7	52
	0937	8.8	268
	1651	4.0	122
	2056	4.9	149
14 Sa	0221	2.9	88
	1003	8.8	268
	1722	3.0	91
	2304	4.9	149
15 Su	0305	4.1	125
	1029	8.8	268
	1754	1.9	58
16 M	0121	5.6	171
	0404	5.4	165
	1055	8.8	268
	1830	0.8	24
17 Tu	0244	6.7	204
	0520	6.4	195
	1119	8.9	271
	1902	-0.4	-12
18 W	0336	7.7	235
	0630	7.2	219
	1148	9.0	274
	1937	-1.4	-43
19 Th	0415	8.6	262
	0736	7.7	235
	1224	9.2	280
	2018	-2.3	-70
20 F	0450	9.2	280
	0834	7.9	241
	1309	9.3	283
	2101	-3.0	-91
21 Sa	0528	9.6	293
	0928	7.8	238
	1402	9.2	280
	2146	-3.2	-98
22 Su	0607	9.9	302
	1024	7.5	229
	1503	9.0	274
	2233	-3.1	-94
23 M	0645	10.0	305
	1125	7.0	213
	1605	8.6	262
	2319	-2.5	-76
24 Tu	0724	10.0	305
	1228	6.3	192
	1715	7.9	241
25 W	0007	-1.4	-43
	0800	10.0	305
	1342	5.4	165
	1830	7.1	216
26 Th	0053	0.0	0
	0838	9.9	302
	1454	4.2	128
	1956	6.3	192
27 F	0145	1.6	49
	0914	9.8	299
	1603	3.0	91
	2142	5.8	177
28 Sa	0235	3.3	101
	0950	9.6	293
	1659	1.9	58
	2345	6.0	183
29 Su	0336	4.9	149
	1025	9.4	287
	1751	0.9	27
30 M	0138	6.9	210
	0449	6.3	192
	1057	9.1	277
	1836	0.1	3
31 Tu	0254	7.9	241
	0614	7.2	219
	1129	8.8	268
	1917	-0.4	-12

Time meridian 120° W. 0000 is midnight. 1200 is noon.
Heights are referred to mean lower low water which is the chart datum of soundings.

Port Townsend Tides
1991 • JANUARY • 1991

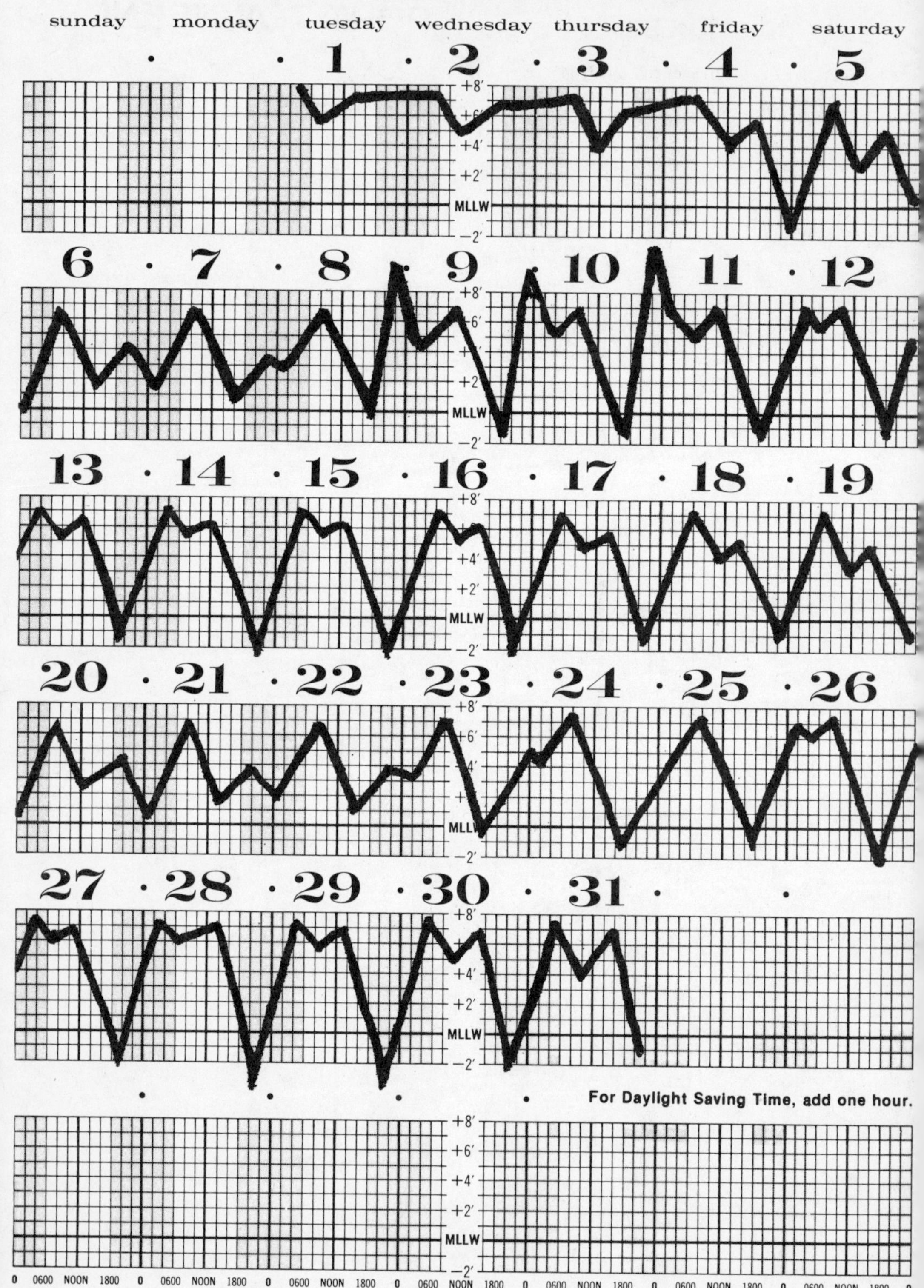

Port Townsend Tides
1991 • FEBRUARY • 1991

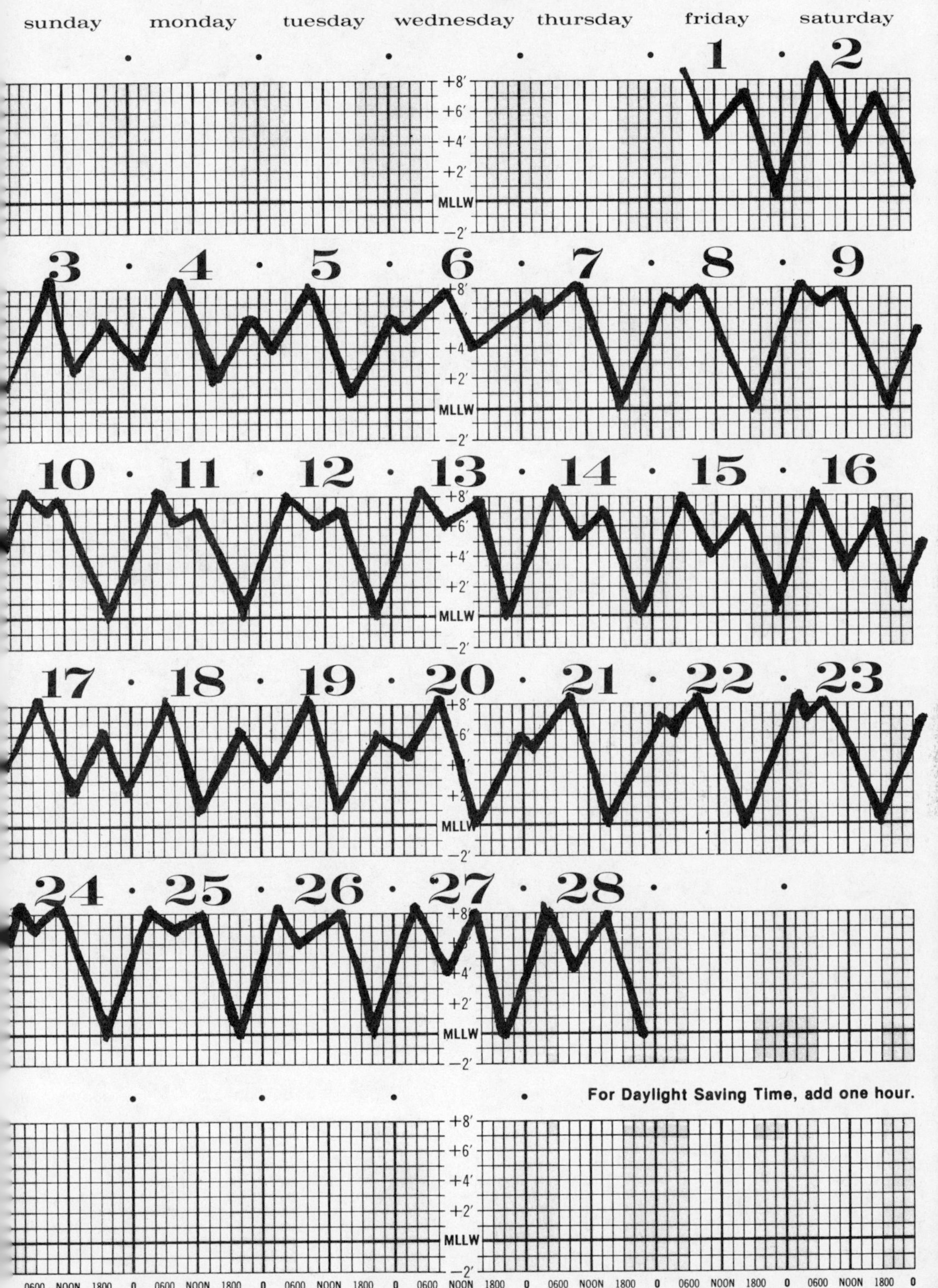

Port Townsend Tides
1991 • MARCH • 1991

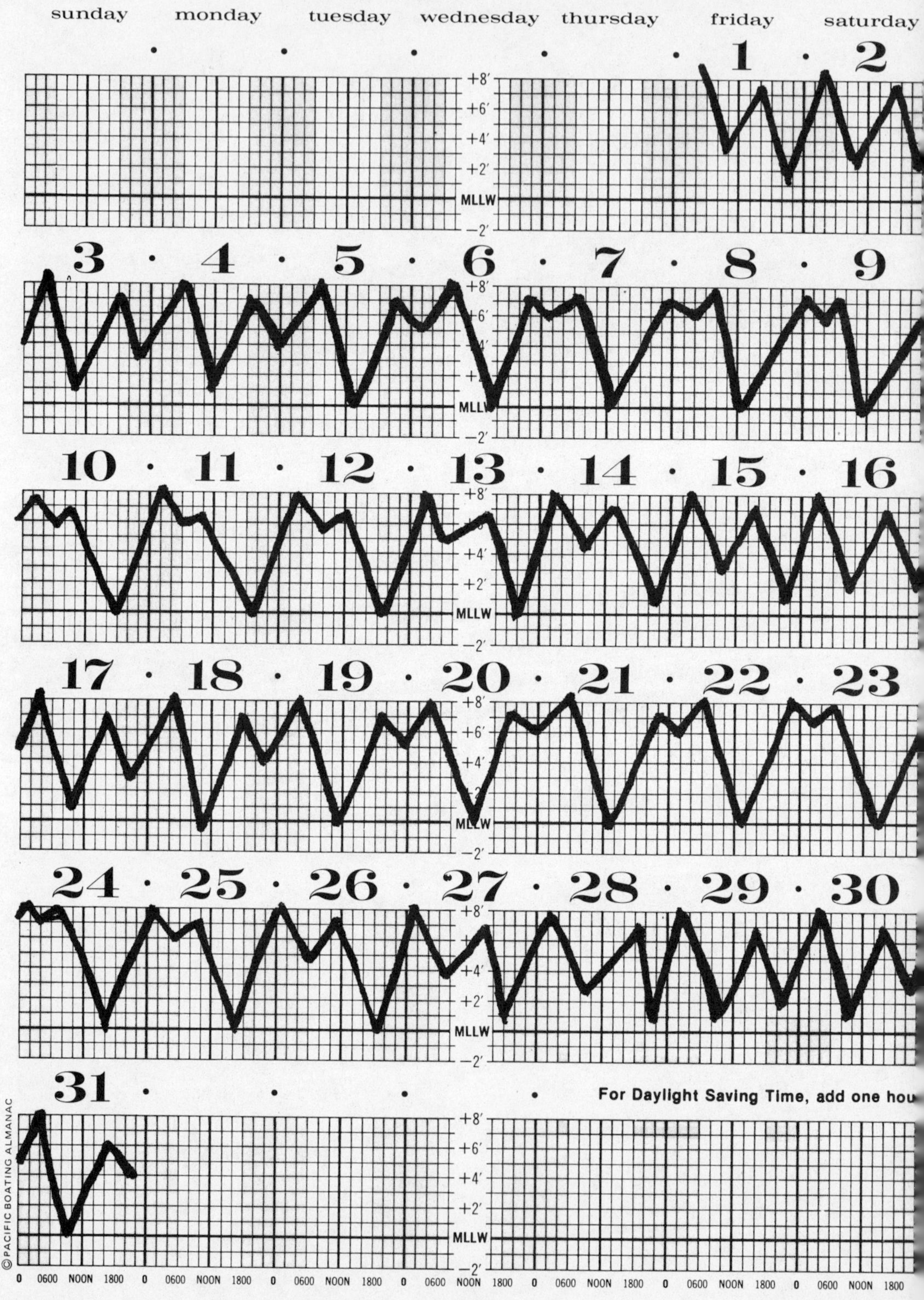

Port Townsend Tides
1991 • APRIL • 1991

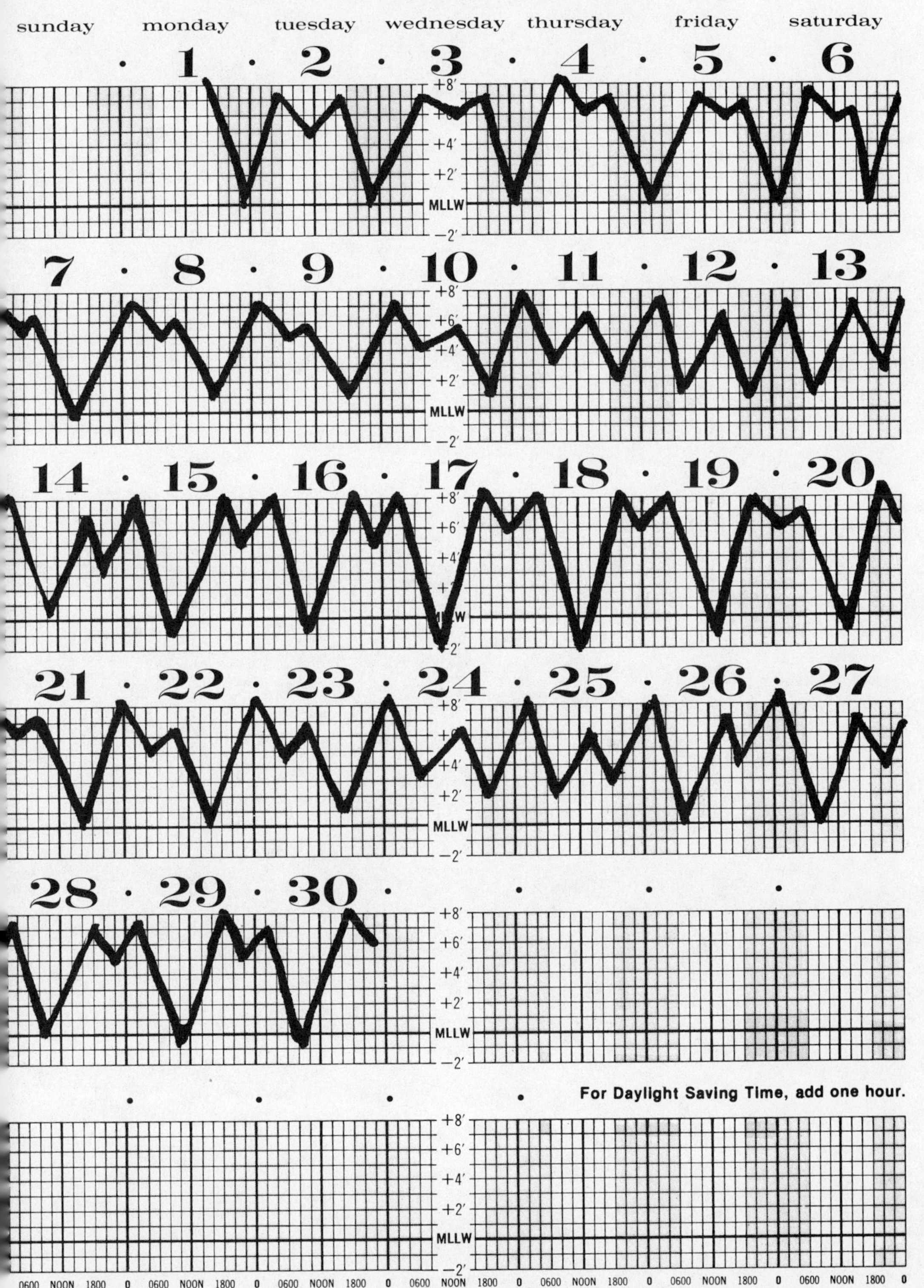

Port Townsend Tides
1991 • MAY • 1991

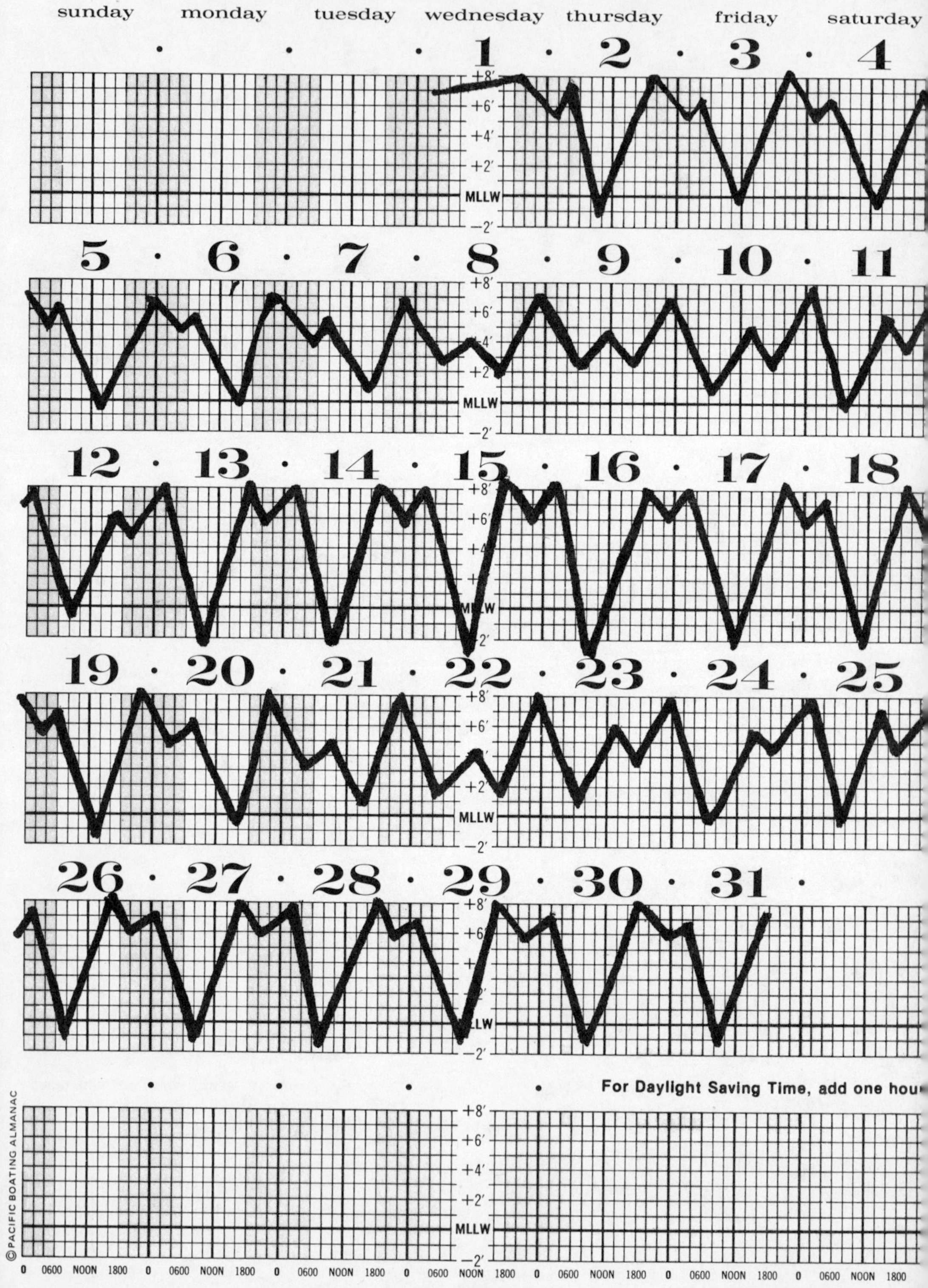

Port Townsend Tides
1991 ● JUNE ● 1991

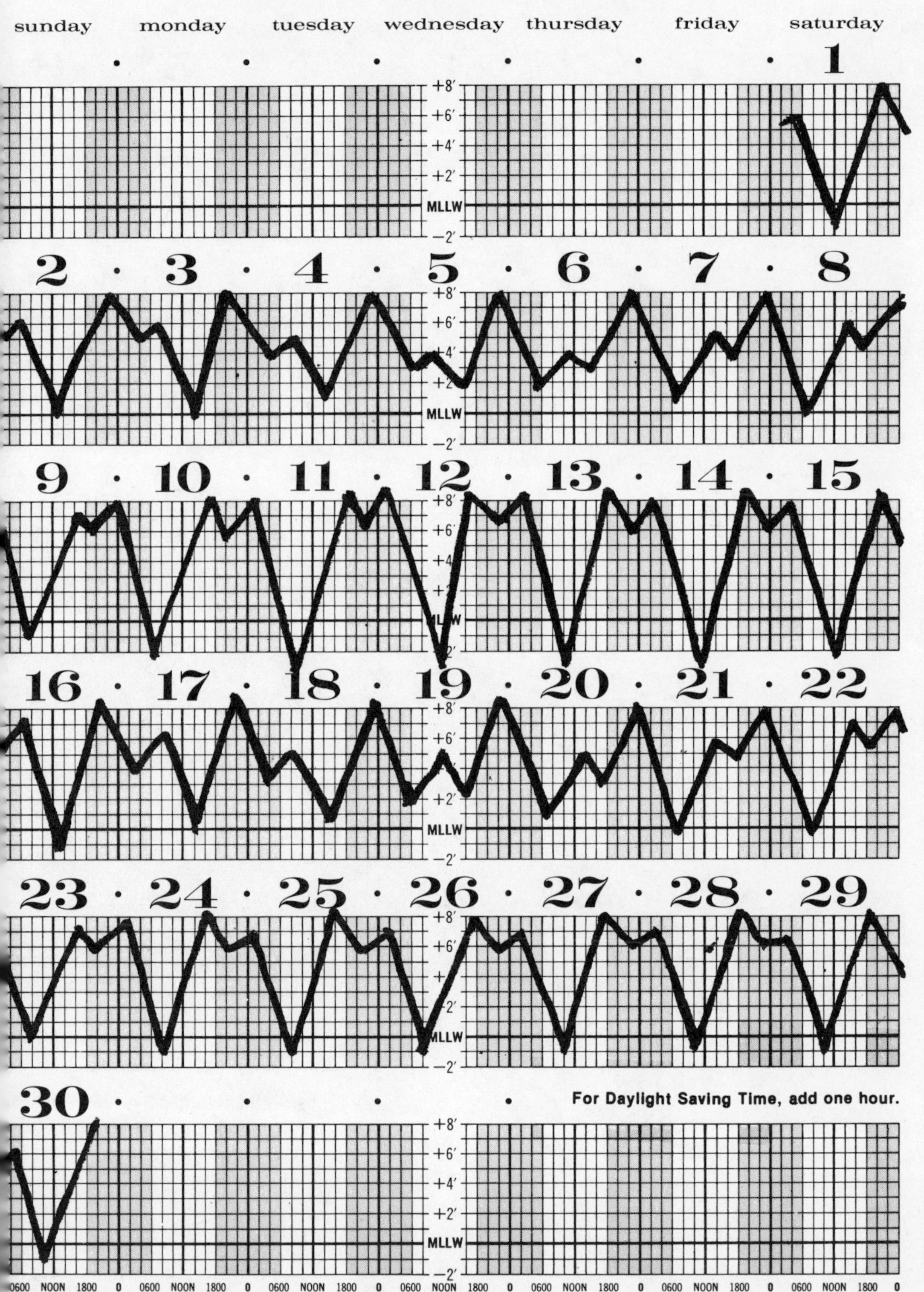

Port Townsend Tides
1991 ● JULY ● 1991

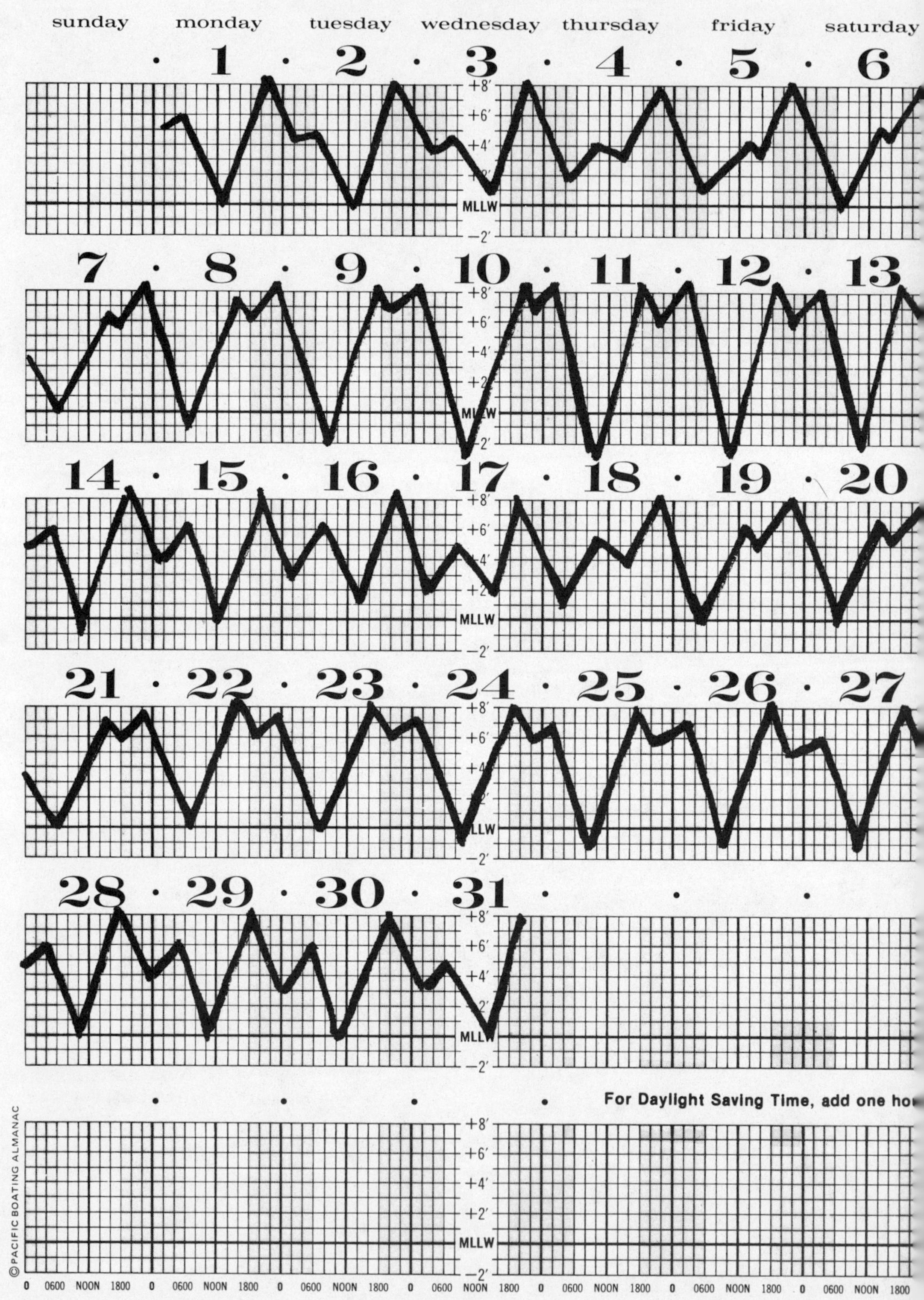

Port Townsend Tides
1991 ● AUGUST ● 1991

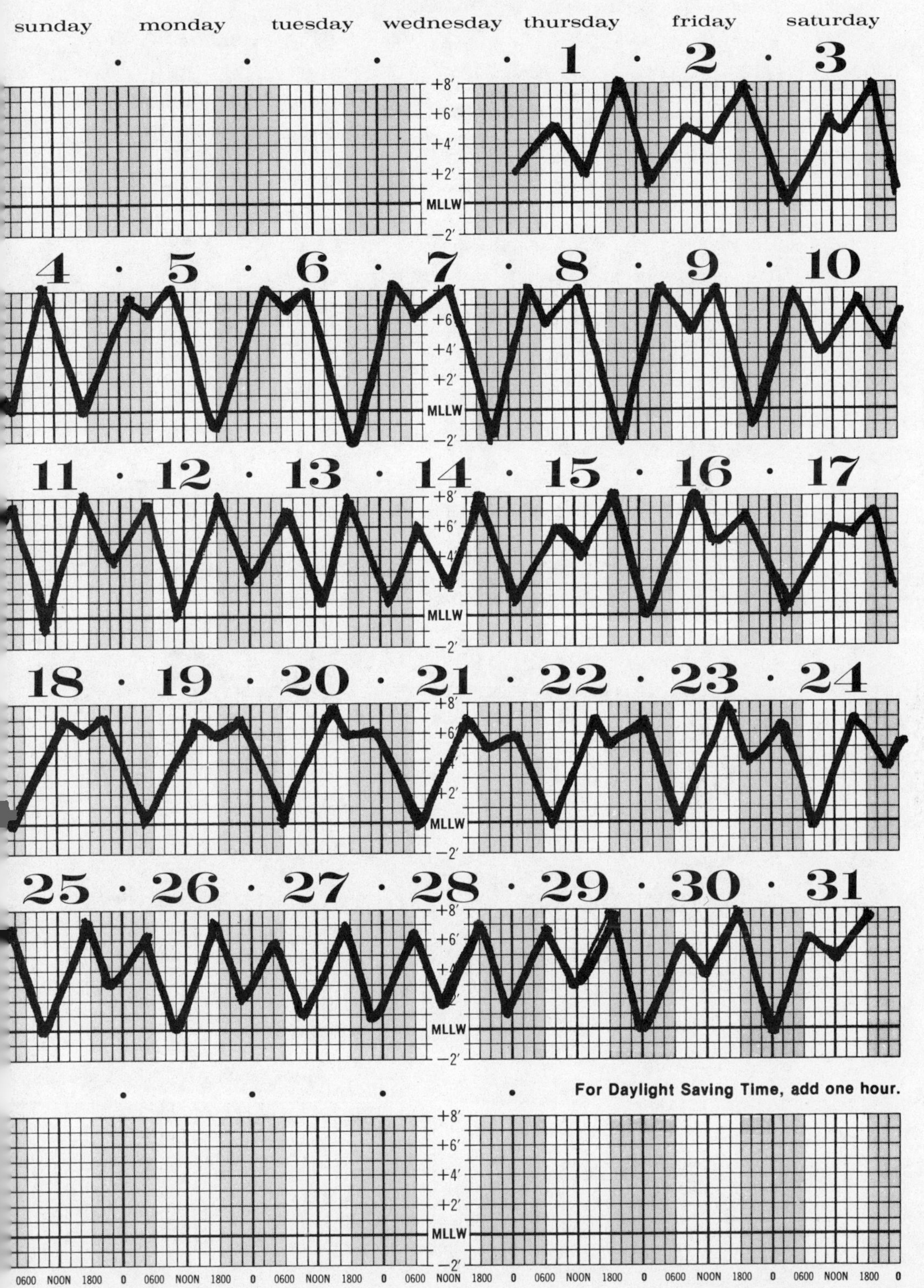

Port Townsend Tides
1991 • SEPTEMBER • 1991

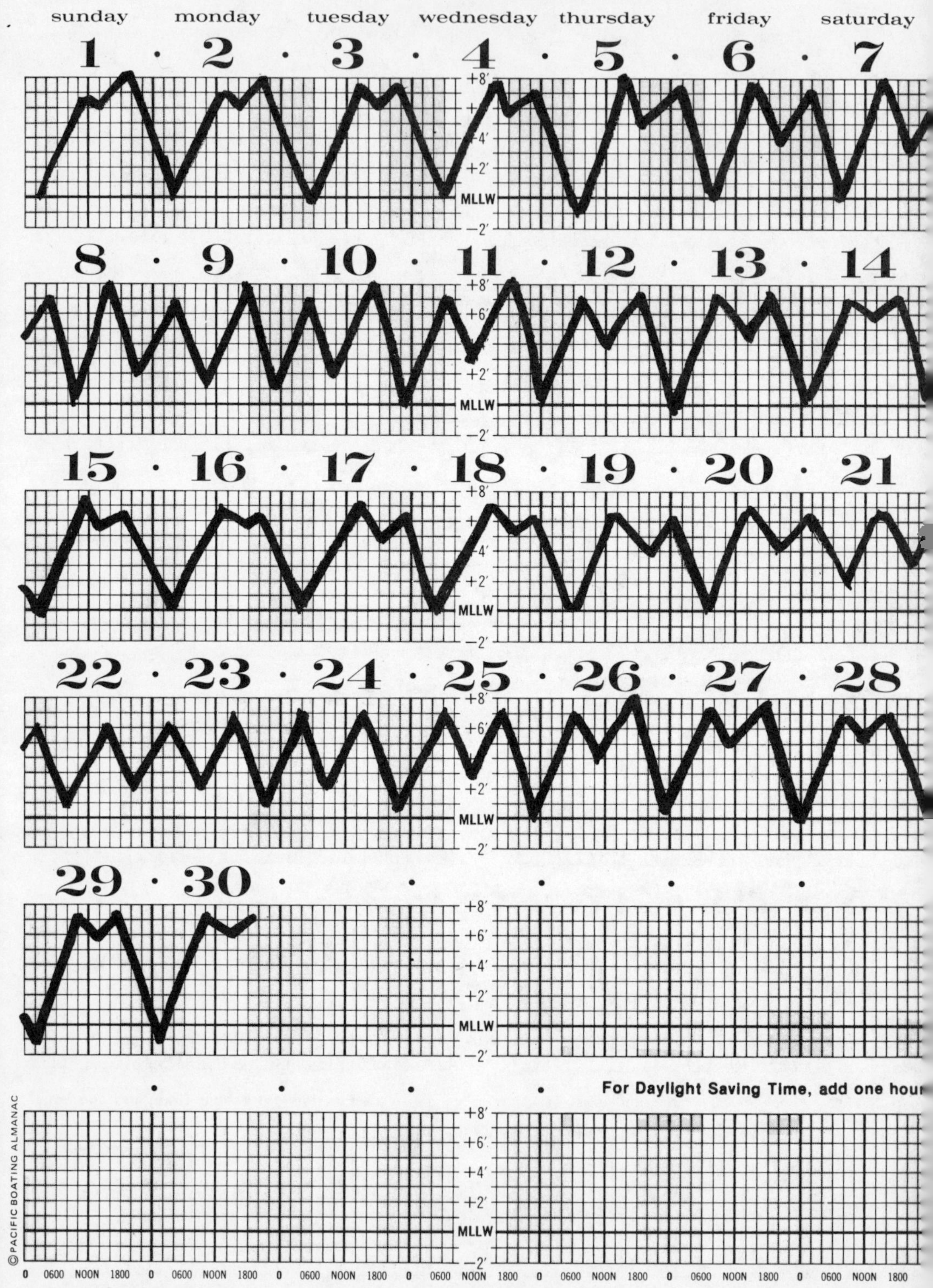

Port Townsend Tides
1991 ● OCTOBER ● 1991

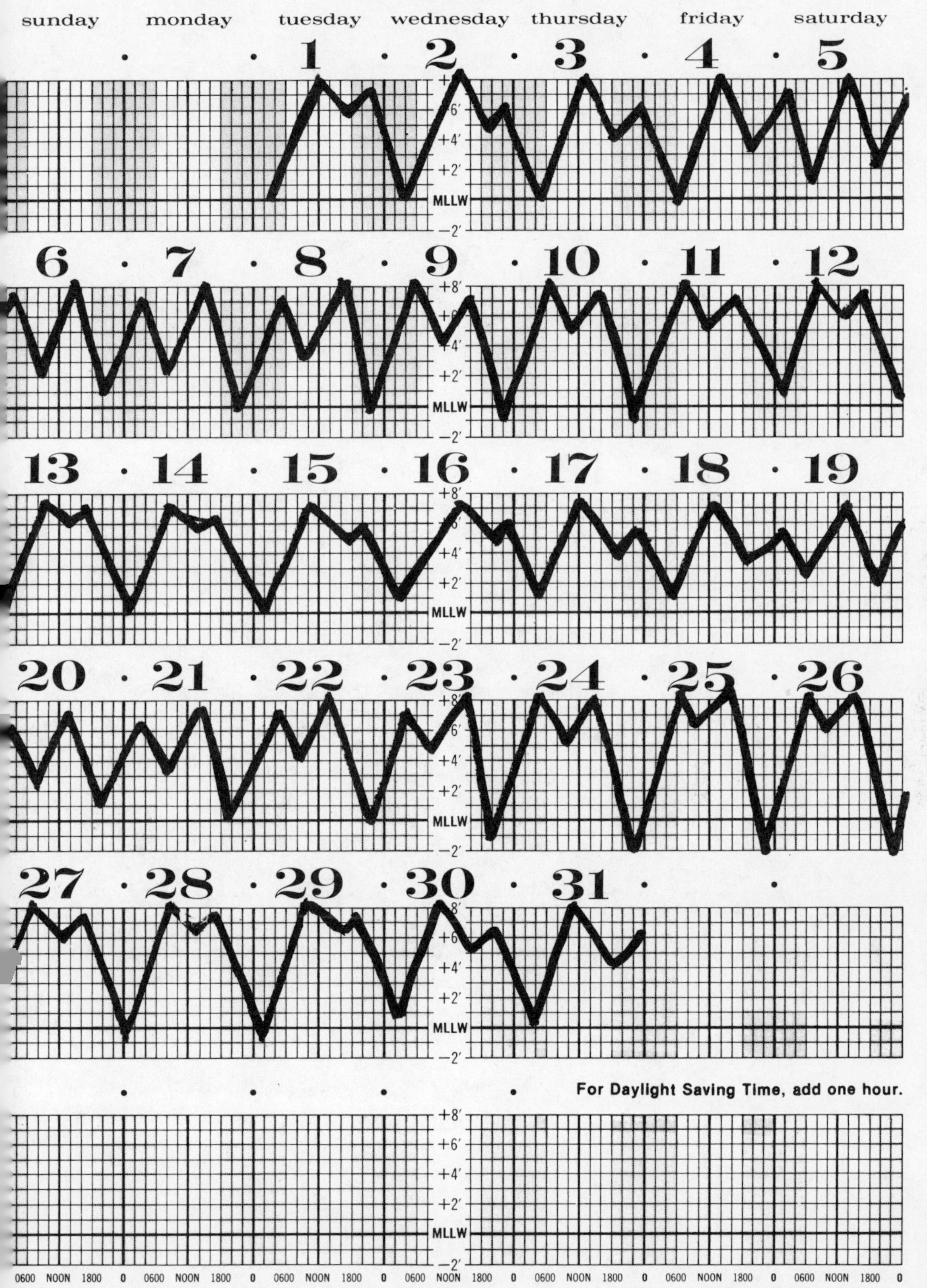

Port Townsend Tides
1991 • NOVEMBER • 1991

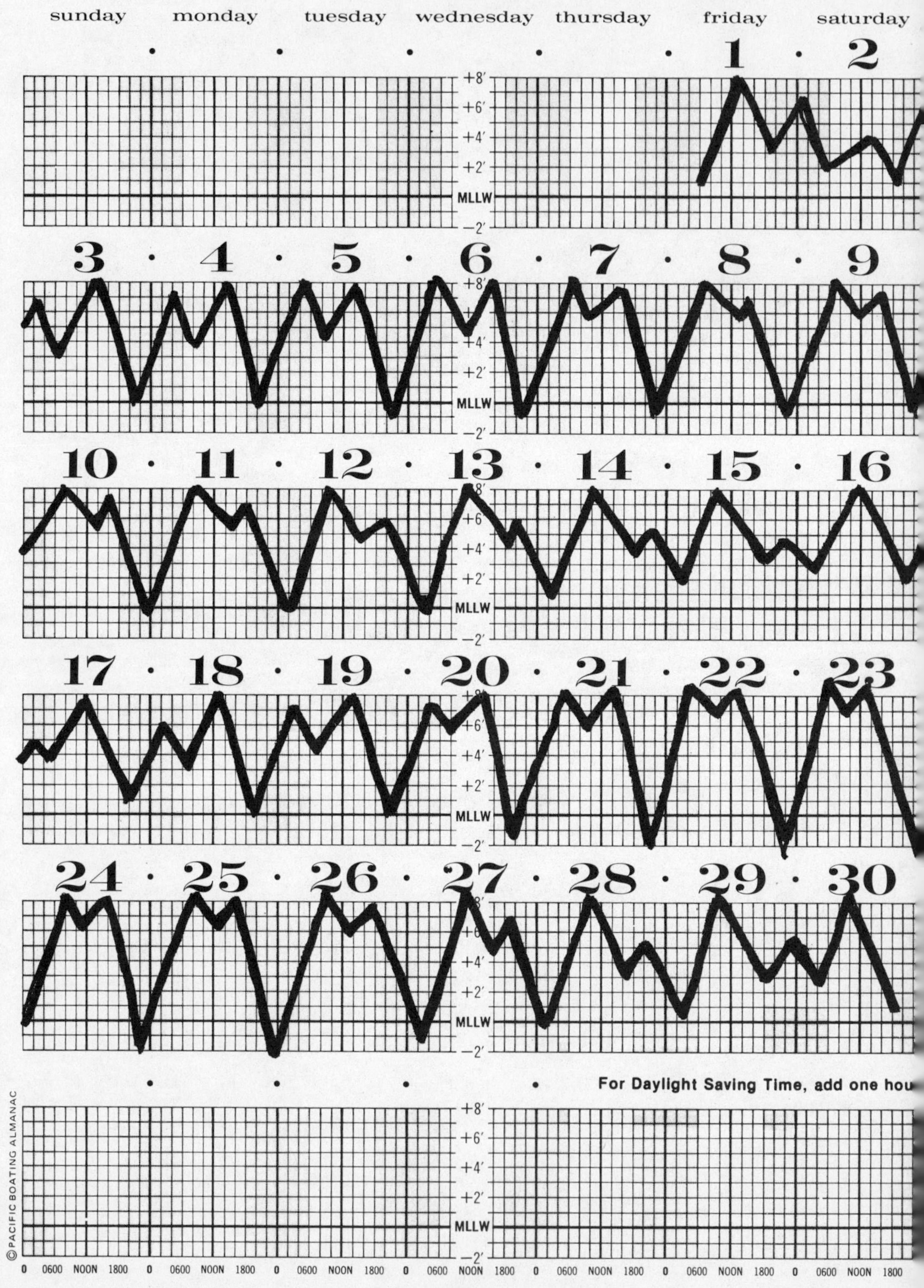

Port Townsend Tides
1991 • DECEMBER • 1991

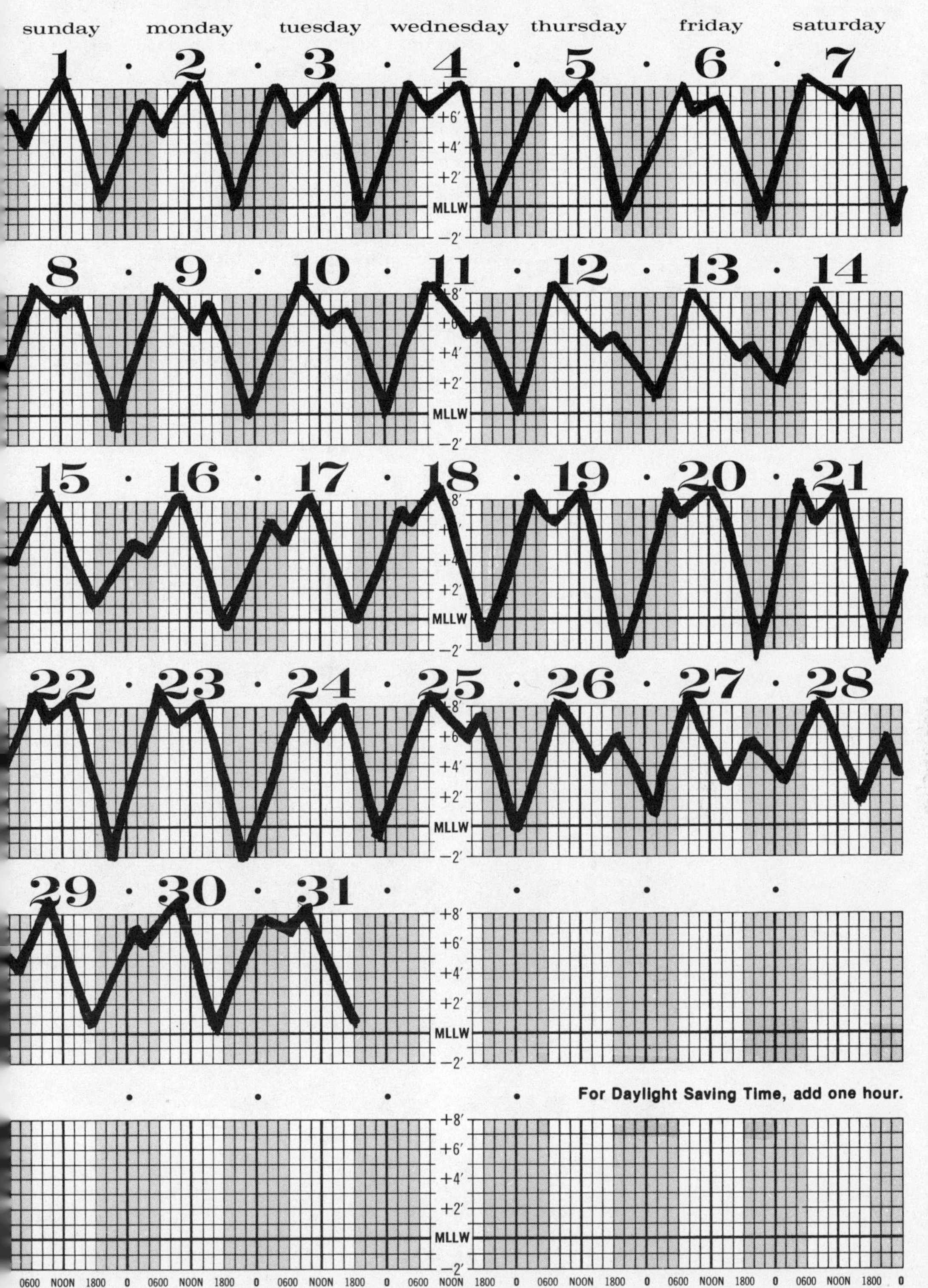

SEATTLE

1991 TIDE TABLES

For Daylight Saving Time, add one hour.

Times and Heights of High and Low Waters

JANUARY

Day	h m	ft	cm	Day	h m	ft	cm
1 Tu	0603	13.3	405	16 W	0617	12.3	375
	1118	7.5	229		1136	7.1	216
	1557	11.5	351		1611	10.2	311
	2316	-3.1	-94		2318	-0.9	-27
2 W	0645	13.4	408	17 Th	0636	12.4	378
	1209	6.8	207		1211	6.5	198
	1659	11.0	335		1653	10.0	305
					2350	-0.5	-15
3 Th	0002	-2.3	-70	18 F	0657	12.5	381
	0721	13.4	408		1247	5.7	174
	1305	6.0	183		1742	9.8	299
	1758	10.4	317				
4 F	0045	-1.1	-34	19 Sa	0022	0.2	6
	0758	13.3	405		0720	12.5	381
	1357	5.1	155		1325	4.9	149
	1903	9.6	293		1835	9.4	287
5 Sa	0130	0.5	15	20 Su	0058	1.2	37
	0834	13.0	396		0747	12.5	381
	1453	4.2	128		1408	4.0	122
	2016	8.8	268		1933	9.1	277
6 Su	0215	2.2	67	21 M	0135	2.5	76
	0912	12.6	384		0815	12.4	378
	1555	3.4	104		1453	3.0	91
	2141	8.2	250		2041	8.7	265
7 M	0303	4.0	122	22 Tu	0217	3.9	119
	0949	12.1	369		0845	12.2	372
	1655	2.5	76		1544	2.0	61
	2321	8.2	250		2203	8.6	262
8 Tu	0359	5.6	171	23 W	0306	5.5	168
	1028	11.6	354		0919	12.0	366
	1753	1.8	55		1641	1.1	34
					2340	8.8	268
9 W	0103	8.7	265	24 Th	0405	7.0	213
	0509	7.0	213		1002	11.7	357
	1108	11.1	338		1740	0.1	3
	1847	1.1	34				
10 Th	0230	9.5	290	25 F	0127	9.6	293
	0633	7.9	241		0528	8.1	247
	1149	10.7	326		1051	11.5	351
	1937	0.4	12		1845	-0.8	-24
11 F	0325	10.4	317	26 Sa	0243	10.6	323
	0757	8.3	253		0657	8.6	262
	1234	10.4	317		1148	11.4	347
	2019	-0.1	-3		1943	-1.6	-49
12 Sa	0411	11.1	338	27 Su	0342	11.5	351
	0857	8.3	253		0818	8.5	259
	1316	10.2	311		1255	11.3	344
	2100	-0.5	-15		2038	-2.2	-67
13 Su	0449	11.6	354	28 M	0424	12.2	372
	0950	8.2	250		0923	8.0	244
	1405	10.2	311		1401	11.2	341
	2136	-0.8	-24		2130	-2.5	-76
14 M	0525	11.9	363	29 Tu	0505	12.7	387
	1026	7.9	241		1017	7.2	219
	1447	10.2	311		1506	11.2	341
	2211	-1.0	-30		2216	-2.3	-70
15 Tu	0553	12.1	369	30 W	0537	13.0	396
	1101	7.6	232		1106	6.2	189
	1529	10.2	311		1608	11.1	338
	2243	-1.1	-34		2301	-1.8	-55
				31 Th	0609	13.1	399
					1151	5.1	155
					1707	10.8	329
					2343	-0.8	-24

FEBRUARY

Day	h m	ft	cm	Day	h m	ft	cm
1 F	0641	13.0	396	16 Sa	0606	12.1	369
	1237	4.2	128		1211	3.6	110
	1803	10.4	317		1747	10.2	311
					2359	1.5	46
2 Sa	0025	0.5	15	17 Su	0627	12.2	372
	0713	12.8	390		1248	2.6	79
	1322	3.3	101		1838	10.1	308
	1903	9.8	299				
3 Su	0107	1.9	58	18 M	0038	2.6	79
	0741	12.5	381		0653	12.1	369
	1410	2.6	79		1327	1.7	52
	2008	9.3	283		1934	9.9	302
4 M	0149	3.5	107	19 Tu	0117	3.8	116
	0813	12.0	366		0723	12.0	366
	1459	2.2	67		1413	1.0	30
	2122	8.9	271		2040	9.6	293
5 Tu	0231	5.0	152	20 W	0202	5.2	158
	0848	11.5	351		0755	11.8	360
	1552	1.8	55		1506	0.4	12
	2251	8.7	265		2158	9.5	290
6 W	0324	6.4	195	21 Th	0251	6.5	198
	0925	10.9	332		0834	11.5	351
	1651	1.6	49		1604	0.0	0
					2332	9.6	293
7 Th	0028	9.0	274	22 F	0400	7.6	232
	0432	7.5	229		0921	11.1	338
	1007	10.3	314		1709	-0.3	-9
	1754	1.3	40				
8 F	0157	9.6	293	23 Sa	0108	10.1	308
	0603	8.2	250		0529	8.3	253
	1056	9.9	302		1027	10.7	326
	1851	0.9	27		1818	-0.6	-18
9 Sa	0259	10.3	314	24 Su	0223	10.8	329
	0740	8.3	253		0708	8.2	250
	1149	9.7	296		1143	10.4	317
	1945	0.5	15		1924	-0.9	-27
10 Su	0342	10.8	329	25 M	0313	11.5	351
	0843	8.0	244		0823	7.4	226
	1255	9.6	293		1302	10.3	314
	2031	0.1	3		2022	-1.0	-30
11 M	0420	11.3	344	26 Tu	0351	12.0	366
	0928	7.6	232		0919	6.4	195
	1348	9.7	296		1415	10.4	317
	2110	-0.1	-3		2115	-0.9	-27
12 Tu	0449	11.5	351	27 W	0427	12.3	375
	1003	7.1	216		1005	5.2	158
	1442	9.8	299		1521	10.6	323
	2148	-0.2	-6		2200	-0.5	-15
13 W	0511	11.7	357	28 Th	0456	12.4	378
	1035	6.4	195		1047	4.0	122
	1527	10.0	305		1622	10.7	326
	2220	-0.2	-6		2245	0.3	9
14 Th	0529	11.9	363				
	1104	5.5	168				
	1614	10.1	308				
	2252	0.2	6				
15 F	0547	12.0	366				
	1136	4.5	140				
	1658	10.2	311				
	2327	0.7	21				

MARCH

Day	h m	ft	cm	Day	h m	ft	cm
1 F	0525	12.4	378	16 Sa	0445	11.4	347
	1128	2.9	88		1059	2.2	67
	1717	10.7	326		1702	10.5	320
	2324	1.3	40		2305	2.5	76
2 Sa	0552	12.2	372	17 Su	0508	11.6	354
	1207	2.0	61		1134	1.1	34
	1811	10.5	320		1751	10.7	326
					2341	3.4	104
3 Su	0003	2.4	73	18 M	0533	11.7	357
	0620	12.0	366		1213	0.1	3
	1245	1.4	43		1843	10.8	329
	1905	10.3	314				
4 M	0042	3.6	110	19 Tu	0020	4.3	131
	0647	11.6	354		0603	11.7	357
	1325	1.1	34		1254	-0.6	-18
	1958	10.0	305		1939	10.8	329
5 Tu	0123	4.8	146	20 W	0105	5.4	165
	0717	11.1	338		0636	11.5	351
	1407	1.0	30		1342	-0.9	-27
	2102	9.7	296		2041	10.6	323
6 W	0209	5.9	180	21 Th	0153	6.4	195
	0749	10.6	323		0713	11.2	341
	1456	1.1	34		1433	-1.0	-30
	2215	9.4	287		2157	10.4	317
7 Th	0301	6.8	207	22 F	0253	7.2	219
	0824	10.0	305		0800	10.7	326
	1551	1.2	37		1533	-0.7	-21
	2342	9.4	287		2319	10.5	320
8 F	0407	7.6	232	23 Sa	0410	7.7	235
	0908	9.5	290		0859	10.1	308
	1653	1.3	40		1641	-0.4	-12
9 Sa	0101	9.7	296	24 Su	0039	10.7	326
	0541	7.9	241		0547	7.5	229
	1007	9.0	274		1022	9.5	290
	1757	1.3	40		1752	0.0	0
10 Su	0207	10.1	308	25 M	0138	11.1	338
	0720	7.7	235		0713	6.7	204
	1120	8.8	268		1155	9.2	280
	1900	1.2	37		1901	0.3	9
11 M	0252	10.5	320	26 Tu	0225	11.4	347
	0821	7.1	216		0819	5.4	165
	1235	8.8	268		1324	9.3	283
	1951	1.0	30		2003	0.7	21
12 Tu	0326	10.8	329	27 W	0303	11.7	357
	0859	6.4	195		0907	4.1	125
	1341	9.0	274		1438	9.7	296
	2037	1.0	30		2056	1.2	37
13 W	0350	11.0	335	28 Th	0337	11.8	360
	0931	5.5	168		0946	2.8	85
	1437	9.4	287		1540	10.1	308
	2113	1.1	34		2142	1.9	58
14 Th	0408	11.2	341	29 F	0407	11.7	357
	1000	4.5	137		1025	1.7	52
	1527	9.7	296		1637	10.5	320
	2151	1.4	43		2224	2.7	82
15 F	0427	11.3	344	30 Sa	0433	11.6	354
	1030	3.4	104		1100	0.8	24
	1614	10.1	308		1728	10.7	326
	2226	1.9	58		2305	3.5	107
				31 Su	0500	11.3	344
					1135	0.2	6
					1815	10.8	329
					2344	4.4	134

Time meridian 120° W.   0000 is midnight.   1200 is noon.
Heights are referred to mean lower low water which is the chart datum of soundings.

1991 TIDE TABLES

SEATTLE

For Daylight Saving Time, add one hour.

Times and Heights of High and Low Waters

APRIL

Day	h m	ft	cm	Day	h m	ft	cm
1 M	0526	11.0	335	16 Tu	0443	11.4	347
	1207	-0.2	-6		1144	-2.0	-61
	1900	10.8	329		1848	11.6	354
2 Tu	0026	5.2	158	17 W	0007	6.0	183
	0554	10.6	323		0518	11.3	344
	1246	-0.2	-6		1227	-2.4	-73
	1949	10.7	326		1944	11.6	354
3 W	0108	5.9	180	18 Th	0059	6.6	201
	0622	10.2	311		0557	11.1	338
	1325	-0.1	-3		1316	-2.3	-70
	2044	10.4	317		2043	11.5	351
4 Th	0153	6.6	201	19 F	0155	7.1	216
	0655	9.8	299		0643	10.5	320
	1409	0.2	6		1410	-1.8	-55
	2142	10.2	311		2148	11.4	347
5 F	0248	7.1	216	20 Sa	0303	7.2	219
	0733	9.3	283		0742	9.8	299
	1500	0.6	18		1508	-1.0	-30
	2251	10.1	308		2254	11.4	347
6 Sa	0357	7.4	226	21 Su	0429	6.9	210
	0822	8.7	265		0857	9.0	274
	1555	1.1	34		1614	-0.1	-3
	2355	10.1	308		2353	11.4	347
7 Su	0527	7.3	223	22 M	0555	6.0	183
	0928	8.2	250		1034	8.4	256
	1658	1.5	46		1723	0.9	27
8 M	0054	10.3	314	23 Tu	0047	11.5	351
	0646	6.7	204		0708	4.7	143
	1054	7.9	241		1217	8.3	253
	1800	1.8	55		1832	1.9	58
9 Tu	0137	10.5	320	24 W	0132	11.5	351
	0738	5.9	180		0800	3.3	101
	1217	8.0	244		1347	8.7	265
	1859	2.1	64		1935	2.8	85
10 W	0209	10.6	323	25 Th	0209	11.5	351
	0817	4.8	146		0845	1.9	58
	1332	8.4	256		1501	9.4	287
	1948	2.4	73		2030	3.6	110
11 Th	0233	10.7	326	26 F	0241	11.3	344
	0849	3.7	113		0921	0.7	21
	1432	9.0	274		1600	10.0	305
	2033	2.9	88		2121	4.3	131
12 F	0254	10.8	329	27 Sa	0311	11.1	338
	0921	2.4	73		0958	-0.1	-3
	1529	9.6	293		1649	10.6	323
	2116	3.4	104		2208	5.0	152
13 Sa	0318	11.0	335	28 Su	0339	10.9	332
	0952	1.0	30		1033	-0.7	-21
	1618	10.3	314		1737	10.9	332
	2159	4.0	122		2250	5.6	171
14 Su	0343	11.1	338	29 M	0404	10.6	323
	1027	-0.2	-6		1105	-1.1	-34
	1707	10.9	332		1820	11.2	341
	2241	4.6	140		2332	6.1	186
15 M	0411	11.3	344	30 Tu	0433	10.3	314
	1103	-1.3	-40		1138	-1.2	-37
	1756	11.4	347		1902	11.3	344
	2322	5.3	162				

MAY

Day	h m	ft	cm	Day	h m	ft	cm
1 W	0012	6.5	198	16 Th	0001	7.1	216
	0505	10.0	305		0446	11.2	341
	1214	-1.2	-37		1209	-3.5	-107
	1944	11.2	341		1942	12.4	378
2 Th	0054	6.8	207	17 F	0056	7.2	219
	0537	9.7	296		0535	10.7	326
	1252	-0.9	-27		1258	-3.0	-91
	2026	11.1	338		2034	12.3	375
3 F	0142	7.0	213	18 Sa	0158	7.0	213
	0612	9.3	283		0630	10.0	305
	1333	-0.5	-15		1350	-2.1	-64
	2117	11.0	335		2129	12.3	375
4 Sa	0239	7.1	216	19 Su	0308	6.5	198
	0654	8.8	268		0743	9.1	277
	1418	0.1	3		1445	-0.8	-24
	2203	10.9	332		2218	12.1	369
5 Su	0342	7.0	213	20 M	0426	5.6	171
	0750	8.2	250		0909	8.2	250
	1506	0.8	24		1545	0.7	21
	2252	10.8	329		2308	12.0	366
6 M	0454	6.5	198	21 Tu	0539	4.3	131
	0902	7.7	235		1049	7.7	235
	1559	1.5	46		1647	2.2	67
	2338	10.8	329		2352	11.8	360
7 Tu	0557	5.6	171	22 W	0642	2.9	88
	1028	7.3	223		1233	7.9	241
	1657	2.4	73		1754	3.6	110
8 W	0011	10.8	329	23 Th	0034	11.6	354
	0649	4.5	137		0734	1.5	46
	1159	7.4	226		1401	8.6	262
	1756	3.2	98		1902	4.8	146
9 Th	0043	10.8	329	24 F	0112	11.3	344
	0731	3.3	101		0818	0.4	12
	1318	8.0	244		1512	9.4	287
	1855	4.0	122		2004	5.7	174
10 F	0112	10.8	329	25 Sa	0146	11.0	335
	0806	1.9	58		0857	-0.5	-15
	1428	8.8	268		1611	10.2	311
	1945	4.7	143		2103	6.3	192
11 Sa	0142	10.9	332	26 Su	0218	10.7	326
	0841	0.4	12		0933	-1.1	-34
	1527	9.8	299		1657	10.8	329
	2041	5.4	165		2152	6.7	204
12 Su	0211	11.0	335	27 M	0250	10.4	317
	0917	-0.9	-27		1008	-1.4	-43
	1620	10.7	326		1739	11.2	341
	2132	6.0	183		2236	7.0	213
13 M	0243	11.2	341	28 Tu	0319	10.2	311
	0957	-2.1	-64		1041	-1.6	-49
	1712	11.4	347		1818	11.4	347
	2221	6.5	198		2319	7.2	219
14 Tu	0319	11.3	344	29 W	0352	10.0	305
	1037	-3.0	-91		1113	-1.7	-52
	1801	11.9	363		1856	11.6	354
	2309	6.9	210				
15 W	0401	11.3	344	30 Th	0001	7.2	219
	1122	-3.5	-107		0427	9.8	299
	1851	12.3	375		1150	-1.6	-49
					1931	11.6	354
				31 F	0043	7.2	219
					0505	9.5	290
					1225	-1.3	-40
					2007	11.6	354

JUNE

Day	h m	ft	cm	Day	h m	ft	cm
1 Sa	0128	7.1	216	16 Su	0150	6.1	186
	0546	9.1	277		0635	9.6	293
	1304	-0.9	-27		1332	-1.5	-46
	2042	11.6	354		2053	12.7	387
2 Su	0221	6.7	204	17 M	0252	5.1	155
	0635	8.6	262		0750	8.8	268
	1343	-0.2	-6		1421	0.1	3
	2117	11.6	354		2135	12.5	381
3 M	0313	6.2	189	18 Tu	0358	4.0	122
	0731	8.0	244		0917	8.0	244
	1427	0.7	21		1513	1.8	55
	2153	11.5	351		2216	12.2	372
4 Tu	0411	5.5	168	19 W	0504	2.8	85
	0843	7.5	229		1052	7.7	235
	1509	1.8	55		1609	3.6	110
	2225	11.4	347		2258	11.8	360
5 W	0504	4.5	137	20 Th	0605	1.6	49
	1006	7.2	219		1235	8.0	244
	1601	3.0	91		1717	5.1	155
	2257	11.3	344		2338	11.4	347
6 Th	0553	3.3	101	21 F	0658	0.6	18
	1134	7.3	223		1405	8.8	268
	1657	4.2	128		1830	6.3	192
	2329	11.2	341				
7 F	0642	1.9	58	22 Sa	0018	11.0	335
	1304	8.0	244		0747	-0.2	-6
	1759	5.4	165		1514	9.6	293
					1940	7.1	216
8 Sa	0003	11.1	338	23 Su	0055	10.6	323
	0724	0.5	15		0830	-0.8	-24
	1426	8.9	271		1610	10.4	317
	1905	6.4	195		2049	7.5	229
9 Su	0039	11.2	341	24 M	0136	10.3	314
	0806	-0.9	-27		0909	-1.2	-37
	1526	10.0	305		1655	10.9	332
	2007	7.1	216		2143	7.6	232
10 M	0119	11.3	344	25 Tu	0214	10.0	305
	0850	-2.2	-67		0945	-1.5	-46
	1623	11.0	335		1732	11.3	344
	2107	7.5	229		2229	7.6	232
11 Tu	0201	11.4	347	26 W	0250	9.9	302
	0933	-3.2	-98		1020	-1.6	-49
	1710	11.7	357		1806	11.5	351
	2203	7.7	235		2307	7.5	229
12 W	0246	11.4	347	27 Th	0328	9.8	299
	1019	-3.8	-116		1053	-1.7	-52
	1755	12.3	375		1836	11.7	357
	2258	7.6	232		2345	7.3	223
13 Th	0338	11.3	344	28 F	0407	9.7	296
	1106	-4.0	-122		1127	-1.6	-49
	1844	12.6	384		1904	11.8	360
	2352	7.3	223				
14 F	0431	11.0	335	29 Sa	0024	6.9	210
	1154	-3.6	-110		0449	9.5	290
	1927	12.8	390		1202	-1.3	-40
					1931	11.8	360
15 Sa	0048	6.8	207	30 Su	0103	6.4	195
	0530	10.5	320		0535	9.1	277
	1243	-2.8	-85		1237	-0.7	-21
	2012	12.8	390		1958	11.9	363

Time meridian 120° W. 0000 is midnight. 1200 is noon.
Heights are referred to mean lower low water which is the chart datum of soundings.

SEATTLE

1991 TIDE TABLES

For Daylight Saving Time, add one hour.

Times and Heights of High and Low Waters

JULY

Day	h m	ft	cm	Day	h m	ft	cm
1 M	0147	5.8	177	16 Tu	0223	3.4	104
	0627	8.7	265		0751	8.9	271
	1313	0.1	3		1355	1.4	43
	2024	11.8	360		2045	12.2	372
2 Tu	0230	5.1	155	17 W	0319	2.5	76
	0722	8.2	250		0914	8.3	253
	1351	1.1	34		1445	3.2	98
	2051	11.7	357		2123	11.8	360
3 W	0319	4.2	128	18 Th	0418	1.7	52
	0831	7.8	238		1044	8.1	247
	1431	2.4	73		1539	4.8	146
	2122	11.6	354		2202	11.3	344
4 Th	0408	3.2	98	19 F	0517	1.1	34
	0946	7.6	232		1223	8.4	256
	1519	3.8	116		1642	6.2	189
	2151	11.5	351		2244	10.8	329
5 F	0457	2.0	61	20 Sa	0619	0.5	15
	1116	7.7	235		1349	9.0	274
	1612	5.2	158		1804	7.2	219
	2228	11.3	344		2330	10.3	314
6 Sa	0551	0.8	24	21 Su	0712	0.0	0
	1248	8.3	253		1459	9.8	299
	1717	6.5	198		1930	7.7	235
	2305	11.2	341				
7 Su	0644	-0.4	-12	22 M	0018	9.9	302
	1415	9.3	283		0801	-0.4	-12
	1829	7.5	229		1551	10.4	317
	2351	11.2	341		2041	7.7	235
8 M	0737	-1.6	-49	23 Tu	0103	9.7	296
	1524	10.3	314		0845	-0.8	-24
	1943	8.0	244		1633	10.9	332
					2131	7.6	232
9 Tu	0040	11.2	341	24 W	0153	9.6	293
	0826	-2.6	-79		0924	-1.0	-30
	1615	11.2	341		1708	11.2	341
	2052	8.0	244		2213	7.3	223
10 W	0135	11.3	344	25 Th	0238	9.6	293
	0915	-3.3	-101		1001	-1.1	-34
	1658	11.9	363		1737	11.4	347
	2152	7.8	238		2248	6.9	210
11 Th	0231	11.3	344	26 F	0321	9.7	296
	1005	-3.6	-110		1033	-1.1	-34
	1740	12.3	375		1801	11.5	351
	2248	7.2	219		2320	6.4	195
12 F	0333	11.2	341	27 Sa	0403	9.6	293
	1053	-3.5	-107		1105	-0.9	-27
	1820	12.6	384		1822	11.6	354
	2340	6.4	195		2354	5.8	177
13 Sa	0433	10.8	329	28 Su	0447	9.6	293
	1138	-2.8	-85		1137	-0.5	-15
	1857	12.7	387		1842	11.6	354
14 Su	0035	5.4	165	29 M	0030	5.0	152
	0536	10.3	314		0533	9.4	287
	1224	-1.7	-52		1212	0.1	3
	1931	12.7	387		1905	11.7	357
15 M	0127	4.4	134	30 Tu	0106	4.2	128
	0640	9.6	293		0625	9.1	277
	1309	-0.3	-9		1245	1.0	30
	2008	12.5	381		1928	11.7	357
				31 W	0148	3.4	104
					0720	8.8	268
					1323	2.2	67
					1954	11.6	354

AUGUST

Day	h m	ft	cm	Day	h m	ft	cm
1 Th	0230	2.5	76	16 F	0325	1.0	30
	0822	8.5	259		1022	8.8	268
	1402	3.5	107		1514	5.8	177
	2023	11.4	347		2105	10.4	317
2 F	0317	1.7	52	17 Sa	0425	0.9	27
	0934	8.3	253		1157	8.9	271
	1448	4.9	149		1621	6.9	210
	2055	11.2	341		2151	9.8	299
3 Sa	0411	0.9	27	18 Su	0528	0.8	24
	1100	8.4	256		1324	9.3	283
	1545	6.4	189		1752	7.5	229
	2134	11.1	338		2243	9.4	287
4 Su	0509	0.1	3	19 M	0631	0.6	18
	1236	8.9	271		1428	9.9	302
	1653	7.3	223		1924	7.5	229
	2221	10.9	332		2345	9.1	277
5 M	0609	-0.7	-21	20 Tu	0729	0.3	9
	1406	9.7	296		1518	10.3	314
	1817	7.9	241		2030	7.2	219
	2319	10.8	329				
6 Tu	0712	-1.5	-46	21 W	0048	9.1	277
	1505	10.6	323		0818	0.1	3
	1941	7.9	241		1554	10.7	326
					2112	6.8	207
7 W	0024	10.7	326	22 Th	0145	9.2	280
	0809	-2.1	-64		0857	-0.1	-3
	1552	11.3	344		1627	10.9	332
	2047	7.5	229		2147	6.2	189
8 Th	0133	10.8	329	23 F	0236	9.4	287
	0900	-2.5	-76		0935	-0.1	-3
	1632	11.8	360		1652	11.0	335
	2144	6.6	201		2216	5.6	171
9 F	0239	10.8	329	24 Sa	0321	9.5	290
	0949	-2.5	-76		1008	0.0	0
	1706	12.1	369		1709	11.1	338
	2235	5.6	171		2247	4.8	146
10 Sa	0341	10.8	329	25 Su	0404	9.7	296
	1038	-2.0	-61		1039	0.4	12
	1739	12.3	375		1727	11.2	341
	2321	4.5	137		2319	3.9	119
11 Su	0444	10.7	326	26 M	0450	9.8	299
	1121	-1.1	-34		1114	0.9	27
	1811	12.3	375		1745	11.3	344
					2351	3.0	91
12 M	0007	3.4	104	27 Tu	0534	9.9	302
	0544	10.4	317		1146	1.7	52
	1205	0.1	3		1805	11.3	344
	1843	12.2	372				
13 Tu	0056	2.4	73	28 W	0027	2.1	64
	0647	9.9	302		0624	9.8	299
	1247	1.5	46		1220	2.6	79
	1916	11.9	363		1830	11.3	344
14 W	0141	1.7	52	29 Th	0102	1.3	40
	0750	9.5	290		0716	9.7	296
	1329	3.1	94		1300	3.7	113
	1948	11.5	351		1856	11.2	341
15 Th	0232	1.3	40	30 F	0144	0.7	21
	0903	9.0	274		0816	9.5	290
	1418	4.5	137		1342	4.9	149
	2027	11.0	335		1928	11.0	335
				31 Sa	0233	0.2	6
					0926	9.4	287
					1432	6.0	183
					2006	10.8	329

SEPTEMBER

Day	h m	ft	cm	Day	h m	ft	cm
1 Su	0328	-0.1	-3	16 M	0432	1.1	34
	1048	9.4	287		1234	9.8	299
	1533	7.0	213		1742	7.3	223
	2053	10.5	320		2201	8.5	259
2 M	0431	-0.4	-12	17 Tu	0538	1.2	37
	1221	9.7	296		1337	10.1	308
	1654	7.6	232		1912	7.0	213
	2154	10.1	308		2320	8.3	253
3 Tu	0541	-0.6	-18	18 W	0643	1.2	37
	1337	10.3	314		1422	10.4	317
	1826	7.6	232		2004	6.4	195
	2307	9.9	302				
4 W	0647	-0.8	-24	19 Th	0036	8.4	256
	1431	10.9	332		0735	1.2	37
	1946	6.9	210		1458	10.6	323
					2043	5.6	171
5 Th	0032	9.9	302	20 F	0139	8.7	265
	0749	-1.0	-30		0821	1.3	40
	1514	11.3	344		1526	10.7	326
	2043	5.9	180		2115	4.8	146
6 F	0148	10.1	308	21 Sa	0234	9.1	277
	0844	-0.8	-24		0859	1.5	46
	1550	11.6	354		1545	10.8	329
	2132	4.6	140		2143	3.8	116
7 Sa	0254	10.3	314	22 Su	0323	9.5	290
	0933	-0.4	-12		0938	1.9	58
	1623	11.8	360		1603	10.8	329
	2217	3.3	101		2212	2.8	85
8 Su	0358	10.6	323	23 M	0407	9.9	302
	1019	0.3	9		1013	2.4	73
	1651	11.9	363		1622	10.9	332
	2259	2.1	64		2240	1.7	52
9 M	0456	10.7	326	24 Tu	0452	10.3	314
	1101	1.3	40		1045	3.0	91
	1721	11.8	360		1641	11.0	335
	2338	1.2	37		2312	0.7	21
10 Tu	0553	10.7	326	25 W	0537	10.6	323
	1143	2.4	73		1124	3.7	113
	1750	11.5	351		1707	11.1	338
					2350	-0.1	-3
11 W	0019	0.5	15	26 Th	0626	10.8	329
	0646	10.5	320		1203	4.6	140
	1228	3.6	110		1734	11.1	338
	1822	11.2	341				
12 Th	0101	0.2	6	27 F	0029	-0.7	-21
	0745	10.2	311		0716	10.8	329
	1310	4.7	143		1245	5.4	165
	1854	10.7	326		1806	11.0	335
13 F	0144	0.2	6	28 Sa	0112	-1.1	-34
	0847	9.9	302		0816	10.7	326
	1359	5.7	174		1330	6.3	192
	1927	10.1	308		1843	10.7	326
14 Sa	0233	0.4	12	29 Su	0200	-1.1	-34
	0956	9.7	296		0924	10.5	320
	1455	6.6	201		1429	7.0	213
	2009	9.5	290		1928	10.3	314
15 Su	0328	0.8	24	30 M	0258	-0.8	-24
	1119	9.6	293		1036	10.5	320
	1607	7.2	219		1541	7.4	226
	2058	9.0	274		2026	9.7	296

Time meridian 120° W. 0000 is midnight. 1200 is noon.
Heights are referred to mean lower low water which is the chart datum of soundings.

1991 TIDE TABLES

SEATTLE

For Daylight Saving Time, add one hour.

Times and Heights of High and Low Waters

OCTOBER

Day	h m	ft	cm	Day	h m	ft	cm
1 Tu	0402	-0.4	-12	16 W	0438	1.7	52
	1152	10.7	326		1231	10.5	320
	1713	7.3	223		1840	6.3	192
	2145	9.2	280		2251	7.7	235
2 W	0512	0.0	0	17 Th	0540	2.2	67
	1252	11.0	335		1313	10.6	323
	1839	6.4	195		1932	5.4	165
	2321	8.9	271				
3 Th	0624	0.4	12	18 F	0019	7.8	238
	1346	11.3	344		0639	2.6	79
	1942	5.2	158		1345	10.7	326
					2004	4.4	134
4 F	0052	9.1	277	19 Sa	0133	8.3	253
	0727	0.9	27		0732	3.0	91
	1425	11.5	351		1410	10.7	326
	2031	3.7	113		2036	3.2	98
5 Sa	0212	9.6	293	20 Su	0231	8.9	271
	0822	1.5	46		0820	3.5	107
	1459	11.6	354		1433	10.8	329
	2115	2.3	70		2107	2.0	61
6 Su	0318	10.1	308	21 M	0325	9.7	296
	0915	2.2	67		0859	4.1	125
	1531	11.6	354		1454	10.9	332
	2155	1.0	30		2135	0.8	24
7 M	0416	10.7	326	22 Tu	0411	10.4	317
	1000	3.0	91		0942	4.6	140
	1600	11.5	351		1518	11.0	335
	2233	0.1	3		2207	-0.3	-9
8 Tu	0509	11.0	335	23 W	0454	11.0	335
	1045	3.9	119		1024	5.2	158
	1630	11.3	344		1545	11.1	338
	2309	-0.6	-18		2240	-1.2	-37
9 W	0558	11.2	341	24 Th	0539	11.5	351
	1127	4.7	143		1105	5.8	177
	1658	11.0	335		1614	11.2	341
	2347	-0.9	-27		2319	-2.0	-61
10 Th	0647	11.2	341	25 F	0628	11.7	357
	1209	5.5	168		1147	6.4	195
	1728	10.6	323		1648	11.2	341
11 F	0026	-0.8	-24	26 Sa	0001	-2.3	-70
	0736	11.1	338		0720	11.9	363
	1255	6.1	186		1236	6.9	210
	1759	10.1	308		1727	11.0	335
12 Sa	0105	-0.6	-18	27 Su	0046	-2.3	-70
	0831	10.8	329		0813	11.8	360
	1344	6.7	204		1328	7.2	219
	1838	9.6	293		1809	10.6	323
13 Su	0149	-0.1	-3	28 M	0136	-1.9	-58
	0927	10.6	323		0912	11.7	357
	1443	7.1	216		1435	7.3	223
	1917	9.0	274		1908	9.9	302
14 M	0239	0.5	15	29 Tu	0232	-1.1	-34
	1033	10.5	320		1014	11.7	357
	1554	7.3	223		1554	7.0	213
	2006	8.4	256		2021	9.1	277
15 Tu	0336	1.1	34	30 W	0334	0.0	0
	1135	10.5	320		1113	11.7	357
	1727	7.0	213		1718	6.1	186
	2120	7.9	241		2157	8.4	256
				31 Th	0441	1.1	34
					1205	11.7	357
					1831	4.8	146
					2341	8.2	250

NOVEMBER

Day	h m	ft	cm	Day	h m	ft	cm
1 F	0552	2.2	67	16 Sa	0533	3.9	119
	1251	11.8	360		1222	11.1	338
	1929	3.2	98		1918	3.3	101
2 Sa	0116	8.7	265	17 Su	0119	8.1	247
	0658	3.2	98		0635	4.8	146
	1332	11.7	357		1251	11.0	335
	2015	1.7	52		1953	2.0	61
3 Su	0234	9.5	290	18 M	0228	9.0	274
	0801	4.1	125		0732	5.6	171
	1407	11.6	354		1320	11.1	338
	2054	0.4	12		2025	0.7	21
4 M	0337	10.3	314	19 Tu	0324	9.9	302
	0857	4.9	149		0823	6.2	189
	1441	11.5	351		1349	11.1	338
	2133	-0.5	-15		2100	-0.6	-18
5 Tu	0434	11.0	335	20 W	0413	10.8	329
	0948	5.6	171		0912	6.8	207
	1509	11.2	341		1420	11.3	344
	2211	-1.2	-37		2136	-1.7	-52
6 W	0521	11.5	351	21 Th	0459	11.6	354
	1033	6.1	186		1001	7.2	219
	1541	10.9	332		1455	11.4	347
	2243	-1.5	-46		2218	-2.6	-79
7 Th	0606	11.8	360	22 F	0541	12.2	372
	1115	6.6	201		1050	7.5	229
	1613	10.6	323		1534	11.5	351
	2320	-1.6	-49		2259	-3.1	-94
8 F	0649	11.9	363	23 Sa	0630	12.6	384
	1157	6.9	210		1137	7.5	232
	1642	10.3	314		1619	11.4	347
	2356	-1.4	-43		2342	-3.2	-98
9 Sa	0731	11.8	360	24 Su	0715	12.8	390
	1242	7.2	219		1228	7.6	232
	1717	9.9	302		1705	11.1	338
10 Su	0033	-1.0	-30	25 M	0028	-2.8	-85
	0813	11.7	357		0804	12.8	390
	1331	7.3	223		1327	7.3	223
	1752	9.4	287		1801	10.5	320
11 M	0115	-0.5	-15	26 Tu	0120	-2.0	-61
	0858	11.5	351		0851	12.7	387
	1429	7.3	223		1431	6.8	207
	1838	8.9	271		1906	9.6	293
12 Tu	0158	0.2	6	27 W	0210	-0.7	-21
	0943	11.4	347		0941	12.6	384
	1532	7.1	216		1544	5.9	180
	1933	8.3	253		2029	8.7	265
13 W	0247	1.1	34	28 Th	0306	0.8	24
	1029	11.3	344		1027	12.5	381
	1645	6.5	198		1700	4.7	143
	2049	7.7	235		2207	8.1	247
14 Th	0336	2.0	61	29 F	0407	2.5	76
	1111	11.2	341		1113	12.3	375
	1747	5.6	171		1805	3.2	98
	2220	7.3	223		2356	8.1	247
15 F	0434	3.0	91	30 Sa	0516	4.1	125
	1150	11.1	338		1157	12.1	369
	1839	4.5	137		1901	1.7	52
	2355	7.5	229				

DECEMBER

Day	h m	ft	cm	Day	h m	ft	cm
1 Su	0137	8.8	268	16 M	0058	8.2	250
	0627	5.4	165		0533	6.2	189
	1238	11.8	360		1138	11.4	347
	1950	0.5	15		1904	1.1	34
2 M	0253	9.8	299	17 Tu	0217	9.2	280
	0738	6.4	195		0642	7.2	219
	1316	11.5	351		1214	11.3	344
	2034	-0.5	-15		1946	-0.2	-5
3 Tu	0352	10.7	326	18 W	0319	10.2	311
	0840	7.0	213		0748	7.9	241
	1352	11.2	341		1252	11.4	347
	2113	-1.1	-34		2030	-1.4	-43
4 W	0444	11.5	351	19 Th	0411	11.2	341
	0937	7.4	226		0850	8.2	250
	1430	10.9	332		1334	11.6	354
	2148	-1.5	-46		2115	-2.4	-73
5 Th	0526	11.9	363	20 F	0454	12.1	369
	1026	7.6	232		0944	8.3	253
	1503	10.7	326		1423	11.7	357
	2224	-1.7	-52		2158	-3.1	-94
6 F	0605	12.2	372	21 Sa	0539	12.7	387
	1109	7.7	235		1037	8.2	250
	1537	10.4	317		1513	11.7	357
	2259	-1.6	-49		2243	-3.4	-104
7 Sa	0640	12.3	375	22 Su	0618	13.1	399
	1150	7.7	235		1129	7.8	238
	1614	10.2	311		1607	11.5	351
	2334	-1.5	-46		2328	-3.3	-101
8 Su	0715	12.3	375	23 M	0659	13.3	405
	1230	7.5	229		1221	7.2	219
	1651	9.9	302		1706	11.1	338
9 M	0011	-1.1	-34	24 Tu	0014	-2.6	-79
	0750	12.3	375		0738	13.3	405
	1315	7.3	223		1317	6.4	195
	1733	9.5	290		1806	10.4	317
10 Tu	0047	-0.6	-18	25 W	0102	-1.4	-43
	0819	12.2	372		0817	13.3	405
	1400	7.0	213		1414	5.4	165
	1822	9.0	274		1918	9.6	293
11 W	0126	0.2	6	26 Th	0150	0.2	6
	0854	12.1	369		0858	13.1	399
	1453	6.4	195		1517	4.3	131
	1918	8.4	256		2037	8.8	268
12 Th	0205	1.2	37	27 F	0239	2.1	64
	0928	12.0	366		0936	12.8	390
	1548	5.7	174		1524	3.1	94
	2027	7.8	238		2213	8.3	253
13 F	0249	2.4	73	28 Sa	0335	4.0	122
	0959	11.8	360		1018	12.4	378
	1641	4.8	146		1730	2.0	61
	2149	7.5	229		2359	8.4	256
14 Sa	0335	3.7	113	29 Su	0441	5.7	174
	1033	11.6	354		1103	12.0	366
	1738	3.6	110		1829	1.0	30
	2321	7.6	232				
15 Su	0430	5.0	152	30 M	0141	9.2	280
	1105	11.5	351		0557	7.0	213
	1821	2.4	73		1145	11.5	351
					1924	0.1	3
				31 Tu	0254	10.2	311
					0723	7.8	238
					1230	11.1	338
					2010	-0.5	-15

Time meridian 120° W. 0000 is midnight. 1200 is noon.
Heights are referred to mean lower low water which is the chart datum of soundings.

San Juan Islands Tides
1991 • JANUARY • 1991

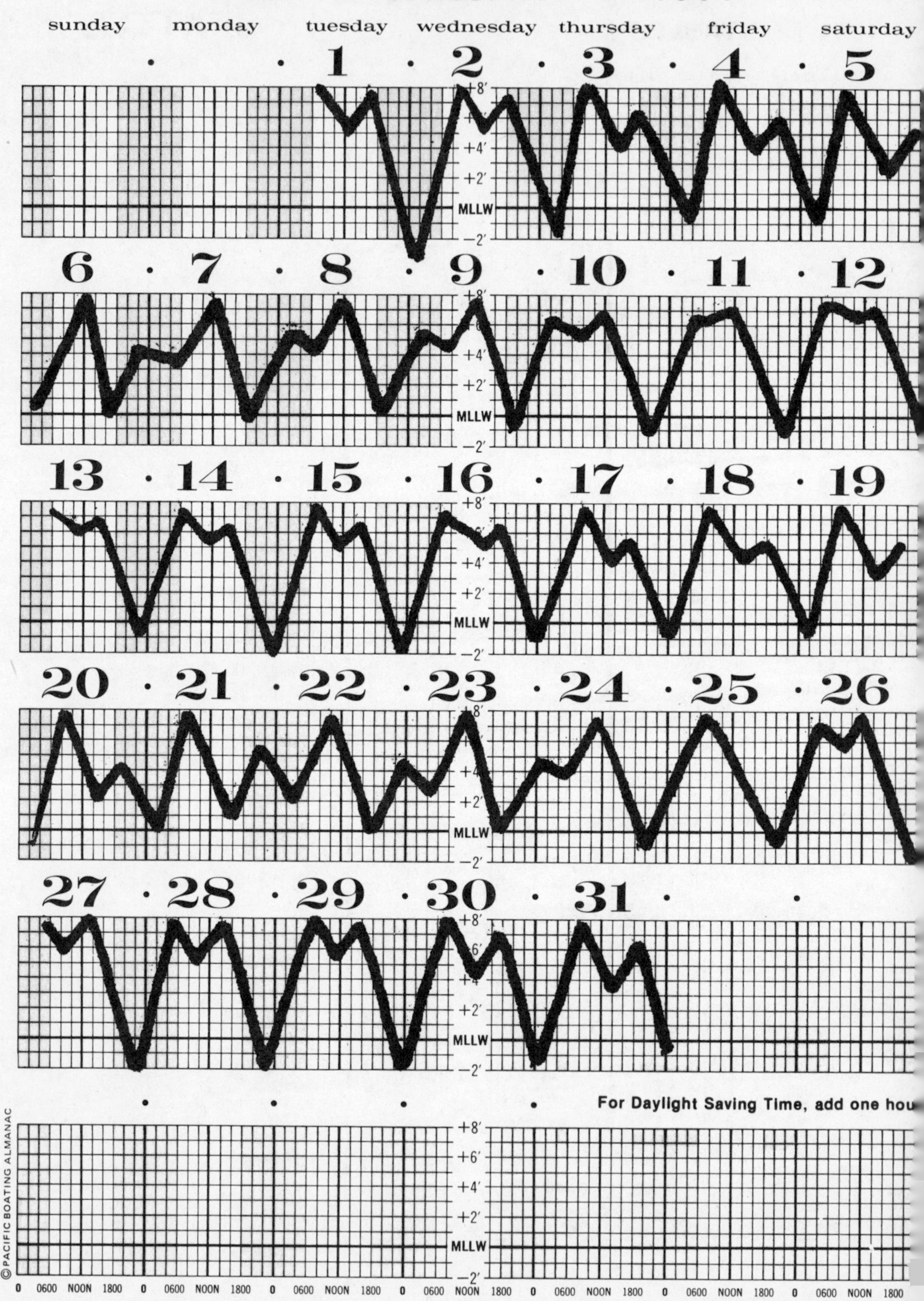

San Juan Islands Tides
1991 • FEBRUARY • 1991

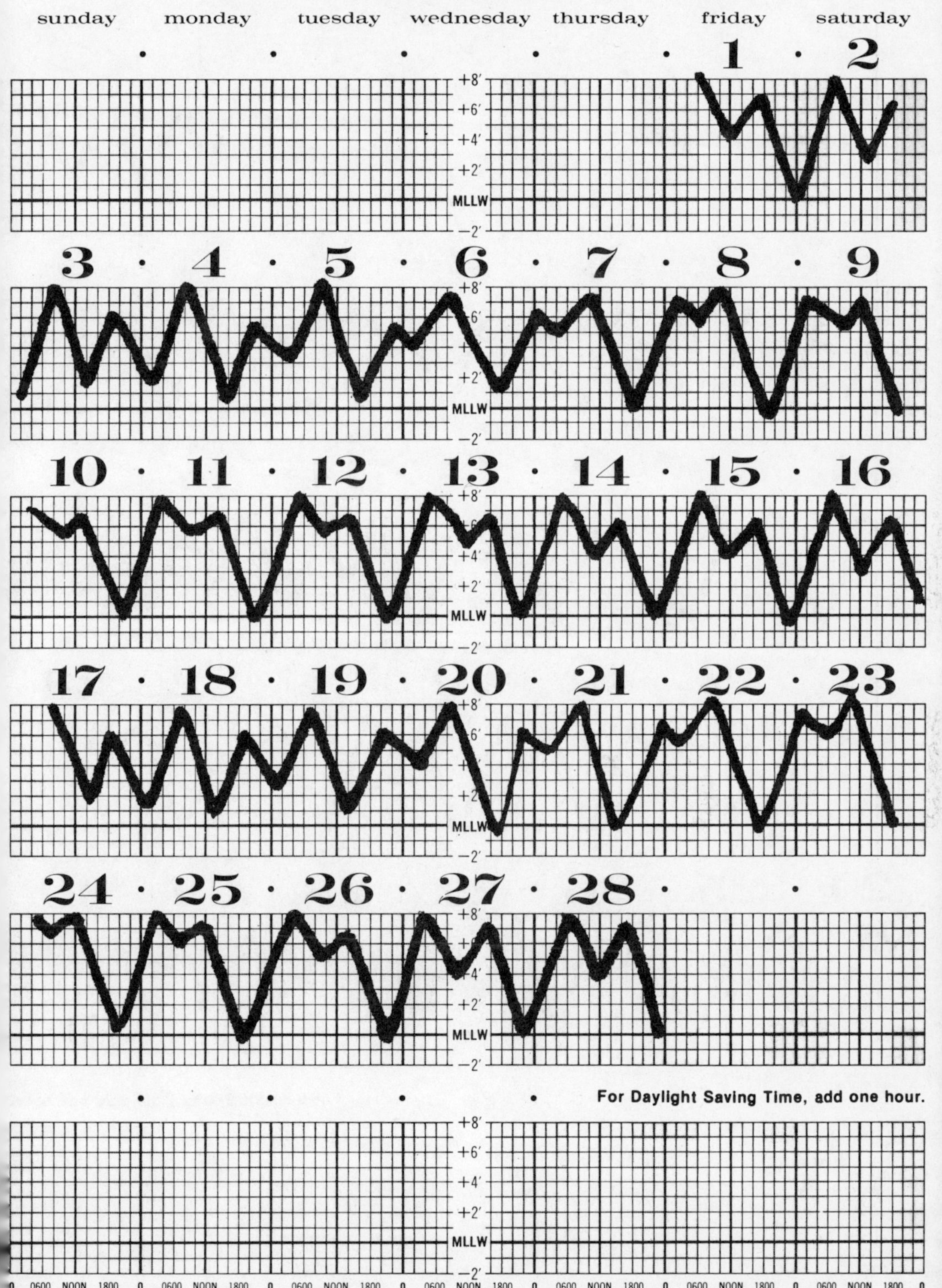

San Juan Islands Tides
1991 ● MARCH ● 1991

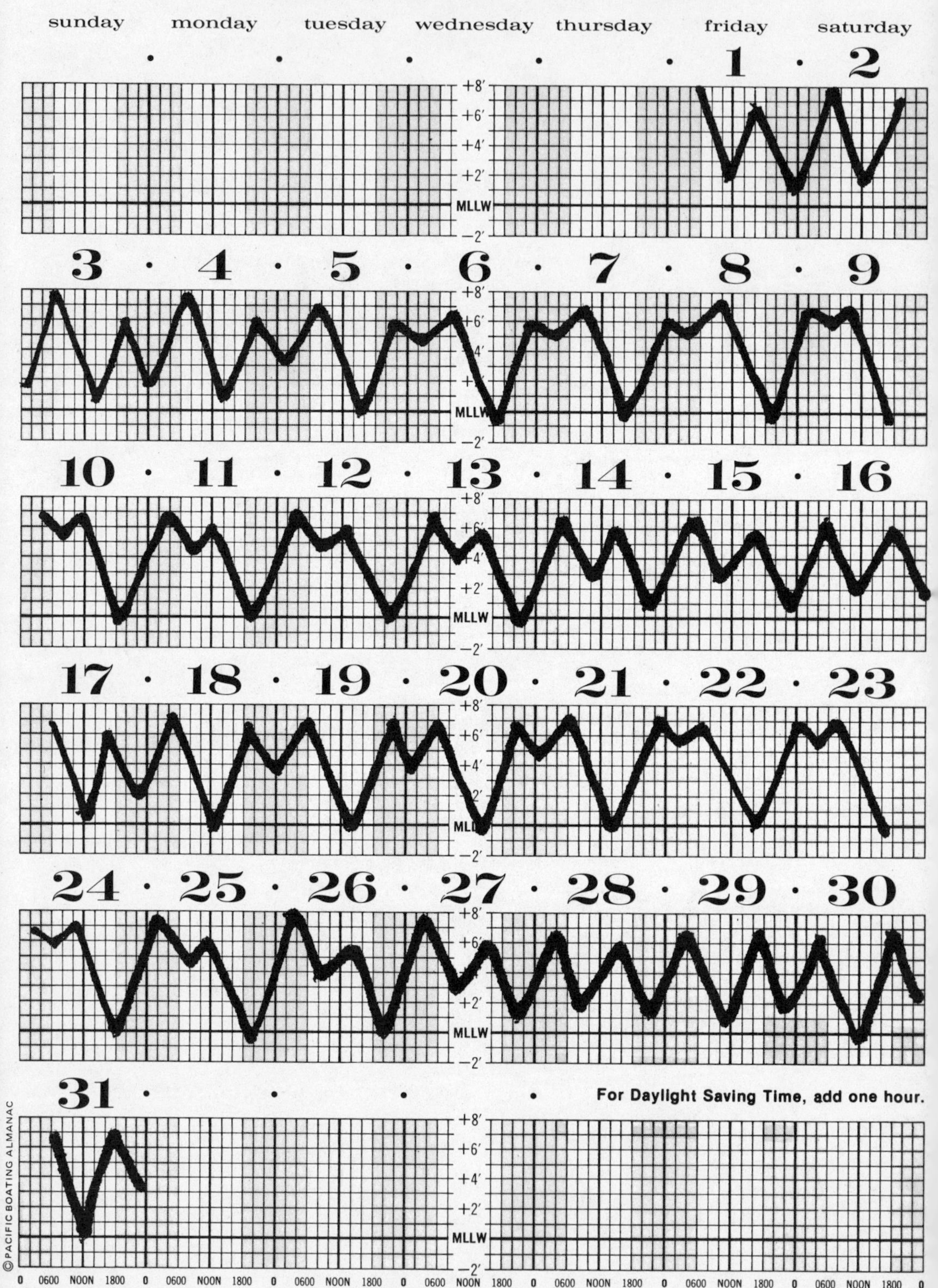

San Juan Islands Tides
1991 • APRIL • 1991

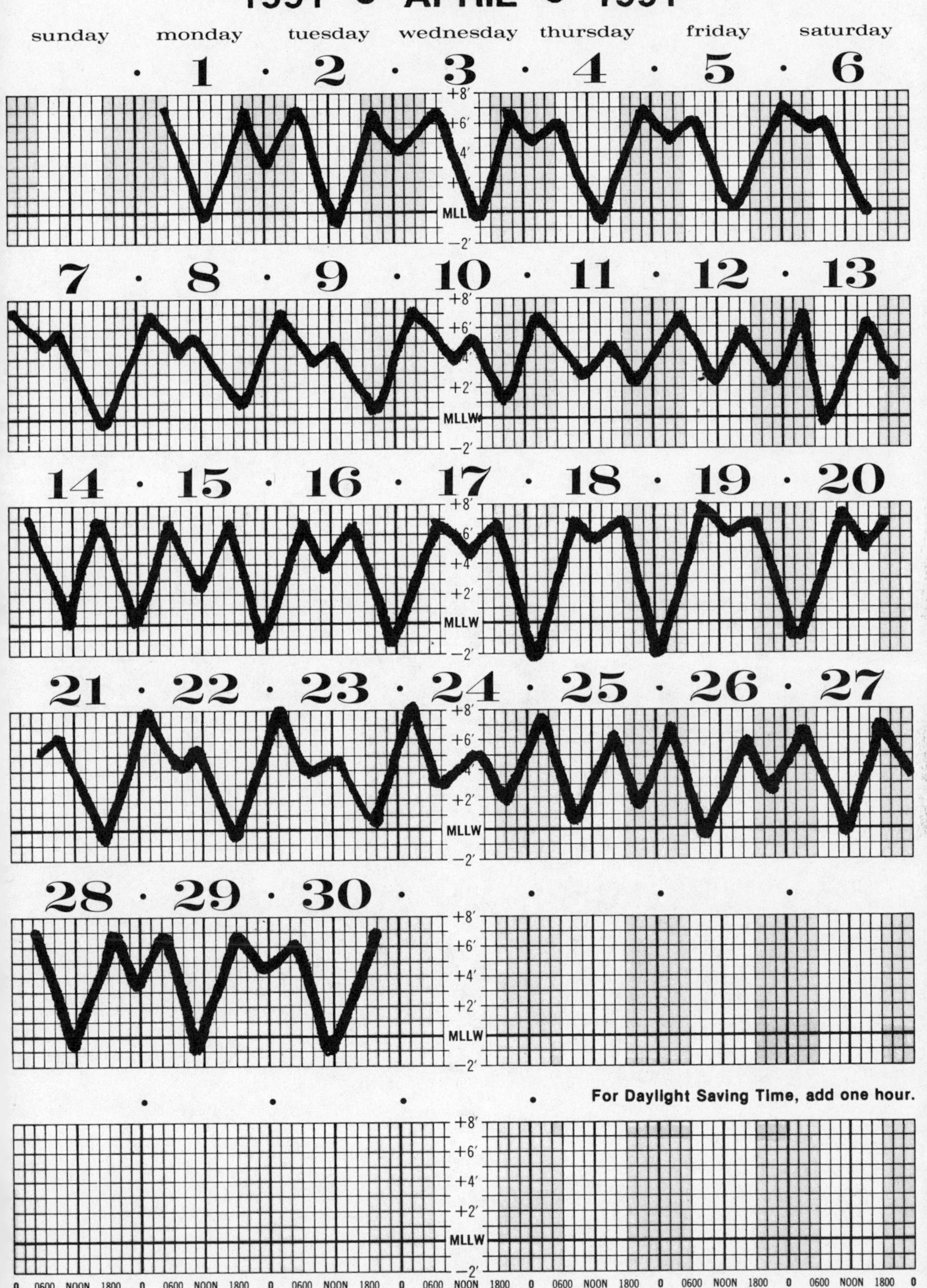

T-103

San Juan Islands Tides
1991 ● MAY ● 1991

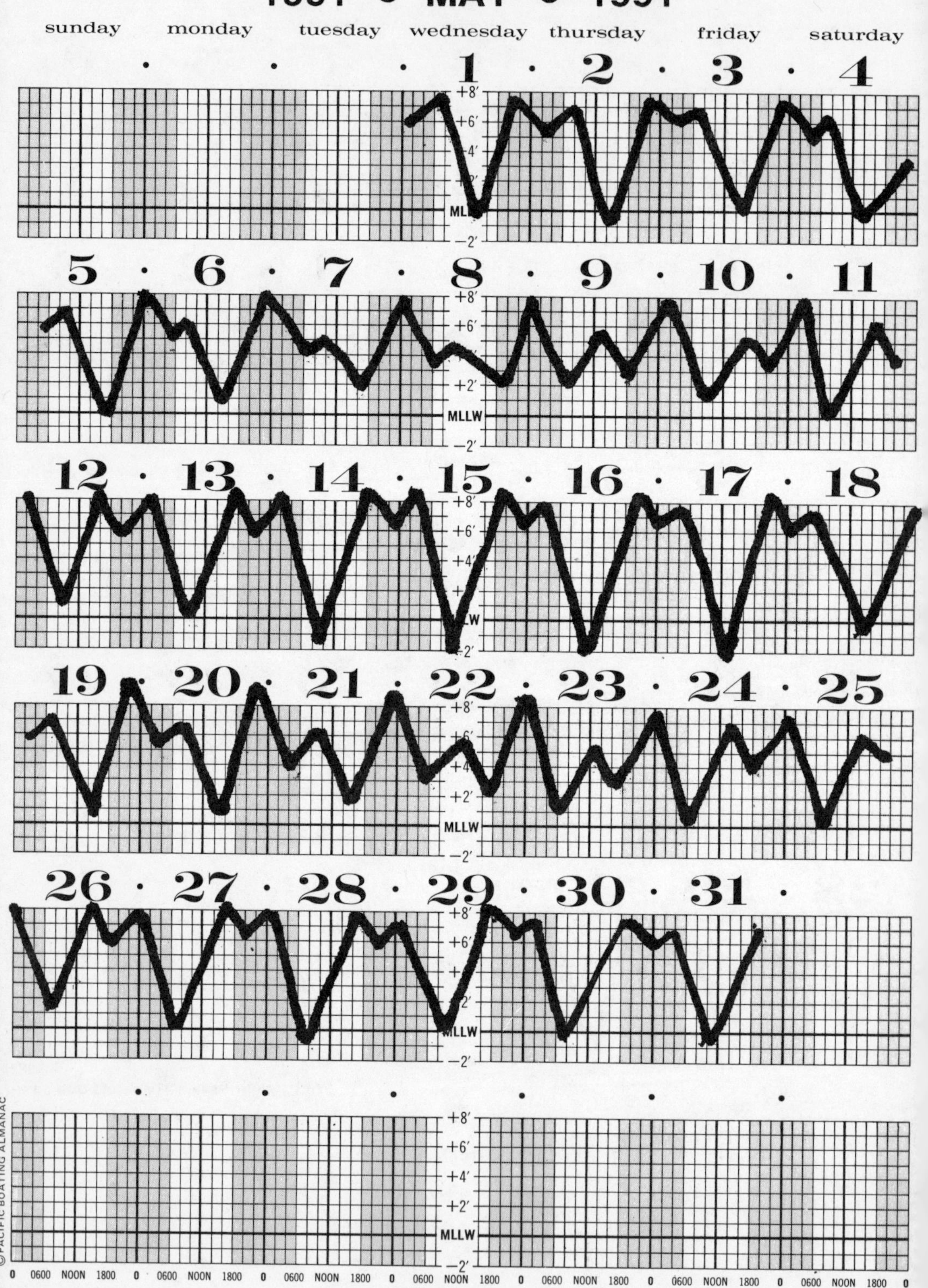

San Juan Islands Tides
1991 ● JUNE ● 1991

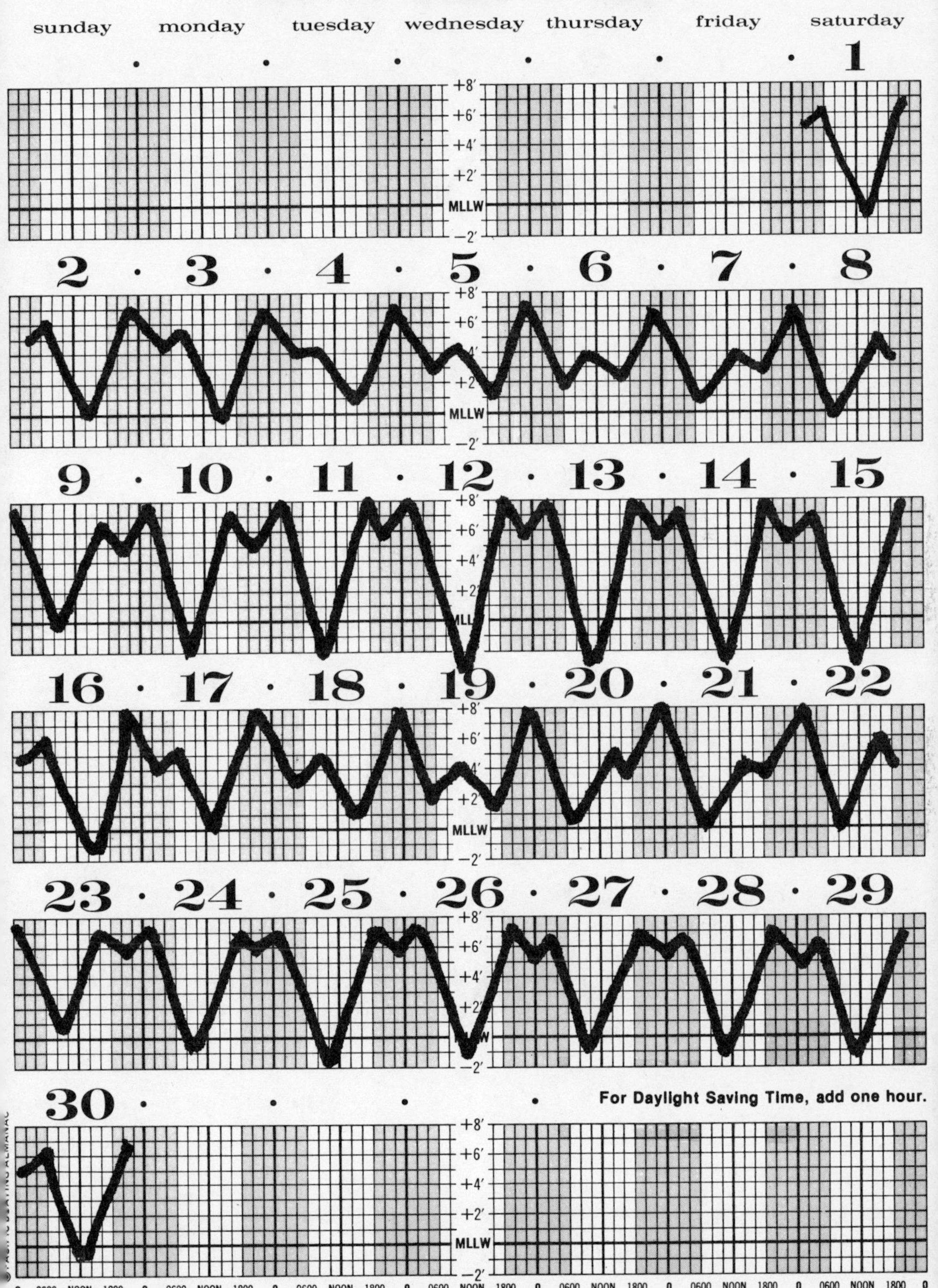

San Juan Islands Tides
1991 • JULY • 1991

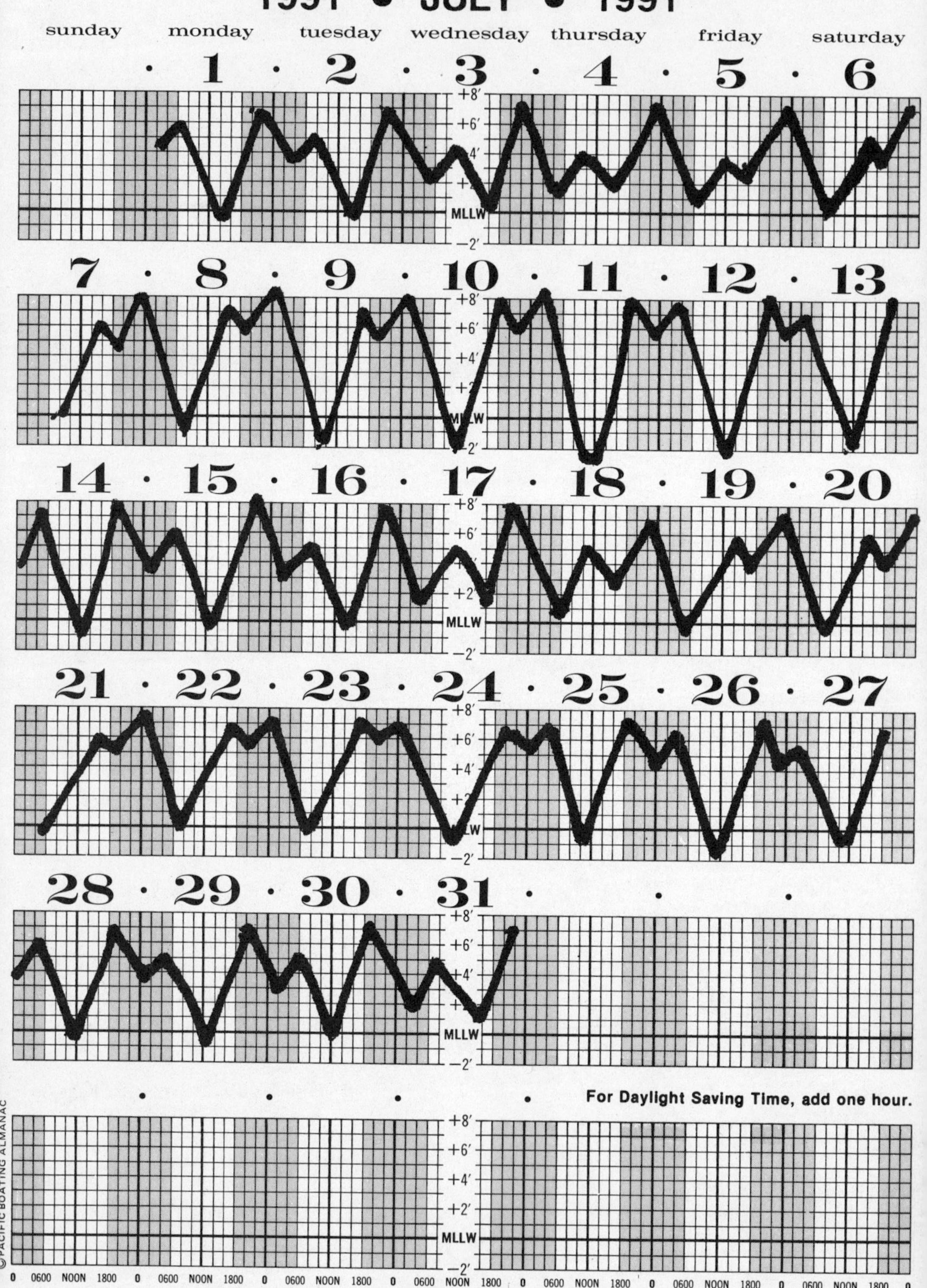

San Juan Islands Tides
1991 ● AUGUST ● 1991

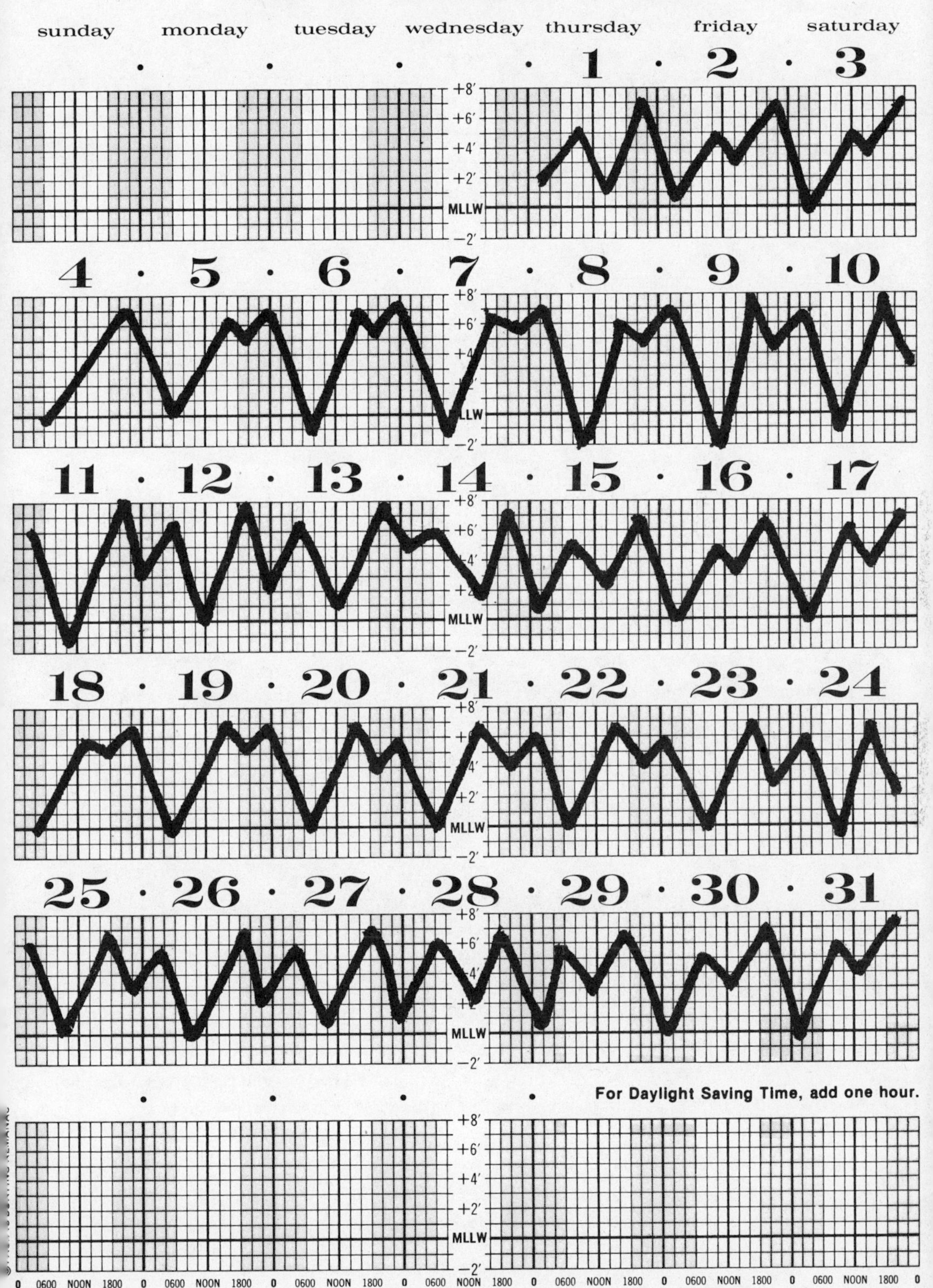

San Juan Islands Tides
1991 • SEPTEMBER • 1991

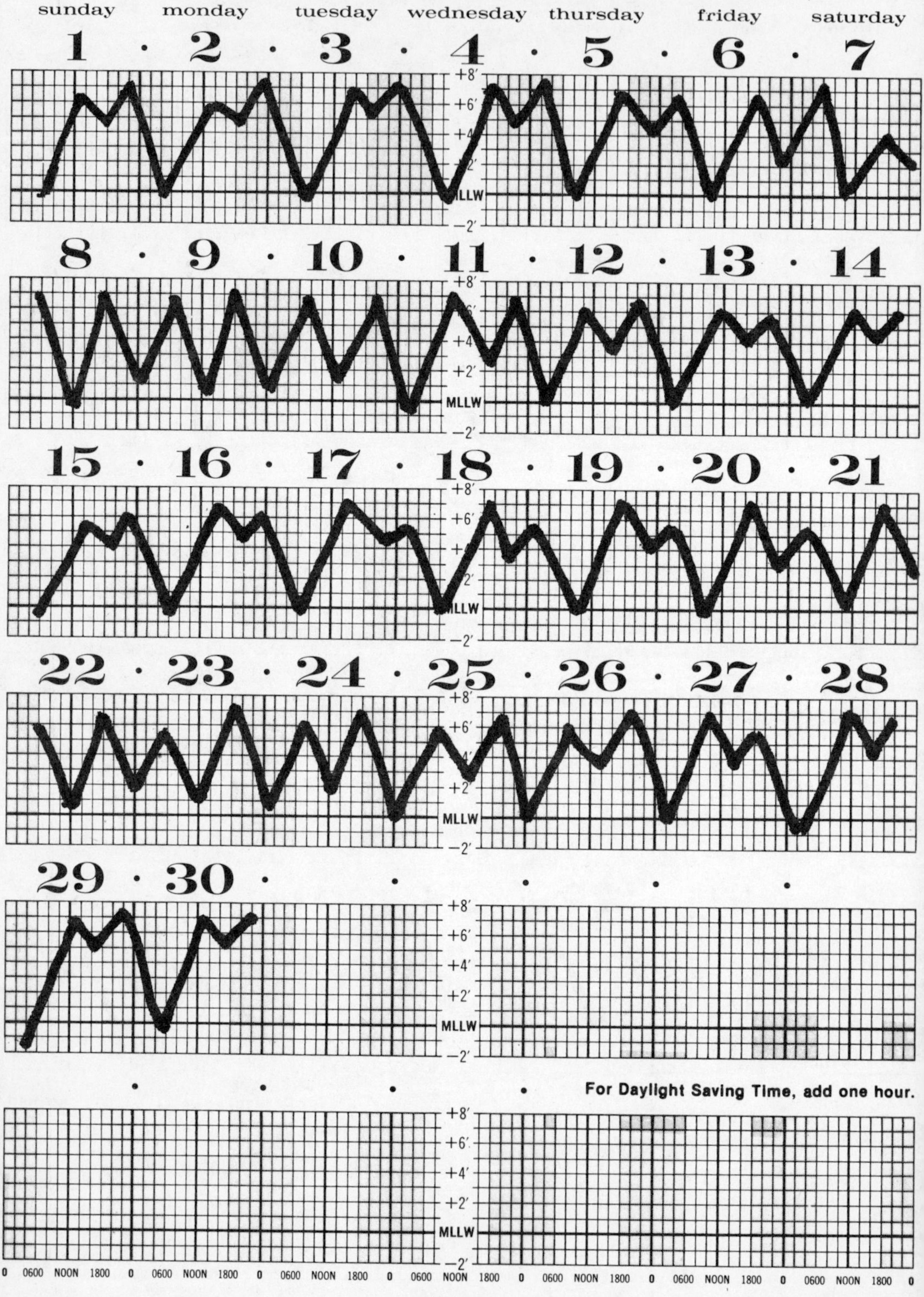

sunday	monday	tuesday	wednesday	thursday	friday	saturday
1	2	3	4	5	6	7
8	9	10	11	12	13	14
15	16	17	18	19	20	21
22	23	24	25	26	27	28
29	30					

For Daylight Saving Time, add one hour.

0 0600 NOON 1800 0 0600 NOON 1800 0 0600 NOON 1800 0 0600 NOON 1800 0 0600 NOON 1800 0 0600 NOON 1800 0 0600 NOON 1800 0

+8′ +6′ +4′ +2′ MLLW −2′

San Juan Islands Tides
1991 ● OCTOBER ● 1991

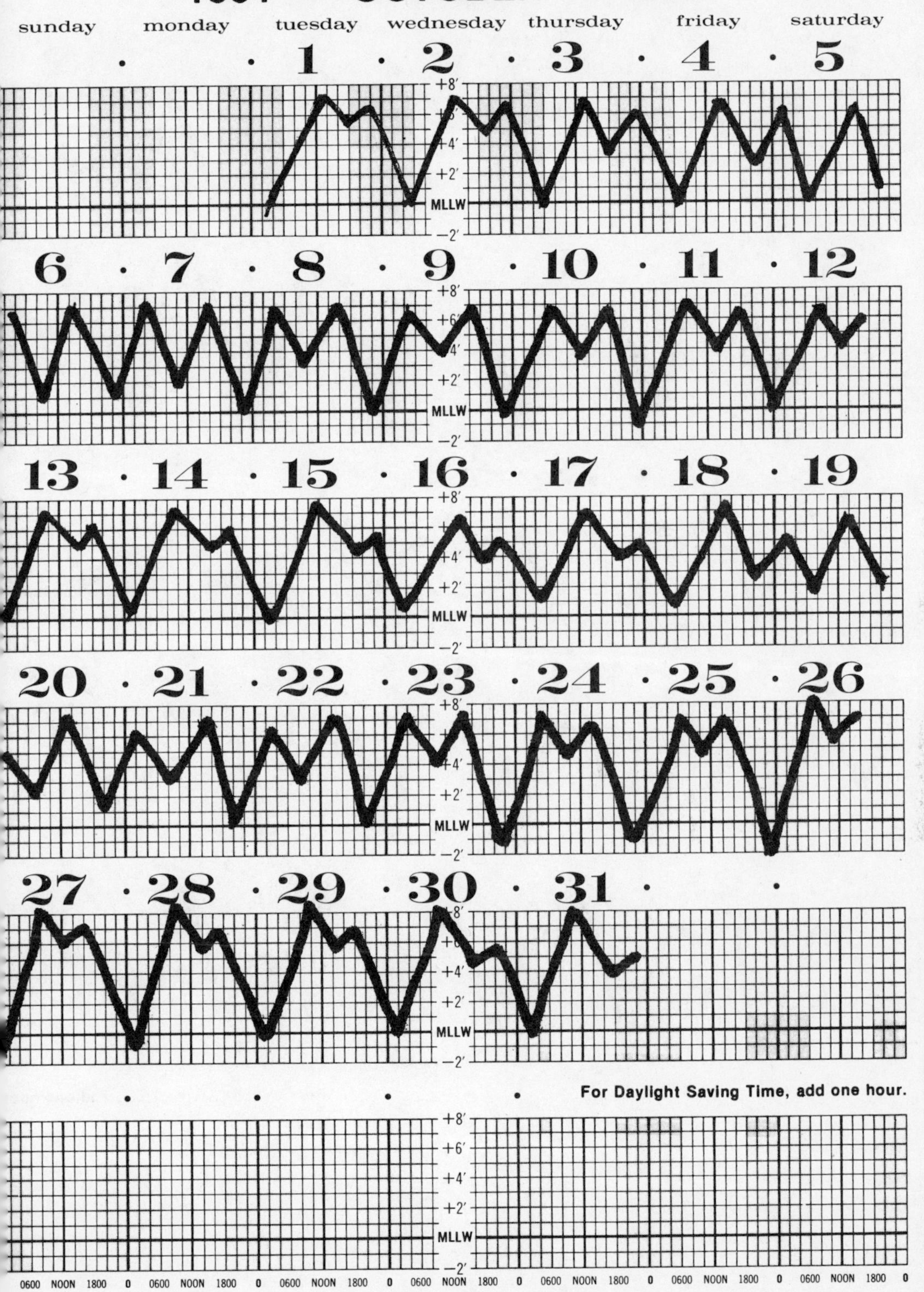

San Juan Islands Tides
1991 • NOVEMBER • 1991

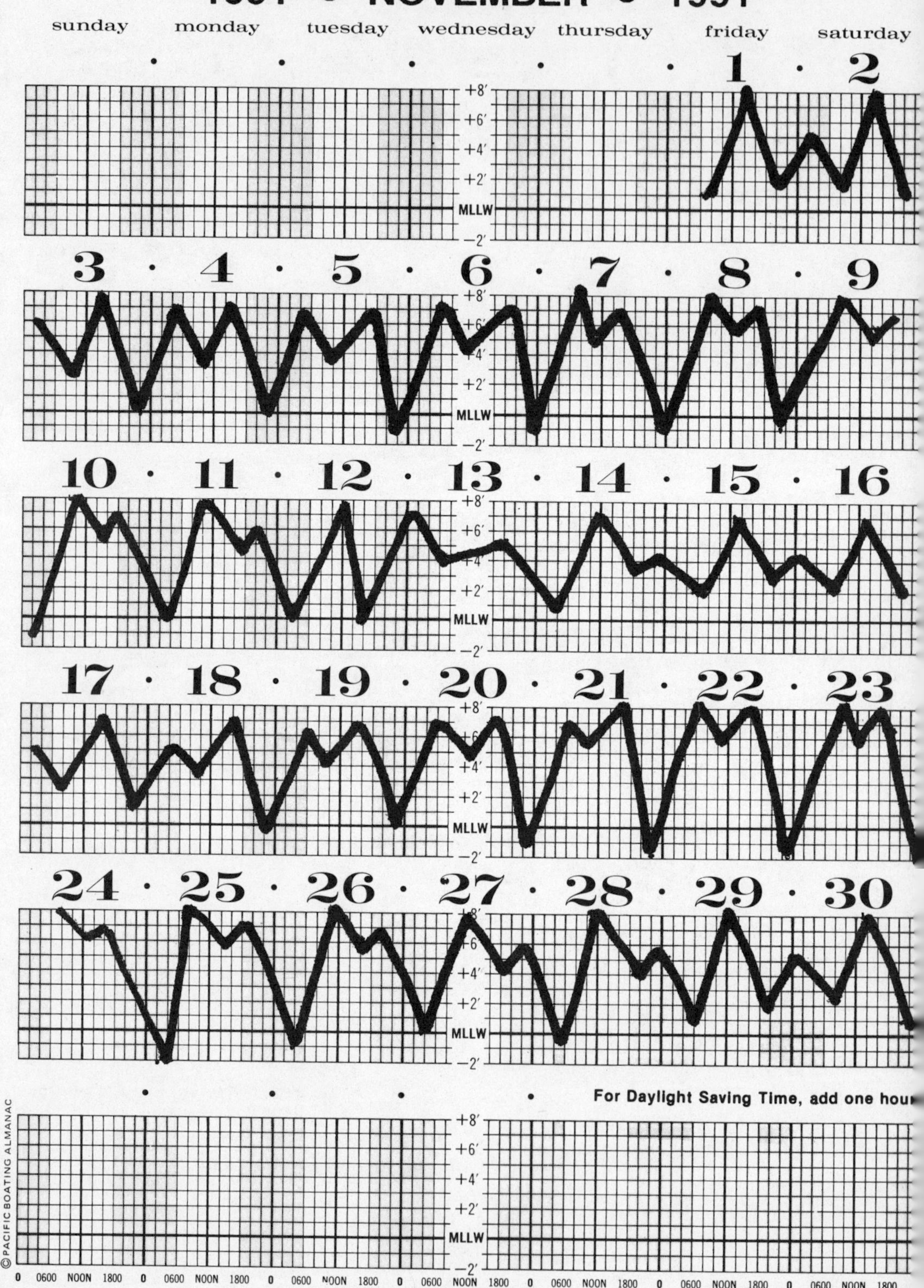

San Juan Islands Tides
1991 • DECEMBER • 1991

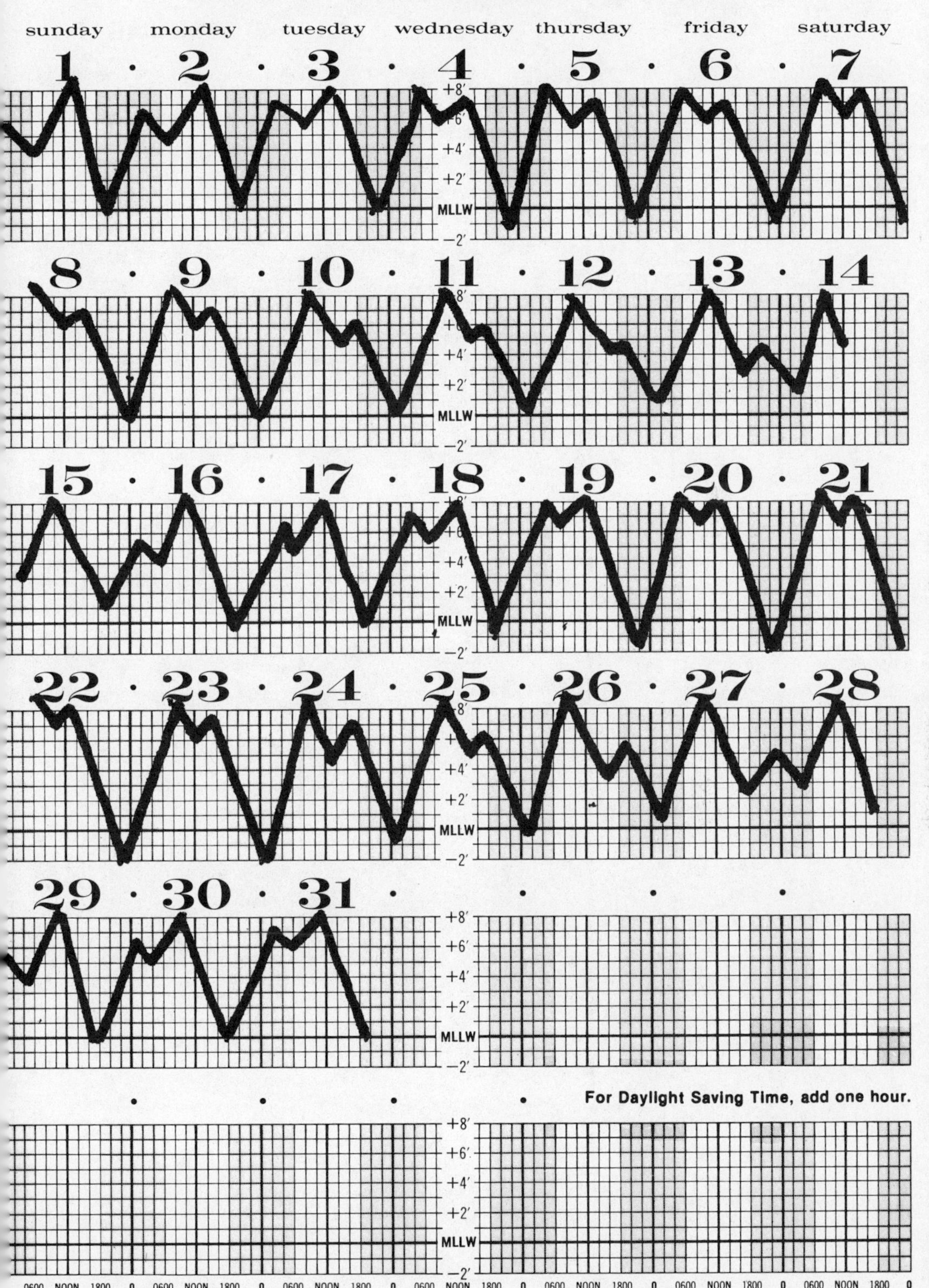

VICTORIA

1991 TIDE TABLES

For Daylight Saving Time, add one hour.

Times and Heights of High and Low Waters

JANUARY

Day	h m	ft	cm	Day	h m	ft	cm
1 Tu	0700	9.0	274	16 W	0720	8.6	262
	0825	8.9	271		0840	8.6	262
	1255	10.3	314		1225	9.2	280
	2140	0.0	.0		2145	1.7	52
2 W	0720	8.9	271	17 Th	0715	8.5	259
	0935	8.6	262		0940	8.2	250
	1400	9.8	299		1315	8.9	271
	2225	0.6	18		2215	2.0	61
3 Th	0740	8.9	271	18 F	0715	8.5	259
	1040	8.1	247		1035	7.8	238
	1500	9.0	274		1405	8.4	256
	2305	1.5	46		2245	2.5	76
4 F	0735	8.8	268	19 Sa	0640	8.5	259
	1155	7.4	226		1130	7.2	219
	1610	8.0	244		1510	7.8	238
	2345	2.6	79		2315	3.2	98
5 Sa	0725	9.0	274	20 Su	0640	8.7	265
	1315	6.6	201		1225	6.5	198
	1725	7.0	213		1640	7.0	213
					2345	4.0	122
6 Su	0020	3.8	116	21 M	0655	8.8	268
	0745	9.1	277		1325	5.7	174
	1500	5.7	174		1810	6.4	195
	1855	6.1	186		2355	5.0	152
7 M	0045	5.0	152	22 Tu	0715	9.1	277
	0810	9.2	280		1430	4.7	143
	1615	4.7	143		2000	5.9	180
					2145	5.8	177
8 Tu	0835	9.2	280	23 W	0735	9.3	283
	1700	3.9	119		1535	3.7	113
9 W	0855	9.2	280	24 Th	0755	9.6	293
	1740	3.2	98		1640	2.8	85
10 Th	0900	9.2	280	25 F	0820	9.9	302
	1815	2.7	82		1735	1.9	58
11 F	0855	9.3	283	26 Sa	0855	10.1	308
	1855	2.3	70		1825	1.1	34
12 Sa	0915	9.4	287	27 Su	0950	10.2	311
	1930	2.0	61		1910	0.7	21
13 Su	0955	9.5	290	28 M	1100	10.2	311
	2005	1.7	52		1955	0.5	15
14 M	1045	9.5	290	29 Tu	0550	8.6	262
	2040	1.6	49		0720	8.4	256
					1220	10.0	305
					2040	0.6	18
15 Tu	1135	9.4	287	30 W	0600	8.4	256
	2115	1.6	49		0830	7.9	241
					1330	9.6	293
					2120	1.1	34
				31 Th	0600	8.3	253
					0930	7.3	223
					1435	9.0	274
					2200	1.9	58

FEBRUARY

Day	h m	ft	cm	Day	h m	ft	cm
1 F	0510	8.5	259	16 Sa	0440	8.2	250
	1025	6.6	201		1010	6.1	186
	1535	8.2	250		1520	7.8	238
	2235	2.8	85		2215	3.6	110
2 Sa	0530	8.7	265	17 Su	0455	8.4	256
	1125	5.9	180		1100	5.3	162
	1635	7.4	226		1620	7.3	223
	2310	3.9	119		2245	4.4	134
3 Su	0600	8.9	271	18 M	0520	8.6	262
	1225	5.2	158		1150	4.6	140
	1745	6.7	204		1730	6.8	207
	2340	5.0	152		2315	5.3	162
4 M	0625	9.0	274	19 Tu	0540	8.9	271
	1330	4.6	140		1240	3.9	119
	1930	6.1	186		1850	6.4	195
	2350	6.0	183		2335	6.2	189
5 Tu	0650	9.0	274	20 W	0605	9.1	277
	1445	4.1	125		1340	3.3	101
6 W	0710	9.0	274	21 Th	0625	9.3	283
	1555	3.6	110		1445	2.7	82
7 Th	0720	8.9	271	22 F	0645	9.4	287
	1650	3.2	98		1600	2.2	67
8 F	0730	9.0	274	23 Sa	0725	9.5	290
	1740	2.9	88		1705	1.8	55
9 Sa	0755	9.0	274	24 Su	0825	9.4	287
	1825	2.6	79		1800	1.6	49
10 Su	0840	9.0	274	25 M	0405	8.3	253
	1905	2.4	73		0520	8.3	253
					0950	9.2	280
					1850	1.5	46
11 M	0940	8.9	271	26 Tu	0415	8.1	247
	1940	2.2	67		0635	7.7	235
					1135	9.0	274
					1935	1.7	52
12 Tu	0600	8.3	253	27 W	0420	7.9	241
	0700	8.3	253		0735	7.0	213
	1055	8.8	268		1250	8.7	265
	2015	2.2	67		2015	2.1	64
13 W	0550	8.1	247	28 Th	0315	7.9	241
	0750	7.9	241		0825	6.2	189
	1225	8.7	265		1355	8.4	256
	2045	2.2	67		2055	2.8	85
14 Th	0530	7.9	241				
	0840	7.4	226				
	1330	8.5	259				
	2115	2.5	76				
15 F	0435	8.0	244				
	0925	6.8	207				
	1425	8.2	250				
	2145	3.0	91				

MARCH

Day	h m	ft	cm	Day	h m	ft	cm
1 F	0330	8.1	247	16 Sa	0300	8.0	244
	0920	5.4	165		0905	4.7	143
	1455	7.9	241		1450	7.5	229
	2130	3.6	110		2105	4.4	134
2 Sa	0355	8.4	256	17 Su	0320	8.2	250
	1005	4.7	143		0950	3.8	116
	1550	7.4	226		1550	7.3	223
	2205	4.5	137		2140	5.2	158
3 Su	0425	8.6	262	18 M	0345	8.5	259
	1055	4.1	125		1030	3.0	91
	1655	7.0	213		1650	7.1	216
	2235	5.5	168		2210	6.0	183
4 M	0450	8.7	265	19 Tu	0410	8.8	268
	1145	3.6	110		1120	2.4	73
	1825	6.7	204		1820	6.9	210
	2300	6.3	192		2240	6.7	204
5 Tu	0515	8.7	265	20 W	0430	8.9	271
	1235	3.4	104		1210	2.0	61
					2225	7.3	223
					2305	7.3	223
6 W	0530	8.6	262	21 Th	0445	9.0	274
	1330	3.2	98		1305	1.8	55
7 Th	0540	8.5	259	22 F	0455	9.0	274
	1435	3.2	98		1410	1.8	55
8 F	0535	8.5	259	23 Sa	0530	8.9	271
	1545	3.1	94		1520	1.9	58
9 Sa	0405	8.4	256	24 Su	0210	8.2	250
	1650	3.1	94		0245	8.2	250
					0630	8.5	259
					1630	2.1	64
10 Su	0400	8.3	253	25 M	0205	8.1	247
	1740	2.9	88		0455	7.7	235
					0810	8.0	244
					1730	2.3	70
11 M	0410	8.1	247	26 Tu	0220	7.9	241
	0625	8.0	244		0600	7.0	213
	0800	8.1	247		1040	7.6	232
	1825	2.9	88		1820	2.7	82
12 Tu	0405	7.9	241	27 W	0145	7.8	238
	0645	7.6	232		0650	6.1	186
	0935	7.9	241		1205	7.5	229
	1900	2.9	88		1900	3.2	98
13 W	0340	7.6	232	28 Th	0140	7.9	241
	0710	7.1	216		0735	5.1	155
	1145	7.7	235		1315	7.3	223
	1935	3.1	94		1945	3.9	119
14 Th	0245	7.6	232	29 F	0200	8.0	244
	0745	6.4	195		0820	4.2	128
	1255	7.7	235		1420	7.2	219
	2005	3.4	104		2020	4.7	143
15 F	0245	7.7	235	30 Sa	0225	8.2	250
	0825	5.6	171		0905	3.4	104
	1355	7.6	232		1520	7.1	216
	2035	3.8	116		2055	5.5	168
				31 Su	0250	8.4	256
					0945	2.8	85
					1635	7.0	213
					2130	6.2	189

Time meridian 120° W. 0000 is midnight. 1200 is noon.
Heights are referred to the Canadian chart datum of soundings. Subtract 2.5 feet (0.8 meter) to refer these levels to the datum of N.O.S. charts.

1991 TIDE TABLES

VICTORIA

For Daylight Saving Time, add one hour.

Times and Heights of High and Low Waters

APRIL

Day	h m	ft	cm	Day	h m	ft	cm
1 M	0315	8.4	256	16 Tu	0235	8.9	271
	1025	2.4	73		1010	0.9	27
	1940	7.2	219		1945	7.5	229
	2205	6.9	210		2140	7.3	223
2 Tu	0335	8.4	256	17 W	0250	9.1	277
	1105	2.2	67		1055	0.6	18
	2105	7.4	226		2100	7.8	238
	2225	7.4	226		2220	7.8	238
3 W	0345	8.4	256	18 Th	0255	9.2	280
	1150	2.2	67		1145	0.6	18
					2210	8.1	247
					2305	8.1	247
4 Th	0320	8.3	253	19 F	0315	9.0	274
	1235	2.3	70		1240	0.9	27
					2300	8.2	250
5 F	0240	8.3	253	20 Sa	0020	8.2	250
	1325	2.6	79		0345	8.6	262
					1340	1.4	43
					2340	8.2	250
6 Sa	0220	8.2	250	21 Su	0225	8.0	244
	1430	2.9	88		0420	8.0	244
					1440	2.0	61
7 Su	0215	8.1	247	22 M	0005	8.1	247
	1535	3.1	94		1545	2.7	82
8 M	0200	7.9	241	23 Tu	0015	8.0	244
	1635	3.3	101		0535	6.3	192
					0925	6.5	198
					1645	3.4	104
9 Tu	0130	7.7	235	24 W	0005	8.0	244
	1725	3.5	107		0615	5.3	162
					1115	6.3	192
					1735	4.1	125
10 W	0110	7.6	232	25 Th	0015	8.0	244
	0640	6.4	195		0650	4.3	131
	1025	6.6	201		1250	6.3	192
	1805	3.8	116		1825	4.9	149
11 Th	0105	7.6	232	26 F	0035	8.2	250
	0700	5.5	168		0730	3.3	101
	1205	6.7	204		1540	6.6	201
	1840	4.2	128		1905	5.7	174
12 F	0110	7.7	235	27 Sa	0100	8.3	253
	0730	4.6	140		0805	2.5	76
	1315	6.8	207		1700	7.0	213
	1915	4.8	146		1945	6.4	195
13 Sa	0125	8.0	244	28 Su	0125	8.4	256
	0805	3.5	107		0845	1.9	58
	1415	6.9	210		1805	7.3	223
	1950	5.4	165		2020	7.0	213
14 Su	0145	8.3	253	29 M	0145	8.4	256
	0845	2.5	76		0920	1.5	46
	1520	7.1	216		1910	7.7	235
	2025	6.1	186		2055	7.5	229
15 M	0210	8.6	262	30 Tu	0155	8.4	256
	0925	1.6	49		1000	1.3	40
	1640	7.2	219		2015	7.9	241
	2100	6.7	204		2125	7.8	238

MAY

Day	h m	ft	cm	Day	h m	ft	cm
1 W	0125	8.5	259	16 Th	0135	9.5	290
	1040	1.3	40		1040	-0.4	-12
					2050	8.3	253
					2210	8.2	250
2 Th	0125	8.4	256	17 F	0210	9.3	283
	1120	1.5	46		1125	0.0	0
					2125	8.4	256
					2325	8.1	247
3 F	0130	8.3	253	18 Sa	0245	8.8	268
	1200	1.7	52		1215	0.6	18
					2200	8.3	253
4 Sa	0110	8.2	250	19 Su	0100	7.8	238
	1240	2.1	64		0320	8.0	244
	2310	8.1	247		1310	1.5	46
					2225	8.3	253
5 Su	1325	2.5	76	20 M	1400	2.5	76
	2320	8.0	244		2230	8.2	250
6 M	1415	3.0	91	21 Tu	0525	6.0	183
	2325	7.9	241		0750	6.1	186
					1455	3.5	107
					2235	8.2	250
7 Tu	1505	3.5	107	22 W	0535	4.9	149
	2330	7.8	238		1010	5.6	171
					1550	4.6	140
					2250	8.3	253
8 W	0700	5.9	180	23 Th	0605	3.8	116
	0755	5.9	180		1410	5.9	180
	1555	4.1	125		1645	5.6	171
	2330	7.8	238		2310	8.4	256
9 Th	0615	5.1	155	24 F	0640	2.9	88
	1055	5.8	177		1535	6.6	201
	1640	4.8	146		1735	6.4	195
	2335	7.9	241		2335	8.4	256
10 F	0635	4.0	122	25 Sa	0715	2.2	67
	1235	6.0	183		1645	7.2	219
	1725	5.4	165		1820	7.1	216
	2350	8.2	250				
11 Sa	0705	2.9	88	26 Su	0000	8.5	259
	1445	6.4	195		0750	1.6	49
	1810	6.1	186		1745	7.7	235
					1905	7.6	232
12 Su	0010	8.5	259	27 M	0010	8.5	259
	0740	1.8	55		0825	1.2	37
	1650	7.0	213		2340	8.6	262
	1855	6.8	207				
13 M	0030	8.9	271	28 Tu	0900	1.0	30
	0825	0.8	24		1945	8.1	247
	1800	7.5	229		2010	8.1	247
	1935	7.4	226		2355	8.7	265
14 Tu	0050	9.2	280	29 W	0940	0.9	27
	0905	0.1	3				
	1905	7.9	241				
	2020	7.8	238				
15 W	0110	9.5	290	30 Th	0020	8.6	262
	0950	-0.3	-9		1015	1.0	30
	2000	8.1	247		2110	8.2	250
	2110	8.1	247		2140	8.2	250
				31 F	0045	8.5	259
					1055	1.2	37
					2120	8.2	250
					2255	8.1	247

JUNE

Day	h m	ft	cm	Day	h m	ft	cm
1 Sa	0105	8.2	250	16 Su	0330	8.2	250
	1130	1.5	46		1150	1.0	30
	2130	8.1	247		2040	8.2	250
2 Su	0025	7.9	241	17 M	0050	6.9	210
	0110	7.9	241		0455	7.2	219
	1205	2.0	61		1235	2.2	67
	2145	8.1	247		2035	8.3	253
3 M	1240	2.5	76	18 Tu	0230	6.0	183
	2155	8.0	244		0625	6.2	189
					1320	3.4	104
					2050	8.4	256
4 Tu	1315	3.2	98	19 W	0410	4.9	149
	2155	8.0	244		0820	5.5	168
					1400	4.6	140
					2115	8.5	259
5 W	1350	3.9	119	20 Th	0500	3.8	116
	2150	8.0	244		1320	5.7	174
					1430	5.7	174
					2145	8.5	259
6 Th	0530	5.0	152	21 F	0540	3.0	91
	0855	5.4	165		2210	8.6	262
	1420	4.7	143				
	2200	8.1	247				
7 F	0535	4.0	122	22 Sa	0615	2.3	70
	2210	8.4	256		2225	8.6	262
8 Sa	0600	2.9	88	23 Su	0655	1.8	55
	2230	8.7	265		2220	8.6	262
9 Su	0640	1.7	52	24 M	0730	1.4	43
	2250	9.1	277		2220	8.7	265
10 M	0720	0.7	21	25 Tu	0805	1.2	37
	2315	9.5	290		2250	8.7	265
11 Tu	0805	-0.1	-3	26 W	0845	1.1	34
	2350	9.8	299		2330	8.7	265
12 W	0850	-0.6	-18	27 Th	0920	1.0	30
	1915	8.2	250		2005	8.1	247
	1950	8.2	250		2035	8.1	247
13 Th	0035	9.8	299	28 F	0015	8.6	262
	0935	-0.7	-21		0955	1.1	34
	1940	8.3	253		2010	8.0	244
	2105	8.2	250		2140	7.9	241
14 F	0125	9.6	293	29 Sa	0055	8.4	256
	1020	-0.5	-15		1030	1.4	43
	2005	8.3	253		2010	8.0	244
	2215	8.0	244		2240	7.7	235
15 Sa	0225	9.0	274	30 Su	0135	8.0	244
	1105	0.1	3		1100	1.7	52
	2030	8.2	250		2015	7.9	241
	2330	7.5	229		2340	7.3	223

Time meridian 120° W. 0000 is midnight. 1200 is noon.
Heights are referred to the Canadian chart datum of soundings. Subtract 2.5 feet (0.8 meter) to refer these levels to the datum of N.O.S. charts.

VICTORIA

1991 TIDE TABLES

Times and Heights of High and Low Waters

JULY

Day	h m	ft	cm	Day	h m	ft	cm
1 M	0205	7.5	229	16 Tu	0025	5.6	171
	1135	2.3	70		0520	6.7	204
	2010	7.9	241		1200	3.3	101
					1905	8.4	256
2 Tu	0045	6.8	207	17 W	0140	4.8	146
	0240	6.9	210		0645	5.9	180
	1205	3.0	91		1235	4.5	137
	2000	8.0	244		1935	8.5	259
3 W	0155	6.1	186	18 Th	0300	4.0	122
	0325	6.1	186		1120	5.7	174
	1230	3.7	113		1255	5.6	171
	2005	8.1	247		2005	8.6	262
4 Th	0305	5.2	158	19 F	0410	3.3	101
	0710	5.5	168		2030	8.6	262
	1255	4.6	140				
	2020	8.2	250				
5 F	0400	4.3	131	20 Sa	0505	2.7	82
	2035	8.5	259		2050	8.5	259
6 Sa	0445	3.2	98	21 Su	0550	2.3	70
	2055	8.8	268		2050	8.5	259
7 Su	0530	2.2	67	22 M	0630	1.9	58
	2115	9.2	280		2105	8.6	262
8 M	0615	1.2	37	23 Tu	0710	1.7	52
	2150	9.5	290		2150	8.6	262
9 Tu	0700	0.4	12	24 W	0750	1.6	49
	2240	9.8	299		2245	8.6	262
10 W	0745	-0.2	-6	25 Th	0825	1.5	46
	2340	9.8	299		1850	7.9	241
					1945	7.9	241
					2350	8.5	259
11 Th	0830	-0.4	-12	26 F	0900	1.5	46
	1830	8.1	247		1850	7.7	235
	1955	8.0	244		2035	7.6	232
12 F	0050	9.6	293	27 Sa	0055	8.3	253
	0915	-0.3	-9		0930	1.7	52
	1850	8.0	244		1845	7.6	232
	2105	7.6	232		2125	7.2	219
13 Sa	0200	9.2	280	28 Su	0155	8.0	244
	1000	0.2	6		1000	2.0	61
	1855	7.9	241		1810	7.6	232
	2210	7.0	213		2215	6.8	207
14 Su	0305	8.5	259	29 M	0250	7.6	232
	1040	1.1	34		1030	2.5	76
	1815	8.0	244		1755	7.7	235
	2315	6.4	195		2305	6.2	189
15 M	0410	7.7	235	30 Tu	0345	7.1	216
	1120	2.1	64		1100	3.1	94
	1835	8.2	250		1805	7.9	241
					2355	5.6	171
				31 W	0450	6.6	201
					1130	3.9	119
					1825	8.1	247

AUGUST

Day	h m	ft	cm	Day	h m	ft	cm
1 Th	0050	4.9	149	16 F	0155	3.4	104
	0605	6.0	183		1850	8.4	256
	1155	4.8	146				
	1845	8.2	250				
2 F	0145	4.2	128	17 Sa	0310	3.1	94
	0740	5.7	174		1910	8.4	256
	0930	5.6	171				
	1905	8.4	256				
3 Sa	0250	3.4	104	18 Su	0420	2.8	85
	1925	8.7	265		1920	8.3	253
4 Su	0355	2.6	79	19 M	0515	2.6	79
	1950	9.0	274		1945	8.3	253
5 M	0500	1.8	55	20 Tu	0600	2.4	73
	2030	9.3	283		1645	8.0	244
					1750	8.0	244
					2035	8.2	250
6 Tu	0555	1.2	37	21 W	0645	2.3	70
	2125	9.4	287		1700	7.9	241
					1830	7.8	238
					2145	8.1	247
7 W	0645	0.7	21	22 Th	0725	2.2	67
	2240	9.4	287		1715	7.6	232
					1910	7.5	229
					2330	8.1	247
8 Th	0730	0.4	12	23 F	0755	2.3	70
	1710	7.8	238		1710	7.4	226
	1855	7.6	232		1945	7.1	216
9 F	0005	9.3	283	24 Sa	0040	8.0	244
	0815	0.5	15		0830	2.4	73
	1715	7.6	232		1610	7.3	223
	2000	7.0	213		2025	6.5	198
10 Sa	0115	9.0	274	25 Su	0135	7.9	241
	0855	1.0	30		0900	2.7	82
	1610	7.7	235		1555	7.4	226
	2100	6.4	195		2110	5.9	180
11 Su	0220	8.5	259	26 M	0225	7.6	232
	0935	1.7	52		0925	3.2	98
	1625	7.9	241		1610	7.6	232
	2200	5.6	171		2150	5.3	162
12 M	0320	7.9	241	27 Tu	0320	7.3	223
	1015	2.6	79		0955	3.8	116
	1655	8.2	250		1630	7.8	238
	2255	4.9	149		2235	4.6	140
13 Tu	0425	7.2	219	28 W	0415	7.0	213
	1050	3.7	113		1025	4.5	137
	1725	8.4	256		1650	8.1	247
	2350	4.2	128		2320	4.0	122
14 W	0535	6.5	198	29 Th	0515	6.6	201
	1125	4.8	146		1055	5.3	162
	1755	8.5	259		1715	8.2	250
15 Th	0050	3.7	113	30 F	0010	3.4	104
	0735	6.0	183		0630	6.3	192
	1150	5.8	177		1120	6.0	183
	1825	8.5	259		1735	8.4	256
				31 Sa	0105	2.9	88
					1750	8.6	262

SEPTEMBER

Day	h m	ft	cm	Day	h m	ft	cm
1 Su	0205	2.6	79	16 M	0315	3.0	91
	1810	8.8	268		1455	8.0	244
2 M	0315	2.2	67	17 Tu	0425	3.0	91
	1855	8.9	271		1500	8.0	244
3 Tu	0430	1.9	58	18 W	0520	3.1	94
	1955	8.8	268		1515	7.8	238
					1820	7.4	226
					2005	7.5	229
4 W	0530	1.6	49	19 Th	0605	3.1	94
	1525	7.8	238		1515	7.5	229
	1655	7.7	235		1840	7.0	213
	2125	8.6	262		2230	7.3	223
5 Th	0620	1.6	49	20 F	0645	3.2	98
	1530	7.6	232		1425	7.4	226
	1810	7.2	219		1905	6.5	198
	2315	8.5	259				
6 F	0705	1.7	52	21 Sa	0000	7.3	223
	1440	7.5	229		0715	3.5	107
	1910	6.4	195		1410	7.4	226
					1935	5.8	177
7 Sa	0030	8.3	253	22 Su	0055	7.3	223
	0745	2.1	64		0750	3.8	116
	1430	7.7	235		1415	7.5	229
	2000	5.5	168		2010	5.1	155
8 Su	0135	8.1	247	23 M	0150	7.3	223
	0830	2.8	85		0815	4.3	131
	1455	7.9	241		1435	7.7	235
	2050	4.7	143		2045	4.2	128
9 M	0240	7.7	235	24 Tu	0245	7.3	223
	0905	3.6	110		0845	4.9	149
	1520	8.2	250		1455	8.0	244
	2140	3.9	119		2125	3.5	107
10 Tu	0340	7.3	223	25 W	0340	7.2	219
	0945	4.6	140		0920	5.5	168
	1550	8.4	256		1515	8.2	250
	2230	3.3	101		2210	2.8	85
11 W	0445	7.0	213	26 Th	0440	7.1	216
	1020	5.5	168		0950	6.1	186
	1620	8.5	259		1540	8.5	259
	2315	2.9	88		2250	2.3	70
12 Th	0625	6.7	204	27 F	0555	7.0	213
	1050	6.3	192		1025	6.8	207
	1650	8.4	256		1555	8.6	262
					2340	1.9	58
13 F	0005	2.7	82	28 Sa	0945	7.4	226
	0950	7.0	213		1050	7.3	223
	1110	7.0	213		1600	8.8	268
	1710	8.4	256				
14 Sa	0100	2.8	85	29 Su	0030	1.8	55
	1720	8.2	250		1605	8.8	268
15 Su	0205	2.9	88	30 M	0130	1.9	58
	1715	8.1	247		1645	8.7	265

Time meridian 120° W. 0000 is midnight. 1200 is noon.
Heights are referred to the Canadian chart datum of soundings. Subtract 2.5 feet (0.8 meter) to refer these levels to the datum of N.O.S. charts.

1991 TIDE TABLES

VICTORIA

For Daylight Saving Time, add one hour.

Times and Heights of High and Low Waters

OCTOBER

Day	h m	ft	cm	Day	h m	ft	cm
1 Tu	0240	2.1	64	16 W	0310	3.4	104
	1305	8.0	244		1245	8.0	244
	1425	8.0	244				
	1755	8.3	253				
2 W	0350	2.3	70	17 Th	0410	3.7	113
	1315	8.0	244		1230	7.9	241
	1630	7.5	229				
	1945	7.8	238				
3 Th	0450	2.6	79	18 F	0500	4.1	125
	1320	7.8	238		1230	7.8	238
	1735	6.7	204		1840	6.1	186
	2215	7.4	226		2255	6.5	198
4 F	0545	3.0	91	19 Sa	0545	4.5	137
	1255	7.8	238		1235	7.8	238
	1825	5.8	177		1855	5.3	162
	2345	7.3	223				
5 Sa	0630	3.5	107	20 Su	0015	6.6	201
	1305	8.0	244		0620	5.0	152
	1910	4.8	146		1245	7.9	241
					1920	4.4	134
6 Su	0100	7.3	223	21 M	0120	6.8	207
	0715	4.2	128		0655	5.5	168
	1330	8.2	250		1300	8.1	247
	1955	3.8	116		1950	3.5	107
7 M	0205	7.3	223	22 Tu	0225	7.0	213
	0755	5.0	152		0725	6.1	186
	1355	8.4	256		1315	8.4	256
	2040	3.0	91		2025	2.5	76
8 Tu	0310	7.3	223	23 W	0325	7.3	223
	0835	5.8	177		0800	6.6	201
	1425	8.5	259		1340	8.7	265
	2120	2.4	73		2105	1.7	52
9 W	0440	7.3	223	24 Th	0605	7.5	229
	0915	6.5	198		0840	7.2	219
	1450	8.6	262		1355	9.0	274
	2205	2.0	61		2145	1.2	37
10 Th	0720	7.5	229	25 F	0725	7.9	241
	0950	7.1	216		0915	7.7	235
	1510	8.6	262		1400	9.2	280
	2245	1.9	58		2230	0.8	24
11 F	0835	7.7	235	26 Sa	0830	8.1	247
	1025	7.6	232		1000	8.1	247
	1520	8.5	259		1410	9.3	283
	2330	2.0	61		2315	0.8	24
12 Sa	1000	8.0	244	27 Su	0935	8.4	256
	1050	7.9	241		1050	8.3	253
	1450	8.4	256		1435	9.2	280
13 Su	0015	2.3	70	28 M	0005	1.1	34
	1415	8.3	253		1025	8.5	259
					1200	8.4	256
					1510	8.9	271
14 M	0105	2.6	79	29 Tu	0100	1.6	49
	1300	8.2	250		1100	8.5	259
					1345	8.2	250
					1545	8.3	253
15 Tu	0205	3.0	91	30 W	0200	2.2	67
	1255	8.1	247		1125	8.4	256
				31 Th	0300	3.0	91
					1130	8.4	256
					1715	6.5	198
					2050	6.7	204

NOVEMBER

Day	h m	ft	cm	Day	h m	ft	cm
1 F	0405	3.8	116	16 Sa	0305	4.9	149
	1125	8.4	256		1100	8.4	256
	1750	5.3	162		1820	5.1	155
	2255	6.4	195		2325	5.9	180
2 Sa	0500	4.7	143	17 Su	0350	5.6	171
	1140	8.5	259		1105	8.5	259
	1830	4.3	131		1830	4.2	128
3 Su	0045	6.5	198	18 M	0250	6.4	195
	0550	5.5	168		0435	6.3	192
	1205	8.7	265		1120	8.7	265
	1905	3.3	101		1855	3.2	98
4 M	0335	7.0	213	19 Tu	0410	7.0	213
	0635	6.3	192		0525	7.0	213
	1230	8.8	268		1135	9.0	274
	1945	2.4	73		1925	2.2	67
5 Tu	0445	7.5	229	20 W	0510	7.6	232
	0720	7.0	213		0615	7.6	232
	1255	8.9	271		1155	9.3	283
	2025	1.8	55		2005	1.3	40
6 W	0550	7.9	241	21 Th	0600	8.1	247
	0800	7.6	232		0700	8.1	247
	1320	9.0	274		1205	9.7	296
	2100	1.4	43		2045	0.5	15
7 Th	0650	8.2	250	22 F	0655	8.5	259
	0845	8.0	244		0750	8.4	256
	1325	9.0	274		1230	9.9	302
	2140	1.3	40		2130	0.1	3
8 F	0745	8.4	256	23 Sa	0740	8.7	265
	0925	8.3	253		0845	8.7	265
	1305	8.9	271		1300	10.0	305
	2220	1.3	40		2210	0.0	0
9 Sa	0845	8.6	262	24 Su	0820	8.9	271
	1005	8.5	259		0950	8.8	268
	1310	8.9	271		1335	9.8	299
	2300	1.6	49		2300	0.3	9
10 Su	0935	8.6	262	25 M	0855	8.9	271
	1100	8.6	262		1100	8.7	265
	1320	8.7	265		1415	9.3	283
	2340	1.9	58		2345	0.9	27
11 M	1010	8.6	262	26 Tu	0925	8.9	271
					1225	8.3	253
					1450	8.6	262
12 Tu	0020	2.4	73	27 W	0035	1.7	52
	1030	8.6	262		0945	8.9	271
					1410	7.6	232
					1515	7.6	232
13 W	0100	3.0	91	28 Th	0120	2.8	85
	1040	8.5	259		0945	8.9	271
					1730	6.4	195
					1905	6.5	198
14 Th	0140	3.6	110	29 F	0210	3.9	119
	1050	8.4	256		0950	9.0	274
					1720	5.3	162
					2130	5.9	180
15 F	0220	4.2	128	30 Sa	0300	5.1	155
	1055	8.4	256		1015	9.1	277
	1850	5.9	180		1745	4.1	125
	2015	5.9	180				

DECEMBER

Day	h m	ft	cm	Day	h m	ft	cm
1 Su	0200	6.3	192	16 M	0940	9.1	277
	0355	6.2	189		1800	3.5	107
	1040	9.2	280				
	1820	3.2	98				
2 M	0330	7.2	219	17 Tu	0955	9.4	287
	0450	7.1	216		1830	2.4	73
	1105	9.3	283				
	1855	2.4	73				
3 Tu	0435	7.9	241	18 W	1015	9.8	299
	0545	7.8	238		1905	1.5	46
	1130	9.3	283				
	1930	1.8	55				
4 W	0530	8.4	256	19 Th	1040	10.1	308
	0635	8.3	253		1945	0.6	18
	1145	9.4	287				
	2010	1.4	43				
5 Th	0625	8.7	265	20 F	1120	10.4	317
	0725	8.7	265		2030	0.1	3
	1130	9.4	287				
	2045	1.2	37				
6 F	0715	8.9	271	21 Sa	1205	10.5	320
	0810	8.8	268		2110	-0.2	-6
	1140	9.4	287				
	2125	1.2	37				
7 Sa	0755	8.9	271	22 Su	0720	8.9	271
	0900	8.9	271		0835	8.9	271
	1210	9.3	283		1255	10.3	314
	2200	1.3	40		2155	0.0	0
8 Su	0830	8.9	271	23 M	0740	8.9	271
	0955	8.8	268		0950	8.6	262
	1240	9.1	277		1350	9.8	299
	2235	1.5	46		2240	0.5	15
9 M	0850	8.8	268	24 Tu	0800	8.9	271
	1100	8.7	265		1100	8.1	247
	1305	8.8	268		1450	9.0	274
	2315	1.9	58		2320	1.3	40
10 Tu	0900	8.8	268	25 W	0755	8.9	271
	1230	8.4	256		1215	7.5	229
	1305	8.4	256		1615	8.0	244
	2345	2.4	73				
11 W	0910	8.8	268	26 Th	0005	2.4	73
					0745	9.1	277
					1340	6.6	201
					1750	6.9	210
12 Th	0015	3.1	94	27 F	0045	3.7	113
	0915	8.7	265		0810	9.3	283
					1525	5.5	168
					1935	6.0	183
13 F	0045	3.8	116	28 Sa	0120	5.0	152
	0920	8.7	265		0840	9.4	287
					1635	4.4	134
14 Sa	0105	4.6	140	29 Su	0910	9.5	290
	0920	8.8	268		1720	3.4	104
	1745	5.4	165				
	2035	5.6	171				
15 Su	0105	5.4	165	30 M	0940	9.5	290
	0930	8.9	271		1800	2.7	82
	1740	4.5	137	31 Tu	1005	9.5	290
					1840	2.2	67

Time meridian 120° W. 0000 is midnight. 1200 is noon.
Heights are referred to the Canadian chart datum of soundings. Subtract 2.5 feet (0.8 meter) to refer these levels to the datum of N.O.S. charts.

VANCOUVER

1991 **TIDE TABLES**

For Daylight Saving Time, add one hour.

Times and Heights of High and Low Waters

JANUARY

Day	h m	ft	cm	Day	h m	ft	cm
1 Tu	0710	16.4	500	16 W	0715	15.3	466
	1215	11.7	357		1230	11.2	341
	1645	14.5	442		1655	13.2	402
2 W	0020	0.5	15	17 Th	0015	2.8	85
	0745	16.6	506		0740	15.4	469
	1310	11.0	335		1310	10.7	326
	1750	14.0	427		1740	13.0	396
3 Th	0105	1.3	40	18 F	0045	3.1	94
	0825	16.6	506		0800	15.5	472
	1410	10.1	308		1350	10.0	305
	1855	13.2	402		1830	12.6	384
4 F	0145	2.5	76	19 Sa	0120	3.8	116
	0900	16.5	503		0825	15.6	475
	1505	9.1	277		1430	9.2	280
	2000	12.3	375		1925	12.1	369
5 Sa	0230	4.1	125	20 Su	0150	4.8	146
	0930	16.3	497		0850	15.6	475
	1605	8.0	244		1515	8.2	250
	2110	11.5	351		2025	11.7	357
6 Su	0310	5.9	180	21 M	0225	6.1	186
	1005	16.0	488		0910	15.5	472
	1705	6.9	210		1600	7.1	216
	2230	10.9	332		2135	11.4	347
7 M	0350	7.8	238	22 Tu	0305	7.7	235
	1035	15.5	472		0940	15.3	466
	1800	6.0	183		1650	6.0	183
					2300	11.4	347
8 Tu	0015	11.0	335	23 W	0350	9.3	283
	0440	9.6	293		1005	15.1	460
	1105	14.9	454		1745	4.9	149
	1850	5.2	158				
9 W	0215	11.8	360	24 Th	0050	11.9	363
	0550	11.1	338		0455	10.8	329
	1135	14.2	433		1040	14.9	454
	1940	4.5	137		1840	3.9	119
10 Th	0340	12.9	393	25 F	0245	12.9	393
	0725	12.0	366		0620	12.0	366
	1205	13.7	418		1125	14.7	448
	2025	4.0	122		1945	3.0	91
11 F	0430	13.8	421	26 Sa	0355	13.9	424
	0855	12.3	375		0800	12.5	381
	1245	13.4	408		1220	14.5	442
	2110	3.6	110		2045	2.2	67
12 Sa	0510	14.5	442	27 Su	0445	14.8	451
	1000	12.3	375		0915	12.4	378
	1330	13.2	402		1330	14.4	439
	2155	3.3	101		2140	1.5	46
13 Su	0545	14.9	454	28 M	0525	15.3	466
	1045	12.2	372		1020	11.9	363
	1425	13.2	402		1450	14.4	439
	2235	3.0	91		2235	1.2	37
14 M	0620	15.1	460	29 Tu	0605	15.7	479
	1120	11.9	363		1115	11.2	341
	1520	13.3	405		1600	14.4	439
	2310	2.7	82		2320	1.2	37
15 Tu	0645	15.2	463	30 W	0640	15.9	485
	1155	11.6	354		1205	10.3	314
	1605	13.3	405		1705	14.2	433
	2345	2.6	79				
				31 Th	0005	1.8	55
					0710	16.1	491
					1255	9.3	283
					1800	13.8	421

FEBRUARY

Day	h m	ft	cm	Day	h m	ft	cm
1 F	0045	2.7	82	16 Sa	0025	4.3	131
	0740	16.1	491		0710	15.0	457
	1345	8.2	250		1315	7.8	238
	1900	13.2	402		1845	13.0	396
2 Sa	0125	4.1	125	17 Su	0100	5.2	158
	0810	16.0	488		0730	15.1	460
	1430	7.2	219		1355	6.8	207
	2000	12.6	384		1935	12.8	390
3 Su	0200	5.7	174	18 M	0135	6.3	192
	0840	15.7	479		0755	15.2	463
	1520	6.3	192		1435	5.8	177
	2105	12.0	366		2035	12.6	384
4 M	0240	7.4	226	19 Tu	0210	7.7	235
	0905	15.3	466		0820	15.1	460
	1605	5.7	174		1520	4.9	149
	2215	11.7	357		2140	12.4	378
5 Tu	0315	9.0	274	20 W	0255	9.1	277
	0930	14.7	448		0845	14.9	454
	1655	5.3	162		1610	4.2	128
	2350	11.8	360		2300	12.5	381
6 W	0405	10.4	317	21 Th	0345	10.5	320
	0955	14.1	430		0915	14.5	442
	1745	5.0	152		1705	3.8	116
7 Th	0140	12.3	375	22 F	0050	12.8	390
	0510	11.6	354		0455	11.6	354
	1020	13.5	411		0955	14.2	433
	1845	4.9	149		1805	3.4	104
8 F	0300	13.0	396	23 Sa	0225	13.5	411
	0705	12.2	372		0630	12.1	369
	1055	13.0	396		1055	13.7	418
	1940	4.7	143		1920	3.2	98
9 Sa	0350	13.6	415	24 Su	0325	14.1	430
	0845	12.1	369		0810	11.9	363
	1150	12.7	387		1215	13.4	408
	2040	4.4	134		2025	2.9	88
10 Su	0435	14.1	430	25 M	0410	14.6	445
	0945	11.8	360		0920	11.2	341
	1310	12.6	384		1350	13.3	405
	2130	4.0	122		2125	2.7	82
11 M	0510	14.3	436	26 Tu	0450	14.9	454
	1020	11.4	347		1015	10.2	311
	1430	12.7	387		1510	13.4	408
	2210	3.7	113		2220	2.7	82
12 Tu	0540	14.5	442	27 W	0525	15.1	460
	1055	11.0	335		1100	9.1	277
	1530	13.0	396		1615	13.6	415
	2250	3.4	104		2305	3.1	94
13 W	0605	14.6	445	28 Th	0555	15.2	463
	1130	10.4	317		1145	7.9	241
	1620	13.1	399		1715	13.7	418
	2320	3.4	104		2345	3.9	119
14 Th	0630	14.8	451				
	1205	9.7	296				
	1705	13.2	402				
	2355	3.7	113				
15 F	0650	14.9	454				
	1240	8.8	268				
	1755	13.1	399				

MARCH

Day	h m	ft	cm	Day	h m	ft	cm
1 F	0620	15.2	463	16 Sa	0545	14.3	436
	1230	6.8	207		1205	6.2	189
	1810	13.6	415		1800	13.4	408
2 Sa	0025	5.0	152	17 Su	0000	6.2	189
	0650	15.2	463		0610	14.5	442
	1310	5.8	177		1240	5.1	155
	1905	13.4	408		1850	13.5	411
3 Su	0100	6.3	192	18 M	0040	7.2	219
	0715	15.0	457		0630	14.6	445
	1350	5.0	152		1320	4.1	125
	2000	13.1	399		1945	13.6	415
4 M	0140	7.6	232	19 Tu	0120	8.3	253
	0740	14.7	448		0700	14.6	445
	1430	4.6	140		1400	3.3	101
	2055	12.9	393		2045	13.6	415
5 Tu	0215	8.9	271	20 W	0200	9.4	287
	0800	14.2	433		0725	14.5	442
	1510	4.4	134		1445	2.8	85
	2200	12.8	390		2150	13.6	415
6 W	0255	10.0	305	21 Th	0255	10.4	317
	0820	13.7	418		0755	14.1	430
	1550	4.5	137		1535	2.7	82
	2315	12.7	387		2305	13.6	415
7 Th	0345	11.0	335	22 F	0355	11.2	341
	0845	13.1	399		0835	13.6	415
	1635	4.7	143		1630	2.9	88
8 F	0045	12.9	393	23 Sa	0030	13.8	421
	0455	11.6	354		0520	11.6	354
	0915	12.6	384		0930	13.0	396
	1735	5.0	152		1740	3.3	101
9 Sa	0155	13.2	402	24 Su	0145	14.0	427
	0710	11.7	357		0705	11.2	341
	1000	12.0	366		1055	12.3	375
	1840	5.1	155		1850	3.7	113
10 Su	0255	13.4	408	25 M	0235	14.3	436
	0835	11.3	344		0820	10.3	314
	1120	11.7	357		1245	12.0	366
	1950	5.1	155		2000	4.0	122
11 M	0340	13.7	418	26 Tu	0320	14.4	439
	0920	10.8	329		0915	9.1	277
	1310	11.6	354		1420	12.2	372
	2045	4.9	149		2100	4.4	134
12 Tu	0415	13.8	421	27 W	0355	14.5	442
	0955	10.1	308		1000	7.8	238
	1430	12.0	366		1530	12.6	384
	2135	4.7	143		2155	4.9	149
13 W	0440	13.9	424	28 Th	0430	14.5	442
	1025	9.3	283		1045	6.5	198
	1530	12.4	378		1630	13.0	396
	2215	4.7	143		2240	5.6	171
14 Th	0505	14.0	427	29 F	0500	14.5	442
	1055	8.4	256		1125	5.4	165
	1620	12.8	390		1725	13.4	408
	2250	4.9	149		2325	6.5	198
15 F	0525	14.2	433	30 Sa	0525	14.4	439
	1130	7.3	223		1200	4.4	134
	1710	13.1	399		1820	13.7	418
	2325	5.4	165				
				31 Su	0005	7.5	229
					0550	14.2	433
					1240	3.7	113
					1910	13.8	421

Time meridian 120° W. 0000 is midnight. 1200 is noon.
Heights are referred to the Canadian chart datum of soundings. Subtract 3.8 feet (1.2 meters) to refer these levels to the datum of N.O.S. charts.

1991 TIDE TABLES

VANCOUVER

For Daylight Saving Time, add one hour.

Time and Heights of High and Low Waters

APRIL

Day	h m	ft	cm	Day	h m	ft	cm
1 M	0040	8.5	259	16 Tu	0020	9.3	283
	0615	14.0	427		0535	14.3	436
	1315	3.2	98		1250	1.7	52
	2000	13.9	424		1955	14.6	445
2 Tu	0120	9.4	287	17 W	0110	10.1	308
	0635	13.7	418		0605	14.3	436
	1350	3.1	94		1335	1.3	40
	2050	13.8	421		2050	14.7	448
3 W	0200	10.2	311	18 Th	0200	10.7	326
	0655	13.3	405		0640	14.0	427
	1425	3.3	101		1420	1.3	40
	2145	13.7	418		2155	14.7	448
4 Th	0245	10.8	329	19 F	0300	11.1	338
	0720	12.8	390		0725	13.4	408
	1500	3.7	113		1510	1.8	55
	2245	13.6	415		2255	14.7	448
5 F	0340	11.2	341	20 Sa	0415	11.2	341
	0745	12.3	375		0820	12.6	384
	1540	4.1	125		1610	2.5	76
	2350	13.5	411				
6 Sa	0505	11.3	344	21 Su	0000	14.7	448
	0820	11.7	357		0545	10.7	326
	1630	4.7	143		0940	11.7	357
					1710	3.5	107
7 Su	0050	13.5	411	22 M	0055	14.7	448
	0710	11.0	335		0710	9.6	293
	0920	11.1	338		1125	11.1	338
	1730	5.2	158		1820	4.6	140
8 M	0145	13.5	411	23 Tu	0140	14.6	445
	0810	10.3	314		0810	8.3	253
	1100	10.7	326		1310	11.0	335
	1840	5.6	171		1930	5.6	171
9 Tu	0225	13.5	411	24 W	0225	14.5	442
	0850	9.5	290		0900	6.9	210
	1300	10.7	326		1435	11.5	351
	1945	5.9	180		2030	6.5	198
10 W	0300	13.6	415	25 Th	0300	14.3	436
	0920	8.5	259		0940	5.5	168
	1425	11.2	341		1545	12.2	372
	2040	6.1	186		2130	7.4	226
11 Th	0330	13.6	415	26 F	0330	14.1	430
	0950	7.4	226		1020	4.4	134
	1525	11.9	363		1645	13.0	396
	2130	6.5	198		2220	8.2	250
12 F	0355	13.7	418	27 Sa	0400	13.9	424
	1020	6.2	189		1055	3.4	104
	1620	12.7	387		1740	13.6	415
	2215	7.0	213		2305	9.0	274
13 Sa	0415	13.8	421	28 Su	0430	13.7	418
	1055	4.9	149		1130	2.8	85
	1715	13.3	405		1830	14.1	430
	2255	7.7	235		2345	9.7	296
14 Su	0440	14.0	427	29 M	0450	13.5	411
	1130	3.6	110		1205	2.4	73
	1805	13.9	424		1915	14.4	439
	2340	8.5	259				
15 M	0505	14.2	433	30 Tu	0030	10.3	314
	1210	2.5	76		0515	13.3	405
	1900	14.3	436		1240	2.3	70
					2000	14.5	442

MAY

Day	h m	ft	cm	Day	h m	ft	cm
1 W	0110	10.7	326	16 Th	0100	11.1	338
	0535	13.0	396		0530	14.2	433
	1315	2.4	73		1315	0.3	9
	2040	14.5	442		2050	15.5	472
2 Th	0150	10.9	332	17 F	0200	11.2	341
	0600	12.7	387		0620	13.6	415
	1345	2.7	82		1405	0.7	21
	2125	14.4	439		2140	15.5	472
3 F	0240	11.1	338	18 Sa	0305	10.9	332
	0630	12.3	375		0720	12.8	390
	1420	3.1	94		1455	1.6	49
	2210	14.3	436		2230	15.5	472
4 Sa	0340	11.1	338	19 Su	0420	10.3	314
	0705	11.7	357		0835	11.9	363
	1500	3.7	113		1545	2.8	85
	2300	14.2	433		2320	15.4	469
5 Su	0500	10.8	329	20 M	0540	9.2	280
	0755	11.1	338		1000	11.0	335
	1540	4.4	134		1640	4.3	131
	2345	14.0	427				
6 M	0625	10.2	311	21 Tu	0005	15.2	463
	0910	10.5	320		0650	7.9	241
	1630	5.2	158		1140	10.6	323
					1740	5.9	180
7 Tu	0025	13.9	424	22 W	0045	14.9	454
	0720	9.3	283		0745	6.5	198
	1055	10.1	308		1320	10.8	329
	1730	6.0	183		1850	7.4	226
8 W	0105	13.8	421	23 Th	0125	14.5	442
	0800	8.3	253		0830	5.1	155
	1245	10.3	314		1450	11.5	351
	1835	6.9	210		2000	8.6	262
9 Th	0135	13.7	418	24 F	0200	14.1	430
	0830	7.1	216		0910	4.0	122
	1410	10.9	332		1605	12.5	381
	1940	7.7	235		2100	9.6	293
10 F	0205	13.7	418	25 Sa	0230	13.8	421
	0905	5.7	174		0950	3.2	98
	1520	11.9	363		1705	13.4	408
	2045	8.4	256		2200	10.3	314
11 Sa	0235	13.7	418	26 Su	0300	13.5	411
	0940	4.3	131		1030	2.6	79
	1620	12.9	393		1750	14.1	430
	2140	9.1	277		2250	10.7	326
12 Su	0305	13.9	424	27 M	0330	13.2	402
	1020	2.9	88		1105	2.2	67
	1720	13.8	421		1835	14.5	442
	2230	9.8	299		2335	11.0	335
13 M	0335	14.1	430	28 Tu	0400	13.1	399
	1100	1.7	52		1140	2.1	64
	1810	14.5	442		1910	14.7	448
	2320	10.4	317				
14 Tu	0410	14.3	436	29 W	0015	11.2	341
	1145	0.8	24		0425	13.0	396
	1905	15.1	460		1215	2.1	64
					1950	14.8	451
15 W	0010	10.8	329	30 Th	0055	11.2	341
	0450	14.4	439		0455	12.8	390
	1230	0.3	9		1250	2.3	70
	1955	15.4	469		2025	14.8	451
				31 F	0140	11.2	341
					0530	12.5	381
					1320	2.6	79
					2100	14.8	451

JUNE

Day	h m	ft	cm	Day	h m	ft	cm
1 Sa	0225	11.0	335	16 Su	0255	10.0	305
	0610	12.1	369		0735	12.6	384
	1355	3.0	91		1435	2.2	67
	2135	14.7	448		2155	15.9	485
2 Su	0320	10.7	326	17 M	0400	8.9	271
	0700	11.5	351		0850	11.7	357
	1430	3.6	110		1520	3.8	116
	2210	14.6	445		2230	15.7	479
3 M	0420	10.1	308	18 Tu	0510	7.7	235
	0800	10.9	332		1010	10.9	332
	1505	4.4	134		1610	5.5	168
	2245	14.5	442		2310	15.3	466
4 Tu	0520	9.3	283	19 W	0610	6.4	195
	0920	10.4	317		1140	10.7	326
	1545	5.4	165		1705	7.4	226
	2315	14.3	436		2345	14.9	454
5 W	0610	8.3	253	20 Th	0705	5.3	162
	1050	10.1	308		1325	11.1	338
	1635	6.6	201		1810	9.0	274
	2345	14.2	433				
6 Th	0655	7.1	216	21 F	0020	14.4	439
	1225	10.4	317		0750	4.3	131
	1735	7.9	241		1500	12.0	366
					1925	10.2	311
7 F	0015	14.1	430	22 Sa	0055	13.9	424
	0740	5.8	177		0840	3.6	110
	1400	11.1	338		1610	12.9	393
	1845	9.1	277		2040	11.0	335
8 Sa	0050	14.0	427	23 Su	0130	13.4	408
	0820	4.4	134		0920	3.1	94
	1520	12.2	372		1705	13.7	418
	2000	10.1	308		2145	11.3	344
9 Su	0125	14.1	430	24 M	0210	13.1	399
	0905	3.1	94		1005	2.7	82
	1625	13.3	405		1745	14.3	436
	2110	10.8	329		2235	11.5	351
10 M	0200	14.2	433	25 Tu	0245	13.0	396
	0950	1.8	55		1040	2.5	76
	1720	14.3	436		1820	14.6	445
	2205	11.3	344		2320	11.4	347
11 Tu	0245	14.4	439	26 W	0325	12.9	393
	1040	0.8	24		1120	2.4	73
	1815	15.0	457		1855	14.7	448
	2305	11.5	351				
12 W	0335	14.5	442	27 Th	0000	11.3	344
	1125	0.2	6		0405	12.9	393
	1900	15.4	469		1155	2.4	73
	2355	11.5	351		1930	14.7	448
13 Th	0425	14.5	442	28 F	0040	11.1	338
	1215	-0.1	-3		0450	12.8	390
	1945	15.7	479		1230	2.5	76
					2000	14.8	451
14 F	0055	11.2	341	29 Sa	0120	10.8	329
	0525	14.1	430		0530	12.6	384
	1300	0.2	6		1300	2.8	85
	2030	15.9	485		2030	14.8	451
15 Sa	0150	10.7	326	30 Su	0200	10.4	317
	0625	13.5	411		0620	12.2	372
	1350	1.0	30		1330	3.2	98
	2110	15.9	485		2055	14.8	451

Time meridian 120° W. 0000 is midnight. 1200 is noon.
Heights are referred to the Canadian chart datum of soundings. Subtract 3.8 feet (1.2 meters) to refer these levels to the datum of N.O.S. charts.

VANCOUVER

1991 TIDE TABLES

For Daylight Saving Time, add one hour.

Times and Heights of High and Low Waters

JULY

Day	h m	ft	cm	Day	h m	ft	cm
1 M	0245	9.9	302	16 Tu	0330	7.3	223
	0710	11.7	357		0850	11.9	363
	1405	4.0	122		1455	5.2	158
	2120	14.8	451		2140	15.5	472
2 Tu	0335	9.1	277	17 W	0425	6.3	192
	0810	11.1	338		1005	11.3	344
	1435	5.0	152		1540	7.0	213
	2145	14.7	448		2210	15.1	460
3 W	0420	8.2	250	18 Th	0520	5.4	165
	0920	10.8	329		1135	11.2	341
	1515	6.2	189		1630	8.8	268
	2210	14.6	445		2245	14.5	442
4 Th	0510	7.2	219	19 F	0615	4.7	143
	1035	10.6	323		1320	11.6	354
	1600	7.6	232		1735	10.2	311
	2240	14.4	439		2320	13.9	424
5 F	0555	6.0	183	20 Sa	0710	4.3	131
	1210	10.9	332		1450	12.4	378
	1655	9.1	277		1900	11.2	341
	2310	14.3	436		2355	13.3	405
6 Sa	0645	4.8	146	21 Su	0800	3.9	119
	1350	11.7	357		1555	13.2	402
	1805	10.3	314		2025	11.5	351
	2345	14.2	433				
7 Su	0740	3.6	110	22 M	0040	12.9	393
	1520	12.7	387		0850	3.6	110
	1930	11.3	344		1640	13.7	418
					2130	11.5	351
8 M	0030	14.3	436	23 Tu	0135	12.8	390
	0835	2.5	76		0940	3.3	101
	1625	13.7	418		1720	14.1	430
	2045	11.7	357		2220	11.4	347
9 Tu	0120	14.4	439	24 W	0230	12.8	390
	0930	1.5	46		1025	3.1	94
	1715	14.5	442		1755	14.3	436
	2150	11.8	360		2300	11.2	341
10 W	0220	14.5	442	25 Th	0325	12.9	393
	1020	0.8	24		1100	2.9	88
	1800	15.0	457		1830	14.3	436
	2250	11.6	354		2335	10.8	329
11 Th	0325	14.5	442	26 F	0410	13.0	396
	1110	0.4	12		1135	2.9	88
	1840	15.4	469		1855	14.4	439
	2345	11.1	338				
12 F	0430	14.4	439	27 Sa	0015	10.4	317
	1200	0.4	12		0455	12.9	393
	1920	15.7	479		1205	3.0	91
					1920	14.5	442
13 Sa	0040	10.4	317	28 Su	0050	9.9	302
	0535	14.0	427		0540	12.7	387
	1245	0.9	27		1235	3.4	104
	1955	15.8	482		1940	14.6	445
14 Su	0135	9.5	290	29 M	0130	9.2	280
	0635	13.4	408		0625	12.4	378
	1330	2.0	61		1305	4.0	122
	2030	15.9	485		2005	14.7	448
15 M	0235	8.4	256	30 Tu	0210	8.5	259
	0740	12.6	384		0720	12.0	366
	1410	3.5	107		1340	4.9	149
	2105	15.8	482		2025	14.7	448
				31 W	0250	7.6	232
					0815	11.7	357
					1410	6.1	186
					2050	14.7	448

AUGUST

Day	h m	ft	cm	Day	h m	ft	cm
1 Th	0330	6.7	204	16 F	0430	4.7	143
	0915	11.5	351		1120	12.0	366
	1450	7.4	226		1600	9.9	302
	2115	14.5	442		2140	13.8	421
2 F	0415	5.8	177	17 Sa	0520	4.6	140
	1030	11.5	351		1255	12.3	375
	1535	8.8	268		1705	10.9	332
	2140	14.4	439		2215	13.1	399
3 Sa	0510	4.9	149	18 Su	0620	4.6	140
	1200	11.7	357		1415	12.8	390
	1635	10.1	308		1845	11.4	347
	2215	14.2	433		2300	12.6	384
4 Su	0605	4.1	125	19 M	0720	4.5	137
	1350	12.3	375		1515	13.2	402
	1745	11.2	341		2020	11.4	347
	2300	14.1	430				
5 M	0705	3.3	101	20 Tu	0000	12.3	375
	1510	13.1	399		0820	4.4	134
	1915	11.8	360		1605	13.5	411
	2355	14.0	427		2115	11.1	338
6 Tu	0810	2.5	76	21 W	0120	12.2	372
	1605	13.9	424		0910	4.1	125
	2040	11.8	360		1640	13.7	418
					2200	10.7	326
7 W	0105	14.0	427	22 Th	0230	12.4	378
	0910	1.9	58		0955	3.9	119
	1650	14.4	439		1715	13.9	424
	2145	11.3	344		2235	10.2	311
8 Th	0225	14.1	430	23 F	0325	12.7	387
	1005	1.4	43		1035	3.8	116
	1730	14.8	451		1740	14.0	427
	2240	10.6	323		2310	9.6	293
9 F	0335	14.1	430	24 Sa	0415	12.9	393
	1055	1.3	40		1110	3.9	119
	1805	15.1	460		1805	14.0	427
	2335	9.7	296		2345	9.0	274
10 Sa	0440	14.1	430	25 Su	0500	13.0	396
	1140	1.7	52		1140	4.2	128
	1840	15.4	469		1825	14.1	430
11 Su	0025	8.6	262	26 M	0020	8.2	250
	0540	13.8	421		0545	12.9	393
	1225	2.6	79		1210	4.7	143
	1910	15.5	472		1845	14.3	436
12 M	0115	7.5	229	27 Tu	0055	7.3	223
	0640	13.4	408		0630	12.8	390
	1305	3.9	119		1240	5.5	168
	1945	15.5	472		1905	14.4	439
13 Tu	0200	6.4	195	28 W	0130	6.4	195
	0740	12.9	393		0720	12.7	387
	1345	5.4	165		1315	6.6	201
	2015	15.3	466		1930	14.4	439
14 W	0250	5.6	171	29 Th	0210	5.6	171
	0845	12.4	378		0815	12.6	384
	1425	7.0	213		1355	7.7	235
	2045	14.9	454		1950	14.3	436
15 Th	0340	5.0	152	30 F	0250	4.8	146
	0955	12.1	369		0915	12.5	381
	1510	8.6	262		1435	8.9	271
	2110	14.4	439		2020	14.2	433
				31 Sa	0335	4.3	131
					1025	12.5	381
					1525	10.1	308
					2050	14.0	427

SEPTEMBER

Day	h m	ft	cm	Day	h m	ft	cm
1 Su	0430	3.9	119	16 M	0515	4.9	149
	1200	12.6	384		1325	13.2	402
	1630	11.0	335		1855	11.2	341
	2135	13.7	418		2205	11.7	357
2 M	0530	3.6	110	17 Tu	0625	5.2	158
	1335	13.1	399		1420	13.3	405
	1755	11.5	351		2010	10.8	329
	2230	13.4	408		2335	11.4	347
3 Tu	0640	3.3	101	18 W	0730	5.3	162
	1440	13.6	415		1510	13.5	411
	1930	11.4	347		2100	10.2	311
	2350	13.1	399				
4 W	0750	3.1	94	19 Th	0120	11.5	351
	1530	14.1	430		0830	5.2	158
	2045	10.8	329		1545	13.5	411
					2135	9.5	290
5 Th	0120	13.1	399	20 F	0230	11.9	363
	0850	2.9	88		0920	5.2	158
	1610	14.4	439		1615	13.6	415
	2140	9.8	299		2205	8.7	265
6 F	0245	13.3	405	21 Sa	0325	12.3	375
	0945	2.9	88		1000	5.3	162
	1645	14.6	445		1640	13.6	415
	2230	8.6	262		2240	7.9	241
7 Sa	0350	13.6	415	22 Su	0415	12.8	390
	1035	3.3	101		1035	5.6	171
	1720	14.8	451		1700	13.7	418
	2315	7.4	226		2310	6.9	210
8 Su	0455	13.8	421	23 M	0500	13.1	399
	1120	4.0	122		1110	6.1	186
	1750	14.9	454		1720	13.8	421
					2345	5.9	180
9 M	0000	6.2	189	24 Tu	0550	13.4	408
	0550	13.8	421		1145	6.8	207
	1205	5.0	152		1740	14.0	427
	1820	14.9	454				
10 Tu	0045	5.2	158	25 W	0020	4.9	149
	0645	13.7	418		0635	13.6	415
	1245	6.3	192		1220	7.7	235
	1850	14.8	451		1805	14.1	430
11 W	0125	4.4	134	26 Th	0055	4.1	125
	0740	13.5	411		0725	13.7	418
	1325	7.6	232		1300	8.6	262
	1915	14.5	442		1830	14.1	430
12 Th	0210	4.0	122	27 F	0135	3.4	104
	0840	13.3	405		0820	13.8	421
	1405	8.8	268		1340	9.5	290
	1945	14.0	427		1855	14.1	430
13 F	0250	3.9	119	28 Sa	0215	3.0	91
	0940	13.1	399		0920	13.7	418
	1450	9.9	302		1430	10.4	317
	2010	13.5	411		1930	13.8	421
14 Sa	0335	4.1	125	29 Su	0305	2.9	88
	1055	13.0	396		1030	13.7	418
	1545	10.7	326		1530	11.0	335
	2035	12.9	393		2010	13.4	408
15 Su	0420	4.5	137	30 M	0400	3.1	94
	1215	13.0	396		1150	13.8	421
	1700	11.2	341		1645	11.3	344
	2115	12.3	375		2105	12.8	390

Time meridian 120° W. 0000 is midnight. 1200 is noon.
Heights are referred to the Canadian chart datum of soundings. Subtract 3.8 feet (1.2 meters) to refer these levels to the datum of N.O.S. charts.

1991 TIDE TABLES

VANCOUVER

For Daylight Saving Time, add one hour.

Times and Heights of High and Low Waters

OCTOBER

Day	h m	ft	cm	Day	h m	ft	cm
1 Tu	0500	3.4	104	16 W	0510	5.6	171
	1300	14.0	427		1315	13.7	418
	1825	11.0	335		1950	9.9	302
	2225	12.2	372		2320	10.5	320
2 W	0610	3.9	119	17 Th	0620	6.2	189
	1355	14.2	433		1355	13.7	418
	1945	10.1	308		2030	9.1	277
3 Th	0015	12.0	366	18 F	0110	10.7	326
	0725	4.3	131		0725	6.6	201
	1440	14.4	439		1430	13.6	415
	2040	8.9	271		2100	8.1	247
4 F	0150	12.2	372	19 Sa	0225	11.3	344
	0825	4.7	143		0825	7.0	213
	1520	14.5	442		1500	13.6	415
	2130	7.5	229		2130	7.1	216
5 Sa	0305	12.7	387	20 Su	0325	12.1	369
	0925	5.3	162		0915	7.4	226
	1555	14.5	442		1525	13.6	415
	2215	6.2	189		2200	5.9	180
6 Su	0410	13.3	405	21 M	0415	12.9	393
	1015	6.0	183		1000	7.9	241
	1625	14.5	442		1550	13.7	418
	2255	4.9	149		2235	4.8	146
7 M	0505	13.8	421	22 Tu	0505	13.6	415
	1100	6.9	210		1040	8.5	259
	1655	14.5	442		1610	13.9	424
	2335	3.9	119		2310	3.7	113
8 Tu	0600	14.1	430	23 W	0555	14.2	433
	1145	7.9	241		1120	9.2	280
	1725	14.3	436		1640	14.0	427
					2345	2.7	82
9 W	0015	3.2	98	24 Th	0640	14.6	445
	0650	14.3	436		1205	9.8	299
	1225	8.8	268		1705	14.2	433
	1750	14.1	430				
10 Th	0050	2.9	88	25 F	0025	2.0	61
	0745	14.4	439		0730	14.9	454
	1305	9.6	293		1250	10.4	317
	1815	13.7	418		1735	14.2	433
11 F	0130	2.9	88	26 Sa	0105	1.7	52
	0835	14.4	439		0825	15.1	460
	1350	10.3	314		1335	11.0	335
	1840	13.3	405		1810	13.9	424
12 Sa	0205	3.2	98	27 Su	0150	1.7	52
	0925	14.2	433		0920	15.1	460
	1440	10.8	329		1435	11.3	344
	1905	12.8	390		1855	13.5	411
13 Su	0245	3.7	113	28 M	0240	2.0	61
	1025	14.0	427		1020	15.1	460
	1540	11.1	338		1545	11.3	344
	1935	12.2	372		1950	12.7	387
14 M	0325	4.3	131	29 Tu	0335	2.8	85
	1125	13.9	424		1120	15.1	460
	1705	11.1	338		1710	10.8	329
	2015	11.5	351		2105	11.9	363
15 Tu	0415	5.0	152	30 W	0430	3.8	116
	1220	13.8	421		1215	15.0	457
	1855	10.6	323		1835	9.7	296
	2130	10.9	332		2250	11.2	341
				31 Th	0540	4.9	149
					1300	15.0	457
					1935	8.3	253

NOVEMBER

Day	h m	ft	cm	Day	h m	ft	cm
1 F	0040	11.2	341	16 Sa	0050	10.3	314
	0650	6.0	183		0605	7.9	241
	1345	14.9	454		1305	14.0	427
	2025	6.8	207		2015	6.9	210
2 Sa	0210	11.7	357	17 Su	0215	11.1	338
	0755	7.1	216		0720	8.8	268
	1420	14.7	448		1335	13.9	424
	2110	5.3	162		2050	5.7	174
3 Su	0325	12.6	384	18 M	0325	12.2	372
	0855	8.0	244		0825	9.6	293
	1455	14.5	442		1405	13.9	424
	2150	4.1	125		2125	4.4	134
4 M	0430	13.5	411	19 Tu	0420	13.3	405
	0950	8.9	271		0920	10.2	311
	1530	14.3	436		1435	14.0	427
	2230	3.1	94		2200	3.2	98
5 Tu	0525	14.2	433	20 W	0510	14.2	433
	1045	9.6	293		1015	10.7	326
	1600	14.1	430		1505	14.2	433
	2310	2.5	76		2240	2.1	64
6 W	0615	14.8	451	21 Th	0600	15.0	457
	1130	10.2	311		1100	11.1	338
	1625	13.9	424		1540	14.4	439
	2345	2.2	67		2320	1.3	40
7 Th	0700	15.1	460	22 F	0645	15.6	475
	1215	10.7	326		1150	11.5	351
	1655	13.6	415		1620	14.5	442
8 F	0020	2.1	64	23 Sa	0005	0.8	24
	0740	15.3	466		0735	15.9	485
	1255	11.0	335		1240	11.6	354
	1720	13.3	405		1700	14.4	439
9 Sa	0055	2.4	73	24 Su	0050	0.6	18
	0825	15.2	463		0820	16.1	491
	1340	11.2	341		1335	11.6	354
	1745	12.9	393		1750	14.0	427
10 Su	0130	2.8	85	25 M	0135	1.0	30
	0905	15.1	460		0910	16.2	494
	1430	11.3	344		1435	11.3	344
	1815	12.4	378		1850	13.2	402
11 M	0205	3.4	104	26 Tu	0220	1.8	55
	0950	14.9	454		0955	16.2	494
	1535	11.1	338		1545	10.6	323
	1855	11.8	360		2000	12.2	372
12 Tu	0240	4.1	125	27 W	0310	3.0	91
	1035	14.8	451		1040	16.1	491
	1655	10.8	329		1705	9.5	290
	1945	11.1	338		2125	11.3	344
13 W	0320	4.9	149	28 Th	0400	4.6	140
	1115	14.6	445		1125	15.9	485
	1815	10.1	308		1815	8.1	247
	2110	10.4	317		2305	10.8	329
14 Th	0405	5.9	180	29 F	0500	6.3	192
	1155	14.4	439		1205	15.6	475
	1910	9.1	277		1910	6.6	201
	2300	10.1	308				
15 F	0500	6.9	210	30 Sa	0050	11.0	335
	1235	14.2	433		0610	8.0	244
	1945	8.1	247		1245	15.3	466
					2000	5.2	158

DECEMBER

Day	h m	ft	cm	Day	h m	ft	cm
1 Su	0230	11.8	360	16 M	0205	11.3	344
	0720	9.4	287		0610	10.2	311
	1320	14.9	454		1215	14.4	439
	2045	4.0	122		2000	4.8	146
2 M	0350	13.0	396	17 Tu	0325	12.5	381
	0830	10.4	317		0735	11.2	341
	1400	14.5	442		1250	14.4	439
	2125	3.1	94		2045	3.6	110
3 Tu	0450	14.0	427	18 W	0425	13.7	418
	0935	11.1	338		0845	11.8	360
	1435	14.1	430		1330	14.5	442
	2205	2.5	76		2130	2.4	73
4 W	0540	14.8	451	19 Th	0515	14.7	448
	1030	11.4	347		0950	12.1	369
	1505	13.8	421		1415	14.6	445
	2245	2.1	64		2215	1.4	43
5 Th	0620	15.3	466	20 F	0600	15.5	472
	1120	11.6	354		1045	12.2	372
	1540	13.6	415		1505	14.8	451
	2320	2.1	64		2300	0.7	21
6 F	0655	15.6	475	21 Sa	0640	16.0	488
	1205	11.7	357		1135	12.1	369
	1610	13.4	408		1600	14.8	451
					2350	0.3	9
7 Sa	0000	2.1	64	22 Su	0720	16.3	497
	0730	15.6	475		1230	11.7	357
	1245	11.6	354		1655	14.5	442
	1645	13.2	402				
8 Su	0030	2.4	73	23 M	0035	0.4	12
	0805	15.6	475		0800	16.6	506
	1330	11.5	351		1325	11.1	338
	1720	12.9	393		1800	14.0	427
9 M	0105	2.8	85	24 Tu	0120	1.1	34
	0840	15.6	475		0840	16.7	509
	1415	11.2	341		1425	10.3	314
	1800	12.4	378		1905	13.1	399
10 Tu	0135	3.4	104	25 W	0205	2.3	70
	0915	15.5	472		0920	16.7	509
	1510	10.8	329		1530	9.2	280
	1850	11.7	357		2015	12.2	372
11 W	0210	4.1	125	26 Th	0250	3.9	119
	0945	15.4	469		0955	16.5	503
	1605	10.2	311		1630	7.9	241
	1950	11.1	338		2135	11.4	347
12 Th	0240	5.1	155	27 F	0335	5.8	177
	1015	15.2	463		1030	16.2	494
	1705	9.4	287		1735	6.6	201
	2105	10.4	317		2305	11.0	335
13 F	0315	6.2	189	28 Sa	0425	7.8	238
	1045	15.0	457		1110	15.8	482
	1755	8.4	256		1830	5.4	165
	2235	10.2	311				
14 Sa	0400	7.5	229	29 Su	0055	11.3	344
	1110	14.8	451		0530	9.6	293
	1840	7.3	223		1145	15.2	463
					1925	4.4	134
15 Su	0020	10.4	317	30 M	0245	12.3	375
	0455	8.9	271		0650	11.0	335
	1140	14.6	445		1225	14.6	445
	1920	6.1	186		2015	3.7	113
				31 Tu	0400	13.4	408
					0815	11.8	360
					1305	14.1	430
					2100	3.1	94

Time meridian 120° W. 0000 is midnight. 1200 is noon.
Heights are referred to the Canadian chart datum of soundings. Subtract 3.8 feet (1.2 meters) to refer these levels to the datum of N.O.S. charts.

Height of Tide at Any Time

Time from the nearest high water or low water

h m	h m	h m	h m	h m	h m	h m	h m	h m	h m	h m	h m	h m	h m	h m	h m
4 00	0 08	0 16	0 24	0 32	0 40	0 48	0 56	1 04	1 12	1 20	1 28	1 36	1 44	1 52	2 00
4 20	0 09	0 17	0 26	0 35	0 43	0 52	1 01	1 09	1 18	1 27	1 35	1 44	1 53	2 01	2 10
4 40	0 09	0 19	0 28	0 37	0 47	0 56	1 05	1 15	1 24	1 33	1 43	1 52	2 01	2 11	2 20
5 00	0 10	0 20	0 30	0 40	0 50	1 00	1 10	1 20	1 30	1 40	1 50	2 00	2 10	2 20	2 30
5 20	0 11	0 21	0 32	0 43	0 53	1 04	1 15	1 25	1 36	1 47	1 57	2 08	2 19	2 29	2 40
5 40	0 11	0 23	0 34	0 45	0 57	1 08	1 19	1 31	1 42	1 53	2 05	2 16	2 27	2 39	2 50
6 00	0 12	0 24	0 36	0 48	1 00	1 12	1 24	1 36	1 48	2 00	2 12	2 24	2 36	2 48	3 00
6 20	0 13	0 25	0 38	0 51	1 03	1 16	1 29	1 41	1 54	2 07	2 19	2 32	2 45	2 57	3 10
6 40	0 13	0 27	0 40	0 53	1 07	1 20	1 33	1 47	2 00	2 13	2 27	2 40	2 53	3 07	3 20
7 00	0 14	0 28	0 42	0 56	1 10	1 24	1 38	1 52	2 06	2 20	2 34	2 48	3 02	3 16	3 30
7 20	0 15	0 29	0 44	0 59	1 13	1 28	1 43	1 57	2 12	2 27	2 41	2 56	3 11	3 25	3 40
7 40	0 15	0 31	0 46	1 01	1 17	1 32	1 47	2 03	2 18	2 33	2 49	3 04	3 19	3 35	3 50
8 00	0 16	0 32	0 48	1 04	1 20	1 36	1 52	2 08	2 24	2 40	2 56	3 12	3 28	3 44	4 00
8 20	0 17	0 33	0 50	1 07	1 23	1 40	1 57	2 13	2 30	2 47	3 03	3 20	3 37	3 53	4 10
8 40	0 17	0 35	0 52	1 09	1 27	1 44	2 01	2 19	2 36	2 53	3 11	3 28	3 45	4 03	4 20
9 00	0 18	0 36	0 54	1 12	1 30	1 48	2 06	2 24	2 42	3 00	3 18	3 36	3 54	4 12	4 30
9 20	0 19	0 37	0 56	1 15	1 33	1 52	2 11	2 29	2 48	3 07	3 25	3 44	4 03	4 21	4 40
9 40	0 19	0 39	0 58	1 17	1 37	1 56	2 15	2 35	2 54	3 13	3 33	3 52	4 11	4 31	4 50
10 00	0 20	0 40	1 00	1 20	1 40	2 00	2 20	2 40	3 00	3 20	3 40	4 00	4 20	4 40	5 00
10 20	0 21	0 41	1 02	1 23	1 43	2 04	2 25	2 45	3 06	3 27	3 47	4 08	4 29	4 49	5 10
10 40	0 21	0 43	1 04	1 25	1 47	2 08	2 29	2 51	3 12	3 33	3 55	4 16	4 37	4 59	5 20

(Left column: Duration of rise or fall, see footnote)

Correction to height

Ft	Ft	Ft	Ft	Ft	Ft	Ft	Ft	Ft	Ft	Ft	Ft	Ft	Ft	Ft	Ft
0.5	0 0	0 0	0 0	0 0	0 0	0 0	0 1	0 1	0 1	0 1	0 1	0 2	0 2	0 2	0 2
1.0	0 0	0 0	0 0	0 0	0 1	0 1	0 1	0 2	0 2	0 2	0 3	0 3	0 4	0 4	0 5
1.5	0 0	0 0	0 0	0 1	0 1	0 1	0 2	0 2	0 3	0 4	0 4	0 5	0 6	0 7	0 8
2.0	0 0	0 0	0 0	0 1	0 1	0 2	0 3	0 3	0 4	0 5	0 6	0 7	0 8	0 9	1 0
2.5	0 0	0 0	0 1	0 1	0 2	0 2	0 3	0 4	0 5	0 6	0 7	0 9	1 0	1 1	1 2
3.0	0 0	0 0	0 1	0 1	0 2	0 3	0 4	0 5	0 6	0 8	0 9	1 0	1 2	1 3	1 5
3.5	0 0	0 0	0 1	0 2	0 2	0 3	0 4	0 6	0 7	0 9	1 0	1 2	1 4	1 6	1 8
4.0	0 0	0 0	0 1	0 2	0 3	0 4	0 5	0 7	0 8	1 0	1 2	1 4	1 6	1 8	2 0
4.5	0 0	0 0	0 1	0 2	0 3	0 4	0 6	0 7	0 9	1 1	1 3	1 6	1 8	2 0	2 2
5.0	0 0	0 1	0 1	0 2	0 3	0 5	0 6	0 8	1 0	1 2	1 5	1 7	2 0	2 2	2 5
5.5	0 0	0 1	0 1	0 2	0 4	0 5	0 7	0 9	1 1	1 4	1 6	1 9	2 2	2 5	2 8
6.0	0 0	0 1	0 1	0 3	0 4	0 6	0 8	1 0	1 2	1 5	1 8	2 1	2 4	2 7	3 0
6.5	0 0	0 1	0 2	0 3	0 4	0 6	0 8	1 1	1 3	1 6	1 9	2 2	2 6	2 9	3 2
7.0	0 0	0 1	0 2	0 3	0 5	0 7	0 9	1 2	1 4	1 8	2 1	2 4	2 8	3 1	3 5
7.5	0 0	0 1	0 2	0 3	0 5	0 7	1 0	1 2	1 5	1 9	2 2	2 6	3 0	3 4	3 8
8.0	0 0	0 1	0 2	0 3	0 5	0 8	1 0	1 3	1 6	2 0	2 4	2 8	3 2	3 6	4 0
8.5	0 0	0 1	0 2	0 4	0 6	0 8	1 1	1 4	1 8	2 1	2 5	2 9	3 4	3 8	4 2
9.0	0 0	0 1	0 2	0 4	0 6	0 9	1 2	1 5	1 9	2 2	2 7	3 1	3 6	4 0	4 5
9.5	0 0	0 1	0 2	0 4	0 6	0 9	1 2	1 6	2 0	2 4	2 8	3 3	3 8	4 3	4 8
10.0	0 0	0 1	0 2	0 4	0 7	1 0	1 3	1 7	2 1	2 5	3 0	3 5	4 0	4 5	5 0
10.5	0 0	0 1	0 3	0 5	0 7	1 0	1 3	1 7	2 2	2 6	3 1	3 6	4 2	4 7	5 2
11.0	0 0	0 1	0 3	0 5	0 7	1 1	1 4	1 8	2 3	2 8	3 3	3 8	4 4	4 9	5 5
11.5	0 0	0 1	0 3	0 5	0 8	1 1	1 5	1 9	2 4	2 9	3 4	4 0	4 6	5 1	5 8
12.0	0 0	0 1	0 3	0 5	0 8	1 1	1 5	2 0	2 5	3 0	3 6	4 1	4 8	5 4	6 0
12.5	0 0	0 1	0 3	0 5	0 8	1 2	1 6	2 1	2 6	3 1	3 7	4 3	5 0	5 6	6 2
13.0	0 0	0 1	0 3	0 6	0 9	1 2	1 7	2 2	2 7	3 2	3 9	4 5	5 1	5 8	6 5
13.5	0 0	0 1	0 3	0 6	0 9	1 3	1 7	2 2	2 8	3 4	4 0	4 7	5 3	6 0	6 8
14.0	0 0	0 1	0 3	0 6	0 9	1 3	1 8	2 3	2 9	3 5	4 2	4 8	5 5	6 3	7 0
14.5	0 0	0 2	0 4	0 6	1 0	1 4	1 9	2 4	3 0	3 6	4 3	5 0	5 7	6 5	7 2
15.0	0 0	0 2	0 4	0 6	1 0	1 4	1 9	2 5	3 1	3 8	4 4	5 2	5 9	6 7	7 5
15.5	0 0	0 2	0 4	0 7	1 0	1 5	2 0	2 6	3 2	3 9	4 6	5 4	6 1	6 9	7 8
16.0	0 0	0 2	0 4	0 7	1 1	1 5	2 1	2 6	3 3	4 0	4 7	5 5	6 3	7 2	8 0
16.5	0 0	0 2	0 4	0 7	1 1	1 6	2 1	2 7	3 4	4 1	4 9	5 7	6 5	7 4	8 2
17.0	0 0	0 2	0 4	0 7	1 1	1 6	2 2	2 8	3 5	4 2	5 0	5 9	6 7	7 6	8 5
17.5	0 0	0 2	0 4	0 8	1 2	1 7	2 2	2 9	3 6	4 4	5 2	6 0	6 9	7 8	8 8
18.0	0 0	0 2	0 4	0 8	1 2	1 7	2 3	3 0	3 7	4 5	5 3	6 2	7 1	8 1	9 0
18.5	0 1	0 2	0 5	0 8	1 2	1 8	2 4	3 1	3 8	4 6	5 5	6 4	7 3	8 3	9 2
19.0	0 1	0 2	0 5	0 8	1 3	1 8	2 4	3 1	3 9	4 8	5 6	6 6	7 5	8 5	9 5
19.5	0 1	0 2	0 5	0 8	1 3	1 9	2 5	3 2	4 0	4 9	5 8	6 7	7 7	8 7	9 8
20.0	0 1	0 2	0 5	0 9	1 3	1 9	2 6	3 3	4 1	5 0	5 9	6 9	7 9	9 0	10 0

(Left column: Range of tide, see footnote)

Sunrise and Sunset, Seattle
1991

Date		42° N. Rise	42° N. Set	44° N. Rise	44° N. Set	46° N. Rise	46° N. Set	48° N. Rise	48° N. Set	50° N. Rise	50° N. Set	52° N. Rise	52° N. Set
		h m	h m	h m	h m	h m	h m	h m	h m	h m	h m	h m	h m
Jan.	1	07 28	16 39	07 35	16 32	07 42	16 25	07 50	16 17	07 59	16 08	08 08	15 59
	6	07 28	16 43	07 35	16 37	07 42	16 30	07 49	16 22	07 58	16 14	08 07	16 05
	11	07 27	16 49	07 34	16 42	07 40	16 36	07 48	16 28	07 56	16 20	08 05	16 11
	16	07 25	16 54	07 31	16 48	07 38	16 42	07 45	16 35	07 52	16 27	08 01	16 19
	21	07 23	17 00	07 28	16 55	07 34	16 49	07 41	16 42	07 48	16 35	07 56	16 27
	26	07 19	17 06	07 24	17 01	07 30	16 56	07 36	16 50	07 42	16 43	07 50	16 36
	31	07 14	17 13	07 19	17 08	07 24	17 03	07 30	16 58	07 36	16 52	07 42	16 45
Feb.	5	07 09	17 19	07 13	17 15	07 18	17 10	07 23	17 06	07 28	17 00	07 34	16 54
	10	07 03	17 26	07 07	17 22	07 11	17 18	07 16	17 14	07 20	17 09	07 26	17 04
	15	06 57	17 32	07 00	17 29	07 04	17 25	07 07	17 22	07 12	17 17	07 16	17 13
	20	06 50	17 38	06 53	17 36	06 56	17 33	06 59	17 29	07 02	17 26	07 06	17 22
	25	06 42	17 45	06 45	17 42	06 47	17 40	06 50	17 37	06 53	17 34	06 56	17 31
Mar.	2	06 35	17 51	06 36	17 49	06 38	17 47	06 40	17 45	06 42	17 43	06 45	17 40
	7	06 26	17 57	06 28	17 55	06 29	17 54	06 31	17 53	06 32	17 51	06 34	17 49
	12	06 18	18 02	06 19	18 02	06 20	18 01	06 21	18 00	06 21	17 59	06 22	17 58
	17	06 10	18 08	06 10	18 08	06 10	18 08	06 10	18 07	06 11	18 07	06 11	18 07
	22	06 01	18 14	06 01	18 14	06 00	18 14	06 00	18 15	06 00	18 15	05 59	18 16
	27	05 52	18 19	05 52	18 20	05 51	18 21	05 50	18 22	05 49	18 23	05 48	18 24
Apr.	1	05 44	18 25	05 43	18 26	05 41	18 28	05 40	18 29	05 38	18 31	05 36	18 33
	6	05 35	18 30	05 34	18 32	05 32	18 34	05 30	18 36	05 27	18 39	05 25	18 41
	11	05 27	18 36	05 25	18 38	05 22	18 41	05 20	18 44	05 17	18 47	05 14	18 50
	16	05 19	18 42	05 16	18 44	05 13	18 47	05 10	18 51	05 06	18 54	05 02	18 58
	21	05 11	18 47	05 08	18 50	05 04	18 54	05 01	18 58	04 56	19 02	04 52	19 07
	26	05 04	18 53	05 00	18 56	04 56	19 01	04 51	19 05	04 47	19 10	04 41	19 15
May	1	04 57	18 58	04 53	19 02	04 48	19 07	04 43	19 12	04 37	19 18	04 31	19 24
	6	04 50	19 04	04 46	19 08	04 40	19 14	04 35	19 19	04 29	19 25	04 22	19 32
	11	04 44	19 09	04 39	19 14	04 34	19 20	04 27	19 26	04 21	19 33	04 13	19 40
	16	04 39	19 14	04 34	19 20	04 27	19 26	04 21	19 33	04 14	19 40	04 06	19 48
	21	04 35	19 19	04 29	19 25	04 22	19 32	04 15	19 39	04 07	19 47	03 58	19 56
	26	04 31	19 24	04 24	19 30	04 17	19 37	04 10	19 45	04 02	19 53	03 52	20 02
	31	04 28	19 28	04 21	19 35	04 14	19 42	04 06	19 50	03 57	19 59	03 47	20 09
June	5	04 26	19 31	04 19	19 38	04 11	19 46	04 03	19 54	03 54	20 04	03 43	20 14
	10	04 24	19 35	04 17	19 42	04 09	19 50	04 01	19 58	03 51	20 08	03 41	20 18
	15	04 24	19 37	04 16	19 44	04 09	19 52	04 00	20 01	03 50	20 11	03 39	20 21
	20	04 24	19 39	04 17	19 46	04 09	19 54	04 00	20 03	03 50	20 13	03 39	20 23
	25	04 25	19 40	04 18	19 47	04 10	19 55	04 01	20 04	03 52	20 13	03 41	20 24
	30	04 27	19 40	04 20	19 47	04 12	19 55	04 04	20 03	03 54	20 13	03 43	20 23
July	5	04 30	19 39	04 23	19 46	04 15	19 53	04 07	20 02	03 57	20 11	03 47	20 22
	10	04 33	19 37	04 26	19 44	04 19	19 51	04 11	19 59	04 02	20 08	03 52	20 18
	15	04 37	19 34	04 31	19 41	04 23	19 48	04 15	19 56	04 07	20 04	03 57	20 14
	20	04 41	19 31	04 35	19 37	04 28	19 44	04 21	19 51	04 13	19 59	04 04	20 08
	25	04 46	19 26	04 40	19 32	04 34	19 39	04 27	19 46	04 19	19 53	04 10	20 02
	30	04 51	19 21	04 45	19 27	04 39	19 33	04 33	19 39	04 26	19 46	04 18	19 54
Aug.	4	04 56	19 16	04 51	19 21	04 45	19 26	04 39	19 32	04 33	19 39	04 25	19 46
	9	05 01	19 09	04 56	19 14	04 51	19 19	04 46	19 24	04 40	19 30	04 33	19 37
	14	05 06	19 03	05 02	19 07	04 57	19 11	04 53	19 16	04 47	19 21	04 41	19 27
	19	05 11	18 55	05 08	18 59	05 04	19 03	04 59	19 07	04 55	19 12	04 50	19 17
	24	05 17	18 48	05 13	18 51	05 10	18 54	05 06	18 58	05 02	19 02	04 58	19 06
	29	05 22	18 40	05 19	18 42	05 16	18 45	05 13	18 48	05 10	18 51	05 06	18 55
Sept.	3	05 27	18 31	05 25	18 33	05 22	18 36	05 20	18 38	05 17	18 41	05 14	18 44
	8	05 32	18 23	05 30	18 24	05 29	18 26	05 27	18 28	05 24	18 30	05 22	18 32
	13	05 37	18 14	05 36	18 15	05 35	18 16	05 33	18 18	05 32	18 19	05 30	18 21
	18	05 43	18 05	05 42	18 06	05 41	18 07	05 40	18 07	05 39	18 08	05 38	18 09
	23	05 48	17 57	05 48	17 57	05 47	17 57	05 47	17 57	05 47	17 57	05 47	17 57
	28	05 53	17 48	05 53	17 48	05 54	17 47	05 54	17 47	05 54	17 46	05 55	17 46
Oct.	3	05 58	17 39	05 59	17 38	06 00	17 37	06 01	17 36	06 02	17 35	06 03	17 34
	8	06 04	17 31	06 05	17 29	06 07	17 28	06 08	17 26	06 10	17 25	06 12	17 23
	13	06 09	17 23	06 11	17 21	06 13	17 19	06 15	17 17	06 18	17 14	06 20	17 12
	18	06 15	17 15	06 18	17 12	06 20	17 10	06 23	17 07	06 26	17 04	06 29	17 01
	23	06 21	17 07	06 24	17 04	06 27	17 01	06 30	16 58	06 34	16 54	06 38	16 50
	28	06 27	17 00	06 30	16 57	06 34	16 53	06 38	16 49	06 42	16 45	06 47	16 40
Nov.	2	06 33	16 54	06 37	16 50	06 41	16 45	06 46	16 41	06 50	16 36	06 56	16 31
	7	06 39	16 48	06 44	16 43	06 48	16 39	06 53	16 34	06 59	16 28	07 05	16 22
	12	06 45	16 42	06 50	16 38	06 55	16 32	07 01	16 27	07 07	16 21	07 14	16 14
	17	06 52	16 38	06 57	16 33	07 02	16 27	07 08	16 21	07 15	16 14	07 22	16 07
	22	06 58	16 34	07 03	16 28	07 09	16 22	07 16	16 16	07 23	16 09	07 31	16 01
	27	07 03	16 31	07 09	16 25	07 16	16 19	07 23	16 12	07 30	16 04	07 39	15 56
Dec.	2	07 09	16 29	07 15	16 23	07 22	16 16	07 29	16 09	07 37	16 01	07 46	15 52
	7	07 14	16 29	07 20	16 22	07 27	16 15	07 35	16 07	07 44	15 59	07 53	15 49
	12	07 18	16 29	07 25	16 22	07 32	16 15	07 40	16 07	07 49	15 58	07 58	15 48
	17	07 22	16 30	07 29	16 23	07 36	16 16	07 44	16 08	07 53	15 59	08 03	15 49
	22	07 25	16 32	07 32	16 25	07 39	16 18	07 47	16 09	07 56	16 01	08 06	15 51
	27	07 27	16 35	07 34	16 28	07 41	16 21	07 49	16 13	07 58	16 04	08 08	15 54
Jan.	1	07 28	16 39	07 35	16 32	07 42	16 25	07 50	16 17	07 59	16 08	08 08	15 59

Local mean time. To obtain standard time of rise or set, see table 5.

Sunrise and Sunset, Anchorage
1991

Date		54° N. Rise h m	54° N. Set h m	56° N. Rise h m	56° N. Set h m	58° N. Rise h m	58° N. Set h m	60° N. Rise h m	60° N. Set h m	62° N. Rise h m	62° N. Set h m	64° N. Rise h m	64° N. Set h m
Jan.	1	08 19	15 48	08 31	15 36	08 46	15 21	09 03	15 04	09 23	14 44	09 50	14 17
	6	08 18	15 54	08 29	15 42	08 43	15 29	08 59	15 12	09 19	14 53	09 44	14 28
	11	08 15	16 01	08 26	15 50	08 39	15 37	08 54	15 22	09 12	15 04	09 35	14 41
	16	08 10	16 10	08 21	15 59	08 33	15 47	08 47	15 33	09 04	15 16	09 24	14 55
	21	08 04	16 19	08 14	16 09	08 25	15 58	08 38	15 45	08 54	15 30	09 12	15 11
	26	07 58	16 28	08 07	16 19	08 17	16 09	08 28	15 57	08 42	15 44	08 59	15 27
	31	07 50	16 38	07 58	16 30	08 07	16 21	08 17	16 10	08 30	15 58	08 44	15 44
Feb.	5	07 41	16 48	07 48	16 41	07 56	16 33	08 05	16 23	08 16	16 13	08 29	16 00
	10	07 31	16 58	07 38	16 52	07 45	16 45	07 53	16 37	08 02	16 27	08 13	16 17
	15	07 21	17 08	07 27	17 03	07 33	16 57	07 40	16 50	07 47	16 42	07 57	16 33
	20	07 10	17 18	07 15	17 14	07 20	17 09	07 26	17 03	07 32	16 56	07 40	16 49
	25	06 59	17 28	07 03	17 24	07 07	17 20	07 12	17 16	07 17	17 11	07 23	17 05
Mar.	2	06 48	17 38	06 50	17 35	06 54	17 32	06 57	17 28	07 01	17 25	07 06	17 20
	7	06 36	17 48	06 38	17 46	06 40	17 43	06 42	17 41	06 45	17 38	06 49	17 35
	12	06 24	17 57	06 25	17 56	06 26	17 55	06 28	17 54	06 29	17 52	06 31	17 50
	17	06 11	18 07	06 12	18 06	06 12	18 06	06 13	18 06	06 13	18 05	06 14	18 05
	22	05 59	18 16	05 59	18 17	05 58	18 17	05 57	18 18	05 57	18 19	05 56	18 20
	27	05 47	18 26	05 45	18 27	05 44	18 29	05 42	18 30	05 40	18 32	05 38	18 35
Apr.	1	05 34	18 35	05 32	18 37	05 30	18 40	05 27	18 42	05 24	18 46	05 20	18 49
	6	05 22	18 44	05 19	18 47	05 16	18 51	05 12	18 55	05 08	18 59	05 03	19 04
	11	05 10	18 53	05 06	18 57	05 02	19 02	04 57	19 07	04 51	19 13	04 45	19 19
	16	04 58	19 03	04 53	19 08	04 48	19 13	04 42	19 19	04 35	19 26	04 28	19 34
	21	04 47	19 12	04 41	19 18	04 35	19 24	04 28	19 32	04 19	19 40	04 10	19 50
	26	04 36	19 21	04 29	19 28	04 22	19 36	04 13	19 44	04 04	19 54	03 53	20 05
May	1	04 25	19 31	04 17	19 38	04 09	19 47	04 00	19 56	03 48	20 08	03 35	20 21
	6	04 15	19 40	04 06	19 48	03 57	19 58	03 46	20 09	03 34	20 22	03 18	20 37
	11	04 05	19 49	03 56	19 58	03 45	20 09	03 33	20 21	03 19	20 36	03 02	20 53
	16	03 57	19 57	03 46	20 07	03 35	20 19	03 21	20 33	03 05	20 49	02 46	21 09
	21	03 49	20 05	03 38	20 16	03 25	20 29	03 10	20 44	02 52	21 03	02 30	21 25
	26	03 42	20 13	03 30	20 25	03 16	20 39	03 00	20 55	02 41	21 15	02 15	21 41
	31	03 36	20 20	03 24	20 32	03 09	20 47	02 52	21 05	02 30	21 27	02 02	21 56
June	5	03 32	20 25	03 19	20 39	03 03	20 54	02 45	21 13	02 21	21 37	01 50	22 09
	10	03 29	20 30	03 15	20 44	02 59	21 00	02 39	21 20	02 15	21 45	01 40	22 20
	15	03 27	20 34	03 13	20 48	02 57	21 04	02 36	21 25	02 11	21 51	01 34	22 28
	20	03 27	20 36	03 13	20 50	02 56	21 07	02 36	21 27	02 09	21 54	01 31	22 32
	25	03 28	20 36	03 14	20 51	02 57	21 07	02 37	21 28	02 11	21 54	01 33	22 32
	30	03 31	20 36	03 17	20 50	03 01	21 06	02 41	21 26	02 15	21 51	01 39	22 27
July	5	03 35	20 33	03 21	20 47	03 06	21 03	02 46	21 22	02 22	21 46	01 48	22 19
	10	03 40	20 30	03 27	20 43	03 12	20 58	02 54	21 16	02 31	21 38	02 00	22 08
	15	03 46	20 25	03 34	20 37	03 20	20 51	03 02	21 08	02 41	21 29	02 14	21 56
	20	03 53	20 18	03 42	20 30	03 28	20 43	03 12	20 59	02 53	21 18	02 29	21 42
	25	04 01	20 11	03 50	20 22	03 38	20 34	03 23	20 48	03 06	21 05	02 44	21 26
	30	04 09	20 03	03 59	20 12	03 48	20 24	03 35	20 37	03 19	20 52	03 00	21 11
Aug.	4	04 17	19 54	04 08	20 02	03 58	20 13	03 46	20 24	03 32	20 38	03 16	20 54
	9	04 26	19 44	04 18	19 52	04 09	20 01	03 58	20 11	03 46	20 23	03 31	20 37
	14	04 35	19 33	04 28	19 40	04 20	19 48	04 10	19 57	04 00	20 08	03 47	20 20
	19	04 44	19 22	04 38	19 28	04 30	19 35	04 22	19 43	04 13	19 52	04 02	20 03
	24	04 53	19 11	04 47	19 16	04 41	19 22	04 34	19 29	04 27	19 37	04 17	19 45
	29	05 02	18 59	04 57	19 04	04 52	19 09	04 46	19 14	04 40	19 20	04 32	19 28
Sept.	3	05 11	18 47	05 07	18 51	05 03	18 55	04 58	18 59	04 53	19 04	04 47	19 10
	8	05 20	18 35	05 17	18 38	05 14	18 41	05 10	18 44	05 06	18 48	05 01	18 52
	13	05 28	18 23	05 26	18 24	05 24	18 27	05 22	18 29	05 19	18 32	05 16	18 35
	18	05 37	18 10	05 36	18 11	05 35	18 12	05 33	18 14	05 32	18 15	05 30	18 17
	23	05 46	17 58	05 46	17 58	05 46	17 58	05 45	17 58	05 45	17 59	05 44	17 59
	28	05 55	17 45	05 56	17 45	05 56	17 44	05 57	17 43	05 58	17 43	05 58	17 42
Oct.	3	06 04	17 33	06 06	17 31	06 07	17 30	06 09	17 28	06 11	17 26	06 13	17 24
	8	06 14	17 21	06 16	17 19	06 18	17 16	06 21	17 13	06 24	17 10	06 27	17 07
	13	06 23	17 09	06 26	17 06	06 29	17 02	06 33	16 59	06 37	16 54	06 42	16 49
	18	06 32	16 57	06 36	16 53	06 41	16 49	06 45	16 44	06 51	16 39	06 57	16 32
	23	06 42	16 46	06 47	16 41	06 52	16 36	06 58	16 30	07 05	16 23	07 12	16 15
	28	06 52	16 35	06 57	16 30	07 04	16 23	07 11	16 16	07 19	16 08	07 28	15 59
Nov.	2	07 01	16 25	07 08	16 18	07 15	16 11	07 23	16 03	07 33	15 53	07 44	15 42
	7	07 11	16 15	07 19	16 08	07 27	16 00	07 36	15 50	07 47	15 39	08 00	15 27
	12	07 21	16 07	07 29	15 58	07 38	15 49	07 49	15 38	08 01	15 26	08 16	15 11
	17	07 30	15 59	07 40	15 50	07 50	15 39	08 02	15 27	08 15	15 14	08 32	14 57
	22	07 40	15 52	07 50	15 42	08 01	15 31	08 14	15 18	08 29	15 02	08 48	14 43
	27	07 48	15 46	07 59	15 36	08 11	15 23	08 25	15 09	08 42	14 52	09 03	14 31
Dec.	2	07 56	15 42	08 08	15 31	08 21	15 17	08 36	15 A02	08 54	14 44	09 17	14 21
	7	08 03	15 39	08 15	15 27	08 29	15 13	08 45	14 57	09 05	14 37	09 30	14 12
	12	08 09	15 38	08 22	15 25	08 36	15 11	08 53	14 54	09 14	14 33	09 41	14 06
	17	08 14	15 38	08 27	15 25	08 41	15 10	08 59	14 53	09 20	14 32	09 48	14 04
	22	08 17	15 40	08 30	15 27	08 45	15 12	09 02	14 54	09 24	14 33	09 52	14 04
	27	08 19	15 43	08 32	15 30	08 46	15 16	09 04	14 58	09 25	14 37	09 53	14 09
Jan.	1	08 19	15 48	08 31	15 35	08 46	15 21	09 03	15 04	09 23	14 43	09 50	14 17

Local mean time. To obtain standard time of rise or set, see table 5.

Moonrise and Moonset, Seattle
1991

Day	JANUARY Rise h m	JANUARY Set h m	FEBRUARY Rise h m	FEBRUARY Set h m	MARCH Rise h m	MARCH Set h m	APRIL Rise h m	APRIL Set h m	MAY Rise h m	MAY Set h m	JUNE Rise h m	JUNE Set h m	Day
1	1756	0850	2047	0831	1936	0653	2202	0621	2252	0604	2315	0746	1
2	1921	0923	2200	0850	2049	0712	2308	0650	2339	0653	2338	0852	2
3	2041	0948	2312	0908	2202	0732	....	0725	....	0749	2358	0959	3
4	2157	1009	....	0929	2312	0754	0009	0809	0017	0851	....	1106	4
5	2310	1028	0022	0952	....	0819	0101	0900	0047	0956	0016	1214	5
6	....	1046	0131	1019	0020	0851	0144	0959	0113	1103	0035	1324	6
7	0020	1105	0236	1052	0124	0929	0219	1103	0135	1211	0054	1438	7
8	0129	1125	0337	1133	0220	1015	0248	1210	0154	1320	0116	1556	8
9	0237	1149	0430	1223	0309	1110	0312	1319	0213	1431	0143	1716	9
10	0344	1218	0515	1322	0349	1212	0333	1429	0232	1545	0217	1837	10
11	0447	1254	0552	1426	0421	1318	0352	1540	0253	1703	0303	1952	11
12	0545	1339	0621	1534	0448	1427	0411	1654	0317	1824	0403	2054	12
13	0636	1432	0646	1644	0510	1538	0431	1811	0348	1946	0516	2142	13
14	0717	1533	0707	1755	0530	1649	0453	1930	0428	2105	0639	2219	14
15	0751	1639	0726	1906	0549	1802	0520	2052	0520	2213	0803	2247	15
16	0819	1748	0744	2018	0608	1916	0553	2212	0625	2307	0924	2311	16
17	0841	1857	0802	2132	0628	2033	0637	2325	0742	2349	1042	2332	17
18	0901	2007	0823	2248	0651	2152	0733	....	0903	....	1156	2351	18
19	0919	2117	0846	....	0719	2312	0841	0026	1023	0020	1308	....	19
20	0937	2229	0916	0006	0755	....	0957	0113	1140	0046	1419	0011	20
21	0955	2342	0953	0124	0841	0028	1116	0150	1255	0107	1528	0032	21
22	1016	....	1043	0238	0940	0136	1234	0218	1407	0127	1636	0056	22
23	1041	0059	1146	0342	1050	0231	1350	0241	1517	0146	1741	0126	23
24	1113	0218	1300	0435	1207	0314	1503	0302	1627	0205	1840	0201	24
25	1155	0337	1421	0515	1326	0348	1615	0321	1737	0227	1932	0244	25
26	1252	0450	1543	0546	1445	0414	1727	0340	1844	0253	2015	0336	26
27	1402	0552	1703	0612	1601	0437	1837	0400	1948	0324	2051	0434	27
28	1523	0641	1821	0633	1716	0456	1947	0423	2045	0402	2119	0537	28
29	1647	0718	....	....	1829	0516	2055	0451	2135	0448	2143	0643	29
30	1810	0747	....	....	1941	0535	2157	0524	2216	0542	2203	0749	30
31	1930	0810	....	....	2053	0556	....	....	2248	0642	....	....	31

Day	JULY Rise h m	JULY Set h m	AUGUST Rise h m	AUGUST Set h m	SEPTEMBER Rise h m	SEPTEMBER Set h m	OCTOBER Rise h m	OCTOBER Set h m	NOVEMBER Rise h m	NOVEMBER Set h m	DECEMBER Rise h m	DECEMBER Set h m	Day
1	2222	0856	2146	1123	2219	1406	2344	1437	0128	1427	0300	1337	1
2	2240	1003	2213	1237	2323	1508	....	1511	0243	1448	0412	1401	2
3	2258	1111	2246	1353	....	1558	0103	1538	0357	1509	0522	1431	3
4	2318	1222	2330	1508	0038	1638	0223	1602	0511	1533	0630	1506	4
5	2342	1335	....	1618	0159	1710	0341	1623	0624	1559	0732	1549	5
6	....	1452	0028	1717	0322	1736	0458	1644	0735	1631	0827	1640	6
7	0012	1611	0139	1805	0443	1759	0614	1706	0842	1709	0913	1737	7
8	0050	1727	0300	1842	0603	1821	0728	1731	0942	1755	0951	1839	8
9	0142	1835	0425	1911	0721	1842	0842	1759	1034	1848	1021	1943	9
10	0248	1930	0550	1936	0837	1905	0952	1833	1117	1947	1046	2048	10
11	0407	2013	0711	1958	0951	1930	1057	1914	1152	2050	1108	2152	11
12	0532	2046	0830	2018	1103	2000	1154	2003	1220	2155	1127	2257	12
13	0657	2112	0946	2040	1210	2036	1242	2058	1244	2300	1146	....	13
14	0819	2135	1100	2103	1311	2120	1321	2159	1304	....	1204	0003	14
15	0938	2155	1212	2129	1404	2211	1353	2303	1324	0005	1224	0111	15
16	1053	2215	1321	2201	1449	2309	1420	....	1342	0112	1247	0221	16
17	1206	2237	1425	2239	1525	....	1442	0009	1402	0220	1315	0335	17
18	1317	2300	1522	2325	1554	0011	1502	0115	1424	0331	1351	0452	18
19	1427	2328	1611	....	1619	0117	1521	0222	1450	0445	1438	0608	19
20	1533	....	1652	0019	1640	0224	1540	0331	1522	0603	1539	0719	20
21	1634	0001	1725	0119	1659	0331	1601	0441	1603	0721	1653	0818	21
22	1729	0042	1752	0223	1718	0439	1624	0555	1657	0835	1815	0905	22
23	1815	0130	1815	0330	1737	0549	1652	0711	1803	0939	1939	0942	23
24	1852	0227	1836	0437	1758	0700	1728	0828	1919	1031	2101	1011	24
25	1923	0329	1854	0545	1822	0814	1813	0944	2040	1112	2221	1036	25
26	1948	0434	1912	0653	1852	0929	1910	1052	2200	1144	2337	1058	26
27	2010	0541	1931	0802	1929	1045	2018	1150	2318	1210	....	1120	27
28	2029	0648	1953	0913	2017	1157	2134	1236	....	1232	0051	1142	28
29	2047	0755	2017	1026	2116	1301	2253	1312	0034	1253	0203	1206	29
30	2105	0902	2048	1141	2226	1354	....	1341	0148	1314	0314	1233	30
31	2124	1011	2128	1255	....	....	0011	1406	....	....	0422	1306	31

Time meridian 120° W. 0000 is midnight. 1200 is noon.

Moonrise and Moonset, Anchorage
1991

Day	JANUARY Rise h m	Set h m	FEBRUARY Rise h m	Set h m	MARCH Rise h m	Set h m	APRIL Rise h m	Set h m	MAY Rise h m	Set h m	JUNE Rise h m	Set h m	Day
1	1738	1103	2146	0928	2045	0741	....	0604	0049	0500	0102	0724	1
2	1928	1110	2319	0929	2218	0742	0025	0612	0149	0545	0109	0850	2
3	2111	1113	....	0930	2351	0744	0153	0628	0225	0653	0113	1016	3
4	2247	1115	0050	0932	....	0747	0307	0659	0244	0814	0116	1141	4
5	....	1117	0221	0936	0123	0753	0358	0752	0254	0941	0118	1307	5
6	0018	1118	0352	0942	0254	0802	0426	0907	0300	1108	0120	1436	6
7	0147	1119	0520	0954	0418	0822	0440	1033	0304	1235	0123	1609	7
8	0316	1121	0638	1019	0524	0900	0448	1202	0306	1402	0127	1749	8
9	0445	1125	0734	1108	0604	1004	0452	1331	0309	1532	0133	1935	9
10	0615	1133	0805	1222	0624	1127	0455	1500	0311	1705	0145	2121	10
11	0740	1149	0819	1349	0635	1256	0457	1630	0314	1844	0208	2247	11
12	0851	1221	0826	1521	0640	1427	0459	1803	0319	2030	0258	2338	12
13	0936	1321	0830	1653	0643	1558	0501	1940	0327	2218	0426	....	13
14	0959	1441	0832	1823	0645	1729	0505	2123	0343	2357	0614	0001	14
15	1010	1611	0834	1953	0647	1900	0510	2310	0417	....	0803	0013	15
16	1016	1743	0835	2124	0648	2035	0521	....	0524	0106	0947	0019	16
17	1019	1913	0836	2258	0651	2213	0541	0055	0702	0140	1125	0023	17
18	1020	2042	0838	....	0654	2356	0626	0222	0848	0157	1258	0026	18
19	1021	2211	0841	0036	0700	....	0745	0314	1032	0205	1429	0028	19
20	1022	2341	0848	0219	0712	0141	0925	0339	1211	0210	1559	0031	20
21	1023	....	0902	0403	0737	0321	1109	0350	1344	0213	1728	0035	21
22	1025	0115	0932	0538	0830	0435	1249	0357	1514	0216	1857	0040	22
23	1029	0254	1037	0642	0957	0515	1425	0401	1643	0218	2022	0049	23
24	1037	0439	1214	0713	1140	0534	1558	0403	1813	0221	2135	0106	24
25	1055	0625	1403	0727	1325	0543	1728	0405	1943	0225	2226	0138	25
26	1137	0755	1550	0734	1506	0548	1858	0407	2112	0231	2255	0231	26
27	1300	0847	1732	0737	1643	0550	2029	0410	2234	0242	2310	0345	27
28	1449	0909	1910	0739	1816	0553	2201	0415	2341	0302	2319	0509	28
29	1641	0919	....	....	1949	0554	2329	0422	....	0340	2324	0635	29
30	1829	0924	....	....	2121	0556	....	0435	0025	0441	2327	0801	30
31	2010	0926	....	....	2253	0559	....	....	0049	0559	....	....	31

Day	JULY Rise h m	Set h m	AUGUST Rise h m	Set h m	SEPTEMBER Rise h m	Set h m	OCTOBER Rise h m	Set h m	NOVEMBER Rise h m	Set h m	DECEMBER Rise h m	Set h m	Day
1	2329	0926	2152	1259	2117	1657	2325	1649	0208	1525	0431	1347	1
2	2331	1050	2159	1435	2226	1756	....	1700	0342	1529	0602	1354	2
3	2333	1216	2210	1614	....	1827	0108	1706	0515	1533	0733	1405	3
4	2336	1345	2234	1752	0002	1843	0249	1711	0648	1538	0900	1422	4
5	2341	1519	2323	1913	0148	1852	0427	1715	0821	1546	1017	1452	5
6	2350	1659	....	2001	0335	1857	0604	1718	0953	1558	1114	1542	6
7	....	1843	0048	2024	0518	1901	0739	1723	1118	1619	1149	1650	7
8	0005	2019	0235	2036	0658	1904	0914	1728	1229	1656	1210	1810	8
9	0039	2128	0426	2043	0835	1908	1048	1737	1319	1753	1222	1933	9
10	0147	2203	0614	2047	1011	1912	1219	1752	1348	1906	1229	2056	10
11	0328	2219	0756	2050	1147	1918	1341	1817	1404	2028	1234	2218	11
12	0520	2228	0935	2053	1320	1928	1444	1901	1414	2152	1238	2340	12
13	0710	2233	1110	2056	1448	1945	1524	2006	1421	2315	1241	....	13
14	0854	2236	1245	2101	1602	2017	1547	2124	1425	....	1245	0102	14
15	1033	2239	1418	2108	1655	2109	1600	2247	1428	0038	1249	0227	15
16	1207	2242	1548	2119	1727	2220	1608	....	1432	0201	1254	0357	16
17	1339	2245	1711	2140	1744	2342	1613	0012	1436	0327	1303	0532	17
18	1511	2250	1817	2218	1754	....	1616	0137	1440	0456	1318	0711	18
19	1641	2258	1901	2319	1800	0108	1620	0302	1447	0631	1347	0848	19
20	1808	2312	1925	....	1804	0234	1623	0427	1459	0811	1443	1005	20
21	1926	2337	1938	0036	1807	0400	1627	0556	1520	0951	1611	1053	21
22	2024	....	1946	0202	1810	0526	1632	0729	1601	1120	1757	1117	22
23	2100	0023	1950	0328	1813	0653	1641	0907	1712	1222	1945	1130	23
24	2119	0131	1953	0455	1817	0823	1655	1047	1848	1255	2130	1139	24
25	2129	0253	1956	0620	1822	0957	1722	1223	2033	1313	2309	1144	25
26	2135	0419	1958	0746	1831	1134	1812	1340	2215	1323	....	1149	26
27	2139	0546	2001	0913	1848	1313	1932	1428	2354	1330	0044	1153	27
28	2141	0711	2004	1043	1919	1443	2110	1453	....	1334	0216	1158	28
29	2143	0836	2010	1217	2018	1550	2252	1507	0128	1339	0348	1204	29
30	2145	1001	2020	1354	2144	1629	....	1515	0300	1343	0519	1213	30
31	2148	1128	2039	1532	....	....	0032	1520	....	....	0647	1227	31

Time meridian 135° W.   0000 is midnight.   1200 is noon.

NOTES

NOTES

NOTES

NOTES

ELECTRONICS
Table of Contents

RADIO EMERGENCY PROCEDURES

THE DISTRESS CALL

The Distress Call has absolute priority over all other transmissions and need not be addressed to any particular station. Any mariner hearing a Distress Call shall immediately cease all transmissions capable of interfering with the distress message and shall continue to listen on the frequency on which the call was heard.

If your vessel is in distress and abandonment is necessary, the radio transmitter should be set for continuous emission to provide rescue vessels and aircraft with a homing signal.

PROPER USE OF DISTRESS, URGENT AND SAFETY SIGNALS

Several instances have been reported of vessels calling MAYDAY to report they were out of gas, lost, having engine trouble, etc. . . and in each case, when questioned, they advised they were in no immediate danger. The use of MAYDAY in this fashion is prohibited. It tends to nullify the importance of this signal and is a violation of Federal Communications Commission (FCC) regulations. In the interest of maritime safety it is imperative that all mariners familiarize themselves with the proper use of radiotelephone signals authorized for the different situations they may encounter.

The following is taken from FCC regulations as to the proper use of the Distress, Urgent and Safety signals by mobile stations.

DISTRESS SIGNAL -- The radiotelephone Distress Signal consists of the word **MAYDAY** spoken three times. This signal indicates that a mobile station is threatened by grave and imminent danger and requests immediate assistance.

URGENT SIGNAL -- The radiotelephone Urgent Signal consists of three repetitions of the words PAN-PAN (Rhymes with DAWN). This signal indicates that the calling stations has a very urgent message to transmit concerning the safety of a ship, aircraft or other vehicle, or the safety of a person.

SAFETY SIGNAL -- The radiotelephone Safety Signal consists of the word SECURITE spoken three times. This signal indicates that the station is about to transmit a message concerning the safety of navigation or giving important meteorological warnings.

RADIOTELEPHONE (VOICE) MESSAGE

Periodically, mariners in distress or having knowledge of another vessel in distress do not give all information required by the International Radio Regulations and by the Federal Communications Commission. This makes it harder to start a search and could very well lead to loss of life. Use of proper format is vital in the transmission of marine distress messages. Clarity and brevity are required. The Coast Guard strongly recommends that the distress message format and transmission procedures be learned by all mariners.

1. If in **DISTRESS** or observing a **DISTRESS** (i.e., when threatened by grave and imminent danger) the Radiotelephone Alarm Signal (if available) should be transmitted for approximately one minute on either 2182 kHz or 156.8 MHz (CHANNEL 16) prior to the **DISTRESS CALL.** The Radiotelephone Alarm Signal consists of two audio tones, of different pitch, transmitted alternately. Its purpose is to attract the attention of persons on watch and shall only be used to announce that a distress call or message is about to follow.

    Then **SPEAK SLOWLY AND CLEARLY CALL: MAYDAY MAYDAY MAYDAY THIS IS** (your vessel's call and name repeated **THREE** times).

    a. **IF ABOARD A VESSEL IN TROUBLE** -- give:
        1) **WHO** you are (your vessel's call sign and name).
        2) **WHERE** you are (your vessel's position in latitude/longitude or true bearing and distance in nautical miles from a widely known geographical point; local names known only in the immediate vicinity are confusing).
        3) **WHAT** is wrong.
        4) Kind of assistance desired.
        5) Number of persons aboard and the condition of any injured.
        6) Present seaworthiness of your vessel.
        7) Description of your vessel -- length, type, cabin, masts, power, color of hull, superstructure and trim.
        8) Your listening frequency and schedule.

    b. **IF OBSERVING ANOTHER VESSEL IN DISTRESS -- give:**
        1) Your position and the bearing and distance of the vessel in difficulty.
        2) Nature of distress.
        3) Description of the vessel in distress (see Item [7] above).
        4) Your intentions, course and speed, etc.
        5) Repeat your radio call sign and name of your vessel and give your listening frequency and schedule.

2. If you need INFORMATION OR ASSISTANCE FROM THE COAST GUARD (other than in a distress), call COAST GUARD on either 2182 kHz or 156.8 MHz (the DISTRESS and CALLING FREQUENCIES). You will then be shifted to a common working frequency allowing the distress frequencies to remain open.

High Seas Weather - Facsimile (FAX)

USCG COMMUNICATION STATION, SAN FRANCISCO FACSIMILE SCHEDULE

Station: San Francisco, CA (call sign NMC) (U.S. Coast Guard)
Service area: Eastern and Central Pacific Ocean

Time (Zulu)	Frequencies (kHz)	Contents of Chart
0145	4344.1, 8680.1, 12728.1 -	(TEST PATTERN)
0150		Surface Forecast Valid 00Z
0200		Sea Forecast Valid 00Z
0300Z	4344.1, 8680.1, 12728.1 -	(TEST PATTERN)
0305		Sea surface Temperature analysis
0315		Sea surface Temperature analysis
0325		Sea weather forecast for 12Z
0335		Sea weather forecast for 12Z
0500	4344.1, 8680.1, 12728.1 -	(TEST PATTERN)
0505		00Z surface analysis
0515		Extended surface analysis
0526		Sea surface temperature
1500	8680.1, 12728.1, 17149.3	(TEST PATTERN)
1505		Sea surface Temperature analysis
1515		Satellite Picture
1715	8680.1, 12728.1, 17149.3	(TEST PATTERN)
1720		12Z Tropical analysis
1730		12Z surface analysis
1740		Satellite Picture
2015	8680.1, 12728.1, 17149.3	(TEST PATTERN)
2020		Radiofacsimile schedule
2030		500MB max wind
2040		Satellite Picture
2330	8680.1, 12728.1, 17149.3 -	(TEST PATTERN)
2335		18Z Tropical analysis
2345		18Z surface analysis

OREGON - WASHINGTON - VHF-FM MARITIME FREQUENCIES

1. Listed below are general frequencies which may be of interest to mariners.

Channel	Frequencies Transmit / Receive		Purpose
6	156.300	156.300	Intership safety
13	156.650	156.650	Bridge to Bridge
14	156.700	56.700	VTS Puget Sound
16	156.800	156.800	Int'l Distress & Calling
22A	157.100	157.100	Coast Guard/Non-Coast Guard liaison with the boating public

VHF-FM Frequencies

FREQUENCY (MHz)

CHANNEL DESIG.	SHIP TRANSMIT	SHIP RECEIVE	INTENDED USE
01	156.050	156.050	Port Operations and commercial
03	156.150	156.150	Port Operations and commercial
63	156.175	156.175	Port Operations and commercial
05	156.250	156.250	Port Operations
06	156.300	156.300	Intership Safety
7A	156.350	156.350	Commercial
08	156.400	156.400	Commercial
09	156.450	156.450	Commercial & Non Commercial
10	156.500	156.500	Commercial
11	156.550	156.550	Commercial
12	156.600	156.600	Port Operations
13	156.650	156.650	Navigational (Bridge to Bridge)
14	156.700	156.700	Port Operations
15	156.750	156.750	Environmental (Receive only)
16	156.800	156.800	Distress, Safety and calling
17	156.850	156.850	State Control
18A	156.900	156.900	Commercial
19A	156.950	156.950	Commercial
20	157.000	161.600	Port Operations
21A	157.050	157.050	US Government Only
22A	157.100	157.100	US Coast Guard Liason
23A	157.150	157.150	US Government Only
24	157.200	161.800	Public Correspondence
25	157.250	161.850	Public Correspondence
26	157.300	161.900	Public Correspondence
27	157.350	161.950	Public Correspondence
28	157.400	162.000	Public Correspondence
65A	156.275	156.275	Port Operations
66A	156.325	156.325	Port Operations
67	156.375	156.375	Commercial
68	156.425	156.425	Non Commercial
69	156.475	156.475	Non Commercial
70	156.525	156.525	Data -Computer Only
71	156.575	156.575	Non Commercial
72	156.625	156.625	Non Commercial
73	156.675	156.675	Port Operations
74	156.725	156.725	Port Operations
77	156.875	156.875	Port Operations
78A	156.925	156.925	Non Commercial
79A	156.975	156.975	Commercial
80A	157.025	157.025	Commercial
81A	157.075	157.075	US Government Only
82A	157.125	157.125	US Government Only
83A	157.175	157.175	US Government Only
84	157.225	161.825	Public Correspondence
85	157.225	161.825	Public Correspondence
86	157.325	161.925	Public Correspondence
87	157.375	161.975	Public Correspondence
88	157.425	162.025	Public Correspondence
88A	157.425	157.425	Commercial
WX1		162.550	Weather (Receive Only)
WX2		162.400	Weather (Receive Only)
WX3		162.475	Weather (Receive Only)

Note: The addition of the letter "A" to the channel number indicates that the ship receive channel used in the United States is different from the one used by vessels and coast stations of other countries. Vessels equipped for U.S. operations only will experience difficulty communicating with foreign ships and coast stations on these channels.

VHF Telephone Channels

Marine Operator channels are monitored 24 hours a day for mariners to place ship-to-shore and ship-to-ship calls. VHF range to marine operator channels often exceeds 50 miles. Call up to the marine operator is made on their working channel listed. Calls to your ship station by the marine operator will first be on Channel 16 and then on the working channel. Mariners are requested to first obtain a marine Identification Number (MIN number) or an account with the telephone stations they plan to be using. There is no monthly charge for telephone service — just a charge each time a call is placed or received.

AREA SERVED	CH.	INFORMATION SOURCE	AREA SERVED	CH.	INFORMATION SOURCE
California			**British Columbia**		
San Diego	28/86	(800) 252-9015	Victoria	26/28	(604) 642-3431
Dana Point	84	(714) 527-1021	Saltspring Island	27	(604) 432-2926
San Pedro	24/26	(800) 252-9015	Nanaimo	26/87	(604) 245-4032
Redondo	27/85/87	(213) 540-5445	New Westminster	23	(604) 432-2926
Santa Barbara	25/86	(805) 963-0511	Vancouver	24/25/26	(604) 273-2309
San Luis Obispo	26	(805) 928-8313		86/88/84	
Monterey Bay	28	(408) 313-2903	Courtenay	23/27	(604) 432-2926
Santa Cruz	27/28	(408) 354-9000	Comox	26	(604) 339-3613
San Francisco	26/84/87/85	(800) 252-9015	Cape Lazo	23	(604) 339-3613
Bodega Bay	25	(800) 252-9015	Kelsey Bay	27	(604) 432-2926
Fort Bragg	28	(800) 252-9015	Sayward	28	(604) 432-2926
Eureka	26	(800) 252-9015	Alert Bay	26/86	(604) 974-5413
Klamath Falls	28	(707) 464-3171	Bull Harbour	26	(604) 432-2926
			Bamfield	27	(604) 432-2926
Inland			Tofino	24	(604) 725-3384
Bakersfield	28	(805) 322-0657	Holberg	26	(604) 432-2926
Fresno	26	(209) 233-8818	Westview	85	(604) 432-2926
Stockton	27/28/86	(415) 542-4720	Calvert Island	84	(604) 432-2926
Redding	28	(916) 241-5624	Bella Bella	25/27	(604) 432-2926
Lake Tahoe	26/28/86	(916) 546-5957	Prince Rupert	26/27	(604) 624-2053
Meadow Lakes	24	(209) 233-8818	Trutch Island	86	(604) 432-2926
Lake Mead	26	(702) 293-3353	Massett	24	(604) 432-2926
			Sandspit	26	(604) 637-5311
Oregon					
Brookings	27	(206) 347-6400	**Southeastern Alaska**		
Coos Bay	25	(206) 347-6400	Ketchikan	28	(907) 276-6811
Newport	28	(206) 242-6789	Ratz Mountain	26	(907) 276-6811
Astoria	24/26	(206) 242-6789	Craig	28	(907) 276-6811
Rainier	28	(206) 242-6789	Petersburg	28	(907) 276-6811
Portland	26	(206) 242-6789	Juneau	26	(907) 276-6811
			Lena Point	28	(907) 276-6811
Washington			Sitka	28	(907) 276-6811
Everett	24	(206) 532-6925	Cape Spencer	28	(907) 276-6811
Averdeen	28	(206) 532-6925			
Cosmopolis	28	(206) 532-6925			
Port Angeles	25	(206) 345-2211			
Bellingham	28/85	(206) 345-2211	Do NOT call BC operators on Channel 16.		
Seattle	25.26	(206) 345-2211			
Tacoma	28	(206) 345-2211	Data by Gordon West		
Olympia	85	(206) 345-2211			
Bremerton	28	(206) 345-2211			

VHF Weather Stations

These stations offer a 100 mile range to 24 hour NOAA weather broadcasts tailored to marine cruising on inland and open waters. There are no stations on the Pacific Coast using weather Channel 3. Canada uses its own weather channel, channel 21 receive, duplex (International 21). Weather warnings will be preceded by an alerting tone to activate special weather monitor receivers. If you hear a steady 10 second tone, listen carefully for the weather warning message.

LOCATION	CHANNEL	LOCATION	CHANNEL
• California		Vancouver	WXBC
San Diego	WX2	Bowen Island	WX3
Los Angeles	WX1	Comox	WX1
Santa Barbara	WX2	Alert Bay	WX, 1 & 2
San Luis Obispo	WX1	Bull Harbour	WX1
Monterey	WX2	Tofino	CH25
San Francisco	WX1	Prince Rupert	WXBC, 1,2 & CH25
Sacramento	WX2	Sandspit	CH25
Point Arena	WX2	Calvent	WX2
Eureka	WX2	Barry Inlet	WX2
Crescent City/Brookings	WX1	Dundas Isl.	WX2
		Klemtu	WX1
• Oregon		Mount Gil	WX2
Salem	WX3	Naden Harbor	WX2
Coos Bay	WX2	Van Inlet	WX1
Eugene	WX2	Eliza	WX1
Newport	WX1		
Astoria	WX2	**• Alaska**	
Portland	WX1	Anchorage	WX1
Brookings	WX1	Cordova	WX1
		Juneau	WX1
• Washington		Ketchikan	WX1
Olympia	WX3	Kodiak	WX1
Yakima	WX1	Petersburg	WX1
Seattle	WX1	Seaward	WX1
Neah Bay	WX1	Sitka	WX1
Cape Flattery	WX1	Valdez	WX1
		Yakutat	WX1
• British Columbia		Nome	WX1
(Scheduled broadcasts		Homer	WX2
only on Channel 21 (161.65)		Wrangell	WX2
Victoria	CH25		

Storm Warnings

VOICE TRANSMISSION OF NWS SAN FRANCISCO WARNINGS AND FORECAST – NORTH PACIFIC

GMT	FREQUENCIES (kHz)	STATION
0000	4403.9, 13107.0,	KMI
0430	4428.7, 8765.4,	NMC
1030	13113.2, 17307.3	NMC
1200	4403.9, 13107.0	KMI
1230	13113.2, 17307.3,	NMC
1630	13113.2, 17307.3	NMC
2230	13113.2, 17307.3,	NMC

To convert Greenwich Mean Time (GMT) to Pacific Standard Time (PST), subtract 8 hours. GMT to Pacific Daylight Savings Time (PDST), subtract 7 hours.

GMT TIME	TRANSMITTING STATION	CARRIER FREQUENCY	BROADCAST TYPE
0103	Group San Diego	157.1 MHz	Notice to Mariners
0203	Los Angeles	157.1 MHz	Notice to Mariners
0333	Monterey	2670 kHz	Weather/Notice to Mariners
0503	Los Angeles	2670 kHz	Weather/Notice to Mariners
1303	Los Angeles	157.1 MHz	Weather/Notice to Mariners
1533	Monterey	2670 kHz	Weather/Notice to Mariners
1615	Monterey & Humbolt	157.1 MHz	Weather/Notice to Mariners
1600	San Francisco	157.1 MHz	Weather/Notice to Mariners
1703	Group San Diego	157.1 MHz	Notice to Mariners
1803	Los Angeles	157.1 MHz	Notice to Mariners
1900	San Francisco	157.1 MHz	Weather/Notice to Mariners
2103	Los Angeles	2670 kHz	Weather/Notice to Mariners
2315	Humbolt	157.1 MHz	Weather/Notice to Mariners
2330	San Francisco	157.1 MHz	Weather/Notice to Mariners
2345	Monterey	157.1 MHz	Weather/Notice to Mariners

MARINE WEATHER FORECAST:

	TELEPHONE NUMBER	OFFICE HOURS (PST)
Los Angeles, CA	(213) 824-7211	8:00 AM - 4:30 PM Weekdays
Los Angeles, CA	(213) 209-7213 (7214)	8:00 AM - 4:30 PM Weekdays
Los Angeles, CA	(213) 477-1463	24 hours daily

Broadcast Notice to Mariners

The stations listed below announce all broadcast on 2182 kHz and 156.80 MHz (Channel 16) and shift to 2670 kHz and 157.10 MHz (Channel 22), on which frequencies the complete boradcast are read. These stations broadcast Notice to Mariners information, on receipt and at the following scheduled times:

GROUP NORTH BEND, OREGON	1003 PST	2203 PST
GROUP ASTORIA, OREGON	0933 PST	2133 PST
GROUP PORTLAND, OREGON	0945 PST	
GROUP PORT ANGELES, WASHINGTON	1015 PST	2215 PST
GROUP SEATTLE, WASHINGTON	1030 PST	2230 PST

HIGH SEAS SSB PHONE SERVICE

FOR PLACING AND RECEIVING PHONE CALLS UP TO 10,000 MILES OUT TO SEA

COAST STATION KMI – CALIFORNIA

ADDRESS: **AT&T**
Station KMI
P.O. Box 8
Inverness, California 94937

FOR TECHNICAL INFORMATION CALL: (415) 669-1055 (COLLECT)

Coast Station	Channel Designation	Coast Station Transmit (Carrier)	Ship Station Transmit (Carrier)
	242	2450.0	2003.0
	248	2506.0	2406.0
	----	2182.0	2182.0
	417	4407.0	4112.6
	416	4403.9	4109.5
	401	4357.4	4063.0
	822	8784.0	8260.1
	809	8743.7	8219.8
	804	8728.2	8204.3
	1229	13,187.6	12,416.8
	1203	13,107.0	12,336.2
	1202	13,103.9	12,333.1
	1201	13,100.8	12,330.0
	1624	17,304.2	16,531.3
	1603	17,239.1	16,466.2
	1602	17,236.0	16,463.1
	2236	22,704.5	22,108.5
	2228	22,679.7	22,083.7
	2223	22,664.2	22,068.2
	2214	22,636.3	22,040.3

(Coast Station: KMI — Point Reyes, California)

CHANNELS 416 -1203

*UTC	TFC	Weather
0000	X	☐
0400	X	
0800	X	
1200	X	☐
1600	X	
2000	X	

☐ Broadcasts of national weather service information.
Note: Traffic lists and weather will be omitted if channel is busy.
* Formerly GMT

TO ARRANGE FOR SERVICE, CALL COLLECT: (201) 631-4165
Or Write: AT&T COMMUNICATIONS MANAGER
High Seas Service
Room 220
201 Littletown Road
Morris Plains, NJ 07950

Aircraft Radio Beacons

These stations will not be found on marine charts. Their locations are approximate and can be pinpointed on an aeronautical chart. Each Aircraft Beacon offers excellent range to exceed 50 miles. Aeronautical weather reports may also be transmitted by these stations.

STATION (I.D.)	FREQUENCY	STATION (I.D.)	FREQUENCY
● California		**● British Columbia**	
Tijuana (TIJ)	398 kHz	Mill Bay (MB)	293 kHz
Tijuana (UN)	381 kHz	Active Pass (AP)	378 kHz
San Diego (AN)	245 kHz	White Rock (WC)	332 kHz
San Diego (SA)	269 kHz	Victoria (YJ)	233 kHz
El Toro (NZJ)	410 kHz	Tofino (AZ)	359 kHz
San Clemente (NUC)	350 kHz	Vancouver (VR)	266 kHz
Long Beach (LG)	233 kHz	Nanaimo (CP)	251 kHz
Los Angeles (IGD)	332 kHz	Estevan Point (EP)	374 kHz
San Nicolas Island (NSI)	203 kHz	Comox (QQ)	400 kHz
Santa Barbara (BA)	338 kHz	Campbell River (BL)	219 kHz
Point Mugu (NTD)	224 kHz	Alert Bay (AL)	335 kHz
Goleta (BA)	338 kHz	Port Hardy (ZT)	242 kHz
Ford Ord (OAR)	236 kHz	Cape Scott (ES)	354 kHz
San Francisco (SFG)	332 kHz	McInnes Island (MS)	380 kHz
Farallon Island (F)	314 kHz	Ethelda (TC)	302 kHz
Hayward (HWD)	351 kHz	Cape St. James (CJ)	292 kHz
Oakland (OAK)	362 kHz	Inlet (Sandspit) (SK)	329 kHz
Arcata (CV)	233 kHz	Lawn Point (LZ)	385 kHz
Gold Beach (GOL)	396 kHz	Prince Rupert (PR)	218 kHz
		● Washington	
		Neah Bay (EBY)	391 kHz
		Ediz Hook (K)	322 kHz
		Kitsap (PWT)	206 kHz
		Crescent (TIW)	375 kHz
		Gray (GRF)	216 kHz
		Seattle (SEA)	362 kHz
		Paine (PA)	396 kHz
		Whidbey Island (NU3)	407 kHz

Data by Gordon West

Radio Beacons for Direction Finding

These stations offer the most accurate signals for direction finding. Each station will send its Morse code identifier for positive station identification. Sequenced radio beacons offer the greatest range, each station taking turns for one minute transmitting a specific identifier. Check your chart for station locations.

BEACON – kHz	SEQUENCE	LAT.N.	LONG. W.	MILES RANGE	SIGNAL
Cape Blanco 304	(V)	42 50.3	124 33.8	100	– – – / (OE)
Cape Arago 304	(I)	43 20.5	124 22.5	50	– · – – (Y)
Yaquina Head 304	(VI)	44 40.6	124 04.7	50	· – – (W)
Cape Kiwanda 320		45 13.0	123 58.2	15	– · – (K)
Columbia River 304	(II)	46 11.1	124 11.0	20	– – ·· (Z)
Cape Disappointment 304	(IV)	46 16.6	124 03.0	50	– – – (O)
Willapa Bay 304	(III)	46 44.0	124 04.6	20	·· – / – (UT)
Cape Flattery 288	(I)	48 23.5	124 44.1	100	· – – · (P)
James Island 288	(II)	47 54.2	124 38.8	50	· – – – / ·· (JI)
Carmanah 288	(III)	48 36 7	124 45.0	35	– ·· (D)
Victoria 233		48 37.8	123 19.0	75	– · – – / ·· – – ·· (YJ)
Amphritrite Point 288	(IV)	48 55.3	125 32.4	50	· – (A)
Point Wilson 314	(II)	48 08.7	122 45.2	30	– – · – (Q)
Smith Island 314	(III)	48 19.1	122 50.5	20	– – · (G)
Race Rocks 314	(IV)	48 17.9	123 31.8	40	· – – – (J)
New Dungeness 314	(V)	48 10.9	123 06.5	30	·· – (U)
(minute silent) 314	(VI)				
Tofino 359		49 02.9	125 42.3	50	– · – – / · – – ·· (YAZ)
Sands Head 296	(I&IV)	49 06.4	123 16 1	20	– – (G)
Sisters Island 296	(III)	49 29.2	124 26.0	30	– – (M)
Point Atkinson 296	(II&V)	49 19.8	123 15.8	30	··· – (V)
Lennard Island 318	(I)	49 06 0	125 55.3	30	– · – (K)
Quatsino 318	(II&V)	50 26.5	128 01.8	50	– ··· (B)
(minute silent) 318	(III)				
Pine Island 318	(IV)	50 58.5	127 43.0	40	· – – · (P)
(minute silent) 318	(VI)				
Langara Island 308	(I)	54 15.4	133 03.5	60	···· (H)
Triple Island 308	(II)	54 17.6	130 52.8	50	– – – (O)
Bonilla Island 308	(III)	53 29.6	130 38.1	60	· – ·· (L)
Chetco River 296		42 02.8	124 16.0	5	– ··· (B)

Radio Beacons for Direction Finding

BEACON – kHz	SEQUENCE	LAT.N.	LONG. W.	MILES RANGE	SIGNAL
Umpqua River 324		43 39.8	124 11.8	20	·· – (U)
Cape Kiwanda 320		45 13.0	123 58.0	50	– · – (K)
Grays Harbor 325		46 54.3	124 07.8	50	– – · (G)
Ediz Hook 322		48 08.4	123 24.1	20	– · – (K)
Whiffin Spit 304		48 21.5	123 42.6		Dashes
Victoria 233		48 38.0	123 19.0	75	– · – –/· – – – (YJ)
Vspr Nrslr 310		48 47.2	125 12.9	5	Dashes
Active Pass		48 52.4	123 17.4	25	· –/· – – · (AP)
Tofino 359		49 03.0	125 42.0	50	– · – –/· –/– – ·· (YAZ)
Estevan Point 374		49 23.0	126 32.5	100	·/· – – · (EP)
Lookout Island 310		49 59.9	127 26.8	10	Dashes
Alert Bay 335		50 35.2	126 55.5	25	· –/· – ·· (AL)
Cape Scott 354		50 47.0	128 25.5	75	– – ··/·/··· (ZES)
Godkin Point 298		50 53.4	127 55.4	10	Dashes
Egg Island 207		51 15.0	127 50.0	25	·· –/·/– – (UEM)
Cape St. James 292		51 56.2	131 01.0	100	– · –/· – – – (CJ)
McInnes Island 380		52 15.1	128 43.2	100	– –/··· (MS)
Ethelda Bay 302		53 03.1	129 41.2	125	–/– · – · (TC)
Sandspit 368		53 11.8	131 56.6	50	– – ··/· – – · (ZP)
Dead Tree 248		53 21.0	131 54.4	25	– – ·· (Z)
Lawn Point 385		53 25.4	131 54.8	45	· – ··/– – ·· (LZ)
Prince Rupert 218		54 15.8	130 25.3	100	· – – ·/· – · (PR)
Scotch Cap 300		54 23.8	164 44.5	100	– – ·· (Z)
Cape Sarichef 290		54 36.0	164 55.7	100	– – –/– (OT)
Guard Island 324		55 26.8	131 52.7	100	· – – – (J)
Cape Decision 318		56 00.1	134 08.1	100	·· –/– (UT)
St. Paul 314		57 09.5	170 11.6	150	···/· – – –/– · – – (SPY)
Five Finger 295		57 16.3	133 37.7	60	– ·· (D)
Cape Spencer 286		58 12.0	136 38.3	200	– (T)
Cape St. Elias 298		59 47.8	144 36.3	150	– – – (O)
Cape Hinchinbrook 292		60 14.3	146 38.8	100	· – – (W)

Amateur Radio (Ham)
MARITIME MOBILE NETS

Meters	Band name	KHz	Zulu	Ends	PST	PDT	Days
15	Inter-American Net	21,415	2030	0	1230	1330	
15	Int'l Maritime Net	21,404	2200	2300	1400	1500	Mon/Fri
20	Seafarers/Maritime Service Net	14,313	200	500	1800	1900	
20	DDD Net-Pacific for Canadians	14,115	400	0	2000	2100	Daily
20	Maritime emergency	13,310	400	1600	800	1900	
20	Pacific Maritime	14,314	500	600	2300	2400	Daily
20	Mariana-Guam	14,310	700	800	2300	2400	Daily
20	So. Pacific	14,315	800	0	0	100	
20	Gunkholers Net-Tulagi	14,328	1000	0	300	200	
20	North Net	14,345	1445	0	745	745	Daily
20	Marqueses	14,340	1545	0	745	845	
20	Atlanta	14,313	1600	1700	800	900	
20	Cal-Hawaii	14,340	1630	0	830	930	
20	DDD Net-Pacific for Canadians	14,115	1730	0	930	1030	Mon/Fri
20	Chaplin Robinson	14,313	1800	2300	1000	1100	Daily
20	Manana	14,340	1630	0	830	930	
20	East Coast Waterway	14,290	2130	0	1330	1430	M-W-F
20	Calif. to So. Pac.	14,285	2300	2310	1500	1600	Mon
20	Calif. to Caribbean	14,285	2310	2320	1510	1620	Mon
40	Carib Net	7158	0	0	1600	1700	
40	East Coast Waterway	7268	1330	0	520	630	Daily
40	Baja Net to LaPaz	7235	1600	1630	810	900	Daily
40	Maritime Mobile	7245	1600	0	800	900	
40	WESCARS	7255	1700	0	900	1000	Daily
40	Serape Net Admirals	7280	1730	0	930	1030	Sun
40	Shamaru/Smitty Hawaii Net	7285	1900	0	1100	1200	
40	West Coast Admirals	7190	2230	2300	1430	1530	Daily
75	So. Pacific	3815	715	0	2315	15	Daily
75	East Coast Waterway	3968	1345	0	545	645	Daily

Gordon West, WB6N0A, may be contacted via the Manana Net, Monday through Friday, 1900 hours ZULU (around 11:00 to 12:00 noon PST) on 14.342, MHz. Contact net control for your call to WB6N0A.

Data by Gordon West

Loran - C

An Electronic long range navigation system that lets you determine your position anywhere in the coverage area...an area that now encompasses 16 million square miles. LORAN - C can tell you where you are, with ¼ mile accuracy and let you return to within 50 to 300 feet of that same spot, time after time. It operates continuously, in all weather. It's accurate, dependable and cost efficient.

LORAN - C

NORTH PACIFIC CHAIN -- 9990

St. Paul, Alaska -- Master	57 09'12.3"N., 170 15'06.8"W.
Attu, Alaska -- Xray	52 49'44.0"N., 173 10'49.0"E.
Port Clarence, Alaska -- Yankee	65 14'40.3"N., 166 53'12.6"W.
Narrow Cape, Alaska -- Zulu	57 26'20.2"N., 152 22'11.3"W.

CENTRAL PACIFIC CHAIN -- 4990

Johnston Island -- Master	16 44'44.0"M., 169 30'31.2"W.
Upolu Point, Hawaii -- Xray	20 14'49.2"N., 155 53'09.7"W.
Kure Island -- Yankee	28 23'41.8"N., 178 17'30.2"W.

NORTHWEST PACIFIC CHAIN -- 9970

Iwo Jima, Volcano 15 -- Master	24 48'03.6"N., 141 19'30.3"E.
Marcus Island --Whiskey	24 17'07.9"N., 153 58'53.2"E.
Hokkaido, Japan --X ray	42 44'37.1"N., 143 43'09.2"E.
Gesashi, Japan --Yankee	26 36'25.0"N., 128 08'56.4"E.
Yap Island, U.S.A. Trust -- Zulu	09 32'45.8"N., 138 09'56.0"E.

U.S. WEST COAST CHAIN -- 9940

Fallon, Nevada -- Master	39 33'06.6"N., 118 49'56.4"W.
George, Washington -- Whiskey	47 03'48.0"N., 119 44'39.5"W.
Middletown, California -- Xray	38 46'57.0"M., 122 29'44.5"W.
Searchlight, Nevada -- Yankee	35 19'18.2"N., 114 48'17.4"W.

CANADIAN WEST COAST CHAIN -- 5990

Williams Lake BC, Canada -- Master	51 57'58.8"N., 122 22'02.2"W.
Shoal Cove, Alaska -- Xray	55 26'20.9"N., 131 15'19.7"W.
George, Washington -- Yankee	47 03'48.0"N., 199 44'39.5"W.
Port Hardy, BC, Canada -- Zulu	50 36'29.7"N., 127 21'29.0"W.

GULF OF ALASKA CHAIN -- 7960

Tok, Alaska -- Master	63 19'42.8"N., 142 48'31.9"W.
Narrow Cape, Alaska -- Xray	57 26'20.2"N., 152 22'11.3"W.
Shoal Cove, Alaska -- Yankee	55 26'20.8"N., 131 15'19.7"W.

EPIRBS

Emergency Position Indicating Radiobeacon (EPIRBs) have saved several lives off the California Coast during the past two years. EPIRBs are effective in situations where it is impossible to establish radio communications. An EPIRB is a simple yet reliable device that can provide the Coast Guard with a location of a vessel or person in distress at sea.

EPIRBS -- are particularly effective when used in tandem with search and rescue satellites (SARSAT). SARSAT monitors distress transmissions from EPIRBs and provides locations to Coast Guard Rescue Coordination Centers. The following table lists the four types of EPIRBs:

CLASS	FREQUENCY	REGULATIONS	DETECTION
A	121.5 & 243.0 MHz VHF-AM	Floatfree. Required on vessels for ocean and coast traders whose route is more than 20 miles from a safe harbor. Energizes automatically when immersed in water.	SARSAT & high altitude air craft.
B	121.5 & 243.0 MHz VHF-AM	Energized manually prior to immersion in water. Use is voluntary. For vessels operating more than 20 miles from the coast.	SARSAT & high altitude air craft.
C	Ch. 16 (156.8 MHz) VHF-FM for 1.5 seconds. Shifts to Ch. 15 (156.75 MHz) for longer periods for direction finding purposes, then re-cycles.	Energized manually prior to immersion in water. Use is voluntary. For vessels operating within 20 miles of the coast. Use by recreational boaters is especially encour-aged.	VHF-FM equipped shore units and other units that routinely monitor Ch. 16, such as Coast Guard aircraft and vessels.
"406"	406 MHz	New commercial system for large boats.	Self I.D. and locate through SARSAT/ COSPAS.

RADAR ASSISTED SEARCH AND RESCUE

Coast Guard search-and-rescue aircraft and surface craft use radar to assist in locating disabled vessels. Wooden and fiberglass vessels are often poor radar targets. Operators of disabled craft that are the object of a search are requested to hoist, as high above the waterline as possible, a radar-reflecting device. If no special radar-reflecting device is aboard, an improvised device consisting of metallic objects of irregular shape can be used. The more irregular the shape, the better will be the radar-reflective quality.

PROCEDURES AND SIGNALS BETWEEN AIRCRAFT AND SURFACE CRAFT FOR DIRECTING SURFACE CRAFT TO THE SCENE OF DISTRESS

The following procedures performed in sequence by an aircraft mean that the aircraft is directing a surface craft toward the scene of a distress incident:
1. Circling the surface craft at least once.
2. Crossing the projected course of the surface craft close ahead at low altitude, opening and closing the throttle, or changing the propeller pitch.
3. Heading in the direction in which the surface craft is to be directed. The surface craft should hoist the international code flag CHARLIE, or use any other signaling means available to indicate its intention to comply.

Crossing the wake of the surface craft close astern at a low altitude while opening and closing the throttle or changing the propeller pitch, means that the assistance of the surface craft is no longer needed.

COAST GUARD DROPPABLE PUMPS

The Coast Guard often provides vessels in distress with emergency pumps by either making parachute drops, by lowering on helicopter hoist, or by delivering by vessel. The most commonly used type of pump comes complete in a sealed aluminum drum about half the size of a 50-gallon oil drum. One single lever on top opens it up. Do not smoke, as there may be gas fumes inside the can. The pump will draw about 140 gallons per minute. Operating instructions are provided inside the pump container.

Racon Radar Beacons
Pacific Coast

LOCATION	LAT N.	LONG W.	CODE	COMMENT
Point Lay, AK	69 44.1	163 00.6	N	Structure-Seasonal
Icy Cape, AK	70 17.3	161 54.5	G	July 1 - Sept. 15
Wainwright, AK	70 36.6	159 51.9	K	
South Skull Cliff, AK	70 54.8	157 37.3	T	
Point Barrow, AK	71 23.2	156 27.2	N	
Cape Simpson, AK	71 03.4	154 43.6	O	
Drew Point, AK	70 51.9	153 54.8	K	
Cape Halkett, AK	70 49.8	152 17.4	M	
Atugaru Point, AK	70 33.3	157 42.5	N	
Colville River, AK	70 28.1	150 37.9	K	
Oliktok Point, AK	70 29.8	149 53.2	G	
Midway Islands, AK	70 29.1	148 21.5	M	
Cross Islands, AK	70 29.7	147 57.5	N	
Bullen Point, AK	70 10.5	146 51.4	K	
Brownlow Point, AK	70 09.6	145 50.6	O	
Seal Rocks, AK	60 09.8	146 50.2	D	on structure
Strait of Juan De Fuca, WA	48 30.6	124 47.0	O	TLS LB "J"
Columbia River, WA	46 11.1	124 11.0	M	LNB "CR"
San Francisco, CA	37 45.0	122 41.5	M	LNB "SF"
Los Angeles, CA	33 42.0	118 14.5	O	

VHF-FM PUBLIC CORRESPONDENCE
CHANNELS BY AREA
North Pacific - BC

Area	Channel	Operator Will Answer
West Coast/	86	Rennell Sound
Queen Charlotte Island	25	Tasu
West Coast/	60	Holberg
Vancouver	27	Winter Harbour
	87	Brooks Peninsula
	23	Estevan Point
	24 & 84	Tofino
	27	Bamfield
	87	Pachena Point
Strait of Juan De Fuca	23	Jordan River
	25	Port Angeles (U.S.A.)
	23 & 24	Everett (U.S.A.)
Dixon Entrance	87	Pearce Island
	85	Dundas Island
	25	Prince Rupert
	27	Prince Rupert
	24	Masset
	28	Langara
Hecate Strait	02	Noble Mtn
	23	Grenville Channel
	24	Hopkins Point
	60	Gil Island
	86	Trutch Island
	64	Louise Island
	85	Tolmie Channel
	87	Swindle Island
	03	Burnaby Island
	24	Cape St. James
Queen Charlotte Sound	24	Bella Coola
	25	Bella Bella
	01	Denny Island
	03	Rivers Inlet
	23 & 84	Calvert Island
	85	Coast Cone (Smith Sound)

Continued

VHF-FM PUBLIC CORRESPONDENCE CHANNELS BY AREA
North Pacific - BC

Area	Channel	Operator Will Answer
Queen Charlotte Strait	02	Cape Caution
	24	Port Hardy
	26	Alert Bay
Johnstone Strait	28	Sayward
Georgia Strait	87	East Thurlow
	01	Chatham Point
	25	Stuart Island
	60	Campbell River
	27	Campbell River
	88	Sarah Point
	85	Powell River
	24	Jervis Inlet
	23	Courtenay
	25	Pender Harbour (Madiera Park)
	86	Sechelt
	87	Nanaimo
	85	West Vancouver
	88	Vancouver
	24	Vancouver
	25 & 26	Vancouver
	23	Vancouver
	86	Vancouver
	27	Victoria
	28	Bellingham (U.S.A.)
	25	Bellingham (U.S.A.)
	86 & 26	Victoria

CANADIAN COAST GUARD
WEST COAST
Scheduled and Continuous Marine Broadcasts

Coast Guard Radio Station	As Scheduled in Radio Aids to Marine Navigation Canadian Coast Guard Frequency and/or VHF Channel	Continuous Marine Forecasts Local Weathers Notices to Shipping
Alert Bay	2054 kHz	161.65 MHz
		162.55 MHz
Comox	2054 kHz	162.55 MHz
Prince Rupert	2054 kHz	161.65 MHz
Tofino	2054 kHz	161.65 MHz
Vancouver	2054 kHz	161.65 MHz
Victoria	2054 kHz	161.65 MHz

ALASKA PUBLIC CORRESPONDENCE

The following channels are operated in Alaska by Alaxcom, Inc. these are non-Coast Guard stations:

	CHANNEL	CALL SIGN	CITY
A	26	WSX 73	Nome
B	28	WHX 353	Togiak
C	28	WAB 902	Unalaska
D	26	WSX 74	Cold Bay
E	24	WHV 399	Egegik
F	26	WHV 403	Dillingham
G	28	WSX 87	Nikishka
H	26	WSX 78	Kodiak
I	26	WAB 903	Diamond Ridge
J	28	WAB 900	Seward
K	27	WHX 428	Whittier
L	28	WAB 901	Valdez
M	26	WSX 77	Cordova
N	24	WHV 829	Yakutat
O	25	WRN 40	Lena Point
P	26	WAB 976	Juneau
Q	24	WHV 825	Manley
R	27	WRN 42	Petersburg
S	28	WRN 41	Ketchikan
T	86	WHV 821	High Mountain
U	25	WAB 956	Craig
V	26	WAB 960	Ratz Mountain
W	28	WRN 43	Sitka
X	26	WAB 975	Cape Spencer

Public Class IIIB Coast Station (VHF Maritime Radio-Telephone)

SEVENTEENTH COAST GUARD DISTRICT
SPECIAL NOTICE TO MARINERS
MARINE INFORMATION BROADCASTS ON VHF-FM

National Weather Service VHF Broadcasts (continous)

| WX1 | | WX3 | |
162.55 MHz		162.40 MHz	
Anchorage	Kodiak	Valdez	Homer
Cordova	Petersburg	Nome	Wrangell
Juneau	Seward		Yakutat
Ketchikan	Sitka		

ALASKA COAST GUARD VHF-FM INFORMATION BCST STATIONS

This is the "U.S. USE ONLY" channel 22A which is not compatible with the international designated channel 22.

22 (157.1 MHz)	BCST TIMES (GMT)	
SITKA		
Mud Bay	0033	0903
	1350	2103
JUNEAU		
Cape Fanshaw/Yakutat	0203	1403
Robert Barron	0303	1503
Althorp Peak	0403	1433
KETCHIKAN		
Zarembo Island/Sukkwan Island	0215	1415
Cape Decision/Mary Island	0233	1433
Gravina Island	0315	1515
VALDEZ		
Valdez Harbor/Naked Island/		
Boswell Bay	0115	0715
	1315	2115
Point Pigot	1333	2133
Cape Hinchinbrook	0133	0733
KODIAK		
Cape Gull/Pillar Mountain/		
Diamond Ridge	0133	1433
Narrow Cape/Rugged Island/		
Sitkinak Dome/ Site Summit/	0530	1630
Tuklung Mountain	0233	1803

SEVENTEENTH COAST GUARD DISTRICT
SPECIAL NOTICE TO MARINERS

Schedule of Marine Weather Broadcasts on Medium/High Freq.

National Weather Service Broadcasts

On March 1, 1987 the National Weather Service implemented a new High Frequency Radio Broadcast Scheduled for marine weather information. This revision was made in response to numerous public comments on the schedule. The biggest change in the schedule is that all broadcasts will be made at the <u>same local time every day regardless of standard (AST) or daylight (ADT) time.</u>
The following VOICE BROADCAST are the upper sideband (USB) 4125 kHz:

LOCATION	STATION	TIME
Annette	KDG58	7:00 AM
Kodiak	WHB29	8:00 AM
Yakutat	KDG91	9:30 AM
Cold Bay	KCI95	10:30 AM
King Salmon	KCI98	11:00 AM
Nome	KCI94	11:30 AM
Annette	KDG58	4:45 PM
Kodiak	WHB29	6:00 PM
Yakutat	KDG91	7:30 PM
Cold Bay	KCI95	8:30 PM
King Salmon	KCI98	9:00 PM
Nome	KCI94	9:30 PM

NOTE: King Salmon broadcasts are seasonal April 1 - Oct. 15.
Cold Bay broadcasts on 2512 kHz (USB) April 1 - Oct. 15 and on 4125 kHz (USB) Oct. 16 - March 30.

Coast Guard High Freq Base Stations

6506.4 kHz (SSB)	(GMT)
COMMSTA Kodiak	0203 1645

To convert from GMT to local time, subtract:

    8 hours for Pacific Standard Time & Alaska Daylight Time
    9 hours for Alaska Standard Time
  10 hours for Aleutian/Hawaiian Standard Time

Canadian Weather Reports

Vancouver	CHQM-AM	1320 kHz
	CHQM-FM	103.5 MHz
	CKNW-AM	980 kHz
	CKWX-AM	1130 kHz
	CKO-FM	96 MHz
	CFUN-AM	1410 kHz
	CJVB-AM	1470 kHz
	CKLG-AM	730 kHz
	CJOR-AM	600 kHz
	CFOX-FM	99 MHz
Victoria	CKDA-AM	1220 kHz
	CFMS-FM	98.30 MHz
	CFAX-AM	1070 kHz
	CJVI-AM	900 kHz
Nanaimo	CHUB-AM	1570 kHz
	CKEG-AM	1350 kHz
Squamish	CISQ-FM	104.9 MHz
Whistler	CISW-FM	102.1 MHz
Pemberton	CISP-FM	104.5 MHz
Prince Rupert	CFPR-AM	860 kHz
Repeater Stations		1150 kHz AM
Alice Arm		1150 kHz AM
Kitimat		101.1 MHz FM
Masset		103.9 MHz FM
Port Clements		102.9 MHz FM
Sandspit		104.9 MHz FM
Stewart		1450 kHz AM
Courtenay	CFCP-AM	1440 kHz AM
Campbell River	CFWB-AM	1490 kHz AM
Powell River	CHQB-AM	1280 kHz AM
Port Hardy	CFNI-AM	1240 kHz AM

ECHOSOUNDER

BACKGROUND

The first echosounder was invented by a man named Reginald A. Fessenden around 1920. Its invention was spurred, in large measure, by the public outcry over the sinking of the passenger liner Titanic in April 1912. That disaster gave rise to a demand for better navigation and communication on the high seas.

Prior to Fessenden's invention, the primary means of determining the depth of the water was to station a man in the bow with a leadline. He would heave the leadline over the side and read the depth of water relative to pieces of string, ribbons or other markers on the line.

Fessenden (1866-1932) was a Canadian/ American/ Bermudan inventor and scientist who is popularly known as the "Father of Marine Electronics." He held more than 600 patents, second only to Thomas A. Edison. He is credited with making the first radiotelephone transmission at Cobb Island, Maryland, in 1900 and inventing the loop direction finder in 1907.

The echosounder grew out of experiments that Fessenden had conducted aboard ship, tapping a hammer against the hull, listening for an echo through an earphone and timing its return with a stopwatch. Using these observations, he developed a flashing-type echosounder, which was in many respects similar to those still used today.

Since then, there have been many advances. It didn't take long for people to realize that you could do a lot more than just measure the depth of the water with an echosounder. You could also learn a great deal about the composition of the bottom and -- more important -- you could "see" what was between your boat and the bottom, namely fish. Much progress was made during the 1950s and 1960s in improving the fish finding characteristics of echosounders and the instruments soon became utterly indispensable for any well-equipped commercial or sports fishing vessel.

Today, there are many types of sounders available, offering an amazing diversity of features and capabilities. You can choose from relatively simple flashing depth indicators, highly sophisticated multi-frequency video fishfinders and everything in between. In the pages that follow, we will discuss some of these basic types, along with their advantages and disadvantages.

Why Can You See Fish?

The soundwaves from the transducer are reflected from discontinuities in the medium in which they travel. These discontinuities may be solid objects or air bubbles. Fish can be detected because their air bladders present such discontinuities. This explains why some very large fish are hard to detect with an echosounder; they may have small air bladders. Tuna, for instance, are notoriously poor echosounder targets. On the other hand, some tiny fish may have proportionally oversized air bladders and these will show up strongly on your echosounder.

BASIC PRINCIPLES

Echosounders are called by a variety of names. Sometimes you'll hear them referred to as fish finders, or recorders, or depth sounders, or just plain sounders. You may even hear them called (incorrectly) "sonars." Although sounders and sonars work on the same principle - measuring distance to an underwater object using sound waves - they are different. Properly speaking, a sounder measures distances straight up and down beneath the bottom of a boat, while sonar is normally used with its transducer directed at an angle from the boat's bottom.

The fundamental idea behind an echosounder is simple. You can measure the distance from your boat to an underwater object by observing the amount of time it takes for a sound wave to bounce off the object back to your boat. Sound travels at a relatively constant speed of 4800 feet per second through the water. Thus, if it takes one second for a sound wave to travel to the bottom and back again, the depth of water is 2400 feet (remember that the sound must travel down and back again).

In a marine echosounder, a device called a "transducer" is used to launch the sound wave through the water. A transducer is an instrument that converts electric energy into sound energy and vice versa. A microphone or loudspeaker, for instance, is a type of transducer. The echosounder transducer is mounted on or in the hull of the boat (more about this subject later). It emits pulses of ultrasonic energy that are higher in frequency than humans or fish can hear, in response to electric impulses from the echosounder. When the sound strikes an object (the bottom or something between the transducer and the bottom) part of this sound is reflected back to the transducer as an echo. The transducer converts this sound wave into an electric impulse, which is sent back to the echosounder's receiver, where it is amplified to a useful level. The echosounder calculates the distance to the object as a function of the time it took for the signal to go down and back.

Note that the transducer doesn't emit a continuous long sound wave. If it did, it would have a difficult time hearing the echo in its own transmitted noise. Instead, it transmits a precisely timed series of pulses, or bursts, of sound and listens in between the pulses.

The basic method of measuring the distance through the water is essentially the same for all echosounders. The differences are in what frequencies they use, how much power they transmit and - most of all - how they display their information.

Please see illustration next page.

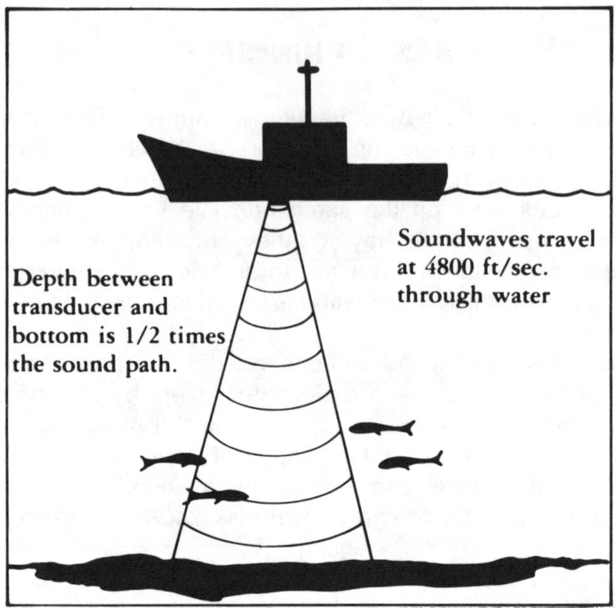

How an Echosounder Works

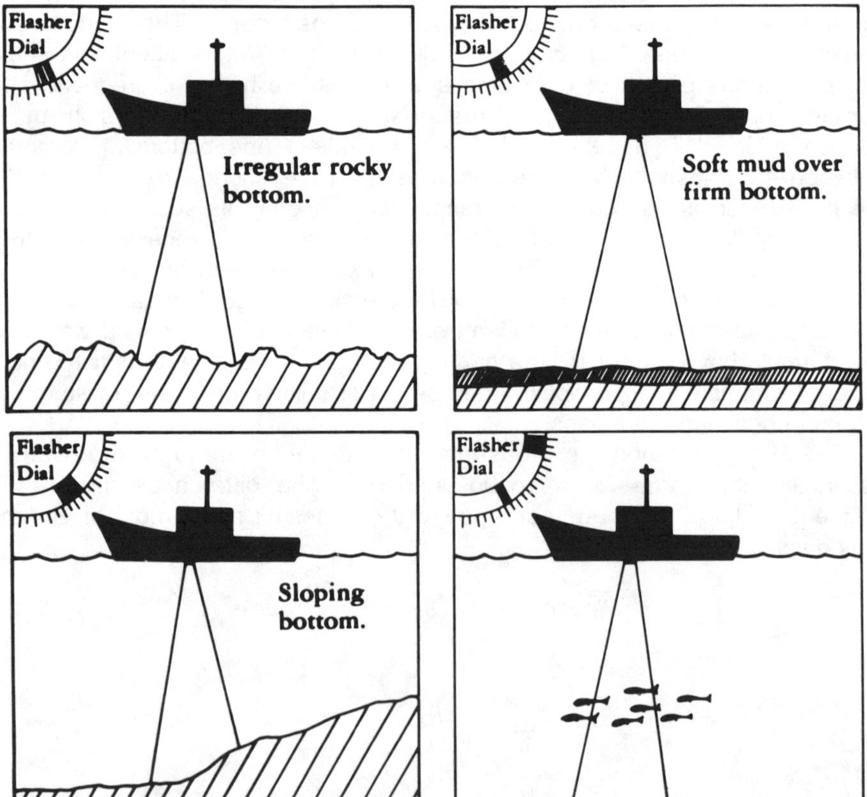

Interpreting a Flashing Sounder Display.

LORAN-C

BACKGROUND

Loran-C is a radionavigation system operating on a frequency of 100 kHz. It uses shore-based transmitters, which broadcast their signals hundreds of miles in all directions. The transmitting stations are organized into chains covering geographical regions. An on-board Loran-C receiver calculates its location by measuring the time differences in signals received from three or more stations in a chain.

Loran is an acronym standing for Long Range Navigation. The modern Loran-C system grew out of an earlier system called Loran-A, which was developed during World War II to meet military requirements. Based on successful wartime experience with Loran-A, the system was expanded during the postwar years. By the end of the 1960s, there were more than 80 Loran-A transmitters serving tens of thousands of mariners.

Loran-A had limitations, however, and work soon began on a successor system that would have longer range and better accuracy. Thus was born Loran-C.

In 1974, the U.S. Government, following an exhaustive survey of all available systems, designated Loran-C as the official government-provided radionavigation aid for the Coastal Confluence Zone. The U.S. Coast Guard embarked on a dramatic expansion of the Fledgling system. As the Loran-C system grew, Loran-A was slowly phased out, and by the early 1980s the changeover was complete.

Loran-C coverage now exists along the entire U.S. and Canadian coastline at least 200 miles to sea, as well as the Great Lakes region and many other parts of the world.

The U.S. Government is committed to maintaining the U.S. Loran-C stations well into the next century. Loran-C will serve as back-up and supplement to the space-based Global Positioning System (GPS) and other satellite-based and land-based radionavigation systems.

WARNING

Loran-C is one of many aids to navigation. The prudent mariner should never depend on any single source of navigation information to the exclusion of others. You should use Loran-C in conjunction with buoys, lights, daymarkers, soundings, radar ranges and other available aids. You should also regularly plot and log Loran-C fixes during open-water navigation.

BASIC PRINCIPLES

The fundamental principle behind Loran-C is that radio waves travel at relatively constant velocities through the air. By measuring the time it takes a radio signal to travel from one point to another, we can accurately calculate the distance as a function of time and radio wave velocity.

To understand how this principle applies to Loran-C, consider the following example. A radio transmitter "M" broadcasts pulsed signals. At precisely timed intervals, this is followed by another pulse from a second station "X". The signals from both stations travel outward in all directions (Figure 1).

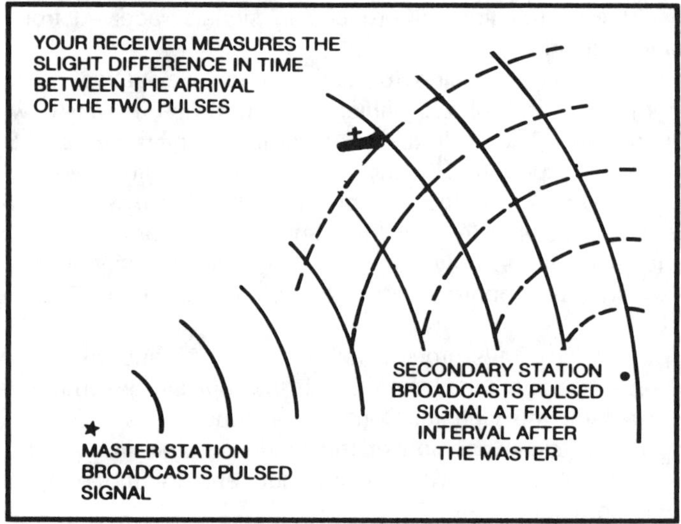

Fig. 1. Broadcast Signals from Master and Secondary

Let's say you are on a boat at point "A" with a radio receiver and a very fast stopwatch. When you receive the first pulse from station "M" you start the stopwatch. You stop it again as soon as the second signal from station "X" gets there, measuring the time within 1/10 of a microsecond. Now look at Figure 2. You can see a series of hyperbolic lines drawn between "M" and "X". These are lines of constant time difference. If you measure a time difference of 13470 microseconds, it will be the same anywhere along the line labelled 13470. This means you are located somewhere on this line. You cannot be anywhere else. In other words, you have defined a navigational line of position, which is no different than one plotted with a compass bearing or radar range.

A "fix" is defined as the intersection of two or more lines of position (LOPs). Thus, to find out exactly where we are on the line 13470, we need to come up with a second LOP.

The second line of position is provided by measuring the time difference between "M" and another transmitter, "Y". In Figure 3 you can see that your location is at the intersection of two lines of position, 13475.3 and 37598.0.

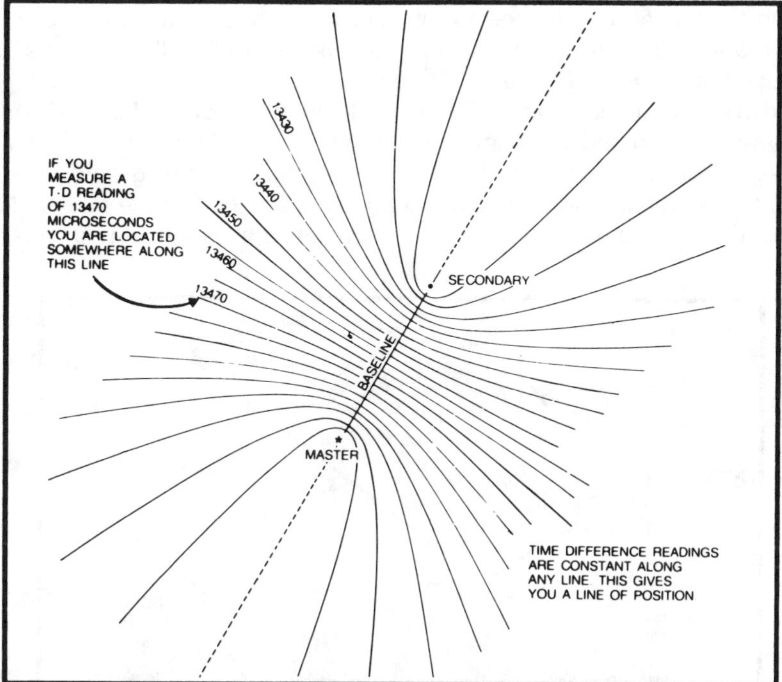

Fig. 2. Hyperbolic Lines of Constant Time Difference.

A modern Loran-C set contains a receiver tuned to listen for the 100 kHz pulses, a very accurate timer and a small computer that processes the information. In its basic form, it simply measures time differences and gives a direct readout of those values in microseconds. This readout is usually called LOPs or T-Ds, for lines of position or time differences. Many modern sets are able to perform other navigational computations as well, such as automatically converting Loran-C lines to latitude-longitude coordinates and calculating courses to destinations or waypoints.

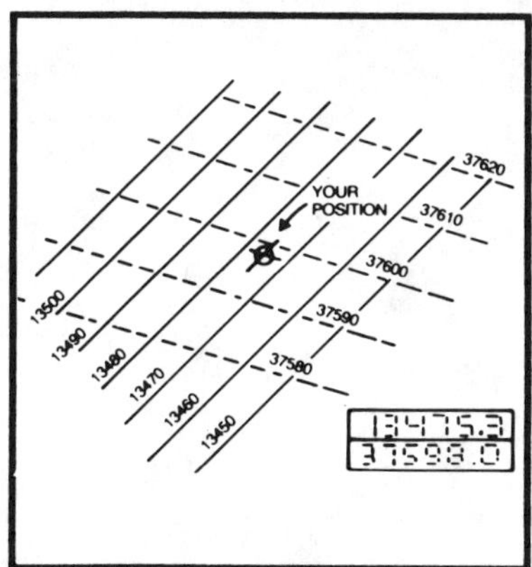

Fig. 3. A Loran-C Fix.

Loran-C stations are organized into chains, consisting of one master and two or more secondary transmitters (sometimes also called "slaves").   A typical chain is shown in Figure 4.

Time difference readings are predictable for any pair of Loran-C stations and they are overprinted on many standard charts by the government mapping authorities.   You can plot your position on the chart by noting time difference readings for the master and any two secondaries and finding the intersection of those two lines.   This normally involves interpolating between plotted lines.

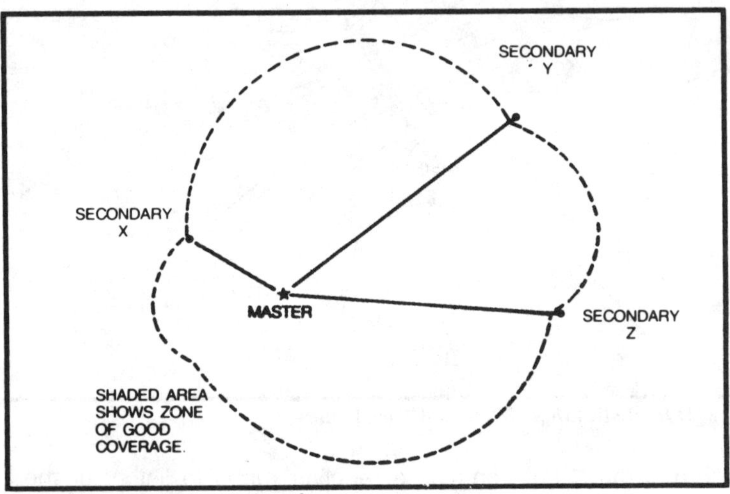

Fig. 4. A Typical Loran-C Chain.

WAYPOINT NAVIGATION

One of the most useful features of a modern Loran-C is its ability to store multiple waypoints, facilitating route planning and accurate navigation from point to point.

Basically, a "waypoint" is any predetermined position to which you wish to steer. It may be a turning point, an event mark, a destination or any other point along your intended track. Generally, a route from one place to another will involve multiple waypoints (see Figure 7).

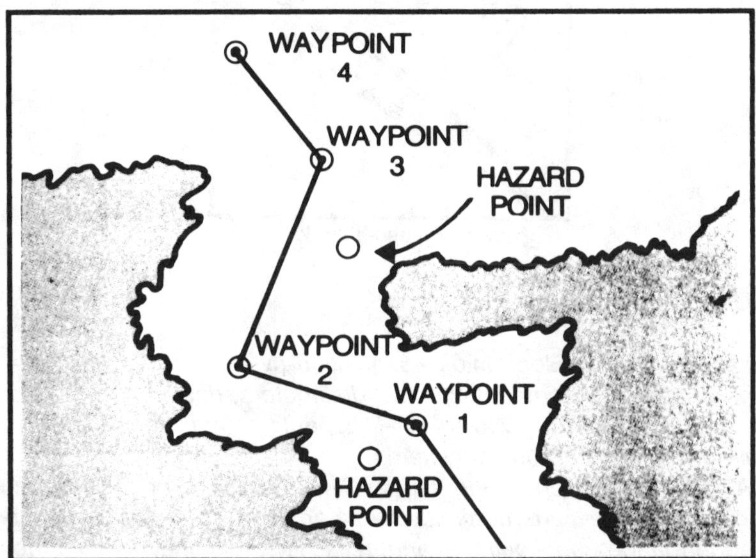

Figure 7. Waypoint navigation

Some Loran-C receivers offer multiple strings of waypoints, which can be tied together into different routes. You can instruct the set to shift automatically from one waypoint to the next as you proceed along your route. This procedure is an advanced function of Loran-C. It can be complicated and you should carefully study your operator's manual for guidance.

Most Loran-C sets can store several waypoints. Some can accept a hundred or more. Following the instructions in your owner's manual, you can enter the coordinates of these locations -- in latitude/longitude of Loran-C T-Ds. Waypoints are normally numbered and to determine the course-to-steer from your current location to any waypoint you simply ask for it by number. Depending on your receiver, you may be able to obtain course-to-steer, distance, time to destination, set and drift. You can often determine the distance to the right or left of track, or cross-track error (see Figure 8). In some cases, course information is presented in either true or magnetic bearings and you should be sure to check which is being used before plotting courses.

WARNING

While your Loran-C set can tell you the *direct* course to steer to any given waypoint, it cannot tell you whether this is a *safe* course to follow. It does not tell you whether there is land or a dangerous reef in the way. You should always plot courses on a nautical chart before following the Loran-C recommended course.

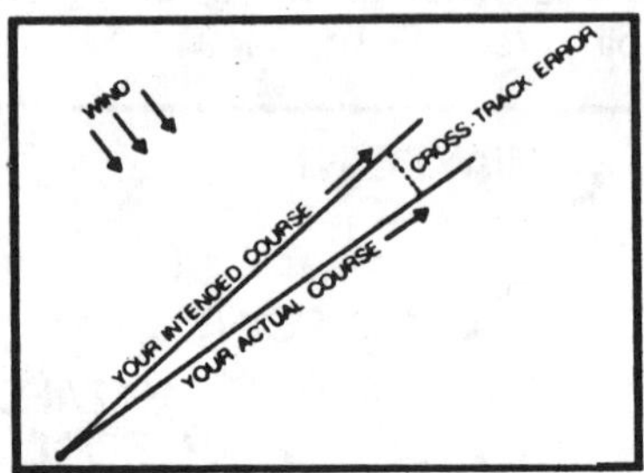

Figure 8. Cross-Track Error

Printed with the permission from the NMEA.

The National Marine Electronics Association (NMEA) is a professional trade association of almost 300 manufacturers, distributors, dealers and others in the industry. It includes firms involved in all aspects of making, selling, installing and repairing marine electronics systems.

NMEA members support the highest standards of professionalism and business ethics. They are committed to continued improvement in product design, performance, applications and reliability, and they work together to sponsor programs that benefit everyone in the marine electronics marketplace. The NMEA has developed the industry's first and only standardized interface protocol for marine electronics, providing a universal digital "language" that permits different items of marine electronics, such as Loran-C receivers and autopilots, to exchange information. The NMEA sponsors seminars and workshops to help educate the user public in safe and proper use of marine electronics, and also sets minimum standards of competence for certified technicians who install and repair marine electronics equipment.

Membership in the NMEA is open to all companies and individuals involved in the marine electronics industry. For more information, call or write:

Ely M. Hamaty, Executive Director
National Marine Electronics Association
P.O. Box 130
Accord, MA 02018 - 0130
(617)878-1723

1991 PACIFIC BOATING Almanac

Burgees of the West

For quick recognition of Western boating clubs.

Aahmes Shrine YC
Oakland, CA

Club de Yates de Acapulco

Aeolian YC
980 Fernside Blvd.
Alameda, CA 94501
Bay Farm Island Bridge
(415) 523-2586

**Aerospace Cruising &
Sailing Club**
Box 92957
Los Angeles, CA 90009

Alamitos Bay YC
7201 E. Ocean Blvd.
Long Beach, CA 90803
(213) 434-9955

Albany Boat Club
820 N. Albany Road.
Albany, OR 97321

Anacapa YC
3821 Vistoria Avenue
Oxnard, CA 93030
(805) 985-9059

Anacortes YC
Box 513
At Cap Sante
Anacortes, WA 98221
(206) 293-5277

Arizona YC
Box 3285
Scottsdale, AZ 85257
(602) 994-1305

Arrow Boat Club
Box 691
Castlegar, B.C.
Location: W. Kootenay Dist.
South Central B.C.

**Assn. of Orange Coast
Yacht Clubs**

**Assn. of Santa Barbara
Channel Yacht Clubs**

**Assn. of Santa Monica Bay
Yacht Clubs**

Astoria YC
P.O. Box 323
Astoria, OR 97103
(206) 325-4725

Auburn Elks YC
1314 Auburn Way North
Auburn, WA 98002
(206) 838-1808

Bahia Corinthian YC
1601 Bayside Drive
Corona del Mar, CA 92625
(714) 644-9530

Balboa Angling Club
A Street
Balboa, CA 92661
(714) 673-6316

Balboa Bay Club
1221 W. Coast Hwy.
Newport Beach, CA 92660
(714) 645-5000

Balboa Island YC
410 Bay Front
Balboa, CA 92662
(714) 673-1070

Balboa YC
1801 Bayside Drive
Corona del Mar, CA 92625
(714) 673-3515

Ballena Bay YC
1150 Ballena Blvd. #151
Alameda, CA 94501
(415) 523-2292

Bay Area Navy Sailing Assn.

**Bay Area Navy Sailing
Assn.**

Bay View Boat Club
489 China Basin St.
San Francisco, CA 94107
(415) 788-9496

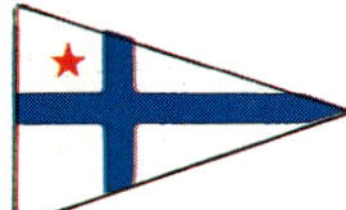

Bellingham YC
2625 Harbor Loop
Bellingham, WA 98225
(206) 733-7390

Bel-Marin Keys YC
#4 Montego Key
Ignacio, CA 94947

Ben Ali Shrine YC
Isleton, CA

Berkeley YC
1 Seawall Drive
Berkeley Marina
Berkeley, CA 94710
(415) 540-9167

Billings Boat Club
P.O. Box 756
Billings, MT 59103

Blue Water Cruising Club
6325 Vermont
Long Beach, CA 90803
(213) 430-3467

Bremerton Boating Club
P.O. Box 2185
Sheridan Park Station
Bremerton, WA 98310

Bremerton YC
2700 Yacht Haven Way
Bremerton, WA 98310
(206) 479-2662

Bridge Marina YC
P.O. Box 1101
Oakley, CA 94561
(415) 757-9971

Buccanneer YC
Box 76
San Pedro, CA 90733

Burrard YC
Box 2870
Stanley Park
Vancouver, B.C.

Cabrillo Beach YC
267 E. 22nd Street
San Pedro, CA 90731
(213) 519-1694

Cactus YC
4825 NE 86th Street
Seattle, WA 98004
(206) 523-7838

Cal Sailing Club
Eshleman Hall
University of California
Berkeley, CA 94710
(415) 527-7245

Caliente Isle YC
P.O. Box 444
Bethel Island, CA 94511

California Yacht Club
4469 Admiralty Way
Marina del Rey, CA 90291
(213) 823-4567

Canadian Forces Sailing Assn.
Esquimalt Squadron
1001 Maplebank Road
Victoria, B.C. V9A 4M2
(604) 385-2646

Canadian Power Squadrons
26 Golden Gate Court
Scarborough, Ontario
(416) 293-2438

Capistrano Bay Yacht Club
34555 Casitas Place
Dana Point, CA 92629
(714) 493-7102

Capital City YC
Box 22, Blue Heron Bay
Victoria, B.C.
(604) 656-4512

Capitol Cruising Club
P.O. Box 1194
Olympia, WA 98501

Captain's Cove YC
S. Arm Fraser River
Vancouver, B.C.
(604) 946-2023

Carling Boat Club of Tacoma
Box 272
Tacoma, WA 98401

Casper Boat Club
Lake Shore Drive
Alcova Lake, WY
P.O. Box 2123
Casper, WY
(307) 472-6922

Catalina Island YC
30 Casino Way
Avalon, CA 90704
(213) 510-0022

Central Oregon Boat Club, Inc.
840 S. Main
Prineville, OR 97754

Cerritos Bahia YC
6289 E. Pacific Coast Hwy.
Long Beach, CA 90803
(213) 598-5051

Channel Cruising Club
22430 Ladeen Avenue
Torrance, CA 90505
(213) 378-6408

Channel Islands Naval YC
Box 4395, USN CBC
Port Hueneme, CA 93401

Channel Islands YC
4100 Harbor Blvd.
Oxnard, CA 93030
(805) 985-6091

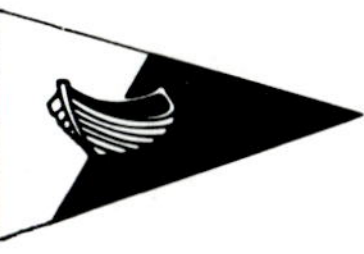

**City of Gig Harbor
The "Maritime City"**
2602 64th St. NW
Gig Harbor, WA 98335
(206) 858-3340

Classic Yacht Assn.
Box 3877
Long Beach, CA 90803

Clear Lake YC
Clear Lake Highlands,
CA 95422
(707) 277-9126

Clover Island YC
P.O. Box 6207
Clover Island
Ft. of Washington St.
Kennewick, WA 99336
(509) 586-9656

Columbia River YC
201 N.E. Tomahawk
Portland, OR 97217
(503) 289-6561

Columbia River Yachting Assn.
1018 NE 68th Street
Vancouver, WA

Coos Bay YC
Box 296
Coos Bay, OR 97420

Corinthian YC
Box 857
Tiburon, CA 94920
(415) 435-4771
Corinthian Island, Belvedere

Corinthian YC
122 Lakeside
Seattle, WA 98107
Pier L Shilshole Marina
Seattle, WA 98107
(206) SU9-1919

Coronado YC
Box 187
1631 Strand Way
Coronado, CA 92118
(619) 435-1848

Coronado Cays YC
Grand Caribe Isle
Coronado, CA 92118
(619) 429-0133

Corsair YC
Box 14777
Long Beach, CA 90814
(213) 467-8117

Cowlitz Boating Club

Coyote Point YC
1820 Coyote Point Drive
San Mateo, CA 94401
(415) 347-6730

Cruiser Haven YC
6649 Embarcadero Drive
Stockton, CA 95209

Dana Point YC
Box 87
24707 Dana Drive
Dana Point, CA 92629
(714) 496-2900

Dana West YC
24601 Dana Drive
Dana Point, CA 92629
(714) 661-1185

Day Island YC
Lakebay, WA 98349
Clubhouse on mainland side
of Day Island Waterway
(206) 564-9982

Dayton YC
413 S. 2nd
Dayton, WA 99328

Del Rey YC
13900 Palawan Way
Marina del Rey, CA 90291
(213) 823-4664

Delta Marina YC
Box 75
100 Marina Drive
Rio Vista, CA 94571

Delta YC
Stockton River Mail
Stockton, CA 95204
(209) 463-6063

Des Moines YC
Box 98362
Des Moines, WA 98188
(206) 878-7220

Diablo Sailing Club
Box 31122
Walnut Creek, CA 94598

Diablo YC
Box 348
Bethel Island, CA 94511
Meetings: Leisure Landing
Bethel Island

Discovery Bay YC
4871 Marina Road
Byron, CA 94514
(415) 634-1210

Dolphin YC
Box 871
Camas, WA 98607
(206) 835-3119
Clubhouse: 34 "A" Street
Washougal, WA 98671

Dos Rios YC
Tr. 1, Box 515
Antioch, CA 94909
(415) 831-8149

Eagle Harbor YC
Box 10905
Bainbridge Island, WA 98110
(206) 842-4309

Eagle Harbour YC
5750 Eagle Barbour Road
W. Vancouver, BC V7W 1P5
(604) 921-7636

Edmonds YC
Box 63
460 Admiral Way
Edmonds, WA 98020

Elkhorn YC
Box 45, Moss Landing
Monterey Bay, CA 95039
(408) 724-3975

Elks YC
2040 Westlake Ave., North
Seattle, WA 98109
(206) 284-5530

Empire Sailing Club
Box 446
2370 Ashe Street
Lakeport, CA 95453
(707) 263-5291

Encinal YC
North Harbor, Pacific Marina
P.O. Box 2953
Alameda, CA 94501
(415) 522-3272

Eugene YC
P.O. Box 2751
Eugene, OR 97402
Clubhouse : Fern Ridge Lake
18 mi. W of Eugene
(503) 485-2100

Everett YC
14th Street Dock
Everett, WA 98201
(206) 259-8178

Fidalgo Yacht Club
1905 Skyline Way
Anacortes, WA 98221
(206) 293-4711

Folsom Lake YC
Box 156
Folsom, CA 95630

Forth Sutter YC
Sacramento, CA

Fox Island YC
P.O. Box 1
Cedrona Cove
Fox Island, WA 98333
(206) 549-2603

Fremont Sailing Club
4920 Sterling Drive
Fremont, CA 94536

Fresno YC
Box 12352
Fresno, CA 93777

Gig Harbor YC
Box 22
Gig Harbor, WA 98335
(206) 858-3578

Golden Gate YC
1 Yacht Club Road
The Marina
San Francisco, CA 94123
(415) 346-2628

Gulf YC
Box 34075, Postal Station
"D" Vancouver 15, B.C.
(604) 987-0864

Hanalei Bay YC
1599 Ala Moana Blvd.
Honolulu, HI 96814
(808) 523-2960

Hat Island YC

Hawaii YC
Box 1739-C
Ala Moana
"Ala Wai Harbor"
Honolulu, HI 96815
(808) 949-4622

Hyden Island YC
12050 N. Jantzen Drive
Portland, OR 97217
(503) 283-4369

Hell's Canyon Boat Club
Riverside Drive
Clarkston, WA
Mail: Box 18
Lewiston, ID 83501

Hidden Harbor YC
285 NW Market Street
Seattle, WA 98107
(206) 789-8591

Hollyburn Sailing Club

Hollywood YC

Hood River YC
Hood River, OR 97031

Houseboat YC
3058 Rocky Point Road
Bremerton, WA 98312

Humboldt YC
P.O. Box 445
Foot of Commercial
Eureka, CA 95501
(707) 445-2148

Hunters Point YC

Huntington Harbour YC
3821 Warner Avenue
Huntington Beach, CA 92645
(213) 592-2186

Imperial Valley Anglers Club
P.O. Box 402
El Centro, CA 92251

International Order of the Blue Gavel

International YC
Box 1165
Drayton Harbor Mall
Blaine, WA 98230
(206) 332-8442

Inverness YC
Box 186
Inverness, CA 94937
(415) 669-9980

Islam Shrine YC
San Francisco, CA

Island Sailing Club
Box 4066
Foster City, CA 94404
E of San Mateo on
San Francisco Bay

Island YC
Alameda Marina
1815 Clement Avenue
Alameda, CA 94501
(415) 521-2980

Jonathan YC
Jonathan Club
850 Palisades Beach Rd.
Santa Monica, CA 90403
(213) 624-0881

Juneau YC
1050 Harborway
Juneau, AK 99801
(907) 586-2911

Kaneohe YC
44-503 Kaneohe
Oahu, HI
(808) 247-4121

Kelowna YC
1414 Water Street
Kelowna, B.C.
(604) 762-3310

Ketchikan YC
Thomas Basin
Ketchikan, AK

King Harbor YC
280 Yacht Club Way
Redondo Beach, CA 90277
(213) 376-2459

Kingston Cove YC
Box 81
Kingston, WA 98346

Kitimat Yacht Club
Box 221
Kitimat, B.C.

Kitsilano YC
2401 Point Grey Road
Vancouver 9, B.C.
(604) 738-1225

Klamath YC
Box 1648
2700 Front Street
Klamath Falls, OR 97601
(503) 882-9106

Ladner YC
Box 82
5011 River Road West
Delta, B.C. (604) 946-4056

Lahaina YC
Box 751
835 Front Street
Lahaina, Maui, HI 96761
(808) 661-3576

Lake Arrowhead YC
One Yacht Club Road
Lake Arrowhead, CA 92352
(714) 337-9052

Lake Chelan Boating Club
Chelan, WA 98816

Lake Chelan YC
Chelan, WA 98816
(509) 687-3429

Lake Havasu YC
Box 2065
Lake Havasu City, AZ 86043
(602) 453-5005

Lake Mead YC
1000 Rockaway Street
Las Vegas, NV 89107
(702) 565-1001

Lake Merced Sailing Club
Harding Road
San Francisco, CA 94132
(415) 753-1101

Lake Merritt Sailing Club
Sailboat House
1520 Lakeside Drive
Lake Merritt
Oakland, CA 94612
(415) 444-3807

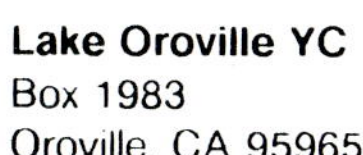

Lake Oroville YC
Box 1983
Oroville, CA 95965

**Lake Washington
Sailing Club**
Sacramento, CA

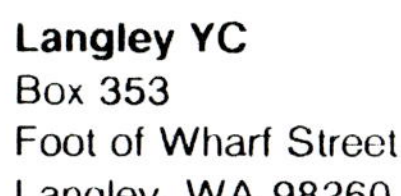

Lakeside YC
1730 Lakeside S.
Seattle, WA 98144

Langley YC
Box 353
Foot of Wharf Street
Langley, WA 98260

Las Vegas YC
Box 2615
Las Vegas, NV 89104

Lido Isle YC
701 Via Lido Sound
Newport Beach, CA 92663
(714) 673-6170

**Little Ships Fleet of
Long Beach**
6286A E Pacific Coast Hwy.
Long Beach, CA 90814

Loch Lomond YC
95 Loch Lomond Drive
San Rafael, CA 94901
(415) 453-9811

Long Beach YC
6201 Appian Way
Long Beach, CA 90803
(213) 598-9401

Longview YC
P.O. Box 1730
Longview, WA 98632

Los Angeles YC
500 Barracuda Street
Terminal Island, CA 90731
(213) 831-1203

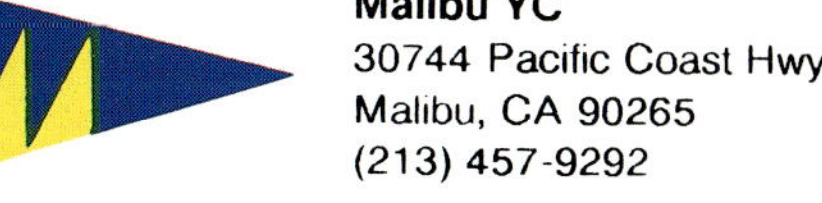

Malibu YC
30744 Pacific Coast Hwy.
Malibu, CA 90265
(213) 457-9292

Maple Bay YC
Box 406
Duncan, B.C. V9L 3X9
(604) 746-4521

Marin YC
24 Summit Avenue
San Rafael, CA 94901

**Marina del Rey Pioneer
Skippers, Inc.**
Boat Owners Assn.
Box 381
Marina del Rey, CA 90921
(213) 821-7614

Marina YC
4333 Admiralty Way
Marina del Rey, CA 90292
(213) 822-0611

The Marlin Club
2445 Shelter Island Drive
San Diego, CA 92106
(619) 222-2502

Martinez YC
P.O. Box 128
Martinez, CA 94553
(415) 228-5450

McNary YC
P.O. Box 435
Hermiston, OR
(503) 567-5603

Meridian YC
1951 Embarcadero Cove
Oakland, CA 94606
(415) 521-1246

**Metropolitan YC
of Oakland**
1853 Embarcadero
Foot of Webster Street
Oakland, CA 94607
(415) 536-7450

Meydenbauer Bay YC
9927 Meydenbauer Way SE
Bellevue, WA 98004
(206) 454-8880

Milltown Sailing Assoc.
Box 2963
Everett, WA 98203
(206) 258-2176

Mission Bay YC
1215 El Carmel Place
San Diego, CA 92109
(619) 488-0501

Mokelumne YC
964 Brannen Island Road
Isleton, CA 95641

Montana Sailing Assn., Inc.
Polson, MT 59860
(406) 549-2934

Monterey Peninsula YC
Box 91, Municipal Pier #2
Monterey, CA 93940
(408) 372-9686

Morro Bay YC
Box 324
541 Embarcadero
Morro Bay, Ca 93442
(805) 772-3981

Multnomah Channel YC
Rt. 1, Box 100
Portland, OR 97231
(503) 283-2257

Nanaimo YC
400 Newcastle Avenue
Box 432
Nanaimo, B.C. V9R 5L3

Navy YC, Long Beach
Naval Station
Long Beach, CA 90802
(213) 547-7285

Neptune Sailing Club
535 Lake Street
Kirkland, WA 98033
(206) 828-2681

Nevada Sailing Club
Box 164
Henderson, NV 89015

Newberg Boat Club
914 E. Fulton Street
Newberg, OR

**Newport Harbor YC &
Newport Harbor YC Anglers**
720 W. Bay Ave.
Balboa, CA 92661
(714) 673-7730

**Newport Ocean Sailing
Assn.**
Box 425
Corona del Mar, CA 92625
(714) 640-1351

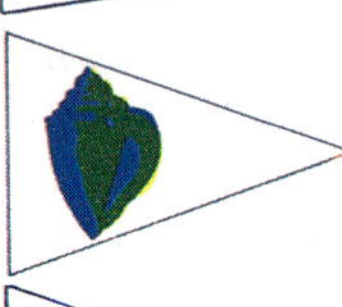

Newport YC
81 Skagit Key
Bellevue, WA 98006
(206) 747-3291

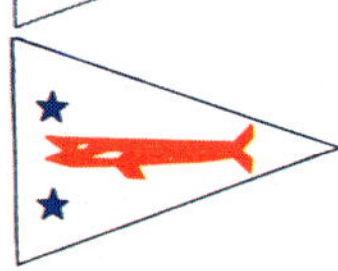

Normandy Cove Boat Club
18915 Marine View Dr. S.W.
Seattle, WA 98166
(206) 242-3778

North Bay YC
40 Point San Pedro Road
San Rafael, CA 94901

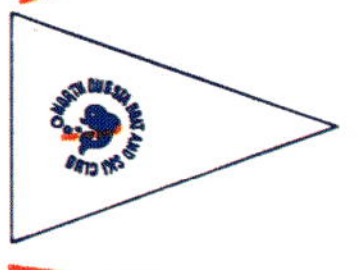

N. Cuesta Boat & Ski Club
Box 202
Paso Robles, CA 93446

**North Pacific Ocean
Racing Assn.**

North Shore Beach and YC
Highway 111
North Shore, CA 92254
(619) 393-3071

**Northern California Power
Cruiser Assn.**

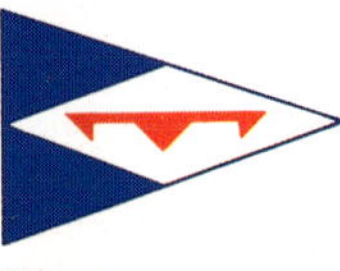

Northwest Multihull Assn.
Box 70413 Ballard Station
Seattle, WA 98107
(206) 747-1167

**Northwest Outboard
Trailer Sailors**
Box 1516
Portland, OR 97207

Oak Harbor YC
Box 121
Oak Harbor, WA 98277

Oakland YC
#1 Pacific Marina
Alameda, CA 94501
(415) 522-6868

**Ocean Racing
Catamaran Assn.**
109 Dolphin Avenue
Seal Beach, CA 90740

Oceanside YC
1950 Harbor Drive North
Oceanside, CA 92054
(714) 722-5751

Offshore Cruising Club
Box 3631
Long Beach, CA 90803
Location: Little Geiger Cove,
Catalina, CA
(818) 577-2293

Olympia Outboard Club
P.O. Box 973
Olympia, WA 98501

Olympia YC
201 N. Simmons Street
Olympia, WA 98501
(206) 357-6767

Orcas Island YC
P.O. Box 121
Eastsound, WA 98245
(206) 376-4018

**Oregon Corinthian
Sailing Assn.**
Box 5434
Portland, OR 97228

**Oregon Federation
of Boaters**
7515 S.W. Miller Hill Road
Beaverton, OR 97007

Oregon Speed Boat Assn.
18775 S.W. Vista Street
Aloha, OR 97405

Orick Boat Club
Box 842
Eureka, CA 95501

**Outboard Boating Club of
Long Beach, Inc.**
Box 3391
Long Beach, CA 90803

Oyster Point YC
911 Marina Drive
S. San Francisco, CA 94080
(415) 873-5144

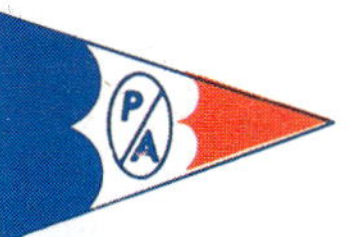

Pacific Anglers
Balboa Bay Club
1221 W. Coast Highway
Newport Beach, CA 92660

**Pacific Coast
Yachting Assn.**

Pacific Corinthian YC
2600 S. Harbor Drive
Oxnard, CA 93030
(805) 985-7292

**Performance Handicap
Racing Fleet**

**Pacific Inter-Club
Yacht Assn.**

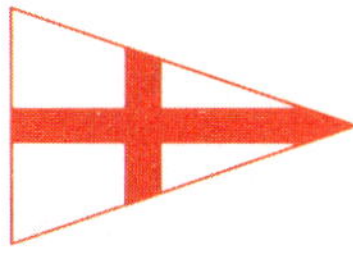

**Pacific International
Yachting Assn.**
308-2230 Cadboro Bay Rd.
Victoria, B.C. V8R 5G9

Pacific Mariners YC
13915 Panay Way
Marina del Rey, CA 90291
(213) 823-9717

Pacific Yacht Club
Hickman AFB (SSH)
c/o Hickam Harbor
Oahu, HI 96553

**Pacific Yacht &
Balloon Club**
Box 1542
Newport Beach, CA 92663

Palo Alto YC
643 Bair Island Road
Redwood City, CA 94603
(415) 361-9458

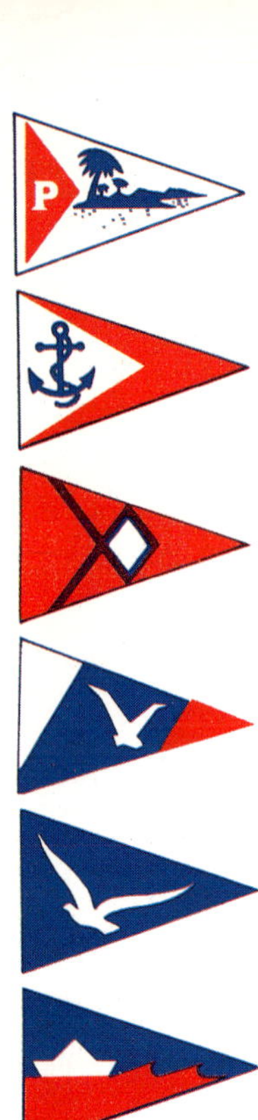

Paradise Harbor YC
233 Trinidad Drive
Tiburon, CA 93920
(413) 435-1652

Pearl Harbor YC
Box 6357
Honolulu, HI 96818

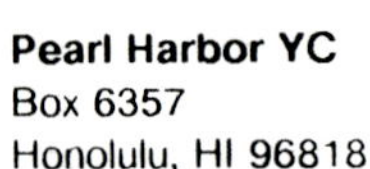

Peninsula Yacht Club
1536 Maple Street
Redwood City, CA 94063
(415) 361-9591

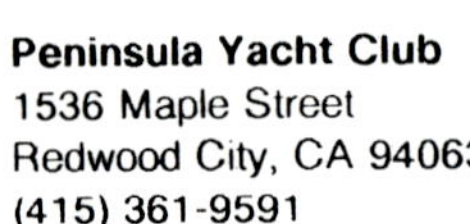

Peninsula Sailing Club
3219 Halverson Avenue
Bremerton, WA 98310

Pierpont Bay YC
1363 Spinnaker Drive
Ventura, CA 93003
(805) 644-6672

Pilchuck Boat Club
Rt. 4, Box 187
Arlington, WA 98223

Pittsburg YC
P.O. Box 971
Pittsburg, CA 94565
(415) 432-1056

Point Dume YC
P.O. Box 8773
Calibasas, CA 91301

Point San Pablo YC
Box 307
Point Richmond Station
Richmond, CA 94807
(415) 620-9690

**Pomona Valley
Sailing Assn.**
Box 2145
Pomona, CA 91766

**Port Angeles Yacht &
Outboard Motorboat Club**
Box 692
Port Angeles, WA 98362
West end of Port Fill,
Port Angeles

Portland Rowing Club
Ft. of SE Harney Street
Portland, OR 97202
(503) 228-1347

Portland YC
1241 NE Marine Drive
Portland, OR 97211
(503) 285-1922

Port Ludlow YC
Box 32
Port Ludlow, WA 98365

Port Madison YC
P.O. Box 10002
Bainbridge Island, WA 98110

Port Orchard YC
721 Bay Street
Port Orchard, WA 98366
(206) 876-9010

Port Sonoma YC
P.O. Box 317
Novato, CA 94948

Port Townsend YC
Box 75
Port Townsend, WA 98368

Poulsbo YC
Box 115
Poulsbo, WA 98370
(206) 779-5991

Presidio YC
Box 29046
Presidio of San Francisco,
CA 94129
(415) 332-2319

**Princess Louisa
International Society**
385 Maple Avenue SW
Renton, WA 98055

Puget Sound YC
2321 N. Northlake Way
Seattle, WA 98103
(206) 634-3733

Quartermaster YC
Box 76
Burton, WA 98013
(206) 463-5350

Queen City YC
2608 Boyer Avenue E.
Seattle, WA 98102
(206) 323-9602

Rainier YC
9094 Seward Park Ave. S.
Seattle, WA 98118
(206) 722-9576

Redondo Beach YC
819 N. Harbor Dr. Bldg. F
Redondo Beach, CA 90277
(213) 314-4838

Richland YC
Comstock Road
at River Point Rd.
Box 314
Richland, WA 99352
(509) 946-6900

Richmond YC
Box 295
Point Richmond, CA 94807
(415) 237-2821

Richmond YC
807 River Road
Richmond, B.C.
(604) 278-1013

Riverside YC
Box 154
Wilsonville, OR 97070

River View YC
Box 22066
Sacramento CA 95822
Location: Islands Marina,
Miner Slough, Ca

Roche Harbor YC
1747 NW 100th
Seattle, WA 98177
(206) 776-6824

Rocky Point YC
Rocky Point Moorage
Rt. 1, Box 276B
North Rocky Point Road
Scappoose, OR 97056
(503) 543-2424

Rogue YC
Box 723
Medford, OR 97501

Rose City YC
3737 NE Marine Drive
Portland, OR 97211
(503) 282-2049

Royal City YC
Foot of Jardine St.,
S. New Westminster, B.C.
(604) 526-6111

Royal Vancouver YC
3811 Point Grey Road
Vancouver 9, B.C.
(604) 224-1344

Royal Victoria YC
3475 Rippon Road
Victoria, B.C.
Tsehum Haven
2031 Swartz Bay
Victoria, B.C.

Sacajewea Boat Club
Box 631
Pasco, WA 99301
Location: Pasco yacht Basin

Sacramento YC
Box 773
W. Sacramento, CA 95961
(916) 371-9850

St. Francis YC
On the Marina
San Francisco, CA 94123
(415) 563-6363

St. Helens YC
Strand Street
St. Helens, OR 97051
(503) 397-0010

**Salem Yacht &
Boating Club**
Box 361
Salem, OR 93701
(503) 363-0067

**San Diego Assn.
of Yacht Clubs**

**San Diego Naval
Sailing Club**
c/o Special Services Dept.
Naval Amphibious Base
Coronado
San Diego, CA 92155
(619) 435-8788

San Diego YC
1011 Anchorage Lane
San Diego, CA 92106
(619) 222-1103

**San Fernando Valley
Sailing Club, Inc.**
P.O. Box 173
Van Nuys, CA 91408
(818) 701-1718

**San Francisco Bay
Sailing Assn.**

San Francisco YC
98 Beach Road
Belvedere, CA 94920
(415) 435-9133

San Joaquin YC
Box 326
Bethel Island, CA 94511
(415) 684-9985

San Jose Sailing Club
Box 5631
San Jose, CA 95150

San Juan Island YC
Box 67
Friday Harbor, WA 98250
(206) 378-3434

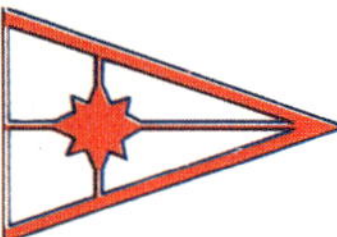

San Leandro YC
Box 551
San Leandro, CA 94577
(415) 351-9666

San Luis YC
Box 247
Avila Beach, CA 93424
(805) 595-9951

San Pedro YC
700 Henry Ford Avenue
Bldg. A-1
Wilmington, CA 90744

San Rafael YC
405 San Francisco Blvd.
Box 821
San Rafael, CA 94915
(415) 459-9828

Santa Barbara Sailing Club
Box 1542
Santa Barbara, CA 93102
(805) 965-4912

Santa Barbara YC
130 Harbor Way, Breakwater
Santa Barbara, CA 93109
(805) 965-8112

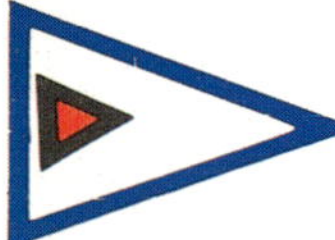

Santa Clara Racing Assn.
Box 82334
San Diego, CA 92138

Santa Cruz YC
Box 454
Santa Cruz, CA 95061
(408) 425-0690

Santa Monica YC
13575 Mindanao Way
Marina del Rey, CA 90292
(213) 827-7692

Sausalito Cruising Club
Box 155
Sausalito, CA 94966

Sausalito YC
Box 267
Sausalito, CA 94966

Sauvie Island YC
Rt. 1, Box 261
Portland, OR 97231

Seal Beach YC
255 Marina Drive
Long Beach, CA 90803
(213) 431-9254

Seattle YC
1807 E. Hamlin Street
Seattle, WA 98112
(206) 325-1000

Sequoia YC
451 Seaport Court, Box 5548
Redwood City, CA 94063
(415) 361-9472

**Semiahmoo Bay
Sailing Club**
14597 Marine Drive
White Rock, B.C.

Shark Island YC
1099 Bayside Drive
Newport Beach, CA 92662
(714) 760-0221

Shasta YC
Box 117
Redding, CA
(707) 238-9954

Shelter Bay YC
Box 1
LaConner, WA 98257

Shelton YC
P.O. Box 453
Shelton, WA 98584
(206) 426-9476

Shilshole Bay YC
2442 NW Market Street #98
Seattle, WA 98107

**Shoreline YC
of Long Beach**
423-D Shoreline Village Dr.
Long Beach, CA 90801
(213) 435-4093

Sierra Sailing Assn.
4724 Pico Avenue
Bakersfield, CA 93306

Silver Gate YC
2091 Shelter Island Drive
San Diego, CA 92106
(714) 222-1214

Sinclair Inlet YC
Box 1197
Port Orchard, WA 98366

**Small Boat Racing Assn.
of Northern California**

**Small Yacht Racing Assn.
of San Francisco Bay**

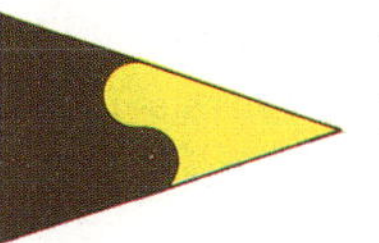

Solano YC
Box 411
Suisun City, CA 94585
(707) 428-9701

South Bay YC
Box 102
Alviso, CA 95002

**South Bay Yacht
Racing Club**
P.O. Box 10967
Marina del Rey, CA 90295

South Coast Corinthian YC
13445 Mindanao Way
Marina del Rey, CA 90291
(213) 823-9027

**Southern California
Cruiser Assn.**

**Southern California
Yachting Assn.**
(818) 988-4965

South Shore YC
2527 West Coast Highway
Newport Beach, CA 92663
(714) 646-3102

Southwestern YC
Box 6397
2702 Qualtrough Street
San Diego, CA 92106
(714) 222-0438

Spindrift YC
Rt. 1, Box 69A
Isleton, CA 95641

Spinnaker YC
Box 1561
San Leandro, CA 94457
(415) 351-9930

Spokane Sailing Club
Spokane, WA

Spokane YC
Box 805
Spokane, WA 99208

Sportsmen Inc. YC
Rt. 1, Box 565
Antioch, CA 94509
(415) 757-9866

Squalicum YC
Box 735
Boathaven, Squalicum
Boat Harbor
Bellingham, WA 98225

Stanwood Camano YC
Box 38
Stanwood, WA 98292
(206) 387-3737

Stillwater YC
Box 561
Pebble Beach, CA 93953

Stockton Sailing Club
South Buckley Cove
4980 Brookside Road
Stockton, CA 95207
(209) 951-5600

Stockton YC
3235 River Drive
Stockton, CA 95204
(209) 946-9259

Sunset Aquatic YC
Box 538
Sunset Beach, CA 90742
(213) 592-2833

Swinomish YC

Tacoma YC
Pt. Defiance
Tacoma, WA 98407
(206) 752-3555

The Dalles YC
Box 775
Ft. of Madison
The Dalles, OR 97058

Three Tree Point YC
Box 281
Seahurst, WA 98062
(206) 623-2503

Tiburon YC
233 Trinidad Drive
Tiburon, CA 94920

Totem YC
Box 1404
Tacoma, WA 98401
(206) 759-9062

Transpacific YC
880 Rosalind Road
San Marino, CA 91108

Tucson Sailing Club
5042 E. Speedway Blvd.
Tucson, AZ 85712

The Tuna Club
Box 526
Avalon, CA 90704
(213) 510-0079

Tsawwassen YC
P.O. Box 1028 Station A
Delta, B.C. V4M 3T2

Tyee YC
2929 NE Marine Drive
Portland, OR 97211
(503) 284-4772

Tyee YC
3229 Fairview Avenue E
Seattle, WA 98102
(206) 323-9440

U.S. Broadbill Club
1600 W. Coast Hwy., #A
Newport Beach, CA 92660
(714) 646-7581

U.S. Coast Guard Auxiliary

U.S. Power Squadrons

UC-Irvine Sailing Assn.
Crawford Hall
Univ. of CA, Irvine
Irvine, CA 92664
(714) 835-5846

University of WA YC
Sub 24 HUB Box 235 FK10
Univ. of Seattle
Seattle, WA 98195

Vagabundos del Mar
P.O. Box 824
Isleton, CA 95641
(707) 374-5511

Vallejo YC
Box 311
Vallejo, CA 94590
(707) 648-9409

Vancouver Cruising Club
1395 Rainbow Drive
North Vancouver, B.C.

Vancouver YC
2006 SE Lieser Road
Washougall, WA 98664
(206) 835-5400

Venice YC
14025 Panay Way
Marina del Rey, CA 90292
(213) 822-6662

Ventura YC
1755 Spinnaker Drive
Ventura, CA 93001
(805) 642-0426

Vernon YC
Box 443
Vernon, B.C.
(604) 545-5518

Victoria Cruising Club
Box 234
McPherson Lounge
Royal Athletic Park
Victoria, B.C.

Viking YC
4224 Marine View Drive
Tacoma, WA 98422

Voyagers YC
2616 "A" Newport Blvd.
Newport Beach, CA 92660
(714) 673-7991

Waikiki YC
1599 Ala Moana
Honolulu, HI
(808) 949-7141

Walla Walla YC
Box 1223
Walla Walla, WA 99362
(509) 547-4946

Wave Toppers YC
Box 70465
Seattle, WA 98107

Weber Point YC
N. Spud Island River Mail
Stockton, CA
Mail: 846 E. Dayton Avenue
Fresno, CA 93704

West Coast YC
Box 2970
Seal Beach, CA 90740

West End Cruising Club
Box 1566
Avalon, CA 90704
(213) 510-0303

Westlake YC
32123 Lindero Canyon Road
Westlake Village, CA 91361
(818) 889-4820

West Seattle YC
Box 16095
Seattle, WA 98116

West Vancouver YC
5854 Marine Drive
West Vancouver, B.C.
(604) 921-7575

Westward Cruising Club
Box 724
Hermosa Beach, CA 90254

West Wind YC
Box 752
Wilmington, CA 90744

Whiskeytown Sailing Club
Box 184
Whiskeytown, CA 96001

Willamette Sailing Club
6336 SW Beaver Avenue
Portland, OR 97201
(503) 289-7731

Willamette YC
948 N. Jantzen
Portland, OR 97217
(503) 289-7731

Windjammers YC
13444 Bali Way
Marina del Rey, CA 90291
(213) 823-2345

**Yacht Racing Assn.
of SF Bay**
Fort Mason Center, Bldg. E
San Francisco, CA 94123
(415) 771-9500

**Yacht Racing Union of
Southern California**

Yakima Valley Boat Club
Box 885
Yakima, WA 98901

Yarrow Bay YC
Box 40
Kirkland, WA 98033
(206) 822-6066